BHAGAVAD GĪTĀ EXPLAINED

Bhagavad Gītā in Its Own Time and Place

Michael Beloved/ Yogi Madhvācārya

Original Sanskrit text :

- Chapters 23 -40 Bhishma Parva, *Mahābhārata*--granted and permitted by John Smith-University of Cambridge, Bhandarkar Oriental Research Institute.

Numbered, four-lined, formatted Sanskrit:

- Marcia & Michael Beloved (April 2008)

Devanagari script:

- Sanskrit 2003 Font

Transliteration:

- URW Palladio ITU font/ ITranslator

Word-for-Word typeset:

- Bernard Adjodha/Michael Beloved

Format assistant:

- Marcia K. Beloved

Cover Feature Art/Design:

- Michael Beloved

Shiva Art

- Sir Paul Castagna

Śrī Śrī Arjuna-Krishna Line Art, Universal Form Art, Śrī Śrī Krishna-Balarāma Art:

- Terri Stokes-Pineda

Adi Shankaracharya Art:

- Prafula Kharsani/Asian Printery

Illustrations of meditation focus:

- Michael Beloved/Sir Paul Castagna

Correspondence
Michael Beloved
3703 Foster Ave
Brooklyn NY 11203
USA

Paul Castagna
P.O.Box 150
Iron Belt WI 54536
USA

Email
axisnexus@gmail.com

ISBN
9781942887997
LCCN
2008907393

Bhagavad Gītā Explained

Bhagavad Gītā in Its Own Time and Place

श्रीभगवानुवाच
लोकेऽस्मिन्द्विविधा निष्ठा पुरा प्रोक्ता मयानघ ।
ज्ञानयोगेन सांख्यानां कर्मयोगेन योगिनाम् ॥ ३.३ ॥

śrībhagavānuvāca
loke'smindvividhā niṣṭhā purā proktā mayānagha
jñānayogena sāṁkhyānāṁ karmayogena yogināṁ (3.3)

The Blessed Lord said: In the physical world, a two-fold standard was previously taught by Me. O Arjuna, my good man. This was mind regulation by the yoga practice of the Sāṁkhya philosophical yogis and the action regulation by the yoga practice of the non-philosophical yogis. (3.3)

Scheme of Pronunciation

Consonants

Gutturals:	क	ख	ग	घ	ङ
	ka	kha	ga	gha	ṅa
Palatals:	च	छ	ज	झ	ञ
	ca	cha	ja	jha	ña
Cerebrals:	ट	ठ	ड	ढ	ण
	ṭa	ṭha	ḍa	ḍha	ṇa
Dentals:	त	थ	द	ध	न
	ta	tha	da	dha	na
Labials:	प	फ	ब	भ	म
	pa	pha	ba	bha	ma

Semivowels:

य	र	ल	व
ya	ra	la	va

Numbers:

०	१	२	३	४	५	६	७	८	९
0	1	2	3	4	5	6	7	8	9

Sibilants:	श	ष	स
	śa	ṣa	sa

Aspirate:	ह
	ha

Vowels:

अ	आ	इ	ई	उ	ऊ	ऋ	ॠ
a	ā	i	ī	u	ū	ṛ	ṝ
ए	औ	ओ	औ	ळ	ॡ	ं	ः
e	ai	o	au	lṛ	lṝ	ṁ	ḥ

Apostrophe ऽ

Table of Contents

Scheme of Pronunciation 4

How to use this book: 7

A note on the diacritical marks and pronounciation: 7

Introduction 8

*CHAPTER 1 Arjuna's Discouragement** 9

*CHAPTER 2 Divine State** 48

*CHAPTER 3 Cultural Activity and Renunciation** 112

*CHAPTER 4 Disciplines of Accomplishment** 148

*CHAPTER 5 Disciplined Use of Opportunities by aYogi ** 182

*CHAPTER 6 Yoga Practice** 206

*CHAPTER 7 Krishna: The Ultimate Reality** 258

*CHAPTER 8 Another Invisible Existence** 280

*CHAPTER 9 The Devotional Attitude** 302

*CHAPTER 10 A Fraction of Krishna's Splendor** 327

*CHAPTER 11 The Universal Form** 366

*CHAPTER 12 The Most Disciplined Yogi** 409

*CHAPTER 13 Material Nature The Person The Living Space** 423

*CHAPTER 14 The Extensive Mundane Reality** 445

*CHAPTER 15 Two Types of Spirits** 463

*CHAPTER 16 Two Types of Created Beings** 475

*CHAPTER 17 Three Types of Confidences** 492

*CHAPTER 18 The Most Secret of All Information** 507

Concluding Remarks 547

Indexed Names of Arjuna 548

Indexed Names of Krishna *549*

Names, Places and Things *552*

Index To Verses: Selected Sanskrit Words *553*

Index to Translation *561*

LIST OF TEACHERS *595*

About the Author *595*

Publications *596*

English Series 596

Meditation Series 598

Explained Series 599

Commentaries 600

Specialty 603

Online Resources *604*

How to use this book:

Make a casual reading of the entire text.

Make a second reading taking note of specific interests.

Make a third reading checking carefully for realisations and applications.

Finally, make an indepth study for integrating Bhagavad Gītā into your life.

A note on the diacritical marks and pronounciation:

Names like Krishna and Arjuna are accepted in common English usage. Their English spellings occur in the translation without diacritical marks.

There is a sanskrit lettering guide on page 4.

***Here are some hints** on how to use the diacritical marks for near-exact pronunciation:*

*Letters with a **dot** below them, should be pronounced while the tongue touches and is released curling slightly at the top of palate.*

*The s sound for ś carries an h with it and is said as the **sh** sound in **she.***

*The s sound for ṣ carries an h with it and is said as the **sh** sound in **shun.***

*The h sound for ḥ carries an echoing sound of the vowel before it, such that **oḥ** is actually **oho** and **aḥ** is actually **aha**.*

*In many Sanskrit words the **y** sound is said as an **i** sound, especially when the y sound preceeds an a. For instance, prāṇāyāma should be praa-**nai**-aa-muh, rather than praa-naa-**yaa**-muh.*

*The **a** sound is more like **uh** in English, while the **ā** sound is like the a sound in **far**.*

*The **ṛ** sound is like the **ri** sound in **ridge**.*

*The **ph** sound is never reduced to an f sound as in English. The **p sound** is maintained.*

*Whenever **h** occurs after a consonant, its integrity is maintained as an air forced sound.*

*If the h sound occurs after a vowel and a consonant, one should let the consonant remain with the vowel which preceeds it and allow the h sound to carry with the vowel after it, such that Duryodhana is pronounced with the d consonant allied to the o before it and the h sound manages the a after it.Say Dur-**yod-ha**-na or Dur-**yod-han**. Do not say Dur-yo-**dha**-na. Separate the d and h sounds to make them distinct. In words where you have no choice and must combine the d and h sound, as in the word dharma. Make sure that the **h sound** is heard as an **air sound pushed out from the throat**. Dharma should never be mistaken for darma. But adharma should be **ad-har-**ma.*

*The **c** sound is **ch,** and the **ch** sound is **ch-h**.*

Introduction

As a philosophical treatise and a religious canon, Bhagavad-Gītā stood the test of time. With the prevalence of literacy, many hundreds of published and unpublished translations and commentaries abound. People find solace in the philosophy of Gītā and existential security in the promises given by Sri Krishna. Gītā was abused and is still subjected to harassment by philosophers and preachers who find it necessary to use it to support their doctrines and claims.

This translation shows what Sri Krishna explained to Arjuna in terms of their cultural situation. At least in so far as the Mahābhārata described.

This translation stands apart from others by its lack of exploitation of the Gītā for missionary or for philosophical purposes. Once you begin reading this, you may be reluctant to put it down. This really can put you in touch with Lord Krishna and with Arjuna, the initially discouraged but later courageous and enlightened warrior.

Most of all, this volume opens the door to understanding the life style of persons who lived in the time of Śrī Krishna. With that clarification, you can methodically and consistently integrate the Gītā.

This is the ***Bhagavad Gītā in Its Own Time and Place,****and it puts you directly in touch with Krishna and Arjuna!*

Regarding the exhaustive Indexes:

All entries ***except*** *those for the Commentary give reference to verse numbers. The last Index which is to the Commentary is the only one which refers to page numbers.*

CHAPTER 1

Arjuna's Discouragement*

धृतराष्ट्र उवाच
धर्मक्षेत्रे कुरुक्षेत्रे
समवेता युयुत्सवः ।
मामकाः पाण्डवाश्चैव
किमकुर्वत संजय ॥ १.१ ॥
dhṛtarāṣṭra uvāca
dharmakṣetre kurukṣetre
samavetā yuyutsavaḥ
māmakāḥ pāṇḍavāścaiva
kimakurvata saṁjaya (1.1)

dhṛtarāṣṭra — Dhritarashtra; uvāca — said; dharmakṣetre — at the place for settling political affairs; kurukṣetre — at Kurukṣetra, a small plain in Punjab, India; samavetā — meeting together; yuyutsavaḥ — being possessed with battle spirit; māmakāḥ — my sons; pāṇḍavāś — the sons of Pāndu; caiva — and indeed; kim — what; akurvata — did so; saṁjaya — Sanjaya

Dhṛtarāṣṭra said: O Sanjaya, being possessed with battle spirit and meeting together, what did my sons and the sons of Pāndu do at Kurukṣetra, the place for settling political affairs? (1.1)

Commentary:

To understand this verse, we will have to go to the *Mahābhārata* to see the circumstances under which Sanjaya spoke the *Gītā* to King *Dhṛtarāṣṭra*. Here is a summary of that story:

> *As the armies assembled, King Dhṛtarāṣṭra consulted the great sage Vyāsaji, who offered him supernatural vision to view the battlefield. Dhṛtarāṣṭra declined to witness the horrors of the civil war and requested instead, to hear of the battle. Vyāsa then gave mystic insight to Sanjaya, who narrated the events to the blind king.*

Being blind, *Dhṛtarāṣṭra* was curious to know what took place at *Kurukṣetra*, the place where the armies faced each other. He could not see. He was reliant on some eye-witness account. He was a politician, but being blind, he had no intention of going to the battlefield. He was reliant on the police work of his sons and friends.

Dhṛtarāṣṭra also had a particular interest in Lord Krishna. He was pleased to know that Krishna was on the battlefield because he admired the Lord. He was always affected by the unique actions of this Divinity, Lord Krishna. From in his mind, *Dhṛtarāṣṭra* peered through his sense of hearing to get news of the warfield.

While reviewing this manuscript, Sriman Ramanand Prasad informed the writer that *Dhṛtarāṣṭra* declined the initial offer of *Śrīla Vyāsadeva* to grant vision of the battle at *Kurukṣetra*. It was not until Bhishma lay wounded on the tenth day of the battle, when Sanjaya returned with that news to King *Dhṛtarāṣṭra*, that the King's interest in the battle was stirred. He then requested Sanjaya to tell how Bhishma fell. And so in the Bhishma Parva of the *Mahābhārata*, the *Bhagavad-Gītā* was told by that disciple of *Vyāsaji*, named Sanjaya.

**The Mahābhārata contains no chapter headings. This title was assigned by the translator on the basis of verse 27 of this chapter.*

संजय उवाच
दृष्ट्वा तु पाण्डवानीकं
व्यूढं दुर्योधनस्तदा ।
आचार्यमुपसंगम्य
राजा वचनमब्रवीत् ॥ १.२ ॥
saṁjaya uvāca
dṛṣṭvā tu pāṇḍavānīkaṁ
vyūḍhaṁ duryodhanastadā
ācāryamupasaṁgamya
rājā vacanamabravīt (1.2)

saṁjaya uvāca — Sanjaya said; dṛṣṭvā — after observing; tu — indeed; pāṇḍavānīkaṁ — Pandava army; vyūḍhaṁ — which was set in battle formation; duryodhanas — Duryodhana, the eldest son of Dhrtarashtra, the crown prince of the Kurus; tadā — at that time; ācāryam — military teacher; upasaṁgamya — approaching; rājā — crown prince; vacanam — remark; abravīt — said

Sanjaya said: Indeed, after observing the Pandava army which was set in a battle formation, the Crown Prince Duryodhana, while approaching the Military Teacher, said this remark: (1.2)

Commentary:

Sanjaya did not reply freely but only as directed by King *Dhṛtarāṣṭra*. This was an urgent matter. Sanjaya could not speak his peace. He spoke as the King desired because he was merely a secretary. Later on in the *Gītā*, Sanjaya, after telling all that Lord Krishna explained, mustered up enough confidence to speak fearlessly. Then he said:

saṁjaya uvāca
ityahaṁ vāsudevasya pārthasya ca mahātmanaḥ
saṁvādamimamaśrauṣam adbhutaṁ romaharṣaṇam
vyāsaprasādācchrutavān etadguhyamahaṁ param
yogaṁ yogeśvarātkṛṣṇāt sākṣātkathayataḥ svayam
rājansaṁsmṛtya saṁsmṛtya saṁvādamimamadbhutam
keśavārjunayoḥ puṇyaṁ hṛṣyāmi ca muhurmuhuḥ
tacca saṁsmṛtya saṁsmṛtyarūpamatyadbhutaṁ hareḥ
vismayo me mahānrājan hṛṣyāmi ca punaḥ punaḥ
yatra yogeśvaraḥ kṛṣṇo yatra pārtho dhanurdharaḥ
tatra śrīrvijayo bhūtir dhruvā nītirmatirmama (18.74-78)

Sanjaya said: In this way, I heard this talk of the son of Vasudeva and the great-souled son of Pṛthā. It is amazing. It causes the hairs to stand on end.

By the grace of Vyasa, I am the one who heard this secret information of the supreme yoga from the Lord of yoga, Krishna, who Himself explained it directly.

O King, remembering repeatedly, this amazing and holy talk between Keśava and Arjuna, I rejoice again and again.

And remembering repeatedly that super-fantastic form of Hari, my astonishment is great, O King, and I excitedly rejoice again and again.

Wherever there exists the Lord of yoga, Krishna, wherever there is the son of Pṛthā, the bowman, there would surely be splendor, victory, prosperity and morality. This is my opinion. (18.74-78)

In the beginning, Sanjaya did not have the courage to speak to *Dhṛtarāṣṭra* like this. For one thing, the King might have ordered his arrest for being a sympathizer in supporting the enemy.

Knowing fully well the seriousness of the situation, and the King's fears, Sanjaya begins this reply by describing what transpired on the side of the King. He did not begin by describing the Pandavas, even though most of the *Gītā* concerns Arjuna's requests and questions to Lord Krishna.

It is of interest, however, to know that Prince Duryodhana made an assessment and became annoyed at the expert lay-out of the Pandava army. He went to his military instructor in a rage and voiced concerns.

Duryodhana, like many a ruler, took advice from military experts. During a battle, a ruler cannot afford to rely on his own judgment. He must consult men who specialize in armaments and battle formations. When Duryodhana viewed the strength of the enemy with displeasure, he went to *Droṇa*, the weapon-projectile instructor.

Duryodhana was excited. *Droṇa* was reserved and relaxed. After all, weapons were his specialty. He was not afraid of battle. To him, combat was a normality. *Droṇa* already knew what the Pandavas did. He trained them, and he knew their capabilities. The information that Duryodhana brought him was boring, to say the least. Still *Droṇa*, a seasoned general, listened as if he was concerned.

There was only one military senior of *Droṇa* on that battlefield. That was Bhishma, the oldest man on the scene. Both of them secretly regarded Duryodhana as a scatter-brain. As politicians, however, they did not disclose this to him.

पश्यैतां पाण्डुपुत्राणाम्
आचार्य महतीं चमूम् ।
व्यूढां द्रुपदपुत्रेण
तव शिष्येण धीमता ॥ १.३ ॥

paśyaitāṁ = paśya + etāṁ = see this; pāṇḍuputrāṇām — of the sons of Pāndu; ācārya — sir; mahatīm — great; camūm — army; vyūḍhāṁ — which is set for combat;

paśyaitāṁ pāṇḍuputrāṇām
ācārya mahatīṁ camūm
vyūḍhāṁ drupadaputreṇa
tava śiṣyeṇa dhīmatā (1.3)

drupada putreṇa — by the son of Drupada; tava — your; śiṣyeṇa — by a student; dhīmatā — by perception

Sir, see this great army of the sons of Pāndu, which is set for combat by your perceptive student, the son of Drupada. (1.3)

Commentary:

This is an insult to *Droṇācārya*. Essentially, Duryodhana informs *Droṇa* that a miscalculation was made when the son of *Drupada* was trained by the teacher. As far as Duryodhana was concerned, *Droṇa* should have known better than to teach the son of an enemy. In human dealings, it is a folly to instruct the son of a competitor. Duryodhana insulted *Droṇa* by diplomatically informing him of his failure to understand that whatever training he would give an enemy could be used against him in the future.

If we were to cut out the diplomacy, Duryodhana said:

Look here, Droṇa! Look here, teacher! You are expert at military techniques but where is your foresight? How is it that you willingly trained the son of an enemy? Drupada is your rival, and still you taught his son Dhṛṣṭadyumna. Now just see! This boy acts as an army engineer for the Pāṇḍavas. They married his sister, Princess Draupadī. What should I do? I have no choice but to rely on you. I ask that you be cautious in selection of students in the future. You imperiled us by teaching these Pāṇḍavas and their friends the military techniques. In any case, I am hopeful that you are still their military superior. I rely on your direction for victory.

अत्र शूरा महेष्वासा
भीमार्जुनसमा युधि ।
युयुधानो विराटश्च
द्रुपदश्च महारथः ॥१.४॥
atra śūrā maheṣvāsā
bhīmārjunasamā yudhi
yuyudhāno virāṭaśca
drupadaśca mahārathaḥ (1.4)

atra — here; śūrā — heroes; maheṣvāsā — great bow men; bhīmārjunasamā — equal to Bhima and Arjuna; yudhi — in battle; yuyudhāno — Yuyudhana; virāṭaś — Virata; ca — and; drupadaś — Drupada; ca — and; mahārathaḥ — the great chariot fighter

Here are heroes, great bowmen, who are equal in battle to Bhima and Arjuna. There is Yuyudhāna, Virāṭa, and Drupada, the great chariot fighter. (1.4)

Commentary:

Duryodhana does not want *Droṇa* to underestimate the power of the Pandavas. He explains that the Pandava forces are equal to his in battle prowess. Citing *Yuyudhāna*, *Virāṭa*, and *Drupada* he alerts the teacher that there are seasoned fighters on the side of the Pandavas. Of course *Droṇa* knew this; but Duryodhana wanted to be sure that his teacher took it seriously

Yuyudhāna is also known as *Sātyaki*, *Dāruka* and Saineya. He functioned as Krishna's charioteer under the usual name of *Dāruka*. He was a *Yadava* by family clan. He happened to be one of the generals in the Pandava army and he killed many Kaurava warriors. It so happened that once he was intimidated by *Bhūriśravā*, a commander for Duryodhana. When he was tired at the end of the day's fight, *Bhūriśravā* managed to throw him down. After doing this, *Bhūriśravā* intended to decapitate *Sātyaki's* body, but Lord Krishna alerted Arjuna. If *Sātyaki's* body was killed, the Pandavas would have been implicated since he fought on their behalf. Arjuna could understood the implications. With lightning speed, he released an arrow that cut off *Bhūriśravā*'s hand. When *Bhūriśravā* reacted by assuming a yoga posture to commit suicide, *Sātyaki* killed him.

Sātyaki is not an ordinary entity. He is an eternal associate of Lord Krishna. As such, his activities have the transcendental touch. He came to this planet as part of Krishna's divine team of actors. He was above any material taint but as it is in this world, even the divine beings commit errors.

Virāṭa was a territorial ruler. He was a very pious, peace-loving person, but he relied heavily on his brother Kichaka, who was an evil, vice-prone, strong-armed man. This Kichaka had a bad habit of taking the wives of others. When he set eye on *Draupadī*, *Bhīma* killed him. It so happened however, that after the death of Kichaka, the Kauravas and Trigartas attacked King *Virāṭa*. It was a plan to intimidate him, to bring him to his knees politically and economically. Susharma intended to subdue him in battle and the Kauravas intended to destroy his economy which stood on a thriving cattle industry.

It went to their bad luck, however. At the time, the five Pandavas were taking shelter at Upaplavya, the capital city of *Virāṭa*, and they assisted the King. Arjuna in particular crushed the pride of the Kauravas by appearing suddenly, and singlehandedly chasing them away from the cattle pastures.

Virāṭa was one of seven commanders in the Pandava army. He was killed by *Droṇa*. *Virāṭa* was a good general but he was no match for *Droṇa* who was a military genius. In the days of the *Mahābhārata*, one who stood in battle before a general like *Droṇa* was, in a way, venturing to the hereafter.

It is said that Bhishma and *Droṇa* were part of the Universal Form of the Supreme Lord, as faces of that supervisory power. Thus, even though they fought on the side that opposed the Pandavas, they were superhuman. They had to be respected by others. When he faced *Droṇa* in battle, *Virāṭa* was doomed.

So long as *Droṇa* acted as a kind teacher to the warriors, they liked him. Everyone respected him always. Whenever he took up his weapons for combat, many warriors scattered out of the way. He was that type of professional warrior.

Drupada was the king of Panchala. He was the father of *Draupadī*, the wife of the Pandavas. *Drupada*'s sons were *Dhṛṣṭadyumna* and *Śikhandī*. It is of interest that *Drupada*'s children indirectly caused the downfall of the Kauravas. *Draupadī* issued a powerful curse on the head of the Kuru leaders. This she did secretly, releasing her potency upon them. A man like Bhishma, who is a superhuman character, cannot be cut down by the curse of an ordinary woman. We have to conclude that *Draupadī* is one of the demigoddesses. It is explained in the *Mahābhārata*, that after leaving her earthly body, she was seen in the heavenly world as a source of good fortune.

King *Drupada* grew up as a friend of *Droṇa*. As boyhood friends both of them studied at the gurukula of the sage Agnivesha. *Drupada* promised to share his ancestral kingdom with *Droṇa*. But later on, he realized that this was a promise made in ignorance.

Droṇa, however, took the promise seriously. When *Droṇa* came to ask *Drupada* for half of the kingdom, *Drupada* said that they were not friends. "How," he asked the begging *Droṇa*, "could a king like me be friends with a pauper like you?" Noting the snobbish, intimidating attitude of *Drupada*, *Droṇa* decided to humble him in the future. Later on, after *Droṇa* instructed the Kauravas and Pandavas, he requested that for their educational fees, they should conquer *Drupada*. This they did and *Droṇa* then took the southern half of

Drupada's kingdom and allowed *Drupada* to govern the northern portion. For this, a deep feeling of resentment developed in *Drupada*. This king conducted a mystic ceremony to get a son who would kill *Droṇa*. That son was born as *Dhṛṣṭadyumna*. As fate would have it, he also had a son named *Śikhandī* who was dual sexed, being male, part of the time, and female, part of the time. Bhishma was mortally wounded during an offensive led by *Śikhandī*.

King *Drupada* brought down the house of the Kauravas through his three children, Princess *Draupadī*, Prince *Dhṛṣṭadyumna*, and the Prince-Princess *Śikhandī*. Might is not everything. A gentleman like *Drupada* wrought havoc for big generals like Bhishma and *Droṇa*.

Dhṛtarāṣṭra was identified as the eldest son of Vichitravirya but it so happened that he was born blind. His actual father was *Śrīla Vyāsadeva* but he was begotten by *Vyāsadeva* through a queen of *Vichitravirya*. This King died at an early age. *Vyāsaji* was *Vichitravirya's* half-brother. *Dhṛtarāṣṭra* bore a grudge against destiny for being the eldest son and simultaneously having a blind body. As such, he was a very discontent man. He felt some hope, however, after his wife Gandhari bore one hundred sons. He felt relieved and tried to use his sons to offset the incapacity.

Dhṛtarāṣṭra was, overall, a kind man but he had a serious defect in that he tried to undermine the Pandavas. As life would have it, *Dhṛtarāṣṭra* was disqualified from ascending the throne. His brother Pandu took it, but Pandu was also checked by providence. He lost his body at an early age. Subsequently, *Dhṛtarāṣṭra* took charge of the kingdom. By the time Pandu's sons grew up, *Dhṛtarāṣṭra* was accustomed to the ruling power. He had no intention of yielding to the Pandavas. That was his mistake. As a result his sons got involved in the war at *Kurukṣetra*, and lost the battle. It was a civil war which could have been avoided if *Dhṛtarāṣṭra* was detached from his sons.

The first name mentioned in the *Bhagavad Gītā* is *Dhṛtarāṣṭra*. He was the one to ask Sanjaya for an eye-witness account. Being empowered by *Śrīla Vyāsaji*, the actual father of *Dhṛtarāṣṭra*, Sanjaya reviewed all events that transpired on the battlefield. Sanjaya was a secretary of the King. In modern terms we may say that he was a Secretary of State. He was a very reasonable man, but he failed at his attempt to impress sense on the King. Though his advice was appreciated by *Dhṛtarāṣṭra*, the heavy-headed King did not apply it. Sanjaya got a good chance to study the nature of politicians. He felt that they were incapable of long-range vision, being too determined for conquest and too rash in reacting to political frustrations. In any case, he did his service to *Śrīla Vyāsadeva* by being on hand as counselor, secretary and friend of the King. Sanjaya realized the divinity of both Krishna and Arjuna and he considered them to be worshippable deities.

Duryodhana was the eldest son of *Dhṛtarāṣṭra* and for all practical purposes, his policies prevailed; his father was reliant on him. Duryodhana was enterprising, but he was a conniving person.

The *Mahābhārata* history is the story of the rivalry between the sons of *Dhṛtarāṣṭra* and those of Pandu. It was a civil conflict. Duryodhana stars in this charade as the villain; Yudhishthira as the pious hero.

The Pandavas were five in number: Yudhishthira, *Bhīma*, Arjuna, Nakula and Sahadeva. The three elders were sons of *Kuntī* and the juniors were sons of *Mādrī*. Both *Kuntī* and *Mādrī* were wives of King Pandu. In his own time, Yudhishthira was the most pious man. In fact, his piety rivals that of Lord Krishna and in some circumstances his purity of intent put to question even the motives of the Lord. He was free of vindictiveness. He was so tolerant that his brothers, particularly *Bhīma*, became irritated with him, when he would not retaliate for wrong-doings. It is seen however, that even as pious an individual as Yudhishthira is provoked in the material world. Even he was egged on and pushed around by circumstances. Eventually, he was compelled to fight for his rights. He was imperiled once in the Battle of *Kurukṣetra* when *Droṇa* planned to kidnap him. Arjuna's son, Abhimanyu, took an action to thwart *Droṇa*. Even though the action was successful, Abhimanyu was killed. The plan worked however, and Yudhishthira was spared from capture by the enemy.

Some people feel that Yudhishthira was a simple-minded devotee, one without complications. This view is false. Yudhishthira was one of the most sophisticated thinkers of his time. He knew mystic formulas and mystic bodily disciplines of yoga, but he was so humble that hardly anyone realized how much of a mystic he was. He hid his expertise and gave people the impression that he was just an ordinary person. He kept his charisma under tight control and did not exhibit himself whimsical.

Yudhishthira was a last-resort man. In a crisis he tried every kind method until at last he would allow his brothers to take disciplinary action. As soon as he got a result he would order them to ease up immediately. He was an ideal ruler. He acted as though he was righteousness personified.

At the end of the war, Lord Krishna advised Yudhishthira to flush Duryodhana out of a lake. Duryodhana mastered some breath restraint techniques. He used these to make his gross body enter a trance under water. King Yudhishthira made a deal with Duryodhana for a fair fight with *Bhīma*. Lord Krishna did not like this idea. He alerted Arjuna that Yudhishthira was too compassionate. Krishna said:

> ***Just see, Arjuna! Your elder brother indulged in a reckless gamble by making this offer to Duryodhana. Suppose Bhīma loses What will happen? It will mean that Duryodhana will again be king. And we may lose what we fought for.***

Despite this feeling, the Supreme Being, Lord Krishna, empowered *Bhīma*. He advised *Bhīma* to disable Duryodhana. Then Yudhishthira became the legitimate ruler of the Kuru country. In the material world, everything is complicated because of the intertwining of past lives. Even a person as great and as saintly as Yudhishthira may be, in some instances, displeasing to the Supreme Lord. We should look to Krishna for advice in every activity. We can never become so perfect that we stop making mistakes. If Yudhishthira was imperfect in some way or another, then we are imperfect to a much greater degree. The only way to compensate for this is to take the advice of the Lord.

Bhīma Pandava was the second son of *Kuntī*. He was a strong-man reputed to have the strength of 10,000 elephants. He was known as Vayuputra, the son of the wind, and as Vrikodara, the man with a wolf's belly. In certain situations, he appeared to be crude. Usually he adhered to the instructions of his elder brother. At one time, when Yudhishthira gambled away his country, personal property, his brothers and himself, *Bhīma* concluded that Yudhishthira was mad. He seriously thought of abandoning his brother. He was calmed by Arjuna.

Bhīma was known to be dangerous on the battlefield. He was much feared by enemy warriors because he fought with any weapon within reach. If there were no weapons, he smashed opponents with bare hands. He killed Kichaka, a famous strong man.

Once Duryodhana showed his thighs to *Draupadī*. He did this to intimidate her since Yudhishthira staked her and lost in a gambling match. Taking affront to this, *Bhīma* swore to break the thighs of Duryodhana. *Bhīma* completed this vow when, after the Battle of *Kurukṣetra*, he broke Duryodhana's thighs in a club fight. Lord Balarama was annoyed at *Bhīma* for doing this. He wanted to discipline *Bhīma*, but Lord Krishna appealed to Balarama to overlook it. Krishna explained that the vicious action of *Bhīma* was offset by Duryodhana's offense to *Draupadī*.

There are many lessons in the *Mahābhārata* literature but an interested reader would need to read the text with proper guidance to form the right conclusions. *Nārada* was not fond of the *Mahābhārata*. He asked *Śrīla Vyāsadeva* to write something better in the form of the *Śrīmad Bhāgavatam*. The problem with the *Mahābhārata* is its stress on human cultural affairs. While the *Śrīmad Bhāgavatam* brings forward the relation between the human being and God, the *Mahābhārata* stresses relations amongst human beings. Still there are great lessons for moral clarification in the *Mahābhārata*.

Droṇa was the son of the sage Bharadvaja. *Droṇa* was born from the semen of the sage but the embryo body did not develop in a woman's womb. The sage once saw a heavenly beauty named Ghritachi. His semen was emitted. He collected it and allowed it to develop in a container.

Droṇa was fortunate to have received from Lord *Paraśurāma* the complete knowledge of weaponry. In those days, one learned skills from a particular teacher as there were no schools like the universities we have today. In addition, the teacher taught the fundamentals. If one completed the training and took up the practice, one could complete the education in the teacher's absence. *Droṇa* was the best military expert of his time; only Bhishma rivaled him. In any case, after he perfected the military skill, *Droṇa* visited the city of the Kurus. Bhishma noted him and immediately hired him as the teacher of the military academy which formed there.

Droṇa's big mistake was to take the kingdom of King *Virāṭa*. He took that kingdom, divided it into two parts, and gave himself one part and *Virāṭa* the other. This was offensive. From this, his death was arranged.

Lord Krishna played a trick on *Droṇa* by having Yudhishthira confirm that *Aśvatthāmā* was dead. *Droṇa* was very attached to his son *Aśvatthāmā*. When he heard this news, he resolved to kill his body by yoga disciplines. He was so expert in *prāṇāyāma* that he could kill his body by breath control if he so desired. After hearing from the reputed, saintly, truth-telling Yudhishthira, that *Aśvatthāmā* was dead, *Droṇa* sat down to do yoga for departure from this world. He was killed on the spot by the son of King *Drupada*. Actually, the elephant by the name of *Aśvatthāmā* was dead. Therefore *Droṇa* was tricked by Lord Krishna. Subsequently, some people have doubts about Krishna's credibility. We must understand, however, that the Lord is the Equalizer. If we trick others, we may be tricked by Him in turn. It is simply the law of compensation.

The two big generals at *Kurukṣetra* were Bhishma and *Droṇa*. These two were not ordinary entities. They were empowered. They were superior souls. Later on, when Lord Krishna considered how to conclude His earthly manifestation, He admitted that he got a great deal of help from Dṛona and Bhishma. We can know for sure that these two entities were part of the supernatural power expressed by Lord Krishna in the Universal Form seen by Arjuna. But in that form, these great souls were also being chastised by the Lord. The wonder of it: In one instance they acted as agents of the Lord and in the other, they were chastised by Him.

Arjuna Pandava is just as famous as Lord Krishna. This is due to the *Bhagavad-Gītā* discourse which transpired between the two. Arjuna was also known as Krishna because of his blackish hair. Arjuna and Lord Krishna used to be together as buddies. At *Kurukṣetra*, Arjuna became respectful in his relationship with the Lord. He accepted Lord Krishna as his spiritual master for all time. There were other authorities in Arjuna's life, but at *Kurukṣetra*, Arjuna disregarded them and heard only Krishna. As the Lord told him:

yadā te mohakalilaṁ buddhirvyatitariṣyati
tadā gantāsi nirvedaṁ śrotavyasya śrutasya ca (2.52)

When from your delusion-saturated mind, your discrimination departs, you will become disgusted with what is to be heard and what was heard. (2.52)

Arjuna was a mystic yogi. He was so expert in the kriyā techniques that he could consciously separate himself from the gross body and travel to the heavenly planets and fight demoniac magicians there. Arjuna was not ordinary. His austerities in *haṭha* yoga were so complete that he attracted Lord Shiva who challenged him in the Himalayas.

As far as combat was concerned, Arjuna was a marksman. He was considered a capable lawman. He was highly respected by the people of his time. Arjuna was attractive to women. Many girls wanted to marry him. He had more than one wife. His favorites were Subhadra, the sister of Lord Krishna, and *Draupadī*, the daughter of King *Drupada*.

As destiny would have it, Arjuna was so irresistibly drawn to Subhadra that he kidnapped her. Lord Balarama was enraged at the audacity of Arjuna. He promised to catch Arjuna and give him a good licking, but Lord Krishna spoke to Lord Balarama and explained that Arjuna was, in fact, the most treasured sweetheart of Subhadra.

From time to time, Arjuna forgot the *Bhagavad Gītā* discourse. In the end, after Lord Krishna's departure from this planet, Arjuna recalled the lecture of the *Gītā*.

deśā-kālārtha-yuktāni hṛt-tāpopaśamāni ca
haranti smarataś cittaṁ govindābhitāni me

As I remember all that Govinda said to me, which was so relevant to the time, place and circumstances, and so effective in relieving the pangs of grief, my heart is overwhelmed. (Śrīmad Bhāgavatam. 1.15.27)

Thus he retrieved himself transcendentally and was shifted into the association of the Supreme Lord. He is an eternal associate of Krishna, so there is never any question that he would remain bound in any material world.

Nakula was the fourth of the Pandavas, as the son of *Mādrī* and King Pandu. He was the most handsome of the lot. In the end, he was criticized by Yudhishthira for some slight vanity regarding his beauty. It is said that he used to cover his face from time to time to prevent women from falling in love with him. He was an expert swordsman and horseman. Shishupala was an enemy of Lord Krishna. But after the *Kurukṣetra* war, Nakula married the daughter of Shishupala and formed an alliance with Shishupala's clan. By that time, Shishupala had passed on.

Sahadeva was the twin of Nakula. He was expert in relating the law of social actions and reactions. Thus King Yudhishthira used to consult with him. Like the other brothers, he was heroic. At *Kurukṣetra*, he fought valiantly.

धृष्टकेतुश्चेकितानः
काशिराजश्च वीर्यवान् ।
पुरुजित्कुन्तिभोजश्च
शैब्यश्च नरपुंगवः ॥१.५॥
dhṛṣṭaketuścekitānaḥ
kāśirājaśca vīryavān
purujitkuntibhojaśca
śaibyaśca narapuṁgavaḥ (1.5)

dhṛṣṭaketuś — Dhṛṣṭaketu; cekitānaḥ — Cekitāna; kāśirājaś — the king of Kāśi; ca — and; vīryavān — valiant man; purujit — Purujit; kuntibhojaś — Kuntibhoja; ca — and; śaibyaś — Śaibya; ca — and; narapuṅgavaḥ — bull among men

There is Dhṛṣṭaketu, Cekitāna, and the Kāśi ruler, that valiant man. There is Purujit and Kuntibhoja and Śaibya, the bull-bodied man. (1.5)

Commentary:

Droṇacharya, the military teacher, the munitions expert and ultimate planner of the battle formations, realized these factors by direct insight. This military teacher performed austerities in his youth. His mystic senses were active. Everything Duryodhana said was stale news. In addition. *Droṇa* had trusted spies who reported on political conditions in the adjacent provinces.

Bhishma also had this ability to know what took place in other locations. He used direct mystic observation and spies. We can just imagine the insight of those men. When a woman by the name of Ambā became angry with Bhishma , and wanted to kill him or engage an assassin for the task, Bhishma had some of his ascetic friends spy on her. At that time the woman successfully petitioned Lord Shiva. Failing to find some person to discipline Bhishma to her satisfaction, she asked Shiva for a male body and for the power to deal with Bhishma in her own way. She got Shiva's assurance about a male body. Then she practiced more yoga austerities and *prāṇāyāma* disciplines. She then gave up her old body and moved on to the subtle world. Bhishma was such a careful man, so calculating and cautious, that he spied on her even in the astral world. He knew exactly when and where she would pick up such a male form. When she appeared again in this world as the daughter-son, transvestite child of King *Drupada* named *Śikhandī*, Bhishma recognized her. Later on when asked by Duryodhana why he was so insistent on not killing a female or a warrior whose body was female at one time or another, he explained how he tracked the transmigration of Ambā.

Duryodhana gave this information to insult the teacher. He wanted to motivate aggressiveness in *Droṇa*. A man like *Droṇa* is not fearful of warfare. Therefore Duryodhana was concerned that his teacher should give up the cool-headed attitude of seasoned warriors. Duryodhana knew well that unless one is irritated sufficiently one cannot kill on a wholesale basis. And this is what he desired. He wanted to wipe out the Pandavas, their allies and all, hoping that after their departure from this world, he would live in peace with the family clan.

At the time of Duryodhana's speech, Droṇacharya considered the irony of life, how he grew up, how he mastered the yoga process and military skill, and how his life evolved. The whole flow of his life was being halted by providence. It appeared to him that even for a great person like himself, a genius of sorts, life was an enigma, a great puzzle to be solved, something odd, something that one never has completely under control, something variant to one's preference. In the background of his mind, there were thoughts of Lord Krishna, Who to him was like a grinding machine, checking and putting every living being through a test. *Droṇa* also remembered his rash action of seizing half of the kingdom of *Drupada*. *Droṇa*'s father was a poor brahmin sage, but the old man was content with his lot. In contrast, *Droṇa* was not satisfied being poor. To get money and property, he criminally attacked King *Drupada* and the Panchala people. As *Droṇa* considered his destiny, Duryodhana brooded on the outcome of the war. He wanted a quick and easy victory.

Droṇa made the mistake of taking half of the kingdom of *Drupada*. He did this because he was young and reactionary at the time. By that act, *Droṇa* caused an energy of resentment to be released. That negative force was used by King *Drupada* to create a son who could kill the body of *Droṇa*. If we commit a wrongdoing, there is a compensatory energy released. This energy is used to form our future destiny. It so happened that ancient brahmins knew how to catch or collect such energy. If the energy could not be acquired easily, the brahmin priests would catch it in the psychic atmosphere, carefully handle it to avoid personal contamination, and use it for their clients in sacrificial ceremonies. If on the other hand, the energy could be collected easily, they would, by special mystic catch-phrases, accumulate it rapidly in mystic containers, and then hurl it to satisfy their clients' needs.

The brahmins who worked for King *Drupada* caught the reactionary energy of *Droṇa*, and offered it to *Dhṛṣṭadyumna* as the means of killing *Droṇa*. *Dhṛṣṭaketu* was the son of this *Dhṛṣṭadyumna*. Duryodhana mentioned these military chiefs to antagonize *Droṇa*. Chekitana was the grandson of *Dhṛṣṭadyumna* and the son of *Dhṛṣṭaketu*. He was king of the Kekayas. Duryodhana mentions his name to irk *Droṇa* into action against the family of King *Drupada*, from whom *Droṇa* had seized half a kingdom. *Kāśirāja*, the King of Kashi, was a powerful ruler. Once Bhishma kidnapped the three daughters of a king of this city and got away with it but the girls were dissatisfied with Bhishma. The King of Kāśi fought for the Pandavas during the war. By mentioning the name of this king, Duryodhana further alerted *Droṇa* that there was great danger since some allies of the Pandavas were people with grievances against either *Droṇa*, Bhishma, the Kuru family, or one of its allies. Purujit is an uncle of the Pandavas, being the brother of their mother *Kuntī*. He was killed by *Droṇa* on the battlefield. Purujit was a devotee of the Lord, but nevertheless his body was killed by *Droṇa*, who was another, more powerful devotee. Kuntibhoja was the foster father of *Kuntī*, whose father was Shura, the King of the Shurasenas, a devotional people. But there was an agreement between Shura and *Kuntī* such that Kuntibhoja died at *Kurukṣetra* in the Kuru civil war. Much detail is not given on the life of Shaibya, the king of the Shibis, but in the Udyoga Parva, 59.161.5, it is said that when General *Dhṛṣṭadyumna* arranged the Pandava battalions, he assigned Shaibya to deal with Kritavarma who fought for Duryodhana.

युधामन्युश्च विक्रान्त
उत्तमौजाश्च वीर्यवान् ।
सौभद्रो द्रौपदेयाश्च
सर्व एव महारथाः ॥ १.६ ॥
yudhāmanyuśca vikrānta
uttamaujāśca vīryavān
saubhadro draupadeyāśca
sarva eva mahārathāḥ (1.6)

yudhāmanyuś — Yudhāmanyu; ca — and; vikrānta — valiant; uttamaujāś — Uttamauja; ca — and; vīryavān — heroic; saubhadro — the son of Subhadra; drāupadeyāś — the sons of Draupadī; ca — and; sarve — all; eva — indeed; mahārathāḥ — champions of chariot warfare

There is the valiant Yudhāmanyu and the heroic Uttamauja. There are the son of Subhadra and the sons of Draupadī, who indeed, are all champions of chariot warfare. (1.6)

Commentary:

Duryodhana had some admiration for the allies of the Pandavas. He dropped his resentment and commented on those whom he admired. Some of these had cordial relationships with him. Some, like the sons of Subhadra and the sons of *Draupadī*, were nephews, of whom he was fond. Still, he could not afford to stop the war merely for these affections which to him, amounted to routine concern for others. He had to press on for victory, to secure the kingdom from the ravages of a family quarrel. It was here at *Kurukṣetra* that he planned to make one last show of superiority over the Pandavas.

Yudhāmanyu and *Uttamauja* are both Panchala chieftains who were killed by *Droṇa* on the battlefield after the *Gītā* was spoken. It is interesting that Duryodhana alerted *Droṇa* to the battle attitude of these men whom *Droṇa* would kill later on the war field.

The son of Subhadra and Arjuna was the famous Abhimanyu, who did something heroic on the battlefield. But soon after, due to inexperience as a warrior, he was cut down by the Kauravas. His death greatly pained his father. Subsequently, by the grace of Lord Krishna, Jayadratha was killed by Arjuna. Abhimanyu imperiled himself by entering the ranks of the Kauravas but he did this and martyred himself to save King Yudhishthira from being captured by Droṇacharya.

The glorious sons of *Draupadī* were Prativindhya, Sutasoma, Shrutakirti, Shatanika and Shrutakarma. They were called the sons of *Draupadī* since each of them was sired by a Pandava in turn. These sons of *Draupadī* fought heroically but they were killed by *Aśvatthāmā* later.

As it is in the material world, there is *tit for tat*, or a licking for an offense, one insult for another, one intimidation for an aggravation. Hardly a man will let any matter rest. Most actions are reactions which should conclude something from the past, but we misunderstand life and interpret every action as fresh assault. This is how we create ongoing complications. This is called *samsāra*, or the dreary, intertwining course of haphazard births and deaths.

अस्माकं तु विशिष्टा ये
तान्निबोध द्विजोत्तम ।
नायका मम सैन्यस्य
संज्ञार्थं तान्ब्रवीमि ते ॥१.७॥

asmākaṁ tu viśiṣṭā ye
tānnibodha dvijottama
nāyakā mama sainyasya
saṁjñārthaṁ tānbravīmi te (1.7)

asmākaṁ — our men; tu — but; viśiṣṭā — distinguished; ye — who; tān — them; nibodha — be informed; dvijottama — O best of the initiates; nāyakā — commanders; mama — of my; sainyasya — of the army; saṁjñārthaṁ — for the sake of giving information; tān — them; bravīmi — I mention; te — to you

But, O best of the initiates, be informed of our men who are distinguished. For the sake of giving information to you, I mention the leaders of my army. (1.7)

Commentary:

The *Gītā* tells us that Arjuna became horribly depressed seeing many friends and relatives on the warfield. Duryodhana made similar observations before the battle and having outgrown his boyish nature. Duryodhana did not buckle under with crippling emotions. Instead he panicked, hurried to his military teacher, and reported the matter. Beginning in this verse, Duryodhana slowly regained confidence.

Considering his army, he assessed that he had warriors who were just as heroic as the Pandavas. He felt he had nothing to fear. There was only one odd personality as far as Duryodhana was concerned. That person was Krishna. Duryodhana had no one on his side to match Lord Krishna. But all the same he took steps to counterbalance that disadvantage by remembering that Lord Krishna promised not to fight on the warfield. Lord Krishna said that He would only give advice. Duryodhana remembered that and took pleasure in that fact. He failed to realize that when the advice of Krishna is used efficiently, it makes even an ordinary man seem just as powerful as the Divinity.

It is interesting that even in the days of the *Mahābhārata* conflict, a Commander-in-Chief like Duryodhana made a roll call to his Chief of Military Staff, *Droṇa*. This procedure is followed today even in Western countries. Even today, the Commander-in-Chief or the President of the country must consult with the Chief-of-Staff of military officers. Tactical decisions are made by the Chief-of-Staff.

भवान्भीष्मश्च कर्णश्च
कृपश्च समितिंजयः ।
अश्वत्थामा विकर्णश्च
सौमदत्तिस्तथैव च ॥ १.८॥

bhavānbhīṣmaśca karṇaśca
kṛpaśca samitiṁjayaḥ
aśvatthāmā vikarṇaśca
saumadattistathaiva ca (1.8)

bhavān — your qualified self; bhīṣmaś — Bhishma; ca — and; karṇaśca — Karṇa; kṛpaś — Kṛpa; ca — and; samitiṁjayaḥ — victorious in battle; aśvatthāmā — Aśvatthāmā; vikarṇaś — Vikarṇa; ca — and; saumadattis — the son of Somadatta; tathaiva — as well; ca — and

There is your qualified self, and Bhishma, Karṇa and Kṛpa who are victorious in battle. There is also Aśvatthāmā, Vikarṇa and the son of Somadatta. (1.8)

Commentary:

As a matter of respect and with great feeling for his teacher, being confident that *Droṇa* was capable of wiping out the Pandavas forces, Duryodhana mentioned his teacher first, addressing the teacher as *bhavān*: Respected Sir, Your Lordship. Droṇacharya was, in fact, a person whose military expertise was not excelled by any other limited person who resided on this planet at the time This was due to practice. The theory of military conquest was known to others but *Droṇa* took the practice of it the furthest. The address of *bhavān*, Your Lordship, is no flattery

Bhishma was regarded as the grandsire of the Kuru family even though he never married nor had children. Being a vowed celibate and being a yogi as well, he maintained resistance to sexual desires and only touched four women in his life, namely his mother, Gangā, and three princesses whom he abducted, known as *Ambā*, *Ambalikā*, and *Ambikā*. These three girls were kidnapped by him for his less heroic half-brother, Vichitravirya. Bhishma, though celibate, was not resistant to political affairs. And this was perhaps his downfall. Resistance to sexual desire is good but if it is not done efficiently, it surfaces in another way as uncontrollable political or paternal desire.

Bhishma and *Droṇa* were the most powerful people of their time. Except for Lord Krishna and Lord Balarama, Who were divine people, not of limited scope, there were hardly any people on the planet who could successfully challenge Bhishma or *Droṇa*. These were very dangerous people from the military viewpoint. Duryodhana is aware of this, thus he anticipated victory. Lord Balarama simply refused to fight at *Kurukṣetra* and that matter was closed. Lord Krishna only agreed to be there as the advisor of Arjuna. To advise Arjuna, Krishna acted as Arjuna's charioteer. Duryodhana was a little worried about the outcome. He was not sure what Krishna's presence on Arjuna's chariot would mean. But he estimated that since Krishna was not fighting, mere advice would do little to bring about a Pandava victory.

Karṇa was a rival and half-brother of Arjuna. *Karṇa* was the first son of *Kuntī*. As it is in this world, moral principles regarding sexual intercourse may overshadow the birth of a child who is born to an unwedded mother. To avoid social disgrace, *Kuntī* put her first son in a container and allowed his infant form to float down a river. He was rescued by a chariot driver and raised by the man's wife, a woman named Rādhā. As in these circumstances, the rejected child usually finds his body's mother and challenges her rejection of him. This happened between *Kuntī* and *Karṇa*, except that *Kuntī* was the one to find *Karṇa* just before the Battle of *Kurukṣetra*. *Kuntī* tried to convince *Karṇa* that it was irregular to fight for Duryodhana. She explained that in actuality the Pandavas were his brothers. But *Karṇa*, though admitting that *Kuntī* was his body's mother, remained faithful to Duryodhana.

Duryodhana did a great favor to *Karṇa* by making him the ruler of a small country named *Aṅga*. This saved *Karṇa*'s pride, so he was appreciative. He could not bring himself to betray Duryodhana. For him, sticking to this principle was a moral accomplishment. On the other hand, *Karṇa* was greatly contaminated by envy of the Pandavas, especially of the fame, manly-attractiveness, and recognized princely birth of Arjuna.

Theoretically, *Karṇa* recognized Lord Krishna as the Supreme Person, but he did not allow that recognition to jolt his loyalty to the Kauravas. That was his mistake. Droṇacharya did not like *Karṇa* because *Karṇa* had cheated his guru, by taking knowledge from *Paraśurāma* under false pretense, assuming a student role in the disguise of a gentle-natured, perceptive, brahmin boy. *Karṇa* was discovered and cursed by *Paraśurāma*. The curse stipulated that an important weapons-invoking procedure would be forgotten at a crucial moment on a battlefield.

By stroke of luck, *Karṇa* pleased the celestial King Indra, who gave him a javelin which was just as dangerous as the weapon-projectile technique deprived of him by *Paraśurāma*. Later, Lord Krishna caused *Bhīma*'s son, Ghatotkacha, to absorb that weapon. It killed the body of Ghatotkacha and he attained the heavenly world for sacrificing his form in that way. Overall, *Karṇa* was Arjuna's competitor and when there was a martial arts display, *Karṇa* duplicated all of Arjuna's feats and performed some other wonders, all to the dismay of the Pandavas. *Karṇa* was empowered by the sun god, but somehow or other he reacted to his mother's rejection of his infant body. Thus his life went off course as he maintained resentment against destiny. At the end, he was killed by Arjuna, shot through on the battlefield as if a common warrior.

Kṛpa is also called *Kṛpācārya* because he was a military instructor of both the Pandavas and the Kauravas. In any case, he was one of the few to survive the war. He helped *Aśvatthāmā* to kill the sons of *Draupadī* and some others who were sleeping after their victory over the Kauravas. This was a controversial matter because later on, *Kṛpācārya* acted as an advisor to Parikshit, the grandson of Arjuna. *Kṛpa* and *Kṛpi*, his twin sister, were children of the sage and sound expert, Sharadvata, who abandoned them. They were brought up by King *Śantanu*, Bhishma's father. *Kṛpa* was basically a peace-loving man and a highly pious and upright living entity who resisted corruption. Even so, he was circumstantially forced to fight for the Kauravas. Such is the way of destiny.

Aśvatthāmā was the son of Droṇacharya and it is said that he still uses a subtle body somewhere in the Himalayas. He mastered the breath nourishment techniques. He is supposed to be promoted in evolution in the next world cycle. We must clarify a point, however: Those who are said to be living for so many hundreds of years in the Himalayas are usually living there in subtle dimension and not on the gross level. Some of them are living in subtle bodies which are resistant to rebirth. Some return there instinctively at the time of death, even though they take numerous gross bodies. For these great yogis, the substantial body is the subtle one; therefore when they say they are going to stay there for a long time, they mean in the subtle form. Materialistic people think superstitiously that it is the gross body that survives for a cycle but it is the subtle one. An accomplished yogi may not even notice the death of his gross form. The death of his earthly body does not disrupt his consciousness nor affect his sense of identity.

There are yogis who are continue the disciplines in subtle bodies, aiming for perfection. Most of them congregate about the Kailash Hill in the Himalayas. Even today, if one has some astral ability, one can meet these yogis to get instructions. As far as yoga is concerned, if one has clear psychic perception one can take an astral guru and acquire the needed techniques from him. One does not have to find a guru in the physical form.

Aśvatthāmā acted irresponsibly after the Battle of *Kurukṣetra*. He murdered the five sons of *Draupadī* while they slept. In any case, he came to his senses later, and took up austerities for compensation. He will be promoted in the mundane evolutionary cycle and be allowed to do much devotional service. *Śrīmad Bhāgavatam* mentions this.

Vikarṇa was an heroic fighter. He was somewhat impartial. This younger brother of Duryodhana let it be known to the Kurus that their act of robbing Yudhishthira in a dice game was wrong. He objected to the idea of disrobing *Draupadī*. He did, however, fight for his relatives at the *Kurukṣetra* battle. He was killed by *Bhīma* who greatly disliked the Kauravas.

The son of Somadatta is *Bhūriśravā*. He was born with a bad energy. His father performed austerities to get a favor from Lord Shiva. There is a misunderstanding even among some educated Vaishnavas, where some feel that Lord Shiva gives favors to people who please him. A great yogi and semi-absolute person like Lord Shiva cannot be involved in giving faulty boons to limited entities. Lord Shiva gives favors because it is his duty.

The idea that Lord Shiva is pleased by badly-motivated austerities is false. Kashyapa Muni explained this truth to his wife Diti. He told her that Lord Shiva is completely detached and has a job to do. If someone performs austerities and builds up enough energy to purchase the fulfillment of desires, he is allowed the fulfillment at his own risk. It is not that Lord Shiva is pleased, but we may interpret it in that way if we are critical of his award-granting capacity.

Bhūriśravā's father had some problem when he was kicked in public by another ruler. He held a grudge for this. Through austerities, he received sufficient power to collect some impious reactions of the offending ruler. He then enthused his son with the negative power. The son was to kick a descendant of his father's victor. This happened when *Bhūriśravā* kicked *Sātyaki* on the Battlefield of *Kurukṣetra*. Lord Krishna did not like the idea of *Bhūriśravā* doing this, and besides, *Bhūriśravā* was about to behead Sātyaki. Lord Krishna then alerted Arjuna that *Sātyaki* was fighting on the side of the Pandavas and should be protected. Arjuna then shot an arrow and cut off *Bhūriśravā's* right hand which was raised to behead *Sātyaki*. After this, *Bhūriśravā* sat down to leave his body by starvation, and in the meanwhile *Sātyaki* recovered and cut off his opponent's head.

Later on, during an in-house fight in the Yadu clan, *Sātyaki* was killed by one of his kinsmen who attacked him when they were drinking rice wine. The attack was made as a reaction to this killing of *Bhūriśravā* when the warrior was in a yoga posture, having renounced military concerns. In the material world, there is always some upset, some contrary circumstance. There are endless cycles of actions, reactions, and counteractions. There can be lasting no peace in this existence.

Duryodhana gave this roll call so that Droṇacharya would place these men in strategic positions. He did not want any of them to leave the battlefield except through the door of death or by victory. In a diplomatic way, he informed the teacher of this. Duryodhana himself did not have the intelligence to arrange the warfield. Still, since the overall responsibility rests with him, he advised the teacher, even though it was, in a sense, a disrespectful approach.

Dhṛtarāṣṭra listened carefully to Sanjaya because he wanted his side to win. He knows of Lord Krishna's superiority, but still, since Krishna pretended to be detached, *Dhṛtarāṣṭra* hoped that the laws of chance would fall in his favor. He knows well that if Krishna was a combatant on the side of the Pandavas, the Kauravas would lose. He thought that since God took a neutral stance, it would be a fair fight, which could very well end in victory.

अन्ये च बहवः शूरा
मदर्थे त्यक्तजीविताः ।
नानाशस्त्रप्रहरणाः
सर्वे युद्धविशारदाः ॥ १.९ ॥
anye ca bahavaḥ śūrā
madarthe tyaktajīvitāḥ
nānāśastrapraharaṇāḥ
sarve yuddhaviśāradāḥ (1.9)

anye — other; ca — and; bahavaḥ — many; śūrā — heroes; madarthe — for my sake; tyakta jīvitāḥ — would give their lives; nānā śastra praharaṇāḥ — wielding various weapons; sarve — all; yuddha viśāradāḥ — being experts in warfare

And many other heroes wielding various weapons, being experts in warfare, would give their lives for my sake. (1.9)

Commentary:

This statement is made to counteract the influence of Lord Krishna and to ward off any fears *Droṇa* might have about the Lord. In terms of warriors and weapons, Duryodhana feels that he is more than a match for the Pandavas, but he is uncertain of the fighting spirit, long-range judgement, and determination of his men. He realized that the combination of Krishna and Arjuna has dangerous.

He felt a sense of insecurity in reference to Lord Krishna's presence on the battlefield. On the emotional level he found himself leaning this way and that way for support. But now he found something that counterbalanced the insecurity any man might feel if God were against him. In the Sanskrit we see the word *madartha*, which is a combination of *mat* (*concerning me, centering about me*) and *artha* (*in my interest, focused on my concerns*).

By situating himself in the providential energy of the concern of other warriors, Duryodhana had safely, but foolishly, counterbalanced Lord Krishna. It is as if he said to *Droṇācārya*:

> *There is only one problem: The fear of Lord Krishna. But there is a way out of this. Even if Krishna is the Supreme Being as some great sages claim, still He can do nothing if He does not participate physically. Just see how many men support me! Many of these people dislike Krishna. One may be the Supreme Person or not be the Supreme Person. What does it matter?*
>
> *Actually, being the Supreme Person is irrelevant in these social situations. Circumstances usually depend on collective support. Without majority power, what can Krishna or Yudhishthira do?*
>
> *If people do not like Krishna, that is His problem. I made friends with these heroic men and the Pandavas did likewise with their allies. That is all there is to it. Insofar as Krishna is God, that is no concern of mine. This is a practical matter. In this affair, I have the greater percentage of followers. My victory is the likelihood. I am not afraid of Krishna He may be God and perhaps He is just a powerful being. How can it be ascertained?*

अपर्याप्तं तदस्माकं
बलं भीष्माभिरक्षितम् ।
पर्याप्तं त्विदमेतेषां
बलं भीमाभिरक्षितम् ॥ १.१० ॥
aparyāptaṁ tadasmākaṁ
balaṁ bhīṣmābhirakṣitam
paryāptaṁ tvidameteṣāṁ
balaṁ bhīmābhirakṣitam (1.10)

aparyāptaṁ- inadequate; tad — this; asmākaṁ — of ours; balaṁ — military force; bhīṣmābhi rakṣitam — supervised by Bhishma; paryāptaṁ — sufficient; tvidam = tu — however + idam - this; eteṣām — of these; balam — military power; bhīmābhirakṣitam — protected by Bhīma

Inadequate is this military force of ours which is supervised by Bhishma. Sufficient, however, is their military power which is protected by Bhīma. (1.10)

Commentary:

This is a reverse statement due to the contrary thinking pattern and emotional fluctuation of Duryodhana. Some people cannot have a steady mind but must waver back and forth between self confidence and uncertainty. On one hand, he projects victory. Most of the warriors are his. He has Bhishma and *Droṇa*, the most experienced generals. But on the other hand, he cannot be certain about the outcome. He hates *Bhīma*, the Pandava who rivaled him. This *Bhīma*, the second Pandava, is not the Commander-in-Chief of the Pandava army, but he is a leading figure on their side. Duryodhana in order to put himself in the forefront, in comparison to this Pandava strong-man, imagined *Bhīma* as the leader.

In any case, Duryodhana cannot help but admire the enterprising and charismatic power of King Yudhishthira, the eldest Pandava. Though exiled for thirteen years, he still amassed a sizeable army.

अयनेषु च सर्वेषु
यथाभागमवस्थिताः।
भीष्ममेवाभिरक्षन्तु
भवन्तः सर्व एव हि ॥१.११॥
ayaneṣu ca sarveṣu
yathābhāgamavasthitāḥ
bhīṣmamevābhirakṣantu
bhavantaḥ sarva eva hi (1.11)

ayaneṣu — in maneuvers; ca — and; sarveṣu — in all; yathā bhāgam — as by assignment; avasthitāḥ — positioned; bhīṣmam — Bhishma; evābhirakṣantu — definitely protect; bhavantaḥ — your honorable master; sarve — all; eva — indeed; hi — certainly

And in all maneuvers, as positioned by assignment, all your honorable masters should definitely protect Bhishma. (1.11)

Commentary:

Arjuna's body was younger than Duryodhana. The generals on the Pandavas' side were not as experienced as *Droṇa* and Bhishma. Still, Duryodhana wanted protection from carelessness. He considered the Pandavas to be rebels to his authority. He reminded *Droṇa* to plan everything carefully, not to take any chances, and to be sure that the aged General Bhishma was not exposed unnecessarily to enemy fire. Everyone respected Bhishma. So long as he lived, Duryodhana's men would be confident. If Bhishma were killed, or if the ranks of his army were to be broken, there might be a panic. His warriors might become fearful and the small Pandava force might strike with fatality.

There was some hostility between *Karṇa* and Bhishma and between others in Duryodhana's army. Bhishma repeatedly insulted *Karṇa*, assessing this marksman as nothing but the son of a chariot driver, a two-bit warrior who had no aristocratic pedigree. Thus Duryodhana desired that his men focus on loyalty to the government and not involve themselves in petty quarrels. This meant adhering to the orders of Bhishma, and protecting Bhishma on all sides. In terms of firing skill, Bhishma may be compared to a human machine gun, but Duryodhana did not desire for any of the enemy to shoot Bhishma from behind. Duryodhana thought, "My grandfather will do everything in his power to drive away these Pandavas. They will be lucky if they are not killed by him. In any case, even though Bhishma will undoubtedly kill thousands of warriors, he should be protected. I want no mishap to affect him. I do not want to explain Bhishma's death to my father, King *Dhṛtarāṣṭra*."

तस्य संजनयन्हर्षं
कुरुवृद्धः पितामहः ।
सिंहनादं विनद्योच्चैः
शङ्खं दध्मौ प्रतापवान् ॥१.१२॥
tasya saṁjanayanharṣaṁ
kuruvṛddhaḥ pitāmahaḥ
siṁhanādaṁ vinadyoccaiḥ
śaṅkhaṁ dadhmau pratāpavān (1.12)

tasya — of him (Duryodhana); saṁjanayan — producing; harṣaṁ — happiness; kuruvṛddhaḥ — the eldest Kuru; pitāmahaḥ — the grandfather; siṁha nādaṁ — a lion-like roar; vinadyo ccaiḥ — sounding a loud; śaṅkhaṁ — conchshell; dadhmau — blew; pratāpavān — voluminously

The eldest Kuru, the grandfather, voluminously blew his conchshell, sounding a loud lion-like roar, thus producing great happiness for Duryodhana. (1.12)

Commentary:

The Kuru elder, Bhishma, understood the fears of Duryodhana. Bhishma drew his own conclusions about defeat or victory but he did not express his views. He was a seasoned warrior, elderly stateman and hardened combatant. He was not the type to enter emotional outbursts. As a matter of duty and to inform everyone that he was willing and able, that he needed no sympathy because of an aged body, that his wits were intact, that he was ready to kill on a wholesale basis, Bhishma sounded his conch which had the peculiar sound of a roaring lion. When he blew the conch, it was the first to be heard on the battlefield. All warriors stopped activities, and looked in his direction.

ततः शङ्खाश्च भेर्यश्च
पणवानकगोमुखाः ।
सहसैवाभ्यहन्यन्त
स शब्दस्तुमुलोऽभवत् ॥१.१३॥
tataḥ śaṅkhāśca bheryaśca
paṇavānakagomukhāḥ
sahasaivābhyahanyanta
sa śabdastumulo'bhavat (1.13)

tataḥ- then; śaṅkhāś- conches; ca — and; bheryaś - kettledrums; ca — and; paṇavānaka gomukhāḥ — cymbals, drums and trumpets; sahasaivā-bhyahanyanta = sahasā- simultaneously + eva — indeed + abhyahanyanta — were sounded; sa — that; śabdas — sound; tumulo — tumultuous; 'bhavat (abhavat)- was

And then the conches and kettledrums, the cymbals, drums and trumpets, were simultaneously sounded. That sound was tumultuous. (1.13)

Commentary:

Bhishma's sounding off was the signal for the other Kaurava warriors to show their battle fervor in a sounding gesture, inviting the Pandavas to prepare for a clash or to run from the battlefield. There was some lack of confidence in the Kaurava army since they preferred that the Pandavas take the peaceful way out, and thus be disinherited from the political and economic assets of the Kurus.

ततः श्वेतैर्हयैर्युक्ते
महतिस्यन्दने स्थितौ ।
माधवः पाण्डवश्चैव
दिव्यौ शङ्खौ प्रदध्मतुः ॥१.१४॥
tataḥ śvetairhayairyukte
mahatisyandane sthitau
mādhavaḥ pāṇḍavaścaiva
divyau śaṅkhau pradadhmatuḥ (1.14)

tataḥ — then; śvetair — with white; hayair — with horses; yukte — harnessed; mahati — in a magnificent; syandane — swif- moving chariot; sthitau — standing; mādhavaḥ — the descendant of Madhu; pāṇḍavaś caiva — and indeed the son of Pāndu; divyau — supernatural; śaṅkhau — two conches; pradadhmatuḥ — blew

Then, standing in a magnificent, swift-moving chariot with white horses harnessed, the descendant of Madhu and the son of Pāndu blew two supernatural conchshells. (1.14)

Commentary:

Duryodhana was on the offensive. Yudhishthira was on the defensive. Bhishma sounded off for Duryodhana, reflecting Duryodhana's bullying mood. Krishna and Arjuna sounded off for Yudhishthira with full confidence that justice would triumph. While Bhishma's conch made a mundane impact, Arjuna's and Krishna's made a psychic register.

पाञ्चजन्यं हृषीकेशो
देवदत्तं धनंजयः ।
पौण्ड्रं दध्मौ महाशङ्खं
भीमकर्मा वृकोदरः ॥१.१५॥

pāñcajanyaṁ hṛṣīkeśo
devadattaṁ dhanaṁjayaḥ
pauṇḍraṁ dadhmau mahāśaṅkha
bhīmakarmā vṛkodaraḥ (1.15)

pāñcajanyaṁ — the conch named Pāñcajanya; hṛṣīkeśo — Krishna; devadattaṁ — a conch named Devadatta; dhanaṁjayaḥ — conqueror of wealthy countries; pauṇḍraṁ — conch named Paundra; dadhmau — blew; mahāśaṅkha — great conch; bhīma karmā — one whose actions are terrible; vṛkodaraḥ — wolf-bellied man

The conchshell named Pāñcajanya was blown by Hṛṣīkeśa, Krishna. The Devadatta conch was sounded by the conqueror of wealthy countries, Arjuna. Bhīma, the wolf-bellied man whose actions are terrible, blew the great conch named Paundra. (1.15)

Commentary:

The history of the *Pāñcajanya* is given in the *Śrīmad Bhāgavatam*, Vishnu *Purāṇa*, and other Vedic literature. Lord Krishna, in the action of rescuing the departed son of his teacher, killed a giant crustacean. Taking the shell of the creature, he used it for a sounding tool. These materially visible acts of the Lord, however, partially reflect His transcendental life. In the previous verse, Sanjaya gave the adjective *divyau* which means psychic, spiritual, transcendental, or supernatural. Despite the mundane history of the *Pāñcajanya*, it has a transcendental counterpart; the act of acquiring a physical shell is a coordination in material nature of a transcendental reality of the Lord. These truths are difficult to grasp. Empowered Vaishnava spiritual masters, like His Divine Grace *Śrīla* Bhaktivedanta Swami, did much to explain these matters.

The *Devadatta* blowing shell of Arjuna also has a mundane history and a transcendental one. Material nature does her best to match up to the transcendental nature and attributes of the supreme and limited entities. This is exactly the tendency of matter. Insofar as she can appease us by matching up, she produces forms and products, but in all cases, she falls short to a degree; she is not capable of a total reproduction.

The three personalities mentioned will be responsible for the most discipline on the *Kurukṣetra* battlefield. These are Lord Krishna, the son of *Devakī*, and Arjuna and *Bhīma*, the sons of Queen *Kuntī* and King Pandu. They replied to Bhishma, disregarding the other warriors. Bhishma was the fountainhead of the Kuru family and without his permission, the civil war could not take place. This reply of Krishna, Arjuna and *Bhīma* is a direct confrontation on the sound level.

Bhīma is mentioned as the terror. He was battle-hungry and did not want a peaceful settlement. Being disgusted with the attitude of the Kauravas, he was ready for action. He could only be satisfied by expressing anger and frustration on the Kurus. Of the five

Pandavas, *Bhīma* was the most vulgar, the most crude, but on occasion, he showed as much finesse as the others. People who were familiar with him knew that he was a rash fellow, who had to be controlled by his elder brother, King Yudhishthira. In regards to eating, it is said that whenever his mother cooked, she sanctified the food and divided it into two equal parts. One half was for herself and the four brothers. The other half was for *Bhīma*. Thus he became known as the man with a wolf's stomach.

During banishment, the Pandavas walked miles on foot. On occasion, *Bhīma* carried them on his shoulders. He fetched them as a light load. The strong-man Kichaka, the brother-in law of King *Virāṭa*, was feared by the Kurus. Even though they wanted to raid the cattle ranches of this king, they refrained from doing so, for fear of Kichaka. But when that strong-man harassed *Draupadī*, *Bhīma* killed him with bare hands. It was *Bhīma* who killed the wrestler-king *Jarāsandha*. *Bhīma* found out during a wrestling challenge with *Jarāsandha* that he had met his match. He admitted this to Krishna: "I cannot kill this man. I tried every death-hold. Somehow or the other, Govinda, this fellow matches me. How may I finish him off?" Taking hints from Krishna, *Bhīma* then ripped Jarasandha's body in half.

Once, *Bhīma* was subdued by a powerful snake in the Himalayan region. When the snake held *Bhīma* in its coils, *Bhīma* tried every method to escape but he could not. It so happened that the soul in that reptilian body functioned as a king named Nahusha in a former life. King Yudhishthira came to the location. He rescued both *Bhīma* and that fallen king. *Bhīma* had a reputation of having the strength of 10,000 elephants. He was one of the strongest men of his time.

अनन्तविजयं राजा
कुन्तीपुत्रो युधिष्ठिरः ।
नकुलः सहदेवश्च
सुघोषमणिपुष्पकौ ॥ १.१६ ॥
anantavijayaṁ rājā
kuntīputro yudhiṣṭhiraḥ
nakulaḥ sahadevaśca
sughoṣamaṇipuṣpakau (1.16)

anantavijayaṁ — name of a conchshell; rājā — king; kuntī putro — son of Kuntī ; yudhiṣṭhiraḥ — Yudhishthira; nakulaḥ — Nakula; sahadevaś — Sahadeva; ca — and; sughoṣa maṇipuṣpakau — names of two conchshells: Sughosha and Manipushpaka

The King, Kuntī's son, Yudhishthira, blew the Anantavijayam. Nakula and Sahadeva blew the Sughosha and Manipushpaka respectively. (1.16)

Commentary:

Sanskrit words have precise meanings. Names given to creatures or objects are usually given with intention. For instance, *anantavijaya* literally means on-going victory or continuous enterprise. We must therefore carefully regard the Sanskrit language and its application in these Vedic literatures. It is a fact that a blind boy may be named Padmalochana, which is to say the lotus-eyed one. Therefore we should check to see if the meaning applies to the person or object which bears it. King Yudhishthira did have on-going victory because he was the person of righteousness. A person of that nature wins out, even if he appears to have lost at the onset of an enterprise.

काश्यश्च परमेष्वासः
शिखण्डी च महारथः ।
धृष्टद्युम्नो विराटश्च
सात्यकिश्चापराजितः ॥ १.१७॥

kāśyaś — King of Kāśi; ca — and; parameṣvāsaḥ — superior bowman; śikhaṇḍī — Śikhandī; ca — and; mahā rathaḥ — great chariot fighter; dhṛṣṭadyumno — Dhṛṣṭadyumna; virāṭaś — Virata; ca — and;

kāśyaśca parameṣvāsaḥ
śikhaṇḍī ca mahārathaḥ
dhṛṣṭadyumno virāṭaśca
sātyakiścāparājitaḥ (1.17)

sātyakiś cā 'parājitaḥ = sātyakiś — Satyaki + ca — and + aparājitas — unconquered one

The King of Kāśi, the superior bowman, and Śikhandī, the great chariot fighter, Dhṛṣṭadyumna and Virata and Sātyaki, the unconquered one, (1.17)

Commentary:

Sanjaya gave King *Dhṛtarāṣṭra* a picturesque idea of the scene. This preparation for an engagement is of interest to retired men and politicians. They enjoy listening to these descriptions of battlefield layouts. One man is attracted to another man's heroism. Some men leave their female companions and go off sporting to enjoy adventurism with other men. It is part of the masculine mystique.

The King of Kashi was not on friendly terms with the Kurus. Bhishma kidnapped three Kashi princesses a long time ago. There was an enmity between their clans. The Kashis sided with the Pandavas. *Śikhandī* was in the Kāśi clan in his past life, but at the time, he had a female body. His mission in this life was to kill Bhishma, but he could not do that unless he was aided by special factors of providence. Providence, however, is so powerful that it may bring down as powerful a person as Bhishma. With the assistance of providence, an ant or mosquito can disfigure an elephant, and a cripple can climb Mount Everest. *Dhṛṣṭadyumna* was there to kill *Droṇa*. His father, *Drupada*, was present as well. Sātyaki is also known as *Dāruka*, Lord Krishna's charioteer at *Dvāraka*.

द्रुपदो द्रौपदेयाश्च
सर्वशः पृथिवीपते ।
सौभद्रश्च महाबाहुः
शङ्खान्दध्मुः पृथक्पृथक् ॥१.१८॥
drupado draupadeyāśca
sarvaśaḥ pṛthivīpate
saubhadraśca mahābāhuḥ
śaṅkhāndadhmuḥ pṛthakpṛthak (1.18)

drupado — Drupada; draupadeyāś — sons of Draupadī; ca — and; sarvaśaḥ — all together, being grouped together; pṛthivī pate — O King of the province; saubhadraś — son of Subhadra; ca — and; mahābāhuḥ — strong-armed; śaṅkhān — conchshells; dadhmuḥ — blew; pṛthak pṛthak — one by one

...O king of the province, Drupada and the sons of Draupadī, being grouped together, and the strong-armed son of Subhadra, blew conchshells in series. (1.18)

Commentary:

As *pṛthivīpate*, ruler of the earth or caretaker of the planet, *Dhṛtarāṣṭra* was flattered by the poetic Sanjaya. In Sanskrit literature, there is much exaggeration in the use of the language. This is an example of it. *Dhṛtarāṣṭra* was only lord of a part of India. He was not lord of the earth. The Kurus were prominent in India. No chieftains in the vicinity took them lightly, but that did not mean that *Dhṛtarāṣṭra* was actually pṛthivīpate, or lord of the entire earth. Some Sanskrit speakers do indulge in this poetic injustice. We must therefore be on the alert for these exaggerations.

Dhṛtarāṣṭra intended, however, to be regarded as lord of the earth. This flattery of Sanjaya is appropriate in satisfying the vanity of the blind king.

We translated *pṛthivīpate* as *king of the province*, rather than the lord of the earth. *Pṛthivī* means earth or a section of it, a province. Thus our translation is accurate. No one in his right mind would consider *Dhṛtarāṣṭra* the king of the entire planet in the days of the

Mahābhārata war. At least the history of the *Mahābhārata* does not attribute this blind king with planetary rulership. In this verse, Sanjaya deliberately stressed *Drupada* and his grandsons who were the sons of *Draupadī*. These were sired by the Pandavas. This brought to *Dhṛtarāṣṭra*'s mind the attempted stripping of *Draupadī* in the senate house of the Kurus. That was an embarassing occurrence to be remembered by the king. By mentioning the son of Subhadra, Sanjaya indicated that even if Krishna did not fight, Krishna's nephew would. This was another itch in the mind of *Dhṛtarāṣṭra*, that lord of a province in India.

स घोषो धार्तराष्ट्राणां
हृदयानि व्यदारयत् ।
नभश्च पृथिवीं चैव
तुमुलो व्यनुनादयन् ॥ १.१९ ॥
sa ghoṣo dhārtarāṣṭrāṇāṁ
hṛdayāni vyadārayat
nabhaśca pṛthivīṁ caiva
tumulo vyanunādayan (1.19)

sa — the; ghoṣo (ghoṣaḥ) — noise; dhārtarāṣṭrāṇāṁ — the men of Dhṛtarāṣṭra; hṛdayāni — emotions; vyadārayat — disrupted; nabhaś — the sky; ca — and; pṛthivīṁ — the earth; caiva — and indeed; tumulo — vibrating sound; vyanunādayan — cause to resonate

The noise disrupted the emotions of the sons of Dhṛtarāṣṭra, and the vibrating sound caused the sky and earth to resonate. (1.19)

Commentary:

Sanjaya used the term dhārtarāṣṭrānām, meaning the sons of *Dhṛtarāṣṭra*, but we have used the translation "of the men of *Dhṛtarāṣṭra*". This phrase applies to male descendants or supporters of *Dhṛtarāṣṭra*. Sanjaya alerted *Dhṛtarāṣṭra* that from the time Arjuna and Krishna blew their divinely-empowered conches and all the other Pandavas and their allies sounded, *Dhṛtarāṣṭra*'s men suffered from a breach of confidence.

अथ व्यवस्थितान्दृष्ट्वा
धार्तराष्ट्रान्कपिध्वजः ।
प्रवृत्ते शस्त्रसंपाते
धनुरुद्यम्य पाण्डवः ॥ १.२० ॥
atha vyavasthitāndṛṣṭvā
dhārtarāṣṭrānkapidhvajaḥ
pravṛtte śastrasaṁpāte
dhanurudyamya pāṇḍavaḥ (1.20)

atha — then; vyavasthitān — in battle formation; dṛṣṭvā — after observing; dhārtarāṣṭrān — the sons of Dhṛtarāṣṭra; kapidhvajaḥ — the man with a monkey insignia; pravṛtte — in the challenge; śastrasaṁpāte — in the clash of weapons; dhanur — bow; udyamya — raising; pāṇḍavaḥ — son of Pāṇḍu

Then after observing the sons of Dhṛtarāṣṭra in battle formation, the man with a monkey insignia, that son of Pandu, raised his bow in the challenge of the clash of weapons. (1.20)

Commentary:

At first, Duryodhana centralized himself. Now, another hero does the very same thing, except that Arjuna was authorized to be prominent. Lord Krishna empowered Arjuna to take charge of the battle but only under Krishna's supervision. When a man is authorized for a moment, an hour, a day or a year, he may take himself seriously during the empowerment. That is what Arjuna did. In the meantime, the warriors forgot Duryodhana.

Authorization by Lord Krishna is a very tricky business. Many of us become carried away when we are authorized, not realizing that the empowerment may be temporary. King

Dhṛtarāṣṭra, the master of that Kuru country, was not particularly inclined to hearing of Arjuna at the time. Still, he listened as stipulated by destiny.

Arjuna was known as *kapidhvajah*, the man whose chariot bore an illustration of a special monkey or *kapi*. This was the supernatural monkey named Hanuman. Like many heroes before and after him, Hanuman is an idolized, legendary figure.

It appears that Arjuna had the authority to stop this war, for if he refused to fight, the Pandava forces would be disempowered, broken down in spirit. Arjuna went forward in his celebrated battle chariot. He wanted to take a close look at the armies.

हृषीकेशं तदा वाक्यम्
इदमाह महीपते ।
सेनयोरुभयोर्मध्ये
रथं स्थापय मेऽच्युत ॥ १.२१ ॥
hṛṣīkeśaṁ tadā vākyam
idamāha mahīpate
senayorubhayormadhye
rathaṁ sthāpaya me'cyuta (1.21)

hṛṣīkeśaṁ — Hṛṣīkeśa, Krishna; tadā — then; vākyam — request; idam — this; āha — he spoke; mahīpate — O Lord of the earth; senayoḥ — of the two armies; ubhayoḥ — of the two; madhye — in the midst; rathaṁ — chariot; sthāpaya — cause to be parked; me — my; 'cyuta = acyuta — unaffected

Then he spoke this request to Hṛṣīkeśa, Krishna: O Lord of the earth, cause my chariot to be parked in the midst of the two armies, O unaffected one, (1.21)

Commentary:

We can already detect Arjuna's confusion, his loss of confidence, and his effort to hide the uncertainty. War was declared. The armies met. In truth, it was not time for observations of the sort Arjuna desired to make. But as the unerring one, the person of perfection, the person who never makes mistakes, Lord Krishna positioned the chariot for a view.

यावदेतान्निरीक्षेऽहं
योद्धुकामानवस्थितान् ।
कैर्मया सह योद्धव्यम्
अस्मिन्रणसमुद्यमे ॥ १.२२ ॥
yāvadetānnirīkṣe'haṁ
yoddhukāmānavasthitān
kairmayā saha yoddhavyam
asminraṇasamudyame (1.22)

yāvad — so that; etān — these; nirīkṣe — I can see; 'haṁ = ahaṁ — I; yoddhu-kāmān — battle-hungry; avasthitān — armed warriors; kair — with whom; mayā — with myself; saha — with; yoddhavyam — should be fought; asmin — in this; raṇasamudyame — in the battle engagement

...so that I can see those battle-hungry, armed warriors, with whom I should fight in this battle engagement. (1.22)

Commentary:

Arjuna speaks to both himself and to Lord Krishna. He will have to re-assess everything before deciding whether to fight or not. He wants to confront the opponents visually, to be sure that they understand the implications. He is unwilling to fight reckless warriors who have not calculated the consequences of conflict. By asking the identity of the opponents, Arjuna, who knows them all too well, suggested that they might have become crazy.

योत्स्यमानानवेक्षेऽहं
य एतेऽत्र समागताः ।
धार्तराष्ट्रस्य दुर्बुद्धेर्
युद्धे प्रियचिकीर्षवः ॥ १.२३ ॥
yotsyamānānavekṣe'haṁ
ya ete'tra samāgatāḥ
dhārtarāṣṭrasya durbuddher
yuddhe priyacikīrṣavaḥ (1.23)

yotsyamānān — those who are about to fight; avekṣe — I wish to observe; 'haṁ = ahaṁ — I; ya — who; ete — these; 'tra = atra — here; samāgatāḥ — assembled together; dhārtarāṣṭrasya — of the son of Dhṛtarāṣṭra; durbuddher — of the evil-minded; yuddhe — in battle; priyacikīrṣavaḥ — desiring to please

I wish to observe these who are to fight, who assembled here desiring to please the evil- minded son of King Dhṛtarāṣṭra, in battle. (1.23)

Commentary:

Arjuna wanted to understand the influence under which the friends, relatives, and allies of *Dhṛtarāṣṭra* came to the battlefield. To him, they seem convinced that they would be fighting for a righteous cause. He wanted to analyze the situation to understand their motivation. It was interesting to Arjuna that these men were eager to kill others even though their leader was the conniving, corrupt son of *Dhṛtarāṣṭra*. Arjuna was baffled by the allowance of providence which permitted these men to come with eagerness, risking their lives for an unjust cause.

संजय उवाच
एवमुक्तो हृषीकेशो
गुडाकेशेन भारत ।
सेनयोरुभयोर्मध्ये
स्थापयित्वा रथोत्तमम् ॥ १.२४ ॥
saṁjaya uvāca
evamukto hṛṣīkeśo
guḍākeśena bhārata
senayorubhayormadhye
sthāpayitvā rathottamam (1.24)

saṁjaya — Sanjaya; uvāca — said; evam — thus; ukto — being addressed; hṛṣīkeśo — Hrisikesa; guḍākeśena — by the thick-haired baron; bhārata — O descendant of Bharata; senayor — of the two armies; ubhayor — of the two; madhye — in the middle; sthāpayitvā — caused to be positioned; rathottamam — best of the chariots

Sanjaya said: O descendant of Bharata, thus being addressed by Arjuna, the thick-haired baron, Krishna, who is known as Hṛṣīkeśa, caused the best of the chariots to be positioned in the midst of the two armies. (1.24)

Commentary:

Lord Krishna agreed to be Arjuna's charioteer. Though He claimed to be the Lord of the universe, Krishna complied with Arjuna's request for chariot service. The Lord watched, knowing fully well that Arjuna's assessment would cause nervousness. Arjuna wanted to be the central figure, to decide whether to proceed with the war or not. Krishna knew all too well that Arjuna entered an emotional trap. A soft-hearted man should not put himself into a position that would trigger cowardice. He should be cautious and allow the iron-willed men to take such a posture. But Arjuna did not care about that. At the time, he felt he was the man of the moment and he regarded Lord Krishna as his cousin and charioteer.

Arjuna took the risk, because Lord Krishna was with him. He had someone to lean on in danger. He could afford to risk himself. He had a reliable and resourceful friend. A son who courts danger when his father is nearby to rescue him, is not exactly stupid but it may be said that he exploits the rescuing power of his parent. A daughter who flirts with boys when her strict mother walks beside her, certainly takes a risk, but she knows that the boys will not advance. So it was, at this moment with Krishna and Arjuna. In a sense Arjuna could afford to fall apart because God was beside him. In becoming confused and depressed, Arjuna will show us what advantage we could have if we get close to Krishna. In *Dvāraka*, Lord Krishna's sons used to take many risks and usually the Lord rescued them. This is the privilege of those who are that close to Lord Krishna.

By complying with Arjuna's request, and signaling the horses to move forward, judging the situation of the armies and finding the best position from which to observe them, Lord Krishna gave Arjuna permission to be the man of the moment. But that was done at Arjuna's risk. If we want to be in an important position and if we want God to place us there, it might be arranged, but such acts of God are done at our risk in terms of the laws of consequence. Arjuna buckled under when the emotional energy which motivated him, caved in and left him sitting on the chariot like a frightened boy.

All the Kurus were descendants of a famous King Bharata of antiquity. Thus Sanjaya addresses *Dhṛtarāṣṭra* as a descendant.

भीष्मद्रोणप्रमुखतः
सर्वेषां च महीक्षिताम् ।
उवाच पार्थ पश्यैतान्
समवेतान्कुरूनिति ॥१.२५॥
bhīṣmadroṇapramukhataḥ
sarveṣāṁ ca mahīkṣitām
uvāca pārtha paśyaitān
samavetānkurūniti (1.25)

bhīṣma droṇa pramukhataḥ — in the presence of Bhisma, Droṇa; sarveṣām — of all these; ca — and; mahīkṣitām — rulers of the earth; uvāca — (Krishna) said; pārtha — O son of Pṛthā; paśyai 'etān — behold them; samavetān — are assembled together; kurūn — Kurus; iti — thus

In the presence of Bhishma, Droṇa and all those rulers of the earth, Krishna said: O son of Pṛthā, behold these Kurus who are assembled here together. (1.25)

Commentary:

King *Dhṛtarāṣṭra* listened keenly to hear Arjuna's response. He knew that whatever Arjuna decided would affect the outcome of the war. But it was not just *Dhṛtarāṣṭra* who wondered. All the warriors on the warfield observed Arjuna. Duryodhana smiled because he knew that Arjuna would be embarrassed to face Bhishma and *Droṇa*. Duryodhana hardly believed that Arjuna would face Bhishma and *Droṇa* in a fierce battle encounter. Arjuna already confronted these Kuru leaders in battle when they seized King *Virāṭa's* cows after Kichaka was killed. In that confrontation Arjuna fought in a sporting spirit without harming any of them. Duryodhana was confident that Arjuna did not possess the callousness of heart required to kill his grandfather Bhishma and his teacher *Droṇa*.

Bhishma was Arjuna's great-uncle. Arjuna's father was Pandu. Pandu's father was *Śrīla Vyāsadeva* whose mother was *Satyavatī*.

Vyāsaji served as a substitute father of Pandu. King Vichitravirya, Bhishma's paternal half-brother, was supposed to be Pandu's father, but Vichitravirya died before producing progeny. His mother, Queen *Satyavatī*, requested Vichitravirya's half-brother, *Vyāsaji*, to sire children in the wombs of Vichitravirya's wives. To authorize this, *Satyavatī* acquired the permission of her stepson who was Bhishma. And this is how Bhishma fit into the picture as the great uncle of Arjuna.

We may understand from this, that the energy to beget a child may be psychically transferred from one prospective father to another. It is possible. Under the circumstance the emotion of fatherhood for a particular entity may be in more than one man, even though only one begets the body of the son. These social incongruencies may occur by acts of providence which are beyond our control. As human beings, we should try our best to maintain moral principles. Social experience teaches that sexual complications create serious problems. Still we have to maintain a broad outlook when providence breaks the moral rules. We should always try to bring ourselves back to morality when we find ourselves off course but we must be prepared to deal sensibly and impartially with sexual complications.

तत्रापश्यत्स्थितान्पार्थः
पितॄनथ पितामहान् ।
आचार्यान्मातुलान्भ्रातॄन्
पुत्रान्पौत्रान्सखींस्तथा ।
श्वशुरान्सुहृदश्चैव
सेनयोरुभयोरपि ॥ १.२६ ॥
tatrāpaśyatsthitānpārthaḥ
pitṝnatha pitāmahān
ācāryānmātulānbhrātṝn
putrānpautrānsakhīṁstathā
śvaśurānsuhṛdaścaiva
senayorubhayorapi (1.26)

tatra apaśyat — there he saw; sthitān — standing; pārthaḥ — the son of Pṛthā; pitṝn — fathers; atha — then; pitāmahān — grandfathers; ācāryān — revered teachers; mātulān — maternal uncles; bhrātṝn — brothers; putrān — sons; pautrān — grandsons; sakhīṁs — friends; tathā — as well as; śvaśurān — fathers-in-law; suhṛdaś = suhṛdaḥ — well-wishing men; caiva — and indeed; senayoḥ — in the two armies; ubhayoḥ — in the both; api — also

The son of Pṛthā saw men who were fathers, grandfathers, revered teachers, maternal uncles, brothers, sons, grandsons, as well as friends, fathers-in-law and well-wishing friends, standing there in both armies. (1.26)

Commentary:

Duryodhana understood the emotional nature of Arjuna. He enjoyed Arjuna's emotional response. To see a soft-hearted man in the midst of such a situation is a miserable sight for a sober person, but for a mean-hearted person like Duryodhana it gave enjoyment. In a sense, Arjuna should not have requested Lord Krishna to bring the chariot into a position from which the generals could be seen in such a mean and bold stance. But from the angle of providence, it had to happen. Arjuna had to experience that sorrow all alone.

Fighting is one type of interaction; affectionate dealings are another. The seasoned warriors like Bhishma and *Droṇa* knew this. These men had already faced such situations. Bhishma had fought and partially subdued his own dear teacher, *Paraśurāma*, the empowered chastiser of rulers. *Droṇa* humbled his own dear friend, *Drupada*. A person like *Droṇa* was a moving killing-machine on any battlefield. In a confrontation, such men suddenly forgot their affections even for their closest relatives. But Arjuna was not like that. He could not instantly dismiss his affections for others. Bhishma and *Droṇa* knew what Arjuna was going through, but they could care less because as seasoned military men, they had no time for youngsters who might have ventured out to fight a man's war. If Arjuna did not have the guts, courage, and whatever else it took to be a fighter, that was his dilemma. He could go back to military school and harden himself further. Arjuna was well-practiced in weaponry but if he lacked emotional control, that was his problem. This is the way Bhishma and *Droṇa* saw it. As Krishna explained to Arjuna elsewhere in the *Gītā*, all of the veteran warriors wanted to see Arjuna fight. If Arjuna were to run away, they would all be disappointed. They would lose admiration of him.

All the same, it does not mean that Bhishma and *Droṇa* were callous, blood-thirsty warriors. These men knew that anyone who panics on the warfield, runs away promptly. It is natural to run in the face of serious threat or danger. Thus Bhishma and *Droṇa* made a calculated display of military power to either scare away or harden Arjuna.

Arjuna made a serious mistake in considering the opponents to be relatives, well-wishers and friends. One should have a certain type of vision in affectionate dealings and the reverse type in battle encounters. It is something like father and son. In some cases the father is affectionate and in others, he may be meaner than a stranger. It all depends on which mood is appropriate to the son's long-range interest. A mature individual knows when to apply affection and when to enforce discipline. If we always want to live in the world of affection, we will be living in imagination only. Affection, indifference, and discipline are the three ways of relations. To achieve certain results, one must know how and when to apply each. Affection alone cannot work in this world because this situation is always changing.

Arjuna may be accused of attachment in this case, but it is more like a lack of preparation. He was not prepared for a civil war. He had a misconception that war meant fighting persons other than relatives and friends. Lord Krishna corrected this faulty thinking of Arjuna.

Interestingly, King *Dhṛtarāṣṭra*, who was up-tight and nervous at the beginning, relaxed at this stage of the discourse with Sanjaya. Knowing the gentle nature of Arjuna, *Dhṛtarāṣṭra* enjoyed this affectionate display of his nephew. He hoped that the battle would have ended with Arjuna's withdrawal from the warfield.

Near the end of the fight when Sanjaya sat alone with *Dhṛtarāṣṭra*, at least so the *Mahābhārata* tells us, *Dhṛtarāṣṭra* relieved himself and explained his frustrations. He told Sanjaya that even though people might have considered him to be foolish, still he had insight. He listed many observations which caused him to lose hope in victory and to know of certain defeat. One of the observations was this:

Dhṛtarāṣṭra said: "When I heard from you, Sanjaya, that Arjuna was overcome with cowardice and sat down on the chariot seat, and then Lord Krishna spoke and showed Arjuna all the worlds within the Universal Form, O Sanjaya, I lost all hope of victory." (Mahābhārata excerpt)

तान्समीक्ष्य स कौन्तेयः
सर्वान्बन्धूनवस्थितान् ।
कृपया परयाविष्टो
विषीदन्निदमब्रवीत् ॥ १.२७॥
tānsamīkṣya sa kaunteyaḥ
sarvānbandhūnavasthitān
kṛpayā parayāviṣṭo
viṣīdannidamabravīt (1.27)

tān — them; samīkṣya — observing; sa — he; kaunteyaḥ — son of Kuntī; sarvān — all; bandhūn — relatives; avasthitān — armored; kṛpayā — with compassion; parayāviṣṭaḥ — overwhelmed by deep; viṣīdann — feeling discouraged; idam — this; abravīt — he said

Observing all his relatives in the armored state, that son of Kuntī was overwhelmed by deep compassion. Feeling discouraged, he spoke this: (1.27)

<u>*Commentary:*</u>

There is no point dressing in a battle array, then going forward, facing the opponents and crying. That is pointless. Lord Krishna explained this to Arjuna in no uncertain terms.

Duryodhana enjoyed this presumption of Arjuna, who came forward without the proper emotional regard. Before fighting one must convert affections into defensive or offensive power. If one is unable to do so, one should not go to a battlefield.

We may wonder why Arjuna felt this sorrow. It was spontaneous but nevertheless motivated. The urge was emotional. It arose because Arjuna was aware of his ability to wipe out many of the Kurus. He was aware of Krishna's supportive presence. He knew that the Kauravas would lose because of descending sinful reactions. Arjuna thought, "These people are making a serious mistake if they expect to be victorious. It would be a miscalculation. They have no power to win because their faulty actions will de-energize them. At the same time, we may not have the courage to discipline them."

Arjuna cried for the stupidity of Duryodhana and his supporters who were determined to fight to the bitter end, giving up all sensibility and reasonableness. Arjuna was sad because he not could be sure that they would have become reformed, even if there was a battle. The battle might be fought. They might give up their bodies and pass on from this world with the same determination and misunderstanding, not grasping that it is better to live in insufficiency by the rules of righteousness than to prosper by unfair means. This was the underlying cause for Arjuna's sorrow. But Arjuna was not God. What was the worth of his view?

दृष्ट्वेमान्स्वजनान्कृष्ण
युयुत्सून्समवस्थितान् ।
सीदन्ति मम गात्राणि
मुखं च परिशुष्यति ॥१.२८॥
dṛṣṭvemānsvajanānkṛṣṇa
yuyutsūnsamavasthitān
sīdanti mama gātrāṇi
mukhaṁ ca pariśuṣyati (1.28)

dṛṣṭvemāṁ — having seen this; svajanān — my people; kṛṣṇa — Krishna; yuyutsūṁ — eager for combat; samavasthitān — standing near; sīdanti — collapse; mama — my; gātrāṇi — legs; mukhaṁ — mouth; ca — and; pariśuṣyati — dries up

Having seen this situation of my own people, standing near, eager for combat, my legs collapse and my mouth dries up. (1.28)

Commentary:

The impetus for fighting has left Arjuna. He sat down. He turned to Krishna to discuss the matter. His attitude changed. He became indifferent to the civil dispute between his brothers and Duryodhana.

Bhīma, Arjuna, and Lord Krishna insisted that there be a fight. Only Yudhishthira was hesitant. Then, at last, after the allies expressed desire for war, Yudhishthira declared it. Now Arjuna experienced a change in attitude in favor of retreating. His nature reacted to the situation in a cowardly manner.

वेपथुश्च शरीरे मे
रोमहर्षश्च जायते ।
गाण्डीवं स्रंसते हस्तात्
त्वक् चैव परिदह्यते ॥१.२९॥
vepathuśca śarīre me
romaharṣaśca jāyate
gāṇḍīvaṁ sraṁsate hastāt
tvak caiva paridahyate (1.29)

vepathuś — trembling; ca — and; śarīre — in the body; me — my; romaharṣaś — bristling of hair; ca — and; jāyate — takes place; gāṇḍīvaṁ — Gāṇḍīva bow; sraṁsate — falls; hastāt — from the hand; tvak — skin; caiva — and indeed; paridahyate — burns

A trembling is in my body and a bristling of my hairs takes place. The Gāṇḍīva bow falls from my hand. Indeed, my skin burns. (1.29)

Commentary:

Arjuna's body reacted in a nervous way. He was unable to control the response. Ancient warriors were supposed to have mastered fear and cowardice in military training and during their first battle encounter. Despite fears, a warrior was supposed to assume a manly posture of courage whereby his normal affection became meaningless even to his own mind.

न च शक्नोम्यवस्थातुं
भ्रमतीव च मे मनः ।
निमित्तानि च पश्यामि
विपरीतानि केशव ॥ १.३० ॥
na ca śaknomyavasthātuṁ
bhramatīva ca me manaḥ
nimittāni ca paśyāmi
viparītāni keśava (1.30)

na — not; ca — and; śaknomy — I can; avasthātuṁ — to remain standing; bhramatīva — as if it wanders; ca — and; me — my; manaḥ — the mind; nimittāni — indications; ca — and; paśyāmi — I perceive; viparītāni — bad; keśava — beautiful-haired one

I cannot remain standing. My mind feels as if it wavers. I perceive bad indications, O beautiful-haired one. (1.30)

Commentary:

These reactionary feelings within the nature of Arjuna are natural for any man who confronts a civil conflict without the proper preparation. The decision to fight should be made before one goes to the battlefield and not after one gets there and observes the belligerent attitude of the opponents. We may study Arjuna's reaction for a better understanding of human nature.

न च श्रेयोऽनुपश्यामि
हत्वा स्वजनमाहवे ।
न काङ्क्षे विजयं कृष्ण
न च राज्यं सुखानि च ॥ १.३१ ॥
na ca śreyo'nupaśyāmi
hatvā svajanamāhave
na kāṅkṣe vijayaṁ kṛṣṇa
na ca rājyaṁ sukhāni ca (1.31)

na — no; ca — and; śreyaḥ — benefit; 'nupaśyāmi = anupaśyāmi — I can imagine; hatvā — killing; svajanam — my folks; āhave — in battle; na — nor; kāṅkṣe — desired; vijayaṁ — victory; kṛṣṇa — O Krishna; na — nor; ca — and; rājyaṁ — political power; sukhāni — good feelings; ca — and

And I can imagine no benefit in killing off my kinfolk in battle. I do not desire victory, O Krishna, or political power, or good feelings. (1.31)

Commentary:

Arjuna searched his mind and feelings and could not find a supportive cause for fighting, especially since the implication was death for relatives. As far as he was concerned, the situation was irrational. Each person has a conscience. Each person may be posted in a position to analyze the outcome of wholesale violence. But that does not mean that each warrior's view has equal worth. It all depends on positions of importance. It may be that Arjuna put himself in a more important position than was due to him. If so, he acted egotistically.

It was a tough position. Arjuna had to deal with his conscience and simultaneously dismiss its conclusions because he was subordinate to a greater authority. He had two leaders over him, his brother Yudhishthira and his cousin Lord Krishna. If he were to resign as a fighter, he would have been blackmailing or intimidating his brother. He would have been denying his fighting service to Lord Krishna. These factors must be considered. In that sense, his objections were irrelevant. The question is: How important was Arjuna? How much should he have allowed himself in terms of refusing an order from Yudhishthira or Lord Krishna? What was the value of his sensitivities?

We may all ask ourselves the same questions after understanding the demands of Krishna in the *Gītā*.

किं नो राज्येन गोविन्द
किं भोगैर्जीवितेन वा ।
येषामर्थे काङ्क्षितं नो
राज्यं भोगाः सुखानि च ॥१.३२॥
kiṁ no rājyena govinda
kiṁ bhogairjīvitena vā
yeṣāmarthe kāṅkṣitaṁ no
rājyaṁ bhogāḥ sukhāni ca (1.32)

kiṁ — what value would there be; no — to us; rājyena — with political control of a nation; govinda — Chief of the cowherds; kiṁ — what use would there be?; bhogair — with enjoyments; jīvitena — with life; vā — or; yeṣām — whose; arthe — in the interest; kāṅkṣitaṁ — was desired; no — of us; rājyaṁ — political control; bhogāḥ — enjoyable aspects; sukhāni — pleasures; ca — and

What value to us would there be with political control of a nation, O Chief of the cowherds? What use would there be with the enjoyable aspects or with life? Those in whose interest, the political control, the enjoyments and pleasures, were desired by us, (1.32)

Commentary:

After taking a position as the master of the war field, the person who would stop or continue the hostilities, Arjuna began to assess the worth of the battle encounter. Like us, he took himself too seriously. He felt that his opinion counted. Every human is plagued with this false application of his or her individuality. But consideration is so much wasted energy when we apply it to a situation for which we are not responsible. In situations where we are merely minor actors, the application of this type of thinking is a waste of energy.

We are not suggesting that a man should not think for himself nor analyze his participation in activities, but one must know that his conclusions may be applied differently to different situations, all depending upon the degree of liabilities. In this situation, there are two people on the Pandavas' side who have to carry the major responsibility for the participation of the Pandava forces. These persons are King Yudhishthira and Lord Krishna. Others are simply subordinates of these two personalities. The considerations of Arjuna have relevance insofar as it might show Arjuna how he would have preferred to arrange the circumstances if he were in charge.

To consider is alright, but we must know how, when, and where to apply the consideration; otherwise we will suffer needless anxiety. By going to the center of the war field in this attitude of being the main man, Arjuna exposed himself to an emotional breakdown that was unnecessary. In any case, we learn from it.

The question as to the value of a kingdom which is acquired through bloodshed, especially bloodshed of relatives and friends, is a question that should have been asked by King Yudhishthira and not by Arjuna. But there is an appropriate question: What would be the value of life which was continued after encouraging members of one's family to continue a corrupt administration? This question greatly foreshadowed and nullified

Arjuna's original idea. Even though a kingdom acquired by judicial violence or disciplinary force, is not as preferable as a country acquired by peaceful conciliation, still, to adjust a corrupted kingdom by force would be better than to walk on with indifference and allow the population to suffer. It is a case of selecting the better of two evils. Failure to apply disciplinary measures when it is one's duty to do so, is a serious crime against God, mankind and material nature. We must be wary about this. Permissiveness toward corruption is a crime.

In regards to the satisfaction a pious man would get by taking a kingdom through disciplinary measures that might include killing of family members and friends, obviously the man would get little joy if any, in doing that. But we must realize that in some activities, satisfaction should not be desired for a result. Only in particular activities should we look for satisfaction and much of what we do should be done as duty only. If we have to get satisfaction for every endeavor, we will put ourselves in a sensitive position and will be able to act only when we anticipate pleasure. This type of pleasure-seeking attitude might be relevant to children but it should be outgrown in adults.

Arjuna asked Lord Krishna about the *bhogāh*, luxuries or relishable pleasures, to be derived from such a battle. It is not that Arjuna was childish, but this is a childish approach nevertheless. An experienced politician should not ask such a question which may be put forward by an excited youth. The mere idea that Arjuna followed his mind over these considerations shows clearly that at the time of his viewing the armies, he was saturated by passionate energies. His assessment was greatly diluted thereby.

Arjuna cited a dilemma or contrary view, a paradox, a yes-and-no affair, a sweet-and-sour experience, a gain-and-loss. He stated that the people for whom the kingdom would be secured were themselves imperiled in the battle. But a mature politician would not view the possibilities in that way. Let us take the example of the death penalty. Let us assume that a man killed a few people. He is then arrested by the police, brought before a court, and found guilty by the due process of law. What next? Is the judge supposed to free him because a psychiatrist suggests that if the accused is executed, a plan for reform would be ineffective?

If the man is killed, he cannot be reformed on this side of existence. But that does not mean that he should be spared the execution. The higher solution to the problem is to reform the man, but the ways of social existence do not necessarily permit the application of a higher solution.

The Kurus were too corrupt to be reformed because their misdeeds strengthened them sufficiently for effective resistance to any reform attempt. Thus they had to face the battle encounter. In other words, in such a situation, the higher solution of reform must be temporarily suspended for the world hereafter or for the life to come as in the case of the convicted murderer.

We cannot settle everything satisfactorily in one life. We should not expect to do so. Arjuna wanted the satisfaction of convincing the Kurus by peaceful means. He was desperate to achieve that. And if he could not, he was willing to sacrifice the moral development of the people who were ruled by the corrupt Kurus. This is a selfishness in Arjuna or in any of us who agree with him. Our decisions in life need to be broadly based. Lord Krishna systematically dismantled and shredded Arjuna's arguments one by one. He striped away all the cuteness of Arjuna.

Arjuna was so concerned about the outcome that he artificially projected himself into the future. He looked around and saw himself emerging as a powerful, happy, aristocratic ruler with no friends and relatives with whom to enjoy victory. This type of petty thinking should be shorn by a competent statesman. If the Pandavas win the battle, the political power will be Yudhishthira's, not Arjuna's. Arjuna would still be an agent of the king even though his service capacity might be that of a governor. The aristocracy will be King Yudhishthira's and so would any resulting happiness. Arjuna would share in that, but to project himself and enjoy that beforehand was to exhibit immaturity.

There is a sharp contrast between this reactionary feeling of Arjuna and that of Bharata, the brother of *Rāma*. When Bharata was offered the kingdom of Ayodhyā and all the aristocratic trappings, he declined. Later on he explained that such power and glory was not suited to his nature. He said that even in imagination, he could not assume such power.

But Bharata is a divinity in the first class, a Godhead person. As such he could make that sort of exacting calculation; while Arjuna, who is in the category of a liberated but limited being, inappropriately takes the egotistic stance.

त इमेऽवस्थिता युद्धे
प्राणांस्त्यक्त्वा धनानि च ।
आचार्याः पितरः पुत्रास्
तथैव च पितामहाः ॥ १.३३ ॥
ta ime'vasthitā yuddhe
prāṇāṁstyaktvā dhanāni ca
ācāryāḥ pitaraḥ putrās
tathaiva ca pitāmahāḥ (1.33)

ta — they; ime — these; 'vasthitā = avasthitā — are armored; yuddhe — in battle formation; prāṇāṁs — lives; tyaktvā — having left aside; dhanāni — financial assets; ca — and; ācāryāḥ — revered teachers; pitaraḥ — fathers; putrās — sons; tathaiva — also; ca — and; pitāmahāḥ — grandfathers

...(they) are armed in battle formation, having left aside their lives and financial assets. These are revered teachers, fathers, sons and also grandfathers, (1.33)

__Commentary:__

Here, Arjuna indirectly asked for consideration. He wanted to be excused. Even if Lord Krishna permitted the battle, Arjuna wanted exemption from it. He indirectly reminded Lord Krishna that fighting against foreigners is easy, but to fight against relatives is perplexing. Arjuna indirectly appealed to Lord Krishna to spare him the task. Arjuna was an ambidextrous marksman who fired arrows with lightning speed. Most of the opponents would have no chance against him. To his mind, the odds of their survival were very slim.

मातुलाः श्वशुराः पौत्राः
स्यालाः संबन्धिनस्तथा ।
एतान्न हन्तुमिच्छामि
घ्नतोऽपि मधुसूदन ॥ १.३४ ॥
mātulāḥ śvaśurāḥ pautrāḥ
syālāḥ saṁbandhinastathā
etānna hantumicchāmi
ghnato'pi madhusūdana (1.34)

mātulāḥ — brothers of mothers; śvaśurāḥ — fathers of wives; pautrāḥ — grandsons; śyālāḥ — brothers-in-law; saṁbandhinas — relatives; tathā — also; etān — them; na — not; hantum — to kill; icchāmi — I desire; ghnato — those who are intent on killing; 'pi = api — even though; madhusūdana — slayer of Madhu

...brothers of our mothers, fathers of our wives, grandsons, brothers-in-law, and also their relatives. O slayer of Madhu, I do not desire to slay them even though they are intent on killing, (1.34)

Commentary:

In so many words, Arjuna asked Lord Krishna to forgive the Kurus. Even if they wanted to kill and were eager to inflict injury, still, Arjuna felt that Lord Krishna, as the Supreme Being, should overlook the offences. To Arjuna's mind, Krishna need not react by compelling Arjuna to hurt or kill them.

अपि त्रैलोक्यराज्यस्य
हेतोः किं नु महीकृते ।
निहत्य धार्तराष्ट्रान्नः
का प्रीतिः स्याज्जनार्दन ॥१.३५॥
api trailokyarājyasya
hetoḥ kiṁ nu mahīkṛte
nihatya dhārtarāṣṭrānnaḥ
kā prītiḥ syājjanārdana (1.35)

api — even; trailokya — of the three sectors, of the universe; rājyasya — political control; hetoḥ — on account of; kiṁ - what; nu — then; mahīkṛte — for the sake of the earth; nihatya — killing; dhārtarāṣṭrān — the sons of Dhṛtarāṣṭra; naḥ — to us; kā — what; prītiḥ — joy; syāj — might it be; janārdana — O motivator of people

...even for political control of the three sectors of the universe, how then for the earth? O motivator of people, what joy should be had by killing the sons of Dhṛtarāṣṭra? (1.35)

Commentary:

Arjuna made the greatest comparison between what might be attained through sovereignty or political power and what might be done to get that authority by killing relatives. He felt that his values were such, whereby he could not fight even if he were offered sovereignty over many planets.

Vedic literature presents a three-fold planetary divide consisting of the lower planets, the earthly middle planets, and the *Svarga* heavenly places. In Arjuna's opinion, none of these were worth the lives of relatives. He placed a very high value on the lives of kinsmen. He then asked if there is anything more desirable which could motivate him to take their lives.

पापमेवाश्रयेदस्मान्
हत्वैतानाततायिनः ।
तस्मान्नार्हा वयं हन्तुं
धार्तराष्ट्रान्स्वबान्धवान् ।
स्वजनं हि कथं हत्वा
सुखिनः स्याम माधव ॥१.३६॥
pāpamevāśrayedasmān
hatvaitānātatāyinaḥ
tasmānnārhā vayaṁ hantuṁ
dhārtarāṣṭrānsvabāndhavān
svajanaṁ hi kathaṁ hatvā
sukhinaḥ syāma mādhava (1.36)

pāpam — sin; evāśrayed = eva — even + āśrayed — should take hold; asmān — to us; hatvaitān = hatvā — having killed + etān — these; ātatāyinaḥ — offenders; tasmān — therefore; nārhā — unjustified; vayaṁ — we; hantuṁ — to kill; dhārtarāṣṭrān — sons of Dhṛtarāṣṭra; svabāndhavān — our relatives; svajanaṁ — our own people; hi — indeed; kathaṁ — how; hatvā — having killed; sukhinaḥ — happiness; syāma — should be; mādhava — descendant of Madhu

Having killed the offenders, sin will take hold of us. Therefore we are not justified to kill the sons of Dhṛtarāṣṭra, our relatives. Having killed our own people, how should we be happy, O descendent of Madhu? (1.36)

Commentary:

Arjuna realized that Krishna had no intentions of stopping the battle. He pleaded using another argument about the evil which would be generated. He felt that in the end, there would be no happiness.

यद्यप्येते न पश्यन्ति
लोभोपहतचेतसः ।
कुलक्षयकृतं दोषं
मित्रद्रोहे च पातकम् ॥ १.३७॥
yadyapyete na paśyanti
lobhopahatacetasaḥ
kulakṣayakṛtaṁ doṣaṁ
mitradrohe ca pātakam (1.37)

yadyapyete = yadi — if + api — even + ete — these; na — not; paśyanti — see; lobhopahata cetasaḥ = lobha — greed + upahata — possessed by + cetasaḥ — thoughts; kulakṣayakṛtaṁ = kula — clan + ksaya — destruction + kṛtaṁ — caused; doṣaṁ — fault; mitradrohe = mitra — friend + drohe — harm; ca — and; pātakam — crime

Even if these persons, their minds being possessed by greed, do not see the fault caused by the destruction of the clan and the crime of hurting a friend, (1.37)

Commentary:

This is the last statement of this nature. After this Arjuna changed his approach in the effort to influence Lord Krishna. If Krishna decided not to participate even as Arjuna's charioteer, King Yudhishthira would have relinquished his claim to the ancestral kingdom and the war may have been averted. Arjuna was hopeful that Krishna would change His view. Even if the Kauravas were a corrupt lot, Arjuna felt no necessity to react.

कथं न ज्ञेयमस्माभिः
पापादस्मान्निवर्तितुम् ।
कुलक्षयकृतं दोषं
प्रपश्यद्भिर्जनार्दन ॥ १.३८॥
kathaṁ na jñeyamasmābhiḥ
pāpādasmānnivartitum
kulakṣayakṛtaṁ doṣaṁ
prapaśyadbhirjanārdana (1.38)

kathaṁ — how; na — not; jñeyam — to be understood; asmābhiḥ — by us; pāpād — from sin; asmān — from this; nivartitum — turn away; kulakṣaya = kula — clan + kṣaya — destruction; kṛtaṁ — caused; doṣaṁ — crime; prapaśyadbhiḥ — by due reason; janārdana — O motivator of human beings

...O motivator of human beings, why, by due reason, should we not understand that we should turn away from this sin, the crime caused by the destruction of the clan? (1.38)

Commentary:

Arjuna focused on the fault of the opponents. First he analyzed himself. When he could not find in himself the will to fight, nor the motivation to be angered, he became critical of the Kauravas. His proposal was this: "There is no point in responding to the faults of these people. O Krishna, let us turn away from this. Allow the government to continue in corruption. Let us live peacefully without responding to the aggression."

कुलक्षये प्रणश्यन्ति
कुलधर्माः सनातनाः ।
धर्मे नष्टे कुलं कृत्स्नम्
अधर्मोऽभिभवत्युत ॥ १.३९॥

kulakṣaye — in destruction of the family clan; praṇaśyanti — vanish; kuladharmāḥ — family traditions; sanātanāḥ — ancient; dharme — in the traditional values; naṣṭe —

kulakṣaye praṇaśyanti
kuladharmāḥ sanātanāḥ
dharme naṣṭe kulaṁ kṛtsnam
adharmo'bhibhavatyuta (1.39)

in the removal; kulaṁ — clan; kṛtsnam — whole; adharmo — lawlessness; 'bhibhavatyuta = abhibhavati — it overpowers + uta — even

In the destruction of the clan, the ancient family traditions vanish. In the removal of the traditional values, the entire clan is overpowered by lawlessness. (1.39)

Commentary:

Arjuna used a different argument. He made a cultural analysis in terms of historic proofs. It is a fact that when a corrupt ruling family is disposed of, the economy may worsen. There was some good and some bad in the Kuru dynasty. Arjuna argued that if the elders were killed, the good policies would go down with the bad ones. The country would become chaotic. In addition, the countries of the allied rulers would be affected.

Arjuna did not think it was worth the risk. Better to have a step-father than no father at all. Better to be ruled by a corrupt government, than not to be governed at all.

अधर्माभिभवात्कृष्ण
प्रदुष्यन्ति कुलस्त्रियः ।
स्त्रीषु दुष्टासु वार्ष्णेय
जायते वर्णसंकरः ॥ १.४० ॥
adharmābhibhavātkṛṣṇa
praduṣyanti kulastriyaḥ
strīṣu duṣṭāsu vārṣṇeya
jāyate varṇasaṁkaraḥ (1.40)

adharmābhibhavat = adharma — lawlessness + abhibhavāt — from predominant; kṛṣṇa — O Krishna; praduṣyanti — are degraded; kulastriyaḥ — the women of the clan; strīṣu — in women; duṣṭāsu — degraded; vārṣṇeya — O clansman of the Vṛṣṇis; jāyate — there arises; varṇasaṁkaraḥ — sexual intermixture of the classes

Due to the predominance of lawlessness, the women of the clan are degraded. In such women, O clansman of the Vṛṣṇis, there arises the sexual intermixture of the classes. (1.40)

Commentary:

This was Arjuna's main argument. If Krishna could have agreed to this contention, Arjuna's desire to desist from the battle would have been fulfilled. The problem with this conclusion of Arjuna, is its validity. It is a fact that when a ruling family is disposed of, or disgraced, the general principles are waived. It may be that the dynasty was corrupt; still, whatever moral principles were maintained by them might deteriorate and the country might sink further in lawlessness.

There are exceptions to this rule, but this is the general history of civilization. Arjuna had a solid argument. When women become sexually loose, there is much cross breeding in terms of intercultural marriages. These instances of sexual familiarity are handled in a haphazard way. The children produced from it, depart from good tradition. Subsequently, they act recklessly and discard the culture of their forebears.

Sriman Ramanand Prasad of American *Gītā* Society has this comment:

All humans are the same race - the human race. The word वर्णसंकरः (varṇa sankarah) may be translated as "children born out of wedlock" The young wives of all the warriors who died on the battle field were generally not allowed to remarry, consequently there was a great possibility of corruption and I think Arjuna was talking about this. Some

Indian brahmanas say that वर्णसंकर: (varṇa sankarah) is "children born of inter-caste marriage" I do not think so. Even Veda Vyāsaji was born out of inter-caste and inter-racial marriage.

Therefore वर्णसंकर: (varṇa sankarah) really means "bastard" and society meets downfall. This is what is happening in a permissive society in America today.

संकरो नरकायैव
कुलघ्नानां कुलस्य च ।
पतन्ति पितरो ह्येषां
लुप्तपिण्डोदकक्रियाः ॥ १.४१ ॥
saṁkaro narakāyaiva
kulaghnānāṁ kulasya ca
patanti pitaro hyeṣāṁ
luptapiṇḍodakakriyāḥ (1.41)

saṁkaraḥ — sexual intermixture; narakāyaiva = narakāya — to hell + eva — indeed; kulaghnānāṁ = kula — clan + ghnānāṁ — destroyers; kulasya — of the clan; ca — and; patanti — are degraded; pitaro — the departed ancestors; hyeṣāṁ = hi — indeed + eṣāṁ — of these; luptapiṇḍodakakriyāḥ = lupta — deprived of + piṇḍa — psychic cakes + udaka — psychic water + kriyāḥ — ceremonial rites

Indeed, the sexual intermixture causes the destroyers of the clan and the clan itself to go to hell. The departed ancestors of those clansmen, being deprived of the psychic cakes and water which are offered ceremonially, are degraded. (1.41)

Commentary:

Arjuna intended to convince Lord Krishna to desist. If Krishna turned away from the battlefield, King Yudhishthira would do likewise, for he used Krishna's opinion as his reference for action. Arjuna explained that if the Kurus were killed in the civil conflict, there would be a sexual imbalance, whereby many widows would link up with men haphazardly. And that, he felt, would ruin the civilization.

Dr. Ramanand Prasad states that:

> *Bastard children generally are a burden to society and they are looked down upon. They have no family values because they do not know who their fathers and grandfathers are.*

Furthermore, Arjuna explained that the departed ancestors would lose their opportunities for rebirth. First they would be deprived of the ghost food that is offered at particular times of the year through the pinda mystic ceremonial procedures.

Secondly, they would lose their opportunities for aristocratic baby forms and might take low-class infant bodies. Such a specter was frightening to Arjuna.

दोषैरेतैः कुलघ्नानां
वर्णसंकरकारकैः ।
उत्साद्यन्ते जातिधर्माः
कुलधर्माश्च शाश्वताः ॥ १.४२ ॥
doṣairetaiḥ kulaghnānāṁ
varṇasaṁkarakārakaiḥ
utsādyante jātidharmāḥ
kuladharmāśca śāśvatāḥ (1.42)

doṣair — with sins; etaiḥ — by these; kulaghnānāṁ — of the family destroyers; varṇasaṁkarakārakaiḥ = varṇasaṁkara — sexual intermixture of classes + kārakaiḥ — by producing; utsādyante — disappeared; jātidharmāḥ — individual skills; kuladharmāś — family duties; ca — and; śāśvatāḥ — long-standing

By the sins of the family destroyers and by the sexual intermixture of the classes, individual skills and traditional family duties disappear. (1.42)

Commentary:

This argument of Arjuna concerns the uprooting of traditional values through which human culture is sustained. It takes centuries to establish such values. They cannot be established in a few generations. After becoming outmoded, it takes centuries to re-establish these. In addition, such values cannot be established by ordinary entities. Selected persons must also be born in a particular time, place and family, to have the sort of impact on history through which the higher cultural values become established again. Understanding this, Arjuna wanted to take no chances. At least he did not want to share in the responsibility of breaking down tradition. Arjuna noted Bhishma, the aged great-grandfather of the Kurus, the man who established and maintained such traditional ways. But Arjuna carefully avoided mentioning any names in verse 37.

yadyapyete na paśyanti lobhopahatacetasaḥ
kulakṣayakṛtaṁ doṣaṁ mitradrohe ca pātakam (1.37)

Even if these persons, their minds being possessed by greed, do not see the fault caused by the destruction of the clan and the crime of hurting a friend, (1.37)

Here Arjuna indirectly stated that people like Bhishma and other elders of the Kuru family were morally desensitized. He felt that their senility or stupidity by virtue of age, should be overlooked.

उत्सन्नकुलधर्माणां
मनुष्याणां जनार्दन ।
नरके ऽनियतं वासो
भवतीत्यनुशुश्रुम ॥ १.४३ ॥
utsannakuladharmāṇāṁ
manuṣyāṇāṁ janārdana
narake 'niyataṁ vāso
bhavatītyanuśuśruma (1.43)

utsanna kula dharmāṇāṁ = utsanna — destroyed + kuladharmāṇāṁ — of family customs; manuṣyāṇām — of men; janārdana — O Kṛṣṇa; narake — in hell; 'niyataṁ = aniyatam — indefinitely; vāso — dwelling; bhavatītyanuśuśruma = bhavati — it is + iti — was developed + anuśuśruma — we heard repeatedly

O Krishna, those who destroy the family customs dwell in hell indefinitely. This was declared repeatedly. (1.43)

Commentary:

Readers of this translation might find that some sentences are awkward but only in terms of our English grammar orientation. The method used in this translation, is to follow the Sanskrit poetic thinking presentation and not to convert into Sanskrit prose and then into English prose. We did not attempt to translate into English first and then to rearrange into English prose. We tried to follow the poet's thinking pattern.

Arjuna did not see a solution by the method of killing off the corrupt Kurus. He thought they would go to hell for causing the confrontation, and that he too would be implicated in the affair, being partially responsible for sending so many fathers to their graves. He knew that he might have to account for killing many fathers who would leave behind widows, who might take to loose connections to fulfill sexual cravings and financial outlays. In addition, sons and daughters might become vice-prone once their fathers died in battle. Arjuna foresaw hell for the corrupt Kurus and for himself as well.

The implication is this: Arjuna desired to be free of implications but the truth is that

Arjuna is already involved. In the next chapter Lord Krishna will cite other scriptural proofs to nullify Arjuna's ideas.

अहो बत महत्पापं
कर्तुं व्यवसिता वयम् ।
यद्राज्यसुखलोभेन
हन्तुं स्वजनमुद्यताः ॥ १.४४ ॥
aho bata mahatpāpaṁ
kartuṁ vyavasitā vayam
yadrājyasukhalobhena
hantuṁ svajanamudyatāḥ (1.44)

aho — O!; bata — what a wonder!; mahat — great; pāpaṁ — sin; kartuṁ — to perform; vyavasitā — committed to; vayam — we; yad — which; rājyasukhalobhena = rājya — aristocratic + sukha — pleasure + lobhena — with greed; hantuṁ — to kill; svajanam — own folks; udyatāḥ — eager for

O! What a wonder! We are committed to perform a great sin, being eager to kill our kinfolk, through greed for aristocratic pleasures. (1.44)

Commentary:

Arjuna cited the disgrace of the conflict. But regardless, material existence itself is a disgrace, not just the undesirable parts of it. Lord Krishna will hammer home this point in the *Gītā*.

यदि मामप्रतीकारम्
अशस्त्रं शस्त्रपाणयः ।
धार्तराष्ट्रा रणे हन्युस्
तन्मे क्षेमतरं भवेत् ॥ १.४५ ॥
yadi māmapratīkāram
aśastraṁ śastrapāṇayaḥ
dhārtarāṣṭrā raṇe hanyus
tanme kṣemataraṁ bhavet (1.45)

yadi — if; mām — me; apratīkāram — unresisting; aśastraṁ — without weapons, unarmed; śastrapāṇayaḥ — those bearing weapons; dhārtarāṣṭrā — sons of Dhṛtarāṣṭra; raṇe — in battle; hanyuḥ — they may kill; tan — this; me — to me; kṣemataraṁ — greater happiness; bhavet — would be

If the weapon-bearing sons of Dhṛtarāṣṭra should kill me in battle, while I was unresisting, and unarmed, this to me would be greater pleasure. (1.45)

Commentary:

Up to this point Arjuna was unable to influence Lord Krishna. Even though the Lord listened without replying, Arjuna sensed that Krishna was determined to have the battle. He gave this final argument. He preferred to die as a martyr.

एवमुक्त्वार्जुनः संख्ये
रथोपस्थ उपाविशत् ।
विसृज्य सशरं चापं
शोकसंविग्नमानसः ॥ १.४६ ॥
evamuktvārjunaḥ saṁkhye
rathopastha upāviśat
visṛjya saśaraṁ cāpaṁ
śokasaṁvignamānasaḥ (1.46)

evam — thus; uktvā — having spoken; arjunaḥ - Arjuna; saṁkhye — in the conflict; rathopastha = ratha — chariot + upastha — seat; upāviśat — sat down; visṛjya — casting aside; saśaraṁ — together with arrow; cāpaṁ — bow; śokasaṁvignamānasaḥ = śoka — sorrow + saṁvigna — overwhelmed + mānasaḥ — heart

Having spoken, Arjuna, who was in the midst of the conflict, sat down on his chariot. Casting aside his arrow and bow, he was overwhelmed with sorrow. (1.46)

Commentary:

Sanjaya concluded the first chapter of the *Bhagavad-Gītā*. At that time, the only hearer of these words was King *Dhṛtarāṣṭra*. We read this some thousands of years after. *Dhṛtarāṣṭra* maintained silence and reflected on the arguments of Arjuna but he was not allowed to reflect much longer. Lord Krishna promptly replied to Arjuna who sat down in that war chariot.

In effect, Arjuna refused to fight. He cast aside his weapons in defiance to the order of Yudhishthira. He resisted the pressures of destiny which brought him to *Kurukṣetra*.

CHAPTER 2

Divine State*

संजय उवाच
तं तथा कृपयाविष्टम्
अश्रुपूर्णाकुलेक्षणम् ।
विषीदन्तमिदं वाक्यम्
उवाच मधुसूदनः ॥२.१॥
saṁjaya uvāca
taṁ tathā kṛpayāviṣṭam
aśrupūrṇākulekṣaṇam
viṣīdantamidaṁ vākyam
uvāca madhusūdanaḥ (2.1)

saṁjaya — Sanjaya; uvāca — said; taṁ — to him; tathā — in this way; kṛpayāviṣṭam — overcome with pity; aśrupūrṇākulekṣaṇam = aśru — tear + pūrṇa — filled + ākula — perplexed + īkṣaṇam — eyes; viṣīdantam — saddened with hopelessness; idaṁ — this; vākyam — response; uvāca — spoke; madhusūdanaḥ — killer of Madhu

Sanjaya said: To him who was overcome with pity, whose eyes were filled with tears, who was perplexed and saddened with hopelessness, the killer of Madhu spoke this response: (2.1)

Commentary:

In an emotionally torn-up condition, Arjuna exhibited infantile behavior. His manliness disappeared. His boyish nature showed through. In that mood he requested guidance from Lord Krishna.

Krishna rescued Arjuna before. Arjuna was already in the habit of getting advice from the Lord in trying circumstances. Lord Krishna had the knack for solving the most difficult problems. Arjuna knew both by instinct and conviction that the Lord would show him a way out of the complexity. By seeing himself as an independent agent, Arjuna placed himself in a very dangerous position. He posed as the master of a situation which he did not have the power to control. When the liabilities were realized by him, his body shivered, his hairs stood on end, his hands lost clasping power, his eyes filled with tears, his emotional energy turmoiled, his intellect was baffled, and his personality felt the limits of its capacity.

Arjuna had the privilege of asking Lord Krishna to drive the chariot forward. Lord Krishna submitted Himself as a chariot driver. The events which led up to this involved a competition between Duryodhana and Arjuna for Krishna's alliance. Here is that story in brief:

**The Mahābhārata contains no chapter headings. This title was assigned by the translator on the basis of verse 27 of this chapter.*

Prince Duryodhana and Arjuna both sought Krishna's alliance in the war. From their respective camps they hurried to Dvāraka, each hoping to meet Krishna. Arriving first and finding Krishna at rest, Duryodhana took a seat near the Lord's head. Arjuna entered soon after and stood at the foot of Krishna's bed. When the Lord awoke, He saw Arjuna first. Krishna inquired of their welfare. Duryodhana said, "It is only fitting that you regard me first. Arjuna and I are equally related to you. You are affectionate to both of us, but I arrived first. By rule of order, you should satisfy my request first."

Krishna replied, "I do not doubt that you came first, but it is Arjuna whom I beheld initially. Since you arrived first and since My eyes rested on Arjuna first, I will assist both of you, equally.

"By policy, the juniors have priority Therefore Arjuna may choose first. I have millions of competent warriors. These may be given to one of you. And I, Myself, without weapons and without fighting consignment, will advise the other. Arjuna, you are entitled to the first selection. You can take either My army or My consultation."

Without hesitation, Arjuna selected Krishna even though Krishna was to be a non-combatant. Duryodhana was exceedingly glad of this choice He got what he wanted, the warriors of Krishna.

After Duryodhana departed, the Lord questioned Arjuna. He said, "Why did you choose Me, knowing that I would carry no weapon nor fight directly?"

Arjuna replied, "Krishna, You can certainly kill the enemy warriors. And I can also defeat them singlehandedly. Your fame and reputation follows You. I am a lover of fame. I always desired that You drive my chariot, and I ask You now to fulfill my desire."

Krishna replied, "O son of Kuntī, it is good that you rate yourself to Me. I agree to be your charioteer." (Summary from Mahābhārata, Udyoga Parva 8)

Once everything was set up for the battle and the warriors confronted each other, Arjuna lost touch with reality. He was pushed over the brink of his limited position as a non-absolute figure. He assumed importance impulsively. This pattern of behavior was exhibited in other circumstances of Arjuna's. He did it again, even after the Battle of *Kurukșetra*. We can understand, therefore, that in the conditioned state we do this repeatedly. Arjuna's one or two mistakes indicate our millions of errors. We are many times worse than Arjuna. We repeatedly overestimate ourselves and forget that we are not absolute. The *Gītā* discusses our highest position as being expressions of the energy of God.

On the other side, we hear that Duryodhana went forward to look at the Pandava army. He evaluated them. Not having the military expertise of Arjuna, he was not as afflicted as Arjuna, nor as emotional. He did not feel that he could be the sole victor. Instead he turned and went to his military instructor to alert the teacher of the crisis. Duryodhana relied on his men, particularly Bhishma and *Droṇa*. In the beginning, Arjuna did no such thing. He relied solely on himself.

One may pass quickly to other verses of the *Gītā* to get to the heart of the matter, but this is the heart of the matter, because this is the turning point. Most of us will not have Lord Krishna standing before us in the crises of life. We have to study this turning point and learn how to rectify ourselves before succumbing to crippling emotions.

By putting himself forward as the master of the situation, as the one indispensible warrior, Arjuna bypassed his eldest brother Yudhishthira. This was a mistake. He was impulsively moved by the circumstances and superseded his brother, the King.

These above are some of the social considerations. We must now change the angle and give the spiritual ones. From the divine view, it did indeed depend on Arjuna and no one else. Even though Arjuna should have extended the courtesy of decision to Yudhishthira, still, Arjuna was the man of the moment. *Droṇa* and Bhishma, the big generals on the battlefield, were thinking of Arjuna because they knew very well that only Arjuna was empowered by destiny to achieve victory for the Pandavas. Arjuna was the only Pandava with the required expertise. This they knew from their experience in fighting him when they tried to rustle the hundreds of cattle of King *Virāṭa*. At that time, Lord Krishna was not physically present. Arjuna did not have an army. He only possessed weapons and a cowardly charioteer named Prince *Bhuminjaya*. But Arjuna defeated the Kurus and put them to flight to save their honor. Bhishma and *Droṇa* knew Arjuna to be a dangerous youngster when it came to military tactics. Still Bhishma understood that in terms of wholesale manslaughter, Arjuna was a youngster. If he was a seasoned gladiator, he would not have been affected by the confrontation. It was of interest to Bhishma, how Lord Krishna would pull Arjuna out of that compassionate nature. The skill of Lord Krishna was greatly admired by Bhishma. When a man is all down and out, mashed-up inside, torn to shreds in his emotions, and chewed up in considerations, it is always interesting to see if anyone could bring him forward to a sensible, functional view. And this is exactly what Lord Krishna did for Arjuna.

The battle was won in the *Gītā* discourse because on that level Lord Krishna rescued Arjuna from the mire of materialistic affections. Arjuna had every right to anticipate victory because that was his power as the intimate associate of Lord Krishna and as the most skilled warrior on the warfield. But Arjuna should have had the courtesy to get formal permission from Yudhishthira before going forward to review the armies. This is the only reason why Arjuna broke down in tears. By sidestepping his eldest brother, the leading Pandava, Arjuna disempowered himself. He put himself up for intimidation by the survival instinct and his limited nature.

Insofar as we function as agents of the Lord, we have to respect certain social arrangements presented by destiny. Otherwise we will be cheated. Lord Krishna can, of course, adjust providence, but normally He does not interfere. Thus, we should express great care, for material nature will resist us if we do not recognize her power. Arjuna will be rescued by Lord Krishna, but that does not mean that we will be rescued in exactly the same way. We should be careful with the social arrangements of material nature and know when to acknowledge these. It takes a bit of humility. We have to shave off the greater portion of our egocentricity.

This *Bhagavad Gītā* translation and purport was written by the grace and order of Lord Balarama of our Śrī Śrī Krishna and Balarama Deities.

Terri Stokes-Pineda

After the *Gītā* was spoken by Krishna, Arjuna became convinced that he should proceed with the battle. He retrieved courage and took weapons again. Then all of the Pandavas and their allies became very happy. This is one of the nicest parts of the *Mahābhārata* where the Pandavas begin to sound off various musical instruments for the second time. The first was in reply to the leonine roaring conchshell of Bhishma. The second uproar was one of sheer happiness and repossession of confidence which depended so much on Arjuna.

But immediately after this, Arjuna's eldest brother, Yudhishthira, suddenly and without any warning, did a strange thing. He decided to honor the social way, tradition. He knew how to respect social superiors. The warriors were struck with wonder at what he did. After all, Lord Krishna already showed the Universal Form, confirming that the Kauravas would be ruined in one way or another. What was the necessity of following social formalities, even in respect to the projected losers? Yudhishthira, the person of righteousness, took off armor, joined his palms in an attitude of submission, and proceeded on foot, going to General Bhishma on the enemy side. Seeing this, Arjuna followed, and so did the other Pandavas. Then Lord Krishna followed as well. Observing this, the principal allies of the Pandavas did likewise. Most of them were confused by this action of Yudhishthira.

Arjuna proceeded quickly, running after Yudhishthira, and so did the other brothers, Lord Krishna and the allied commanders. Arjuna then questioned Yudhishthira as they proceeded. He said, "What is this about? What are you doing, O King? You left us to approach the enemy warriors. What is your intention, O lord of our lives?"

But the King did not reply. *Bhīma* then questioned. He said, "Where are you going, Ruler of rulers? You took off armor. You approach the enemy unarmed. You left aside your brothers. What is the motive, O King?'"

Nakula Pandava questioned. He said, "You are my eldest brother. O relation of the Bharata family, seeing your action in removing armor and approaching the enemy, I am worried.Tell us what you intend, O King."

Sahadeva Pandava said, "When these hostile battalions, terrible and numerous, are here before us, where do you intend to go, O King?

But Yudhishthira did not reply. He merely kept on. Lord Krishna, seeing the perplexity of the brothers and the allies, spoke to ease their troubled hearts. He said, "His intentions are understood by Me. Hear of it! Having honored the social superiors, namely Bhishma, *Droṇa*, *Kṛpa* and *Śalya*, he will fight thereafter. It is the tradition. A man who respects social superiors can be victorious. Even if such a man then fights those very same superiors, he may defeat them. This is the ancient belief."

But just as Lord Krishna said this, the Kaurava army let out a loud groan of, "What is this?" Duryodhana interpreted Yudhishthira's action in his own way. He said that Yudhishthira was a cowardly man who approached Bhishma to get pardon.

In any case, Yudhishthira went to Bhishma to offer respects and to ask for a way of killing Bhishma. And he regarded Droṇa, *Kṛpa* and *Śalya* in the same way. Lord Krishna then took the opportunity to talk to *Karṇa* who was to fight for Duryodhana. And then something strange occurred. Duryodhana's brother, Yuyutsū, left the Kaurava army just as in the *Rāmāyāṇa*, *Vibhīṣaṇa* suddenly left *Rāvaṇa's* government. *Yuyutsū* went over to fight for Yudhishthira. On that occasion, Yudhishthira was blessed by the elders, but *Śalya* told him that if he had not honored the social superiors, he would have been cursed to lose at *Kurukṣetra*. These are social considerations but as long as we are in the material world, we should give them due consideration.

Madhusūdana is used here as a title of Lord Krishna. This title is selected here by Sanjaya who was aware of other pastimes of the Lord. We may study the significance of this special title of the Blessed Lord. Arjuna was *kṛpayāviṣṭam* or overcome with pity. He was *viṣīdantam* or despairing, impotent and full of worry. He lost manliness, decisiveness and sober vision. He forgot mission, strength, objectives and duty. At the end of the previous creation, the demigod *Brahmā* lost track of his objectives and began to lose track of his scientific knowledge of how to create the universe and maintain order among all the creatures. *Brahmā*'s mind drifted into sleep. At the time, the two demons *Madhu* and *Kaiṭabha* emerged all of a sudden from Lord Garbhodakashayi Vishnu, the Lord of our local universe. They wanted to kill *Brahmā* or at least retrieve and transfer his technical knowledge to their own minds. Since there were no books or manuals on how to create planets and creatures, everything was reliant on the knowledge within *Brahmā*'s mind. These two demons planned to get the information. They were about to spring on *Brahmā* when Krishna killed them. Thus he got the name Madhusudana.

In commenting on this verse, our associate, Sir Paul Castagna, stated that Arjuna was the conduit for many of the emotions and sentiments of many of the players on the field. He explained that Arjuna was a "seasoned" warrior, both by bodily age and by his celebrated past. "Arjuna, he said, "only appeared to have acted out of character because he did not express his experience but rather, the experience of those around him." These are the views of Mr. Castagna.

श्रीभगवानुवाच
कुतस्त्वा कश्मलमिदं
विषमे समुपस्थितम् ।
अनार्यजुष्टमस्वर्ग्यम्
अकीर्तिकरमर्जुन ॥ २.२ ॥
śrībhagavānuvāca
kutastvā kaśmalamidaṁ
viṣame samupasthitam
anāryajuṣṭamasvargyam
akīrtikaramarjuna (2.2)

śrī bhagavān — the Blessed Lord; uvāca — said; kutastvā = kutas — how + tvā — to you; kaśmalam — sickly emotion; idaṁ — this; viṣame — at a crucial time; samupasthitam — come; anāryajuṣṭam — not suitable for a cultured man; asvargyam — not facilitating heaven in the hereafter; akīrtikaram — causing disgrace; arjuna — O Arjuna

The Blessed Lord said: How has this sticky emotion come to you at a crucial time? It is not suitable for a cultured man. It does not facilitate heaven in the hereafter. It causes disgrace, O Arjuna. (2.2)

Commentary:

Arjuna mentioned some seemingly valid points and quoted sufficiently from scripture to back up his cause, but in this verse Lord Krishna rejected the proposal. In the *Gītā*, some of Arjuna's original pleas to Lord Krishna are not even answered. Some are answered indirectly. Some are not dealt with at all. Those questions and doubts of Arjuna which had to do with considering the body as the soul, did not even appear in the mind of Lord Krishna.

Usually we ask questions from the practical level, which is the bodily level of considering every creature to be his or her body. Such questions form most of our inquiry but in spiritual circles such questions actually have no standing. Instead of answering the mundane questions of Arjuna, Lord Krishna puts Arjuna to question regarding the hero's assumption of sickly emotions. The Lord wanted Arjuna to dispel those moods promptly. *Kaśmalam* means an impurity in the nature which caused an emotional breakdown, resulting in a warped perception of reality and in forgetting one's place in an activity. Instead of dealing with the conditions of such impotency, Lord Krishna wanted to banish it entirely.

In a gist, the Lord indicated that Arjuna should not ask those stupid questions which were brought up in Chapter One of the *Gītā*, but should instead explain how he got from being a cultured human being to a sickly emotional man. By addressing Arjuna as *anārya*. Lord Krishna intimidated His friend as being other than a cultured fellow, as being a stupid, uneducated, ill-cultured somebody. This was Arjuna's fault because Arjuna allowed himself to degenerate to that.

By by-passing Yudhishthira and going directly to the battle front and peering into the enemy ranks there, Arjuna became victimized by his affections for General Bhishma, his great uncle. Once he saw that man, affections flowed between them and Arjuna became crippled within.

That kind of impulsive behavior was not preferred by Lord Krishna. The Lord reminded Arjuna that he would be barred entry into the heavens, the Swarga places of the angelic world. Krishna thought the behavior of Arjuna was debilitating.

When we succumb to this kind of emotional outburst, we need to review the intentions. Is it to acquire a good reputation and to acquire merit as a godly man?

क्लैब्यं मा स्म गमः पार्थ
नैतत्त्वय्युपपद्यते ।
क्षुद्रं हृदयदौर्बल्यं
त्यक्त्वोत्तिष्ठ परंतप ॥२.३॥
klaibyaṁ mā sma gamaḥ pārtha
naitattvayyupapadyate
kṣudraṁ hṛdayadaurbalyaṁ
tyaktvottiṣṭha paraṁtapa (2.3)

klaibyaṁ — cowardly behavior; mā — not; sma — in fact; gamaḥ — should entertain; pārtha — O son of Pat̤ha; naitat — not this; tvayyupapadyate = tvayi — in your + upapadyate — is suitable; kṣudraṁ — degrading; hṛdayadaurbalyaṁ — emotional weakness; tyaktvottiṣṭha = tyaktva — give up + uttiṣṭha — stand up; paraṁtapa — scorcher of the enemy

O son of Pṛthā, you should not entertain cowardly behavior. This is not suitable for you. Give up this degrading emotional weakness. Stand, O scorcher of the enemy.(2.3)

Commentary:

The tendency for cowardly behavior and the resulting impulsive weakness are part of the scope of material existence. It is something that is permanently a part of the downward progression of destructive emotions. It is part of the insecurity we feel in connection with material bodies. This is also an expression of our limitations as puny spiritual beings. Still Lord Krishna asked Arjuna to dispel or rather to ignore these feelings.

Arjuna was attacked by weakening emotions in two ways; materially and spiritually. From the material angle he bypassed his eldest brother and went beyond the front lines to make an observation which should have been made only after consultation with King Yudhishthira. By superseding his brother, he subjected himself to the emotional energies of Bhishma, *Droṇa*, and other experienced warriors who knew well that a youngster like Arjuna would hesitate if he stopped to consider the slaughter to come.

From the spiritual angle Arjuna put himself forward as the most significant person on the battlefield. This was the objection raised to us by Dr. Vinay Kumar, regarding Arjuna's rash behavior. Of course, we are all like Arjuna in that arrogant aspect, even more so than he. We always try to take charge of any opening in history even if it is not suited to us exactly.

Arjuna was the most significant warrior but only on the basis of support from Yudhishthira, Lord Krishna, *Droṇa* and Bhishma. If we subtract the influence of these people from his life, Arjuna would be reduced considerably. Thus he was arrogant to move forward, forgetting their contributions to his life. He felt that he was indispensible as the focal warrior. But even if they did not object to his pride, he subjected himself to the law of disempowerment. He lost his courage automatically. His manliness was converted to boyish fear. To justify the feeling, he cited scripture in order to divert Lord Krishna.

In the *Gītā*, there is much explanation on devotion to Krishna, but this writer will depart from the habit of whitewashing every verse with that devotional approach. We will instead stick to the *Gītā* as it developed, only bringing in devotion when Krishna mentioned it. Our motive for composing this translation and commentary is to give the *Bhagavad-Gītā its own time and place*. Readers may get some insight of the circumstances under which *Bhagavad-Gītā* was delivered. A reader should consider the relevance to our times

Arjuna is addressed by Lord Krishna as *Arisūdana*, slayer of the enemy, chastiser of the foes. In modern language he would be called a lawman, sheriff, or chief policeman of King Yudhishthira. He used to go out on missions to capture rebels and to subdue insubmissive rulers. By addressing Arjuna in this way, Lord Krishna reminded him of the duty to King Yudhishthira. Arjuna could not afford to get himself wrapped up in personal sentiments at this time when Yudhishthira depended on him to serve as a lawman.

It is interesting that Lord Krishna expected Arjuna to shed his emotional breakdown at the spur of the moment, just like that, without allowing any time for it to subside. This gives us some idea of God's expectations. God, Krishna, feels that so long as we are cultured human beings, we are not supposed to succumb to these weakening moods. Krishna used the term *anārya-juṣṭam* in text 2 and *hṛdaya-daurbalyam* in this verse. These are very cutting terms *anārya-juṣṭam* means, not for a man of honor, for the low class people, for the vulgar humans. *Hṛdaya-daurbalyam* means: weakness of spirit, not having any guts, being cowardly, lacking courage, possessed of emotional weakness, devoid of manliness. In this way, Lord Krishna used some heavy terms to intimidate Arjuna, to bring the hero back to a valiant mood.

अर्जुन उवाच
कथं भीष्ममहं संख्ये
द्रोणं च मधुसूदन ।
इषुभिः प्रतियोत्स्यामि
पूजार्हावरिसूदन ॥२.४॥
arjuna uvāca
kathaṁ bhīṣmamahaṁ saṁkhye
droṇaṁ ca madhusūdana
iṣubhiḥ pratiyotsyāmi
pūjārhāvarisūdana (2.4)

arjuna — Arjuna; uvāca — said; kathaṁ — how; bhīṣmam — Bhisma; ahaṁ — I; saṁkhye — in battle; droṇaṁ — Droṇa; ca — and; madhusūdana — O killer of Madhu; iṣubhiḥ — with arrows; pratiyotsyāmi — I will attack; pūjārhāv arisūdana = pūjārhāu — worthy of reverence + arisūdana — killer of the enemy, Krishna

Arjuna said: How will I attack in battle, Bhishma and Droṇa, who are worthy of reverence, O Krishna? (2.4)

Commentary:

Arjuna was unable to apply the instruction of Lord Krishna. Krishna told him to push off the cowardly feelings and stand for combat, but Arjuna could not comply. Arjuna now explains his position in more detail. Arjuna challenged Bhishma before when Bhishma and the other Kaurava heroes tried to confiscate the cattle of King *Virāṭa*, but that was not a civil war. The *Kurukṣetra* confrontation was a serious civil conflict. It would involve actual killing, not just threatening and sportive display of valor. Arjuna explained to Lord Krishna that the possibility of killing Bhishma or *Droṇa* was completely out of the question. He could not imagine himself as their executioners.

To Arjuna, it was a contradiction to hold someone in reverence and then to kill that person in face-to-face combat. Bhishma was not as childish as Arjuna. In his life he faced great warriors, even his seniors and teachers like *Paraśurāma*. He fought them to a finish. When *Paraśurāma* threatened to chastise Bhishma if Bhishma did not marry the girl *Ambā*, Bhishma told *Paraśurāma* to arm himself and meet at the battlefield. Even though *Paraśurāma* was his teacher and a powerful divine person, Bhishma stood ground and fought. Bhishma had no qualms like Arjuna. Later on in this chapter, Lord Krishna explained to Arjuna that Bhishma, *Droṇa* and the other elders would be disappointed if Arjuna did not stand ground. Thus Lord Krishna revealed Arjuna's misconception about these social matters.

गुरूनहत्वा हि महानुभावान्
श्रेयो भोक्तुं भैक्ष्यमपीह लोके
हत्वार्थकामांस्तु गुरूनिहैव
भुञ्जीय भोगान्रुधिरप्रदिग्धान् ॥२.५॥

gurūn — the revered teachers; ahatvā — not killing; hi — in fact; mahānubhāvān — great-natured; śreyo — better; bhoktuṁ — to eat; bhaikṣyamapīha = bhaikṣyam — begging + api — also + iha — here; loke — on earth; hatvārthakāmāṅs = hatvā — having

gurūnahatvā hi mahānubhāvān
śreyo bhoktuṁ bhaikṣyam
apīha loke
hatvārthakāmāṁstu gurūn
ihaiva
bhuñjīya bhogān rudhira-
pradigdhān (2.5)

killed + artha — on the basis of + kāmān — impulsive desires; tu — but; gurūn — revered teachers; ihaiva = iha — here + eva — indeed; bhuñjīya — I would enjoy; bhogān — luxuries; rudhirapradigdhān = rudhira — bloody + pradigdhān — stained

In fact, it is better to eat by begging in this world than by killing the revered teachers who are great-natured. But having slain the venerable teachers on the basis of impulsive desires, I would enjoy blood-stained luxuries here on earth. (2.5)

Commentary:

Arjuna looked ahead and saw a dismal future. He considered begging to be better, but as Lord Krishna would point out, Arjuna could not settle for a beggar's means. Arjuna acted as a beggar many times before. When the Pandavas were banished to the forest for twelve years, they lived as beggars. During that twelve year period, Arjuna traveled with monks as a wandering ascetic. He knew something about the condition of the ascetics who wandered here and there without a means of livelihood. Still Lord Krishna would not allow Arjuna to follow that life style. Arjuna had a duty and he wants to adopt the beggar's way as an escape only.

Arjuna does, however, have a good point. It is a warning to one and all that we may decide to beg for food before killing relatives to get an inheritance. One should impose austerity on himself before trying to put others in difficulty. Before *Dhṛtarāṣṭra*, Pandu and Vidura were born, Bhishma did single-handedly establish and manage the Kuru government. Some obligation was due to him. To kill him just to acquire the kingdom would be a crime for any junior relative. It is a good argument, except that God, Lord Krishna, wanted to get rid of Bhishma. If Bhishma is old, and if he should be respected, then God is older and He should be honored even more. Lord Krishna will bring out the other aspects of the argument in subsequent verses and we will gradually understand the absurdity of Arjuna's proposals.

Arjuna was thinking that the battle was taking place about him, as part of his planning. But actually, Arjuna was to fight not to secure some ancestral property and power, but to serve his elder brother and Lord Krishna. When we look at the picture from that angle, all of Arjuna's arguments begin to lose significance. The motives he cited are a distortion of his actual role as defense minister in the government of his elder brother. It will be Krishna's task to put Arjuna in the proper perspective by reducing Arjuna's self-imposed centralization and putting Arjuna in his place as a mere servant of destiny.

न चैतद्विद्मः कतरन्नो गरीयो
यद्वा जयेम यदि वा नो जयेयुः ।
यानेव हत्वा न जिजीविषामस्
तेऽवस्थिताः प्रमुखे धार्तराष्ट्राः ॥२.६॥
na caitadvidmaḥ kataranno garīyo
yadvā jayema yadi vā no jayeyuḥ
yāneva hatvā na jijīviṣāmas
te'vasthitāḥ pramukhe
dhārtarāṣṭrāḥ (2.6)

na — not; caitad — and this; vidmaḥ — we know; kataran — which of the alternatives; no = nah — for us; garīyo — is better; yad — which; vā — other; jayema — we should conquer; yadi — if; vā — or; no = naḥ — to us; jayeyuḥ — they should triumph over; yān — who; eva — indeed; hatvā — having killed; na — us; jijīviṣāmas — we desire to outlive; te — they; 'vasthitāḥ = avasthitāḥ — stand armed; pramukhe — before us; dhārtarāṣṭrāḥ — the sons of Dhṛtarāṣṭra

And this we do not know, which of the alternatives is better; whether we should conquer or if they should triumph over us. It concerns these sons of Dhṛtarāṣṭra who stand armed before us, and whom we would not desire to outlive, if they are killed. (2.6)

Commentary:

Arjuna mused to himself mostly. His line of reasoning was faulty. For proper answers, we must have proper questions, proper conclusions, and proper considerations. If we are badly motivated, our questions will be absurd. An authority cannot answer questions which are based on nonsensical ideas. Lord Krishna ignored some ideas of Arjuna. Others He regarded in one verse only. But Krishna situated Arjuna in the right attitude of seeing reality. The Lord systematically explained the operations of reality.

Though presented as a collective matter by Arjuna, this battle was not really a "*we*" affair. It was a hassle between King Yudhishthira and King *Dhṛtarāṣṭra*. It concerned the two of them only. Except for Lord Krishna, the other persons on the battlefield were relations or allies of these two men. Lord Krishna was there as the manifest divine supervisor. Arjuna served Yudhishthira, whose army would either conquer or be defeated. The irony of it! Those whose deaths he would engineer were the very same people with whom he would want to associate after the battle. They stood before him, these men of *Dhṛtarāṣṭra*.

When we look at the situation from this perspective, the whole matter changes, as it becomes not Arjuna's problem, but Yudhishthira's. Arjuna is then free to be himself as a warrior for the King, rather than be burdened with crippling emotions. It was not worthwhile for Arjuna to fight, if he were the King. But he was not. And as a lawman for the King, he had to decide whether to continue the service as a government agent or to quit his job.

It is interesting, however, that even as great a person as Arjuna got to a place within his nature, from where he weighed the factors in favor of enjoyment. He wanted to allow corruption to continue just so he could enjoy the association of relatives. This means that he was visibly affected by the social life he shared with the Kurus. He wanted to overlook injustice while continuing that sweet association. Corruption is not worth the while. If a man can sacrifice his pleasures to eliminate it, he certainly should. A little corruption increases to a tremendous amount if we do not curb it.

कार्पण्यदोषोपहतस्वभावः
पृच्छामि त्वां धर्मसंमूढचेताः
यच्छ्रेयः स्यान्निश्चितं ब्रूहि तन्मे
शिष्यस्तेऽहं शाधि मां त्वां प्रपन्नम्
॥२.७॥

kārpaṇyadoṣopahata-
svabhāvaḥ
pṛcchāmi tvāṁ dharma-
saṁmūḍhacetāḥ
yacchreyaḥ syānniścitaṁ
brūhi tanme
śiṣyaste'haṁ śādhi māṁ
tvāṁ prapannam (2.7)

kārpaṇyadoṣopahatasvabhāvaḥ = kārpaṇya — mercy-prone + doṣa — faulty weakness + upahata — overcome + svabhāvaḥ — my feelings (a person being afflicted with inappropriate mercy, a compulsive mercy-prone man); pṛcchāmi — I ask; tvāṁ — you; dharmasaṁmūḍhacetāḥ = dharma — sense of duty + saṁmūḍha — clouded by confusion + cetāḥ — mind (one whose sense of duty is clouded by confusion of mind); yacchreyaḥ = yac (yad) — which + chreyaḥ (śreyaḥ) — is better; syān — it should be; niścitaṁ — for certain; brūhi — tell; tan — this; me — to me; śiṣyas — student; te — of yours; 'haṁ = ahaṁ — I; śādhi — instruct; māṁ — me; tvāṁ — you; prapannam — submission

As a mercy prone man, overcome by these feelings of pity, with my sense of duty clouded by mental confusion, I ask You to tell me with certainty, what is preferable. I am a student of Yours. Instruct me, who submit to You. (2.7)

Commentary:

Though he had reservations, Arjuna resigned himself to Lord Krishna. Admitting confusion, he asked for advice. There is a similarity, whereby some disciples pretend to be completely surrendered to a guru. In some cases, a petty-minded, popularity-crazed spiritual master actually becomes fooled, thinking that he has genuine followers. In some cases a disciple hides reservations so effectively that the master promotes him to a powerful position in the spiritual society. Then later on, that disciple works against the guru and causes the society to come crashing down.

In the case of Lord Krishna and Arjuna, Krishna was fully aware of Arjuna's incomplete surrender. He will systematically disentangle Arjuna's reservations.

A spiritual master needs to understand in advance that a disciple cannot surrender absolutely. It is impossible. Reservations will be there in the mind of the disciple. These may be revealed one by one in a slow process. They might be solved out. Human beings, even the sincere ones, learn how to play the game of surrender to a guru, for without being submissive, they get nothing from an authority. But that does not mean that their hearts are easily won. As we shall see, Arjuna asked many more questions and at a certain point even asked Lord Krishna to show proof of authority. If in the time of Lord Krishna, people doubted His divinity, then we can just imagine their doubts about a guru.

न हि प्रपश्यामि ममापनुद्याद्
यच्छोकमुच्छोषणमिन्द्रियाणाम् ।
अवाप्य भूमावसपत्नमृद्धं
राज्यं सुराणामपि चाधिपत्यम् ॥२.८॥

na hi prapaśyāmi mamāpanudyād
yacchokamucchoṣaṇam indriyāṇām
avāpya bhūmāvasapatnam ṛddhaṁ
rājyaṁ surāṇāmapi cādhipatyam (2.8)

na- not; hi- in fact; prapaśyām- I see; mamāpanudyād = mama- of me + apanudyāt -- should remove; yac (yad) — which; chokam (śokam) — sadness; ucchoṣaṇam — absorbs; indriyāṇām — sensual enthusiasm; avāpya — acquiring; bhūmāvasapatnam = bhūmau — on earth + asapatnam — unrivaled; ṛddham — prosperity; rājyaṁ — rulership; surāṇām — of the angelic kingdom; api — also; cādhipatyam = ca — and + adhipatyam — sovereignty

In fact, I do not see, what would remove the sadness that absorbs my enthusiasm, even unrivaled rulership and prosperity on earth or sovereignty over the angelic kingdom. (2.8)

Commentary:

As Arjuna gave objections, we can comprehend his hopelessness in the vision of the battle before him. It does not matter what is presented to us by destiny; if we enter a state of emotional confusion, we will be unable to make the proper decisions. Analysis must be made from the proper position, otherwise the conclusions drawn will be incorrect. Arjuna was, however, right to ask for a remedy that could remove his sadness. The unhappiness came over him with such pressure that he imagined its continuation forever. He thought that unhappiness would hamper his ability to enjoy himself either in this world or in the hereafter.

संजय उवाच
एवमुक्त्वा हृषीकेशं
गुडाकेशः परंतप ।
न योत्स्य इति गोविन्दम्
उक्त्वा तूष्णीं बभूव ह ॥२.९॥
saṁjaya uvāca
evamuktvā hṛṣīkeśaṁ
guḍākeśaḥ paraṁtapa
na yotsya iti govindam
uktvā tūṣṇīṁ babhūva ha (2.9)

saṁjaya — Sanjaya; uvāca — said; evam — thus; uktvā — having appealed to; hṛṣīkeśaṁ — Kṛṣṇa; guḍākeśaḥ — Arjuna; paraṁtapa — scorcher of enemies; na — not; yotsya — I will fight; iti — thus; govindam — chief of the cowherds; uktvā — having spoken; tūṣṇīṁ — silently; babhūva — became; ha — indeed

Sanjaya said: O Dhṛtarāṣṭra, scorcher of enemies, after appealing to Krishna, Arjuna said to Govinda, the chief of cowherds, "I will not fight." Having said this, he became silent. (2.9)

Commentary:

King *Dhṛtarāṣṭra* was not the legitimate ruler of the country, yet he functioned as the King. Decisions which pertained to political matters had to be cleared by him or Bhishma. In those days, Bhishma was relaxed and *Dhṛtarāṣṭra* was active. *Dhṛtarāṣṭra*, who used a blind body, relied heavily on his 100 sons who were headed by the eldest, named Duryodhana. Even though blind, *Dhṛtarāṣṭra* was, in fact, the eldest of the substitute sons of King Vichitravirya. Though disqualified because of birth defect, he still nourished grandeurs of being the King .These thoughts motivated him to rely on his petty-minded sons.

Sanjaya knew of the political ambitions of *Dhṛtarāṣṭra*, but he did not agree to the King's views. As a human being, Sanjaya could not help but be sarcastic to the King every now and then. Human tendency does not permit a man to remain silent on every occasion; even the most gentle people lose composure from time to time. In this verse, Sanjaya changed his tone of speech in order to give King *Dhṛtarāṣṭra* some good news, which was in fact, only bad news for the King. It was good news because Arjuna almost collapsed under the pressure of affection directed to him by Bhishma, *Droṇa*, other elderly men, as well as from their wives who were not on the battlefield but whose emotional powers flowed to Arjuna on the psychic plane.

It was bad news because *Dhṛtarāṣṭra* would take secret pleasure in Arjuna's depression; then he would be snapped out of the enjoyment by Lord Krishna's removal of Arjuna's dejection. Sanjaya tactfully alerted *Dhṛtarāṣṭra* not to take Arjuna's collapse too seriously. He did this by addressing Arjuna as *paramtapa*, marshal for the law breakers. Arjuna's job was to curb lawbreakers like *Dhṛtarāṣṭra* and his sons.

In the end, Sanjaya gave *Dhṛtarāṣṭra* full freedom to draw his own conclusions. He said, "This is what Arjuna said to Lord Govinda, Krishna, the protector of the cowherd settlement." In mentioning Krishna's childhood background, Sanjaya applied a touch of sarcasm by suggesting that it was unusual for a cowherd to be advising the most important warrior on the *Kurukṣetra* battlefield.

तमुवाच हृषीकेशः
प्रहसन्निव भारत ।
सेनयोरुभयोर्मध्ये
विषीदन्तमिदं वचः ॥२.१०॥

tam — to him; uvāca — spoke; hṛṣīkeśaḥ — Kṛṣṇa; prahasan — smiling; iva — like; bhārata — O descendant of Bharata; senayoḥ — of the two armies; ubhayoḥ — of both; madhye — in the middle; viṣīdantam —

tamuvāca hṛṣīkeśaḥ
prahasanniva bhārata
senayorubhayormadhye
viṣīdantamidaṁ vacaḥ (2.10)

dejected; idaṁ — this; vacaḥ — speech

Then, in the middle of both armies, Krishna, who was smiling, spoke this speech to the dejected Arjuna. (2.10)

Commentary:

Arjuna was perplexed but Lord Krishna was cool-headed and smiling to boot, as if there were no crisis whatsoever. *Dhṛtarāṣṭra* was given a little time to think.

श्रीभगवानुवाच
अशोच्यानन्वशोचस्त्वं
प्रज्ञावादांश्च भाषसे ।
गतासूनगतासूंश्च
नानुशोचन्ति पण्डिताः ॥२.११॥
śrībhagavānuvāca
aśocyānanvaśocastvaṁ
prajñāvādāṁśca bhāṣase
gatāsūnagatāsūṁśca
nānuśocanti paṇḍitāḥ (2.11)

śrī-bhagavān — the Blessed Lord; uvāca — said; aśocyān — that which should be regretted; anvaśocas — mourned; tvaṁ — you; prajñāvādāṁś — intelligent statements; ca — and; bhāṣase — you express; gatāsūn — departed souls; agatāsūṁś — those not departed; ca — and; nānuśocanti = na — not + anuśocanti — mourn; paṇḍitāḥ — educated men

The Blessed Lord said: You mourned for that which should not be regretted. And you expressed intelligent statements, but the educated persons mourn neither for the embodied or departed souls.(2.11)

Commentary:

By addressing Lord Krishna as *Bhagavān*, Sanjaya reminded *Dhṛtarāṣṭra* that Krishna is the Person of Confidence, the Supreme Person. There can be no doubt as to His determination and capacity. There might be some doubt about Arjuna's but not about Krishna's. Insofar as Arjuna takes shelter of Krishna, there was no doubt either. *Dhṛtarāṣṭra* should stop hoping against reality or wishing that Arjuna's collapse would last indefinitely.

This verse eleven is Lord Krishna's third statement in the *Gītā*. It is one of intimidation and insult. But this is what is took to get Arjuna to change for the better.

Arjuna mourned for the projected death of the warriors as well as for the sorrow which their surviving families might endure. But Krishna stated that such a condition of life should not be regretted. At least the intelligent people, who are aware of reality, would not indulge in such lamentation. Arjuna cited very intelligent statements from the scriptures but he misapplied them. The sentiment for bodily damage is there but an educated person who is conversant with spiritual reality does not allow the feelings of pity to overcome him.

The material body has sympathies but that does not mean that the soul should accommodate these. Some of these feelings should be ignored. Some should be suppressed. Some may be expressed after due consideration. We should not allow our nature to express itself freely at all times. Since we are influenced by material nature, the sentiments must be checked very carefully.

If the material body and the soul were one homogeneous unit, then there would be no need to discriminate in favor of the soul. We must sort all feelings carefully to determine which are spiritually beneficial. We should resist some mental and bodily urges. In the time of Lord Krishna, the educated people were conversant with samkhya, a philosophy of life which stresses the subtle under-basis. The samkhya experts stick to the underlying causes, the subtle impetuses. Samkhya yogis transcended the mundane situation by seeing the psychic substrata.

Lord Krishna insulted Arjuna for improvement. Such an insult is in a sense, the greatest honor that a spiritual master can pay a disciple. It means that the authority recognizes that the disciple has better sense and can make more mature judgments.

न त्वेवाहं जातु नासं
न त्वं नेमे जनाधिपाः ।
न चैव न भविष्यामः
सर्वे वयमतः परम् ॥२.१२॥
na tvevāhaṁ jātu nāsaṁ
na tvaṁ neme janādhipāḥ
na caiva na bhaviṣyāmaḥ
sarve vayamataḥ param (2.12)

na — no; tvevāhaṁ = tv (tu) — in fact + eva — alone + ahaṁ — I; jātu — ever; nāsaṁ = na — not + āsaṁ — I did exist; na — nor; tvaṁ — you; neme = na — nor + ime — these; jana-adhipāḥ — rulers of the people; na — not; caiva — and indeed; na — nor; bhaviṣyāmaḥ — we will exist; sarve — all; vayam — we; ataḥ - from now; param — onwards

There was never a time when I did not exist, nor you, nor these rulers of the people. Nor will we cease to exist from now onwards. (2.12)

Commentary:

An objection might be raised by the staunch followers of Lord Krishna that in this verse Lord Krishna could not have implied that His body might be ruined, even though He would definitely state that the bodies of the warriors would be and that their souls would survive and live on as spiritual units always did. However, we must check the Sanskrit to see what Lord Krishna actually said. In the fourth line of the verse we see the word *vayam*. In the third line we see the word *bhaviṣyāmah*. This means, *we will exist*. It is the first person plural, future tense in Sanskrit grammar.

In this verse, Lord Krishna laid the foundation for the whole *Gītā* discourse insofar as He would teach samkhya yoga or *buddhi* yoga. The teaching of this verse is the basis of the samkhya philosophy. Lord Krishna ridiculed Arjuna for not integrating the samkhya teachings into his practical life. At a certain point the Lord said;

eṣā te'bhihitā sāṁkhye buddhiryoge tvimāṁ śṛṇu
buddhyā yukto yayā pārtha karmabandhaṁ prahāsyasi (2.39)

As explained in the Sāṁkhya philosophy, this vision is the insight, but hear of its application in yoga practice. Yoked with this insight, O son of Pṛthā, you will avoid the complications of action. (2.39)

Arjuna overlooked the facts of the samkhya experience. He replaced that vision of reality with the cultural view which is serviceable while one has a material body and must get along with worldly people but which is useless in the future and final scene when the soul is compelled to leave its body.

A basic misconception is corrected here: A person is not identical to his material body. Here Lord Krishna established that life means the life of the soul or undying principle in the body which will leave the body at the time of death. If life means that undying principle, then death of the body is no cause for lamentation. Arjuna's idea that the men, especially his elders, would cease to live after their bodies were ruined at *Kurukṣetra*, is a cultural view only. Even though that view is functional and realistic, there is another more basic truth. Krishna wanted Arjuna to apply that deeper consideration.

Krishna stressed to Arjuna that his existence do not rely on the body nor on being in the Kuru family. This in no way implies that a human being should impulsively kill his own body or that of others. As soon as one realizes that the life within the body must leave the body at the time of death, one should consider the value of the body. Since a body has value it is wrong to kill it unjustifiably. In addition, the justification for killing a body had better be good enough to satisfy God and material nature, otherwise one will face negative reactions. The mere idea that the soul will continue living beyond the body puts the soul in a position of being liable for irresponsible acts. Its survival assures that it can and will be identified even after the body dies. It will be tagged for criminal acts. When we have the full idea of reincarnation, we do not act whimsically.

Lord Krishna advocated reincarnation openly but He does not give us the right to act irresponsibly. Nor should we act sentimentally without considering the future. Arjuna's argument is destroyed in this one verse of the *Gītā*. His presentation was based on the false premise that the life of the body is the essential factor and that the death of it ruins the life factor. Actually if we are looking for one verse, this particular verse would be sufficient. Here Lord Krishna may have stopped His talk with Arjuna, but the subject matter is much more complicated as we shall read.

देहिनोऽस्मिन्यथा देहे
कौमारं यौवनं जरा ।
तथा देहान्तरप्राप्तिर्
धीरस्तत्र न मुह्यति ॥२.१३॥
dehino'sminyathā dehe
kaumāraṁ yauvanaṁ jarā
tathā dehāntaraprāptir
dhīrastatra na muhyati (2.13)

dehinaḥ — of the embodied soul; 'smin = asmin — in this; yathā — as; dehe — in the body; kaumāraṁ — in childhood; yauvanam — in youth; jarā — in old age; tathā — so in sequence; dehāntaraprāptir = deha — body + antara — another + prāptiḥ — acquirement; dhīraḥ — wise person; tatra — on this topic; na — not; muhyati — is confused

As the embodied soul endures childhood, youth and old age, so another body is acquired in sequence. The wise person is not confused on this topic. (2.13)

Commentary:

The sequence of events which we know as childhood, youth, maturity and old age is endured by creatures as the natural course of material life. It is not what we desire. We want eternal youth. But we accept the course of the body's growth and deterioration as reality. We are resigned to this, as being unalterable. But there is another natural sequence of events; that of taking one body after another, on and on and on.

An ordinary man is somewhat familiar with the changes between birth and death. But the wise, far-seeing, deeply-perceiving men know of the change between death and birth. The changes between death and birth, which are a mystery to ordinary people, are plainly seen by the reality-piercing mystics. Arjuna based his argument on the ordinary vision which is calculated in terms of the changes between the birth of a body and the death of it, but Lord Krishna wanted Arjuna to have the broader view which included the vision of what happens between the death of one body and the birth of another one.

We lack the mystic vision. Thus we are unable to see what happens to the subtle life which passes from the body. Krishna invited us to develop that mystic perception to free ourselves from the limited cultural view. For an intelligent conversation, we need to speak of the subtle life and the soul who is the source of it. The body merely indicates the subtle existence.

There may be doubts about the changes we endure after the death of a body. But until we can develop mystic perception, we cannot challenge the statements of Krishna. The course taken for the development of this view is the samkhya yoga system which results in the development of keen mystic insight. The regulation of that insight is called *buddhi* yoga.

मात्रास्पर्शास्तु कौन्तेय
शीतोष्णसुखदुःखदाः ।
आगमापायिनोऽनित्यास्
तांस्तितिक्षस्व भारत ॥२.१४॥
mātrāsparśāstu kaunteya
śītoṣṇasukhaduḥkhadāḥ
āgamāpāyino'nityās
tāṁstitikṣasva bhārata (2.14)

mātrāsparśāḥ — mundane sensations; tu — but; kaunteya — O son of Kuntī; śītoṣṇasukhaduḥkhadāḥ = śīta — cold + usna — heat + sukha — pleasure + duḥkha — pain + dāḥ — causing; āgamāpāyino = āgama — coming + apāyinaḥ — going; 'nityās = anityāḥ — not manifested continually; tāṁs — them; titikṣasva — you should cope; bhārata — O man of the Bharata family

O son of Kuntī, mundane sensations which cause cold and heat, pleasure and pain, do come and go. Cope with them, O man of the Bharata family. (2.14)

Commentary:

King *Dhṛtarāṣṭra* listened as Sanjaya repeated the discourse between Krishna and Arjuna. As the supreme mystic, Lord Krishna knew that *Dhṛtarāṣṭra* would hear the discourse. Krishna addressed Arjuna as Kaunteya, meaning the son of the old Queen *Kuntī*. Later on in this verse, the Lord addressed Arjuna as man or descendant of the *Bhārata* family. *Bharata* was a distant ancestor of Arjuna. By addressing Arjuna as an affiliate of a woman in the first part of the verse, the Lord indicated that sentiments come from womanly influence, while the life of discrimination comes from manly view point.

Arjuna stressed the materialistic moods that we endure. Lord Krishna acknowledged these moods, but He said that we should realize their impermanence. Moods are felt and then forgotten. Arjuna became crippled and depressed because he focused too strongly on moods, instead of letting them arise and subside while being detached from them.

यं हि न व्यथयन्त्येते
पुरुषं पुरुषर्षभ ।
समदुःखसुखं धीरं
सोऽमृतत्वाय कल्पते ॥२.१५॥
yaṁ hi na vyathayantyete
puruṣaṁ puruṣarṣabha
samaduḥkhasukhaṁ dhīraṁ
so'mṛtatvāya kalpate (2.15)

yaṁ — whosoever; hi — indeed; na — not; vyathayantyete = vyathayanti — afflict + ete — these mundane sensations; puruṣaṁ — that person; puruṣarṣabha — O bull among men; samaduḥkhasukhaṁ — steady in miserable and enjoyable conditions; dhīraṁ — wise man; so — he; 'mṛta tvāya = amṛtatvāya — to immortality; kalpate — is fit

O bull among men, these mundane sensations do not afflict the wise man who is steady in miserable or enjoyable conditions. That person is fit for immortality. (2.15)

Commentary:

Lord Krishna addressed Arjuna as *puruṣarṣabha* which means, *bull among men*. Among the warriors, Arjuna was noted as a bull among men, but he was not classed as a samkhya yogi or *buddhi* yogi. He was noticeably affected by misery and pleasure. His strongman reputation did not apply to emotional regulation. He would be schooled in that area by Lord Krishna.

For the first time, Lord Krishna mentioned the *dhīra* or the man of steady consciousness, the man who identified the permanent feature of consciousness and who does not lose sight of this permanence even when there is happiness or distress. The permanent feature of consciousness is there, regardless, but a socially-involved person loses the focus of it and takes to the moody variations which fluctuate around it. The egotistic or assertive feature of individuality can move or be moved from one plane of consciousness to another. The *dhīra* or man of steady consciousness, restricts himself to the steady levels which will be described by Lord Krishna in this and other chapters of the *Bhagavad-Gītā*.

नासतो विद्यते भावो
नाभावो विद्यते सतः ।
उभयोरपि दृष्टोऽन्तस्
त्वनयोस्तत्त्वदर्शिभिः ॥२.१६॥
nāsato vidyate bhāvo
nābhāvo vidyate sataḥ
ubhayorapi dṛṣṭo'ntas
tvanayostattvadarśibhiḥ (2.16)

nāsato = na- no + asatas - of the non-substantial things; vidyate- there is; bhāvo- enduring existence; nābhāvo = na — no + abhāvaḥ — lack of existence; vidyate — there is; sataḥ — substantial things; ubhayoḥ — of the two; api — also; dṛṣṭaḥ — perceived; 'ntas = antaḥ — certainty; tvanayos = tu — but + anayoḥ — of these two; tattvadarśibhiḥ = tattva — reality + darśibhiḥ — by mystic powers

Of the non-substantial things, there is no enduring existence. Of the substantial things, there is no lack of existence. These two truths were perceived with certainty by the mystic seers of reality. (2.16)

Commentary:

The mystic seers of reality, the *tattvadarśis*, the reality-seeing people, are the Upanishad sages who, while living a simple forest life, reserved themselves for mystic research. The conclusions of these sages are well-known. Their views were recorded in the Upanishads. Here Lord Krishna used the term *'ntas (antas)*, meaning that this was well-known in the time of Arjuna and was a firm conclusion. Why then, did Arjuna leave aside this information and take up a cultural view?

Arjuna, like many of us, was satisfied with theoretical conclusions, without gaining direct experience. As long as we rely on scriptural statements, but have no personal experience of the truths described, we cannot have a firm footing.

Particularly in this modern age, great spiritual masters content themselves with scriptural theory which they explain in great detail as if they experienced the truths recently, while in fact, they have only understood the wording and concepts, but have not in their current lives experienced the realities. Some spiritual masters claim that in their past lives they did all research, practiced the yoga, and completed the needed disciplines. "Thus," they explain, "we do not need to see the direct evidence again." If, as in the case of Arjuna, one forgets the experience of his previous lives and only clings to theory, he may become emotionally crippled.

It is laziness and laziness alone that inspires us to be content with mere theory of spiritual life, thus avoiding specific practices which yield direct results. Lord Krishna directly condemned Arjuna for not grounding himself in the Vedic education system which was established by the Upanishadic sages. Arjuna knew the theory of it, but he was short on its integration.

Arjuna's ideas were false as the Lord indicated. Arjuna's view that the material bodies of his relatives just came into existence from nowhere and would be killed in the battle, was a shallow conclusion, devoid of direct insight. It sprung from mystic blindness. Even if we can prove that the body is important, we should go further to show the basic existence, which has even more importance. That basis is the actual factor of interest and not the body itself. If there were no basis that transcended and outlived the body, and that existed before the body visibly appeared, then the body itself would be of no value and should not be lamented. The composite parts of the body may be broken down into various gross and subtle materials. The materials which came together to form the body will be relinquished in nature at the time of death. There is no point in clinging unduly to a body. We cling because our energy is invested in it and we are afraid of being released from it. We merely want to keep the investment going, but the laws of nature will not permit its indefinite continuation. These truths were known with certainty by the mystic seers of reality, the Upanishadic sages.

अविनाशि तु तद्विद्धि
येन सर्वमिदं ततम् ।
विनाशमव्ययस्यास्य
न कश्चित्कर्तुमर्हति ॥२.१७॥
avināśi tu tadviddhi
yena sarvamidaṁ tatam
vināśamavyayasyāsya
na kaścitkartumarhati (2.17)

avināśi — indestructible; tu — indeed; tad — that factor; viddhi — know; yena — by which; sarvam — all; idaṁ — this world; tatam — is pervaded; vināśam — destructible; avyayasyāsya of the everlasting principle; na — no; kaścit — anyone; kartum - to accomplish; arhati — can

Know that indestructible factor by which all this world is pervaded. No one can accomplish the destruction of that everlasting principle. (2.17)

Commentary:

Lord Krishna gave Arjuna a brief course in the Upanishadic wisdom which was established by great sages. Some of these sages believed in God as a person. Some believed in an impersonal primal cause. In either case, both groups agreed that there was a non-diminishing factor, a permanent energy which serves as the background for temporary appearances. Today we know this factor as the *ātma* or soul. Lord Krishna does not use the word *ātma* nor the word *puruṣa* in this verse, but rather He followed the line of reasoning and mystic research of the sages.

The technical term *avināśi* means what is indestructible, what is not to be lost or diminished, what remains after disintegration.

If we observe a living body and trace it for many years, it will eventually perish, at least from the physical perspective. But if we keep track of the subtle part of that body, the psychology, we will find that a part of it survives the death of the body. That part is said to be irreducible and permanent. It always survives the manifestations that are formed about it.

To understand this, we may take some help from the modern scientists. They proved that matter can neither be created nor destroyed. Of course, they are talking about the most basic form of matter. The visible forms are adjusted in and out of visibility, but the basic energy cannot be reduced or increased. It can only be shifted or transferred. Scientists of the modern era are still trying to find the ultimate particle. At one time they thought it was the atom. Some ancient Indian sages considered that also. Now the scientists are saying that it is not the atom, for within the atom they discovered more minute parts. At the present time, the physicists are not certain about the irreducible material factor.

On the other side of the argument, there is the transcendental spiritual factor which, to the material scientist, is for the most part, an irrelevant consideration. But this is exactly where these scientists are wrong. On the transcendental side, we also have an irreducible factor which is described in this verse as being *avināśi* or non-diminishing.

This statement of Lord Krishna, that the basic power is the non-diminishing factor and that the universe is pervaded by it, can be re-stated in a personal way, to read that the soul is the basic-part of any living form. The universe is pervaded by numerous souls who comprise part of the sum total spiritual energy. Their destruction cannot be accomplished by Arjuna or anyone else. Thus the arrogance of Arjuna is shown. He felt that he could get rid of the souls of Bhishma, *Droṇa*, and the other commanders at *Kurukṣetra*.

अन्तवन्त इमे देहा
नित्यस्योक्ताः शरीरिणः ।
अनाशिनोऽप्रमेयस्य
तस्माद्युध्यस्व भारत ॥२.१८॥
antavanta ime dehā
nityasyoktāḥ śarīriṇaḥ
anāśino'prameyasya
tasmādyudhyasva bhārata (2.18)

antavanta — terminal; ime — these; dehā — bodies; nityasyoktāḥ = nityasya — of the eternal + uktāḥ — it is declared; śarīriṇaḥ — of the embodied soul; anāśinaḥ — of the indestructible; 'prameyasya = aprameyasya — of the immeasurable; tasmāt — therefore; yudhyasva — fight; bhārata — O descendant of Bharata

It is declared that the bodies of the eternal, indestructible, immeasurable embodied soul are terminal. Therefore fight, descendent of the Bharatas. (2.18)

<u>*Commentary:*</u>

Lord Krishna takes the line of spiritual research carried out by the Upanishadic sages long ago. The word *avināśi* occurs in its variation as *anāśino*. Other technical terms are: *nityasya, of the eternal, concerning that eternal principle*; *'prameyasya, (aprameyasya), of the immeasurable, concerning the irreducible item that cannot be absorbed by a lower force*. These aspects of the soul are mentioned. Thus we understand that the Upanishadic sages were tracing the soul by analyzing its qualities.

By asking Arjuna to draw a conclusion (*tasmād*), to think it over, Lord Krishna indicated that Arjuna should fight with a view that the person in the body will survive anyway. With a bit of sarcasm, the Lord addressed Arjuna by his cultural identity, his temporary identity, as a famous member of the Bharalta family.

य एनं वेत्ति हन्तारं
यश्चैनं मन्यते हतम् ।
उभौ तौ न विजानीतो
नायं हन्ति न हन्यते ॥२.१९॥
ya enaṁ vetti hantāraṁ
yaścainaṁ manyate hatam
ubhau tau na vijānīto
nāyaṁ hanti na hanyate (2.19)

ya — who; enaṁ — this embodied soul; vetti — concludes; hantāraṁ — the killer; yaścainaṁ = yas — who + ca — and + inam — this embodied soul; manyate — thinks; hatam — is killed; ubhau — both; tau — two viewers; na- not; vijānītaḥ- understood; nāyaṁ = na — not + ayam — this embodied soul; hanti — kill; na — nor; hanyate — can be killed

Both viewers do not understand, namely: He who concludes that the embodied soul is the killer and he who thinks that the embodied soul is killed. The embodied soul does not kill nor can he be killed. (2.19)

Commentary:

This statement is contradictory from the social angle of vision but it is perfect in terms of the theoretical and practical conclusions of the samkhya philosophy. From the social or materialistic view, we can see plainly that when one creature kills another, the killer survives while the killed creature perishes.This is a fact on the cultural plane. However, Lord Krishna departed from that level to show Arjuna the higher realities.

To follow the Lord's line of reasoning we must return to texts 16 and 17 where He cited the seasoned conclusions of the Upanishadic sages. These statements are not very difficult to understand if we would just part from the cultural view.

nāsato vidyate bhāvo'nābhāvo vidyate sataḥ
ubhayorapi dṛṣṭo'ntas tvanayostattvadarśibhiḥ (2.16)
avināśi tu tadviddhi yena sarvamidaṁ tatam
vināśamavyayasyāsya na kaścitkartumarhati (2.17)

Of the non-substantial things, there is no enduring existence. Of the substantial things, there is no lack of existence. These two truths were perceived with certainty by the mystic seers of reality. (2.16)

Know that indestructible factor by which all this world is pervaded. No one can accomplish the destruction of that everlasting principle. (2.17)

This means that we are not seeing correctly, when we think that a baby had no existence before. A baby consists of several eternally-existing factors which have merged together to form a visible but temporary object. The unity of the baby form is temporary but composite parts of that unity are from before.

All the same, we perceive wrongly if we think that future babies come from nowhere. A baby body is formed from already existing materials, but that formation is hidden from the cultural view. Still, the infant form did not arise from nowhere. This was known with certainty by the ancient seers of reality who perceived what occurred on the mystic plane.

All the creature forms are comprised of certain eternally-existing factors. These factors are non-diminishing. They cannot really disappear. The factors remain in existence eternally. Of these, one factor is most important, the core-self. No one can destroy that principle. No one can hamper its eternal nature. When the reduction or deterioration of the material form is noticed at the time of death, the core-self is not reduced.

Let us look at verse 19 again.

ya enaṁ vetti hantāraṁ yaścainaṁ manyate hatam
ubhau tau na vijānīto'nāyaṁ hanti na hanyate (2.19)

Both viewers do not understand, namely: He who concludes that the embodied soul is the killer and he who thinks that the embodied soul is killed. The embodied soul does not kill nor can he be killed. (2.19)

If we think that we have killed a creature or that we can be killed, we have made a miscalculation. The first mistake involves thinking that the creature which came into existence is one whole item. It is not. The second mistake is to think that the thinker in the creature form is identical with the other parts of the body. The third mistake is to feel that the thinker and the other parts which made up the form are unified forever.

In each creature form there are eternal factors. Regardless of the healthy, unhealthy or dead conditions, these non-diminishing factors are eternal. One eternal part of one body cannot kill an eternal part of another form.

When presenting his arguments in the beginning of the discourse, Arjuna claimed that he was speaking from an educated angle, but here Lord Krishna reduced Arjuna to being a misinformed man. Arjuna thought that he could kill Bhishma and *Droṇa* but Krishna declared that he could kill no one. Nor is there a risk that anyone could kill Arjuna. We understand, however, that these statements of the Lord do not apply to our cultural view. From the ordinary perception the human being known as Bhishma would be killed and so would *Droṇa* or Arjuna or whoever would be fatally wounded on that battlefield. But that is not the point because Arjuna cried on the basis of a projected loneliness which arose from thinking that he would no longer be able to relate to Bhishma and *Droṇa*. And it is false to think that after a body dies or disintegrates into basic elements, the soul who used that body would not be able to relate to a person who remained behind in this world.

In fact, a departed soul takes another bodily form through psychic affection with his future parents. Arjuna is an informed person but he forgot the psychic level and took the cultural view alone.

न जायते म्रियते वा कदा चिन्
नायं भूत्वा भविता वा न भूयः ।
अजो नित्यः शाश्वतोऽयं पुराणो
न हन्यते हन्यमाने शरीरे ॥२.२०
na jāyate mriyate vā kadā cin
nāyaṁ bhūtvā bhavitā vā na bhūyaḥ
ajo nityaḥ śāśvato'yaṁ purāṇo
na hanyate hanyamāne śarīre (2.20)

na — not; jāyate — is born; mriyate — dies; vā — either; kadācin — at any time; nāyaṁ = na — nor + ayaṁ — this embodied soul; bhūtvā — having been; bhavitā — will be; vā — or; na — not; bhūyaḥ — again; ajo — birthless; nityaḥ — perpetual; śāśvataḥ — eternal; 'yaṁ = ayaṁ - this; purāṇaḥ — primeval; na- not; hanyate — is killed; hanyamāne — in the act of killing; śarīre — in the body

This embodied soul is not born, nor does it die at any time, nor having existed will it not be. Being birthless, eternal, perpetual and primeval, it is not slain in the act of killing the body. (2.20)

Commentary:

The whole world is spellbound by the birth of baby forms. Many who speak of reincarnation, know very little about it. Unless we understand the details of reincarnation, we cannot be successful in spiritual life. One may be a believer in God, in Krishna, or in any other divinity; still one cannot be freed from material existence unless one integrates and practically lives out the idea of reincarnation. Arjuna lost the psychic perception but he quickly regained it in the *Gītā*. We will have to make much effort to develop that vision.

Birth of a baby form is a fact. That is a cultural reality. However, it is not the entire information. In that baby form, a soul is present and certain eternal materials are also present. The combination of those materials in a new configuration is a fact but the newness of the person within the combination is a falsity. A baby is an old person appearing again in a new body. The imperishable aspect was listed by its quality in text 17 as *avināśi* which means *the factor which cannot be diminished or reduced*. It is the constant factor. This factor is moving from body to body. Reduction or disintegration has to do with the various elements which are brought together to form or disintegrate a body. These elements cannot stay together eternally.

Stated simply: We are fighting the laws of nature. We desire to reverse an irreversible factor. Material nature will not allow any of the material forms to remain in a configuration permanently. This is something that we fight daily. As a result we are suffering. Our emotional struggles involve a fight against this one law of nature. It is a losing battle, but we are fighting it anyway, in a game of survival. We are losing at every step but we keep fighting.

Lord Krishna asserted that if a person was ever recognized in history, that person cannot ever be reduced, but must continue existing. This means that all historic personalities are still existing. But that does not mean that their cultural forms are. No! The forms are dead, dying or approaching the stage of decay. The personalities who used those forms are still living on the psychic plane. Obviously our cultural vision is slanted to the gross level. If we could miraculously shift it to the psychic plane, we would agree with Krishna.

It appears that Lord Krishna always considered the psychic level. He gave that view top priority over the gross reality. To understand Krishna we have to shift to His perception. This is what Arjuna did at *Kurukṣetra*. Interestingly, from their history in the *Mahābhārata*, we see that Bhishma and *Droṇa* were well aware of the psychic plane. Still they understood that Arjuna was immature in that view and they played a game on him, trying to keep him focused on the cultural level in order to discourage him from fighting. Lord Krishna neutralized their effect on Arjuna, and brought the hero to the spiritual plane.

वेदाविनाशिनं नित्यं
य एनमजमव्ययम् ।
कथं स पुरुषः पार्थ
कं घातयति हन्ति कम् ॥२.२१॥
vedāvināśinaṁ nityaṁ
ya enamajamavyayam
kathaṁ sa puruṣaḥ pārtha
kaṁ ghātayati hanti kam (2.21)

vedāvināśinaṁ = veda — knows + avināśinaṁ — indestructible; nityaṁ — eternal; ya = yaḥ — who; enam — this; ajam — not born, birthless; avyayam — imperishable; kathaṁ — how; sa = saḥ — he; puruṣaḥ — person; pārtha — O son of Partha; kaṁ — whom; ghātayati — causes to kill; hanti — kills (directly); kam — whom

O son of Pṛthā, how can the person who knows this indestructible, eternal, birthless and imperishable principle, cause someone to be killed or even kill someone directly? (2.21)

Commentary:

Here Lord Krishna, the Supreme Being, graciously explained the essentials of spiritual understanding. The question of how a spiritually-educated man can kill or plan the killing of the super-living principle, may be answered in this way: We can certainly feel that we would kill that super-living principle if we only understand reincarnation mentally but have not experienced it consciously.

Mental understanding of spiritual life is just the beginning. It gives only partial protection from illusion. Spiritual masters the world over may fool us into thinking that mental understanding is spiritual life, but this is just a trick. So many of us believe in reincarnation but act as if we are these bodies anyway. Mental understanding of spiritual truths does not give liberation.

The super-living principle is the soul. The living form that we see culturally is the body. The soul will continue. The psychic energies will leave the body at the time of death. These energies will remain invisible as they always were. No one has seen electricity traveling down a covered wire, but we have seen a light bulb show that hidden power. Still, we understand that the unseen electricity energizes the bulb. The unseen soul energizes the body. A defective bulb does not imply that electricity is absent. And a dead body only implies that due to injury or disease, the form can no longer respond to the energizing power of the hidden soul.

Everything we explained so far has to do with understanding this theoretically. This theory does not free our readers from the bodily concept of life. It does, however, affect the strong belief in material existence. This is the first step.

वासांसि जीर्णानि यथा विहाय
नवानि गृह्णाति नरोऽपराणि ।
तथा शरीराणि विहाय जीर्णा;न्य्
अन्यानि संयाति नवानि देही ॥२.२२॥
vāsāṁsi jīrṇāni yathā vihāya
navāni gṛhṇāti naro'parāṇi
tathā śarīrāṇi vihāya jīrṇāny
anyāni saṁyāti navāni dehī (2.22)

vāsāṁsi — clothing; jīrṇāni — worn out; yathā — as when; vihāya — discarded; navāni — new; gṛhṇāti — takes; naro = naraḥ — person; 'parāṇi = aparāṇi — others; tathā — so; śarīrāṇi — bodies; vihāya — abandoned; jirṇāny = worn-out; anyāni — others; saṁyāti — encounters; navāni — new; dehī — the embodied soul

As when discarding old clothing, a person takes new garments, so the embodied soul abandons old bodies taking new ones. (2.22)

Commentary:

This comparison is easy for advanced souls, but for the ordinary minds it is difficult. It is a reasonable argument but the difficulty is the verification of it by direct experience. Even if Lord Krishna sees how the souls transmigrate, still, our vision of it remains to be accomplished. How can we see it? Are we supposed to accept His word only without ever being able to verify it?

To show the distinction between the surviving soul and his present cultural identity, Lord Krishna called the cultural person a nara, a human creature. He addressed the surviving soul as a *dehi*, a body-prone entity, a person who is different from bodies, but who always requires bodies. Arjuna's confusion sprang from a confusion of these two factors. There is a clear distinction between the dehi, or the body-prone person, and the deham, or body of that person. When the two are combined we get a *nara* or living human being. In the case of animals, the combination of body and soul is also there, resulting in a creature of a different species.

The verb *vihāya* means to cast away, to leave, abandon or forsake. We must, at some point, part with a garment or with a body. It is not that we voluntarily do it. Generally, we are reluctant to be separated but we must regardless. Even in the case of a garment, a man might be so attached to an old, worn-out shoe that he wears it in a shabby condition. For instance, the heel of the shoe might have worn out. Still the owner might use it on a rainy day merely because he is more attached to it than to a better piece of footwear. This is all due to strong attachment. If we can be so attached to a shoe, then we can just imagine our attachment to a body.

Once the body-prone, bound living entity becomes familiar with a certain form, he will, more than likely, cling to it for dear life, even if it has a deadly disease. People cling tenaciously to old, shaky, diseased, terrible-looking forms.

But no matter how attached a man might be, material nature forces him to part with his favorite shoe or body. He has no choice. Our attachment to the body does not protect us from the separating power of nature. Eventually we must leave that form.

नैनं छिन्दन्ति शस्त्राणि
नैनं दहति पावकः ।
न चैनं क्लेदयन्त्यापो
न शोषयति मारुतः ॥२.२३॥

nainaṁ = na — not + enaṁ — this; chindanti — pierce; śastrāṇi — weapons; nainaṁ = na — not + enaṁ — this; dahati — burns; pāvakaḥ — fire; na — not; cainaṁ = ca — and +

nainaṁ chindanti śastrāṇi
nainaṁ dahati pāvakaḥ
na cainaṁ kledayantyāpo
na śoṣayati mārutaḥ (2.23)

enaṁ — this; kledayantyāpo = kledayanti — soak + āpo = āpaḥ — water; na — nor; śoṣayati — dry out; mārutaḥ — the wind

Weapons do not pierce, fire does not burn, and water does not wet, nor does the wind dry that embodied soul. (2.23)

Commentary:

Arjuna stated that the *naras* or human beings were at risk of being killed but Lord Krishna disagreed. Let us see if Arjuna is correct. Insofar as the human being is a combination of the body and soul, Arjuna is definitely incorrect. Only a part of the *nara* or human being could be killed. That part is the body. The soul cannot be destroyed.

Arjuna was incorrect in thinking that he could wipe out Bhishma, *Droṇa* and other influential personalities. Certainly, these politicians would be checked to some degree but their influence would remain to a greater extent. Besides, the memory of their worldly acts and their continued psychic influence will have to be contended with.

अच्छेद्योऽयमदाह्योऽयम्
अक्लेद्योऽशोष्य एव च ।
नित्यः सर्वगतः स्थाणुर्
अचलोऽयं सनातनः ॥२.२४॥
acchedyo'yamadāhyo'yam
akledyo'śoṣya eva ca
nityaḥ sarvagataḥ sthāṇur
acalo'yaṁ sanātanaḥ (2.24)

acchedyaḥ — not to be pierced; 'yam = ayam — this; adāhyo = adāhyaḥ — not to be burnt; 'yam = ayam — this; akledyo = akledyaḥ — not to be moistened; 'śoṣya = aśoṣya — not to be dried; eva — indeed; ca — and; nityaḥ — eternal; sarvagataḥ — penetrant of all things; sthāṇuḥ — a permanent principle; acalo = acalaḥ — unmoving; 'yaṁ = ayaṁ — this; sanātanaḥ — primeval

This embodied soul cannot be pierced, cannot be burnt, cannot be moistened and cannot be dried. And indeed, this soul is eternal. It can penetrate all things. It is a permanent principle and is stable and primeval. (2.24)

Commentary:

The history of the soul is very, very old, as old as existence itself. But this, in no way, implies that the soul himself is aware of his eternity. Modern scientists dig up skulls which they believe to be several millions of years old, but that does not mean that the skulls themselves are aware of their resistance to deterioration. The limited entities are not capable of keeping track of their eternity. Being able to exist naturally and being aware of one's existence are two separate factors. An entity who exists may not be aware of itself objectively. This is why we should not reject the notion of reincarnation.

We may study this by considering the situation of trees. A tree may stand for ten years but that does not mean that it kept track of its growth pattern. It has not. The growth continues impulsively. This means that there can be growth without self-awareness. A man can objectively observe the growth of a tree but the vegetation can neither gauge itself nor another tree. Similarly, the Supreme Being can and does observe our transmigrations but we are unable to sort out such soul movements. Though we are fixed portions of reality, we are only aware of the shifty phases we experience in certain bodies. Although we cannot be displaced, we act as if we are parts of an insecurity. Our history goes back for all eternity but we participate in the struggle for survival as if we were temporary.

अव्यक्तोऽयमचिन्त्योऽयम्
अविकार्योऽयमुच्यते ।
तस्मादेवं विदित्वैनं
नानुशोचितुमर्हसि ॥२.२५॥
avyakto'yamacintyo'yam
avikāryo'yamucyate
tasmādevaṁ viditvainaṁ
nānuśocitumarhasi (2.25)

avyakto = avyaktaḥ — undisplayed; 'yam = ayam — this; acintyo = acintyah — unimaginable; 'yam = ayam — this; avikāryo = avikāryaḥ — unchanging; 'yam = ayam — this; ucyate — it is declared; tasmāt — therefore; evaṁ — thus; viditvainaṁ = viditva — knowing + enaṁ — this; nānuśocitum = na — not + anuśocitum — to lament; arhasi — you should

This embodied soul is undisplayed, unimaginable, and unchanging. Therefore knowing this, you should not lament. (2.25)

Commentary:

Vyakta means manifested, or displayed. This means something that is easily seen by human beings or animals; something that is easily sensed, something that is gross. *Avyakta* means something that is unmanifested, existing but difficult to sense, something that we cannot pinpoint; something that is beyond the reach of human senses. On the basis of the soul's resistance to detection, people conclude that it does not exist.

Something that cannot be pin-pointed cannot be targeted. Something that cannot be computed cannot be figured out. Arjuna claimed to have scriptural knowledge. Krishna insulted him by stating that if he understood these scriptural truths, he would not have lamented.

अथ चैनं नित्यजातं
नित्यं वा मन्यसे मृतम् ।
तथापि त्वं महाबाहो
नैनं शोचितुमर्हसि ॥२.२६॥
atha cainaṁ nityajātaṁ
nityaṁ vā manyase mṛtam
tathāpi tvaṁ mahābāho
nainaṁ śocitumarhasi (2.26)

atha — furthermore; cainaṁ = ca — and + enaṁ — this; nityajātaṁ = nitya — continually + jātam — being born; nityaṁ — continually; vā — or; manyase — you think; mṛtam — dying; tathā 'pi = tathā — so + api — also; tvaṁ — you; mahābāho — strong-armed men; nainaṁ = na — not + enaṁ — this; śocitum arhasi = śocitum — to mourn + arhasi — you can

And furthermore if you think that this embodied soul is continually being born or continually dying, even so, O strong-armed man, you should not lament. (2.26)

Commentary:

Lord Krishna digressed to show that even from Arjuna's viewpoint, sorrow is unwarranted. If the person is eternally being born as a baby, then there is no reason to lament his death. He would be born again in a new body sooner or later.

If, on the other hand, we believe that he is eternal but we state that his eternality is subjected to lapses of existence, then still we have no need to lament since the lapses cannot last forever and since all others would be subjected to existential suspension as well. The truth concerning the body and soul must be accepted sooner or later. We are destined to face the reality of it at the time of death. Thus there is no reason to cry for one another, nor to lament for ourselves.

जातस्य हि ध्रुवो मृत्युर्
ध्रुवं जन्म मृतस्य च ।
तस्मादपरिहार्येऽर्थे
न त्वं शोचितुमर्हसि ॥२.२७॥
jātasya hi dhruvo mṛtyur
dhruvaṁ janma mṛtasya ca
tasmādaparihārye'rthe
na tvaṁ śocitumarhasi (2.27)

jātasya — of that which is born; hi — infact; dhruvo = dhruvaḥ — certain; mṛtyur = mṛtyuḥ — death; dhruvaṁ — certain; janma — birth; mṛtasya — of that which is dead; ca — and; tasmādaparihārye = tasmāt — therefore + aparihārye — in what is unavoidable; 'rthe = arthe — in the assessment; na — not; tvaṁ — you; śocitum — to lament + arhasi — you should

In fact, of that which is born, death is certain; of that which is dead, birth is certain. Therefore in assessing what is unavoidable, you should not lament. (2.27)

<u>Commentary:</u>

The two ways of manifestation were discussed according to the view of the ancient samkhya philosophers. Lord Krishna asserted their opinion, that any entity who experiences the birth of a body will, in due course, experience the death of it. And the same entity will have a birth or appearance elsewhere.

Even though we cannot perceive the birth of a person who passed on, we should know for sure that the person will appear somewhere else. He or she may not appear on this earthly level, but would be manifested somewhere, somehow. The eternality of the soul is a certainty. That is the opinion of the experienced mystics and Lord Krishna.

We may have a problem: We may understand this philosophy or accept it without question, and still we may find that we live as though we are our bodies. When pain and discomfort affect the body, the soul acts as if it is the body. How can we change this? Obviously, no amount of theoretical knowledge, even from Lord Krishna, can affect us as much as the direct experience of the truths. Such experience is therefore the final word in the matter. There is a difference between Arjuna and most people who heard the *Gītā* after him. Arjuna was an accomplished yogi long before he went to *Kurukṣetra*. For him, this is a refresher course. He experienced the truths but had forgotten. He is different to someone who hears the *Gītā* and who has not gone through the mystic experience of conscious separation from the body.

We have had an upsurge of interest in the *Gītā* by many Western youths who had psychic experiences using psychedelic drugs and narcotics. These youths were able to relate to the *Gītā* but since their experience was based on drugs and not on disciplinary mystic development, as described in the *Gītā*, most of them could not properly carry through with the realizations gained.

In the revelation of Lord Krishna's controlling powers, Arjuna saw Lord Krishna's historic grasp on the world, but a devotee today must read about that and settle for his imaginative idea of what was shown to Arjuna. Would it be possible for Lord Krishna to reveal how He controls the world at this present time? For Arjuna it was an immediate revelation. Can or will Lord Krishna show His grasp on the world right now, with the people and places that we are in touch with at this moment?

अव्यक्तादीनि भूतानि
व्यक्तमध्यानि भारत ।
अव्यक्तनिधनान्येव
तत्र का परिदेवना ॥२.२८॥

avyaktādīni = avyakta — undetected + ādīni-beginnings of a manifestation; bhūtāni — living beings; vyakta madhyāni = vyakta — visible + madhyāni — interim states; bhārata — O descendant of Bharata; avyakta nidhanāny eva = avyakta —

avyaktādīni bhūtāni
vyaktamadhyāni bhārata
avyaktanidhanānyeva
tatra kā paridevanā (2.28)

undetected + nidhanāni — ends of a manifestation + eva — again; tatra — there; kā — what; paridevanā — complaint

The living beings are undetected in the beginning of a manifestation, visible in the interim stages, and are again undetected at the end of a manifestation. What is the complaint? (2.28)

Commentary:

For cultural living, even the cultural living of devotees and spiritually-minded people, there is no need to pry into these unseen origins. In fact, many persons who claim to be devotees of Krishna, even spiritual masters who represent the Lord, avoid prying into unseen origins. Some of them are not interested since they feel that Krishna will award salvation regardless of what they do. But Arjuna was informed of these mystic matters.

Lord Krishna did not tell Arjuna that experiences of these unseen factors were irrelevant to Arjuna's devotional life, nor that Arjuna should wait until the time of death. Arjuna had to get his sickening moods in order, recap his mystic experience attained through yoga austerities, and then apply himself to fight on the battlefield.

The life during the interim states between the birth of a body and the death of it, was stressed by Arjuna in his arguments. Lord Krishna minimized that and stressed the psychic side.

Krishna explained how a soul lives before the body was born and how it lives after the body dies. Without considering this, without seeing the continuation of the life of the soul beyond death as well as its life before birth, Arjuna will not be able to fight with detachment.

आश्चर्यवत्पश्यति कश्चिदेनम्
आश्चर्यवद्वदति तथैव चान्यः ।
आश्चर्यवच्चैनमन्यः शृणोति
श्रुत्वाप्येनं वेद न चैव कश्चित् ॥२.२९॥
āścaryavatpaśyati kaścidenam
āścaryavadvadati tathaiva cānyaḥ
āścaryavaccainamanyaḥ śṛṇoti
śrutvāpyenaṁ veda na caiva kaścit (2.29)

āścaryavat — wonderful; paśyati — perceives; kaścidenam = kaścid — someone + enam — this; āścaryavad — fantastic; vadati — describes; tathai 'va = tathā — so + eva — indeed; cānyaḥ = ca — and + anyah — another person; āścaryavaccainam = āścaryavat — amazing + ca — and + enam — this; anyaḥ — another; śṛṇoti — hears; śrutvāpyenaṁ = srutva — having heard + api — also + enaṁ — this; veda — knows; na — not; caiva = ca — and + eva — in fact; kaścit — anyone

Someone perceives this embodied soul as being wonderful. Another person describes it as amazing. Another hears of it as being fantastic. And even after hearing this, no one knows this embodied soul in fact. (2.29)

Commentary:

The visible portion of the soul's life is usually perceived by the actions of his material body. This portion has some amazement to it, but only in exceptional individuals who make an impact on world history. Others are simply regarded as ordinary. The invisibility before birth and the invisibility after death is amazing for all souls. They share in that transcendental nature. And it does not matter if a man is important or not. All of us have that nature. This is the wonder of the soul. It existed before the body was manifested. It continues to exist after the body deteriorates. In that sense, we are all amazing.

If, merely as a statement, we find this to be a fascination, then how wonderful it would be, if we were to experience that consciously. Suppose by revelation, we experienced the souls who await rebirth. Suppose we saw them directly. How would that vision affect our mentality?

At the end of the Battle of Kurukṣetra there was great lamentation by the widows and relatives of the slain warriors. *Śrīla Vyāsadeva* and Lord Krishna arranged for them to see the departed souls in the hereafter. What a wonderful experience!

As Lord Krishna said, some of us, even after hearing from authoritative sources, still do not understand how the soul can exist without a body. By authoritative sources we refer to those who realized this by experience, not merely by a conceptual understanding of the *Gītā*. We have to hear from one who experienced this. Ideally, the Gita should be understood by experience and not merely by the wording and the ideas or mental concepts formed by that hearing.

देही नित्यमवध्योऽयं
देहे सर्वस्य भारत ।
तस्मात्सर्वाणि भूतानि
न त्वं शोचितुमर्हसि ॥२.३०॥
dehī nityamavadhyo'yaṁ
dehe sarvasya bhārata
tasmātsarvāṇi bhūtāni
na tvaṁ śocitumarhasi (2.30)

dehī — embodied soul; nityam — eternally; avadhyo = avadhyaḥ — non-killable; 'yaṁ = ayaṁ — this; dehe — in the body; sarvasya — of all, in all cases; bhārata — O descendant of Bharata; tasmāt — therefore; sarvāṇi — all; bhūtāni — beings; na — no; tvaṁ — you; śocitumarhasi = śocitum — to mourn + arhasi — should

In the body, in all cases, this embodied soul is always non-killable, O descendant of Bharata. Therefore you should not mourn for any of these beings. (2.30)

Commentary:

Lord Krishna again addressed Arjuna as *Bhārata*. This means a descendant of *Bharata*, a man of the *Bhārata* family, a person carrying on the *Bhārata* family traditions, or plainly a person with the *Bhārata* surname. In those days, a man of the *Bhārata* family was supposed to be educated in both cultural skills and mystic experience. By addressing Arjuna as Mister *Bhārata*, Lord Krishna tactfully intimidated the warrior.

Here the word *dehi* is used. This term means the embodied one, the person using a mundane form. Even the soul using an animal body is a *dehi*. It means the body-prone personality.

Even the souls in animal bodies are invincible, not subjected to fatality. Our shifty existence on the cultural plane is not significant because we will survive those changes and will continue existing in some other way.

स्वधर्ममपि चावेक्ष्य
न विकम्पितुमर्हसि ।
धर्म्याद्धि युद्धाच्छ्रेयोऽन्यत्
क्षत्रियस्य न विद्यते ॥२.३१॥

svadharmam — your assigned duty; api — also; cāvekṣya = ca — and + avekṣya — looking, mentally considering; na — no; vikampitum — to consider alternatives; arhasi — you should; dharmyād = dharmyāt

svadharmamapi cāvekṣya
na vikampitumarhasi
dharmyāddhi
yuddhācchreyo'nyat
kṣatriyasya na vidyate (2.31)

— from righteousness; dhi = hi — indeed; yuddhācchreyo = yuddhāt — from battle + chreyo = śreyas — better; 'nyat = anyat — other; kṣatriyasya — of the son of a king; na — no; vidyate — there is

And considering your assigned duty, you should not look for alternatives. In fact, for the son of a king, there is no other duty which is better than a righteous battle. (2.31)

Commentary:

In one stroke, Lord Krishna rejected Arjun's idea of changing his role in life, changing duty. Arjuna was a government official for King Yudhishthira. He was not a forest ascetic but he wanted to try for an alternative life style as an ascetic. At one time Arjuna spent part of a year practicing strict austerities and he mastered the ascetic disciplines. That course of asceticism was recommended by *Śrīla Vyāsadeva* in order to reinforce the strength of King Yudhishthira. Upon completion of the practice, Arjuna returned to government service. Just as today the government might send an employee to take a special course at a university, so Arjuna was sent to live the ascetic life. On another occasion Arjuna was absent from his brothers for a year. During that time he traveled with wandering ascetics. In addition, the Pandavas lived with ascetics in their infant years. Arjuna had friends in the ascetic community. He knew he could live with them quite easily. Still it was not an alternative at this point in his life.

Arjuna backed away from emotional relations which were threatened by the confrontation at *Kurukṣetra*. If the battle was canceled, the impurity of these emotions would remain. One goes to a teacher like *Droṇa* to take knowledge from him. This is the essential motive but one invariably plays the role of a submissive servant even though at heart, one may simply want to get techniques from the teacher. One plays huggy-huggy, lovey-dovey with a grandfather like Bhishma because one wants to tap into his life experience, to benefit from his prestige and property. All this was the pain that Arjuna avoided. He began to disown his claim to the political power and legacy of the Kurus. He began to praise people like *Droṇa*, saying that he would not fight against them. But Lord Krishna would have nothing of it. As the Lord explained further on in the *Gītā*, He came to the battlefield to enforce time, to make all men face their faults then and there.

Arjuna' s idea that forest life was devoid of violence, cannot be accepted by anyone who has lived for long in ashramas or in any isolated spiritual community. Even there, we experience verbal conflicts and power struggles which are just as painful as battlefield encounters. In fact, many persons run away from spiritual communities because the emotional pain of confrontations they experienced with spiritual masters and co-disciples, is too hard to bear. As we stated in the beginning of this commentary of the *Gītā*, Arjuna made a mistake when he came forward to review the enemy ranks without taking permission from King Yudhishthira. Lord Krishna reminded Arjuna of dharma, duty as a member of a political family. Arjuna had duties in that Kuru clan. He was not to avoid these. The combat which Arjuna shunned was the very thing most suited to his destiny.

यदृच्छया चोपपन्नं
स्वर्गद्वारमपावृतम् ।
सुखिनः क्षत्रियाः पार्थ
लभन्ते युद्धमीदृशम् ॥२.३२॥

yadṛcchayā — by a stroke of luck; copapannaṁ = ca — and + upapannam — made available; svargadvāram = svarga — heaven + dvāram — gate; apāvṛtam — is open; sukhinaḥ — thrilled, happy; kṣatriyāḥ

yadṛcchayā copapannaṁ
svargadvāramapāvṛtam
sukhinaḥ kṣatriyāḥ pārtha
labhante yuddhamīdṛśam (2.32)

— warriors; pārtha — O son of Pṛthā; labhante — get; yuddham — battle opportunity; īdṛśam — such

And by a stroke of luck, the gate of heaven is opened. Thrilled are the warriors who get such a battle opportunity, O son of Pṛthā. (2.32)

Commentary:

As the son of *Pṛthā* or *Kuntī*, Arjuna had some obligation to live a glorious life on earth, through which his mother would reach the celestial worlds. A mother may rely on the earthly accomplishments of her son, either for her rebirth on earth or her ascension to a subtle paradise. Princess *Pṛthā* became a queen at a young age, but she was dispossessed and had to rely on the Kurus after her husband, King Pandu, passed away. Since the earthly companionship with her husband was cut short, *Kuntī* was reliant on her three sons, namely Yudhishthira, *Bhīma* and Arjuna, each of whom were obligated to do something worthwhile for the benefit of their mother. A son has value to his mother but has even more worth if his father passes on at an early age. This is why Lord Krishna addressed Arjuna here as *Pārtha*, the son of *Pṛthā*. He tactfully reminded Arjuna of the obligations to *Kuntī*.

Providence moves at its own pace; sometimes it accelerates unexpectedly; sometimes it moves slowly. As such, a man should be ready to grab an opportunity when it arises. In some lives, a man hardly gets a chance to put his mark on history but in other lives, opportunity might come easily.

अथ चेत्त्वमिमं धर्म्यं
संग्रामं न करिष्यसि ।
ततः स्वधर्मं कीर्तिं च
हित्वा पापमवाप्स्यसि ॥२.३३॥
atha cettvamimaṁ dharmyaṁ
saṁgrāmaṁ na kariṣyasi
tataḥ svadharmaṁ kīrtiṁ ca
hitvā pāpamavāpsyasi (2.33)

atha — now; cet — if; tvam — you; imaṁ — this; dharmyaṁ — appropriate duty; saṁgrāmaṁ — warfare; na — not; kariṣyasi — will conduct; tataḥ — then; svadharmaṁ — own duty; kīrtiṁca = kīrtiṁ — reputation + ca — and; hitvā — having neglected; pāpam — sin, fault; avāpsyasi — will acquire

Now if you do not conduct this righteous war, then, by neglecting your duty and reputation, you will acquire a fault. (2.33)

Commentary:

Sadly to say, acting has hazards but backing away from opportunity is also risky. Arjuna could not avoid combat without incurring a fault. Lord Krishna used a Sanskrit term: *pāpam*, meaning transgression, a fault, a punishable act, a reactive situation.

Arjuna was trapped. What should he do? If he acted, there were risks as he pointed out in Chapter One. If he did not act there were hazards as Lord Krishna explained. The solution obviously was to submit to Lord Krishna and get expert advice.

Lord Krishna mentioned a purely cultural consideration. This might seem to be a contradiction in the *Gītā* discourse. He said: *tatah svadharmam kīrtim ca*, which means, *then, your own duty and glory*. These aspects of Arjuna's life, though cultural, were related to Arjuna's intellectual consideration. This is why they were mentioned by Krishna at this time. We must deal with cultural life. The approach is to apply spiritual experience to cultural situations. We must work our way through the cultural setting. We have no choice.

To handle a situation expertly we need to apply spiritual disciplines and experiences every step of the way.

अकीर्तिं चापि भूतानि
कथयिष्यन्ति तेऽव्ययाम् ।
संभावितस्य चाकीर्तिर्
मरणादतिरिच्यते ॥२.३४॥
akīrtiṁ cāpi bhūtāni
kathayiṣyanti te'vyayām
saṁbhāvitasya cākīrtir
maraṇādatiricyate (2.34)

akīrtiṁ — downfall; cāpi = ca — and + api — also; bhūtāni — the people; kathayiṣyanti — will speak; te — of you; 'vyayām = avyayām — continually; saṁbhāvitasya — for an honored man; cākīrtir = ca — and + akīrtiḥ — loss of reputation; maraṇād = maraṇāt — than the loss of body; atiricyate — is harder to bear

The people will speak of your downfall continually. And for an honored man, the loss of reputation is harder to bear than the loss of his body. (2.34)

Commentary:

This is another cultural consideration being given by Lord Krishna. This is presented because Arjuna was concerned about his reputation, which he thought would be damaged, if he fought against elderly men like Bhishma and *Droṇa*. Lord Krishna explained that the result would be the opposite of what Arjuna anticipated. Instead of being liked, Arjuna would be shunned if he turned away. Instead of becoming happy as an ascetic, Arjuna would become miserable for losing the reputation as a great fighter and law man. For a hero, the death of his body is a smaller concern than the loss of popularity.

भयाद्रणादुपरतं
मंस्यन्ते त्वां महारथाः ।
येषां च त्वं बहुमतो
भूत्वा यास्यसि लाघवम् ॥२.३५॥
bhayādraṇāduparataṁ
maṁsyante tvāṁ mahārathāḥ
yeṣāṁ ca tvaṁ bahumato
bhūtvā yāsyasi lāghavam (2.35)

bhayād = bhayāt — because of fear; raṇād = raṇāt — from the excitement of battle; uparataṁ — withdraw from; maṁsyante — they think; tvāṁ — you; mahārathāḥ — great warriors; yeṣāṁ — of whom; ca — and; tvaṁ — you; bahumato = bahumataḥ — high opinion; bhūtvā — had; yāsyasi — you will come; lāghavam — insignificance

The great warriors will think that because of fear, you withdrew from battle. And to those who held a big opinion, you will appear to be insignificant. (2.35)

Commentary:

Arjuna thought that he would be appreciated for not fighting but Lord Krishna explained that this was a miscalculation. Arjuna would have received the opposite result, of being considered an amateur, boyish, cowardly warrior. Arjuna thought that people would have appreciated his non-violent stance but Lord Krishna explained that instead they would speak of his cowardice. His reputation would be diminished. His image would be tarnished. They would dismiss him as being unmanly.

अवाच्यवादांश्च बहून्
वदिष्यन्ति तवाहिताः ।
निन्दन्तस्तव सामर्थ्यं
ततो दुःखतरं नु किम् ॥२.३६॥

avācyavādāṁśca = avācya — not to be said, slurred + vādān — words, saying + ca — and; bahūn — many; vadiṣyanti — will speak; tavāhitāḥ = tava — about you + ahitāḥ — enemies; nindantas — laughed at; tava — of

avācyavādāṁśca bahūn
vadiṣyanti tavāhitāḥ
nindantastava sāmarthyaṁ
tato duḥkhataraṁ nu kim (2.36)

you; sāmarthyaṁ — capability; tato = tataḥ — from that; duḥkhataraṁ — greater grief; nu — but; kim — what

The enemies will say many slurs about you, thus laughing at your capability. But, what would be a greater grief than this? (2.36)

<u>Commentary:</u>

Apart from the drop in prestige, Arjuna would be subjected to criticism. He did have enemies, people whom he chastised previously; people who disliked him for no cause. These persons would ridiculed him using profanities. And that would be heard painfully by Arjuna.

हतो वा प्राप्स्यसि स्वर्गं
जित्वा वा भोक्ष्यसे महीम् ।
तस्मादुत्तिष्ठ कौन्तेय
युद्धाय कृतनिश्चयः ॥२.३७॥
hato vā prāpsyasi svargaṁ
jitvā vā bhokṣyase mahīm
tasmāduttiṣṭha kaunteya
yuddhāya kṛtaniścayaḥ (2.37)

hato = hataḥ — be killed; vā — either; prāpsyasi — you will achieve; svargaṁ — angelic world; jitvā — having conquered; vā — or; bhokṣyase — you will enjoy; mahīm — the nation; tasmād = tasmāt — therefore; uttiṣṭha — stand up; kaunteya — O son of Kuntī; yuddhāya — to battle; kṛtaniścayaḥ — be decisive

Either be killed and achieve the angelic world or having conquered, enjoy the nation. Therefore stand up and be decisive, O son of Kunti. (2.37)

<u>Commentary:</u>

Rather than run from the battlefield, Arjuna was to take either alternative of being killed by or of killing the enemy. In either case there would be a favorable reward for him according to cited rules. Arjuna said that he would go to hell for killing relatives, but Krishna disagreed, and said that Arjuna, if he were victorious, would enjoy political power and the country's resources, Arjuna was afraid of facing hell regardless of the outcome.

Arjuna thought that if he went to the forest, he would avoid the sins of warfare, but Lord Krishna explained that this view was flawed. In the forest, Arjuna would incur a sin for neglecting duty

सुखदुःखे समे कृत्वा
लाभालाभौ जयाजयौ ।
ततो युद्धाय युज्यस्व
नैवं पापमवाप्स्यसि ॥२.३८॥
sukhaduḥkhe same kṛtvā
lābhālābhau jayājayau
tato yuddhāya yujyasva
naivaṁ pāpamavāpsyasi (2.38)

sukhaduḥkhe = sukha — happiness + duḥkhe — in distress; same — in the same emotions; kṛtvā — having regard; lābhālābhau — gains or losses; jayājayau — victory or defeat; tato = tataḥ — them; yuddhāya — to battle; yujyasva — apply yourself; naivaṁ = na — not + evaṁ — thus; pāpam — sin,demerit; avāpsyasi — you will get

Having regarded happiness, distress, gains, losses, victory and defeat, as the same emotions, apply yourself to battle. Thus you will get no demerit. (2.38)

Commentary:

In the cultural setting we are besieged by happy, plain and distressful moods. Plain moods are sobering, non-sensational or boring. Happiness may be intense, mild or stimulating. These moods come upon us naturally by the currents of material nature and the degree of our stupidity. The moods can be minimized and reduced, but they cannot be eliminated altogether. Still, Lord Krishna recommended detachment. This detachment is not an artificial mental state which might be assumed merely by hearing what Krishna said, but it is the detachment developed by the yogis after much yoga and discipline. This yoga is itself described by the Lord in the *Gītā*. Yoga is His word for it, not this writer's.

An artificial detachment based on the theoretical knowledge alone does not protect us from the varying moods. It only gives us a pretense of immunity from destructive emotions. Thus we cannot rely on any religious system that merely gives faith and theoretical understanding.

Krishna explained that if Arjuna acted in a detached manner, there would be no consequences. It is seen that in modern times, many persons assumed a theory-based detachment, acted, and then discovered that they were not protected from unfavorable reactions. Thus *naivam pāpam avāpsyasi* cannot mean the application of an artificial, non-yogically-attained detachment.

This immunity from sinful reaction only applies to activities that are directly authorized by Lord Krishna, not to activities that are directly authorized by a devotee of Krishna but which are not approved by the Lord. It is not every opinion of a great devotee that is approved by the Lord. We see here that Lord Krishna did not endorse any of Arjuna's views in Chapter One. All of Arjuna's ideas are scripturally based and sensible but still Lord Krishna systematically rejected them. In the enemy ranks, there were devotees also, elevated men like Bhishma. But Lord Krishna did not approve of all their ideas even though He recognized their devotion and loyalty to Him.

Unless one is personally covered by Lord Krishna at every moment, there is absolutely no guarantee that one's activities will be approved by Him. Our individual nature is there even if we are in the direct presence of Lord Krishna as Arjuna was on the chariot.

A Krishna-believing, Krishna-following monk who commits sinful or immoral acts which are hostile to society but which he passes off as being something for Lord Krishna, may not get the approval of the Lord. Krishna's disapproval would be revealed when an unfavorable reaction appears. We will, however, hear more from Lord Krishna on this matter and get clarification on these issues.

एषा तेऽभिहिता सांख्ये
बुद्धिर्योगे त्विमां शृणु ।
बुद्ध्या युक्तो यया पार्थ
कर्मबन्धं प्रहास्यसि ॥२.३९॥
eṣā te'bhihitā sāṁkhye
buddhiryoge tvimāṁ śṛṇu
buddhyā yukto yayā pārtha
karmabandhaṁ prahāsyasi (2.39)

eṣā — this; te — to you; bhihitā = abhihitā — stated; sāṁkhye — in sāṁkhya philosophy; buddhir = buddhiḥ — insight; yoge — in yoga discipline; tvimām = tu — but + imāṁ — this; śṛṇu — hear; buddhyā — with the insight; yukto = yuktaḥ — yoked; yayā — by which; pārtha — O son of Pṛthā; karmabandhaṁ — complication of action; prahāsyasi — you will avoid

As explained in the Sāṁkhya philosophy, this vision is the insight, but hear of its application in yoga practice. Yoked with this insight, O son of Pṛthā, you will avoid the complication of action. (2.39)

Commentary:

Buddhi yoga means insight yoga, because *buddhi* means insight. In Sanskrit *buddhi* does not mean and never meant devotion. To stress this insight, Lord Krishna repeated the word in its prepositional Sanskrit phrasing as *buddhyā* in line three. Please check this. He did not use the word *bhakti. Bhakti* is stressed in the *Gītā* as we will see later on, but here the stress is on insight gained by a man through the disciplines of the samkhya philosophers of Arjuna's time.

This was the solution given to Arjuna to overcome emotional sickness. This was the only solution given to him directly for that particular problem. Arjuna had other problems but his emotional sickness was to be cured by this process.

The next inquiry about this verse is: How are we supposed to attain proficiency in samkhya vision whereby we would always be in touch with that discriminative insight or as Lord Krishna stated in Sanskrit, *buddhyā yukto yayā*? We will have to wait to see what method Lord Krishna gave for attaining this.

नेहाभिक्रमनाशोऽस्ति
प्रत्यवायो न विद्यते ।
स्वल्पमप्यस्य धर्मस्य
त्रायते महतो भयात् ॥२.४०॥

nehābhikramanāśo'sti
pratyavāyo na vidyate
svalpamapyasya dharmasya
trāyate mahato bhayāt (2.40)

nehābhikramanāśo = na — not + iha — in this insight + abhikrama — endeavor + nāśo (nāśaḥ) — loss; asti — it is; pratyavāyo = pratyavāyaḥ — reversal; na — not; vidyate — there is; svalpam — a little; apy = api — even; asya — of this; dharmasya — of righteous practice; trāyate — protects; mahato = mahataḥ — from the great; bhayāt — from danger

In this insight, no endeavor is lost nor is there any reversal. Even a little of this righteous practice protects from the great danger. (2.40)

Commentary:

As it is with every verse of the *Gītā*, especially with the crucial verses, various *Gītā* translators and commentators stress different parts and give entirely different meanings. Even the authorities in disciplic succession from Krishna have variant translations and stress different ideas. A reader of the *Gītā* should study the Sanskrit of the text carefully but if he can not, he may take a translation at face value or reject it outright, according to his inclination for or against a particular translator. This translation will undoubtedly meet with great opposition but there is no translation that was not rejected by someone.

This translation is meant to keep everything in line with the context of the text and not to separate anything, nor to use anything to capture followers or create a world wide organization. We just want to clarify the *Gītā* in its own time and place, with or without respect to what we are doing today or what we require of the *Gītā* in these modern times. Thus we will make no attempt to lessen the *Gītā*, to dilute the heavy-duty messages nor to change any meanings in a positive or negative way. The fault of the impersonalist translators is their attempt to reduce Krishna to being a mere manifestation of God or being a mere spokesperson for the Supreme Brahman. In doing so, they twist the *Gītā*. Our opposition to them is based on a simple rule: One should merely give the *Gītā* as it was given to Arjuna. And if one wants to write a different philosophy, he should do it separately, rather than try to derail the *Gītā*. If Lord Krishna positioned Himself as the Lord in a very big way, then it is best that we say He did so, even if we do not agree with His declarations. But we should not declare that He did not present Himself as the Absolute Truth. Nor should we indicate that He said this and meant something else. He was dead serious about what He said and to back up His high-sounding words, He showed the Universal Form. Arjuna became convinced. Even if we believe that it was just an apparition, just as Duryodhana felt, then still, we should plainly state what Krishna declared.

In the case of devotional commentators, there is a more serious problem in that on the devotional side, commentators might try to erase or foreshadow parts of the *Gītā* that concern some yogas which do not seem to be *bhakti yoga* but which were explained by Lord Krishna and which form the ground base of the *Gītā*.

In the previous verse, *Śrīla* Sridhara Deva Gosvami, the Gaudiya Math authority, gave a rare purport of just a short commentary which was left for us by *Śrīla* Bhaktivinoda Thakur (see The Hidden Treasure of the Sweet Absolute, p. 32):

Śrīla Sridhara Deva Gosvami's Commentary:

> ***"It will be shown herein that buddhi yoga is a singular path. When this buddhi yoga is seen to be limited by the ideal of action, it is known as karma yoga; when it extends beyond karma up to the utmost limit of knowledge, it is known as jñana yoga, or samkhya yoga; and when, transcending the limitations of both jñana and karma, it touches bhakti, or devotion, it is then known as bhakti yoga, or perfectly pure and complete buddhi yoga." — Srila Bhaktivinoda Thakur***

Here we see clearly that *Śrīla* Bhaktivinoda Thakura identified that the application of *buddhi* yoga to *bhakti yoga*, makes for a perfectly pure and complete *buddhi* yoga. This is technical. It does show, however, that there is a distinction to be made between *buddhi* yoga and other forms of yoga until the *buddhi* is applied to any of the other forms.

Some other Vaishnava acharyas, however, become disturbed to hear of anything except *bhakti yoga*. They feel that all other yogas are antagonistic to *bhakti*. These views, however, are one consideration and what Krishna said to Arjuna is another. Krishna directly told Arjuna to take up *buddhi* yoga. It is the first yoga recommended by Lord Krishna. It means *buddhi* yoga as defined and cultivated in the samkhya system of philosophy of Arjuna's time. No one in his right mind can deny that Lord Krishna directly recommended this *buddhi* yoga.

Up to this point in the *Gītā*, this is the only yoga that was directly recommended. It cannot be denied by any of the commentators. Furthermore, Lord Krishna said that it protects from great danger (*mahatah bhayāt*). The word *dharmasya* is used in the verse and not the word *bhakti* or *bhakti yoga*. It is futile to try to twist the word *dharmasya* It means duty according to one's caste. In the time of Arjuna, caste distinction was very strict in India. Arjuna was in the warrior caste. He had to stick to his *dharma*, or duty, in that caste. He wanted to desist and change the caste to the brahmin category because brahmins have no military obligations. Lord Krishna did not approve of it. Furthermore, Lord Krishna told Arjuna that if he stuck to his caste and performed that duty with the detachment of a samkhya yogi, he would be protected from danger. There is not a scrap of evidence anywhere in the Sanskrit thus far, to this point in the *Gītā*, to suggest that Lord Krishna was telling Arjuna to become a *bhakta* of Krishna or to serve Krishna here as a devotee. The instruction to be a *bhakta* will occur later, but it is not here and it is important for us to understand this. We do not want to be misled by a guru who wants us to leave our duty and go off to an ashrama to follow him in the name of following Krishna's instructions. The instructions are clear. Arjuna was to stay on as a warrior and serve his brother, Yudhishthira, in that war. It was Yudhishthira's war against their relatives in a civil conflict. Arjuna wanted to run to an ashrama or to join a group of ascetics. He did this before as it is described vividly in the rest of the *Mahābhārata* of which the *Gītā* is a part. Ignorance of the *Mahābhārata* is a great cause for our confusion about the *Gītā*. It may cause us to be misled by others who take the *Gītā* out of its place in the *Mahābhārata* and apply it randomly to other situations. Krishna did not allow Arjuna to leave his occupational duty, his *dharmasya*. To understand the word *dharmasya*, we have to go back to text 33:

atha cettvamimaṁ dharmyaṁ saṁgrāmaṁ na kariṣyasi
tataḥ svadharmaṁ kīrtiṁ ca hitvā pāpamavāpsyasi (2.33)

Now if you do not conduct this righteous war, then, by neglecting your duty and reputation, you will acquire a fault. (2.33)

It is clear that dharma is duty. It is the thing Arjuna was running from. In his case, it was the warrior's work of fighting at *Kurukṣetra*. This is also cleared up in text 31:

svadharmamapi cāvekṣya na vikampitumarhasi
dharmyāddhi yuddhācchreyo'nyat kṣatriyasya na vidyate (2.31)

And considering your assigned duty, you should not look for alternatives. In fact, for the son of a king, there is no other duty which is better than a righteous battle. (2.31)

Therefore we need not hunt around for any explanation. It is clear.

Some other technical words are *mahatah bhayāt*, the great fear. What is the great fear? In the previous verse, it is described as *karmabandha*, the bondage or liability that comes from either performing attached activities or not performing duties at all. Different men in different castes or designations, may perform their duties with attachment or may desist from their duties and get varying types of reactions in material nature. But for Arjuna, the reaction was indicated by Arjuna himself in verse 43 of Chapter One:

utsannakuladharmāṇāṁ manuṣyāṇāṁ janārdana
narake 'niyataṁ vāso bhavatītyanuśuśruma (1.43)

O Krishna, those who destroy the family customs dwell in hell indefinitely. This was declared repeatedly. (1.43)

Lord Krishna gave definite knowledge of this great fear elsewhere in the *Gītā*. For the time being, we should remember that it comes about by either of two decisions of a duty-bound man: Either acting with a sense of attachment or deciding not to act at all. Either of these will cause a great fear to manifest in the life of the performer.

A man adds to himself by performing his duty fittingly with an attitude of the samkhya yogi. He takes away from himself or imperils his future by performing his duty with attachment or by avoiding the duty altogether.

व्यवसायात्मिका बुद्धिर्
एकेह कुरुनन्दन ।
बहुशाखा ह्यनन्ताश्च
बुद्धयोऽव्यवसायिनाम् ॥ २.४१ ॥
vyavasāyātmikā buddhir
ekeha kurunandana
bahuśākhā hyanantāśca
buddhayo'vyavasāyinām (2.41)

vyavasāyātmikā — intentional determination; buddhir = buddhih — technical insight; ekeha = eka — one view + iha — in this instance; kurunandana — O dear man of the Kuru family; bahuśākhā — many offshoots; hyanantāś = hi — in fact + anantāḥ — endless; ca — and; buddhayo = buddhayaḥ — views; 'vyavasāyinām = avyavasāyinām — of the person with many hopes

When a person's intentional determination is guided by technical insight, he experiences one view, O dear man of the Kuru family. But the views of a person with many hopes are diverse and endless. (2.41)

Commentary:

Here again in this verse we see *buddhih* and *buddhaya* which are mentioned in text 39. This is again stressed. If Lord Krishna meant something else, He would have used different terms. He directly stressed *buddhi* or intellectual insight as contrasted to an intellectual outlook which has *bahuśākhā* or many imaginary hopes and diversions.

The technical terms are *vyavasāyātmikā*, or intentional determination, and *avyavasāyinām* or unstable mental outlook. These are states of the intellect. When the intellect is on the lower planes, it is affected by the impure emotions and it acts and reacts accordingly. But when it reaches the plane of detachment that is attained by the perfected samkhya yogis, it reaches state of certainty in the vision of reality which was described by Lord Krishna earlier when He explained the truths realized by the Upanishadic sages who declared in ancient times. That reality is permanent. Its non-visibility does not deny it. It is there as the background of all visibility even though we may not see it.

यामिमां पुष्पितां वाचं
प्रवदन्त्यविपश्चितः ।
वेदवादरताः पार्थ
नान्यदस्तीति वादिनः ॥ २.४२ ॥
yāmimāṁ puṣpitāṁ vācaṁ
pravadantyavipaścitaḥ
vedavādaratāḥ pārtha
nānyadastīti vādinaḥ (2.42)

yām — which; imām — this; puṣpitāṁ — poetic; vācaṁ — quotation; pravadantyavipaścitaḥ = pravadanti — they proclaim + avipaścitaḥ — ignorant reciters; vedavādaratāḥ — enjoying Vedic Sanskrit poetry; pārtha — O son of Pṛthā; nānyad = na — not + anyat — anything; astīti = asti — it is + iti — thus; vādinaḥ — saying

This is poetic quotation which the ignorant reciters proclaim, O son of Pṛthā. Enjoying the Vedic verses, they say there is no other written authority. (2.42)

Commentary:

The *vedavādis* are those who enjoy the poetic word formations of the Vedic Sanskrit verses. These are sung with or without the accompaniment of music and it sounds very enjoyable, relaxing and assuring to a person with a sensuous mentality. Instead of focusing on the meaning and analyzing these, the *vedavādis* focus mostly on the sounds. The Upanishadic sages who were appraised as being *tattvadarśih*, reality-perceiving persons, did go beyond the Vedas to actually discover the spiritual reality that is beneath this material world. This is why they were appraised by Lord Krishna, who quoted and approved their conclusions:

nāsato vidyate bhāvo'nābhāvo vidyate sataḥ
ubhayorapi dṛṣṭo'ntas tvanayostattvadarśibhiḥ (2.16)

Of the non-substantial things, there is no enduring existence. Of the substantial things, there is no lack of existence. These two truths were perceived with certainty by the mystic seers of reality. (2.16)

Even today, there are many Hindus who follow these *vedavādis* just as if Lord Krishna had not stated this verse to Arjuna long ago. Even Hindus who hear this verse and understand its meaning and who are impulsively drawn to the Vedic rituals, disregard this verse and go on with the conviction that no other scripture and no other sensual experience is greater than the particular part of the Veda of their choice.

It appears that as great a person as Arjuna was affected by the Vedic hymns which are, more or less, guidelines on becoming successful as a living being in the material world. These Vedic hymns do not, in any way, hint at liberation from material bondage. The verses by Arjuna in Chapter One which are being criticized by Lord Krishna, are as follows:

kulakṣaye praṇaśyanti kuladharmāḥ sanātanāḥ
dharme naṣṭe kulaṁ kṛtsnam adharmo'bhibhavatyuta (1.39)
adharmābhibhavātkṛṣṇa praduṣyanti kulastriyaḥ
strīṣu duṣṭāsu vārṣṇeya jāyate varṇasaṁkaraḥ (1.40)
saṁkaro narakāyaiva kulaghnānāṁ kulasya ca
patanti pitaro hyeṣāṁ luptapiṇḍodakakriyāḥ (1.41)
doṣairetaiḥ kulaghnānāṁ varṇasaṁkarakārakaiḥ
utsādyante jātidharmāḥ kuladharmāśca śāśvatāḥ (1.42)
utsannakuladharmāṇāṁ manuṣyāṇāṁ janārdana
narake 'niyataṁ vāso bhavatītyanuśuśruma (1.43)

In the destruction of the clan, the ancient family traditions vanish. In the removal of the traditional values, the entire clan is overpowered by lawlessness. (1.39)

Due to the predominance of lawlessness, the women of the clan are degraded. In such women, O clansman of the Vṛṣṇis, there arises the sexual intermixture of the classes. (1.40)

Indeed, the sexual intermixture causes the destroyers of the clan and the clan itself to go to hell. The departed ancestors of those clansmen, being deprived of the psychic cakes and water which are offered ceremonially, are degraded. (1.41)

By the sins of the family destroyers and by the sexual intermixture of the classes, individual skills and family duties disappear. (1.42)

O Krishna, those who destroy the family customs dwell in hell indefinitely. This was declared repeatedly. (1.43)

At a glance there seems to be nothing wrong with these rules of cultural living. But if we look closely at the last verse, we will find a discrepancy. It all depends on the type of family tradition. If the family is corrupt, the reformer of it, if he is a pious ruler, will not go to hell. In any case, in verse 42, Arjuna quotes correctly. If traditional rules and proper family behavior are affected, for the better or worse, the elders of the family are disempowered. This is, however, a risk that must be taken in dealing with corruption.

In the world, there will be corruption. It must be dealt with, even at the risk of upsetting some good traditions. It is better to amputate a diseased limb than to have it ruin the entire body. King *Dhṛtarāṣṭra* was told in the *Mahābhārata* that one may sacrifice one village for a country, or one son for a family.

Arjuna quoted scripture in a lopsided way. Krishna condemned his selection of verses in text eleven of this Chapter Two:

Śrībhagavānuvāca
aśocyānanvaśocastvaṁ prajñāvādāṁśca bhāṣase
gatāsūnagatāsūṁśca nānuśocanti paṇḍitāḥ (2.11)

The Blessed Lord said: You mourned for that which should not be regretted. And you expressed intelligent statements. (2.11)

Even today many pandits follow the nice-sounding Vedic mantras. They are considered to be ritual technicians but Lord Krishna categorizes them as *avipaścitas*, ignorant people without vision. The vision they lack is one acquired by a person who went through the yoga practices and mastered the yoga system. Such a person can see as the samkhya philosophers did, as described by Krishna Himself in this chapter. These ritual technicians might talk about reincarnation of the soul but in truth they do not understand it in the least. They have no conscious experience of it. Their faith rests on mundane cultural activities which have to do with this one life, and they advise their clients accordingly.

Being terribly afraid of the yoga austerities and the brain-racking samkhya philosophy, people go to these ritual experts repeatedly just as if Lord Krishna had never denounced them.

A similar occurrence manifested itself in some devotional societies, whereby a spiritual master convinces his followers that there is nothing more than the theoretical understanding of mystic portions of the scriptures. Such devotees follow such a course, thinking that all spiritual truths will be revealed to them at the time of death. They also say that there is no other way of salvation and that spiritual truths cannot and should not be realized, except theoretically, until the time of death. Their teachers, though supportive of Lord Krishna, carefully deny what is recommended by Lord Krishna in verse 41 as *vyavasāyātmikā buddhir*

Arjuna had some theoretical understanding of scripture but it was not enough to cause him to act transcendentally. He had to get direct experience beyond hearing. Arjuna saw the Universal Form and relocated his consciousness to the spiritual level from where he viewed the lower realities in the proper perspective. Hearing is just the beginning. One has to go further to get direct experience.

कामात्मानः स्वर्गपरा
जन्मकर्मफलप्रदाम् ।
क्रियाविशेषबहुलां
भोगैश्वर्यगतिं प्रति ॥ २.४३ ॥
kāmātmānaḥ svargaparā
janmakarmaphalapradām
kriyāviśeṣabahulāṁ
bhogaiśvaryagatiṁ prati (2.43)

kāmātmānaḥ — people of a sensuous nature; svargaparā — people intent on going to the swarga (angelic) world; janmakarmaphalapradām = janma — rebirth + karma — cultural act + phala — pay-off + pradām — offering; kriyāviśeṣabahulāṁ = kriyā — ceremonial rites + viśeṣa — specific + bahulāṁ — various; bhogaiśvaryagatiṁ = bhoga — enjoyment + aiśvarya — political power + gatiṁ — aim; prati — toward

Those reciters, being people of a sensuous nature, being intent on going to the Svarga angelic world, offering such rebirth as payoff for cultural activities, make themselves busy in various specific ceremonial rites, and focus on enjoyment and political power. (2.43)

Commentary:

The Vedic reciters mentioned are loyal to the Vedas but only in a superficial way. They have no intention of performing the austerities through which the Vedic knowledge becomes realized. Subsequently, they misapply knowledge just as Arjuna did in Chapter One, when he tried to use the Vedic statements to convince Lord Krishna to stop the battle. And it is the same with devotees of Lord Krishna who only hear but do not realize in actual experience what was heard and who remain satisfied by that hearing alone, feeling it to be the actual experience. Though they get the knowledge of the *Gītā*, they cannot apply it properly because it is a theoretical, imaginative experience only.

Lord Krishna first cited the Upanishadic sages in text 16 of this chapter as the *tattvadarśih* to distinguish them from the *vedāvadis*. The difference is this: Both the *tattvadarśih* or experienced mystics and the *vedāvadis* or the theoretical believers, do believe in Veda, but the *tattvadarśih* have gone a step further to perceive the truth beyond a mere hearing from the authorities. Arjuna also mentioned that he heard from the authorities. He mentioned that in text 44 of Chapter One, by the term *anuśuśruma*, meaning that he heard it from the authorized disciplic succession, by *paramparā*. And still Lord Krishna rejected what Arjuna said, telling him that he spoke words which described experience, but that he was inexperienced himself.

To nullify Arjuna, Lord Krishna spoke of the seers who directly experienced the reality of the Vedas and noted their conclusions, one of which is stated in text 16 of this chapter. So long as the followers of the Vedas and its supportive scriptures remain *kāmātmānah*, on the sensuous plane of life, and *svargaparā*, being desirous of going to the heavenly world to enjoy good food, nice forms and opulences, they will continue to glorify the theoretical aspect of these scriptures and continue discouraging others from making an all-out effort for directly experiencing the truths which are being described in the Vedic literature. It has to do with a disbelief. They feel that no one can directly experience the realities spoken of by great devotees like Shuka and *Nārada*. As a result, even though they are in a spiritual society which glorifies *Nārada* and Shuka, still they remain time-bound as creatures who are after enjoyment and political power (*bhogaiśvaryagatam*).

Lord Krishna is highly displeased with this approach to the Vedic religion. He wants us to take up the disciplines which will free us from this convention (*janmakarmaphala*).

भोगैश्वर्यप्रसक्तानां
तयापहृतचेतसाम् ।
व्यवसायात्मिका बुद्धिः
समाधौ न विधीयते ॥२.४४॥
bhogaiśvaryaprasaktānāṁ
tayāpahṛtacetasām
vyavasāyātmikā buddhiḥ
samādhau na vidhīyate (2.44)

bhogaiśvaryaprasaktānāṁ = bhoga — pleasure + aiśvarya — power + prasaktānāṁ — of the attached, of the prone; tayāpahṛtacetasām = tayā — by this + apahṛta — captivated + cetasām — idea; vyavasāyātmikā = vyavasāya — focused determination + ātmikā — self; buddhiḥ — intellect; samādhau — in meditation; na — not; vidhīyate — is experienced

Being absorbed by this way of life, pleasure-prone and power-seeking people, are captivated by this idea. Thus in meditation, the self-focused intellect is not experienced by them. (2.44)

Commentary:

If the thinker does not control his intellect and life power, he will be controlled thereby. Being hypnotized by his psychic apparatus, he will be forced to act in a way that is contrary to spiritual well-being. The *Gītā* will elaborate on the inner realm where the psychic apparatus operates.

There cannot be an agreement between the sense-prone and sense-resistant people. They will disagree forever. The sense-prone man has the senses for his master, while the sense-resistant one has the senses to regulate. That is the difference.

त्रैगुण्यविषया वेदा
निस्त्रैगुण्यो भवार्जुन ।
निर्द्वंद्वो नित्यसत्त्वस्थो
निर्योगक्षेम आत्मवान् ॥ २.४५ ॥
traiguṇyaviṣayā vedā
nistraiguṇyo bhavārjuna
nirdvaṁdvo nityasattvastho
niryogakṣema ātmavān (2.45)

traiguṇya — three mood; viṣayā — phases; vedā — Vedas; nistraiguṇyo = nistraiguṇyaḥ — without the three moody phases; bhavārjuna = bhava — be + arjuna — Arjuna; nirdvandvo = nirdvandvaḥ — without fluctuation; nityasattvastho = nityasattvasthaḥ = nitya — always + sattva — reality + sthaḥ — fixed; niryogakṣema — without grasping and possessiveness; ātmavān — soul-situated

Three moody phases are offered by the Vedas. Be without the three moods, O Arjuna. Be without the moody fluctuations. Be always anchored to reality. Be free from grasping and possessiveness. (2.45)

Commentary:

Lord Krishna diplomatically gave His disapproval of the parts of the Vedas which have to do with a conditioned response to material nature. The three approaches are designed for persons who are dull-witted, enthusiastic, or piously-inclined. But the motivation of these people is explained in text 43, either to go to the Swarga world or to take rebirth in this world in a family where much luxury and political supremacy can be cultivated. This is the sum and substance of those who are sensually-inclined.

This does not mean the other man or the non-devotee. It means any of us, devotees or non-devotees, who want materialistic prosperity and political powers.

The Vedas are for the most part, a manual for functioning efficiently on the cultural level of life, but as far as liberation is concerned, the Vedas do not expound much. The first writings which stressed liberation were the Upanishads. This is why Lord Krishna gave His stamp of approval to that. Some sections of the Upanishads are theistic. Some are not. But since those scriptures were recorded by the mystic pioneers, credit was attributed by Lord Krishna.

If we study the *Vālmīki Rāmāyaṇa* we will see that the Upanishadic sages existed even then. We hear of this in the pastimes of King *Rāma* when He toured around the *Pampa* hilly area. He met some great sages and their accomplished disciples in that region. These great sages were doing the mystic research by yogic disciplines and *Rāma* was pleased with their endeavors. Some of the practices of those great sages are described in the *Gītā* . In the time of Krishna the reference was not to modern yogis but to the ancient yogis during and after the *Rāmāyāṇa* era. If we go back to the *Vālmīki Rāmāyaṇa*, we will get more understanding about the teachings elaborated by Lord Krishna in the *Gītā*.

It is a general procedure for Hindus to take shelter in the Vedic sacrifices which pass under the name of a *havan* or *agnihotra* fire sacrifice. But these procedures are the remnants of an Age when everything a man needed to do was sanctified before a sacrificial fire. Nowadays, this procedure is not as effective. Still, Hindus the world over, pursue it, even though it is put to question in these statements of Krishna.

Arjuna is directly advised to get himself away from this self-seeking attitude . The word is *nistraiguṇya*. *Nis* means, *without* or *to be without*, and *traiguṇya* means the three general moods of material nature.

Lord Krishna put restrictions on Arjuna in no uncertain terms, beginning with an exemption from the influence of the moods of material nature, then continuing to an indifferent attitude to pleasure and pain, as well as being fixed in the constancy of the individual consciousness, being freed from craving and being self-controlled. Essentially, this means that Arjuna was not to reach out to the modes of material nature but was, instead, to be situated in spiritual consciousness beyond the cultural plane. And still, Krishna expected that Arjuna would act on the cultural level as a law man for King Yudhishthira. These demands of the Lord may seem unreasonable but they were placed on Arjuna. We will see how Lord Krishna instructed Arjuna about the implications of this detached mood while working through circumstances on the cultural plane.

यावानर्थ उदपाने
सर्वतः संप्लुतोदके ।
तावान्सर्वेषु वेदेषु
ब्राह्मणस्य विजानतः ॥२.४६॥
yāvānartha udapāne
sarvataḥ saṁplutodake
tāvānsarveṣu vedeṣu
brāhmaṇasya vijānataḥ (2.46)

yāvān — as much; artha — importance; udapāne — in a well; sarvataḥ — in all directions; saṁplutodake = saṁpluta — flowing + udake — in water; tāvān — so much; sarveṣu — in the entire; vedeṣu — in the Vedas; brāhmaṇasya — of a brahmin; vijānataḥ — perceptive

For as much importance as there is in a well when suitable water flows in all directions, so much worth is in the entire Vedas for a perceptive brahmin. (2.46)

Commentary:

Lord Krishna depreciated the Vedas in this verse where He compared the Vedas to a water well. A well has value when suitable water is scarce but if one stands in a deep, wide, pure, clean, fresh water lake, he has no need for a well. Similarly, the elementary Vedic information has great value to one if he has no mystic insight. But as soon as we develop that vision, we are no longer limited to the Vedic information.

It is for this reason, that there is an ongoing contention between the experienced mystic devotees and those devotees who have little or no clairvoyance and who rely on scripture only. The mystically-blind devotees rely on scriptural concepts from which they derive a faulty understanding. Arjuna quoted the Vedic literature in Chapter One but his quotations were misapplied. He lost the mystic insight at the time of viewing the warriors. Once his vision was restored, he saw things in an entirely different way, in agreement with what Lord Krishna described.

The theory of scripture is a big event for those who have no direct insight to the scriptural truths and who cannot penetrate the limitations and compromises of scripture. But these theories and their purposes are penetrated by one who has mystic perception.

Lord Krishna identified the man with mystic insight as *vijānatah*. This Sanskrit word is derived from the root word *jña*, "to know. " Krishna used another word, *brāhmaṇasya*, which means "of or for a brahmin."

कर्मण्येवाधिकारस्ते
मा फलेषु कदाचन ।
मा कर्मफलहेतुर्भूर्
मा ते सङ्गोऽस्त्वकर्मणि ॥२.४७॥
karmaṇyevādhikāraste
mā phaleṣu kadācana
mā karmaphalaheturbhūr
mā te saṅgo'stvakarmaṇi (2.47)

karmaṇyevādhikāraste = karmaṇi — in performance + eva — alone + adhikāraḥ — command, privilege + te — your; mā — not; phaleṣu — in the aftermath of consequences; kadācana — at any time; mā — not; karmaphalahetur = karmaphala — a result + hetur (hetuh) — motivation; bhūr = bhūḥ — be; mā — not; te — your; saṅgo = sangah — attachment; 'stv = astu — should be; akarmaṇi — non-action, idleness

The command is yours while performing, but not at any time in the aftermath of consequences. Do not be motivated by a result, nor harbor an attachment to idleness. (2.47)

Commentary:

After describing the mystic vision of the samkhya yogis and speaking of the application of it in social affairs, Lord Krishna explained the functional technique.

One may study this technique and apply it immediately.

We must understand, however, that for consistent application, one will have to perform the austerities. One may apply it, but he will not be able to do it consistently unless he is an empowered soul. He will, of necessity, do it only part of the time. After all, unless one has the experience of the mystic vision and unless one is continuously situated in it, one will have to rely on the cultural view from time to time; then one will fall from the spiritual level into the material cultural mix-up.

After one begins the process and discovers that he cannot apply it consistently, he should begin searching for more effective austerities. By stipulating that the command is ours, only when we perform and not when the consequences come, Lord Krishna took something away from us. At least, we may feel deprived, if we are used to chasing results. A human being works for an employer, not just to work but for a result in the form of money. Now Lord Krishna suggested that we reverse our outlook. A child behaves in a desirable way not just to behave but to get a gift, some allowance or pleasing response from parents. Lord Krishna proposed something to the contrary. This advice of the Lord is, essentially, against human nature. Some preachers try to glamorize this verse of the *Gītā*. They speak of *karma yoga*, selfless service, and pretend that such an action is human, but that cannot be the fact. Most of us do not live in this way which is recommended by Krishna. Arjuna had difficulty applying this process, what to speak of modern people. It is just not human. It is certainly divine but it is not human. Human beings are motivated by projected results. This is exactly so. Lord Krishna said that we should not form a habit of doing this (*mā karmaphalahetur bhūr*). But we already formed the habit. It is deeply engrained.

Lord Krishna recommended that we not become reluctant to do duty. But if our duty is not palatable, if we anticipate that it will not give a favorable result, how will we be motivated to do it? Arjuna had this problem when his knees buckled up as soon as he saw that the consequences of the battle were not to his liking. If there is a desirable reward, a child might exhibit good behavior, but if no reward is projected, he may be reluctant to cooperate.

Obviously this idea of Krishna is revolutionary and essentially anti-human. Something divine, yes, but not human. We will have to be transformed before we can do this consistently.

योगस्थः कुरु कर्माणि
सङ्गं त्यक्त्वा धनंजय ।
सिद्ध्यसिद्ध्योः समो भूत्वा
समत्वं योग उच्यते ॥२.४८॥

yogasthaḥ kuru karmāṇi
saṅgaṁ tyaktvā dhanaṁjaya
siddhyasiddhyoḥ samo bhūtvā
samatvaṁ yoga ucyate (2.48)

yogasthaḥ- in yoga attitude; kuru — do perform; karmāṇi — actions; saṅgaṁ — attachment to crippling emotions; tyaktvā — having abandoned; dhanaṁjaya — conqueror of wealthy countries; siddhyasiddhyoḥ — to success or failure; samo = samaḥ — attitude of indifference; bhūtvā — be; samatvaṁ — indifference; yoga — yogic practice; ucyate — it is said

So perform actions in the yoga mood. Attachment to crippling emotions should be abandoned, O conqueror of wealthy countries. Be indifferent to success or failure. It is said that indifference denotes yoga. (2.48)

Commentary:

Please note *yogasthah yoga—sthah*, meaning to be situated in yoga discipline. *Dhanamjaya* means conqueror or winner of wealth, a person who is victorious over wealthy provinces. Arjuna was that, as a government agent of Yudhishthira. This meant that Arjuna went on military expeditions to conquer, subdue, or intimidate foreign people. This history of Arjuna and his brothers is described vividly in the *Mahābhārata*. Whenever King Yudhishthira became determined to set himself up as the main ruler of an area, he performed special worship ceremonies and then sent his brothers out to obtain the allegiance of neighboring provinces. Those rulers and their people who rejected Yudhishthira's sovereignty were intimidated, and if they did not come to their senses, they were subdued with military strength.

Bhishma, the elder of the Kuru family, was a capable statesman. He singlehandedly ruled the family after the death of his father, King *Śantanu*. Bhisma established a wide reputation for the Kuru people. Their power was feared. Arjuna, as a member of the dynasty, was one of its field marshalls

Saṅgam means attachment to sweet social association. But here Lord Krishna advised Arjuna to *tyaktvā*, or abandon it. Again Lord Krishna quoted the ancient samkhya authorities (*ucyate*), indicating His approval of their view on these matters. For success or failure, Krishna advised that Arjuna place no stress on the outcome. Instead he should be indifferent so that if circumstances suited his plan, he should not become elated; if conditions were a reversal, he should not become depressed.

Readers should note that yoga is again stressed in line four, where Lord Krishna defined the application of yogic discipline. *Śrīla* Bhaktivedanta Swami, that great Vaishnava acharya of modern times, summarily dismissed yoga practice by his definition which minimized it. He asked in writing, "And what is yoga?" And he replied, "Yoga means to concentrate the mind upon the Supreme by controlling the ever-disturbing senses." However, we will have to see what Lord Krishna Himself said about yoga.

दूरेण ह्यवरं कर्म
बुद्धियोगाद्धनंजय।
बुद्धौ शरणमन्विच्छ
कृपणाः फलहेतवः ॥२.४९॥
dūreṇa hyavaraṁ karma
buddhiyogāddhanaṁjaya
buddhau śaraṇamanviccha
kṛpaṇāḥ phalahetavaḥ (2.49)

dūreṇa — by far; hyavaraṁ = hi — surely + avaraṁ — inferior + karma — cultural action; buddhiyogād = buddhiyogāt — intellectual discipline through yoga; dhanaṁjaya — victor of wealthy countries; buddhau — mystic insight; śaraṇam — location of confidence; anviccha — put; kṛpaṇāḥ — low and pathetic; phalahetavaḥ — people motivated for a result

Surely, cultural action is by far inferior to intellectual discipline through yoga. O victor of wealthy countries. One should take shelter in mystic insight, for how pathetic are those who are motivated by the promise of results.(2.49)

Commentary:

Arjuna's conventional way of acting is contrasted to Krishna's recommendation for action on the basis of the reality-piercing vision. In that vision, one is required to see the soul of others. One must also be willing to discipline anyone even if it means hurting the body, because this is exactly what Arjuna will have to do at *Kurukṣetra*. Have any of our readers ever heard that the *Gītā* is a book about non-violence? O, the falsity of that view! No one can read the *Gītā* through and through nor the *Mahābhārata* of which the *Gītā* is a tiny part and form the opinion that the *Gītā* advocates non-violence. It does not. It advocates non-violence to the soul even at the expense of violence to the body. The *Gītā* is the prime advocate of judicial violence to the body for the benefit of the soul. In addition, this non-violence to the soul is not a sentimental type of emotion. It is based on the reality-piercing vision, which Lord Krishna has naturally, but which was attained in the times of Lord Krishna by the samkhya yogis.

Here again in this text, it is plain that for the solution to his emotional problems and the resulting depression of mind, Krishna recommended one method to Arjuna, that of *buddhi* yoga. Line two begins, *buddhi yogāt*; line three begins, *buddhau*. This is being repeated throughout this section of the chapter.

Lord Krishna then attacked weak-minded people as being *kṛpanāh*, which is an insultive description of someone as being pitiable, despicable and low, not having a high cultural background, not understanding what to do for honor. These people, He said, are motivated by a projected result (*phalahetavah*). Needless to say Lord Krishna has systematically insulted human nature, which is, in fact, result-motivated. We are the people He described in line four, who are result-motivated, who need favorable consequences every step of the way, and who become crippled-up, refusing to act if we do not see something desirable in the outcome.

बुद्धियुक्तो जहातीह
उभे सुकृतदुष्कृते ।
तस्माद्योगाय युज्यस्व
योगः कर्मसु कौशलम् ॥२.५०॥
buddhiyukto jahātīha
ubhe sukṛtaduṣkṛte
tasmādyogāya yujyasva
yogaḥ karmasu kauśalam (2.50)

buddhiyukto = buddhiyuktaḥ — a person disciplined by the reality-piercing insight; jahātīha = jahāti — he discards + iha — here; ubhe — both; sukṛtaduṣkṛte — pleasant and unpleasant work; tasmād = tasmāt — therefore; yogāya — to yoga; yujyasva — take yourself to; yogaḥ — yogic mood; karmasu — in performance; kauśalam — skill

A person who is disciplined by the reality-piercing insight discards in each life both pleasant and unpleasant work. Therefore take to the yogic mood. Yoga gives skill in performance. (2.50)

Commentary:

We must again face the terms *buddhi* and yoga. This is being stressed over and over. Arjuna's problem was his susceptibility to weakening emotion. This advice was for his removal from that state of mind and transference to the reality-piercing insight through which he could consider the spiritual welfare of the warriors.

Lord Krishna directly orders Arjuna: Take to yoga procedure, *yogāya yujyasva*. Here the skill of performance is defined as *yogah karmasu* or applying the yogic mood while performing a duty.

In truth, pleasant and unpleasant results come, mostly on the basis of our past life and not just on present actions or decisions. Here lies our confusion. We usually assess everything in terms of what we know of the present life. A man may be paid a government check for something he did five years ago, but he might falsely interpret that the check is a payment for current services. This would be a mistake. We make this mistake because we crave results for our present actions. Destiny, however, does not necessarily respond to our current acts in the present and might respond in the distant future. If we interpret every favorable or unfavorable circumstance as the result of a present act, we will form many false opinions and act haphazardly.

कर्मजं बुद्धियुक्ता हि
फलं त्यक्त्वा मनीषिणः।
जन्मबन्धविनिर्मुक्ताः
पदं गच्छन्त्यनामयम् ॥२.५१॥
karmajaṁ buddhiyuktā hi
phalaṁ tyaktvā manīṣiṇaḥ
janmabandhavinirmuktāḥ
padaṁ gacchantyanāmayam (2.51)

karmajaṁ — produced by actions; buddhiyuktā — disciplined mystic seers; hi — indeed; phalaṁ — result; tyaktvā — having abandoned; manīṣiṇaḥ — wise people; janmabandhavinirmuktāḥ = janma — rebirth + bandha — bondage + vinirmuktāḥ — freed from; padaṁ — place; gacchanty = gacchanti — go; anāmayam — misery-free

Having abandoned the results which are produced by actions, and being freed from the bondage of rebirth, those wise people, the disciplined mystic seers, go to the misery-free place. (2.51)

<u>*Commentary:*</u>

The wise men, the samkhya mystics, do observe the consequences of action but they do not crave pleasant circumstances and they are not repelled by unpleasant events. That is the difference between their attitude and ours. In the hereafter, they attain a world that is free from emotional misery (*anāmayam*). The samkhya experts go (*gacchanti*) to that special place (*padam*).

Śrīla Bhaktivedanta Swami, our Vaishnava spiritual master, gave *yogāya* as, *for the sake of devotional service*. He gave yogah as *Krishna Consciousness* in verse 50. In this verse, he gave *buddhi*-yuktah as, *being done with devotional service*. For *manīṣiṇah* in this verse, he gave, *devotees who are great sages*. However, we will have to stick to Krishna's definition. In this chapter *manīṣiṇah* was already defined by Krishna. *Buddhi*-yoga will be defined by Krishna in Chapter Three.

The *manīṣiṇah* or wise men are described in verse 15 as *dhīram*, in verse 16 as *tattvadarśih*, and as those persons expert in samkhya, in verse 39.

Insofar as we are going to stick to Krishna's meanings and stay in the original presentation, we will have to accept this. We must understand clearly that Lord Krishna referred to the Upanishadic sages whose conclusions were given in text 16. The Lord did not even refer to a devotee of His own time but drew from history of the ancient forest ascetics who went (*gacchati*) to the *anāmayam padam*, the disease-free, pain-free place.

At first Lord Krishna told Arjuna about the *Swarga* heavenly location, or about staying in this world as a successful ruler. That was in verse 32 with the words *svargadvāram* (the entrance of heaven), and in verse 37 with *prāpsyasi svargam* (you will get to heaven) and *bhokṣyase mahīm* (enjoy the earth). But now Lord Krishna, for the first time in the *Gītā*, directly talks of an alternative destination in the hereafter that is different to Swarga or heaven. That is the disease-free, pain-free place, the *anamayam padam*. Arjuna himself mentioned another place in the hereafter which he called hell or *narakāya* in text 42 and *narake* in text 44. He said that departed ancestors (*pitarah*) and the aggressors who destroy family members were destined for that place.

Arjuna's idea was to live nicely in this world. In Chapter One he did not think of the heavenly world nor of this disease-free, pain-free, trouble-free place Krishna mentioned.

Arjuna, however, speculated on the value of the three worlds, *trailokya*, in text 35, saying that it was not worth the fight, especially if it involved killing people like Bhishma and *Droṇa*. Thus far, we encountered this world and three other locations in the hereafter, namely hell, the Swarga angelic places, and the trouble-free places attained by the sages who have the reality-piercing vision. As students of the *Gītā*, we should note these locations.

यदा ते मोहकलिलं
बुद्धिर्व्यतितरिष्यति ।
तदा गन्तासि निर्वेदं
श्रोतव्यस्य श्रुतस्य च ॥२.५२॥
yadā te mohakalilaṁ
buddhirvyatitariṣyati
tadā gantāsi nirvedaṁ
śrotavyasya śrutasya ca (2.52)

yadā — when; te — you; mohakalilaṁ — delusion-saturated mind; buddhir (buddhiḥ) — discrimination; vyatitariṣyati — departs; tadā — then; gantāsi — you will become; nirvedaṁ — disgusted; śrotavyasya — with what is to be heard; śrutasya — what was heard; ca — and

When from your delusion-saturated mind, your discrimination departs, you will become disgusted with what is to be heard and what was heard. (2.52)

Commentary:

Lord Krishna indicated here that as soon as Arjuna's intellect (*buddhi*) is removed from the confusion of his mind space (*mohakalilam*), then Arjuna would see clearly and not be affected by what he heard previously from the inexperienced Vedic reciters. And so long as Arjuna would remain in clarity of the intellect, he would not be affected by them either. But rather, he would become disgusted (*nirvedam*) with the religious figureheads who lectured on the basis of a theoretical understanding of the Vedic wording but who had no mystic experience and thus could not understand the actual purpose of the Veda.

By lack of mystic insight, these reciters use the words of the Vedas and simultaneously attach materialistic meanings based on their mundane experiences only. They pass this off as transcendence. The Vedic learning stresses hearing from these religious authorities but if an authority does not have a reality-piercing intellect, his words bear a departure from the truth and he misleads followers. He certainly uses the words of the Veda but he has no connection with the actual meaning. Thus whatever he says makes no impact on the mind of a truly enlightened man but it hypnotizes and fascinates the ordinary folks.

श्रुतिविप्रतिपन्ना ते
यदा स्थास्यति निश्चला ।
समाधावचला बुद्धिस्
तदा योगमवाप्स्यसि ॥२.५३॥
śrutivipratipannā te
yadā sthāsyati niścalā
samādhāvacalā buddhis
tadā yogamavāpsyasi (2.53)

śrutivipratipannā = śruti — scriptural information + vipratipannā — false, misleading; te — you; yadā — when; sthāsyati — will remain; niścalā — unmoving, steady; samādhāvacalābuddhis = samādhau — in deep meditation; acalā — without moving, stable; buddhis (buddhiḥ) — intelligence; tadā — then; yogam — yoga discipline; avāpsyasi — will master

When rejecting misleading scriptural information, your intelligence remains steady without moody variation, being situated in deep meditation, you will master the yoga disciplines. (2.53)

Commentary:

As Vedic tradition would have it, hearing from a religious authority in the disciplic succession from an established god or from God, is paramount. Nearly every sect in India stresses this paramparā tradition. But something as good as a disciplic succession is regularly misused as we will read what Krishna told Arjuna about the breakdown in the teaching tradition.

Generally there are four leading authorities, namely: Lord Krishna (Vishnu), Lord *Brahmā*, Lord Shiva and Goddess *Lakṣmī* In addition, there are sub-authorities such as *Sūrya*, *Durgā*, *Gaṇesh* and *Agnideva*. It all depends on which part of India and which religious tradition. And it depends on the level of development and traditional influences that prevail over a man. In the Western countries the main influence is Lord Jesus Christ. In comparison to the Vedic way, Jesus, however, is recent.

The idea is that no one should be accepted as an authority unless he can prove that he is in the disciplic succession from one of the four authorities. But this idea is misused on occasion. Even if one can prove the lineage, how will he prove that he has mystic insight as described by Lord Krishna? How can he prove that he is *tattvadarśih*? How can we know if a man is actually seeing directly or is merely repeating from scripture through a compulsion or through faith?

Recently some of this direct mystic perception was minimized. Even some of the Vaishnava acharyas proudly stated that it was important only to repeat what was heard from Vedic sources. Here in the *Gītā* such an opinion is denied by none other than Lord Krishna. Here, Arjuna is told that he should remove his intelligence from the confusion produced in his mind by the theoretical explanation of authorized but mystically-blind teachers of his time. The technical word, *śruti*, is used. This word is usually thrown here and there by authorities to stabilize their positions as being men who repeat only what the Vedic literature says. But here Lord Krishna, the self-proclaimed Lord of the Veda, says to reject *vipratipannā*, the *sruti*, the revelation given by those who do not have the direct mystic experience that is behind the original Vedic recitation.

Krishna discussed Arjuna's clarity which should be without moody variations, in deep consideration with a stable intelligence, without any sort of sentimental appraisal of what is recited from scripture. Then Lord Krishna assured that Arjuna would attained the work-skill yielded by full yoga practice (*yogam avāpsyasi*).

This statement by the Lord is clear. It has left no room for those who merely repeat without first having mastered the mystic insight which correlates with the original Vedic statement.

It will be difficult to go a step further in the *Gītā* if we are unwilling to accept the implication of what Lord Krishna said here. Most modern preachers, even those who are devotees of Lord Krishna, are not actually approved by the Blessed Lord. They lack the qualification since they overlooked the process of the samkhya yogis, a process that Lord Krishna described hereafter. Unless a man is a master of the samkhya process, he is not qualified to be a preacher. He misleads the public, even if he preaches in the name of Lord Krishna.

What is samkhya yoga? How is it mastered? We will have to get the answer from Lord Krishna. Unless He gives it, we are left without definition and may fall victim to anyone who might say: *It is this. It is that. It could be this. It could be that.*

In Chapter One, texts 29 and 30, Arjuna described his weakened condition. He made statements describing bodily nervousness. In reference to his mind, he said, *bhramatīva ca me manah*. This is Sanskrit poetry. The prose Sanskrit would read *manah me iva ca bhramati* which means: this mind of mine wanders uncontrollably.

At this time, Arjuna did not have a problem being a devotee of Krishna. He was a devotee. His problem was to control his mind in the interest of what Krishna requested. It was a mental problem. The Lord gave Arjuna the direct remedy for mind problems which is samkhya philosophy and the samkhya process of mind control.

In verse 53, Lord Krishna advised that Arjuna's mind be put into such a condition that his intellect (*buddhir*) would be stabilized (*niścalā*). We are repeatedly shown that the solution to Arjuna's mental wavering was to control his mind, and the process recommended was the one used by the samkhya yogis. For all practical purposes, we can stop reading the *Gītā* right here. At this point, Lord Krishna thoroughly dealt with Arjuna's original problem when Arjuna experienced a nervous breakdown. But we shall read that it is not that simple. The *Gītā* continues.

We want our readers to understand clearly that up to this point, Arjuna's original request for assistance from Krishna and for answers to the questions of fighting or not fighting is given completely. Except for a crash course in samkhya yoga, Arjuna has the complete answer to his problem of mental wavering, and the resulting physical weakness he experienced when he saw both armies. With this in mind, we will continue the *Gītā*.

अर्जुन उवाच
स्थितप्रज्ञस्य का भाषा
समाधिस्थस्य केशव ।
स्थितधीः किं प्रभाषेत
किमासीत व्रजेत किम् ॥ २.५४ ॥
arjuna uvāca
sthitaprajñasya kā bhāṣā
samādhisthasya keśava
sthitadhīḥ kiṁ prabhāṣeta
kimāsīta vrajeta kim (2.54)

arjuna — Arjuna; uvāca — said; sthitaprajñasya — of the person who is situated in clear penetrating insight; kā — what; bhāṣā — description; samādhisthasya — one who is anchored in deep meditation; keśava — Keśava, Kṛṣṇa; sthitadhīḥ — one who is steady in objectives; kiṁ — whom; prabhāṣeta — should speak; kim — how; āsīta — should sit; vrajeta — move; kim — how

Arjuna said: In regards to the person who is situated in clear, penetrating insight, would you please describe him? Speak of the person who is anchored in deep meditation, O Keśava Krishna. As for the man who is steady in objectives, how would he speak? How would he sit? How would he act? (2.54)

Commentary:

Here Arjuna shows a lack of confidence in himself as being a person of steady transcendental insight. Lord Krishna appraised Arjuna as being capable of such a state but Arjuna did not have the self-confidence. Arjuna exposed the whole issue by asking Lord Krishna to describe a person who had those qualities on a consistent basis. This helps us considerably. This leaves no room for speculation and gives each of us the chance to see exactly what Krishna meant. No man needs to clarify this for Krishna. Krishna spoke for Himself and told Arjuna what He meant.

It appears that Arjuna could not uplift himself immediately. He wanted the Lord to elaborate on the issue of how one may recognize a man who is in steady consciousness.

The question of how the man speaks is important because Krishna condemned the speech of those who do not have the proficiency of a samkhya yogi but who still speak from Veda. Arjuna wanted to know the difference between the man of insight and the others who merely rattle off Veda without having had the transcendental experience of the truths. If a man of mystic means recites a Vedic verse, and a man without mystic ability recites it, what would the difference be? Since they are both speaking the same lines from the Vedic recitation, how would we sense the difference? These are important considerations in a religious world where we are told that a man from a religious sect or organization is qualified merely because he is willing to recite verbatim what he was told by his authority. How do we know if this man is qualified or not? Will he mislead us, just as Arjuna was misled by the authorities who instructed him in Veda and brought him to an emotionally-crippling condition at *Kurukṣetra* where he got the contrary result of being unwilling to serve Krishna and complete duties?

Prajña means vision or mental insight. *Sthita* means steady. Arjuna had an unsteady (*acalā*) mind (*manas*) as he described in Chapter One. Now he asks for a description of a person of steady insight, steady intellectual application of the experience. In two lines of this verse the word for steady is mentioned: *sthita* (line 1), *stha* (line 1), and *sthitadhīh* (line 2). All of these are in relation to the mind and intellect.

श्रीभगवानुवाच
प्रजहाति यदा कामान्
सर्वान्पार्थ मनोगतान् ।
आत्मन्येवात्मना तुष्टः
स्थितप्रज्ञस्तदोच्यते ॥२.५५॥
śrībhagavānuvāca
prajahāti yadā kāmān
sarvānpārtha manogatān
ātmanyevātmanā tuṣṭaḥ
sthitaprajñastadocyate (2.55)

śrī bhagavān — the Blessed Lord; uvāca — said; prajahāti — abandons; yadā — when; kāmān — cravings; sarvān — all; pārtha — O son of Pṛthā; manogatān — escapes from mental dominance; ātmanyevātmanā = ātmani — in the spirit + eva — only + ātmanā — by the spirit; tuṣṭaḥ — being self-content; sthitaprajñastadocyate = sthitaprajñaḥ — one whose insight is steady + tadā — then + ucyate — is identified

The Blessed Lord said: When someone abandons all cravings, O son of Pṛthā, and escapes from mental dominance, being self-content, then that person is identified as one with steady insight. (2.55)

Commentary:

Initially Arjuna wanted help to get himself in order, to get his courage reinstated, to see things in the proper light, to again be himself as the staunch, strong-armed lawman of Yudhishthira. But Arjuna extended the inquiries for an elaboration on a different topic. The question of how Krishna would describe a man of insight is answered completely in this verse, but Lord Krishna gave more information, after which Arjuna asked for more clarification.

To find a man of insight, we must first look for a person who left behind all cravings (*sarvān kāmān*). He must be centered in spiritual identity, not centered in his mind merely. He must have transcended or gone out of the influence of his mind (*manogatan*) and be self-situated in spiritual identity (*ātmany evātmanā*), so that he finds satisfaction (*tuṣṭah*) on that spiritual plane, to such a degree that he feels no compulsion to be influenced by the mind for sensual fulfillment. If we can find such a man, we have found a man of insight, a *sthitaprajña*. This is the person Arjuna was to be if he were to serve his function at *Kurukṣetra*. Arjuna was chastised by Lord Krishna because impurities had come over him, making him leave his steady intelligence and take shelter in his pleasure-oriented mind. The implication is that even a devotee has to strive to be a man of steady insight.

दुःखेष्वनुद्विग्नमनाः
सुखेषु विगतस्पृहः ।
वीतरागभयक्रोधः
स्थितधीर्मुनिरुच्यते ॥२.५६ ॥
duḥkheṣvanudvignamanāḥ
sukheṣu vigataspṛhaḥ
vītarāgabhayakrodhaḥ
sthitadhīrmunirucyate (2.56)

duḥkheṣvanudvignamanāḥ = duḥkheṣv (duḥkheṣu) — in miserable conditions + anudvigna — free from worries + manāḥ — mind; sukheṣu — in good conditions; vigataspṛhaḥ — free from excitement; vītarāgabhayakrodhaḥ = vīta — steps aside + rāga — passion + bhaya — fear + krodhaḥ — anger; sthitadhīr = sthitadhīḥ — steady in meditation; munir = muniḥ — wise man; ucyate — is said to be

Furthermore, someone who in miserable conditions remains free from worries, and who in good conditions remains free from excitement, who steps aside from passion, fear and anger, and who is steady in meditation is considered to be a wise man. (2.56)

Commentary:

Here the word *sthita* is again used but in conjunction with *dhīr* which means meditation, consideration, deep thought, deep mental relaxation. Here also *munir* is used which means sage. Lord Krishna could have used the word *bhakti* but He did not because He is not talking about a devotee here. He is speaking about anyone, regardless of whether the man is a devotee or not. Any man or even a man who is not religiously-inclined at all, can be a *muni* and can be *sthitadhīr* or steady in consideration. It all depends on the man's mental approach to life and the austerities he practiced which give him a non-sentimental approach to life's perplexities.

Many of the Upanishadic sages reached the stage of *sthitadhīr*, of being steady in consideration, of having their minds become stabilized in soul consciousness, of not having their minds anchored in unsteady, impulsive cravings brought on by the senses. Some of these sages were not particularly devotional.

Arjuna is a devotee. Just as he used a chariot, and other warriors who were not devotees of Krishna also used chariots, so a person can use yoga and master mental control without being a devotee.

Insofar as a man may take up mind control practices at the order of Lord Krishna by the Lord's recommendation in the *Gītā*, that man engages in the devotional service of self-purification. But if a man takes it up haphazardly or for ulterior motives he may still, if he applies himself, become a mental master without being a devotee. In one sense, mind control practices are one thing and devotional service to Krishna is another matter. But in another sense, mind control can fall under the heading of being *bhakti yoga* or devotion to Krishna. It all depends on the motivation.

If, however, a man mastered mind control, doing it for a bad motive, and if after some time he becomes a devotee of Krishna, Lord Krishna might require him to use his mental mastery in divine service. Then the mastery becomes an asset for devotion to Krishna. In this way we may distinguish between a skill and its usage in the service of the Lord.

The definition in this verse applies to devotees and non-devotees. It applies to any man from anywhere from any discipline, even a military man. Any person who can remain steady-minded in bad circumstances, free from craving in good times, who can side-step passionate energy and impulsive fits of anger, is a man of steady determination. He can be called a *muni* but this does not necessarily mean that he is a devotee of Lord Krishna.

यः सर्वत्रानभिस्नेहस्
तत्तत्प्राप्य शुभाशुभम् ।
नाभिनन्दति न द्वेष्टि
तस्य प्रज्ञा प्रतिष्ठिता ॥२.५७॥
yaḥ sarvatrānabhisnehas
tattatprāpya śubhāśubham
nābhinandati na dveṣṭi
tasya prajñā pratiṣṭhitā (2.57)

yaḥ- who; sarvatrā — in all circumstances; anabhisnehaḥ — without crippling affections; tattat = tad tad-this or that; prāpya- meeting; śubhāśubham — enjoyable and disturbing factors; nābhinandati = na — not + abhinandati — excited; na — nor; dveṣṭi — distressed; tasya — his; prajñā — reality-piercing consciousness; pratiṣthitā - is established

A person who, in all circumstances, is without crippling affections, who, when meeting enjoyable or disturbing factors, does not get excited nor distressed, his reality-piercing consciousness is established. (2.57)

Commentary:

Except for the reality-piercing consciousness (*prajña pratiṣţhitā*), we may apply the title of being "cool-headed" to this type of man. But many men are cool-headed about contrary or favorable circumstances, and still they do not have the reality-piercing consciousness. They have simply learnt how not to be disturbed by certain circumstances. They have learnt to take life as it is for whatever it is. They have become callous even to their own emotions. Many men ingest alcohol, smoke cigarettes or marijuana, or take some type of drug and become callous to life, but these people do not have the reality-piercing consciousness. Unless we know the process used by the samkhya yogis to attain their type of cool-headedness, we will not understand how to distinguish between a cool-headed callous man and the cool-headed sage or *muni* whom Krishna describes.

Jñā indicates knowledge. Usually this indicates theoretical information, book knowledge, but in some cases, depending on what the writer or speaker intended, *jñā* means wisdom. When *pra* is added to *jñā*, giving *prajñā*, wisdom, deep consideration is the direct meaning. There is no question that it might mean book knowledge or theory. It means the experience and the resulting wisdom one gets from applied knowledge.

यदा संहरते चायं
कूर्मोऽङ्गानीव सर्वशः।
इन्द्रियाणीन्द्रियार्थेभ्यस्
तस्य प्रज्ञा प्रतिष्ठिता ॥२.५८॥
yadā saṁharate cāyaṁ
kūrmo'ṅgānīva sarvaśaḥ
indriyāṇīndriyārthebhyas
tasya prajñā pratiṣṭhitā (2.58)

yadā — when; saṁharate — pulls; cāyaṁ = ca — and + ayam — this; kūrmo = kūrmaḥ — tortoise; 'ṅgānīva = aṅgānīva = aṅgāni — limbs + iva — like, compared to; sarvaśaḥ — fully; indriyāṇīndriyārthebhyas = indriyani — senses + indriyarthebhyaḥ — attractive things; tasya — his; prajñā — reality-piercing vision; pratiṣṭhitā — is established

When such a person pulls fully out of moods, he or she may be compared to the tortoise with its limbs retracted. The senses are withdrawn from the attractive things in the case of a person whose reality-piercing vision is established. (2.58)

Commentary:

A result of yoga proficiency is indicated. This portion of yoga practice is called pratyāhār. It will be described more in the *Gītā*. We will get a direct understanding of what was done by the ancient sages. In pratyāhār the student learns how to pull in sensuous energies just the way the tortoise retracts its limbs and shuts down its acting and sensing organs for a time. And just as the tortoise remains in its shell safely and listens, so the meditating sage remains in his energies and observes his psyche.

As a tortoise's limbs come out of its body and are visibly seen, so the sensual powers of a living entity come out of the psyche and protrude into the environment searching for enjoyable things (*indriyārtha*). However, we do not normally see how this energy protrudes. It takes mystic vision to see a psychic action. This mystic vision is called *vyavasāyātmikā buddhi* in texts 41 and 44 of this chapter.

Many many sages and yogis and other mental disciplinarians developed this power to varying degrees. Some of them were devotees. In fact, some devotees of the Blessed Lord do not have this power, while others do. This process of sense withdrawal may take years to master. We naturally seek sense pleasure. To withdraw from sensual stimuli is in a sense, most unnatural. Still it is recommended by Lord Krishna. Arjuna had some difficulty because his emotional energy expressed itself too powerfully through his optic nerves. After viewing the Kuru warriors, he could no longer keep himself in order. He admitted in Chapter One, text 30, that he could not even hold himself together. He said: *na ca śaknomy avasthātum, No, I am not able to keep myself in order.*

When we allow energy to surge through the senses in too great a volume, we lose control. Thus we need to learn how to withdraw the senses so that we can counterbalance the outward, impulsive force.

विषया विनिवर्तन्ते
निराहारस्य देहिनः।
रसवर्जं रसोऽप्यस्य
परं दृष्ट्वा निवर्तते॥ २.५९॥
viṣayā vinivartante
nirāhārasya dehinaḥ
rasavarjaṁ raso'pyasya
paraṁ dṛṣṭvā nivartate (2.59)

viṣayā = viṣayāḥ — temptations; vinivartante — turn away; nirāhārasya — from (without) indulgence; dehinaḥ — of the embodied soul; rasavarjaṁ = rasa — memory or mental flavor of past indulgences + varjaṁ — except for, besides; raso = rasah — memories (mental flavors); 'pyasya = apyasya = apy (api) — even + asya — of him; paraṁ — higher stage; dṛṣṭvā — having experienced; nivartate — leaves

The temptations themselves turn away from the disciplinary attitude of an ascetic, but the memory of previous indulgences remain with him. When he experiences higher stages, those memories leave him. (2.59)

Commentary:

For those who want to transcend the lower tendencies, this verse gives the key technique of experiencing higher stages (*param dṛṣṭvā*). We cannot drop a bad habit unless we first cultivate a higher one (*param*). As the Lord explained, if we apply a severe austerity against a certain bad habit, our attitude of severity will itself cause the temptations to go away for a while, but the memory of the former indulgences will remain with us to bring us back to the lower behavior.

A two-stage process is required; one of restraint and one of a cultivated higher habit. If we use restraint only, we will be haunted by the memory of the bad habit, and if we simply want a higher habit without applying an austerity, we will fail also. Both processes must be put into effect; that of restraint from the bad habit and application of a higher one.

Nirāhārasya usually means fasting but it also means any type of restraint or limitation of a habit. We may fast from an addictive food that ruins our body. We may restrain from an addictive habit that ruins our behavior. This is all restraint.

यततो ह्यपि कौन्तेय
पुरुषस्य विपश्चितः।
इन्द्रियाणि प्रमाथीनि
हरन्ति प्रसभं मनः ॥२.६०॥
yatato hyapi kaunteya
puruṣasya vipaścitaḥ
indriyāṇi pramāthīni
haranti prasabhaṁ manaḥ (2.60)

yatato = yatataḥ — concerning an aspiring seeker; hyapi = hi — indeed + api — also; kaunteya — son of Kuntī; puruṣasya — of the person; vipaścitaḥ — of the discerning educated; indriyāṇi — the senses; pramāthīni — tormenting; haranti — seize, adjust; prasabhaṁ — impulsively, by impulse; manaḥ — mentally

Concerning an aspiring seeker, O son of Kuntī , concerning a discerned educated person, the senses do torment him. By impulses, the senses do adjust his mentality. (2.60)

Commentary:

Here the Lord admited that even a spiritual seeker, even an educated man (*vipaścitah*), will have trouble controlling the senses. The senses will torment him. They will, on occasion, adjust his mentality towards degradation. Arjuna was such a wise man but he was carried off into delusion by what he saw at *Kurukṣetra*.

By admitting that a wise man may be periodically degraded, Lord Krishna indirectly pledged to give any of us who strive, a technique for self-reform from crippling attacks within our nature.

तानि सर्वाणि संयम्य
युक्त आसीत मत्परः।
वशे हि यस्येन्द्रियाणि
तस्य प्रज्ञा प्रतिष्ठिता ॥२.६१॥
tāni sarvāṇi saṁyamya
yukta āsīta matparaḥ
vaśe hi yasyendriyāṇi
tasya prajñā pratiṣṭhitā (2.61)

tāni — these; sarvāṇi — all (senses); saṁyamya — restraining; yukta — yogically disciplined; āsīta — should sit; matparaḥ — focused on Me, on My interest; vaśe — in control; hi — indeed; yasyendriyāṇi = yasya — of whom + indriyāṇi — of the sensuality; tasya — of him; prajñā — vision; pratiṣṭhitā — anchored

Restraining all these senses, being disciplined in yoga practice, an ascetic should sit, being focused on Me. The vision of a person whose sensuality is controlled, remains anchored in reality. (2.61)

Commentary:

This is the first verse of the *Gītā* where Lord Krishna directly advocated His interest. At first, the Lord merely preached about the difference between the body and the soul, stressing the eternal nature of the soul. Then He explained how Arjuna could remove himself from confusion and situate himself in soul consciousness beyond a wavering mentality. Here the Lord entirely advocated His own interest. This is the first direct instruction about devotion to Krishna. Lord Krishna directly says *mat* (with Me, Krishna) as the highest interest (*parah*). This is deliberate because in text 59, the Lord suggested that we substitute a higher experience (*param*). Now He indicates that His interest is that higher reality.

The *prajña pratiṣṭhitā* (the man of steady spiritual insight) is advised to focus on Lord Krishna's idea, Lord Krishna's interest. This is the application of *buddhi* yoga to *bhakti yoga*, as contrasted to *buddhi* yoga by itself or as contrasted to *buddhi* yoga being done for any other motive.

ध्यायतो विषयान्पुंसः
सङ्गस्तेषूपजायते ।
सङ्गात्संजायते कामः
कामात्क्रोधोऽभिजायते ॥२.६२॥
dhyāyato viṣayānpuṁsaḥ
saṅgasteṣūpajāyate
saṅgātsaṁjāyate kāmaḥ
kāmātkrodho'bhijāyate (2.62)

dhyāyato = dhyāyataḥ — considering; viṣayān — sensual objects; puṁsaḥ — a person; saṅgas — attachment; teṣupajāyate = teṣu — in them + upajāyate — is born, is created; saṅgāt — from attachment; saṁjāyate — is born; kāmaḥ — craving; kāmāt — from craving; krodho = krodhah — anger; 'bhijāyate = abhijāyate — is derived

The act of considering sensual objects, creates in a person, an attachment to them. From attachment comes craving. From this craving, anger is derived. (2.62)

Commentary:

Further details were given. This is a most merciful act of Lord Krishna. What we experience in a flash, something impulsive, something we can hardly control, is being shown to us in slow motion so that we can understand how to root it out. All sensual problems would be washed away if we stop at the point of consideration of sensual desire. By consideration or deliberation of sensual treats, sensual delights and cravings, we create a sense of attachment. We thereby empower the senses to dominate the psyche.

Once there is an attachment, we can reverse the process by first considering the bad effects of the action. But if the action is completed, if we failed to restrain ourselves, a craving will develop. If at the point of craving, we fail to stop, we will either satisfy the impulse and take the reactions, or we will become frustrated and manifest anger towards the person or force that frustrated us.

For an advanced individual, the key is to stop early in consideration and to divert the mind to the higher spiritual experience (*param*) or to Krishna's interest (*matparah*). But for an ordinary man, the consideration of the bad reactions is the usual way of curbing the self from the sensually-motivated acts.

The method used depends on our stage of advancement and the type of saintly association we have. An ordinary man who has no facility of saintly association, cannot use the method of substituting a higher habit or of putting in place the highest habit, which is the interest of the Lord. That man learns the hard way. This hard way is his best teacher at this stage. In that method he considers a sensual object, he becomes attached to it, he craves it, he endeavors to enjoy it, he gets it or does not get it, he enjoys it or he is kept at a distance from it. And then at last, he suffers a bad consequence or a full frustration. In either case, whether he enjoys it or not, there will be an undesirable reaction. He learns from that bad consequence and in time, after repeatedly being subjected to the harassments of nature, he relents and seeks out a saintly associate.

In contrast, an ordinary man who has some saintly association will use the hard method in part and the best method in part. The best method is that of hearing from a superior soul and complying with his advice. The superior in this case must give advice that is in agreement with what Krishna recommended in the *Gītā*.

In the hard method, a man considers a sensual delight, he develops an attachment to it, he begins to go after it, and then he catches himself in the act of craving and endeavoring; he realizes his weakness and decides to consult his saintly friend or teacher. Then, on the basis of saintly advice, he stops himself and returns to the normal sober consciousness without moody fluctuations and random cravings.

There is a difference between a saintly friend and a saintly teacher, but in some cases, the same person serves in both capacities. In others, one person serves as the teacher and another as the friend. Certain confidential aspects which have to do with our shame, can only be revealed to a saintly friend. Lord Krishna used to act as the divine friend of Arjuna, but at *Kurukṣetra* when that relationship proved to be ineffective to motivate Arjuna, the Lord switched to the teaching role. Later on, the friendly mood was expressed again.

The method of instant substitution is the most wonderful way of getting out of a sensual trap. But only after long practice does this procedure become a reality. Otherwise we make many mistakes in preliminary stages.

Advanced souls use the substitution method directly or by the help of superiors. Lord Krishna discussed this method of substitution in detail. We must understand, however, that Lord Krishna granted two types of higher substitution, not one. The first is to institute a higher habit (*param*). The second and the superior method is to institute the higher habit of Krishna's interest or idea (*matparah*). The application of either of these is better than continued craving and its reactions.

क्रोधाद्भवति संमोहः
संमोहात्स्मृतिविभ्रमः ।
स्मृतिभ्रंशाद्बुद्धिनाशो
बुद्धिनाशात्प्रणश्यति ॥२.६३॥
krodhādbhavati saṁmohaḥ
saṁmohātsmṛtivibhramaḥ
smṛtibhraṁśādbuddhināśo
buddhināśātpraṇaśyati (2.63)

krodhād = krodhāt — from anger; bhavati — becomes (comes); saṁmohaḥ — delusion; saṁmohāt — from delusion; smṛti — conscience + vibhramaḥ — vanish; smṛtibhraṁśād = smṛtibhraṁśāt = smṛti — memory, judgement + bhraṁśāt — from fading away; buddhināśo = buddhināśaḥ = buddhi —discerning power + nāśaḥ — lose, affected; buddhināśāt = buddhi — discernment + nāśāt — from loss, from being affected; praṇaśyati — is ruined

From anger, comes delusion. From this delusion, the conscience vanishes. When he loses judgment, his discerning power fades away. Once the discernment is affected, he is ruined. (2.63)

Commentary:

Sometimes anger subsides of its own accord. Then a man behaves properly. But if the anger remains in force, he does develop some very crazy ideas. Anger has its own force. Thus it drives a man to live out offensive fantasies. The man then loses good sense and social training. His sense of right and wrong disappears. He reaches a stage of not caring about the consequences. Then he acts irresponsibly.

रागद्वेषवियुक्तैस्तु
विषयानिन्द्रियैश्चरन् ।
आत्मवश्यैर्विधेयात्मा
प्रसादमधिगच्छति ॥२.६४॥
rāgadveṣaviyuktaistu
viṣayānindriyaiścaran
ātmavaśyairvidheyātmā
prasādamadhigacchati (2.64)

rāgadveṣaviyuktais = rāga — cravings + dveṣa — disliking + viyuktaiḥ — discontinued; tu — if, however; viṣayān — attractive objects; indriyaiścaran = indriyaiḥ — by the senses + caran — interacting; ātmavaśyair = ātmavaśyaiḥ — disciplined person; vidheyātmā — a well-behaved person; prasādam — grace of providence; adhigacchati — gets

If, on the other hand, cravings and dislikings are continued and the attractive objects and senses continue interaction, a disciplined person who is usually well-behaved, gets the grace of providence. (2.64)

Commentary:

This is in contrast to the man who allows his consideration of sensual delights to motivate him. He becomes degraded by imagining sensual rewards. He is lowered by craving. If he gets fulfillment, he indulges until he becomes weary. By this repeated process, he develops an addiction which turns into an ugly vice.

If, however, he is prevented from satisfying the craving, he becomes frustrated. This frustration, if not accepted by him, turns into anger against society. The anger turns into unreasonable thinking patterns. Such thinking destroys his sense of morality. The loss of morality causes reckless action and irresponsibility, which carry consequences.

As an alternative, Lord Krishna instructed that we stop the craving and its hazards which include frustration, anger, irresponsible action, and consequences. He proposed that we learn to stop craving and disliking. *Yukta* means to join to something, to link up with something. *Viyukta* means the opposite, to disconnect with something, to move away from something. The suggestion is that the craving and disliking are not properties of the soul, but rather are properties of the energies that are near the soul. Lord Krishna suggested that we stop linking with the energies and remain detached internally. He indicated that even if we are detached, we may have to tolerate the senses and their linkage with objects. He said in verse 59 that the sense objects (*viṣayā*) which usually attract a man will turn away from (*nivartate*) him if he becomes a sensual disciplinarian. Even though they turn away, they will return to test him. In some instances, he will have to allow his body to engage with them anyway. But Lord Krishna suggested that the man cautiously go ahead if he is circumstantially forced to do so. He should act it out with detachment from inner feelings which urge him to enjoy or dislike the encounter.

This advice is directly relevant to Arjuna but we can benefit from it too. Arjuna had to face sense objects in the forms of the relatives who were before him as military combatants. In that case, it was emotionally painful and not enjoyable; it was something unfavorable. But Krishna advised Arjuna to be detached from the repulsive feelings and to proceed with a task that was being circumstantially forced on him.

Prasādam is mentioned in this verse and we have listed this as *the grace of providence*. This grace was explained to the writer directly by Lord Krishna of our Sri Sri Krishna-Balarama Deities.

We must face our destiny as Arjuna did. We should practice self-restraint on a consistent basis (*ātmavaśyair*). We need to be persons who are self-subdued, gentle towards life and providence (*vidheyātmā*). With those qualities, we qualify for the divine grace. Lord Krishna explained that *prasadam* (the grace of providence) may come as His personal act upon a soul. But He mentally stated to this commentator:

"Usually, divine grace comes automatically by the all-surrounding personal and impersonal energies which act favorably in the life of a well-behaved, disciplined person. One does not have to be My devotee to get this grace of providence, but the recipient must be disciplined and well-behaved at the time of reception."

प्रसादे सर्वदुःखानां
हानिरस्योपजायते ।
प्रसन्नचेतसो ह्याशु
बुद्धिः पर्यवतिष्ठते ॥२.६५॥
prasāde sarvaduḥkhānāṁ
hānirasyopajāyate
prasannacetaso hyāśu
buddhiḥ paryavatiṣṭhate (2.65)

prasāde — the grace of providence producing spiritual peace of mind; sarvaduḥkhānāṁ = sarva — all + duḥkhāṇāṁ — of the emotional distresses; hānir = hāniḥ — cessation, end; asyopajāyate = asya — of him + upajāyate — is produced; prasannacetaso = prasannacetasaḥ = prasanna — peaceful + cetasaḥ — of mind; hyāśu = hy (hi) — indeed + āśu — at once; buddhiḥ — intelligence; paryavatiṣṭhate — becomes stable.

By the grace of providence, all the emotional distresses cease for him. Being of a pacified mind, his intelligence at once, becomes stable. (2.65)

Commentary:

The nature of that providential fortune (*prasādam*) may be understood by studying the effects of it. If a man is shielded by it, his emotional distresses cease; he is relieved from anxieties and their resulting emotional pains. Being of a pacified mind, his intelligence (*buddhih*) will remain steady and constant in its outlook on life. Again, Lord Krishna explained to Arjuna how to get out of the mental confusion and emotional turmoil that affected this great hero on the battlefield.

नास्ति बुद्धिरयुक्तस्य
न चायुक्तस्य भावना ।
न चाभावयतः शान्तिर्
अशान्तस्य कुतः सुखम् ॥२.६६॥
nāsti buddhirayuktasya
na cāyuktasya bhāvanā
na cābhāvayataḥ śāntir
aśāntasya kutaḥ sukham (2.66)

nāsti = na — no + asti — is; buddhir = buddhiḥ — proper discernment; ayuktasya — of the uncontrolled person; na — not; cāyuktasya = ca — and + ayuktasya — of the uncontrolled person; bhāvanā — concentration; na — not; cābhāvayataḥ = ca — and + abhāvayataḥ — a person lacking concentration; śāntir = śāntiḥ — peace; aśāntasya — lacking emotional stability; kutaḥ — how is it to be achieved; sukham — happiness

In comparison, never is there proper discernment in an uncontrolled person. He is not capable of concentration. One who lacks concentration cannot get inner peace. For one who lacks emotional stability, how will happiness be achieved? (2.66)

Commentary:

A law of psychology is declared here. While we are uncontrolled, we lose discernment. The proper discrimination leaves us. We become incapable of proper concentration. Without this concentration (*bhāvanā*) we plan haphazardly and impractically. We get no peace or appreciation.

A schizophrenic is a person who is habitually insecure, being emotionally unstable. Such a person gets no real happiness. We do find, however, that an emotionally disturbed person gets a false happiness. To distinguish real happiness, Krishna used the word *śāntir* which means the superior happiness that comes from proper consideration and decision-making, as opposed to *aśāntasya*, a disturbed state which might produce an imaginary joy.

इन्द्रियाणां हि चरतां
यन्मनोऽनुविधीयते ।
तदस्य हरति प्रज्ञां
वायुर्नावमिवाम्भसि ॥२.६७॥
indriyāṇāṁ hi caratāṁ
yanmano'nuvidhīyate
tadasya harati prajñāṁ
vāyurnāvamivāmbhasi (2.67)

indriyāṇāṁ — of the senses; hi — indeed; caratāṁ — wandering; yan = yad — when; mano = manaḥ — the mind; 'nuvidhīyate = anuvidhīyate — is prompted; tadasya = tad — that + asya — of it; harati — it utilizes; prajñāṁ — of the discernment; vāyur = vāyuḥ — the wind; nāvam — a ship; ivāmbhasi = iva — like + ambhasi — in the water

When the mind is prompted by the wandering senses, it utilizes the discernment, just as in water, the wind handles a ship. (2.67)

Commentary:

This directly applies to Arjuna's situation but we can also apply it to our daily condition. Arjuna allowed his senses to range over the enemy ranks and to assess what would happen if there was a battle. His mind then presented a picture of fatalities. This presentation was based on projected probabilities which were gaged by comparing the battle skills of warriors. Arjuna did this using the excuse of having to make an assessment. He said:

hṛṣīkeśaṁ tadā vākyam idamāha mahīpate
senayorubhayormadhye rathaṁ sthāpaya me'cyuta (1.21)
yāvadetānnirīkṣe'haṁ yoddhukāmānavasthitān
kairmayā saha yoddhavyam asminraṇasamudyame (1.22)
yotsyamānānavekṣe'haṁ ya ete'tra samāgatāḥ
dhārtarāṣṭrasya durbuddher yuddhe priyacikīrṣavaḥ (1.23)

Then he spoke this request to Hṛṣīkeśa, Krishna: O Lord of the earth, cause my chariot to be parked in the midst of the two armies, O unaffected one,

...so that I can see those battle-hungry, armed warriors, with whom I should fight in this battle engagement.

I wish to observe these who are to fight, who assembled here desiring to please the evil- minded son of King Dhṛtarāṣṭra, in battle. (1.21-23)

In making such an assessment, Arjuna subjected himself to random influences. His mind then projected the probabilities. This was improper for Arjuna. He was not supposed to regard that. In any case, putting aside Arjuna's presumptions, Lord Krishna showed that Arjuna should not put himself at odds with providence. By opposing providence, Arjuna opened himself to illusions. He lost track of discernment (*prajñām*). His mind, like a strong wind, pushed his intellect, which was compared to a rudderless boat.

For us the meaning is clear. If we allow the senses to range over objects unrestrictedly, especially over objects which invoke our affections, our mind will empower the senses to crave pleasant associations with the objects. The mind will then push our intellect in an undesirable direction. Thus we return to Lord Krishna's declaration in text 62, where He explained that the act of considering sensual objects creates an attachment for them. This is enacted by the mind. If we allow the mind to consider on its own, we will be ruined thereby.

तस्माद्यस्य महाबाहो
निगृहीतानि सर्वशः ।
इन्द्रियाणीन्द्रियार्थेभ्यस्
तस्य प्रज्ञा प्रतिष्ठिता ॥२.६८॥

tasmād — therefore; yasya — of the person who; mahābāho — O powerful Arjuna; nigṛhītāni — retracts; sarvaśaḥ — in every interaction; indriyāṇīndriyārthebhyas =

tasmādyasya mahābāho
nigṛhītāni sarvaśaḥ
indriyāṇīndriyārthebhyas
tasya prajñā pratiṣṭhitā (2.68)

indriyāṇi — sensual feelings + indriyārthebhyaḥ — of the attractive objects; tasya — his; prajñā — discernment; pratiṣṭhitā — remains constant

Thus, O Arjuna, concerning the person who, in every interaction retracts the sensual feelings from the attractive objects; his discernment remains constant. (2.68)

Commentary:

Arjuna is being addressed sarcastically as *mahābāho*, powerful man, mighty-armed man, but even though he was that powerful materially, he was a weakling on the emotional level. His mind proved to be the controller on that plane of his existence. Lord Krishna sarcastically contrasts Arjuna's gross bodily posture to that of a sensually-resistant, mind-controlling man (ā*tmavasyair vidheyatma*, 2.64) who is powerful on the mental and emotional levels even though he might be a physical weakling. The process of retracting the sensual feelings from the pursuit of their objects (*indriyāṇīndriyārthebhyas*) is called *pratyāhār*. We mentioned this before. Lord Krishna will give further details. Here we can get a hint of the process. It is sufficient at this point to understand that the only way to have a constant and steady discernment is to keep the sensual energy under control, so that it does not pursue sense objects haphazardly. Ideally, the mind should not be allowed to control the senses on its own. The most difficult part of this retraction process is the application of restraint to all senses simultaneously, as Lord Krishna described. He says *sarvaśah*, which means on all sides, in all respects, on all levels through which it could be expressed. This is quite a task for any human being.

या निशा सर्वभूतानां
तस्यां जागर्ति संयमी ।
यस्यां जाग्रति भूतानि
सा निशा पश्यतो मुनेः ॥२.६९॥
yā niśā sarvabhūtānāṁ
tasyāṁ jāgarti saṁyamī
yasyāṁ jāgrati bhūtāni
sā niśā paśyato muneḥ (2.69)

yā — which; niśā — void; sarvabhūtānāṁ — all ordinary people; tasyāṁ — in this; jāgarti — is perceptive; saṁyamī — the sense-controlling person; yasyāṁ — in what; jāgrati — is exciting; bhūtāni — the masses of people; sā — that; niśā — is void; paśyato = paśyataḥ — of the perceptive; muneḥ — of the sage

The sense-controlling person is perceptive of that which is void to the ordinary people. What is exciting to the masses of people is void to the perceptive sage. (2.69)

Commentary:

The disciplined man is described here as a man of restraint, a man who is always involved in self-control, a *samyamī*. This type of man is found in all spheres of life, not just in the devotional circles. By using the word *muni*, Lord Krishna spoke of a man who is aware of spiritual disciplines. Again, such a man who is a *muni* may or may not be a devotee of Lord Krishna, but he must have some spiritual interest and be involved in mind control and self control for spiritual improvements. This is why he is called a sage or *muni*.

The sages or *munis* accept the challenges of life and work their way through these methodically, not for a projected result, but to play their part in the world's history. Arjuna is being indicated as an ordinary man because he tried to avoid the challenges of his life at *Kurukṣetra*. He wanted to discontinue the engagement. Still he presented himself in the beginning as a man of knowledge, a man conversant with scripture and its application. Lord

Krishna showed Arjuna the contrast between an ordinary man and a wise individual.

In addition, Arjuna wanted to go to the forest and projected himself there with enthusiasm but Lord Krishna indicated that a wise man would not be enthusiastic to make that choice. A wise man would see nothing delightful in such an alternative.

Arjuna was contrary in using the words of the wise men and acting like an ordinary man. He was misusing scripture, applying high-sounding words to his ordinary response on the war field. Lord Krishna objected when He told Arjuna:

śrībhagavānuvāca
aśocyānanvaśocastvaṁ prajñāvādāṁśca bhāṣase
gatāsūnagatāsūṁśca nānuśocanti paṇḍitāḥ (2.11)

The Blessed Lord said: You mourned for that which should not be regretted. And you expressed intelligent statements. (2.11)

Here Arjuna spoke the words of the pandits, the educated people of the Vedic era, but he acted like a commoner (*anārya*, 2.2). Mr. Winthrop Sargeant, who used much of *Śrīpad Rāmānuja's* explanation of the *Bhagavad Gītā*, gave the most exacting note regarding this verse. He wrote that '"the sage who sees perceives the light of the *ātman*, which is dark as night to others, while the others see the light of the senses which is dark as night to the sage". (The *Bhagavad Gītā*, Sargeant, p. 154)

This note is within the context of the *Gītā* in its own time and place, and is qualified by the preceeding verse, text 68.

आपूर्यमाणमचलप्रतिष्ठं
समुद्रमापः प्रविशन्ति यद्वत् ।
तद्वत्कामा यं प्रविशन्ति सर्वे
स शान्तिमाप्नोति न कामकामी ॥ २.७० ॥
āpūryamāṇamacalapratiṣṭhaṁ
samudramāpaḥ praviśanti yadvat
tadvatkāmā yaṁ praviśanti sarve
sa śāntimāpnoti na kāmakāmī (2.70)

āpūryamāṇam — becoming filled; acala — not moving about + pratiṣṭham — remaining stationary; samudram — the ocean; āpaḥ — the waters; praviśanti — they enter; yadvat — in which; tadvat — similarly; kāmā = kāmāḥ — cravings; yaṁ — whom; praviśanti — enter, arise; sarve - all; sa — he; śāntim — true satisfaction; āpnoti — gets; na — not; kāmakāmī — one who craves for every desire

Becoming filled, not flowing about, remaining stationary, the ocean absorbs the waters that enter it. Similarly, a person who remains calm when cravings arise gets true satisfaction, but not the person who craves for every desire. (2.70)

Commentary:

This is another sarcastic remark. Arjuna did not remain calm but became agitated. His energy began to flow out of him in such great proportions that he lost vital strength, sat down and began trembling as his eyes brimmed with tears. If he were on that occasion, a truly wise man, he would have kept composure.

There is a very important point made here that was stressed also in text 64. Even for a wise man, there will be some agitation but the wise man does not allow the agitation to overrule him. He controls its force by depriving it of attention. But the weaker person contemplates and/or considers the emotional disturbances and thus feeds the weakness, causing it to get the better of his nature.

The passionate energies might stir a little in a wise man, but they are quelled, put to silence, by his detachment from his own feelings. But the weaker human beings are affected by moods in every instance.

We need to rid ourselves of the tendency of trying to fulfill every desire that arises in the psyche. Most of these desires should be allowed to subside of their own accord. We should not give impetus to them unless we first determine their spiritual worth.

The *kāmakāmī* is the person who feels compelled to chase after every desire, to try to fulfill every urge. *Kāma* means lust or sensual urge. *Kāmī* means a person who is lusty or sensually motivated by nature. Lord Krishna insists that we curb the lusty nature.

विहाय कामान्यः सर्वान्
पुमांश्चरति निःस्पृहः ।
निर्ममो निरहंकारः
स शान्तिमधिगच्छति ॥ २.७१ ॥
vihāya kāmānyaḥ sarvān
pumāṁścarati niḥspṛhaḥ
nirmamo nirahaṁkāraḥ
sa śāntimadhigacchati (2.71)

vihāya — rejects; kāmān — cravings; yaḥ — who; sarvān — all; pumāṁścarati = pumān — person + carati — acts; niḥspṛhaḥ — free of lusty motivation; nirmamo = nirmamaḥ — indifferent to possessions; nirahaṁkāraḥ — free from impulsive assertion; sa — he; śāntim — contentment; adhigacchati — attains

The person who rejects all cravings, whose acts are free of lusty motivation, who is indifferent to possessions, who is free of impulsive assertion, attains contentment. (2.71)

Commentary:

The key point is to ignore certain desires or cravings which arise in our nature. These features of our energy may continue but we must learn how to resist them, how to ignore their pressing, demanding impulses. In the case of Arjuna, he may have averted the crippling sensations by ignoring them in the beginning and by not considering the possibilities more and more.

Once we subject ourselves to these moods, we are moved by a lusty motivation. We act haphazardly without deliberation. We spoil our destiny.

Being indifferent to possessions (*nirmamo*), being indifferent to the feeling of *mine* or *this is mine,* applies to both manifested and non-manifested possessions. But manifested possessions are of two kinds: Those which are self-propelled and those which are propelled by other agencies. For instance, a car is propelled by other agencies but a turtle can move on its own.

By studying the attitude of the samkhya yogis, one can come to understand, at least intellectually, that all possessions are owned in a very relative sense. A man is allowed to possess an item on a conditional basis only. He should remain detached and should be slightly indifferent to his own personal feelings as well. Since he is not absolute, he has no alternative but to take himself lightly. He is not the Supreme Being. And he is not that essential to universal life.

A man should also be free from the tendency of making claims for everything that he does in life. *Ahamkāra* is a combination of two words, *aham* and *kāra*. *Aham* means I. *Kāra* means doing, making, creating. *Nirahamkāra* means, *not to be involved deeply,* in the sense of, *I am doing this; I am doing that.*

Every man has to take help from the material elements, from the social situation, from the universal situation and from the supernatural agency. There is no question of making any absolute or total claim on anything.

एषा ब्राह्मी स्थितिः पार्थ
नैनां प्राप्य विमुह्यति ।
स्थित्वास्यामन्तकालेऽपि
ब्रह्मनिर्वाणमृच्छति ॥२.७२॥

eṣā brāhmī sthitiḥ pārtha
naināṁ prāpya vimuhyati
sthitvāsyāmantakāle'pi
brahmanirvāṇamṛcchati (2.72)

eṣā - this; brāhmī - divine; sthitiḥ — state; pārtha - son of Pṛthā; naināṁ = na - not + enāṁ - this; prāpya — does have; vimuhyati — is stupefied; sthitvā — is fixed; 'syāṁ = asyāṁ — in this; antakāle — at the time of death; 'pi = api — also; brahma — divinity + nirvāṇam — full stoppage of mundane sensuality; ṛcchati — attains

This divine state is required, O son of Pṛthā. If a man does not have this, he is stupefied. At the time of death, the full stoppage of mundane sensuality and the attainment of divinity is attained by one who is fixed in this divine state. (2.72)

Commentary:

Brāhmī sthitih is the spiritual level. First Lord Krishna spoke of the *sthitaprajña* when Arjuna asked about a man of steady insight (*sthitaprajñas* 2.54). In texts 57, 58, and 61, Lord Krishna spoke of *prajña pratiṣṭhita*. This is the first mention of *brāhmī sthitih*. There is a vast difference between *sthitaprajñas* and *brāhmī sthitih*. *Sthitaprajñas* refers to being situated firmly in one's own experience. Stated simply, *sthitaprajñas* means being situated in discriminatory wisdom. It is something personal, based on natural or developed mystic insight. But *brāhmī sthitih* means being situated on the spiritual level of the soul, being integrated there and being unaffected at the time by the material situations. In the *sthita prajña*, one still uses the mind but in the proper way, while in the *brāhmī sthitih* one looks away from the mind directly through the soul to the spiritual level that is beyond these material manifestations.

The *brāhmī sthitih* and the related state of *brahma nirvāṇam* are available to both devotees and non-devotees of Krishna. It is not limited to devotees. In fact, in this chapter, Lord Krishna gave such a broad-based process that He stressed Himself only once in text 61, saying *matparah*, being intent on Me (on Krishna Himself). Otherwise the Lord gives a process that can be used even by those spiritualists who are not interested in focusing to Him.

The destination of *brahma nirvāṇam* is broad-based. It applies to Krishna's devotees and others who are not interested in surrendering to Krishna. Arjuna surrendered to Krishna fully, but there are others who are not inclined to that.

One may attain a spiritual level of life beyond this material situation by following this process described. Some of these levels do not afford the facility of being with Krishna, but they are spiritual levels nevertheless.

Nirvāṇa is a word that was made popular by Lord Buddha. He stressed that everyone should try to stop, to end, to blow out this material existence and all that it involves. Nirvāṇa means that a man has brought his material existence to an end. He is done with it. He has terminated his involvements. He has no intentions of congregating with us again in the material world. He eliminated his material interest, choking off all his material tendencies and short-cutting his interest in our history.

Brahmanirvāṇa means that the man had not only ended his material history, but he entered into the brahman level as well. But there is a range of levels in the brahman world. We will hear of this later on from Lord Krishna. Once a man is situated permanently on the spiritual platform, he will, at the time of death of the present body, reach one of the spiritual levels in the vast range of spiritual existence.

In a sense, we can see that Lord Krishna was unconcerned as to whether the warriors died or not. Krishna did everything within His power to convince Arjuna to fight, to remove Arjuna's hesitation. This is the last argument in this chapter. Lord Krishna offered something besides victory and an earthly kingdom or death in battle and the heavenly world. He offered detached action and a spiritual destination. He indirectly reassured Arjuna that in such a situation, one does not have to worry about reactions because there will be *nirvāṇa*, the extinguishing of all these actions and reactions. If one attains this spiritual position, he does not have to deal with the mundane histories through which perplexities of destiny are hurled before a man.

CHAPTER 3

Cultural Activity and Renunciation*

अर्जुन उवाच
ज्यायसी चेत्कर्मणस्ते
मता बुद्धिर्जनार्दन ।
तत्किं कर्मणि घोरे मां
नियोजयसि केशव ॥ ३.१ ॥
arjuna uvāca
jyāyasī cetkarmaṇaste
matā buddhirjanārdana
tatkiṁ karmaṇi ghore māṁ
niyojayasi keśava (3.1)

arjuna — Arjuna; uvāca — contested; jyāyasī — is better; cet = ced — if; karmaṇaḥ — than physical action; te — your; matā — idea; buddhirjanārdana = buddhiḥ — mental action + janārdana — motivator of men; tatkiṁ = tat (tad) — them + kiṁ — why; karmaṇi — in action; ghore — in horrible; māṁ — me; niyojayasi — you urge; keśava — handsome-haired one

Arjuna contested: O motivator of men, if it is Your idea that the mental approach is better than the physically-active one, then why do You urge me to commit horrible action, O handsome-haired One? (3.1)

Commentary:

First Arjuna summarized what the Lord told him; that the mental approach to problems is better than the impulsive, active one. But Lord Krishna did not mean a mental approach without action even though Arjuna seemed to think that this was the Lord's view.

Arjuna then said that if that was the Lord's opinion in reality, he felt that the Lord contradicted Himself by proposing silent reflection and then urging Arjuna to combat. This is Arjuna's confusion. Arjuna felt at this point that Krishna spoke of contemplation without action. But this is not what Krishna meant. A disciple may from time to time confuse his views with those of the spiritual teacher. The words used by the teacher may be the same as those used by the disciple but the meanings might be variant. A disciple should free himself from his own meanings in order to grasp the explanations of a teacher. Otherwise, there will be undue disagreement.

Lord Krishna referred to a mental approach followed by prompt and effective action as contrasted to a non-mental approach which is replaced only by an impulsive activity. One has to get the mind under control, then direct the mind as it directs the life energies. One should not let the mind run free. An uncontrolled mind falls under the control of the impulsive life energies which make the body act in an irresponsible way.

**The Mahābhārata contains no chapter headings. This title was assigned by the translator on the basis of verse 4 of this chapter.*

व्यामिश्रेणैव वाक्येन
बुद्धिं मोहयसीव मे ।
तदेकं वद निश्चित्य
येन श्रेयोऽहमाप्नुयाम् ॥ ३.२ ॥
vyāmiśreṇaiva vākyena
buddhiṁ mohayasīva me
tadekaṁ vada niścitya
yena śreyo'hamāpnuyām (3.2)

vyāmiśreṇaiva = vyāmiśreṇa — with this two-way + iva — like this; vākyena — with a proposal; buddhiṁ — intelligence; mohayasīva = mohayasi — you baffle + iva — like this; me — of me; tad — this; ekaṁ — one; vada — tell; niścitya — surely; yena — by which; śreyo = śreyaḥ — the best; 'ham = aham — I; āpnuyām — I should get

You baffle my intelligence with this two-way proposal. Mention one priority, by which I would surely get the best result. (3.2)

Commentary:

Arjuna thought it was a two-way proposal but it was not. Lord Krishna clarified this. The misunderstanding occurred because Arjuna did not grasp the meanings of the words used by Krishna. Arjuna thought that the Lord's meanings were similar to his own. It was not a two-way proposal but a singular plan of action used formerly by the accomplished samkhya yogis who considered in terms of reality and then acted promptly. Though he misunderstood, Arjuna asked for clarification.

श्रीभगवानुवाच
लोकेऽस्मिन्द्विविधा निष्ठा
पुरा प्रोक्ता मयानघ ।
ज्ञानयोगेन सांख्यानां
कर्मयोगेन योगिनाम् ॥ ३.३ ॥
śrībhagavānuvāca
loke'smindvividhā niṣṭhā
purā proktā mayānagha
jñānayogena sāṁkhyānāṁ
karmayogena yoginām (3.3)

śrī bhagavān — the Blessed Lord; uvāca — said; loke — in this physical world; 'smin = asmin — in this; dvividhā — of the two-fold; niṣṭhā — standard; purā — previously; proktā — was taught; mayā — by me; 'nagha = anagha — O blameless one, good man; jñānayogena — mind regulations by yoga practice; sāṁkhyānāṁ — of the Sāṁkhya philosophical yogis; karmayogena — action regulation by yoga practice; yoginām — of the non-philosophical yogis

The Blessed Lord said: In the physical world, a two-fold standard was previously taught by Me. O Arjuna, my good man. This was mind regulation by the yoga practice of the Sāṁkhya philosophical yogis and the action regulation by the yoga practice of the non-philosophical yogis. (3.3)

Commentary:

Readers should note lines 4 and 5 as follows:

jñānayogena sāṁkhyānāṁ karmayogena yoginām

Both the ancient samkhya sages and the ancient ascetics were yogis, but the samkhyas were more advanced, having passed the elementary stages of yoga practice. They progressed to concentration, contemplation and trance states. The elementary yogis were those who were still on the stages of *āsana* postures and *prāṇāyāma* breath nutrition. The advanced yogis did the *āsana* and breath procedures but they were also proficient at the higher mystic stages. It is not that the ancient samkhya yogis were merely philosophers like some modern jñana yogis who have no yoga proficiency. Even in cases like that of the sage *Vasiṣṭha* who is a famous jñana yogi from the ancient days, there is a record of *āsana* and *prāṇāyāma*. We should not allow modern commentators to pretend that these ancient samkhya yogis knew the theory of spirituality and applied themselves to concentration, contemplation and trance only. In Chapter Six, text 3, this is explained further:

āruruksormuneryogaṁ karma kāraṇamucyate
yogārūḍhasya tasyaiva śamaḥ kāraṇamucyate (6.3)

For a philosophical man who strives for yoga expertise, cultural activity is recommended. For one who has mastered yoga already, the tranquil reserved method is the means. (6.3)

We proceeded to Chapter Six to show that Lord Krishna clarified what He meant in this verse, that the neophytes of spirituality were advised to take to activity; the advanced ones were to use the mystic process in full.

Both neophytes and the advanced practitioners must be active, but the neophytes are more active on the physical level, while the advanced souls maneuver more on the mystic plane. This means that a society that is established to assist neophytes will not have much facility for the advanced person. And one that caters for the advanced ones may be inappropriate for neophytes. Spiritual life is not static; it is dynamic. Krishna said that He taught these two processes of mind and body regulation, namely, thinking regulation and action regulation.

The neophytes, even in those days, did the *āsana* postures as well as the breath nutrition techniques, but those neophytes acted much on the physical level while the advanced persons performed more on the mystic plane and less on the physical plane, except in special circumstances.

न कर्मणामनारम्भान्
नैष्कर्म्यं पुरुषोऽश्नुते ।
न च संन्यसनादेव
सिद्धिं समधिगच्छति ॥३.४॥
na karmaṇāmanārambhān
naiṣkarmyaṁ puruṣo'śnute
na ca saṁnyasanādeva
siddhiṁ samadhigacchati (3.4)

na — not; karmaṇām — concerning cultural activity; anārambhān — not being involved; naiṣkarmyaṁ — freedom from cultural activity; puruṣo = puruṣaḥ — a person; 'śnute = aśnute — attains; na — not; ca — and; saṁnyasanādeva = saṁnyasanād (saṁnyasanāt) — from renunciation + eva — alone; siddhiṁ — spiritual perfection; samadhigacchati — achieves

A man does not attain freedom from cultural activity merely by not being involved in social affairs. And not by renunciation alone, does he achieve spiritual perfection. (3.4)

Commentary:

Lord Krishna clears up the misunderstanding of Arjuna who felt that if he did not act, he would avoid bad results. Here the Lord makes it clear that even if one avoids an unpleasant act, one may still get a bad consequence. Many people feel that if they turn away from an unpleasant act, they would be saved the reactions which would be due if the act were performed. But that is not necessarily true.

From the other angle, it is also false to think that if we renounce everything and do nothing, we will attain perfection. We hear of Gautama Buddha, how he sat down, did nothing physically, and attained perfection, but this does not mean that the same success will be ours if we follow in his footsteps. We might get a more entangling result than the one we tried to avoid in the first place. Buddha preached after he reached the spiritual perfection he aspired for. In the end, he had to act by preaching. He had to influence others and thus set into motion a new chain of obligations to followers.

One may try his best to oversimplify the means and methods of reality, but his conclusions may not tally with the truth. And thus he will, of necessity, be victimized by providence.

न हि कश्चित्क्षणमपि
जातु तिष्ठत्यकर्मकृत् ।
कार्यते ह्यवशः कर्म
सर्वः प्रकृतिजैर्गुणैः ॥३.५॥
na hi kaścitkṣaṇamapi
jātu tiṣṭhatyakarmakṛt
kāryate hyavaśaḥ karma
sarvaḥ prakṛtijairguṇaiḥ (3.5)

na — no; hi — indeed; kaścit — anyone; kṣaṇamapi = kṣaṇam — a moment + api — also; jātu — ever; tiṣṭhatyakarmakṛt = tiṣṭhati — exists + akarmakṛt — not acting; kāryate — caused to act; hyavaśaḥ = hi — indeed + avaśaḥ — against their wishes; karma — vibration; sarvaḥ — everyone; prakṛtijair = prakṛtijaiḥ — produced by material nature; guṇaiḥ — variations of mundane energy

No one, even momentarily, ever exists without vibration. By the variations of mundane energy in material nature, everyone, even against their wishes, is forced to perform. (3.5)

Commentary:

This does not give us much leeway. This one statement of the *Gītā* has considerably reduced the projected scope of our free will. Here *prakṛtijair guṇaih* is mentioned as being the moody variations within material nature. *Kāryate* means any impulsive urge, an act performed regardless of our liking or disliking the matter.

By this statement, every creature (*sarvah*) must act according to the influences which come upon him from material nature. Arjuna's incapacity of sitting down on the chariot was an act of not acting. If completed, it would carry consequences. It occurred because Arjuna was prevailed upon by certain moody variations (*guṇaih*) of mundane energy (*prakṛtijair*). As long as we are situated in material nature, we will be motivated by it in varying degrees. But if we get out or transcend it, and still have a material body or subtle form, its influence will be lessened considerably.

कर्मेन्द्रियाणि संयम्य
य आस्ते मनसा स्मरन् ।
इन्द्रियार्थान्विमूढात्मा
मिथ्याचारः स उच्यते ॥३.६॥
karmendriyāṇi saṁyamya
ya āste manasā smaran
indriyārthānvimūḍhātmā
mithyācāraḥ sa ucyate (3.6)

karmendriyāṇi — bodily limbs; saṁyamya — restraining; ya = yaḥ — who; āste — sits; manasā — by the mind; smaran — remembering; indriyārthān — attractive objects; vimūḍhātmā = vimūḍha — deluded + ātmā — self; mithyācāraḥ — deceiver; sa — he; ucyate — it is declared

A person who, while restraining his bodily limbs sits, with the mind remembering attractive objects, is a deceiver. So it is declared. (3.6)

Commentary:

This criticism applied to Arjuna's plan to go to the forest, abandoning duty on the war field. Suppose Arjuna was to contemplate spiritual life as the ascetics did in his time; still he would have thought of his warring friends and enemies. He would have put his bodily limbs and senses under restraint, but his mind would have raved on with the ideas, picturizations and feelings pertaining to the unresolved Kuru conflict. Thus Arjuna would have deceived others into thinking that he assumed contemplative life, while in fact, he would have been deeply involved on the mental plane.

Unresolved social matters do haunt a retired man who ran away from duties. The energies of the unresolved affairs and the thoughts of the related people reach that man with greater intensity. Instead of meditating, he thinks of the problems more and more and he applies himself to mental resolutions. But since it cannot be settled mentally, he impulsively leaves the isolation and returns to the location where he can resolve the differences and fulfill the obligations. It is best, therefore, to get advice from a superior person who knows how to bring social hassles to conclusion. Then one may progress easily to meditation. The complicated energies in a man's life do not leave him merely because he went into isolation. They follow him wherever he may go.

Arjuna wanted to leave the chariot, the weapons, Krishna's association, his friends and the confrontation. He did not consider that the problems would follow wherever he would roam. The isolation would itself cause an intensification of the mental hostilities. And a peaceful, thought-free meditation would elude him.

यस्त्विन्द्रियाणि मनसा
नियम्यारभतेऽर्जुन ।
कर्मेन्द्रियैः कर्मयोगम्
असक्तः स विशिष्यते ॥३.७॥

yastvindriyāṇi manasā
niyamyārabhate'rjuna
karmendriyaiḥ karmayogam
asaktaḥ sa viśiṣyate (3.7)

Yas (yaḥ) — whosoever; tvindriyāṇi = tv (tu) — however + indriyāṇi — the senses; manasā — by the mind; niyamyārabhate = niyamya — controlling + ārabhate — endeavors; 'rjuna — Arjuna; karmendriyaiḥ — by the limbs; karmayogam — regulating his work by yoga practice; asaktaḥ — without attachment; sa = saḥ — he; viśiṣyate — is superior

However, whosoever endeavors to control the senses by the mind, O Arjuna, and who restricts the limbs through regulating his work by yoga practice, without attachment, is superior. (3.7)

Commentary:

This person, the sense energy controller, is superior to the man who goes to an isolated place and who fails to regulate his mental and emotional powers. The contrast is made in relation to the internal nature or the psyche of the individual and not in contrast to the external actions of the body. A man may be involved externally in a questionable way and still be superior to a person who lives peacefully but whose internal posture is faulty. The Lord hints to Arjuna that going to the forest for a peaceful life would not necessarily imply that Arjuna may do something better, but staying on to complete duties in a perceptive, detached mood, would be superior.

Niyamya in the second line means controlling or subduing. This word stresses the motive for the discipline. The intention should be to control the impulsive energies. One may carefully regulate the senses by the mind for other reasons, such as to increase sensual indulgence. A man may, for instance, save his money for many months in order to spend it later in a casino. In that case, his motive was the desire to risk the funds in a gambling venture. Thus in life, we always use discipline or restraint for various purposes but this particular yoga practice is performed to subdue the mind and the senses for the sake of controlling impulsive urges.

In this verse, Lord Krishna gave His definition of *karma yoga*. This definition is different to the general view of *karma yoga* where a person feels that if he works hard, saves up some money and then gives it to a religious cause, he is performing *karma yoga*. We do not see such a definition here. Modern gurus who are anxious for funds, may encourage followers to give large donations either from government approved or questionable business practices. They declare this to be *karma yoga*.

Karma yoga by Lord Krishna's definition in this verse means a procedure for disciplining the senses while performing one's duty. Arjuna, for instance, was to perform such *karma yoga* by staying on the battlefield, disciplining his cowardly impulses, and fighting with detachment. *Karma yoga* is: Working or functioning (*karma*) with discipline (*yoga*). What has that got to do with giving money to a religious organization? How has it come to mean that I will get a large income, compute my taxes at the end of the fiscal year and cream off a portion of my income for my preferred religious society? How has it come to mean that if I have an illicit business, I perform *karma yoga* by giving all or some of the criminally-earned money to a spiritual teacher or society?

If *karma yoga* means giving that sort of money to a religious cause, Lord Krishna would have told Arjuna to fight hard, take the riches of the warriors and offer it to the forest ascetics who had spiritual communities. In that act, the offering would have been the motive for fighting. But this is not the case. And the *karma* yogi described here is superior to the pretensive ascetic described in verse 6. That, however, does not mean that in every case the karmi yogi is superior to a practicing ascetic.

नियतं कुरु कर्म त्वं
कर्म ज्यायो ह्यकर्मणः ।
शरीरयात्रापि च ते
न प्रसिध्येदकर्मणः ॥३.८॥
niyataṁ kuru karma tvaṁ
karma jyāyo hyakarmaṇaḥ
śarīrayātrāpi ca te
na prasidhyedakarmaṇaḥ (3.8)

niyataṁ — moral; kuru — do; karma — cultural duty; tvaṁ — you; karma — performance; jyāyo = jyāyaḥ — better; hy akarmaṇaḥ = hi — indeed + akarmaṇaḥ — than non-action; śarīrayātrāpi = śarīra — body + yātrā — maintenance + api — even; ca — and; te — your; na — not; prasidhyet — could be achieved; akarmaṇaḥ — without activity

Moral action should be done by you. Performance is better than non-performance. Even the maintenance of your body could not be achieved without activity. (3.8)

Commentary:

Arjuna was, in effect, sitting idle on the chariot, stalling for time and decision-making. While he did this, time moved on. His opportunity for glory was slipping away. Idleness, however, is part and parcel of our conditioned nature. Sometimes we feel at ease in it. Sometimes we feel in total harmony with it. Still it is not in our interest. As spirits, we are energetic, not static. When our enthusiasm is absorbed by material nature, a dullness of mind and a laziness of body comes over us.

Niyatam means what is enjoined or standardized, what is normally acceptable. Arjuna felt he was in an emergency; thus he gave good reasons for avoiding the duties. Lord Krishna alerted him that the killing of warriors by another warrior is duty.

In line 3, the word *te* means *your*. Lord Krishna told Arjuna that he, Arjuna, could not maintain his body without activity. Even if Arjuna were to go to the ascetic life style, he would endeavor. It was inevitable. Ascetics in the time of Arjuna performed yoga *āsana* postures and various chores just to maintain their bodies and residences.

Akarmanah means, *that inaction*. When contrasted to idleness, it may seem that idleness is better than destructive work, but idleness also bears an unfavorable reaction. On occasion, destructive work is better than idleness since the benefit is a lesson learnt. Idleness merely postpones the display of a person's imperfection. One does not improve merely by remaining idle. It is by endeavoring that one learns. The soul is the energetic principle in the creation. It is supposed to be dynamic.

One might feel that meditation and contemplation involves a considerable reduction in work but this is only on the gross level. If one tries to meditate and does not act on the mystic plane to control the impulses, his meditation will be useless.

यज्ञार्थात्कर्मणोऽन्यत्र
लोकोऽयं कर्मबन्धनः ।
तदर्थं कर्म कौन्तेय
मुक्तसङ्गः समाचर ॥३.९॥

yajñārthātkarmaṇo'nyatra
loko'yaṁ karmabandhanaḥ
tadarthaṁ karma kaunteya
muktasaṅgaḥ samācara (3.9)

yajñārthāt = *yajña* — *religious fulfillment and ceremony* + *ārthāt* — *for the sake of; karmaṇo* = *karmaṇaḥ* — *from action; 'nyatra* = *anyatra* — *besides; loko* = *lokaḥ* — *world; 'yaṁ* = *ayam* — *this; karmabandhanaḥ* — *something bound by action; tadartham* = *tad* — *this* + *arthaṁ* — *purpose, value; karma* — *cultural activity; kaunteya* — *son of Kuntī; muktasaṅgaḥ* — *freedom from attachment; samācara* — *act promptly*

Besides action for religious fulfillment and ceremony, this world, is action-bound. Act for the sake of religious fulfillment and ceremony, O son of Kuntī. Be free from attachment. Act promptly. (3.9)

Commentary:

The technicality of actions is explained in this verse, namely, to determine whether a particular activity is a genuine religious function or is truly supportive of one. Once we determine this, we may act or divert ourselves accordingly. By this rule, all activity which is not genuine or which is not directly supportive of true religion, will become an implication for the actors. This includes a non-activity or an avoidance or refusal to act. Both action and non-action are action. Enthusiasm or laziness produces particular types of actions which bring on particular consequences according to the time and place.

Lying down to sleep is an action. It is not an inaction. Meditation or remaining still for some time is action. The result of a good rest is renewed enthusiasm. Good rest is an action.

As far as genuine religion is concerned, anything can be called a genuine religion by a religious leader or by his followers but a truly genuine religion is not dependent on being labeled by an authority. In fact, any authority might misuse his prestige by labeling a non-religious act as a religious activity. A religious act is not necessarily an act performed by a member of a genuine religion, but rather it is a God-inspired act performed by anyone from any religious or non-religious organization. It may be performed willfully, habitually, accidentally, or unconsciously. And most of all, a member of a genuine religion may not perform genuinely religious acts all of the time. He may deviate periodically just as a criminally-minded man may do something that is genuinely religious on occasion.

Whatever a person does that is not genuinely religious creates negative implications. These acts lead to further implication of other reactive acts. Arjuna was advised by Lord Krishna to act on the battlefield in terms of genuine religion, to be free of attachment, and to act promptly, seizing the opportunity of serving the Divine Lord.

Sridhara Maharaja, the Gaudiya Vaishnava Acarya, gave *yajñārthat* as "selfless duty offered unto Lord Vishnu". However, we will have to stick to the Sanskrit and the meaning in the context of what Lord Krishna said. Sridhara Maharaja did clarify that *yajña* pertains to sacrifices which were offered under the directions of the devas or demigods. He directly stated that *prajāpatih* in the next verse, is Lord *Brahmā*, the demigod creator.

For this translation, we gave yajñartha as religious fulfillment and ceremonies, without stipulating these for Lord Vishnu. *Yajña* does mean Lord Vishnu as *Śrīla* Bhaktivedanta stated, but *yajña* also has other meanings. The most common meaning is genuine religious ceremonies of Vedic origin which usually include a fire sacrifice. But these ceremonies are offered to any of the devas or supernatural authorities, including the *devadevah* or the Lord of the supernatural people, Lord Vishnu. In fact, in the Vedic era, as we can tell from the hymns of the four Vedas, Lord Vishnu was not especially highlighted for these sacrifices, but rather Indra and other *deva* supernaturals were.

It is not just a matter of the opinion of this writer or any other, nor is it a matter of missionary zeal because it is clarified in the next four verses, as we shall read. The point is: If a man does something that is not covered by supernatural authorities, he will be forced to take the liabilities, regardless of whether the action is good or bad. If he acts on his own without a commission from one of the supernatural people, he must deal with consequences and react accordingly in a purposeful or haphazard way. In a sense, this is a deadly trap. If we act by ourselves, we are implicated further and since we do not have an all-knowing vision, we are bound to err. On the other hand, if we act for a supernatural person, we must be certain that we are actually inspired by him, otherwise the particular supernatural might issue a disclaimer and negative reactions will come to us in due course of time. Since we do not remember past lives, we respond unconsciously to most reactions, and thus become further implicated. Still, the solution is not one of laziness or inaction. For as explained, inaction is another form of action that brings on distasteful consequences.

The only way out is to get advice from someone who can see all the options and direct us in the best course. This is what Arjuna did at *Kurukṣetra* by placing his life in Krishna's hands. But how can we get in touch with Krishna to that extent? Or can we trust any religious authority, or even this writer? It is seen that religious authorities do make mistakes. They do from time to time, give the wrong advice to disciples. Who can we trust? Lord Krishna made Himself available to His dear friend and disciple, Arjuna, but is He available to us in the same way? These are serious considerations.

सहयज्ञाः प्रजाः सृष्ट्वा
पुरोवाच प्रजापतिः ।
अनेन प्रसविष्यध्वम्
एष वोऽस्त्विष्टकामधुक् ॥३.१०॥
sahayajñāḥ prajāḥ sṛṣṭvā
purovāca prajāpatiḥ
anena prasaviṣyadhvam
eṣa vo'stviṣṭakāmadhuk (3.10)

sahayajñāḥ — along with religious fulfillment and ceremony; prajāḥ — first human beings; sṛṣṭvā — having created; purovāca = pura — long ago + uvāca — said; prajāpatiḥ — procreator Brahmā; anena — by this; prasaviṣyadhvam — may you produce; eṣaḥ — this; vo = vaḥ — your; 'stviṣṭakāmadhuk = astviṣṭakāmadhuk = astu — may it be + iṣṭakāmadhuk — for granting desires

Long ago, having created the first human beings, along with religious fulfillment and ceremonies, the Procreator Brahmā said: By this worship procedure, you may be productive. May it cause the fulfillment of your desires. (3.10)

Commentary:

This statement of Lord Krishna defies all modern evidence regarding the evolution of man from the ape. Undoubtedly, we see a plain, obvious, and visible connection between the ape, primitive man and modern man, but that connection is overrated by the anthropologists. This is due to their lack of mystic insight.

Just as today, there are different grades of human beings appearing even in the same nation or in the same family, so formerly there were different grades appearing without any sort of immediate or remote connection. Thus the anthropological view is simply an effort to oversimplify a very complicated process. By erasing or banishing the mystic content of the creation, a grave mistake is being made in forming so many conceptions which are totally misleading. But insofar as we are mystically-blind and resistant to the development of our psychic selves, we will continue with this ignorance of the difference between the subtle body and the gross one. We need not even talk about the difference between the soul and body. That differential is too vast for our crippled spirituality to comprehend. We should at least grasp the variation between the subtle dream body and the earthly one. A great effort should be made by educated people to grasp the substantiality of the dream form that is used every time the gross body sleeps. This is the beginning of spiritual life for modern man.

Here we are informed of the Vedic version of creation, the view that was held before Lord Krishna's appearance. He simply restates it. Long, long ago (*pura*) the *Prajāpati*, Demigod *Brahmā*, the potent creator of creatures and planets, did create *yajñah* or genuine religious ceremonies, and the human beings (*prajāh*) who were to perform these. After this, *Brahmā* instructed those original human beings, the great sages, his sons, that they should perform the religious ceremonies as he stipulated. By that performance, their needs were to be fulfilled. *iṣṭakāmadhuk* means someone or something that gives us what we really desire. In those ancient times, which were long, long ago, these sons of *Brahmā*, the great sages, did not have petty desires. Being high-minded, they were, for the most part, free from perversion .Thus most of their desires were harmonious with the divine will.

देवान्भावयतानेन
ते देवा भावयन्तु वः ।
परस्परं भावयन्तः
श्रेयः परमवाप्स्यथ ॥३.११॥
devānbhāvayatānena
te devā bhāvayantu vaḥ
parasparaṁ bhāvayantaḥ
śreyaḥ paramavāpsyatha (3.11)

devān — supernatural rulers; bhāvayatānena = bhāvayatā — may you cause to flourish + anena — by this procedure; te — they; devā — the supernatural rulers; bhāvayantu — may they bless you; vaḥ — you; parasparaṁ — each other; bhāvayantaḥ — favorably regarding one another; śreyaḥ — well-being; param — highest; avāpsyatha — you will achieve

By this procedure, you may cause the supernatural rulers to flourish. They, in turn, may bless you. In favorably regarding each other, the highest well-being will be achieved. (3.11)

Commentary:

This information means that initially, the leading human beings cultivated a relationship with the supernatural people. Those leading human beings were mentally conceived sons of *Brahmā* who did not remain on the celestial level, but who descended to take on super-fine earthly forms.

Those who remained on the celestial level, being content with celestial bodies, and who had no urges to come down to the earthly plane, were the devas, or demigods. These supernaturals were to regulate the existence of all other persons who took appearance in the material world and who used gross forms.

As described by *Brahmā*, there was to be an affectionate relationship between the humans and the celestials, but the humans were to be subordinate. They were to act as advised. Then, by cooperating with the orders of the supernaturals, they would get an easy living on earth. For communication with the supernaturals, a sector of human beings, the mystics or brahmins, were produced and these persons were supposed to act as mediators between mankind and the agents of God.

More information about the mind-born sons of *Brahmā* and about his creation of the supernatural engineers is given in texts like the *Śrīmad Bhāgavatam*. Interested readers should pursue their study to that book. It is sufficient for the average reader to know that these verses of *Bhagavad Gītā* are verified elsewhere in the Vedic literature. Here Lord Krishna uses a scriptural reference from the Vedic texts of His time.

इष्टान्भोगान्हि वो देवा
दास्यन्ते यज्ञभाविताः ।
तैर्दत्तानप्रदायैभ्यो
यो भुङ्क्ते स्तेन एव सः ॥३.१२॥
iṣṭānbhogānhi vo devā
dāsyante yajñabhāvitāḥ
tairdattānapradāyaibhyo
yo bhuṅkte stena eva saḥ
(3.12)

iṣṭān — most desired; bhogān — enjoyable people and things; hi — indeed; vo = vaḥ — to you; devā — supernatural rulers; dāsyante — they will give; yajñabhāvitāḥ — manifested through prescribed austerity and religious ceremony; tair = taiḥ — by those; dattān — given items; apradāyaibhyo = apradāya — not offering + ebhyaḥ — to them; yo = yaḥ — who; bhuṅkte — enjoys; stena — a thief; eva — only; saḥ — he

The supernatural rulers, being manifested through prescribed austerity and religious ceremony, will, indeed, give you the most desired people and things. Whosoever does not offer those given items to them, but who enjoys these, is certainly a thief. (3.12)

<u>Commentary:</u>

Here the underlying basis for the resentments of life are clearly explained by *Brahmā* to the first human beings. First *Brahmā*, the prime celestial engineer, created the devas or supernatural demigods. Then he created the planets and creatures. However, there was a circular system of desiring, getting fulfillment of realistic desires and again going back to the supernatural people to find out what should be done with the yields or fulfillments. However, people, especially pious Hindus who follow this system, fall into a trap of petitioning the supernaturals, then getting yields, and finally using the yields at leisure without consulting the demigods. When this is done, adverse reactions ensue. It may be asked: What is the purpose of worshipping these devas for something if one must, in turn, go again to the devas with the persons or items for more consultation? This is a very good question.

Obviously the whole procedure is a trap meant to utilize our human nature and keep us under, as stooges of the devas. Otherwise, if it were not so, we would ask for something, get it, and do whatever we wanted without consultation and without reaction. But this is not how the system was initially designed. If I petition a shop keeper for a pound of sugar, if I receive the sweet crystals and pay him the stipulated price, why should I return to ask how to use the product for the shopkeeper's satisfaction? Obviously I am not inclined to that. I purchased the sugar because I wanted to enjoy it. But here we are informed that *Brahmā* told his mind-born sons that if they did that, they would be regarded as thieves (*stena*).

The question remains and it is a persistent one that we must solve satisfactorily if we are to improve our relationship with Krishna: How are we to ask for something from God and then in turn, go back to God to ask Him what we should do with the acquired item? In other words, what are we to do with our desires if we find that when we return to the supernaturals with the yields, they tell us to do something that is contrary to what we intended?

Such a system would only work under one condition: Our initial desires must be in complete harmony with that of the supernatural people, which means that if we are at variance with them or if we see things differently, there will be conflict. We will be regarded as thieves and will be treated as having stolen the items. O, what a system!

According to the procedure given by *Brahmā*, we get an idea that those mind-born sons of his were highly-evolved, completely detached human beings. They were capable of conforming to such rules whereby they would ask for something in a religious ceremony, then work honestly for that item or have it produced instantly, as the case may be, then take the yield with a detached mood, then offer it again in a ceremony to the supernaturals and get their instruction on how to use it.

This means that the only desire those sages had, was to get these items for the religious ceremony. They did not have desires for usage of items but relied on the celestials to provide the instructions once the yields manifested. In our case, however, we have the desire for usage and we could care less about the religious ceremonies or the instruction of the supernaturals.

According to this, responsible living involves detecting the needs of the supernaturals, petitioning them for these things, getting the items instantly or gradually by honest endeavor, then again going to the devas for counsel on usage. O, what an adjustment that is for our human nature!

Interestingly, just one week ago, we were inclined to installing a picture form of the goddess Sarasvati in our home temple area. We were studying some musical techniques in playing two drums, the dholak and tabla. When we approached the demigoddess, we had the usual human attitude of asking her to assist us in this learning but she looked with a very callous regard. Seeing this, we toned down our attitude and gradually under her influence, we assumed a new mood of, "Please teach us these instruments so that we can serve you." After this, the goddess assumed a very pleasing mood.

At the time, we realized that it was our duty to make ourselves available as her student and servant. She was in charge. We were to assist her.

It appears, therefore, that our human side can be convened to what *Brahmā* requested of his mind-born sons in the very beginning. Such an adjustment will take some time, however, because we are oriented to the selfish way, the way of trying to imitate the supernatural controllers. We want to be controllers in our own right, to evolve to a point of being bosses. We have no intention of being servants or stooges forever. If anything, we act as stooges for a time but only with a motive to replace our masters.

यज्ञशिष्टाशिनः सन्तो
मुच्यन्ते सर्वकिल्बिषैः ।
भुञ्जते ते त्वघं पापा
ये पचन्त्यात्मकारणात् ॥ ३.१३ ॥

yajñaśiṣṭāśinaḥ santo
mucyante sarvakilbiṣaiḥ
bhuñjate te tvaghaṁ pāpā
ye pacantyātmakāraṇāt (3.13)

yajñaśiṣṭāśinaḥ = yajñaśiṣṭa — sanctified items used after a religious ceremony + āśinaḥ — utilizing; santo = santaḥ — virtuous souls; mucyante — they are released; sarvakilbiṣaiḥ — from all faults; bhuñjate — consume; te — they; tvaghaṁ = tv (tu) — but + aghaṁ — impurity; pāpā — wicked people; ye — who; pacantyātmakāraṇāt = pacanti — prepare + ātma — self + kāraṇāt — for the sake of

(Krishna continued): The virtuous people who utilize the items after they are sanctified by prescribed ceremony, are released from all faults. But the wicked ones who prepare for their own sake, consume their own impurity. (3.13)

Commentary:

As far as a bill of rights is concerned, this verse is perhaps one of the most important verses in the *Bhagavad Gītā*. This verse concerns not only our relationship with the Supreme Lord, but also with the in-between authorities, the supernatural demigods. *Śrīla* Bhaktivedanta Swami with all missionary zeal, gave *santah* as, *the devotees of the Lord* but *Śrīla* Sridhara Maharaja gave the plain meaning, *saintly persons*. We gave, *virtuous souls,* in compliance with what Sridhara Maharaja gave in his translated verse. In all honesty, the word *santah* cannot mean devotees of the Lord unless we state that all worshippers of the demigods are devotees. And in fact, at the time of *Brahmā*'s declaration of these rules of consumption, the devotees of the devas or demigods were indeed all devotees of the Lord, for then there were only the mind-born, super-perceptive sons of *Brahmā*. But the devotees of the demigods in today's environment are a variant lot. Only some are devotees of the Lord. *Śrīla* Bhaktivedanta Swami gave all of them the benefit of the doubt by categorizing all of them as devotees. This is in their favor, for he blessed them in this wonderful way for the potential of reaching Lord Krishna and being claimed by Him.

This rule of consumption, being an important stipulation, was and is taken very seriously by the demigods. Any man who complies with this rule in part or whole is marked as being worthy of a certain degree of security. He is regarded as being virtuous.

Bhuñjate means: they enjoy or they eat, they consume or they utilize. *Pacanti* means: they cook or they digest. In this reading we listed it as: *they consume*. According to these rules of consumption, the world is not a consumer economy or a place of human dominion, but rather, it is a world of benevolent dictatorship of the demigods. The earthly people are expected to honor the devas, the supernaturals, work to acquire yields, then return to the supernaturals for direction on the usage of the yields. This is different from needing something, asking God or an agent of God, acquiring the item and using it as one desires. According to this view, we are not ever supposed to have any desires of our own, but must always look towards God or the agents of God for a mission in terms of their needs.

The word *pacanti* means *they cook*, but we listed it as *they prepare*. This is in keeping with the overall use of *yajña* sacrificial ceremony. Such sacrificial ceremonies usually concern food offerings to the supernaturals but in some cases they do not. For instance, in some cases, a person offers items into the sacrifice for military purposes. In other cases nothing visible is offered. We will hear more of the various types of yajñas in other verses of the *Gītā*. Commentators usually restrict this *yajña* to *stoma* or *agnistoma* sacrifices, but Lord Krishna did not do so. Readers are asked to bear on with the writer until we reach the portion where Lord Krishna will describe more of the types of sacrifices that might be offered and the various types of yields that are produced. It is a fact, however, that even Lord Krishna stressed the eating aspect of the sacrifices. This is shown in the next verse.

अन्नाद्भवन्ति भूतानि
पर्जन्यादन्नसंभवः ।
यज्ञाद्भवति पर्जन्यो
यज्ञः कर्मसमुद्भवः ॥३.१४॥

annād=annāt- from nourishment; bhavanti- are produced; bhūtāni - the creatures; parjanyād = parjanyāt — from rain clouds; anna — nourishment; saṁbhavaḥ — originated; yajñād = yajñāt — from prescribed austerity and religious

annādbhavanti bhūtāni
parjanyādannasaṁbhavaḥ
yajñādbhavati parjanyo
yajñaḥ karmasamudbhavaḥ (3.14)

ceremony; bhavati — exists; parjanyo = parjanyaḥ — rain; yajñaḥ — prescribed austerity and religious ceremony; karma — cultural action; samudbhavaḥ — is caused

The creatures are produced from nourishment. From rain clouds, nourishment originated. From prescribed austerity and religious ceremony, rain clouds are produced. And prescribed austerity and religious ceremony are caused by cultural activities. (3.14)

Commentary:

A chain of causes and effects is listed. If we begin with the cause it would be action (*karma*). From that, a particular type of action, the religious ceremony, is produced. This is *yajñah*. From this ceremony of effective procedure, rain comes or *Parjanya*, the rain deity, acts to materialize rain clouds. From that moisture, vegetation grows and food is produced.

Anna means food. That is the general meaning. On the broader basis, *anna* means yield. Thus from action, a formal presentation for a request is made. From that formality, favorable conditions manifest. These favorable conditions may or may not include a favorable weather pattern. It may be willing workers who have a favorable attitude or even unwilling workers who are pressured by time and destiny to work and produce regardless of their attitude. From this effort, a product is produced. But at the point of production, *Brahmā* instructed that we take the manufactured or produced items to the supernaturals to ask of them the purpose of the said item.

Lord Krishna stressed that cultural activity (*karma*) is the cause of all this. The whole world moves on the basis of cultural activity, either of God's, the agents of God, or the dependent entities who are supervised by God and His agents. But action is the basis. Arjuna wanted to be inactive. Lord Krishna showed that some sort of action is required for production.

कर्म ब्रह्मोद्भवं विद्धि
ब्रह्माक्षरसमुद्भवम् ।
तस्मात्सर्वगतं ब्रह्म
नित्यं यज्ञे प्रतिष्ठितम् ॥३.१५॥
karma brahmodbhavaṁ viddhi
brahmākṣarasamudbhavam
tasmātsarvagataṁ brahma
nityaṁ yajñe pratiṣṭhitam (3.15)

karma — cultural activity; brahmodbhavaṁ = brahma — the Veda + udbhavaṁ — produced; viddhi — be aware; brahmākṣarasamudbhavam = brahma — Supreme Spirit + akṣara — the unaffected spiritual reality + samudbhavam — produced; tasmāt — hence; sarvagataṁ — all-pervading; brahma — spirit person; nityaṁ — always; yajñe — in prescribed austerity and religious ceremony; pratiṣṭhitam — is situated

Cultural activity is produced from the Personified Veda. The Personified Veda comes from the unaffected Supreme Spirit. Hence the all-pervading Supreme Spirit is always situated in prescribed austerity and religious ceremony. (3.15)

Commentary:

The general translation of this verse given by the Gaudiya Vaishnava acharyas is that the prescribed activities are handed down in the Vedas. These Vedas were produced by *Brahmā* who is mentioned in text 10 as *Prajāpati* (the Lord of the creatures). But Swami Bhaktivedanta Prabhupada gave *Prajāpati* as Lord Vishnu, who is the Lord of *Brahmā*. It is not a point of contention, however, because Lord *Brahmā* did as he was inspired when he told the first humans how they were to relate to the demigods. *Brahmā* was just an agent.

Śrīla Bhaktivedanta rightly pointed out that the Lord of the creatures is Vishnu. Vishnu is the Deity behind the scenes Who employs *Brahmā*. In the *Śrīmad Bhāgavatam*, this is confirmed when *Nārada* asked *Brahmā* about his origin. *Brahmā* admitted that he was motivated by Somebody Else, by Vishnu.

The driving force behind everything is, ultimately, Lord Vishnu. There is no doubt about it. The point cannot be counteracted by anyone, regardless of whether we are for or against the Vaishnava cause. If we follow the line of the Vedas down to the *Purāṇas*, and the *Gītā* of the *Mahābhārata*, we must admit this. It cannot be avoided.

Karma brahmodbhavam means that initially, action was produced by the Personified Veda, Lord *Brahmā*. *Nityam yajñe pratiṣṭham* means that the all-pervading spirit is always situated in genuine procedures of yield. In other words, no satisfactory result can come unless the all-pervading spirit supervises the production. Insofar as the material world is concerned, Lord Vishnu is the originator.

The limited spirits are located here and there, everywhere in the material creation, but this place was produced by Lord Vishnu. He has the ultimate responsibility for it. This cannot be denied. Even though the limited individual spirits are part of the sum total reserve of imperishable energy (*akṣara*), still, none of them have the power to produce this world. Thus, even though they act in this world after its production, we must recognize Lord Vishnu, the Godhead.

Lord Krishna of our Sri Sri Krishna-Balarama Deities asked us to explain that *karma* in this verse means any action. It is not restricted to action which is stipulated by demigod *Brahmā* in the Vedas. But it does include these in the whole range of actions which are compliant with or deviant from the stipulations of *Brahmā*.

However, if we find an activity which is compliant with what *Brahmā* stipulated, compliant with Veda, we can know for certain that such an act or such a procedure is genuinely religious and has the all-pervading spirit, the Supervising Supreme Lord, as its original inspirer or basis. This clearly distinguishes an act by a limited entity that is deviant and one that is compliant under *Brahmā*'s Vedic protection plan. More clarification of this work plan is given in the next verse.

एवं प्रवर्तितं चक्रं
नानुवर्तयतीह यः ।
अघायुरिन्द्रियारामो
मोघं पार्थ स जीवति ॥३.१६॥

evaṁ pravartitaṁ cakraṁ
nānuvartayatīha yaḥ
aghāyurindriyārāmo
moghaṁ pārtha sa jīvati (3.16)

evaṁ — thus; pravartitaṁ — perpetuated; cakraṁ — circular process; nānuvartayatīha = na — not + anuvartayati — cause to be perpetuated + iha — on earth; yaḥ — who; aghāyurindriyārāmo = aghāyurindriyārāmaḥ = aghāyuḥ — malicious + indriyārāmaḥ — sensually-happy person; moghaṁ — worthless; pārtha — son of Pṛthā; sa = saḥ — he; jīvati — lives

O son of Pṛthā, a person who does not cause this circular process to be perpetuated here on earth, lives as a malicious, sensually-happy and worthless person. (3.16)

Commentary:

By this definition, most of the human beings are ungrateful. It may be that we were not educated in the process laid down by *Brahmā*, but still our life method is described here as being *mogham*, or worthless, *indriyārāmas*, or reckless, and *aghāyus* or vicious towards ourselves, the other humans, the lower creatures, the supernatural people and the Supreme Lord.

It must mean also that there is an allowance for our deviant life style. Otherwise there would be no facility for us to deviate. Lord Krishna categorized us as being ungrateful because we do not assist in turning the circular process of invoking the supernaturals, endeavoring for a yield, returning the yield in a religious ceremony, getting the instruction from the supernaturals, executing it, and then being satisfied with whatever they award. What a system Krishna described! And how unfortunate we are to His view. Later on in the *Gītā* He gave details of how He enthuses the creation and causes even the rebellious entities to have acting energy. In that way He described Himself as the Lord of everything that be.

यस्त्वात्मरतिरेव स्याद्
आत्मतृप्तश्च मानवः ।
आत्मन्येव च संतुष्टस्
तस्य कार्यं न विद्यते ॥३.१७॥
yastvātmaratireva syād
ātmatṛptaśca mānavaḥ
ātmanyeva ca saṁtuṣṭas
tasya kāryaṁ na vidyate (3.17)

yastvātmaratireva = yas (yaḥ) — who + tv (tu) — but + ātma — spiritual self + ratir (ratiḥ) — pleased + eva — surely; syāt — should be; ātmatṛptaśca = ātma — self + tṛptaḥ — satisfied + ca — and; mānavaḥ — a human being; ātmanyeva = ātmany (ātmani) — in the self + eva — only; ca — and; saṁtuṣṭaḥ — content; tasya — of him; kāryaṁ — cultural duty; na — no; vidyate — it is experienced

A person who is spiritually-pleased, self-satisfied and internally-content, has no cultural duties. (3.17)

Commentary:

This statement of spiritual self-satisfaction of the spirit soul was indicated in Chapter Two by Lord Krishna when the Lord described the eternal nature of the soul. As an everlasting principle, the spirit does not need to endeavor for anything, at least not insofar as its existence is automatically maintained, regardless of its circumstantial position. At all times, the spirit is spirit. At all times, the spirit is in touch with the brahman or spiritual level of existence. But that does not mean that the spirit realizes this. For the realization, he must take a course of disciplines.

The spirit is a reality unto itself. This is why Lord Krishna spoke of its self-satisfaction. The spirit is so essential as a part of existence that it was not created at any stage, not even by God. But it does have an eternal relationship with God at all stages of existence.

The soul or *ātma*, the spirit, is so subtle that he may not even realize his own substantiality. This is the problem. Therefore material existence is an advantage to him in that it takes him out of that ignorance of himself and puts him into a condition of imagined survival, so that he may make a mock endeavor to exist comfortably. This is all afforded for self-realization.

Tṛptas and *samtuṣṭah* normally mean satisfied, pleased or content, but since *ātmaratis* is used it must be applied to spiritual satisfaction. *Ātma* means the spirit and *deha* means the body. When satisfaction is applied to the body, it is mundane, but when it is applied directly and exclusively to the spirit, it is of a transcendental nature, being entirely different to what satisfies the body.

This spiritual self-satisfaction is also popularly called *ānanda* or blissful, spiritual happiness. We will hear more of it from Lord Krishna.

नैव तस्य कृतेनार्थो
नाकृतेनेह कश्चन ।
न चास्य सर्वभूतेषु
कश्चिदर्थव्यपाश्रयः ॥३.१८॥

naiva tasya kṛtenārtho
nākṛteneha kaścana
na cāsya sarvabhūteṣu
kaścidarthavyapāśrayaḥ
(3.18)

naiva = na — not + eva — indeed; tasya — regarding him; kṛtenārtho = kṛtena — with action + artho (arthaḥ) — gain; nākṛteneha = na — not + akṛtena — with non-action + iha — in this case; kaścana — anyone; na — not; cāsya = ca — and + asya — of him; sarvabhūteṣu — in all mundane creatures; kaścit — any; arthavyapāśrayaḥ = artha — purpose + vyapāśrayaḥ — depending

The person who does not aspire for gain in an action or in an inaction, is not reliant on any mundane creature. (3.18)

Commentary:

This definition gives us some idea of how to judge a person's contentment to determine whether it is mundane or spiritual. A man might claim spiritual happiness but how can people know if he is truthful? Krishna gave a way to test. It is not what a man says about his happiness, but it is how he is motivated. If he is result-motivated, yield-conscious, then he is not situated in that spiritual happiness. It would be a different type of happiness, no matter what he says.

Kṛtenārtha means trying to get something (*artha*) from an action (*karma*), but every-action will have a result or yield. Even Lord Krishna expects a certain result from Arjuna and from the Battle of *Kurukṣetra*. Therefore, we cannot get rid of yield or result. It will be there. Nor can we get rid of our nature which compels us to act for reward. The mystery is solved by remembering what Lord Krishna told Arjuna about approaching the supernaturals for a mission. A man must be spiritually-situated within his nature to such a degree that he can afford to consult with the supernaturals and work for them on every occasion, free of charge, free of requiring a reward. Obviously, hardly any of us can act in this selfless way.

A man cannot, at any stage, just artificially or by hoping and praying or chanting or whatever, reach this level of spiritual satisfaction. It is impossible because our tendencies do not change that easily. We usually act on the basis of a result-motivated action. We are essentially yield-conscious. When we cannot easily perceive a reward, we refuse to act. A person's body, mind and emotions slow down as soon as he does not see the promised or imagined reward. We also regard each other as result-motivated beings. Even in the highest spiritual societies, children are encouraged with sweets and adults are pampered with cherished foods and rewards to keep them motivated. Who can deny this?

It is exactly so. Arjuna behaved like this in the beginning when he refused to act. He became paralyzed because he could not see an enjoyable result. He said, "No, Krishna, I cannot fight."

तस्मादसक्तः सततं
कार्यं कर्म समाचर ।
असक्तो ह्याचरन्कर्म
परमाप्नोति पूरुषः ॥३.१९॥

tasmādasaktaḥ satataṁ
kāryaṁ karma samācara
asakto hyācarankarma
paramāpnoti pūruṣaḥ (3.19)

tasmād = tasmāt — therefore; asaktaḥ — unattached; satataṁ — always; kāryaṁ — duty, required tasks; karma — action; samācara — perform; asakto = asaktaḥ — unattached; hyācarankarma = hy (hi) — indeed + ācaran — executing + karma — action; param — the highest stage; āpnoti — gets; pūruṣaḥ — a person

Therefore, being always unattached, perform the action which is your duty. By being detached and executing the required tasks, a person gets the highest stage. (3.19)

Commentary:

This status of being unattached at every step is not our situation in the conditioned stage, but it can be attained. Certainly!

Śrīla Bhaktivedanta Swami, our Vaishnava authority, gave *param* as *the Supreme*, but *Śrīla* Sridhara Maharaja gave *pure devotion of the highest type* and an alternate meaning of *the ultimate maturity of selfless action*.

We are in favor of the alternate one by Sridhara Maharaja. This meaning is completely in harmony with what Krishna explained to this point. He discussed selfless action, having to do with being perfectly situated in the everlasting spiritual nature of the soul and not having to hanker for mundane energies, being so rich in spirituality that one can afford to work continuously and freely for the supernatural people and the Supreme Lord.

कर्मणैव हि संसिद्धिम्
आस्थिता जनकादयः ।
लोकसंग्रहमेवापि
संपश्यन्कर्तुमर्हसि ॥३.२०॥

karmaṇaiva hi saṁsiddhim
āsthitā janakādayaḥ
lokasaṁgrahamevāpi
saṁpaśyankartumarhasi (3.20)

karmaṇaiva = karmaṇa — by cultural activities + eva — alone; hi — indeed; saṁsiddhim — perfection; āsthitā — attained; janakādayaḥ = janaka — Janaka + ādayaḥ — beginning with; lokasaṁgrahamevāpi = loka — world + saṁgraham — maintenance + eva — only + api — only; saṁpaśyan — seeing mentally; kartum — to act; arhasi — you should

Beginning with Janaka, perfection was attained by cultural activities alone. Seeing the necessity for world maintenance, you should act. (3.20)

Commentary:

This King Janaka was the father of *Sītādevī*, the wife of Lord *Rāma*. He was famous for having worked his way to perfection by perfectly executing his duty in the mood of the accomplished samkhya yogis. This mood was described in detail in the previous and present chapters.

By making this comparison, Lord Krishna encouraged Arjuna to fight as Janaka did. Sometimes we hear that the *Gītā* advocates non-violence but if we mean that it preaches an absolute non-violence to the material body, we have a misconception.

The example of Janaka is there, in that he did violence to the unruly. The *Gītā* teaches non-violence towards the soul only, even at the expense of the body. It never teaches in any verse full non-violence to the body. The mere idea that Lord Krishna incited Arjuna to fight even after Arjuna broke down in tears after assuming a passive stance, reveals the tone of the *Gītā*.

Janaka and kings like him forged their way to spiritual perfection by acting in the world and yet maintaining spiritual consciousness during involvements. Some of these kings mastered the samkhya process before assuming rulership. Some perfected the practice while ruling. It is not that they performed perfectly without mastering the samkhya process of detachment.

King Janaka was well known in his time. He was respected by masterful yogis like Vasishtha, the spiritual master of King Dasharatha, and by Vishvamitra, Lord Rāma's ballistics teacher who was a masterful yogi himself.

Janaka was himself a master of yoga practice but he performed his kingly duties anyway and applied his highly developed spirituality to worldly affairs and so forged his way to perfection without escaping from cultural duties.

The question is: Why does Lord Krishna feel that Arjuna could perform as well as Janaka? The answer is simple: Arjuna, too, like King Janaka, perfected the yoga austerities prior to the Battle of *Kurukṣetra*. The history of his austerities is given in the *Mahābhārata*. We will give a summary of those austerities so that readers can understand why Krishna felt that Arjuna was on par with Janaka and could apply himself like an accomplished samkhya yogi on the battlefield.

When King Yudhishthira was banished from the Kuru capital for thirteen years, there was a time when this king considered how he might regain the kingdom. While the Pandavas lived in the forest, Śrīla *Vyāsadeva*, the actual grandfather of Yudhishthira, came there. After being questioned by Yudhishthira, Vyāsaji recommended that Arjuna go to the Himalayas to perform certain austerities and to reach Lord Shiva and the Indra demigod, so that Arjuna could procure celestial weapons. Taking lessons from *Vyāsaji*, Yudhishthira taught Arjuna the austerities. Later on, Arjuna completed this. The description is in the Vana Parva. Once King Yudhishthira explained to Arjuna that all weaponry skill was invested in Bhishma, *Drona*, *Krpa* and *Aśvatthāmā*. The Pandavas had to strive to get more education on weaponry. Yudhishthira then passed on to Arjuna some information about how Arjuna would see all the dimensions in this world and by that, meet the various supernatural controllers, and get military techniques from them which would surpass the knowledge of the Kauravas. After Arjuna got this information, which was originally given to Yudhishthira by *Vyāsaji*, Arjuna left and travelled to the north. He reached the sacred Himavat where the celestials reside and met Indra who was disguised as a blazing ascetic. Indra told Arjuna to seek the blessings of Lord Shiva and then return.

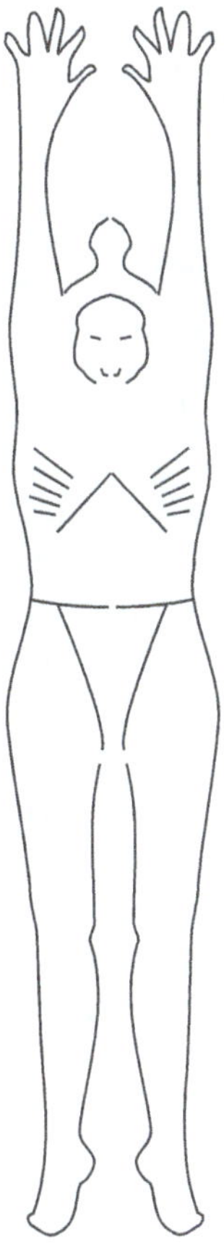

So Arjuna went further north to a Himalayan peak and began severe austerities.

Everyone who knows something about the Himalayas knows fully well that they are very icy. But in the time of Arjuna, the climate was more favorable. In any case, Arjuna began his austerities. His garments were made of grass straw and deerskin. He passed the first month eating fruit on every fourth night. This means that in the first month he ate fruit on seven or eight occasions. In the second month, he ate fruit every seventh day which means about four times only during that month. In the third month he ate only once every two weeks, meaning twice during the month. In the fourth month he lived on air alone with arms raised without support and balanced on his tiptoes. This particular posture is called *taḍāsana* palm tree.

Now anyone who knows anything about yoga knows fully well that Arjuna was practicing the highest stage of *prāṇāyāma* yoga. It is not that Arjuna was performing a religious fast or the twice per month ekādaśi fast. Arjuna was a master of *prāṇāyāma* nutrition. He did not need solid food or any type of earthly nourishment once he set himself seriously to practice. A person of that nature can very well follow in the footsteps of King Janaka.

The austerities of Arjuna caused the mountain to shake and smoke. Shiva then went in the guise of an aborigine hunter to check on Arjuna. A fight arose between them over a boar which each claimed as target. Arjuna was ultimately defeated and received Shiva's blessings and the gift of the Gandiva bow. Arjuna then went to Indra's celestial planet and received many other supernatural weapons needed to defeat the Kauravas in the pending war.

Readers should study this story and draw their own conclusions about why Lord Krishna compared Arjuna to Janaka and so incited Arjuna to realize that he could perform spiritually even on a battlefield in a civil war in which he would injure and kill relatives and friends, without having guilty feelings and incurring reactions.

In the Battle of *Kurukṣetra*, Arjuna was to act promptly, getting himself off the emotional plane, putting himself on the spiritual level, and setting an example by following Krishna's directions in terms of doing violence to any material body for the sake of the soul, who used it.

यद्यदाचरति श्रेष्ठस्
तत्तदेवेतरो जनः ।
स यत्प्रमाणं कुरुते
लोकस्तदनुवर्तते ॥३.२१॥
yadyadācarati śreṣṭhas
tattadevetaro janaḥ
sa yatpramāṇaṁ kurute
lokastadanuvartate (3.21)

yadyad — whatever; ācarati — does; śreṣṭhaḥ — the greatest; tattad = tad tad — this and that; evetaro (evetaraḥ) = eva — only + itaraḥ — the others; janaḥ — perform; sa = saḥ — he; yat — what; pramāṇaṁ — trend; kurute — establishes; lokastadanuvartate = lokaḥ — the world + tad — that + anuvartate — pursues

Whatever a great person does, for that only, others aspire. Whatever trend he establishes, the world pursues. (3.21)

<u>*Commentary:*</u>

As the Lord told Arjuna in Chapter Two, text 32;

yadṛcchayā copapannaṁ svargadvāramapāvṛtam
sukhinaḥ kṣatriyāḥ pārtha labhante yuddhamīdṛśam (2.32)

And by a stroke of luck, the gate of heaven is opened. Thrilled are the warriors who get such a battle opportunity, O son of Pṛthā. (2.32)

Arjuna should take the opportunity to fight heroically. And besides, if Arjuna assumed a detached mood, it would inspire others to do likewise, to free themselves from the same type of emotional muddlement which afflicted Arjuna when his knees buckled under. If Arjuna were to serve Krishna as the agent of the Lord for chastising the unruly Kauravas, then others might be inspired for righteous life style from his example.

न मे पार्थास्ति कर्तव्यं
त्रिषु लोकेषु किंचन ।
नानवाप्तमवाप्तव्यं
वर्त एव च कर्मणि ॥३.२२॥
na me pārthāsti kartavyaṁ
triṣu lokeṣu kiṁcana
nānavāptamavāptavyaṁ
varta eva ca karmaṇi (3.22)

na — not; me — of me; pārthāsti = pārtha — O son of Pṛthā + asti — is; kartavyaṁ — should be done; triṣu — in the three divisions; lokeṣu — in the universe; kiṁcana — anything specific; nānavāptamavāptavyaṁ = na — not + anavāptam — not attained + avāptavyam — to be acquired; varta — I function; eva — yet; ca — and; karmaṇi — in cultural activities

For Me, O son of Pṛthā, there is nothing specific that must be done in the three divisions of the universe. And there is nothing that I have not attained nor should acquire, and yet I function in cultural activities. (3.22)

Commentary:

The question: "What is the benefit for Lord Krishna?" is answered here in part. The complete answer will be given later on. After all, there must be some benefit for the Lord, but it is not something mundane nor is it a sensual craving. Lord Krishna spoke of it in Chapter Four. In this chapter leading statements are given.

This statement is in response to Arjuna's remark in Chapter One:

aho bata mahatpāpaṁ kartuṁ vyavasitā vayam
yadrājyasukhalobhena hantuṁ svajanamudyatāḥ (1.44)

O! What a wonder! We are committed to perform a great sin, being eager to kill our kinfolk, through greed for aristocratic pleasures. (1.44)

Lord Krishna cleared Himself of any motivation to share in the spoils of the war. His interest is not wealth and political power (*rājyasukha*).

There is a technicality, however, because Lord Krishna must act in this world. God has to act and God has to motivate others to perform as we will read in another verse. But God does not have to act impulsively or under the force of consequences as we do. He does not have to be part of the consequential life we are living but He may enter into it and rectify us as a matter of duty since the overall responsibility is His. Some seem to think that He is free to act or not to act but such a statement is a rationalization only, in an effort to justify a false idea, or to enjoy thinking of God as being totally independent of such duties. God must create the world to give us opportunity for progress. And He must help us to progress spiritually. He does have self-imposed duties which are stipulated by His very nature of being the fully-responsible Supreme Being. Lord Krishna will, Himself, explained this in the *Gītā*.

Krishna's work is free from the fruitive or rewarding-hankering urges that mobilize us. That is the difference. This is one of the main reasons why the great sages follow Krishna. It is due to His hanker-free attitude.

यदि ह्यहं न वर्तेयं
जातु कर्मण्यतन्द्रितः ।
मम वर्त्मानुवर्तन्ते
मनुष्याः पार्थ सर्वशः ॥३.२३॥
yadi hyahaṁ na varteyaṁ
jātu karmaṇyatandritaḥ
mama vartmānuvartante
manuṣyāḥ pārtha sarvaśaḥ (3.23)

yadi — if; hyahaṁ = hy (hi) — perchance + ahaṁ — I; na — not; varteyaṁ — should perform; jātu — ever; karmaṇyatandritaḥ = karmaṇy (karmaṇi) — in work + atandritaḥ — attentively; mama — of me, my; vartmānuvartante = vartma — pattern + anuvartante — they follow; manuṣyāḥ — human beings; pārtha — O son of Pṛthā; sarvaśaḥ — in all respects

If perchance, I did not perform attentively, then all human beings, O son of Pṛthā, would follow Me in all respects. (3.23)

Commentary:

This is a direct reason for the acting part played by the Lord. Here Lord Krishna explained this in all seriousness. It is a responsibility of the Supreme Being to set the proper example since the dependent limited spirits can only idolize and follow behind the Lord. God acts freely, but He is well aware of responsibilities. The connection is that the agents of God, persons like Arjuna, must cooperate with the Lord to assist in His soul saving work.

उत्सीदेयुरिमे लोका
न कुर्यां कर्म चेदहम् ।
संकरस्य च कर्ता स्याम्
उपहन्यामिमाः प्रजाः ॥३.२४॥
utsīdeyurime lokā
na kuryāṁ karma cedaham
saṁkarasya ca kartā syām
upahanyāmimāḥ prajāḥ (3.24)

utsīdeyur = utsīdeyuh — would perish; ime — these; lokā — worlds; na — not; kuryāṁ — I should engage; karma — cultural activity; cedaham = cet — if + aham — I; saṁkarasya — of the social chaos; ca — and; kartā — producer; syām — I should be; upahanyām — I should destroy; imāḥ — these; prajāḥ — creatures

If I should not engage in cultural activity, these worlds would perish. And I would be a producer of social chaos. I would have destroyed these creatures. (3.24)

Commentary:

Lord Krishna's motives are directly spelled out in these verses and was explained further in Chapter Four, where the Lord gave more details. Arjuna wanted a reason to fight. Now he is told of the basis of the responsibility.

God is so essential to the universal situation that if He did not enthuse energy into the world, it would go out like a blown light bulb. And as He stated, He would be responsible for the ensuing chaos. The Lord did not want to be the cause of chaos and social confusion (*samkarasya*). Arjuna was the first to mention confusion (*varṇasamkārah*) in Chapter One, text 41, but Arjuna spoke of confusion after the battle. Lord Krishna is concerned about universal chaos (*lokā samkarah*) and not just a battle aftermath, nor the limited crisis of the Kauravas thereafter.

In text 23 of this chapter, the word *atandritah* occurs. This means alert, unwearied, carefully, vigilant, and responsible. In trying to strip Lord Krishna of His rational (*cit*) nature and in trying to attribute Him with only His spiritual pleasure (*ānanda*), some say that He does all this for His sweet pleasure. But the rational nature or the sober, responsible feature of the Lord functions just as well as His spiritual pleasure. Both have their applications. In the material world, the sober, responsible nature has an importance in terms of assisting us to become free of gross ignorance.

सक्ताः कर्मण्यविद्वांसो
यथा कुर्वन्ति भारत ।
कुर्याद्विद्वांस्तथासक्तश्
चिकीर्षुर्लोकसंग्रहम् ॥३.२५॥
saktāḥ karmaṇyavidvāṁso
yathā kurvanti bhārata
kuryādvidvāṁstathāsaktaś
cikīrṣurlokasaṁgraham (3.25)

saktāḥ — attached; karmaṇyavidvāṁso = karmaṇyavidvāṁsaḥ = karmaṇi — in activities + avidvāṁsaḥ — unintelligent; yathā — as; kurvanti — they act; bhārata — O son of the Bharata family; kuryād = kuryāt — he should perform; vidvāṁs — the wise person; tathāsaktaś = tathā — so + asaktaḥ — detached; cikīrṣur = cikīrṣuḥ — intending to do; lokasaṁgraham = loka — society + saṁgraham — maintenance

As the unintelligent people perform with attachment to cultural activity, O son of the Bharata family, so the wise person should act, but in a detached manner, for the maintenance of society. (3.25)

Commentary:

The contrast between the foolish and the wise is shown. This relates to the stipulation of *Brahmā* that the humans should first consult with the supernaturals, then work under their direction for yields, then go back to the supernaturals when the yields come and get instruction for usage. But the foolish persons will not do this. They, being impulsively involved (*saktah*) in the activities (*karmani*), cannot stop to consult with the supernaturals. They act wildly without superior guidance. And who are these foolish people (*avidvāms*)? They are you and me, the reward-motivated, hankering individuals.

Since we do not have a developed contemplative tendency, we must work our way out of material existence. The Lord sends His agents like Arjuna to show us how to keep working and still become detached along the way. We instinctively go through the motions of work and gradually by association with Arjuna and others like him, we develop detachment. By this, we develop an interest in the yoga disciplines of the samkhya yogis. And then after many, many lives, we would become genuine human beings like the mind-born sons of *Brahmā*.

After explaining His responsibility for the world, Lord Krishna advised the wise men (*vidvāms*) to work for social order. Krishna expects the wise men to be responsible. He praised King Janaka and others who willingly and enthusiastically cooperated with Him.

न बुद्धिभेदं जनयेद्
अज्ञानां कर्मसङ्गिनाम् ।
जोषयेत्सर्वकर्माणि
विद्वान्युक्तः समाचरन् ॥ ३.२६ ॥
na buddhibhedaṁ janayed
ajñānāṁ karmasaṅginām
joṣayetsarvakarmāṇi
vidvānyuktaḥ samācaran (3.26)

na — *not; buddhibhedaṁ* = *buddhi* — *intelligence* + *bhedaṁ* — *breaking (broken intelligence, indetermination); janayet* — *should produce; ajñānāṁ* — *of the simpletons; karmasaṅginām* — *of those attached to action; joṣayet* — *should inspire to be satisfied; sarvakarmāṇi* — *all actions; vidvān* — *the wise person; yuktaḥ* — *disciplined; samācaran* — *performing*

One should not produce indetermination in the minds of the simpletons. A wise person should inspire them to be satisfied by action. The wise one should be disciplined in behavior. (3.26)

Commentary:

A stricture is given for the wise men who know that impulsive work is implicating and not liberating. Impulsive work does not lead one out of material existence but into it, in a deeper, more captivating way. Still, knowing this, a wise man who is detached, should not rashly try to alert the common people to their foolishness.

Ideally, every man should take up the disciplines of the samkhya yogis. Until one does so, one will remain as a *kāmakāmī*, a sensually-motivated, reward-grabbing person. Still, people cannot suddenly shift from materially-binding activities to spiritually-freeing ones. They must do so gradually through long association. A wise man must therefore befriend them and gradually convince them to curb the reward-grabbing profile. Then they will, in the course of time, become contemplative and detached.

Even though work, especially battlefield work, is fraught with danger and is troublesome, both physically and emotionally, Lord Krishna rejected Arjuna's proposal to give up duties. The Lord suggested that Arjuna work in a detached mood. In the *Gītā*, Arjuna was the one to state that the Kauravas were short-sighted people who wanted to fight impulsively without assessing the consequences. He said:

yadyapyete na paśyanti lobhopahatacetasaḥ
kulakṣayakṛtaṁ doṣaṁ mitradrohe ca pātakam (1.37)
kathaṁ na jñeyamasmābhiḥ pāpādasmānnivartitum
kulakṣayakṛtaṁ doṣaṁ prapaśyadbhirjanārdana (1.38)

Even if these persons, their minds being possessed by greed, do not see the fault caused by the destruction of the clan and the crime of hurting a friend,

...O motivator of human beings, why, by due reason, should we not understand that we should turn back from this sin, the crime caused by the destruction of the clan? (1.37-38)

Here Arjuna addressed the Kauravas as *lobhopahata-cetasah*, people with greed-oriented consciousness. He addressed himself and his men as being *jñeyam pāpād*, being sensible regarding faults, recognizing what was wrong. But Lord Krishna said that even so, the Pandavas were not to run away but were to fight just as enthusiastically as the Kauravas. The Pandavas were to do so with detachment, without hankering for rewards, and for the purpose of serving Lord Krishna in His mission of keeping order in human society.

As the Vaishnava authorities have always contended, the entire *Gītā* is directed in a way to show that everyone should surrender to Krishna. Now we see that their idea is correct, since all the ideas of Lord Krishna thus far are converging into a surrender to Him, in the performance of the devotional service of helping the Lord with His responsibilities.

The direct meaning for Arjuna is that he was not to leave the battlefield, nor to act in a way that would motivate other warriors to renounce the battle. After all, most of the other warriors did not have a history of the gruesome austerities Arjuna endured. Arjuna was to fight just as intended but his mood of combat was to be different. His external stance of fighting would be similar to the Kauravas, but the similarity would stop there because his attitude would be diametrically opposed to theirs. Instead of fighting to gain a country, money and political control, he would fight to establish a righteous government.

प्रकृतेः क्रियमाणानि
गुणैः कर्माणि सर्वशः ।
अहंकारविमूढात्मा
कर्ताहमिति मन्यते ॥ ३.२७॥
prakṛteḥ kriyamāṇāni
guṇaiḥ karmāṇi sarvaśaḥ
ahaṁkāravimūḍhātmā
kartāhamiti manyate (3.27)

prakṛteḥ — of the primal mundane energy; kriyamāṇāni — performed; guṇaiḥ — by the variations; karmāṇi — actions; sarvaśaḥ — in all cases; ahaṁkāravimūḍhātmā = ahaṁkāra — falsely-asserted identity + vimūḍha — confused + ātmā — self; kartāham = kartā — performer + aham — I; iti — thus; manyate — he thinks

In all cases, actions are performed by variations of the primal mundane energy. But the identity-confused person thinks: "I am the performer." (3.27)

Commentary:

Some Vaishnava commentators and their followers understand this to mean that action of conditioned beings is under the jurisdiction of material nature but not the action of unconditioned souls nor those of Lord Krishna. They attribute a special transcendence to the actions of the Lord or the actions of empowered divine agents and their assistants. However, this verse is Krishna's direct speech to Arjuna and it supersedes anything that any of the commentators might say, which is inconsistent. In line 2, we find the word *sarvaśah*, which means in all cases, in entirety. *Śrīla* Bhaktivedanta Swami has given an entirely different meaning for the words as *all kinds of*, but we are compliant with Sridhara Maharaja who gave the meaning of, *in all ways*.

Even Lord Krishna must make a material impact if He is to have an effect on our gross attitude in this world. Even He, picked up a gross chariot wheel, once, during the Battle of *Kurukṣetra*, to do gross damage to General Bhishma. All the mundane activities, regardless of whether they are performed by the Supreme Lord or by the limited entities, involve the use of the mundane energy (*prakṛteh*). But the technicality concerns not the use of the energy but the motive in such use. This was already discussed in the previous verses where Lord Krishna spoke of acting for the welfare of the world in terms of His mission and in acting for the sake of cravings as in the case of our conditioned selves. In either case, such actions involve mundane energies, and it is so in all cases (*sarvaśah*).

Variations in the power of material nature (*guṇah*) are expressed through three general classifications as dulling, enthusing or clarifying influences. The lowest are the dulling ones, the median are the enthusing ones, the highest are the clarifying ones. The divine people do use matter. They certainly do. They use it when they have to relate to the matter-attracted entities.

Certain preachers try to protect the integrity of God by stating that God does not handle matter. But there is no necessity to spare God such pains because God is not affected even when He handles matter. He is that transcendental. In our case, we are affected by a slight touch of the materials. God is different. He should not be gauged by our limitations. We do God no favor by declaring that He does not use matter, especially since He certainly does when relating to lowly beings who cannot be educated by Him, except through the use of the material energies.

The identity-confused persons feel that they are the prime movers in this world. They feel that they are the permanent features here. They are influenced by and used by material nature. They are not as directive of matter as they would like to be. But Lord Krishna and His assistants are directive. Their position in relationship to matter is one of a greater degree of control. But Theirs is not an absolute control because material nature is an eternal reality unto itself. Even for the divine people, there is some adjustment that must be made in dealing with matter because of matter's inherent qualities. Still the divinities display the greatest percentage of control.

A confused entity feels that he has more control than he is capable of. Thus he miscalculates greatly and becomes more and more involved in a struggle to release himself from the reactions forced on him by material nature. But the Lord does not become entangled in that way, while His assistants like Arjuna become a little entangled periodically and are abruptly released by the grace of the Lord.

तत्त्ववित्तु महाबाहो
गुणकर्मविभागयोः।
गुणा गुणेषु वर्तन्त
इति मत्वा न सज्जते ॥३.२८॥
tattvavittu mahābāho
guṇakarmavibhāgayoḥ
guṇā guṇeṣu vartanta
iti matvā na sajjate (3.28)

tattvavit — reality-perceiving person; tu — but; mahābāho — O powerful man; guṇakarmavibhāgayoḥ = guṇa — moods of nature + karma — action + vibhāgayoḥ — in two-fold basis; guṇa — the variation of material nature; guṇeṣu — in the variations of material nature; vartanta — they interact; iti — thus; matvā — having thought; na — no; sajjate — is attached

But, O powerful man, having considered that variations of material nature interact with variations of material nature, the reality-perceiving person is not attached to action. (3.28)

Commentary:

The *tattvavit* is the person who perceives reality as it is. *Tattva* means reality. Reality is independent of our perception or understanding of it. It does not make accommodation for our misconceptions. It is totally independent of our assessments.

As stated by Lord Krishna, the single, most powerful motivator in this world is material nature (*prakṛteh*). This cannot be denied. But as an offshoot of this, there are moods of material nature. The actions are enacted under the influence or through the manifestations of these moods. Thus from material nature, we get moods. From the moods, actions are manifested. Actions, however, are not purely material. The moods of nature are purely material but the actions are a combination of spiritual power and those mundane influences.

Understanding that material nature is a powerful influence, the *samyamīs* (disciplined sages) do not become attached to anything. Material nature is a non-reliable energy. A sober person does not put his trust in it. He does not become attached to such a shifty influence.

प्रकृतेर्गुणसंमूढाः
सज्जन्ते गुणकर्मसु।
तानकृत्स्नविदो मन्दात्
कृत्स्नविन्न विचालयेत् ॥ ३.२९ ॥
prakṛterguṇasaṁmūḍhāḥ
sajjante guṇakarmasu
tānakṛtsnavido mandāt
kṛtsnavinna vicālayet (3.29)

prakṛter = prakṛteḥ — of subtle material nature; guṇasaṁmūḍhāḥ = guṇa — variations of material nature + saṁmūḍhāḥ — deluded people; sajjante — they are attached; guṇakarmasu — in the mood-motivated activities; tān — them; akṛtsnavido = akṛtsnavidaḥ — partially-knowing; mandāt — foolish people; kṛtsnavin — the person who understands the whole reality; na — not; vicālayet — should unsettle

Those who are deluded by the variations of material nature are attached to mood-motivated activities. The person who understands the reality should not unsettle those foolish people who have partial insight. (3.29)

Commentary:

The *kṛtsnavit* are those in complete knowledge of the whole. Previously Lord Krishna addressed them as the *tattvadarśis*. In this case, however, there is a subtle distinction. The *tattvadarśis* are those great souls who are reserved from worldly life and who, if they were in the social flow of history, would see circumstances in real divine terms. But the *kṛtsnavits* are those who are active or world-participating *tattvadarśis*. They are on the scene just as common people are; they are involved socially, but they see the reality as they participate. King Janaka, who was cited in text 20, was such a person. Krishna suggested that Arjuna follow the example of that ancient king.

The rule is this: So long as a reality-perceiving man is in the social flow, he should act like Janaka. He should participate with a detached mood. If he cannot become involved, he should go into isolation as prescribed elsewhere in the *Gītā*. If he is in the flow of history, he is prohibited from encouraging worldly people to be lazy or to act as if they were contemplative yogis or ascetics. Instead he is supposed to act in a way that spurs them on but he should do so with a detached mood, observing how they function and advising them how to remove faulty actions, replacing these with pious activities and high-class devotional services. All this is described in great detail by Lord Krishna.

The *akṛtsnavida* are the people who have no knowledge of reality or who have little information about it. They are prone to miscalculation because they are stupefied by the modes of material nature (*guṇasammūḍhāh*). These modes operate within their minds and feelings, manifesting as impractical ideas and impulsive cravings.

It is important to understand that these people cannot be freed instantly. There is no point in thinking that any of them can, all of a sudden, become contemplative ascetics. It was explained by Lord Krishna elsewhere that a man is impulsively driven by tendencies. He can be freed but only gradually. He must work his way out of it. He cannot jump out of it suddenly. We have seen and heard of souls who suddenly and permanently removed themselves from the influence of material nature, but these were great souls in their previous lives. Their sudden departure from worldliness was not really a rapid conversion, but was rather a sudden awakening back into their natural condition of being seers of reality (*tattvadarśis*).

In that sense, persons like Gautama Buddha, who all of a sudden departed from a life of luxury and who attained spiritual enlightenment abruptly, did not set an example for others. Such people, like Buddha, produced by their life style, a most rare display of abrupt spirituality. The average person will be thoroughly and surely frustrated if he were to follow the course taken by Buddha. He had better take the course shown by persons like King Janaka, the history-participating *tattvadarśis*, or the *kṛtsnavidas*.

मयि सर्वाणि कर्माणि
संन्यस्याध्यात्मचेतसा ।
निराशीर्निर्ममो भूत्वा
युध्यस्व विगतज्वरः ॥३.३०॥
mayi sarvāṇi karmāṇi
saṁnyasyādhyātmacetasā
nirāśīrnirmamo bhūtvā
yudhyasva vigatajvaraḥ (3.30)

mayi — to me; sarvāṇi — all; karmāṇi — working power; saṁnyasyādhyātmacetasā = saṁnyasya — entrusting + adhyātmacetasā — by meditation on the Supreme Spirit; nirāśīr — from cravings; nirmamo = nirmamaḥ — indifferent to selfishness; bhūtvā — being; yudhyasva — do fight; vigatajvaraḥ = vigata — departed + jvaraḥ — feverish mood

All your working power should be entrusted to Me. On the Supreme Spirit, you should meditate. Being free from cravings, indifferent to selfishness, do fight. Be a man whose feverish mood has departed. (3.30)

Commentary:

This is similar to what *Brahmā* told his mind-born sons. He instructed that they approach the agents of the Lord for directions. In this case, the Lord Himself directly tells a human being to surrender the working power (*karmāṇi*). Arjuna was to act after consulting Krishna, Who would direct him in the use of his power. If we look at this from our view, it means that Krishna wants us to ignore all impulsion. Instead of acting as our nature directs, Krishna desires that we reserve the acting power and use it as He recommended.

In the second line of the verse, He supported this idea by instructing that we think of (*cetasā*) the Supreme Spirit, Himself (*ādhyātma*). This is in contrast to dwelling on everything else that we encounter in material nature.

Lord Krishna mercifully and informatively laid out the conditions of mind and feelings under which we could consistently report to Him for instructions on how to use our acting power without yield-motivated cravings and without possessiveness. This is a complete renunciation of the conditioned nature. Obviously, such an accomplishment would be gradual. The Lord gave various methods of attaining it. Arjuna was to get rid of the emotional level which affected him when he saw the two armies in the reckless battle mood. Arjuna quickly complied with that instruction because he was a great soul who was capable of a sudden reversal of the conditioned weakened mentality. But what is practical for Arjuna may not be accomplished that easily by others

ये मे मतमिदं नित्यम्
अनुतिष्ठन्ति मानवाः ।
श्रद्धावन्तोऽनसूयन्तो
मुच्यन्ते तेऽपि कर्मभिः ॥३.३१॥
ye me matamidaṁ nityam
anutiṣṭhanti mānavāḥ
śraddhāvanto'nasūyanto
mucyante te'pi karmabhiḥ (3.31)

ye — whosoever; me — My; matam — idea; idam — this; nityam — constantly; anutiṣṭhanti — they apply; mānavāḥ — human beings; śraddhāvanto=śraddhāvantaḥ — having faith; 'nasūyanto = anasūyantaḥ — not complaining; mucyante — are freed; te — they; 'pi = api — also; karmabhiḥ — from the consequences of actions

Those human beings, who believe My idea, constantly applying it, having faith, not complaining, are freed from the consequences of action. (3.31)

Commentary:

A technique is given here by Lord Krishna, but this one is for souls who are expert in soul control and behavioral disciplines. Elsewhere in the *Gītā*, the Lord will give more elementary methods. It is informative, however, to know that we must first believe in this idea of the Lord. We are required to have faith in His assurances. Krishna particularly says Me, *matam*, which means: *My view, My idea, My plan, My scheme of things*. In addition, we should prevent ourselves from grumbling or complaining. This will be quite an accomplishment for any of us. Even Arjuna grumbled about having to fight and he is a great soul capable of performing like King Janaka.

If however, we can practice this partially or perfectly, we would be free from consequences of actions proportionately. The clarification is: All actions, even those of Lord Krishna, or of His agents and then assistants, do carry reactions. But an actor is free from the liabilities if he complies with Krishna as explained in the verse. Material nature will react regardless of whether the actor is a divinity, an agent of the divine, or a rebel towards the supreme will. Only those persons who act for the Lord as instructed by Him, are free from liabilities. This applies to both kind and vicious acts. All actions bring consequences which bind the actor if he is not sanctioned by the Lord and if he is not acting on behalf of the Lord. In addition we must realize that a materially-kind act may be harmful to the spirit and a materially-vicious one, may assist it. Actions are not to be gauged only by their material impact. This will be clarified in other parts of the *Gītā*.

Actors are forewarned, however, that actions done by the advice of divine or human personalities, will bear consequences for the actor if such are done by the actor for the actor. Let us understand this. If one has a plan of action or if one consciously or unconsciously pretends to act for the Lord, while in fact, one acts for himself, then even if he took advice from the Lord, the agent of the Lord, or the scripture, he must face the liabilities.

To escape liabilities, two requirements must be met, namely:

1. *The advice of the Lord or of His agent or the scripture, must be procured.*
2. *The act must be the expressed will of the Lord for the actor to serve on behalf of the Lord.*

A compliance with this has nothing to do with being in a spiritual society or religious organization. A man of good standing in such an organization may assume that he is acting for the Lord, while in fact, he may be acting for himself. He may have even procured the advice or sanction of the Deity of the Lord, or of a divine agent, or of the scripture, but if the act was for himself he must face the liabilities. Thus indeed, the laws of consequences face us at every step when we are not 100% in touch with the divine will as servants of that power.

Spiritual masters the world over, those believing in Krishna and those who do not regard Him, may play with these rules. Their disciples may sing their glories confidently for a long time to come but none of them can actually bypass these procedures. No one can waive these, but naive disciples may be fooled because they cannot see into the distant future to understand the connection between actions of this life and delayed reactions which are to come in another.

ये त्वेतदभ्यसूयन्तो
नानुतिष्ठन्ति मे मतम् ।
सर्वज्ञानविमूढांस्तान्
विद्धि नष्टानचेतसः ॥३.३२॥
ye tvetadabhyasūyanto
nānutiṣṭhanti me matam
sarvajñānavimūḍhāṁstān
viddhi naṣṭānacetasaḥ (3.32)

ye — who; tvetad = tv (tu) — but + etad — this; abhyasūyanto = abhyasūyantaḥ — discrediting; nānutiṣṭhanti = na — not + anutiṣṭhanti — they practise; me — My; matam — idea; sarvajñānavimūḍhāṁs = sarva — all + jñāna — insight + vimūḍhāṁs — muddled; tān — them; viddhi — know; naṣṭān — jinxed; acetasaḥ — senseless

Know that those who discredit this instruction and do not practice My ideas, being of muddled insight, are jinxed and senseless. (3.32)

Commentary:

This means that if we do not follow the Lord's instruction, we may still get a yield or result, but our lives will be haphazard. We will not be able to consolidate on what we achieve. Being crazed and senseless, psychotic and schizophrenic, our plans will bring ruination sooner or later, even though we may prosper for a time. Since we may not see how material nature functions, we will miscalculate and will be baffled at some point.

There is a key to this verse, however, that of resenting the instructions of the Lord. This is connected to what *Brahmā* said to his mind-born sons about first consulting the supernatural controllers. If we resent following this process of consultation, we are bound to suffer sooner or later.

It may be natural to feel uneasy about these stipulations which for the most part are a threat to our desired independence. Still we should check our feelings and consider the benefits offered; freedom from the liabilities is a big benefit for any limited being. The liabilities are a serious risk to our continued happiness.

Sir Paul Castagna repeatedly brought it to our attention that these conditions laid down by Lord Krishna are hard to hear and the stipulations put on by the Lord or by *Brahmā* are unreasonable when we consider our natural condition as yield-hungry beings or reward-seeking creatures. However, Sir Paul and all the beings whom he represents, should still consider the advantages of Krishna's offer as contrasted to the disadvantages which go with the so-called independent way. As will be proven by the Lord, our independence is myth. It simply does not exist. What we call independence is just the accustomed dependence on material nature.

सदृशं चेष्टते स्वस्याः
प्रकृतेर्ज्ञानवानपि ।
प्रकृतिं यान्ति भूतानि
निग्रहः किं करिष्यति ॥३.३३॥
sadṛśaṁ ceṣṭate svasyāḥ
prakṛterjñānavānapi
prakṛtiṁ yānti bhūtāni
nigrahaḥ kiṁ kariṣyati (3.33)

sadṛśam — according to; ceṣṭate — one acts; svasyāḥ — from one's own; prakṛter = prakṛteḥ — from material nature; jñānavān — wise man; api — also; prakṛtiṁ — material nature; yānti — they submit; bhūtāni — the creatures; nigrahaḥ — restraint; kiṁ — what; kariṣyati — will do

A human being, even a wise man, acts according to his material nature. The creatures submit to the material nature. What will restraint do? (3.33)

Commentary:

Arjuna felt that he could leave the battlefield and adopt an ascetic life permanently but Lord Krishna repeatedly explained that such an attempt would ultimately fail. A law of psychology is stated here: An individual usually acts on the basis of his normal response to material nature. It does not matter if he is wise or foolish. He will still act by habit. Due to long association with material nature, a certain stance towards her developed. A human acts in certain ways repeatedly. Later on in the *Gītā*, Lord Krishna explained how material nature feeds upon or takes nourishment from the living entities. The connection with material nature is one of intimate victimization. At least it is so while we are conditioned. The Lord stated that in comparison, the normal responses will override restraint. If Arjuna were to go to the forest, he would return to fight to fulfill normal tendency. Previously when Arjuna took to ascetic life, his motivation was to gain power to fight the Kauravas. If he went to the forest during the battle, he would not be successful because his nature would assert itself. Thus he would return to be a combatant.

There is a way out of the dilemma but it is not the way of escape. One has to stand ground and perform with detachment, just as the ancient King Janaka did. That is the only way. Then gradually, one may alter deep-seated tendencies. It took King *Viśvāmitra* thousands of years of adjustment to change his nature. He performed some very difficult austerities to accomplish the transformation. Our acquired nature cannot be changed abruptly. If Lord Krishna admits this, then no man, no preacher, no religious leader can prove the contrary. Lord Krishna has the most persuasive power, the most saving grace. If He admits that our nature can only be changed gradually and that an abrupt process will not work, then He indirectly informed us of the necessity to apply improvements steadily. It will take consistent effort to change. Restraint must be used but we should not expect the restraint to work abruptly. It will only work gradually over an extended period. There are cases of sustained abrupt releases from the influence of material nature but such histories are spectacular and rare.

इन्द्रियस्येन्द्रियस्यार्थे
रागद्वेषौ व्यवस्थितौ ।
तयोर्न वशमागच्छेत्
तौ ह्यस्य परिपन्थिनौ ॥३.३४॥
indriyasyendriyasyārthe
rāgadveṣau vyavasthitau
tayorna vaśamāgacchet
tau hyasya paripanthinau (3.34)

indriyasyendriyasyārthe = indriyasya — of a sense organ + indriyasya — of a sense organ + arthe — in an attractive object; rāgadveṣau = rāga — the response of liking + dveṣau — the response of disliking; vyavasthitau — deep-seated; tayor = tayoḥ — of these two; na — not; vaśam — power; āgacchet — should be influenced; tau — two; hyasya = hy (hi) — indeed + asya — of him; paripanthinau — two hindrances

The response of liking or disliking that is felt between a sense and an attractive object, is deep-seated. One should not be influenced by the power of these two moods. They are hindrances. (3.34)

Commentary:

Another method of transcending the feelings and ideas that emanate from material nature is given. This is another approach which we might use to gradually transcend and overcome material nature on an individual basis.

The response of a particular sense organ to a favored sense object can be predicted because the feeling occurs over and over. It is ingrained. For instance, a man's tongue likes sugar and a cow's tongue likes grass. This can be predicted. We do not have to test this. When in a romantic mood, one partner likes the sexual polarity of the other. This is obvious. But Lord Krishna advised that to change our nature we should avoid the encouraging and discouraging responses of the senses. This means that the tongue of a man will like sugar and dislike a bitter medicine, but the man must practice detachment from the liking or disliking selections.

The sensual polarity is a hindrance to our quest for freedom from materialistic dominance. This does not mean, however, that a time will come when the tongue will not like sugar. A devotee should develop detachment from the sensual selections. The soul should break the reliance on sensual dictation. It should develop an independence whereby it can direct the tongue to something sweet or something bitter for the overall benefit of the body, rather than to gorge on sweet foods only and ruin the body. Unless there is detachment, we cannot cultivate a resistance to the moods of material nature nor to the negative and positive polarity of sensual responses.

श्रेयान्स्वधर्मो विगुणः
परधर्मात्स्वनुष्ठितात् ।
स्वधर्मे निधनं श्रेयः
परधर्मो भयावहः ॥३.३५॥
śreyānsvadharmo viguṇaḥ
paradharmātsvanuṣṭhitāt
svadharme nidhanaṁ śreyaḥ
paradharmo bhayāvahaḥ (3.35)

śreyān — better; svadharmo = svadharmaḥ — one's righteous duty; viguṇaḥ — imperfect; paradharmāt — than the righteous duty of another; svanuṣṭhitāt = sv (su) — good, great + anuṣṭhitāt — than done; svadharme — in one's righteous duty; nidhanaṁ — death; śreyaḥ — it is better; paradharmo = paradharmaḥ — righteous duty of another; bhayāvahaḥ = bhaya — risk + āvahaḥ — bringing on

Better to do one's righteous duty imperfectly, than to do the duty of another with great efficiency. Death is better in the course of one's duty but the task of another is risky. (3.35)

Commentary:

Arjuna wanted to take a contemplative course, so as to avoid his life's duty as a lawman and warrior. Lord Krishna alerted him to the risks involved. For a man to become injured in the discharge of his duty is more beneficial for his soul's future, than for him to do the job of another with great efficiency. Doing the work of another brings on a psychic danger (*bhayāvahah*). It is risky. We will hear more of that risk in other verses of the *Gītā*. If in the process of assisting another, one neglects his duty, he subjects himself to supernatural disapproval and thus imperils his destiny in the same or the next life.

As stated in this chapter, the supernaturals have some expectations of the human beings. If we plan a contrary course, we may receive a backlash. This presents a certain danger. In addition, we will have to deal with those human beings and departed souls who become displaced by our neglect of obligations. All this might be too much for any of us to bear.

अर्जुन उवाच
अथ केन प्रयुक्तोऽयं
पापं चरति पूरुषः ।
अनिच्छन्नपि वार्ष्णेय
बलादिव नियोजितः ॥ ३.३६ ॥
arjuna uvāca
atha kena prayukto'yaṁ
pāpaṁ carati pūruṣaḥ
anicchannapi vārṣṇeya
balādiva niyojitaḥ (3.36)

arjuna — Arjuna; uvāca — said; atha — then; kena — by what?; prayukto = prayuktaḥ — forced; 'yaṁ = ayam — this; pāpaṁ — evil; carati — commits; pūruṣaḥ — a person; anicchannapi = anicchan — unwilling + napi (api) — even; vārṣṇeya — family man of the Vṛṣṇis; balād = balāt — from force; iva — as if; niyojitaḥ — compelled

Arjuna said: Then explain, O family man of the Vṛṣṇis, by what is a person forced to commit an evil unwillingly, just as if he were compelled to do so? (3.36)

Commentary:

Lord Krishna explained some ideal concepts but Arjuna presents the practical side. Everything Lord Krishna said followed a logical pattern. His views seem functional, but Arjuna wondered about our normal routine. In addition, the Lord admitted that according to the general condition, we human beings act by typical responses. Even the wise men act in a predictable way. Krishna said that we are influenced by material nature. She prompts us. So what can restraint accomplish in comparison to this great hold, nature exercises over us?

If material nature grips us and if our puny will power is minor, how can we ever break the pattern of impulsive behavior?

Arjuna is correct in asking about the force which urges us to act against spiritual interest. What is that power (*kena*)? How can it be transcended? Actually, Lord Krishna answered the question by citing material nature as the subtle energy that deludes us. But that answer was not detailed enough.

श्रीभगवानुवाच
काम एष क्रोध एष
रजोगुणसमुद्भवः ।
महाशनो महापाप्मा
विद्ध्येनमिह वैरिणम् ॥ ३.३७ ॥

śri bhagavān — the Blessed Lord; uvāca — said; kāma — craving; eṣa — this; krodha — anger; eṣa — this; rajoguṇasamudbhavaḥ = rajo (rajaḥ) — passion + guṇa — emotion + samudbhavaḥ — source; mahāśano

śrībhagavānuvāca
kāma eṣa krodha eṣa
rajoguṇasamudbhavaḥ
mahāśano mahāpāpmā
viddhyenamiha vairiṇam (3.37)

(mahāśanaḥ) = mahā — great + aśana — consuming power; mahāpāpmā = mahā — much + pāpmā — damage; viddhyenam = viddhi — recognize + enam — this; iha — in this case; vairiṇam — enemy

The Blessed Lord said: This force is craving. This power is anger. The passionate emotion is the source. It has a great consuming power and does much damage. Recognize it as the enemy in this case. (3.37)

Commentary:

A direct answer is given by Lord Krishna. He claimed that strong desire (*kāma*) or anger (*krodha*) which are produced of the passionate mood of material nature, causes a man to commit spiritually-destructive acts.

Krishna attributed the passionate mode of nature as having great consuming power for the energies of the soul. It does a tremendous amount of damage or deterioration to the energies of the soul by getting the person to contribute to evil acts (*pāpmā*). As human beings, we live by desires, by yearnings. We know ourselves as desires and yearnings. How are we to stop?

धूमेनाव्रियते वह्निर्
यथादर्शो मलेन च ।
यथोल्बेनावृतो गर्भस्
तथा तेनेदमावृतम् ॥ ३.३८॥
dhūmenāvriyate vahnir
yathādarśo malena ca
yatholbenāvṛto garbhas
tathā tenedamāvṛtam (3.38)

dhūmenāvriyate = dhūmena — by smoke + āvriyate — is obscured; vahnir = vahniḥ — the sacrificial fire; yathā — similarly; 'darśo = ādarśaḥ — mirror; malena — with dust; ca — and; yatholbenāvṛto = yatholbenāvṛtaḥ = yatho (yatha) — similarly + ulbena — by skin + āvṛtaḥ — is covered; garbhaḥ — embryo; tathā — so; tenedam = tena — by this + idam — this; āvṛtam — is blocked

As the sacrificial fire is obscured by smoke, and similarly as a mirror is shrouded by dust or as an embryo is covered by skin, so a man's insight is blocked by the passionate energy. (3.38)

Commentary:

Just as we use earthly food and earthly bodies, some entities ingest types of fire and use fire as a body. *Vanih* is the supernatural ruler who controls those entities. He conveys genuine sacrificial offerings to other supernatural authorities.

Human beings may conduct a sacrificial ceremony to petition a supernatural authority. For this a sacrificial priest is required but if the priest is not qualified or if the time and circumstance for a ceremony are improper, the fire does not burn properly and the ceremony does not give the proper yield. In that case, there will be some smoke which will obscure the flame.

Similarly, a mirror's ability to give reflection is affected by the layer of dust that covers the sheen. An embryo cannot look out because a membrane of skin prohibits the view. The soul lives within the mind which houses the intellect. But if he becomes passionate, his intellect becomes obscured. His plans become impractical and he suffers accordingly.

A man should apply the recommendation in the previous verse; Recognize the passionate force as the enemy. Take steps to curtail its influence.

आवृतं ज्ञानमेतेन
ज्ञानिनो नित्यवैरिणा ।
कामरूपेण कौन्तेय
दुष्पूरेणानलेन च ॥३.३९॥
āvṛtaṁ jñānametena
jñānino nityavairiṇā
kāmarūpeṇa kaunteya
duṣpūreṇānalena ca (3.39)

āvṛtam — is adjusted; jñānam — discernment; etena — by this; jñānino = jñāninaḥ — educated people; nityavairiṇā = nitya — eternal + vairiṇā — by the enemy; kāmarūpeṇa = kāma — yearning for various things + rūpeṇa — by the sense or form of; kaunteya — son of Kuntī; duṣpūreṇānalena = duspūreṇa — is hard to satisfy + analena — by fire; ca — and

The discernment of educated people is adjusted by their eternal enemy which is the sense of yearning for various things. O son of Kuntī, the lusty power, is as hard to satisfy as it is to keep a fire burning. (3.39)

Commentary:

In the time of Krishna and Arjuna, education included a spiritual orientation. At that time, even the warriors had spiritual understanding. They got some training in yoga disciplines and ceremonial procedures. Still, some ancient scholars deviated, from proper behavior. This occurred through the eternal enemy, the constant weakness, the lusty energy which produces a sense of longing for persons and things. As one cannot satisfy a fire because its consumption of fuel is perpetual, so one cannot satisfy the sense of longing. As soon as one fulfills one desire, another emerges to occupy the sense of longing.

इन्द्रियाणि मनो बुद्धिर्
अस्याधिष्ठानमुच्यते ।
एतैर्विमोहयत्येष
ज्ञानमावृत्य देहिनम् ॥३.४०॥
indriyāṇi mano buddhir
asyādhiṣṭhānamucyate
etairvimohayatyeṣa
jñānamāvṛtya dehinam (3.40)

indriyāṇi — the senses; mano = manaḥ — the mind; buddhir = buddhiḥ — the intelligence; asyādhiṣṭhānam = asya — if this + adhiṣṭhānam — warehouse; ucyate — it is authoritatively stated; etair = etaiḥ — with these; vimohayatyeṣa = vimohayaty (vimohayati) — confuses + eṣa — this; jñānam — insight; āvṛtya — is shrouded; dehinam — embodied soul

It is authoritatively stated that the senses, the mind and the intelligence are the combined warehouse of the passionate enemy. By these faculties, the lusty power confuses the embodied soul, shrouding his insight. (3.40)

Commentary:

Lord Krishna indicated that the senses, the mind and the intelligence are the avenues through which the modes of material nature function to influence the spirit in a degrading direction. But it is also factual that without these mundane senses, mind and intelligence, we cannot make spiritual progression. In our present condition we need these tools to progress spiritually, to gain self-realization, the awareness of what we really are.

These three, the senses, mind, and intelligence, operate on the energy of *prāṇa* which is a super-fine mundane energy. But this energy has a three-fold effect as being dulling, enthusing, or clarifying. When it is enthusing it is especially dangerous since it drives us to perform irresponsible acts. When it is dulling it stops our activity. When it is clarifying it promotes responsibility.

So long as we consider ourselves to be the body (*dehinam*), we will remain under the power of the modes and will be shuffled around by their variations. If we are lucky, we may fall under the clarifying mode, the one that promotes righteous activities. But if we are unlucky, we are victimized by the enthusing or dulling energies. In any case, there is no independence. Relatively speaking, a man with clarity has the most preference. Even he is influenced but he can make a better choice of what destiny places before him. He cannot create anything original but must select from what destiny offers to him.

It is important that we understand this lack of independence. Many preachers fool us by stating that we have a choice or that we are free to do whatever we desire. This is untrue. No limited person has freedom at any time. It simply does not exist, at least not in the material world. We may understand this by taking the example of a man in a modern department store. In the large cities of the developed countries there are large stores which sell a wide variety of merchandise. Still, the selection of any commodity is limited. In addition, a man can only select from what is available. Even if he has sufficient money to make a special order, the request must be practical in terms of raw material available. If he wants a helicopter that travels at 100 miles per hour, he may order it because such a flying machine is available, but if he wants an aircraft that travels at the speed of light, he cannot select it. His so-called freedom is checked. He is free to choose what is offered by providence at the particular time.

One's insight and memory are enhanced by clarifying modes of nature. One can make the best selection from that level. In the passionate mode, one hankers for a particular item regardless of whether it is serviceable or not. In passion, one's selective skill is curtailed. In the dulling mode, the limitation increases further.

A human being cannot be free because he does not have the equipment of the Personality of Godhead, the equipment which is required to make the proper selection. A human being is greatly handicapped.

There was a man who met a fine woman but he did not want to marry her. Still, the woman adored him. And she worshipped and worshipped a supernatural woman to attain him. She prayed, "I will do anything to get him. I will give all my pious credits from my past life in exchange for marrying him. If only I could get this one man as my husband, then surely I will worship you, O goddess, for the rest of my life."

And she yearned and yearned but she did not realize that the passionate energy is not as selective as the clarifying mode. She relied on yearning and it misled her by showing that one man and no other. It greatly magnified the value of that man in her eyes. After some time, the man yielded and her desire was fulfilled. But she discovered that the man was not as affectionate as desired. This is passion. When we rely on the passionate energy it shows us one or two of the choices. It greatly magnifies these and makes every other alternative seem insignificant. And so we are misled.

तस्मात्त्वमिन्द्रियाण्यादौ
नियम्य भरतर्षभ ।
पाप्मानं प्रजहिह्येनं
ज्ञानविज्ञाननाशनम् ॥ ३.४१ ॥
tasmāttvamindriyāṇyādau
niyamya bharatarṣabha
pāpmānaṁ prajahihyenaṁ
jñānavijñānanāśanam(3.41)

tasmāt — thus; tvam — you; indriyāṇyādau = indriyāṇi — senses + ādau — initially; niyamya — regulating; bharatarṣabha — powerful man of the Bharata family; pāpmānaṁ — degrading power; prajahi — squelch, destroy; hyenaṁ = hy (hi) — certainly + enaṁ — this; jñānavijñānanāśanam = jñāna — knowledge + vijñāna — discernment + nāśanam — ruining

Thus regulating the senses initially, you should, O powerful man of the Bharata family, squelch this degrading power which ruins knowledge and discernment. (3.41)

Commentary:

The mind and intelligence may have their plans but these cannot be executed without the help of the senses. In fact, the senses are the stooges of the mind. The mind itself is the stooge of the intelligence. But as it is, relationships do become inverted. A director may be directed by subordinates. Sometimes the senses direct the mind and the mind in turn, directs the intelligence. The soul, who is supposed to control these psychic tools, is driven to act impulsively, thus becoming liable for faulty activities.

If the sensual enthusiasm is retracted, there would be no impulsive action since the energies will be unable to move the body. If one squelches or gradually and steadily retracts the sensual enthusiasm, one would be free from impulsive action. Lord Krishna gave a strong reason to curb the senses. Unless we get a strong reason we will be disinclined to the discipline since the senses entice and give enjoyment. It is costly enjoyment, but we overlook the costs. Despite the suffering that follows, we feel that it is worth the risk. Still the Lord gave us the reason to curtail it, since it ruins our hard-earned knowledge and discernment. *Vimoha* (confusion) is a very good reason for curbing the senses. We should agree with Krishna on this one point and begin the process of restricting the sensual influence that makes us impulsive.

इन्द्रियाणि पराण्याहुर्
इन्द्रियेभ्यः परं मनः ।
मनसस्तु परा बुद्धिर्
यो बुद्धेः परतस्तु सः ॥३.४२॥

indriyāṇi parāṇyāhur
indriyebhyaḥ paraṁ manaḥ
manasastu parā buddhir
yo buddheḥ paratastu saḥ (3.42)

indriyāṇi — the senses; parāṇyāhur = parāṇi — are energetic; āhur (āhuḥ) — the ancient psychologists say; indriyebhyaḥ — the senses; paraṁ — more energetic; manaḥ — the mind; manasas — in contrast to the mind; tu — but; parā — more sensitive; buddhir = buddhiḥ — the intelligence; yo = yaḥ — which; buddheḥ — in reference to the intelligence; paratas — most sensitive; tu — but; saḥ — he, the spirit

The ancient psychologists say that the senses are energetic, but in comparison to the senses, the mind is more energetic. In contrast to the mind, the intelligence is even more sensitive. But in reference, the spirit is most elevated. (3.42)

Commentary:

Psychology in the time of Lord Krishna was researched and expounded by the Upanishadic sages. They were quoted in Chapter Two by Lord Krishna. The advanced ones were known as masters of samkhya philosophy. *Āhur* means: they said, they declared, they established authoritatively.

According to these sages, the senses are energetic but the mind in comparison is even more alive. The intelligence is even more active than the mind. But the most sensitive is the thinker itself, the *ātma*.

When we contrast these in terms of sensitivity we can see that the soul can give the most direct and most refined sort of pleasure. Thus it is demeaning for the soul to look to the other principles for enjoyment. Since the soul is the most refined of the components, it may look to itself before it looks to any lower principle for enjoyment. This was recommended in the previous verse which discussed spiritual self-satisfaction. Lord Krishna proved that direct spiritual self-satisfaction is better than intellectual, mental or sensual joy.

एवं बुद्धेः परं बुद्धा
संस्तभ्यात्मानमात्मना ।
जहि शत्रुं महाबाहो
कामरूपं दुरासदम् ॥ ३.४३ ॥

evaṁ buddheḥ paraṁ buddhvā
saṁstabhyātmānamātmanā
jahi śatruṁ mahābāho
kāmarūpaṁ durāsadam (3.43)

evaṁ — thus; buddheḥ — than the intelligence; paraṁ — higher; buddhvā — having understood; saṁstabhyātmānamātmanā = saṁstabhya — keeping together + ātmānam — the personal energies+ ātmanā — by the spirit; jahi — uproot; śatruṁ — enemy; mahābāho — O powerful man; kāmarūpaṁ — form of passionate desire; durāsadam — difficult to grasp

Thus having understood what is higher than intelligence, keeping the personal energies under control of the spirit, uproot, O powerful man, the enemy, the form of passionate desire which is difficult to grasp. (3.43)

Commentary:

This advice is direct. Arjuna could apply it instantly because he had disciplinary training. Lord Krishna would tell us more before we could apply this advice of His.

The difficulty will be to sort out the spirit from the intelligence, mind and senses. We should learn from Lord Krishna how to maintain the distinctions from moment to moment. Anytime we experience a blur or confusion regarding identity, we will be prone to the lower influence.

Lord Krishna in His usual casual mood with His perfect sense of humor, addressed Arjuna as *mahābāho* which means *mighty-armed, powerful man*. But Arjuna will have to apply power on the psychological level if he wants to conquer the psyche. He was a strong man physically but he would need psychological power, the type acquired by the samkhya yogis. With that soul strength, he could curb the psyche.

CHAPTER 4

Disciplines of Accomplishment*

श्रीभगवानुवाच
इमं विवस्वते योगं
प्रोक्तवानहमव्ययम् ।
विवस्वान्मनवे प्राह
मनुरिक्ष्वाकवेऽब्रवीत् ॥४.१॥
śrībhagavānuvāca
imaṁ vivasvate yogaṁ
proktavānahamavyayam
vivasvānmanave prāha
manurikṣvākave'bravīt (4.1)

śrī bhagavān — the Blessed Lord; uvāca — said; imaṁ — this; vivasvate — to Vivasvat; yogaṁ — yogic skill of controlling personal energies; proktavān — having explained; aham — I; avyayam — perpetual; vivasvān — Vivasvat; manave — to Manu; prāha — explained; manur = manuḥ — Manu; ikṣvākave — to Ikṣvāku; 'bravīt = abravīt — imparted

The Blessed Lord said: I explained to Vivasvat, this perpetual teaching of controlling the personal energies through yoga. Vivasvat explained it to Manu. Manu imparted it to Ikṣvāku. (4.1)

Commentary:

After laying out the process of the samkhya yogis and showing how it was applied by King Janaka and others, Lord Krishna explained that He is the ultimate source of the knowledge. Students usually look back to predecessors who were pioneers of engineering. Arjuna is being told that Lord Krishna was Himself the original teacher of the ancient kings and ascetics.

Patañjali in his *Yoga Sūtras* also reached back and brought to the attention of readers, some of the qualities of the original teacher. He said:

sa eṣaḥ pūrveṣām api.guruḥ kālena anavacchedāt

He, this particular person, being unconditioned by time, is the guru even of the ancient teachers, the authorities from before. (Yoga Sutras 1.26)

Patañjali did not name that Supreme Lord but only listed His attributes as:

kleśa karma vipāka āśayaiḥ aparāmṛṣṭaḥ puruṣaviśeṣaḥ Īśvarah

The Supreme Lord is that special person who is not affected by troubles, actions, developments or by subconscious motivations. (Yoga Sūtras 1.24)

**The Mahābhārata contains no chapter headings. This title was assigned by the translator on the basis of verse 32 of this chapter.*

The yoga that was explained to Vivasvat was explained by Lord Krishna in Chapters Two and Three. It was the skill mastered by the forest ascetics and which was practiced in practical life by persons like King Janaka. It is nothing else. We cannot project some other knowledge or system because we have to accept this within the context of the *Gītā*. Some modern commentators destroy the context of the *Gītā* by suggesting that something else was taught but in the first line of the verse, *yogam* was listed as the subject and that yoga was already described by Lord Krishna in brief. The application of it to worldly life or to the political life of the ancient kings who knew of it, was also described in Chapter Three.

Śrīla Bhaktivedanta Swami referred us to the *Mahābhārata*, Santi Parva 348.51-52 to verify this statement about the transfer of the techniques and information. There are many Vedic literatures that verify this. However, in the *Mahābhārata* some volumes list it in text 349 of the Santi Parva. There it is explained that during the seventh birth of *Brahmā*, Garbhodakashayi Vishnu gave the information and techniques to *Brahmā*, who in turn, educated one of his mentally-conceived sons named *Dakṣa*. *Dakṣa* gave it to *Āditya*, the solar deity. It was from the solar deity that *Vivasvat* obtained it. This *Vivasvat* gave it to his son *Manu*, who gave it to his son, *Ikṣvāku*. Lord Krishna claimed that He supervised these transmissions.

The importance of this verse is two-fold. First the information is passed on with great care from teacher to student, beginning with the Supreme Lord, then going to *Brahmā*, the planetary creator. Secondly, the information was passed on to saintly rulers who were submissive to the system established by *Brahmā*. But a parallel succession from the Lord also passed through saintly ascetics like *Nārada* Muni. This is why the *Gītā* listed the two types separately as passing through the samkhya yogis and passing through the mystic kings like Janaka.

Even though the knowledge is the same and the techniques of yoga are exactly the same in each case, the way of life and application of the disciplines to life vary in each case. The saintly ascetics retreat from worldly life while the saintly rulers become involved with detachment.

It is a mistake to become convinced that this yoga teaching is not aṣṭanga yoga. It is that very discipline. If one follows contrary suggestions, one will be misled. If one is serious about the *Gītā* he should research further in the Puranic histories to find out exactly what yoga austerities *Manu* and others performed. Some modern preachers are all too eager to replace the word *yoga* in line 1 with the words *bhakti yoga* or with the word *bhakti* or even with whatever theoretical explanation of devotion (*bhakti*) or religion (dharma) they propagate.

एवं परंपराप्राप्तम्
इमं राजर्षयो विदुः ।
स कालेनेह महता
योगो नष्टः परंतप ॥४.२॥
evaṁ paramparāprāptam
imaṁ rājarṣayo viduḥ
sa kāleneha mahatā
yogo naṣṭaḥ paraṁtapa (4.2)

evam — thus; paramparāprāptam = paramparā — a series of teachers + prāptam — received; imaṁ — this; rājarṣayo = rājarṣayaḥ — yogi kings; viduḥ — they knew; sa = saḥ — it; kāleneha = kālena — in time + iha — here on earth; mahatā — long; yogo = yogaḥ — yogic discipline; naṣṭaḥ — was lost; paraṁtapa — O burner of enemy forces

Thus, received through a series of teachers, the yogi kings knew this skill of controlling the personal energies. After a long time, here on earth, this yoga application was lost, O burner of enemy forces. (4.2)

Commentary:

Even though the succession through ascetic kings was lost, the one through the non-political ascetics was intact. But the non-political ascetics were unable to reform the line through the kings Thus Lord Krishna begins the succession for kings afresh, with Arjuna as his disciple. Arjuna was an ascetic prince. The succession through kings was still there, but the rulers lost their ascetic touch and were deviant. Thus Lord Krishna began that succession through Prince Arjuna. In the next verse, Krishna will explain why He selected Arjuna.

The transfer of this knowledge passes through two types of persons, those who are ascetic and those who are political.

This yogic discipline was already defined briefly in Chapters Two and Three. No one should superimpose another meaning just to superficially update the *Gītā* to modern times. The system of yoga being discussed is the one practiced by the ancient samkhya yogis and the one mastered by the Upanishadic sages who lived before and during the time of Lord Krishna

Thus, the Upanishadic views cannot be left out of the *Gītā*. Krishna included many of their conclusions in His discourse with Arjuna.

It is also stated that at times some forest ascetics who were in the disciplic succession approached certain saintly kings to enter that branch of the succession which specialized in the application of yoga to social and political affairs. It is known that once Gautama approached King Pravahana Jaivali:

taṁ ha ciraṁ vasetyājñapāyancakāra
taṁ hovāca yathā mā tvaṁ gautamāvado
yatheyaṁ na prāktvattaḥ purā vidyā
brāhmaṇāngacchati tasmādu sarveṣu lokeṣu
ksatrasyaiva praśāsanamabhūditi tasmai hovāca

The King advised him: "You should stay here for a long time."

At the end of the period, the king said, "Even as you told me, O Gautama, prior to you, this political science of governing (praśānam) was never transmitted to brahmins. This is why the teaching belonged to the rulers in earlier times in all countries. "

Then the king instructed Gautama. (Chandogya Upanishad 5.3.7)

स एवायं मया तेऽद्य
योगः प्रोक्तः पुरातनः ।
भक्तोऽसि मे सखा चेति
रहस्यं ह्येतदुत्तमम् ॥४.३॥

sa evāyaṁ mayā te'dya
yogaḥ proktaḥ purātanaḥ
bhakto'si me sakhā ceti
rahasyaṁ hyetaduttamam (4.3)

sa = saḥ — it; evāyaṁ = eva — indeed + ayam — this; mayā — by me; te — to you; 'dya = adya — today; yogaḥ — yoga technique; proktaḥ — is explained; purātanaḥ — ancient; bhakto = bhaktaḥ — devoted; 'si = asi — you are; me — of me; sakhā — friend; ceti = ca — and + iti — thus; rahasyaṁ — confidential teaching; hyetad = hi — truly + etad — this; uttamam — best

Today, this ancient yoga technique is explained to you by Me, since you are devoted to Me and are My friend. Indeed, this is confidential and is the best teaching. (4.3)

Commentary:

It appears that even though one may be a king and may be versed in the yoga disciplines, one cannot use the information properly unless one is devoted to Lord Krishna (*bhakto 'si me*) and is a dear friend of the Lord (*sakhā*). Thus the transmittance is spoilt if one is not in touch with Krishna as described. Lord Krishna stressed Himself. We cannot avoid Him. If we take Him out and propose that anyone can understand the knowledge regardless of their affiliation or non-affiliation with the Lord, we would have destroyed the *Gītā*. As we proceed through the *Gītā*, Lord Krishna will put Himself more and more in the forefront of everything.

Other warriors at *Kurukṣetra* may have wondered why Krishna did not give them attention. He showered grace on Arjuna. Why was Arjuna singled out? Krishna answered that complaint. Line two reads: *yogah proktah purātanah*. If we follow the wording exactly, it means: *"The yoga declared, is ancient*." This means that Krishna explained the same yoga which Garbhodakashayi Vishnu explained to *Brahmā*. This yoga cannot be modernized or changed.

अर्जुन उवाच
अपरं भवतो जन्म
परं जन्म विवस्वतः ।
कथमेतद्विजानीयां
त्वमादौ प्रोक्तवानिति ॥४.४॥
arjuna uvāca
aparaṁ bhavato janma
paraṁ janma vivasvataḥ
kathametadvijānīyāṁ
tvamādau proktavāniti (4.4)

arjuna — Arjuna; uvāca — said; aparaṁ — later; bhavato = bhavataḥ — Your Lordship; janma — birth; paraṁ — earlier; janma — birth; vivasvataḥ — Vivasvat; katham — how; etad — this; vijānīyāṁ — I should understand; tvam — you; ādau — in the beginning, before; proktavān — having explained; iti — thus

Arjuna said: Your Lordship's birth was later. The birth of Vivasvat was earlier. How should I understand that You explained this before? (4.4)

Commentary:

Lord Krishna made a big claim, stating that He began an information and technique transmission, long, long ago, when some ancient ascetic kings ruled the earth. It is said that these kings even had celestial jurisdiction and that their forebear was *Āditya*, a legendary solar engineer. Even so, if we accept what the Lord said at face value, how are we to understand that He instructed an ancestor of Vivasvat, a very ancient ruler?

The implication is, of course, that Lord Krishna is following His own way of thinking and not ours. He thought of activities performed many thousands of years before.

श्रीभगवानुवाच
बहूनि मे व्यतीतानि
जन्मानि तव चार्जुन ।
तान्यहं वेद सर्वाणि
न त्वं वेत्थ परंतप ॥४.५॥

śrī bhagavān — the Blessed Lord; uvāca — said; bahūni — many; me — of Me; vyatītāni — transpired; janmāni — births; tava — your; cārjuna = ca — and + arjuna — Arjuna; tānyahaṁ = tāny (tāni) — them + aham — I; veda — I recall; sarvāṇi — all;

śrībhagavānuvāca
bahūni me vyatītāni
janmāni tava cārjuna
tānyahaṁ veda sarvāṇi
na tvaṁ vettha paraṁtapa (4.5)

na — not; tvaṁ — you; vettha — you remember; paraṁtapa — O scorcher of the enemies

The Blessed Lord said: Many of My births transpired, and yours, Arjuna. I recall them all. You do not remember, O scorcher of the enemies. (4.5)

Commentary:

We may accept or reject this answer, but this is what Krishna said in response to Arjuna's inquiry about Krishna's inception of a systematic teaching which was transmitted to some celestial and earthly kings. This particular statement appears to be one of supreme arrogance on Krishna's part. It was known to the warriors on the battlefield that Lord *Nārāyaṇa* taught Demigod *Brahmā*. How could Krishna, a human being, claim to be identical with that Supreme Lord?

Lord Krishna has not only asserted memory of ancient events but He denied Arjuna that recall. Krishna exalted Himself above everyone else. He reduced Arjuna to being a limited being with no scope for detailed memory of past lives. Krishna said that He knows (*veda*) but Arjuna does not know (*na vettha*).

अजोऽपि सन्नव्ययात्मा
भूतानामीश्वरोऽपि सन् ।
प्रकृतिं स्वामधिष्ठाय
संभवाम्यात्ममायया ॥४.६॥
ajo'pi sannavyayātmā
bhūtānāmīśvaro'pi san
prakṛtiṁ svāmadhiṣṭhāya
saṁbhavāmyātmamāyayā (4.6)

ajo = ajaḥ — birthless; 'pi = api — even though; sann = san — being; avyayātmā = avyaya — imperishable + ātmā — person; bhūtānām — of the creatures; īśvaro = īśvaraḥ — Lord; 'pi = api — even; san — being; prakṛtiṁ — material energies; svām — my own; adhiṣṭhāya — controlling; saṁbhavāmyātmamāyayā = sambhavāmy (saṁbhavāmi) — I become visible + ātma — self + māyayā — by supernatural power

Even though I am birthless and My person is imperishable, and even though I am the Lord of the creatures, by controlling My material energies, I become visible by My supernatural power. (4.6)

Commentary:

Birthlessness and imperishability are attributed to the limited souls also, but there is a distinction between them and Lord Krishna. For one thing, the limited beings are not the Lord (*īśvaro*).

In stating that His material energies (*prakṛtim svām*) are controlled (*adhiṣṭhaya*), Lord Krishna separated Himself from the limited persons, some of whom cannot control their relationship with their allotment of material nature and some of whom cannot fully control their spiritual nature unless they take controlling assistance from a divine being

Some Vaishnava acharyas excluded material nature from being a part of the personal energies of the Lord. *Śrīla* Bhaktivedanta Swami, our Vaishnava authority, gave *prakṛtih* as *transcendental form*. Sridharadeva Maharaja gave *personal spiritual identity of truth, auspiciousness and beauty*. However, the literal meaning of prakṛtim is *nature*. Generally, prakṛtim means *material nature*. Here, Lord Krishna used the term *svam* which means *my own*. We gave *material energies* for *prakṛtim*. And these include the material nature because Lord Krishna claims to be the ultimate possessor and controller even of matter.

This verse is a key one in understanding the Lord's manifestation of a body which could be seen through material eyeballs and which interacted materially. A spiritual body or transcendental form cannot directly interact with a gross material form. Lord Krishna interacted materially in His own time with devotees like Arjuna and with bad rulers like Kamsa.

This commentator will not try to spare the Lord the pains of using a material body. In keeping with this verse, we will explain that Krishna's forms, His transcendental and material ones, come into our view transcendentally or materially by Krishna's supernatural power (*ātmamāyayā*). He does manifest a material form, but that body is under His control (*adhiṣţhāya*). It is produced from His personal reserve of material energy and not from the vast endless mundane power at large. In our case, a material body is produced by certain laws of consequences and through our dependence on the Lord, for we are neither original nor resourceful enough to handle the material energy effectively.

There is another distinction between ourselves and the Lord. Both the Lord and our limited selves have transcendental forms. His has a human-like appearance, though vastly beautiful and superior. Our spiritual forms go through adaptations under the pressure put on by material nature. Our transcendental forms have no limbs and senses in a human-like configuration. But rather, it merely glows in a spark-like appearance. Its face, arms and legs are yet to be manifested. Thus Krishna has that spiritual human-like form which we endeavor to develop. This is the vast distinction between ourselves and the Lord.

For one reason or the other, some Vaishnava authorities insist on saying that Krishna used no material body, but this is totally untrue. Lord Krishna certainly did. We must understand that His use of such a body is an assertion of His divinity and not a denial of it. If God uses a material body, He does not become less than God. In fact, He then asserts Himself with more proof of divinity. We are grossly aware. His contact with the earthly level is His mercy to reveal divine power. God cannot be screened off from this world, nor barred entry here, nor be denied a material form if He wants to develop and use one. After all, He has His own range of material and spiritual energies which are reserved for His usage (*prakṛtim svām*).

He uses His own supernatural power (*ātmamāyayā*) to manifest a body or an apparition (*sambhavāmi*) into any dimension at any time or in any place. He is not limited to the spiritual level. He can use mundane materials if He so desires. But His preference is the transcendental one.

He is birthless and imperishable and so are we. But the difference is that we are uncertain about eternity. Our status is put to question when we make contact with material nature. His is not. That was proven at *Kurukṣetra* where Krishna used a material form along with His transcendental body, but He was not lowered by the material one. He did not lose the spiritual perspective while projecting that material body. And this is why Lord Krishna made a clear distinction between Himself and Arjuna in the previous verse. He explained that He could remember all those previous births, but Arjuna could recall none of it.

यदा यदा हि धर्मस्य
ग्लानिर्भवति भारत ।
अभ्युत्थानमधर्मस्य
तदात्मानं सृजाम्यहम् ॥४.७॥

yadā yadā — whenever; hi — indeed; dharmasya — of righteousness; glānir = glāniḥ — decrease; bhavati — it is; bhārata — O son of the Bharata family; abhyutthānam — increasing; adharmasya —

yadā yadā hi dharmasya
glānirbhavati bhārata
abhyutthānamadharmasya
tadātmānaṁ sṛjāmyaham (4.7)

of unrighteousness, of wickedness; tadā — then; 'tmānaṁ = ātmānaṁ — My self; sṛjāmyaham = sṛjāmy (sṛjāmi) — show + aham — I

Whenever there is a decrease of righteousness, O son of the Bharata family, and when there is an increase of wickedness, then I show Myself. (4.7)

Commentary:

Many translators of *Gītā* think that whenever there is reduction in piety and a corresponding increase in impiety, the Lord personally appears. They propagate this idea on the basis of line four of this verse: *tadātmānam sṛjāmyaham*. If we take this verse word for word into English, it would read, *Then, by My own self, I do produce*. From this, some commentators deduce that Krishna will appear personally in every case of worldwide degradation. This view is erroneous, being based on a lack of information about Krishna's material energies (*prakṛtim svām*), His own self (*ātmāna*) and His supernatural power (*ātmamāyayā*).

The Lord can motivate limited beings to serve Him in a rescuing or reforming capacity. He does not have to come Himself. Arjuna is an example of a limited person who was empowered to rectify a bad political situation. It does take the personal action of Lord Krishna, however, but that personal act may manifest as the act of another personality. And we can gauge a man's empowerment by the effects of his activities.

Another important aspect is the timing of these manifestations. We hear in the Vedic literature that the world had to bear the atrocities of demons like Hiranyakashipu and *Rāvaṇa* for a very long time before Krishna acted to eliminate these tyrants. In the case of deviant super-kings like Kartavirya, the world had to endure their offenses for some time before divine agents prevailed to bring order. We should not, therefore, try to squeeze into this verse, some other meaning, nor try to assure followers that Krishna said He would come Himself. His only assurance is that His personal power would be manifested. That power can be displayed through the body of any other living entity. Krishna is that penetrant.

परित्राणाय साधूनां
विनाशाय च दुष्कृताम् ।
धर्मसंस्थापनार्थाय
संभवामि युगे युगे ॥४.८॥
paritrāṇāya sādhūnāṁ
vināśāya ca duṣkṛtām
dharmasaṁsthāpanārthāya
saṁbhavāmi yuge yuge (4.8)

paritrāṇāya — to protecting; sādhūnāṁ — of the saintly persons; vināśāya — to destruction; ca — and; duṣkṛtām — of the wicked people; dharmasaṁsthāpanārthāya = dharma — righteousness + saṁsthāpana — the establishing of + arthāya — for the sake of; saṁbhavāmi — I come into visible existence; yuge yuge — from era to era

To protect the saintly people, to destroy the wicked ones, and to establish righteousness, I come into the visible existence from era to era. (4.8)

Commentary:

Lord Krishna's involvement in the created mundane situation is thoroughly explained in this verse. This one verse is frequently quoted in lectures about Lord Krishna. It explains the Lord's reasons for manifesting personal energies in social situations.

The three factors of protecting the saints, disciplining the criminals and establishing righteousness are the three parts of a delicate balance. The saintly persons represent the clarifying power of material nature and the criminals represent the alluring and dulling power. When the balance of these two forces tilt in the direction of world-wide irresponsibility, something is done to shift it towards clarity. Wicked behavior is manifested through crime and vice. The Lord teaches the principles of righteousness and inspires devotees like Arjuna to act in an exemplary way.

Sambhavāmi means "I come into being". But this translation gives, "I come into visible existence", since the Lord either comes directly or sends a capable agent to show His energy. In either case, His personal energy is involved in rectifying a spiritually and morally worn-down humanity. As we will hear, Lord Krishna showed Arjuna the adjustments made on the supernatural level to remove the crimes and vices of the Kuru family. This was shown in the vision of the Universal Form.

जन्म कर्म च मे दिव्यम्
एवं यो वेत्ति तत्त्वतः ।
त्यक्त्वा देहं पुनर्जन्म
नैति मामेति सोऽर्जुन ॥४.९॥
janma karma ca me divyam
evaṁ yo vetti tattvataḥ
tyaktvā dehaṁ punarjanma
naiti māmeti so'rjuna (4.9)

janma — visitation; karma — deed; ca — and; me — of me; divyam — supernatural; evaṁ — thus; yo = yaḥ — who; vetti — realizes; tattvataḥ — in truth; tyaktvā — abandoning; deham — body; punarjanma = rebirth; naiti = na — not + eti — goes; mām — to Me; eti — goes; so = saḥ — he; 'rjuna = arjuna — Arjuna

One who knows My supernatural visitation and deeds, who truly realizes this while abandoning his body, does not go for rebirth. He goes to Me, O Arjuna. (4.9)

Commentary:

Punarjanma naiti means, *again to rebirth, he does not go*. Krishna declares that if we can actually understand (*vetti tattvatah*) His divine birth and actions (*janma karma ca me divyam*), then we would not be subjected to a rebirth that is forced on us by the consequential destiny. This concludes the Lord's discourse in the previous chapter where He told Arjuna that a person who acts with detachment as King Janaka did, is not subjected to liabilities nor is that individual forced into particular wombs by lusty pressure nor by whimsical supernatural agency, nor by the reactive ways of material nature.

The magic of it! Just by thoroughly understanding Lord Krishna's visitation and actions as He explained, a man becomes free from having to take these haphazard and implicating rebirths.

The birth of Lord Krishna (*janma*), we gave as *visitation*. It is not a birth in the usual sense. As Krishna explained, He controls His material energies. He is not subjected to haphazard influences.

Krishna spoke of the devotee going to Krishna. What does that mean? Some commentators from the Vedanta groups say that the devotee will go to the brahman, the spiritual energy, to be one with that spiritual power. But we will have to let Lord Krishna explain what He means.

To stress the knowing factor of His birth, Lord Krishna added the word *tattvatah* to the word *vetti*. The indication is that one should know by experience. If one knows about this divine visitation and the activities of Krishna only by a theoretical study, he will not get the result intended.

वीतरागभयक्रोधा
मन्मया मामुपाश्रिताः ।
बहवो ज्ञानतपसा
पूता मद्भावमागताः ॥४.१०॥
vītarāgabhayakrodhā
manmayā māmupāśritāḥ
bahavo jñānatapasā
pūtā madbhāvamāgatāḥ (4.10)

vītarāgabhayakrodhā = vīta — gone + rāga — craving + bhaya — fear + krodhā — anger; manmayā — think of Me; mām — Me; upāśritāḥ — rely on; bahavo = bahavaḥ — many; jñānatapasā — by austerity/education; pūtā — purified; madbhāvam — my level of existence; āgatāḥ — attained

Many, whose cravings, fear and anger are gone, who are totally focused on Me, who are purified by austerity and education, attained My level of existence. (4.10)

Commentary:

Krishna told Arjuna of the ancient lineage of kings who were educated by Him and who practiced the austerities He recommended. Now the Lord assures Arjuna that there were many others besides Janaka, Vivasvat, *Manu* and *Ikṣvāku*. These fortunate persons achieved Krishna's level of existence (*madbhāvam*). What, therefore, is so special about getting Krishna's love?

The removal of cravings, fears and anger is a sufficient cause for being attracted to Lord Krishna. As the Lord stated, the cravings cause the soul to lose control of his subtle energies, making him a puppet of the senses. Fears and dangers are removed by experiencing the eternity of the soul. It is necessary to distinguish the various parts of the psyche. We need to separate ourselves from the temporary energies which comprise mental and emotional energy. The angers are removed when we begin to see like the reality-perceiving sages. Then we do not miscalculate about the wonders of nature. Being reliant on Lord Krishna and doing what He says, we do not perform reckless activity.

Pūtā (becoming purified) applies to our intellect being cleared of passionate and dulling energies and our own soul being released from the hypnosis of misinterpretation.

Here, in the *Gītā*, we reach a turning point where the Lord definitely puts Himself at the forefront as the pivot of spirituality. There is nobody else standing at this position in the *Gītā*, only Krishna. Let us follow to see how He substantiated the claim for full reliance on Him.

ये यथा मां प्रपद्यन्ते
तांस्तथैव भजाम्यहम् ।
मम वर्त्मानुवर्तन्ते
मनुष्याः पार्थ सर्वशः ॥४.११॥
ye yathā māṁ prapadyante
tāṁstathaiva bhajāmyaham
mama vartmānuvartante
manuṣyāḥ pārtha sarvaśaḥ (4.11)

ye — who; yathā — as; māṁ — me; prapadyante — they rely; tāṁs = tan — them; tathaiva = tathā — so + eva — indeed; bhajāmyaham = bhajāmy (bhajāmi) — relate to + aham — I; mama — my; vartmānuvartante = vartma — course of an action + anuvartante — are affected; manuṣyāḥ — human beings; pārtha — son of Pṛthā; sarvaśaḥ — everywhere

As they rely on Me, so I relate to them, O son of Pṛthā. All human beings, everywhere, are affected by My course of action. (4.11)

Commentary:

The bestowal of Krishna's affection is in proportion to a person's reliance on Him. Again we are left to ask about the value of His affections. Krishna will explain that value elsewhere in the *Gītā*.

Krishna also claimed that somehow or the other His procedures (*vartma*) affect all men. His rules apply universally (*sarvaśah*). We should keep an open mind, giving Krishna an opportunity to verify this.

Krishna's rules are strict. If a person rejects His ideas, He declared in text 32 of Chapter Three that such an individual becomes muddled, crazy, and senseless. We will have to get proof of this.

काङ्क्षन्तः कर्मणां सिद्धिं
यजन्त इह देवताः ।
क्षिप्रं हि मानुषे लोके
सिद्धिर्भवति कर्मजा ॥४.१२॥
kāṅkṣantaḥ karmaṇāṁ siddhiṁ
yajanta iha devatāḥ
kṣipraṁ hi mānuṣe loke
siddhirbhavati karmajā (4.12)

kāṅkṣantaḥ — wanting; karmaṇām — of ritual action; siddhiṁ — success; yajanta — they worship; iha — here on earth; devatāḥ — supernatural authorities; kṣipraṁ — quickly; hi — indeed; mānuṣe — in the humans; loke — in the world; siddhir = siddhiḥ — fulfillment; bhavati — there is, comes to be; karmajā — produced of ritual action

Wanting their ritual action to succeed, people in the world, worship the supernatural authorities. Quickly in this human world, there is fulfillment which comes from ritual action. (4.12)

Commentary:

This is a sarcastic remark to the warriors at *Kurukṣetra*, who by their tradition, performed ceremonial rites before the battle. After pushing Himself up as the Supreme Authority and suggesting that anyone who bypasses or ignores Him, will be frustrated, Lord Krishna berated and minimized the blessing received by people who worship the various Vedic deities (*devatāh*). Even today, Hindus the world over, take resort of worshipping the gods, but here, thousands of years ago, Lord Krishna minimized and sarcastically regarded the practice. Are we to assume that all those persons worshipping the numerous Vedic deities are crazy?

First the Lord mentioned that in the beginning of the creation *Brahmā*, the supervisor of the Vedic deities, instructed his mentally-conceived sons to take up ritual worship. He advised them to do so in consultation with their supernatural superiors only and not to desire independently or impulsively. *Brahmā* placed what we might consider to be a heavy or weighty restriction upon those mind-born sons of his. But when the regulation of *Brahmā* deteriorated, people followed his advice in part only, asking for what they desired and consulting the supernaturals about their impulsive needs. They gradually and certainly, rejected the part of the instruction having to do with holding their working energy in reserve and using it as advised by the celestial people.

In the time of Lord Krishna people had great confidence in this system of getting desires fulfilled through Vedic rituals. It is claimed in some of the *Purāṇas* that a particular king named *Purūrava*, the husband of Urvashi, started the process of asking for things impulsively. Here is a statement from the *Śrīmad Bhāgavatam* regarding this:

purūravasa evāsīt trayī tretā-mukhe nṛpa
agninā prajayā rājā lokaṁ gāndharvaṁ eyivān

O King, at the beginning of Treta era, Purūrava inaugurated a ritual ceremony. Thus Purūrava, who considered the sacrificial fire his son, was able to go to the Gandharva angelic world as he desired. (Bhag. 9.14.49)

But Lord Krishna did not like *Purūrava's* technique. He took this opportunity to ridicule it. He indicated that it was a sweet-sour process, one of fulfillment and frustration simultaneously. There is no doubt that Lord Krishna will Himself take the liability for frustrating these worshippers of the multi-demigods as Krishna tries to establish Himself as the ultimate authority, the one and only Supreme Personality.

चातुर्वर्ण्यं मया सृष्टं
गुणकर्मविभागशः ।
तस्य कर्तारमपि मां
विद्ध्यकर्तारमव्ययम् ॥४.१३॥

cāturvarṇyaṁ mayā sṛṣṭaṁ
guṇakarmavibhāgaśaḥ
tasya kartāramapi māṁ
viddhyakartāramavyayam (4.13)

cāturvarṇyaṁ — the four career categories; mayā — by me; sṛṣṭaṁ — instituted; guṇa - habit; karma - work tendency; vibhāga — distribution; śaḥ — by; tasya — of it; kartāram — creator; api — also; māṁ — me; viddhyakartāram = viddhy (viddhi) — know + akartāram — one not required to act; avyayam — eternal

According to the distribution of habits and work tendencies, the four career categories were instituted by Me. Know that I am never required to participate. (4.13)

Commentary:

Varṇa is not a complicated Sanskrit word. It can be translated into any language since it applies to a universal division of human beings in terms of their work tendencies and the related inclinations. The four career specializations are a generalization, which puts each individual into a contemplative, administrative, business-oriented, or servile class. Each human being has predominant tendencies that function best when doing certain work. This is called the *varṇa*.

Social scientists the world over, agree that the human species is related to all other species through the chain of evolution, but they focus on the material body and feel that life is a progression of bodies. Even from that faulty view, the work tendencies of men may be traced to certain animal backgrounds. These can be traced to a primal creator or to material nature as the ultimate source. In either case, we may admit that whatever we are today or whatever inclination we would manifest in the future, is based on the original source.

Krishna claimed that even though He created and established the system of work division, still He is exempt from it. He does not have to play the employment game. It is a fatiguing game for those who are transmigrating since their position in any society is based on skill and performance. We are scared of the intimidations that come by insufficient education and the ensuing poverty. But Krishna said that He is totally exempt from this worrisome situation. If in a certain birth, we have insufficient education, we may be subjected to poverty. Krishna said that He is exempt from such misfortunes.

न मां कर्माणि लिम्पन्ति
न मे कर्मफले स्पृहा ।
इति मां योऽभिजानाति
कर्मभिर्न स बध्यते ॥४.१४॥

na māṁ karmāṇi limpanti
na me karmaphale spṛhā
iti māṁ yo'bhijānāti
karmabhirna sa badhyate (4.14)

na — not; māṁ — me; karmāṇi — actions; limpanti — they entrap; na — not; me — of me; karmaphale — in a pay-off; spṛhā — desire; iti — thus; māṁ — me; yo = yaḥ — who; 'bhijānāti = abhijānāti — understands; karmabhir = karmabhih — by actions; na — not; sa = saḥ — he; badhyate — is entrapped

Actions do not entrap Me. The desire for payoff is not in Me. The person who understands this is not entrapped by action. (4.14)

Commentary:

Krishna refuted various ideas that people had about Him. These views were propagated by skeptics who doubted His divinity.

There is a rule that for better or worse, actions affect a man. Actions which give a favorable result are preferred. Those which give an unfavorable one are shunned. But in either case, there is entrapment. The individual is tagged for consequences of his actions, which are in fact, induced by material nature. As the Lord explained, unless a man applies consistent detachment, he cannot overcome the good or the bad reactions. Lord Krishna went so far in glorifying Himself that He declared immunity for any individual who, at the time of death, understands Him as He presented Himself in the *Gītā*. According to Krishna, such a person is not subjected to consequential rebirth.

एवं ज्ञात्वा कृतं कर्म
पूर्वैरपि मुमुक्षुभिः ।
कुरु कर्मैव तस्मात्त्वं
पूर्वैः पूर्वतरं कृतम् ॥४.१५॥
evaṁ jñātvā kṛtaṁ karma
pūrvairapi mumukṣubhiḥ
kuru karmaiva tasmāttvaṁ
pūrvaiḥ pūrvataraṁ kṛtam (4.15)

evaṁ — thus; jñātvā — having understood; kṛtaṁ — done; karma — functional work; pūrvair = pūrvaiḥ — by the ancient rulers like Janaka; api — even; mumukṣubhiḥ — by those who desire liberation; kuru — perform; karmaiva = karma — cultural acts + eva — indeed; tasmāt — therefore; tvaṁ — you; pūrvaiḥ — by the yogi kings like Janaka; pūrvataraṁ — before; kṛtam — performed

Having understood this conclusion, functional work was done, even by the yogi kings who desired liberation. Therefore you should perform cultural acts, just as it was done before. (4.15)

Commentary:

Understanding the supremacy of Krishna, His exemption from complications of destiny and His superiority over all the other individuals, ancient seers took Krishna's advice, completed their duties in a detached mood and eventually, by His grace, transcended material existence and gained release from rebirths. The Lord pleaded with Arjuna to act in the way of King Janaka and those ascetic rulers who cooperated in the divine purposes and worked for world improvement as stipulated by Krishna.

But since Lord Krishna is not included in the history of King Janaka, or any of those ancient kings, how are we to fit Krishna into that era? If Krishna appeared before, who was He in the time of any of those kings? What was His name during those visitations? Or did He merely inspire others to act on His behalf while He remained unmanifest?

किं कर्म किमकर्मेति
कवयोऽप्यत्र मोहिताः ।
तत्ते कर्म प्रवक्ष्यामि
यज्ज्ञात्वा मोक्ष्यसेऽशुभात् ॥४.१६॥
kiṁ karma kimakarmeti
kavayo'pyatra mohitāḥ
tatte karma pravakṣyāmi
yajjñātvā mokṣyase'śubhāt (4.16)

kiṁ — what; karma — action; kiṁ — what; akarmeti = akarma — no action + iti — thus; kavayo = kavayaḥ — eloquent philosophers; 'py = api — even; atra — in this matter; mohitāḥ — confused; tat — this; te — to you; karma — action; pravakṣyāmi — I will discuss; yaj = yad — which; jñātvā — knowing; mokṣyase — you will be freed; aśubhāt — from undesirable circumstances

What is action? What is not an action? Even eloquent philosophers are confused on this subject. I will discuss the subject of action with you. Knowing this, you will be freed from undesirable circumstances. (4.16)

Commentary:

As the Lord said, even the eloquent philosophers (*kavayas*) are confused (*mohitah*) as to whether an action is an action or if a restraint is an inaction. Even they have some difficulty determining the intricacies of material existence. Is a stationary object capable of a mobile effect? Does a mobile object have a stationary effect? How are we to know?

कर्मणो ह्यपि बोद्धव्यं
बोद्धव्यं च विकर्मणः ।
अकर्मणश्च बोद्धव्यं
गहना कर्मणो गतिः ॥४.१७॥
karmaṇo hyapi boddhavyaṁ
boddhavyaṁ ca vikarmaṇaḥ
akarmaṇaśca boddhavyaṁ
gahanā karmaṇo gatiḥ (4.17)

karmaṇo = karmanaḥ — of action; hyapi = hy (hi) — indeed + api — also; boddhavyaṁ — should be known; boddhavyaṁ — should be recognized; ca — and; vikarmaṇaḥ — inappropriate action; akarmaṇaś = akarmaṇaḥ — no action + ca — and; boddhavyaṁ — should be understood; gahanā — difficult to comprehend; karmaṇo = karmaṇaḥ — of action; gatiḥ — the course

Indeed, appropriate action should be known and one should also recognize the inappropriate type. The effect of no action should be understood. The course of action is difficult to comprehend. (4.17)

Commentary:

Appropriate action and inappropriate action are not easy to determine. For the most part, we live by a trial-and-error process. We hope that our actions would produce favorable results. Even so, one man's favor is another creature's misfortune. Lord Krishna intended to impart to Arjuna the ability to determine what is right or wrong in any given circumstance. Arjuna thought that a non-violent stance was appropriate, that people would appreciate him for it, but Krishna showed that Arjuna was mistaken (*aśubhāt*).

From the discourse thus far, we can know for certain that even inaction may bring bad consequences. It is not a solution to sit down or to restrain oneself necessarily. It all depends on the situation and what is required as divine duty. Lord Krishna did admit, however, that it is difficult (*gahanā*) to understand the intricacies of action. Krishna must educate us before we can be freed from faultiness. Thus far, He did not impart the technique though He discussed some of the austerities and the resulting benefit attained by the ancient ascetics and masterful kings like Janaka.

कर्मण्यकर्म यः पश्येद्
अकर्मणि च कर्म यः ।
स बुद्धिमान्मनुष्येषु
स युक्तः कृत्स्नकर्मकृत् ॥४.१८॥
karmaṇyakarma yaḥ paśyed
akarmaṇi ca karma yaḥ
sa buddhimānmanuṣyeṣu
sa yuktaḥ kṛtsnakarmakṛt (4.18)

karmaṇyakarma = karmaṇy (karmaṇi) — in performance + akarma — non-action; yaḥ — who; paśyed = paśyet — he should see; akarmaṇi — in non-action; ca — and; karma — action; yaḥ — who; sa = saḥ — he; buddhimān — wise person; manuṣyeṣu — of human beings; sa = saḥ — he; yuktaḥ — skilled in yoga; kṛtsnakarmakṛt = kṛtsna — all + karmakṛt — action performance

He who perceives the non-acting factor in a performance and sees an acting factor when there is no action, is the wise person among human beings. He is skilled in yoga and can perform all actions. (4.18)

Commentary:

What exactly is the impotent factor in action? What is the potency in inaction? Only God can tell us or the wisest of human beings, those reality-perceiving *tattvadarśis* and their acting counterparts, the saintly kings like Janaka. Besides these, no man can understand these statements of Lord Krishna.

We can at least understand that for one man to perform, another man or another supernatural force, person or power must have motivated the performer. That force may be non-active while utilizing the working power of the motivated man. We can also understand that when nothing is done, the effect of neglect is manifested. Or, stated differently, some forces may disempower an energy or energetic personality.

We can understand this verse if we learn from a *buddhimān* (person of great wisdom). Here *bhakti* or devotion to Krishna is not stressed. This concerns *buddhi*. This refers to Chapters Two and Three of the *Gītā* concerning the development of the reality-perceiving intellect (*buddhi*) which was developed by the samkhya yogis in the time of Lord Krishna and which was used to solve the problems of worldly life by the mystically-perceptive kings like Janaka.

The stress is on the development of spiritual vision which is not necessarily reliant on devotion to Krishna. The soul itself has this vision regardless of his affinity to any spiritual authority. For instance, even if a man is hostile to the government of his country, even if he is not particularly patriotic and is declared a rebel, still his body may have two eyes. He has this equipment as part of his material form. It is not reliant on loyalty to his country. Similarly, the *buddhi*, or intellect of a man, may be developed so that he can, to a greater degree, perceive all relevant factors of reality, at least insofar as he may understand the reactions that usually take place within material nature. The soul itself has a *buddhi* (intellect) and regardless of its alignment with a supernatural or divine personality, that mystic tool of vision is there. It is clouded, however, by an attached mood. If one applies detachment, he may perceive reality and live in harmony with nature.

यस्य सर्वे समारम्भाः
कामसंकल्पवर्जिताः ।
ज्ञानाग्निदग्धकर्माणं
तमाहुः पण्डितं बुधाः ॥४.१९॥
yasya sarve samārambhāḥ
kāmasaṁkalpavarjitāḥ
jñānāgnidagdhakarmāṇaṁ
tamāhuḥ paṇḍitaṁ budhāḥ (4.19)

yasya — one whom; sarve — all; samārambhāḥ — endeavors; kāmasaṁkalpa varjitāḥ = kāma — desire + saṁkalpa — intention + varjitāḥ — not mixed into; jñānāgni dagdha karmāṇaṁ = jñāna — knowledge + āgni — fiery force + dagdha — burnt, destroyed + karmāṇaṁ — action; tam — him; āhuḥ — call; paṇḍitaṁ — learned man; budhāḥ — wise man

He for whom desires and intentions are not mixed into his endeavors, who destroyed reactionary work by the fiery force of his knowledge, he, the wise men call a pandit or learned man. (4.19)

Commentary:

Varjitāh, a technical word in this verse, means, *left out, excluded, relinquished, or abandoned*. We have used, *restricted within his nature*. We are discussing a psychic action. This type of action cannot be seen externally except through an indirect gross action or an indirect gross neglect.

Careful study of this verse takes us back to the explanation given by Lord Krishna, regarding the instructions *Brahmā* gave his mentally-conceived sons. *Brahmā* told them to restrain themselves and to act only after consultation with the supernatural authorities who were to regulate their working energy. After explaining this to Arjuna, Lord Krishna gradually introduced Himself as the Supreme Person. He suggested that a man's ability be regulated by His instruction of what a man should do.

We may look at this verse from another angle to see if we could contain our natural energies. How could we reserve their expressive capacity for use under direction of Lord Krishna? Reservation of sensual power causes a build-up of the impulsive energies. This accumulation could be enriching, or maddening, all depending on our capacity for the austerity. If it is enriching, the reserve of energy would act like a fire to burn any reactions which may come when we act under Krishna's direction.

This will not burn our previous misdeeds, however. It would harden us emotionally and make us somewhat impervious to adverse reactions and pleasurable rewards that are due from haphazard acts in past lives.

Some commentators gave another meaning to this verse. They believe that all of a sudden, a man's misdeeds from all past lives would be burnt up by his energy reserve and his newly assumed Krishna-directed activities. But that is a construed meaning. There is nothing in the Sanskrit to cover previous or future haphazard acts. This verse applies to acts performed when a man restricts himself from his own inner urgings, retains and reserves his acting energies and impulses, and acts only after he consults with Krishna or alternately an empowered agent. The man must act in harmony with Krishna's desires; the burning action is applied to consequences of Krishna-inspired acts and not to other activities of the past, present or future.

In this respect, we offer a clarification to Sir Paul Castagna, who spent many years trying to understand the implications of this verse and who disbelieved the general commentaries of some Vaishnava preachers. Mr. Castagna was distrustful of preachers who said that all acts committed by a devotee after he surrenders to Krishna and to their authority, would be devoid of reactions. Mr Castagna is right if his idea is that the coverage does not extend that far. In fact, the coverage applies only to those acts which are in total harmony with the desires of the Lord. Let us go over the details step by step, so that we may get a clear understanding of this verse.

Adventure, enterprises or undertakings are natural for human beings. Indeed, even the animals are involved in this. The universe is involved in an adventure, even though most of the entities neither understand the overall scheme or the small part they are required to play in the universal drama. Nevertheless, the tendency of enterprise is there. Desires or cravings are there. In fact, in nature there is a part which is itself a tendency of craving. This part of the nature will crave regardless. Unless it is held in check, it will brood on an item and yearn for it. Intentions are there but an intention is different from a motivation. Let us assume that a man wants a child. If his desire for a child is strong, he will have to get a female companion. Once he gets the partner, he must impregnate to beget the child in her body. Now in that case, if the woman questions his intention, he may say, I intend to impregnate." But if she asks him for a motivation, he may reply, "I want a child." There is a clear distinction between intention and motivation. Both of these are important. They arise from particular places within psychic nature.

Lord Krishna cited the wise man (*budhāh*) who is credited as being educated (*paṇḍitam*) if he can consistently check within himself the expressions of enterprise, adventure, desires, cravings and intentions. If such a man can act as instructed by the Supreme Lord or by a rightly-situated agent of the Lord, the actions will themselves consume the reactions they produce. Such a person lives with a safe psychic ecology. His existence is clear, risk-free, dirtless, antiseptic, and non-hazardous to himself and others, at least from the spiritual viewpoint.

The process of stiffling, muffling, restricting and not allowing the expression of one's active energies, is a mystic act, even though the results may manifest physically.

Only those effects which come as a reaction to divinely-inspired acts are burnt (*dagdha*) by the perception of the mystically-superior actions, described in this verse. Other acts of a man are not covered by this guarantee. In addition, a man does not have to be in touch with Krishna consciously to get the benefits listed in this verse, but he does have to choke off his inner nature and not allow it to express itself impulsively and he must be inspired by a supernatural agency which is in touch with the divine will. Then he will surely be covered by the guarantee.

त्यक्त्वा कर्मफलासङ्गं
नित्यतृप्तो निराश्रयः ।
कर्मण्यभिप्रवृत्तोऽपि
नैव किंचित्करोति सः ॥४.२०॥
tyaktvā karmaphalāsaṅgaṁ
nityatṛpto nirāśrayaḥ
karmaṇyabhipravṛtto'pi
naiva kiṁcitkaroti saḥ (4.20)

tyaktvā — given up; karmaphalāsaṅgaṁ = karma — action + phala — pay-off + āsaṅgam — attachment, quest; nityatṛpto (nityatṛptaḥ) = nityaḥ — always + tṛptaḥ — satisfied; nirāśrayaḥ — not dependent; karmaṇy = karmaṇi — in performance; abhipravṛtto = abhipravṛttaḥ — proceeding, functioning; 'pi = api — even; naiva = na — not + eva — indeed; kiṁcit — anything; karoti — does; saḥ — he

Giving up the quest for a payoff from actions, being always satisfied, not depending on anything, he does nothing at all even while performing. (4.20)

Commentary:

Thus far in the *Gītā*, Lord Krishna stuck to the argument that Arjuna should fight despite the unfavorable consequences which Arjuna listed in Chapter One. Some of these consequences were not speculations of Arjuna but were standard facts about the aftermath of any civil war. Lord Krishna never denied some of those points even though He told Arjuna that the projection about honor was a miscalculation. Arjuna felt that he would be honored more if he avoided war but Krishna disagreed. However, in other areas, Lord Krishna did not say a word. For instance, Arjuna said that there would be many widows after the war and that many of the women would be spoilt by caste inter-breeding. Arjuna imagined other horrors such as the loss of dear friends. But Krishna dismissed all that, stating that those warriors who fought courageously would go to heaven or would live on by conquest.

Devotion to Krishna will be stressed in other parts of the *Gītā*, but up to this point, the main idea is that Arjuna should fight in a detached mood, not depending on a favorable outcome. He should perform his duty and not worry about the results. Thus Krishna urged Arjuna to perform.

निराशीर्यतचित्तात्मा
त्यक्तसर्वपरिग्रहः ।
शारीरं केवलं कर्म
कुर्वन्नाप्नोति किल्बिषम् ॥४.२१॥

nirāśīr — without hoping; yatacittātmā = yata — reserved + citta — thought + ātmā — spirit; tyaktasarvaparigrahaḥ = tyakta — giving up + sarva — all + parigrahaḥ —

nirāśīryatacittātmā
tyaktasarvaparigrahaḥ
śārīraṁ kevalaṁ karma
kurvannāpnoti kilbiṣam (4.21)

tendency for grasping; śārīraṁ — body; kevalaṁ — alone; karma — action; kurvan — functioning; nāpnoti = na — not + āpnoti — acquire; kilbiṣam — fault

Without hoping, being reserved in thought and spirit, giving up all tendency for grasping, using the body effectively for action, he does not acquire a fault. (4.21)

Commentary:

If Arjuna was still bothered by the implication of battle, if he still felt uneasy about fighting and had an aching conscience, the Lord spoke to remove such a contention in Arjuna's soul. By citing King Janaka, the Lord proved conclusively that it was possible to perform police work and still attain perfection while doing so. But one would have to consistently apply a mood which was devoid of hopes, being reserved in psychology, such that the thinking and feeling energies were totally conserved. One would have to abandon the sense of grasping and use the body effectively or precisely (*kevalam*) for action, functioning as destined. Then one would not develop such guilt and remorse when dealing with relatives in the performance of duty.

यदृच्छालाभसंतुष्टो
द्वंद्वातीतो विमत्सरः ।
समः सिद्धावसिद्धौ च
कृत्वापि न निबध्यते ॥४.२२॥
yadṛcchālābhasaṁtuṣṭo
dvaṁdvātīto vimatsaraḥ
samaḥ siddhāvasiddhau ca
kṛtvāpi na nibadhyate (4.22)

yadṛcchā — by chance; lābha — benefit; saṁtuṣṭaḥ — satisfied; dvandvātīto (dvandvātītaḥ) = dvandva — likes and dislikes + atītaḥ — ignoring; vimatsaraḥ — free from envy; samaḥ — even-minded; siddhāv = siddhau — in success; asiddhau — in failure; ca — and; kṛtvā — having performed; 'pi = api — also; na — no; nibadhyate — is implicated

Being satisfied by benefit which comes by chance, ignoring likes and dislikes, being free from envy, even-minded in success and failure, and having performed, a man is still not implicated. (4.22)

Commentary:

The historic participation of kings like Janaka is explained. These reality-perceptive persons maintained freedom from envy, and were steady in their attitude towards success and failure. They functioned efficiently in pleasant or unpleasant duties. If, by chance, a benefit came, they were unexcitedly satisfied with it. They did not hanker for particular results. This is how they gained immunity from implications and liabilities. Even if an implication arose, they faced it and performed with detachment. Since they acted for the Supreme Lord or His agent, they simply returned to such authorities with the perplexities. Taking solutions from Krishna or from His agent, they were not baffled by contrary outcomes.

गतसङ्गस्य मुक्तस्य
ज्ञानावस्थितचेतसः ।
यज्ञायाचरतः कर्म
समग्रं प्रविलीयते ॥४.२३॥

gatasaṅgasya = gata — gone + saṅgasya — of attachment; muktasya — of the liberated person; jñānāvasthitacetasaḥ = jñāna — knowledge + avasthita — established + cetasaḥ — of an idea; yajñāyācarataḥ = yajñāya — for

gatasaṅgasya muktasya
jñānāvasthitacetasaḥ
yajñāyācarataḥ karma
samagraṁ pravilīyate (4.23)

austerity and religion + ācarataḥ — doing; karma — action; samagraṁ — completely; pravilīyate — cancels

Concerning a person whose attachment is finished, who is liberated, whose idea is established in knowledge, any of his action which is done solely for austerity and religion, does cancel completely. (4.23)

Commentary:

It is obvious that Lord Krishna intended for Arjuna to fight. Many of these verses point in that direction of Krishna taking away Arjuna's fears about the outcome of the battle. The philosophy here is that of the Upanishadic sages and the samkhya yogis who were prominent in the time of Arjuna and Lord Krishna. These statements are the conclusions of those authorities.

One cannot be successful at this process if he assumes detachment artificially as many modern followers of the *Gītā* do. The detachment must be consistently applied. It must be integrated into one's consciousness (*cetasah*). Otherwise, one will act in genuine detachment in one instant and act in false detachment in the next, and will be implicated.

Only a person who is a naturalist at this process will have all his activities melt away without consequences (*samagram praviliyat*).

ब्रह्मार्पणं ब्रह्महविर्
ब्रह्माग्नौ ब्रह्मणा हुतम् ।
ब्रह्मैव तेन गन्तव्यं
ब्रह्मकर्मसमाधिना ॥४.२४॥
brahmārpaṇaṁ brahmahavir
brahmāgnau brahmaṇā hutam
brahmaiva tena gantavyaṁ
brahmakarmasamādhinā (4.24)

brahmārpaṇaṁ = brahma — spiritual existence + arpaṇam — ceremonial articles; brahma — spiritual existence; havir = haviḥ — sacrificial ingredients, ghee; brahmāgnau = brahma — spiritual existence + agnau — in fire; brahmaṇā — by the qualified brahmin priest; hutam — offering oblations; brahmaiva = brahma — spiritual existence + eva — indeed; tena — by him; gantavyaṁ — to be attained; brahmakarmasamādhinā = brahma — spiritual existence + karma — activity + samādhinā — by meditative contact

Spiritual existence is the basis of his ceremonial articles. It is the foundation of sacrificial ingredients. The perceptive priest pours the stipulated items into the fiery splendor of spiritual existence. It is the spiritual existence which is attained by a person who keeps contact with the spiritual level while acting. (4.24)

Commentary:

This is in support of *Brahmā*'s order to his mentally-conceived sons. They were to perform certain Vedic sacrifices that were recommended by their father, the sub-lord of the creation. Lord Krishna supports the Vedic sacrifices which were performed by a perceptive priest who mastered the samkhya yoga system and attained maturity in the reality-piercing vision described in Chapters Three and Four.

The Lord said that the sacrificial articles used, as well as the offerings and the act of pouring substances like the ghee, all this, is of the nature of that spiritual existence, but only on the condition that the brahmin priest is genuinely mystic and is loyal to the original stipulations of *Brahmā*, the creator god. The detail of how the mystic priest kept in touch with the spiritual level is not given. But we heard that he reserved his energies for usage by the directions of the supernatural people who are the agents of *brahma*.

We gave "spiritual existence" for the word Brahman.

The term *samādhinā* means, *by meditation, by contemplating, by thinking, or by considering deeply*. When a man keeps in touch with the spiritual level or with supernatural authorities who are on the subtle plane, he will, of necessity, act from that platform and his actions will not be of a mundane origin.

दैवमेवापरे यज्ञं
योगिनः पर्युपासते ।
ब्रह्माग्नावपरे यज्ञं
यज्ञेनैवोपजुह्वति ॥४.२५॥
daivamevāpare yajñaṁ
yoginaḥ paryupāsate
brahmāgnāvapare yajñaṁ
yajñenaivopajuhvati (4.25)

daivam — to a supernatural authority; evāpare = eva — indeed + apare — some; yajñaṁ — austerity and religious ceremony; yoginaḥ — yogis; paryupāsate — practise; brahmāgnāv = brahmāgnau — in the fiery brilliance of spiritual existence; apare — others; yajñaṁ — austerity and religious ceremony; yajñenaivopajuhvati = yajñena — by austerity and religious ceremony; eva — indeed + upajuhvati — they offer

Some yogis perform austerity and religious ceremony in relation to a supernatural authority. Others offer austerity and religious ceremony as the sacrifice into the fiery brilliance of spiritual existence. (4.25)

Commentary:

This verse requires some understanding of Vedic religious ceremonies. Sridharadeva Maharaja, a great Gaudiya Math acharya of these modern times, gave clarification. He listed the following meanings for the Sanskrit words in his Śrīmad *Bhagavad Gītā* translation and commentary (see The Hidden Treasure of the Sweet Absolute, p. 79.)

- *yoginaḥ - karma yogis, those who execute spiritual life by the path of action; daivam yajñaṁ eva -of sacrifice intended only for the demigods headed by Indra; apare - other jñāna-yogīs; upajuhvati - invoke in sacrifice; yajñaṁ — the soul, jivātmā, as the element tvam, representing the butter of sacrifice; brahma-agnau - unto the Supersoul, Paramatma, as the element of tat, representing the sacrificial fire; yajñena eva - simply by vibrating the praṇava mantra, oṁkāra*

He translated this verse as follows:

Other karma-yogīs perform sacrifice in the worship of demigods such as Indra and Varuna. Other jñana-yogīs, simply by vibrating the praṇava mantra, omkāra, offer the individual soul (as the sacrificial clarified butter) unto the Supersoul (as the sacrificial fire). (Sweet Absolute, p. 81)

Sridhara's meaning for this verse is very clear; the word *yogīnah* in line two means, *those persons who take Vedic ritual of sacrifices very seriously*. As he indicated in his vocabulary, these sacrifices are mainly meant for the celestial king, Indra, a supernatural being who controls the *svarga* heavenly places. Thus, we can see that the word *yogi* in this verse does not refer at all to yogis who practice *āsana* or *prāṇāyāma* but to aspirants who are striving for spiritual perfection through the performance of Vedic ritualistic ceremonies. Such people, however, are heading to the *svarga* heavenly places only. They will not be reaching the transcendental places. Indra has no jurisdiction over such realms. The worship of Indra culminates in reaching the *svarga* angelic world which is a mundane paradise only.

Lord Krishna mentioned *yajñam* to Indra and the other devatas or demigods, but He discouraged the process. Elsewhere in the *Gītā*, Krishna directly condemns this.

The worshippers of these multi-demigods continue on and on, endlessly with rituals, just as if the *Bhagavad Gītā* had no meaning whatsoever. In contrast to them are the *jñana*-yogis who also do not practice yoga *āsana* postures and *prāṇāyāma* nutrition, but who may have practiced earlier in their lives or in previous lives. These *jñana*-yogis were headed by Swami Vivekananda in modern times. Their idea is clearly stated here as indicated by the meaning of Sridharadeva Maharaja. They do not bother to waste their time with Vedic sacrifices like the god-appeasing Hindus. Instead they aspire for direct contact with the spiritual plane. Putting aside the sacrificial utensils, the sacrificial fire, the ghee, *samāgri* and such items, bypassing the brahmin priest, they consider the spiritual effulgence to be the fire and themselves to be the ghee to be offered. By sheer will power, they try to push themselves out of material existence into the spiritual atmosphere. In this way they make an effort to sacrifice their individuality (*jīvātma*) into the fire of either the sum total spiritual energy or the Personality of Godhead, according to their impersonal or personal views.

Sridharadeva Maharaja gave the *paramātma* Supersoul as the symbolic fire of sacrifice, but some of the jñana yogis do not believe in the Supersoul The respected Sridharadeva has expressed the Vaishnava bias, intending to convert hard-core *jñana* yogis into *bhakti* yogis, or devotees of Krishna. However, the Sanskrit does not directly indicate the *paramātma* Supersoul. Nor does it indicate exclusively the use of *praṇava*, the *omkāra* sound. Lord Krishna, unlike Sridharadeva Maharaja, who revealed much of this verse, did not limit this verse to the modern proposals. Krishna left the verse wide open. He will fill in the spaces by showing the various paths to spirituality (*brahma*). *Paramātma* is just one of the paths.

This verse is important to show the distinction between the two essential paths of spirituality offered by the Vedic system. The first and more elementary one is that of remaining as a materialistic man and just offering a small portion of the yields into a sacrificial fire from time to time. This relates to *Brahmā*'s original instruction to his mentally-conceived sons. The second path is a radical departure from that instruction. It is meant to put an end to material existence. Persons on that final path do not focus on yields or mundane items but shed all concerns and apply themselves for deliverance.

The second path, though not recommended by *Brahmā* in the beginning, did emerge from *Brahmā*'s body as his mentally-produced sons, the Kumaras. They advocated a way of self-realization which was practiced by others at a later date. Some other sons of *Brahmā* were materialistic. Some like the Kumaras, were resistant to mundane existence. And some others applied themselves in a cultural way while developing spirituality side by side.

To this point the Lord gave some destinations for the living entities. Let us revise the listing: The earth, the *svarga* heavenly places, the hells, and the trouble-free spiritual places.

Arjuna indicated that there are living beings in the upper, median and lower planetary systems of this material world. He acknowledged the ghostly planes where the ancestors hover in subtle bodies. In the time of Arjuna, Vedic astronomers categorized planets in terms of a northerly-southerly configuration. Locations north of the earth were considered higher. Southern ones were considered to be below the earth. The planets in the middle were considered median.

The Lord used *brāhmīsthitih* and *brahmanirvāṇam* in text 72 of Chapter Two. But these are broad terms covering the entire spiritual realm. These terms leave much to be defined. They are too vague, to say the least. Thus every *Gītā* commentator tried to explain what he felt Krishna intended. But Lord Krishna explained the terms elsewhere in the *Gītā*.

In this verse, two paths are indicated. One allows the human beings to promote material existence in the authorized way, as agents of the supernatural sub-creators. The other terminates one's material existence, whether in cooperation with or in defiance to the subcreators. In the beginning of the creation *Brahmā*'s first mentally-conceived sons were the four Kumaras. They were resistant to him and declined to support material existence. They were inclined to self realization by mental analysis and mystic insight. Later on, some other mind-born sons of *Brahmā* were produced. They were inclined to expanding mundane social life. In a sense, the two groups of entities are diametrically opposed, but there is a way for their mutual benefit and cooperation.

श्रोत्रादीनीन्द्रियाण्यन्ये
संयमाग्निषु जुह्वति ।
शब्दादीन्विषयानन्ये
इन्द्रियाग्निषु जुह्वति ॥४.२६॥
śrotrādīnīndriyāṇyanye
saṁyamāgniṣu juhvati
śabdādīnviṣayānanye
indriyāgniṣu juhvati (4.26)

śrotrādīnīndriyāṇy = śrotrādīnīndriyāṇi = śrotra — hearing + ādīni — and related aspects + indriyāṇi — senses; anye — others; saṁyamāgniṣu = saṁyama — restraint + agniṣu — in the fiery power; juhvati — they offer; śabdādīn = śabda — sound + ādīn — and so on; viṣayān — sensual pursuits; anye — others; indriyāgniṣu — in the fiery energy of sensuality; juhvati — they offer

Other yogis offer hearing and other sensual powers into the fiery power of restraint. Some offer sound and other sensual pursuits into the fiery sensual power. (4.26)

Commentary:

These processes of discipline mentioned by Krishna, beginning in verse 24, continuing through verse 33, are very important. These are the general classifications of the authorized systems of penance. For completion of this *Gītā* study, we should recall these systems again and again, since Lord Krishna spoke more of them in other chapters. In verse 34, just after Krishna enumerated these procedures, He asked Arjuna to surrender to the spiritual masters. We will hear of this shortly.

Brahmā's idea about offering yields to the supernatural people is not the only way to offer sacrifice. Vedic fire sacrifices are merely one way of austerity. Other methods are listed here. The benefit of each, will be explained elsewhere. These methods, however, are more or less actions of the subtle body or of the causal body or of the soul directly. As such they are not subjected to an easy rating. That is the cause of their unpopularity.

How does one offer the hearing, seeing, smelling, tasting and touching senses into the fiery power of restraint (*samyamāgniṣu*)? Perhaps we can reply that only God, only Krishna knows. But that is an evasive answer.

How does one offer sounds, forms and flavors into the fiery sensual power itself (*indriyāgniṣu*)? The experts of the process know.

सर्वाणीन्द्रियकर्माणि
प्राणकर्माणि चापरे ।
आत्मसंयमयोगाग्नौ
जुह्वति ज्ञानदीपिते ॥४.२७॥
sarvāṇīndriyakarmāṇi
prāṇakarmāṇi cāpare
ātmasaṁyamayogāgnau
juhvati jñānadīpite (4.27)

sarvāṇīndriyakarmāṇi = sarvāṇi — all + indriyakarmāṇi — sensual actions; prāṇakarmāṇi = prāṇa — breath function + karmāṇi — activities; cāpare = ca — and + apare — some; ātmasaṁyamayogāgnau = ātmasaṁyama — self-restraint + yogāgnau — in fiery yoga austerities; juhvati — they offer; jñānadīpite = jñāna — experience + dīpite — illuminated

Some ascetics subject the sensual actions and the breath function to self-restraint by fiery yoga austerities, which are illuminated by experience. (4.27)

Commentary:

Here again, we find another type of sacrifice. These ascetics try to bypass the gross material existence and make a short cut to liberation. The sensual actions (*indriyakarmāṇi*) and the breath functions (*prāṇa karmāṇi*) are restrained by some ascetics who, by a strong sense of spirituality (*ātma*), curtail and reserve the use of the sensual and impulsive powers and offer these into the practice of yoga *āsana* postures and *prāṇāyāma* purification processes. They are inspired (*dīpite*) by mystic experience (*jñāna*) yielded from their practices.

द्रव्ययज्ञास्तपोयज्ञा
योगयज्ञास्तथापरे ।
स्वाध्यायज्ञानयज्ञाश्च
यतयः संशितव्रताः ॥४.२८॥
dravyayajñāstapoyajñā
yogayajñāstathāpare
svādhyāyajñānayajñāśca
yatayaḥ saṁśitavratāḥ (4.28)

dravya — property + yajñās — austerity and religious ceremony; tapo (tapaḥ) — self denial + yajñā — austerity and religious ceremony; yoga —eight-part yoga process + yajñāḥ — austerity and religious ceremony; tathāpare = tathā — as well as + apare — some others; svādhyāyajñānayajñāśca = svādhyāya — study of the Veda + jñāna — knowledge + yajñāḥ — austerity and religious ceremony + ca — and; yatayaḥ — ascetics; saṁśitavratāḥ = saṁśita — strict + vratāḥ — vows

Persons whose austerity and religious ceremony involve the control of material possession, those whose austerity and religious life involve some self-denial, as well as some others whose penance and religious procedure is the eight-part yoga discipline, and those whose austerity and religious ceremony is the study of the Veda and the acquirement of knowledge, all these are regarded as ascetics with strict vows. (4.28)

Commentary:

There is always an attempt by spiritual masters of repute to draw a line on what a man should do to restrict himself. Here Lord Krishna gave more than one process. Beginning with the first recommendation given by *Brahmā* to his mind-born sons, the Lord listed off many disciplines. The choice discipline given by the Lord thus far was the one of the samkhya yogis. It appears, however, that they used more than one discipline or more than one combination of disciplines. The attempt of some spiritual masters, to restrict what we do for salvation, is an attempt to keep us under their individual influences only. Ultimately, a man must find a discipline that is suited to his nature. He may not progress through a general procedure. One method that works well for one individual may not give the same success to another. A serious ascetic must search out the various techniques until he finds a process that gives him effective control over vices. In addition, a process which serves at one stage, may not serve well at a higher level. An ascetic might have to abandon one discipline to move further.

The urgency of any man's spiritual development rests with the man himself. The gurus or spiritual experts of various processes are more or less concerned with their missionary activities, their showmanship and their popularity. A seeker should fend for himself and determine what is in his best interest by judging how his vices are curbed or expanded by a process.

One ascetic might find it expedient to renounce, donate, surrender or sacrifice property (*dravyayajñās*). For him, this would give spiritual advancement while for another man, that effort may give no result whatsoever. Thus, if one joins a spiritual group that specializes in renunciation of property, one will advance as much as that discipline may allow. An ascetic may get great benefit from performing yoga *āsana* postures and other technical yoga practices (*yogayajñās*), or by curbing his diet by fasting (*tapoyajñā*), but that might help only at a certain stage or it may be developed into a more technical aspect of the same practice. It all depends on the individual level of advancement.

Some do Vedic recitation of mantras on and on and on, endlessly, through prayer bead chanting (*japa*), or through ritualistic prayers (*svādhyāya*). But even this discipline might be outgrown or may develop to a more advanced level. One should not become stagnant in a practice.

Another system is the sacrifice of knowledge (*jñānayajñā*), whereby one ignores his learning and keeps his mind away from imagination and plans. One tries to maintain thoughtlessness while serving a particular spiritual master or performing a particular austerity like fasting, singing devotional songs, saying devotional prayers, controlling the breathing, or doing yoga postures.

Each of these disciplines has one thing in common: Stipulated vows, exacting promises and pre-set determination (*samsitavratah*). Only a determined ascetic can test to see if the process gives the desired result.

Someone may take a vow to fast for a day or two but he may not complete it. Someone may take a vow to refrain from sexual intercourse for three days or a week, but he might indulge anyway. Someone may take a vow to chant a particular prayer, but he may not observe it. In all cases, however, the attempt is made. The person discovers his or her capacity for the austerity.

अपाने जुह्वति प्राणं
प्राणेऽपानं तथापरे ।
प्राणापानगती रुद्ध्वा
प्राणायामपरायणाः ॥४.२९॥
apāne juhvati prāṇaṁ
prāṇe'pānaṁ tathāpare
prāṇāpānagatī ruddhvā
prāṇāyāmaparāyaṇāḥ (4.29)

apāne — in exhalation; juhvati — they offer; prāṇam — inhalation; prāṇe — in inhalation; 'pānaṁ = apāṇaṁ — in exhalation; tathāpare = tathā — similarly + apare — others; prāṇāpāna gatī = prāṇa — energizing air + apāna — de-energizing air + gatī — channel; ruddhvā — restraining; prāṇāyāmaparāyaṇāḥ = prāṇa — inhaling + āyāma — regulating + parāyaṇāḥ — intent

Some offer inhalation into the exhalation channels; similarly others offer the exhalation into the inhalation channels, thus being determined to regulate the channels of the energizing and de-energizing airs. (4.29)

Commentary:

Apāne juhvati prāṇam means that the recharged blood surges in the veins. This occurs in the gross body. To understand this one should know physiology. Usually the veins carry exhausted blood. The arteries transport recharged blood. The blood charger is the lung. The pump which circulates the blood is the heart. In terms of nutrition, the most important organ in the body is the lung. People feel that the stomach and intestines are the most important organs of nutrition, but this is incorrect. Only the *prāṇāyāma* yogis stress the lung as the essential organ of nutrition.

Usually the veins carry only exhausted blood which is laden with carbon dioxide, but the *prāṇāyāma* yogis learn how to push out that exhausted blood by sending recharged blood into the veins. This is mastered after long, consistent practice under the guidance of great yogis.

Prāṇāyāma yoga causes an action in the subtle body but it begins with a physical effort. The subtle and gross forms are interlocked. A physical action affects the subtle form as well.

The procedure for putting surcharged blood into the veins is the first step in *prāṇāyāma* practice. But this first step might take years to achieve. It all depends on the direction received from an advanced teacher and the intensity and care taken with the practice. The *prāṇa* is fresh air on the physical level, but it is solarized subtle air on the astral or subtle plane. The *apāna* is the carbon dioxide and other heavy gases on the gross level and it is lunarized, moon-charged subtle air on the astral plane. In the beginning of *prāṇāyāma* practice, one has to consider everything in terms of oxygen and carbon dioxide. At a later stage of practice, one sees the physiology of the subtle body and perfects the practice on a higher plane.

It is interesting to note that all great Vaishnavas in the time of Lord Krishna were masters of the process given in this verse. But in the modem setting, the Vaishnava teachers, shun the *prāṇāyāma* practice and have, for the most part, outlawed it. This writer, however, had success in these processes. And for that, we are indebted to our *Śrī Śrī* Krishna Balarama Deities and to Lord Shiva, the master of the yogis.

In the second line of the verse, we read *prāṇe'pānam tathāpare* which means that on the physical level, the *apāna* or carbon dioxide energy is pushed into the pranic or oxygen surcharged channels. This is not as complicated as it sounds. This stage is only attained at the advanced levels of *prāṇāyāma* practice. Many writers comment on this verse even though they know absolutely nothing about *prāṇāyāma* practice. Their theoretical understanding is misleading to readers. They cannot be blamed, however. In writing commentaries, an author may cheat readers by giving purely theoretical explanations. Many commentators use this trick.

A yogi does not push the *apāna* or carbon-dioxided blood into his arteries. He purifies the body to such an extent that his carbon-dioxided blood is itself surcharged with oxygen. When he reaches a stage of bodily purity, he pushes the blood in the veins backwards into the arteries. This is done by certain muscular locks and stretches which cause the reversal.

At the advanced stages, he takes lunarized moonlight or surcharged energy into the subtle form, instead of using subtle carbon dioxide. In a normal human body, carbon dioxide is used for various purposes. If it is not sufficiently produced as a waste gas in the body, one increases it by smoking cigarettes, chewing tobacco, drinking coffee, taking narcotics, drinking liquor, taking vinegar, and numerous other practices. Meat consumption helps to increase the carbon dioxide. In the yoga practice, one desires to reduce this carbon dioxide to nil.

When all the carbon dioxide is exhaled, the blood in the veins and arteries is surcharged with clean air. At that stage one gets the power through locks and stretches to reverse the channels. The greatest benefit, however, is in the subtle body. Even though, externally, the practice of yoga concerns the gross form, this is an appearance only. The actual benefit is in the subtle body. When the subtle body is cleaned out and subdued, the causal plane is reached in actuality.

This writer is in a Vaishnava disciplic succession, but after reaching the advanced stages of kundalini yoga by the process bhastrika *prāṇāyāma*, kriyās, and mudras, we can say with all confidence that unless one masters the *prāṇāyāma* as the ancient Vaishnava yogis did, one cannot attain perfection. We know what the Vaishnava acharyas say and what the modern Vaishnava scriptures recommend but we must speak clearly on this issue. The ancient yogis like *Nārada*, Shuka, *Vyāsaji* and others were masters of the *prāṇāyāma* practices. The former requirements for salvation have not changed one bit. The idea that the requirements changed to suit our times is an inducement to start the spiritual process. It is nothing but an encouragement. One cannot attain perfection without practicing the austerities performed by the ancient Vaishnava ascetics. It is impossible. But one cannot understand this until he takes up those ancient practices, advances through them, and then looks back to his previous condition on the so-called easy paths for our era.

The greatest misconception about *prāṇāyāma* is transmitted by the modern experts of the process. They speak of *prāṇāyāma* as breath control. One great yogi, *Śrī* Paramhamsa Yogananda, a *kriyā* technique master, did alert seekers that *prāṇāyāma* mean surcharging of the body, especially of the subtle form. But if we want to understand what a yogi does in the practices, we have to begin thinking of breath nutrition.

These yogis learn how to increase breath nutrition and progressively decrease intestinal food. They simply switch to more breath nutrition. It is not that they are restraining the breath but rather they are restraining the body's tendency to limit the breath.

First a yogi surcharges his gross body with oxygen and his subtle body with pranic subtle air. When the body has an excess of that and when all the gross and subtle carbon dioxide is driven out, he then stops or slows the breathing. Thus it is not that he restrained the breath but rather he increased the breath nutrition considerably. When he is free from the need to breathe, he meditates and enters *samādhi*. For the time being, his mind is freed from the task of inhalation and exhalation. His life force is freed from the task of gasping for breath every few seconds. His mind becomes stilled to a degree and he makes detailed observations of the mental shifts which ruin clarity and self-realization.

The major accomplishment, however, is to shift the focus of consciousness from the gross form to the subtle one, then to the causal one and then to the spirit soul and then to supreme objectives. Neophyte *bhakti* yogis and some spiritual masters feel that they can shift from the gross body to the spiritual level merely by understanding the theory of these practices but that is a completely false idea. The result of this fallacy is their continued focus on the physical plane. They cannot shift abruptly from the physical to the spiritual. And that is why *prāṇāyāma* is necessary. First we curb our physical diet, then we curb it even more, but we can only curb it if we increase breath intake. Without increasing breath intake, one will have to wait until the body gets older when it cannot digest properly or when a disease forces one to curtail foods. Restricted eating for health reasons or because of old age is not the same as restricted eating because of breath increase.

If we cannot increase breath nutrition, our attachment to gross food will remain. It will go with us at the time of death. The result will be the assumption of another gross body in the process of time by the grace of destiny. That is the result we will achieve from our religious practice. If we are unable to shift from the gross focus now, we will not be mastering it, all of a sudden, at the time of death. We may think so or our spiritual master may assure us, but it will not occur because the law of habit will assert itself.

अपरे नियताहाराः
प्राणान्प्राणेषु जुह्वति ।
सर्वेऽप्येते यज्ञविदो
यज्ञक्षपितकल्मषाः ॥४.३०॥

apare — others; niyatāhārāḥ — persons restrained in diet; prāṇān — fresh air; prāṇeṣu — into the previous inhalations; juhvati — impel; sarve — all; 'pyete (apyete) = apy (api) — also + ete — these; yajñavido = yajñavidaḥ — those who know the value of an act of

apare niyatāhārāḥ
prāṇānprāṇeṣu juhvati
sarve'pyete yajñavido
yajñakṣapitakalmaṣāḥ (4.30)

sacrifice; yajñakṣapitakalmaṣāḥ = yajña — austerity and religious ceremony + kṣapita — destroyed, removed + kalmaṣāḥ — impurities

Others who were restrained in diet, impel fresh air into the previously inhaled air. All these ascetics whose impurities were removed by austerity and religious ceremony understand the value of an act of sacrifice. (4.30)

Commentary:

Whatever a commentator may say that is inconsistent with what Krishna said, is loaded with motivation to stop a human being from taking up other practices besides the one the teacher advocates. And this is a cheating process. It is up to the seeker to protect the self from it.

The discipline mentioned in this verse as food restraint, controlled and reduced diet (*niyatāhārāh*), was taught to this writer by many yogis but it was Swami Shivananda of Rishikesha who stressed this to the writer in the astral world years ago. In fact, we can only explain this verse because he first expounded it. He used to say, "Eat less, breathe more." Of course, such an instruction means absolutely nothing to a person who is not familiar with *prāṇāyāma* breath nutrition methods. One may reason that if the oxygen in the bloodstream is increased, a person would automatically eat less. But actually this is not so.

Many years ago, this writer thought he knew something about the practice. He took steps to increase the oxygen in the body by bhastrika *prāṇāyāma* but when he did so, he found to his dismay that the food intake of the body increased drastically. The result he desired was not attained. Here is the reason: First of all, if one increases the air intake alone, one will increase the appetite of the body. The increased air will cause the body to desire more food to bind with the air. Food and air are combined to form red corpuscles. Thus if one increases the air, he will develop a very powerful digestive system. His appetite will increase. This is, of course, a healthy process, but it is not the result a yogi desires.

A yogi desires reduction in food intake without bringing on ill health to the body. To do this he must increase the breath intake and change the food items so that the stools of the body have reduced foul odor. And that is the most closely guarded secret in yoga practice.

To become restrained in diet as stated in this verse, does not mean to fast on certain sacred days. It has nothing to do with that. It has to do with finding the foods which cause a reduction in the odor of stools in the body. If one can discover or find out from a master of the process what these foods are, and if one can eat such foods and greatly reduce stool odor, one masters the practice.

यज्ञशिष्टामृतभुजो
यान्ति ब्रह्म सनातनम्।
नायं लोकोऽस्त्ययज्ञस्य
कुतोऽन्यः कुरुसत्तम ॥४.३१॥
yajñaśiṣṭāmṛtabhujo
yānti brahma sanātanam
nāyaṁ loko'styayajñasya
kuto'nyaḥ kurusattama
(4.31)

yajñaśiṣṭāmṛtabhujo = yajñaśiṣṭāmṛtabhujaḥ = yajñaśiṣṭa — the physical result of a sacrifice + amṛta — the psychological enjoyment + bhujaḥ — enjoying; yānti — they go; brahma — to the spiritual region; sanātanam — primeval; nāyaṁ = na — not + ayam — this; loko = lokaḥ — world; 'sty = asty (asti) — is (properly utilized); ayajñasya — of a person who performs no austerity or religious ceremony; kuto = kutaḥ — how can it be?; 'nyaḥ = anyaḥ — other; kurusattama — best of the Kurus

Those who enjoy the physical and psychological results of a sacrifice, go to the primeval spiritual region. This world is not properly utilized by those who do not perform austerity or religious ceremony. How then can the other world be, O best of the Kurus? (4.31)

Commentary:

There is no statement here that in this age, a human being cannot perfect any of the disciplines listed off in verses 24 through 29. Many authorities say that these disciplines are outdated and cannot be followed successfully by any man today. These disciplines are very practical if a person applies himself seriously. It may be that only a few people can perfect these austerities, but those few people should not be discouraged merely because the masses are unable to do it. In fact, purity can be transferred to human society only through these austerities. It is austerities alone that bring lasting purity. It is austerities which directly set a man on the proper course. We refer readers to a statement made by Lord Vishnu to *Brahmā* in the beginning of the creation when *Brahmā* was baffled about duties. The Lord said:

pratyādiṣṭaṁ mayā tatra tvayi karma-vimohite
tapo me hrdayarti sākṣād ātmāhaṁ tapaso 'nagha
sṛjāmi tapasaivedaṁ grasāmi tapasā punaḥ
bibharmi tapasā viśvaṁ vīryaṁ me duścaraṁ tapaḥ

You were instructed by Me at the time when you were duty-confused. Penance in relation to Me, is My very being. It is inner energy. I am the person of penance, O sincere one.

I produce the creation by penance. I withdraw it by a penance later on. I maintain it by penance. The cosmic exhibition is a display of penance only. (Śrīmad Bhāgavatam. 2.9.23-24)

It is the same in the *Gītā*. Arjuna was told to apply a penance to his emotional nature, to control his impulsive tendencies and fight. He was not being told to chant the names of the Lord. Chanting the holy names of the Lord has its specific time and place, but it cannot replace the application of specific penances which yield specific results in the discharge of social or devotional duties.

We cannot in the undisciplined state, suddenly go to the kingdom of God. One can only go if he becomes purified sufficiently. His nature must be altered away from humanity towards divinity. That is accomplished mostly by austerity. Even in Arjuna's case, the recommendation was restraint of the sensual nature so that he could change his attitude and fight in agreement with Krishna's scrutinizing ideas.

एवं बहुविधा यज्ञा
वितता ब्रह्मणो मुखे ।
कर्मजान्विद्धि तान्सर्वान्
एवं ज्ञात्वा विमोक्ष्यसे ॥४.३२॥
evaṁ bahuvidhā yajñā
vitatā brahmaṇo mukhe
karmajānviddhi tānsarvān
evaṁ jñātvā vimokṣyase (4.32)

evaṁ — thus; bahuvidhā — many types; yajñā — disciplines of accomplishment; vitatā — expounded; brahmaṇo = brahmaṇaḥ — of spiritual existence; mukhe — in the mouth; karmajān — action-produced; viddhi — know; tān — them; sarvān — all; evaṁ — thus; jñātvā — having realized; vimokṣyase — you will be freed

Many types of disciplines of accomplishment were expounded in the mouth of the spiritual existence. Know them all to be produced from action. Realizing this, O Arjuna, you will be freed. (4.32)

Commentary:

Brahmaṇo mukhe means, *in the mouth of the spiritual existence, the speaking face of the primal cause*. According to some Vedanta experts, no one can really claim to be the one and only face of the Absolute. They even minimized Lord Krishna by saying He is just one such face and that there are others. According to their view, Lord Krishna has no monopoly as a spokesman for the Supreme Absolute. Of course, in the *Gītā* and elsewhere, Lord Krishna established Himself as the Absolute Truth. In the *Gītā*, Arjuna said that he heard of Krishna's supremacy, from *Nārada*, *Vyāsaji* and others.

In any case, this brahmaṇo mukhe or speaking face of the Absolute Truth, of *brahman*, was defined already in the *Gītā* in Chapter Three, verse 10:

sahayajñāḥ prajāḥ sṛṣṭvā purovāca prajāpatiḥ
anena prasaviṣyadhvam eṣa vo'stviṣṭakāmadhuk (3.10)

Long ago, having created the first human beings, along with religious fulfillment and ceremonies, the Procreator Brahmā said: By this worship procedure, you may be productive. May it cause the fulfillment of your desires. (3.10)

Here the word *prajāpatih* identities that speaking face of the Absolute who produced the Vedas. He is *Brahmā*, the sub-creator god. If we are following the Vedic system as believers or even as skeptics, we should accept that *Brahmā* is the *brahmaṇo mukhe*, the speaking face of the original spiritual energies.

Now if *Brahmā* did establish the disciplines, why is it that he objected to the performance of austerities by the four Kumaras in the very beginning? The answer is this: Even though *Brahmā* is responsible for manifesting the sum total destiny, his personal desires are only part of the sum total nature. But he is impregnated with the motives of others. Thus in the beginning he wanted to satisfy his own nature but he was impulsively producing other aspects of the sum total universal destiny even against his will. In all cases, however, some action was required to manifest the primeval ideas. Arjuna was to understand this. By acting, Arjuna would be freed; not by hesitation nor by avoidance of duty.

Each of the disciplines, even the mystic ones, are actions. Not one of them is an inaction. But to those who are mystically blind, non-physical actions appear to be inactions.

Brahmā is not the only mouthpiece of the Absolute Truth but he is a primal one. He was the first to direct others who were manifested after him. *Brahmā* himself, however, was directly told by Lord Garbhodakashayi Vishnu, at least so we are told in the Vishnu *Purāṇa*, *Bhāgavata Purāṇa* and other authoritative Vedic scriptures. The Kumaras themselves are listed as empowered agents of Ishwara, Lord Krishna. It is said.:

sa eva prathamaṁ devaḥ kaumāraṁ sargam āśritaḥ
cacāra duścaraṁ Brahmā brahmacaryam akhaṇḍitam

He, alone at first, the God of this universe, produced the Kumāras, who underwent a severe discipline by the power of spiritual energy and for the purpose of realizing the Absolute Truth. They did this continually. (Śrīmad Bhāgavatam. 1.3.6)

Here we get news that the Kumaras were empowered as spokespersons of the Absolute Truth (*brahma*). They proved it by *brahmāchārya*, disciplines and actions (*ācārya*) which caused them to focus on and realize that primeval spiritual nature (*brahma*). By this, the first person in the universe, the Supreme Lord, Garbhodakashayi Vishnu, then *Brahmā* and then the Kumaras and others after them, were speaking with spiritual power, dictating how we are to realize the spiritual nature. All these systems of penances which give various advantages are activated by action (*karma-jān*).

By stating this, Lord Krishna again urged Arjuna to act. Every man should act his way out of a difficult situation. There is no point in not facing destiny, nor in adapting non-action as an act of evasion. Non-action has its time and place, but if misapplied, it causes more complications.

श्रेयान्द्रव्यमयाद्यज्ञाज्
ज्ञानयज्ञः परंतप ।
सर्वं कर्माखिलं पार्थ
ज्ञाने परिसमाप्यते ॥४.३३॥
śreyāndravyamayādyajñāj
jñānayajñaḥ paraṁtapa
sarvaṁ karmākhilaṁ pārtha
jñāne parisamāpyate (4.33)

śreyān — better; dravyamayād = dravyamayāt — than property; yajñāj = yajñāt — than control and ritual regulation; jñānayajñaḥ = jñāna — theoretical knowledge and primitive practical knowledge + yajñaḥ — control and ritual regulation; paraṁtapa — scorcher of the enemy; sarvaṁ — all; karmākhilaṁ = karma — activity + akhilaṁ — without exception; pārtha — son of Pṛthā; jñāne — as conclusion; parisamāpyate — is realized completely

Better than property control and its ritual regulation is knowledge control and its ritual regulation, O scorcher of the enemy. Every activity without exception, O son of Pṛthā, is realized as a conclusion in the final analysis. (4.33)

Commentary:

Here we see a piece of sarcasm. Arjuna is being addressed as *paramtapa* which means, *scorcher of the enemies*. That was his reputation. But even though he could control and regulate the rebels who were not related to him, he was unable to handle his deviant relatives. And he did break down emotionally, proving that, at the crucial moment, he could not bring himself to regulate his own mind and emotions.

After listing the various standard disciplines through which the ancient seers approached the Absolute Truth, the Spiritual Source Energies, Lord Krishna compared the results of the regulatory actions. Beginning with the gross material elements (*dravyamayāt*), Krishna showed the value of each type of restriction.

Property control is an external action but within the nature there is another type of property, subtle stuff, psychic energy. This is consciousness. Consciousness is realized intellectually as knowledge of subject matters.

Theoretical knowledge gives a false satisfaction. If it is not converted into experience, it is useless. Knowledge should produce practical results and not be theoretical without effective practice . And from such practices one can draw the proper conclusions.

तद्विद्धि प्रणिपातेन
परिप्रश्नेन सेवया ।
उपदेक्ष्यन्ति ते ज्ञानं
ज्ञानिनस्तत्त्वदर्शिनः ॥४.३४॥
tadviddhi praṇipātena
paripraśnena sevayā
upadekṣyanti te jñānaṁ
jñāninastattvadarśinaḥ (4.34)

tad — this; viddhi — know; praṇipātena — by submitting as a student; paripraśnena — by asking questions; sevayā — by serving as requested; upadekṣyanti — they will teach; te — you; jñānaṁ — knowledge; jñāninaḥ — those who know; tattvadarśinaḥ — perceptive reality-conversant sages

This you ought to know. By submitting yourself as a student, by asking questions and by serving as requested, the perceptive reality-conversant teachers will teach you the knowledge. (4.34)

Commentary:

Every method described in verses 25 through 30 can be learned from any teacher who is adept at it and who developed mystic sensual perception for perceiving the hidden aspects of reality. To be a student one should submit oneself for learning, ask questions and serve as requested. There is no stipulation here about honored worship of a guru or treating him as if he were God. The submission is one as a student approaching submissively for an education and a practical technique.

यज्ज्ञात्वा न पुनर्मोहम्
एवं यास्यसि पाण्डव ।
येन भूतान्यशेषेण
द्रक्ष्यस्यात्मन्यथो मयि ॥४.३५॥
yajjñātvā na punarmoham
evaṁ yāsyasi pāṇḍava
yena bhūtānyaśeṣeṇa
drakṣyasyātmanyatho mayi (4.35)

yaj = yad — which; jñātvā — having known; na — not; punar — again; moham — delusion; evaṁ — thus; yāsyasi — you succumb; pāṇḍava — O son of Pāndu; yena — by which; bhūtāny = bhūtāni — living beings; aśeṣeṇa — without exception, all; drakṣyasy = drakṣyasi — you will perceive; ātmany = ātmani — in the self; atho — then; mayi — in me

Having known that experience, you will never again succumb to delusion, O son of Pāndu. By that experience, you will perceive all beings in relation to yourself and then in relation to Me. (4.35)

Commentary:

Lord Krishna gave a very broad application in this verse. He indicated that all the disciplines listed in texts 24 through 33 should be mastered. However, it is greatly narrowed down to the experiences of the samkhya yogis mentioned in Chapter Two and to the saintly kings like Janaka who have the samkhya vision even though they functioned culturally.

There is something definite in the result to be achieved. Once we get the vision, we will know it since our consideration of all other living beings will be consistent with Lord Krishna's. More details of this divine vision is given elsewhere.

अपि चेदसि पापेभ्यः
सर्वेभ्यः पापकृत्तमः ।
सर्वं ज्ञानप्लवेनैव
वृजिनं संतरिष्यसि ॥४.३६॥
api cedasi pāpebhyaḥ
sarvebhyaḥ pāpakṛttamaḥ
sarvaṁ jñānaplavenaiva
vṛjinaṁ saṁtariṣyasi (4.36)

api — even; ced — if; asi — you are; pāpebhyaḥ — of the culprits; sarvebhyaḥ — of all; pāpakṛttamaḥ — most wicked; sarvaṁ — all; jñānaplavenaiva = jñāna — experience + plavena — by conveyance + eva — indeed; vṛjinaṁ — bad tendencies; saṁtariṣyasi — you will overcome

Even if you were the most wicked of the culprits, you will overcome all bad tendencies by the conveyance of this experience. (4.36)

Commentary:

This is more appraisal of the samkhya experience mentioned in previous chapters. It pertains to nothing else. By that experience a man, even if he is the most evil person, would be conveyed beyond the level of imperfections and be able to transcend or shed off bad traits.

यथैधांसि समिद्धोऽग्निर्
भस्मसात्कुरुतेऽर्जुन ।
ज्ञानाग्निः सर्वकर्माणि
भस्मसात्कुरुते तथा ॥४.३७॥
yathaidhāṁsi samiddho'gnir
bhasmasātkurute'rjuna
jñānāgniḥ sarvakarmāṇi
bhasmasātkurute tathā (4.37)

yathaidhāṁsi = yathā — as + idhāṁsi (edhāṁsi) — firewood; samiddho = samiddhaḥ — set on fire; 'gnir = agnir — fire; bhasmasāt kurute — it reduces to ashes; 'rjuna (arjuna) = Arjuna; jñānāgniḥ = jñāna — realize knowledge + agniḥ — fiery potency; sarvakarmāṇi = sarva — all + karmāṇi — actions; bhasmasāt kurute — it reduces to nothing; tathā — so

As when wood is set on fire, it is reduced to ashes, O Arjuna, so the fiery potency of realized knowledge reduces all actions to nothing. (4.37)

Commentary:

This is a description of the condition of a man who effectively transcended material existence and relocated to the spiritual level. Even though such a person may have a material body and may function culturally as Janaka and other capable rulers, still that individual would be free from implications. His actions would not produce any binding force to keep him in the mundane evolutionary cycle. He would be free to travel to the transcendental places during the life span of his body and also after its death.

The example of fire and wood is appropriate. Just as fire reduces wood to ashes, so a wise man with the reality-perceiving vision would, by that piercing view, act to destroy for himself, the implications of actions.

न हि ज्ञानेन सदृशं
पवित्रमिह विद्यते ।
तत्स्वयं योगसंसिद्धः
कालेनात्मनि विन्दति ॥४.३८॥
na hi jñānena sadṛśaṁ
pavitramiha vidyate
tatsvayaṁ yogasaṁsiddhaḥ
kālenātmani vindati (4.38)

na — nothing; hi — indeed; jñānena — with direct experience; sadṛśaṁ — compared with; pavitram — purifier; iha — in this world; vidyate — is relevant; tat — that realization; svayaṁ — himself; yogasaṁsiddhaḥ = yoga — yoga practice + saṁsiddhaḥ— perfected; kālenātmani = kālena — in time + ātmani — in the self; vindati — he locates

Nothing, indeed, can be compared with direct experience. No other purifier is as relevant in this world. That man who himself is perfected in yoga practice, will in time, locate the realization in himself. (4.38)

Commentary:

Yogasamsiddhah means perfection (*samsiddhah*) in yoga. *Śrīla* Bhaktivedanta Swami translated yoga as devotion in this verse, but we will have to note what he said and then return to what Krishna said in the previous chapters. Krishna did not list yoga as devotion but as a series of disciplines which were listed in texts 24 through 33 and in other parts of the chapters we covered thus far.

Nothing can be compared with direct experience because every other thing is something that the person has not directly perceived. Until he can perceive it in reality, it is in someone else's experience or someone's theoretical presentation. There is no purifier that can be rated side by side with personal experience and the correct interpretation of it.

This verse states that a man has to experience the reality for himself. He has to understand where he fits in to the overall picture, especially in relation to other beings. Unless a man understands this, he is bound to live at odds with the world. A reality-perceiving man sees his actual position in the overall scheme and becomes spiritually happy in that vision. He does not become God as some philosophers proclaim, but rather he finds his rightful place in reference to the other limited persons and in reference to the unlimited God.

श्रद्धावाँल्लभते ज्ञानं
तत्परः संयतेन्द्रियः ।
ज्ञानं लब्ध्वा परां शान्तिम्
अचिरेणाधिगच्छति ॥४.३९॥

śraddhāvāṁllabhate jñānaṁ
tatparaḥ saṁyatendriyaḥ
jñānaṁ labdhvā parāṁ śāntim
acireṇādhigacchati (4.39)

śraddhāvān — one who has faith; labhate — he gets; jñānaṁ — the experience; tatparaḥ = tad — that + paraḥ — being devoted to; saṁyatendriyaḥ = saṁyata — restraining + indriyaḥ — sensual energy; jñānaṁ — experience; labdhvā — having acquired; parāṁ — supreme; śāntim — peace; acireṇādhigacchati = acireṇa — quickly + adhigacchati — goes

One who has faith, gets the experience. Being devoted to restraining the sensual energy, having acquired the experience, he goes quickly to the supreme peace. (4.39)

Commentary:

The seekers must have faith (*śraddhavān*) in the teacher or teachers (*jñāninah*) and in the process given. Faith in the teacher gives one the power to believe what the teacher says. Faith in the process gives one the courage to practice the austerity. Since consistent experience comes mainly through the austerity, the practice of it is essential.

Once some experience is gained, one may use it to gain further control of the senses. That gives even higher experience. One rapidly attains the supreme peace (parām śāntim) in that way. This supreme peace, however, was not described in detail. To avoid speculation, we will read closely to understand more. It does have to do with being in harmony with reality, as the Upanishadic sages were and as the saintly kings practiced.

अज्ञश्चाश्रद्दधानश्च
संशयात्मा विनश्यति ।
नायं लोकोऽस्ति न परो
न सुखं संशयात्मनः ॥४.४०॥

ajñaścāśraddadhānaśca
saṁśayātmā vinaśyati
nāyaṁ loko'sti na paro
na sukhaṁ saṁśayātmanaḥ (4.40)

ajñaścāśraddadhānaśca = ajñaḥ — ignorant person + ca — and + aśraddadhānaḥ — faithless person + ca — and; saṁśayātmā = saṁśaya — doubtful + ātmā — self; vinaśyati — is degraded; nāyaṁ = na — not + ayaṁ — this; loko = lokaḥ — world; 'sti = asti — is; na — not; paro = paraḥ — beyond the physical world; na — not; sukhaṁ — in happiness; saṁśayātmanaḥ = saṁśaya — doubting + ātmanaḥ — for the self

The ignorant person, the faithless one who is doubtful, is degraded. Neither this physical world, nor the dimensions beyond this, nor happiness, is for the person who is doubtful. (4.40)

Commentary:

The happiness (*sukham*) in this verse is the same happiness described in the previous verse as supreme peace (*parām śāntim*). It is not the regular sensual happiness that we crave on the lower planes. *Parām*, or supreme, indicates that it is a spiritual grade of joy of *brahman* origin. A doubtful man who is doubtful of what Krishna said may find happiness in this world but he will not find the supreme spiritual joy. After passing from his material body, he will not find it in the hereafter either. He will become frustrated in objectives, all because his idea does not conform to reality.

योगसंन्यस्तकर्माणं
ज्ञानसंछिन्नसंशयम् ।
आत्मवन्तं न कर्माणि
निबध्नन्ति धनंजय ॥४.४१॥
yogasaṁnyastakarmāṇaṁ
jñānasaṁchinnasaṁśayam
ātmavantaṁ na karmāṇi
nibadhnanti dhanaṁjaya (4.41)

yogasaṁnyastakarmāṇaṁ = yoga — yoga technique + saṁnyasta — renounced + karmāṇaṁ — action; jñānasaṁchinnasaṁśayam = jñāna — realized knowledge + saṁchinna — removed + saṁśayam — doubt; ātmavantaṁ — self-composed; na — no; karmāṇi — cultural activities; nibadhnanti — they bind; dhanaṁjaya — O conqueror of wealthy countries

Cultural activities do not implicate a person whose actions are renounced through techniques developed in yoga practice, whose doubt is removed by realized knowledge and who is self-composed, O conqueror of wealthy countries. (4.41)

Commentary:

Śrīla Bhaktivedanta Swami gave yoga as, *devotional service in karma yoga.* In his translation the word *yoga* and its meaning entirely disappeared. Sridhara Maharaja, the Gaudiya Math authority who was based in India as the main acharya after the disappearance of *Śrīla* Bhaktisiddhanta Sarasvati, gave *yoga-samnyasta-karmāṇam,* as, *one who has ceased all actions in accordance with the path of sannyāsa or abnegation, only after practising niṣkama karma-yoga, the path of selfless action.*

We will, however, stick to the Gita to get the meaning of the word *yoga.* We already received hints but there will be more. Whatever modern Vaishnava authorities say that is consistent with the text, must be accepted.

It is important to observe that Lord Krishna spoke of renunciation of motivated actions by the process of yoga and not just of the renunciation of actions. We have to find out why He stressed doing so by the process of yoga. Some modern seekers renounce or try to renounce their motivated actions when they are criticized or intimidated by preachers, or when they want to join a spiritual society in which such renunciation is a requirement for membership, but that sort of renunciation fails because it is not done by yoga.

To remove doubts; the recommendation is *jñāna* which we give as *realized knowledge.* The usual meaning of *jñana,* is knowledge, but knowledge itself cannot do much to save a man unless the knowledge is derived from personal experience and not from theoretical information. Theory and the mastership of it does not save a man from doubts. One must also be *ātmavantam* which means self-composed or rather, detached from one's mind, senses and intellect and situated mostly in his soul rather than in the psychic organs which are so necessary for usage by the soul. Then after achieving all this, a man who acts, is free from implications. Such a man is free to go on to the spiritual atmosphere regardless of whether he is a devotee of Lord Krishna or not. It does not necessarily apply to devotees of Krishna alone. Even a man from another religion like a Buddhist or Christian or even a man who does not believe in any supreme being can achieve that state of detachment from material nature and be saved from implications.

तस्मादज्ञानसंभूतं
हृत्स्थं ज्ञानासिनात्मनः ।
छित्त्वैनं संशयं योगम्
आतिष्ठोत्तिष्ठ भारत ॥४.४२॥
tasmādajñānasaṁbhūtaṁ
hṛtsthaṁ jñānāsinātmanaḥ
chittvainaṁ saṁśayaṁ yogam
ātiṣṭhottiṣṭha bhārata (4.42)

tasmād = *tasmāt* — *therefore; ajñānasaṁbhūtaṁ* = *ajñāna* — *ignorance* + *saṁbhūtaṁ* — *produced by; hṛtsthaṁ* — *lodged in your being; jñānāsinā* = *jñāna* — *realized knowledge* + *asinā* — *by the cutting effect; 'tmanaḥ* = *ātmanaḥ* — *of yourself; chittvainaṁ* = *chittva* — *having severed entirely* + *enaṁ* — *this; saṁśayam* — *doubt; yogaṁ* — *to yogic technique; ātiṣṭhottiṣṭha* = *ātiṣṭha* — *resort to* + *uttiṣṭha* — *make a stand; bhārata* — *man of the Bharata family*

Therefore having severed entirely, with the cutting instrument of realized knowledge, this doubt that comes from the ignorance lodged in your being, resort to yogic technique and make a stand, O man of the Bharata family! (4.42)

Commentary:

We again return to Lord Krishna's prime objective which is to make Arjuna stand ground and fight at *Kurukṣetra*. The Lord directly tells Arjuna to use the benefit of his former yoga practice and to get up and fight (*yogam ātiṣṭhottiṣṭha*). Arjuna is to use the psychological benefits of his former yoga practice and then fight just as King Janaka and others did, which means to fight with an emotionally-hardened attitude in detachment from mundane affections, only looking at the spiritual advantage to be derived by the parties involved.

A clear distinction is made between Krishna and Arjuna, between Krishna and any limited being. Krishna does not have the *ajñāna*, or ignorance, innately situated (*stham*) in the central being (*hṛt*). But the limited souls do. Therefore they have to use the realized knowledge (*jñāna*) to remove or cut out (*asinā*) that ignorance. Thus the necessity of yoga disciplines on our part. Being naturally super-conscious, Lord Krishna does not need yoga.

CHAPTER 5

Disciplined Use of Opportunities by aYogi *

अर्जुन उवाच
संन्यासं कर्मणां कृष्ण
पुनर्योगं च शंससि ।
यच्छ्रेय एतयोरेकं
तन्मे ब्रूहि सुनिश्चितम् ॥५.१॥
arjuna uvāca
saṁnyāsaṁ karmaṇāṁ kṛṣṇa
punaryogaṁ ca śaṁsasi
yacchreya etayorekaṁ
tanme brūhi suniścitam (5.1)

arjuna — Arjuna; uvāca — said; saṁnyāsaṁ — renunciation of involvement; karmaṇām — of social activity; kṛṣṇa — Krishna; punar — again; yogaṁ — the application of yoga austerities to worldly life; ca — and; śaṁsasi — you approved; yacchreya = yad — which + chreya (śreyaḥ) — better; etayor = etayoḥ — of these two; ekaṁ — one; tan — this; me — to me; brūhi — tell; suniścitam — with certainty

Arjuna said: You approved renunciation of social activity and also mentioned the application of yoga to worldly life. Which one of these is better? Tell me this with certainty. (5.1)

Commentary:

To Arjuna's mind Lord Krishna spoke of two paths in the preceding chapters. They were:

1. *samnyāsam karmaṇām—the total renunciation of social activity*
2. *yogam—the various disciplines which were known as yoga in the time of Krishna and Arjuna*

These two procedures of living appeared to be contradictory to Arjuna. Since Krishna appraised both, Arjuna asked for the best one. He could not, at the time Chapter Four was spoken to him, decide what to do. Trusting Krishna, he wanted the Lord to make the selection.

If we read Chapters Two, Three, and Four carefully, we will understand that Lord Krishna wanted Arjuna to apply the skill of detachment in the field of action. Or stated differently, to apply the skill of the emotional maturity one gains from yoga practice, into the worldly life. But Arjuna did not see this consistency at the time of hearing Chapter Four.

Arjuna already practiced the yoga disciplines as the *Mahābhārata* history shows, but he failed to apply the skills to his worldly life when facing the armies. Krishna urged Arjuna to apply that emotional maturity and mystic outlook.

**The Mahābhārata contains no chapter headings. This title was assigned by the translator on the basis of verse 2 of this chapter.*

श्रीभगवानुवाच
संन्यासः कर्मयोगश्च
निःश्रेयसकरावुभौ ।
तयोस्तु कर्मसंन्यासात्
कर्मयोगो विशिष्यते ॥५.२॥
śrībhagavānuvāca
saṁnyāsaḥ karmayogaśca
niḥśreyasakarāvubhau
tayostu karmasaṁnyāsāt
karmayogo viśiṣyate (5.2)

śrī-bhagavān — the Blessed Lord; uvāca — said; saṁnyāsaḥ — total renunciation of social opportunities; karmayogaśca = karmayogaḥ — disciplined use of social opportunities by a yogi + ca — and; niḥśreyasakarāv = niḥśreyasa — ultimate happiness + karāv (karau) — leading to; ubhau — both; tayos — of the two; tu — but; karmasaṁnyāsāt — than the renunciation of cultural activity; karmayogo = karmayogaḥ — disciplined use of social opportunities by a yogi; viśiṣyate — is better

The Blessed Lord said: Both methods, the total renunciation of social opportunities and the disciplined use of opportunities by a yogi, lead to ultimate happiness. But of the two aspects, the disciplined use of opportunities in a yogic mood is better than total renunciation of cultural activity. (5.2)

Commentary:

Following Arjuna's line of reasoning, Lord Krishna gave a preference. He clarified that He meant the application of yoga to worldly life and not a contrast between yoga and worldly life.

If we contrast the two, then Lord Krishna said that *karma yoga*, or action that is performed by a man who has perfected yoga, is better than renunciation without action. Let us consider this from another angle: A man cannot really perform *karma yoga* unless he mastered yoga. And a man who takes to renunciation would have done so for the purpose of perfecting the disciplines of yoga. This would mean, therefore, that an actual *karma* yogi is already proficient in yoga.

Persons like King Janaka and even Arjuna already performed and perfected yoga practice before acting in the world in responsible positions. In those days, aristocratic boys attended private schools where the essentials of yoga were taught.

Just as modern boys become educated before getting a job and functioning as adults, so these ancient aristocratic boys, the princes like Arjuna, attended yoga training schools. Thus they developed emotional detachment and sharpened mystic insight.

However this answer to Arjuna's question is just that only. It is an answer for Arjuna and it is not an answer for all persons in all times and places. Lord Krishna did not give Uddhava the same answer. For Arjuna, *karma yoga* as practiced by King Janaka was the ideal path at that time of Arjuna's life. Later on Arjuna and his brothers would be advised by *Nārada* Muni, a reliable agent of the Lord, to abandon the path of *karma yoga* and to assume the path of renunciation, *sannyāsa*.

ज्ञेयः स नित्यसंन्यासी
यो न द्वेष्टि न काङ्क्षति ।
निर्द्वंद्वो हि महाबाहो
सुखं बन्धात्प्रमुच्यते ॥५.३॥
jñeyaḥ sa nityasaṁnyāsī
yo na dveṣṭi na kāṅkṣati
nirdvaṁdvo hi mahābāho
sukhaṁ bandhāt pramucyate (5.3)

jñeyaḥ — to be known; sa = saḥ — he; nityasaṁnyāsī = nitya — consistent + saṁnyāsī — a renouncer of social opportunities; yo = yaḥ — who; na — not; dveṣṭi — dislikes; na — not; kāṅkṣati — craves; nirdvandvo = nirdvandvaḥ — indifferent to opposite features; hi — indeed; mahābāho — O strong-armed man; sukhaṁ — easily; bandhāt — from implication; pramucyate — is freed

Indeed, a person who neither dislikes nor craves, who is indifferent to opposite features, should be recognized as a consistent renouncer, O strong-armed man. He is easily freed from implication. (5.3)

Commentary:

For standard meaning, *nitya* means, *eternal* or *perpetual*. We gave, *consistent*. A man who is consistently renounced, not now and then, nor periodically, but in all of his undertakings, easily slips away from the implications of his activities.

The key is his indifference to opposite features (*nirdvandvo*), particularly to his liking and disliking moods. Due to detachment, he can think clearly and use the reality-piercing intellect (*buddhi*). This was the technique used by those ancient kings like Janaka. Unless a man can apply himself like those experts of detachment, he should not be called a *karma* yogi as defined in the *Gītā*.

सांख्ययोगौ पृथग्बालाः
प्रवदन्ति न पण्डिताः ।
एकमप्यास्थितः सम्यग्
उभयोर्विन्दते फलम् ॥५.४॥
sāṁkhyayogau pṛthagbālāḥ
pravadanti na paṇḍitāḥ
ekamapyāsthitaḥ samyag
ubhayorvindate phalam (5.4)

sāṁkhyayogau = sāṁkhya — Sāṁkhya ideas + yogau — and yoga practices; pṛthagbālāḥ — simple-minded people; pravadanti — they describe; na — not; paṇḍitāḥ — the perceptive speakers; ekam — one; apy = api — even; āsthitaḥ — practiced; samyag — correctly; ubhayor = ubhayoḥ — of either; vindate — one gets; phalam — result

It is the simple-minded people, not the perceptive speakers, who say that Sāṁkhya ideas and yoga practices are separate. Even if one method is practised correctly, the practitioner gets the result of either. (5.4)

Commentary:

Arjuna saw a contrast in the two practices but Lord Krishna indirectly said that Arjuna was naive, and childish (*bālāh*). It appears that even though Arjuna was expert in yoga practices, he did not master the application to worldly life. As such, he was not yet on par with the functional kings like Janaka. He was like a boy who learnt mathematics and then became confused in its application to financial concerns.

In terms of spiritual perfection, however, both yoga and samkhya yoga can give perfection, provided they are proficiently mastered. We should get Lord Krishna's complete definition for the two terms, namely, samkhya and yoga. Since we are not living in the time of Lord Krishna we will have to learn from the Vedic literatures what those practices were in their own time and place, as contrasted to the meaning of these terms today.

If commentators use different definitions, it would mean that their explanations are variant. If we are serious about understanding the *Gītā* as Lord Krishna delivered it, we must identify the exact methods of these practices.

यत्सांख्यैः प्राप्यते स्थानं
तद्योगैरपि गम्यते ।
एकं सांख्यं च योगं च
यः पश्यति स पश्यति ॥५.५॥

yat — whatever; sāṁkhyaiḥ — by the Sāṁkhya experts; prāpyate — is attained; sthānaṁ — the level; tad — that; yogair = yogaiḥ — by the yogis; api — also; gamyate — is reached; ekaṁ — one; sāṁkhyaṁ —

yatsāṁkhyaiḥ prāpyate sthānaṁ
tadyogairapi gamyate
ekaṁ sāṁkhyaṁ ca yogaṁ ca
yaḥ paśyati sa paśyati (5.5)

Samkhya; ca — and; yogaṁ — yoga; ca — and; yaḥ — who; paśyati — perceived; sa = saḥ — he; paśyati — sees

The level obtained by the Sāṁkhya experts is also reached by the yogis. Sāṁkhya and yoga are essentially one. He who perceives that really sees. (5.5)

Commentary:

Mathematics at school and mathematics at a commercial concern are the same. Still there is a tiny bit of difference since one involves just an academic simplicity of learning and the other involves the practicing complexity of application. Still there is a continuity (*ekam*) in the two. They are related.

संन्यासस्तु महाबाहो
दुःखमाप्तुमयोगतः ।
योगयुक्तो मुनिर्ब्रह्म
नचिरेणाधिगच्छति ॥५.६॥
saṁnyāsastu mahābāho
duḥkhamāptumayogataḥ
yogayukto munirbrahma
nacireṇādhigacchati (5.6)

saṁnyāsaḥ — renunciation of opportunity; tu — indeed; mahābāho — O mighty man; duḥkham — difficulty; āptum — to obtain; ayogataḥ — without yoga-proficiency; yogayukto = yogayuktaḥ — yoga-proficient; munir = muniḥ — sage; brahma — spiritual level; nacireṇādhigacchati = nacirena — in no span of time + adhigacchati — reaches

Renunciation of opportunities is difficult to attain without yoga practice, O mighty man. In the nick of time, a yoga-proficient sage reaches the spiritual plane. (5.6)

Commentary:

True renunciation is consistent application of detachment. This is difficult to attain if one has not perfected the yoga disciplines. It can be done but it is extremely rare to find a person who is expert at detachment and who has not mastered yoga. The divine beings like Krishna act with natural detachment without any yoga practice, but they are the exceptions. They do not have lapses of memory. Their super-consciousness is readily adaptable to any circumstance.

Arjuna wanted to act perfectly without using his acquired yogic detachment, but he could not do so. Lord Krishna brought to Arjuna's attention that he must apply that emotional maturity gained through yoga practice. Arjuna would view the *Kurukṣetra* situation in the yogic way. Arjuna's approach was like that of a school boy who wants to manage bank's concerns without using the mathematical proficiency developed during the school years. Of course, a few individuals might manage finances even if they have not gone to school but these few are the geniuses. Most people will have to apply schooling. And if a man has no schooling, he would have to take a course before he could function proficiently.

योगयुक्तो विशुद्धात्मा
विजितात्मा जितेन्द्रियः ।
सर्वभूतात्मभूतात्मा
कुर्वन्नपि न लिप्यते ॥५.७॥

yogayukto = yogayuktaḥ — one proficient in yoga; viśuddhātmā — one of purified self; vijitātmā — one who is self-controlled; jitendriyaḥ — one who has conquered his senses; sarvabhūtātmabhūtātmā = sarva — all + bhūta — being + ātma — self + bhūta — being + ātmā — self (sarvabhūtātmabhūtātmā - one

yogayukto viśuddhātmā
vijitātmā jitendriyaḥ
sarvabhūtātmabhūtātmā
kurvannapi na lipyate (5.7)

who feels related to all beings); kurvan — acting; api — even; na — not; lipyate — is implicated

A person who is proficient in yoga, whose soul is purified, who is self-controlled, who conquered his senses, whose self feels related to all beings, is not implicated when acting. (5.7)

Commentary:

This type of *karma yoga* cannot be performed by a person who is not purified in his nature, in his psychology (*viśuddhātmā*). This is why the ancient kings like Janaka became proficient in yoga. The specialty of yoga practice is that it gives purification of the *guṇas* (modes of material nature) to which we are adapted. Each man has a portion of material nature as his sectioned-off lower self or psyche. Unless that portion is purified, one cannot consistently reach the spiritual plane. And it is not a matter of wishful thinking either. One has to take definite steps in the yoga to master this. Arjuna went through this formerly and yet he became re-contaminated. What can be said of the modern men who have never in present life taken up yoga? How can such men be *karma* yogis by the definition of the *Gītā*?

नैव किंचित्करोमीति
युक्तो मन्येत तत्त्ववित् ।
पश्यञ्शृण्वन्स्पृशञ्जिघ्रन्
अश्नन्गच्छन्स्वपञ्श्वसन् ॥५.८॥
naiva kiṁcitkaromīti
yukto manyeta tattvavit
paśyañśṛṇvanspṛśañjighrann
aśnangacchansvapañśvasan (5.8)

naiva = na — not + eva — indeed; kiṁcit— anything; karomīti = karomi — initiate + iti — thus; yukto = yuktaḥ — proficient in yoga; manyeta — he thinks; tattvavit — knower of reality; paśyañśṛṇvan = paśyan — seeing + śṛṇvan — hearing; spṛśañjighrann = spṛśan — touching + jighran — smelling; aśnan — eating; gacchan — walking; svapañśvasan = svapan — sleeping + śvasan — breathing

"I do not initiate anything." Being proficient in yoga, this is what the knower of reality thinks. While seeing, hearing, touching, smelling, eating, walking, sleeping and breathing, (5.8)

Commentary:

From the modern perspective, we may ask what or who sees, hears, touches, smells, eats, walks, sleeps, and breathes? If it is not the person who has a body, then who or what does all of this? A theoretical answer would be that the life force or the automatic nervous system does this. Which of us ever experiences sufficient separation from the life force to objectively perceive it? This is why yoga practice was required as a prerequisite. It is through such practice that the ancients easily perceived this. There are other ways, however. *Patañjali* in his *Yoga Sūtras* listed other methods:

janma auṣadhi mantra tapaḥ samādhijāḥ siddhayaḥ

> ***The mystic skills are produced through taking birth in particular species, or by taking drugs, or by reciting special sounds, or by physical bodily austerities or by the continuous effortless linkage of the attention to a higher concentration force, object or person. (Yoga Sūtra 4.1)***

Thus a man, without any endeavor in this present life, might have a mystic perfection. Another might develop mystic vision by taking herbs such as marijuana or chemicals like LSD or special beverages which were used for Vedic sacrifices. Another might do so by particular chants and sounds, another by austerities, and yet another by profound meditations. However, thus far in the *Gītā*, Lord Krishna acknowledged yoga and the resulting profound meditations of the samkhya experts.

Many hippies went to spiritual masters who came to the Western countries from India. These hippies used drugs like marijuana, LSD, and heroin. From their mystic experiences, they understood that the actions like eating, hearing, and sleeping were being conducted by the *prāṇa* or the subtle energy in the body. These hippies also reached states of consciousness through which they understood that they were not the initiators of any activities. But after their experiences, when they returned to normal consciousness, they lost touch with the higher vision. Yoga is special since one who proficiently practices, does not lose the higher perception.

प्रलपन्विसृजन्गृह्णन्
उन्मिषन्निमिषन्नपि ।
इन्द्रियाणीन्द्रियार्थेषु
वर्तन्त इति धारयन् ॥५.९॥
pralapanvisṛjangṛhṇann
unmiṣannimiṣannapi
indriyāṇīndriyārtheṣu
vartanta iti dhārayan (5.9)

pralapan — talking; visṛjan — evacuating; gṛhṇan — holding; unmiṣan — opening the eyelids; nimiṣan — closing the eyelids; api — also; indriyāṇīndriyārtheṣu = indriyāṇi — senses + indriyārtheṣu — in the attractive objects; vartanta — interlock; iti — thus; dhārayan — considers

...while talking, evacuating, holding, opening and closing the eyelids, he considers, "The senses are interlocked with the attractive objects." (5.9)

Commentary:

These qualifications of a *karma* yogi are important if we are to understand what sort of person King Janaka was and what sort of person Arjuna became after Krishna showed him how to apply the yoga practice.

In our normal worldly consciousness, we do not perceive life in this way. That is an honest fact. We would have to take up a process through which that adjustment in consciousness is made consistently, before we can perform *karma yoga* like King Janaka. To realize in fact, that the senses are interlocked with their objects, the soul would have to be objectively detached from a body and all of its sensual desires. Such a separation is a mystic act. It cannot be realized consistently, without performing certain austerities through which we come to sort out the differences between ourselves and the various subtle mechanisms we are interlocked with.

ब्रह्मण्याधाय कर्माणि
सङ्गं त्यक्त्वा करोति यः ।
लिप्यते न स पापेन
पद्मपत्रमिवाम्भसा ॥५.१०॥
brahmaṇyādhāya karmāṇi
saṅgaṁ tyaktvā karoti yaḥ
lipyate na sa pāpena
padmapatramivāmbhasā (5.10)

brahmaṇy = brahmaṇi — on the spiritual level; ādhāya — putting on, focused on; karmāṇi — actions; saṅgaṁ — attachment; tyaktvā — having discarded; karoti — he acts; yaḥ — who; lipyate — affected; na — not; sa = saḥ — he; pāpena — by necessary violence; padmapatram = padma — lotus + patram — leaf; ivāmbhasā = iva — just as + ambhasā — by water

Being focused on the spiritual level, discarding attachments, his acts are not defiled by necessary violence, just as a lotus leaf is not affected by water. (5.10)

Commentary:

Some Vaishnava acharyas gave *brahmaṇi* as *the Supreme Lord*. We gave the original meaning as *the spiritual level*. *Brahman* is a broad term meaning the spiritual plane of life and all that is there in pristine glory. This includes the Supreme Lord. Usually, devotees of Krishna perceive the brahman spiritual level in terms of Krishna's personal influence, but others who are not attracted to Krishna may attain spiritual zones where they experience no relationship to Krishna. Since Lord Krishna did not stress Himself in this verse as He does elsewhere, I did not interpose His name here.

Pāpena means, *by sin*, or *by an evil act*. We gave *by necessary violence*. Necessary violence is that violence which is judicially administered for reforming an offender. It is the violence Lord Krishna motivated in Arjuna, for Arjuna to hurt bodies for the benefit of souls. Such violence appears to be a sin (*pāpam*), but in fact, it is not. In any case, for such judicial discipline there are reactions, but the person who is spiritually-situated is not degraded by the negative effects. This verse does not mean, as some commentators suggest, that a spiritually-situated man can commit a sinful act and be saved from the reaction. This directly applies to Arjuna's situation. It was Arjuna who recognized the sin of killing relatives and friends. Let us review his words:

pāpamevāśrayedasmān hatvaitānātatāyinaḥ
tasmānnārhā vayaṁ hantuṁ dhārtarāṣṭrānsvabāndhavān
svajanaṁ hi kathaṁ hatvā sukhinaḥ syāma mādhava (1.36)

Having killed the offenders, sin will take hold of us. Therefore we are not justified to kill the sons of Dhṛtarāṣṭra, our relatives. Having killed our own people, how should we be happy, O descendent of Madhu? (1.36)

Arjuna was afraid of the reaction for the evil (*pāpam*) of killing relatives. Krishna replied directly in this verse that if Arjuna were to remove his soul from the modes of material nature (*guṇās*) and relocate it to the spiritual level (*brahman*), then no sin would manifest, if Arjuna proceeded to wound and kill enemy warriors who were members of a corrupt dynasty. It is necessary violence that is discussed here; violence perpetrated by the Supreme Being, Krishna, Who, as a matter of duty, deals out justice when He comes to the human plane. This does not mean that a religious man or a religious group can perpetrate violence or sinful acts and escape. It means that in cases where judicial justice is done, reactions will not degrade the executioner if that person is spiritually situated when he executes the law. This is the only condition under which this verse applies, this and no other.

The example of the lotus leaf will suffice. Water falls on it but does not penetrate it. The reactions may or may not come to an agent of justice, but they do not cling to him. If, however, the agent deviates and misuses power, then he will face reactions which will affect him. It is not that he is protected in every activity. The protection holds only for acts which are motivated from the spiritual level as justice acts which compensate for previous wrongs.

कायेन मनसा बुद्ध्या
केवलैरिन्द्रियैरपि ।
योगिनः कर्म कुर्वन्ति
सङ्गं त्यक्त्वात्मशुद्धये ॥५.११॥

kāyena — with the body; manasā — with the mind; buddhyā — with the intellect; kevalair = kevalaiḥ — alone; indriyair = indriyaiḥ — by the senses; api — even; yoginaḥ — yogis; karma — cultural activity; kurvanti — they perform;

kāyena manasā buddhyā
kevalairindriyairapi
yoginaḥ karma kurvanti
saṅgaṁ tyaktvātmaśuddhaye (5.11)

saṅgaṁ — attachment; tyaktvā — having discarded; 'tmaśuddhaye = ātmaśuddhaye = ātma — self + śuddhaye — towards purification

With the body, mind and intellect, or even with the senses alone, the yogis, having discarded attachment, perform cultural acts for self-purification. (5.11)

Commentary:

The two paths mentioned in Chapters Two and Three are described in brief in this verse. The one used by the ancient yoga-trained kings like Janaka is the usage of the body, mind and intelligence with detachment from the cultural plane, without implications. The path used by the mystic yogis who are not actively involved in human affairs is the mystic one on the super-sensual plane (indriyair). These mystics are in the process of relocating their focus to the subtle level. This is why Lord Krishna used the term *kevalair*, which means *merely*, *alone* or *only with*. To function exclusively on the subtle plane, one must advance beyond the need for a gross body and brain *(kāyena manasā buddhyā)*.

The most important term in this verse, however, is *'tmaśuddhaye (ātmaśuddhaye)*, self-purification. This means purification of the *ātma*, or soul. To purify the *ātma*, one must first free the *ātma* from the body, mind, intelligence, and life force. The life force is not directly mentioned in this verse, but it is present in the word *indriyair* because it is the life force that energizes the senses. It is not the mind nor the soul which energizes the senses directly, but it is the life force. Unless the body, mind, intelligence, and life force are purified, there is no question of purification of the soul. Those who feel that the soul could detach himself from the body-mind complex suddenly, are in great ignorance.

The attachment between the soul and his material energy is so deep that unless that energy is purified, the soul cannot be freed from material existence. He will not have the power to move himself one step from matter unless he purifies the subtle material energy in the psyche.

युक्तः कर्मफलं त्यक्त्वा
शान्तिमाप्नोति नैष्ठिकीम् ।
अयुक्तः कामकारेण
फले सक्तो निबध्यते ॥५.१२॥
yuktaḥ karmaphalaṁ tyaktvā
śāntimāpnoti naiṣṭhikīm
ayuktaḥ kāmakāreṇa
phale sakto nibadhyate (5.12)

yuktaḥ — proficient in yoga; karmaphalaṁ — reward of cultural activity; tyaktvā — having abandoned; śāntim — peace; āpnoti — obtains; naiṣṭhikīm — steady; ayuktaḥ — a person not proficient in yoga; kāmakāreṇa — by action which is motivated by desire; phale — in result; sakto = saktaḥ — attached; nibadhyate — is bound

The person who is proficient in yoga, and who abandons the rewards of cultural activity, obtains steady peace. The person who is not proficient in yoga, being attached to results, is bound by desire-motivated action. (5.12)

Commentary:

This preaching by Lord Krishna is being stressed and over-stressed. Lord Krishna's primal objective is to get Arjuna to pick up bow and arrows, resume a warrior's attitude, and fight. Verse after verse, we see that Lord Krishna urged Arjuna. Here again, Krishna sarcastically insulted Arjuna, suggesting that Arjuna is undisciplined, is influenced by cravings for affection from relatives, and wants good results in terms of enjoying life with the Kurus no matter what they do. But Krishna warned Arjuna that he would be bound up in unfavorable consequences. Arjuna should abandon any idea about living happily with the Kurus. He should fight and obtain steady soberness of mind and the resulting existential security, being at peace with God even if it meant being shunned by family members.

सर्वकर्माणि मनसा
संन्यस्यास्ते सुखं वशी ।
नवद्वारे पुरे देही
नैव कुर्वन्न कारयन् ॥५.१३॥
sarvakarmāṇi manasā
saṁnyasyāste sukhaṁ vaśī
navadvāre pure dehī
naiva kurvanna kārayan (5.13)

sarvakarmāṇi = sarva — all + karmāṇi — actions; manasā — with the mind; saṁnyasyāste = saṁnyasy (saṁnyasi) — renouncing + āste — he sits; sukhaṁ — happily; vaśī — director; navadvāre = nava — nine + dvāre — in the gate; pure — in the city; dehī — the embodied soul; naiva = na — not + eva — indeed; kurvan — acting; na — nor; kārayan — causing activity

Renouncing all action with the mind, the embodied soul resides happily within as the director in the nine-gated city, neither acting or causing activity. (5.13)

Commentary:

This statement applies to the two types of transcendentalists listed so far, namely, the mystics who are not actively involved in history and those administrators who are participating. Both of these are active, but externally the mystics appear to be inactive. Since he functions mostly through the subtle body, a mystic is very much involved. But if we have no mystic vision, we may consider him to be a non-participant.

In either case, that of the mystic and that of the active, qualified transcendentalist, one single factor qualifies either of them for being *tattvadarśis*, reality-perceiving personalities. That is their clear understanding that the actions of their bodies, even those of the subtle forms, are being motivated by the resultant energies. Their soul energy is involved by necessity, but they are not the prime movers. They themselves are being motivated. The city, or body of nine openings (*navadvāre pure*), is the material body, but it is also the subtle form which has the same nine openings. These nine openings are the two eyes, two ears, two nostrils, one mouth, a genital and anus. This was well-documented by the Upanishadic sages and was well understood by the samkhya yogis, long, long before the time of Lord Krishna. As the director (*vaśī*) of that body, the living entity is merely an energy supplier with a token position as the master of the residence. He does not have absolute control over anything. He is bombarded with influences on all planes. In such a situation, realizing his helplessness, he has three choices: Either to be happy, sad, or indifferent. After all, if you are not in charge and if you are not going to be within the near or remote future, then what should be your attitude?

We are helplessly involved in having a body, mind, intelligence, and a set of sensual equipments which function impulsively. If even Janaka and his peers could not be in absolute control of their subtle forms, how can we ?

न कर्तृत्वं न कर्माणि
लोकस्य सृजति प्रभुः ।
न कर्मफलसंयोगं
स्वभावस्तु प्रवर्तते ॥५.१४॥

na — not; kartṛtvaṁ — means of action; na — nor; karmāṇi — actions; lokasya — of the creatures; sṛjati — he creates; prabhuḥ — the Lord; na — nor; karmaphalasaṁyogaṁ = karma — action + phala — consequence +

na kartṛtvaṁ na karmāṇi
lokasya sṛjati prabhuḥ
na karmaphalasaṁyogaṁ
svabhāvastu pravartate (5.14)

saṁyogaṁ — cyclic connection; svabhāvaḥ — inherent nature; tu — but; pravartate — it causes

The Lord does not create the means of action, or the actions of the creatures, or the action-consequence cycle. The inherent nature causes this. (5.14)

Commentary:

There was some difficulty in translating this verse. At first, we followed the meaning given by our Vaishnava spiritual master, His Divine Grace A.C. Bhaktivedanta Swami. The technicality has to do with the word *prabhu*. This word means master, lord, supervisor. *Śrīla* Bhaktivedanta gives it as *the master of the city of the body*, as the *dehi* of the previous verse. *Dehi* means *embodied spirit*. However, the Gaudiya Math authority, *Śrīla* Sridhara Maharaja, gave *prabhu* as *the Supreme Lord*. And the exacting grammatical translator, Winthrop Sargeant, gave *the Lord, the Mighty One, the ātman or self*. Sanskrit dictionaries gave, *the Lord* or *the limited embodied soul*.

In this particular verse, however, it means the Supreme Lord. In verse 13, Lord Krishna described the soul and his body, but in this verse, there is a contrast between the Supreme Lord and His so-called body, the *loka* or the universe. In either case, that of the soul or of the Supreme Lord, the situation is described as being very similar. That prabhu here means the Supreme Lord, will be confirmed later on when we hear of the Universal Form.

However, readers are asked to take careful note of what our Vaishnava authority said in his *Bhagavad-Gītā As It Is*. His purport clears off any illusions a limited person might have about absolutely possessing a body.

In this verse, many theories of many men are shredded to bits by Lord Krishna. He begins with *na*, which means: *no, not, or not possible*. He says that the Lord of the world (*prabhu*) does not create (*sṛjati*) the destiny nor the activities of people. Still many preachers say that the Lord does this. We are therefore left to ask this most important question: If the Lord does not, then who or what does? And the answer is already given in the last line by the term *svabhāvas* which means that whatever transpires, is being enacted by inherent or innate forces. In addition, the Lord said that He is not responsible for the action-consequence cycle (*karmaphalasamyogam*). Some years ago a great yogi, Swami Yogeshwarananda, explained this verse in India and people were shocked by what he said. He explained that in the case of any mundane destiny there is no direct involvement by the Lord since the mere proximity of the Lord to the material creation is sufficient for all possible agitation. He claimed that destiny transpired automatically on the basis of the interacting primeval energies (*prāṇa*) along with the particles of *brahman*, the spirit souls, and that the Lord was not directly involved, nor was it necessary for Him to directly wield the energies. This hard talk of the Swami got him a bad name and people began to think he was atheistic.

Of course, he was correct. This verse confirms it. Here Lord Krishna easily and definitely put the blame for all of this agitation upon *svabhāvas*, the inherent nature of individuals and energies involved in any given situation, whether it be local or universal.

नादत्ते कस्यचित्पापं
न चैव सुकृतं विभुः ।
अज्ञानेनावृतं ज्ञानं
तेन मुह्यन्ति जन्तवः ॥५.१५॥

nādatte = na — not + ādatte — perceives; kasyacit — of anyone; pāpaṁ — evil consequence; na — not; caiva = ca — and + eva — indeed; sukṛtaṁ — good reaction; vibhuḥ — the Almighty God; ajñānenāvṛtaṁ = ajñānena —

nādatte kasyacitpāpaṁ
na caiva sukṛtaṁ vibhuḥ
ajñānenāvṛtaṁ jñānaṁ
tena muhyanti jantavaḥ (5.15)

by ignorance + avṛtam — shrouded; jñānaṁ — knowledge; tena — through which; muhyanti — they are deluded; jantavaḥ — the people

The Almighty God does not receive from anyone, an evil consequence nor a good reaction. The knowledge of this is shrouded by ignorance through which the people are deluded. (5.15)

Commentary:

This has to be the ultimate disclaimer given by any of the powerful personalities who appeared in human history or who claimed to be God. As we shall read further in the *Gītā*, Lord Krishna claimed Himself as the Lord of lords, the God of gods. But He issued this disclaimer which is a very bothersome statement. Hardly a preacher dares to repeat this verse for fear that the entire congregation would run away, but this is exactly what Krishna said: "The Supreme Person does not receive anyone's sins (*pāpam*) nor anyone's virtuous acts (*sukṛtam*)." He, the Supreme Person, is fabulous and all-powerful (*vibhuh*), making our pious acts and sins unnecessary for Him. We can neither defile nor enhance Him. It is by ignorance (*ajñānena*) only that we think otherwise. Krishna said that we have a shrouded discrimination through which we derive false ideas.

ज्ञानेन तु तदज्ञानं
येषां नाशितमात्मनः ।
तेषामादित्यवज्ज्ञानं
प्रकाशयति तत्परम् ॥५.१६॥
jñānena tu tadajñānaṁ
yeṣāṁ nāśitamātmanaḥ
teṣāmādityavajjñānaṁ
prakāśayati tatparam (5.16)

jñānena — by experience; tu — however; tad — this; ajñānaṁ — ignorance; yeṣāṁ — of whom; nāśitam — removed; ātmanaḥ — of the self; teṣām — of them; ādityavaj = ādityavat — like the sun; jñānam — revelation; prakāśayati — causes to appear; tat — that; param — Supreme Truth (explained in two previous verses)

However, for those, in whose souls the ignorance is removed by experience, that revelation will cause the Supreme Truth to appear distinctly like the sun. (5.16)

Commentary:

Direct clarity is proof of a transcendental process. One may go on hearing from a spiritual master for millions of years, or even reading the *Bhagavad-Gītā*; still if one does not acquire direct perception, one has not experienced the supreme reality (*tat param*) as described in the two proceeding verses (5.14-15).

It is essential, therefore, that a disciple place a stipulation on himself to endeavor for personal perfection. His soul has its own spiritual sense which can develop into transcendental vision. He is obligated to improve his condition. The spiritual master also has an obligation to lead the disciple in that direction and to insist that the disciple take up the needful austerities through which the material attraction is greatly reduced. The spiritual energies should be conserved from material interest and the increased reserve power should be directed to the transcendence.

At the present time, in our conditioned state, all the spiritual capacities of the soul are either restricted or stunted. This is due to the soul power being diverted in the mundane direction. There is a strong, almost irresistible pull between the soul and the mundane energies. Breaking this attraction requires a special austerity. A man can say what he likes, believe what he desires, and follow whatever spiritual master or Deity he prefers, but until he can stop the wastage of energies, he will never have any consistent transcendental experience. The heart of the problem is the wastage of soul energies which pour out into the material world, making the spirit soul impoverished in spirituality.

The sun-like experience (*ādityavajjñānam*) will not arise if we are tired out and dissipated by a mundane focus. We must first curtail and then cease altogether the mundane attraction. This is called the state of *brahma nirvāṇa* which was mentioned at the end of Chapter Two.

eṣā brāhmī sthitiḥ pārtha naināṁ prāpya vimuhyati
sthitvāsyāmantakāle'pi brahmanirvāṇamṛcchati (2.72)

This divine state is required, O son of Pṛthā. If a man does not have this, he is stupefied. At the time of death, the full stoppage of mundane sensuality and the attainment of divinity is attained by one who is fixed in this divine state. (2.72)

तद्बुद्धयस्तदात्मानस्
तन्निष्ठास्तत्परायणाः ।
गच्छन्त्यपुनरावृत्तिं
ज्ञाननिर्धूतकल्मषाः ॥५.१७॥
tadbuddhayastadātmānas
tanniṣṭhāstatparāyaṇāḥ
gacchantyapunarāvṛttiṁ
jñānanirdhūtakalmaṣāḥ (5.17)

tadbuddhayaḥ — those whose intellects are situated in that supreme truth; tadātmānaḥ — those whose spirits are focused on that supreme truth; tanniṣṭhāḥ — those whose reference is that supreme truth; tatparāyaṇāḥ — those who aspire to that supreme truth as the highest reality; gacchanty (gacchanti) — go + apunar — never again + āvṛttim — rebirth; jñana — experience + nirdhūta — removed + kalmaṣāḥ — faults

Those whose intellects are situated in that Supreme Truth, whose souls are focused on it, whose basic reference is that, whose faults are removed by the experience, who aspire to that as the highest reality, never go again to rebirth. (5.17)

Commentary:

Up to Chapter Five, Lord Krishna did not stressed devotion to Himself. Such devotion was mentioned but the stress is on the emotional maturity and the spiritual outlook of those who were experts at yoga practice either through prolonged forest life or through training in the youth and the application of it in government administration. Krishna did not name any of these ancient yogis except to title them as the samkhyas, but He did name some administrators, like *Manu* and Janaka.

In the next chapter, namely Chapter Six, Lord Krishna will elaborate on the system of the samkhya yogis. After going through that chapter, we should have no doubts about that process. To this point in the *Gītā*, there is little stress on devotion to Lord Krishna.

To separate the intellectual understanding from the actual experience, Lord Krishna mentioned both the intellectual view and the soul experience by giving separate terms for each. *Tadbuddhyas* means that a person directly perceives the supreme truth (*tat param*), as described in verses 14 and 15 of this chapter. *Tadātmānas* means when the person experiences the supreme reality. Thus, those who have only an intellectual understanding of the supreme reality, are left aside. They are not qualified for exemption from rebirth. It does not matter what their spiritual masters told them nor what they believe; if they have not experienced directly, they do not qualify. They must be both intellectually comprehending (*buddhi tadbuddhayas*) and soul experienced (*tadātmānas*).

In addition, their consistent reference point (*tanniṣṭhāh*) must be that supreme reality.

They must aspire to that spiritual reality (*tatparāyanāh*). Then they will never again (*apunar*) return to this world, and their faults (*kalmaṣāh*) are removed by the transcendental experience.

विद्याविनयसंपन्ने
ब्राह्मणे गवि हस्तिनि ।
शुनि चैव श्वपाके च
पण्डिताः समदर्शिनः ॥५.१८॥
vidyāvinayasaṁpanne
brāhmaṇe gavi hastini
śuni caiva śvapāke ca
paṇḍitāḥ samadarśinaḥ (5.18)

vidyāvinayasaṁpanne = vidyā — learning + vinaya — trained + saṁpanne — accomplished; brāhmaṇe — in a brahmin; gavi — in a cow; hastini — in an elephant; śuni — in a dog; caiva = ca — and + eva — indeed; śvapāke — in a dog-flesh eater; ca — and; paṇḍitāḥ — scripturally-conversant mystic seers; samadarśinaḥ = sama — common factor + darśinaḥ — observing

In a learned, trained, accomplished brahmin, in a cow, an elephant, a dog, or a dog-flesh eater, the scripturally-conversant mystic seers observe a common factor. (5.18)

Commentary:

Of the materially-embodied creatures, the learned, trained accomplished brahmin is the highest. A spiritually-experienced person is called a pandit, but the modern meaning of pandit is someone who is expert in Vedic rituals regardless of spiritual experience. By theory, a ritual expert is supposed to be a first-class mystic who can see the supernatural people in the subtle world, but time has worn down the definition and reduced it to a person who is expert in Sanskrit or Hindi pronunciations and the ritual procedures of Vedic rites. By modern tradition, a man is considered a brahmin if his father is a brahmin or if his family lineage was traceable to an ancient brahmin sage. By this system of *gotra* or family checking, every man is traceable to one of the mind-born sons of *Brahmā*, who in the beginning of time, produced the first womb-born bodies. These sons of *Brahmā* are listed in the *Śrīmad Bhāgavatam*:

marīcī .atryaṅgirasau pulastyaḥ pulahaḥ kratuḥ
bhṛgur vasiṣṭho dakṣaś ca daśamas tatra nāradaḥ

Marīci. Atri, Aṅgirā, Pulastya, Pulaha, Kratu, Bhṛgu, Vasiṣṭha, Dakṣa, and the tenth son, Nārada, were thus born.(Śrīmad Bhāgavatam 3.12.22)

Even if one is in a demoniac family, still, one's body is traceable to one of these sages. Thus, one must have *gotra* or ancestral connections with one of the mind-born sons of *Brahmā*. For instance, demons like *Rāvaṇa* were against the Vedic system established by *Brahmā* but still, *Rāvaṇa's* body was traceable to *Pulastya Muni* who is *Brahmā*'s son. Thus, in a Vedic ceremony, the ritual priest usually asks the sacrificial performer to declare his body's connection with *Brahmā*.

Samadarśinah means: *same seeing* or *same vision*. Some commentators interpret that the soul in each body is the same soul. Others think that the soul in each body is the supreme soul or the Supersoul. And others feel that all souls in all bodies are part of one soul which is reflected differently in each body. They explain that it is like a sun in the sky being reflected in different ponds. In that case, the reflections, though appearing differently, are of the same sun.

The writer, in trying to put the *Gītā* in its own time and place, left all such explanations in their places. *Samadarśinah* means: *observing the same type of reality in each of the forms of a brahmin, cow, elephant, dog or dog-flesh eater*. In each of these forms there is the same type of soul and this is seen by the mystically-perceptive people. In each of these forms we have material nature. In each contact with material nature, there is an adjustment of her energies depending on the resultant influences which bear upon a soul. The brahmin does not see the same person in each of these forms but he sees the same type of soul with the same elevating or depressing influences of subtle and gross matter.

The common factor in each of these forms is the *ātma* or limited soul. Some commentators give the *paramātma* or Supersoul since He is the ultimate director. He transmits Himself into every living being. However, the same type of *ātma* or limited soul is in each body, but each of the souls are different individuals, while the *paramātma* or Supersoul is the same individual Lord. In this verse, the vision of the pandits, or the spiritually-experienced persons, is described. They see the same type of soul with the same sort of elevating or degrading potential in each of the creature forms.

The distinction is made between the Supersoul and the soul. The Supersoul makes a slight contact with the causal level and does not, except in special occasions, spread His influences any lower. But the soul registers himself mostly on the subtle and gross levels. Generally, the conditioned souls are more aware of their individuality on the subtle and gross levels. They lose self-focus on the causal plane or beyond. A learned brahmin can become a dog-flesh eater and a cannibal can become a brahmin. The one can be degraded and the other elevated, all depending on the pressures of destiny that bear on either. They are that similar. If a light is placed in a room with reflectors, its influence will increase, but if the same light is relocated to a dungeon, it will not show as much radiance.

The individual limited entities have about the same spiritual brilliance, but the varying influences of material nature cause them to appear higher or lower. In the case of the *paramātma*, there is no comparison between Him and the limited souls. He is like the sun. They are like so many fireflies which can never produce enough light to rival His brilliance. Still, the limited beings have their little radiance which is suppressed in material nature.

इहैव तैर्जितः सर्गो
येषां साम्ये स्थितं मनः ।
निर्दोषं हि समं ब्रह्म
तस्माद्ब्रह्मणि ते स्थिताः ॥५.१९॥
ihaiva tairjitaḥ sargo
yeṣāṁ sāmye sthitaṁ manaḥ
nirdoṣaṁ hi samaṁ brahma
tasmādbrahmaṇi te sthitāḥ (5.19)

ihaiva = iha — here in this world + iva (eva) — indeed; tair = taiḥ — by those; jitaḥ — conquered; sargo = sargaḥ — birth; yeṣāṁ — of whom; sāmye — in impartiality; sthitaṁ — established; manaḥ — mind; nirdoṣaṁ — faultless; hi — indeed; samaṁ — equally disposed; brahma — pure spirit; tasmāt — therefore; brahmaṇi — on the pure spiritual plane; te — they; sthitāḥ — established

Here in this world, birth is conquered by those whose minds are established in impartiality. Indeed, pure spirit is faultless and equally disposed. Therefore they are established on the pure spiritual plane. (5.19)

Commentary:

The philosophy of the Upanishads is carefully interwoven in the *Gītā* thus far, especially in Chapters Three and Four. Dr. Sambidananda Das, Bhaktisastri, a commissioned disciple of *Śrīla* Bhaktisiddhanta Sarasvati, stated conclusively in his *"History and Literature of the Gaudiya Vaishnavas"*, that the Chandogya Upanishad mentions Lord Krishna as the son of *Devakī* and as the disciple of Ghora Angirasa, who instructed Lord Krishna in the doctrine. Dr Sambidananda states that the teachings Krishna learnt from Ghora Angiras are more or less the same as that which Krishna taught to Arjuna in the *Gītā*.

Sargo means *appearance, birth, formation*. Insofar as he can, a brahmin controls or regulates his birth. He is not absolute. He can only regulate insofar as the puny soul can handle material nature. By purifying his psychic energies and taking shelter of the Supreme Lord he increases the chance of remaining unaffected by matter.

Of the modes of material nature, the mode of goodness is the best, but this mode causes a fall to passion and ignorance. A wise man therefore takes to the brahmin or spiritual level because it is flawless and gives an impartial view.

न प्रहृष्येत्प्रियं प्राप्य
नोद्विजेत्प्राप्य चाप्रियम् ।
स्थिरबुद्धिरसंमूढो
ब्रह्मविद्ब्रह्मणि स्थितः ॥५.२०॥
na prahṛṣyetpriyaṁ prāpya
nodvijetprāpya cāpriyam
sthirabuddhirasaṁmūḍho
brahmavidbrahmaṇi sthitaḥ
(5.20)

na — not; prahṛṣyet — should become excited; priyaṁ — dear item or favorable circumstance; prāpya — having attained; nodvijet = na — no + udvijet — should detest; prāpya — having obtained; cāpriyam = ca — and + apriyam — something unpleasant; sthira — stable; buddhiḥ — intelligent; asaṁmūḍho = asammūḍhaḥ — without confusion; brahmavid — a person who continually experiences the spiritual reality; brahmaṇi — on the spiritual plane; sthitaḥ — situated

Having attained a desired item or favorable circumstance, a person should not become excited. Having attained something unpleasant, he should not detest it. With stable intelligence, without confusion, a person who continually experiences the spiritual reality, remains situated on the spiritual plane. (5.20)

Commentary:

Using the Upanishadic philosophy, Lord Krishna instilled in Arjuna the idea of not shuddering nor hesitating because of an unpleasant possibility. He urged Arjuna to reach the spiritual place (*brahmaṇi*) from which one could act in a battle and be spared reactions. Arjuna was instructed to be *brahmavid* or *brahman-knowing, spirit-aware*. He should not rejoice when getting a pleasing item (*priyam*). We must note also that besides quoting the Upanishadic authorities, Lord Krishna claimed to be the original teacher of these techniques and ideas.

This *karma yoga* is that type of action performed by one who was schooled by the Upanishadic sages and who took to worldly activities later, thus applying the emotional security gained by the yoga procedure.

बाह्यस्पर्शेष्वसक्तात्मा
विन्दत्यात्मनि यत्सुखम् ।
स ब्रह्मयोगयुक्तात्मा
सुखमक्षयमश्नुते ॥५.२१॥
bāhyasparśeṣvasaktātmā
vindatyātmani yatsukham
sa brahmayogayuktātmā
sukhamakṣayamaśnute (5.21)

bāhya — external; sparśeṣv (sparśeṣu) — sensation; asakta — not attachéd; ātmā — soul; vindatyātmani = (vindati) — finds + ātmani — in the spirit; yat — who; sukham — happiness; sa = saḥ — he; brahmayogayuktātmā = brahma — spiritual plane + yoga — yoga process; yukta — linked + ātmā — spirit; sukham — happiness; akṣayam — non-fluctuating; aśnute — makes contact with

The person who is not attached to the external sensations, who finds happiness in the spirit, whose spirit is linked to the spiritual plane through yoga process, makes contact with the non-fluctuating happiness. (5.21)

Commentary:

The general objective of the Upanishadic sages was to reach *brahman*. The process used by them in the advanced stage was called *brahma-yoga* as stated in this verse. They aimed at getting out of material existence altogether, to attain the non-fluctuating spiritual happiness (*sukham akṣayam aśnute*). Later on when Buddhism developed, many people took to that religion, hoping for freedom from material existence by extinction of their active individuality (*nirvāṇa*). Long before the Buddha, the process of extinction of one's material existence (*svayā prakṛti*, 7.20) was known to the Upanishadic sages. *Brahman* is the general aim of all transcendentalists.

Brahman means whatever there is on the spiritual plane. *Brahma yoga* means specifically: the mystic means of reaching that level. While some modern people take to *brahma yoga* directly by practicing meditation as their preliminary and final process, the ancient sages more intelligently and definitely began with physical yoga, the *prāṇāyāma* breath nutrition and then at last, concentration, meditation, and body trance. After Buddhism became popular in India, the yoga process became foreshadowed as people began to think that yoga was unnecessary. Buddhism suggested that they could bypass yoga and practice meditation directly. However, most Buddhists are not as successful as the Buddha. The history of Buddha's techniques in austerities was never fully revealed. After the Buddha, Shankaracharya came and powerfully reversed the influence of Buddha. And after Shankaracharya, many Vaishnava acaryas tried to their utmost to erase the influence of Shankara.

Śrī Ādiśankarācārya

It seems, however, that the influence of the Upanishadic sages, that of Buddha, that of Shankara, as well as that of powerful Vaishnava acaryas like Śrī Madhvācārya, all persisted side by side in human society. Neither of these have completely nullified the other.

Up to this point in the *Gītā*, Lord Krishna recommended the process of the Upanishadic sages at least insofar as that helps a living entity to attain emotional maturity and to face duties in life. Still, some modern spiritual masters in disciplic succession from Krishna, carefully avoid the Upanishads. In fact, many of them minimized the process of *brahma yoga*.

Finding the people in a condition of helpless attachment (*sakta*) to external sensations (*bāhyasparśeṣv*), the Vaishnava teachers recommend the usage of the external world as an offering to Lord Krishna. But this verse recommends detachment (*asakta*) from such an external situation and a re-focus on the spiritual place directly, not by a round-about way of focusing on matter with intentions of procuring and offering it to the Supreme Lord. Here the method of focus is the mystic method perfected through hard-core yoga. The soul is supposed to reach the spiritual plane by mystic action and not by the round-about way suggested by some Vaishnava authorities.

Instead of imagining or actually getting some enjoyment by material activities which are to be offered to the Lord, Krishna spoke of directly reaching (*aśnute*) the non-fluctuating spiritual happiness (*sukham akṣayam*). This happiness is unadulterated and not mixed up with material sensations.

A distinction must be made between mundane sensual happiness and spiritual sensual happiness. The spiritual type continuously exists on the spiritual plane as an entirely independent enjoying energy (*ānanda*). Spiritual happiness is comprised of continuous spiritual joy, while material pleasure is dependent on particular combinations of the modes of material nature. The spiritual pleasure is there and the problem is how to contact it. But the material pleasure is formulated by our activities under particular influences of the modes of nature.

In the case of sanctified material offerings to the Lord, the devotee will have to deal with the mixture of spiritual and material happiness. He should sort that out for his own sake. But if he reaches the spiritual level exclusively, he does not have to sort out the lower happiness. Once he becomes familiar with the spiritual type, he would not confuse it with the material pleasure.

Some Vaishnava teachers, however, are suspicious of this process of *brahma yoga*, since they say that it is devoid of spiritual variety. But that contention does not stand. Even in the neophyte stage of being a devotee of Krishna, one has to deal with this steady, non-variant (*akṣayam*) spiritual happiness. A neophyte who is afraid of it, often mistakes varieties of material happiness for spiritual joy. He then commits many self-righteous acts in the name of devotion to Krishna and thus becomes baffled in the spiritual process.

In truth, a devotee must re-focus on this spiritual plane by *brahma yoga*. He has no choice. He must become anchored there for some time to retrieve his spirituality which is currently absorbed in material energy. When he is solidly situated there, he can move on to the unadulterated spiritual variety which is so much advertised by the Vaishnavas. The so-called spiritual pleasure enjoyed by neophyte Vaishnavas is simply a high grade of material enjoyment—that and nothing else. One cannot, in the impure stage, reach any spiritual level to enjoy happiness.

Lord Krishna rightly used the term *brahmaṇi sthitah (5.20)*. For each seeker the place reached in the exclusive spiritual plane would depend on the individual's level of advancement. And this has to do with his natural or developed spiritual sense perception. Living entities who have no spiritual limbs and senses except for a spherical, glowing spiritual shape and a general spiritual-sensing capacity, cannot, all of a sudden, develop spiritual limbs and senses. For them, it will take some time. Thus each soul who reached the level of brahman, the spiritual plane, may reach there in a different way and may be distinctly or indistinctly perceptive, all depending on their development. Unless we deliberately re-focus (*yuktātmā*) ourselves there, success will elude us and we will again take another material body.

ये हि संस्पर्शजा भोगा
दुःखयोनय एव ते ।
आद्यन्तवन्तः कौन्तेय
न तेषु रमते बुधः ॥५.२२॥

ye — which; hi — indeed; saṁsparśajā — coming from sensual contact; bhogā — pleasures; duḥkhayonaya = duḥkha — pain + yonayaḥ — sources; eva — indeed; te — they; ādyantavantaḥ = ādy (ādi) — beginning + anta — ending + vantaḥ

ye hi saṁsparśajā bhogā
duḥkhayonaya eva te
ādyantavantaḥ kaunteya
na teṣu ramate budhaḥ (5.22)

— possessed with; kaunteya — O son of Kuntī; na — never; teṣu — in them; ramate — delights; budhaḥ — a wise person

The pleasures that come from sensual contacts are sources of pain. They have a beginning and ending, O son of Kuntī. A wise person never delights in them. (5.22)

Commentary:

This was a warning to Arjuna not to try to continue enjoying his relations with the Kurus. Such affectionate relationships inevitably produce painful responses at one stage or another. The wise man *(budhah)* does not get involved in family affections. He performs his duty but does not indulge too deeply in family concerns. He knows the limitations of such relationships. Most family concerns are a false play of relationships which have no lasting value. For instance, in one life one may be a grandfather to a particular entity and in the next life, be the son of the same entity.

As a grandfather, one may take himself very seriously as an elder. When that same person is converted into a grandson, he takes the infantile role very seriously also. The whole range of these convertible affections is an exposure of our gross ignorance. In all cases of materially-formed relations, there will be some emotional pain. An experienced man who is seasoned in the samkhya philosophy and the related disciplines, remains detached from the pleasure stage. An experienced man anticipates this dual response of nature and deliberately reduces the pleasurable feelings, thus curtailing the after-pain responses.

Ramate means to really enjoy oneself or as modern people say, *to get it on* or *to have much fun*, but the wise man knows well that material nature gives an equally painful response for an expanded enjoyment. Therefore he avoids the cycle of impulsive emotions.

शक्नोतीहैव यः सोढुं
प्राक्शरीरविमोक्षणात् ।
कामक्रोधोद्भवं वेगं
स युक्तः स सुखी नरः ॥५.२३॥
śaknotīhaiva yaḥ soḍhuṁ
prākśarīravimokṣaṇāt
kāmakrodhodbhavaṁ vegaṁ
sa yuktaḥ sa sukhī naraḥ (5.23)

śaknotīhaiva = śaknoti — can + iha — here on earth + iva (eva) — indeed; yaḥ — who; soḍhuṁ — to endure; prāk — before; śarīravimokṣaṇāt = śarīra — body + vimokṣaṇāt — from leaving; kāmakrodhodbhavaṁ = kāma — craving + krodha — anger + udbhavaṁ — basis; vegaṁ — impulsion; sa = saḥ — he; yuktaḥ — discipline; sa = saḥ — he; sukhī — happy; naraḥ — human being

The person who, before leaving the body, endures the craving-based, anger-based impulsions, is disciplined. He is a happy human being. (5.23)

Commentary:

The force (*vegam*) of desire and anger cannot be stopped entirely. It arises even in the mind and feelings of an experienced man. For that matter, even the Personality of Godhead, even Lord Krishna, was seen to display some desire and anger. This is because of natural force (*vegam*). But the difference is the ability to contain such an impulsion. The Personality of Godhead is expert at its control and so are the experienced sages.

Real happiness in the material world does not mean the fulfillment of desires, but rather the contentment that comes from detachment while doing one's duty. To act in a composed way even when the force within is converted into anger, causes the anger energy to be reconverted into soberness. But a man cannot restrain himself until he learns to cling to the spiritual plane.

The Upanishadic sages performed special austerities to change their impulsive gross and subtle bodies. Nowadays, seekers avoid such penances and still expect the same results attained by the ancient sages. Some spiritual masters assure us that we will get the same result. It is seen, however, that the modern seekers do not attain the same goal. It is simply a pretense. The subtle nature does not change by any easy method but only by the proper austerities which must be performed in this life or in some future time here on earth or elsewhere in some other subtle or gross situation. The modern easy religions are merely preparations for the life of austerities. They are not replacements for these.

The patient endurance of craving-based and anger-based emotions is not just a matter of wishing for inner peace. It is applied consistently only when one's material nature is transmuted. For liberation or for spiritual purity, the living entity does have to purify the portion of material nature he utilizes. At the time of death, the subtle material nature follows the soul to the world hereafter. If it is not transmuted and purified by a powerful penance, it will again take the soul to another gross body. It cannot be changed by wishful thinking.

योऽन्तःसुखोऽन्तरारामस्
तथान्तर्ज्योतिरेव यः ।
स योगी ब्रह्मनिर्वाणं
ब्रह्मभूतोऽधिगच्छति ॥५.२४॥

yo'ntaḥsukho'ntarārāmas
tathāntarjyotireva yaḥ
sa yogī brahmanirvāṇaṁ
brahmabhūto
'dhigacchati (5.24)

yo = yaḥ — who; 'ntaḥsukho = antahsukhaḥ — he who is happy within; 'ntarārāmas = antarārāmas — he who is spiritually delighted; tathāntarjyotir (tathāntarjyotiḥ) = tathā — as a result + antarjyotiḥ — he who has brilliant consciousness within; eva — indeed; yaḥ — who; sa = saḥ — he; yogī — yogi; brahmanirvāṇaṁ — stoppage of disturbing sensuality and attainment of constant spirituality; brahmabhūto = brahmabhūtaḥ — absorption on the spiritual plane; 'dhigacchati = adhigacchati — he attains

The person who is happy within, who is spiritually delighted and as a result, experiences the brilliant consciousness, he, that yogi, experiences the stoppage of disturbing sensuality and attains constant spirituality in absorption on the spiritual plane. (5.24)

Commentary:

The state of *brahmanirvāṇam* is again mentioned. This was first presented in Chapter Two, text 72. Thus far in the *Gītā*, devotional service to Lord Krishna is not stressed. That will be stressed in other chapters. The main thrust so far, is to get Arjuna to the spiritual level in psychological isolation from material existence, so that he can function in the material world as a divine agent. Arjuna was supposed to banish human emotions and deal with the Kurus in a detached manner. Having removed himself from the mundane social level, Arjuna was supposed to see everything in spiritual terms and so reduce life to a spiritual equation. For him, and any other warrior who could reach the spiritual plane (*brahmabhūto*), the acts of killing warriors would cause no disturbance due to the constant focus on the spiritual level.

लभन्ते ब्रह्मनिर्वाणम्
ऋषयः क्षीणकल्मषाः ।
छिन्नद्वैधा यतात्मानः
सर्वभूतहिते रताः ॥५.२५॥

labhante — they attain; brahmanirvāṇaṁ — cessation of material existence and a simultaneous absorption in spirituality; ṛṣayaḥ — the seers; kṣīṇakalmaṣāḥ = kṣīṇa — terminates + kalmaṣāḥ — sins, faults; chinnadvaidhā = chinna — removed +

labhante brahmanirvāṇam
ṛṣayaḥ kṣīṇakalmaṣāḥ
chinnadvaidhā yatātmānaḥ
sarvabhūtahite ratāḥ
(5.25)

dvaidhā — doubts; yatātmānaḥ = yata — restrained + ātmānaḥ — souls; sarvabhūtahite = sarva — all + bhūta — creatures + hite — in welfare; ratāḥ — joy

Those seers whose sins and faults are terminated, whose doubts are removed, whose souls are restrained, who find joy in regarding the welfare of the creatures, attain a cessation of their material existence and a simultaneous absorption in spirituality. (5.25)

Commentary:

The cessation of one's material existence does not mean the end of existence but it does mean the end of social involvements in the material world and a lack of communication with those who are still involved in material transactions. Insofar as we are materially-absorbed, anyone who ended off his material existence is lost to us forever. But if we switched over to spiritual absorption, we could communicate with any soul who is situated anywhere, either in the material or spiritual atmospheres.

The concept of an extinguishment of one's material nature and the non-continuation of individuality after that, is a false one. It is not possible to kill off one's individuality. But it is possible to remove the polarization of it which causes the attachment in material nature. It all depends on the condition of the life force. Without life force, the soul cannot relate to the material world. The life force is made up of the *prakṛti* or the subtlest grade of material energy. Unless we act through that force, we cannot be tagged for mundane liabilities. Those who have transcended this world have in effect finished out or abolished their mundane life force. The mystery is: How is this done?

This commentary was written to guide readers to Krishna's methods of curbing and finally eliminating the need for mundane life force.

कामक्रोधवियुक्तानां
यतीनां यतचेतसाम् ।
अभितो ब्रह्मनिर्वाणं
वर्तते विदितात्मनाम् ॥५.२६॥
kāmakrodhaviyuktānāṁ
yatīnāṁ yatacetasām
abhito brahmanirvāṇaṁ
vartate viditātmanām (5.26)

kāmakrodhaviyuktānāṁ = kāma — desire + krodha — anger + viyuktānāṁ — of the separation from; yatīnāṁ — of the ascetics; yatacetasām — of those whose thinking is restrained; abhito = abhitaḥ — very close; brahmanirvāṇaṁ — cessation of material existence, assumption of enlightened spirituality; vartate — it is; viditātmanām — of those who understand the spiritual self

The cessation of material existence and assumption of enlightened spirituality is soon to be attained by those ascetics whose thinking is restrained, who understand the spiritual self,and are separated from desire and anger. (5.26)

Commentary:

Sages who are done with material existence, no longer relate to us. Their assistance to us is, for the most part, nil. But those souls who are close to closing off their material existence are very useful to us. They can tell us something about the soul because they are knowers of the spiritual self (*viditātmanām*).

Such great sages are not impulsively connected to desire and anger in their material nature. As such they are detached from the survival tendency. In fact their desire and anger are purged out of their energy while ours is integrated into it. These great sages are called *yatīnām*, which means ascetics. They are involved in *yatacetasām* which is complete stoppage of random thinking. In these regards, we quote *Patañjali*, the author of the Yoga Sūtra. He declared:

yogaḥ cittavṛtti nirodhaḥ

The skill of yoga is demonstrated by the conscious non-operation of the vibrational modes of the mento-emotional energy.

Patañjali is sometimes ridiculed by some Vaishnava teachers but we accredit him with giving us a summary of the objectives of the Upanishadic sages who are indicated here by Lord Krishna and who practiced in the forest at the time of Krishna's advent. The question as to, who would tell us about the soul, is answered in this verse. Lord Krishna explained that those who are close to (*abhito*) ending off their material existence, are qualified to lecture. Someone who has passed beyond the subtle and gross material energy cannot tell us, because we are not equipped to hear in that superfine spiritual way. But someone who is just about to depart can explain much to us.

स्पर्शान्कृत्वा बहिर्बाह्यांश्
चक्षुश्चैवान्तरे भ्रुवोः ।
प्राणापानौ समौ कृत्वा
नासाभ्यन्तरचारिणौ ॥५.२७॥

sparśānkṛtvā bahirbāhyāṁś
cakṣuścaivāntare bhruvoḥ
prāṇāpānau samau kṛtvā
nāsābhyantaracāriṇau (5.27)

sparśān — sensual contact; kṛtvā — having done; bahir = bahiḥ — external; bāhyāṁś = bāhyān — excluded; cakṣuścaivāntare = cakṣuś — visual focus + ca — and = eva — indeed + antare — in between; bhruvoḥ — of the two eyebrows; prāṇāpānau — both inhalation and exhalation; samau — in balance; kṛtvā — having made; nāsābhyantaracāriṇau = nāsa — nose + abhyantara — within + cāriṇau — moving

Excluding the external sensual contacts, and fixing the visual focus between the eyebrows, putting the inhalation and exhalation in balance, moving through the nose, (5.27)

Commentary:

Procedures like the one above are no longer recommended by most of the spiritual masters who claim to represent Lord Krishna in the authorized disciplic succession. The procedure of gazing from within to the middle of the eyebrows is now confined mostly to *kriyā* yoga and meditation practices The one of observing air flow within the nostrils is confined to *prāṇāyāma* practices. *Bhakti yoga* or devotional disciplinary life, as it is generally known today, is devoid of these practices.

The control of the visual sense is very important in the quest for life force control. Unless one controls the visual sense, there is no question of bringing the impulsive actions to a complete halt. And without doing this, there can be no spiritual perfection, since the soul would remain conditioned by mundane survival impulses. All the senses are dangerous outlets for the life force, but the visual sense is especially prominent. So long as the soul is habituated to this visual sense, he cannot turn about within and control the life force, but rather he will be directed by it. In the practice of gazing between the eyebrows one first gazes with the split attention which flows down the optic nerves. Then, some time after, when one achieves some stability in concentration, one retracts the two channels of energy flow and gazes with a singular attention.

Split visual energy from core-self to eyes

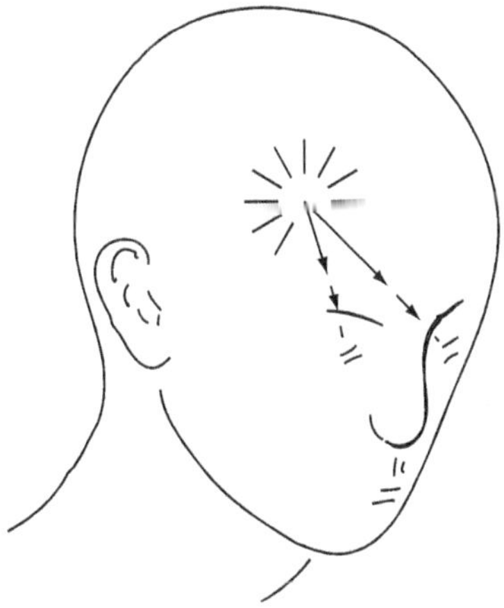

Optical energy withdrawal into core-self

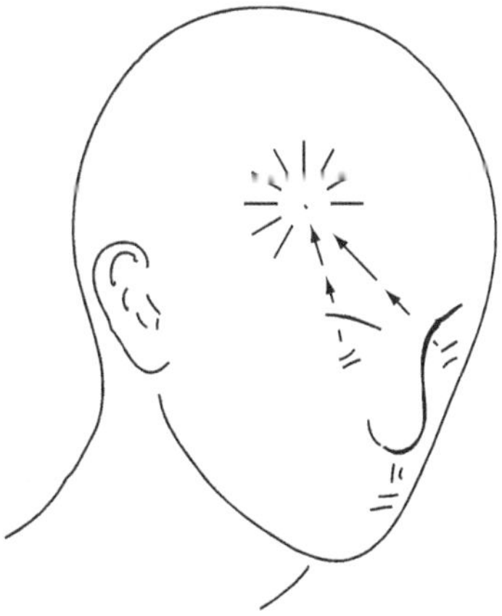

Optical focus through eyes to brow chakra

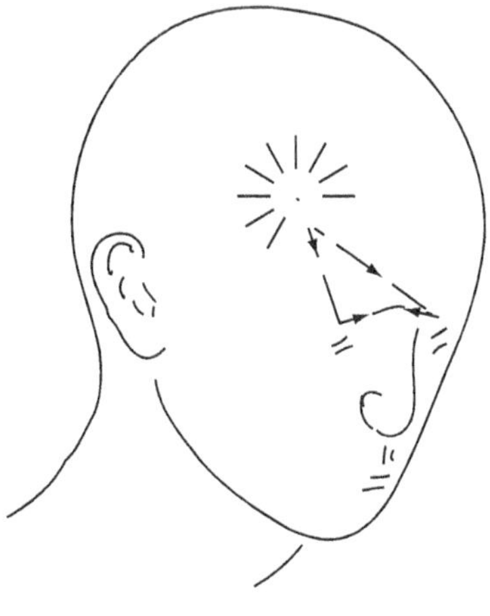

Optical energy withdrawn from brow chakra through eyes to core-self

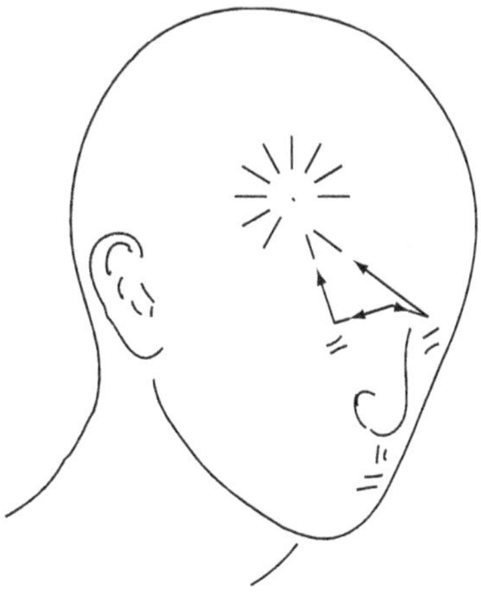

Core-self's attention direct to brow chakra

Attention withdrawal through brow chakra into core-self

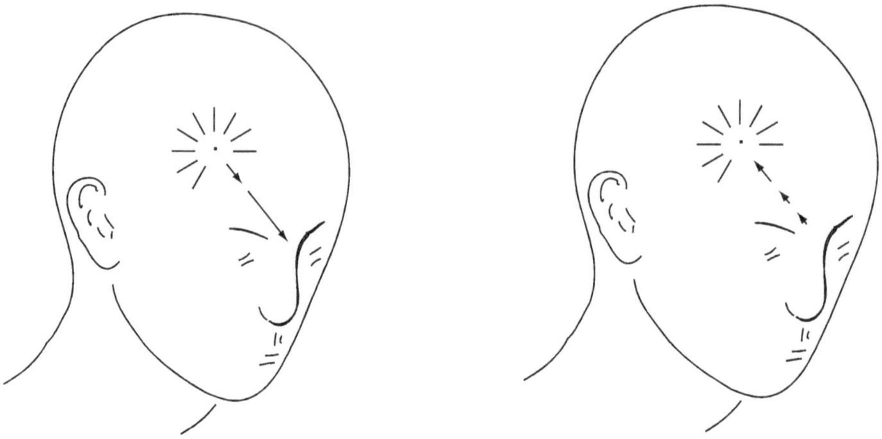

But those who meditate on that brow chakra and who do not take up *prāṇāyāma*, or who have not mastered it, do not achieve perfection in the practice. Their life energy remains contaminated. For success in the practice one has to clean up the subtle body by flushing out the *apāna* air and replacing it with nutritious pranic air. This is all part of the *prāṇāyāma* process. This is why *prāṇāyāma* is mentioned in this verse.

यतेन्द्रियमनोबुद्धिर्
मुनिर्मोक्षपरायणः ।
विगतेच्छाभयक्रोधो
यः सदा मुक्त एव सः ॥५.२८॥
yatendriyamanobuddhir
munirmokṣaparāyaṇaḥ
vigatecchābhayakrodho
yaḥ sadā mukta eva saḥ (5.28)

yatendriyamanobuddhir = yata — controlled + indriya — sensual energy + mano (manah) — mind + buddhiḥ — intelligence; munir = muniḥ — wise person; mokṣaparāyaṇaḥ - one who is dedicated to achieving liberation; vigatecchābhayakrodho = vigata — gone away + icchā — desire + bhaya — fear + krodho (krodhaḥ) — anger; yaḥ — who; sadā — always; mukta — liberated; eva — indeed; saḥ — he

...the wise man, who is dedicated to achieving liberation, whose sensual energy, mind and intellect are controlled, whose desire, fear and anger are gone, is liberated always. (5.28)

Commentary:

Mokṣaparāyaṇah is someone who is dedicated to becoming liberated by any possible means — in one way or another. It is a person who rakes his brain and spends most of his time seeking and pursuing the aim of liberation. This does not imply that he is after a relationship with God, but it is indicated that those who want such a relationship and who also are desperately seeking liberation are included as *mokṣaparāyaṇah*.

Any person who is destined by his endeavor to become liberated in the near future, is a *mokṣaparāyaṇah*. Of those who want such an abrupt release from material existence, some admire Krishna, some admire other divine personalities. Some are not attached to anyone besides themselves. Regardless, they are all listed here under the term of *mokṣaparāyaṇah*. For success in such a venture, one must be rid of desire, fear and anger. This means that one's life must be completely curbed and purified. Desire, fear and anger are motivated by life force. These are not motivated by the mind or soul but rather the mind and soul are used by the life force to express its tendencies. We need not argue about the method of life force control and purification. Our concern is that it must be completed before a person is rated as a *mokṣaparāyaṇah*.

When *yata* is added to *indriyamanobuddhir*, we get *yatendriyamanobuddhir*, which means: ascetic control of the senses, mind and intellect. This is controlled through yoga practice, *prāṇāyāma*, and related disciplines.

भोक्तारं यज्ञतपसां
सर्वलोकमहेश्वरम् ।
सुहृदं सर्वभूतानां
ज्ञात्वा मां शान्तिमृच्छति ॥५.२९॥
bhoktāraṁ yajñatapasāṁ
sarvalokamaheśvaram
suhṛdaṁ sarvabhūtānāṁ
jñātvā māṁ śāntimṛcchati (5.29)

bhoktāraṁ — enjoyer; yajñatapasāṁ — of the religious ceremonies and austerities; sarvalokamaheśvaram = sarva — all entire + loka — world + maheśvaram — Supreme God; suhṛdaṁ — friend; sarvabhūtānāṁ — of all creatures; jñātvā — recognizing; māṁ — me; śāntim — spiritual peace; ṛcchati — attains

Recognizing Me, as the enjoyer of religious ceremonies and austerities, the Supreme God of the entire world, the friend of the creatures, he attains spiritual peace. (5.29)

Commentary:

We gave, *sacrificial disciplines* for *yajñatapasām*. This is perhaps a departure from the meaning given by most *Gītā* commentators. We followed two rules to give that meaning. The first relates to the Sanskrit word compounds whereby in *yajñatapasām*, *yajña* is an adjective and *tapasām* is a noun. In addition, we have not given *yajña* as a noun meaning, *for Vedic sacrifices or Vedic ritualistic ceremonies*. This is in keeping with what Lord Krishna said in Chapter Four, verses 24-33, where He does not limit *yajña* or sacrifice to ritual or fire sacrifices. I ask readers to review these words of Lord Krishna and to see that *yajña*, as Krishna meant the word, is not limited to ritual ceremonies but is extended even to the spiritual self into the untinged spiritual existence (*brahman*). Lord Krishna even spoke of offering one's exhalation into inhalation as a type of sacrifice (4. 24).

After speaking of the broader means of attaining spiritual existence, Lord Krishna narrowed down the recommendation to Himself only, as the super-controller of the world (*sarvalokamaheśvaram*). The indication is that the majority of the Upanishadic sages were interested in Lord Krishna as their ultimate friend and shelter. At least this is the claim of Krishna. He specifically mentions their recognition (*jñātvā*) of Him. We must agree with the Vaishnava acharyas who stress this point over and over throughout their *Gītā* commentaries. We will have to offer our respects to their firm conclusions about the *Gītā* as being centralized on Krishna.

CHAPTER 6

Yoga Practice*

श्रीभगवानुवाच
अनाश्रितः कर्मफलं
कार्यं कर्म करोति यः ।
स संन्यासी च योगी च
न निरग्निर्न चाक्रियः ॥६.१॥
śrībhagavānuvāca
anāśritaḥ karmaphalaṁ
kāryaṁ karma karoti yaḥ
sa saṁnyāsī ca yogī ca
na niragnirna cākriyaḥ (6.1)

śrī bhagavān - the Blessed Lord; *uvāca* — said; *anāśritaḥ* — not relying on; *karmaphalaṁ* — result of an action; *kāryaṁ* — obligation; *karma* — action; *karoti* — he fulfills; *yaḥ* — who; *sa* = *saḥ* — he; *saṁnyāsī* — renouncer; *ca* — and; *yogī* — yogi; *ca* — and; *na* — not; *niragnir* = *niragniḥ* — without a fire ceremony; *na* — nor; *cākriyaḥ* = *ca* — and + *akryaḥ* — lacking physical activities

The Blessed Lord said: A person who fulfills obligatory action, without depending on the result of the action, is a renouncer, and a yogi, not the one who is without a fire ceremony or who lacks physical activity. (6.1)

Commentary:

In several places of the Vedic literature it is recommended that a renunciant or *sannyāsi* give up the Vedic fire (*niragnir*). Such a man is not supposed to be tagging along behind a priest or pandit to get favors from the supernatural people, nor to patronize annual festivals and the like. He is supposed to be freed from the numerous ceremonial obligations. In the end, such a man is supposed to go to an unknown place where his relatives are conspicuous by their absence. He is supposed to give up his body there in peace without the fuss of grieving relatives. Here Lord Krishna puts to question those suggestions of the Vedic literature. This is one problem with the *Gītā* and with Lord Krishna. In some instances, He supports the Vedic tradition. In others, he derides it.

While the renouncer or *sannyāsi* usually takes his vow when his body reaches an elderly age, a yogi usually starts early. It is difficult to begin yoga *āsana* postures in an old body. Such a young man, the yogi, usually avoids social activities (*akriyah*). He does perform yoga exercises with precision and care but he avoids worldly life and lives in isolation from society. In this verse. Lord Krishna puts a question to such yogis.

We get the message here that one should renounce or curtail the interest in worldly activities in terms of trying to exploit or enjoy these, but one should complete his duties of life regardless. We will hear more and more of this throughout the *Gītā*. Lord Krishna hammered away at Arjuna's desire to leave the battlefield. Krishna was against that plan of Arjuna. He tried to convince the hero to remain and deal with the situation at *Kurukṣetra* in a manly way, but with detachment and mental clarity. Arjuna must fulfill the obligation (*kāryam karma karoti*). At least that is what Krishna desired.

**The Mahābhārata contains no chapter headings. This title was assigned by the translator on the basis of verse 12 of this chapter.*

We heard many of the Vaishnava acharyas either say or write that one should stay at his duty of life and cultivate spirituality, particularly Krishna consciousness, as the particular teacher defines it. This point is asserted by Lord Krishna. Even though the Lord does not assert Himself in this verse, He did establish Himself in the last verse of the previous chapter. Throughout the *Gītā* we will see that gradually Lord Krishna pushed Himself forward as the ultimate goal of life.

यं संन्यासमिति प्राहुर्
योगं तं विद्धि पाण्डव ।
न ह्यसंन्यस्तसंकल्पो
योगी भवति कश्चन ॥६.२॥

yaṁ saṁnyāsamiti prāhur
yogaṁ taṁ viddhi pāṇḍava
na hyasaṁnyastasaṁkalpo
yogī bhavati kaścana (6.2)

yaṁ — that which; saṁnyāsam — renunciation; iti — thus; prāhur = prāhuḥ — the authorities define; yogaṁ — applied yoga; taṁ — it; viddhi — know; pāṇḍava — Arjuna Pandava; na — not; hy = hi — indeed; asaṁnyastasaṁkalpo = (asaṁnyastasaṁkalpaḥ) = asaṁnyasta — without renunciation + saṁkalpaḥ — intention; yogī — yogi; bhavati — becomes; kaścana — anyone

That which the authorities define as renunciation, know it as applied yoga, O Arjuna Pandava. Indeed, no one becomes a yogi without an intention for renunciation. (6.2)

Commentary:

This verse is a direct answer to Arjuna's question in the last chapter. After trying to reason with Arjuna and dealing with the subject in the way Arjuna presented it, Lord Krishna now directly attacks Arjuna's misunderstanding about renunciation and yoga. In this case, the stress is not on yoga *āsana* postures but on advanced *karma yoga*, the type of yoga that was performed by King Janaka.

There is a bit of difference between yoga practice and yoga application. Yoga means certain bodily postures, breath nutrition methods, and subtle body control techniques. *Karma yoga* or yoga as it may be applied in the life of an administrator or worldly-involved man, means to maintain a sense of detachment while acting in the world. We have to recognize this distinction. In all cases of yoga and its applications, we must understand this difference. Arjuna indicated, that to his mind, Krishna's instructions were dualistic or contradictory. But Arjuna was confused. In one instance, the Lord recommended that Arjuna think deeply about the Kuru conflict and in another instance, the Lord told him to act efficiently like King Janaka. Arjuna considered this to be a dualistic instruction. Thus, in this verse, the Lord asserted that a reserved way of thinking (*samnyasa*) is not necessarily contrary to a controlled way of acting (*karma yoga*). Let us review Arjuna's original question:

arjuna uvāca
saṁnyāsaṁ karmaṇāṁ kṛṣṇa.punaryogaṁ ca śaṁsasi
yacchreya etayorekaṁ tanme brūhi suniścitam (5.1)

Arjuna said: You approved renunciation of social activity and also mentioned the application of yoga to worldly life. Which one of these is better? Tell me this with certainty. (5.1)

Lord Krishna's first reply was:

śrībhagavānuvāca
saṁnyāsaḥ karmayogaśca niḥśreyasakarāvubhau
tayostu karmasaṁnyāsāt karmayogo viśiṣyate (5.2)

The Blessed Lord said: Both methods, the total renunciation of social opportunities and the disciplined use of opportunities by a yogi, lead to ultimate happiness. But of the two aspects, the disciplined use of opportunities in a yogic mood is better than total renunciation of cultural activity. (5.2)

In the first line of Krishna's reply, the two aspects in question are mentioned: *samnyāsah karmayogaśca*. This is why we explained that in this verse under consideration (6.2), the term yogam means *karma yoga*. It does not mean yoga practice in ā*sanas*, *prāṇāyāma*, *kriyās* and *bandhas*. We must understand this.

A practicing yogi who is learning to perfect yoga disciplines, is not a practical yogi like Janaka who mastered the practice and then returned to complete worldly duties with detachment. In fact, not all of the yogis who performed disciplines have to return to worldly life. Some of them are not required to do so. Only some like Janaka and Arjuna have to return to act out some political or social role in the world. Only these have to demonstrate *karma yoga* or the application of yoga maturity to worldly life. Those yogis who have no worldly obligations to complete, would be fools to venture into the world and get involved just for the sake of it. They should instead, push on with practice, perfect it, and attain higher worlds (*lokas*) by mystic transference.

Sometimes those who have to take up worldly duties become envious of those who have no obligations. They start missionary activities and blacklist the reserved yogis. But this is all part of envy. In the case of Arjuna, we see that he understood the risk of worldly application of yoga. He understood it all too well, but Lord Krishna did not allow Arjuna to run off to be with the forest ascetics who had no duties at *Kurukṣetra*. These forest ascetics were not required to gain their spiritual perfection by fighting like Janaka and Arjuna.

In addition we have to realize that the modern exponents of *karma yoga* who say that it can be performed even without having a proficiency in yoga practice, are for the most part not talking about this higher *karma yoga* of the *Gītā*, but rather about their own idea of the matter or about a lower stage of *karma yoga* which is described in chapter 12. There is absolutely no evidence whatsoever to show that the higher *karma yoga* can be performed by a person who is not already proficient in yoga practice. Yoga practice is the prerequisite. Renunciation itself is not the prerequisite but true renunciation develops after becoming proficient.

At this point in the *Gītā*, I ask my readers to allow me to explain the difference between those who use yoga in worldly life and those who apply the practice for transference to higher worlds. We may take the case of mathematics. Some boys who study mathematics will be required to use the knowledge in other areas of life. Banking is not mathematics, but it involves the use of it. Similarly persons like Janaka and Arjuna had to apply their yoga schooling to administrative and judicial concerns. This is the application of yoga to the political field.

Lord Krishna explained that He, as the Supreme Teacher, taught this science of applied yoga to the politicians formerly. The meaning is clear. In the time of Lord Krishna and before, wherever the Vedic way of life was functioning, boys who were destined for political life first went to a yoga school. But later on, they did not necessarily continue the yoga disciplines even though they used the emotional maturity, the detached attitude of mind they attained by yoga practice. A boy who studies mathematics may use a small part of the learning later in a bank job. Another boy who studied the same subject and who later begins a farm enterprise, may use his training in a way that makes it difficult to see the connection between this job and his former schooling. He may, for instance, plan his farm operations in a very efficient way, and even though the connection may not be obvious, his efficient planning may be a result of the mathematical learning in school days. In other words, the efficiency of his planning may have come from the logical and systematic outlay of mathematics.

But another boy who went through the same course at the same time may have gone on to be a mathematics teacher or a physics researcher, where he actually uses advanced mathematics on a daily basis. This boy is like the yogi who does not return to worldly life but who stays on in the forest to further his education instead of concluding the learning and then applying it in another career. We can see here that the boys who left the course should not envy or resent the boy who continued with mathematics, but this is exactly what happens. These spiritual groups that attract persons who want to apply yoga maturity are often envious and critical of those groups which attract those who will remain with yoga practice to the end and will not leave their practice to enter worldly life. In fact, most of the spiritual groups which attract persons who want to apply yoga practice, rather than perfect yoga, usually attract people who never did nor ever will take up yoga, at least not in the same lifetime. Some who are attracted took up yoga and became frustrated and left the practice before attaining proficiency.

But as the Lord said, if a man has no intention (*saṁkalpa*) for renunciation, he cannot become a practical yogi. In other words, unless one is actually hardened by yoga practice, he cannot be successful in his bid to be a practical yogi or a *karma* yogi.

At this point in the *Gītā*, we can rest on the subject of *karma yoga*. It will be mentioned again and again, but up to this point, we should have a clear understanding of how it was defined at the time of Lord Krishna.

Modern *karma yoga* is different to this ancient standard which is the application of yoga practice to worldly life. In the ancient definition, one had to be schooled in yoga practice before he could become a *karma* yogi. In other words, the word yogi has meaning in the *karma yoga* of the past but today a *karma* yogi is a man who has not done yoga but who postures himself with detachment in the worldly field.

आरुरुक्षोर्मुनेर्योगं
कर्म कारणमुच्यते ।
योगारूढस्य तस्यैव
शमः कारणमुच्यते ॥६.३॥

āruruksormuneryogaṁ
karma kāraṇamucyate
yogārūḍhasya tasyaiva
śamaḥ kāraṇamucyate (6.3)

ārurukṣor = ārurukṣoḥ — of one who strives; muner = muneḥ — of a philosophical man; yogaṁ — yoga expertise; karma — cultural activity; kāraṇam — the means; ucyate — it is remembered; yogārūḍhasya — of one who mastered yoga; tasyaiva = tasya — of him + iva (eva) — indeed; śamaḥ — tranquil method; kāraṇam — the means; ucyate — it is remembered

For a philosophical man who strives for yoga expertise, cultural activity is recommended. For one who has mastered yoga already, the tranquil reserved method is the means. (6.3)

Commentary:

We may think that a man who desires proficiency in yoga should take up the process seriously and the man who is expert should enter the field of activity. This was the idea of *Prahlād*. It is said that he once met a yoga master (*yogārūḍha*) who fed himself like a python (see *Śrīmad Bhāgavatam*, Canto 7, Chapter 13). This yogi lay on the ground day and night and accepted whatever foodstuffs came, just as a python remains in one place until an edible creature arrives.

Prahlād noticed, however, that this yogi had the fat body of a well-fed, materialistic man. He graciously challenged the yogi, hinting that the ascetic should use his spiritual sense of security for the welfare of others.

The yogi told *Prahlād* of the motivation for living in that easy-going, anti-social way. He explained that material happiness was an illusion and that real happiness is found only where material involvement comes to a complete halt. He refused to change his lifestyle.

In the end, *Prahlād* understood that ultimately, a perfect person has no worldly obligation.

Prahlād did not like the idea that this yogi should live in the reserved method (*śamah*), not participating in history (*karma*). Most modern Vaishnava acharyas share this view of *Prahlād*. Some of them even become hostile to yogis. But here in the *Gītā*, Lord Krishna does not display a disliking for them; rather He is supportive. But He objects to it for Arjuna's development.

In this verse, there is a complication but we may take it step by step to understand the complexity. A man who strives and who is a philosophically-minded person, and who wants to gain proficiency in yoga, cannot all of a sudden or should not all of a sudden, take to yoga in fullness, since by doing so, he would be neglecting other duties and would become known as radical or as an irresponsible escapist. Such a man may continue participation, using the action methods of *karma yoga* in the fashion of King Janaka. This however, does not mean that every man can do this.

Some modern advocates of *karma yoga* twist this verse and suggest that every modern man can do this. They overlook one word: *muneh*. A *muneh* is a philosopher. The man must at least be a philosopher. And he must also take up yoga practice gradually. He will not become an expert yogi just by doing *karma yoga* or by being mentally detached from worldly life. But on the other hand, a person who is proficient in yoga practice and whose destiny does not dictate a return to worldly involvement, should take to the reserved tranquil method of simple living, high thinking, and advanced yoga disciplines.

We must understand that the man who is striving cannot be successful at *karma yoga* unless he takes up or continue his yoga practice in spare time.

यदा हि नेन्द्रियार्थेषु
न कर्मस्वनुषज्जते ।
सर्वसंकल्पसंन्यासी
योगारूढस्तदोच्यते ॥६.४॥

yadā hi nendriyārtheṣu
na karmasvanuṣajjate
sarvasaṁkalpasaṁnyāsī
yogārūḍhastadocyate (6.4)

yadā — when; hi — indeed; nendriyārtheṣu = na — not + indriyārtheṣu — in attractive objects; na — not; karmasv = karmasu — in performance; anuṣajjate — feels attached; sarvasaṁkalpasaṁnyāsī = sarvasaṁkalpa — all motivations + saṁnyāsī — discarding; yogārūḍhas — proficient in yoga practice; tadocyate = tada — then + ucyate — it is said

Indeed, when having discarded all motivations, a person feels no attachment to attractive objects nor to performance, he is said to be proficient in yoga practice. (6.4)

Commentary:

Tadocyate, an abbreviated form of *tada ucyate*, means, *at that stage it is said*, or, *then it is declared*. These declarations were made by the Upanishadic sages. Sir Paul Castagna, who with Dr. Ramanand Prasad, reviewed the manuscript of this translation and commentary, advocated the need for a *Gītā* which applies to modern times. This *Gītā* which is an effort to show the *Gītā* in its own time and place, reveals the situation in the time of

Lord Krishna. Even though we may want to get away from that ancient setting and put the *Gītā* into modern relevance, let us note that here in Chapter Six, Lord Krishna kept quoting the Upanishadic sages. He kept asserting the opinions of the ancient ascetics.

There are many readers of the *Gītā*, but how many of them know the Upanishads? How many of them know that Lord Krishna took schooling from some Upanishadic sages and learned the Upanishads thoroughly? Furthermore, how many devotees of Krishna realize that Krishna established His *Gītā* discourse on the basis of information presented by the sages of the Upanishadic era? It is not that Krishna learnt something from these sages. In the *Gītā*, Lord Krishna dismisses all educational limitations by presenting Himself as the teacher of the ancient solar kings like *Ikṣvāku*. But we cannot deny that He used the Upanishads as the basis of the *Gītā*. The first hint was given in Chapter Two:

nāsato vidyate bhāvo'nābhāvo vidyate sataḥ
ubhayorapi dṛṣṭo'ntas tvanayostattvadarśibhiḥ (2.16)

Of the non-substantial things, there is no enduring existence. Of the substantial things, there is no lack of existence. These two truths were perceived with certainty by the mystic seers of reality. (2.16)

Śrīmad Bhāgavatam tells us what Krishna and Balarāma learnt when He was at the boarding school of *Śrīpad* Sandipani Muni. Here is a verse:

tayor dvija-varas tuṣṭaḥ śuddha-bhāvanuvṛttibhiḥ
provāca vedān akhilān saṅgopaniṣado guruḥ

That best of brahmanas, the spiritual master Sandīpani, was satisfied with Their submissive behavior, and thus he taught Them the entire Vedas, together with their six corollaries and the Upanishads.(Śrīmad Bhāgavatam 10.45.33)

In addition, the Chandogya Upanishad informs us:

taddhai tad ghora āṅgirasaḥ
kṛṣṅāya devakīputrāyoktvovā cāpipasā
eva sa babhūva so 'ntavelayāmetattrayaṁ
pratipadyetākṣitamas yac yutamasi
prāṇa saṁśitamasīti tatraite dve ṛcau bhavataḥ

Ghora Angirasa explained this well-known information to Devakī's son Krishna and said, "Such a knower should, at the time of death, repeat these three coded sentences: **You, O soul, are imperishable. You, O soul, are unchangeable. You, O soul, are the subtle essence."** ***(Hearing that instruction,) Krishna became satisfied. There are two Rig Veda verses in regards to this. (Ch.Up.3.17.6)***

We must also keep in mind the claim of Lord Krishna where He stated that He is the supreme teacher of the application of yoga and that the solar deity and his descendants were taught the knowledge in a disciplic succession. Krishna promised to establish the knowledge again in the political families through Arjuna. Let us review the verse in consideration:

sa evāyaṁ mayā te'dya yogaḥ proktaḥ purātanaḥ
bhakto'si me sakhā ceti rahasyaṁ hyetaduttamam (4.3)

Today, this ancient yoga technique is explained to you by Me, since you are devoted to Me and are My friend. Indeed, this is confidential and is the best teaching. (4.3)

The key word in the verse being discussed is given only as part of a compound word. That key word is *artha*, which means interest or exploitive value. *Indriyārthesu* means, *in the objects of the senses,* or, *in the exploitive value of those things which are pursued by the senses.*

Yogāruḍhas means, *the culmination of yoga practice,* or, *the results of proficient yoga practice.*

These descriptions are all suited to answer Arjuna's question about a sagely man. Let us review that question:

arjuna uvāca
sthitaprajñasya kā bhāṣā samādhisthasya keśava
sthitadhīḥ kiṁ prabhāṣeta kimāsīta vrajeta kim (2.54)

Arjuna said: In regards to the person who is situated in clear, penetrating insight, would you please describe him? Speak of the person who is anchored in deep meditation, O Keśava Krishna. As for the man who is steady in objectives, how would he speak? How would he sit? How would he act? (2.54)

This verse explains that until a seeker reached the stage of detachment, where he finds no exploitive value in sense objects or in worldly participation, he should not take fully to contemplative life (*śamah*) but should instead work out (*karma*) his destiny while continuing practice. But those seekers who have no exploitive needs should take to contemplative life and overcome all urges for material existence (*brahma-nirvanam*, 2.72).

The eight stages of yoga are: *yama, niyama, āsana, prāṇāyāma, pratyāhāra, dhāranā, dhyāna*, and *samādhi*. One who is free from exploitive needs can complete these in a jiffy in one life, by steady application in one stage after another. But other seekers who have exploitive needs cannot do so. Ideally, they should, like Arjuna and King Janaka, practice the first stages of *yama, niyama, āsana, prāṇāyāma*, and *pratyāhāra* in their youth; then return to worldly obligations where they apply their emotional maturity to worldly life. When these obligations are somewhat completed, and their exploitive needs are to a greater degree extinguished, they should take to the advanced stages of *dhāranā, dhyāna*, and *samādhi* to complete yoga and to attain spiritual tranquility (*śamah*, 6.3).

उद्धरेदात्मनात्मानं
नात्मानमवसादयेत् ।
आत्मैव ह्यात्मनो बन्धुर्
आत्मैव रिपुरात्मनः ॥६.५॥
uddharedātmanātmānaṁ
nātmānamavasādayet
ātmaiva hyātmano bandhur
ātmaiva ripurātmanaḥ (6.5)

uddhared = uddharet — should elevate; ātmanā — by the self; 'tmānaṁ = ātmānam — the self; nātmānam = na — not + ātmānam — the self; avasādayet — should degrade; ātmaiva = ātmā — self + eva — only; hyātmano = hyātmanaḥ = hy (hi) — indeed + ātmanaḥ — of the self; bandhur = bandhuḥ — friend; ātmaiva = ātmā — self + eva — as well; ripur = ripuḥ — enemy; ātmanaḥ — of the self

One should elevate his being by himself. One should not degrade the self. Indeed, the person should be the friend of himself. Or he could be the enemy as well. (6.5)

Commentary:

A limited entity can only do so much to help himself but if the self-help is neglected, hardly a man can assist him. If it were the grace of the Lord only and if nothing else were required, this appeal of the Lord that we lift up (*uddhared*) ourselves, would not be made by Krishna. It is obvious that self effort is a major part of our salvation from degradation.

The little effort of a limited entity is greatly magnified by the grace of the Lord, but a lack of that endeavor provides an opening for the degrading energies in material nature.

Thus the limited entities must protect themselves and then the Lord's grace takes effect in their lives.

A person becomes the enemy of his own energies if he makes no effort to keep himself aloof in the ocean of material existence. He should not be reluctant to maintain prestige as a spiritual being. He should do everything in his power to keep the spiritual profile in order. If push comes to shove, as we modern people say, or if there is a conflict of interest between our spiritual self and our material energies, then we should sacrifice or restrict the materialism. That is the gist of it. Otherwise we will be degraded (*avasādayet*).

Every limited entity has a quota of material energy at his disposal. This means that we are responsible for the use and abuse of that portion. Therefore, we cannot really lump all the liabilities on the Supreme Lord. The Lord is the Master of the sum total reality but that does not mean that He is personally responsible for our small quota; rather He is an overseer, a supervisor of a vast array of persons and energies. In the final analysis, we should see to our own interest but we should do this under His direction.

A small-time living entity, a just-about-nothing, cannot really afford to be on his own, at least not completely. We must keep in touch with the Blessed Lord to get a certain existential protection. Otherwise, we will of necessity, by our limited purview, make stupid mistakes, miscalculating and repeatedly regretting the effects of our folly.

बन्धुरात्मात्मनस्तस्य
येनात्मैवात्मना जितः ।
अनात्मनस्तु शत्रुत्वे
वर्तेतात्मैव शत्रुवत् ॥ ६.६ ॥
bandhurātmātmanastasya
yenātmaivātmanā jitaḥ
anātmanastu śatrutve
vartetātmaiva śatruvat (6.6)

bandhur = bandhuḥ — friend; ātmā — personal energies; 'tmanas = ātmanas — of the self; tasya — of him; yenātmaivātmanā = yena — by whom + ātmā — self + eva — indeed + ātmanā — by the self; jitaḥ — subdued; anātmanas — of one who is not self-possessed; tu — but; śatrutve — in hostility; vartetātmaiva = varteta — it operates + ātmā - self + eva — indeed; śatruvat — like an enemy

The personal energies are the friend of the person by whom those energies are subdued. But for one whose personality is not self-possessed, the personal energies operate in hostility like an enemy. (6.6)

Commentary:

To befriend (*bandhur*) one's nature, one does not become friendly with it, but controls it. Controlling the nature, however, is not just a matter of brute force. Controlling something has more to do with understanding the nature of its operation than with using brute force. Still, brute force is involved in certain phases of self-control. After all, everything has an inherent (*svabhāvah*) mood or tendency that will be resistant to influences. Therefore some brute force will be required but beyond that one must be expert in knowing the nature of one's nature.

Some feel that when something is understood one should just supply the needs of the said understood subject, but this is a great misunderstanding put forward by people who have neither authority nor purpose. For instance, Lord Krishna understood Arjuna quite well but that did not mean that the Lord allowed Arjuna to do what he wanted. Krishna knew that Arjuna was limited and that Arjuna could not see spiritually at all times. Still the Lord used some intimidation and insult to motivate Arjuna. But Krishna also assisted Arjuna with the desire to fight at *Kurukṣetra*, to kill off relatives and get away with it scot-free. That part of Arjuna's plan was fulfilled by Krishna.

The implication is that we must be prepared to be curbed or adjusted by the Lord and by the superior souls. We should not expect them to accommodate and pamper us.

If we do not subdue our material nature, our spiritual nature, and the psychic connection between the two, we will act as self-enemies (*anātmanas*). We need to control our material nature and spiritual nature as well. We cannot become friendly with ourselves by allowing our natures to function freely. We can only befriend (*bandhur*) ourselves by controlling the psychological powers (*ātmanā jitah*).

जितात्मनः प्रशान्तस्य
परमात्मा समाहितः ।
शीतोष्णसुखदुःखेषु
तथा मानावमानयोः ॥ ६.७॥
jitātmanaḥ praśāntasya
paramātmā samāhitaḥ
śītoṣṇasukhaduḥkheṣu
tathā mānāvamānayoḥ (6.7)

jitaātmanaḥ — of the self-controlled person; praśāntasya — of the person who is peaceful; paramātmā — the directive part of the self; samāhitaḥ — composed; śītoṣṇasukhaduḥkheṣu = śīta — cold + uṣṇa — heat + sukha — pleasure + duḥkheṣu — in pain; tathā — also; mānāvamānayoḥ = māna — honor + avamānayoḥ — in dishonor

The directive part of a self-controlled, peaceful person remains composed in the cold, heat, pleasure, pain, and also in honor and dishonor. (6.7)

Commentary:

Dualistic situations of good and bad weather, pleasant and unpleasant feelings, being appreciated and being shunned, continue even in the life of a saintly, self-realized man, for that is the unalterable course of destiny.

Material nature decreases her harassments of a saintly, self-realized man but she does not stop the irritations altogether. Due to having reformed his lower nature, a saintly person is not offended by the presumptions of material nature. Some commentators indicated that *samāhitah* means, *merged with the paramātmā (Supersoul),* but this cannot be. In all cases, we must recognize the individual limited entity for what he is and not merge him with anyone or anything. The communication is very intimate in trance consciousness (*samādhi*), but that does not mean that there is a seamless mergence. Getting close to someone, even to God, is not a mergence, but a very, very close communication. The soul cannot lose its individual nature, even when its consciousness is tranced out of this world or relocated into the spiritual energy.

Readers are cautioned by me, however, that even though the term *paramātmā* usually means Supersoul or Supreme Soul, it does not mean that in this verse. The Gaudiya Math authority, Sridhara Deva Maharaja, does not give the Supersoul meaning in this verse. Please study his meaning below, where he deliberately separated *param* from *ātmā* and linked *param* with *samāhitah*.

➢ *jitātmanah — for the yogi who has conquered the mind; praśāntasya — who is free from attraction and aversion; śītā uṣṇa sukha duhkheṣu — in cold and heat, happiness and unhappiness; tathā mānāvamānayoh — and in honor and insult; ātmā—the soul; bhavet— is; param-samāhitah— situated in the deep absorption of yogic trance. (The Hidden Treasure of the Sweet Absolute, p. 106)*

The two words of the first line of this verse, *jitātmanah* and *praśāntasya*, are in the genitive case, the *of,* possessive case. And *paramātmā* is in the nominative or subjective case. Param in this verse indicates not the Supersoul but rather the directive part of the psyche of the ordinary limited soul. This directive part is supposed to control the other parts of the psyche, since through such control the personal energies befriend rather than antagonize the person.

These personal energies consist of the mental faculties and emotional powers. These are listed in the *Bhagavad Gītā* under the following names:

indriyāṇi parāṇyāhur indriyebhyaḥ paraṁ manaḥ
manasastu parā buddhir yo buddheḥ paratastu saḥ (3.42)
evaṁ buddheḥ paraṁ buddhvā saṁstabhyātmānamātmanā
jahi śatruṁ mahābāho kāmarūpaṁ durāsadam (3.43)

The ancient psychologists say that the senses are energetic, but in comparison to the senses, the mind is more energetic. In contrast to the mind, the intelligence is even more sensitive. But in reference, the spirit is most elevated.

Thus having understood what is higher than intelligence, keeping the personal energies under control of the spirit, root out, O powerful man, the enemy, the form of passionate desire which is difficult to grasp. (3.42-43)

Here also the word *param* occurs as a term of comparison of one higher power over another. And it is on this basis, in this context, that I translated *param* in this verse

ज्ञानविज्ञानतृप्तात्मा
कूटस्थो विजितेन्द्रियः ।
युक्त इत्युच्यते योगी
समलोष्टाश्मकाञ्चनः ॥६.८॥
jñānavijñānatṛptātmā
kūṭastho vijitendriyaḥ
yukta ityucyate yogī
samaloṣṭāśmakāñcanaḥ (6.8)

jñānavijñānatṛptātmā = jñāna — knowledge + vijñāna — realized experience + tṛpta — content + ātmā — self; kūṭastho = kūṭasthaḥ — stable; vijitendriyaḥ = vijita - subdued + indriyaḥ — sensual energy; yukta — disciplined in yoga; ityucyate = ity (iti) — thus + ucyate — is called; yogī — yogi; samaloṣṭrāśmakāñcanaḥ = sama — same + loṣṭra — lump of clay + aśma — stone + kāñcanaḥ — gold

The yogi who is satisfied with knowledge and realized experience, who is stable and who has conquered his sensual energy, who regards a lump of clay, a stone or gold in the same way, is said to be disciplined in yoga. (6.8)

Commentary:

Kūṭastho means unchanging or stable. This refers to the great sages who remain riveted to the spiritual plane at all times, never drifting their focus from there, even when there is intense-pleasure or intolerable pain. Generally, a living entity is focused in the material world. Even though one's spirit remains in touch with the spiritual plane, one's attention may not be focused there. It is by chance, that an ordinary man may focus on the spiritual level. But for an advanced entity, it is the opposite feature. By chance, he transfers his attention to the mundane plane. Thus the ordinary man and the advanced entity have variant views. The ordinary person considers material nature as the reference for life, while the advanced soul considers the spiritual level as the standard. These two views were depicted in the beginning of the *Gītā* with Arjuna giving the ideal mundane consideration and Lord Krishna rejecting that as a form of ignorance.

Lord Krishna spoke of the yogi without stressing that such a yogi has to be a devotee of His. Later on, we will come to understand that Krishna means the yogi devotee. These yogis are the highest transcendentalists. There are many *bhaktas* (devotees) of Krishna who are against yoga practice. They cannot understand Krishna's stress on yoga. Throughout the *Gītā*, the direct and indirect indications lead to the conclusion that the yogi devotee is foremost. Why does Lord Krishna stress the yogi? Because the yogi is *kūţastho*. He is anchored on the spiritual plane. It is something definite for him. It is not a chance affair. In addition, the yogi has subdued the senses by a thorough yoga practice. He is a *vijita* or a conqueror of the senses.

In this verse, the word yogi appears in line 3 and if the word *bhakta* was placed there, we would have some problem understanding the verse. Why? Because *bhakta* means any kind of devotee of Krishna, even one who is not anchored on the spiritual plane.

A man does not have to be a conqueror of his senses to be a devotee or *bhakta*. Oh no! He can be materialistic. He can be a weakling in sense control and still be a devotee. But to be a yogi in truth, he must have the qualifications mentioned in this verse. And to be a yogi *bhakta* he must be both a yogi and a devotee. Some modern Vaishnava acharyas tilted the definition of a yogi *bhakta*; they changed the meaning to indicate that one just needs to be intellectually conversant with the *Gītā*, *Śrīmad Bhāgavatam*, *Chaitanya Charitamrita* and the allied scriptures, and also be competent at Vaishnava Deity worship ceremonies and have some charm for attracting disciples. In the time of Lord Krishna, a yogi *bhakta* was actually a devotee who was expert in yoga practice. And yoga practice meant *āsana*, *prāņāyāma*, and mental concentration as explained in the *Gītā*, and as explained to Uddhava by Lord Krishna in the *Śrīmad Bhāgavatam*.

In this translation, we are disregarding the modern definition. Our intention is to present the *Gītā* in its own time and place. Of course this does not mean that we are disrespecting the conclusions of the modern acharyas, but it does indicate that we want to get the substance of the *Gītā* in terms of what Krishna said to Arjuna and not in terms of how it was adjusted for modern times.

To an ancient yogi, or ancient yogi *bhakta*, a lump of clay, a stone, or gold could be well regarded evenly because the ancient definition involved a greater degree of detachment from material affairs. And such an ancient yogi was not the same as an ancient *karma* yogi like Janaka. Persons like Janaka were not yogis in terms of this verse because they had to keep their eye on government gold. But forest ascetics like *Vyāsaji* and Shuka could afford to regard gold as a sort of yellow stool because it was not required that they run a government and be in state administration. Even so, the modern, tilted definition of a yogi *bhakta* is a world apart from the ancient one, even from the ancient definition of a *karma* yogi. While the ancient yogi *bhakta* and *karma* yogi had to know yoga in detail, the modern yogi *bhakta* and *karma* yogi are required to know the theory and not the practice of yoga.

A further distinction is made between the ancient yogi *bhakta* and *karma* yogi. It is explained repeatedly in the Vedic literature that the ancient *karma* yogis had to enter the stage of vanaprastha to complete their austerities in older bodies. Many kings like Prithu, did in elderly bodies, return to forest life to finish up yoga practice. These ancient *karma* yogis did not aim at perfection directly from the active social life but only from the passive social stage after retirement. Even in the time of Lord Krishna, this was done by King Yudhishthira. And a pretender *karma* yogi, King *Dhŗtarāşţra*, also did this, as he was urged by Vidura to complete the vanaprastha stage of yoga practice in retirement. On the other hand, there are only a few examples of a forest yogi *bhakta* like *Vyāsaji* or Shuka who performed *karma yoga* to attain perfection. *Paraśurāma* may be cited as one, who though born as the son of a brahmin, took up the *karma yoga* tasks of a ruler and disciplined other leaders of the ruling caste.

सुहृन्मित्रार्युदासीन
मध्यस्थद्वेष्यबन्धुषु ।
साधुष्वपि च पापेषु
समबुद्धिर्विशिष्यते ॥६.९॥
suhṛnmitrāryudāsīna
madhyasthadveṣya bandhuṣu
sādhuṣvapi ca pāpeṣu
samabuddhirviśiṣyate (6.9)

suhṛnmitrāryudāsīna = suhṛn (suhṛd) — friend + mitra — acquaintance + ary (ari) — enemy + udāsīna — indifferent; madhyasthadveṣyabandhuṣu = madhyastha — evenly disposed + dvesya — enemy + bandhuṣu — to kinsmen; sādhuṣv = sādhuṣu — in saintly people; api — also; ca — and; pāpeṣu — in sinful people; samabuddhir = samabuddhiḥ — one who exhibits balanced judgement; viśiṣyate — be regarded with distinction

A person who is indifferent to friend, acquaintance, and enemy, who is evenly-disposed to enemies and kinsmen, who exhibits balanced judgment towards saintly people or sinful ones, is to be regarded with distinction. (6.9)

Commentary:

An ancient yogi *bhakta* could afford to regard people in this impartial way because he had no political interest. Being apart from social concerns, not grabbing a place in history, not trying to form a religious sect, such a devotional ascetic regarded friends and enemies alike. He did not have to polarize his followers in order to make them feel that they were better than everyone else. He did not require large donations from rich patrons and followers. He did not have to stoop to anyone for contributions.

योगी युञ्जीत सततम्
आत्मानं रहसि स्थितः ।
एकाकी यतचित्तात्मा
निराशीरपरिग्रहः ॥६.१०॥
yogī yuñjīta satatam
ātmānaṁ rahasi sthitaḥ
ekākī yatacittātmā
nirāśīraparigrahaḥ (6.10)

yogī — yogi; yuñjīta — should concentrate; satatam — constantly; ātmānam — on the self; rahasi — in isolation; sthitaḥ — situated; ekākī — alone; yatacittātmā = yata - controlling + citta - thinking + ātmā — self; nirāśīr — without desire; aparigrahaḥ — without possessions.

In isolation, the yogi should constantly concentrate on the self. Being alone, he should be of controlled thinking and subdued self without desire and without possessions. (6.10)

Commentary:

Lord Krishna defined the term yogi. He explained basic yoga practice. This definition is of value since some modern commentators whitewash the definition and substitute their own meanings for the words yoga and yogi. We are not questioning their motives. Their intentions may be in our interest, but we want to understand the *Gītā* as it was delivered to Arjuna. It may be argued that this is the definition of the early stages of yoga practice, but even so, let us look and see what was required in yoga:

- Concentration on his own soul (*yuñjīta ātmānam*)
- Isolation (*rahasi ekākī*)
- Controlled thinking and controlled feelings (*yatacittātmā*)
- Having no desires or cravings (*nirāśīr*).
- Being without possessions or worldly responsibilities (aparigrahah)

The last requirement in the verse, that of being without possessions or responsibilities, disqualified a *karma* yogi, even an ancient one. The ancient and modern *karma* yogis have to deal with possessions and responsibilities, in the form of properties and dependents. But while a modern *karma* yogi may never have become proficient in yoga practice, an ancient one was required to have expertise.

Some modern Vaishnava acharyas shun the first requirement which is *yuñjīta ātmānam* (concentration on one's own soul). It is a long argument between the Vaishnavas and the Shankarites. It is a common belief that the first person who instructed the Indians to separate the *Bhagavad Gītā* from the *Mahābhārata* was Śrīpad Shankaracharya, the greatest exponent of impersonalism ever to preach in India. Even today, his influence prevails. But the Vaishnavas in their effort to erase his impact, have set themselves at a safe distance from soul concentration, even the soul focus which is advocated in the *Gītā*. There is a great fear that if a man takes to soul focus, he might begin thinking that he is God or that he does not need God or that there is no God, or that he himself has suddenly become God. Thus many Vaishnava authorities push off the process of soul focus. But it is required as part of yoga practice as yoga is defined in the *Gītā*.

We may clarify, however, that soul focus only means the retrieval of the greater portion of the attention that is invested in the mind, the life force, and the senses. Instead of doling out vast quantities of psychic energy to the mind, life force and senses, the individual restricts these psychic tools. He conserves the psychic energy, re-directs it to himself, the soul, and tries to realize what he is. It is not a contrast between God and the limited soul but rather between the limited soul and his psychic equipments. Those who feel that the soul focus means competing with God or reducing God, are very much mistaken. Thus the Vaishnava acharyas have every right to condemn them in no uncertain terms. But when the Vaishnava leaders ridicule even those seekers who pursue soul focus in the proper way, they are being counter-productive. They work against the very *Gītā* they are so protective of.

Controlled thinking and controlled feelings (*yatacittātmā*) are described by modern Vaishnavas in a different way. They feel that the thinking cannot be controlled absolutely and that we should not try to achieve a total reduction in the thinking process nor try to freeze the mind in trance consciousness (*samādhi*). They feel that one should not try to suppress nor terminate the feelings, but should instead express them in a Krishna-centered way with Krishna-centered emotions. In terms of thinking, they acclaim that the thinking process serves nicely if one diverts the mind to Krishna pastimes and missionary activities.

However, the ancient process is a bit different from what we are told by these modern Vaishnava teachers. In the ancient process, one controls the thinking and feeling impulses to an almost absolute degree. Then, if one still has much time to live in his body, he transfers himself to thinking and feeling in relation to the Divinity. He does not in the beginning apply his contaminated mind and feelings to the Lord. First he purifies the mind and life force. Then he applies himself purely to the divine personalities and their activities. This is a course of austerities which can be performed by selected individuals for the complete purification of the mind and life force.

Having no desire or cravings (*nirāśīr*) is a state that develops after long, long yoga practice. Arjuna realized the difficulty of accomplishing such a state. He told Krishna that to control the roving mind was more difficult than to stop the blowing wind. And the modern Vaishnavas stuck to that verse to inform us that we should not even think of such absolute control of the psyche.

Being without possession and worldly responsibilities is accepted by the leading devotees who greatly simplify the lives of their followers, especially those who live in temples and ashramas. This is one aspect that is not neglected nor tilted by modern Vaishnava leaders. However, it is seen that for missionary purposes and for the establishment and continuation of their organizations, possessions become a necessity and worldly responsibilities for the wives and children of followers, must be faced. Thus they are forced to compromise the principle of non-possessiveness.

शुचौ देशे प्रतिष्ठाप्य
स्थिरमासनमात्मनः ।
नात्युच्छ्रितं नातिनीचं
चैलाजिनकुशोत्तरम् ॥ ६.११ ॥
śucau deśe pratiṣṭhāpya
sthiramāsanamātmanaḥ
nātyucchritaṁ nātinīcaṁ
cailājinakuśottaram (6.11)

śucau — in clean; deśe — in place; pratiṣṭhāpya — fixing; sthiram — firm; āsanam — seat; ātmanaḥ — of his self; nātyucchritaṁ = na — not + atyucchritaṁ — too high; nātinīcam = na — not + atinīcam — too low; cailājinakuśottaram = caila - cloth + ajina — antelope skin + kuśa — kusha grass + uttaram — underneath

In a clean place, fixing for himself a firm seat which is not too high, not too low, with a covering layer of cloth, antelope skin and kusha grass underneath, (6.11)

Commentary:

This is a description of yoga, not one of applied yoga. As we stated, applied yoga and yoga are different. The physical practice of yoga concerns *āsana* postures, but the application of it in social affairs, is subtle. Formerly, students of yoga went to a virgin forest or a sanctified place to practice. Yoga was not practiced in busy cities nor in public at busy temples, but in an isolated place away from the social scene. The yogi was supposed to be by himself (*ātmanah*) or with his teacher who was a forest ascetic.

तत्रैकाग्रं मनः कृत्वा
यतचित्तेन्द्रियक्रियः ।
उपविश्यासने युञ्ज्याद्
योगमात्मविशुद्धये ॥ ६.१२ ॥
tatraikāgraṁ manaḥ kṛtvā
yatacittendriyakriyaḥ
upaviśyāsane yuñjyād
yogamātmaviśuddhaye (6.12)

tatraikāgraṁ = tatra — there + ekāgram — single-focused; manaḥ — mind; kṛtvā — having made; yatacittendriyakriyaḥ = yata - controlled + citta — thought + indriyakriyaḥ — sense energy; upaviśyāsane = upaviśya — seating himself + āsane — in a posture; yuñjyād = yuñjyāt — should practice; yogamātmaviśuddhaye = yogam — to yoga discipline + ātma — self + viśuddhaye — to purification

...being there, seated in a posture, having the mind focused, the person who controls his thinking and sensual energy, should practise the yoga discipline for self-purification. (6.12)

Commentary:

Here we are given the abstract purpose of yoga practice as *ātmaviśuddhaye* (self-purification). Modern Vaishnava teachers try to say that unless yoga is designed for God realization in terms of Krishna consciousness, it is bogus. They stress that the single-pointed concentration should be to Krishna only. Usually, they cite a verse which states that concentration should be on Lord Vishnu or Krishna. Elsewhere in the *Gītā*, Lord Krishna does say that a devotee or even a yogi devotee should concentrate on Him, on Krishna Himself. Thus the idea stressed by the Vaishnava authorities is confirmed in no uncertain terms in the *Gītā*.

However, in this particular verse, this is not stated by Krishna. He does not specify where the single-pointed concentration should be placed. He states directly that the yoga practice, at least the preliminary stage, should be for self-purification.

Tatraikāgram is a combination of two words, namely *tatra* and *ekāgram*. *Ekāgram manah* means one-pointed mental concentration. No specification is given since in the beginning, a yoga teacher may assign his students various internal or external objects for concentration. The object might not be Lord Vishnu. For instance, Lord Krishna in text 27 of the previous chapter gave one such concentration point which is within the physical and subtle bodies:

sparśānkṛtvā bahirbāhyāṁś cakṣuścaivāntare bhruvoḥ
prāṇāpānau samau kṛtvā nāsābhyantaracāriṇau (5.27)

Excluding the external sensual contacts, and fixing the visual focus between the eyebrows, putting the inhalation and exhalation in balance, moving through the nose. (5.27)

In text 10 of this chapter. He gave another such focus as the soul itself:

yogī yuñjīta satatam ātmānaṁ rahasi sthitaḥ
ekākī yatacittātmā nirāśīraparigrahaḥ (6.10)

In isolation, the yogi should constantly concentrate on the self. Being alone, he should be of controlled thinking and subdued self without desire and without possessions. (6.10)

In addition, we heard in Chapter Four from texts 24 through 33, of the standard focus points, ideas or conceptions. These are all given at various stages of the process of self-purification (*ātmaviśuddhaye*). We are told, however, by some of the prominent Vaishnava leaders that such advice of Krishna applied only in the times of Krishna. Such a statement, however, puts Krishna to question as to why He recommended something at the end of *Dvāpara Yuga* which would be that obsolete soon after in the *Kali Yuga*.

Yoga practice as it is described here means mastership of *āsana haṭha* yoga postures, isolation from human society, simplicity of living to the extent of using natural material like kuśa grass, animal skins and hand-woven cloth. It involves single-pointed concentration according to the advice of a yoga teacher, tight control of the imagination (*yatacitta*) and the reduction in gross sensual activity (*indriyakriyas*). Incidentally, mind control involves one-pointed concentration but sense control or sensual energy and feelings control, involves *prāṇāyāma* practices which were explained in a previous verse (5.27). Self-purification is attained by introspection which leads to *samādhi* trance consciousness, hence the necessity to have mastered the *āsana* postures and the *prāṇāyāma* breath nutrition techniques.

समं कायशिरोग्रीवं
धारयन्नचलं स्थिरः ।
संप्रेक्ष्य नासिकाग्रं स्वं
दिशश्चानवलोकयन् ॥ ६.१३ ॥
samaṁ kāyaśirogrīvaṁ
dhārayannacalaṁ sthiraḥ
saṁprekṣya nāsikāgraṁ svaṁ
diśaścānavalokayan (6.13)

samam — balanced; kāyaśirogrīvaṁ = kāya — body + śiro (śiraḥ) — head + grīvam — neck; dhārayan — holding; acalam — without movement; sthiraḥ — steady; saṁprekṣya — gazing at; nāsikāgraṁ = nāsikā — nostril + agram — tip; svam — own; diśaścānavalokayan = diśaḥ — the directions + ca — and + anavalokayan — not looking

Holding the body, head and neck in balance, steady without movement, gaze at the tip of the nose, not looking in any other direction. (6.13)

Commentary:

The sitting posture required here is the *padmāsana* lotus pose. Only in that sitting posture can the body, head and neck remain erect in a straight line without motion. The technique of staring at the tip of the nose is called *nāsikāgram*. Lord Krishna added the word *svam* which means, *one's own*. So this concentration point is within the body.

Some yogi masters feel that *nāsikāgram* means staring from within to the center of the eyebrows at the chakra there. Some others feel that it is exactly as stated, being at the tip or point of the nose.

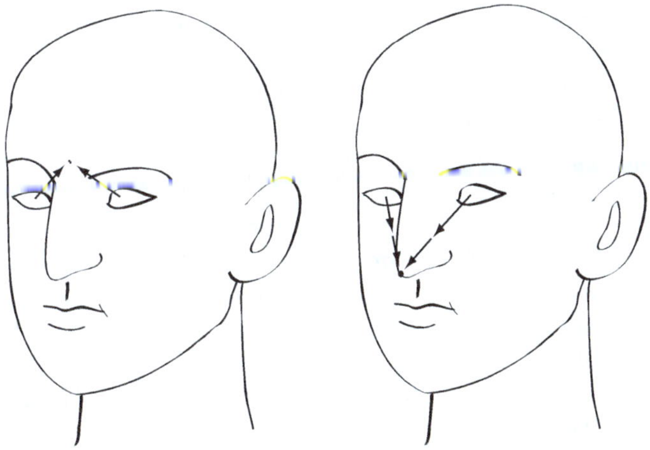

We inform readers, however, that both practices have particular purposes. Staring at the tip of the nose activates the base chakra known as *mūlādhāra* spot where kundalini shakti is anchored. Steady concentration on the brow chakra (*ajña*) compresses the mind and intellect and gives increased psychic perception. In addition, staring at the top of the nose bridge gives an adept direct control of the sexual urge by controlling the pubococcygeus muscle.

These practices are not meant to turn any limited soul into God but only to help with self-purification (*ātma-viśuddhaye*) in the effort for self-perfection or to become godly and fit for divine association.

प्रशान्तात्मा विगतभीर्
ब्रह्मचारिव्रते स्थितः ।
मनः संयम्य मच्चित्तो
युक्त आसीत मत्परः ॥६.१४॥
praśāntātmā vigatabhīr
brahmacārivrate sthitaḥ
manaḥ saṁyamya maccitto
yukta āsīta matparaḥ (6.14)

praśāntātmā = praśānta — pacified + ātmā — self; vigatabhīr (vigatabhīḥ) = vigata - gone away + bhīḥ — fear; brahmacārivrate — in the vow of sexual restraint; sthitaḥ — established; manaḥ — mind; saṁyamya — controlling; maccitto = maccittaḥ — though fixed on Me; yukta — disciplined; āsīta — should sit; matparaḥ — devoted to Me

With a pacified self, free from fears, with a vow of sexual restraint firmly practised, with mind controlled and having Me in his thought with his mind concentrated, he should sit, being devoted to Me as the Supreme Objective. (6.14)

Commentary:

Praśāntātmā means ***a spiritually peaceful self***. Some modern people misunderstand this, thinking that it means a substituted material type of sensual happiness. But *praśānta* means to be at peace with God. A man may be happy sensually and still be at odds with the Lord. Until we become more compatible with God, our peace of mind is superficial. God gave an allowance for variations in desires even to the extent that we may do something hostile to Him and still feel happy. But this type of happiness is not *praśānta*. A yogi who has accomplished himself, gone away from social complications, scaled down his material hankerings, properly understood his limitations and has decided not to exploit the material nature can afford to be at peace with God. The rest of us cannot. We are simply not prepared for such a loss of opportunity to exploit material nature. At the present time, material nature, has great significance. It is the one place where we have a foothold. Until we become greatly experienced in the frustration resulting from tangling with nature, we will not be able to attain a quieted self. And this is, perhaps, the only reason why modern Vaishnava leaders suggest that we not even attempt the practice.

This is a description of the *Bhagavad-Gītā* in its own time and place, but we must, from time to time, think of the relevance of the *Gītā* to our time. How much of the *Gītā* can we put into practice? How far should we go in underrating and shrinking the meaning of the words of the *Gītā*? What will be gained by such a reduction? Can we shrink down the meanings and get the same result gained by the ancient sages? These are questions that require careful consideration.

Vigatabhīr means ***freedom from fear***. But we cannot have that so long as we are involved in worldly activities with any degree of attachment. Mundane attachment has fear as its counterpart. We cannot separate it conveniently. It goes with the way of material living. An isolated yogi who is done with material hankerings, whose nature is matured and cured away from the exploitive tendency that we are so eager to display, is as fearless as he is detached from any need for mundane association.

Brahmacārivrate means *in the vow of a brahmacāri*, but the word *brahmacārin* is said to have a common and technical meaning. The common meaning is, *a student of a brahmin, a student of a spiritually-cultured teacher*. The technical meaning is ***a celibate student of a spiritually-cultured teacher*** or any person who adopts the lifestyle which affords him continuous focus on brahman, on spiritual reality. Vrata is a ***vow*** or discipline. Most commentators agree that a brahmacarin is one who adopts a vow of celibacy or who, by virtue of a youthful body, developed no sexual urge and who lives under the direction of a spiritually-conversant teacher.

The indication is, therefore, that a yogi is not supposed to have a wife. Thus we are left with a puzzle. How then was *Śrīla Vyāsaji*, the writer of the *Gītā*, considered a yogi? The answer is simple. The verse applies specifically to a student yogi, a person who practices yoga during the student years. It was customary in the time of Krishna, for boys to go to a spiritual teacher, just as children go to private boarding schools today. For persons like *Vyāsaji* who were householders and who were therefore conscious of the sexual urge, the word *brahmacāri* applies with a more technical meaning, as a person who adopts a lifestyle which is specifically designed for the pursuit of *Brahman*, the Supreme Cause. Such a householder brahmacari did not regard his wife as a sexual object. And he exhibited the quality of *aparigrahah*, being shorn of possessions, living very simply, only having the bare necessities and not allowing his wife to accumulate much nor influence him to develop a luxurious life.

Manah samyamya means ***a controlled mind***. This implies having an already controlled mind; not trying to control the mind. The yogi must already be expert in mind control by yoga practice. He should have perfected concentration, contemplation and trance, which is the freezing of the mind on higher planes of consciousness.

And lastly, *maccitto* and *matparah* mean **focus of the thinking element on Krishna** and **devotion to Krishna**. In this respect, we can do nothing but agree with the Vaishnavas. They defined meditation as a determined focus on the lotus feet of Krishna.

युञ्जन्नेवं सदात्मानं
योगी नियतमानसः ।
शान्तिं निर्वाणपरमां
मत्संस्थामधिगच्छति ॥६.१५॥

yuñjannevaṁ sadātmānaṁ
yogī niyatamānasaḥ
śāntiṁ nirvāṇaparamāṁ
matsaṁsthāmadhigacchati (6.15)

yuñjan — disciplining; evaṁ — as described; sadā — continuously; 'tmānaṁ = ātmānam — himself; yogī — yogi; niyatamānasaḥ — one who has a subdued mind; śāntiṁ — spiritual security; nirvāṇaparamāṁ = nirvāṇa - extinction of mundane affinity + paramām — highest living state; matsaṁsthām — existentially positioned with Me; adhigacchati — achieves

Disciplining himself continuously as described, the yogi who has a subdued mind, experiences spiritual security. He achieves the extinction of mundane affinity as he simultaneously attains the highest living state. He achieves an existential position with Me. (6.15)

Commentary:

After the appearance of Gautama Buddha, the word *nirvāṇa* assumed a mysterious aspect. It is used and overused in the transcendental societies. Generally a Vaishnava avoids this word, even though it appears so often in these *Gītā* verses. The reason is simple. After the Buddha, the word assumed an impersonal and Godless aspect. The Buddha did not mention devotion to a personal God. His main concern was to free himself and others from material existence. His idea was to end misery at all costs. To avoid the connotations which the Buddha put on the word *nirvāṇa*, the Vaishnavas keep their distance from the word, even though it is part and parcel of the *Gītā* vocabulary. The meanings of the word in the *Gītā* are quite different from the meaning suggested by Buddha.

After the Buddha, the respected Śrīmad Shankaracharya stressed another word. That is mukti or liberation from the material existence, but Shankara did not give us a scorn for Vedic rites, nor for Vedic deity worship. Shankara made his constructive criticism of these but he did not reduce their value.

The two words *nirvāṇa* and mukti are avoided by Vaishnavas. They stress instead, Vaikuntha and *bhakti. Nirvāṇa* means the extinction of social involvement. It may be contrasted to *nirvaha* which means to complete or to carry on, to become more involved. Most of us are interested in *nirvaha*. We want to complete something mundane, or to extend what we already started. Those who do not want to serve anyone and who are afraid of any type of involvement, consider *nirvāṇa* to be a complete ending off, a state through which all relationships are terminated. But those who want to continue service and who are much desirous of spiritual association see *nirvāṇa* as a complete ending of material involvements and a relative increase of spiritual associations. Besides these two types of persons, there are those who think that spiritual association is imaginary. They feel that mundane relationships are the ultimate use of affections. These are therefore called *samsāris*, people interested in repeated births and deaths. This group of materialistic souls feel that mundane existence is worth the pain of it.

Those who want liberation from material bondage but who feel that associative life is risky and who have the energy and determination, try to put out their existence, the way one would put out a fire. That is their meaning for *nirvāṇa*. But those who want salvation in association with the Supreme Lord Krishna or with any other person who is conceived of as being perfect and divine, regard *nirvāṇa* as being a final exit from the material world and a permanent entrance into the kingdom of God. In either case, the *Gītā* applies it. The *Gītā* is not polarized. In the *Gītā*, there is room for every type of salvationist but we must agree that in particular verses, Lord Krishna stressed Himself and presented Himself as the supreme objective.

In the first line of this verse, the term *ātmānam* is used, but this cannot mean that a yogi is left unto himself alone, otherwise the focus on Krishna as mentioned in the previous verse would be meaningless. With all reason, we must understand that the limited soul cannot be left alone. He has to deal with the all-surrounding reality on one level or another, either on the mundane or spiritual planes, or the cross worlds between the two. The environment cannot be avoided. In the *Gītā* Lord Krishna repeatedly stressed the value of self-focus even though some Vaishnava acharyas carefully bypass this and even discourage it. Self-focus in the *Gītā* does not mean that there is no other focus. It does not mean that there is no God focus .Krishna directly presents Himself as the ultimate focus. For instance, we hear from Lord Krishna about the order of *Prajāpati*. But immediately after mentioning that, Krishna suggested that we should follow no other supernatural person but Himself. He does not overlook the focus on the higher personalities, even though there are strong suggestions by Him that we substitute Him in the place of all others. Later on in the *Gītā*, when Lord Krishna showed the Universal Form, He directly and finally installed Himself. This was quite a bold move, for a historic personality to put Himself before human society as the ultimate and final replacement for all divinities ever worshipped by men. Somehow or the other Lord Krishna did that.

Ātmānam, or the soul himself, cannot be ignored. We must deal with ourselves. As stated by the Lord, yoga is essential for the purpose of self-purification. This cannot be ignored. One must continually (*sadā*) discipline (*yunjan*) himself (*ātmānam*) if he wants to reach the spiritual plane either as a devotee of Krishna or otherwise. Even if one is a devotee of Krishna, he will not be able to get a permanent relocation to the spiritual world of Krishna unless he is completely purified. Self-discipline is stressed because when someone else, even a guru, disciplines the disciple, that is just the beginning. Until the disciple takes up the spiritual practice in earnest, he cannot make permanent progress. In that sense, those spiritual masters who convey that their disciples can be freed merely by their grace, are cheating. The grace, blessings and well-wishes of a spiritual master are an essential part of the salvation process, but the personal effort of the disciple for the removal of bad habits and spiritually-destructive tendencies are an essential portion too. The guru must do his part and the disciple as well.

Niyatamānasah is a subdued mind. In the time of Krishna, one curbed such a mind by practicing *prāṇāyāma* to curb the life energy that stimulates the mind. Modern Vaishnava teachers usually have no interest in *prāṇāyāma* but try to curb the mind by japa chanting. Formerly, however, it was realized that the mind is goaded and stirred by the life force. As a woman is impregnated by a man and becomes pregnant regardless of whether she desires a child or not, so the mind becomes impelled if it is stirred by the life force. Thus, in the Upanishadic times, the sages controlled the life force by mastering breath energy.

Even before the time of Lord Krishna, these methods were well practiced. For instance, long, long ago in the time of Lord Rama, the son of King Dasharatha, the forest ascetics mastered *prāṇāyāma*. In the Aranya Kanda, Canto VI, we are told of some ascetic practices of various sages who greeted Sri *Rāma* at the hermitage of Sharabhanga. We list these verbatim from the translation of *Śrīmad Vālmīki Rāmāyaṇa* published by *Gītā* Press of Gorakhpur, India. The various sages included:

> ***. . . (those) who washed the utensils after their meals (keeping nothing for another time), those who lived on the sun's or moon's rays, those who powdered grains by stones, many ascetics living on leaves, those using teeth as the mortar and pestle, others doing penance in neck-deep water, those using limbs of the body alone for bed, those without bed, those enjoying no respite from their religious observances, sages living on water alone, others on air alone, those having sky as the only roof, those sleeping on the altar, those dwelling on high altitudes, those who controlled their senses, those who used to wear wet clothes, those doing japa, those devoted to penance, those doing the penance of sitting in the middle of four fires, with the sun (the fifth) overhead, all possessed of brahmic lustre, and with their mind concentrated through steadfast practice of yoga—these ascetics approached Rāma in the hermitage of Sarabhanga. (2-6, p.661)***

Modern Vaishnava teachers, however, bring it to our attention that we are in a different time cycle. They say that we cannot perform such austerities. This statement of theirs, however, is not absolute. This writer had some success with similar austerities. He cannot stand before an audience and say that it is impossible. He does, however, agree that it is impossible for most people.

Śāntim means *spiritual security* but modern pandits usually bless their vice-prone audiences with *śāntim* as if such a thing can be had by materialistic devotees. Such cheating abounds and there is absolutely nothing we can do to stop it. *Śāntim*, however, cannot be attained by a materialistic person who is not self-realized and who is not separated from the worldly situations. Materialistic involvement means the absence of *śāntim*. This is why the yogis go to an isolated place.

Nirvāṇaparamām means *the ending off, the termination of material existence and the full assumption of life in the undiluted spiritual existence (paramām)*. But Lord Krishna established Himself at the end of all this by His words of *matsamsthām adhigacchati*, stating that such a person who focuses on Him, who relies on Him, goes to His situation in the spiritual sky.

नात्यश्नतस्तु योगोऽस्ति
न चैकान्तमनश्नतः ।
न चातिस्वप्नशीलस्य
जाग्रतो नैव चार्जुन ॥ ६.१६ ॥
nātyaśnatastu yogo'sti
na caikāntamanaśnataḥ
na cātisvapnaśīlasya
jāgrato naiva cārjuna (6.16)

nātyaśnatas = na — not + atyaśnatas — of too much eating; tu — but; yogo = yogaḥ — yoga; 'sti = asti — it is; na — not; caikāntam = ca — and + ekāntam — solely; anaśnataḥ — of not eating at all; na — not; cātisvapnaśīlasya = ca — and + atisvapna - too much sleeping + śīlasya — of habit; jāgrato = jāgrataḥ — of staying awake; naiva = na — nor + eva — indeed; cārjuna = ca — and + arjuna — Arjuna

But Arjuna, yoga practice does not consist of eating too much. And it is not the practice of not eating at all, nor the habit of sleeping too much nor staying awake either. (6.16)

Commentary:

Yoga practice is not a general religious process. Since yoga requires isolation, it cannot be a general religious system. Thus the idea that yoga was suited formerly and that it is not agreeable today, is unfounded. Yoga was never suited to social living in the materialistic or cultural way. Yoga was always a system apart from the general life style.

Overeating is not yoga, neither is undernourishment; neither is oversleeping or unnecessarily staying awake. Here is why: The idea of yoga is self-purification. Let us keep this in mind. That was told to us in verse 12:

tatraikāgraṁ manaḥ kṛtvā yatacittendriyakriyaḥ
upaviśyāsane yuñjyād yogamātmaviśuddhaye (6.12)

...being there, seated in a posture, having the mind focused, the person who controls his thinking and sensual energy, should practise the yoga discipline for self-purification. (6.12)

In the initial stages, yoga concerns itself with the purification of the gross body, the purification of the mind, the purification of the life force, the purification of the subtle body, and the purification of the causal form, in that order; then finally, the purification of the soul. In the beginning, a yogi might feel that he can, all of a sudden, purify the soul, but as he practices he realizes that this cannot be done abruptly. He has to start with the physical body. Here is the question: If I am not my physical body, if I am a spirit, then why do I have to purify my physical form? The answer is simply this: You do not have to purify your physical body but you must consider whether you can effectively transcend the physical form without purifying it. If you cannot, you will have to purify it.

The next question is: If I am required to purify my physical form and I do not have sufficient energy to do so because my body is too old and it will soon pass away, then what is my position? Your position is this: You will have to take another physical body and purify that one by yoga practice in the next life. Yoga practice may be unnecessary for those who can effectively transcend the physical form. But even these superior souls may have to practice it. Here is why: If a man cannot perfect yoga practice in a gross body, how will he perfect a more subtle practice like mind and life energy control? If we cannot control something physical, how can we control something that exists only in the psychic world? It is easier to control something physical than it is to regulate a subtle object. The people who claim to have transcended the body even though they have not controlled it, are for the most part, pretenders.

There is, however, a reason why most of us are reluctant to take up yoga practice. It is simply this: We are lazy. We want results by exercising our will power only. We do not want to exert any other energy. We want something in return for nothing. We want God to serve us with perfection while we go on with the normal course of our lives. The most austerity we want to perform in this age, is to call on the name of God. In other words, the sum total austerity we would commit ourselves to, is the manipulation of our tongues, vocal cords, lips and mouth cavity in God's glorification. We do not want to lift a finger for self-purification.

When a man has completed self-purification, he becomes fit for liberation and divine association. Otherwise his plans for divine life are for the most part an imagination only. At first, soul purification may seem to a seeker, to be mind purification, but when one makes an effort at mind purification one discovers that the mind cannot be purified unless the intellect is purified. The intellect cannot be purified unless one has mystic communication with the higher levels of life. This cannot be achieved unless the life force is purified.

Someone may not realize that he has a subtle body. He may not experience himself as the subtle form but only as the gross form. And still, he may speak of transcending the gross body and going to the kingdom of God at the time of death. This is all imaginary. There is no validity in this. It is simply a series of fairy tales. If our religious process is powerful, then why is it that we cannot even realize the next higher body, the subtle one?

As one woman recently told the writer, "*I do not know what my soul is. To tell you the truth, I want to ask you: Where is my soul?* " She was honest. She made progress. If the seeker cannot know his subtle form distinctly, he cannot know his soul either. If we cannot perceive something as limited as the subtle body, then what is the question of perceiving the soul?

One religious man who spent years going to temples and chanting the names of God, singing the praises of God, asked the writer this question: "*What is the soul? I was never able to figure out what my soul is.*"

Religious leaders the world over, from every major religious group, proceed year after year, day after day, with this same cheating process of entertaining the childish people without bringing them into self-realization. It is so pathetic. Even though there is little we can do to change this, we are thoroughly disgusted with it. Every day a new religious leader emerges with the same trick as before. So many of these leaders are influence peddlers.

Too much eating is not part of yoga practice. Yoga practice aims at curtailing the eating process. The idea is to reduce the attention that goes to the gross body so that the energy invested in that body is reduced. The conserved energy is then invested in a discipline which is recommended by a spiritual master. Increased food consumption means increased attention to the body which means that the soul will, by impulsion, invest more consciousness into the body.

Increased eating means an increase of the fat or muscle content of the body. In yoga practice, however, at least initially, there is an increase in food intake. This is not due to greed. This is due to increased digestive ability of the body. Such increases in food do not cause an increase in fat or muscle, since the body does not take in more than it needs even if the yogi overeats. Due to strong digestive power and good circulation, a practicing yogi does not have bodily weight increases even if he overeats. But as soon as he stops the practice of *āsana* and *prāṇāyāma* combined, his body may become obese if he overeats.

Muscle content does not increase in the body of a practicing yogi but certain muscles become more developed and others become more relaxed. Certain muscles dissolve away or decrease in size. An increase in eating in the initial stages of yoga practice is no problem for the yogi. Soon after there is an increase, there will be a reduction as the practice becomes more consistent and the blood circulation in the body becomes more efficient.

Under-eating, however, is a danger to the yogi in the initial stages. But under-eating, by the standards of worldly people, is excellent for the yogi in the advanced stages. Thus under-eating in the advanced stages is not a violation of the rule in this verse. In the advanced stages, two factors contribute to increased nutrition in the body. These are efficient circulation and increased breath nutrition. These offset the under-eating of gross food. Since the yogi increased circulation and breath nutrition, his under-eating or reduction in food intake is not really a reduction but is actually an increase in nutrition. By eating less food, breathing much more air, and having his circulation increased tremendously, he actually increases his nutritional intake.

On the other hand, those who reduce their food intake and observe haphazard fasting and who do not practice *prāṇāyāma* nor do yoga *āsana* consistently, do punish themselves unnecessarily.

While the food is somewhat easy to control, sleeping is much more difficult to curb. Sleeping regulations simply do not work unless one becomes regulated in his work, rest and eating. All these must be carefully regulated before sleep can be controlled. Work includes sexual activity. Sexual activity, strenuous endeavor, and overtaxing mental work can cause excessive drowsiness. As long as the sexual urge is not curbed, drowsiness cannot be curbed by a natural means, but it can be regulated by drinking, chewing, injecting or inhaling stimulants. The use of stimulants, however, is contrary to yoga practice.

Sleep is the most complicated mechanism to control. Sleep is regulated by the life force. Overeating contributes to excessive sleep. When one overeats, his bodily organs must work harder to process the excess food. This results in a fatigued life energy which is only replenished in sleep. The most dangerous cause of excessive sleep in human beings is excessive sexual activity. For children it is different. They sleep excessively if they are allowed to play excessively. This excessive play is a form of strenuous activity. It tires out the life force and thus brings on sleep through which the life force is rejuvenated.

Too little sleep overtaxes the life force and causes it to react by producing mental instability and erratic sleep. After a session of too little sleep, a person oversleeps to compensate. In the advanced stages of yoga practice, one loses his interest in sleep and becomes unconcerned about it. Whenever the body sleeps, one switches to a psychic level and continues activities there. Thus an advanced yogi might appear to oversleep, while in fact, he travels to another level of consciousness and remains awake there.

These matters of shifting the focus of consciousness may seem incredible, but if one takes to the practice and experiences it for himself, he begins to understand. Yoga gives gradual but consistent results. It takes many years to reap the benefit of a consistent yoga practice.

युक्ताहारविहारस्य
युक्तचेष्टस्य कर्मसु ।
युक्तस्वप्नावबोधस्य
योगो भवति दुःखहा ॥६.१७॥
yuktāhāravihārasya
yuktaceṣṭasya karmasu
yuktasvapnāvabodhasya
yogo bhavati duḥkhahā (6.17)

yuktāhāravihārasya = yukta — regulated + āhāra — eating + vihārasya — of leisure; yuktaceṣṭasya = yukta — disciplined + ceṣṭasya — of endeavor; karmasu — in duties; yuktasvapnāvabodhasya = yukta — disciplined + svapna - sleep + avabodhasya — of waking; yogo = yogaḥ — yoga practice; bhavati — is; duḥkhahā — distress-removing

For a person who is regulated in eating and in leisure, who is disciplined in the endeavor of duties, who is moderate in sleeping and waking, for him, the yoga practice is a distress-remover. (6.17)

Commentary:

Here the benefit of yoga practice is described. Yoga, therefore, is not designed as a set of gymnastics. For the serious ones, yoga removes many mundane distresses (*duhkhahā*).

Yoga removes physical and psychic pains. It works on the physical, mental and emotional levels. It helps the soul to curb his life force which is the principal cause of physical and psychological irregularities.

यदा विनियतं चित्तम्
आत्मन्येवावतिष्ठते ।
निःस्पृहः सर्वकामेभ्यो
युक्त इत्युच्यते तदा ॥६.१८॥
yadā viniyataṁ cittam
ātmanyevāvatiṣṭhate
niḥspṛhaḥ sarvakāmebhyo
yukta ityucyate tadā (6.18)

yadā — when; viniyataṁ — tightly controlled; cittam — thought; ātmany = ātmani — in the spiritual core self; evāvatiṣṭhate = eva — alone + avatiṣṭhate — is attentive; niḥspṛhaḥ — free from desire; sarvakāmebhyo (sarvakāmebhyaḥ) = sarva — all + kāmebhyaḥ — from cravings; yukta — proficient in yoga; ity = iti — thus; ucyate — is said; tadā — then

When with tightly controlled thought, he is attentive to his spiritual core self alone, being freed from desires and from all cravings, he is said to be proficient in yoga. (6.18)

Commentary:

This is another description of the result of yoga practice. By these statements, we can judge a yogi or a person who claims to be self-controlled. Some persons exhibit such control from birth. Thus they do not require yoga practice to show this. It is said that the South Indian saint Ramana Maharshi was like this. And there were others who became famous in that way. In some cases these saints are not professed devotees of the Supreme Lord but rather they may become advocates of an open spiritual existence without any implied service to a Divinity.

It is said that we cannot tightly control our minds because the mind is restless by nature. But the possibility of such mind control was recognized by Lord Krishna. This is why He used the word *viniyatam*. *Yatam* means control and when *vini* is put as a prefix, it means tightly-controlled. So we must accept the possibility if we believe in the *Gītā*.

Ātmany evāvatiṣṭhate means being situated (*avatiṣṭhate*) in the soul alone (*ātmany eva*). But this can be misinterpreted to mean that the soul focus is the ultimate aim. For instance, Sri Ramana Maharshi, who was a remarkable personality with a deep realization of spiritual nature, did teach that soul focus was the ultimate aim. But recently, a few months ago, when I spoke to him in the astral world, he said, *"I only made one mistake. I did not stress Lord Krishna enough. I was too attached to self-happiness. I should have gone further and directed people to Krishna."*

By the definition of the *Gītā*, self-focus cannot mean that the soul or the self is absolute or that the soul is the soul's ultimate companion. Soul focus in the *Gītā* is intended to get the conditioned entities to leave aside material nature for a time, so that they can realize that self-happiness is superior to mundane sensual pleasure. It is a contrast between the soul and the psychic tools of pleasure, not between the soul and God. Some commentators twist the *Gītā* and use it to support their idea of the soul being an absolute principle unto itself.

Krishna wants us to properly realize that the soul is more important than the psychic tools like the mind and the senses. We should not sacrifice our spiritual interest for sensuality. That is the lesson of the *Gītā*. Thus in the beginning one should become anchored to self-focus to realize that consciousness of the soul is a higher, more secured existence, than perception on the psychic and physical planes. At the present time, the lower levels are necessary but we should be disciplined in the use of these, or we will become degraded by lower tendencies which cause us to adapt ourselves to lower life forms.

Eventually, we have to develop self-focus with the proper intention. Then we can understand that gross and subtle sensuality are of a lower grade than soul pleasure. In the ultimate analysis, the association of the Personality of Godhead is the highest joy but we cannot reach that level if we do not understand that the soul itself is higher than the psychic pleasures, and that the Lord is higher than the soul. This is why Ramana Maharshi expressed his regret to me. He indicated that he was waiting for an opportunity to take another body through which he would preach the *Bhagavad Gītā* as Krishna intended it to be, acting then as a powerful agent to bring people to realize the glory of the Blessed Lord.

Until a living entity sees the futility and utility of mundane existence as Krishna sees it, he cannot become free from material existence. Ramana Maharshi is an example of a saintly person who saw the futility of material existence, but he did not at the time, understand its proper utility according to Lord Krishna. Here in the *Gītā*, Lord Krishna explained the proper advantage to be gained from this world, as well as the disadvantage or risk of being involved here.

यथा दीपो निवातस्थो
नेङ्गते सोपमा स्मृता ।
योगिनो यतचित्तस्य
युञ्जतो योगमात्मनः ॥६.१९॥
yathā dīpo nivātastho
neṅgate sopamā smṛtā
yogino yatacittasya
yuñjato yogamātmanaḥ (6.19)

yathā — as; dīpo = dīpaḥ — lamp; nivātastho (nivātasthaḥ) = nivāta — windless + sthaḥ — situated; neṅgate = na — not + iṅgate — flickers; sopamā = so (sāḥ) — this + upamā — in comparison; smṛtā — recalled; yogino = yoginaḥ — of the yogi; yatacittasya — of a person whose thinking is restrained; yuñjato = yuñjataḥ — of practising; yogam — yoga; ātmanaḥ — of the self

This comparison is recalled: A lamp in a windless place which does not flicker, and a yogi of controlled thought who performs disciplines in relation to the spiritual self. (6.19)

Commentary:

There is no hint here that Lord Krishna dislikes this self-focus as He Himself described it in the *Gītā*. Some modern Vaishnava teachers, however, convey the impression that self-focus is undesirable and misleading. It must be, therefore, that there is a risk involved in self-focus. To protect us from becoming atheistic or impersonal, the Vaishnava leaders divert us from these verses of the *Gītā*. But Lord Krishna said what He said. It is up to the individual seekers to use or abuse these statements of the Blessed Lord. We do, however, have His blessing to be successful in self-focus insofar as it will bring us to the realization that the lower pleasures are worthless.

A modern man can just imagine the evolutionary status and mental stability of the ancient yogis who were so accomplished as to be accredited as having achieved what is described in this verse. We can only appreciate and admire those sages from a historic distance. All glories unto them, wherever they may be!

यत्रोपरमते चित्तं
निरुद्धं योगसेवया ।
यत्र चैवात्मनात्मानं
पश्यन्नात्मनि तुष्यति ॥६.२०॥

yatroparamate = yatra — where + uparamate — it stops; cittaṁ — thinking; niruddhaṁ — restraint; yogasevayā = yoga — yoga discipline + sevayā — by practice; yatra — where; caivātmanā = ca — and + eva — indeed + ātmanā — by the self; 'tmānaṁ = ātmānam — the self; paśyan —

yatroparamate cittaṁ
niruddhaṁ yogasevayā
yatra caivātmanātmānaṁ
paśyannātmani tuṣyati (6.20)

seeing; ātmani — in the self; tuṣyati — is satisfied

At the place where being restrained by yoga practice, thinking stops, and at the place where the yogi perceives the self by the self, he is satisfied in the self. (6.20)

Commentary:

In Chapter Two, text 54, Arjuna asked some questions of Lord Krishna. These verses are an answer to those questions. Let us review Arjuna's inquiry:

arjuna uvāca
sthitaprajñasya kā bhāṣā samādhisthasya keśava
sthitadhīḥ kiṁ prabhāṣeta kimāsīta vrajeta kim (2.54)

Arjuna said: In regards to the person who is situated in clear, penetrating insight, would you please describe him? Speak of the person who is anchored in deep meditation, O Keśava Krishna. As for the man who is steady in objectives, how would he speak? How would he sit? How would he act? (2.54)

The spirit soul itself is worthy of its own association so we can just imagine the value of the Supreme Lord Who is the ultimate focus of all selves. The contrast between the psychic equipments and the soul, shows that the soul is superior. And in a contrast between the Lord and the limited soul, the Lord is superior. The soul, therefore, should not sacrifice his spiritual awareness for mundane moods. But this is exactly what it does in the conditioned state. Thus, when again the soul discovers the high value of itself, it becomes very happy. Some who discover their high self-value do not go on to become devotees of Lord Krishna. This is because their initial impetus was to get free from the dominating influence of material nature; they were not aware of the Lord's glories at the time of their self-realization. But even those people do, in the process of time, become attracted to Krishna. To save seekers from the mishap of not being attracted to the Lord, the Vaishnava authorities graciously spread His glories by hook or crook, so that even if one is self-attracted, one may hear of the Lord and develop an affinity for divine association. In the *Śrīmad Bhāgavatam, Nārada* Muni said that just by hearing of the Lord from some great souls and just by taking the remnants of their foodstuffs, he was irresistibly attracted, so much that even though he went through this course of self-realization in self-satisfaction, he stuck to the attraction of Krishna and became perfected in the divine association.

Besides these considerations, an important aspect of self-realization was explained by Krishna--- that of the location of the soul when thinking stops. Some great preachers claim that thinking never stops, but these advocates of continuous thinking need to explain the words *uparamate* and *niruddham*, which give stress to complete cessation of thoughts (*cittam*). The point is: Where (*yatra*) is the soul located when this occurs?

सुखमात्यन्तिकं यत्तद्
बुद्धिग्राह्यमतीन्द्रियम् ।
वेत्ति यत्र न चैवायं
स्थितश्चलति तत्त्वतः ॥६.२१॥

sukham — happiness; ātyantikaṁ — continuous; yat= yad — which; tad — this; buddhigrāhyam — grasp by the intellect; atīndriyam — beyond the mundane senses; vetti — he knows; yatra — whereabout; na

sukhamātyantikaṁ yattad
buddhigrāhyamatīndriyam
vetti yatra na caivāyaṁ
sthitaścalati tattvataḥ (6.21)

— *not; caivāyam = ca — and + eva — indeed + ayam — this; sthitaścalati = sthitaḥ — established + calati — he shifted; tattvataḥ — the reality*

He knows the whereabouts of that continuous happiness, which is grasped by the intellect and which is beyond the mundane senses. And being established, he does not shift from that reality. (6.21)

Commentary:

Nowadays people consider the normal consciousness of a gross body to be boring and dull. But this normal consciousness is a facet of the Supreme Reality. There is spiritual pleasure, but in the material world, that aspect is replaced by mundane happiness which is limited. *Ānanda* is an endless spiritual joy but it is not available to the souls who are focused in the material direction.

Mundane happiness is limited. Modern people try to extend the limitations of it by inducing happiness by sensual stimulation. Some people try to find happiness by meditation or by some other psychic discipline. Unending happiness is the most sought-after experience in the material world. We may wonder how a person can shift himself away from soberness since that soberness is a feature of spirituality. The answer is that by drugs, music, movies and other sensually-stimulating ways, the living entity can intensify his material focus and distance himself from spirituality.

The material energy has a very subtle aspect called *prāṇa, pradhāna* or *prakṛti*. These Sanskrit terms mean *very, very subtle cosmic energy*. By bringing on more material focus, a living entity can take himself away from soberness, but in doing so, he does not reach *ānanda* (spiritual happiness), but rather he reaches a subtler or grosser state of matter. He may, however, falsely interpret that shift in awareness as something spiritual.

When, by the proper spiritual austerities, a yogi shifts from the normal sober level to a higher spirituality, he is put in touch with the spiritual pleasure potency. His intellect, finding that superior happiness, holds on to it. The intellect scribes or etches into the mind or the memory, that joyful experience. Then a repeated effort is made to regain that enjoyment.

For instance, let us take the romantic experience. After a young man or young woman has a romance, the intellect etches that into the mind and it continuously searches after such experiences. Similarly, when the intellect finds the spiritual joy on the spiritual level, it remembers how the soul journeyed mystically or psychically to that spiritual plane. It urges the soul to return there repeatedly. This explains why some yogis become so attached to meditation or trance consciousness. The sweetness of the spiritual happiness is attractive to a materially-afflicted soul who found it through yoga austerities.

As stated by the Lord, after becoming established (*sthitas*) in this spiritual happiness, the yogi does not shift off *(na calati)* from there. He learns where it is located in his psyche. He continuously remains in touch with it. This is the level of *brahma bhūta*, the spiritual plane.

One difference between yoga practice and the other spiritual disciplines is indicated here. There are definite reasons why the ancient sages left aside all other processes of self-realization and stuck to yoga. It is due to the definiteness of yoga. Through yoga, one becomes familiar with the mystic landscape. One gets direct experience of how to go to the higher levels at the time of death. *Vetti yatra* means that the yogi knows where the spiritual happiness is located. Of course, this spiritual happiness is not the fullness of spiritual life. Still, if a yogi persists in yoga practice, he learns the exact location of the various subtle, causal, spiritual and super-spiritual levels.

Some non-yogi seekers try to pretend that it is not important to know these levels. They cite *Gītā*, particularly the location verse about the yogis who use the course of the sun or moon to go to higher worlds, but such talk is useless. One clings to ignorance merely because he does not know a fact, not because there is a value in not knowing. The same preachers who deride the yogi's familiarity with the psychic and spiritual places, know their town, village, or city, quite well. They use physical geography. But since they have not performed the austerities, they do not know the mystic terrain. Arjuna knew it well and so did King Yudhishthira. The *Mahābhārata* history states that. Śrīla *Vyāsadeva* knew it. *Nārada* knew it. Shuka knew it.

यं लब्ध्वा चापरं लाभं
मन्यते नाधिकं ततः ।
यस्मिन्स्थितो न दुःखेन
गुरुणापि विचाल्यते ॥६.२२॥
yaṁ labdhvā cāparaṁ lābhaṁ
manyate nādhikaṁ tataḥ
yasminsthito na duḥkhena
guruṇāpi vicālyate (6.22)

yaṁ — which; labdhvā — having attained; cāparaṁ = ca — and + aparaṁ — other; lābhaṁ — attainment; manyate — he thinks; nādhikam = na — not + adhikam — greater; tataḥ — than that; yasmin — which; sthito = sthitah — established; na — not; duḥkhena — by distress; guruṇāpi = guruṇā — by deep + api — also; vicālyate — is drawn away

And having attained that, he thinks there is no greater attainment. Being established in that, he is not drawn away, even by deep distress. (6.22)

Commentary:

Arjuna asked Lord Krishna about the man who was situated in clear penetrating insight (*sthitaprajñasya*, 2.54). This verse replies to that inquiry. After the man reaches the spiritual plane and experiences the happiness there, he then develops a reference point for true happiness. He becomes reluctant to engage in material activities for pleasure's sake. Such a man may appear to be serious to those who are enjoying themselves in the material world. Sometimes, even neophyte transcendentalists fail to understand such a man. They feel that he is too strict as a non-participant in material existence.

After spending many births in material forms and getting manhandled by the laws of material nature, which take their exact cutting strokes in the form of destiny, an experienced soul feels relieved to find the happiness of the spiritual plane. But that does not mean that such a spiritually-happy, wise man has settled up with the Lord. On the contrary, his problems now commence in earnest. He will have to return to the material scene to be a spiritual leader and to help Lord Krishna with the world's responsibilities. Many such persons who find that unending spiritual happiness (*sukham ātyantikam*) become terribly disappointed to hear that they must again come back into the material social scene to preach and share the realization.

तं विद्याद्दुःखसंयोग -
वियोगं योगसंज्ञितम् ।
स निश्चयेन योक्तव्यो
योगोऽनिर्विण्णचेतसा ॥६.२३॥

tam — this; vidyād = vidyāt — let it be understood; duḥkhasaṁyoga = duḥkha — emotional distress + saṁyoga — emotional identity with; viyogaṁ — separation; yogasaṁjñitam = yoga — mastery of yoga + saṁjñitam — recognized as; sa = saḥ — this; niścayena — with determination; yoktavyo =

tam̐ vidyādduḥkhasam̐yoga -
viyogam̐ yogasam̐jñitam
sa niścayena yoktavyo
yogo'nirviṇṇacetasā (6.23)

yoktavyaḥ — to be practiced; yogo = yogah — yoga; 'nirviṇṇacetasā (anirviṇṇacetasā) = anirviṇṇa — not depressed + cetasā — with thought

Let it be understood that this separation from emotional distress is the mastery of yoga. This yoga is to be practised with determination and without depressing thought. (6.23)

<u>*Commentary:*</u>

In the beginning, yoga practice means isolation from social hassles. Either by instinct from a past life or by being harassed presently, a person may take to yoga practice. There are various reasons for practicing yoga. When one finds a teacher, one takes shelter under him safely in the beginning. Later on, however, after one practices, material nature in liaison with living entities to whom one is obligated, produces strong forces of destiny which may move one away from the shelter of the teacher. At that point, one's yoga disciplines may prove their worth in the form of detachment from adversity and hellish conditions.

There is hostility that one faces when he turns away from social relationships. This comes in the form of intense hatreds from the conditioned entities who were former associates. They, sensing that one might be slipping out of their grip, develop strong grasping attitudes and fight to keep one from being liberated.

It is at this point that one is required to apply the technique which is mentioned in this verse. Lord Krishna told Arjuna: "This information I will give you (*tam*), let it be understood thoroughly (*vidyād*)." Krishna mentioned this because Arjuna was just at the point where he needed to apply the techniques which would free him of associations which deterred him from the execution of duties. The related Kauravas and their friends pressured Arjuna emotionally, causing him to lose enthusiasm for duty. Arjuna fought back internally and converted their crippling energies into the power of discipline, through which he twanged his bow and released arrows on the battlefield.

Arjuna got emotional distress, much of which was directed to him by relatives who wanted him to run away, but Arjuna was unable to separate himself from their bad feelings. Instead he unified (*samyoga*) himself with it and was crippled. He had to convert that lazy energy into the fire of discipline. Arjuna did practice yoga. He perfected the *āsana* and *prāṇāyāma* procedures. When he performed austerities in the Himalayas, he stood on tiptoes with arms raised, completely nourished his body with breath, and entered a trance state. While Arjuna's body was in *samādhi* trance, he left in a super-fine subtle form and visited the *Swarga* paradise, the place where the Indra demigod presides.

Arjuna was not like most of the modern followers of Krishna who are not yogis and do not have such expertise but who pretend that they could, by a mental decision, become detached. Arjuna's form was, for the most part, purified. His contamination was trivial. Many modern devotees are not purified and the transcendence they pretend to have, is trivial. Lord Krishna advised Arjuna to show yoga expertise by applying the technique of instant detachment from crippling emotions.

संकल्पप्रभवान्कामांस्
त्यक्त्वा सर्वानशेषतः ।
मनसैवेन्द्रियग्रामं
विनियम्य समन्ततः ॥६.२४॥

sam̐kalpaprabhavān = sam̐kalpa — motive + prabhavān — produced; kāmām̐s — cravings; tyaktvā — having abandoned; sarvān — all; aśeṣataḥ — without exception; manasaivendriyagrāmam̐ = manasā — by mind +

saṁkalpaprabhavānkāmāṁs
tyaktvā sarvānaśeṣataḥ
manasaivendriyagrāmaṁ
viniyamya samantataḥ (6.24)

eva — indeed + indriyagrāmaṁ — the total sensual energy; viniyamya — controlling; samantataḥ — completely

Abandoning without exception, all desires which are produced from motivation, and completely restraining the total sensual energy by the mind, (6.24)

Commentary:

Sankalpa means intentions. We gave, motive. The deeper intentions are the motives. These are the origins of desires. If one can realize his deeper intentions, he could be freed from desires or he could work to fulfill desires in a very practical and honest way. Some intentions, however, do not originate in the soul. They are emitted from the life force. Since the soul needs the assistance of the life force, he becomes implicated. To gain material experience, the soul must keep in touch with the psychic equipments like the mind, intellect, and life force. Once a sufficient quantity of experience is gained, the soul returns to its normal spiritual nature and forms a comparison. Certain conclusions about material existence are then drawn. This process was indicated in Chapters Two and Three as the samkhya way of thinking and reasoning.

At some stage of this mundane existence, either now or in the distant future, a living entity will have to abandon the material cravings.

The physical and psychic senses evolved out of the mind energy. These senses can be directed transcendentally. Still, one must at some stage, retract the energy that surges through the mind to energize the senses. Material senses are an indirect application of the attentive powers. What we require is a direct perception whereby the soul power is converted to a seeing, hearing, smelling, tasting and touching spiritual form.

शनैः शनैरुपरमेद्
बुद्ध्या धृतिगृहीतया ।
आत्मसंस्थं मनः कृत्वा
न किंचिदपि चिन्तयेत् ॥ ६.२५ ॥
śanaiḥ śanairuparamed
buddhyā dhṛtigṛhītayā
ātmasaṁsthaṁ manaḥ kṛtvā
na kiṁcidapi cintayet (6.25)

śanaiḥ śanair (śanaiḥ) — little by little; uparamed = uparamet — should withdraw from sensual activity; buddhyā — by intelligence; dhṛtigṛhītayā = dhṛti — firmness + gṛhītayā — grasped; ātmasaṁsthaṁ = ātma — spiritual self + saṁsthaṁ — fixed; manah — mind; kṛtvā — having made; na — not; kiṁcit — anything; api — even; cintayet — should think

...little by little, with a firm grasp by the intelligence, he should withdraw from sensual activity. Having made his mind to be fixed on the spiritual self, he should not think of anything. (6.25)

Commentary:

The motivated, desire-based actions cannot stop abruptly. It will take some time. But if one steadily applies the braking force as described in the *Gītā*, step by step, little by little, stage by stage, with patience and determination, the desires will gradually decrease. The bad motivation will be exposed. One will develop the habit of self-correction. One should keep stifling off desires, finding their motives, analyzing these and eradicating them one by one. This may seem to be a long, drawn-out and detailed process, but we are making extraneous endeavors for many other things which are not in our spiritual interest. Why should salvation be easier to achieve than anything else? Salvation is worth the effort. Why complain if it requires prolonged endeavor?

Many modern devotees desire to use the intelligence alone to get the personal energies under control. They do not want to include yoga practice. In other words, they only want to think their way out of the maze of material existence. But they may not be allowed. It is not that simple. One has to use the physical, intellectual, and emotional parts of the personal energies to extricate oneself from material existence. If it were just a matter of thinking, Lord Krishna would not have lectured so extensively on the yoga process. We must remember that Arjuna did cultivate yoga expertise. His application of it, was not imaginary. He actually mastered it before fighting at *Kurukṣetra*.

The Lord said that one should think of nothing. However, even though this means a blank mind devoid of mundane conceptions, it does not apply to spiritual reality. Lord Krishna instructed the yogi to think of Him. In text 14 of this chapter we read: *manah samyamya maccitto*.

Maccitto means thinking of Krishna, having thoughts fixed on Krishna. But according to the occasion and the stage of practice, one may also have a plain mind, observing the sober feature of consciousness. And that is also described in the *Gītā* as the process of clearing the mind of mundane ideas, then reaching the plane of sober consciousness, then getting in touch with Lord Krishna for directions on how to keep in association with Him and how to serve Him.

When the mind is penned in, it is restricted from being urged on by the life force. Once this is achieved, the senses stay calm and do not drive the soul for risky sensuality.

यतो यतो निश्चरति
मनश्चञ्चलमस्थिरम् ।
ततस्ततो नियम्यैतद्
आत्मन्येव वशं नयेत् ॥ ६.२६ ॥
yato yato niścarati
manaścañcalamasthiram
tatastato niyamyaitad
ātmanyeva vaśaṁ nayet (6.26)

yato yato = yataḥ yataḥ — wherever; niścarati — wanders away; manaścañcalam = manas — mind + cañcalam — drifting; asthiram — unsteady; tatastato = tatastataḥ — from there; niyamyaitad = niyamya — restrain + etad — it; ātmany (ātmani) — in the self; eva — indeed; vaśam — control; nayet — should direct

To wherever the unsteady, drifty mind wanders, from there he should restrain it. He should direct the mind to control it in the self. (6.26)

Commentary:

We must again stress that these verses about self-focus are in reference to the mind's constant drifting to inferior objects. These are not encouragements to avoid a focus on the Lord. Yoga is very productive if this is remembered. Yoga is a great aid and an accelerator if one remembers this during concentration and contemplation.

If a devotional yogi bypasses this self-focus, he will fail at his devotional practice, due to lack of quality focus on the Lord. A materialistic focus is quite insufficient and it will always be so. Thus the alternative is to get the mind under control, to strive hard, to pressure the mind into desirable patterns. The mind does not really yield to the so-called easy processes. If hard-core yoga processes fail, then other easier systems will fail in a bigger way.

Certain commentators have twisted these parts of the *Gītā*, suggesting that this self-focus is the ultimate aim. Lord Krishna presents self-focus only as the alternative to the lower mundane focus, as the intermediate stage and not as the final accomplishment.

The advice given in this verse is repeated again in the *Gītā* when Arjuna said that to control the mind was even more difficult than trying to control the wind. The advice is: One must have a standard focus for the mind. This standard focus is given by a spiritual master who is adept in yoga and who gives one individualized instruction. The prescribed self-focus may be a point in the body like the space between the eyebrows, or it may be a Deity form of the Lord, or a sound vibration.

One practices concentration on that point or subject. Whenever the mind drifts, one should retrieve it and bring it back under the control of the soul. The given place or subject of concentration for mind control changes as one advances, but the objective, which is to control the mind, does not change until the mind has yielded sufficiently. Eventually one reaches a stage where the subject is himself, the soul. This is the stage being described here, but this is not the final stage. It is, however, a key stage, since the self will have to deal with itself no matter what subject becomes its focus.

Self-focus is meant to make the self understand its value in reference to the lower energies which it usually pursues. But first, the mind must be trained to obey the self. If the mind is not trained, it will wander like a wild animal. Every time the mind wanders, the self will stray behind it, just as a farmer must go after his animals when they wander here and there in a forest. This wandering process must be brought to a complete halt in the advanced stages.

The mind drifts by two forces: One is external and the other is internal. The external force is the numerous sense objects. The internal one is the life force. To control access to the external world, a yogi goes into isolation. That settles this problem. In isolation, his mind does not have much access to the sense objects. The mind calms down after a few days because there is no external attraction to aggravate the sensual urge. Still, however, the quieted sensual urge will be there.

The mind will calm down but it will still be urged by the life force from within. And this is where the yoga *kriyās* are applied. Many people follow this Swami and that Swami and begin to meditate without doing yoga and many thousands of these meditators are fooling themselves. For the non-yogi, the life force cannot be curbed by meditation and mantras alone. It is impossible. It can only be curbed completely when yoga is added. Thus, even if one goes into isolation, he can sit as long as he likes, or he can chant for millenniums and the mind will still be urged in the wrong direction by the life force. The life force is curbed by yoga practices. This is why the ancient sages took up yoga. This is why Krishna explained yoga in the *Gītā* and devoted so many verses to the description of its benefits.

In the *Gītā*, in reference to this same drifting of the mind, Lord Krishna said that if a man goes into isolation and then continues to think of sense objects, he is a pretender. But some commentators feel that the isolated yogi has the fault of remembering the old sense objects. Therefore their idea is that if one can wash out these memories, one would be freed. They suggest that one should chant a mantra to baffle the mind and erase the old memories. This is, however, a very simple and incomplete approach to the problem.

The mind is stirred by subconscious energy and by the life force. Even if a seeker could clean out all the old mental impressions from millions and millions of previous births, he would still have to deal with the urges of the life force and this is why yoga became necessary in the process of salvation.

प्रशान्तमनसं ह्येनं
योगिनं सुखमुत्तमम् ।
उपैति शान्तरजसं
ब्रह्मभूतमकल्मषम् ॥ ६.२७॥

praśāntamanasaṁ = *praśānta* — *psychologically pacified* + *manasaṁ* — *mind; hyenaṁ* = *hy* (*hi*) — *indeed* + *enam* — *him; yoginaṁ* — *yogi; sukham* — *happiness; uttamam* — *superior; upaiti* — *experiences;*

praśāntamanasaṁ hyenaṁ
yoginaṁ sukhamuttamam
upaiti śāntarajasaṁ
brahmabhūtamakalmaṣam (6.27)

śāntarajasaṁ = śānta — calmed + rajasam — emotion; brahmabhūtam — spiritual level; akalmaṣam — free from bad tendencies

Indeed, being psychologically pacified, the yogi, whose emotions are calmed, who is on the spiritual plane, who is free from bad tendencies, experiences superior happiness. (6.27)

Commentary:

Sukham uttamam is usually given as supreme happiness. That is the literal meaning. However, *uttamam* also means a superior grade. It is misleading to suggest that the self-satisfaction which comes from spiritual self-focus is the supreme happiness. It is merely a happiness of a superior grade in reference to the mundane happiness which is derived from pleasant mundane sensations.

Bhagavad Gītā does not recommend self-focus and the resulting self-satisfaction as the ultimate aim, but only as the intermediate aim for self-stability and for self-worth over the value of material nature. We will still have to rate the devotional relationship with the Supreme Lord as the best of all sensations.

Rajasam means passions or emotions. This is a technical term for the life force which is the source of all these passions or emotions. Even though in the conditioned state we regard these emotions as soul feelings, they are not seen as such from the liberated level. These emotions spring from the life force. They must be purified before one can become free from material bondage.

Dormant mundane emotions are different to pacified (*śānta*) mundane energy. The pacified type is a purer energy used by ascetics who are proficient in the ancient yoga practices in the *Gītā*.

When the emotions are in dormancy they are not purified. They are simply in storage, awaiting expression. Dormant, low energy emotions have bad tendencies (*akalmasam*) within them. A yogi is trained to purify himself of low energy and to relocate himself to a higher, purer emotional level, where the energy is devoid of bad tendencies. A question arises as to why the yogi cannot transfer himself to the higher plane without having to purify the lower emotions. The answer is: Unless he first purifies the lower energy he can neither perceive nor really desire to be in the purified state. And if by some sheer grace, he was transferred out of the lower condition, he would, by habit or tendency, return there.

A man who is used to residing in a dirty slum cannot maintain himself in a hygienic aristocratic setting. But if he endeavors and keeps his shanty in a neat state, he can manage himself quite well if he is relocated to a luxurious place. Great yogis like Saubhari and *Viśvāmitra* abandoned yoga *kriyā* practices but only temporarily. They were overcome by dormant impurities when they were lax and felt that they attained the perfection of practice. But later on they cleaned out their natures completely and relocated to the spiritual environment. These two yogis are ridiculed by some preachers but that is simply the preachers' sarcasm and envy.

There are so many impurities in the nature, that one is apt to move forward and then be set back in stages. But the serious, determined yogi who is done with material exploitation reinstates himself in the practice every time there is a setback. We heard from Lord Krishna that the mind is to be retrieved every time it drifts. Need we hear more of this?

युञ्जन्नेवं सदात्मानं
योगी विगतकल्मषः ।
सुखेन ब्रह्मसंस्पर्शम्
अत्यन्तं सुखमश्नुते ॥ ६.२८ ॥
yuñjannevaṁ sadātmānaṁ
yogī vigatakalmaṣaḥ
sukhena brahmasaṁsparśam
atyantaṁ sukhamaśnute (6.28)

yuñjan — applying yoga disciplines; evaṁ — thus; sadā — constantly; 'tmānaṁ = ātmānam — the self; yogī — yogi; vigatakalmaṣaḥ — free from faults; sukhena — easily; brahmasaṁsparśam — constanting the spiritual plane; atyantaṁ — endless; sukham — happiness; aśnute — attains

Applying the yoga disciplines constantly to the self, the yogi being freed from faults, easily contacting the spiritual plane, attains endless happiness. (6.28)

Commentary:

This stress on endless happiness (*atyantam sukham*)of the spiritual plane (*brahman*) is not a contrast to devotion. It is meant to pull the conditioned being away from the material world. In the material world, there is an attraction to pleasing sensation. So long as we are attracted by that, we cannot muster up enough enthusiasm to pursue spiritual life. If, however, by the divine association of Krishna or by the saintly association of a great soul, we make contact with the spiritual plane (*brahmasamsparśam*), we would evaluate the material sensations as being inferior.

There is a catch, however. The undeveloped living entity is originally a portion of that blissful spiritual energy. It is not that he is something else. He is a speck of that energy. How then has he become confused regarding his self-identity? How has he become insecure? Furthermore, we may understand, at least intellectually, that his current insecurity is imaginary. If, at any stage, his eternality were at risk, the whole idea of spiritual life would be meaningless. Spiritual life is merely an attempt to recapture, reinforce, and further develop spirituality. The living entity is already eternal. His endeavors for spiritual life are an attempt to recapture glory or at least to become aware that such glory exists.

The baffling energies, the mundane potencies, keep the living entity confused about his self-identity. It draws the soul's attention away from itself. Thus self-focus is required in the initial stages.

Kalmasah means faults, imperfections or blemishes. The living entity does have its eternal status as a part of the overall eternity, but that does not mean that it is aware of its status as an eternal being. It is not. It is quite limited in assessments. On the other hand, the Supreme Being knows the possibilities At least that is the claim made by Krishna in the *Gītā*. When the living entity is put into the material creation by the Supreme it is put to the test to find its limitations. Due to a limited outlook it is said to be full of faults. Gradually, however, it comes to realize that there is no embarrassment in being limited. It then scales down its self-image and becomes practical with its capacity. This is called the removal of faults (*akalmasah*).

Even though the Supreme Being puts the limited entities in touch with material nature, the limited entities do remain in touch (*samsparśam*) with the spiritual nature (*brahman*) throughout the duration of material existence. They always remain in touch. But one cannot be aware of his contact with the spiritual level if he is focused on the material plane. His focus on the material energy robs him of spiritual self-awareness.

Those living entities who are not in the material creation and who live subjectively on the spiritual level of *brahman* are not entirely free from the material energy. The material potency is adjacent to the brahman spiritual energy as well, but it has no activity or expression there in the spiritual energy. Thus the entities in that energy are continuously absorbed in that endless happiness (*atyantam sukham*) which is rediscovered here by the yogis.

In that sense, we cannot blame the Lord for material nature's influence over us. He is responsible for manifesting material nature in a tangible way, but He is not responsible for our affinity to it, since we were always in touch with it anyway. In the *Gītā*, the Lord issued a disclaimer in this regard (5.15). We should carefully consider that.

In a sense, our implication in material nature is a great mystery that can only be settled by our individual attentiveness to the recovery, establishment, and further development of spirituality. The objectivity gained in being in the material existence is good if it is applied to that vital recovery. Otherwise, as the Buddha alerted us, such objectivity serves as a source of misery.

The constant (*sadā*) application (*yuñjan*) of yoga disciplines is required to recover ourselves but unfortunately it has to be done individually. This is why people do not like yoga. They prefer instead, a farce in the form of a collective bid for liberation. *Gītā* explains that for yoga one has to go into isolation, by himself without a group. The guru must instruct in the particular discipline but the disciple must himself, take up the austerity and work for cleansing. In material life, if one can afford it, he hires a servant to do the menial tasks but in spiritual life, the menial work of cleaning up one's tendencies must be done by oneself. The guru can only set an example and provide advice.

सर्वभूतस्थमात्मानं
सर्वभूतानि चात्मनि ।
ईक्षते योगयुक्तात्मा
सर्वत्र समदर्शनः ॥६.२९॥
sarvabhūtasthamātmānaṁ
sarvabhūtāni cātmani
īkṣate yogayuktātmā
sarvatra samadarśanaḥ (6.29)

sarvabhūtastham — existing in all mundane creature forms; ātmānaṁ — spirit; sarvabhūtāni — all creatures; cātmani = ca — see + ātmani — in the self; īkṣate — he sees; yogayuktātmā — one who is proficient in yoga; sarvatra — in all cases; samadarśanaḥ — seeing the same

With a spirit existing in every creature, and with every creature based on a spirit, a person who is proficient in yoga, perceives the same existential arrangement in all cases. (6.29)

Commentary:

This is a choice verse. Most of the yogis like this particular verse which sums up the resulting vision of an accomplished ascetic. *Samadarśanah* means seeing the same thing in all cases (*sarvatra*). However, this verse was greatly misunderstood. The enthusiasm of the commentators in regards to this verse, has to do not so much with the spiritual perception described, but rather with the promise of that equal vision. Some yogis desperately try to attain that equality of vision. They feel uncomfortable with the disparities of material existence.

In an effort to equalize all things, even God, some yogis use this verse to explain their belief that all entities are one and that all are either the equivalent of or the substratum of God or the Supreme Reality.

This commentator, however, is set apart from all this. Readers are now requested to consider the explanation of this verse with great care and patience:

Bhūta means *body* or *being*. The word body, however, usually is understood in the limited way as a material body. Even though a living material body is a *bhūta*, still the word has a broader meaning. *Bhuta* means a mundane form either of a gross or subtle or causal description. It is not limited to the gross level we perceive. For instance, a living body is a *bhūta*. But if that specific body dies, the surviving invisible subtle form is also a *bhūta*. And if that subtle form were destroyed, what would remain as a causal form would be a *bhūta*.

In any or all of these forms, there is spirit. Spirits are the basis of form. God is the overall supervisor but the actual direct basis of the individual forms is the individual spirits who predominate in them. We can understand this by studying the modern situation of automobile ownership. The manufacturer is certainly the master of all cars produced by his factory, but he does not drive every vehicle personally. The vehicles are controlled by the individual users. They are the basis. Even though a manufacturer invented and produced the vehicle, he is still not the basis. Let us consider this further. The manufacturer makes the vehicles on the basis of a need of the potential users. So even in the formative state, the potential users of those cars are the basis. Even though the users neither invent nor produce cars, still they are the basis because the manufacturer creates the item on the basis of the need of those users.

The Supreme Lord produces the creature forms, but this is done on the basis of our needs. In the *Gītā*, Lord Krishna states flatly that He does not want nor does He ever need anything in the material world. We may then ask: Why does He claim to create the world? Why should someone create something that He does not desire? The answer: A responsible person must fulfill the legitimate needs of dependants. It is his duty.

The yogi who developed the mystic vision by yoga austerity, begins to see mystically that in each configuration of gross creature forms, there is a spirit. He also sees that the same spirit is the basis of the form. This does not mean that all the forms are one nor that all the souls or spirits are one. We do not endorse that opinion which became popular. But rather it means that there is a similar act of a soul as a possessor and a basic user of each of the forms. All the users of individual cars are not one nor are all cars one, nor are the ideas in the minds of the users all one, but rather, there is a common factor of having one driver for each car.

Each body has special hookup points whereby any spirit can be connected psychically to the subtle equipments or nervous system for using that particular form. This is compared to cars which have seats, steering wheels and other suitable equipments which make the vehicles serviceable to human beings. After he sees the similarities, the yogi becomes happy to know that the same existential arrangement is available within a species.

यो मां पश्यति सर्वत्र
सर्वं च मयि पश्यति ।
तस्याहं न प्रणश्यामि
स च मे न प्रणश्यति ॥६.३०॥
yo māṁ paśyati sarvatra
sarvaṁ ca mayi paśyati
tasyāhaṁ na praṇaśyāmi
sa ca me na praṇaśyati (6.30)

yo = yaḥ — who; mām — me; paśyati — sees; sarvatra — in all forms; sarvam — all creatures; ca — and; mayi — in Me; paśyati — sees; tasyāham = tasya — his + aham — I; na — never; praṇaśyāmi — I am out of range; sa = saḥ — he; ca — and; me — my; na — never; praṇaśyati — he is out of view

To him who sees Me in all forms and who sees all creatures in reference to Me, I am never out of range, and he is never out of My view. (6.30)

Commentary:

The previous verse and this verse are linked. Thus we will have to bow down to those great Vaishnava teachers who claimed that the *Gītā* is Krishna-centered, meant for devotees of Krishna and for the development of devotion to the Lord. The truth is: Once a man directly sees by mystic vision that all subtle, gross and causal bodies (*bhūtas*) are being operated by spirits and that the designs of these bodies are similarly accommodated for easy operation by spirits, that person must also see or realize that there is a Supreme Spirit (*paramātma*) who provides the equipment.

If we can understand the similarity in design of a particular type of automobile, then we naturally begin to perceive the one manufacturer. As soon as a yogi gets that direct mystic perception by the opening up of his psychic vision through yoga austerities, his vision intensifies and he sees the Supersoul. This Supersoul is described in great detail in other verses of the *Gītā*. This particular verse is the first that gives a direct hint of the Supersoul. Lord Krishna presented Himself as that Supreme Person.

If the yogi does not advance further, after seeing the similarity of the bodies, he may never realize what is described in this verse. Thus, he may never come to understand how the Supersoul functions. A man who realizes that a particular type of car has a similar design in all cases, may stop there and not go any further to realize that there must be a common manufacturer.

Many yogis and sages reach this point, stop their austerities, become famous, and preach on the basis of their limited mystic perception. They declare to the world that all the bodies are of the same type and all the souls are the same and that every person is equal to every other person with equal access to the body equipments. This sort of conclusion is absurd.

The word *mām* in the first line means, *me*. It is also a pronoun. However, we gave, *my influence*. This pronoun also means, *what pertains to me,* or, the expression of my influence. *Mayi* in the second line means, *in me*, but we gave, *in reference to me*. It is not that a man sees the manufacturer with every vehicle but rather he sees the influence, the inventive power and the creative ability of the manufacturer. The influence of the producer travels wherever the product goes. These bodies carry the imprint of the Supreme Personality. Even an inferior car, even a wrecked vehicle, has the imprint of the manufacturer. Even an animal body, even a deformed human one, even a sickly or dead one, has the stamp of the Supersoul.

An advanced mystic can see that influence directly. Even though a viewer on a city street cannot see the car manufacturer and can only surmise his influence, a yogi, by mystic vision, directly sees both the influence of the Lord and the Lord Himself. Others who do not have that mystic capacity may rely on their belief in the Lord.

The mystic yogi sees the influence of the Lord and the Lord notices him. As the yogi looks to the Lord, the Lord observes him.

सर्वभूतस्थितं यो मां
भजत्येकत्वमास्थितः ।
सर्वथा वर्तमानोऽपि
स योगी मयि वर्तते ॥६.३१॥

sarvabhūtasthitam — existentially situated in all creatures; yo = yaḥ — who; mām — Me; bhajaty = bhajati — he honors; ekatvam — in harmony; āsthitaḥ — established; sarvathā — in various circumstances;

sarvabhūtasthitaṁ yo māṁ
bhajatyekatvamāsthitaḥ
sarvathā vartamāno'pi
sa yogī mayi vartate (6.31)

vartamāno = vartamānaḥ — existentially situated; 'pi = api — although; sa = saḥ — he; yogī — yogi; mayi — in Me; vartate — he remains in touch

Although moving in various circumstances, the yogi who is established in that harmony, who honors Me as being existentially situated in all creatures, remains in touch with Me. (6.31)

Commentary:

This is another verse of the *Gītā* that is warped considerably by some commentators who are not so much interested in Lord Krishna as they are in unity with the whole reality. For them, however, such a unity is an imaginative escape from individuality and its burdensome responsibilities. *Ekatvam* means *oneness* because *eka* means *one*. We have *harmony*. Some translators give *unity* or *oneness*. We have carefully avoided the use of those terms, because of the misleading connotations which are inconsistent with the rest of the *Gītā*.

A person may perceive a widespread existential situation and still not see any God nor Krishna, Who claims to be God. It is possible. In fact, many philosophers perceive the existence without God and without an individual like Krishna claiming Himself as the Supreme Person. This verse, however, only covers those philosophers who see Krishna in the way Lord Krishna presents Himself in the *Gītā*. Such persons must pay honor to Krishna in the way recommended by Him. Such seers are said to be established in harmony with Krishna. Krishna remains the same Krishna. The mystic yogi remains himself. But the yogi experiences a harmony or non-obstructiveness, an intimate agreement with Krishna's ideas. All his misgivings about God give way to a detailed understanding of the mercy and sensibility of the Divinity. Thus in whatever way he acts, the mystic devotee stays in communication with Krishna at all times and in all places.

आत्मौपम्येन सर्वत्र
समं पश्यति योऽर्जुन ।
सुखं वा यदि वा दुःखं
स योगी परमो मतः ॥६.३२॥
ātmaupamyena sarvatra
samaṁ paśyati yo'rjuna
sukhaṁ vā yadi vā duḥkhaṁ
sa yogī paramo mataḥ (6.32)

ātmaupamyena = ātma — self + aupamyena — by reference; sarvatra — in all cases; samaṁ — similarity; paśyati — he sees; yo = yaḥ — who; 'rjuna = arjuna — Arjuna; sukhaṁ — pleasurable sensations; vā — or; yadi — regardless; vā — or; duḥkhaṁ — painful sensations; sa = saḥ — he; yogī — yogi; paramo = paramaḥ — highest; mataḥ- considered as

He who, in reference to himself, sees the same facilities in all cases, regardless of pleasure or painful sensations, he, O Arjuna, is considered as the highest yogi. (6.32)

Commentary:

The similarity described in this verse is not the same as that described in the two previous verses. This similarity has to do with our response to pleasant and unpleasant sensations (*sukham vā yadi vā duhkham*). In an example of a car, its manufacturer and user, all of the users will react in almost the same way in a car accident. Each user sits at a certain distance from the steering wheel. A head-on collision will cause a particular type of damage to the chest and head of each driver. Similarly, because we are hooked up to the psychic equipments which are hooked up to the nerves of the body, pleasant and unpleasant sensations produce similar responses in each of us.

If, for instance, a boy is tickled under the armpit, he will laugh even if he does not desire to be happy, or even if there is no apparent reason for a jolly mood. This is because of the design of the body and its ability to produce pleasing sensations by certain stimulations. Why, therefore, does Krishna single out this yogi merely because he perceives the similarity? The answer is: Such a yogi understands quite well that he can be degraded. He does not go around telling the other limited souls that they can be God or that they do not need God or that there is no God. At the same time, he does not advocate a cheapened approach to God's association. He knows quite well that attaining perfection takes much endeavor. A man who endured a head-on collision knows quite well that every user of a car can be subjected to a horrifying collision. As such he becomes humble in his use of vehicles. He heeds the warnings of the manufacturer. He does not, at any stage, feel absolutely safe in an automobile. He is always aware of the hazards of driving.

It does not require much austerity to understand that we can become degraded but it does require much austerity to perceive that directly by mystic perception. Who can see directly that he can take a dog's body, or a mouse's, or a germ's, or a tree's form? This is not easy to view. At the time of the awakening of that mystic vision, where one sees that he can become degraded, he does develop a deep respect for the Supreme Being. He no longer maintains a high status of himself. He no longer pitches himself against the Almighty. He knows quite well that birth in a lower species is a possibility.

अर्जुन उवाच
योऽयं योगस्त्वया प्रोक्तः
साम्येन मधुसूदन ।
एतस्याहं न पश्यामि
चञ्चलत्वात्स्थितिं स्थिराम् ॥६.३३॥
arjuna uvāca
yo'yaṁ yogastvayā proktaḥ
sāmyena madhusūdana
etasyāhaṁ na paśyāmi
cañcalatvātsthitiṁ sthirām (6.33)

Arjuna — Arjuna; uvāca — said; yo = yah — who; 'yaṁ = ayaṁ — this; yogas — yoga practices; tvayā — by you; proktaḥ — explained; sāmyena — by comparative similarity; madhusūdana — O slayer of Madhu; etasyāhaṁ = etasyā — of this + aham — I; na — not; paśyāmi — see; cañcalatvāt — due to shiftiness; sthitiṁ — position; sthirām — standard

Arjuna said: O slayer of Madhu, due to a shifty vision, I do not see this standard position of a comparatively similar view which is yielded by this yoga practice, declared by You. (6.33)

<u>Commentary:</u>

This is another greatly misunderstood statement of the *Gītā*. Generally translators stay clear of the last two Sanskrit words. Or they interpret these without considering the statement Lord Krishna made just before Arjuna asked this question. *Sthitim* means, *situation, place or foundation*. *Sthirām* means, *a fixed situation, something permanent*. But Arjuna spoke of the fixed vision Lord Krishna described. We gave *sthitim sthirām* as, *the standard position*. Let us now review what Lord Krishna described as that standard position:

sarvabhūtasthamātmānaṁ sarvabhūtāni cātmani
īkṣate yogayuktātmā sarvatra samadarśanaḥ (6.29)

With a spirit existing in every creature, and with every creature based on a spirit, a person who is proficient in yoga, perceives the same existential arrangement in all cases. (6.29)

According to this same explanation of Krishna, the vision is developed by the advanced practice of yoga:

yogī yuñjīta satatam ātmānaṁ rahasi sthitaḥ
ekākī yatacittātmā nirāśīraparigrahaḥ (6.10)

In isolation, the yogi should constantly concentrate on the self. Being alone, he should be of controlled thinking and subdued self without desire and without possessions. (6.10)

This chapter has to do with yoga and yogis. Many modern Vaishnava authorities carefully leave aside or gloss over this chapter because it is not meant for devotees who avoid the yoga which is described in texts 10-12 of this chapter. We must understand this before we proceed. In addition, one should know well that Arjuna did perform such yoga. He was not yoga-resistant.

Samyena is the important term for understanding Arjuna's question. The great Vaishnava commentator *Śrīla* Bhaktivedanta Swami gave *generally* as the meaning of *samyena*. But Sridhara Maharaja, the Gaudiya authority, gave, *equal vision of one's own and others' happiness and distress*. We gave, *a comparatively similar view of all creatures*. Before a reader becomes confused with these different wordings he should go to the *Gītā* itself. Arjuna queried about Krishna's statement. Let us see where Lord Krishna used the word previously:

jñānavijñānatṛptātmā kūṭastho vijitendriyaḥ
yukta ityucyate yogī samaloṣṭāśmakāñcanaḥ (6.8)
suhṛnmitrāryudāsīna madhyasthadveṣya bandhuṣu
sādhuṣvapi ca pāpeṣu samabuddhirviśiṣyate (6.9)

The yogi who is satisfied with knowledge and realized experience, who is stable and who has conquered his sensual energy, who regards a lump of clay, a stone or gold in the same way, is said to be disciplined in yoga.

A person who is indifferent to friend, acquaintance, and enemy, who is evenly-disposed to enemies and kinsmen, who exhibits balanced judgment towards saintly people or sinful ones, is to be regarded with distinction. (6.8-9)

sarvabhūtasthamātmānaṁ sarvabhūtāni cātmani
īkṣate yogayuktātmā sarvatra samadarśanaḥ (6.29)

With a spirit existing in every creature, and with every creature based on a spirit, a person who is proficient in yoga, perceives the same existential arrangement in all cases. (6.29)

The Lord spoke of vision whereby one sees a similar value in clay, a stone or gold (6.8), and a similar discrimination towards friends and enemies (6.9), and finally a similar view of how the individual souls are situated in reference to their particular bodies (6.29).

Even though he was an expert yogi, Arjuna lost that vision and became relocated into the cultural view which is full of disparities and prejudices in the struggle for survival. He plainly admitted that he did not have (*na pasyāmi*) the vision. He was not seeing things in that way, whereby there was a comparatively similar view of all creatures as Krishna described. But Arjuna went a step further to trace his lack of the higher vision to the shiftiness (*cañcalatvāt*) of the mind.

चञ्चलं हि मनः कृष्ण
प्रमाथि बलवद्दृढम् ।
तस्याहं निग्रहं मन्ये
वायोरिव सुदुष्करम् ॥६.३४॥
cañcalaṁ hi manaḥ kṛṣṇa
pramāthi balavaddṛḍham
tasyāhaṁ nigrahaṁ manye
vāyoriva suduṣkaram (6.34)

cañcalam — unsteady; hi — indeed; manaḥ — the mind; kṛṣṇa — Krishna; pramāthi — troubling; balavat — impulsive; dṛḍham — resistant; tasyāham = tasya — of it + aham — I; nigraham — controlling; manye — I think; vāyor = vāyoḥ — of the wind; iva — compared to; suduṣkaram — very difficult to accomplish

Unsteady indeed is my mind, O Krishna. It is troublesome, impulsive and resistant. I think that controlling it is comparable to controlling the wind. It is very difficult to accomplish. (6.34)

Commentary:

This is a very practical and true statement that no human being can deny, but it is out of place because Lord Krishna first of all explained the yoga practice and then explained the result of that practice as having a controlled mind. In other words, Lord Krishna did not expect that a man would control his mind without having gone through yoga disciplines.

Normally, the mind is unsteady, impulsive and resistant, but it is not so for a proficient yogi. A question arises, however, as to why a proficient yogi like Arjuna had difficulty with moods. The answer is: Arjuna lost touch with his proficiency. This was due to being in association with the worldly Kurus and others who were not applying the yoga practice. Subsequently, Arjuna began to live in the same impulsive way as most humans do. Up to this point in the *Gītā*, Lord Krishna preached about the application of yoga. Krishna even cited rulers like Janaka who applied it to worldly life. The first statement of Krishna directing Arjuna to apply that yoga, occurred in Chapter Two:

yogasthaḥ kuru karmāṇi saṅgaṁ tyaktvā dhanaṁjaya
siddhyasiddhyoḥ samo bhūtvā samatvaṁ yoga ucyate (2.48)

So perform actions in the yoga mood. Attachment to crippling emotions should be abandoned, O conqueror of wealthy countries. Be indifferent to success or failure. It is said that indifference denotes yoga. (2.48)

buddhiyukto jahātīha ubhe sukṛtaduṣkṛte
tasmādyogāya yujyasva yogaḥ karmasu kauśalam (2.50)

A person who is disciplined by the reality-piercing insight disregards in each life both pleasant and unpleasant work. Therefore take to the yogic mood. Yoga gives skill in performance. (2.50)

The comparison of the wind to the mind applies to one who has not mastered yoga or one who mastered it, but who forgot how to apply it for mind control. It does not apply to a proficient yogi. To such a yogi, mind control is effortless and easy. The description of the uncontrolled mind is given in line two: *pramāthi balavad dṛḍham*. Readers should study the meanings of these Sanskrit terms:

pramāthi— agitating, causing trouble, harassing, scattering;
balavad— strong, powerful, impulsive, demanding;
dṛḍham— resistant, obstinate, intense, hard fixed, non-yielding.

If we recall Arjuna's questions when he saw a contradiction in Krishna's directive, that on one hand, he be a yogi and on the other hand, he act in the world, we can see that Arjuna did not master the application of yoga practice. Even though he got the proficiency in yoga he did not get the proficiency in its application to practical life. He was not, when he first came to *Kurukṣetra*, as adept as King Janaka in the application of yoga. This means that we may master yoga and still not know how to apply it to social conditions. Thus, even for its application, a teacher is required. Arjuna had Lord Krishna for a teacher. That was Arjuna's fortune.

The big puzzle for modern devotees is this: Can a modern devotee who has no mastery of yoga develop the expertise of detached action as King Janaka and others did? Arjuna could not apply himself. He had to be trained by Lord Krishna. Readers may recall when Krishna promised to train Arjuna:

sa evāyaṁ mayā te'dya yogaḥ proktaḥ purātanaḥ
bhakto'si me sakhā ceti rahasyaṁ hyetaduttamam (4.3)

Today, this ancient yoga technique is explained to you by Me, since you are devoted to Me and are My friend. Indeed, this is confidential and is the best teaching. (4.3)

श्रीभगवानुवाच
असंशयं महाबाहो
मनो दुर्निग्रहं चलम्।
अभ्यासेन तु कौन्तेय
वैराग्येण च गृह्यते ॥६.३५॥
śrībhagavānuvāca
asaṁśayaṁ mahābāho
mano durnigrahaṁ calam
abhyāsena tu kaunteya
vairāgyeṇa ca gṛhyate (6.35)

śrībhagavān — the Blessed Lord; uvāca — said; asaṁśayam — undoubtedly; mahābāho — O powerful man; mano = manah — the mind; durnigraham — difficult to control; calam — unsteady; abhyāsena — by practice; tu — however; kaunteya — O son of Kuntī; vairāgyena — by the indifference to response; ca — and; gṛhyate — it is restrained

The Blessed Lord said: Undoubtedly, O powerful man, the mind is difficult to control. It is unsteady. By practice, however, O son of Kuntī, by indifference to its responses, also, it is restrained. (6.35)

Commentary:

The secret to mind control is given here as practice in the application of yoga discipline (*abhyāsena*) and by the indifferent attitude towards mental impulses (*vairāgyena*). The question is: Are we willing to accept such a solution to the problem of mind control? Let us consider the full solution which is given in brief by Lord Krishna. First we must learn yoga and become proficient in it. This should be done in isolation. Then we would have to get a yogi tutor in disciplic succession from Lord Krishna to teach us how to apply the yoga training in worldly life. Then we would be expert at mind control even in a civil conflict. At least, readers must accept that this is the specific solution of mind control for Arjuna.

असंयतात्मना योगो
दुष्प्राप इति मे मतिः ।
वश्यात्मना तु यतता
शक्योऽवाप्तुमुपायतः ॥६.३६॥
asaṁyatātmanā yogo
duṣprāpa iti me matiḥ
vaśyātmanā tu yatatā
śakyo'vāptumupāyataḥ (6.36)

asaṁyatātmanā = asaṁyata —indisciplined + ātmanā — by the self; yogo = yogaḥ — yoga; duṣprāpa — difficult to master; iti — thus; me — my; matiḥ — opinion; vaśyātmanā = vaśya — disciplined + ātmanā — by the self; tu — however; yatatā — by endeavor; śakyo = śakyaḥ — possible; 'vāptum = avāptum — to acquire; upāyataḥ — by effective means

For the undisciplined person, yoga is difficult to master. This is My opinion. For the disciplined one, however, by endeavor, it is possible to acquire the skill by an effective means. (6.36)

Commentary:

The *samyata* is the disciplined person and the *asamyata* is the indiscipline human being. These terms were indicated in verse 69 of Chapter Two where we see the word *samyamī*:

yā niśā sarvabhūtānāṁ tasyāṁ jāgarti saṁyamī
yasyāṁ jāgrati bhūtāni sā niśā paśyato muneḥ (2.69)

The sense-controlling person is perceptive of that which is void to the ordinary people. What is exciting to the masses of people is void to the perceptive sage. (2.69)

The term for a controlled man is *vaśyātmanā*, but that term was indicated before in text 26 of Chapter Five by the word yati. In this verse of Chapter Six, we ask readers to note the term *yatatā* which means *by endeavor, by striving*. According to this, mind control is not possible without personal endeavor at yoga. There is no statement here to say that it is possible by God's grace alone or by the mercy of a guru alone. Practice and detachment from sensuality are given in the previous verse, and now personal striving is stressed. But no specific method is given; rather the Lord said *by an effective method* (*upāyatah*). Krishna did list the standard disciplines in Chapter Four, texts 24-33. They yielded particular types of sense, mind, or emotional control for human beings.

अर्जुन उवाच
अयतिः श्रद्धयोपेतो
योगाच्चलितमानसः ।
अप्राप्य योगसंसिद्धिं
कां गतिं कृष्ण गच्छति ॥६.३७॥
arjuna uvāca
ayatiḥ śraddhayopeto
yogāccalitamānasaḥ
aprāpya yogasaṁsiddhiṁ
kāṁ gatiṁ kṛṣṇa gacchati (6.37)

arjuna — Arjuna; uvāca — said; ayatiḥ — indisciplined person; śraddhayopeto = śraddhayopetaḥ = śraddhayā — by faith + upetaḥ — has got; yogāccalitamānasaḥ = yogāc (yogāt) — from yoga practice + calita — deviated + mānasaḥ — mind; aprāpya — not attain; yogasaṁsiddhiṁ — yoga proficiency; kāṁ — what; gatiṁ — course; kṛṣṇa — Krishna; gacchati — he goes

Arjuna said: What about the undisciplined person who has faith? Having deviated from yoga practice, having not attained yoga proficiency, what course does he take, O Krishna? (6.37)

Commentary:

This is a very good question. Another relevant inquiry is: What is achieved by those who have not mastered yoga disciplines and who, therefore, cannot apply yoga to practical life because they never did learned the practice? What is the situation of a modern devotee who has no proficiency in yoga or its application? Where does he stand?

As contrasted to the *yati* (disciplined man), we have the *ayatih* (uncontrolled man), but in this case, Arjuna specifically asks about an uncontrolled man who practiced yoga as described in this chapter but who has not mastered the technique of its application to social affairs.

This uncontrolled neophyte yogi is the one who has faith (*śraddhayā*) but who, due to a lack of proficiency, deviates from the disciplines. This person had faith in yoga and in its results, and he took up the practices, but before he became proficient, his mind influenced him to deviate to sensuality.

It appears that Arjuna realized that he deviated from the practice by failing to apply himself with detachment at *Kurukṣetra*. Thus, Arjuna described his own condition in this verse.

कच्चिन्नोभयविभ्रष्टश्
छिन्नाभ्रमिव नश्यति ।
अप्रतिष्ठो महाबाहो
विमूढो ब्रह्मणः पथि ॥६.३८॥
kaccinnobhayavibhraṣṭaś
chinnābhramiva naśyati
apratiṣṭho mahābāho
vimūḍho brahmaṇaḥ pathi (6.38)

kaccin = kaccid — is he; nobhayavibhraṣṭaś = na — not + ubhaya — both + vibhraṣṭaḥ — lost out; chinnābhram = chinna — faded + abhram — cloud; iva — like; naśyati — lost; apratiṣṭho = apratiṣṭhaḥ — without foundation; mahābāho — O Almighty Kṛṣṇa; vimūḍho = vimūḍhaḥ — baffled; brahmaṇaḥ — of the spirituality; pathi — on the path

Is he not like a faded cloud, lost from both situations, like being without a foundation? O Almighty Krishna: He is baffled on the path of spirituality. (6.38)

Commentary:

What a pitiful statement! Just imagine a man who practiced the austerities of yoga, but failed because he was pressured to desist by mental influence. He is diverted. He loses his reputation as a student yogi. He is rejected as a worldly man as well. What is his position? In both worlds, that of the ascetics and that of the worldly people, he is shunned.

A faded cloud? It was there showing itself. But then there was a dissipating influence. It vanished. Where did it go? Did no one protect it?

Readers are asked to note that Arjuna did not limit this inquiry to devotees of Krishna. He did not say the bhaktas of Krishna, nor the yogi *bhakta*, but rather, anyone who was on the path to the transcendence (*brahmaṇah*).

एतन्मे संशयं कृष्ण
छेत्तुमर्हस्यशेषतः।
त्वदन्यः संशयस्यास्य
छेत्ता न ह्युपपद्यते ॥६.३९॥
etanme saṁśayaṁ kṛṣṇa
chettumarhasyaśeṣataḥ
tvadanyaḥ saṁśayasyāsya
chettā na hyupapadyate (6.39)

etan = etad — this; me — of mine; saṁśayam — doubt; kṛṣṇa — Krishna; chettum — remove; arhasy = arhasi — you can; aśeṣataḥ — without reminder, fully; tvadanyaḥ = besides you; saṁśayasyāsya = saṁśayasya — of doubt + asya — of this; chettā — remover of doubt; na — not; hy (hi) — indeed; upapadyate — he exists

You can, O Krishna, remove this doubt of mine fully. Besides You, no other remover of doubt, exists here. (6.39)

Commentary:

Chettā means a cutter or a person who cuts up doubts about the spiritual path. We gave, *remover of doubt*. It is interesting that after five chapters, Chapter Two through Chapter Six, Arjuna is still in a troubled area. What will it take to convince him to fight, to apply his yoga skill for detachment, and still be free from sinful reactions? He would gain some reputation as a transcendentalist by fighting, and he would also acquire some social prestige since people would respect him just as they honored King Janaka.

Arjuna felt that no one but Lord Krishna could remove his doubts. What a statement! Many other qualified persons were present at *Kurukṣetra*. Still Arjuna did not have confidence in them as he did in Lord Krishna. Does this mean that Lord Krishna must personally free the devotee? Or is Arjuna being particular?

श्रीभगवानुवाच
पार्थ नैवेह नामुत्र
विनाशस्तस्य विद्यते ।
न हि कल्याणकृत्कश्चिद्
दुर्गतिं तात गच्छति ॥ ६.४० ॥
śrībhagavānuvāca
pārtha naiveha nāmutra
vināśastasya vidyate
na hi kalyāṇakṛtkaścid
durgatiṁ tāta gacchati (6.40)

śrībhagavān — the Blessed Lord; uvāca — said; pārtha — O son of Pṛthā; naiveha = na — either + eva — indeed + iha — here on earth; namutra = na — nor + amutra — above in the celestial regions; vināśaḥ — loss; tasya — his; vidyate — it is realized; na — not; hy (hi) — indeed; kalyāṇakṛt — performer of pious acts; kaścid — anyone; durgatiṁ — into misfortune; tāta — O ideal one; gacchati — goes down permanently

The Blessed Lord said: O son of Pṛthā, it is realized that neither here on earth nor above in the celestial regions, does the unaccomplished yogi lose his skill. Indeed, O dear Arjuna, no performer of virtuous acts, goes down permanently into misfortune. (6.40)

Commentary:

Here is another verse of the *Gītā* that is greatly misused by spiritual masters who take this verse out of its time and place and force it into the modern setting created by spiritual teachers for their disciples. Whether the guarantees of the modern spiritual masters will stand the test of time or whether these will fail is to be seen, but we know that in the time of Krishna this guarantee applied to the well-intended ascetic who took to yoga practice with great faith and then fell away for a time. The persons who are covered under the insurance policy of this verse are described by Arjuna himself in text 37 as *ayatih śraddayopeto* and as *yogăccalatimānasah* and as *aprāpya yogasamsiddhim*. Lord Krishna did not apply this statement to others. Elsewhere in the *Gītā*, coverage is given for other types of devotees or ascetics. Those who qualify for the guarantee of this verse must have the qualities listed:

- *ayatih* — an ascetic who has not controlled his mind, senses and life energy.
- *śraddhayā*— an ascetic who has faith in the yoga disciplines, who believes the process would yield the stipulated results
- *yogācalatimānasah*— a person whose mind or determination of mind, moved away from yoga practice
- *aprāpya yogasamsiddhim* — a person who has not attained the perfection of yoga.

We must therefore identify that ascetic who was performing yoga, who then was diverted from the practice and resumed worldly life, but who had full faith that the disciplines would bring about his purification. This particular verse does not stipulate that this person has to be a devotee of Lord Krishna. There is no word to indicate that, not even the word *śraddhayā* (full faith or confidence). That confidence in this verse applies to the process of yoga and not to the Lord Himself. Elsewhere in the *Gītā* we will see verses which are descriptive of faith in Krishna exclusively. Arjuna is a case of an ascetic who had no proficiency in the application of yoga to worldly life. Lord Krishna took up the task of being Arjuna's teacher of yoga application. This is clearly stated in Chapter Four. In fact, *Bhagavad Gītā* is the preliminary course given to Arjuna by Krishna and the completion of the training was given during the *Kurukṣetra* Battle.

Just last week, we received a letter from an individual who accused Lord Krishna of double talk and of giving faulty guarantees in the *Gītā*. The fact is, however, that we are yet to find any such faulty promise. It may be, however, that modern spiritual masters who exploit the *Gītā*, do give such guarantees to cover their toned-down, substituted disciplines which are, in fact, a fraud.

If someone substituted a modern process that is suitable to modern people, we cannot blame Lord Krishna. We must check to see if the promise of Lord Krishna applied in its own time and place.

The assurance in this verse is that a person who falls from yoga practice at some stage, will not, if he had strong faith and sincerity at the time of his mishap, lose his status socially or spiritually. Just as Arjuna fell away from the application of yoga because of strong impulses within his mind, and just as Lord Krishna reinstated him, so an ascetic yogi will be reinstated at a later date. He will gain socially and be allowed to continue the practice.

प्राप्य पुण्यकृताँल्लोकान्
उषित्वा शाश्वतीः समाः ।
शुचीनां श्रीमतां गेहे
योगभ्रष्टोऽभिजायते ॥ ६.४१ ॥
prāpya puṇyakṛtāṁllokān
uṣitvā śāśvatīḥ samāḥ
śucīnāṁ śrīmatāṁ gehe
yogabhraṣṭo'bhijāyate(6.41)

prāpya — obtaining; puṇyakṛtām — of the performer of virtuous acts; lokān — celestial places; uṣitvā — having lived; śāśvatīḥ — many, many; samāḥ — years; śucīnām — of the purified person; śrīmatām — of the prosperous person; gehe — in the social circumstance; yogabhraṣṭo = yogabhraṣṭaḥ — fallen from yoga; 'bhijāyate = abhijāyate — is born

After obtaining the celestial places where the virtuous souls go, having lived there for many, many years, the fallen yogi is born into the social circumstances of the purified and prosperous people. (6.41)

Commentary:

In one statement we hear that the yogi was elevated after death to the celestial places where the virtuous souls (*punyakṛtām*) go, but in the same verse we hear that the yogi had fallen (*yogabhraṣṭo*). Thus the elevation to the mundane heavens is considered to be lower than the completion of yoga practice.

By this statement of Lord Krishna, we understand that the ancient yogis who did not complete their practice and who fell away from it, did go on to the higher regions where the pious celestials live. They stayed there for many, many years and then they were attracted to this earthly location, being pulled into a family of righteous, blessed persons. Despite the fault of these yogis, they did achieve a higher place at the time of death. Then they returned to earth in good families. In this way, Lord Krishna explained that they did not lose their standing. Modern spiritual masters give this same assurance to their disciples, even though the disciples are not performing the disciplines of the ancient ascetics. Thus it rests with destiny to prove whether the promises of these gurus are fraudulent or not.

In a religion like Christianity, preachers assure their congregations that by following that system they will go to heaven at the time of death to be with God forever. But here we see that in the time of Lord Krishna, as great a person as Krishna only promised the aspiring ascetics of His time that they would be transferred to the heavens to be in association with pious celestial people and then would again come back to this earth. It is a wonder that modern people, intelligent as they are, believe the contrary assurances of modern teachers.

अथ वा योगिनामेव
कुले भवति धीमताम् ।
एतद्धि दुर्लभतरं
लोके जन्म यदीदृशम् ॥ ६.४२ ॥
atha vā yogināmeva
kule bhavati dhīmatām
etaddhi durlabhataraṁ
loke janma yadīdṛśam (6.42)

atha vā — alternately; yoginām — of the yogi; eva — indeed; kule — in the family situation; bhavati — is born; dhīmatām — of the enlightened people; etad — this; dhi = hi — indeed; durlabhataram — difficult to attain; loke — in this world; janma — birth; yad — which; īdṛśam — such

Alternately, he is born into a family of enlightened people. But such a birth is very difficult to attain in this world. (6.42)

<u>Commentary:</u>

We get specific information here. As in every insurance contract there are clauses. First Lord Krishna stated that the fallen yogi would not lose out in yoga practice, nor in the social stance; then He explained that the ascetics would be elevated at the time of death and would go to the celestial worlds where the pious angelic people reside. They would stay there for a long, time, and then they would feel an attraction to pious earthly parents.

The first families listed are those who are righteous and blessed. But such families are distinguished from the second type of family, which is the highest type of birth in the material world; that of having parents who are wise in transcendence (*dhīmatām*). Such a birth, Lord Krishna said, is very difficult to acquire (*durlabhataram*).

तत्र तं बुद्धिसंयोगं
लभते पौर्वदेहिकम् ।
यतते च ततो भूयः
संसिद्धौ कुरुनन्दन ॥ ६.४३ ॥
tatra taṁ buddhisaṁyogaṁ
labhate paurvadehikam
yatate ca tato bhūyaḥ
saṁsiddhau kurunandana (6.43)

tatra — there; tam — it; buddhisaṁyogam — cumulative intellectual interest; labhate — inspired with; paurvadehikam — from a previous birth; yatate — he strives; ca — and; tato = tataḥ — from that time; bhūyaḥ — again; saṁsiddhau — to perfection; kuru-nandana — O dear son of the Kurus

In that environment, he is inspired with the cumulative intellectual interest from a previous birth. And from that time, he strives again for yoga perfection, O dear son of the Kurus. (6.43)

<u>Commentary:</u>

To those persons who took a new body and who did not complete yoga practice in the former birth, this is a reassuring statement. But it is also a very hard statement made by the Lord. First of all, not all persons who took up yoga and fell down, will be going to the places where the pious celestials live, and not all those who are transferred to such a place will be staying there for many, many years. Some may experience those blissful regions for a split second at the time of death; some for a day, some for a week, and some for a year. It depends on the amount of practice one executed before the body died. It is greatly dependent also on one's mentality, either to enjoy celestial life or to push on for full perfection.

Arjuna was interested in the celestial regions. This is why Lord Krishna explained that outcome. If the intention of the yogi is to go to the celestial places and if he cultivated sufficient practice, he would go there. But if he had no intention, he would not go there even if his body died before he completed the practice. Rather, he would take another body or go to a celestial place where yoga practice would be continued. The location (loka) cited by Lord Krishna in this verse is not where celestial yogis live but rather is a nice place where pious entities who are not inclined to yoga reside. There is a history in the Vedic literature of yogis who refused to go to that celestial place. Mudgal is one of the cases cited in the *Mahābhārata*. He was to lose his body. When the time of death drew near, the Indra demigod sent an escort for Mudgal's glowing celestial body but Mudgal declined, stating that he was not interested in going to any place from which he would again fall back to the earth. He said that he would rather remain on the earth and continue the practice for full perfection. Mudgal then got a life extension and perfected the practice before going to the spiritual worlds.

Still, we may ask what might happen to other yogis who did not get a life extension and who, on one hand, passed on without desiring the celestial life. Where would such a yogi go? The answer is: He will remain in the earthly region in an astral form until he gets another earthly body. He will also take his birth in a family of righteous, blessed people or in a family of practicing yogis. He will take his birth quickly rather than after many, many years of enjoyment in the angelic paradises.

Yogis who did not fall away from their practice, but who, at the time of death, are greatly advanced, and who are not particularly attracted to being on earth but who want to continue the austerities, may go to worlds that are higher than the angelic paradises. These worlds are mentioned in the Vedic literature as Maharloka, Janaloka, Tapaloka, and Brahmaloka. Such planets have communities of ascetics who continue the practices in super-fine subtle forms.

In regards to the yogi Lord Krishna described, the person takes a new body as indicated and then all of a sudden he is inspired by past austerity. But the memory of it may not be objective. He might just feel an inclination towards yoga. By using the term *labhate* which means *he is inspired with*, Lord Krishna tactfully informed that the memory of the practice is awakened by divine grace. Due to long absence from austerities, the memory of the practice stays deep in the subconscious. Only by special mercy and under special circumstances, is it re-awakened. Therefore, either a powerful guru or the Lord Himself, would prevail to re-awaken that tendency in the ascetic.

In fact, in cases of this nature, we see that some persons take a new body and begin to aspire for material opulence, which is a clear indication that he was living in luxurious surroundings in the heavenly regions. He becomes baffled here on earth since in heaven, the opulence came without endeavor and on earth, one has to exploit and scheme to acquire luxuries.

After getting that grace from the Lord, or from a spiritual master, the disciple must strive again with renewed interest. Otherwise, he will sink down in material existence, at least for a time, until he again becomes disgusted with mundane degradation.

पूर्वाभ्यासेन तेनैव
ह्रियते ह्यवशोऽपि सः ।
जिज्ञासुरपि योगस्य
शब्दब्रह्मातिवर्तते ॥ ६.४४॥
pūrvābhyāsena tenaiva
hriyate hyavaśo'pi saḥ
jijñāsurapi yogasya
śabdabrahmātivartate (6.44)

pūrvābhyāsena = pūrva — previous + abhyāsena — by practice; tenaiva = tena — by it + eva — indeed; hriyate — he is motivated; hy (hi) — indeed; avaśo = avaśaḥ — without conscious desire; 'pi = api — even; saḥ — he; jijñāsuḥ — persistently inquiring; api — even; yogasya — of yoga; śabdabrahmātivartate = śabda — spoken description + brahma — spiritual reality + ativartate — instinctively sees beyond (śabdabrahma — Vedas)

Indeed, by previous practice, he is motivated, even without conscious desire. He who persistently inquires of yoga, instinctively sees beyond the Veda, the spoken description of the spiritual reality. (6.44)

Commentary:

Even though the yogi is urged on without conscious desire, he still needs to have the memory of his former practice ignited within the consciousness. This is done by supernatural power, either by the Lord, by a supernatural person or by a spiritual master who may be using a physical body. The memory arises as a tendency, usually, or as an interest in yogic, philosophical, psychic, or religious matters. Once it surfaces, the momentum of it builds up and it replaces his interest in the luxury life he enjoyed on the higher planets. In the case of those who did not go to the heavenly worlds, and who stayed for a short time on the astral plane waiting to get another earthly form, their memory also must be ignited. In the interim state and when they enter a womb, the memory of their practice might be foreshadowed. As a result, they have to cancel out their childhood conditioning once they get the new body. For all these souls, austerities come naturally as compared to those who have little or no previous practice.

These yogis do see beyond the Vedic recitations and the theoretical information from the scriptures which is greatly misunderstood by those who have little or no mystic perception. As Lord Krishna indicated in Chapter Two, the sweetly-sounding poetic recitations of the Vedas are misleading. The pandits who glorify it, may lack mystic perception:

yāmimāṁ puṣpitāṁ vācaṁ pravadantyavipaścitaḥ
vedavādaratāḥ pārtha nānyadastīti vādinaḥ (2.42)

This is poetic quotation which the ignorant reciters proclaim, O son of Pṛthā. Enjoying the Vedic verses, they say there is no other written authority. (2.42)

The Vedas are highly extolled. They are not to be derided by an ordinary human being, but Lord Krishna claimed to be extraordinary and beyond the jurisdiction of *Brahmā*, the supernatural author of the Vedas. Lord Krishna said:

traiguṇyaviṣayā vedā nistraiguṇyo bhavārjuna
nirdvaṁdvo nityasattvastho niryogakṣema ātmavān (2.45)

Three moody phases are offered by the Vedas. Be without the three modes, O Arjuna. Be without the moody fluctuations. Be always anchored to reality. Be free from grasping and possessiveness. (2.45)

In addition. Lord Krishna predicted that Arjuna would give up attachment for the Vedic recitation (*śabdabrahma*) and would see reality directly, instead of trying to view it conceptually by hearing from the Vedas, imagining what was heard, and then believing the imagined concept:

yadā te mohakalilaṁ buddhirvyatitariṣyati
tadā gantāsi nirvedaṁ śrotavyasya śrutasya ca (2.52)

When from your delusion-saturated mind, your discrimination departs, you will become disgusted with what is to be heard and what was heard. (2.52)

Many modern preachers indulge in the act of intellectually understanding a scripture, even the *Bhagavad Gītā*. Accepting their intellectual picturization as reality, they talk convincingly. These preachers have no mystic experience but simply learn to repeat what their teacher said. In some cases, the teacher speaks from imagination and not from actual experience. In this way, a whole series of misunderstandings are transmitted from an authority to his disciples and further on, to others. This leads to a series of conceptual distortions. The yogi goes beyond this theory. He gets direct experience. Instead of looking at the map of material and spiritual life, which is laid out in the Vedic literatures, he tries to reach the reality. But he checks the map for references. Yoga, therefore, is highly specialized. And this is why so much of the *Gītā* speaks of it. Let us listen to what Lord Krishna had to say about mere hearing from the Vedas:

śrutivipratipannā te yadā sthāsyati niścalā
samādhāvacalā buddhis tadā yogamavāpsyasi (2.53)

When rejecting misleading scriptural information, your intelligence remains steady without moody variation, being situated in deep meditation, with a stable intelligence, you will master the yoga disciplines. (2.53)

This speaks for itself. Of course, one would be the greatest fool to deride the Vedas as Lord Krishna did. After all, until we are totally freed from this creation of *Brahmā*, we had better be careful before we criticize his Vedas. Still, we should understand that such a map of spiritual and material life, such a manual for mundane existence, is an indication. We should not prostitute the Vedas by merely imagining what they described. We should try to develop psychic and spiritual senses to see reality, and then check with the Vedas to verify and gauge our process.

प्रयत्नाद्यतमानस्तु
योगी संशुद्धकिल्बिषः ।
अनेकजन्मसंसिद्धस्
ततोयाति परां गतिम् ॥६.४५॥
prayatnādyatamānastu
yogī saṁśuddhakilbiṣaḥ
anekajanmasaṁsiddhas
tatoyāti parāṁ gatim (6.45)

prayatnāt — from steady effort; yatamānaḥ — consistently controlled; tu — but; yogī — yogi; saṁśuddha — thoroughly cleansed; kilbiṣaḥ — bad tendencies; anekajanmasaṁsiddhas = aneka — not one + janma — birth + saṁsiddhaḥ — perfected; tato = tataḥ — from then onwards; yāti — reaches; parāṁ — supreme; gatim — goal

From a steady effort and a consistently controlled mind, the yogi who is thoroughly cleansed of bad tendencies, who is perfected in many births, reaches the supreme goal. (6.45)

Commentary:

Samśuddhakibiṣah is the act of being thoroughly cleansed of bad tendencies. The yogi is able to clean his character by the process of steady effort at the disciplines of yoga and a consistently-controlled mind. There are many other methods recommended here and there but this is the way of yogis. And though he is not perfected in one birth (*anekajanmasamsiddhas*), still, after his struggle for perfection, he reaches the supreme goal. Preachers sometimes use this statement of Lord Krishna to deride the path of yoga, to criticize it as being long and arduous, but let us see how Krishna rated it.

तपस्विभ्योऽधिको योगी
ज्ञानिभ्योऽपि मतोऽधिकः ।
कर्मिभ्यश्चाधिको योगी
तस्माद्योगी भवार्जुन ॥६.४६॥
tapasvibhyo'dhiko yogī
jñānibhyo'pi mato'dhikaḥ
karmibhyaścādhiko yogī
tasmādyogī bhavārjuna (6.46)

tapasvibhyo = tapasvibhyaḥ — to the other types of ascetics; 'dhiko = adhikaḥ _ — is superior; yogī — yogi; jñānibhyo = jñānibhyaḥ — to the masters of the philosophical theory; 'pi = api — also; mato = mataḥ — is considered to be; 'dhikaḥ = adhikaḥ — is superior; karmibhyaḥ — to the ritual performers; cādhiko (cādhikaḥ) = ca — and + adhikaḥ — is better than; yogī — yogi; tasmād = tasmāt — hence; yogī — yogi; bhavārjuna = bhava — be + arjuna — Arjuna

The yogi is superior to other types of ascetics; he is also considered to be superior to the masters of philosophical theory, and the yogi is better than the ritual performers. Hence, be a yogi, Arjuna. (6.46)

Commentary:

This is Krishna's opinion. We can take, twist it or leave it. The tapasvis are the ascetics, those who specialize in penances of all sorts. We got a listing of these in Chapter Four, texts 24-33. *Jñanis* are those who are trying to get out of the material world by mere thinking. Even those who study the *Gītā* and who make no other endeavor but an intellectual one are *jñanis*. The karmis are those who are attached to rituals. They feel that they can attain everything, even spiritual perfection, by Vedic ritualistic ceremonies. They are neither interested in thinking their way out of the material world nor in working with the body in yoga postures and breath nutrition techniques. But Lord Krishna gave the opinion that the yogi is superior to these.

The most interesting thing about the path of devotion to Krishna and about the devotees who take to that path, is that most of them do not realize that the devotees are divided into four types as listed in this verse, namely, devotees who take to austerities like fasting or refraining from sense enjoyment, devotees who study scriptures and lecture intensively, devotees who are attached to rituals, either as Deity worship with fire sacrifice or without it, and who are attached to the mantras used in such ceremonies. And lastly, devotees who are attached to yoga practice.

There is one limitation that we face in devotional societies. That is: Who started the society? Was he a yogi devotee, a ritual-mantra-liking devotee, a studious devotee, or a penance-liking devotee? The answer to this question describes the type of society formed by that spiritual leader. Arjuna was advised to be a yogi devotee. At least that was considered as the highest in the time of Lord Krishna.

योगिनामपि सर्वेषां
मद्गतेनान्तरात्मना ।
श्रद्धावान्भजते यो मां
स मे युक्ततमो मतः ॥६.४७॥
yogināmapi sarveṣāṁ
madgatenāntarātmanā
śraddhāvānbhajate yo māṁ
sa me yuktatamo mataḥ (6.47)

yoginām — of the yogis; api — also; sarveṣāṁ — of all these; madgatenāntarātmanā = madgatena — attracted to me + antarātmanā — with his soul; śraddhāvān — full of faith; bhajate — worships; yo = yaḥ — who; mām — me; sa = saḥ — he; me — to me; yuktatamo = yuktatamaḥ — most devoted; mataḥ — is regarded

Of all yogis, the one who is attracted to Me with his soul, who worships Me with full faith, is regarded as being most devoted to Me. (6.47)

<u>Commentary:</u>

There are many types of yogis, many types of *tapasvis*, many types of *jñanis*, and many types of *karmis*. But, of all these, the yogi who is soul-to-Supersoul attracted to Lord Krishna and who honors Him as requested in the *Gītā*, is regarded by the Lord as being most devoted to Him. Each devotee has a dominant tendency that places him in one of the four categories.

CHAPTER 7

Krishna: The Ultimate Reality*

श्रीभगवानुवाच
मय्यासक्तमनाः पार्थ
योगं युञ्जन्मदाश्रयः ।
असंशयं समग्रं मां
यथा ज्ञास्यसि तच्छृणु ।७.१॥
śrībhagavānuvāca
mayyāsaktamanāḥ pārtha
yogaṁ yuñjanmadāśrayaḥ
asaṁśayaṁ samagraṁ māṁ
yathā jñāsyasi tacchṛṇu (7.1)

śrībhagavān — the Blessed Lord; uvāca — said; mayy = mayi — in Me; āsaktamanāḥ — attention absorbed in; pārtha — O son of Pṛthā; yogam — yoga; yuñjan — practicing; madasrayah = mad — on me + āśrayah — being dependent; asaṁśayaṁ — without doubt; samagraṁ — fully; māṁ — Me; yathā — as; jñāsyasi — you will know; tac = tad — this; chṛṇ = śṛṇu — hear

The Blessed Lord said: With attention absorbed in Me, O son of Pṛthā, practicing yoga, being dependent on Me, you will know of Me fully without a doubt. Hear of this. (7.1)

Commentary:

The description of yoga practice was given in Chapter Six. The application of yoga was described, at least insofar as it was taught in the disciplic succession from Krishna. Janaka, an ancient ascetic king, was given as an example. Krishna assured that He would again, as He did previously, establish the training whereby persons who were already adept in yoga practice could learn its application to worldly life.

Many Vaishnava preachers minimize the yoga practice of the *Gītā*. They substitute *bhakti*, devotion to Krishna, as yoga's replacement. But in the *Gītā* itself, devotion to Krishna is there in its own right without being a replacement for yoga. If we are to regard the *Gītā* in its own time and place, we must include yoga. After giving the description of yoga Lord Krishna explained that devotion to Him is required. He does not sandblast yoga out of the *Gītā* and paint over its practice with *bhakti* (devotion). But rather the Lord will now add *bhakti* to that undercoating or foundation of yoga. On the foundation of yoga, He will now build the beautiful house of *bhakti*. Some modern commentators say, however, that *bhakti* does not need yoga.

**The Mahābhārata contains no chapter headings. This title was assigned by the translator on the basis of verse 7 of this chapter.*

This Chapter Seven begins with *mayy (mayi)* which means, *in Me*. *Me* refers to Krishna Himself and not to anything indirect. In this chapter, Lord Krishna will begin to thrust Himself more and more into the picture. He discussed self-purification (*ātmaśuddhaye*). He showed how the purified soul can become attached to Him. Purification is actually a tall order for any contaminated living being, but it is preliminary. In this respect, we must agree with those Vaishnava teachers who keep stressing that devotion to Krishna is the ultimate objective. Even though they minimize purification and even though they push aside the yogic method of achieving that, we must agree that in the final analysis, the purified person is supposed to turn to Krishna, to be irresistably attracted to Krishna, and to work in a way that pleases and satisfies Krishna.

Āsaktamanāh means a person whose mind is attached or absorbed in a particular object. It indicates a strong emotional attachment. But here, Lord Krishna spoke of a purified soul who was purified by yoga austerities. Readers may recall that at the end of Chapter Six, Lord Krishna rated this devotee as the highest devotee. A purified person who uses purified energy or new energy that is not contaminated, is different from an impure person. The attachment for Krishna may be there in both cases, but the quality of the affection is completely different.

In line two, Lord Krishna again mentioned the foundation of austerities as *yogam yuñjan* (practicing yoga). Modern commentators like to slice it out of the way or say that it means devotional activities and the regulative life in ashrams where devotional and missionary service are practiced.

Madāśraya means: being dependent on Me, on Krishna. Here Krishna says nothing about being dependent on a guru nor on the brahman spiritual energy. He does not even mention *brahmanirvāṇa* which was mentioned before, but He directly substitutes Himself as the primal objective of the purified yogi.

He speaks of knowing Him (*jñāsyasi mām*). We will have to accept the fact that from here on in the *Gītā* Lord Krishna will be putting Himself more and more into the limelight, under the spotlight, as the ultimate aim of spiritual life and as the direct aim of the devotee yogis.

ज्ञानं तेऽहं सविज्ञानम्
इदं वक्ष्याम्यशेषतः ।
यज्ज्ञात्वा नेह भूयोऽन्यज्
ज्ञातव्यमवशिष्यते ॥७.२.
jñānaṁ te'haṁ savijñānam
idaṁ vakṣyāmyaśeṣataḥ
yajjñātvā neha bhūyo'nyaj
jñātavyamavaśiṣyate (7.2)

jñānam- information; te — to you; 'ham = aham -I; savijñānam — with experience; idam — this; vakṣyāmy(vakṣyāmi)- I will explain; aśeṣataḥ — without deleting anything; yaj = yad — which; jñātvā — having known; neha = na — not + iha — in this world; bhūyo = bhūyaḥ — further; 'nyaj = anyat — other; jñātavyam — to be discovered; avaśiṣyate — is left

I will explain the information and give the experience to you without deleting anything. Having known that, no other experience would be left to be discovered in this world. (7.2)

Commentary:

Lord Krishna intended to impart the experience to Arjuna. This is why the word vijñānam is mentioned. This means that Krishna will mystically put Arjuna in touch with the experiences which underlie the information given. Unless a spiritual master can put the disciple in touch with the experiences, a mere theoretical layout or imaginative presentation produces a distortion in the mind of the disciple. The greatest mishap is the lack of experience of the spiritual master. If the spiritual master draws from book information and from spoken information only, he is unfit to be a guru but the disciple might not be perceptive enough to know that. In the last chapter Lord Krishna spoke of those disciples who have the instinct for yoga practice. The Lord said:

pūrvābhyāsena tenaiva hriyate hyavaśo'pi saḥ
jijñāsurapi yogasya śabdabrahmātivartate (6.44)

Indeed, by previous practice, he is motivated, even without conscious desire. He who persistently inquires of yoga, instinctively sees beyond the Veda, the spoken description of the spiritual reality. (6.44)

Such a man transcends theoretical information of spiritual matters (*śabda brahma*). He detects a spiritual master who has only mastered scriptural theory, but has not experienced the reality which it represents.

मनुष्याणां सहस्रेषु
कश्चिद्यतति सिद्धये ।
यततामपि सिद्धानां
कश्चिन्मां वेत्ति तत्त्वतः ॥७.३॥
manuṣyāṇāṁ sahasreṣu
kaścidyatati siddhaye
yatatāmapi siddhānāṁ
kaścinmāṁ vetti tattvataḥ (7.3)

manuṣyāṇām — of human beings; sahasreṣu — in thousands; kaścid — someone; yatati — strives; siddhaye — to psychological perfection; yatatām — of those who endeavor; api — even; siddhānām — of those who are perfected; kaścin = kaścid — someone; mām — me; vetti — comprehends; tattvataḥ — in truth

Someone, in thousands of human beings, strives for psychological perfection. Of those who endeavor, even of those who are perfected, someone knows Me in truth. (7.3)

Commentary:

The question is: If the human beings are not striving for perfection, then, what are they aiming for? Obviously only the Lord could provide an unbiased answer. Only He has that universal vision to see exactly where every individual soul is heading.

We do know, however, that if we do not understand ourselves, our spirits, then certainly we cannot comprehend the Supreme Self, the Supreme Soul. Most human beings accept themselves as their most recent material body. They are not even aware of any previous bodies. A few of them consider themselves as subtle forms. These are mostly yogis, mystics, devotees and spiritualists. But even these hardly understand or perceive the causal form. Only a few yogis reach the causal level at the time of death. Of these, many of them feel that spiritual consciousness is absolute. They aim no further than to situate themselves into spiritual consciousness. They take to *samādhi* trance to dissolve the psychic equipments which connect us to the subtle and gross bodies. Of these great yogis, only one or two get a hint to worship Krishna as He stipulates.

If we cannot comprehend a spiritual form with spiritual limbs and senses, being imperishable and infallible and living in a spiritual environment with other imperishable forms, then we cannot understand what Krishna told Arjuna. The whole basis of the *Gītā* has to do with Krishna's world. Ultimately that is what He advertised to human society. But if we cannot understand our own spirit, we cannot understand Krishna's either.

भूमिरापोऽनलो वायुः
खं मनो बुद्धिरेव च ।
अहंकार इतीयं मे
भिन्ना प्रकृतिरष्टधा ॥७.४॥
bhūmirāpo'nalo vāyuḥ
khaṁ mano buddhireva ca
ahaṁkāra itīyaṁ me
bhinnā prakṛtiraṣṭadhā (7.4)

bhūmir = bhūmiḥ — solid substance; *āpo = āpaḥ* — liquid substance; *'nalo = analaḥ* — flames; *vāyuḥ* — gas; *kham* — space; *mano = manaḥ* — mindal energy; *buddhir = buddhiḥ* — intelligence; *eva* — indeed; *ca* — and; *ahaṁkāra* — initiative; *itīyam = iti* — thus + *iyam* — this; *me* — My; *bhinnā* — apportioned; *prakṛtir = prakṛtiḥ* — mundane energy; *aṣṭadhā* — eight-sectioned

Solid substance, liquid substance, flame, gas, space, mindal energy, intelligence, and initiative are My apportioned, eight-sectioned mundane energy. (7.4)

Commentary:

An important clarification is made here by the term *prakṛti*, the sum total material nature which is manifested into eight parts. Outside the material creation, the *prakṛti* (mundane power) is manifested in only one way, that of a static eternal potency.

The eightfold differentiation of the material energy exists only in this type of creation which is a sectioned-off, isolated world. *Ahamkāra* is usually translated as false ego. We gave initiative. *Ahamkāra* pertains to any good or bad application of the spirit soul's attention to the mundane potencies. In that sense, everything in the material world is a demonstration of misplaced consciousness. We have, therefore, given the English as *initiative*, the mere desire to interact for any mundane cause.

Mr. Winthrop Sargeant, who gave a grammatically-sound translation of the *Bhagavad Gītā* and who quoted from the Vaishnava authority *Rāmānujācārya*, gave *self consciousness* for *ahamkāra*. However, *ahamkāra* means self consciousness in the material creation in reference to any form of supernatural or gross matter. There is self consciousness outside of the material world. Therefore self consciousness itself is not a special aspect of this manifestation, even though a faulty self consciousness or a misplaced, insecure one, is.

अपरेयमितस्त्वन्यां
प्रकृतिं विद्धि मे पराम् ।
जीवभूतां महाबाहो
ययेदं धार्यते जगत् ॥७.५॥
apareyamitastvanyāṁ
prakṛtiṁ viddhi me parām
jīvabhūtāṁ mahābāho
yayedaṁ dhāryate jagat (7.5)

apareyam = apara — inferior + *iyam* — this; *tv = tu* — but; *anyām* — another; *prakṛtiṁ* - energy; *viddhi* — know; *me* — of Me; *parām* — higher; *jīvabhūtām* — the hosts of individual spirits; *mahābāho* — O strong man; *yayedam = yaya* — through which + *idam* — this; *dhāryate* — is sustained; *jagat* — universe

That is inferior. But, O strong man, know of My other higher energy which consists of the hosts of individual spirits, through which this universe is sustained. (7.5)

Commentary:

On the basis of this statement, many *Gītā* commentators say that the living entity, the *ātma*, is a part of God or that he is a part and parcel of God. But until we know what each of the commentators meant by "God", it is difficult to determine if they are in harmony with the *Gītā*. Superficially agreeing with what Krishna says is not as important as understanding what He presents. One may agree but such agreement might be with mental reservation or with a motivation, especially if it is done to make a claim as Krishna's spokesman or to accredit one's view as being similar to Krishna's.

In the materialistic stage of life and in the imaginative theoretical stage of spiritual life, one can hardly agree with Lord Krishna. After all, we heard in Chapter One that Arjuna had basic disagreements. Even though they were so friendly with each other, still Krishna and Arjuna disagreed. But Arjuna asked for clarification. Once he got that, he agreed.

In the *Gītā*, Lord Krishna explained that we are in His influence and He is out of our psyche but some commentators feel that we are in Krishna and Krishna is in us. They do not understand that Krishna is speaking of His influence and the energy field of our psyche. Here in this verse, Krishna does not say that we are part of His personality but rather that we do comprise His superior potency. But hardly a man wants to accept this. It would be disappointing to hear that we are just a part of God's energy, if someone already told us that we were a part of God directly. What does it mean to be a part of someone's energy? Is that a demeaning position?

Some translators feel that the eightfold, divided material nature (*bhinnā prakṛtir aṣṭadhā*) is Krishna's nature but it is Krishna's energy, and not His nature. And it is only one type of energy. Material nature is a nature only in the sense that it absorbs our spiritual power.

The limited souls are listed in this verse as the other (*anyām*) energy (*prakṛtim*). But the adjective *parām* is given to explain that the entities are the highest of the energies which are owned by Krishna. Thus the question remains as to whether this is an insult from Krishna. What does He mean by categorizing us as the superior energy? Is He not a personality? Why has He listed us as an energy?

There is, however, a bright side to this statement of Krishna. He accredits us as sustaining (*dhāryate*) the universe (jagat). We can take pride in that. He gave us at least that much credit. But the statement about our being a superior energy is mysterious. What does it mean for one personality to be the energy of another?

एतद्योनीनि भूतानि
सर्वाणीत्युपधारय ।
अहं कृत्स्नस्य जगतः
प्रभवः प्रलयस्तथा ॥७.६॥
etadyonīni bhūtāni
sarvāṇītyupadhāraya
ahaṁ kṛtsnasya jagataḥ
prabhavaḥ pralayastathā (7.6)

etadyonīni = etad — this + yonīni — multiple origins; bhūtāni — the creatures; sarvāṇīty = sarvāṇi — all + ity (iti) — thus; upadhāraya — understand; aham — I; kṛtsnasya — of the entire; jagataḥ — of the universe; prabhavaḥ — cause of production; pralayaḥ — cause of the destruction; tathā — as well

This higher energy functions as the multiple origins of all creatures. Understand this. I am the cause of production as well as destruction of the entire universe. (7.6)

<u>Commentary:</u>

Even though He is the overall producer (*prabhavah*), still He said that the living entities (*jīvabhūtām*) are the source of the various creature forms. It is a direct statement since the term *yonīni* is used. This means wombs or origins. We living entities are the functional basis for the creation of the creature forms. Even though there is a producer of cars, the users themselves are the cause of the vehicles. Due to his sensitivity to the users' needs, the manufacturer creates the cars to satisfy his sense of responsibility. The bodies we use are not designed to be used by the Lord, but rather, by us only.

As the producer (*prabhavah*) and wrecker (*pralayas*) of the universal situation (*kṛtsnasya jagat*), the Lord has the final say in everything. But rarely does He assert authority and so people say that there is no God. To assert Himself, Lord Krishna appeared at *Kurukṣetra*. Let us review two related verses from Chapter Five:

sarvakarmāṇi manasā saṁnyasyāste sukhaṁ vaśī
navadvāre pure dehī naiva kurvanna kārayan (5.13)
na kartṛtvaṁ na karmāṇi lokasya sṛjati prabhuḥ
na karmaphalasaṁyogaṁ svabhāvastu pravartate (5.14)

Renouncing all action with the mind, the embodied soul resides happily within as the director in the nine-gated city, not acting nor causing activity.

***The Lord does not create the means of action, nor the actions of the creatures, nor the action-consequence cycle. But the inherent nature causes this.* (5.13-14)**

We may ask: If Krishna is the overseer and the ultimate producer, why does He not take the responsibility for the whimsical acts of our bodies? Who asked Him to produce these bodies? If a car user did not create the car and if it was produced without his asking, why should he be blamed for reckless driving?

मत्तः परतरं नान्यत्
किञ्चिदस्ति धनंजय ।
मयि सर्वमिदं प्रोतं
सूत्रे मणिगणा इव ॥७.७॥

mattaḥ parataraṁ nānyat
kiṁcidasti dhanaṁjaya
mayi sarvamidaṁ protaṁ
sūtre maṇigaṇā iva (7.7)

mattaḥ — than myself; parataram — higher, nānyat = na — not + anyat — other; kiṁcid — anything; asti — is; dhanaṁjaya — O conqueror of rich countries; mayi — on Me; sarvam — all; idam — this; protam — strong; sūtre — on a thread; maṇigaṇā — pearls; iva — like

O conqueror of rich countries, no other reality is higher than Myself. All this existence relies on Me, like pearls strung on a string. (7.7)

Commentary:

The two realities identified as material nature and the limited entities, are realities unto themselves. These factors are eternally existing in their primeval forms. Lord Krishna claimed that He is higher than either of these. He said that He is the basic shelter of the other factors. Pearls have their independent existence apart from a thread but their suspension and order relies on the thread. The limited entities are eternal, regardless of how they feel about Krishna or regardless of whether they are accept Him or not. Material nature, in its essence, is also eternal. Insofar as these interact, the Lord is the ultimate controller. All the interaction occurs under His supervision. At least this is the claim of Lord Krishna.

रसोऽहमप्सु कौन्तेय
प्रभास्मि शशिसूर्ययोः ।
प्रणवः सर्ववेदेषु
शब्दः खे पौरुषं नृषु. ॥७.८॥

raso'hamapsu kaunteya
prabhāsmi śaśisūryayoḥ
praṇavaḥ sarvavedeṣu
śabdaḥ khe pauruṣaṁ nṛṣu(7.8)

raso = rasaḥ — taste; 'ham = aham — I; apsu — in water; kaunteya — O son of Kuntī; prabhāsmi = prabhā — light + asmi — I am; śaśisūryayoḥ — of the sun and moon; praṇavaḥ — of the sacred syllable Om; sarvavedeṣu — in all the Vedas; śabdaḥ — sound; khe — in the atmosphere; pauruṣam — manliness; nṛṣu — in men

I am represented as taste in water, O son of Kuntī . I am signified as light in the moon and sun, as the sacred syllable *Om* in all the *Vedas*, as the sound in the atmosphere, as the manliness in men. (7.8)

Commentary:

After explaining that His influence is permanently situated in the material manifestation, Krishna explained how we can detect His power. By taking hints from these lessons of how to appreciate Lord Krishna's influence in the material world, one can learn how to be aware of Krishna even in this location.

पुण्यो गन्धः पृथिव्यां च
तेजश्चास्मि विभावसौ ।
जीवनं सर्वभूतेषु
तपश्चास्मि तपस्विषु ॥७.९॥

puṇyo gandhaḥ pṛthivyāṁ ca
tejaścāsmi vibhāvasau
jīvanaṁ sarvabhūteṣu
tapaścāsmi tapasviṣu (7.9)

puṇyo (puṇyaḥ)- wholesome; gandhaḥ odor; pṛthivyām- in the earth; ca - and; tejaḥ — brilliance: cāsmi= ca — and + asmi — I am; vibhavasau — in the sun; jīvanam — life; sarvabhūteṣu — in all creatures; tapaścāsmi = tapaḥ — austerity + ca — and + asmi — I am; tapasviṣu — in the ascetics

I am represented as wholesome odor in the earth. I am sensed by the brilliance in the sun, by the life in all creatures. I am indicated by the austerity of the ascetics. (7.9)

Commentary:

The *Śrīmad Bhāgavatam* is the supportive and illustrative text for the *Bhagavad Gītā*. Whatever seems theoretical or merely conceptual in the *Gītā* is illustrated in the lives of personalities in the *Śrīmad Bhāgavatam*. As the *Gītā* was spoken by the Lord, the Bhāgavatam was spoken about the Lord and His great devotees. There is an example of how the great sages studied the austerity of an ascetic and then concluded that these austerities were performed to please God. It was the case of *Brahmā*, the creator of the planets. It is said that once he was approached by *Nārada* Muni. *Nārada* addressed *Brahmā*, asking of the person *Brahmā* communicated with in meditations. At the time, the sages were not aware of any supreme person except *Brahmā*. Thus when they saw him engaged in introspective penance, they concluded that He worshipped another or at least tried to communicate with someone in another dimension. Here is what *Nārada* said to *Brahmā*:

sa bhavān acarad ghoraṁ yat tapaḥ susamāhitaḥ
tena khedayase nas tvaṁ parā-śaṅkaṁ ca yacchasi

Still, you confound us, because with the utmost deliberation, you perform severest austerities; thus causing us doubts as to whether there is someone who is greater than you. (Śrīmad Bhāgavatam. 2.5.7)

Observing the life energy (*jīvanam*) of the creatures is another way of detecting the Supreme Lord. Even though a product is used by others who do not have the capacity to invent the item, still we can sense the existence of the manufacturer. The limited entities cannot create their own material bodies without the assistance of the Supreme Lord. And the life energy in the bodies is impulsive and involuntary, operating with or without respect to the will of the limited souls. Thus we can see that the Supreme Lord is in the background. Ultimately, His influence supersedes all.

Observing sunshine is a common way of sensing the influence of the Lord. Many simple-minded people assumed the existence of God merely by observing the sun, moon, and stars.

Even without having scientific knowledge, people assumed the glory of God. Even though God's subtle influences require much mystic insight to perceive, His existence is not a very difficult idea to formulate. After observing the fragrance of uncontaminated earth, people speak of the good earth and thank God for it. Merely by smelling the earth, tilling and farming it, people have assumed that there is a God.

बीजं मां सर्वभूतानां
विद्धि पार्थ सनातनम् ।
बुद्धिर्बुद्धिमतामस्मि
तेजस्तेजस्विनामहम् ॥७.१०॥
bījaṁ māṁ sarvabhūtānāṁ
viddhi pārtha sanātanam
buddhirbuddhimatāmasmi
tejastejasvināmaham (7.10)

bījam — primary cause; mām — Me; sarvabhūtānām — of all creatures; viddhi — know; pārtha — O son of Pṛtha; sanātanam — primeval; buddhir = buddhiḥ — intelligence; buddhimatām — of the geniuses; asmi — I am; tejaḥ — splendor; tejasvinām — of the splendrous things; aham — I

Know me as the primeval, primary cause of all creatures, O son of Pṛthā. I can be inferred as the intelligence of the geniuses and glimpsed by the splendor of the splendorous things. (7.10)

Commentary:

Bhūtānām means the creature forms in the mundane world. These include the subtle mundane beings. All subtle or causal mundane configurations which emanate from or are formed on the basis of the spirits, are *bhūtānām* forms. The term *bhūta* means any of the subtle or gross material elements in formation.

Lord Krishna described Himself as the *bījam* (primary cause) of these forms. He, the Supreme Lord, was the first to perceive mundane forms. He established a Universal Form through which He supervises universal activities. He described Himself as being the primeval source (*sanātanam*).

Krishna's existence can be inferred by the intelligence of the geniuses, but He is not liable for their pious or sinful acts. Ultimately, all liability rests with Him. He will, in due course, summarize everything satisfactorily. The initial act of genius (*buddhimatām*) was the Lord's. That was the act of creating the mundane world. Thus, all other geniuses are secondary sources of the resourceful power. The *tejas* (splendrous wonders) of the world do indicate Krishna's existence. He is the first of creators, the first of thinkers.

बलं बलवतां चाहं
कामरागविवर्जितम् ।
धर्माविरुद्धो भूतेषु
कामोऽस्मि भरतर्षभ ॥७.११॥
balaṁ balavatāṁ cāhaṁ
kāmarāgavivarjitam
dharmāviruddho bhūteṣu
kāmo'smi bharatarṣabha (7.11)

balam — strength; balavatām — of the strong; cāham = ca — and + aham — I; kāmarāgavivarjitam = kāma — selfish desires + rāgavivarjitam — free from passionate urges; dharmāviruddho = dhārmaviruddhaḥ = dharma — Vedic rules of morality + aviruddhaḥ - not opposed to; bhūteṣu — in creatures; kāmo = kāmaḥ — romance; 'smi = asmi — I am; bharatarṣabha — powerful son of the Bharatas

I am indicated as the strength of the strong, which is free from selfish desire and passionate urges. I am supportive of romance which is not opposed to the Vedic rules of morality, O powerful son of the Bharata family. (7.11)

Commentary:

Administrative power that is free from restrictive lusty powers (*kāma*) and from blind passionate desire (*rāga*) is an expression of the caring interest of the Supreme Lord. This particular power of the Lord is invested in the mighty creatures (*balavatām*) who are supposed to care for their dependents and guard them from cultural follies. The Supreme Lord is addressed as the Almighty because He has the most sovereignty. As Krishna explained in Chapter Four, He comes out into the material world to establish social order.

All of the creatures have their *pecking order* or system of seniority. Usually the superiors take control of the inferiors. Some human beings make an endeavor to equalize every man and woman under the banner of civil liberties, but the system of existence defines disparities. As such we must look to the Lord to understand how to use administrative power. When such power is surcharged with lust and craving, the user unconsciously prepares himself for rash reactions. It is said that discretion is the better part of valor. Might should be guided with good sense or the mighty ones will imperil themselves by neglect of the law of fairness. Most commentators discuss the restriction on sexual love in terms of human beings, but in this verse, the term *bhūteṣu* means, *in the creatures,* or, *in the beings. Bhūteṣu* is taken to mean an earthly creature form which we can perceive with an earthly body, but *bhūteṣu* actually means any mundane creature form. In fact, all subtle creature forms which are made of mundane energy are included in *bhūteṣu.* Krishna is supportive of sexual affections which are not opposed to the Vedic religious principles.

ये चैव सात्त्विका भावा
राजसास्तामसाश्च ये ।
मत्त एवेति तान्विद्धि
न त्वहं तेषु ते मयि ॥७.१२॥
ye caiva sāttvikā bhāvā
rājasāstāmasāśca ye
matta eveti tānviddhi
na tvahaṁ teṣu te mayi (7.12)

ye — which; caiva — and indeed; sāttvikā — perceptive clarity; bhāvā — states of being; rājasāḥ — enthusiasm; tāmasāśca = tāmasāḥ — depression + ca — and; ye — which; matta — from Me; eveti = eva — indeed + iti — thus; tān — them; viddhi — know; na — not; tv = tu — but; aham — I; teṣu — in them; te — they; mayi — on Me

Regarding the states of being, which are perceptive clarity, enthusiasm, and depression, know that they are produced by Me. But I am not based in them. They are dependent on Me. (7.12)

Commentary:

Krishna claimed to be the original producer not only of well-being and enthusiasm, but of reductions. These three states are endured by us in material existence. In the pure spiritual environment, depression does not play a part; only clarity of perception and enthusiasm are experienced. In the material world, all three states are based on potent mundane energy. This energy is called *prakṛti* in the *Gītā* but in the Upanishads, it is also categorized as *prāṇa*, which is the same *prakṛti* in a state of activation, made usable to us by the grace of the Supreme Being.

In this verse, Lord Krishna segregated Himself from the limited beings, by stating that even though the *prakṛti* energies do rely on His energization (*mayi*), He is not based (*na tu aham*) in them in the least.

त्रिभिर्गुणमयैर्भावैर्
एभिः सर्वमिदं जगत् ।
मोहितं नाभिजानाति
मामेभ्यः परमव्ययम् ॥७.१३॥
tribhirguṇamayairbhāvair
ebhiḥ sarvamidaṁ jagat
mohitaṁ nābhijānāti
māmebhyaḥ paramavyayam (7.13)

tribhir = tribhiḥ — by three; guṇamayair = guṇamayaiḥ — by mundane influence produced; bhāvair = bhāvaiḥ — by states of being; ebhiḥ — by these; sarvam — all; idam — this; jagat — world; mohitam — stupified; nābhijānāti = na — not + abhijānāti — recognizes; mām — Me; ebhyaḥ — than these; param — higher; avyayam — unaffected

All this world is stupefied by the three states of being, which are produced by the mundane influence. The world does not recognize Me, Who is higher than these energies and Who is unaffected. (7.13)

Commentary:

It is suggested here that due to a stupification by the three-fold influence of material nature (*tribhih guṇamayaih bhāvaih*) we cannot recognize Krishna. At least many warriors on the battlefield were not seeing Krishna in the way Krishna presented Himself to Arjuna. They were seeing Him as a human being, powerful, but limited in one way or the other. Krishna pushed Himself forward with these godly attributes. He explained that material nature blurred the vision of the limited viewers. As the *avyayam*, the unchanging principle which is not affected by material nature, Krishna distinguished Himself from the limited selves.

दैवी ह्येषा गुणमयी
मम माया दुरत्यया ।
मामेव ये प्रपद्यन्ते
मायामेतां तरन्ति ते ॥७.१४॥
daivī hyeṣā guṇamayī
mama māyā duratyayā
māmeva ye prapadyante
māyāmetāṁ taranti te (7.14)

daivī — supernatural; hy = hi — indeed; eṣā — this; guṇamayī — quality-controlled; mama — of Me; māyā — magical display; duratyayā — difficult to transcend; mām — Me; eva — indeed; ye — who; prapadyante — they rely on; māyām — bewitching energy; etām — this; taranti — they can see beyond; te — they

Indeed this quality controlled illusion of Mine is supernatural and difficult to transcend. Only those who rely on Me, can see beyond this bewitching energy. (7.14)

Commentary:

A big solution is presented here in the word *daivī* which means divine, heavenly or supernatural. Material nature is also supernatural. It extends into the psychic or subtle and further into the causal level which underlines the subtle plane. If it were just a physical accomplishment, it would be an easy attainment.

Daivī also means that whatever is under discussion is being regulated by the *devas* or *devatās*, the supernatural people. It is not just a natural force without personal regulation. And that makes it even more difficult to understand.

Lord Krishna made a big claim, stating that only by reliance on Him, (*mam eva ye prapadyante*) can we transcend or go beyond material nature's influence. Furthermore, we are left to consider the situation of other saviors. If Krishna alone (*eva*) can do this, then what is the position of authorities of the various religions which flourish all over the world? Krishna claims to have total monopoly on salvation. What about the promises of other saviors?

न मां दुष्कृतिनो मूढाः
प्रपद्यन्ते नराधमाः ।
माययापहृतज्ञाना
आसुरं भावमाश्रिताः ॥७.१५॥
na māṁ duṣkṛtino mūḍhāḥ
prapadyante narādhamāḥ
māyayāpahṛtajñānā
āsuraṁ bhāvamāśritāḥ (7.15)

na — not; mām — Me; duṣkṛtino = duṣkṛtinaḥ — evil-doers; mūḍhāḥ — confused; prapadyante — they take shelter; narādhamāḥ — lowest of human beings; māyayāpahṛtajñānā = māyayā — by misconception + apahṛta — erased + jñānā — discrimination; āsuram — corrupted; bhāvam — existence; āśritāḥ — attached

The confused evildoers, the lowest of human beings, those whose discrimination is erased by misconceptions, do not take shelter of Me. They are attached to a corrupted existence. (7.15)

Commentary:

Lord Krishna was rejected by some in His own time. He is rejected by many today. Here He gave an explanation for why people disregard Him. He claimed that their intelligence is bedazzled by misconceptions which arise from the complicated influences of material nature. Subsequently, they do not rely on Krishna as suggested and they become attached to a degraded existence (*āsuram*).

चतुर्विधा भजन्ते मां
जनाः सुकृतिनोऽर्जुन ।
आर्तो जिज्ञासुरर्थार्थी
ज्ञानी च भरतर्षभ ॥७.१६॥
caturvidhā bhajante māṁ
janāḥ sukṛtino'rjuna
ārto jijñāsurarthārthī
jñānī ca bharatarṣabha (7.16)

caturvidhā — four kinds; bhajante — worship; mām — Me; janāḥ — people; sukṛtino = sukṛtinaḥ — good people; 'rjuna = arjuna — Arjuna; ārto = ārtaḥ — distressed person; jijñāsur = jijñāsuḥ — inquisitive person; arthārthī — needy person; jñānī — informed person; ca — and; bharatarṣabha — O bullish man of the Bharata family

Four kinds of good people worship Me, O Arjuna: the distressed one, the inquisitive one, the needy one, and the informed one, O bullish man of the Bharata family. (7.16)

Commentary:

Lord Krishna categorized His devotees as having virtuous tendency (*sukṛtino*). *Sukṛta* means doing good, being benevolent, being pious, and being virtuous. In the previous verse, those who do not display a positive attraction to Krishna were tagged as being *āsuram* or wicked, demoniac, corrupted.

तेषां ज्ञानी नित्ययुक्त
एकभक्तिर्विशिष्यते ।
प्रियो हि ज्ञानिनोऽत्यर्थम्
अहं स च मम प्रियः ॥७.१७॥
teṣāṁ jñānī nityayukta
ekabhaktirviśiṣyate
priyo hi jñānino'tyartham
ahaṁ sa ca mama priyaḥ (7.17)

teṣām — of these; jñānī — the informed man; nityayukta — constantly disciplined in yoga; ekabhaktir = ekabhaktiḥ — one who is singularly devoted; viśiṣyate — is distinguished; priyo = priyaḥ — fond; hi — indeed; jñānino = jñāninaḥ — of the informed person; 'tyartham = atyartham — very; aham — I; sa = sah — he; ca — and; mama — of Me; priyaḥ — fond

Of these, the informed man who is constantly disciplined in yoga, being singularly devoted, is distinguished indeed. I am fond of this person and he is fond of Me. (7.17)

Commentary:

Of all His devotees Lord Krishna singled out the *jñāni*, the informed, mystically-experienced devotee, as being the very best. But that informed devotee must exhibit singular interest in being devoted to Krishna (*ekabhaktih*).

Thus devotion is distinguished from spiritual knowledge and spiritual experience. One may be a devotee of Krishna and be somewhat ignorant of the spiritual truths described in the *Gītā*. One may be a devotee and be partially aware of these realities.

To be the highest devotee, one must be singularly devoted to Him, be conversant with the *Gītā* information and be directly experienced in the realities Krishna explained to Arjuna. Persons who lack that understanding are also regarded as devotees if they exhibit some positive devotion (*bhakti*) to Krishna.

उदाराः सर्व एवैते
ज्ञानी त्वात्मैव मे मतम् ।
आस्थितः स हि युक्तात्मा
मामेवानुत्तमां गतिम् ॥७.१८॥
udārāḥ sarva evaite
jñānī tvātmaiva me matam
āsthitaḥ sa hi yuktātmā
māmevānuttamāṁ gatim (7.18)

udārāḥ — exalted; sarva — all; evaite = eva — indeed + ete — these; jñānī — informed person; tv = tu — but; ātmaiva = ātmā — personal self + eva — indeed; me — of Me; matam — is considered; āsthitaḥ — situated with; sa = saḥ — he; hi — truly; yuktātmā — one who is disciplined in yoga practice; mām — Me; evānuttamām = eva — indeed + anuttamām — supreme; gatim — objective

All these are exalted people. But the informed one is considered to be my personal representative. Indeed, he who is disciplined in yoga practice, is situated with Me as the Supreme Objective. (7.18)

Commentary:

The devotional attraction (*bhaktih*) to Krishna is what qualifies a person as a devotee. Anyone who resorts to or relies upon Krishna is rated as being exalted among the creatures. But the informed devotee who communicates intimately with the Lord and whose existence is steadied on Krishna as the Supreme Objective (*anuttamām gatim*) is the foremost of the devotees and the foremost of the human beings in Krishna's estimation.

As Krishna puts Himself forward as the Supreme over everyone and everything else, He likewise puts His devotees as being the best of human beings.

बहूनां जन्मनामन्ते
ज्ञानवान्मां प्रपद्यते ।
वासुदेवः सर्वमिति
स महात्मा सुदुर्लभः ॥७.१९॥
bahūnāṁ janmanāmante
jñānavānmāṁ prapadyate
vāsudevaḥ sarvamiti
sa mahātmā sudurlabhaḥ (7.19)

bahūnām — of many; janmanām — of births; ante — at the end; jñānavān — the informed devotee; mām — Me; prapadyate — surrenders to; vāsudevaḥ — son of Vasudeva; sarvam — everything; iti — thus; sa = saḥ — he; mahātmā — great soul; sudurlabhaḥ — hard to locate

At the end of many births, the informed devotee surrenders to Me, thinking that the son of Vasudeva is essential to everything. Such a great soul is hard to locate. (7.19)

Commentary:

Of the informed devotees, a few are on the verge of terminating their material existences (*bahūnām janmanām ante*). These greatly experienced souls form the conclusion that Lord Krishna, the son of Vasudeva, is the cause of the material manifestations. But there are others who are not devotees and who aspire for the end of their transmigration. They do not come to the same conclusion.

कामैस्तैस्तैर्हृतज्ञानाः
प्रपद्यन्तेऽन्यदेवताः ।
तं तं नियममास्थाय
प्रकृत्या नियताः स्वया ॥७.२०॥
kāmaistaistairhṛtajñānāḥ
prapadyante'nyadevatāḥ
taṁ taṁ niyamamāsthāya
prakṛtyā niyatāḥ svayā (7.20)

kāmaiḥ — by desires; taistair = taihtaiḥ — by whose, by these, contrary; hṛtajñānāḥ — persons whose experience is overshadowed; prapadyante — they plead with; 'nyadevatāḥ = anyadevatāḥ = anya — other + devatāḥ — supernatural rulers; taṁtam — this or that; niyamam — religious procedures; āsthāya — following; prakṛtyā — by material nature; niyatāḥ — restricted; svayā — by their own

Persons whose experience was overshadowed by contrary desires, plead with other supernatural rulers, following this or that religious procedure, being restricted by their own material nature. (7.20)

Commentary:

In putting Himself forward as the Supreme Lord, in bypassing and minimizing all other Vedic deities who were being worshipped in His time, Lord Krishna found it necessary to explain why some go to the other lords for their needs. Even in the time of Lord Krishna, even in His direct presence, some people went to other supernatural lords to fulfill desires. There was definitely a tension at *Kurukṣetra*, as Krishna tried to put Himself ahead of all supernatural people of the time.

How can we lift ourselves away from the weighty influences of material nature and move more in His direction? Arjuna was weighed down by mundane influences and even by his family attachment to persons who were resistant to Lord Krishna and who were relied on other supernatural people for victory at *Kurukṣetra*. But Arjuna was delivered suddenly. Can we, all of a sudden, place our confidence in Krishna?

A very technical Sanskrit term which is perhaps very disturbing, is *prakṛtyā svayā*. It literally means, *their own material natures*. Some commentators carefully stride away from this since they do not want to be trapped into endless question and answer sessions by critical audiences. Previously, Lord Krishna spoke about His own material nature or His own energies under the term *prakṛtim svām* (4.6).

Some Vaishnava commentators, including our Vaishnava authority, *Śrīla* Bhaktivedanta Swami, have carefully worked around Lord Krishna's use of these two terms, namely; *prakṛtim svām* (4.6) and *prakṛtyā* svayā (7.20). Why is it that these Vaishnava authorities gave *prakṛtim* in Chapter Four, verse 6, as "transcendental form" and *prakṛtyā* in Chapter Seven, verse 20, as "nature"? Serious readers may settle that question for themselves. We know this: In either use of the terms *prakṛtim* and *prakṛtyā*, the qualifying pronouns, *svām* and *svayā*, must be taken into consideration.

This we know for sure: Lord Krishna explained that He controls His relationship with material nature. When He comes into this world or is manifested here materially so that He can be seen using a body that is visible on the worldly level, He regulates that manifestation of material nature. But the living entities are for the most part regulated by (*niyatās*); held down by, controlled by, or influenced by their affiliation with material nature.

In either case, that of the Lord or of the limited entities, material nature (*prakṛti*) is involved. I feel no necessity to convert the word *prakṛti* into any other meanings, even those given by our Vaishnava teachers. When Krishna mentioned His own *prakṛti*, He used the term *adhiṣṭhāya* (4.6); but in reference to us, He used the term *niyatāh* . So there is no necessity to dodge His involvement with material nature or His usage of a material form for Himself.

Adhiṣṭhāya means to govern, to control, or more precisely to stand over, to keep in position. But *niyatāh* means to be subdued by, to be governed by, to be restricted by. It is the exact opposite in our case in the relationship with material nature.

यो यो यां यां तनुं भक्तः
श्रद्धयार्चितुमिच्छति ।
तस्य तस्याचलां श्रद्धां
तामेव विदधाम्यहम् ॥७.२१॥
yo yo yāṁ yāṁ tanuṁ bhaktaḥ
śraddhayārcitumicchati
tasya tasyācalāṁ śraddhāṁ
tāmeva vidadhāmyaham (7.21)

yo yo = yaḥ yaḥ — whoever; yāṁ yām- whatever; tanum — deity form; bhaktaḥ - devotedly worship; śraddhayārcitum = śraddhayā — with belief + arcitum — to worship; icchati - desires; tasya — of him; tasyācalām = tasya — of him + acalām - unwavering; śraddhām — confidence; tām — it; eva — indeed; vidadhāmy = vidadhāmi — allow; aham — I

I grant unwavering faith to anyone, who with belief, wants to worship any worshipable deity form. (7.21)

<u>*Commentary:*</u>

The allowance for deviant worship of other supernatural beings or of ordinary wonders or even of imagined objects is explained here by Krishna in His own way. Krishna listed both animate objects of worship (*yo yo*) and the inanimate ones (*yām yām*). He covers the entire range of adorations and superstitions. Wherever we place our confidence (*śraddhām*), He may allow us to rely on that person or object.

But why does Krishna put Himself in the picture so essentially? Why does He state that He allows, bestows or grants to us (*vidadhāmi*) the capacity to express our confidence or faith in something other than Himself? Is Krishna personally aware of every case of everyone's expression of faith?

स तया श्रद्धया युक्तस्
तस्या राधनमीहते ।
लभते च ततः कामान्
मयैव विहितान्हि तान् ॥७.२२॥
sa tayā śraddhayā yuktas
tasyā rādhanamīhate
labhate ca tataḥ kāmān
mayaiva vihitānhi tān (7.22)

sa = saḥ — he; tayā — with this; śraddhayā — by faith; yuktaḥ — endowed; tasyārādhanam = tasya — of this + ārādhanam — worshipfully petitioning a deity; īhate — thinks of; labhate — gets; ca — and; tataḥ — from that; kāmān — desires; mayaiva = maya — by Me + eva — indeed; vihitān — permitted; hi — truly; tān — them

Being endowed with this confidence, he thinks of worshipfully petitioning the deity and gets from that source, his desires, as those fulfillments are permitted by Me. (7.22)

Commentary:

Lord Krishna, again, placed Himself between us and our objectives. Here He presented Himself as the ultimate wish-fulfiller. The process of placing our confidence in a supernatural person or wonderful object, is well understood by the advanced human beings. Particularly in the field of religion, preachers, spiritual teachers and others understand this very well. Some of them exploit us on the basis of our impulsive need to worship. But Krishna says that He permits the reliance.

Ārādhanam means forceful worship, or an irresistable pull of attraction. Some objects, some people do have that sort of power over us. And we use terms like fantastic, and charismatic to describe these.

Lord Krishna permits it, but elsewhere in the *Gītā*, He issued a disclaimer for the responsibilities involved. Thus He permits as He claims, but at our expense. If we place our confidence in the right person at the right time and place, then we gain. Otherwise, it is a lesson learned by unfavorable reactions which we receive.

अन्तवत्तु फलं तेषां
तद्भवत्यल्पमेधसाम् ।
देवान्देवयजो यान्ति
मद्भक्ता यान्ति मामपि ॥७.२३॥
antavattu phalaṁ teṣāṁ
tadbhavatyalpamedhasām
devāndevayajo yānti
madbhaktā yānti māmapi (7.23)

antavat — something with an end, short-lived; tu — but; phalam — results; teṣām — of them; tad — this; bhavaty = bhavati — it is; alpamedhasām — of those with little intelligence; devān — supernatural rulers; devayajo = devayajaḥ — those who worship the supernatural rulers; yānti — go; madbhaktā — those who worship Me; yānti — go; mām — to Me; api — surely

But for those with little intelligence, the result is short-lived. The worshippers of the supernatural rulers go to those gods. Those who worship Me, surely go to Me. (7.23)

Commentary:

Lord Krishna reduced most human beings as blank idolaters, fools as it were, who cannot see what they are doing and who approach other powerful persons or fantastic objects which do them no lasting good. This one verse is a general insult to humanity. As Lord Krishna insulted Arjuna in Chapter Two, addressing Arjuna as a nit-wit, a screw-ball, as it were, *anārya* (2.2), He leveled a direct insult at humanity here. Krishna reduced all other supernatural lords or gods to being short-sighted and not capable of acting in our long-ranged interest. One gets the idea that Krishna feels that only His advice is worthwhile. He said that the results achieved from the others are temporary and are for people like ourselves who have petty understanding (*alpamedhasām*)

But the main point is that whatever or whosoever we worship, attracts us, and that same principle or person becomes the force that draws us. Krishna makes the claim for His devotees. His devotees go to Him for what they need and they keep going to Him, while others go to the particular supernatural person or force upon whom they resort for blessings.

Some commentators explain that Krishna's devotees go to His transcendental place, and attain a nature like His, while the devotees of other Vedic gods go to the respective places of these supernaturals.

This verse, however, is one that is carefully avoided by many Indian pandits who do not want to scare audiences. Many Indians are attracted to multiple gods like *Gaṇeśa*, Shiva, *Durgā*, *Kālī*. *Sūrya*, Indra, *Satya Nārāyaṇa*, Hanuman, *Rāma*, and many other gods who are worshipped in the whole range of Hinduism. Instead of repeating this verse verbatim, some pandits carefully avoid this verse. They do not mention it in public, since many Hindus who like other parts of the *Gītā*, have no intentions of abandoning the worship of multiple gods. Even today, educated Hindus may welcome a visitor into their homes, with statements of: "Come in. We worship all the gods. We do not neglect any. All of them are God."

अव्यक्तं व्यक्तिमापन्नं
मन्यन्ते मामबुद्धयः ।
परं भावमजानन्तो
ममाव्ययमनुत्तमम् ॥७.२४॥
avyaktaṁ vyaktimāpannaṁ
manyante māmabuddhayaḥ
paraṁ bhāvamajānanto
mamāvyayamanuttamam (7.24)

avyaktam — that which is beyond the sensual range; vyaktim — that which is grossly perceived; āpannam — within range, limited; manyante — they think; mām — Me; abuddhayaḥ — unintelligent ones; param — higher; bhāvam — being; ajānanto = ajānantaḥ — not realizing; mamāvyayam = mama — of Me + avyayam — imperishable; anuttamam — supermost

Though I am beyond their sensual range, the unintelligent think of Me as being limited to their gross perception. They do not realize My higher existence which is imperishable and supermost. (7.24)

Commentary:

Lord Krishna has again leveled another insult at humanity. This statement applies to every human who cannot and does not rate Lord Krishna as He presented Himself in the *Gītā*. *Manyante mām abuddhayah* refers to the average human being who cannot see Krishna as He presented Himself to Arjuna. Such a person, you or me, just cannot directly perceive that divine nature Krishna described. In addition, even if we are attracted to Krishna, still we have to see through our own sensuality. Whatever He presents that defies our sensual range, is left for us to accept by belief only. Until we achieve some higher sensuality, our vision will not be a perfect match with Krishna's. Every man must look through his own eyes. Even Arjuna could not, at first, see what Krishna spoke of. Was Arjuna not a devotee at the time? He certainly was. And still he could not see. Still, some modern devotees and their leaders pretend that they are seeing with Krishna eye to eye but their vision is an imaginative, imperfect idea of what Krishna said. Until we get the divine vision which was granted to Arjuna, we cannot see Krishna in truth even though we might have some slight idea and may be attracted to Him and be open-minded towards Him. Anyone may have an open mind to Krishna's ideas, but being able to directly perceive what He described, is an entirely different matter.

We are these stupid people, the *abuddhayah*, who have not developed the reality-piercing vision which was described in great detail in Chapters Two, Three, and Four. But are we not devotees? We may be. But that is not the key requirement for having that direct vision.

The first line reads: *avyaktam vyaktim āpannam*. Taken literally this means: *avyaktam*— a form which cannot be seen; *vyaktim*— a form which can be plainly seen; *āpannam*— assumed, taken on, became. Krishna said that when He comes into the material world and is seen as an historic personality, we assume that He arrived from nowhere and then became a human body just as we consider ourselves to have come into being. The first line was already explained by Lord Krishna Himself in Chapter Two. Let us return to the place where

Krishna explained this:

avyaktādīni bhūtāni vyaktamadhyāni bhārata
avyaktanidhanānyeva tatra kā paridevanā (2.28)

The living beings are undetected in the beginning of a manifestation, visible in the interim stages, and are again undetected at the end of a manifestation. (2.28)

Readers are asked to note that the same terms, *vyaktim* and *avyaktam*, are used there previously. It appears that Lord Krishna greatly resented opinions which indicated that He was not manifested before His human form became visible, and that He was perhaps just a human body. He disliked a thought which He explained in 2.26:

atha cainaṁ nityajātaṁ nityaṁ vā manyase mṛtam
tathāpi tvaṁ mahābāho nainaṁ śocitumarhasi (2.26)

And furthermore if you think that this embodied soul is continually being born or continually dying, even so, O strong-armed man, you should not lament. (2.26)

Even though Krishna appeared as a human historic person, He wants to be categorized differently. Following His line of thinking, we are to assume therefore, that even though Krishna took birth as a baby, grew up as a cowherd boy, assumed political importance as the son of Vasudeva, He is entirely different to everyone else. We are not to assume that He came from nowhere (*avyaktam*) and then became manifested (*vyaktim*) as a human personality, as we did or as any other creature of this world does, without any comprehensive memory of past existences. But rather, we should acknowledge that He lived before, always lived, always will live, and always remembers Who He was before and whom He taught before.

śrībhagavānuvāca
bahūni me vyatītāni janmāni tava cārjuna
tānyahaṁ veda sarvāṇi na tvaṁ vettha paraṁtapa (4.5)

The Blessed Lord said: Many of My births transpired, and yours, Arjuna. I recall them all. You do not remember, O scorcher of the enemies. (4.5)

Most of the Vaishnava commentators dismiss the idea of a material body of Lord Krishna. According to their view, there was no such body, but evidence to the contrary occurs in the *Mahābhārata*. And *Śrīmad Bhāgavatam* also mentions a mundane body of Krishna, even though some Vaishnava commentators take great pains to bypass or explain away the relevant verses.

Here in this *Gītā* verse, however, the manifested human or ordinary historic body of Krishna is distinguished from His whole self which is called *param bhavam* and which is described as being *avyayam anuttamam*. Besides the limited body which was visible to ordinary people, there is higher being (*param bhāvam*), which is imperishable and unsurpassed (*avyayam anuttamam*). We should understand that Krishna did have that limited edition of a human body and still He was the entirety of what He described for Himself in the *Gītā*. He restricted Himself on certain occasions. He assumed a limited form to be seen by our sensuality.

The problem of whether God could take a material body or not, is an old one. It is a question each religion faced and dealt with in one way or another. Some modern religions like Christianity carefully discarded this question by stating that God is a spirit and that He has nothing to do with material manifestation. Christianity, however, answered the question in a very humane way by presenting the human body of the only begotten son of God, who is said to have assumed a physical form and then resumed a divine one miraculously. Exactly how a person with a divine form could have that form converted into a physical one as the son of Mary and then have it reconverted into a divine one after that physical one was killed is a great mystery. But this is Christian doctrine. Thus in Christianity, the question of God taking on a human form was carefully and neatly disposed of. We were given instead a more human approach, which in one swipe, protected God from descent and also maintained His honor by the production of a converted human form for His only begotten son, who was supposed to be with Him in the very beginning in a divine form.

Other religions may not have so expertly dealt with the matter of the possibility or impossibility of God taking a human form but in the Vedic setting, we do have the idea of the *avatār* or incarnation of the Godhead. The word *avatār* means: *one who came down, descended or entered.*

However, some Vedantists, hailing themselves as having reached the end (*anta*) of knowledge (*veda*), say that the *avatār* is not the absolute truth but is only a reflection or spokesperson of it. In that way they have saved themselves from explaining how it could be possible for a God to descend in a physical body that was visible to the physical senses of the human beings. But other Vedantists, those who believe in the *Gītā*, say that God does descend.

The issue is this; Does God accept material bodies? Perhaps such an issue could never be settled satisfactorily. But each reader has to decide for himself. If God does not take on a human, earthly body from time to time, then how will human beings ever get any hints of His features and actions?

नाहं प्रकाशः सर्वस्य
योगमायासमावृतः ।
मूढोऽयं नाभिजानाति
लोको मामजमव्ययम् ॥७.२५॥
nāhaṁ prakāśaḥ sarvasya
yogamāyāsamāvṛtaḥ
mūḍho'yaṁ nābhijānāti
loko māmajamavyayam (7.25)

nāham = na — not + aham — I; prakāśaḥ — visible; sarvasya — of everyone; yoga — yogically self-controlled + māyā — mystic power + samāvṛtaḥ — shielded; mūḍho = mūḍhaḥ — stupified; 'yam = ayam — this; nābhijānāti = na — not + abhijānāti — recognizes; loko = lokaḥ — population; mām — Me; ajam — not subjected to birth shocks; avyayam — not liable to existential pressures of change

I am not visible to everyone, because I am shielded by My yogicly, self-controlled mystic powers. This stupefied population does not recognize Me as not being subjected to shocks of birth and not being liable to existential pressures of change. (7.25)

Commentary:

Lord Krishna explained that He is not recognized by everyone because He has Himself under a mystic shield, which prevents the deluded and confused people from understanding His identity. Who are these deluded people? He explained who they were in previous verses, stating that they could not properly assess Him and could not be attracted to Him positively because they were bogged down by their weighty but useless considerations under the influence of material nature. Instead of going to Him for shelter and relying on Him as stipulated, they go, instead, to other supernatural persons or forces and have some petty desires fulfilled. They cannot recognize Krishna Who is continuous in memory of past births (*ajam*) and Who is sustaining to Himself and to everything else, as described. Since they rely either on themselves, on material nature or on limited supernaturals, they are doomed to failure. At least this is the view expressed by Lord Krishna.

वेदाहं समतीतानि
वर्तमानानि चार्जुन ।
भविष्याणि च भूतानि
मां तु वेद न कश्चन ॥७.२६॥
vedāhaṁ samatītāni
vartamānāni cārjuna
bhaviṣyāṇi ca bhūtāni
māṁ tu veda na kaścana (7.26)

vedāham = veda — know + aham — I; samatītāni — the departed souls; vartamānāni — the living creatures; cārjuna = ca — and + arjuna — Arjuna; bhaviṣyāni — those who are to be born; ca — and; bhūtāni — creatures; mām — Me; tu — but; veda — recognizes; na — not; kaścana — anyone

I know the departed souls and the living creatures, O Arjuna, as well as those beings who are to be born. But no one recognizes Me. (7.26)

Commentary:

Lord Krishna distinguished Himself from the rest, from us, the limited beings, by stating that He knows about our condition in the departed, embodied and soon-to-be embodied states. Those who are embodied are using earthly bodies at the moment. Those who are departed are those who are neither using an earthly body nor are in the process of having baby forms formulated for them. They hover in the ghostly or subtle plane of life. Those who are soon-to-be embodied are those who have entered the bloodstream of a would-be parent. In the process of time, within moments, hours, days, months or years, they would emerge from a parent's form in an infant body.

Krishna claimed that He knows all living entities. He said that no one knows about Him unless, of course, He reveals Himself or volunteers the information. This is an answer to the question of why people do not know Krishna; He has not made Himself visible to them. For the time being, He is shielded by His self-controlled mystic power which cannot be penetrated by a limited being.

इच्छाद्वेषसमुत्थेन
द्वंद्वमोहेन भारत ।
सर्वभूतानि संमोहं
सर्गे यान्ति परंतप ॥७.२७॥
icchādveṣasamutthena
dvaṁdvamohena bhārata
sarvabhūtāni saṁmohaṁ
sarge yānti paraṁtapa (7.27)

icchādveṣasamutthena = icchā — liking + dveṣa — disliking + samutthena — through the urge; dvandvamohena = dvandva — two-fold sensuality + mohena — by the delusive influence; bhārata — O man of the Bharata family; sarvabhūtāni — all beings; saṁmoham — delusion; sarge — at the beginning of the creation; yānti — they are influenced by; paraṁtapa — O scorcher of the enemy

O man of the Bharata family, at the beginning of any creation, all beings are influenced by delusion through the urge of liking or disliking and by the delusive influence of the two-fold sensuality. So it is, O scorcher of the enemy. (7.27)

Commentary:

The key word in this verse is *sarge*. *Sarge* means, *at birth, at the beginning of creation, at the occurrence of a dimensional change, at the start of a circumstantial change*. It appears that whenever there is a new birth or a new circumstance, we are affected by dual forces which pull us here and there through natural attraction or repulsion to objects. While one creature is happy under one circumstance, another is sad for the same condition. A cactus thrives in a desert region while other plants whither away. But if the cactus is moved to a tropical area where there is sufficient rain, it might not thrive as well. Thus the response is in part due to the environment and in part due to our own prejudiced expectations. In the *Gītā*, Lord Krishna has, all along, suggested that we harden ourselves against this dual polarity by becoming detached from the liking and disliking impulses.

The advice of Lord Krishna is practical. A limited entity cannot at any stage change the complete environment but he can adjust his nature. The effort lies with him to do something to help himself from these liking and disliking tendencies which send him here and there, headlong into confusion. Any environment he enters, has forces within it, which might bring on a liking and disliking mood alternately. And he must, for sanity, protect himself, not so much from the environment, but rather, from his own reactionary impulses. This he must do by subduing the senses and the life energy which surges to enliven the sense organs. It was for this purpose that the ancient Upanishadic sages took to isolation in an attempt to study their psyche and then to adopt effective ways of controlling it.

येषां त्वन्तगतं पापं
जनानां पुण्यकर्मणाम् ।
ते द्वंद्वमोहनिर्मुक्ता
भजन्ते मां दृढव्रताः ॥७.२८॥
yeṣāṁ tvantagataṁ pāpaṁ
janānāṁ puṇyakarmaṇām
te dvaṁdvamohanirmuktā
bhajante māṁ dṛḍhavratāḥ (7.28)

yeṣām — of whom; tv = tu — but; antagatam = anta — terminated + gatam — gone; pāpam — sinful propensity; janānām — of people; puṇyakarmaṇām — of persons of righteous actions; te — they; dvandvamohanirmukta = dvandva — two-fold + moha — delusion + nirmuktā — free from; bhajante — worship; mām — Me; dṛḍhavratāḥ — those who maintain firm vows of austerity

But those people whose sinful propensities are terminated, whose actions are righteous, who are free from the two-fold delusion, who are maintaining firm vows of austerity, do worship Me. (7.28)

Commentary:

The persons addressed above are those who are among Krishna's devotees. While in previous chapters, Lord Krishna mentioned others who were being purified but who were not necessarily His devotees, here He distinguished the advanced devotees. Those devotees are people like Markandeya Rishi, who was singled out by Krishna as being the most advanced among the *jñāni*, mystically-experienced followers.

The tie between their worship of Krishna with firm vows (*dṛḍhavratāh*) and their termination of sinful propensities (*antagatam pāpam*) is the freedom they get from self-destructive tendencies. The big item is the termination of sinful propensities. This does not occur by mere mind control but by life energy control. A devotee of Krishna whose life energy is not under control cannot stick to firm vows no matter how hard he may try. His impure tendencies will cause him to deviate.

Purified actions come about automatically for a person whose sinful propensities are terminated. His life energies are cleared up. But those who are not so pure, show pure actions periodically. However, those who show it now and again, and who do not have a purified life energy, are not steady at good character. And this is how they are detected. A process of salvation is recognized not by its ability to promise everything to the follower but by its ability to deliver whatever it promises to yield.

जरामरणमोक्षाय
मामाश्रित्य यतन्ति ये ।
ते ब्रह्म तद्विदुः कृत्स्नम्
अध्यात्मं कर्म चाखिलम् ॥७.२९॥
jarāmaraṇamokṣāya
māmāśritya yatanti ye
te brahma tadviduḥ kṛtsnam
adhyātmaṁ karma cākhilam (7.29)

jarāmaraṇamokṣāya = jarā — bodily deterioration + maraṇa — bodily death + mokṣāya — to permanent release; mām — Me; āśritya — being dependent; yatanti — strive; ye — who; te — they; brahma — spiritual existence; tad — this; viduḥ — they know; kṛtsnam — complete; adhyātmam — Supreme Self; karma — cultural activity; cākhilam = ca — and + akhilam — entirely

Those who, being dependent on Me, strive for permanent release from bodily deterioration and death, know this spiritual existence completely, as well as the Supreme Spirit and the value of cultural activity. (7.29)

Commentary:

This verse applies to the rare advanced devotees of Krishna who are within the *jñānī* category as described. Some transcendentalists advocated *brahman* (complete spiritual existence) but not all of them speak of reliance on Krishna (*māmāśritya*). Thus some who are attracted to the complete, unadulterated, *brahman* (spiritual energy) are not necessarily devotees of Krishna. This verse applies to His devotees only. To desire release from bodies which bear old age and death is to desire release from the material energy completely. And it would mean also, wanting release from one's own material nature or from the portion of material nature's life energies which carry the soul life after life in a subtle and causal body. Such a feat is an extraordinary accomplishment for any limited entity. Such souls are very rare. We know that Markandeya Rishi is said to be such a great entity and there are others like *Narāda* Muni, King Priyavrata and Dhruva.

Some modern Vaishnavas minimize the striving element, replacing it entirely with the grace factor. But this verse stresses *yatanti*, which means that they strive or are striving for release. The attraction to material nature is causeless. The living entity must realize this and then work for self-purification to get beyond the need for material nature. With the Lord's assistance, if he strives sufficiently, he gains release. The requirements are very high because such a devotee must also be aware of the Supreme Spirit (*adhyātman*) and of the whole range of activities which may bind or liberate a limited entity.

साधिभूताधिदैवं मां
साधियज्ञं च ये विदुः ।
प्रयाणकालेऽपि च मां
ते विदुर्युक्तचेतसः ॥७.३०॥
sādhibhūtādhidaivaṁ māṁ
sādhiyajñaṁ ca ye viduḥ
prayāṇakāle'pi ca māṁ
te viduryuktacetasaḥ (7.30)

sādhibhūtādhidaivam = sa — with + adhibhūta — Lord of mundane beings + adhidaivam — Lord of the supernatural rulers and powers; mām — Me; sādhiyajñam = sa — with + adhiyajñam — Supreme Master of religious discipline; ca — and; ye — who; viduḥ — they know; prayāṇakāle — at the time of final departure from the body; 'pi = api — even; ca — and; mām — Me; te — they; vidur = viduḥ — know; yuktacetasaḥ — those with concentrated mental focus

Those who know Me as the Lord of mundane beings, Lord of the supernatural rulers and powers, and Supreme Master of religious disciplines, and who know Me even at the time of the final departure from the body, are the ones who know Me with concentrated mental focus. (7.30)

Commentary:

In the previous verse and in this verse, Lord Krishna identified Himself as the Supreme Self, as the Lord of mundane beings, as the Lord of the supernatural people and powers, and as the Supreme Master of the religious ceremonies and disciplines. Arjuna will ask for more substantiation of these claims.

Krishna explained that a devotee who is aware of divine supremacy as He described it, and who maintains a steady absorption in consciousness upon Krishna in the desired way, would be released from material existence. It is amazing that anyone could reduce the path set forth by Krishna in the *Gītā* as being something easy. When we hear of the requirements for those who reached the end of their material existence (*antagatam*) by the method of Krishna Consciousness, we are frightened by the higher requirements which many of us surely cannot reach, at least not in this life. The total absorption required is a high, very demanding and complete discipline (*yajñam*).

CHAPTER 8

Another Invisible Existence*

अर्जुन उवाच
किं तद्ब्रह्म किमध्यात्मं
किं कर्म पुरुषोत्तम ।
अधिभूतं च किं प्रोक्तम्
अधिदैवं किमुच्यते ॥८.१॥
arjuna uvāca
kiṁ tadbrahma kimadhyātmaṁ
kiṁ karma puruṣottama
adhibhūtaṁ ca kiṁ proktam
adhidaivaṁ kimucyate (8.1)

arjuna — Arjuna; uvāca — said; kim — what; tad — this; brahma — spiritual reality; kim — what; adhyātmam — Supreme Soul; kim — what; karma — cultural activity; puruṣottama — Supermost Personality; adhibhūtam — sum total gross reality; ca — and; kim — what; proktam — authoritatively described as; adhidaivam — Supreme Supernatural Person and Power; kim — what; ucyate — is described

Arjuna said: What is this spiritual reality? What is the Supreme Soul? What is cultural activity, O Supermost Personality? Concerning the sum total gross reality, how is that described authoritatively? And speaking of the Supreme Supernatural Person and Power, what is that described to be? (8.1)

Commentary:

The last two verses of Chapter Seven were so concentrated and required so much understanding by a limited entity, that even Arjuna did not understand them completely when he heard from Krishna. Before Krishna continued the discourse, Arjuna asked for more clarification. Even today, people in India and elsewhere do not know where the *brahman* is. Even though we hear about it, the most we know, is that one group of transcendentalists advocate it as the Supreme. Others minimize it as being non-personal. But it is doubtful if even the advocates understand it. Some say that it cannot be explained thoroughly because it transcends reason and words.

Arjuna asked about it: *kim tad brahma*. This is to say: What (*kim*) is this (*tad*) spirituality (*brahman*)? Yes, we are behind Arjuna urging him to ask the question again and again until we get some definite idea of this. Since Krishna claimed to know everything, He ought to give a satisfactory answer. What is that spiritual reality?

In verses 29 and 30 of Chapter 7, Krishna identified Himself as the *adhyātman*, the Supreme or Primal Soul. But Arjuna might have missed that because the Lord did not pause between the verses and only at a second glance or after consideration would Arjuna realize that *adhyātman* in verse 29 applies to *mām* (Krishna) in verse 30. Krishna already said that He is the one, but Arjuna persisted with the question anyway. Arjuna pushed for a complete answer and Krishna will show the Universal Form to prove it.

**The Mahābhārata contains no chapter headings. This title was assigned by the translator on the basis of the verse above*

Arjuna asked about actions. Unless one understands these, there is absolutely no hope that one could get out of material existence. One's affiliation with material nature would promote further mundane involvement on and on, endlessly. One would be drawn back repeatedly into material existence without ever coming to an ending point (*antagatam*).

Arjuna addressed Lord Krishna as *puruṣottama*, the Supermost (*uttama*) of the Personalities (*puruṣa*). But if Arjuna really understood what that address meant he would not have asked Krishna about the identity of the Supreme Soul. He addressed Krishna in this way both as a way of respect and for clarification.

Arjuna asked about the Lord of the sum total reserve of subtle and gross material elements. Who could that person be? What is the size of the body of such a personality? How does he control such an extended reality? Arjuna inquired of the Lord of the supernatural persons and powers. What sort of potency would that person possess? What sort of resistance to the supreme will does He tolerate from others?

अधियज्ञः कथं कोऽत्र
देहेऽस्मिन्मधुसूदन ।
प्रयाणकाले च कथं
ज्ञेयोऽसि नियतात्मभिः ॥८.२॥
adhiyajñaḥ kathaṁ ko'tra
dehe'sminmadhusūdana
prayāṇakāle ca kathaṁ
jñeyo'si niyatātmabhiḥ (8.2)

adhiyajñaḥ — Supreme Regulator of religious ceremonies and disciplines; katham — how; ko = kaḥ — who; tra = atra — here; dehe — in the body; 'smin = asmin — in this; madhusūdana — O slayer of Madhu; prayāṇakāle — at the time of departure from the body; ca — and; katham — how; jñeyo = jñeyaḥ - to be known; 'si = asi — you are; niyatātmabhiḥ = niyata — subdued + ātmabhiḥ — by persons

Who is the Supreme Regulator of religious ceremonies and disciplines? How is He located here in this body, O killer of Madhu? And how, at the time of departure from the body, are You to be known by those persons who are subdued? (8.2)

Commentary:

The common meaning for *yajña* is sacrifice, Vedic fire sacrifice. We used a seemingly new meaning: religious disciplines. In Chapter Four, verses 24 through 33, Lord Krishna used that meaning by including various types of sacrifices (*evam bahuvidhā yajñā*, 4.32) which included the common meaning. Arjuna wanted to know about the Supreme Regulator of the disciplines. He wanted to know how that Person was located in the human body.

Lord Krishna spoke of how the advanced devotees become absorbed in Him at the time of death. Arjuna wanted some more details. He identified those advanced devotees as the *niyatātmas*, persons with controlled (*niyata*) personality (*ātma*).

श्रीभगवानुवाच
अक्षरं ब्रह्म परमं
स्वभावोऽध्यात्ममुच्यते ।
भूतभावोद्भवकरो
विसर्गः कर्मसंज्ञितः ॥८.३॥
śrībhagavānuvāca
akṣaraṁ brahma paramaṁ
svabhāvo'dhyātmamucyate
bhūtabhāvodbhavakaro
visargaḥ karmasaṁjñitaḥ (8.3)

śrībhagavān — the Blessed Lord; uvāca — said; akṣaram — unaffected; brahma — spiritual reality; paramam — supreme; svabhāvo = svabhāvaḥ — personal nature; 'dhyātmam = adhyātmam — supreme soul; ucyate — it is said; bhūtabhāvodbhavakaro = bhūtabhāva — existence of mundane forms + udbhava — production + karo (karaḥ) — causing; visargah — creative power; karmasaṁjñitaḥ = karma — cultural activity + saṁjñitaḥ — is known

The Blessed Lord said: The spiritual reality is unaffected and supreme. The Supreme Soul is described as a personal existence Who causes the production of the mundane world. Cultural action is known as creative power. (8.3)

Commentary:

These are very terse answers but we will get more details elsewhere in the *Gītā*. Such subject matter was taught by the Upanishadic sages to their disciples while their discipoles attended the small private schools held by those teachers. We heard that Lord Krishna also attended such a school. He was sent there by His father, Prince Vasudeva. What Krishna and Balarama learnt is described in brief in the *Śrīmad Bhāgavatam*:

tayor dvija-varas tuṣṭaḥ śuddha-bhavānuvṛttibhiḥ
provāca vedān akhilān saṅgopaniṣado guruḥ
sa-rahasyaṁ dhanur-vedaṁ dharmān nyāya-pathāṁs tathā
tathā cānvīkṣikīṁ vidyāṁ rāja-nītiṁ ca ṣaḍ-vidhām

Being pleased with Their pure-minded attitude, that best of the initiated brahmins, Their spiritual teacher, taught Them the entire Vedas along with the related sciences and Upanishads,

...along with the science of archery with its secrets, as well as the knowledge in the books on righteous behavior, the methods of logic and the six-fold political science. (10.45.33-34)

It is also said that Lord Krishna got specific spiritual information from sage Ghora Angiras:

taddhai tad ghora āṅgirasaḥ
kṛṣṇaya devakīputrāyoktvovā cāpipāsa
eva sa babhūva so 'ntavelāyāmetattrayaṁ
pratipadyetāksitamas yac yutamasi
prāṇa saṁśitamasīti tatraite dve ṛcau bhavatah

Ghora Angirasa explained this well-known information to Devaki's son Krishna and said, "Such a knower should, at the time of death, repeat these three coded sentences; "You, O soul, are imperishable. You, O soul, are unchangeable. You, O soul, are the subtle essence." (Hearing that instruction), Krishna became satisfied. There are two Rig Veda verses in regards to this. (Chandogya Upanishad. 3.17.6)

The Upanishadic sages established the existence of the brahman, the spiritual reality. They described it extensively in their teachings. Thus it was unusual for Arjuna to ask for clarification on it. Even though it was described, the description concerned something that was vague to human understanding and abstract to human senses. And from that angle, Arjuna had every right to ask for clarification.

Even the laws of nature which affect gross reality are sometimes forgotten by us. How then can we be aware of spiritual factors which affect that which we cannot perceive?

For a description of *brahman*, Lord Krishna gave *akṣaram* and *paramam*. *Akṣaram* means that which is imperishable and eternal, that which cannot be altered, adjusted or affected. *Paramam* means that which is supreme. Again, these descriptions do not explain everything about *brahman*. These two terms alone are insufficient for our understanding, but they do give us some idea. The word *brahman* was translated in many ways. This writer gives "spiritual reality". We gave this on the basis of the overall description of it in the *Bhagavad Gītā*. This spiritual reality is said to be imperishable and was regarded as the basis of everything we perceive.

The Supreme Spirit, or Primal Person, the *adhyātman*, is said to be located within the psyche or the subtle compartment (*svabhāva*) in which the soul is housed in the material creation. It is said that He, the Primal Person, is the originator of all psyches or subtle compartments. Lord Krishna explained this in more detail in His description of the Supersoul. Action, which Arjuna inquired of, was defined as a creative power of all visible potency, *visargah. Visargah*, however, may apply to subtle potency which cannot be seen through physical vision.

अधिभूतं क्षरो भावः
पुरुषश्चाधिदैवतम् ।
अधियज्ञोऽहमेवात्र
देहे देहभृतां वर ॥८.४॥
adhibhūtaṁ kṣaro bhāvaḥ
puruṣaścādhidaivatam
adhiyajño'hamevātra
dehe dehabhṛtāṁ vara (8.4)

adhibhūtam — sum total gross reality; kṣaro = kṣaraḥ — ever-changing; bhāvaḥ — nature; puruṣaścādhidaivatam = puruṣa — master of the world + ca — and + adhidaivatam — Lord of the Supernatural rulers and powers; adhiyajño = adhiyajñaḥ — the Supreme Regulator of religious ceremonies and disciplines; 'ham = aham — I; evātra = eva — indeed + atra — here; dehe — in the body; dehabhṛtām vara — O best of the embodied souls

The sum total gross reality is ever-changing nature. The master of the world is the Lord of the supernatural rulers and powers. O best of the embodied souls, I, Who exist here in the body, am the Supreme Regulator of religious ceremonies and disciplines. (8.4)

Commentary:

By using the word *kṣaro*, Lord Krishna described the primal substance of the world, the material energy in all its forms and shapes, as being ever-changing and temporary, as being unstable, not reliable. He labeled the Lord of the supernaturals as a person, as *puruṣa*, and not as an impersonal spiritual energy. His view is that supernatural people are supervised by the Supreme Person. Lord Krishna then identified Himself (*'ham or aham)* as the Supreme Regulator of religious disciplines (*yajña*). This was established in Chapter Seven and elsewhere.

For some readers, there might be a problem of evidence. For all this self-acclaim by Lord Krishna, sufficient evidence is not shown. Thus far, His word only was given.

अन्तकाले च मामेव
स्मरन्मुक्त्वा कलेवरम् ।
यः प्रयाति स मद्भावं
याति नास्त्यत्र संशयः ॥८.५॥
antakāle ca māmeva
smaranmuktvā kalevaram
yaḥ prayāti sa madbhāvaṁ
yāti nāstyatra saṁśayaḥ (8.5)

antakāle — at the end of life; ca — and; mām — Me; eva — in particular; smaran — remembering; muktvā — giving up; kalevaram — body; yaḥ — who; prayāti — departs the body; sa = saḥ — he; madbhāvam — My condition of existence; yāti — is elevated; nāsty (nasti) = na — not + asti — is; atra — here; saṁśayaḥ — doubt

If at the end of one's life, one recalls Me in particular, as one gives up the body, one is elevated to My condition of existence. There is no doubt about this. (8.5)

Commentary:

Even though *eva* is a minor word in Sanskrit, it has the most importance in this verse as being: *in particular, especially, only, alone*.

The memory of Krishna must have that quality of singularness and one must know Krishna sufficiently, just as Arjuna knew Krishna. To be elevated to Krishna's condition of existence (*madbhāvam*) is not an ordinary achievement for any living being in this world.

यं यं वापि स्मरन्भावं
त्यजत्यन्ते कलेवरम् ।
तं तमेवैति कौन्तेय
सदा तद्भावभावितः ॥८.६॥
yaṁ yaṁ vāpi smaranbhāvaṁ
tyajatyante kalevaram
taṁ tamevaiti kaunteya
sadā tadbhāvabhāvitaḥ (8.6)

yaṁ yam - whatever; vāpi = va — or + api — also; moreover; smaran — recalling; bhāvam — texture of existence; tyajaty = tyajati — abandons; ante — in the end; kalevaram - the body; taṁtam - that that; evaiti = eva - indeed + eti — is projected; kaunteya - O son of Kuntī; sadā - always; tad — that + bhāva — status of life + bhāvitaḥ — being transformed

Moreover, whatever texture of existence is recalled when a person abandons his body in the end, to that same type of life, he is projected, O son of Kuntī, always being transformed into that status of life. (8.6)

Commentary:

This is not a very promising outlook, since it would depend not on our religious faith, nor on our hopes for salvation, but on the actual state of consciousness at the time of death. The texture of existence we recall at that crucial time would determine the type of existence we would be projected into in the hereafter and also the type of life we would get in the next location. By stating *sadā*, that it is always like this, Lord Krishna left no room for fanciful hopes.

तस्मात्सर्वेषु कालेषु
मामनुस्मर युध्य च ।
मय्यर्पितमनोबुद्धिर्
मामेवैष्यस्यसंशयः ॥८.७॥
tasmātsarveṣu kāleṣu
māmanusmara yudhya ca
mayyarpitamanobuddhir
māmevaiṣyasyasaṁśayaḥ (8.7)

tasmāt — therefore; sarveṣu — at all; kāleṣu — at times; mām — Me; anusmara — remember; yudhya — fight; ca — and; mayy = mayi — on Me; arpitamanobuddhir (arpitamanobuddhiḥ) = arpita — anchor + manobuddhiḥ — mind and intelligence; mām — to Me; evaiṣyasy (evaiṣyasi) = eva — indeed + eṣyasi — will be with; asaṁśayaḥ — without doubt

Therefore, at all times, remember Me and fight. Anchor your mind and intelligence on Me. You will be with Me without doubt. (8.7)

Commentary:

This is the advice for those who want to attain a condition of existence that is similar to Lord Krishna's. We must remember that insofar as we do not have experience of these truths, it would be our faith in Krishna only that would keep us believing His ideas in the *Gītā*. In this Chapter Eight, however, there is a big turning point in the *Gītā*, as more and more, Lord Krishna puts Himself forward as the one and only worthy focus of attention. He repeatedly stressed Himself to Arjuna.

अभ्यासयोगयुक्तेन
चेतसा नान्यगामिना ।
परमं पुरुषं दिव्यं
याति पार्थानुचिन्तयन् ॥८.८॥
abhyāsayogayuktena
cetasā nānyagāminā
paramaṁ puruṣaṁ divyaṁ
yāti pārthānucintayan (8.8)

abhyāsa — practice;. yoga — yoga; yuktena — by discipline; cetasā — by the mind; nānyagāminā = na — not + anya —other + gāminā — by venturing outward; paramam — supreme; puruṣam — person; divyam — divine; yāti — one goes; pārthānucintayan = pārtha — son of Pṛthā + anucintayan — deeply meditating

With a mind that does not venture outwards, which is disciplined by yoga practice, a person goes to the divine Supreme Person, while deeply meditating, O son of Pṛthā. (8.8)

Commentary:

This verse is a return to the topic of mind focus, thought focus, and meditation on the Supreme Person. Here Lord Krishna did not mentioned Himself. He substituted the *paramam puruṣam divyam* (the Divine Supreme Person). In other words, He accredited even those meditators who are not particularly meditating on Him, but who instead focus on the Divine Supreme Person, Whoever that may be. Of course, Krishna repeatedly identified Himself with, and suggested that He is the Supreme Person. But in this verse, He did not specify Himself.

कविं पुराणमनुशासितारम्
अणोरणीयांसमनुस्मरेद्यः ।
सर्वस्य धातारमचिन्त्यरूपम्
आदित्यवर्णं तमसः परस्तात् ॥८.९॥
kaviṁ purāṇamanuśāsitāram
aṇoraṇīyāṁsamanusmaredyaḥ
sarvasya dhātāram acintyarūpam
ādityavarṇaṁ tamasaḥ parastāt
(8.9)

kavim — the person who knows everything; purāṇam — the most ancient; anuśāsitāram — the supreme supervisor; aṇor (aṇoḥ)- than the atom; aṇīyāṁsam — more minute; anusmared (anusmaret)- should meditate on; yaḥ — who; sarvasya — of all; dhātāram supporter; acintya — unimaginable + rūpam — form; ādityavarṇam = āditya —radiance + varṇam — category; tamasaḥ — grossness; parastāt — distinct form

He who meditates on the Person Who knows everything, the most ancient of people, the Supreme Supervisor, the most minute factor, the one with unimaginable form, with a radiant body, free of grossness, (8.9)

Commentary:

A tremendous amount of leeway is given for meditation on the Supreme Spirit. Even if one cannot accept Krishna as the Supreme Lord, one should meditate on the Supreme Spirit as fitting the description above. One may or may not believe in Lord Krishna but this advice to meditate on the Supreme Person is beneficial for anyone.

As *kavim*, that Supreme Person must be the know-it-all, the omniscient one. He must be the most ancient person even though His form must not be aged and wrinkled. He must be the Supreme Supervisor. He must be able to penetrate the most minute of things. He must be the supporter of all and His form must be unimaginable. He must be radiant and free from grossness.

प्रयाणकाले मनसाचलेन
भक्त्या युक्तो योगबलेन चैव ।
भ्रुवोर्मध्ये प्राणमावेश्य सम्यक्
स तं परं पुरुषमुपैति दिव्यम् ॥८.१०॥
prayāṇakāle manasācalena
bhaktyā yukto yogabalena caiva
bhruvormadhye prāṇam āveśya samyak
sa taṁ paraṁ puruṣamupaiti divyam (8.10)

prayāṇakāle — at the time of death; manasācalena = manasā — by the mind + acalena- by unwavering; bhaktyā — with devotion; yukto = yuktaḥ — connected; yogabalena — with psychological power developed through yoga practice; caiva = ca — and + eva — indeed; bhruvor = bhruvoḥ — of the two eyebrows; madhye — in the middle; prāṇam — energizing breath; āveśya- having caused to enter; samyak — precisely; sa = saḥ — he; tam - this; param — supreme; puruṣam- person; upaiti — he goes; divyam — divine

...and that meditator who even at the time of death, with an unwavering mind, being connected devotedly, with psychological power developed through yoga practice, and having caused the energizing breath to enter between the eyebrows with precision, goes to the Divine Supreme Person. (8.10)

Commentary:

In this and the two previous verses, some leeway is given to the meditators who do not necessarily call on Krishna or know Krishna as He described Himself to Arjuna, but who know of the unnamed Supreme Spirit as defined in the previous verse and elsewhere in the *Gītā*. Thus Lord Krishna does make space in the *Gītā* for meditators who seek out the Supreme Being by the attributes specified.

The standard methods used by the meditators in the time of Lord Krishna are explained in the *Gītā*. These are time-proven procedures through which serious ascetics got association with the Supreme Divine Person.

Yogabalena means by the strength of yoga practice which consists of *āsana* postures, *prāṇāyāma* breath nutrition techniques and finally mystic concentration and meditation. The *prāṇāyāma* breath nutrition techniques are indicated by the terms in the third line: *bhruvor madhye prāṇam āveśya samyak.*

This means that the life energy (*prāṇam*) is centered precisely through (*āveśya samyak*) the middle of the eyebrows (*bhruvor madhye*). This *prāṇāyāma* concentration technique is applied while performing such *mudrās* as *yoni, unmani, and sambhavi*. This cannot be done successfuly unless one has mastered it before the time of death. It takes some years to master these techniques. The successful use of these procedures is possible when the yogi retracts all of his spinal gyrating centers and pulls all such energy into his brain. In the advanced stages, this is done mentally but initially one has to train the life energy to obey the commands. This takes years. This particular technique became very popular in the Western countries after the appearance of Sri Paramhamsa Yogananda, a *kriyā* master in the lineage of Sri Lahiri Mahasaya.

We can know, however, from this verse of the *Gītā*, that despite the criticism which comes from many Vaishnava teachers, the *kriyā* masters use a procedure which is recognized and authorized in the *Gītā*. In fact, many of the *kriyā* masters do not accept Krishna wholely and solely as Krishna presented Himself to Arjuna, but in this verse, a leeway is given by Lord Krishna to these yogis, who, even though they may not accept His declarations, can aim for the association of the Divine Supreme Personality (*paramam puruṣam divyam*).

One thing is certain, however: Those *kriyā* yogis will not be associating with the

Supreme Spirit unless they have *bhaktyā yukto*, applied steadfast devotion to the Supreme Personality as described. The mystic yogis who do not accept Krishna as Krishna presents Himself, but who sincerely apply consistent devotion *(bhaktyā yukto)* to Lord Vishnu, Lord *Nārāyaṇa*, or even for Lord Shiva, the Master of the Yogis, will get success.

यदक्षरं वेदविदो वदन्ति
विशन्ति यद्यतयो वीतरागाः ।
यदिच्छन्तो ब्रह्मचर्यं चरन्ति
तत्ते पदं संग्रहेण प्रवक्ष्ये ॥८.११॥
yadakṣaraṁ vedavido vadanti
viśanti yadyatayo vītarāgāḥ
yadicchanto brahmacaryaṁ caranti
tatte padaṁ saṁgraheṇa pravakṣye
(8.11)

yad — which; akṣaram — imperishable; vedavido = vedavidaḥ — knowers of the Veda; vadanti — they described; viśanti — they enter; yad — which; yatayo = yatayaḥ — ascetics; vītarāgāḥ — free from cravings; yad — which; icchanto = icchantaḥ — desiring; brahmacaryam — life of celibacy; caranti — they follow; tat = tad — this; te — to you; padam — process; saṁgraheṇa — in brief; pravakṣye — I will explain

I will briefly explain the process to you, which the knowers of the Veda describe as imperishable, which the ascetics who are free from cravings enter and who desiring to be transferred there, they follow a life of celibacy. (8.11)

Commentary:

This is more information on what the *kriyā* yogis do. Some of these yogis do not focus on the Supreme Spirit as described in the previous three verses. Instead they focus on the *brahman* which is listed in this verse as the *akṣaram*, the imperishable unaffected energy. Thus, that is also the location. Some Vaishnavas brand this location as the impersonal energy, the *brahman* effulgence. They shun it and take steps to discourage anyone from approaching it. However, we will hear from Lord Krishna on this matter. He told Arjuna that He would explain what these yogis practice. A technical word, *brahmācārya*, is listed as part of the requirement to be met by those ascetics. This is usually translated as celibacy. It is, however, more than celibacy because it means practice which reinforces the focus on the *brahman* (spiritual energy). And for celibacy, it means yoga austerities which move the sexual hermones up through the body away from the sexual organs of the body. This is celibacy through *āsana* and *prāṇāyāma* practices.

सर्वद्वाराणि संयम्य
मनो हृदि निरुध्य च ।
मूर्ध्न्याधायात्मनः प्राणम्
आस्थितो योगधारणाम् ॥८.१२॥
sarvadvārāṇi saṁyamya
mano hṛdi nirudhya ca
mūrdhnyādhāyātmanaḥ prāṇam
āsthito yogadhāraṇām (8.12)

sarvadvārāṇi = sarva — all + dvārāṇi — entrances; saṁyamya — controlling; mano = manaḥ — mind; hṛdi — in the core of consciousness; nirudhya — confining; ca — and; mūrdhny = mūrdhni — in the brain; ādhāyātmanaḥ = ādhāya — situating + ātmanaḥ — of the soul; prāṇam — energizing breath; āsthito = āsthitaḥ — remain fixed; yogadhāraṇām — yoga concentration

Controlling all openings of the body, and restricting the mind in the core of consciousness, situating the energizing energy of the soul in the brain, remaining fixed in yoga concentration, (8.12)

Commentary:

This practice applies to yogi devotees of Krishna and yogis who are not devotees of Krishna but who are aiming at the Supreme Person as described. Many modern devotees of Krishna who are on the popular path of Krishna consciousness, scoff at persons who practice these yogic methods. But here in the *Gītā*, the Lord does not express a dislike for it. Some modern Vaishnava teachers propagate the idea that no true devotees of Krishna would use any such method but the *Gītā* does not say this.

The word *hṛdi* is usually translated as heart, but it also means central consciousness. As it applies here, *hṛdi* does not mean the physical heart. The process of placing the life force in the skull (*murdhny ādhāyātmanah prāṇam*) is known as *kuṇḍalinī* yoga but some consider it as a *kriyā* practice or as an advanced *haṭha* yoga practice. Others see it as a part of *prāṇāyāma* practice.

These processes cannot be learned unless one has the direction of a person who mastered the process, but that person may not be using a physical body. If by the grace of the Lord and by the benefit of past births, one has keen mystic perception, he can learn these from a yoga master who has no physical body but who resides in the astral world. The yoga master must descend at least to the astral level to assist the neophyte yogis. For those without mystic perception, their only alternative, if they are seriously interested, is to find an expert who has a physical body. Such yogi experts, however, are rare. They are very hard to find. Most yogis do not become this advanced in the practice.

By a twist of planetary fate, most modern devotees of Krishna lost interest in the yoga they might have practiced in past lives. In fact, most of the devotees are hostile to yoga. They are quite satisfied hearing scripture, chanting recommended Holy Names of the Lord, and doing service to support the preaching mission of their teachers. Whatever is required for such a preaching mission is considered as devotional service by modern devotees. But it is seen, that sometimes, certain activities which pass this way are proven to be deviant.

Still there are a few *bhakti* yogis who practice yoga. But these are few and far between. Due to the general hostility they face from their devotional friends, they are usually hidden from view, since otherwise they are affected by drastic criticism from the non-yogi devotees who are in the majority.

ओमित्येकाक्षरं ब्रह्म
व्याहरन्मामनुस्मरन् ।
यः प्रयाति त्यजन्देहं
स याति परमां गतिम् ॥८.१३॥
omityekākṣaraṁ brahma
vyāharanmāmanusmaran
yaḥ prayāti tyajandehaṁ
sa yāti paramāṁ gatim (8.13)

om — the uttered sound om; ity = iti — thus saying; ekākṣaram — one syllable; brahma — spiritual reality; vyāharan — chanting; mām — Me; anusmaran — meditating on; yaḥ — who; prayāti — passes on; tyajan — renouncing; deham — body; sa = saḥ — he; yāti — attains; paramām — supreme; gatim — objective

...uttering *Om,* the one-syllable sound which represents the spiritual reality, meditating on Me, the yogi who passes on, renouncing the body, attains the highest objective. (8.13)

Commentary:

Here again, Lord Krishna put Himself forward as the objective even of these yogis. Even though some modern Vaishnavas dismiss yoga as being irrelevant to salvation, still it was mentioned by Krishna at the close of the *Dvāpara Yuga*, just before the *Kali* era began.

After elaborating on what the yogis do, Lord Krishna again presented Himself as the focus. He particularly said *mām anusmaram*, which means, *meditating, thinking or remembering Me (Krishna)*. In this verse, we do not get any details of the highest objective, the *paramām gatim*, but there is information elsewhere.

अनन्यचेताः सततं
यो मां स्मरति नित्यशः ।
तस्याहं सुलभः पार्थ
नित्ययुक्तस्य योगिनः ॥८.१४॥
ananyacetāḥ satataṁ
yo māṁ smarati nityaśaḥ
tasyāhaṁ sulabhaḥ pārtha
nityayuktasya yoginaḥ (8.14)

ananyacetāḥ — one whose mind does not go to another focus; satatam — perpetually; yo = yaḥ — who; mām — Me; smarati — he remembers; nityaśaḥ — constantly; tasyāham = tasya — to him + aham — I; sulabhaḥ — easy to reach; pārtha — O son of Pṛthā; nityayuktasya — of one who is constantly disciplined in yoga; yoginaḥ — of the devotee

He whose mind does not go to another focus at any time, who thinks of Me constantly, for that yogi who is constantly disciplined in yoga, I am easy to reach, O son of Pṛthā. (8.14)

Commentary:

We heard that the path of the yogis is most difficult and when we study the austerities the yogis perform, we can easily understand why this is said. But this is a statement of the ease with which some yogis reach Krishna. Some commentators gave "devotee" for the word *yoginah*, but if we follow this discourse carefully, we can see that this Sanskrit word applies to yogis. At least that is the context of the word *yoginah* in this verse. This verse is interpreted differently according to the missionary aims of the various commentators but if we want to understand it in its own place in the text, we must follow the preceding verses and not twist the meaning.

Yogis who are practiced at mind control and who have mastered that process, who do not allow their minds to go anywhere else (*ananya*) and who constantly think of Lord Krishna as described in the previous verse (*mām anusmaram*), reach Krishna easily. This is obvious because these yogis have the surest method of perfection. They have the most consistent and definite course. It is hardly likely that they would be distracted. What we are discussing here, is their steady focus on Krishna with devotion.

Devotion to Krishna is everything if the devotee is purified, but if he is not, his devotion will not take him to the spiritual locations of Krishna but rather it will keep him in the material world as a devotee of Krishna perpetually, at least until he becomes purified. The process of yoga, as stated before in the *Gītā*, is a specific process for purification of the psyche and the life energy. Because of that purity, the yogis find it easy to reach Krishna in the spiritual places which are beyond this material world. An impure devotee cannot reach Krishna there because the impurities will keep him in the material atmosphere. But if permitted, he may reach Krishna here in this material setting.

मामुपेत्य पुनर्जन्म
दुःखालयमशाश्वतम् ।
नाप्नुवन्ति महात्मानः
संसिद्धिं परमां गताः ॥८.१५॥

mām — Me; upetya — approaching; punarjanma — rebirth; duḥkhālayam = duḥkha — misery + ālayam — location; aśāśvatam — shifty; nāpnuvanti = na — not + apnuvanti — subjected to; mahātmānaḥ —

māmupetya punarjanma
duḥkhālayamaśāśvatam
nāpnuvanti mahātmānaḥ
saṁsiddhiṁ paramāṁ gatāḥ (8.15)

great souls; saṁsiddhim — perfect; paramām — supreme; gatāḥ — gone

Approaching me in this way, those great souls who went to supreme perfection are not subjected to rebirth in this shifty, miserable location. (8.15)

Commentary:

Again we remain in the context of this chapter and of the verses preceding this one, to know that Krishna is speaking of those fully-accomplished, yogi devotees. Some translators take these special verses and apply them to other types of devotees according to various missionary objectives. But if we want to understand *Gītā*, in its own time and place, as Arjuna heard it and applied it, we must stick to the text.

These great souls (*mahātmānah*) are yogi devotees, not others, not even great politicians and martyrs of India who, in these modern times, carry the title *mahātma* to their names. A contrast is given between this miserable, shifty, material place and that of the supreme location. According to Lord Krishna, once these yogi devotees attain the spiritual location, they do not return to this shifty place.

आ ब्रह्मभुवनाल्लोकाः
पुनरावर्तिनोऽर्जुन ।
मामुपेत्य तु कौन्तेय
पुनर्जन्म न विद्यते ॥८.१६॥
ā brahmabhuvanāllokāḥ
punarāvartino'rjuna
māmupetya tu kaunteya
punarjanma na vidyate (8.16)

ā — up to; brahmabhuvanāl = brahmabhuvanāt — to Brahmā's world; lokāḥ — populations; punarāvartino = punarāvartinaḥ — subjected to repeated birth and death; 'rjuna = arjuna — Arjuna; mām — Me; upetya — approaching; tu — but; kaunteya — O son of Kuntī; punarjanma — impulsion of rebirth; na — not; vidyate — is experienced

Up to Brahmā's world, the populations are subjected to repeated births and deaths, O Arjuna. But in approaching Me, rebirth is not experienced, O son of Kuntī. (8.16)

Commentary:

This is one of the most frequently quoted verses of the *Gītā*. It is especially dear to devotees of Krishna. But this verse applies to those devotees of Krishna or devotees of the Supreme Spirit as Krishna defined, who reached an existential status that is near to (upetya) Krishna. The existential status must also be their living condition and not just their hope for salvation.

Any devotee of Krishna who has only a hope for salvation and who in his existential condition, is greatly reliant on material nature, even while believing in Krishna, will be subjected to rebirth. And the same applies to those who are not devotees of Krishna but who are devotees of the Supreme Spirit as described by Krishna in this chapter.

There is a world of difference between a devotee of Krishna and a non-devotee, but insofar as a man might not be a devotee of Krishna but might be a devotee of the Supreme Spirit as described by Krishna, that man is covered under certain guarantees stated by Krishna in the *Gītā*. There is also a world of difference between the advanced devotees of Krishna who have reached to an existential living situation that is near to that of the Lord and those devotees who are still living in existential dimensions which are under *Brahmā*'s jurisdiction.

But who is *Brahmā*? *Brahmā* is the local galactic creator or the local god of this world. He is the person who created the planets and the first creature forms merely by his will power. At least that is what we are told in the Vedic literature. According to that explanation of creation, all material planets in the universe are dependent on the mental energy of *Brahmā*. If he goes to sleep or if he passes away, then all these worlds which we see, are ruined. Beings in such a world are subjected to dimensional slips of their manifest existences. And that makes the place very insecure (*aśāśvatam*, 8.15)

The claim of Krishna is fantastic. He appeared in *Brahmā*'s creation and appears to be one of the results of *Brahmā*'s creative powers, and still He claims to be beyond *Brahmā*'s capacity and to transcend *Brahmā*'s creative monopoly. He claims to be outside of *Brahmā*'s control and to be non-reliant on and independent of *Brahmā*'s mental power.

If we accept what Krishna states, we are presently in a hairy-scary situation of being reliant on a limited god, on *Brahmā*, a person who cannot maintain the security forever and who will, of necessity, allow us to slip here, and slip there, existentially.

सहस्रयुगपर्यन्तम्
अहर्यद्ब्रह्मणो विदुः ।
रात्रिं युगसहस्रान्तां
तेऽहोरात्रविदो जनाः ॥८.१७॥
sahasrayugaparyantam
aharyadbrahmaṇo viduḥ
rātriṁ yugasahasrāntāṁ
te'horātravido janāḥ (8.17)

sahasra — one thousand + yuga — time cycle + paryantam — limit; ahar — day; yad — which; brahmaṇo = brahmaṇaḥ — of Brahmā; viduḥ — they know; rātrim — night; yugasahasrāntāṁ = yuga — time cycle + sahasra — one thousand + antam — end; te — they; 'horātravido (ahoratravidaḥ) = ahoratra — day and night + vidaḥ — knowers; janāḥ — people

Those who know the day of Brahmā, which has a limit of one thousand time cycles, and the night of Brahmā, which ends in a thousand time cycles, are the people who know day and night. (8.17)

Commentary:

The reckoning of time by the astrologers of Krishna's era is quite different from the figures of time by modern scientifically-minded astronomers. An elaborate study is required for anyone who seeks to understand how the Vedic time scale was calculated. Many doubts arise as to whether these calculations are speculative or not. Modern people look for concrete proof in the form of something they can see physically either directly with the eye of the human body or indirectly with the aid of modern scientific instruments. Thus there is a conflict between the ancient Vedic method and the modern scientific one.

It will suffice, however, for us to understand that *Brahmā* is supposed to be the creator of everything perceivable within this universe. Galaxies or star systems are regarded merely as levels of worlds within *Brahmā*'s creation. And *Brahmā* is seen as a sub-agent of God. The qualities of God mentioned in text 9 of this chapter are generally accepted in the Vedic fold but the name of that God is not agreed on. Some say it is Krishna, as Krishna professes. Others say it is Vishnu and that Krishna is merely Vishnu's incarnation. Others say that it is *Nārāyaṇa*. Others say that it is Shiva. The opinions vary. But the function of God is accepted by all who are believers in a Supreme Personality.

Bhagavad Gītā is part of the *Mahābhārata* history. This text is consistent with the *Śrīmad Bhāgavatam*, wherein *Brahmā* is presented as a sub-creator. According to that text, *Brahmā* lives for one hundred celestial years and then his subtle body dies. But at the end of each of his days he goes to sleep. And when he does, these lower worlds are temporarily ruined. As soon as he arises the next morning, these worlds are re-created afresh. *Brahmā*'s planet and others that are near to his are not destroyed during his daily slumber, but they are totally ruined at the end of his 100 years of subtle life.

Readers who feel that these descriptions in the Vedic literature are so much of a myth or legend, need not despair. This *Gītā* translation is not a missionary work. This is simply an attempt to understand the *Gītā* in its own time and place. Thus we try to understand the information as it was presented in its own historic setting. We can understand the life of *Brahmā* by studying the life of a powerful capitalist. Such a person may order the shutdown of his factory at the end of each work day. For all practical purposes, we may say that the business collapses at the end of each work day and is re-established at the beginning of the next day. But at the end of the life of the capitalist, the business is ruined permanently. The workers who were dependent on him would be inconvenienced by a lack of salary. During the day of such a capitalist, the work shifts in the factory might be divided into two parts just as *Brahmā*'s day was divided into four, hundred-era time-blocks. And the night of the capitalist would be timed, even though activity would have stopped during his slumber.

Śrīla Bhaktivedanta Swami, our Vaishnava authority, gave the following figures:

Satya Yuga	1,728,000 years
Tretā Yuga	1,296,000 years
Dvāpara Yuga	864,000 years
Kali Yuga	432,000 years

He wrote that the four yugas (eras), in rotation of 100 times, comprise of one day of *Brahmā* and the same numbers comprise of *Brahmā*'s night. Furthermore, he wrote that *Brahmā*'s life of one hundred years is 311 trillion and 40 million earthly years.

When we consider that Lord Krishna told Arjuna of discourses with the solar king some thousands and thousands of years before Krishna's *Dvāpara* Yuga appearance, it is not fantastic for Krishna to describe the vast time-stretch of *Brahmā*'s life. If we follow Krishna's idea of Himself as well as His view of everyone else, it is easy to see how He could discuss these matters as if they were simple arithmetic. Readers are reminded to keep an open mind in terms of studying the *Gītā* in its own time and place.

अव्यक्ताद्व्यक्तयः सर्वाः
प्रभवन्त्यहरागमे ।
रात्र्यागमे प्रलीयन्ते
तत्रैवाव्यक्तसंज्ञके ॥८.१८॥
avyaktādvyaktayaḥ sarvāḥ
prabhavantyaharāgame
rātryāgame pralīyante
tatraivāvyaktasaṁjñake (8.18)

avyaktād = avyaktāt — from the invisible world; vyaktayaḥ — the visible world; sarvāḥ — all; prabhavanty = prabhavanti — they are produced; aharāgame — at the beginning of Brahmā's day; rātryāgame — at the beginning of Brahmā's night; pralīyante — they are reverted back; tatraivāvyaktasaṁjñake = tatra — at the time + eva — indeed + avyakta — invisible world + saṁjñake — is understood as

When the day of Creator Brahmā begins, all this visible world is produced from the invisible world. When his night comes, the manifested energies are reverted back into the invisible world. (8.18)

Commentary:

This is one thing that we can understand since the law of conservation of energy is visible to us even grossly. We see that a small seed exploits some earth and expands to potential. But parts of the plant revert back out of manifestation as it grows. And ultimately, the plant perishes and all the materials repose to the earth.

We are somewhat familiar with the visible world but what do we know about the invisible world (*avyakta*)? We know this much: The manifested energies come from that invisible world or as we commonly say, the energies seem to come from nowhere, from an abstract source. Thus when they are disintegrated, they again return to that invisible foundation. The great modern scientist Albert Einstein baffled the world with his understanding of the integration and disintegration of matter. He produced the formula $E=mc^2$: indicating that total energy in an object can be realized if the object or the vibrations within the object were impelled at a speed which is equivalent to the speed of light multiplied by itself or the speed of light squared. But this fancy formula simply means that the total energy of a visible form (*vyakta*) is converted out of visible existence or is thoroughly disintegrated if all particles in the body were to be subjected to a very high speed beyond the speed of light squared, and it is possible to slow down some of these energies. They are slowed down when we perceive them materially. We can just imagine the speed of vibration of the spiritual energies which are beyond this material scope. Albert Einstein, for all he was, could not even imagine something existing beyond the speed of light squared. At least he understood that from the material viewpoint, such things might well not exist or at least they could not be exploited by human beings.

भूतग्रामः स एवायं
भूत्वा भूत्वा प्रलीयते ।
रात्र्यागमेऽवशः पार्थ
प्रभवत्यहरागमे ॥८.१९॥

bhūtagrāmaḥ sa evāyaṁ
bhūtvā bhūtvā pralīyate
rātryāgame'vaśaḥ pārtha
prabhavatyaharāgame (8.19)

bhūtagrāmaḥ — multitude of beings; sa = saḥ — this; evāyam = eva — indeed + ayam — this; bhūtvā bhūtvā — repeatedly manifesting; pralīyate — is shifted out of visibility; rātryāgame — at the arrival of Brahmā's night; 'vaśaḥ = avaśaḥ — happening naturally; pārtha — O son of Pṛthā; prabhavaty = prabhavati — it comes into existence; aharāgame — on the onset of Brahmā's day

O son of Pṛthā, this multitude of beings which is repeatedly manifested, is naturally shifted out of visibility at the arrival of each of Brahmā's nights. It again comes into existence at the onset of Brahmā's day. (8.19)

Commentary:

This production of existence has nothing to do with the spirit or the *ātma*. And it should not be confused with that. We should not feel that the *ātma* is created by *Brahmā* or by the master of *Brahmā*, by God. In fact, the *ātma* is self-existent. It is not created. However, the manifested forms used by the *ātma* are definitely created under God's supervision. There is no doubt about that. But there is also a law of material existence which operates automatically to baffle the *ātma* or spirit. This law is indicated here by the impulsive, cyclic way of manifestation and demanifestation (*'vaśal, avaśah*).

The selves are self-existent, but they do have affectionate relationships with the Lord and with each other. Still, that does not mean that these relationships are exactly the same as that of a father who begets a body for a son in the womb of a woman nor with that of a father who exhibits a vulgar sexual love for his wife. The relationships are there on the spiritual plane but they are lacking in the vulgar context with which we are so familiar in the material world. In a sense, consciousness is affection. Therefore, relationships are natural for the living entities, one to another and from each of them individually to the Lord or to an empowered agent of the Divinity. But in the material world, vulgarity comes into play. And this is detrimental to the sanity of the living entities.

During *Brahmā*'s days, the world revolves as we observe but the world we perceive, is merely one such place. Other creations exist side by side with this one without ever clashing into this one. This is why they are not detected. All of these worlds which are produced by *Brahmā* depend on the mind of *Brahmā*. Thus when he sleeps, they perish. They actually become non-manifested but their essential energies are retrieved into the primal material potency and the spirits who utilized them are also retrieved back into spiritual existence from whence they originated.

How can we ascertain this? Can this be proven? Can a man see this as clearly as he sees the sun, the moon, or his material body? The answer is, of course: No, he cannot see it in that way. First he will have to equip himself with the necessary vision. And if he is not equipped, he will be left with a belief or disbelief. *Gītā* will state, however, that Arjuna was shown the mysteries of these creations. At least there is a history that one person, Arjuna, was shown this on request. While he viewed, others viewed as well. They viewed directly. We may view by the way of imagining what Arjuna experienced. Lord Krishna used a special word: *'vaśah (avaśah)*, which means that this takes place automatically. Material nature has a certain way in which it operates. More details of this will be given elsewhere as we progress through this information.

The multitude of beings of which we are a part, are manifested first on the level of ideation. This is called the causal plane. From there, they are manifested on the subtle plane which is the level of invisible, particle forms. These are forms of light and radio wave energy. From that plane, the physical forms are produced. But all these manifestations are repeatedly adjusted on and on until the night of *Brahmā* comes. Then the physical and subtle existence is destroyed. During the night of *Brahmā*, the causal forms, the forms of ideation, remain intact. At the dawn of his day, the causal bodies serve as the basis for the creation of new subtle forms. And those new subtle bodies resemble the old ones which were destroyed. The causal forms of ideation act as blueprints for the production of new subtle bodies in the exact configuration used in the last creation.

All this takes place automatically by the interaction of various potencies, but with some supervision of the Lord. However, it is not that the conditioned entities have any free will in the matter. They are under the influence of various energies at all times. Since they rely on material nature, their ideas are tarnished.

परस्तस्मात्तु भावोऽन्यो
ऽव्यक्तोऽव्यक्तात्सनातनः ।
यः स सर्वेषु भूतेषु
नश्यत्सु न विनश्यति ॥८.२०॥

parastasmāttu bhāvo'nyo
'vyakto'vyaktātsanātanaḥ
yaḥ sa sarveṣu bhūteṣu
naśyatsu na vinaśyati (8.20)

paraḥ — high; tasmāt — than this; tu — but; bhāvo = bhāvaḥ — existence; 'nyo = anyaḥ — another; 'vyakto = avyaktaḥ — invisible; 'vyaktāt = avyaktāt — than the unmanifest state of the dissolvable creation; sanātanaḥ — primeval; yaḥ = which; sa = saḥ — it; sarveṣu — in all; bhūteṣu — in creation; naśyatsu — in the disintegration; na — not; vinaśyati — is disintegrated

But higher than this, there is another invisible existence, which is higher than the primeval unmanifested states of this dissolvable creation. When all these creatures are disintegrated, that is not affected. (8.20)

Commentary:

A clear distinction between the manifested material world, the unmanifested basis of the material world, and the other place (*parah tasmāt*) is made in this verse. First we have the material world, the visible creation. But much of this creation is invisible to our present senses. The entire scope of the causal, subtle, and gross material creation is a manifested existence, even though much of it is invisible to us. And beyond that there is the primeval unmanifested state of the material energy which is termed as *'vyaktāt (avyaktāt) sanātanah*. But this primeval basis, though imperishable in itself, is different from the other existence mentioned by Krishna which He says is higher.

अव्यक्तोऽक्षर इत्युक्तस्
तमाहुः परमां गतिम् ।
यं प्राप्य न निवर्तन्ते
तद्धाम परमं मम ॥८.२१॥
avyakto'kṣara ityuktas
tamāhuḥ paramāṁ gatim
yaṁ prāpya na nivartante
taddhāma paramaṁ mama (8.21)

avyakto = avyaktaḥ — invisible world; 'kṣara = akṣara — unalterable; ity = iti — thus; uktaḥ — is declared; tam — it; āhuḥ — authorities say; paramām — supreme; gatim — objective; yam — which; prāpya — attaining; na — not; nivartante — return here; tad — that; dhāma — residence; paramam — supreme; mama — My

That invisible world is unalterable, so it is declared. The authorities say that it is the supreme objective. Attaining that, they do not return here. That place is My supreme residence. (8.21)

Commentary:

We remind readers that there are two unmanifested existences being listed. Both of these are beyond the dimensions which manifest in the material world. The higher of the two is now described as being Krishna's supreme residence (*dhāma paramam mama*), and as being the place where the great sages relocate permanently.

पुरुषः स परः पार्थ
भक्त्या लभ्यस्त्वनन्यया ।
यस्यान्तःस्थानि भूतानि
येन सर्वमिदं ततम् ॥८.२२॥
puruṣaḥ sa paraḥ pārtha
bhaktyā labhyastvananyayā
yasyāntaḥsthāni bhūtāni
yena sarvamidaṁ tatam (8.22)

puruṣaḥ — person; sa = saḥ — this; paraḥ — supreme; pārtha — O son of Pṛthā; bhaktyā — by a devotional relationship; labhyaḥ — attainable; tv = tu — but; ananyayā — not by any other; yasyāntaḥsthāni = yasya — of which + antaḥsthāni — existing within; bhūtāni — beings; yena — by which; sarvam — all; idam — this; tatam — energized

That Supreme Person, O son of Pṛthā, is attainable through a devotional relationship and not by any other means. Within His influence, all beings exist. By Him, all the universe is energized. (8.22)

Commentary:

This is another verse where Lord Krishna gave leeway for anyone to reach the Supreme Person even if one does not agree that Krishna is that special personality. In either case, one has to reach Krishna or that Supreme Person by a devotional relationship. More details will be given elsewhere in the *Gītā*. Krishna informs us that all beings have a standing in this world by the influence (*yasyāntahsthāni*) of the Supreme Person (*puruṣah parah*). The entire universe is pervaded by His energies which maintain the world.

The Supreme Person mentioned in this verse was described in texts 8 and 9 of this chapter:

abhyāsayogayuktena cetasā nānyagāminā
paramaṁ puruṣaṁ divyaṁ.yāti pārthānucintayan (8.8)
kaviṁ purāṇamanuśāsitāram aṇoraṇīyāṁsamanusmaredyaḥ
sarvasya dhātāram acintyarūpam ādityavarṇaṁ tamasaḥ parastāt (8.9)

With a mind that does not venture outwards, which is disciplined by yoga practice, a person goes to the divine Supreme Person, while deeply meditating, O son of Pṛthā.

He who meditates on the Person Who knows everything, the most ancient of people, the Supreme Supervisor, the most minute factor, the one with unimaginable form, with a radiant body, free of grossness, (8.8-9)

यत्र काले त्वनावृत्तिम्
आवृत्तिं चैव योगिनः ।
प्रयाता यान्ति तं कालं
वक्ष्यामि भरतर्षभ ॥८.२३॥
yatra kāle tvanāvṛttim
āvṛttiṁ caiva yoginaḥ
prayātā yānti taṁ kālaṁ
vakṣyāmi bharatarṣabha (8.23)

yatra — where; kāle — in time; tv = tu — but; anāvṛttim — not return; āvṛttim — return; caiva = ca — and + eva — indeed; yoginaḥ — yogis; prayātā — departing; yānti — go; tam — this; kālam — time; vakṣyāmi — I will tell; bharatarṣabha — O bullish man of the Bharata family

O bullish man of the Bharata family, I will tell you of the departure for the yogis who do or do not return. (8.23)

Commentary:

Yoginah means *the yogis*, but many commentators change the meaning to give credence to their missionary objectives. A biased commentator may deliberately scratch out the word *yoginah* and give a translation that applies to persons in his religious group, even though such persons do not practice yoga as a discipline. Readers are alerted that this and related verses, pertain to yogis who have mystic expertise. Others cannot use the methods described because their souls have no thrust towards locations which are beyond this earthly place. It is not the religion we profess nor the salvation promised by a scripture, but rather our actual mind-set and our ability to transcend this earthly place. These aspects must be realistic before we can travel beyond this earthly place or this universe, at the time of death.

अग्निर्ज्योतिरहः शुक्लः
षण्मासा उत्तरायणम् ।
तत्र प्रयाता गच्छन्ति
ब्रह्म ब्रह्मविदो जनाः ॥८.२४॥
agnirjyotirahaḥ śuklaḥ
ṣaṇmāsā uttarāyaṇam
tatra prayātā gacchanti
brahma brahmavido janāḥ (8.24)

agnir = agniḥ — summer season; jyotir = jyotiḥ — bright atmosphere; ahaḥ — daytime; śuklaḥ — bright moonlight; saṇmāsā — six months; uttarāyaṇam — the time when the sun appears to move north; tatra — at that time; prayātā — departing; gacchanti — they go; brahma — to the spiritual location; brahmavido = brahmavidaḥ — knowers of the spiritual dimension; janāḥ — people

The summer season, the bright atmosphere, the daytime, the bright moonlight, the six months when the sun appears to move north; if at that time, they depart the body, those people who know the spiritual dimension, go to the spiritual location. (8.24)

Commentary:

This only applies to persons who are trained in yoga. Others who are not trained in yoga may rarely leave the earthly atmosphere. This particular method of soul travel is explained in the Upanishads.

Brahmavido means the *brahman*-knowing personalities. But these persons must also be yogis (*yoginah*). If a person knows *brahman* theoretically and does not or did not practice yoga to actually experience the *brahman* spiritual reality, he will not be able to relocate at the time of death.

Readers may check the Upanishads to see the conclusions of the sages who lived in the time of Lord Krishna. And we remind you that Krishna did attend the *gurukula* boarding school of some of these Upanishadic sages, particularly Sandipani Muni and Ghora Angiras. The information in this verse matches a statement in the Chandogya Upanishad:

atha yadu caivāsmicchavyam kurvanti
yadi ca nārciṣamevābhisam-
āpūryamāṇapakṣamāpuryamāṇa-pakṣādyānṣaḍudaṅṅeti
māsām stanmāsebhyaḥ saṁvatsaram
sarv-atsarādādityamādityāccandramasaṁ
candramaso vidyutam tatpuruṣo 'mānavaḥ
sa unānbrahma gamayatyeṣa devapayo brahmapatha
etena pratipadyamānā imaṁ mānavamāvartaṁ nāvartante nāvartante

Now regarding such persons, regardless of whether the cremation rites are performed or not, they go to the light, from the light to the day, from the day to the bright fortnight, from that to the six months during which the sun rises toward the north, from that to the year, from the year to the sun, from the sun to the moon, from the moon to lightning. A spiritual person causes them, who exist there, to realize the spiritual existence. This is the path to the celestial world and the path to the spiritual plane. Those who go by this path do not return to this human cyclic existence. They do not return. (Chandogya Upanishad 4.15.5)

However, this is a more gradual process than it appears. Let us see another related verse from the same scripture:

tadya ittham viduḥ ye ceme'ranye sraddhā tapa ityupāsate
te' rciṣamabhisambhavantyarciṣco'harahna
āpuryamāṇapakṣamāpuryamānapakṣādyānsaḍudaṅṅeti māsām stān
māsebhyaḥ saṁvatsaraṁ saṁvatsarādādityamādityāc candramasaṁ candramaso
vidyutaṁ tatpuruṣo' mānavaḥ sa enānbrahma gamayatyeṣa devayānaḥ it

Among them (the departed spirits), those who know the ritual process and those who are devoted to the faith and practiced in austerity in the forest, they travel to the light, from the light to the day, from the day to the bright fortnight, from the bright fortnight to those six months during which the sun moves to the north, from these to the sun's yearly course, from the yearly course to the sunlight and from the sunlight to the moon, from the moon to the lightning. A divine person causes them to realize the spiritual existence. This is the path to reach the supernatural controllers. (Chandogya Upanishad 5.10.1 -2)

Readers can check these scriptures carefully and draw their own conclusions. One may also do some more research by checking the *Bṛhadāraṇyaka Upaniṣad.*

Some commentators paint a dull picture of these yogic accomplishments. They state that one does not have to become a yogi to attain salvation but could attain it even without performing the yoga disciplines.

धूमो रात्रिस्तथा कृष्णः
षण्मासा दक्षिणायनम् ।
तत्र चान्द्रमसं ज्योतिर्
योगी प्राप्य निवर्तते ॥८.२५॥
dhūmo rātristathā kṛṣṇaḥ
ṣaṇmāsā dakṣiṇāyanam
tatra cāndramasaṁ jyotir
yogī prāpya nivartate (8.25)

dhūmo = dhūmaḥ — smoky, misty or hazy season; rātris — night time; tathā — as well as; kṛṣṇaḥ — the dark moon time; saṇmāsā — six months; dakṣiṇāyanam — the time when the sun appears to move south; tatra — at that time; cāndramasam — moon; jyotir = jyotiḥ — light; yogī — yogi; prāpya — attaining; nivartate — is born again

The smoky, misty or hazy season, as well as in the night-time, the dark-moon time, the six months when the sun appears to move south; if the yogi departs at that time, he attains moonlight, after which he is born again. (8.25)

Commentary:

Yogī prāpya nivartate means that the aspiring yogi will comeback to this earthly place or to some parallel earthly dimension to use another material body. Let us see a corresponding statement in the Chandogya Upanishad:

atha ya ime grāma iṣṭapūrte dattamityupāsete te dhūmamabhisambhavanti
dhūmādrākriṁ rātreraparapakṣamaparapakṣādyān ṣaṅdakṣinaiti
māsāṁ stānnaite saṁvatsaramabhiprāpnuvanti

māsebhyaḥ pitṛlokaṁ pitṛlokādākāsamākāsāccandramasameṣa
somo rājā taddevānāmannaṁ taṁ devā bhakṣayanti

tasminyāvatsampātamuṣitvāthaitamevadhvānaṁ punarnivartante
yathetamākāśamākāśādvāyuṁ vayurbhūtvā dhūmo bhavati dhūmo bhūtvā-bhram bhavati

abhraṁ bhūtvā megho bhavati megho bhūtvā pravarṣati ta iha vrīhiyavā
oṣadhivanaspatayastilamāṣā iti jāyante' to vai khalu durniṣpṛtaraṁ
yoyo hyannamatti yo retaḥ siñcati tadbhūyu eva bhavati

tadya iha ramaṇīyacaraṇā ahhyāśo ha yatte ramaṇīyāṁ
yonimāpadyeranbrāhmaṇayonim vā kṣanniyayoniṁ va vaiśyayoniṁ
vātha va iha kapūyacaraṇā abhyāśo ha yatte kapūyāṁ
yonimāpadyerañśvayoniṁ va sūkarayoniṁ va caṇḍalayoniṁ va

athaitayoḥ payorna katareṇacana tānīmani
kṣudrāṇyasakṛdāvartīni bhūtāni bhavanti jāyasva
mrirasvetyetattṛtīyaṁ sthānaṁ tenāsau loko na sampūryate
tasmājjugupseta tadeṣa śokaḥ (5.10.3-8)

But those who, while living in villages, practice religious ceremonies, do welfare activities and give charity, go to the smoky region, from the smoky zone, to the darkish places, from the darkish places they travel along with the darkness of the dark fortnight moon, from there to those months during which the sun travels southward. From there they do not reach the sun's yearly course.

From the sun's southern course, they travel to the place of the departed forefathers, from there to the outer space. From outer space to the moon. This is the place of King Soma. And soma beverage is the food of the deities. This soma beverage is what the deities eat.

Staying in that place till they expire their rights to live there, they return again by the same way as they came. They come to outer space and from space to the earthly atmosphere. Having become earthly air, they become water vapor. Having become water vapor, they become a white mist.

Having become a white mist, they become a cloud. Having become a cloud, they fall as rain. Then they are born in this world as rice or barley, herbs and trees, sesame plants, and beans. But the release from these is more difficult, for they become like the person who eats the food and sows the seed.

Among them, those who have godly disposition quickly reach a good womb, the womb of a brahmin or of an administrator or of a mercantile parent. But those who have evil disposition, quickly reach a wicked parent or the womb of a dog or hog or cannibalistic human being.

By neither of these two paths (of living on this planet or living on the moon), do they go (out of the material world). They keep repeatedly revolving, being born as small creatures subject to being addressed, "Be born - die." This is the third state. Therefore that region of the moon is never filled up. Hence one should be disgusted with it. There is a verse regarding this.

(Chandogya Upanishad 5.10.3-8)

In these verses, we see that the situation was extended to others besides yogis. It applied to the ritualistic householders who believe in the Vedas. We get great detail of the course they take. However, in the *Gītā*, these verses apply to the yogis. There is a vast difference between a yogi and the other types of elevationists.

शुक्लकृष्णे गती ह्येते
जगतः शाश्वते मते ।
एकया यात्यनावृत्तिम्
अन्ययावर्तते पुनः ॥८.२६॥
śuklakṛṣṇe gatī hyete
jagataḥ śāśvate mate
ekayā yātyanāvṛttim
anyayāvartate punaḥ (8.26)

śuklakṛṣṇe — light and dark; gatī — two paths; hyete = hy (hi) — indeed + ete — these two; jagataḥ — of the universe; śāśvate — perpetual; mate — is considered; ekayā — by one; yāty = yāti — goes away; anāvṛttim — not return; anyayāvartate = anyayā — by other + āvartate — comes back; punaḥ = punar — again

The light and the dark times are two paths which are considered to be perpetually available for the universe. It is considered so by the authorities. By one, a person goes away not to return; by the other he comes back again. (8.26)

<u>*Commentary:*</u>

According to some commentators, there is yet another path which is indicated in the following verse. However, such a proposal is totally absurd. Even our Vaishnava spiritual master indicated this other path but we are sorry to say that after a close check of the *Gītā*, we have not found an alternative path. The reason is this: A person leaving the earthly environment must travel from this place in a certain way to reach the spiritual provinces. There might be a difference in the immediacy of the arrival on the spiritual places or the speed of travel, but the direction of travel is the same in all cases since the celestial geography is the same.

In addition, it is not merely a matter of faith in a particular religion. Faith or confidence alone, cannot take a man to the spiritual world because his innate developed mundane tendencies will keep him earth-bound. He must therefore deliberately purify himself away from the mundane nature. Then he may depart freely. This purificatory process is the specialty of the yogis. It is not an accident that in all of these verses, Lord Krishna used words which directly mean "the yogis". But some disagree and say that Lord Krishna gave an alternate course in the next two verses; but there is no evidence to support such proposals, which are simply slogans.

नैते सृती पार्थ जानन्
योगी मुह्यति कश्चन ।
तस्मात्सर्वेषु कालेषु
योगयुक्तो भवार्जुन ॥८.२७॥
naite sṛtī pārtha jānan
yogī muhyati kaścana
tasmātsarveṣu kāleṣu
yogayukto bhavārjuna (8.27)

naite = na — not + ete — these two; sṛtī — two paths; pārtha — O son of Pṛthā; jānan — knowing; yogī — yogi; muhyati — is confused; kaścana — at all; tasmāt — therefore; sarveṣu — in all; kāleṣu — in times; yogayukto = yogayuktaḥ — disciplined in yoga practice; bhavārjuna = bhava — be + arjuna — Arjuna

Knowing these two paths, O son of Pṛthā, the yogi is not confused at all. Therefore at all times, be disciplined in yoga practice, O Arjuna. (8.27)

Commentary:

Somehow or the other, some translators translated the word *yogī* in line two to mean *devotee*. But no one explains why Lord Krishna did not use the word *bhakta*, which is the word for *devotee*. Why is it that in the previous verse, he used yogi? And then He uses yogi in this verse and also in the next. When Krishna used the word yogi in the previous verse, some commentators found it convenient to give *yogī* as yogi, but now, all of a sudden, *yogī* might be translated as *devotee*. This is a problem.

We will, however, stick to the word yogi, because we want to understand *Gītā* in its own time and place. Lord Krishna directly told Arjuna to be disciplined in yoga at all times (*yogayukto*). But how could Arjuna do that on a battlefield where he would not be practicing postures and *prāṇāyāma* breath methods? This was how: He would follow the examples of people like King Janaka who studied yoga, became somewhat proficient in it, then took administrative duties and applied the emotional detachment and maturity gained from the yoga practice.

Readers may recall that Krishna promised to teach Arjuna the application of yoga to worldly life, just as Krishna said He taught the sun god in some distant past.

वेदेषु यज्ञेषु तपःसु चैव
दानेषु यत्पुण्यफलं प्रदिष्टम् ।
अत्येति तत्सर्वमिदं विदित्वा
योगी परं स्थानमुपैति चाद्यम् ॥८.२८॥

vedeṣu — from study of the Vedas; yajñeṣu — from religious ceremonies and disciplines; tapaḥsu — from austerities; caiva — and indeed; dāneṣu — from scripturally-recommended acts of charity; yat = yad — which; puṇyaphalam — good result;

vedeṣu yajñeṣu tapaḥsu caiva
dāneṣu yatpuṇyaphalaṁ
pradiṣṭam
atyeti tatsarvamidaṁ viditvā
yogī paraṁ sthānamupaiti
cādyam (8.28)

pradiṣṭam — described; atyeti — goes beyond; tat — this; sarvam — all; idam — this; viditvā — having known; yogī — yogi; param — supreme; sthānam — state; upaiti — goes; cadyam = cā — and + adyam — primal

The yogi, having known all this, goes beyond the good results which are derived from study of the Veda, beyond religious ceremonies and disciplines, beyond austerities and beyond offering scripturally-recommended gifts in charity. He goes to the Supreme Primal State.

Commentary:

The last line directly states, *yogi param sthānam upaiti cādyam*; that the yogi goes to the primal supreme state. He does this by becoming completely detached from *punya* (pious merits). But these services are the aim of some Hindus. Why then, did Krishna belittle *punya*? The answer is: Motivated *punya* brings a soul back into the earthly plane.

By the path of Vedic recitation, by doing Vedic religious ceremonies or performing austerities with an aim to acquire pious credits, and by giving in charity with an aim for benefit, a man exposes his bad motivation and his strong continued interest in exploiting the material creation. But a yogi gets beyond this.

All these people, the yogis and the religiously-inclined people, may or may not be devotees of Krishna. Therefore the stress is not on being a devotee, since one might be a devotee and be inclined to *punya* (pious credits) for luxury and power in the material world. The stress is on detachment. In fact, one may or may not be a devotee and still might be taking up the process of yoga to gain the detachment described.

As we stated, Bhishma was a successful yogi who used the path of light. That is described in the *Mahābhārata* and the *Bhāgavata Purāṇa*. Readers who have a serious interest should pursue the study of these books.

CHAPTER 9

The Devotional Attitude*

श्रीभगवानुवाच
इदं तु ते गुह्यतमं
प्रवक्ष्याम्यनसूयवे ।
ज्ञानं विज्ञानसहितं
यज्ज्ञात्वा मोक्ष्यसेऽशुभात् ॥९.१॥
śrībhagavānuvāca
idaṁ tu te guhyatamaṁ
pravakṣyāmyanasūyave
jñānaṁ vijñānasahitaṁ
yajjñātvā mokṣyase'śubhāt (9.1)

śrībhagavān — the Blessed Lord; uvāca — said; idam — this; tu — but; te — to you; guhyatamam — most secret; pravakṣyāmy = pravakṣyāmi — I will explain; anasūyave — to one who is not cynical; jñānam — knowledge; vijñānasahitaṁ = vijñāna — experienced + sahitam — with; yaj = yad — which; jñātvā — having known; mokṣyase — you will be freed; 'śubhāt = aśubhāt — from impurity

The Blessed Lord said: But I will explain to you who are not cynical, the most secret truths, the knowledge with the experience, which having known, you will be freed from impurities. (9.1)

Commentary:

Whatever Lord Krishna considered to be the most secret knowledge was explained to Arjuna because Arjuna displayed a certain standard of behavior in reference to Krishna. Arjuna was not cynical towards the Lord. *Asūyave* refers to a person who is envious of another or who has a cynical attitude towards what another person explains. But *anasūyave* means one who does not have such a negative mood. Arjuna had the qualification for being a good student of any teacher. He was dear to all who instructed him. He had a submissive attitude towards *Droṇa* and Bhishma who were teachers in other fields of learning.

Anasūyave means that Arjuna had an accepting attitude, an open mind towards what Lord Krishna said. He was not doubting or being cynical. He wanted to understand the Lord's ideas. In Chapter Four, Lord Krishna explained the various types of disciplinary methods for self-purification. Then the Lord spoke of learning these techniques from the spiritual masters of each of the disciplines. The requirements for a student were explained:

tadviddhi praṇipātena paripraśnena sevayā
upadekṣyanti te jñānaṁ jñāninastattvadarśinaḥ (4.34)

This you ought to know. By submitting yourself as a student, by asking questions, by serving as requested, the perceptive reality-conversant teachers will teach you the knowledge. (4.34)

**The Mahābhārata contains no chapter headings. This title was assigned by the translator on the basis of verse 26 of this chapter.*

Arjuna's attitude of *praṇipātena*, humble submission, gentleness towards the teacher and being open-minded to hear what the teacher explained, being free from a cutting, rasping, judging perspective, gave Arjuna the ability to learn quickly from any teacher. If we have such an attitude towards a teacher, the teacher will give us even more than we asked for (*paripraśnena*). The teacher will bless us, giving us knowledge, and open the way for us to gain direct experience of what was conceptualized.

Mokṣyase 'śubhāt (*mokṣyase aśubhāt*) means a release from impurities. In this case, it is a release from impurities in judgment (*jñānam vijñānasahitam*). Faulty judgment leads to faulty conclusions. This leads to faulty actions which bring on negative consequences, which in turn, evoke rash reactions in a never-ending cycle of complications.

राजविद्या राजगुह्यं
पवित्रमिदमुत्तमम् ।
प्रत्यक्षावगमं धर्म्यं
सुसुखं कर्तुमव्ययम् ॥९.२॥
rājavidyā rājaguhyaṁ
pavitramidamuttamam
pratyakṣāvagamaṁ dharmyaṁ
susukhaṁ kartumavyayam (9.2)

rājavidyā — ultimate information; rājaguhyam — greatest secret; pavitram — purifier of consciousness; idam — this; uttamam — transcendental; pratyakṣa — by direct experience; avagamam — understood; dharmyam — the principle of religion; susukham — very happy; kartum — to execute; avyayam — everlasting.

This is the ultimate information, the greatest secret, the purifier of consciousness. It is plain to see, righteous, easy to practise and thoroughly consistent. (9.2)

<u>Commentary:</u>

We should take Krishna's word for it, just as Arjuna did. We should open our minds, hear what Krishna presents, and try to put ourselves into an attitude of submission whereby we may get direct experience of what He describes.

Of great interest to us, is the ease of this practice *(susukham kartum).* Easy to practice? How could it be easy to practice? Most people avoid it. Most people do not perceive it. And still, the Lord said that it is easy to practice.

अश्रद्दधानाः पुरुषा
धर्मस्यास्य परंतप ।
अप्राप्य मां निवर्तन्ते
मृत्युसंसारवर्त्मनि ॥९.३॥
aśraddadhānāḥ puruṣā
dharmasyāsya paraṁtapa
aprāpya māṁ nivartante
mṛtyusaṁsāravartmani (9.3)

aśraddadhānāḥ — having no faith; puruṣā — people; dharmasyāsya = dharmasya — of the righteous behavior + asya — of this; paraṁtapa — stern subduer of the enemy; aprāpya — not attaining; mām — to Me; nivartante — they are born again; mṛtyusaṁsāravartmani = mṛtyu — death + saṁsāra — cyclic rebirth + vartmani — in the course

People who have no faith in this righteous behavior, who have not attained Me, are born again in the cyclic course of death and rebirth, O stern subduer of the enemy. (9.3)

<u>Commentary:</u>

The threatening overtone of this verse cannot be denied, but Lord Krishna made it clear that His association is attained under certain conditions only. Misbehavior puts a spirit at a distance from Him.

मया ततमिदं सर्वं
जगदव्यक्तमूर्तिना ।
मत्स्थानि सर्वभूतानि
न चाहं तेष्ववस्थितः ॥९.४॥
mayā tatamidaṁ sarvaṁ
jagadavyaktamūrtinā
matsthāni sarvabhūtāni
na cāhaṁ teṣvavasthitaḥ (9.4)

mayā — by Me; tatam — pervaded; idam — this; sarvam — all; jagad = jagat — world; avyaktamūrtinā = avyakta — invisible + mūrtinā — by form; matsthāni — standing on Me, surviving on Me; sarvabhūtāni — all beings; na — not; cāham = ca — and + aham — I; teṣv = teṣu — in them; avasthitaḥ — standing on, surviving on

This world is pervaded by My invisible form. All beings survive on My energy but I am not surviving on theirs. (9.4)

Commentary:

The *avyaktamūrtinā* is something real (*mūrtinā*), but it is invisible, abstract, and imperceptible (*avyakta*). It is inconceivable. We may accept it on the basis of confidence in Krishna. In time we might perceive it with supernatural eyes.

Lord Krishna presented a one-sided, influential relationship. He pervades but is not pervaded. He influences but is not influenced. The beings exist in His energy, but He is not in their field of consciousness.

न च मत्स्थानि भूतानि
पश्य मे योगमैश्वरम् ।
भूतभृन्न च भूतस्थो
ममात्मा भूतभावनः ॥९.५॥
na ca matsthāni bhūtāni
paśya me yogamaiśvaram
bhūtabhṛnna ca bhūtastho
mamātmā bhūtabhāvanaḥ (9.5)

na — not; ca — and; matsthāni — standing on Me, surviving on Me; bhūtāni — beings; paśya — behold; me — My; yogam = yoga — psychological power; aiśvaram — supremacy; bhūtabhṛn = bhūtabhṛt — sustaining beings; na — not; ca — and; bhūtastho = bhūtasthaḥ — existing on the beings; mamātmā = mama — My + ātmā — self; bhūtabhāvanaḥ — causing beings to be

And the created beings are not existing on Me. Behold My psychological supremacy. While sustaining the beings and not existing on them, I Myself cause them to be. (9.5)

Commentary:

In English language, we call this a paradox, a contradiction, something that appears illogical and hard to believe. If this is true, then it violates the rules of association.

On one hand, the beings are in Krishna's influence but on the other hand, He says that they are not in His consciousness. Thus, what does He really mean? If someone is in another's influence, the subject is automatically within the scope of the other's consciousness, otherwise there is no meaning to the statement that he is under the other's purview ."Behold." Krishna said. "Just see My glory. I influence these beings and still they are not really within My personal consciousness. I give them association but I do not absorb theirs."

यथाकाशस्थितो नित्यं
वायुः सर्वत्रगो महान् ।
तथा सर्वाणि भूतानि
मत्स्थानीत्युपधारय ॥९.६॥

yathākāśasthito = yathākāśasthitaḥ = yathā — as + ākāśa — space + sthitaḥ — situated; nityam — always; vāyuḥ — wind; sarvatrago = sarvatragaḥ — everywhere going, pervasive; mahān —

yathākāśasthito nityaṁ
vāyuḥ sarvatrago mahān
tathā sarvāṇi bhūtāni
matsthānītyupadhāraya (9.6)

powerful; tathā — so; sarvāṇi — all; bhūtāni — beings; matsthānīty (matsthānīti) = matsthānī — exist under Me + iti — thus; upadhāraya — consider thoroughly

As the powerful wind is always situated in space and is pervasive, so all beings exist under My influence. Consider this thoroughly. (9.6)

Commentary:

Mahān means *mightily, powerfully, with much power.* As permitted, the living entities travel about powerfully. As the wind pervades everything, so the living entities move about, trying to exploit whatever they perceive.

सर्वभूतानि कौन्तेय
प्रकृतिं यान्ति मामिकाम् ।
कल्पक्षये पुनस्तानि
कल्पादौ विसृजाम्यहम ॥९.७॥
sarvabhūtāni kaunteya
prakṛtiṁ yānti māmikām
kalpakṣaye punastāni
kalpādau visṛjāmyaham (9.7)

sarvabhūtāni — all beings; kaunteya — son of Kuntī; prakṛtim — material nature; yānti — retrogress into; māmikām — my own; kalpakṣaye — at the end of a day of Brahmā; punas = punar — again; tāni — they; kalpādau — at the beginning of a day of Brahmā; visṛjāmy = visṛjāmi — I produce; aham — I

O son of Kuntī, all beings retrogress into My own material nature at the end of Brahmā's day. I produce them again at the beginning of Brahmā's next day. (9.7)

Commentary:

This verse of the *Gītā* is very controversial. It has the key to understanding Krishna's view of our situation in and out of material nature. Our Vaishnava spiritual master has, for some reason, translated this verse in a special way. We give his translation as follows:

> *O son of Kuntī, at the millennium, every material manifestation enters into My nature, and at the beginning of another millennium, by My potency I again create. (Bhagavad-Gītā As It Is, 9.7)*

The technicality has to do with the word *prakṛti* which he gave as meaning, *nature,* in this verse and meaning, *material nature,* in the following verse 8. However, readers of the *Gītā* will have to decide for themselves what to believe since Lord Krishna is not standing before us as He stood before Arjuna. We ask serious students of the *Gītā* to study the *Gītā* within the context of the *Gītā* itself. That will give the clearest understanding.

In contrast to *Śrīla* Bhaktivedanta's translation, the Gaudiya Math authority, *Śrīla* Sridhara Deva Maharaja, gave this translation:

> ***O son of Kuntī, at the universal cataclysm, the multitude of beings are merged in My illusory nature, known as maya. And with the beginning of the new millennium, I create all the distinct species again. (The Hidden Treasure of the Sweet Absolute, 9.7)***

We are in favor of Sridhara Maharaja's translation because it is consistent in the use and meaning of the word *prakṛti.* We stated in the first line of the translation that all beings are based on material nature. This does not mean that the souls or spirits are based on material nature. It means that the *bhūtānis* or mundane forms which include the physical, subtle and causal bodies, are based on material nature, *prakṛti.* These forms are retracted into the invisible material energy at the end of the creative cycle. But Lord Krishna put in the word *māmikām* which means, *my, mine, my own*. In this way. He claimed material nature as one of His energies. He puts Himself forward as the owner of mundane potency.

And again in the new manifestation, the distinct forms are manifested again. Sridhara Maharaja clarified this by stating that Krishna creates all the distinct species again. We know, of course, that Krishna directs others like *Brahmā* and *Manu* to do this.

प्रकृतिं स्वामवष्टभ्य
विसृजामि पुनः पुनः ।
भूतग्राममिमं कृत्स्नम्
अवशं प्रकृतेर्वशात् ॥९.८॥
prakṛtiṁ svāmavaṣṭabhya
visṛjāmi punaḥ punaḥ
bhūtagrāmamimaṁ kṛtsnam
avaśaṁ prakṛtervaśāt (9.8)

prakṛtim — material nature; svām — own; avaṣṭabhya — supported on, founded on; visṛjāmi — I produce; punaḥ punaḥ — repeated, again and again; bhūtagrāmam — the multitude of beings; imam — this; kṛtsnam — whole; avaśam — powerless; prakṛter = prakṛteḥ — of material nature; vaśāt — in respect to the potency

On the foundation of material nature, I repeatedly produce this whole multitude of beings, which is powerless in respect to the potency of material nature. (9.8)

Commentary:

The material nature is supportive of its own manifested situation but only so long as Krishna's will and power are involved. At least this is the understanding Krishna conveys in the *Gītā*. If either the Lord or material nature were removed, the material creation would collapse. Both are necessary for the continuation of the manifested material world. Even though the world keeps changing, still its continuation in tangible forms depends on the Lord and on the primal mundane energy, the *prāṇa*, the subtle elements.

At the same time, the conditioned souls who use the various gross, subtle and causal forms, are drastically affected by the charm of material nature. Their deliverance occurs only by special action of someone who is completely resistant to the mundane potency. Krishna claims that He is that Someone.

न च मां तानि कर्माणि
निबध्नन्ति धनंजय ।
उदासीनवदासीनम्
असक्तं तेषु कर्मसु ॥९.९॥
na ca māṁ tāni karmāṇi
nibadhnanti dhanaṁjaya
udāsīnavadāsīnam
asaktaṁ teṣu karmasu (9.9)

na — not; ca — and; mām — Me; tāni — these; karmāṇi — cultural acts; nibadhnanti — they bind; dhanaṁjaya — conqueror of rich countries; udāsīnavad = udāsīnavat — indifferently; āsīnam — sitting, being situated; asaktam — unattached; teṣu — in these; karmasu — in cultural actions

And these cultural activities do not bind Me, O conqueror of rich countries. Since I am situated indifferently, I remain unattached to the activities. (9.9)

Commentary:

Again Lord Krishna set Himself apart from everyone. He claims immunity from the charms of material nature. Even though everyone else is charmed, including the supernatural controllers, Lord Krishna says that He is not. We find a bit of sarcasm in the address of Arjuna as *dhanamjaya* (conqueror of wealthy countries). Arjuna was a conqueror but he was subdued by the emotions of material nature.

मयाध्यक्षेण प्रकृतिः
सूयते सचराचरम् ।
हेतुनानेन कौन्तेय
जगद्विपरिवर्तते ॥९.१०॥
mayādhyakṣeṇa prakṛtiḥ
sūyate sacarācaram
hetunānena kaunteya
jagadviparivartate (9.10)

mayādhyakṣeṇa = mayā — with Me + adhyakṣeṇa — as supervisor; prakṛtiḥ — material nature; sūyate — produces; sacarācaram — moving and non-moving things; hetunānena = hetunā — by cause of + anena — by this; kaunteya — son of Kuntī; jagad = jagat — world; viparivartate — operates

With Me as the supervisor, material nature produces moving and nonmoving things. By this cause, O son of Kuntī, the universe operates. (9.10)

Commentary:

Lord Krishna again put Himself forward as the most essential cause of the creation. Citing His position as the overseer, He said that material nature produces living and non-living things into tangible manifestation. And this is the reason why the universe persists. Of course, we may believe or disbelieve this. But Krishna stated it to Arjuna.

अवजानन्ति मां मूढा
मानुषीं तनुमाश्रितम् ।
परं भावमजानन्तो
मम भूतमहेश्वरम् ॥९.११॥
avajānanti māṁ mūḍhā
mānuṣīṁ tanumāśritam
paraṁ bhāvamajānanto
mama bhūtamaheśvaram (9.11)

avajānanti — they hold a low opinion; mām — Me; mūḍhā — the foolish people; mānuṣīm — human; tanum — body; āśritam — having assumed; param — higher; bhāvam — being; ajānanto = ajānantaḥ — not knowing; mama — of Me; bhūtamaheśvaram = bhūta — being + maheśvaram — Almighty God

The foolish people, not knowing My higher existence as the Almighty God of the beings, hold a low opinion of Me as having a human body. (9.11)

Commentary:

As the *bhūtamaheśvaram*, the Great Lord of all beings, on physical, psychic and causal planes. Lord Krishna feels that we should all honor Him. But He said we hold a low opinion of Him because we are foolish (*mūḍha*).

The problem here is that we do not have the direct vision to see Krishna as described. How do we know for sure that He is the *bhūtamaheśvaram*, the Great Lord of all beings?

मोघाशा मोघकर्माणो
मोघज्ञाना विचेतसः ।
राक्षसीमासुरीं चैव
प्रकृतिं मोहिनीं श्रिताः ॥९.१२॥
moghāśā moghakarmāṇo
moghajñānā vicetasaḥ
rākṣasīmāsurīṁ caiva
prakṛtiṁ mohinīṁ śritāḥ (9.12)

moghāśā — people with vain hopes; moghakarmāṇo = moghakarmāṇaḥ — people with purposeless actions; moghajñānā — people with incorrect information; vicetasaḥ — without discrimination; rākṣasīm — wicked; āsurīm — devilish; caiva — and indeed; prakṛtim — mode of material nature; mohinīm — deluding feature; śritāḥ — relying on

Persons with vain hopes, purposeless actions, and incorrect information, who lack discrimination, being wicked and devilish, rely on the deluding feature of material nature. (9.12)

Commentary:

According to these proposals, there are three types of reliance in material nature. The most degrading of these is described as *prakṛtim mohinīm*. If we rely on, or resort to (*śritāḥ*) this portion of the material power, we will exhibit wicked and devilish qualities.

Material nature's influence is more than physical. It is psychological and conceptual. Thus we should be aware of it. Regardless of our acceptance of Krishna as *bhūtamaheśvaram*, the greatest Lord or the Supreme Lord of all beings, we can still know for certain that we experience the influence of material nature physically, psychologically, and conceptually. This influence bears upon us and pushes us impulsively.

Prakṛtim is usually translated as nature. But this translator gave, *material nature*, just to be consistent with some other information given elsewhere in the *Gītā*. The term *mohinīm* qualifies *prakṛtim* to show that it is the bewildering portion of material nature. The whole range of influence of material nature is, in a sense, bewildering, but a particular aspect is most confusing. Readers who doubt this meaning of *prakṛtim* should study the definitions of material nature which are given by Lord Krishna in Chapter Eighteen of the *Bhagavad Gītā*. A summary statement is given in verse 40 of that chapter:

na tadasti pṛthivyāṁ vā divi deveṣu vā punaḥ
sattvaṁ prakṛtijairmuktaṁ yadebhiḥ syāttribhirguṇaiḥ (18.40)

There is no object on earth nor even in the subtle mundane domains, which can exist without these three modes which were produced from material nature. (18.40)

महात्मानस्तु मां पार्थ
दैवीं प्रकृतिमाश्रिताः ।
भजन्त्यनन्यमनसो
ज्ञात्वा भूतादिमव्ययम् ॥९.१३॥

mahātmānastu māṁ pārtha
daivīṁ prakṛtimāśritāḥ
bhajantyananyamanaso
jñātvā bhūtādimavyayam (9.13)

mahātmānaḥ — great souls; tu — but; mām — Me; pārtha — son of Pṛthā; daivīm — supernatural; prakṛtim — material energy; āśritāḥ — being reliant; bhajanty = bhajanti — they worship; ananyamanaso = ananyamanasaḥ — persons whose minds do not deviate; jñātvā — knowing; bhūtādim — originator of beings; avyayam — constant factor

But great souls, being reliant on the supernatural level of material nature, worship Me, without deviation, knowing Me as the originator of beings, the constant factor. (9.13)

Commentary:

The *mahātmānas* are those who have direct experience of Krishna. These are not the people who heard of Krishna in words and descriptions but who have not directly experienced Krishna's greatness. These are the *tattvadarśih*, reality-perceiving devotees of Krishna. Arjuna was such a person since he got sensual revelation of Krishna.

In the previous verse the Lord described those persons who were reliant on the deluding, bewitching portion of material nature. Now He goes directly to the highest level of human beings. Some commentators do not translate *prakṛti* as material nature but rather as nature, giving daivi *prakṛtim* as *divine nature* or as *godly, divine nature*. However, we gave, *the supernatural level of material nature*. We want to remain in the context. Readers are asked to re-check verse 7.I4 of the *Gītā*. where Lord Krishna first mentioned the *daivī* quality of material nature. There we read:

daivī hyeṣā guṇamayī mama māyā duratyayā
māmeva ye prapadyante māyāmetāṁ taranti te (7.14)

Indeed this quality controlled illusion of Mine is supernatural and difficult to transcend. Only those who rely on Me, can see beyond this bewitching energy. (7.14)

No translator in his right mind would say that this *daivī hi esa guṇamayī* refers to divine nature because the words *guṇa*mayī, *māyā*, *durataya*, *māyām*, *etām*, and *taranti* would be difficult to erase. These words directly mean material nature. It cannot be denied. Thus there is no need to alter the meaning of *daivī* at this point in the *Gītā*. We must stick to it as it was presented. Further on in the *Gītā* we will hear more about material nature and understand why this translator's meanings are appropriate. For now, however, we present verse 14.6:

tatra sattvaṁ nirmalatvāt prakāśakamanāmayam
sukhasaṅgena badhnāti jñānasaṅgena cānagha (14.6)

Regarding these influences, the clarifying one is relatively free from perceptive impurities. It is illuminating and free from disease, but by granting an attachment to happiness and to expertise, it captivates a person, O sinless one. (14.6)

In this verse, even material nature is listed as having a portion of energy which is *sattvam*, reality-yielding, and *prakāśakam*, illuminating or enlightening. It is important to understand that the material energy itself is simultaneously capable of providing delusion or enlightenment. It can assist in our bid for perfection. It can help us in perceiving the Lord. It is not the total nor final influence but initially, it gives a start.

The recognition (*jñātvā*) of Lord Krishna as *bhūtādim*, the first person Who initiated this creation with all its various conceptual, psychological, and physical forms, and as the *avyayam*, the constant factor behind all the manifestations, is attained only by those who are fully enlightened and who are in fact having that sort of revealing experience. For the time being, we should have an open approach to these declarations.

The purpose of material nature is revealed in no uncertain terms. She has a good purpose which is to reveal the Supreme Person, or at least to introduce us to the Divinity. Material nature, therefore, though on one hand a bewitching force, is on the other, a clarifier. And if material nature had no such power or if she could not be accredited in that way, we would have to question the sanity of the Creator. But if material nature is capable of giving us that first revelation of the Divine Supreme Being, then this creation is worth the while.

सततं कीर्तयन्तो मां
यतन्तश्च दृढव्रताः ।
नमस्यन्तश्च मां भक्त्या
नित्ययुक्ता उपासते ॥९.१४॥
satataṁ kīrtayanto māṁ
yatantaśca dṛḍhavratāḥ
namasyantaśca māṁ bhaktyā
nityayuktā upāsate (9.14)

satatam — always; kīrtayanto = kīrtayantaḥ — glorifying; mām — Me; yatantaśca = yatantaḥ — endeavoring + ca — and; dṛḍhavratāḥ = dṛḍha — firm + vratāḥ — vows; namasyantaśca = namasyantaḥ — paying respects to + ca — and; mām — Me; bhaktyā — with devotion; nityayuktā = nitya — always + yuktā — disciplined; upāsate — worship

Always glorifying Me, endeavoring with firm vows, paying respect to Me with devotion, being always disciplined, they worship Me. (9.14)

Commentary:

These persons are described in the previous verse as *mahātmānas*, persons whose *ātmānas* (spirits) are *mahā* (great). While living in the material world, these great souls are, to a degree, reliant on material nature. But they take recourse (*āśritāh*) to the supernatural (*daivīm*), uncontaminated part of material nature (*prakṛtim*).

A distinction is made here between those devotees who are not in material nature and those who reside here and who must relate to material nature to a degree. As we will hear elsewhere in the *Gītā*, Krishna stated that the material nature has everyone covered in the material world, everyone, that is, but Krishna. But the great souls in the mundane creation, take shelter in the highest, uncontaminated energy of material nature which is the daivi *prakṛti*. Apart from that they also rely on Lord Krishna or alternately on the Supreme Person Who is defined in verse 9 of Chapter Eight:

kaviṁ purāṇamanuśāsitāram aṇoraṇīyāṁsamanusmaredyaḥ
sarvasya dhātāram acintyarūpam ādityavarṇaṁ tamasaḥ parastāt (8.9)

He who meditates on the Person Who knows everything, the most ancient of people, the Supreme Supervisor, the most minute factor, the one with unimaginable form, with a radiant body, free of grossness, (8.9)

The verse under discussion, *Gītā* 9.14, is frequently quoted by the devotees of Krishna but it applies, not to every devotee of the Lord, but to the *mahātmānas* described in this, the previous, and other verses of the *Gītā*. Others cannot glorify the Lord in that pure way because they have not reached the stage of reliance on the *daivī* potency of material nature. They are still relying on the lower modes of passion and ignorance and as such they cannot maintain firm vows. Taking a firm vow is one thing and maintaining oneself in such discipline is an entirely different matter which is reliant on the pure or impure condition of the life energy in the body. This life energy is thoroughly and completely mundane. It cannot be made transcendental at all, even though some teachers pretend that it might be. The life energy can only be upgraded by switching its energy intake to the *daivī prakṛti* (uncontaminated mundane potency). Unless we can switch this energy in that way, we will not be able to maintain vows.

As far as devotion (*bhaktyā*) is concerned, it would rely on the quality. This verse is a description of a high quality of devotion. The perpetual or continuous worship of the Lord (*satatam kīrtayanto mām*) can only be carried by one with full purity. Otherwise it is not possible because the lower modes do not permit a devotee to worship continuously even if he lives at a temple or resides with a spiritual master. One can certainly give others the impression of continuous, perpetual worship of the Lord, but unless one is checked on the psychic side of life, there can be no guarantee that the worship is thorough and continuous.

This is not meant as a discouragement towards impure devotion or worship in the impure stages but it is a clarification of why devotees deviate from the path and why, even if they hope and aspire, they do not get the results attained by great souls like *Nārada* and Dhruva. A cheap, scrappy but highly glorified and advertised brand of devotion will not take one to the higher stages but it will give one a foothold on the lower levels of the devotional path. And if one does not pick himself up from there and improve himself, he will get nowhere. Cheap versions of devotion are a mercy offer of great souls who come down to preach and who realize that our spiritually impoverished condition prohibits us from reaching the high stages. But still, these allowances are the beginning stage, from which we must push ourselves forward, on and on, until we reach the level of a real *mahātmāna*.

ज्ञानयज्ञेन चाप्यन्ये
यजन्तो मामुपासते ।
एकत्वेन पृथक्त्वेन
बहुधा विश्वतोमुखम् ॥९.१५॥
jñānayajñena cāpyanye
yajanto māmupāsate
ekatvena pṛthaktvena
bahudhā viśvatomukham (9.15)

jñānayajñena = jñāna — concept + yajñena — by discipline; cāpy (capi) = ca — and + api — also; anye — others; yajanto = yajantaḥ — performing regulated worship; mām — Me; upāsate — they worship; ekatvena — with the singular basis; pṛthaktvena — as variety; bahudhā — variously shown; viśvatomukham — facing all levels

By the discipline of concepts, others do perform regulated worship of Me as the Singular Basis and as the Variety, facing all levels of reality simultaneously. (9.15)

Commentary:

The sacrifice which consists of dealing with theoretical conceptions of spiritual life and which may evolve into actual experience to clear away the accumulated misconceptions, was mentioned as one of the approved methods in Chapter Four of the *Gītā*:

dravyayajñāstapoyajñā yogayajñāstathāpare
svādhyāyajñānayajñāśca yatayaḥ saṁśitavratāḥ (4.28)

Persons whose austerity and religious ceremony involve the control of material possession, those whose austerity and religious life involve some self-denial, as well as some others whose penance and religious procedure is the eight-part yoga discipline, and those whose austerity and religious ceremony is the study of the Veda and the acquirement of knowledge, all these are regarded as ascetics with strict vows. (4.28)

The path of a *jñāna* yogi is a conceptual path. Therefore it is branded as a path of mental speculation, a path of formulating conceptions about absolute truth. Since our perception is imperfect and since our sensual apparatus has limited range, the conceptions formed in our minds are faulty. The conceptual path, however, is one of the approved paths. That is what Krishna said:

śreyāndravyamayādyajñāj jñānayajñaḥ paraṁtapa
sarvaṁ karmākhilaṁ pārtha jñāne parisamāpyate (4.33)

Better than property control and its ritual regulation is knowledge control and its ritual regulation, O scorcher of the enemy. Every activity without exception, O son of Pṛthā, is realized as a conclusion in the final analysis. (4.33)

When, however, the path of conceptual discipline (*jñānayajña*) evolves to one of actual experiences, the *jñāni* (mental speculator) as he is critically and scornfully called, begins to clear away misconceptions and correct errors of judgment. He gets closer to the Supreme Being. He realizes that he must submit to the Supreme Person. He comes to understand that the ideas of that Supreme Lord are the basis for the overall reality. He surrenders and agrees to be educated by the Lord. And so, after many births and deaths, he attains the divine association.

Our Vaishnava authority, *Śrīla* Bhaktivedanta Swami, that great preacher of Krishna consciousness in these modern times, did condemn the path of *jñāna* yoga in no uncertain terms But we must understand that some persons cannot advance except through this path. It all depends on the acquired nature of the individual. No matter what path a man assumes, if he keeps progressing, he will ultimately reach divine association. Thus, it is not so much the path but the rate of progression. A lower path is outstrided by one who progresses while a higher path may stagnate one who is lazy and complacent.

Lord Krishna has again put Himself forward by identifying Himself as the focus, even of those who rely on formulated conceptions of the Absolute Truth. These conceptions are indicated in brief by the following Sanskrit terms:

ekatvena — by oneness of all energies, forms and powers
pṛthaktvena — by the multiplicity of all energies, forms, and powers
bahudhā viśvatomukham — as the multiple controller who regulates all aspects on all planes in material existence

In modern times, those who worship the Oneness are usually called Advaita Vedantists. They believe in a Oneness of everything. They do not necessarily believe that there is a distinct Supreme Person but rather that everyone is a part of a sum total Oneness (*ekatva*). But even those persons are being claimed here by Krishna as worshipping Him (*māmupāsate*).

अहं क्रतुरहं यज्ञः
स्वधाहमहमौषधम् ।
मन्त्रोऽहमहमेवाज्यम्
अहमग्निरहं हुतम् ॥९.१६॥
ahaṁ kraturahaṁ yajñaḥ
svadhāhamahamauṣadham
mantro'hamahamevājyam
ahamagniraham hutam (9.16)

aham — I; kratur — Vedic ritual; aham — I; yajñaḥ — sacrificial ceremony; svadhāham = svadhā — sanctified offering + aham — I; auṣadham — medicinal herb; mantro = mantraḥ — sacred sound; 'ham = aham — I; evājyam = eva — indeed + ājyam — ghee; aham — I; agnir = agniḥ — fire; aham — I; hutam — oblation

I am represented as the Vedic ritual. I may also be seen as the sacrificial ceremony or as the sanctified offering. I may be regarded as the medicinal herb. I may be seen as the ghee, fire or oblation given. (9.16)

Commentary:

This verse is taken very seriously by those who follow Vedic rituals and who think that these ceremonies are the sum total process for spiritual perfection. We must, however, see this verse in the overall presentation of the *Gītā*. Elsewhere in the *Gītā*, the same Lord Krishna who identified Himself with the Vedic procedure, did condemn the same.

These sacrifices are much reliant on the motive of the performer. If the motive is approved by Lord Krishna, then He is part and parcel of the ceremony, but if the motive is for temporary results, Krishna is only indirectly connected and the performer must rely on other supernatural people or powers.

पिताहमस्य जगतो
माता धाता पितामहः ।
वेद्यं पवित्रमोंकार
ऋक्साम यजुरेव च ॥९.१७॥

pitāham = pitā — father + aham — I; asya — of this; jagato = jagataḥ — of the universe; mātā — mother; dhātā — creator; pitāmahaḥ — grandfather; vedyam — subject to be known; pavitram — purifier; oṁkāra — sacred syllable

pitāhamasya jagato
mātā dhātā pitāmahaḥ
vedyaṁ pavitramoṁkāra
ṛksāma yajureva ca (9.17)

Om; ṛk — Rig Veda; sāma — Sāma Veda; yajur — Yajur Veda; eva — indeed; ca — and

I am the father of this universe, the mother, the creator, the grandfather, the subject of education, the purifier, the sacred syllable *Om*, the *Rig*, *Sama*, and *Yajur Vedas*. (9.17)

Commentary:

Here, Lord Krishna presented Himself as the God, the ultimate Deity. He replaced every other authority with Himself. He accredited Himself as the father, mother, producer, and grandfather of the universe.

According to a belief in the time of Lord Krishna, the demigod *Brahmā* is the father of the planets and creatures. *Brahmā*'s father is supposed to be *Nārāyaṇa*, Who is also known as Garbhodakashayi Vishnu. The mother of the world is supposed to be the demigoddess *Durgā Devī*. The producer of the cosmic space and the materials within it, is supposed to be Maha Vishnu, the source of *Brahmā*'s father. But now Lord Krishna claims Himself to be all of these.

As the Christians pointed out repeatedly, there are too many of these gods, Gods, Deities, and Lords in Hinduism. But Lord Krishna reduced the scope of such multiple gods to Himself alone.

The three Vedas listed, the Rig, Sama, and Yajur, do not acknowledge Krishna openly as Krishna presents Himself in the *Gītā*. For that matter, modern followers of the Vedas do not stress Lord Krishna at all. The Vedas usually split up the worship in terms of the functions of the various supernaturals. The Supreme God is not stressed in the Vedas as Krishna stressed Himself in the *Gītā*. But regardless, Lord Krishna identifies Himself with the Vedas.

गतिर्भर्ता प्रभुः साक्षी
निवासः शरणं सुहृत् ।
प्रभवः प्रलयः स्थानं
निधानं बीजमव्ययम् ॥९.१८॥
gatirbhartā prabhuḥ sākṣī
nivāsaḥ śaraṇaṁ suhṛt
prabhavaḥ pralayaḥ sthānaṁ
nidhānaṁ bījamavyayam (9.18)

gatir = gatiḥ — objective; bhartā — supporter; prabhuḥ — master; sākṣī — observer; nivāsaḥ — existential residence; śaraṇaṁ — shelter; suhṛt — friend; prabhavaḥ — origin; pralayaḥ — cause of universal disintegration; sthānam — foundation; nidhānam — reservoir of energies; bījam — case; avyayam — non-deteriorating

I am the objective, the supporter, the master, the observer, the existential residence, the shelter, the friend, the origin, the cause of universal integration, the foundation, the reservoir of energies, and the non-deteriorating cause. (9.18)

Commentary:

Apart from a blind religious faith in Krishna and a confidence in what He portrays Himself to be, the only thing left is to get direct evidence. What will we do if we do not get the evidence? Others have made similar claims for themselves even in the Vedic literature. There are other scriptures. What about the gods or God of other religions? Which of them is actually the Supreme? And for which of them are these claims validated? What is the evidence to support such a claim of Krishna?

He presented Himself as the primal objective, the supporter of the world, the final master of everyone, the continuous observer or judging mind over the world, the existential residence of everything, the shelter, the friend, the origin, the cause of universal collapse, the foundation of the world, the reservoir of energies, and the non-deteriorating cause. What else could be said about Him? If nothing else, and until we get direct evidence, what He states so far is impressive. For a historic personality to make such a claim is stupendous.

तपाम्यहमहं वर्षं
निगृह्णाम्युत्सृजामि च ।
अमृतं चैव मृत्युश्च
सदसच्चाहमर्जुन ॥९.१९॥
tapāmyahamahaṁ varṣaṁ
nigṛhṇāmyutsṛjāmi ca
amṛtaṁ caiva mṛtyuśca
sadasaccāhamarjuna (9.19)

tapāmy (tapāmi)- I produce heat; aham — I; aham — I; varṣam — rainfall; nigṛhṇāmy = nigṛhṇāmi — I withhold; utsṛjāmi — I release; ca — and; amṛtam — relatively-long life span of the celestial bodies; caiva — and indeed; mṛtyus- quick death of earthly bodies; ca — and; sad = sat — eternal life; asac = asat — short-term existence; cāham = ca — and + aham — I; arjuna — Arjuna

I produce heat. I withhold and release rainfall. I arrange the relatively-long life span of celestial bodies and the quick death of the earthly ones, as well as the short-term existence and eternal life. (9.19)

Commentary:

By these explanations, Lord Krishna placed a personal levy on just about everything. But what is the proof of such control of every detail of circumstances? Who has seen a human-like person controlling the sun, the moon, the stars, the weather conditions, the life span of the earthly bodies and the displacements we endure by being in one place today and in another some time after?

त्रैविद्या मां सोमपाः पूतपापा
यज्ञैरिष्ट्वा स्वर्गतिं प्रार्थयन्ते.।
ते पुण्यमासाद्य सुरेन्द्रलोकम्
अश्नन्ति दिव्यान्दिवि देवभोगान् ॥९.२०॥
traividyā māṁ somapāḥ pūtapāpā
yajñairiṣṭvā svargatiṁ prārthayante
te puṇyamāsādya surendralokam
aśnanti divyāndivi devabhogān
(9.20)

traividyā — knowers of the three Vedas; mām — Me; somapāḥ — soma drinkers; pūta — reformed; pāpā — bad tendencies; yajñaiḥ — with sacrificial procedures; iṣṭvā — worshiping; svargatim — path of heaven; prārthayante — they desire; te — they; puṇyam — merit based; āsādya — attaining; surendra — king of the angelic people; lokam — world; aśnanti — they enjoy; divyān — angelic; divi — in the astral region; devabhogān — celestial delights

The knowers of the three *Vedas,* the soma drinkers, and those who are reformed of bad tendencies, worship Me with sacrificial procedures. They desire to be transferred to heaven. Attaining the merit-based world of Surendra, the king of the angelic people, they enjoy celestial delights in the astral region. (9.20)

Commentary:

These persons who worship the demigod Indra (or Surendra) may not worship Krishna. In any case, Lord Krishna claims Himself as their ultimate Deity. For success on such a path to an astral paradise, one needs to read the Vedas with great faith, establish procedures for the extraction of juice from the soma plants, perform elaborate rituals, and take up strict vows for ceremonial bathing, sexual restraint, periods of isolation and fasting as recommended by a knowledgeable brahmin priest. If all conditions are met and circumstances go in one's favor, one will, at the time of death, go to an angelic paradise for some time. When the heavenly holiday is over, one resumes life on earth, through assumption of an embryo.

ते तं भुक्त्वा स्वर्गलोकं विशालं
क्षीणे पुण्ये मर्त्यलोकं विशन्ति ।
एवं त्रयीधर्ममनुप्रपन्ना
गतागतं कामकामा लभन्ते ॥९.२१॥

te taṁ bhuktvā svargalokaṁ viśālaṁ
kṣīṇe puṇye martyalokaṁ viśanti
evaṁ trayīdharmam anuprapannā
gatāgataṁ kāmakāmā labhante (9.21)

te — they; tam — it; bhuktvā — having enjoyed; svarga — angelic paradise; lokam — world; viśālam — multi-dimensional; kṣīṇe — in being exhausted; puṇye — in pious merit; martyalokam — world of short life-duration; viśanti — they enter; evam — thus; trayī — three Vedas; dharmam — injunctions for righteous life style; anuprapannā — adhering to; gatāgatam — going away and coming back; kāmakāmā — those who aspire for pleasures and luxuries; labhante — they get the opportunity

Having enjoyed the multi-dimensional, angelic paradise world, exhausting their pious merits, they enter the world of short-life duration. Thus adhering to the tri-part Vedic injunctions for righteous life style, those who aspire for pleasures and luxuries get the opportunity to go to heaven and come back to the earth again. (9.21)

Commentary:

Previously Lord Krishna indicated that this process of working hard to qualify for a journey to paradise was not to His liking. But here, the Lord said that He is actually the person Whom the paradise-yearners worship. At one point, Lord Krishna even chided Arjuna by pointing out that if Arjuna died while fighting, he would go to the *Swargaloka* place to live in luxurious circumstances there. But from the overall view, it appears that Lord Krishna does not like this process even though He claimed to have created it.

In this verse we find the word *kāmākāmā*, and in Chapter Two a related word was given in the form of *kāmakāmī*:

āpūryamāṇamacalapratiṣṭhaṁ samudramāpaḥ praviśanti yadvat
tadvatkāmā yaṁ praviśanti sarve sa śāntimāpnoti na kāmakāmī (2.70)

Becoming filled, not flowing about, remaining stationary, the ocean absorbs the waters that enter it. Similarly, a person who remains calm when cravings arise gets true satisfaction, but not the person who craves for every desire. (2.70)

There Lord Krishna indicated that such a person who impulsively desires, cannot have any spiritual peace and existential security. Such people, He indicated, are full of anxieties over trivial aspects. They are very nervous and unstable. They have little understanding of spiritual reality.

Of great interest, however, is the hint Lord Krishna gave, as evidence of this heavenly course taken by the successful ritualists. He cited their going, returning, and aspiring for luxury. In other words, because they came from the *Swarga* luxurious paradises, they strive for luxuries when they get an earthly body. Their minds are so stained by the luxurious conditions of the angelic places that even though they forgot the celestial life, their subconscious attachment to luxury motivates them to strive for aristocracy when they assume human life.

अनन्याश्चिन्तयन्तो मां
ये जनाः पर्युपासते ।
तेषां नित्याभियुक्तानां
योगक्षेमं वहाम्यहम् ॥९.२२॥
ananyāścintayanto māṁ
ye janāḥ paryupāsate
teṣāṁ nityābhiyuktānāṁ
yogakṣemaṁ vahāmyaham (9.22)

ananyāś — to no other person; cintayanto = cintayantaḥ — keeping the mind attuned to; mām — Me; ye — who; janāḥ — people; paryupāsate — they worship; teṣām — concerning them; nityābhiyuktānāṁ = nitya — always + abhiyuktānām — of those who cultivate yoga disciplines; yogakṣemam — welfare; vahāmy = vahāmi — I tend to; aham — I

I tend to the welfare of the persons who worship Me and no other person, who keep their minds attuned to Me, and who always cultivate the yoga disciplines. (9.22)

Commentary:

According to how much a man tends to Krishna's ideas, that much Krishna supervises the life of that person. Krishna tends to the welfare of the devotees in proportion to the devotees submissiveness to Him.

If we adapt a false concept of Krishna's ideas, He will not protect us as promised. If our spiritual master transmits to us a false idea of what Krishna said, Krishna will not support it. Let us take, for example, this writer. He made an effort to clarify some of Krishna's ideas, but if he transmits a false view, then he will be responsible for misleading others. If on the other hand, he transmits proper knowledge that is consistent with what Krishna said, and if the reader's mind changes that into a false view, then the reader himself is mostly responsible; the writer is liable to a degree and must, if the opportunity presents itself, help that reader come to the proper understanding.

It is not the words, but the ideas behind the words. Since words have variant meanings, we need to get a clear understanding of Krishna's ideas,. Even the same words may have variant meanings for different people. It is essential to get the ideas which are the core of the issue.

A basic sketch of a great devotee of the Lord is given here. Krishna provides for that devotee's welfare and supervises his circumstances. It is not that Krishna becomes his servant, but rather, Krishna becomes the devotee's guardian, just as a parent would provide the affectionate and disciplinary needs of a child. Krishna provides affection or discipline according to the time, place, and righted welfare of a particular devotee. Nor does such a devotee dictate to Krishna nor whimsically suggest to Krishna what should be done. This role of Krishna, as protector of a devotee, is a responsible, sober, parental mood towards the devotee.

The requirements for the devotee, by which he falls under this parental protection plan, are listed elsewhere in the *Gītā*. An interested person should study the *Gītā* and find those statements. One must be careful, however, not to substitute contrary ideas.

Let us review the requirements given in this verse. The devotee must:

- *ananyāś cintayanto mām — Not (an) have any other (anyāś) ideas (cintayanto) besides Krishna (mām) and Krishna's interest as described in the Gītā.*
- *paryupāsate— worship Krishna as recommended in the Gītā.*
- *nityābhiyuktānām— always (nitya) be steady in the yoga disciplines (abhiyuktānām) by which one can remain in association with Krishna.*

Then Lord Krishna will see to the devotee's welfare by giving the affections and disciplines which foster spiritual nature and which brings the devotee closer and closer to the Lord.

येऽप्यन्यदेवता भक्ता
यजन्ते श्रद्धयान्विताः ।
तेऽपि मामेव कौन्तेय
यजन्त्यविधिपूर्वकम् ॥९.२३॥
ye'pyanyadevatā bhaktā
yajante śraddhayānvitāḥ
te'pi māmeva kaunteya
yajantyavidhipūrvakam (9.23)

ye — who; 'py = api — even; anyadevatābhaktā = anya — other + devatā — supernatural rulers + bhaktā — worshipping; yajante — they do prescribed ceremonies and disciplines; śraddhayānvitāḥ = śraddhayā — with faith + anvitāḥ — with; te — they; 'pi = api — also; mām — Me; eva — indeed; kaunteya — son of Kuntī; yajanty = yajanti — they do prescribed ceremonies and disciplines; avidhipūrvakam — not by the recommendation

Those who, with religious ceremonies, disciplines and faith, devotedly worship other supernatural rulers, indirectly petition Me, O son of Kuntī, although they do not perform the ceremonies and disciplines by My recommendation. (9.23)

Commentary:

The keywords in this verse are *yajanti* and *avidhipūrvakam*. *Yajanti* is not just worship, but rather particular ritual worship which is recommended in the Vedic scriptures. A person may, however, consider that modern religions like Christianity, might be covered as being a ritual worship to the supernatural Jesus Christ. In any case, Krishna said that any such worship which is done with great confidence (*śraddhayānvitah*) and which goes directly to and is accepted or considered by a supernatural being (*deva*) is, in a sense, being directed to Krishna but not in the way that Krishna recommends (*avidhipūrvakam*).

So what is the status of such a person who is a devotee (*bhakta*) of some other supernatural being (deva)? And how far should we proceed in the worship of spiritual masters who insist that we adore them, praise them, and formally worship them because they introduced us to the idea of worshipping Krishna? As we go through the *Gītā*, the stress on worshipping such spiritual masters is only there in a few verses, but some of these authorities make themselves into a replacement for Krishna or into equivalents of their Lord.

अहं हि सर्वयज्ञानां
भोक्ता च प्रभुरेव च ।
न तु मामभिजानन्ति
तत्त्वेनातश्च्यवन्ति ते ॥९.२४॥
ahaṁ hi sarvayajñānāṁ
bhoktā ca prabhureva ca
na tu māmabhijānanti
tattvenātaścyavanti te (9.24)

aham — I; hi — truly; sarvayajñānām = sarva — all + yajñānām — of religious ceremonies and disciplines; bhoktā — the person who appreciates; ca — and; prabhur = prabhuḥ — master; eva — indeed; ca — and; na — not; tu — but; mām — Me; abhijānanti — they recognize; tattvenātaś = tattvena — by reality + ataḥ — hence; cyavanti — they deviate form the path of virtue; te — they

Indeed I am the Master of all religious ceremonies and disciplines and I am the person Who should appreciate such procedures. But they do not recognize Me; hence they deviate from the path of virtue. (9.24)

Commentary:

As the *bhoktā*, the Person Who appreciates, Lord Krishna presents Himself as the prabhu or master of religious interest. He claims that all disciplinary worship procedures (*sarvayajñānām*) should be directed to Him as He stipulates. This brings us again to the focal idea in the *Gītā*: That of Krishna presenting Himself as the ultimate objective.

The word *cyuta* means, *fallen, slipped, shifted, or deviated*. We gave, *failed*. The idea is that anyone who does not approach Krishna, as He stipulates, and who uses himself in a way that is opposed to His recommendations, will ultimately fail in spiritual progression.

Earlier in the *Gītā*, the Lord admitted that people get good luck or some yields from worshipping the other supernaturals, but He said that the results were short-ranged and temporary. Now He says that the whole scope of such worship is a frustration, a serious mistake (*cyuta*).

यान्ति देवव्रता देवान्
पितॄन्यान्ति पितृव्रताः ।
भूतानि यान्ति भूतेज्या
यान्ति मद्याजिनोऽपि माम् ॥९.२५॥
yānti devavratā devān
pitṝnyānti pitṛvratāḥ
bhūtāni yānti bhūtejyā
yānti madyājino'pi mām (9.25)

yānti — they go; devavratā — those who satisfy the supernatural rulers; devān — supernatural rulers; pitṝn — pious ancestors who exist as departed spirits; yānti — go; pitṛvratāḥ — those who satisfy the pious ancestors; bhūtāni — the ghostly spirits; yānti — go; bhūtejyā — those who satisfy the ghosts; yānti — they go; madyājino = madyājinaḥ — those who satisfy Me; 'pi = api — surely; mām — Me

Those who satisfy the supernatural rulers, go to those authorities. Those who satisfy the pious ancestors, associate with such departed spirits. Those who try to satisfy the ghosts, go to those beings. Those who try to satisfy Me, surely approach Me. (9.25)

Commentary:

It is interesting how Lord Krishna has disowned every other authority but Himself. He systematically distinguished Himself from all other adorable persons for all times. To Him, there is a distinction between Himself and every other person who takes worship from human beings. Some say that everything is one or that all the gods are one, or that Krishna, Shiva, Vishnu, and *Brahmā* are one. Here Krishna presents a totally segregated view. He not only separates Himself from the departed souls, but from the devas (demigods) of Hinduism as well.

पत्रं पुष्पं फलं तोयं
यो मे भक्त्या प्रयच्छति ।
तदहं भक्त्युपहृतम्
अश्नामि प्रयतात्मनः ॥९.२६॥
patraṁ puṣpaṁ phalaṁ toyaṁ
yo me bhaktyā prayacchati
tadahaṁ bhaktyupahṛtam
aśnāmi prayatātmanaḥ (9.26)

patram — leaf; puṣpam — flowers; phalam — fruit; toyam — water; yo = yaḥ — who; me — Me; bhaktyā — with devotion; prayacchati — he offers; tad — that; aham — I; bhaktyupahṛtam = bhakty (bhakti) —devotional + upahṛtam — given; aśnāmi — I accept; prayatātmanaḥ = prayata — disciplined, purified + ātmanaḥ —from the person

I do accept that given devotion from a disciplined, purified person who offers Me a leaf, flower, fruit or water with a devotional attitude. (9.26)

Commentary:

Prayata means: restrained, self-subdued, holy, pious, devoted, purified by austerities. It is a person who keeps the organs of the senses and the psychology of the mind, feelings and expressions under control. If such a person, being devoted to Krishna, offers a leaf, flower, fruit or some water, Krishna said that He would take it from the devotee.

A broader application of this verse was given by many other commentators, but it is doubtful if Lord Krishna really accepts the offering granted by undisciplined, impious devotees. Unless one has his psychology under disciplinary control, his offering to the Lord would be impure and there would be a question of whether the offerings were accepted or not. Of course, anyone in any established religious society, can tell the public that his offerings are accepted, but how can this be verified? Even a great *sannyāsi* spiritual master may say that his are, but how can we be sure? How can we know for certain that Krishna actually took the offerings? Is it merely our faith that induces Krishna to accept? What is the singular factor by which we can be assured?

To protect themselves from distorted interpretations of this verse, readers should get a reliable Sanskrit dictionary to check the word *prayata*. One has to check *yata* which occurs in the Sanskrit dictionaries as *yam*[1]. Then one must check that root word with the *pra*[2] prefix. Some Vaishnava commentators overlook or reduce the meaning of the word and stress the word *bhaktyā* which is in line 2. If Lord Krishna meant *bhaktyā* alone without *prayata*, then He would not have added this word.

Some commentators suggest that Lord Krishna as Lord Chaitanya deleted the *prayata* requirement and further substantiated the *bhaktyā* factor, but such a proposal is absurd. What they are saying, in effect, is that the original *Gītā* should be discarded and a new *Gītā* be written that is suitable to their view of the suggestions of Lord Chaitanya. And thus one must decide for himself, how he will interpret this verse.

यत्करोषि यदश्नासि
यज्जुहोषि ददासि यत् ।
यत्तपस्यसि कौन्तेय
तत्कुरुष्व मदर्पणम् ॥९.२७॥
yatkaroṣi yadaśnāsi
yajjuhoṣi dadāsi yat
yattapasyasi kaunteya
tatkuruṣva madarpaṇam (9.27)

yat = yad — what; karoṣi — you do; yad — what; aśnāsi — you eat; yaj = yad — what; juhoṣi — you present ceremonially; dadāsi — you gave away; yat = yad — what; yat = yad — what; tapasyasi — you perform as a discipline; kaunteya — son of Kuntī; tat = tad — that; kuruṣva — do; madarpaṇam — offering to Me

Whatever you do, whatever you eat, whatever you present ceremonially, whatever you give away, whatever you perform as a discipline, O son of Kuntī, do that as an offering to Me. (9.27)

Commentary:

This is an instruction to Arjuna but many Vaishnava authorities apply this instruction to their followers, telling their followers that whatever they do, whatever they eat, whatever they present ceremonially, whatever they give away, whatever restriction they observe, should be done as an offering to Krishna. However, there is no assurance that Krishna extended this offer to anyone whose character was not like Arjuna's.

[1]यम् [2]प्र

The question is: What harm would there be if someone of a distorted character, were to offer these aspects of his life to Krishna? The answer is: There is a danger in that such a person might believe that the offerings were being accepted in truth. And thus he would suffer from a self-righteous attitude and risk himself in spiritual stagnation. He would not develop an inch further if he felt that he was on par with Arjuna, or that his offerings were pure enough to be accepted by Krishna.

Unless one is close to Krishna existentially and is as exalted as Arjuna, it is doubtful whether this statement of the *Gītā* is applicable to oneself. Suppose I am a devotee of Krishna and I do immoral acts for missionary purposes. Are these impure acts accepted by Krishna? Will Krishna actually accept the money I derive from such acts? Or will I face baffling reactions in the future?

Suppose I desire to eat flesh. Will Krishna accept that if I first offer it to Him? Or suppose I am a vegetarian but I am a glutton or a sugar addict. Will my attitude towards food affect the preparations of food offerings to Krishna? Will Krishna accept a religious ceremony if I do it with pride, flaunting myself on the public? Will Krishna accept it if I am distracted while worshipping?

Will Krishna approve of my fasting, if before fasting I gorge my belly and if after fasting, I stuff to my throat at a feast? Are all of these aspects approved by Krishna? The answer, of course, must be given by Lord Krishna Himself. If we cannot find an answer in the *Gītā*, we need not look anywhere for any adjusted conclusion. If Krishna gave no answer, He left this topic unclarified. But if the answer is in the *Gītā*, we should locate and examine it.

शुभाशुभफलैरेवं
मोक्ष्यसे कर्मबन्धनैः ।
संन्यासयोगयुक्तात्मा
विमुक्तो मामुपैष्यसि ॥९.२८॥
śubhāśubhaphalairevaṁ
mokṣyase karmabandhanaiḥ
saṁnyāsayogayuktātmā
vimukto māmupaiṣyasi (9.28)

śubhāśubha- good and bad; phalair (phalaiḥ) -with consequences; evam — thus; mokṣyase — you will be liberated; karmabandhanaiḥ — from the implications of action; saṁnyāsa — renunciation; yoga — yoga; yukta — disciplined; ātmā — self; vimukto = vimuktaḥ — liberated; mām — Me; upaiṣyasi — you will attain

Thus you will be liberated from good and bad consequences and from the implications that come from action. Being liberated by the discipline of yoga as it was applied to renunciation, you will come to Me. (9.28)

Commentary:

The previous verse, as well as this one, applies specifically to Arjuna and to devotees who are on par with Him. This writer cannot in all honesty, apply this verse to any others, nor to himself. The exalted status of Arjuna is shown in the *Gītā*, when Krishna said that since Arjuna was His dear friend, since Arjuna was not envious of Him, was not rivaling towards Him, He would explain the most confidential information. It appears that since the time of Arjuna, many devotees of Krishna who are not on par, eased themselves into these guarantees which were given to Arjuna.

Both in this and the previous verse, the Lord used the second person singular which means *you* (Arjuna), while in many other verses he used the third person, meaning *he* (any person or a particular type of person described). We must observe that in these two verses, Arjuna was singled out by the use of *you*.

Samnyāsa yoga, the yoga of renunciation, is a special aspect of self-discipline which was developed in the days of Krishna for students who performed yoga and then either returned to worldly life to function in a detached mood or remained as ascetics and did not participate in worldly obligations. Those who returned to complete worldly obligations were called *tyāgis* and the life-long ascetics were called *samnyāsis*. Arjuna was to be an ideal *tyāgi* like the yogi-king Janaka.

Arjuna gets a personal assurance that if he would act on the battlefield with the sort of detachment King Janaka exhibited, he would be free of all implications and even later on, he would go to Krishna and be near to Krishna existentially, thus benefiting from the spiritual security that is natural to Krishna.

समोऽहं सर्वभूतेषु
न मे द्वेष्योऽस्ति न प्रियः ।
ये भजन्ति तु मां भक्त्या
मयि ते तेषु चाप्यहम् ॥९.२९॥
samo'haṁ sarvabhūteṣu
na me dveṣyo'sti na priyaḥ
ye bhajanti tu māṁ bhaktyā
mayi te teṣu cāpyaham (9.29)

samo = samaḥ — equally disposed; 'ham = aham — I; sarvabhūteṣu — to all beings; na — not; me — of Me; dveṣyo = dveṣyaḥ — shunned; 'sti = asti — is; na — not; priyaḥ — especially dear; ye — who; bhajanti — they worship; tu — but; mām — Me; bhaktyā — with devotion; mayi — in Me; te — they; teṣu — in them; cāpy = cāpi — and too; aham — I

I am equally disposed to all beings. No one is shunned by Me nor is anyone especially dear to Me. But those who worship Me with devotion are My favorite and I am special to them too. (9.29)

Commentary:

This statement of Krishna was supported by practical acts. After all, any person can say that he is equally disposed to his friends, enemies, lovers and despisers, but on the practical level, this is difficult to manifest. For a better understanding of this verse, we would require to consider the history of Lord Krishna, to see exactly how He treated friends and what sort of reaction He gave to enemies. Readers are referred to the *Śrīmad Bhāgavatam*, Tenth Canto, where Krishna's life story is given. We should not, however, overlook His statement about favoring those who worship Him in devotion.

अपि चेत्सुदुराचारो
भजते मामनन्यभाक् ।
साधुरेव स मन्तव्यः
सम्यग्व्यवसितो हि सः ॥९.३०॥
api cetsudurācāro
bhajate māmananyabhāk
sādhureva sa mantavyaḥ
samyagvyavasito hi saḥ (9.30)

api — also; cet = ced — if; sudurācāro = sudurācāraḥ — wicked person; bhajate — worships; mām — Me; ananyabhāk — without being devoted to another; sādhur = sādhuḥ — saintly; eva — indeed; sa = sah — he; mantavyaḥ — should be considered; samyag = samyac — correctly; vyavasito = vyavasitaḥ — decided; hi — indeed; saḥ — he

If a wicked person worships Me without being devoted to any other authority, he is considered saintly, for he decided correctly. (9.30)

Commentary:

This particular verse is a favorite of those devotees who are addicted to immoral or sinful acts. Some of them use this verse to extract badly-needed respect from others. They claim that since they are worshipping Krishna, everyone should regard them as great devotees. They expect that everyone will forget their history or current criminal acts and realize that they are rightly focused and accredited by Lord Krishna.

Some missionaries deliberately advertise this statement to attract criminal elements, whom they exploit to get easy money or vicious favors. Some use this statement to preach against those who are critical of questionable followers who perpetrate criminal acts in the name of Krishna or of a religious society. Such interpretations of this verse are a perversion, however, and the advocates will not be spared the rash reactions that come from material nature.

When broken into parts, the word *sudurācāro* gives: *su* — very; *dur* — bad, wicked; *ācāra* — doer. Thus this word means: a very bad personality, someone with a criminal history. If the word-prefix *su* was not used, it would be a mild word referring to anyone who misbehaved but who does not have a criminal record. This statement, however, does not say that such a criminal should continue vicious or immoral acts, nor that his criminal acts will be devoid of consequences. It only states that such a man who worships (*bhajate*) Lord Krishna should be considered as a saintly person and he is rated as being rightly focused in the act of worshipping and being attentive to Krishna.

The interpretation of this verse made by some, whereby they say that it implies that such a man is fully protected by Krishna from sinful reactions and from continued sinful acts, is artificial because the verse does not state that. But it would be wrong not to give the man due respect for that part of his life which has to do with the worship of Krishna. One should not use this verse to victimize the public nor to extract artificial credits and respects from others. After all, if a man has a criminal history, and he does become a devotee, why does he not become humble and repentant? The answer is this: He took shelter of the Lord to escape reactions without wanting to change sincerely. But in some cases a man wants to change, but cannot, because his old nature hangs onto him and does not release him, even though he made a decision for reform. Thus he resumes sinful activities and pulls down the spiritual master and preaching mission that he is affiliated with. Still, because he once decided (*vyavasito*) to worship (bhajate) Lord Krishna, he has a credit for being saintly or good-natured (*sadhur*) in that regard.

क्षिप्रं भवति धर्मात्मा
शश्वच्छान्तिं निगच्छति ।
कौन्तेय प्रतिजानीहि
न मे भक्तः प्रणश्यति ॥९.३१॥
kṣipraṁ bhavati dharmātmā
śaśvacchāntiṁ nigacchati
kaunteya pratijānīhi
na me bhaktaḥ praṇaśyati (9.31)

kṣipram — quickly; bhavati — he becomes; dharmātmā — a person whose character is virtuous; śaśvacchāntim = śaśvac (śaśvat) — eternal + chāntim (śāntim) — spiritual peace; nigacchati — he experiences; kaunteya — son of Kuntī; pratijānīhi — take note!; na — not; me — of Mine; bhaktaḥ — devotees; praṇaśyati — is ruined permanently

He quickly becomes a person whose character is virtuous. He experiences the eternal spiritual peace. O son of Kuntī, take note of it! No devotee of Mine is ruined permanently. (9.31)

Commentary:

This is one of the most profound verses in the *Gītā*. We may ask whether Lord Krishna can actually support such a guarantee. One man recently wrote the writer about this verse. But he complained bitterly, that perhaps this verse was a farce issued by Krishna. However, I pointed out to him that he may have read a distorted or missionary-motivated translation. I asked him to carefully check the Sanskrit.

What is the basis of this statement? Did Arjuna ask Lord Krishna a question which had to do with a doubt, and did Krishna state this to remove that uncertainty about His doctrine and promises? Was this a defensive statement by Lord Krishna because He made bold claims presenting Himself to be the best of the supernaturals? In the first place, this verse does not mean that a devotee of Krishna will not sink down or will not fall down, or will not see hell, but it does mean that he will not be in trouble on a permanent or ongoing basis. Krishna implies here that He will keep track of the devotee and will, over a period of time, get that devotee in order. It means nothing more.

Some preachers, being biased by their missionary aims, might say something else, but what they say may not withstand the test of time. And in fact, as we analyze the Sanskrit and the match of this statement with other verses of the *Gītā*, we will find Lord Krishna's meaning and be able to separate ourselves from the phony promises of enthusiastic but exploitive missionaries.

The word *pratijānīhi* comes from the root *pratijñā* which means: *To promise, confirm, state, affirm, assert, know, be aware of, learn, comprehend, understand, know to be,* and *consider*. Readers, therefore, can form their own opinion as to which of these meanings apply. Arjuna asked Lord Krishna previously:

arjuna uvāca
ayatiḥ śraddhayopeto yogāccalitamānasaḥ
aprāpya yogasaṁsiddhiṁ kāṁ gatiṁ kṛṣṇa gacchati (6.37)
kaccinnobhayavibhraṣṭaś chinnābhramiva naśyati
apratiṣṭho mahābāho vimūḍho brahmaṇaḥ pathi (6.38)
etanme saṁśayaṁ kṛṣṇa chettumarhasyaśeṣataḥ
tvadanyaḥ saṁśayasyāsya chettā na hyupapadyate (6.39)

Arjuna said: What about the undisciplined person who has faith? Having deviated from yoga practice, having not attained yoga proficiency, what course does he take, O Krishna?

Is he not like a faded cloud, lost from both situations, like being without a foundation? O Almighty Krishna: He is baffled on the path of spirituality.

You can, O Krishna, remove this doubt of mine fully. Besides You, no other remover of doubt, exists here. (6.37-39)

Lord Krishna then replied:

śrībhagavānuvāca
pārtha naiveha nāmutra vināśastasya vidyate
na hi kalyāṇakṛtkaścid durgatiṁ tāta gacchati (6.40)

The Blessed Lord said: O son of Pṛthā, it is realized that neither here on earth nor above in the celestial regions, does the unaccomplished yogi lose his skill. Indeed, O dear Arjuna, no performer of virtuous acts, goes down permanently into misfortune. (6.40)

Krishna gives some more information regarding Arjuna's question about a person who endeavors in the spiritual direction, in the direction of self and mind control, and who fails at the process. Lord Krishna assured that even if a man is not a yogi, even if he were not striving for sense and mind control, if he is carried away by his previous bad habits, still, even if the man is wicked, if he is focused on worshipping *(bhajate)* Krishna, he should be considered to be a good man *(sadhur)*.

Obviously, Lord Krishna asserted that an aspiring yogi who strives on the spiritual path, may go to the heavenly planets, and then return to this earthly place to continue his progress. The progress is not lost. It is the progress that Lord Krishna speaks about. A person's effort at spiritual improvement will not be lost permanently even if he falls away from spiritual disciplines. He will resume and continue. Lord Krishna will make sure that he does.

Let us review what Krishna said about those endeavoring yogis, because the guarantee that applies to the criminally-minded persons who have turned to Krishna cannot be any better of a guarantee than that which is given in bold print for the sincere souls who have no record of vicious acts.

prāpya puṇyakṛtāṁllokān uṣitvā śāśvatīḥ samāḥ
śucīnāṁ śrīmatāṁ gehe yogabhraṣṭo'bhijāyate(6.41)
atha vā yogināmeva kule bhavati dhīmatām
etaddhi durlabhataraṁ loke janma yadīdṛśam (6.42)
tatra taṁ buddhisaṁyogaṁ labhate paurvadehikam
yatate ca tato bhūyaḥ saṁsiddhau kurunandana (6.43)
pūrvābhyāsena tenaiva hriyate hyavaśo'pi saḥ
jijñāsurapi yogasya śabdabrahmātivartate (6.44)

After obtaining the celestial places where the virtuous souls go, having lived there for many, many years, the fallen yogi is born into the social circumstances of the purified and prosperous people.

Alternately, he is born into a family of enlightened people. But such a birth is very difficult to attain in this world.

In that environment, he is inspired with the cumulative intellectual interest from a previous birth. And from that time, he strives again for yoga perfection, O dear son of the Kurus.

Indeed, by previous practice, he is motivated, even without conscious desire. He who persistently inquires of yoga, instinctively sees beyond the Veda, the spoken description of the spiritual reality. (6.41-44)

Krishna claimed that by taking shelter of Him, even the criminally-minded people get the taste of the eternal spiritual peace (*śaśvacchāntim*). They experience this. When they compare this to the happiness of worldly life, they find the old sensual enjoyment to be shallow. As such they become attached to the spiritual security in Krishna's association and they strive to remain in His company. But due to the momentum of criminal acts, they are again drawn away from Krishna, but temporarily. This is the point here. Such people will certainly see hell, undoubtedly. But in time, they will be reformed by Krishna.

Readers should pay specific attention to the word *ananyabhāk* in the previous verse 30. This means that the criminally-minded person must worship (*bhajate*) Krishna (*mām*) and no other person (*ananyabhāk*).

Therefore, those criminally-minded people who do worship others and who are not completely focused on Krishna, are not covered in this guarantee. A missionary may give the guarantee to anyone who has a criminal record and who offers some criminally-acquired money but unless such a man becomes totally absorbed in the worship of Krishna, as Krishna defines it and not as the missionary might have defined it in a deviant or adjusted way, he will not be covered by this guarantee.

मां हि पार्थ व्यपाश्रित्य
येऽपि स्युः पापयोनयः ।
स्त्रियो वैश्यास्तथा शूद्रास्
तेऽपि यान्ति परां गतिम् ॥९.३२॥
māṁ hi pārtha vyapāśritya
ye'pi syuḥ pāpayonayaḥ
striyo vaiśyāstathā śūdrās
te'pi yānti parāṁ gatim (9.32)

mām — Me; hi — indeed; pārtha — son of Pṛthā; vyapāśritya — by relying on; ye — who; 'pi = api — also; syuḥ — they should be; pāpayonayaḥ — persons from sinful parentage; striyo = striyaḥ — women; vaiśyāḥ — businessmen; tathā — even; śūdrās — laborers; te — they; 'pi = api — also; yānti — they move towards; parām — supreme; gatim — goal

O son of Pṛthā, by relying on Me, even persons from sinful parentage, even women, businessmen, even laborers, do move towards the supreme goal. (9.32)

Commentary:

The hinge is reliance on Krishna, taking shelter in Krishna, and allowing the resultant divine influence to work in a person's life. The effect of Krishna's association is a revolutionary adaptation to the divine ideas of the Lord and to the resultant disciplinary life and its attainment.

There is a bias here, however, in that Lord Krishna first mentioned the criminal, the *sudurācāro*; then He mentions four other types of disadvantaged persons, making a total of five categories. The four are:

- *pāpayonayah--- persons born from evil parentage*
- *striyo--- women*
- *vaiśyās--- merchants, commercial farmers, contenders and others whose occupation caused their minds to be possessed of commerce.*
- *śudrās--- unskilled laborers or skilled laborers with low income, poverty stricken members of the population, people without aristocracy.*

किं पुनर्ब्राह्मणाः पुण्या
भक्ता राजर्षयस्तथा ।
अनित्यमसुखं लोकम्
इमं प्राप्य भजस्व माम् ॥९.३३॥
kiṁ punarbrāhmaṇāḥ puṇyā
bhaktā rājarṣayastathā
anityamasukhaṁ lokam
imaṁ prāpya bhajasva mām (9.33)

kim — how; punar — more again, more accessible; brāhmaṇāḥ — brahmins; puṇyā — piously-inclined; bhaktā — devoted; rājarṣayaḥ — yogi kings; tathā — also; anityam — temporary; asukham — miserable; lokam — world; imam — this; prāpya — having acquired; bhajasva — devote yourself; mām — Me

How much more accessible then, is it for the piously-inclined brahmins and yogi kings? Having acquired an opportunity in this temporary, miserable world, you should devote yourself to Me. (9.33)

Commentary:

This ultimatum by Krishna, that Arjuna had better devote (*bhajasva*) himself to Krishna, is given as an alternative to a continued existence in this temporary and miserable world (*anityam asukham lokam*). How Arjuna acquired an opportunity to act in this miserable place is not explained, but the urgency of getting out of this place is surely addressed.

The yogi kings are those kings who had training in yoga and then learnt the application of it to worldly life, just as King Janaka did. These are persons like Arjuna who were schooled in the application of an already-learnt yoga practice except that Arjuna was trained on the spot by Lord Krishna. Arjuna learned yoga from others but Krishna gave him the technique of its application.

In contrast to those yogi-kings, rulers, and princes, there are the piously-inclined brahmins (*brāhmaṇāh puṇyā*), who do not apply themselves to worldly life as much as the administrators do but who live simply with a greatly curtailed, material involvement.

मन्मना भव मद्भक्तो
मद्याजी मां नमस्कुरु ।
मामेवैष्यसि युक्त्वैवम्
आत्मानं मत्परायणः ॥९.३४॥
manmanā bhava madbhakto
madyājī māṁ namaskuru
māmevaiṣyasi yuktvaivam
ātmānaṁ matparāyaṇaḥ (9.34)

manmanā — one whose mind is fixed on Me; bhava — be; madbhakto = madbhaktaḥ — being devoted to Me; madyājī — performing ceremonial worship of Me; mām — to Me; namaskuru — make obeisance; mām — Me; evaiṣyasi = eva — indeed + esyasi — you will come; yuktvaivam = yuktva — disciplined + evam — thus; ātmānam — self; matparāyaṇaḥ — with Me as the Supreme Objective

With the mind fixed on Me, being devoted to me, performing ceremonial worship to Me, make obeisance to Me. Being thus disciplined, with Me as the Supreme Objective, you will come to Me. (9.34)

Commentary:

At this point in the discourse, we can see that Lord Krishna completely put Himself in the center of everything as the immediate and ultimate aim of life. This verse is a very famous one. Anyone who heard *Gītā* lectures must have heard this verse being repeated again and again. By the repeated use of personal pronouns, indicating Himself: *man, mad, mad, mam, mam*, and *mat*; Lord Krishna stressed the focus of Himself.

By this recommendation, we should put our minds on Krishna, be devoted to Him, offer ceremonial worship, make reverence, be steady and consistent in these procedures, and devote our souls to Him with the intent of gaining His association and tending His interests.

CHAPTER 10

A Fraction of Krishna's Splendor*

श्रीभगवानुवाच
भूय एव महाबाहो
शृणु मे परमं वचः ।
यत्तेऽहं प्रीयमाणाय
वक्ष्यामि हितकाम्यया ॥१०.१॥
śrībhagavānuvāca
bhūya eva mahābāho
śṛṇu me paramaṁ vacaḥ
yatte'haṁ prīyamāṇāya
vakṣyāmi hitakāmyayā (10.1)

śrī bhagavān — the Blessed Lord: uvāca — said; bhūya — again; eva — indeed; mahābāho — O powerful man; śṛṇu — hear; me — from Me; paramam — supreme; vacaḥ — information; yat = yad — which; te — to you; 'ham = aham — I; prīyamāṇāya — to one who is beloved; vakṣyāmi — I will explain; hitakāmyayā — desiring your welfare

The Blessed Lord said: Again, O powerful man, hear from Me of the supreme information. Desiring your welfare, I will explain it, O beloved one. (10.1)

Commentary:

As promised, Lord Krishna gave the complete course of how to apply yoga practice. This teaching is the teaching Krishna claimed to have passed on to the yogi-kings like Janaka. As stated, the disciplic succession that passed through those kings to their sons was disrupted. Krishna wanted to re-establish it through Arjuna.

It appears that in the course of time, some of the brahmins lost track of the application of yoga to worldly life. It is said in the Chandogya Upanishad that a brahmin named Gautama got the knowledge of how to apply yoga from a king named Pravahana Jaivali.

Generally these kings transmitted the techniques to their sons, the princes, but on occasion, they taught others. Originally, however, the brahmins themselves were to teach this information to the administrators, just as empowered entities like *Paraśurāma* passed on the technique to others; but on occasion the rulers who become expert, taught humble, inquisitive brahmins. It is even said that once Shuka went to meet a King Janaka to learn of this application of yoga to worldly life.

In the Chandogya Upanishad, we hear that at a certain point in history, this knowledge of the application of yoga to worldly life was not even given to the brahmins.

taṁ ha ciraṁ vasetyājñapāyancakāra
taṁ hovāca yathā mā tvaṁ gautamāvado
yatheyaṁ na prāktvattaḥ purā vidyā
brāhmaṇāngacchati tasmādu sarveṣu lokeṣu
ksatrasyaiva praśāsanamabhūditi tasmai hovāca

**The Mahābhārata contains no chapter headings. This title was assigned by the translator on the basis of verse 41 of this chapter.*

The King advised him: "You should stay here for a long time."

At the end of the period, the king said, "Even as you told me, O Gautama, prior to you, this political science of governing (praśānam) was never transmitted to brahmins. This is why the teaching belonged to the rulers in earlier times in all countries. "

Then the king instructed Gautama. (Chandogya Upanishad 5.3.7)

न मे विदुः सुरगणाः
प्रभवं न महर्षयः .
अहमादिर्हि देवानां
महर्षीणां च सर्वशः ॥१०.२॥
na me viduḥ suragaṇāḥ
prabhavaṁ na maharṣayaḥ
ahamādirhi devānāṁ
maharṣīṇāṁ ca sarvaśaḥ (10.2)

na — not; me — of Me; viduḥ — they know; suragaṇāḥ — the supernatural rulers; prabhavam — the origin; na — nor; maharṣayaḥ — great yogi sages; aham — I; ādir = ādiḥ — source; hi — in fact; devānām — of the supernatural rulers; mahārṣīnām — of the great yogi sages; ca — and; sarvaśaḥ — in all respects

The supernatural rulers do not know My origin, nor do the great yogi sages. In all respects, I am the source of the supernatural rulers and the great yogi sages. (10.2)

Commentary:

This is a hint. No limited person can really understand Krishna in full. It is up to Krishna to reveal Himself. One can know Krishna to some degree, depending on one's categorical status in reference to the Lord, but since He is the source of the production of the world, He cannot be known in full. Insofar as we may get from Him some concept or direct experience of His nature and productions, we may understand.

This statement is in part, a defense being put up by Lord Krishna to explain why the supernatural controllers and great sages did not declare His glories openly. They did not know Him. To finalize this, Lord Krishna displayed the Universal Form. We have to understand that these declarations of Krishna are to an extent, appalling not only to people in our own time, but to people in the time of Krishna who believed that Lord Shiva was God or that Lord *Nārāyaṇa* was God, or that Lord *Brahmā* was God, or that Lord Surya or Lord Vishnu was God. Krishna showed proof because His declaration was disruptive to the religious beliefs of His time.

Lord Krishna berated the supernatural controllers and the earthly authorities, the great sages. Some of them despised Him; some did not think much of Him. These supernatural people like Lord Shiva and Lord Vishnu had already gained popularity among mankind. Lord Shiva, in particular, was known from ancient times. He made an impact on the earth's history. Now Krishna would make His mark and convince the people that He is supreme. It is seen, however, that even today, many Indians are still uncertain about Krishna's position as the Supreme. They are still talking about all of the gods and putting Krishna in the heap as one of the deities.

यो मामजमनादिं च
वेत्ति लोकमहेश्वरम् ।
असंमूढः स मर्त्येषु
सर्वपापैः प्रमुच्यते ॥१०.३॥

yo = yaḥ — who; mām — Me; ajam — birthless; anādim — beginningless; ca — and; vetti — knows; lokamaheśvaram — Almighty God of the world; asaṁmūḍhaḥ — unconfused, perceptive; sa = saḥ — he; martyeṣu — of

yo māmajamanādiṁ ca
vetti lokamaheśvaram
asaṁmūḍhaḥ sa martyeṣu
sarvapāpaiḥ pramucyate (10.3)

those who use perishable bodies; sarvapāpaiḥ — from all faults; pramucyate — is freed

Of those who use perishable bodies, the one who regards Me as birthless and beginningless and who knows that I am the Almighty God of the world, is the perceptive person. He is freed from all faults. (10.3)

Commentary:

This is more than a matter of a mere belief in Lord Krishna, even though a belief may start one out on the path of knowing about, seeking out, and getting Krishna's association. A mere belief in Krishna, a mere mental understanding of a description of the words and guarantees of the *Gītā*, a mere feeling of affection towards Krishna, will not free one from all evils. It is thoroughly misleading to assure an audience or a group of disciples that simply by hearing such a description and accepting it, they will be free from all faults. Many senior devotees of Krishna make this blunder and mislead those who are trying to get some divine association.

Vetti means to know inside out, to know thoroughly by experience. It is not the kind of knowledge that is passed on in disciplic succession whereby the spiritual master himself has no experience but has only heard and then formed a mental conception and developed an emotional feeling without actually experiencing these attributes of Krishna.

Inexperienced spiritual masters do cheat their followers by passing on such information in the theoretical or imaginative form to assure hearers that such a transmission is the total message. *Vetti* means knowing to the degree of experiencing. If one has actually experienced Lord Krishna as the Supreme Lord of the world, just as Arjuna did when he saw the Universal Form, then one is released from all faults, not otherwise.

As the government of a country does not recognize the currency of a man who prints his own money, so the laws of material nature do not honor the guarantee of these cheating spiritual masters who have not experienced and who in turn give their followers imaginative ideas about Krishna. These commentaries are certainly conceptual but there is a difference. This writer does not give the readers the view that they can be freed from sins by the concepts. The concepts are given as an impetus to earn direct experience from Lord Krishna. We will read of Arjuna's direct experience of knowing (*vetti*) Krishna as the Supreme Lord of the world (*lokamaheśvaram*).

Some preachers claim that it is not important to see the Universal Form. They stress that it is fearful and that we should try to get to the loving side of Krishna. But unless one sees the Universal Form, one cannot properly appreciate Lord Krishna. Spiritual masters, whether they are in good standing in the Vaishnava tradition or not, are so much of a rip-off, a fraud, when they cheat their disciples by downplaying the importance of the Universal Form which was seen by Arjuna. If it was an unnecessary revelation, why did Krishna show it? This they cannot explain. They can merely bypass this in order to call so many naieve human beings into their following. But the concept of Krishna that such followers enjoy, is not the real Krishna. The real Krishna is not that easy to attain.

Both the limited souls and Krishna are birthless (ajam) and beginningless (*anādim*). Why then, did Krishna stress this about Himself? The answer is hinted at in line 3 by the term *asammūḍhah*. Krishna is not confused at any time. The limited souls, though birthless and beginningless, do become confused about spirituality, but Krishna claimed an exemption for Himself, and He gave proof of that in the *Gītā*. Of course, so much of *Gītā* must be accepted on the basis of mere belief, because the revelation of the Universal Form and other visions seen by Arjuna cannot be seen by others who do not qualify. Until such time, we will have to settle for a belief, but we should not fool ourselves nor let anyone trick us into thinking that merely by such a belief in the words of the *Gītā*, we are freed from all sins.

बुद्धिर्ज्ञानमसंमोहः
क्षमा सत्यं दमः शमः ।
सुखं दुःखं भवोऽभावो
भयं चाभयमेव च ॥१०.४॥
buddhirjñānamasaṁmohaḥ
kṣamā satyaṁ damaḥ śamaḥ
sukhaṁ duḥkhaṁ bhavo'bhāvo
bhayaṁ cābhayameva ca (10.4)

buddhir = buddhiḥ — intelligence; jñānam — knowledge; asaṁmohaḥ — non-confusion, sanity; kṣamā — patience; satyam — truthfulness; damaḥ — self-control; śamaḥ — tranquility; sukham — pleasure; duḥkham — pain; bhavo = bhavaḥ — existence; 'bhāvo = abhāvaḥ — non-existence; bhayam — fear; cābhayam = ca — and + abhayam — fearlessness; eva — indeed; ca — and;

Intelligence, knowledge, sanity, patience, truthfulness, self-control, tranquility, pleasure, pain, existence, non-existence, fear, fearlessness... (10.4)

Commentary:

These aspects and the ones listed in the verse below are attributed as Krishna's production. These aspects are an overview of the various factors which make up material existence. Some are positive. Others are negative.

अहिंसा समता तुष्टिस्
तपो दानं यशोऽयशः ।
भवन्ति भावा भूतानां
मत्त एव पृथग्विधाः ॥१०.५॥
ahiṁsā samatā tuṣṭis
tapo dānaṁ yaśo'yaśaḥ
bhavanti bhāvā bhūtānāṁ
matta eva pṛthagvidhāḥ (10..5)

ahiṁsā — non-violence; samatā — impartiality; tuṣṭiḥ — contentment; tapo = tapaḥ — austerity; dānam — charity; yaśo = yaśaḥ — fame; 'yaśaḥ = ayaśaḥ — infamy; bhavanti — are; bhāvā — existential conditions; bhūtānām — of the beings; matta — from Me; eva — alone; pṛthagvidhāḥ — multiple

...non-violence, impartiality, contentment, austerity, charity, fame and infamy, are multiple existential conditions, which are derived from Me alone. (10.5)

Commentary:

Insofar as Lord Krishna can prove that He is the Supreme Lord, we can accept that these aspects of existence were caused in His act of starting the material world. For those of us who accept Krishna's declarations with caution, we may take these aspects as being manifested by the Supreme Absolute Truth. In either case, the Primal Cause should be credited with having started the mundane creation. It is appropriate that we look to the Primal Cause, regardless of whoever, or whatever we assume that person or force to be.

Persons who refuse to accept Lord Krishna as the Supreme Lord or who have doubts about Krishna as the Ultimate Authority, do so because they lack faith in His authority. Unless one gets the revelation Arjuna got, one's ideas of Krishna are for the most part, reliant on faith in Him or a lack of confidence in Him. A human being is limited and circumspect by objective experiences. Those who have no experience of the revelation Krishna gave to Arjuna and who have no belief in the descriptions of it, form variant ideas. But Krishna allowed that anyone may accept and aim for the Supreme Spirit as defined in

Chapter Eight, text 9. Readers who have difficulty accepting these declarations of Krishna should carefully study the description Krishna gave of the Supreme Spirit.

kaviṁ purāṇamanuśāsitāram aṇoraṇīyāṁsamanusmaredyaḥ
sarvasya dhātāram acintyarūpam ādityavarṇaṁ tamasaḥ parastāt (8.9)

He who meditates on the Person Who knows everything, the most ancient of people, the Supreme Supervisor, the most minute factor, the one with unimaginable form, with a radiant body, free of grossness, (8.9)

If we believe Krishna and also have the revelation Arjuna got, even in part, then we may reach the state of consistent confidence in Krishna.

A careful study of the *Gītā* gives us a better idea of what we should discover about Krishna. It is a lead on, a sort of map of the way of discovery of these glories of Krishna or glories of the Supreme Spirit as our belief and faith permits.

One must, however, agree to honor Krishna for His level of superior intelligence in presenting this information of the *Gītā*. The information is very logical, philosophical and revealing in particular ways. The *Gītā* is a well-considered presentation. There is no doubt about it. This is why many intelligent persons who do not even believe in Krishna as He presents Himself, do study the *Gītā*. These persons sidestep, what they consider to be, the arrogance of Krishna and carefully go on to the philosophy of life and layout of existence that Krishna presented. They do not deal with Krishna's declarations of supremacy. They do not take that seriously, but they do pay strict attention to His philosophy and analysis of the mundane world.

Intelligence (*buddhir*, 10.4) is present everywhere in the mundane creation in both the moving and non-moving forms, in chemicals and in inert or the so-called dead materials. This intelligence is shown by the reactive nature of each item we find in the creation. The most intelligence, however, is seen in the overall interaction of the whole universal situation. On the local level, intelligence is manifested in different proportions in different creatures. A man's ability to grasp a subject shows the application of intelligence. *Bhagavad Gītā* teaches that despite the disparities, the intelligence of the limited entities is just about equal. It is said that a saintly man sees the true equality of all souls. He recognizes the soul in the various creature forms and understands that their potential for development is similar.

Knowledge for theory and knowledge in practice is *jñānam*. But knowledge in practice, which is experience, is superior to knowledge in theory which one acquires without practice. There are two types of **knowledge**, namely that which is formulated based on practice and that which is formulated in the mind on the basis of hearing from a true or untrue source. The knowledge which is based on practice, on experience, is far superior to the conceptual type which is based on hearing, reading and conceptualizing. Hearing and reading are faulty processes of learning, since by hearing, one forms various misconceptions. This occurs because one depends on the mind.

When a man hears something, his mind does not accept it as it is, for the mind, by its very nature, has to reference incoming ideas to those which are already lodged in the memory. Even if one hears from a true source, he is apt to form misconceptions. Hearing is greatly accredited by spiritual authorities, but actually, hearing is very faulty if it is not backed by an experience which illustrates what is heard. Arjuna, for example, heard from Krishna about the variation between considering an action and acting. But Arjuna developed a misconception about it. Lord Krishna clarified that considering an action and then acting, is not a contradiction. Hearing itself, therefore, is a very imperfect way of receiving information but if hearing is backed by an experience which shows the actual truth, then hearing becomes complete and perfect.

Sammohah is confusion or illusion. *Asammohas* (10.4) is clarity or **sanity**. As we will hear from Krishna, material nature itself provides a basis for both confusion and clarity, all depending on which type of energy we utilize. The clarifying energy is called the *sattva guṇa* energy. The confusing mode is called the *rajo guṇa*. The dulling mood is termed as the *tamo guṇa*. A superior clarity comes from the spiritual plane of existence which is beyond the material modes. So long as a soul is involved with the material nature, he may select which of the modes he will utilize or which he may be influenced by. In utilizing the material modes, an aspiring soul is required to use a greater percentage of clarifying energies and the least of the confusing or dulling types.

One cannot become free from the lower modes merely by conceptions or by promises of spiritual teachers and scriptures. One must make a separate endeavor to purify the subtle energy in the psyche and to insure that a more purified subtle energy is used in the operation of the mind and senses. This is why *āsanas* and *prāṇāyāma* have importance. This is why yoga is described by Lord Krishna as being the cause of soul purification:

tatraikāgraṁ manaḥ kṛtvā yatacittendriyakriyaḥ
upaviśyāsane yuñjyād yogamātmaviśuddhaye (6.12)

...being there, seated in a posture, having the mind focused, the person who controls his thinking and sensual energy, should practise the yoga discipline for self-purification. (6.12)

A man must purify his mind and life energy, not his mind alone. Senses which are enthused by an impure life force cannot become purified merely by looking at sanctified objects. The main problem is not the outer world, but the inner energy or life force which drives the senses. An impure life force may seek out and find satisfaction in purified, clean, sanctified objects but that does not mean that the life force itself becomes cleansed by perceiving pure items. The inner content of the life force must be changed and its usage of impure energy from the lower modes, must be changed also.

The idea that one's senses will be purified by outer means is a fool's concept only. Many people accept such a view and go on with their spiritual life in the false hope that they will get salvation. At the end of the body, however, the soul must carry his impure life energy and be bogged down by its bad habits and so be drawn back into other material forms according to the profile of the impure life energy.

Clarity stays far away from a man whose life force is impure. For him, the seeing instrument, which is the mind and intellect, does not afford the clarity required for correct decisions. The mind itself is a minor problem when compared to the life force. In the yoga system, there is talk about mind and sense control. And modern people do have a little understanding about mind control and sensual restrictions. But they hardly understand life energy control. One may control the mind as much as he likes and he may restrict the senses also, but still, the impure life energy will do the devil's work in motivating vices and new forms of impulsive sensuality. We get a hint from Lord Krishna:

karmendriyāṇi saṁyamya ya āste manasā smaran
indriyārthānvimūḍhātmā mithyācāraḥ sa ucyate (3.6)

A person who, while restraining his bodily limbs, sits with mind remembering attractive objects, is a deceiver. So it is declared. (3.6)

A seeker cannot jump from the material level to the spiritual one suddenly. Even though one might have a flash of enlightenment or a flash of genuine spiritual enthusiasm, it does not last. One returns to his basic level and must work his way upwards through the modes of material nature. When the seeker has continually resituated himself in a higher mode, in a gradual and sure process of changing lower habits permanently, he gradually reaches the spiritual plane.

Ksamā (10.4) means **patience** or forbearance. This has to do more with destiny than with social relations. Insofar as social relations are a tool of destiny, patience applies, but otherwise, the main effort is to be patient with destiny. As energetic beings, we are eager to get on with the fulfillment of our constructive and destructive desires, but destiny regulates how we might fulfill these. And we must, if we want an easy course, work along with destiny. Destiny will not give any living entity full facility at any time. We only get partial facility with periods of success and periods of failure. A perceptive and humble person must accept all of these positively, knowing well that he is a limited being with a limited scope.

Satyam (10.4) has a broad and narrow meaning. Some meanings are: true, real, genuine, honest, sincere, truthful, faithful, virtuous and upright. The narrow meaning is the one which applies to our human social condition and the broad one has to do with the reality that transcends our humanity.

For social purposes, truth means speaking the truth and living in a way that sponsors truthfulness. **Truthfulness** is more than a vow, more than a moral principle. It has to do with the permission of providence. Unless providence permits a man, he cannot be truthful no matter how he aspires to be honest. If a man really wants to be truthful, he should aim, not at a vow of truthfulness, but to put himself in a position whereby truthfulness is sponsored by his lifestyle. He should put himself in a non-defensive position in relation to destiny. If we are in opposition to destiny or if we are in a situation which poses an irritation to destiny, truthfulness will vanish. Vows have their limitations. On the lower stages, one who takes a vow of truthfulness, must deal with the resulting pride. But on the higher levels when one sees the limitations, one does not take any vow but instead works to be humble towards providence. He pleads with providence to simplify his existential needs, so that no occasion for untruthfulness may arise.

Beyond the social uses of truthfulness, there is a broader aspect. The English equivalent of this superior truthfulness is reality. For both the liars and the truth-tellers, reality is there as a contrasting factor which must be faced. Reality transcends opinions. In one sense, reality is destiny. Reality is absolute.

Damah (10.4) is **self-control**. But self-control is not possible until all the psychic equipments are controlled. The self is the last object to be controlled. First we must control grosser things like the body, the emotions, the sensual impulses, the thinking impulses, the mindal compartment. Until these are under control there is no question of self-control. Despite theories and promises in various religious books, a man cannot control himself unless he gets his psychic equipment under a near-absolute regulation. The self is motivated by the psychic equipments. Its control of itself cannot be consistent if it is constantly goaded by the psychic urges. Therefore these must be brought under control by specific means. Each of the psychic tools are controlled by a particular discipline. This is why we find that a spiritual master might exhibit control in one aspect of spirituality and be unrestrained in another.

One spiritual master might have a very disciplined mind but may have loose and impulsive emotions. Another might have some restraint over his emotions but his impractical sense of reason might assume a domineering aspect over him. While yet another might have his sensuality under control but his thinking energy might be unrestrained. This occurs because each of the psychic tools requires a particular discipline.

Some spiritual masters, however, like to fantasize about the discovery of a complete process which curbs everything by a single procedure. But there is no such method. Each of the equipments are particular and requires a particular type of restraint, according to their particular types of energies consumed.

It may be said that putting gasoline in a car will rectify its stalled condition, but that only applies if all the essential parts are in order. If for instance, the transmission is faulty, gasoline will not repair that fault. One has to attend to the particular problem and give it the appropriate solution. There is no point in discussing self control until all the psychic equipments are curbed completely, since if even one of the equipments is unrestrained, it may motivate the senses and cause the soul to act impulsively. Here are two *Gītā* verses that help us to understand this:

yatato hyapi kaunteya puruṣasya vipaścitaḥ
indriyāṇi pramāthīni haranti prasabhaṁ manaḥ (2.60)

Concerning an aspiring seeker, O son of Kuntī , concerning a discerned educated person, the senses do torment him. By impulsions the senses do adjust his mentality. (2.60)

indriyāṇāṁ hi caratāṁ yanmano'nuvidhīyate
tadasya harati prajñāṁ vāyurnāvamivāmbhasi (2.67)

When the mind is prompted by the wandering senses, it utilizes the discernment, just as in water, the wind handles a ship. (2.67)

Śamah is inner **tranquility**, the absence of passionate feeling within the psyche. This occurs naturally or by endeavor. Those who rely on its natural occurrence and who are not spiritually advanced, become victims of passion periodically. A very advanced personality need make no endeavor to quell his passion but we certainly must try our best to bring the passionate nature under control. We should purify our inner energies, clarify our objectives, improve character and scale down desires. This gives more facility of expression for our peaceful nature.

Sridhara Deva Gosvami has given *damah* as *control of the external senses*, and *śamah* as *control of the internal senses* (The Hidden Treasure of the Sweet Absolute, p. 173). These types of control are related. External control concerns social behavior. Internal control is more important than the external type but an effort on the external level does affect us internally and can assist in the quest for good behavior. If, however, we misuse external control, it has a counter-productive effect.

Sukham and *duhkham* (10.4) are **pleasure** and **pain**. This includes physical, mental and emotional adjustment. These are part and parcel of material existence because this existence is temporary. In Chapter Thirteen, Lord Krishna explained that we, the limited entities, are subjected to such pleasures and pain in the material world. It is due to our connection to the mind because we are harnessed by and wired to the mind.

In actuality the soul has nothing to do with pleasures and pains, but as long as one is hooked up to a subtle body, one will have to endure it. It is an indirect response but in the conditioned stage, the soul is affected. By assigning Himself as the cause of this pleasure and pain, Lord Krishna indicated that none of the limited entities are responsible for their condition of being in material nature, because none of them created the material world nor were instrumental in putting themselves in touch with the active mundane energy. The initial actions are God's only. And therefore ultimately, it is all His responsibility.

There are many well-meaning but poorly-informed preachers who state that it is our fault, but when asked about the creator of the material world, they become silent. Or they state that God created it and gave us a choice of following His instruction or disobeying. They fail to explain how a fully-responsible, fully-perceptive God could give the partially-responsible, partially perceptive entities that kind of absolute choice. The connections between God, the limited entities and material nature are not as simple as these preachers assume it to be. Our task is purification. From purification, comes clarification. From clarification, comes recognition of the realities that face us and from that recognition comes the proper decision. A man never qualifies for the divine service until he becomes purified. But he may act out a mock devotion before he reaches that stage.

Bhavo 'bhāvo is *bhavah* and *abhāvab* (10.4). In Sanskrit, words change according to particular sound-adjusting rules called sandhi rules. By these rules, the *ah* of *bhavah* can be changed to *o* and the *a* of *abhavah* can be dropped and replaced with an apostrophe. *Bhavah* and *abhāvah* mean: being and non-being, or **existing** and **not existing**, or appearing and not appearing.

The fundamental teaching of Lord Krishna in Chapter Two, is the eternal nature of the soul. As such the death of a body, does not mean the death of a soul. For appearance in one place, one must have a suitable form, otherwise, those who use forms in that location and who do not have clear psychic perception would not detect one. For the gross detection, a soul or spirit must use a detectable form. When we see its form, we can say it is existing. But if it does not use a form, we say that it is not existing.

The soul's existence is asserted to an absolute degree in the *Gītā*, but his appearance and disappearance through forms is also explained by Lord Krishna. In this verse, Krishna claimed that He has the monopoly on the appearance and disappearance of the forms of the various limited entities.

Bhayam cābhayam (10.4) means **fear** and **fearlessness**. The absence of fear or fearlessness is manifested as innocence or courage. *Cābhayam* is a combination of two Sanskrit words: *ca* and *abhayam*. *Ca* means *and*. *Abhayam* means *without fear*. A limited being cannot control his fear and fearlessness absolutely. He can only control himself in familiar surroundings. He does not have the ability to control himself beyond that. Only God has that type of power to be absolutely fearless. For that matter, one of the aspects of God is fearlessness, while everyone else has some degree of fear. The fear, however, is not manifested under all conditions. It is felt under certain conditions of uncertainty. Thus Krishna, since He presented Himself as the Supreme Person, accredited Himself as the cause of fear and fearlessness.

Ahimsā is **non-violence**. *himsā* means violence or injury. When *a* is put before *himsā*, the meaning is reversed. Since Mahatma Gandhi became famous, the word *ahimsā* became popular but the idea of non-violence did not begin with Gandhi. Others propagated it. Even today, it remains a popular sentiment.

Bhagavad Gītā does not propagate non-violence to the body at the expense of the soul, but it does advocate in absolute terms, non-violence to the soul, even at the expense of the body. Thus we see that Krishna urged Arjuna to wipe out the Kauravas and assured Arjuna that the death of their bodies was good for the benefit of their souls, while the continuation of those forms was ruinous and would have been a violence to one and all.

Samatā means: sameness, likeness, similarity, **impartiality**, fairness, or to treat someone as an equal. The *Gītā* preaches this by advocating that an advanced soul see the similarity in potential of all limited entities and see that they are provided with opportunities for living in various species of life, and that the laws of nature apply to each of them fairly. A man should understand that his situation is not unique. The situation of those who are situated in higher or lower positions, is not necessarily unique either. It all depends on one's categorical status. If one is a limited entity, he has an almost equal chance of improving himself if he strives for purification; otherwise, if he neglects his development, he will remain in his current status or be degraded. When a limited entity realizes that he has the same potential of other successful limited beings, he loses the envy of others. His existence becomes simplified.

As we heard in the *Gītā*, Lord Krishna presented Himself as being unique, as being special, as being absolute, and as being the one and only Final Authority. There is no sense in envying Krishna, since none of the limited beings will ever match Him. But in comparison to each other, the limited ones in similar categories have similar potential.

Tuṣṭih means **contentment**. Without contentment, one cannot be free from hankerings and anxieties. A person who is habitually discontent cannot be happy even in the material world. He certainly cannot attain spiritual peace or *śānti*, spiritual security. Contentment comes from submitting to one's destiny and allowing destiny to take its course. If one tries to fight destiny, he may get a false satisfaction but his mind will be full of fear and anxieties, because he is limited, and will, sooner or later, be frustrated by fate. We may contest some of the ideas of the *Gītā*, especially Krishna's suggestions. If we do not agree with His views in those regards, we may still take hints from Him on how to satisfy the Supreme Spirit or the primal cause.

Tapo means penance or religious **austerities**, but there are other Sanskrit words that denote austerity. *Tapo*, however, also means burning, heating, distressing, causing some pain or discomfort. Therefore tapo means the kind of austerity which involves some discomfort, some type of endeavor, especially austerities which affect the life energy in the body. In the time of Lord Krishna, the Upanishadic sages and other ascetics engaged in yoga *āsana* postures and *prāṇāyāma* practices which were considered as *tapo*. We already gave some history of Arjuna's asceticism in the Himalayas. Many spiritual masters advocate that yoga and *prāṇāyāma* are no longer necessary. They say that we can get the same results that the sages got from that sort of austerity, by easier methods. But this has not been proven conclusively. Many people who follow these spiritual masters and believe what they say, do not know the result attained by great sages. Still, they are believing what they are told, even though they have not checked to see if they are getting the same benefit. In any case, it rests with the particular seeker to judge the method given.

Dānam is **charity**. This type of charity is charity that is recommended in the Vedic scriptures. These stipulate that a gift should be given to the proper person at the proper time and in the proper place. Even the animals are worthy of charity on occasion. In presenting Himself as the Supreme Being, Lord Krishna makes a claim as being the cause of charity. The Supreme Cause is ultimately, the source of all productions.

Money and goods, however, are not the only commodities which may be given in charity. One good gift of charity is education. Another good gift is caring concern which helps foster a good character and a basic sense of security in others. The focus on charity as money or as monetary donations is a greatly distorted conception pushed by wealthy individuals who seek fame by donating money. These persons, however, do distribute their sins along with their money. When a poor man takes something from a rich man, the poor fellow accepts some of the sin of the wealthy donor. The gift carries the crime which was committed in its accumulation. Thus, poor persons usually remain in a condemned existence by their acceptance of such gifts. Unless a wealthy individual has got his wealth by purely pious and fair means, his gifts are donations of sin only. He merely uses such occasions to gain a good reputation, while in fact, he is worthy of ill-repute.

In modern times, some wealthy individuals feel that if their money is acquired by government approval, it is sin-free. This is a misconception. Many business practices which are approved by a government are sin-formulated and sin-yielding. Thus we cannot judge the sinful or sinless quality of money by government regulations. It is up to the individual poor man to decide what he should do with such gifts of charity which are, in fact, gifts of sin. Recently one rich man told the writer that the *Bhagavad Gītā* was supportive of a person enjoying his good providence. He thought that whatever we get by the grace of providence is ours to enjoy. But the gifts of providence are mostly deposits of providence given to us for safekeeping. This person considered, however, that these items were given for enjoyment or exploitation, or at least for our decision-making. But this is not consistent with the philosophy of the *Gītā*.

Something is given by providence, not for our enjoyment, but for our safekeeping until we can receive further instruction of what to do with it. A very small portion of what we get is actually for our enjoyment and that portion is so minute as to be negligible. Most of it is meant to be in our safekeeping and to be passed on to others at a later date. But if we assume the attitude of enjoyers, we make many mistakes and sink our teeth into things that do not belong to us, thus forestalling salvation and causing all sorts of unfavorable conditions in future lives.

What can we actually give to another? What have we produced? What indeed have we created? We are those people who came into the creation after it was created and who found materials here. We are those souls who take help and inspiration from many other sources. How can we make a claim to originality?

Yaśo is **fame**. Popularity actually belongs to the originator of the material creation, the Lord of the world. But there is a distribution of fame according to special acts performed by anyone in any part of the creation. In most cases, however, fame leads to ruination. The temptation to act for fame is a real factor in the existence of a limited entity. By nature, each limited person wants to be known, to be the focus of attention, to be loved or remembered by everyone.

If a man can, if he is that modest and humble, he should ward off the fame that comes to him and direct it to the Supreme Person. It is seen that even some empowered agents of the Lord have difficulty warding off fame. They stand in their positions of popularity, lord it over people and create a false legitimacy, whereby they pose as agents of the Lord and take for themselves even the fame that rightly belongs to God. Such is our miserable condition as human beings. The sickness of a human being, his emotional and mental impurities, knows no bounds.

'yaśah is an abbreviated form of the word *ayaśah* which means ***infamy**, bad reputations, or disrepute.* There is ample room for that in the material creation. A bad reputation follows a man even to the world hereafter, where he faces the consequences of vicious acts even after his material body dies. Both fame and infamy follow a man wherever he may go. Each man is accountable to the living entities in general, to material nature, and to the Supreme Spirit.

Insofar as He can substantiate His claim as the Lord of the world, the primal creator, motivator, and destroyer, Lord Krishna is ultimately responsible for everything that occurs. But that does not mean that He will directly absorb the liabilities. Material nature herself acts to balance out the tensions. She does this by shifts of energies which bring discomfort to one group and comfort to another.

Inasmuch as a rich man is actually the ultimate producer of a project, so Lord Krishna presents Himself as the proprietor of the world. But as the rich man is not directly responsible for a fire or any other disaster that may occur at the project, so Lord Krishna issues disclaimers for the responsibilities that occur in the dealings between the limited entities and material nature.

महर्षयः सप्त पूर्वे
चत्वारो मनवस्तथा ।
मद्भावा मानसा जाता
येषां लोक इमाः प्रजाः ॥१०.६॥
maharṣayaḥ sapta pūrve
catvāro manavastathā
madbhāvā mānasā jātā
yeṣāṁ loka imāḥ prajāḥ (10.6)

mahārṣayaḥ — great yogi sages; sapta — seven; pūrve — in ancient times, of old; catvāro = catvāraḥ — four celibate boys; manavaḥ — primal sexually-disciplined procreators; tathā — also; madbhāvā — coming from Me; mānasā — mentally; jātā — produced; yeṣāṁ — of whom; loka — universe; imāḥ — these; prajāḥ — creatures

The seven great yogi sages of old, the four celibate boys, and also the primal sexually-disciplined procreators come from Me, being produced mentally. From them, the creatures of this universe evolved. (10.6)

Commentary:

Sridhara Deva Gosvami listed the seven great sages of old as *Marīci, Atri, Angira, Pulastya, Pulaha, Kratu*, and *Vasiṣṭa*. He gave the four who are grouped together as *Sanaka, Sanandan, Sanat-Kumara and Sanātana*. According to *Śrīla* Sridhara Deva Gosvami, these four are known as *brahmarśis*. The *Manus* are fourteen in number. They procreate through disciplined sexual indulgence, not for the pleasure of it but as a duty to the Supreme Lord and by the order of *Brahmā*, their father.

Lord Krishna claimed that He mentally produced (*mānasā jātā*) these seven, four, and fourteen authorities. This means that these forms were produced by will power only and not from sexual intercourse. Later on, disciplined sexual intercourse was used by the first *Manu*. However, the Vedic literatures are unanimous in their presentation of *Brahmā* as the mental father of these authorities. Someone by the name of Garbhodaka Vishnu, Who is also called Hiranyagarbha or *Nārāyaṇa*, is listed as the sire of *Brahmā*, having produced *Brahmā*'s body by a natural process using will power and development of potencies. The claim of Krishna to have directly produced the seven, four and fourteen authorities, may be put to question as a contradiction to the information in the *Purāṇa*s, even in the Bhāgavat *Purāṇa*.

However, it must be that Krishna's will and authority overrides *Brahmā*'s. *Brahmā*'s action must be a shadow act of Krishna's intention. We may understand this by observing the sprouting action of a seed. When planted, it transforms itself into a plant. But the seed itself was produced with potencies. The seed did not produce its own capacity. Therefore it is not the actual producer. We would have to retrace history to find the original tree and then we would have found the real producer indeed. Thus, this statement is another example of Krishna's presentation of Himself as the root cause, the foundation, even of personalities, even of the gods like *Brahmā*. It is, therefore, a question of proof. What is the proof that Krishna is actually the root cause that He claims to be?

We get a hint here, however, that the mental production of progeny is a special feature of God and His creator-son *Brahmā*. It appears that no one else was able to reproduce in that way. In addition, it appears that only certain entities, the empowered special ones who are very close to the Supreme Being, can be manifested in the material creation mentally,.

एतां विभूतिं योगं च
मम यो वेत्ति तत्त्वतः ।
सोऽविकम्पेन योगेन
युज्यते नात्र संशयः ॥१०.७॥
etāṁ vibhūtiṁ yogaṁ ca
mama yo vetti tattvataḥ
so'vikampena yogena
yujyate nātra saṁśayaḥ (10.7)

etām — this; vibhūtim — divine glory; yogam — yoga, extensive mystic discipline; ca — and; mama — of My; yo = yaḥ — who; vetti — experience; tattvataḥ — in reality; so = saḥ — he; 'vikampena = avikampena — by consistent; yogena — by yoga practice; yujyate — is harmonized with; nātra = na — not + atra — here; saṁśayaḥ — doubt

Whosoever experiences in reality, this divine glory and extensive mystic discipline of Mine, becomes harmonized with Me by consistent yoga practice. There is no doubt about this. (10.7)

Commentary:

So far the proof is lacking. In a sense, anyone could have studied the Vedic literature and then made a claim to be the Overlord of everyone and everything. Thus we require proof. Arjuna will challenge Krishna on this matter.

Many of the Vaishnava authorities of the modern era have, in many of these verses, translated the word *yoga* as devotion or devotional service, but we have stuck to the original since we are presenting the *Gītā* in its own time and place. If Krishna wanted to say *devotion*, He would have used the word *bhakti*, but He is consistently using the word yoga in its various Sanskrit noun forms. We saw His definition of yoga practice and His stress of it as a basic discipline even for the rulers of society like Arjuna and Janaka.

One cannot realize (*vetti tattvatah*) this divine glory (*vibhūtim*) and extensive mystic discipline (*yogam*) unless it is revealed, or unless one practices yoga austerities to purify the soul in preparation for divine vision. In Arjuna's case, he did perform the yoga disciplines and did also have the revelation in a sudden drastic act of Krishna on the battlefield. At least that is what we are told in the *Mahābhārata* of which *Gītā* is an essential part.

The seven great sages, the four which are grouped together and the Manus, are all expert yogis. These personalities practiced yoga in the past and present creative cycles. They left their bodies through advanced yoga techniques. It is a wonder, therefore, that yoga is being foreshadowed by some commentators, even by those who hail in the disciplic succession from Krishna.

Yujyate in the fourth line means: *He is joined, he is united, he is yoked*. Some commentators claim that this means: He is turned into the Supreme Being. But even though this is an opinion, it is not consistent with the statements of the *Gītā*. In the *Gītā*, we are told that never will the soul lose its individual status. When Arjuna saw the Universal Form, he proclaimed that no one can merge with Krishna. Krishna stood alone as the Supreme Source, the Supreme Personality, Whose views are ultimate.

We gave the word *harmonize* for *yujyate*, to remain consistent with the tone of the *Gītā*. '*vikampena* yogena is *avikampena* yogena. The word yoga is there and we will not change it. Yoga was defined by Krishna in the *Gītā* and there is no verse or line of the Sanskrit where Krishna defines yoga as devotion. But we do see that when the yoga discipline is applied to devotion, we get *bhakti yoga*. In other words, when a person applies his *bhakti* or devotional affections in the disciplined way he cultivated by yoga practice, it is called *bhakti yoga*.

When another person applies his mentality in the disciplined culture he developed by yoga practice, it is called *jñāna* yoga. And when another person applies his working energy or administrative governing skill in the culture of yoga, then we have *karma yoga*. Arjuna therefore was advised to follow Janaka on the path of *karma yoga*. He was told to follow the disciplined administrators because that was his service to society. Persons like *Nārada* are yogi bhaktas in practice. Persons like the four sages are grouped together as *Jñāna* yogis in practice. Persons like Arjuna and Janaka are *karma* yogis in practice.

Nārada is a yogi *bhakta* because he mastered yoga practice and applied his affections, loves and concerns for the Supreme Lord with the disciplinary and purificatory skill he acquired by yoga. Others who love Krishna and who do not have the yoga expertise are not genuine yogi bhaktas, but they are devotees of Krishna nevertheless.

Arjuna is also a yogi *bhakta*, but his specialty is *karma yoga* while *Nārada* is a 100% *bhakti yoga* specialist. Arjuna applied his working energy with discipline and did so because he loved and respected Krishna, but *Nārada* applied his affectionate energies directly and was not obligated to work as an administrator.

अहं सर्वस्य प्रभवो
मत्तः सर्वं प्रवर्तते ।
इति मत्वा भजन्ते मां
बुधा भावसमन्विताः ॥ १०.८ ॥

ahaṁ sarvasya prabhavo
mattaḥ sarvaṁ pravartate
iti matvā bhajante māṁ
budhā bhāvasamanvitāḥ (10.8)

aham — I; sarvasya — of all; prabhavo = prabhavaḥ — originator; mattaḥ — from Me; sarvam — everything; pravartate — proceeds; iti — thus, in this way; matvā — having thought; bhajante — they worship; mām — Me; budhā — intelligent person; bhāvasamanvitāḥ = bhāva — states of being, meditative ability + samanvitāḥ — endowed with

I am the originator of all. From Me, everything proceeds. Thinking of Me in this way, the intelligent persons, who are endowed with meditative ability, worship Me. (10.8)

Commentary:

In our own time, we may apply this to any devotee of Krishna but in the time of Krishna, this applied to the great yogis like *Nārada* and others, who went through *āsanas* and *prāṇāyāmas* and who, by those bodily, mental, and emotional disciplines, became proficient in meditation (*bhāvasamanvitāh*). The history of *Nārada*'s austerities are described elsewhere in Vedic literature.

It is not that *Nārada* performs such austerities now, for in the time of Krishna, the same *Nārada* used to visit Lord Krishna, but there is no record of austerities at that time. He already attained perfection and was maintaining it continuously. However, the contention that modern devotees did, like *Nārada*, perform these austerities in their past lives, is put to question. It is not proven conclusively. There is no concrete evidence. In fact, many of the leading modern devotees fall by the wayside of spiritual life. We hear from day to day, how they either leave or are pushed out of their parent societies for some discrepancy, when their old habit returned to claim them or urge them to behave improperly.

Some contend that the world proceeds naturally from the *brahman*, the sum total spiritual energy, but here Lord Krishna uses the pronoun *aham*, which means, *I*. He refered to Himself as the cause of the world. The participation of *brahman*, however, is not denied by Krishna but its importance is reduced. It is given a subsidiary role as a co-participant with material nature.

मच्चित्ता मद्गतप्राणा
बोधयन्तः परस्परम् ।
कथयन्तश्च मां नित्यं
तुष्यन्ति च रमन्ति च ॥१०.९॥
maccittā madgataprāṇā
bodhayantaḥ parasparam
kathayantaśca māṁ nityaṁ
tuṣyanti ca ramanti ca (10.9)

maccittā — those who think of Me; madgataprāṇā — those who concentrate the life energy onto Me; bodhayantaḥ — enlighten; parasparam — one another; kathayantasca = kathayantaḥ — speaking of + ca — and; mām — of Me; nityam — constantly; tuṣyanti — they are content; ca — and; ramanti — they are happy; ca — and

Those who think of Me, who concentrate the life energy on Me, who enlighten one another and speak of Me constantly, are content and happy. (10.9)

Commentary:

Maccittā are those who think of Krishna. But there are other qualifications listed, such as *madgataprāṇa*, those who have concentrated or have sent (*gata*) their life energy (*prāṇa*) to or on Krishna (mad). These persons must also be enlightening one another (*bodhayantah parasparam*) about Krishna. And they must speak of Him constantly (*nityam*). Then they are content and happy by this conjoint process.

Madgataprāṇa is given other meanings in other commentaries but we ask serious readers to study the meanings of the words *prāṇa* and *gata*. The combination of *gataprāṇa* usually means a dead body or a body from which the life energy (*prāṇa*) is gone (*gata*). Readers are also asked to consider that the focus of the life energy (*prāṇa*) by *prāṇāyāma* is part of the yoga process which was used in the time of Lord Krishna. And it was described in the *Gītā* previously. Please let us stick to the consistent meanings of the *Gītā* in its own time and place, even if we cannot apply these techniques in our lives today. In this way we understand the *Gītā* as it was delivered to Arjuna. There is nothing wrong with realizing that we cannot do exactly as Krishna instructed, but we should not superimpose something else and think that the adjusted procedure was explained to Arjuna.

तेषां सततयुक्तानां
भजतां प्रीतिपूर्वकम् ।
ददामि बुद्धियोगं तं
येन मामुपयान्ति ते ॥१०.१०॥
teṣāṁ satatayuktānāṁ
bhajatāṁ prītipūrvakam
dadāmi buddhiyogaṁ taṁ
yena māmupayānti te (10.10)

teṣām — of these; satatayuktānām = satata — constantly + yuktānām — of the disciplined; bhajatām — of the worshippers; prītipūrvakam — with affection; dadāmi — I give; buddhiyogam — technique of insight yoga, application of yoga to the use of intelligence; tam — it; yena — by which; mām — Me; upayānti — they draw near; te — they

Of those who are constantly disciplined, who worship with affection, I give the technique by which they draw near to Me. (10.10)

Commentary:

Buddhi yoga was explained in great detail in Chapters Three and Four. It is the application of yoga to the cultivation and improvement of the intellect, to bring the intellect to the plane of clarity in clear mystic insight. Unless one has this mystic insight he cannot see beyond the gross material plane. *Buddhi* yoga is not an understanding in the mind nor an ability to follow concepts intellectually The result of having mastered *buddhi* yoga is the withdrawal of the *buddhi* (intellect) from the mundane level and the location of it on the spiritual plane for direct vision and experience there. This is a mystic process. It is only attained by curbing the mind through yoga practice. As long as the mind can wander by its desire, one cannot attain the results of *buddhi* yoga.

Buddhi yoga is an important aspect of yoga practice. *Āsana* postures may appear to be a purely physical accomplishment but nothing is further from the truth, since a living physical body has the subtle and causal forms interlocked into it. The *āsana* postures, if done properly, move one to the subtle plane and help one to curb the subtle body. The next stage is that of *prāṇāyāma* which is a process of getting the life energy curbed. Unless this energy is curbed, attempts at the mind control by various means, turn out to be a failure, because the life energy is in a unique position to motivate the mind impulsively.

It does not matter what spiritual group a man is affiliated with nor what method of mind control he uses, if his life energy is impure, he will fall away from vows and practices. That is definite. At some stage, one needs to understand this. One should take definite steps to curb the life force (*prāṇa*).

Buddhi yoga cannot be accomplished at any time until the life force is curbed because the mind and the intellect are affected by the life force. The condition of the life force determines one's ability to remain steadfast in religious vows (*satatayuktānām*).

Worshipping with affection is easy because every person has affection. It is there, but again, the affections (*prīti*) are affected by the life force. Impure affections do not bring a person closer to Krishna or any other divine personage. One has to keep the life force clean and then the mind and affections can be directed properly. Otherwise, the process is preliminary and it will not give the promised results.

If *buddhi* yoga has no value in reference to *bhakti yoga*, it would not be stressed by Krishna. Some commentators have carefully disposed of *buddhi* yoga as a distinct process by converting *buddhi* yoga to *bhakti yoga*. We remind readers again that *buddhi* yoga is the application of yoga to curbing the intellect, to transform it into spiritual perception. *Bhakti yoga* is the application of yoga to our affections or devotions (*prīti*) so that our affections can be regulated, be purified completely, and be fit for relationships with the divine persons.

When all this is said and done, we can go toward or be near (*upayānti*) Krishna.

तेषामेवानुकम्पार्थम्
अहमज्ञानजं तमः ।
नाशयाम्यात्मभावस्थो
ज्ञानदीपेन भास्वता ॥१०.११॥
teṣāmevānukampārtham
ahamajñānajaṁ tamaḥ
nāśayāmyātmabhāvastho
jñānadīpena bhāsvatā (10.11)

teṣām — of them; evānukampārtham = eva — indeed + anukampā — assistance + artham — interest; aham — I; ajñānajam — ignorance produced; tamaḥ — stupefying influence of material nature; nāśayāmy = nāśayāmi — I caused to be banished; ātmabhāvastho = ātmabhāvasthaḥ — situated in the self; jñānadīpena = jñāna — knowledge, realized + dīpena — with light, with insight (jñānadīpena — with realized insight); bhāsvatā — clear, shining, clarity of consciousness

In the interest of assisting them, I who am situated within their beings, cause the ignorance, produced by the stupefying influence of material nature, to be banished by their clear realized insight. (10.11)

Commentary:

Apart from giving the technique of *buddhi* yoga, Lord Krishna gives assistance to those serious ascetics who are addressed in these verses. This assistance is given to others in various proportions but these verses are addressed to specific ascetics. We have to stay within the context and not spread the guarantees to those who are not specifically mentioned.

The ignorance born of the dark mode of material nature is an intellectual blindness. This is connected to the development of the same *buddhi* yoga, which removes this mental and intellectual lack of vision. This is not a gross darkness like the darkness of night. It is a darkness within the mind, a psychological lack of insight. And it is cleared up by *buddhi* yoga.

Ātmabhāvastho is a combination of three words, namely *ātma* (the spirit), *bhāva* (the being), and *stho* (situated). Krishna indicated that He is stationed or situated in the being of the spirit. And from that existential plane, He causes the ignorance to be removed. *Jñānadīpena* is usually translated as *the lamp of knowledge*. But it is not book information. Nor is it merely a matter of hearing from a spiritual master.

Jñānadīpena is the internal purified intellect gained by virtue of *buddhi* yoga, so that one sees directly the revelation and does not rely on written or spoken information. By using the term *bhāsvatā*, which means "brilliantly shining, clarifying", Krishna stressed the actual experience. We will see that Arjuna will get such a clarifying (*bhāsvatā*) experience shortly when he is shown the Universal Form.

अर्जुन उवाच
परं ब्रह्म परं धाम
पवित्रं परमं भवान् ।
पुरुषं शाश्वतं दिव्यम्
आदिदेवमजं विभुम् ॥ १०.१२ ॥
arjuna uvāca
paraṁ brahma paraṁ dhāma
pavitraṁ paramaṁ bhavān
puruṣaṁ śāśvataṁ divyam
ādidevamajaṁ vibhum (10.12)

arjuna — Arjuna; uvāca — said; param — supreme; brahma — spiritual reality; param — supreme; dhāma — refuge; pavitram — reformer; paramam — supreme; bhavān — You, O Lord; puruṣam — person; śāśvatam — eternal; divyam — divine; ādidevam — Primal God; ajam — birthless; vibhum — one whose influence spreads everywhere

Arjuna said: Hail to You Who are the Supreme Reality, the Supreme Refuge, the Supreme Reformer, O Lord. You are the eternal divine Person, the Primal God Who is birthless, and Whose influence spreads everywhere. (10.12)

Commentary:

Up to this point. Lord Krishna presented no solid proof. Arjuna stated Krishna's glories. At this point, a sudden feeling of surrender was experienced by Arjuna. He experienced a change of attitude. Thus he declared this. These declarations are strictly from the position of acceptance of Krishna as the Supreme Being, as the awesome Godhead.

Even though Arjuna had no solid proof in the *Gītā* thus far, except for Krishna's thorough expounding of some philosophies, still it appears that Arjuna went through a profound change. His attitude towards Krishna in Chapter One was different.

We may or may not accept Arjuna's new condition. After all, Arjuna is stunned by Krishna's repeated bombardments of perfect answers to Arjuna's doubts and questions. How do we know that Arjuna is not mystified?

Arjuna made a big claim for Krishna by declaring Krishna as *param brahma*. According to an ancient theory of *Vedānta*, *param brahma* is not a personality at all but is rather, a supreme power from which the persons arise. Thus, how could Arjuna all of a sudden, address Krishna as the Supreme Power, as the Ultimate Reality (*parambrahma*)? This one statement of Arjuna caused many eyebrows to move in wonder. People wonder whether Arjuna was simply overwhelmed by Krishna's influence which bore upon him on that battlefield of *Kurukṣetra*. Why, all of a sudden, did Arjuna address Krishna, the son of *Devakī*, a person with a history of birth in the human species, as the Supreme Reality? What will this do to the conclusions of great sages who did not realize nor recognize Krishna in that way?

Krishna did declare Himself as the Supreme Refuge (*param dhāma*), as the one person Who is to replace all supernatural persons and forces. Krishna did deliberately present Himself as such. But why, all of a sudden, has Arjuna accepted Krishna in this way? We recall that when Krishna stated that He taught the solar deity, Arjuna questioned by asking how Krishna could have done that since such an incident belonged to antiquity.

Arjuna was right to address Krishna as *pavitra*, a purifier, cleanser, savior or reformer. But to address Krishna as the Foremost Reformer, was another matter. What is the evidence? Every disciple may think that his spiritual master is the foremost reformer. Any student might think that his teacher is the greatest instructor. But how are we to verify this? Elsewhere in the Vedic literatures, others described their teachers or deities as the foremost and supreme. What is the proof regarding Krishna?

आहुस्त्वामृषयः सर्वे
देवर्षिर्नारदस्तथा ।
असितो देवलो व्यासः
स्वयं चैव ब्रवीषि मे ॥१०.१३॥
āhustvāmṛṣayaḥ sarve
devarṣirnāradastathā
asito devalo vyāsaḥ
svayaṁ caiva bravīṣi me (10.13)

āhuḥ — they declare; tvām — You; ṛṣayaḥ — yogi sage; sarve — all; devarṣir = devarṣiḥ — supernatural yogi sage; nāradaḥ — Narada; tatha — as well as; asito devalo —Asita Devala; vyāsaḥ — Vyāsa; svayam — your own self; caiva = ca — and + eva — indeed; bravīṣi — You state; me — to Me

All the yogi sages, as well as the supernatural yogi sage Narada, Asita Devala, and Vyasa declare this of You. And You Yourself state this to me. (10.13)

Commentary:

Arjuna heard about the glories of Krishna from some reputed sages. Then at *Kurukṣetra* he heard the same from Lord Krishna directly. *Nārada* was well-known in the time of the Kurus as a supernatural sage who descended from the celestial world. *Nārada* is said to have appeared even to the demon King, Kamsa, who was killed by Krishna. It is a question of reliability. Who were those sages? Why should we accept their testimony?

Nārada's history is legendary. There is no gross proof. He did not have a gross parentage. According to *Nārada*, his last human parentage was in a previous time cycle when he was the son of a maidservant. After that, he took his parentage from *Brahmā*, the creator sub-God. He appeared by the desire of *Brahmā* and not by the usual sexual association of a man and woman. *Nārada* explained his unusual appearance to *Vyāsaji* in Canto One of the *Śrīmad Bhāgavatam*. The description is incredible. Asita Devala is also of supernatural origin.

Vyāsaji had physical birth. These were great sages and religious authorities of the time. Of the three, *Vyāsaji* was the grandfather of Arjuna. *Vyāsaji* sired Arjuna's father, Pandu. But

Vyāsaji did that upon the request of Queen *Satyavatī*, on behalf of the departed King Vichitravirya, who was *Vyāsaji*'s half-brother. *Vyāsaji*'s father was Parashar Muni who was a great sage of renown and a composer of scripture. He is accredited as the author of the Vishnu *Purāṇa*. *Śrīla Vyāsadeva* was a writer in the tradition of his father. He is author of the *Mahābhārata* of which the *Gītā* is a part. He wrote the *Śrīmad Bhāgavatam* and other Vedic literatures of importance. *Vyāsadeva*'s mother was Queen *Satyavatī*, Arjuna's grandmother. Vichitravirya was *Vyāsadeva*'s half-brother on their mother's side. *Vyāsadeva* is a reliable source. He was highly educated and proficient in yoga austerities. He and his son Shuka were mystics.

सर्वमेतदृतं मन्ये
यन्मां वदसि केशव ।
न हि ते भगवन्व्यक्तिं
विदुर्देवा न दानवाः ॥१०.१४॥
sarvametadṛtaṁ manye
yanmāṁ vadasi keśava
na hi te bhagavanvyaktiṁ
vidurdevā na dānavāḥ (10.14)

sarvam — all; etad — this; ṛtam — true; manye — I believe; yan = yad — which; mām — me; vadasi — you say; keśava — O Keśava; na — not; hi — indeed; te — to you; bhagavan — O Blessed Lord; vyaktim — form; vidur = viduḥ — they know; devā — the supernatural rulers; na — nor; dānavāḥ — descendants of Danu, enemies of the supernatural rulers

All that You say to me is true. I believe it, O Keśava. Indeed it is not possible to understand You, O Bhagavan, Blessed Lord. Neither the supernatural rulers nor their enemies, the descendants of Danu, can know Your form. (10.14)

Commentary:

At this point, there is still no concrete proof about Krishna's divinity. With concurrence of great sages, Arjuna accepted everything that Krishna told him. Then Arjuna said, "I believe whatever You said about Yourself."

The contention that Krishna's body is material, is now addressed by Arjuna. First of all, Arjuna used the word *vyaktim* which means something that our material senses consider to be substantial. We understand that whatever is perceived by our material senses is temporary. This is our experience. Thus Arjuna says *vyaktim*, something that we can see. So the question as to Krishna's form is brought up here. This is a big question. After all, if Krishna appeared as the son of *Devakī's* body, just as any other child appears in this world, then how can Krishna make such claims as He did? But Arjuna said further that even Krishna's grossly manifested form (*vyaktim*) was unknown to the demigods (*vidur devā na*). This means that the supernatural gods (*devas*) do not know (na vidur) that physically-manifested (*vyaktim*) form of Lord Krishna. But still the proof is lacking. At this point, even Arjuna believes and accepts what Krishna said about Himself.

Arjuna therefore proposes that whatever the supernatural people or the supernatural devils may say about Krishna, that is inconsistent with Krishna's declaration of Himself or with what *Nārada*, Asita Devala or *Vyāsaji* stated, would be false.

स्वयमेवात्मनात्मानं
वेत्थ त्वं पुरुषोत्तम ।
भूतभावन भूतेश
देवदेव जगत्पते ॥१०.१५॥

svayam — yourself; evātmanā = eva — indeed + ātmanā — by yourself; 'tmānam = ātmānam — yourself; vettha — you know; tvam — you; puruṣottama — Supreme Person; bhūtabhāvana — one who sustains the

svayamevātmanātmānaṁ
vettha tvaṁ puruṣottama
bhūtabhāvana bhūteśa
devadeva jagatpate (10.15)

existence of all others; bhūteśa — Lord of created beings; devadeva — God of the gods; jagatpate — Lord of the universe

You alone know Yourself, O Supreme Person, O maintainer of the creatures, O Lord of the created beings, O God of gods, O Lord of the universe. (10.15)

Commentary:

Arjuna has, at this point, completely given himself over to Krishna's views. Up to this point, everything is on the plane of belief and sheer faith in Lord Krishna. Arjuna had some supernatural experiences with Lord Krishna prior to the battle of *Kurukṣetra*. He had faith in Krishna but just before the battle when Arjuna performed austerities, he exhibited faith in others like Indra and Shiva. Thus Arjuna's faith was spread between different personalities.

Arjuna declared that only Krishna knew Himself (*svayam evātmanā'tmānam*). He hailed Krishna as *puruṣottama*, the best or highest of the personalities, as *bhūtabhāvana*, the person causing the well-being of all creatures or *bhūtas*, as *bhūteśa*, the *īśa* or Lord of all beings, as *devadeva*, the God of the gods, and as *jagatpate*, the Master of the world.

वक्तुमर्हस्यशेषेण
दिव्या ह्यात्मविभूतयः ।
याभिर्विभूतिभिर्लोकान्
इमांस्त्वं व्याप्य तिष्ठसि ॥१०.१६॥
vaktumarhasyaśeṣeṇa
divyā hyātmavibhūtayaḥ
yābhirvibhūtibhirlokān
imāṁstvaṁ vyāpya tiṣṭhasi (10.16)

vaktum — to describe; arhasy = arhasi — you can; aśeṣeṇa — without deleting anything, thoroughly; divyā — supernatural; hy = hi — in truth; ātmavibhūtayaḥ — wondrous manifestations of Yourself; yābhir = yābhiḥ — by which; vibhūtibhir = vibhūtibhiḥ — wondrous manifestations; lokān — worlds; imāṁs — these; tvam — you; vyāpya — pervading; tiṣṭhasi — you are situated

Please describe thoroughly, Your supernatural wondrous manifestations by which You pervade these worlds and are situated in them. (10.16)

Commentary:

Vaktum means "to talk". It does not mean to reveal directly. It means, rather, to speak of, to discuss. Arjuna wanted to hear more details about Krishna's supernatural (*divya*) personal forms. These forms may not be visible to our material senses, but we may assume that they were visible on some plane of existence.

By using the word *bhūtayas*, Arjuna indicated that these forms must be substantial on some level but since they were *vibhūtibhih*, wonderful, and to an extent inconceivable to human beings, Krishna would have to speak of them extensively to get us to understand His position.

कथं विद्यामहं योगिंस्
त्वां सदा परिचिन्तयन् ।
केषु केषु च भावेषु
चिन्त्योऽसि भगवन्मया ॥१०.१७॥
kathaṁ vidyāmahaṁ yogiṁs
tvāṁ sadā paricintayan
keṣu keṣu ca bhāveṣu
cintyo'si bhagavanmayā (10.17)

katham — how; vidyām — I will know; aham — I; yogin — O mystic master; tvām — You; sadā — constantly; paricintayan — meditating; keṣukeṣu — in what, in what; ca — and; bhāveṣu — in aspects of existence; cintyo = cintyah — to be considered; 'si = asi — You are; bhagavan — Blessed Lord; mayā — by me

How will I know You, Mystic Master, O Yogi? Is it by constantly meditating? In what aspects of existence are You to be considered by Me, O Blessed Lord? (10.17)

Commentary:

Further explanations by Lord Krishna about His self-declared glories would not help the factor of accepting what Krishna said about Himself. Thus Arjuna asked for some revelation.

"What is the method by which we may know You?" he asked.

If we look at this from another angle, Arjuna requested a method of verification. Is it by meditation or by deep consideration (*paricintayan*)? From what level of thought or what level of existence (*bhāveṣu*) are we to visually observe these self-declarations? Arjuna addressed Krishna as the mystic person, the yogin. In Sanskrit, *yogims* is a sound adjustment of the word *yogin*, which means: O yogi, O mystic personality, O expert of the yoga disciplines.

विस्तरेणात्मनो योगं
विभूतिं च जनार्दन ।
भूयः कथय तृप्तिर्हि
शृण्वतो नास्ति मेऽमृतम् ॥ १०.१८॥

vistareṇātmano yogaṁ
vibhūtiṁ ca janārdana
bhūyaḥ kathaya tṛptirhi
śṛṇvato nāsti me'mṛtam (10.18)

vistareṇātmano (vistareṇātmanaḥ) = vistareṇa — with detail + ātmanaḥ — of Yourself; yogam — yoga, self-disciplinary methods and the resultant mystic power; vibhūtim — splendrous form; ca — and; janārdana — O motivator of the people; bhūyaḥ — more; kathaya — explain; tṛptir = tṛptiḥ — final satisfaction; hi — indeed; śṛṇvato = śṛṇvataḥ — of hearing; nāsti = na — not + asti — is; me — of me; 'mṛtam = amṛtam — sweetness

Explain in more detail about Your self-disciplinary methods and the resultant mystic power and of Your splendorous form, O motivator of the people. There is no final satisfaction for me in hearing Your sweet words. (10.18)

Commentary:

It is not every man who would be fascinated with Krishna's description of Himself but Arjuna was. Arjuna was bamboozled just by hearing the glories of Lord Krishna. Every word sounded exhilarating and pleasant to the ears of Arjuna. Some modern day scholars, however, are not impressed. They consider Krishna's talk to be so much of a well-composed boast, either of Krishna or of the composer of *Mahābhārata*. In discussing the *Gītā* with one Westerner, the writer was told by the man:

"Please deal fairly with the Gītā. It is not an ordinary book. There is much to be had from it in terms of a philosophical outlook. But deal with the contradictions, such as Krishna's ego problem. Krishna made some very outlandish claims, as you know. How are these statements to be substantiated? What about similar claims in other Vedic scriptures made by Shiva or Durgā? It is either that these Purāṇic stories are myths or clashing stories without a set conclusion. What do we do with Durgā's Universal Form and Shiva's and others who are competing in the Vedic religions?

"In one part of India," he continued, "we hear that Krishna is God. Then in another part, another authority says that Shiva is God. Then in yet another part we hear that it is Durgā. There are scriptures to support each claim. Each one of the Vedic deities has heroic stories to back the claim. Each has a devotee like Arjuna proclaiming glories. What should be the conclusion?"

This writer, however, is not here to prove anything. We are merely trying to understand the *Gītā* in its own time and place. And readers who are interested may read on. Krishna's proof of Himself is Krishna's problem. We are not a missionary. The purpose of our work is not to convert others. This is a simple effort to understand what Krishna told Arjuna at *Kurukṣetra*.

For *yogam* in line one, we gave, *self-disciplinary methods and the resultant mystic power.* We do not suggest by this that Krishna must perform yoga, but we do state that Krishna Himself explained some of His self-disciplinary methods and the resultant mystic power which is expressed in the material world in the form of the unalterable supreme will and its allowances for deviations. We do hear, however, in both the *Mahābhārata* history and in the *Śrīmad Bhāgavatam*, that Lord Krishna and His brother, *Balarāma*, used a process of yoga when the time came for Them to depart from this gross vision. We also heard in the *Vālmīki Rāmāyāṇa* that Lakshman did the same. Thus, yoga is also used by divine personalities.

Some Vaishnavas, however, object and state differently. Interested readers may do their own research and draw conclusions. It is clear from our day-to-day experience, that God rarely reveals His glories. Otherwise we would see God in plain view. Why is there so much of an effort to reach God? Why are there so many prayers, chants, austerities, and other endeavors in the effort to reach God? Some sort of discipline is involved with being able to see God, otherwise God would be available to plain vision. Even Arjuna was eager to hear something of God, to experience the glories of God. Initially Arjuna's attitude to the Lord was different. At first, he pleaded with Krishna to listen and to accept some social ideas.

श्रीभगवानुवाच
हन्त ते कथयिष्यामि
दिव्या ह्यात्मविभूतयः ।
प्राधान्यतः कुरुश्रेष्ठ
नास्त्यन्तो विस्तरस्य मे ॥१०.१९॥
śrībhagavānuvāca
hanta te kathayiṣyāmi
divyā hyātmavibhūtayaḥ
prādhānyataḥ kuruśreṣṭha
nāstyanto vistarasya me (10.19)

śrībhagavān — the Blessed Lord; uvāca — said; hanta — listen; te — to you; kathayiṣyāmi — I will talk of; divyā — supernaturally; hy = hi — truly; ātmavibhūtayaḥ — own wondrous forms; prādhānyataḥ — most prominent; kuruśreṣṭha — O best of the Kuru clan; nāsty (nāsti) = na — not + asti — is; anto = antaḥ — limit; vistarasya — to the influence; me — My

The Blessed Lord said: Listen, I will talk to you of the most prominent of my supernatural manifestations, O best of the Kuru clan, for there is no limit to My influence. (10.19)

Commentary:

After Arjuna's pleading and pleading for an elaborate description, Lord Krishna agreed but only to describe the prominent, supernatural forms through which He is manifested and through which His glories are indicated.

Some commentators gave *divya* as *divine* but we give *supernatural*. The word divine applies mostly to forms that are imperishable. We gave *supernatural* which applies to the imperishable or the perishable. Everything imperishable is supernatural and those perishable objects which are wonderful or super-ordinary are also supernatural. In this case, *divya* is an adjective which describes the Sanskrit compound word *ātmavibhūtayah*. *Ātma* (the self) means Krishna's self. *Vibhūtayah* in this case means: that which is wonderful, but which was seen or sensed on the material plane.

This is consistent with the word *vyaktim* in text 14 of this chapter. *Vyaktim* means something that we can perceive or regard from our present condition.

अहमात्मा गुडाकेश
सर्वभूताशयस्थितः ।
अहमादिश्च मध्यं च
भूतानामन्त एव च ॥१०.२०॥
ahamātmā guḍākeśa
sarvabhūtāśayasthitaḥ
ahamādiśca madhyaṁ ca
bhūtānāmanta eva ca (10.20)

aham — I; ātmā — self; guḍākeśa — sleep-regulator; sarvabhūtāśayasthitaḥ = sarva — all + bhūta — beings + āśaya — mystic resting place + sthitaḥ — situated in; aham — I; ādiśca = ādiḥ — beginning + ca — and; madhyam — middle; ca — and; bhūtānām — of the beings; anta — end; eva — indeed; ca — and

O sleep regulator, I am the person Who is situated in the mystic resting place of all beings. I am responsible for the beginning, middle, and end of all beings. (10.20)

Commentary:

Arjuna was reputed as a *gudākeśa*, a sleep controller. He perfected *āsana* and *prāṇāyāma* procedures for transcending bodily consciousness. He could leave his body consciously and enter other dimensions. He met Shiva, Indra and other supernatural beings in that way. By controlling the life force in the body, a soul can take control of the sleep impulse which dulls the body. To control the life force, one must take control of its main diet which is air intake. The technique is *prāṇāyāma* practice. No other method works as effectively in controlling the life force.

Krishna rightfully addressed Arjuna as the conqueror of sleep, masterful controller of the sleep impulse of the body, master of *prāṇāyāma* and *āsana* yoga. Krishna discussed something that Arjuna could understand by direct experience. That was the factor of how Krishna is situated in all beings. Only a masterful yogi can understand this directly. Others understand this by conception and belief only and not by experience. Krishna mentioned His claims without giving direct proof. Up to this point we wait to get direct proof or at least to hear that Arjuna received that. We ask readers to hold on. Over the years, explaining from *Bhagavad Gītā*, we were confronted repeatedly by the doubts of others. They challenged, "What is the proof?" We can say at this point that direct proof must come from Krishna because the declarations are His.

Generally translators state that the Supersoul (*antaryāmi*) is situated in the heart of the physical body. We tried repeatedly to correct this misconception. Usually the word *hṛdaya* is used. *Hṛdaya* is usually translated as *heart, center, or source*. However in line two of this verse, we are given an alternate word, namely, *āśaya*, which means: a bed chamber, resting place, asylum, place of residence, abode, retreat, seat of feelings, heart, and mind. These are all meanings. This location is in the subtle body. It is not in the physical form. The living entity, the soul, is not that reliant on a material body for shelter. In the material world, the living entity first takes up residence in the causal form which is located mystically in the center of the chest of a living physical body. Though located there, it is not physical. It is a very subtle cove or resting chamber, just as the word *āśaya* indicated. Krishna stated that He is also in that cove, situated there along with the individual soul in each causal form.

आदित्यानामहं विष्णुर्

ādityānām — of the Adityas; aham — I; viṣṇur = viṣṇuḥ — Vishnu; jyotiṣām — of

ज्योतिषां रविरंशुमान् ।
मरीचिर्मरुतामस्मि
नक्षत्राणामहं शशी ॥१०.२१॥
ādityānāmahaṁ viṣṇur
jyotiṣāṁ raviraṁśumān
marīcirmarutāmasmi
nakṣatrāṇāmahaṁ śaśī (10.21)

lights; ravir = raviḥ — the sun; aṁśumān — radiant; marīcir = marīciḥ — Marici; marutām — of the thunderstormers; asmi — I am; nakṣatrāṇām — of the stars; aham — I; śaśī — the moon

Of the Ādityas, I am Vishnu. Of lights, I am represented by the radiant sun. Of the thunderstormers, I am represented by Marīci. Of the stars, I am signified by the moon. (10.21)

Commentary:

In text 19, we translated *divya* as *supernatural*. We explained that divine cannot be used because this word indicates pure spiritual reality which is not temporary. Furthermore, the term *ātmavibhūtayah* means Krishna's wonderful productions which we can perceive; *bhūta* means something normal that we can perceive; *vibhūta* means something spectacular but which is material to an extent or which is manifested materially. The manifested portion of something spectacular is temporary. This does not mean that the hidden source (*avyakta*) of that manifested object is temporary.

Readers should know that there are divine objects but these cannot be seen directly with mundane senses. However, mundane objects are an indication of the divine. Insofar as a divine object can indicate itself in the material world, the indication is temporary. It will not last because the laws of material nature do not permit this. An example is the human body. Even though we assume it is something ordinary, the human body is spectacular, something supernatural. But it will not last. It does, however, indicate that there is something divine which produced it. That divine object is not visible to our mundane senses and it will never be.

In trying to push on their missions, some preachers indicated that some mundane objects are divine. We must be wary of this dogma. It may be a good slogan in terms of making converts but it is an absolutely worthless doctrine.

Since Lord Krishna intended to explain His prominent, supernatural, mundane productions, we cannot expect a description of the divine objects in the divine world. In fact, Arjuna requested to hear more talk of the fantastic objects in the material world. Lord Krishna presented Himself as being the Lord of all that can be, as the Super Producer of everything. Arjuna pleaded for some confirmation. This is given by Lord Krishna. As we stated repeatedly, the verbal proof is not sufficient. Lord Krishna would give a revelation of exactly how He controls and produces these prominent factors.

In the final analysis, however, a reader of the *Gītā* is left to form his own conclusion. The bare truth is: Unless Krishna can show each and everyone that revelation that He is said to have shown Arjuna, each person is left to his own mental and sentimental devices, to either accept what is written or to reject it. One may, however, still carry on his life with an open mind, waiting for the day when he can accept it fully or when he can get the revelation directly. To date, few of the converts into the Krishna religions have had the direct revelations experienced by Arjuna. Of course, modern people do not have the qualifications of Arjuna. And no matter how much they profess a belief in Krishna, they fail to come to par with Arjuna in austerities, accomplishments, usefulness to Krishna and the overall pattern of direct, friendly dealing with this Lord Krishna. And to make matters worse, we do not see

Krishna walking physically on the earth as Arjuna did. Krishna is not sitting side by side, chatting with us physically as He did with Arjuna.

This reduces the possibilities considerably. And it leaves the evidence on the higher planes of life. Even if someone says, "Yes. Krishna stands beside me as He did for Arjuna," the person cannot produce Krishna physically as Krishna was there with Arjuna, as described in the *Mahābhārata*. Some spiritual masters can surely say, "Yes. Krishna speaks to me directly." But another person may or may not believe because he cannot see Krishna physically. He cannot approach, touch or concur with Krishna as Arjuna did.

There are Deity forms of Krishna which are pictures and sculptured forms, but these have no obvious human habits such as sitting, walking about, eating and so on. Thus, unless a person accepts a spiritual master at his word, or unless a person has keen mystic perception, the statements of a spiritual master about communication with these religious forms is put to question.

And finally, what about the validity of the text? The question was asked repeatedly by persons over the centuries, as to whether the *Gītā* was just written as a legend by a shrewd writer. Depending on a reader's background and sentiment, he may take some of these factors into consideration in dealing with the *Gītā*. Our approach in the commentary is to use an open mind and to look in an unbiased way at the evidence presented. As with all historic data, the presentation is accepted if it seems reasonable and if it does not grossly violate our sense of faith in the events described.

Most of the names mentioned in this part of the *Gītā*, are Vedic. Unless a reader knows the Vedic histories, he cannot understand their significance to Arjuna. Thus we will provide brief biographic information as we progress.

The *Ādityas* were the sons of Aditi. According to Vedic history, they are still living, since they have celestial bodies. These sons are listed in the *Śrīmad Bhāgavatam*:

athātah śrūyatāṁ vaṁśo yo 'diter anupūrvaśaḥ
yatra nārāyaṇo devaḥ svāmsenāvātarad vibhuḥ
vivasvān aryamā pūṣā tvaṣṭātha savitā bhagah
dhātā vidhātā varuṇo mitraḥ śatru urukramaḥ

Now bear this description of the family of Aditi in timely order. In that family, God Nārāyaṇa supernaturally appeared through a parallel part of His personality. The sons of Aditi were Vivasvān, Aryamā, Pūṣā, Tvaṣṭā, Savitā, Bhaga, Dhātā, Vidhātā, Varuṇa, Mitra, Śatru and Urukrama. (Śrīmad Bhāgavatam. 6.6.38-39)

Of these twelve sons of Aditi, the *Gītā* mentioned four, namely *Vivasvān, Aryamā, Varuṇa* and *Urukrama*, the one mentioned as the Vishnu of the *Ādityas*. His popular name is *Vāmana* and He is the Divine Personality Who dealt with the supernatural rebel leader named *Bali*, the son of *Virocana*.

Without diverting readers too far from the *Gītā*, we inform that the Vedic literature described Vishnu, *Nārāyaṇa*, Krishna and Shiva as having certain supernatural and spiritual powers through which these divine personalities express parallel personalities of themselves. By this idea, some of these parallel forms are full expressions of the original divine personality, while some are partial expressions. As the sun produces light continually, so these divine personalities are said to produce parallel forms. We know that any energy which is expressed by the sun and which moves away from the solar fire, becomes diminished in time and loses radiance. But in the case of these Divinities, it is said that Their personal expansions or personal parallel forms do not lose potency. Urukrama Vishnu is described as being *svāmsenāvātarad vibhuh*, the supernatural manifestation of the parallel part of the God *Nārāyaṇa* (*nārāyaṇa devah*). Thus he is not considered to be a full parallelism of that God. The word *vibhuh* indicates that he was visible to people on a material planet.

These sons of Aditi listed are also credited with solar powers for producing suns. Thus we hear of *Vivasvān* in Chapter Four of the *Gītā*, when Krishna told Arjuna that He taught the supernatural people of the solar families. In the *Gītā*, only the names of these ancient kings are given and it does not state anywhere that they were solar kings, but commentators have stated that on the basis of information from other places in the Vedic literature. We must remember that the *Gītā* is a small part of the extensive *Mahābhārata* history, where the details of these legendary solar people are given. In the time of Arjuna, people believed that there were solar kings on the sun planet and that these supernatural personalities established families on earth. The Egyptians and other ancient people like the Mayans had similar beliefs. Modern people might consider all this to be pure legend or myth, but we are not concerned with such opinions in this translation. We are just going through this to see what was presented to Arjuna and upon which cultural basis Arjuna understood it.

There are different versions about the origins of the Maruts. *Śrīmad Bhāgavatam* tells us that there are 49 of them. There was to be one son of Diti, but the embryo was split by Indra into 49 parts. After becoming friends of Indra, they were given positions as storm creators, supernatural weather men, who assist Indra.

Diti and Aditi were sisters. It is said that they have celestial bodies. The sons of Diti, the Maruts, are cousins of Indra, who is the son of Aditi. Krishna claimed that Marīci, the leading Marut, best represents Him. In the time of Arjuna, these celestial deities were prominent. The Indians performed many daily ceremonies invoking these. Thus to Arjuna, these names were impressive, even though to us, in this modern setting, it is not as convincing. As one man told the writer, "Let us get on with the philosophy of the *Gītā*. We do not see these personalities. For all we know they might be legends only. The philosophy is useful, so let us ignore the legends."

However, we should try to understand the *Gītā*, as Arjuna received it. Arjuna became more and more impressed with Krishna on the basis of Krishna's philosophical conclusions as well as the cultural and traditional factors. If we only see the philosophical part, it will be difficult to understand why Arjuna was so impressed.

This particular discourse of Lord Krishna, where He highlights Himself as being the origin of all spectacular people and objects, is part of the training of Krishna consciousness. If one has a competent Vaishnava teacher, he trains one in how to perceive Lord Krishna through mundane objects and through great historic personalities, by realizing that Krishna empowered these or shared glory with these. This is called Krishna consciousness on the mundane plane of life. Of lights, a devotee should see Krishna as being represented by the sun which is the most brilliant object to our normal sense perception. Of lights in the night sky, one should see the moon as being representative of Krishna. This training gives one the ability to attach all importance to Krishna.

वेदानां सामवेदोऽस्मि
देवानामस्मि वासवः ।
इन्द्रियाणां मनश्चास्मि
भूतानामस्मि चेतना ॥१०.२२॥
vedānāṁ sāmavedo'smi

vedānām — of the Vedas; sāmavedo = sāmavedaḥ — Sāma Veda; 'smi = asmi — I am; devānām — of the supernatural rulers; asmi — I am; vāsavaḥ — Vāsava Indra; indriyāṇām — of the senses; manaścāsmi = manas — mind +

devānāmasmi vāsavaḥ
indriyāṇāṁ manaścāsmi
bhūtānāmasmi cetanā (10.22)

ca — and + asmi — I am; bhūtānām — of the creature forms; asmi — I am; cetanā — consciousness

Of the *Vedas*, I am represented by the Sāma Veda. Of the supernatural rulers, I am represented as Vāsava Indra. Of the senses, I am represented as the mind. In creature forms, I am represented as consciousness. (10.22)

Commentary:

The philosophy of Krishna in this part of the *Gītā* is this: Krishna presented Himself as the very best, most glorious aspects of the material creation.

The Vedas are the original Sanskrit text. No other Sanskrit scriptures are as old as the Vedas. Originally, there was one Veda which was transmitted by speech only. The first of the written Vedas is said to be the Rig Veda which is supposed to contain the essence of all other parts. However, the four main Vedas are the Rig, Sama, Yajur, and Atharva.

The Sama Veda is mainly concerned with hymns for Vedic sacrificial ceremonies and Krishna identifies Himself with that text. Lord Krishna identifies Himself with Indra who is also known as *Vāsava*. Indra is the main deity of glorification in the Sama Veda which is sung by the angelic beings at Indra's court.

Of the senses, Krishna identified with the mind, which holds the key position in reference to the senses. Even though the mind is influenced by the senses, it regulates the flow of information which the senses compose. Of the energies in creature forms, Krishna is represented by consciousness, which is the prime factor in living bodies.

रुद्राणां शंकरश्चास्मि
वित्तेशो यक्षरक्षसाम् ।
वसूनां पावकश्चास्मि
मेरुः शिखरिणामहम् ॥१०.२३॥
rudrāṇāṁ śaṁkaraścāsmi
vitteśo yakṣarakṣasām
vasūnāṁ pāvakaścāsmi
meruḥ śikhariṇāmaham (10.23)

rudrāṇām — of the cosmic destroyers; śaṁkaraścāsmi = śaṁkaraḥ — Shankara Shiva + ca — and + asmi — I am; vitteśo = vitteśaḥ = Kubera; yakṣarakṣasām — of the Yakshas and Rakshas; vasūnām — of the Vasus; pāvakaścāsmi = pāvakaḥ — Pavāka + ca — and + asmi — I am; meruḥ — Meru; śikhariṇām — of the mountains; aham — I

Of the cosmic destroyers, I am represented by the Shankara Shiva. Of the Yakshas and Rakshas, I am best represented as Vittesha Kubera. Of the Vasus, I am represented by Pāvaka Agni. Of the mountains, I am represented as Mount Meru. (10.23)

This explanation of the glories of Lord Krishna cannot be appreciated without an understanding of the Vedic literature. The gist of it, is that Krishna identifies Himself with the best, the greatest and principal wonders in the creation. The Rudras are the supernatural destroyers who are capable of demolishing the creation set up by Demigod *Brahmā*. It is said that in the beginning, they emerged through *Brahmā*'s body, through an expression of his frustration in trying to create. At the time, they, the Rudras, began to dismantle the creation. They had the power to do so. They are natural demolishers of whatever *Brahmā* produces.

As their father, *Brahmā* instructed them to desist. When asked for a purpose or duty, *Brahmā* instructed that they go to the forest and perform austerities for the benefit of the creation. Krishna states that Shankara, the leader of the destroyers, represents Him.

Vitteśa is popularly known as *Kuvera*. He is known as the supernatural in charge of the natural resources, especially precious stones and minerals. He is attributed as the patron deity of the seas, being in charge of the wealth of the oceans. Generally, the Yakshas are said to live north of India in the Himalayan regions. The Rakshas are said to live in the south. *Rāvaṇa*, the villain of the *Rāmāyāṇa*, was a king of the Rakshas who lived in a country to the south of India.

The *Vasus* are a class of supernatural regulators, who are said to control certain material elements. They are eight in number. *Pāvaka*, chief of these, is popularly known as *Agnideva*, the fire deity.

Meru is the mountain of gold mineral. It is the most prominent of the mountains listed in the Vedic literature.

पुरोधसां च मुख्यं मां
विद्धि पार्थ बृहस्पतिम् ।
सेनानीनामहं स्कन्दः
सरसामस्मि सागरः ॥१०.२४॥
purodhasāṁ ca mukhyaṁ māṁ
viddhi pārtha bṛhaspatim
senānīnāmahaṁ skandaḥ
sarasāmasmi sāgaraḥ (10.24)

purodhasām — of the family priest; ca — and; mukhyam — chief; mām — me; viddhi — know; pārtha — son of Pṛthā; bṛhaspatim — Bṛhaspati; senānīnām — of the commanders; aham — I; skandaḥ — Skanda; sarasām — of the seas; asmi — I am; sāgaraḥ — the ocean

O son of Pṛthā, know Me as being represented by Brihaspati, the chief of the family priests. Of military commanders, I am represented by Skanda. Of the seas, I am symbolized by the ocean. (10.24)

Commentary:

From the perspective of modern languages like English, French, or Spanish, Sanskrit is to an extent, different. Most of the Vedic scriptures and histories are written in Sanskrit poetry. As a result, the sentence order is complicated. The question may be asked: Did Krishna speak the Sanskrit in this poetic meter or did He speak in prose? Since every sentence of some Vedic literatures are in Sanskrit poetry, are we to believe that every speaker spoke in Sanskrit poetry?

Or are we to rely on the authenticity of the writer, if perhaps he did convert some prose speech into poetry? Even for a writer who loyally converted the speaker's words into poetry, the thought structure of the speaker would have been adjusted. In any case, most translations of the *Gītā*, even those which hail in disciplic succession from Krishna, which are professed to be the most genuine, are in fact, in prose. The usual system of translation is to convert the Sanskrit poetic word-order into a prose word-order, and then to translate into English prose.

The first popular English translation was one by Sir Edwin Arnold which was titled, Song of God. This particular translation was poetic, but it is doubtful if it followed the Sanskrit poetry exactly. Recently an acquaintance questioned as to why a beautiful Sanskrit poem like the *Gītā* was converted into a prose dialogue by translators. Here is a reply: The thinking order of Sanskrit poetry is completely different from that of English poetry. Let us take the first two lines of this verse only. These are the words in the given order with their exact meanings and parts of speech:

- *purodhasām — of the priest / noun in the possessive genitive case*
- *ca — and / conjunction*
- *mukhyam —the chief / noun object accusative case*
- *mām — me / pronoun object accusative case*
- *viddhi — know / imperative verb 2nd person singular*
- *partha — O son of Prtha / noun exclamation vocative case*
- *bṛhaspatim —Bṛhaspati / noun object accusative case*

Those who desire that the *Gītā* be read as a poem and who are from an English-speaking background, should take note of the poetic sentence which would be in English as follows:

Of the priest and the chief me know O son of Pṛthā Brihaspati.

Now how can we make a poetic sentence in English with these words as they are? How would we know which is the subject, which is the object, and how the words are related? In English, even the poetry is in variation to this. Sanskrit language combines prepositions into noun forms by changing the original noun form such that a thinker of Sanskrit has to know what each word ending means and which prepositions are combined into the altered forms. In English, we directly use the prepositions independently. If we were to complete an English prose sentence out of the words above, it would have to be:

O son of Pritha, know me (represented by) Brihaspati, the chief of the priests.

Sanskrit is different to English. Sanskrit poetry is not just poetry as we understand it in English. It is quite possible to put any word anywhere in a Sanskrit sentence, since almost every word is self-contained grammatically. Most Sanskrit words are not reliant on other words nor on a particular location in a sentence. For instance, the word *bṛhaspatim* means that *bṛhaspati* must be the object of the sentence. But in an English sentence, if we put Brihaspati in a particular place it might be the subject, all depending on where it was located in reference to the verb. In Sanskrit, this rule does not apply because the *m* ending in *bṛhaspatim* makes it an object in the sentence. This, therefore, creates the necessity of changing word order when translating.

The above paragraphs were written to explain some facts of Sanskrit language to a few persons who are interested in the changes made in the word order when Sanskrit is translated into English.

Brihaspati is reputed as being a supernatural priest who lives in the celestial world and who officiates as the family priest for Indra, a ruler of the angelic hosts. Skanda is reputed as the commander of the military forces of the angelic people. Since his mothers were the Karttikas, He is also known as Karttikeya. He was adopted by Lord Shiva and Goddess *Durgā*.

महर्षीणां भृगुरहं
गिरामस्म्येकमक्षरम् ।
यज्ञानां जपयज्ञोऽस्मि
स्थावराणां हिमालयः ॥१०.२५॥
maharṣīṇāṁ bhṛgurahaṁ
girāmasmyekamakṣaram
yajñānāṁ japayajño'smi
sthāvarāṇāṁ himālayaḥ (10.25)

maharṣīṇām — of the great yogi sages; bhṛgur = bhṛguḥ — Brigu; aham — I; girām — of spoken words; asmy = asmi — I; ekamakṣaram — one-syllable sound; yajñānām — of the religiously-motivated disciplines; japayajño = japayajñaḥ — the discipline of uttering prayers; 'smi = asmi — I am; sthāvarāṇām — of the stationary objects; himālayaḥ — Himalaya

Of the great yogi sages, Bhrigu is one whom I am best represented by. Of the spoken words, I am represented by the one-syllable sound. Of the religiously-motivated disciplines, I am represented best by the discipline of uttering prayers. Of stationary objects, I am best represented by the Himalayas. (10.25)

Commentary:

In the time of Arjuna, a rishi was a sage with a record of perfected yoga austerities. Such a person had accurate mystic perception. This is a great contrast to many modern day sages and spiritual masters who have no credit of perfecting the yoga disciplines and who are, for the most part, masters of theory only without any direct spiritual experience.

The great sage Bhrigu is supposed to be using a supernatural body, but it is written that he used to appear on this planet.

The special one-syllabled or lettered word (*ekam akṣaram*) is the *om* sound which is known as *omkār* and *praṇava*. This sound was supposed to be repeated before every Vedic hymn but its usage has decreased in modern times. For that matter many modern Vaishnava acharyas do not attach as much importance to this sound as it is given in the *Gītā*, the Vedas and the Upanishads.

Yajña is usually translated as fire sacrifice, but in the *Gītā*, *yajñām* is more than a fire sacrifice. Readers are asked to check in Chapter Four, texts 22 through 33, to see Krishna's broader meanings. In that usage, *Yajña* applies to any of the purificatory-motivated disciplines.

Lord Krishna substantiated the view of the Vaishnava acharyas that japa, the discipline of uttering sacred sounds, is representative of Lord Krishna Himself. Of course, the sound mentioned here, the *girām*, is *om* and not the other sounds or hymns or songs used by the various Vaishnava groups. But essentially we cannot argue the point since Krishna is represented by the japa process of chanting the holy names of God, even though *om* is mentioned specifically here just before japa is discussed. In the time of Arjuna, the *gāyatrī*, *Sama* Veda hymn, and *om* were the stressed mantras. Of the stationary objects, Lord Krishna gave the Himalayan Mountains.

अश्वत्थः सर्ववृक्षाणां
देवर्षीणां च नारदः ।
गन्धर्वाणां चित्ररथः
सिद्धानां कपिलो मुनिः ॥१०.२६॥
aśvatthaḥ sarvavṛkṣāṇāṁ
devarṣīṇāṁ ca nāradaḥ
gandharvāṇāṁ citrarathaḥ
siddhānāṁ kapilo muniḥ (10.26)

aśvatthaḥ — sacred fig tree; sarvavṛkṣāṇāṁ = sarva — all + vṛksāṇām — of trees; devarṣīṇām — of the celestial supernatural yogi sages; ca — and; nāradaḥ — Narada; gandharvāṇām — of the supernatural singers; citrarathaḥ — Citraratha; siddhānām — of the perfected souls; kapilo = kapilaḥ — Kapila; muniḥ — yogi philosopher

Of all trees, I am best represented by the Ashvattha sacred fig tree. Of the supernatural yogi sages, I am represented by Narada. Of the supernatural singers, it is Chitraratha; of the perfected souls, the yogi philosopher Kapila. (10.26)

Commentary:

Another aspect of the Sanskrit language is the periodic absence of verbs. In English, the verb takes an important place in a sentence since the subject and object are determined mostly by their position in reference to the verb, but in Sanskrit some verbs are implied only. Thus a translator has some leeway for including verbs in a translation. But it is not an unlimited license. In Sanskrit, the content is there. A translator should stick to it and not distort, twist, nor derail the original meanings and intention.

In India, by tradition and by scriptural authority, the ashvattha (holy fig tree) is considered sacred. Thus Krishna identified Himself with that vegetation. *Nārada* is supposed to be the foremost of the celestial sages. He is rated as a sage even in the supernatural community, even at the celestial place of the creator-devotee *Brahmā*. *Nārada*'s history in the Vedic literatures is extensive. It is perhaps a fact that no other sage is as popular and instrumental as *Nārada*.

Nārada is said to have visited this earthly place while Lord Krishna was visible on this planet. But *Nārada* is supposed to have a spiritual body. The technique of how he is manifested to material vision and to mundane supernatural vision is a mystery.

The Gandharvas are angelic singers, choristers. And Chitraratha is the reputed leader of these. Of the munis or sages, some are perfected and some are striving for mastership. Of the perfected ones, Kapila Rishi, the son of Devahuti, has the authority to present Himself as a Divinity. He is the founder of the samkhya philosophy which was indicated in Chapter Three and which was practiced routinely by ascetics in the time of Krishna and Arjuna.

उच्चैःश्रवसमश्वानां
विद्धि मामममृतोद्भवम् ।
ऐरावतं गजेन्द्राणां
नराणां च नराधिपम् ॥१०.२७॥
uccaiḥśravasamaśvānāṁ
viddhi māmamṛtodbhavam
airāvataṁ gajendrāṇāṁ
narāṇāṁ ca narādhipam (10.27)

uccaihśravasam — the supernatural horse Uccaihśrava; aśvānām — of the horses; viddhi — know; mām — me; amṛtodbhavam = amṛta — a sweet celestial sea + udbhavam — born from; airāvatam — Airāvata; gajendrāṇām — of kingly elephants; narāṇām — of men; ca — and; narādhipam — King of men

Of horses, know Me as represented by the supernatural horse Uccaihśrava, which was born of the sweet celestial sea. Of the kingly elephants, know Me as represented by Airāvata, and know Me as the King of men. (10.27)

Commentary:

In these aspects and features, Lord Krishna singled out the most prominent as being the best reflection of His authority or glory. This is a training in Krishna consciousness, given to Arjuna and to us as well. If we desire to think of Krishna always, even when viewing or considering things of a mundane quality, we may consider Krishna as He presents Himself in this chapter.

The horse Uchchaihshravah is said to have been born from an ocean of a supernatural beverage which is used by the celestials to keep their bodies in youthfulness. *Airāvata*, a leader elephant, also appeared from that ocean. Of the males, Lord Krishna identified Himself with the emperor or the most powerful ruler.

आयुधानामहं वज्रं
धेनूनामस्मि कामधुक् ।
प्रजनश्चास्मि कन्दर्पः
सर्पाणामस्मि वासुकिः ॥१०.२८॥
āyudhānāmahaṁ vajraṁ
dhenūnāmasmi kāmadhuk
prajanaścāsmi kandarpaḥ
sarpāṇāmasmi vāsukiḥ (10.28)

āyudhānām — of weapons; aham — I; vajram — supernatural thunderbolt; dhenūnām — of cows; asmi — I am; kāmadhuk — supernatural Kamadhuk cow; prajanaścāsmi = prajanas — begetting + ca — and + asmi — I am; kandarpaḥ — Kandarpa, the god of romance; sarpāṇām — of serpents; asmi — I am; vāsukiḥ — Vāsuki

Of weapons, I am compared to the Vajra supernatural thunderbolt. Of cows, I am represented as the supernatural Kamadhuk. And in the case of begetting, I am represented by Kandarpa, the god of romance. Of serpents, I am represented by Vāsuki. (10.28)

Commentary:

The *Vajra* is a supernatural weapon said to be used by King Indra, the ruler of the angelic people. It is said that he operates this *vajra* to produce lightning flashes, rain, storm clouds, and other natural phenomena.

Kāmadhuk, like the previous Uchchaihshravah and *Airāvat*, was produced from the ocean of supernatural beverages, somewhere on a higher planet, at least so the *Purāṇas* state. One of the *Kāmadhuk* species of cows is said to have lived on this planet as the cow of *Vasiṣṭha Muni*. This magical cow was the source of contention between that sage and King *Viśvāmitra*. The cow had such supernatural powers, that from her dung, she created an army which destroyed the army of the offensive king.

Kandarpa is known as *Kāma, Pradyumna, Ananga* and *Smara* He is the supernatural person in charge of affectionate energies. And he is said to induce human beings to express parental affections through which progeny is produced.

Vāsuki is the king of snakes. This serpent is associated with the celestial people and assisted them in a joint venture with their opponents, for churning a supernatural sea on a higher planet.

अनन्तश्चास्मि नागानां
वरुणो यादसामहम् ।
पितॄणामर्यमा चास्मि
यमः संयमतामहम् ॥ १०.२९ ॥
anantaścāsmi nāgānāṁ
varuṇo yādasāmaham
pitṝṇāmaryamā cāsmi
yamaḥ saṁyamatāmaham (10.29)

anantaścāsmi = anantaḥ — Ananta + ca — and + asmi — I am; nāgānām — of supernatural snakes; varuṇo = varuṇaḥ — Varuṇa; yādasām — of the aquatics; aham — I; pitṝṇām — of the piously-departed ancestors; aryamā — Aryamā; cāsmi = ca — and + asmi — I am; yamaḥ — Yama; saṁyamatām — of the subduers; aham — I

I am represented by Ananta among the supernatural snakes. I am represented by Varuṇa, among the aquatics. Among the piously-departed spirits, I am represented by Aryamā. Of the subduers, I am represented by Yama. (10.29)

Commentary:

Both *Vāsuki*, of the previous verse, and Ananta, of this verse, are snakes. *Vāsuki*, however, is a snake from a hellish planet while Ananta is said to be of divine origin. Both are supernatural creatures but *Ananta* is listed as one of the incarnations of Godhead. According to this idea, snake forms are also present in the transcendental world, the Kingdom of God, but they are not vicious as those of this existence.

Varuṇa is attributed as the patron deity of waters. *Aryamā* is the supervisor of the piously-departed forefathers who await rebirth. *Yama* is the controller of the sinfully-departed spirits who are chastised in the ghostly hellish regions.

Yama and *Aryamā* are supernatural people but they are realistic to the departed spirits. *Śrīla* Sridhara Deva Maharaja explained in his translation that *Vāsuki* is one of the single-headed poisonous snakes, while *Ananta*, as a *Nāga*, is a multi-headed, non-poisonous snake.

प्रह्लादश्चास्मि दैत्यानां
कालः कलयतामहम् ।
मृगाणां च मृगेन्द्रोऽहं
वैनतेयश्च पक्षिणाम् ॥ १०.३० ॥
prahlādaścāsmi daityānāṁ
kālaḥ kalayatāmaham
mṛgāṇāṁ ca mṛgendro'haṁ
vainateyaśca pakṣiṇām (10.30)

prahlādaścāsmi = prahlādaḥ — Prahlāda + ca — and + asmi — I am; daityānām — of the titan descendants of Diti; kālaḥ — time; kalayatām — of the monitors; aham — I; mṛgāṇām — of the animals; ca — and; mṛgendro = mṛgendraḥ — king of the beasts; 'ham = aham — I; vainateyaśca = vainateyaḥ — son of Vinata + ca — and; pakṣiṇām — of the birds

And I am represented as Prahlāda among the titan descendants of Diti, as time of the monitors, as the king of beasts among the animals, as the son of Vinata among the birds. (10.30)

Commentary:

The *Daitya* Titans are the powerful sons of *Diti*. These were hostile towards *Diti's* nephews, the *Ādityas*. The *Ādityas* are the sons of *Aditi*. These *Ādityas* are supernatural controllers who supervise in a godly way. The *Daityas* resist the godly influence. Even though *Prahlāda* took birth in the rebel clan of the *Daityas*, he was godly.

Of the monitors, none surpasses time. In the *Gītā*, Krishna identified Himself with that supreme force. Of the beasts He identified Himself with the lion. Interestingly it is said that Krishna appeared as the lionine-man incarnation, *Narasingha*. This *Narasingha* killed Prahlada's father.

The son of Vinata is *Garuḍa*, a powerful, giant devotee-bird, who serves as a flying carrier for Lord Vishnu. The Vishnu *Purāṇa* positions Lord Krishna as an incarnation of Vishnu but that text was composed by Parashar Muni, the father of *Śrīla* Vyasadeva, the writer of the *Gītā*. According to the *Gītā* and the *Śrīmad Bhāgavatam*, Lord Krishna is not an incarnation of Vishnu. He is the source of Vishnu, but He assumed Vishnu's responsibilities from time to time. *Śrīmad Bhāgavatam* informs, that on occasion, Lord Krishna rode the *Garuḍa* bird.

पवनः पवतामस्मि
रामः शस्त्रभृतामहम्।
झषाणां मकरश्चास्मि
स्त्रोतसामस्मि जाह्नवी ॥ १०.३१ ॥
pavanaḥ pavatāmasmi
rāmaḥ śastrabhṛtāmaham
jhaṣāṇāṁ makaraścāsmi
srotasāmasmi jāhnavī (10.31)

pavanaḥ — the wind; pavatām — of the cleansers; asmi — I am; rāmaḥ — Rāma; śastrabhṛtām — of the weapon carriers; aham — I; jhaṣāṇām — of sea monsters; makaraścāsmi = makaraḥ — shark + ca — and + asmi — I am; srotasām — of rivers; asmi — I am; jāhnavī — daughter of Jahnu

Among the cleansers, I am best represented by the wind. Of the weapon carriers, I am best represented by Rāma. Of the sea monsters, I am represented by the shark. Of the rivers, I am represented by Jahnu's daughter. (10.31)

Commentary:

As a general purifier, nothing is more efficient than the wind. Sridhara Maharaja gave Lord *Paraśurāma* as *Rāma* but *Śrīla* Bhaktivedanta Swami gave Lord *Rāma*, the son of King Dasharatha of Rāmāyāṇa fame. Both *Paraśurāma* and *Rāma*, are rated as incarnations of Godhead. *Paraśurāma* is rated as an empowered personality only, while Lord *Rāma* is rated as a parallel divine form of Lord Krishna, as a Godhead Personality. *Paraśurāma* destroyed twenty-one generations of the warrior clans. He killed Karttavirya Arjuna, who was reputed as being more powerful than *Rāvana*, who was killed by *Rāma*. In comparison, however, *Paraśurāma* challenged and was subdued by *Rāma*, the son of Dasharatha.

Of the sea creatures, Krishna is best represented by the shark, and of the rivers, He rated Himself to the Ganga or the Ganges, which is known as the daughter of the sage Jahnu.

सर्गाणामादिरन्तश्च
मध्यं चैवाहमर्जुन ।
अध्यात्मविद्या विद्यानां
वादः प्रवदतामहम् ॥१०.३२॥
sargāṇāmādirantaśca
madhyaṁ caivāhamarjuna
adhyātmavidyā vidyānāṁ
vādaḥ pravadatāmaham (10.32)

sargāṇām — of creations; ādir = ādiḥ — formation; antaśca = antaḥ — ending + ca — and; madhyam — continuation; caivāham = ca — and + eva — indeed + aham — I; arjuna — Arjuna; adhyātmavidyā — knowledge of the Supreme Soul; vidyānām — of sciences; vādaḥ — conclusion; pravadatām — of the logicians; aham — I

Of creations, I am represented by the formation, continuation and ending. O Arjuna, of the sciences, I am knowledge of the Supreme Soul. I am represented by the conclusion of the logicians. (10.32)

Commentary:

The material creation has a beginning, continuation and ending. We experience this on a minute scale from day to day. In our bodies we see a continuation but we can also anticipate an ending and assume that there was a beginning. Krishna spoke of *sargāṇām*, the created objects. These begin, persist for a time, and then lose configuration. He claimed that this process of formation, continuation and ending represents Him. In education, the knowledge of the soul is important. The information of the Supreme Soul is the most important. Since Krishna presented Himself as that Supreme Person (*ādhyātma*), He is the experience of that knowledge. He claimed that the conclusions (*vādah*) of the eloquent speakers represent Him.

अक्षराणामकारोऽस्मि
द्वंद्वः सामासिकस्य च ।
अहमेवाक्षयः कालो
धाताहं विश्वतोमुखः ॥१०.३३॥
akṣarāṇāmakāro'smi
dvaṁdvaḥ sāmāsikasya ca
ahamevākṣayaḥ kālo
dhātāhaṁ viśvatomukhaḥ (10.33)

akṣarāṇām — of letters; akāro = akāraḥ — the letter A; 'smi = asmi — I am; dvandvaḥ — two-word compound; sāmāsikasya — of the word combinations; ca — and; aham — I; evākṣayaḥ = eva — indeed + akṣayaḥ — infinite; kālo = kālaḥ — time; dhātāham = dhātā — Dhātā Brahmā + aham — I; viśvatomukhaḥ — one who faces all directions, four-faced

Of letters, I am represented by the letter A. Of the word combinations, I am represented by the two-word compound. I am comparable to infinite time. I am represented by Dhātā, the four-faced Brahmā.(10.33)

Commentary:

A is the first letter of the Sanskrit alphabet. It is written as अ.

The dvandva are the two-word compounds. An example is *viśvatomukhah* which is a combination of *viśvatah* and *mukhah*. *Viśvatah* is the original form of *viśvato* which is an abbreviation form. *Viśvatah* means on all sides or in all directions. *Mukhah* means face. *Viśvatomukhah* means the person who faces all directions. Lord Krishna identified Himself with *Brahmā*, who is the person with four faces, perceiving all directions simultaneously. Krishna rated Himself to ongoing, non-stopping, eternal time.

मृत्युः सर्वहरश्चाहम्
उद्भवश्च भविष्यताम् ।
कीर्तिः श्रीर्वाक्च नारीणां
स्मृतिर्मेधा धृतिः क्षमा ॥ १०.३४
mṛtyuḥ sarvaharaścāham
udbhavaśca bhaviṣyatām
kīrtiḥ śrīrvākca nārīṇāṁ
smṛtirmedhā dhṛtiḥ kṣamā
(10.34)

mṛtyuḥ — death; sarvaharaścāham = sarvaharaḥ — all-devouring + ca — and + aham — I; udbhavaśca = udbhavaḥ — origin + ca — and; bhaviṣyatām — of things which are to be produced; kīrtiḥ — Kīrti, goddess of fame; śrīr = śrīḥ — Shri, goddess of fortune; vāk — Vāk, goddess of speech; ca — and; nārīṇām — of women; smṛtir = smṛtiḥ — Smṛti, goddess of recollection; medhā — Medhā, goddess of counsel; dhṛtiḥ — Dhṛti, goddess of faithfulness; kṣamā — Kṣamā, goddess of patience

I am represented as all-devouring death. I am the foundation of things that are to be produced. And among women, I am represented by Kīrti, the goddess of fame, Śrī, the goddess of fortune, Vāk, the goddess of speech, Smṛti, the goddess of recollection, Medhā, the goddess of counsel, Dhṛti, the goddess of faithfulness and Kṣama, the goddess of patience. (10.34)

Commentary:

Mṛtyuh is a supernatural being who causes death of mundane bodies. Thus, this comparison with Krishna applies to the concept of death and the supernatural who spreads it. In accordance with what He said, Lord Krishna stated that He is the foundation of future productions.

Most commentators give *nārīṇām* as *of feminine things*. *Nārīṇām* also means *of women*. Most commentators give *kīrtih, śrīr, vāk, smṛtir, medhā, dhṛtih*, and *kṣamā* as qualities of women. We have used the personal meanings, listing these as the names of the various goddesses who exhibit the greatest percentage of these qualities.

Sridhara Deva Maharaja translated the last lines of this verse as follows:

Of ladies, I am the seven qualities of a good wife — grace, beauty, perfect speech, remembrance, intelligence, patience and forgiveness. (The Hidden Treasure of the Sweet Absolute, p. 194)

The Vedic literatures do tell us, however, that initially these qualities were first expressed by particular goddesses of the particular names which the qualities indicated.

बृहत्साम तथा साम्नां
गायत्री छन्दसामहम् ।
मासानां मार्गशीर्षोऽहम्
ऋतूनां कुसुमाकरः ॥ १०.३५॥
bṛhatsāma tathā sāmnāṁ
gāyatrī chandasāmaham
māsānāṁ mārgaśīrṣo'ham
ṛtūnāṁ kusumākaraḥ (10.35)

bṛhatsāma — Brihat Sāma Melody; tathā — also; sāmnām — of the Sāma Veda chants; gāyatrī — Gayatri; chandasām — of the poetic hymns; aham — I; māsānām — of months; mārgaśīrṣo = mārgaśīrṣaḥ — November-December lunar month; 'ham = aham — I; ṛtūnām — of seasons; kusumākaraḥ — spring

Of the Sāma Veda chants, the Brihat Sāma melody represents Me. Of the poetic hymns, I am the Gayatri. Of months, I am best represented by the November-December lunar month. Of the seasons, I am best compared to Spring. (10.35)

Commentary:

Śrīla Bhaktivedanta Swami and Sridhara Deva Maharaja concur that Brihat Sama of the *Sama* Veda is sung to Lord Indra, the supervisor of the *Swārgaloka* angelic place. That particular melody glorifies Indra.

The *Gāyatrī* mantra is considered to be most important of the Rig Veda hymns. It is the most popular and most used of the mantras.

In the Vedic calendar, the months are calculated according to the moon cycle. Thus the month of *mārgaśīrśo* corresponds to the latter part of November and early December. Krishna compared Himself to that period, as well as to the spring.

द्यूतं छलयतामस्मि
तेजस्तेजस्विनामहम् ।
जयोऽस्मि व्यवसायोऽस्मि
सत्त्वं सत्त्ववतामहम् ॥ १०.३६ ॥
dyūtaṁ chalayatāmasmi
tejastejasvināmaham
jayo'smi vyavasāyo'smi
sattvaṁ sattvavatāmaham (10.36)

dyūtam — gambling skill; chalayatām — of the swindlers; asmi — I am; tejaḥ — splendor; tejasvinām — of the splendid things; aham — I; jayo = jayaḥ — victory; 'smi = asmi — I am; vyavasāyo = vyavasāyaḥ — endeavor; 'smi = asmi — I am; sattvam — reality; sattvavatām — of the real things; aham — I

I am represented as the gambling skill of the swindlers. I am compared to the splendor of the splendid things. I am compared to victory and endeavor. I am the reality of the realistic things. (10.36)

Commentary:

It is interesting that Lord Krishna compared Himself to the gambling skill of the swindlers. What an interesting comparison! It means that Krishna is smarter than the smartest man and could outwit anyone. There is much evidence in Krishna's life story in the *Śrīmad Bhāgavatam* to support this claim. That a person can claim to be God and compare Himself to the trickery of swindlers, is quite interesting.

In keeping with what He said about Himself, Krishna compared Himself to the splendor of the splendid things. He rated Himself to victory, endeavor and reality.

वृष्णीनां वासुदेवोऽस्मि
पाण्डवानां धनंजयः ।
मुनीनामप्यहं व्यासः
कवीनामुशना कविः ॥ १०.३७ ॥
vṛṣṇīnāṁ vāsudevo'smi
pāṇḍavānāṁ dhanaṁjayaḥ
munīnāmapyahaṁ vyāsaḥ
kavīnāmuśanā kaviḥ (10.37)

vṛṣṇīnām — of the Vrishnis; vāsudevo = vāsudevaḥ — the son of Vasudeva; 'smi = asmi — I am; pāṇḍavānām — of the Pandavas; dhanaṁjayaḥ — Arjuna; munīnām — of the yogi philosophers; apy = api — also; aham — I; vyāsaḥ — Vyasa; kavīnām — of poets; uśanā — Ushana; kaviḥ — respected poet

Of the Vṛṣṇis, I am the son of Vasudeva. Of the Pāṇḍavas, I am represented by Arjuna. Of the yogi philosophers, I am compared to Vyāsa. Of the poets, I am represented by the respected poet Uśanā. (10.37)

Commentary:

In the Vrishni family, Lord Krishna acted as the son of Vasudeva and thus served that family in a social capacity. In the family of the Pandavas, Lord Krishna was best represented as Arjuna, the famous conqueror of the wealthy provinces, the foremost marksman of his time. Of the sages, Krishna is best represented as *Vyāsaji*, the compiler of the *Mahābhārata*, of which the *Bhagavad Gītā* is a part. Of the poetic geniuses, Krishna is represented by Ushana, who is also known as Pandit Shukracharya. Ushana was such a poetic genius that he could revive a dead body by instantly composing poetic medicinal sound frequencies.

दण्डो दमयतामस्मि
नीतिरस्मि जिगीषताम् ।
मौनं चैवास्मि गुह्यानां
ज्ञानं ज्ञानवतामहम् ॥ १०.३८॥
daṇḍo damayatāmasmi
nītirasmi jigīṣatām
maunaṁ caivāsmi guhyānāṁ
jñānaṁ jñānavatāmaham (10.38)

daṇḍo = daṇḍaḥ — authority to punish; damayatām — of the rulers; asmi — I am; nītir = nītiḥ — morality; asmi — I am; jigīṣatām — of those seeking victory; maunam — silence; caivāsmi = ca — and + eva — indeed + asmi — I am; guhyānām — of secrets; jñānam — knowledge; jñānavatām — of those who know; aham — I

Of rulers, I am the authority to punish. For those seeking victory, I may be compared to the means of morality; of secrets, I am represented by silence. In wise men, I am represented as knowledge. (10.38)

Commentary:

Krishna compares himself to legal procedure and its resulting effect in the form of chastisement. He compares Himself to morality, which is the means of attaining long-lasting victory. And of the secrets, he is representative of silence. He may be regarded as the wisdom of wise men.

यच्चापि सर्वभूतानां
बीजं तदहमर्जुन ।
न तदस्ति विना यत्स्यान्
मया भूतं चराचरम् ॥ १०.३९॥
yaccāpi sarvabhūtānāṁ
bījaṁ tadahamarjuna
na tadasti vinā yatsyān
mayā bhūtaṁ carācaram (10.39)

yac = yad — which; cāpi = ca — and + api — also; sarvabhūtānām — of all created beings; bījam — origin point; tad — that; aham — I; arjuna — Arjuna; na — not; tad — that; asti — is; vinā — without; yat = yad — which; syān = syāt — should be; mayā — through My influence; bhūtam — existing; carācaram — active or stationary

And O Arjuna, I am the origin of all created beings. There is nothing active or stationary which could exist without My influence. (10.39)

Commentary:

This, an extensive description of comparative wonders, is the course of elementary Krishna consciousness, given directly to Arjuna. It has to do with keeping Krishna in view by rating various supernatural and spiritual wonders to the qualities which Krishna attributed to Himself. Most of these comparisons were of mundane objects. Thus, since the objects selected were mostly mundane, this is a practical form of Krishna consciousness. Interested readers can, if they so desire, study this and apply the formulas.

नान्तोऽस्ति मम दिव्यानां
विभूतीनां परंतप ।
एष तूद्देशतः प्रोक्तो
विभूतेर्विस्तरो मया ॥१०.४०॥
nānto'sti mama divyānāṁ
vibhūtīnāṁ paraṁtapa
eṣa tūddeśataḥ prokto
vibhūtervistaro mayā (10.40)

nānto (nāntaḥ) = na — no + antaḥ — end; 'sti = asti — is; mama — of My; divyānām — of the supernatural; vibhūtīnām — manifestations; paraṁtapa — burner of enemy forces; eṣa — this; tūddeśataḥ = tu — but + uddeśataḥ — for a sample; prokto = proktaḥ — explained; vibhūter = vibhūteḥ — of the opulences; vistaro = vistaraḥ — of the spreading, extensive; mayā — by Me

There is no end to My supernatural manifestations, O burner of the enemy forces. This was explained by Me as a sampling of My extensive opulence. (10.40)

Commentary:

Some commentators gave *divyānām vibhūtīnām* as, *of divine manifestations*. We have used the word supernatural since most of the descriptions given by Krishna for this elementary Krishna consciousness, have to do with gross temporary objects or occurrences. Most of the subjects mentioned are impressive but they are temporary nevertheless. Though He considers it to be a sampling or indication of His influences, still the description is expansive from our view.

यद्यद्विभूतिमत्सत्त्वं
श्रीमदूर्जितमेव वा ।
तत्तदेवावगच्छ त्वं
मम तेजोंऽशसंभवम् ॥१०.४१॥
yadyadvibhūtimatsattvaṁ
śrīmadūrjitameva vā
tattadevāvagaccha tvaṁ
mama tejoṁśasaṁbhavam (10.41)

yad yad — what, whatever; vibhūtimat — fantastic; sattvam — real object; śrīmad = śrīmat — prosperous; ūrjitam — powerful; eva — indeed; vā — or; tat tad = tat tat — this, that, any case; evāvagaccha = eva — indeed + avagaccha — realize; tvam — you; mama — of Me; tejo = tejaḥ — splendor; 'ṁśasaṁbhavam (aṁśasaṁbhavam) = aṁśa — fraction + saṁbhavam — origin

You should realize that whatever fantastic existence, whatever prosperous or powerful object there is, in any case, it originates from a fraction of My splendor. (10.41)

Commentary:

As if to top it off, Lord Krishna made this final statement. Having presented Himself in full as the Cause of all causes, having referenced Himself to the most spectacular things in our day to day experience, He accredited Himself as being very, very wonderful in terms of expressing just a fraction of His splendor as the basis of the material creation. If this is a fraction, what is a completion?

Krishna gave no allowance for exceptions in terms of the fantastic, the luxurious and the resourceful. Whatever mundane object we might encounter, whether it be animate or inanimate, is to be regarded as a trifle in comparison to His total power.

अथ वा बहुनैतेन
किं ज्ञातेन तवार्जुन ।
विष्टभ्याहमिदं कृत्स्नम्
एकांशेन स्थितो जगत् ॥१०.४२॥

athavā — but; bahunaitena = bahunā — with extensive + etena — with this; kim — what is the value?; jñātena — with information; tavārjuna = tava — of you + arjuna — Arjuna; viṣṭabhyāham =

atha vā bahunaitena
kiṁ jñātena tavārjuna
viṣṭabhyāhamidaṁ kṛtsnam
ekāṁśena sthito jagat (10.42)

viṣṭabhya — supporting + aham — I; idam — this; kṛtsnam — entire; ekāṁśena = eka — one + aṁśena — by a fraction; sthito = sthitaḥ — based, standing; jagat — world

But Arjuna, what is the value of this extensive information? As the foundation, I support this entire universe with a fraction of Myself. (10.42)

Commentary:

To Lord Krishna as He represented and viewed Himself, this information of elementary Krishna consciousness is not of great significance, but it is most essential to our understanding of how He regarded Himself. Unless we can begin where we are in material existence, and trace the influence of Krishna as described, we would not understand Him in truth. Assuming that His declarations are valid, we may still require proof.

The explanation in this chapter is vital. It is our starting point in understanding Krishna from a conceptual view. It is the beginning of our Krishna conscious path. It is not a direct perception, but only a reasonable and logical system of comparison. But it is an initiation into the process of Krishna consciousness.

It is fantastic that an historic person made such a claim. We can just imagine how Krishna felt about Himself, if He regarded these influences as being fractional. If this is a fraction, how does He feel about His complete energy? If He supports the material world with just one expression of His divine selves, then what is the full expression of His divine personalities?

The only aspect which is missing, is proof. The next chapter gives that. Let us review it.

CHAPTER 11

The Universal Form*

अर्जुन उवाच
मदनुग्रहाय परमं
गुह्यमध्यात्मसंज्ञितम् ।
यत्त्वयोक्तं वचस्तेन
मोहोऽयं विगतो मम ॥ ११.१ ॥
arjuna uvāca
madanugrahāya paramaṁ
guhyamadhyātmasaṁjñitam
yattvayoktaṁ vacastena
moho'yaṁ vigato mama (11.1)

arjuna = Arjuna: uvāca — said; madanugrahāya — kindness to me, as a matter of mercy to me; paramaṁ — highest; guhyam — private; adhyātmasaṁjñitam = adhyātma — Supersoul + saṁjñitam — known as; yad — which; tvayoktaṁ = tvaya — by you + uktam — explained; vacaḥ — lecture; tena — by this; moho = mohaḥ — delusion; 'yam = ayam — this; vigato = vigataḥ — departed; mama — of me (11.1)

Arjuna said: As a matter of mercy to me, the highest, most private information of the Supreme Soul was explained by You in this lecture. Subsequently, the delusion departed from me. (11.1)

Commentary:

Anugrahāya or mercy, divine favor, divine grace to any limited entity, is a very rare bestowal. Somehow, by chance, this writer came in touch with such mercy in the form of some revelations given to him while writing this *Gītā* translation and commentary. But Arjuna got the full divine grace by having Lord Krishna directly before him at *Kurukṣetra*. As the Vaishnava acharyas stressed all along, one cannot make a great leap forward spiritually without the divine grace.

The information about the soul (*ātma*) is important. That information is difficult to attain and it is even more difficult to experience and realize. But the information about the Supreme Soul (*adhyātmasaṁjñitam*) is the most difficult to gain. The realization and experience of it, is very, very difficult to acquire. It has to be bestowed by the Supreme Being Himself. It comes by revelation.

Arjuna claimed that just by hearing this information, his delusion was dissipated (*vigato*). Such is the potency of the words of Krishna.

**The Mahābhārata contains no chapter headings. This title was assigned by the translator on the basis of verse 16 of this chapter.*

भवाप्ययौ हि भूतानां
श्रुतौ विस्तरशो मया ।
त्वत्तः कमलपत्राक्ष
माहात्म्यमपि चाव्ययम् ॥ ११.२ ॥
bhavāpyayau hi bhūtānāṁ
śrutau vistaraśo mayā
tvattaḥ kamalapatrākṣa
māhātmyamapi cāvyayam (11.2)

bhavāpyayau = bhava — origin + apy (api) — also + ayau — ruination; hi — indeed; bhūtānām — of the beings; śrutau — both were heard; vistaraśo = vistaraśaḥ — in detail; mayā — by me; tvattaḥ — from you; kamalapatrākṣa = kamala — lotus + patra — petal + akṣa — eyed; māhātmyam — majestic glory; api — also; cāvyayam = ca — and + avyayam — eternally

The description of the origin and ruination of the beings was heard in detail by me, O Person Whose eyes are shaped like lotus petals. You also described Your eternal majestic glory. (11.2)

Commentary:

After hearing details of the glories of Krishna, Arjuna began to admire Krishna, Who was known as *kamalapatrākṣa*, the Person with lotus petal-shaped eyes. At this stage, Arjuna's admiration increased. Lord Krishna's concise description of the origin and dissolution of the beings, as well as the description of His eternal majesty, was wondrous to hear.

एवमेतद्यथात्थ त्वम्
आत्मानं परमेश्वर ।
द्रष्टुमिच्छामि ते रूपम्
ऐश्वरं पुरुषोत्तम ॥ ११.३ ॥
evametadyathāttha tvam
ātmānaṁ parameśvara
draṣṭumicchāmi te rūpam
aiśvaraṁ puruṣottama (11.3)

evam — thus; etad — this; yathāttha = yathā — as + attha — you explain; tvam — you; ātmānam — yourself; parameśvara — O Supreme Lord; draṣṭum — to see; icchāmi — I wish; te — your; rūpam — form; aiśvaram — majesty; puruṣottama — O Supreme Person

This is as You explained about Yourself, O Supreme Lord. I wish to see Your Majestic Form, O Supreme Person. (11.3)

Commentary:

This is a request for final evidence. If Krishna could substantiate with direct evidence, all doubts could be removed. Arjuna was, at this time, strictly concerned with how Krishna controlled the mundane creations, especially how Lord Krishna would reverse the odds at *Kurukṣetra*, where the Pandavas had the smaller of the two armies. Thus Arjuna asked specifically for a showing of Krishna's majestic form (*rūpam aiśvaram*).

This showing of the majestic form, has meaning for those of us who are earthbound, persons who are presently identifying with material existence and who cannot perceive the transcendence but get hints by hearing of it from the mystic visionaries. We need to know how Krishna controls this world. If Krishna can prove the self-declarations, then doubts about His supremacy would cease.

In Krishna's time, some persons did not accept Him even after being shown a display of majesty. But others did accept Him. Regardless of our mood of acceptance or rejection of the evidence, it ought to be displayed to substantiate His claim.

मन्यसे यदि तच्छक्यं
मया द्रष्टुमिति प्रभो ।
योगेश्वर ततो मे त्वं
दर्शयात्मानमव्ययम् ॥११.४॥
manyase yadi tacchakyaṁ
mayā draṣṭumiti prabho
yogeśvara tato me tvaṁ
darśayātmānamavyayam (11.4)

manyase — you think; yadi — if; tac = tad — that; chakyam = sakyam — possible; mayā — by me; draṣṭum — to see; iti — thus; prabho — O Lord; yogeśvara — Master of yoga technique; tato = tataḥ — then; me — to me; tvam — you; darśayātmānam = darśayā — make it be seen + ātmānam — self; avyayam — eternal

If You think that it is possible for me to see this, O Lord, Master of the yoga technique, then make me see You in that Eternal Form. (11.4)

Commentary:

Arjuna's exceptional quality as a disciple of Lord Krishna is shown here by his pleasant submissive appeal. Whatever Krishna claimed to be, could not be seen by the eyes of a physical body and Arjuna did not have the mystic penetration to verify it. Thus he asked Krishna to provide the vision, to make him see how Krishna controlled the social situations.

श्रीभगवानुवाच
पश्य मे पार्थ रूपाणि
शतशोऽथ सहस्रशः ।
नानाविधानि दिव्यानि
नानावर्णाकृतीनि च ॥११.५॥
śrībhagavānuvāca
paśya me pārtha rūpāṇi
śataśo'tha sahasraśaḥ
nānāvidhāni divyāni
nānāvarṇākṛtīni ca (11.5)

śrībhagavān — the Blessed Lord; uvāca — said; paśya — see; me — My; pārtha — son of Pṛthā; rūpāṇi — forms; śataśo = śataśaḥ — hundred; 'tha = atha — or; sahasraśaḥ — thousand; nānāvidhāni — variously manifested; divyāni — supernatural; nānāvarṇākṛtīni = nānā — various + varṇa — color + ākṛtīni — shapes + ca — and

The Blessed Lord said: O son of Pṛthā, see My forms in the hundreds or rather in the thousands, variously manifested, supernatural and of the various colors and shapes. (11.5)

Commentary:

Without hesitation, Krishna showed Arjuna His influences and the various forms He manifested to control the world and its various dimensions. The vision was sudden, fantastic and awesome.

पश्यादित्यान्वसून्रुद्रान्
अश्विनौ मरुतस्तथा ।
बहून्यदृष्टपूर्वाणि
पश्याश्चर्याणि भारत ॥११.६॥
paśyādityānvasūnrudrān
aśvinau marutastathā
bahūnyadṛṣṭapūrvāṇi
paśyāścaryāṇi bhārata (11.6)

paśyādityān = paśya — look at + ādityān — supernatural rulers; vasūn — Vasus; rudrān — supernatural destroyers; aśvinau — two supernatural doctors; marutaḥ — supernatural stormers; tathā — also; bahūny = bahūni — many; adṛṣṭapūrvāṇi = adṛṣta — unseen + pūrvāṇi — before; paśyāścaryāṇi = paśya — view + āścaryāṇi — wonders; bhārata — O relation of the Bharata family

Look at the supernatural rulers, the supernatural destroyers, the two supernatural doctors and the supernatural stormers. View many wonders which were unseen before, O relation of the Bharata family. (11.6)

Commentary:

The *Ādityas* are the supernatural sons of Aditi. These personalities are said to control the elements, particularly the sun, moon and weather. The *Vasus* are assistants to those *Ādityas*. The Rudras are fearsome destroyers who can cause planetary or galactic havoc but who restrain their destructive powers. The Ashvinis are celestial horsemen with supernatural powers of healing. The Maruts are storm-wielders who function supernaturally under the direction of Indra, who is one of the *Ādityas*.

These supernatural people were well-known in the time of Arjuna. If we were to put this into modern perspective, it would be that Arjuna saw how Lord Krishna controlled the sun planet, the moon, the weather, and the atmosphere. It would mean that Krishna displayed control of the planetary and galactic disintegration.

By addressing Arjuna as a relation of the *Bhārata* family, Lord Krishna indicated that on the supernatural level there are powerful families like the *Ādityas*. They wield a supernatural political control, just as the *Bhārata* dynasty wielded earthly power.

इहैकस्थं जगत्कृत्स्नं
पश्याद्य सचराचरम् ।
मम देहे गुडाकेश
यच्चान्यद्द्रष्टुमिच्छसि ॥११.७॥
ihaikasthaṁ jagatkṛtsnaṁ
paśyādya sacarācaram
mama dehe guḍākeśa
yaccānyaddraṣṭumicchasi (11.7)

ihaikastham = iha — here + ekastham — situated in one reality; jagat — universe; kṛtsnam — entire; paśyādya = pasya — see + adya — now; sacarācaram — with active and inactive; mama — of Me; dehe — in the body; guḍākeśa — O conqueror of sleep; yac = yad — what; cānyad = cānyat = ca — and + anyat — other; draṣṭum — to see; icchasi — you desire

Here, O conqueror of sleep, you see the entire universe with all active and inactive manifestations, situated as one reality, in My body. And observe any other manifestations which you desire to see. (11.7)

Commentary:

Guḍākeśa, a name of Arjuna, means both *curly-haired one* or *conqueror of sleep*. It is a compound word. The meaning varies according to how the compound is split: *guḍā-keśa* means, *curly-haired one*, while *guḍāka-īsa* means, *conqueror of sleep*. In the *Mahābhārata*, Arjuna is addressed as curly-haired one when being identified or described by bodily features. Either meaning applies to Arjuna.

Mama dehe means, *in my mundane body*. Of course, that body was a gigantic mundane form and it was supernatural (*divyāni*, 11.5). Krishna told Arjuna to look within it and see whatever could be conceived of, as a part of the sum total material manifestation.

न तु मां शक्यसे द्रष्टुम्
अनेनैव स्वचक्षुषा ।
दिव्यं ददामि ते चक्षुः
पश्य मे योगमैश्वरम् ॥११.८॥ ॥

na — not; tu — but; mām — Me; śakyase — you can; draṣṭum — to see; anenaiva = anena — by this + iva (eva) — indeed; svacakṣuṣā — with your vision; divyam — supernatural; dadāmi — I give; te — to you; cakṣuḥ —

na tu māṁ śakyase draṣṭum
anenaiva svacakṣuṣā
divyaṁ dadāmi te cakṣuḥ
paśya me yogamaiśvaram (11.8)

sight; paśya — look at; me — Me; yogam — mystic power; aiśvaram — majesty

But you cannot see with your vision. I give you supernatural sight to look at My mystic majesty. (11.8)

Commentary:

At first Lord Krishna displayed the mystic majesty, just as Arjuna requested, but Arjuna could not see the vision. Krishna then gave Arjuna supernatural sight. This means that we cannot see the revelation of the divine unless supernatural senses are made available to us. This greatly limits the possibility of a direct perception of Krishna's controlling power.

Two aspects are shown here. First, one cannot see the vision of Krishna's power grasp unless Krishna reveals it. And secondly, one requires supernatural vision. It means, therefore, that even if one has the supernatural vision, he would not see Krishna's controlling power unless he was allowed to.

संजय उवाच
एवमुक्त्वा ततो राजन्
महायोगेश्वरो हरिः ।
दर्शयामास पार्थाय
परमं रूपमैश्वरम् ॥ ११.९ ॥
saṁjaya uvāca
evamuktvā tato rājan
mahāyogeśvaro hariḥ
darśayāmāsa pārthāya
paramaṁ rūpamaiśvaram (11.9)

saṁjaya — Sanjaya; uvāca — said; evam — thus; uktvā — having said; tato = tataḥ — then; rājan — O King; mahāyogeśvaro = mahāyogeśvaraḥ — the great master of yoga; hariḥ — Hari, the God Vishnu; darśayāmāsa — reveals; pārthāya — to the son of Pritha; paramam — supreme; rūpam — form; aiśvaram — supernatural glory

Sanjaya said: O King, having said that, the great Master of yoga, Hari, the God Vishnu, revealed to the son of Pṛthā, the Supreme Form, the supernatural glory. (11.9)

Commentary:

Krishna gave Arjuna supernatural vision. He allowed Arjuna to use that sight, by which control of the supernatural world could be seen. Sanjaya alerted King *Dhṛtarāṣṭra* that the greatest of the masters of yoga, the greatest mystic of all times, Krishna, then revealed how the world was controlled.

Sanjaya addressed Lord Krishna as Lord Hari which is a name used in those days for Lord Vishnu. This was to alert King *Dhṛtarāṣṭra* that Krishna did indeed have the power to give Arjuna that supernatural sight. It was no falsity. Inasmuch faith as *Dhṛtarāṣṭra* had in Lord Vishnu, so much faith he should have had in Krishna. At least this is what Sanjaya implied.

In the time of Krishna and Arjuna, Lord Vishnu, who is known as Lord Hari and as Lord *Nārāyaṇa* as well as by other names, was recognized in that part of India as the God of this world. He was considered to be the father of *Brahmā*, the planetary creator. Thus Sanjaya identified Lord Krishna as Lord Vishnu incarnate.

In the *Bhagavad Gītā*, and in the *Bhāgavata Purāṇa*, Lord Krishna and the sages, *Nārada* and *Vyāsaji*, declared Lord Krishna as the source of Lord Vishnu, but some people in the time of Lord Krishna, even some sages like the father of *Śrīla Vyāsadeva*, felt that Lord Krishna was Lord Vishnu incarnate. Even Krishna's foster father felt this way as this was suggested to him by the mystic priest, Gargacharya.

अनेकवक्त्रनयनम्
अनेकाद्भुतदर्शनम् ।
अनेकदिव्याभरणं
दिव्यानेकोद्यतायुधम् ॥११.१०॥
anekavaktranayanam
anekādbhutadarśanam
anekadivyābharaṇaṁ
divyānekodyatāyudham (11.10)

anekavaktranayanam = aneka — countless + vaktra — mouth + nayanam — eye; anekādbhutadarśanam = aneka — countless + adbhuta — wonders + darśanam — vision; anekadivyābharaṇaṁ = aneka — countless + divya — supernatural + ābharaṇam — ornament; divyānekodyatāyudham = divya — supernatural + aneka — countless + udyata — uplifted + āyudham — weapon

Countless mouths, eyes, wondrous visions, countless supernatural ornaments, supernatural uplifted weapons, (11.10)

Commentary:

The Universal Form which Arjuna saw was multi-personal, with each supernatural person having senses, clothing, decorations, and weapons for defending the supreme will. Arjuna was to understand that conflict transpired on the supernatural as well as the earthly level. There are conflicts even in the celestial world. And our struggles here, are sensed by the supernatural people.

दिव्यमाल्याम्बरधरं
दिव्यगन्धानुलेपनम् ।
सर्वाश्चर्यमयं देवम्
अनन्तं विश्वतोमुखम् ॥११.११॥
divyamālyāmbaradharaṁ
divyagandhānulepanam
sarvāścaryamayaṁ devam
anantaṁ viśvatomukham (11.11)

divyamālyāmbaradharam = divya — supernatural + mālya — garland + ambara — garment + dharam — wearing; divyagandhānulepanam = divya — supernatural + gandha — perfume + anulepanam — ointment; sarvāścaryamayam = sarvaścarya — all wonder + mayam — made of; devam — God; anantam — infinite; viśvatomukham — facing all directions

...wearing supernatural garlands and garments, with supernatural perfumes and ointments, appearing all wonderful, the God appeared infinite as He faced all directions. (11.11)

Commentary:

We heard that God is omnipotent, omniscient, and omnipresent. God's omnipotence would mean that He has all power at His disposal and He can invoke powers that we cannot conceive of. His omniscience means that He is aware of everything that transpires. He can make a personal appearance at any location if He so pleases. There are as many dimensions as there are variant frequencies of radio and light energy. And He can function in or manifest Himself in any of these. But even though we know this or we hypothesize on this, still we do not have the full experience of it. Arjuna, however, got the experience to understand the wonderful mystic majesty of God *(yogam* aiśvaram *11.8, paramam rūpam aiśvaram 11.9).*

The multi-personalities seen by Arjuna were personal forms. None of them was a scattered, depersonalized, general energy. They wielded different degrees of power and kept various sections of the creation under control.

दिवि सूर्यसहस्रस्य
भवेद्युगपदुत्थिता ।
यदि भाः सदृशी सा स्याद्
भासस्तस्य महात्मनः ॥११.१२॥
divi sūryasahasrasya
bhavedyugapadutthitā
yadi bhāḥ sadṛśī sā syād
bhāsastasya mahātmanaḥ(11.12)

divi — in the sky; sūryasahasrasya = sūrya — sun + sahasrasya — of one thousand; bhaved = bhavet — should be; yugapad — at once; utthitā — risen; yadi — if; bhāḥ — brilliance; sadṛśi — such; sā — it; syād — it might be; bhāsaḥ — of brightness; tasya — of it; mahātmanaḥ — of the great personality

Imagine in the sky, a thousand suns, being at once risen together. If such a brilliance were to be, it might be compared to that Great Personality. (11.12)

Commentary:

Sanjaya saw the vision that was seen by Arjuna. It was not Arjuna alone who saw the vision. Others saw it, especially some supernatural people. Others on the battlefield, persons like Bhishma and *Droṇa*, who were great mystic yogis and who were devotees of Krishna, also saw that Universal Form. Even though they did not desist from the battle after seeing the vision, they perceived it.

Sanjaya, however, wanted to give King *Dhṛtarāṣṭra* some idea of the radiant majesty of the apparition. He compared it to the rising of a thousand suns. Of course, *Dhṛtarāṣṭra* was born into a blind body and therefore, to him, this concept of the sun was imaginary. In any case, Sanjaya tried his best to give the King some idea of Krishna's supernatural power.

For Krishna to claim to be God is one factor. For Him to actually be God in truth is a wonderful reality. For Him to manifest His power into our human circumstance is an entirely different matter. People harbor doubts about the existence of God because of God's seeming inability to come down to the earthly level. Injustices, at least injustices as we perceive them, pass by us every day and we do not see how God corrects and adjusts all of these. It appears that God is not there. Therefore Sanjaya wanted to impress upon *Dhṛtarāṣṭra*, that God's power was shown on the battlefield.

तत्रैकस्थं जगत्कृत्स्नं
प्रविभक्तमनेकधा ।
अपश्यद्देवदेवस्य
शरीरे पाण्डवस्तदा ॥११.१३॥
tatraikasthaṁ jagatkṛtsnaṁ
pravibhaktamanekadhā
apaśyaddevadevasya
śarīre pāṇḍavastadā (11.13)

tatraikastham = tatra — there + ekastham — one position; jagat — universe; kṛtsnam — entire; pravibhaktam — divided; anekadhā — in many ways; apaśyad = apaśyat — he saw; devadevasya — of the God of gods; śarīre — in the body; pāṇḍavas — Arjuna Pandava; tadā — then

There the entire universe existed as one reality divided in many ways. Arjuna Pandava then saw the God of gods in that body. (11.13)

Commentary:

According to *Mahābhārata* history, Sanjaya remained on the battlefield until the day that Bhisma was fatally wounded. Then he left and went to the court of King *Dhṛtarāṣṭra* to report on the fall of the great general, that Grandsire of the Kuru family. Though Bhishma was respected as a grandsire, he did not desire progeny. Since the death of his father, King *Śantanu*, he was the guardian of the family. This is why he was respected as the Elder. Sanjaya was on the battlefield when Krishna showed Arjuna the Universal Form. But Sanjaya also had the mystic insight of the reality-piercing sages. He was blessed by his spiritual master, *Śrīla Vyāsadeva*, to have it. *Vyāsaji* told *Dhṛtarāṣṭra* that Sanjaya would narrate the incidences of the battle by accurate mystic perception.

Tatraikastham is a word compound. When sorted it gives: *tatra*—there; *eka*— one; *stham*—place. The meaning is: situated in one place, situated in one position, situated there in one location, standing together in one place.

The location was the universal body that emerged as an apparition from Krishna's two-handed form which stood near to Arjuna on the battlefield. It was not the battlefield that was the location, but Krishna's body (*deha*, 11.7). Wherever the two-handed Krishna went, that supernatural form of super-subtle personalities journeyed with Him.

ततः स विस्मयाविष्टो
हृष्टरोमा धनंजयः ।
प्रणम्य शिरसा देवं
कृताञ्जलिरभाषत ॥ ११.१४॥
tataḥ sa vismayāviṣṭo
hṛṣṭaromā dhanaṁjayaḥ
praṇamya śirasā devaṁ
kṛtāñjalirabhāṣata (11.14)

tataḥ — then; sa = saḥ — he; vismayāviṣṭo = vismayāviṣṭaḥ — one who is amazed; hṛṣṭaromā — one whose hair is bristled; dhanamjayaḥ — Arjuna, conqueror of rich countries; praṇamya — bowing; śirasā — with the head; devam — God; kṛtāñjalir = kṛtāñjaliḥ — making reverence with palms pressed for prayers; abhāsata — he spoke

Then he, who was amazed, whose hair bristled, Arjuna, the conqueror of rich countries, bowing his head to the God, with palm pressed for prayers, spoke. (11.14)

Commentary:

Over the centuries, many hundreds and thousands of commentators, speakers, and readers of the *Bhagavad Gītā* paid attention to this verse. This is perhaps the only verse that gives solid proof of the experience of Arjuna. In this verse, we see a gross bodily reaction to something Arjuna considered as awe-inspiring. The bristling of hairs was mentioned in Chapter One of the *Gītā*, in reference to Arjuna's fear when he saw relatives, in the fighting mood. After that, Arjuna calmed down and began inquiring of the samkhya philosophy. Everything went well, until Krishna said that He started a teaching that passed to *Vivasvān*, the legendary solar king. Arjuna asked for proof. Krishna provided some wording only, putting Arjuna in his place, bringing it to his attention that he was a limited being of limited recall and that he could not verify what occurred in the hoary past, even though Krishna claimed for Himself full recall. Thereafter, the conversation continued with Arjuna asking a question here and there.

When Arjuna asked Krishna about His control over the world, Lord Krishna gave some details but there was no revelation. Finally, Arjuna asked for a revelation, saying that if it were possible, Krishna should allow him to see the mystic majesty described. At first Krishna began displaying that wondrous power but Arjuna did not respond to the display because he could not see it. Krishna then gave Arjuna the ability to view the apparition. If Arjuna did not see something wonderful, his hairs would not have bristled and he would not have been in wonderment. It was a shocking view. It induced an attitude of reverence (*praṇamya*, *kṛtāñjalih*).

Persons who are doubtful of the divinity of Lord Krishna need to consider this one verse of the *Gītā*, since if any verses are there, this particular verse would solidify one's faith in Krishna or leave it in suspension, all depending on how one considers Arjuna's reaction.

Another aspect is this: If we have no faith in the story and if we feel that it is merely a fantasy of a religious writer, then we have to admit that the writer was courteous to include Arjuna's reaction in this one verse. This verse is undoubtedly a verse that requires deep consideration.

Many, many artists considered how to illustrate this verse of Arjuna and Krishna on the chariot and Arjuna bowing down to the Lord, while seeing the display of the Universal Form expanded from Krishna's body *(mama dehe).*

For those of us who accept this as evidence, the only question left is: Could anyone else get this revelation? Nearly every man wants to see the spectacle. Will Krishna show this to any other person? Generally, the modern Vaishnava teachers play down the possibility of any person other than Arjuna seeing this Universal Form. They do not place any emphasis on our vision of the revelation. In fact, many of them dismiss it as being unnecessary, since they say it has little to do with cultivating love for Krishna. They contend that it might discourage one's love of God.

However, Lord Krishna does not minimize this. When He said that the details of that power were not important, Arjuna pressed on for direct evidence. Arjuna's conventional love for Krishna was affected by the vision. Arjuna gave up his friendly mood and adopted the reverential posture.

This commentator, however, has this to say on the subject: The friendship of Arjuna before seeing the Universal Form was a contaminated, impure one. It was somewhat offensive. After getting the revelation, Arjuna realized the value of Lord Krishna as the Supreme God, the Over-Lord of the world. Thereafter, by the grace of Krishna, Arjuna resumed a friendly mood but with purified emotions. This development shows clearly that until we have this experience, our relationship with the Lord will continue to be an impure one.

Lord Krishna proved Himself as an able spiritual master by taking Arjuna through that reverential attitude and then bringing him back to friendship but to a new friendship which was devoid of false egoism, which was genuine, and which was not motivated with a mood of wanting to use or subordinate Krishna. The vision of the Universal Form is most healing and reforming. It helps the devotee to overcome the last bit of emotional impurity. It is necessary. It may be difficult to achieve such a vision, but the difficulty does not make it unnecessary.

Some teachers make a big outcry about the fearfulness of the Universal Form, saying that such a display extinguishes one's devotional love. However, these preachers have not gone through the experience. They are simply imagining what it would be like to go through it. It would be impossible to be liberated unless one passes through this experience.

In the beginning, this experience is fearful and the fearfulness increases as the experience expands but at a certain stage, the fearfulness goes away. The devotee *Prahlāda*, for example, was not afraid of the awesome, fearful God-form which killed his father. Fear of the Universal Form is there because we have impurities. If our motives were harmonious with Krishna's, such a form would produce no fear. The Lord's disciplinary mood is a cause of fear because we violate the laws of nature and try to rebuff the Supreme Will.

Terri Stokes-Pineda

अर्जुन उवाच
पश्यामि देवांस्तव देव देहे
सर्वांस्तथा भूतविशेषसंघान् ।
ब्रह्माणमीशं कमलासनस्थम्
ऋषींश्च सर्वानुरगांश्च दिव्यान् ॥ ११.१५॥
arjuna uvāca
paśyāmi devāṁstava deva dehe
sarvāṁstathā bhūtaviśeṣasaṁghān
brahmāṇamīśaṁ kamalāsanastham
ṛṣīṁśca sarvānuragāṁśca divyān
(11.15)

arjuna — Arjuna; uvāca — said; paśyāmi — I see; devāṁs — spiritual rulers; tava — your; deva — O God; dehe — in the body; sarvāṁs — all; tathā — as well as; bhūtaviśeṣasaṁghān = bhūta — being + viśeṣa — variety + saṁghān — assembled; brahmāṇam — Lord Brahmā; īśam — Lord; kamalāsanastham = kamala — lotus + āsana — seat + stham — situated; ṛṣīṁśca = ṛṣīn — yogi sages + ca — and; sarvān — all; uragāṁśca = uragān — serpents + ca — and; divyān — supernatural

Arjuna said: I see the supernatural rulers in Your body, O God, as well as all varieties of beings assembled there, Lord Brahmā, who is lotus-seated, all the yogi sages and the supernatural serpents. (11.15)

Commentary:

Tava in line 1 is a pronoun meaning *of you*. We gave *under your control* for the meaning in this verse. Arjuna was looking to see if he could find the legendary, planetary, creator-god *Brahmā*, who sits on a lotus flower. To him, this vision was evidence that Krishna was indeed the Master of the supernatural people.

Besides, even the sages and the supernatural serpents, which could not be controlled by limited beings, were being controlled by Krishna in that Universal Form. From the human view, supernatural serpents might seem mythical but we must remember that the subtle body is a reality even for animals. Even the animals have subtle forms. This is why they are encountered in dreams which concern the realities and illusions of the subtle world. Thus it is quite possible that Arjuna saw the *uragānśca divyan* (supernatural serpents).

In that respect, we can accept this as being more than a matter of belief. If Arjuna got the ability to view the psychic existence, then he would have seen many species in their subtle or super-subtle forms.

Some authoritative translators give *īśam* in this verse as, *Lord Shiva*. *Īśam* is a special title of Lord Shiva, but *īśam* also means *lord* or *master*. Lord Shiva is mentioned as a Rudra in verse 22 of this chapter. In this verse, the three words *brahmāṇam*, *īśam*, and *kamalāsanastham* apply to Lord *Brahmā*, the creator-god whose special seat is a lotus flower. Lord Shiva is different because *Brahmā* begins the creation whereas the Rudras are manifested thereafter. Lord Shiva is more powerful than *Brahmā* and yet, *Brahmā* begins the creation. Each of them is *īśam* (Lord) but *Brahmā* is the one who uses a lotus seat.

अनेकबाहूदरवक्त्रनेत्रं
पश्यामि त्वां सर्वतोऽनन्तरूपम् ।
नान्तं न मध्यं न पुनस्तवादिं
पश्यामि विश्वेश्वर विश्वरूप ॥ ११.१६ ॥

anekabāhūdaravaktranetram = aneka — countless + bāhu — arm + udara — belly + vaktra — face + netram — eye; paśyāmi — I see; tvām — you; sarvato = sarvataḥ — all directions; 'nantarūpam = anantarūpam = ananta — infinite + rūpam — form; nāntam = na — not + antam — end; na —

anekabāhūdaravaktranetraṁ
paśyāmi tvām sarvato'nantarūpam
nāntaṁ na madhyaṁ na punastavādiṁ
paśyāmi viśveśvara viśvarūpa
(11.16)

not; madhyam — middle; na — no; punas = punar — again even; tavādim = tava — of you + ādim — beginning; paśyāmi — I observe; viśveśvara — O Lord of all; viśvarūpa — form of everything

There are countless arms, bellies, faces, and eyes. I see You in all directions, O person of infinite form. There is no end, middle, or even a beginning of You. I observe You, O Lord of all, O Form of everything. (11.16)

Commentary:

To Arjuna, the form included everything that was possible as an individual existence in the material world. He could see numberless arms, bellies, faces and eyes. As he gazed in the distance with supernatural eyes, he saw no limit. He concluded that it was infinite. All of the form was personal. It was multi-dimensional. He could not discern an ending, middle, or beginning. Everything evolved within the influence of the form. He could not calculate the extent of it.

किरीटिनं गदिनं चक्रिणं च
तेजोराशिं सर्वतो दीप्तिमन्तम् ।
पश्यामि त्वां दुर्निरीक्ष्यं समन्ताद्
दीप्तानलार्कद्युतिमप्रमेयम् ॥ ११.१७॥
kirīṭinaṁ gadinaṁ cakriṇaṁ ca
tejorāśiṁ sarvato dīptimantam
paśyāmi tvāṁ durnirīkṣyaṁ samantād
dīptānalārkadyutim aprameyam
(11.17)

kirīṭinam — crowned; gadinam — armed with a club; cakriṇam — bearing a discus; ca — and; tejo — splendor; rāśim — a mass; sarvato = sarvataḥ — on all sides; dīptimantam — shining wondrously; paśyāmi — I see; tvām — you; durnirīkṣyam — difficult to behold; samantāt — in entirety; dīptānalārkadyutim = dīpta — blazing + anala — fire + arka — sun + dyutim — effulgence; aprameyam — immeasurable

This Form is crowned, armed with a club, bearing a discus, a mass of splendor on all sides, shining wondrously with immeasurable radiance of the sun and blazing fire. I see You in entirety, You Who are difficult to behold. (11.17)

Commentary:

Even though the form was manifold with many personalities, and their individual forms with powers, still there was the central figure, Krishna Himself, with a primal discus, primal club, with splendor, shining wondrously. That Primal Personality had a shining effulgence that could not be measured. It was more than any of the other supernatural figures displayed. It was predominant, though it shared the glory of the overall configuration.

त्वमक्षरं परमं वेदितव्यं
त्वमस्य विश्वस्य परं निधानम् ।
त्वमव्ययः शाश्वतधर्मगोप्ता
सनातनस्त्वं पुरुषो मतो मे ॥ ११.१८॥

tvam — you; akṣaram — imperishable; paramam — supreme; veditavyam — to be revealed; tvam — you; asya — of it; viśvasya — of all; param — ultimate; nidhānam — shelter; tvam — you; avyayaḥ —

tvamakṣaraṁ paramaṁ veditavyaṁ
tvamasya viśvasya paraṁ nidhānam
tvamavyayaḥ śāśvatadharmagoptā
sanātanastvaṁ puruṣo mato me
(11.18)

imperishable; śāśvatadharmagoptā = śāśvata — eternal + dharma — law + goptā — guardian; sanātanaḥ — most ancient; tvam — you; puruṣo = puruṣaḥ — person; mato = mataḥ — thought; me — of me

You are the indestructible Supreme Reality, to be revealed. You are the ultimate shelter of all. You are the imperishable, eternal guardian of law. It seems to me that You are the most ancient person. (11.18)

Commentary:

Prior to this revelation, Arjuna's belief in the glory of Krishna was based on hearing from persons like *Nārada, Vyāsaji, Asita Devala*, and Krishna Himself. Now Arjuna's belief in what was heard from those reliable sources, is substantiated by experience. Arjuna's name is now added to the list of those who directly saw Krishna's supremacy.

By attributing Lord Krishna as the indestructible, supreme item of research, Arjuna gave the opinion that the personality of Krishna is itself an object of scientific education. He felt that Krishna should be known (*veditavyam*).

Arjuna experienced Krishna as the supreme resting place and the imperishable guardian of eternal law. Seeing Lord Krishna as the supreme law upholder (*dharmagoptā*), Arjuna felt safe and secure in accepting Krishna's directions about settling the civil war. Arjuna no longer regarded his opinion of morality to be on par with or to be counter-effective towards the opinions of Krishna. In the Universal Form, Krishna had the most power, the most responsibility, and the overall supervisory control.

अनादिमध्यान्तमनन्तवीर्यम्
अनन्तबाहुं शशिसूर्यनेत्रम्
पश्यामि त्वां दीप्तहुताशवक्त्रं
स्वतेजसा विश्वमिदं तपन्तम् ॥ ११.१९ ॥
anādimadhyāntam anantavīryam
anantabāhuṁ śaśisūryanetram
paśyāmi tvāṁ dīptahutāśavaktraṁ
svatejasā viśvamidaṁ tapantam
(11.19)

anādimadhyāntam = an — without + ādi — beginning + madhya — middle + antam — end; anantavīryam = ananta — unlimited + vīryam — manly power; anantabāhuṁ = ananta — unlimited + bāhum — arm; śaśisūryanetram = śaśi — moon + sūrya — sun + netram — eye; paśyāmi — I see; tvām — you; dīptahutāśavaktraṁ = dīpta — blazing + hutāśa — oblation-eating + vaktram — mouth; svatejasā — with Your splendor; viśvam — universe; idam — this; tapantam — heating

You who are without beginning, middle, or ending, Who has infinite manly power, Who has unlimited arms, Who has the sun and moon as Your eyes, I see You, with the blazing oblation-eating mouth, heating this universe with Your Own splendor. (11.19)

Commentary:

This glorification is to the Universal Form as a whole and to Lord Krishna as He is situated as the central figure. As a whole, the form was spectacular but it was obvious to Arjuna that Lord Krishna was the central feature Who regulated all other supernatural people and their powers.

It appeared to Arjuna that the sun and moon served as visualizing searchlights for Krishna. In trying to analyze the form, Arjuna, even with a supernatural mind and supernatural senses, could not assess the beginning, middle, or end. Everything was within the reach of the form's supernatural arms. The central personality of the form as well as the other subordinate persons, had oblation-eating mouths which blazed for consumption of desired eatables. And the splendor functioned as the energizing force of the world.

द्यावापृथिव्योरिदमन्तरं हि
व्याप्तं त्वयैकेन दिशश्च सर्वाः ।
दृष्ट्वाद्भुतं रूपम् उग्रं तवेदं
लोकत्रयं प्रव्यथितं महात्मन् ॥ ११.२० ॥
dyāvāpṛthivyoridam antaraṁ hi
vyāptaṁ tvayaikena diśaścasarvāḥ
dṛṣṭvādbhutaṁ rūpam ugraṁ tavedaṁ
lokatrayaṁ pravyathitaṁ mahātman (11.20)

dyāvāpṛthivyor = dyāvāpṛthivyoḥ — of heaven and earth; idam — this; antaram — space between; hi — indeed; vyāptam - pervaded; tvayaikena = tvaya — by you + ekena - alone; diśaḥ — directions; ca — and; sarvāḥ — all; dṛṣtvā — having seen + adbhutam — marvelous; rūpam — form; ugram — terrible; tavedam = tava — your + idam — this; lokatrayam = loka — world + trayam — three; pravyathitam — trembling; mahātman — O great personality

In all directions, the space between heaven and earth is pervaded by You alone. Seeing Your marvelous Form, of a terrible feature, the three worlds tremble, O great Personality. (11.20)

Commentary:

Some are of the opinion that only Arjuna saw the Universal Form. But the famous Vaishnava *Acarya*, *Śrīla* Bhaktivedanta Swami, gave a short purport to this verse in which he stated that: *dyāvāpṛthivoh* (the space between heaven and earth) and *lokatrayam* (three worlds) are significant words in this verse because it appears that not only Arjuna saw this, but others in other dimensions also viewed it. He wrote: "The vision was not a dream. All who were spiritually awake with the divine vision saw it." (*Bhagavad Gītā As It Is, p. 556*) Arjuna was of the opinion that Krishna had, by displaying that form, caused the universal situation to be endangered. Krishna, in Arjuna's view, caused a trembling. It is a fact, however, that an experience of one person is not necessarily felt by others.

We must remember that regardless of what Arjuna said of his experience, there was testimony given to Arjuna by *Nārada* and *Vyāsaji* who were reputed sages in the time of Krishna. This evidence must be considered when regarding what Arjuna said about Krishna and what Krishna said about Himself.

अमी हि त्वा सुरसंघा विशन्ति
केचिद्भीताः प्राञ्जलयो गृणन्ति ।
स्वस्तीत्युक्त्वा महर्षिसिद्धसंघाः
स्तुवन्ति त्वां स्तुतिभिः पुष्कलाभिः ॥ ११.२१ ॥
amī hi tvā surasaṁghā viśanti
kecidbhītāḥ prāñjalayo gṛṇanti
svastītyuktvā maharṣisiddhasaṁghāḥ
stuvanti tvāṁ stutibhiḥ puṣkalābhiḥ (11.21)

amī — those; hi — truly; tvā — you; surasaṁghā = sura — supernatural ruler + saṁghā — groups; viśanti — they enter; kecid — some; bhītāḥ — terrified; prāñjalayo = prāñjalayaḥ — bowing with palms pressed together; gṛṇanti — they offer praise; svastīty = svastīti = sv (su) — suitable + asti — there be + iti — thus; uktvā — saying; maharṣisiddhasaṁghāḥ = mahārṣi — great yogi sages + siddha — perfected yogis + saṁghāḥ — groups; stuvanti — they praise; tvām — you; stutibhiḥ — with glorification; puṣkalābhiḥ — with lavish

Those groups of supernatural rulers enter You. Some being terrified, bowing with palms pressed together, offer praise. "May everything be suitable," they say. The groups of great yogi sages and perfected yogis praise You with lavish glorification. (11.21)

Commentary:

Here is the evidence that Arjuna saw others who viewed the form just as he perceived it. But those assembled supernatural controllers, the great sages, and the perfected persons, were trying to pacify the central figure of the form. The supernatural controllers or demigods were terrified. The great sages and perfected personalities tried to pacify Krishna, the Central Personality. They said, "*svasti;* Hail to You. Okay, everything will be adjusted to suit You."

The indication here is that before Arjuna was shown the form, the supernatural controllers were not in anxiety about Krishna. He was not considered to be that important. They did not feel that they had to adjust their ideas to suit His plan. They did not take Krishna to be that Supreme Authority. After Krishna revealed His supreme power, they had no alternative but to realize then and there, Who He was and what He demanded of them. They were terrified because, in Krishna's view, they neglected duties. Krishna came to the human world to rectify a morally worn-down and spiritually-reduced situation for which the supernatural people were accountable. Previously they did not think that Krishna could affect them. When they became aware of Krishna's threatening power, they were frightened.

Seeing the situation and sensing the danger of the irritation and its effects on the universal situation, the sages and perfected entities who had no reason to be afraid of Krishna, began to pacify Him, telling Him that everything would be adjusted in the nick of time.

There is still, however, much room for doubt and skepticism. Arjuna was under a vision, an apparition. How do we know that he is not under a magical spell? Or that he is not hallucinating without understanding what was perceived? How are we to be assured that this is not taking place only in Arjuna's mind? It is possible to misinterpret a limited vision as a universal experience.

Many, many persons, even commentators, even some who are awed by the descriptions given here, have doubts about this. Some, however, even though they do not care much about this vision which requires religious faith and conviction in Krishna, go on to the philosophical truths of the *Gītā* and accept the ones that seem reasonable to their understanding. But if we accept the philosophy of Krishna and reject, in part or total, Krishna's presentation of Himself as God, we are in effect accepting some of Krishna's ideas, while rejecting His claim of Himself as the Supreme Being.

Persons who accept ideas of Krishna and who reject Krishna's presentation of Himself as the Supreme God, are simply taking those opinions which suit their understanding. In other words, when we take His philosophy and reject His self-glory, we are borrowing or taking from Him to reinforce our ideas.

Interestingly, even a devotee of Krishna may do this to his Lord Those who are opposed to Krishna's supremacy and who comment on the *Gītā*, are being hypocritical, but a devotee may steal from Krishna also. The central point of the *Gītā*, is not Krishna's philosophy, but it is rather the point of controversy as to whether Krishna is merely a human historic character or the God Personality.

रुद्रादित्या वसवो ये च साध्या
विश्वेऽश्विनौ मरुतश्चोष्मपाश्च ।
गन्धर्वयक्षासुरसिद्धसंघा
वीक्षन्ते त्वां विस्मिताश्चैव सर्वे ॥
११.२२॥

rudrādityā vasavo ye ca sādhyā
viśve'śvinau marutaścoṣmapāśca
gandharvayakṣā surasiddhasaṁghā
vīkṣante tvām vismitāś caiva sarve (11.22)

rudrādityā = rudra — supernatural destroyers + ādityāḥ — supernatural rulers; vasavo = vasavaḥ — Vasus, assistants to supernatural rulers; ye — who; ca — and; sādhyā — Sādhya, guardian angels; viśve — Vishvadeva supernatural priests; 'śvinau = aśvinau — two primal supernatural doctors; marutaścoṣmapāś = marutaḥ — supernatural stormers + ca — and + uṣmapāḥ — spirits who take vapor bodies; ca — and; gandharvayakṣāsurasiddhasaṁghā = gandharva — celestial musicians + yakṣa — spirits guarding natural resources + asura — supernatural rebels + siddha — perfected souls + saṁghā — groups; vīkṣante — they behold; tvām — you; vismitāścaiva = vismitāḥ — amazed + ca — and + iva (eva) — indeed; sarve — all

The supernatural destroyers, the supernatural rulers, the assistants to those rulers, these and the Sādhya guardian angels, the Vishvadeva supernatural priests, the two primal supernatural doctors, the supernatural stormers, the spirits who take vapor bodies, the groups of celestial musicians, the spirits guarding natural resources, the supernatural rebels and the perfected souls, behold You. And they are all amazed. (11.22)

Commentary:

The mystery of the Universal Form is indicated. The form was not seen by anyone until Krishna showed it to Arjuna. Are we to believe that Krishna's supremacy was a hidden factor until that time? Does this mean that Krishna's Godhood was not known by the supernatural people.

The Rudras are supernatural destroyers. These are a class of entities who are capable of demolishing the creation, but who conceal their power. The *Ādityas* are the sons of Aditi. They are the functional gods of the world. Being in charge of the sun and moon, they wield environmental dominance but they function from a supernatural level. They maintain weather and the various aspects which affect creature behavior. The Vasus are assistants to the *Ādityas*. The Vishvadevas are another group of assistants to the *Ādityas*.

They work on a more personal level with individual human beings while the *Vasus* work on a broader planetary scale, not being too particular about individuals. The *Sādhyas* are supernatural beings who perform ritual ceremonies for the Daityas. The Ashvinis are the two supernatural doctors. The Maruts are supernatural weathermen who serve the leading *Āditya* named Indra. They control stormy weather. The *Uṣmapās* are the forefathers who hover in the hereafter in the realm where water vapor is used to create subtle forms. Sometimes we see the vapor bodies they produce in clouds or mist. The Gandharvas are celestial musicians and singers. The Yakshas are the attendants of Kubera, a supernatural person who controls natural resources.

The Asuras are demoniac sorcerers. The Siddhas are the perfected spiritualists who remain in the material world for one reason or another. All these, as Arjuna observed, were amazed to discover that Krishna, the historic human being, was their Supreme Controller.

रूपं महत्ते बहुवक्त्रनेत्रं
महाबाहो बहुबाहूरुपादम् ।
बहूदरं बहुदंष्ट्राकरालं
दृष्ट्वा लोकाः प्रव्यथितास्तथाहम्॥ ११.२३ ॥
rūpaṁ mahatte bahuvaktranetraṁ
mahābāho bahubāhūrupādam
bahūdaraṁ bahudaṁṣṭrākarālaṁ
dṛṣṭvā lokāḥ pravyathitās tathāham
(11.23)

rūpam — form; mahat — great; te — your; bahuvaktranetram = bahu — many + vaktra — mouth + netram — eye; mahābāho — O mighty-armed Person; bahubāhūrupādam = bahu — many + bāhu — arm + ūru — thigh + pādam — foot; bahūdaram = bahu — many + udaram — belly; bahudaṁṣṭrākarālam = bahu — many + daṁṣṭrā — teeth + karālam — terrible; dṛṣṭvā — having seen; lokāḥ — the world; pravyathitāḥ — trembling; tathā — as well as; 'ham = aham — I

O mighty-armed Person, having seen Your great Form with many mouths and eyes, and many arms, thighs, and feet, many bellies and many terrible teeth, the worlds tremble as well as I. (11.23)

Commentary:

The claim that only Arjuna saw that specific form displayed by Krishna, is here refuted by Arjuna himself. *Dṛṣṭvā lokāh* in the fourth line means, *the world having seen*, or, *the beings of the world having seen*. It may be contested, however, that everyone may not have seen this as thoroughly as Arjuna did but every living being might have felt insecure as a result of Arjuna's experience. In any case, according to Arjuna, all beings experienced a trembling or shaking, a nervous type of insecurity (*pravyathitās*) at the time.

It is definite that the supernatural people, the powerful demoniac magicians, and the perfected beings, saw the form visually as Arjuna did. *Śrīla* Bhaktivedanta Swami wrote that those who were spiritually awake saw the Form.

After this, Arjuna asked Lord Krishna to desist. Krishna suggested to Arjuna that there was no necessity for a detailed description of divine glories. But Arjuna pushed on for evidence. He got what he requested in the form of this apparition. Arjuna then requested that Krishna stop the display immediately since it was a threat to everyone except for Lord Krishna. Those who were unaware of Krishna's Godhood and who had the supernatural perception, found out about Krishna at that time. Others who did not have supernatural vision, sensed a great danger.

नभःस्पृशं दीप्तमनेकवर्णं
व्यात्ताननं दीप्तविशालनेत्रम् ।
दृष्ट्वा हि त्वां प्रव्यथितान्तरात्मा
धृतिं न विन्दामि शमं च विष्णो ॥ ११.२४ ॥
nabhaḥspṛśaṁ dīptamanekavarṇaṁ
vyāttānanaṁ dīptaviśālanetram
dṛṣṭvā hi tvāṁ pravyathitāntarātmā
dhṛtiṁ na vindāmi śamaṁ ca viṣṇo
(11.24)

nabhaḥspṛśaṁ = nabhaḥ — sky + spṛśaṁ — touching, extending; dīptam — glowing; aneka — many; varṇam — colors; vyātta — open; ānanam — mouths; dīpta — glowing; viśāla — very great; netram — eyes; dṛṣṭvā — seeing; hi — certainly; tvām — You; pravyathita — perturbed; antaḥ — within; ātmā — soul; dhṛtim — steadiness; na — not; vindāmi — I have; śamam — mental tranquility; ca — also; viṣṇo — O Lord Viṣṇu.

Having seen You, sky extending, blazing, multi-colored, with gaping mouths and blazing vast eyes, there is a shivering in my soul. I find no courage, nor stability, O God Vishnu. (11.24)

Commentary:

Many reputable persons identified Krishna as Lord Vishnu. Krishna Himself claimed to be the source of that God of this world. But despite His claims many persons considered Him to be either identical with or empowered by Lord Vishnu. This was the view of Nanda Gopa, the cowherd man of Vrindavana who served as Krishna's foster father. It was the view of Krishna's father, Vasudeva, as well. Others like *Nārada* and *Vyāsadeva* were of the view that Krishna was simultaneously identical with and productive of Lord Vishnu.

After seeing Krishna display that wonderful supernatural power and seeing the response of the powerful supernatural people, like Lord Shiva and Lord *Brahmā*, Arjuna had to address Lord Krishna as God Vishnu.

In the time of Arjuna, some people felt that Vishnu, *Brahmā*, or Shiva were individually or collectively the God of the world. Some were uncertain as we can understand from a close scrutiny of the Vedic histories. There were different versions of how the creation came about. The people in the area where Arjuna lived were aware of some of these versions. In some, Shiva was regarded as the ultimate originator. In others, Vishnu was, and yet in others, *Brahmā* was. In those scriptures which advocated Vishnu as foremost of the supernatural people, it is described that Vishnu originated the world and then produced *Brahmā* who continued the creation and supervised it, while Lord Shiva assisted *Brahmā* by regulating the transmigrations of the various limited souls who exploit the places and resources. It is said that in the beginning there was Vishnu alone. While the creation transpires. He remains unseen in the background. In the end. He alone survives the universal destruction. Thus Arjuna identified Lord Krishna with Lord Vishnu. From the looks of Lord Krishna in the Universal Form and in His human appearance, the features of that Vishnu were evident.

Seeing that superform and realizing Who Krishna was, Arjuna lost courage and security. He felt very, very small and dispensible. His footing of security in the material world was undermined. He lost reference and value. His importance which caused him to order Krishna to the center field and which prompted him to view the warriors, was forgotten. He was there as someone without importance. Even to Arjuna, the display of the Universal Form was a danger, a threat to his mundane existence, a frightening apparition.

Many devotees of Krishna shun this Universal Form. They openly despise it and discourage persons from reading this part of the *Bhagavad Gītā*. Since such a display scares a devotee like Arjuna, this form is shunned by many devotees.

In this description of Arjuna, there is no mention of any supernatural ladies; not even the spouses of Vishnu, *Brahmā* and Shiva were mentioned. This description is that of a supernatural, masculine alliance formed around Krishna with the power based in Krishna as the Lord of the personalities.

दंष्ट्राकरालानि च ते मुखानि
दृष्ट्वैव कालानलसंनिभानि ।
दिशो न जाने न लभे च शर्म
प्रसीद देवेश जगन्निवास ॥११.२५॥
daṁṣṭrākarālāni ca te mukhāni
dṛṣṭvaiva kālānalasaṁnibhāni
diśo na jāne na labhe ca śarma
prasīda deveśa jagannivāsa (11.25)

daṁṣṭrā— teeth; karālāni — terrible; ca — also; te — Your; mukhāni — faces; dṛṣṭvā — seeing; eva — thus; kāla-anala — the fire of death; sannibhāni — as if; diśaḥ — the directions; na — not; jāne — I know; na — not; labhe — I obtain; ca — and; śarma — grace; prasīda — be pleased; deva-īśa — O Lord of all lords; jagat-nivāsa — O refuge of the worlds

And seeing Your Form with many mouths, having terrible teeth, glowing like the fire of universal destruction, I cannot determine the cardinal points. I do not find any peace of mind. Have mercy, O Lord of the gods, Abode of the universe. (11.25)

Commentary:

Sanskrit dictionaries gave the word *śarma* as *pleasure, happiness, delight, comfort and refuge*. Sri Sridhara Deva Gosvami, a Vaishnava acarya, gave, *peace of mind*. Arjuna could not find any emotional or mental stability while viewing that Universal Form of Krishna. The Form was too serious, too disciplinarian, too critical of any deviation from supreme will. It was a threat to the individual and collective puny wills of the limited beings. It appeared to be very critical, judgmental and reactive. Arjuna was a dear friend and cousin of Krishna but no such joviality was indicated in the central Krishna of the Universal Form.

अमी च त्वां धृतराष्ट्रस्य पुत्राः
सर्वे सहैवावनिपालसंघैः ।
भीष्मो द्रोणः सूतपुत्रस्तथासौ
सहास्मदीयैरपि योधमुख्यैः ॥११.२६॥
amī ca tvāṁ dhṛtarāṣṭrasya putrāḥ
sarve sahaivāvanipālasaṁghaiḥ
bhīṣmo droṇaḥ sūtaputrastathāsau
sahāsmadīyairapi yodhamukhyaiḥ
(11.26)

amī — those; ca — and; tvāṁ — you; dhṛtarāṣṭrasya — of Dhṛtarāṣṭra; putrāḥ — sons; sarve — all; sahaivāvanipālasaṁghaiḥ = saha — with + eva — indeed+avāvanipāla — rulers of the earth + saṁghaiḥ — with groups; bhīṣmo = bhīṣmaḥ — Bhishma; droṇaḥ — Droṇa; sūtaputraḥ — Karna, son of the charioteer; tathāsau = tathā — as well as + asau — that; saha — along with; asmadīyaiḥ — with ours; api — also; yodhamukhyaiḥ — with chief warriors

And those, all the sons of Dhṛtarāṣṭra, along with the groups of rulers, Bhishma, Droṇa, as well as that son of the charioteer, along with our men and also our chief warriors, are in contrast to You. (11.26)

Commentary:

The charioteer's son is *Karṇa*, who was one of the generals on the side of Arjuna's enemies, the Kauravas. *Karṇa*, an illegitimate son of Arjuna's mother, *Kuntī*, was competitively hostile towards Arjuna.

In viewing the Universal Form, Arjuna looked to see his own situation. What he saw in the Universal Configuration was different to what was taking place on the battlefield at that time, even though later, during the battle, it was verified. It appears, therefore, that he saw the future in the Universal Form. On the existential plane where the Form was manifested, the warriors were being mangled to death by Lord Krishna and His various assistants. We may wonder if the warriors had some sort of parallel counterpart that they were unaware of. What exactly did Arjuna see? Was it an hallucination? Was it merely a piece of projected mysticism of Lord Krishna? Since the sons of *Dhṛtarāṣṭra* were still alive and well, standing before Arjuna on the battlefield, who were the parallel people being mangled and harassed by the Universal Form? What was the connection between the mangled warriors in the apparition and the parallel forms of warriors who stood at ease, unhurt on the battlefield?

वक्त्राणि ते त्वरमाणा विशन्ति
दंष्ट्राकरालानि भयानकानि ।
केचिद्विलग्ना दशनान्तरेषु
संदृश्यन्ते चूर्णितैरुत्तमाङ्गैः ॥११.२७॥

vaktrāṇi — mouths; te — your; tvaramāṇā — speedily; viśanti — they enter; daṁṣṭrākarālāni = daṁṣṭrā — teeth + karālāni — dreadful; bhayānakāni — fearful; kecid (kecit) — some; vilagnā — clinging:

vaktrāṇi te tvaramāṇā viśanti
daṁṣṭrākarālāni bhayānakāni
kecidvilagnā daśanāntareṣu
saṁdṛśyante cūrṇitair uttamāṅgaiḥ
(11.27)

daśanāntareṣu = daśana — tooth + antareṣu — in between; saṁdṛśyante — they are seen; cūrṇitaiḥ — with crushed; uttamāṅgaiḥ — with heads

They speedily enter Your fearful mouths, which have dreadful teeth. Some cling between the teeth. They are seen with crushed heads. (11.27)

Commentary:

This ghastly vision of the fight between the Universal Form of Krishna and the supernatural forms of the allied warriors, is a mystery. On the earthly plane, those warriors used healthy bodies, while they waited to engage in the civil war. And on another level, a higher one, the supernatural plane, they were being chastised, hurt, chewed, burnt, and killed in various ways. How is it that the psychic forms were being destroyed by the Universal Configuration and the earthly forms were still in a healthy condition on this level, only to be destroyed some days later Why was there a time delay? And why were those parallel people chewed up on the supernatural level while the earthly counterparts were killed by weaponry on the earthly plane? What is the correlation between the supernatural and the physical?

On the earthly level, Krishna was a non-combatant, appearing merely as a human charioteer. But on the supernatural plane. He displayed Himself as the chief personality in a horrifying, antagonistic Godhead. Previously Krishna displayed another phase of that dreadful Universal Form to Duryodhana. Arjuna was not the first one to see it as some people think. Arjuna was the first one to see this particular phase of the Form. It was active. It had a transforming history. Duryodhana saw another historic part of it. When Duryodhana saw the Form, he dismissed it as an apparition only. Duryodhana had some difficulty correlating the vision he saw with the earthly reality. But Arjuna was convinced by the Form and seemed to think that there was a connection.

यथा नदीनां बहवोऽम्बुवेगाः
समुद्रमेवाभिमुखा द्रवन्ति ।
तथा तवामी नरलोकवीरा
विशन्ति वक्त्राण्यभिविज्वलन्ति ॥११.२८॥
yathā nadīnāṁ bahavo'mbuvegāḥ
samudramevābhimukhā dravanti
tathā tavāmī naralokavīrā
viśanti vaktrāṇyabhivijvalanti (11.28)

yathā — as; nadīnāṁ — of the rivers; bahavo — bahavaḥ — many; 'mbuvegāḥ = ambuvegāḥ — water currents; samudram — sea; evābhimukhā = eva — indeed + abhimukhā — facing towards; dravanti — they flow; tathā — so; tavāmī = tava — of you + amī — those; naralokavīrā = nara — man + loka — world +vīrā — heroes; viśanti — they enter; vaktràni — mouths; abhivijvalanti — they are flaming

As the water currents of many rivers flow to the sea, so the earthly heroes enter Your mouths, which are flaming. (11.28)

Commentary:

In that vision the heroes, many of them, were being burnt to death as they approached the mouths of the various figureheads in that Universal Form. On one hand, the warriors were combating the supreme will, but on the other, the supreme will was welcoming their challenges and sucking them into its flaming mouths for their destruction. To Arjuna the warriors were helplessly being pulled into those fiery openings.

यथा प्रदीप्तं ज्वलनं पतंगा
विशन्ति नाशाय समृद्धवेगाः ।
तथैव नाशाय विशन्ति लोकास्
तवापि वक्त्राणि समृद्धवेगाः ॥ ११.२९ ॥
yathā pradīptaṁ jvalanaṁ pataṁgā
viśanti nāśāya samṛddhavegāḥ
tathaiva nāśāya viśanti lokās
tavāpi vaktrāṇi samṛddhavegāḥ (11.29)

yathā — as; pradīptaṁ — blazing; jvalanaṁ — fire; pataṁgā — moths; viśanti — enter; nāśāya — to destruction; samṛddhavegāḥ — with great speed; tathaiva = tathā — so + iva (eva) — indeed; nāśāya — to ruination; viśanti — enter; lokāh — worlds; tavāpi = tava — you + api — also; vaktrāṇi — mouths; samṛddhavegāḥ — with great speed

As moths speedily enter a blazing fire to destruction, so to ruination, the worlds enter Your mouths with great speed. (11.29)

Commentary:

In the view of Arjuna, in the apparition shown to him by Lord Krishna, everything personal and impersonal in the world was being drawn into the mouths of these supernatural faces of the Universal Form. They were going there to their destruction in a forceful, drawing energy which flowed between them and the Form.

लेलिह्यसे ग्रसमानः समन्ताल्
लोकान्समग्रान्वदनैर्ज्वलद्भिः ।
तेजोभिरापूर्य जगत्समग्रं
भासस्तवोग्राः प्रतपन्ति विष्णो ॥ ११.३० ॥
lelihyase grasamānaḥ samantāl
lokānsamagrānvadanair jvaladbhiḥ
tejobhirāpūrya jagatsamagraṁ
bhāsastavogrāḥ pratapanti viṣṇo (11.30)

lelihyase — you lick; grasamānaḥ — swallow; samantāt — from all sides; lokān — the worlds; samagrān — all; vadanaiḥ — with mouths; jvaladbhiḥ — with flaming; tejobhiḥ — with splendor; āpūrya — filling; jagat — universe; samagraṁ — all; bhāsaḥ — rays; tavogrāḥ = tava — your + ugrāh — horrible; pratapanti — burns; viṣṇo — O Lord Vishnu

You lick, swallowing from all sides, all the worlds with Your flaming mouths, filling the universes with splendor. Your horrible blazing rays burn it, O Lord Vishnu. (11.30)

Commentary:

There remains a question of how to correlate this Universal Form to our situation and to that of the warriors who stood before Krishna and Arjuna on the battlefield. How were the warriors to realize this Form? How were they to understand its supernatural actions?

From the description of what Arjuna saw, it appears that the supernatural mouths were eating up those human beings who approached with hostile intentions. They were being eaten to death on the supernatural level. We have hardly heard of any such thing in the Vedic literature, except of cannibalistic demons like *Kumbhakarṇa*, the giant cannibal who was the brother of *Rāvaṇa*. When he became angry enough, he ate warriors by the handfuls.

Besides the Form's cannibalistic trends, we hear also of its fiery power to burn up the world with blazing rays. The Vedic literature usually described Lord Vishnu as the preserver of the world. Usually, Lord Shiva's *Bhairava* aspect and Goddess *Durgā's Kālī* aspect are attributed with ghastly features, but here Arjuna testified to a ghastly apparition of Krishna.

आख्याहि मे को भवानुग्ररूपो
नमोऽस्तु ते देववर प्रसीद ।
विज्ञातुमिच्छामि भवन्तमाद्यं
न हि प्रजानामि तव प्रवृत्तिम् ॥ ११.३१ ॥
ākhyāhi me ko bhavānugrarūpo
namo'stu te devavara prasīda
vijñātumicchāmi bhavantamādyaṁ
na hi prajānāmi tava pravṛttim
(11.31)

ākhyāhi — explain; me — to me; ko = kaḥ — who; bhavān — respected person; ugrarūpo — ugrarūpaḥ — of terrible form; namo = namaḥ — homage; 'stu = astu — may it be; te — to you; devavara — best of the gods; prasīda — have mercy; vijñātum — to understand; icchāmi — I want; bhavantam — Your lordship; ādyaṁ — primal person; na — not; hi — indeed; prajānāmi — I know; tava — your; pravṛttim — intention

Explain to me who You are, O respected Person of terrible form. I gave my homage to You, O best of gods. Have mercy! I want to understand You, O Primal Person. I do not know Your intention. (11.31)

Commentary:

Having asked for a visionary experience of Krishna's controlling power over the world, Arjuna is now burdened with the responsibility of calling off the apparition. It was real enough to scare him and to scare the supernatural people who viewed it simultaneously with him. Arjuna, therefore, began to plead with the multi-Form. At this point, he has lost track of his chariot-driving friend Krishna. He only saw the ghastly apparition.

Formerly, Arjuna argued with Krishna, hesitated, threw out some fits like a spoiled child. Arjuna stalled and diddle-daddled. After seeing the Universal Form, his childishness vanished. Arjuna asked for Krishna's intentions.

श्रीभगवानुवाच
कालोऽस्मि लोकक्षयकृत्प्रवृद्धो
लोकान्समाहर्तुमिह प्रवृत्तः ।
ऋतेऽपि त्वा न भविष्यन्ति सर्वे
येऽवस्थिताः प्रत्यनीकेषु योधाः ॥ ११.३२ ॥
śrībhagavānuvāca
kālo'smi lokakṣayakṛt pravṛddho
lokānsamāhartumiha pravṛttaḥ
ṛte'pi tvāṁ na bhaviṣyanti sarve
ye'vasthitāḥ pratyanīkeṣu yodhāḥ
(11.32)

śrī bhagavān — the Blessed Lord; uvāca — said; kālo = kālah — time-limit; 'smi = asmi — I am; lokaksayakrt = loka — world + ksaya — destruction + kṛt — causing; pravṛddho = pravṛddhaḥ — mighty; lokān — worlds; samāhartum — to annihilate; iha — here; pravṛttaḥ — appeared; ṛte — without; 'pi = api — also; tvāṁ — you na — not, cease; bhaviṣyanti — they will live; sarve — all; ye — who; 'vasthitāḥ = avasthitāḥ — armored; pratyanikeṣu — on both armies; yodhāḥ — warriors

The Blessed Lord said: I am the time limit, the mighty world-destroying Cause, appearing here to annihilate the worlds. Even without you, all the armored warriors, in both armies will cease to live. (11.32)

Commentary:

Krishna, as the central figure in that Universal Form, informed Arjuna of the intentions to wipe out the warriors. Even without Arjuna's cooperation, Krishna intended to deprive them of their bodies. On the supernatural level, they were burnt by flames from His mouths. Those who were flame-resistant and who persisted into His mouths were chewed up. As Time, Krishna was the final argument, the ultimate victor. He stated His intentions clearly as the annihilation of the world (*lokān samāhartum*). He intended to destroy the civilization of the Kurus. Previously Arjuna refused to cooperate in such a violent venture. Therefore he is told by the Form that even if he did not cooperate, the Supreme would prevail in one way or another.

तस्मात्त्वमुत्तिष्ठ यशो लभस्व
जित्वा शत्रून्भुङ्क्ष राज्यं समृद्धम् ।
मयैवैते निहताः पूर्वमेव
निमित्तमात्रं भव सव्यसाचिन् ॥ ११.३३ ॥
tasmāttvamuttiṣṭha yaśo labhasva
jitvā śatrūnbhuṅkṣva rājyaṁ samṛddham
mayaivaite nihatāḥ pūrvameva
nimittamātraṁ bhava savyasācin (11.33)

tasmāt — therefore; tvam — you; uttiṣṭha — stand; yaśo = yaśaḥ — glory; labhasva — get; jitvā — having conquered; śatrūn — enemies; bhuṅkṣva — enjoy; rājyaṁ — country; samṛddham — prosperous; mayaivaite = mayā — by me + eva — indeed + ete — these; nihatāḥ — supernaturally-destroyed; pūrvam — already; eva — indeed; nimittamātraṁ = nimitta — agent + mātraṁ — only; bhava — be; savyasācin — O ambidextrous archer

Therefore you should stand up! Get the glory! Having conquered the enemies, enjoy a prosperous country. These fellows are supernaturally disposed by Me already. Be only the agent, O ambidextrous archer. (11.33)

Commentary:

This repeats what Krishna told Arjuna in the beginning of their discourse. Readers may recall:

hato vā prāpsyasi svargaṁ jitvā vā bhokṣyase mahīm
tasmāduttiṣṭha kaunteya yuddhāya kṛtaniścayaḥ (2.37)

Either be killed and achieve the angelic world or having conquered, enjoy the nation. Therefore stand up and be decisive, O son of Kunti. (2.37)

Obviously Lord Krishna was not concerned with Arjuna's personal sentiment about non-violence or violence, but rather He wanted to use Arjuna's marksmanship to wipe out the opponents on the battlefield.

Krishna wanted Arjuna to jump out of himself, shed his feelings and values, and be an agent of the Universal Form. To Krishna, Arjuna was only (*mātram*) or merely an instrument (*nimitta*). Otherwise Arjuna had little value. And Arjuna's friendship with the Lord was scrapped for the time being, postponed, or suspended as it were.

द्रोणं च भीष्मं च जयद्रथं च
कर्णं तथान्यानपि योधवीरान् ।
मया हतांस्त्वं जहि मा व्यथिष्ठा
युध्यस्व जेतासि रणे सपत्नान् ॥ ११.३४ ॥
droṇaṁ ca bhīṣmaṁ ca jayadrathaṁ ca
karṇaṁ tathānyānapi yodhavīrān
mayā hatāṁstvaṁ jahi mā vyathiṣṭhā
yudhyasva jetāsi raṇe sapatnān (11.34)

droṇaḥ — Droṇa; ca — and; bhīṣmaṁ — Bhishma; ca — and; jayadrathaṁ — Jayadratha; ca —and; karṇaṁ — Karṇa; tathānyān = tathā — as well as; anyān — others; api — also; yodhavīrān — battle heroes; mayā — by me; hatāṁ — supernaturally hurt; tvaṁ — you; jahi — physically kill; mā — not; vyathiṣṭhā — hesitate; yudhyasva — fight; jetāsi — you will conquer; raṇe — in battle; sapatnān — enemies

Droṇa, Bhishma, Jayadratha, and Karṇa, as well as other battle heroes, were supernaturally hurt by Me. You may physically kill them. Do not hesitate. Fight! You will conquer the enemies in battle. (11.34)

Commentary:

In Krishna's view, Arjuna must have had some fear of losing to *Droṇa*, his martial teacher; Bhishma, his aged grand-uncle who was the most experienced warrior on the battlefield; *Jayadratha*, the warrior king of Sindhesha; *Karṇa*, Arjuna's antagonistic eldest half-brother who was empowered by the solar deity; as well as other battle heroes of renown. If there was any fear of these powerful warriors, Lord Krishna assured Arjuna that those men were already hurt on the supernatural plane.

Insofar as the supernatural parallel forms of those men were the basis of power of the earthly forms of the same, those men were already dead for all practical purposes. Those men had battled against the will of Krishna but they lost on the supernatural plane. Their failure on the earthly plane would follow even if Arjuna did not support Krishna. Still, Krishna desired that Arjuna serve. For Arjuna, such killing was to be a divine service to help Krishna with His self-appointed task of rectifying corrupt governments.

There are some who feel that Krishna asserted an egotistic will-power. Some feel that Krishna should have settled the dispute by peaceful means. But from the vision of the Universal Form, as seen by Arjuna, it appears that the opponents were hostile to Krishna's ideas. They fought to the finish.

संजय उवाच
एतच्छ्रुत्वा वचनं केशवस्य
कृताञ्जलिर्वेपमानः किरीटी ।
नमस्कृत्वा भूय एवाह कृष्णं
सगद्गदं भीतभीतः प्रणम्य ॥११.३५॥
saṁjaya uvāca
etacchrutvā vacanaṁ keśavasya
kṛtāñjalirvepamānaḥ kirīṭī
namaskṛtvā bhūya evāha kṛṣṇaṁ
sagadgadaṁ bhītabhītaḥ praṇamya
(11.35)

saṁjaya — Sanjaya; uvāca — said; etat — this; śrutvā — having heard; vacanaṁ — speech; keśavasya — of the handsome-haired Krishna; kṛtāñjalil— offering respects with joined palms; vepamānah — trembling; kirīṭī — Arjuna, the crowned one; namaskṛtvā = namaḥ — obeisances + krtvā — having made; bhūya — again; evāha = eva — indeed + aha — said; kṛṣṇaṁ — Kṛṣṇaṁ; sagadgadaṁ — stutteringly; bhītabhītaḥ — very frightened; praṇamya — prostrations

Sanjaya said: Having heard the speech of the handsome-haired Krishna, Arjuna, the crowned one, who was trembling, offered respect with joined palms. Bowing again, he stutteringly, with much fright and prostrations, spoke to Krishna. (11.35)

Commentary:

Arjuna was still in a state of shock when Krishna asked him to abandon all fear and fight regardless of how Arjuna felt about the Kurus. Arjuna's supernatural eyes were still open. He could still see that Universal Form. The shock of it prevailed. Previously, he assumed that Krishna was another historic human being. Now he discovered something different. The living display of that supernatural level of existence in which Krishna was seen as the Supreme Person with supreme disciplinary power, was a little too much for Arjuna. As a limited being, he was fearful of that supreme power. His body, face, and mouth were shaking. He bowed down again and again.

अर्जुन उवाच
स्थाने हृषीकेश तव प्रकीर्त्या
जगत्प्रहृष्यत्यनुरज्यते च ।
रक्षांसि भीतानि दिशो द्रवन्ति
सर्वे नमस्यन्ति च सिद्धसंघाः ॥११.३६॥

arjuna uvāca
sthāne hṛṣīkeśa tava prakīrtyā
jagatprahṛṣyatyanurajyate ca
rakṣāṁsi bhītāni diśo dravanti
sarve namasyanti ca siddhasaṁghāḥ
(11.36)

arjuna — Arjuna; uvāca — said; sthāne — in position; hṛṣīkeśa — masterful controller of the senses; tava — your; prakīrtyā — by fame; jagat — universe; prahṛṣyati — rejoices; anurajyate — is delighted; ca — and; rakṣāṁsi — demons; bhītāni — terrified; diśo = diśaḥ — directions; dravanti — they flee; sarve — all; namasyanti — they will reverentially bow; ca — and; siddhasaṁghāḥ — groups of perfected souls

Arjuna said: Everything is in position, O Hṛṣīkeśa, masterful controller of the senses. The universe rejoices and is delighted by Your fame. The demons being terrified, flee in all directions. All the groups of perfected souls will reverentially bow to You. (11.36)

Commentary:

Arjuna said that the groups of perfected persons (*siddhasamghāh*) would, in the near future, bow (*namasyanti*) to Lord Krishna. Before the display of the Universal Power, many ascetics in the celestial world were uncertain about Krishna's position in the supernatural government. But Arjuna felt that after seeing the Universal Form and seeing how Krishna was controlling everyone and everything, the perfected people would agree to what Krishna said about Himself and what *Nārada*, *Asita Devala*, and *Vyāsaji* said about Krishna.

We know today, however, that these views of Arjuna were incorrect, because Krishna was not accepted by everyone even after He displayed the Universal Form. Even though Arjuna saw everyone else peering at the Form, some who peered did not see it in the visually convincing way that Arjuna experienced. Some only felt it. Some did not see it visually, even though to Arjuna's supernatural vision, everyone was seeing it and reacting to it. Arjuna said that he saw demons fleeing away in fear. Those who were hostile to Krishna and who were on the battlefield right there before Arjuna, did not run away, at least not on the physical level. The battle was fought after the display. Many stood their ground to the finish. Some of the entities did not experience Krishna's supremacy as Krishna portrayed it to Arjuna. They had, in one sense, transcended any fears they had of Krishna and kept on with their objections to His ideas.

Even in India today, many Hindus do not accept Lord Krishna as Krishna presented Himself in the *Gītā*. The *Gītā* is accepted on a world-wide basis as a great philosophical discourse, but Krishna as the Person of the Absolute Truth, is not accepted uniformly. Outside of India there are other religions like Christianity and Islam which persist with separate ideas of a Supreme God.

Arjuna testified that the universe (*jagat*) or whole world, at least these human beings on this planet, rejoiced and were delighted by Krishna, but we see that even in India, some religious groups become offended when they are asked to accept Krishna in this way. In the western countries, there is a stiff opposition. Part of the opposition was produced by immature devotees of Krishna who presented Krishna in a haphazard way and who committed many reckless or criminal acts in the name of Krishna. But even when there is no blemish on the missionaries who advocate Krishna, there is a strong resistance.

कस्माच्च ते न नमेरन्महात्मन्
गरीयसे ब्रह्मणोऽप्यादिकर्त्रे ।
अनन्त देवेश जगन्निवास
त्वमक्षरं सदसत्तत्परं यत् ॥ ११.३७॥

kasmācca te na nameran mahātman
garīyase brahmaṇo'pyādikartre
ananta deveśa jagannivāsa
tvamakṣaraṁ sadasattat paraṁ yat (11.37)

kasmāt — why; ca — and; te — to you; na — not; nameran — they should bow; mahātmān — O great soul; garīyase — greater; brahmaṇaḥ — than Brahmā; 'pi = api — also; ādikartre - ādi — original + kartre — to the creator; ananta — infinite; deveśa — lord of the gods; jagan (jagat) — universe + nivāsa — resort; tvam — you; akṣaraṁ — imperishable basis of energies; sat — sum total permanent life; asat — sum total temporary existence; tatparaṁ — that which is beyond; yat = yad — whatever

And why should they not bow to You, O great soul, original creator, Who is also greater than Brahmā, Who is the infinite Lord of the gods, the resort of the world? You are the imperishable basis of energies, the sum total permanent life, the sum total temporary existence, and whatever is beyond all that. (11.37)

Commentary:

Arjuna thought that it made good sense, that everything was in position (*sthāne*, 11.36) as it should be with the supernatural controllers bowing down to Krishna, and with the demoniac entities fleeing from Him, with the celestial people rejoicing that Krishna established His authority and took steps to bring the world to order. Arjuna now understood the nature of Krishna as Krishna explained because Arjuna viewed through supernatural eyeballs and saw directly what Krishna, *Nārada*, *Asita Devala*, and *Vyāsaji* testified to.

त्वमादिदेवः पुरुषः पुराणस्
त्वमस्य विश्वस्य परं निधानम् ।
वेत्तासि वेद्यं च परं च धाम
त्वया ततं विश्वमनन्तरूप ॥ ११.३८॥

tvamādidevaḥ puruṣaḥ purāṇas
tvamasya viśvasya paraṁ nidhānam
vettāsi vedyaṁ ca paraṁ ca dhāma
tvayā tataṁ viśvamanantarūpa (11.38)

tvam — you; ādidevaḥ — first God; puruṣaḥ — spirit; purāṇaḥ — most ancient; tvam — you; asya — of it; viśvasya — of the universe; paraṁ — supreme; nidhānam — refuge; vettāsi = vettā — knower + asi — you are; vedyaṁ — that which is to be known; ca — and; paraṁ — ultimate; ca — and; dhāma — sanctuary; tvayā — by you; tataṁ — pervaded; viśvam — universe; anantarūpa — Person of Infinite Form

You are the First God, the most ancient spirit. You are the knower, You are the supreme refuge of all the worlds. You are that which is to be known. You are the ultimate sanctuary. By You, the universe is pervaded, O Person of Infinite Form. (11.38)

Commentary:

It is interesting that after seeing the Universal Form, Arjuna's attitude to Krishna took a drastic turn. When he first saw the warriors and asked Krishna to take him to the centerfield, Arjuna viewed Krishna as his cousin, casual friend and charioteer. Arjuna asked Krishna to put his chariot in a key position from which he could view the armies. When Arjuna got to that place, Lord Krishna told him to look at the Kurus who assembled in a fighting spirit. Arjuna looked out and then broke down in tears.

Now he regards this situation differently. To him, at this stage of development, Krishna was the **location**; Krishna Himself was the place of that supernatural multi-form.

Everywhere Krishna would go, the whole cosmic situation would move with Him. He carried all personalities around with Him like a sun forcibly pulling planets of a solar system.

To Arjuna, Krishna was the Person who understood what happened. And Krishna was the Education which was worth receiving.

वायुर्यमोऽग्निर्वरुणः शशाङ्कः
प्रजापतिस्त्वं प्रपितामहश्च ।
नमो नमस्तेऽस्तु सहस्रकृत्वः
पुनश्च भूयोऽपि नमो नमस्ते ॥ ११.३९ ॥
vāyuryamo'gnirvaruṇaḥ
śaśāṅkaḥ
prajāpatistvaṁ prapitāmahaśca
namo namaste'stu
sahasrakṛtvaḥ
punaśca bhūyo'pi namo
namaste (11.39)

vāyuḥ — Vāyu wind regulator; yamo = yamaḥ — Yama, Death Supervisor; 'gniḥ = agniḥ — Agni fire controller; varuṇaḥ — Varuṇa, Master of the waters; śaśāṅkaḥ — Śaśāṅka moon lord; prajāpatiḥ — procreator Brahmā; tvaṁ — you; prapitāmahaḥ — father of Brahmā; ca — and; namo = namaḥ — obeisances: namaḥ — obeisances repeated; te — to you; 'stu = astu — let it be; sahasrakṛtvaḥ — a thousand times made; punasca = punaḥ (punar) — again + ca — and; bhūyo = bhuyaḥ — again; 'pi = api — also; namo = namaḥ — obeisances repeated; te — to you

You are represented by Vāyu, the wind regulator; Yama, the death supervisor; Agni, the fire controller; Varuṇa, the master of the waters; Śāśaṅka, the moon Lord; Procreator Brahmā; and you are the father of Brahmā. Obeisances unto You a thousand times repeatedly. Again and again, honor to You! (11.39)

This idea of Krishna superseding all the established Vedic deities, was not begun by Arjuna. As he said, he heard of this from *Nārada*, *Vyāsaji*, and *Asita Devala* who were reputed ascetics of their time. By direct experience, Arjuna said this with conviction. From what Arjuna saw, these Vedic deities depended on Krishna and were empowered by Him.

From what Arjuna saw in that Universal Form, power went out from Krishna to all other authorities. Their activities were regulated by that empowerment.

नमः पुरस्तादथ पृष्ठतस्ते
नमोऽस्तु ते सर्वत एव सर्व ।
अनन्तवीर्यामितविक्रमस्त्वं
सर्वं समाप्नोषि ततोऽसि सर्वः ॥ ११.४० ॥
namaḥ purastādatha pṛṣṭhataste
namo'stu te sarvata eva sarva
anantavīryāmitavikramastvaṁ
sarvaṁ samāpnoṣi tato'si sarvaḥ
(11.40)

namaḥ — reverence; purastāt — from in front; atha — and then; pṛṣṭhataḥ — from behind; te — to you; namo = namaḥ — obeisances; 'stu = astu — let there be; te — to you; sarvata — on all sides; eva — also; sarva — sum total reality; anantavīryāmitavikramaḥ = ananta — infinite + vīrya — power + amita — immeasurable + vikramaḥ — might; tvaṁ — you; sarvaṁ — everything; samāpnoṣi — you penetrate; tato = tataḥ — thus, in that sense; 'si = asi — you are; sarvaḥ — everything

Reverence to You from the front, from behind. Let there be obeisances to You on all sides, O sum total Reality. You are infinite power, immeasurable might. You penetrate everything. In that sense, You are Everything. (11.40)

Commentary:

Arjuna genuinely felt that Lord Krishna, as the sum total Reality (*sarva*), as the location of Reality (*dhāma*), as the person of infinite power (*anantavīrya*) and the person of immeasurable might (*amitavikramas*), was deserving of reverence from every side. In

Arjuna's view, thousands and thousands of those obeisances were due to Krishna.

सखेति मत्वा प्रसभं यदुक्तं
हे कृष्ण हे यादव हे सखेति.।
अजानता महिमानं तवेदं
मया प्रमादात्प्रणयेन वापि ॥ ११.४१ ॥

sakheti matvā prasabhaṁ yaduktaṁ
he kṛṣṇa he yādava he sakheti
ajānatā mahimānaṁ tavedaṁ
mayā pramādāt praṇayena vāpi (11.41)

sakheti = sakhā — friend + iti — such as; matvā — considering; prasabhaṁ — impulsively; yat — whatever; uktaṁ — was said; he — hey; kṛṣṇa — Kṛṣṇa; he — hey; yādava — family man of the Yadus; he — hey; sakheti = sakhā — buddy + iti — thus; ajānatā — through ignorance; mahimānaṁ — majestic supernatural glory; tavedaṁ = tava — your + idam — this; mayā — by me; pramādāt — from familiarity; pranayena- with affection; vāpi = va — or + api — even

Whatever was said impulsively, considering You as a friend, such as, "Hey, Krishna! Hey, family man of the Yadus! Hey, buddy!" was done by me through ignorance of Your majestic supernatural glory or even by affectionate familiarity. (11.41)

Commentary:

Arjuna apologizes for his neglect (*pramādāt*) of Lord Krishna, giving a twofold reason as being ignorant of Krishna's supremacy and being familiar with Krishna. It is said that if one loses touch with the affectionate mood, one is unable to love Krishna. But spiritual affection may be different from a relationship based on a social connection with a divinity. The spiritual friendly relationship would not have the element of confusion or presumptuousness (*pramadāt*) in it .

Arjuna realized that his affection for the Lord was inappropriate. He pleaded with Krishna to show the supernatural glories, for he sensed that only by seeing those, would he be freed from the offence.

यच्चावहासार्थमसत्कृतोऽसि
विहारशय्यासनभोजनेषु ।
एकोऽथ वाप्यच्युत तत्समक्षं
तत्क्षामये त्वामहमप्रमेयम् ॥ ११.४२ ॥

yaccāvahāsārthamasatkṛto'si
vihāraśayyāsanabhojaneṣu
eko'tha vāpyacyut tatsamakṣaṁ
tatkṣāmaye tvām aham aprameyam (11.42)

yat — that; cāvahāsārtham = ca — and + avahāsa — joking + artham — intention; asatkṛto = asatkṛtaḥ — disrespectfully; 'si = asi — you are; vihāraśayyāsanabhojaneṣu = vihāra — play + śayyā — couch + āsana — sitting + bhojaneṣu — in dining; eko = ekaḥ — alone, privately; 'thavāpi = athavāpi = athava —nor + api — also; acyuta — O infallible Kṛṣṇa; tatsamakṣaṁ — before the public; tat — that; kṣāmaye — I ask forgiveness; tvām — of you; aham — I; aprameyam — one who is boundless

And with intent to joke, You were disrespectfully treated, while playing, while on a couch, while sitting, while dining privately or even in public, O infallible Krishna. For that I ask forgiveness of You Who are boundless. (11.42)

Commentary:

This is a sincere plea for pardon. Certain behavioral restrictions apply in friendly dealings with an authority. Thus Arjuna sincerely regretted his familiar treatment of Lord Krishna. With inappropriate regard for the Lord, Arjuna tried to exploit Krishna. The Lord in turn, endured such rudeness of Arjuna. When Arjuna was cornered off by the same contaminated emotions that caused him to be offensive to Krishna, he sought help from the Lord.

Every living entity takes service from God. There is no doubt about that. God does more service to the living entities than they can ever render to Him. Still a limited entity should not try to manipulate the Lord. He should not try to be the center of service but should instead keep himself centralized on the Lord, and be busy about the Lord's interest.

When we are materially affectionate and still want to be devotees of the Lord, we try to manhandle the Lord, to cause Him to serve our sentimental needs. But such needs are neither in our interest nor the Lord's. It is merely one step in the direction of degradation. Arjuna admitted that it was for the sake of joking (*cāvahāsārtham*) that he offended the Lord. It was a joke and nothing else. There was no other way to regard it. When an allowance is given by the Lord for friendship, the devotee should not attempt to convert the relationship to make the Lord a stooge. The friendship should be maintained and developed in a wholesome way for the congeniality of the Lord and the devotee, without the devotee trying to infringe on the supreme value of the Lord. And if the devotee makes some mistake, he should not become offended if the Lord chastises him. When we still have some degree of impurity, discipline is our life-line to sanity.

पितासि लोकस्य चराचरस्य
त्वमस्य पूज्यश्च गुरुर्गरीयान् ।
न त्वत्समोऽस्त्यभ्यधिकः कुतोऽन्यो
लोकत्रयेऽप्यप्रतिमप्रभाव ॥ ११.४३ ॥
pitāsi lokasya carācarasya
tvamasya pūjyaśca gururgarīyān
na tvatsamo
'styabhyadhikaḥ kuto'nyo
lokatraye'pyapratim aprabhāva
(11.43)

pitāsi = pitā — father + asi — you are; lokasya — of the world; carācarasya — of the moving and non-moving; tvam — you; asya — of this; pūjyaśca = pūjyaḥ — worshipable + ca — and; guruḥ — spiritual master; garīyān — gravest; na — not; tvatsamo = tvatsamaḥ = tvat (tvam)—you + samaḥ — similar, like; 'sti = asti — there is; abhyadhikaḥ — greater; kuto = kutaḥ — how; 'nyo = anyaḥ — other; lokatraye — in the three partitions of the universe; 'pi = api — also; apratimaprabhāva — person of uncomparable splendor

You are the father of the world, of the moving and non-moving objects. You are the worshipable and gravest spiritual master. There is none like You in the three partitions of the universe. How could anyone be greater, O person of uncomparable splendor? (11.43)

Commentary:

It was Krishna Who declared that He was the existential superior to everyone. He said that He was the first teacher of those legendary ancient kings who had yoga proficiency and who Krishna claimed were trained by Him in the application of yoga to worldly life. Now Arjuna asked if anyone can be compared with Krishna. There is none like Krishna. Arjuna placed his complete confidence in Lord Krishna.

तस्मात्प्रणम्य प्रणिधाय कायं
प्रसादये त्वामहमीशमीड्यम् ।
पितेव पुत्रस्य सखेव सख्युः
प्रियः प्रियायार्हसि देव सोढुम् ॥ ११.४४ ॥
tasmātpraṇamya praṇidhāya kāyaṁ
prasādaye tvāmahamīśamīḍyam
piteva putrasya sakheva sakhyuḥ
priyaḥ priyāyārhasi deva soḍhum
(11.44)

tasmāt — therefore; praṇamya — bowing with reverence; praṇidhāya — lying down; kāyaṁ — body; prasādaye — I ask mercy; tvām — you; aham — of you; īśam — Lord; īḍyam — to be praised; piteva = pitā — father + eva — as; putrasya — of a son; sakheva = sakhā — friend + eva — as; sakhyuḥ — of a chum; priyaḥ — beloved; priyāyārhasi = priyāya — to a lover + arhasi — you should; deva — O God; soḍhum — to be merciful

Therefore, bowing with reverence, lying my body down, I ask for mercy of You, O Lord Who is to be praised. As a father to a son, as a friend to his chum, as a beloved to a lover, You should be merciful, O God. (11.44)

Commentary:

Others made obeisances to Krishna. From the report of Arjuna, even the celestial people, even the supernatural controllers, were making prostrations. Of course, in the state of reverential frenzy and the resulting shock of the awe-inspiring Universal Form, a critic may say that Arjuna hallucinated and projected fear on what he saw in the apparition. But Arjuna did made this comment previously:

amī hi tvā surasaṁghā viśanti kecidbhītāḥ prāñjalayo gṛṇanti
svastītyuktvā maharṣisiddhasaṁghāḥ stuvanti tvāṁ stutibhiḥ puṣkalābhiḥ (11.21)

Those groups of supernatural rulers enter You. Some being terrified, bowing with palms pressed together, offer praise. "May everything be suitable," they say. The groups of great yogi sages and perfected yogis praise You with lavish glorification. (11.21)

This attitude of Arjuna of asking mercy from Krishna, asking for forgiveness for the offense of trying to subordinate Lord Krishna, is different from the offensive friendly attitude he had before. In this new mood, the purified Arjuna asked for a friendly relationship but one in which Krishna is regarded affectionately as the provider or source of the relationship, rather than being regarded casually as the minor factor in it. Thus the vision of the Universal Form produced this purification in Arjuna. It was a crucial revelation. It was necessary for him, since Arjuna did not come out of the impurity merely by the nine chapters of lectures he heard from Lord Krishna. In Chapter One, Arjuna did most of the talking. In Chapters Two through Ten, nine chapters in all, Lord Krishna lectured extensively. Arjuna did submit himself to Lord Krishna as a student but Arjuna was not convinced of every declaration. This is because Arjuna could not see those truths directly. The vision of the Universal Form, however, clarified the issue of Krishna's claims.

अदृष्टपूर्वं हृषितोऽस्मि दृष्ट्वा
भयेन च प्रव्यथितं मनो मे ।
तदेव मे दर्शय देव रूपं
प्रसीद देवेश जगन्निवास ॥११.४५॥
adṛṣṭapūrvaṁ hṛṣito'smi dṛṣṭvā
bhayena ca pravyathitaṁ mano me
tadeva me darśaya deva rūpaṁ
prasīda deveśa jagannivāsa (11.45)

adṛṣṭapūrvaṁ = adṛṣṭa — never seen + pūrvaṁ — previously; hṛṣito = hṛṣitaḥ — delighted; 'smi = asmi — I am; dṛṣṭvā — having seen; bhayena — with fear; ca — and, but; pravyathitaṁ — trembling; mano = manaḥ — mind; me — my; tat — that; eva — indeed; me — to me; darśaya — to see; deva — O God; rūpaṁ — God-form; prasīda — have mercy; deveśa — Lord of gods; jagannivāsa — shelter of the world

Seeing what was never seen before, I am delighted but my mind trembles with fear. Now, O God, cause me to see the God-form. Have mercy, O Lord of the gods, shelter of the world. (11.45)

Commentary:

One part of Arjuna was delighted (*hṛṣito*) and another part, his mind (*mano*), trembled with fear (*bhayena*). How could it be that he had such dualistic feelings towards the apparition?

Addressing Lord Krishna as, "O God (*deva*), O Lord or Master of gods (*deveśa*), O shelter or abode of the universe (*jagannivāsa*)", Arjuna requested to see the God-body of Krishna (*rūpa*). But which God-body does Arjuna request to see? In the next verse, Arjuna will clarify the request.

Arjuna was unable to switch his vision. Initially, before the fantastic revelation, he could not switch himself from the vision of his material body, and now he is unable to switch himself from the special supernatural sight through which he viewed the apparition.

किरीटिनं गदिनं चक्रहस्तम्
इच्छामि त्वां द्रष्टुमहं तथैव ।
तेनैव रूपेण चतुर्भुजेन
सहस्रबाहो भव विश्वमूर्ते ॥ ११.४६ ॥

kirīṭinaṁ gadinaṁ cakrahastam
icchāmi tvāṁ draṣṭumahaṁ tathaiva
tenaiva rūpeṇa caturbhujena
sahasrabāho bhava viśvamūrte
(11.46)

kirīṭinaṁ — form which wears a crown; gadinaṁ — form which is armed with a club; cakrahastaṁ — form with a disc in hand; icchāmi — I wish; tvāṁ — you; draṣṭum — to see; aham — I; tathaiva = tathā — as requested + eva — indeed; tenaiva = tena -with this + eva — indeed; rūpeṇa — with the form; caturbhujena — with four arms; sahasrabāho — O thousand-armed person; bhava — become; viśvamūrte — person of universal dimensions

I wish to see You wearing a crown, armed with a club, and with a disc in hand, as requested. Please become that four-armed form, O thousand-armed Person, O Person of universal dimensions. (11.46)

Commentary:

We can identify the vision Arjuna requested. He wanted to see the fabulous four-armed form of Divinity, which in the time of Krishna was considered to be the form of God. This form was shown to *Vasudeva* and *Devakī*, the siring parents of Lord Krishna. This is a divine form with four arms. In one hand there is a club, in another a discus, in another a conch, and in another a flower. Arjuna gave positive identification by the term *caturbhujena*, which means *with four arms*. In the previous verse, he identified this form as the God (deva), the Lord of the gods (*deveśa*), and the shelter of the cosmic environment (*jagannivāsa*). In the time of Krishna and Arjuna, this form was known as *Nārāyaṇa*, Vishnu, the father of *Brahmā*.

It is interesting that Arjuna, even though he had supernatural vision, could not see this Form. This means that the supernatural vision awarded him to see the Universal Form (*viśvamurte*) was insufficient for seeing the four-armed form. Arjuna, in this verse, did not address Lord Krishna's human form as the chariot driver, but rather as Lord Krishna, the central figure in the Universal Form. He specifically petitioned the thousand-armed one (*sahasrabāho*), the all-encompassing Form (*viśvamūrte*).

Initially Arjuna asked the chariot driver Krishna to show him the proof of the universal and local control. This request was fulfilled. Then Arjuna asked the central person of the Universal Form to show him the four-armed divinity. At this stage, Arjuna will get divine vision. The vision he got initially was supernatural vision. And to see the four-handed spiritual body of God, he would require divine vision. The four-armed form is not mundane or supernaturally mundane. It is more than a psychic form. However, Arjuna stated that it was the four-armed form he saw some time before. This is indicated by the word tathaiva in the second line of this verse. This means that Arjuna did have the divine vision before.

श्रीभगवानुवाच
मया प्रसन्नेन तवार्जुनेदं
रूपं परं दर्शितमात्मयोगात् ।
तेजोमयं विश्वमनन्तमाद्यं
यन्मे त्वदन्येन न दृष्टपूर्वम् ॥ ११.४७॥
śrībhagavānuvāca
mayā prasannena tavārjunedaṁ
rūpaṁ paraṁ darśitam ātmayogāt
tejomayaṁ viśvamanantam ādyaṁ
yanme tvadanyena na dṛṣṭapūrvam
(11.47)

śrī bhagavān — the Blessed Lord; uvāca — said; mayā — by me; prasannena — by grace; tavārjunedaṁ = tava — to you + arjuna — Arjuna+ idam — this; rūpaṁ — form; param — supreme; darśitaṁ — manifested; ātmayogāt — from my yoga power; tejomayaṁ — made of supernatural energy; viśvam — universal; anantam — infinite; ādyaṁ — primal; yat — which; me — my; tvadanyena = tvad — besides you + anyena — by any other; na — not; dṛṣṭapūrvam = dṛṣṭa — seen + pūrvam — before

The Blessed Lord said: By My grace to you Arjuna, this Supreme Form was manifested from My yoga power. This Form of Mine which is made of supernatural energy, being universal, infinite and primal, was never seen by any other person besides you. (11.47)

Commentary:

Arjuna was not the first devotee nor person to see a Universal Form of Krishna, but he was the first to see that particular phase of the Form. That particular aspect was of interest to the celestial people and to some of the generals on the war field. They wanted to know Krishna's plans.

Since Krishna was a noncombatant, they wanted to know how He intended to secure victory for His friends, the Pandavas. They had a small army and were facing some great odds, challenging a powerful military force, which was organized and commanded by seasoned generals like Bhisma and *Droṇa*, men who had more military expertise than Arjuna.

It is said that Duryodhana had already seen the Universal Form of Krishna but the phase of the form seen by him did not include the biting and burning of the Kauravas. Krishna did, however, show Duryodhana a phase of the form which revealed that Krishna was in a position to influence the gods in whom Duryodhana worshipped. But Duryodhana rejected the vision, feeling that Krishna produced the apparition to make him change his mind about not giving any territory to the Pandavas.

Arjuna was not the first devotee to see the Universal Form, but he was the first devotee to see the destruction of the Kauravas by burning, chopping, squeezing and chewing actions on the supernatural level.

Of great interest, is the word *ātmayogāt*, which literally means, *from my yoga*. In this case, *yoga* means *mystic power*. To verify that this meaning is correct we need to understand the next word which qualifies it. That is *tejomayam*. This word means *made of My brilliance,* or *My splendor,* or *My charismatic energy*. As Arjuna saw previously, the central figure of that Universal Form produced a splendor from which everything was being created and through which everything was being influenced and maintained.

kirīṭinaṁ gadinaṁ cakriṇaṁ ca.tejorāśiṁ sarvato dīptimantam
paśyāmi tvāṁ durnirīkṣyaṁ samantād dīptānalārkadyutim aprameyam (11.17)

This Form is crowned, armed with a club, bearing a discus, a mass of splendor on all sides, shining wondrously with immeasurable radiance of the sun and blazing fire. I see You in entirety, You Who are difficult to behold. (11.17)

anādimadhyāntam anantavīryam anantabāhuṁ śaśisūryanetram
paśyāmi tvāṁ dīptahutāśavaktraṁ svatejasā viśvamidaṁ tapantam (11.19)

You who are without beginning, middle, or ending, Who has infinite manly power, Who has unlimited arms, Who has the sun and moon as Your eyes, I see You, with the blazing oblation-eating mouth, heating this universe with Your Own splendor. (11.19)

lelihyase grasamānaḥ samantāl lokānsamagrānvadanair jvaladbhiḥ
tejobhirāpūrya jagatsamagraṁ bhāsastavogrāḥ pratapanti viṣṇo (11.30)

You lick, swallowing from all sides, all the worlds with Your flaming mouths, filling the universes with splendor, Your horrible blazing rays burn it, O Lord Vishnu . (11.30)

Some commentators insist that this *ātmayogāt* is *yogamāyā*, but that is a vague term which needs to be clarified. Here, however, it is clear that the effulgence or brilliance of the central personality, the huge Krishna form, was producing the *teja* (supernatural radiance). Even Sanjaya saw that radiance and identified it as a light which might be compared to a thousand suns:

divi sūryasahasrasya bhavedyugapadutthitā
yadi bhāḥ sadṛśī sā syād bhāsastasya mahātmanaḥ(11.12)

Imagine in the sky, a thousand suns, being at once risen together. If such a brilliance were to be, it might be compared to that Great Personality. (11.12)

Lord Krishna explained what He meant by *tejomaya* in verse 41 of Chapter Ten:

yadyadvibhūtimatsattvaṁ śrīmadūrjitameva vā
tattadevāvagaccha tvaṁ mama tejoṁśasaṁbhavam (10.41)

You should realize that whatever fantastic existence, whatever prosperous or powerful object there is, in any case, it originates from a fraction of My splendor. (10.41)

From this evidence, *yogamayāt*, *ātmamayāt* and *tejomayam* means, *the emanating energy from the body of that central figure of Krishna in that Universal Form.* Arjuna described that effulgence of Krishna as a blazing radiance.

kirīṭinaṁ gadinaṁ cakriṇaṁ ca tejorāśiṁ sarvato dīptimantam
paśyāmi tvāṁ durnirīkṣyaṁ samantād dīptānalārkadyutim aprameyam (11.17)

This form is crowned, armed with a club, bearing a discus, a mass of splendor on all sides, shining wondrously with immeasurable radiance of the sun and blazing fire. I see You in entirety, You Who are difficult to behold.. (11.17)

nabhaḥspṛśaṁ dīptamanekavarṇaṁ vyāttānanaṁ dīptaviśālanetram
dṛṣṭvā hi tvāṁ pravyathitāntarātmā dhṛtiṁ na vindāmi śamaṁ ca viṣṇo (11.24)

Having seen You, sky extending, blazing, multi-colored, with gaping mouths and blazing vast eyes, there is a shivering in my soul. I find no courage, nor stability, O God Vishnu . (11.24)

Ātmayogāt may appear to be different from the *ātmayogam*, which is the teaching of applied yoga to worldly life. But there is a correlation. In that Universal Form, Arjuna did ask Lord Krishna for His intentions. After feeling scared and after hearing the perfected entities tell Krishna, *svasti*, to settle down, to be calm, to be assured that everything would be alright and that everything would be adjusted by Krishna's desire, Arjuna tried to extract from Krishna His intentions. Krishna then replied:

śrībhagavānuvāca
kālo'smi lokakṣayakṛt pravṛddho lokānsamāhartumiha pravṛttaḥ
ṛte'pi tvāṁ na bhaviṣyanti sarve ye'vasthitāḥ pratyanīkeṣu yodhāḥ (11.32)
tasmāttvamuttiṣṭha yaśo labhasva jitvā śatrūnbhuṅkṣva rājyaṁ samṛddham
mayaivaite nihatāḥ pūrvameva nimittamātraṁ bhava savyasācin (11.33)
droṇaṁ ca bhīṣmaṁ ca jayadrathaṁ ca karṇaṁ tathānyānapi yodhavīrān
mayā hatāṁstvaṁ jahi mā vyathiṣṭhā yudhyasva jetāsi raṇe sapatnān (11.34)

The Blessed Lord said: I am the time limit, the mighty world-destroying Cause, appearing here to annihilate the worlds. Even without you, all the armored warriors, in both armies will cease to live.

Therefore you should stand up! Get the glory! Having conquered the enemies, enjoy a prosperous country. These fellows are supernaturally disposed by Me already. Be only the agent, O ambidextrous archer.

Droṇa, Bhishma, Jayadratha, and Karṇa, as well as other battle heroes, were supernaturally hurt by Me. You may physically kill them. Do not hesitate. Fight! You will conquer the enemies in battle. (11.32-34)

This means the *matyogam* or teaching that was transmitted in the succession of saintly kings like *Manu* and which was exemplified in the life of King *Janaka*. Here is the evidence:

Lord Krishna described Himself as being the motivator in the form of Time and as being the instigator of a summary reaction in which Arjuna would be instrumental (*nimittamātram 11.33*). This goes back to the same instruction which Krishna gave to Arjuna in Chapter Four of the *Gītā*, when Krishna said that He would teach Arjuna what was taught to *Vivasvāt*, *Manu*, *Ikṣvāku* and others. Thus we see that Krishna's yoga, *matyoga*, *ātmayoga*, is the high-class *karma yoga* of the *Gītā*. It is not to be confused with the modern descriptions of *bhakti yoga* which means temple life or services to a spiritual master. It is a service performed to Krishna in helping Him with His mission of maintaining world order and it was taught to rulers who had the ways and means of controlling governments.

Śrībhagavānuvāca.
imaṁ vivasvate yogaṁ proktavānahamavyayam
vivasvānmanave prāha manurikṣvākave'bravīt (4.1)
evaṁ paraṁparāprāptam imaṁ rājarṣayo viduḥ
sa kāleneha mahatā yogo naṣṭaḥ paraṁtapa (4.2)
sa evāyaṁ mayā te'dya yogaḥ proktaḥ purātanaḥ
bhakto'si me sakhā ceti rahasyaṁ hyetaduttamam (4.3)

The Blessed Lord said: I explained to Vivasvat, this perpetual teaching of controlling the personal energies through yoga. Vivasvat explained it to Manu. Manu imparted it to Ikṣvāku.

Thus, received through a series of teachers, the yogi kings knew this skill of controlling the personal energies. After a long time, here on earth, this yoga application was lost, O burner of enemy forces.

Today, this ancient yoga technique is explained to you by Me, since you are devoted to Me and are My friend. Indeed, this is confidential and is the best teaching. (4.1-3)

न वेदयज्ञाध्ययनैर्न दानैर्
न च क्रियाभिर्न तपोभिरुग्रैः ।
एवंरूपः शक्य अहं नृलोके
द्रष्टुं त्वदन्येन कुरुप्रवीर ॥११.४८॥

na vedayajñādhyayanairna dānair
na ca kriyābhirna tapobhirugraiḥ
evaṁrūpaḥ śakya ahaṁ nṛloke
draṣṭuṁ tvadanyena kurupravīra (11.48)

na — not; vedayajñādhyayanaiḥ = veda — Veda + yajñā — by sacrificial ceremonies + adyayanaiḥ — by education; na — nor; danaiḥ — by charity as recommended in the Vedic literature; na — not; ca — and; kriyābhiḥ — by special ritual acts; na — not; tapobhiḥ — by austerities; ugraiḥ — by strenuous; evam — as such; rūpaḥ — form; śakya = śakye — can; ahaṁ — I; nṛloke — in the world of human beings; draṣṭuṁ — to see; tvadanyena = tvad — except you + anyena — by another; kurupravīra — great hero of the Kurus

Not by Vedic sacrificial ceremonies, nor by Vedic education, not by offering charity as recommended in the Vedic literatures and not by special ritual acts, nor by strenuous austerities, can I be seen in such a form in this world of human beings except through the method used by you, O great hero of the Kurus. (11.48)

Commentary:

Here is a complete denial by Krishna of every method besides the one Arjuna used. Arjuna appealed to Lord Krishna to reveal Himself. Arjuna questioned Krishna for details of Krishna's controlling influence. When Krishna's supremacy was still not obvious, Arjuna pleaded for a revelation. He wanted to be shown the supremacy visually. Then Lord Krishna revealed the Universal Form.

Pleading for the revelation was one part of the reason why Arjuna saw it. The other more important part is Arjuna's envy-free relationship with Krishna. Arjuna was near and dear to Lord Krishna, as the Lord described;

sa evāyaṁ mayā te'dya yogaḥ proktaḥ purātanaḥ
bhakto'si me sakhā ceti rahasyaṁ hyetaduttamam (4.3)

Today, this ancient yoga technique is explained to you by Me, since you are devoted to Me and are My friend. Indeed, this is confidential and is the best teaching. (4.3)

śrībhagavānuvāca
idaṁ tu te guhyatamaṁ pravakṣyāmyanasūyave
jñānaṁ vijñānasahitaṁ yajjñātvā mokṣyase'śubhāt (9.1)

The Blessed Lord said: But I will explain to you who are not cynical, the most secret truths, the knowledge with the experience, having known, you will be freed from impurities. (9.1)

bhaktyā tvananyayā śakya ahamevaṁvidho'rjuna
jñātuṁ draṣṭuṁ ca tattvena praveṣṭuṁ ca paraṁtapa (11.54)

By undistracted devotion only, O Arjuna, can I be known, seen in reality, and communicated with, O scorcher of enemies. (11.54)

That nearness and dearness to Krishna is the key qualification of anyone who wants to see the Universal Form as Arjuna did. Many of us who are for Krishna and many who are indifferent or against Krishna, may want to see the Form but since we are not as near and dear as Arjuna, our vision of it, is hardly likely.

मा ते व्यथा मा च विमूढभावो
दृष्ट्वा रूपं घोरमीदृङ्ममेदम् ।
व्यपेतभीः प्रीतमनाः पुनस्त्वं
तदेव मे रूपमिदं प्रपश्य ॥ ११.४९ ॥
mā te vyathā mā ca vimūḍhabhāvo
dṛṣṭvā rūpaṁ ghoramīdṛṅmamedam
vyapetabhīḥ prītamanāḥ punastvaṁ
tadeva me rūpamidaṁ prapaśya
(11.49)

mā — not; te — of you; vyathā — should tremble; mā — not; ca — and; vimūḍhabhāvo = vimūḍhabhāvaḥ — confused state; dṛṣṭvā — having seen; rūpam — form; ghoram — ghastly; īdṛn = īdṛḥ — such; mamedam = mama — of my + idam — this; vyapetabhīḥ = vyapeta — freed from + bhīḥ — fear; prītamanāḥ — cheerful in mind; punaḥ — again; tvam — you; tat — you; eva — indeed; me — of me; rūpam — form; idam — this; prapaśya — look at

You should not tremble or be confused after seeing this, My ghastly form. Be free from fear and be cheerful of mind. Again look at this form of Mine. (11.49)

Commentary:

Even though Arjuna got some supernatural vision and viewed the Universal Form, he could not free himself from the limitations of his individuality. He maintained a subtle fear of the Form. It is amazing that Arjuna remained time-bound to a degree and fearful, too, of the supreme will and the supreme controlling power of Lord Krishna, even after he was transferred into that supernatural view.

Lord Krishna requested Arjuna to free himself from fearful trembling and confusion, and to be cheerful of mind. Arjuna did experience some cheer when he stated that everything was in order as the celestial people were rejoicing and the demons were fleeing from fear. But along with this, Arjuna maintained his identity as a limited being with a limited material body and so he was frightened.

As requested, Krishna showed Arjuna the four-handed divine form, the form which is recognized as Lord Vishnu. In the time of Arjuna, devotees considered Lord Vishnu to be the Primal God. He was said to be four-handed, bearing a lotus flower, conch, discus and club.

For viewing that divine form, Arjuna was given divine vision, which was different from the supernatural psychic eyes that he was granted for viewing the gigantic bodies which comprised the Form.

संजय उवाच
इत्यर्जुनं वासुदेवस्तथोक्त्वा
स्वकं रूपं दर्शयामास भूयः ।
आश्वासयामास च भीतमेनं
भूत्वा पुनः सौम्यवपुर्महात्मा ॥ ११.५० ॥
saṁjaya uvāca
ityarjunaṁ vāsudevas tathoktvā
svakaṁ rūpaṁ darśayāmāsa bhūyaḥ
āśvāsayāmāsa ca bhītamenaṁ
bhūtvā punaḥ saumyavapur
mahātmā (11.50)

Saṁjaya — Sanjaya; uvāca — said; iti — thus; arjunam = Arjuna; vāsudevaḥ — Kṛṣṇa, the son of Vasudeva; tathoktvā= tathā — thus + uktvā — having said; svakaṁ — his own; rūpaṁ — divine form; darśayāmāsa — he revealed; bhūyaḥ — again; āsvāsayāmāsa — he caused to be calm; ca — and; bhītam — frightened person; enam — this; bhūtvā — having assumed; punaḥ = punar — again; saumyavapuḥ = saumya — pleasing + vapuḥ — attractive appearance; mahātmā — great person

Sanjaya said: Krishna, the son of Vasudeva, having said this to Arjuna, revealed His own Divine Form. And once again that great person assumed the pleasing, attractive form and caused the frightened Arjuna to be calm. (11.50)

Commentary:

Two forms were shown to Arjuna in this and the previous verse: the four-handed divine form which Arjuna desired to see and then the form that was already seen by Arjuna as the human form which drove the chariot.

After showing that four-armed form as requested, Lord Krishna again resumed His two-armed form which was beautiful. By using the term *svakam*, which meant Krishna's own divine form, Sanjaya alerted King *Dhṛtarāṣṭra*, that the four-armed form displayed was Krishna's primal four-handed Vishnu Godhead form. This was an important point to be made to the King, while explaining that Lord Krishna, the friend of Arjuna, was the Primal Vishnu, the Primal God.

The narration between Sanjaya and *Dhṛtarāṣṭra* took place some ten or eleven days after the battle began, after Bhisma was morally wounded on the battlefield. But at that time, Sanjaya, by spiritual and supernatural insight, could see the revelation given to Arjuna afresh.

Some Vaishnava authorities claim that the *saumyavapuh*, gentle-featured form, pertains to Krishna's divine two-handed form but that contention is to be considered carefully by reading the rest of this chapter. In the first place, Arjuna did not ask Lord Krishna to show His divine two-armed form. At no time did Arjuna ask for this, but rather he first asked for the Universal Form and for the divine four-armed form.

At no point did Arjuna ask for the divine two-armed form of Krishna. By the same token, we must realize that Arjuna got supernatural vision to see the Universal Form and then he was given a spiritual vision to see the four-handed, divine form. After that, it is said that Krishna again resumed His normal human appearance, recognized by Arjuna as a cousin and friend. *Bhūtvā punah* means that Krishna again became the normal, human Krishna with whom Arjuna was so familiar.

Some Vaishnava commentators, however, insist that this two-armed form of Krishna is a divine form and not a human form; even though it appears to be human, they insist that it is divine.

अर्जुन उवाच
दृष्ट्वेदं मानुषं रूपं
तव सौम्यं जनार्दन ।
इदानीमस्मि संवृत्तः
सचेताः प्रकृतिं गतः ॥ ११.५१ ॥
arjuna uvāca
dṛṣṭvedaṁ mānuṣaṁ rūpaṁ
tava saumyaṁ janārdana
idānīmasmi saṁvṛttaḥ
sacetāḥ prakṛtiṁ gataḥ (11.51)

arjuna — Arjuna; uvāca — said; dṛṣṭvedaṁ = dṛṣṭvā — having seen + idam — this; mānuṣaṁ — human; rūpaṁ — form; tava — of you; saumyam — gentle; janārdana — O motivator of human beings; idānīm — now; asmi — I am; saṁvṛttaḥ — satisfied; sacetāḥ — with mind; prakṛtiṁ — to human nature, to normal condition; gataḥ — gone back, returned

Arjuna said: Seeing this gentle, human-like Form of Yours, O Janardana, motivator of human beings, I am satisfied with my mind returned to the normal condition. (11.51)

Commentary:

The human-like form seen by Arjuna was the same form Krishna used as the charioteer of Arjuna before the revelation. This is not a divine form. If it were, Arjuna would have required special eyes to see it. It is merely Krishna's special physical form. Lord Krishna explained that His material form is different from that of everyone else's. However, this point is thoroughly denied by some Vaishnava acharyas. For some reason, the Vaishnavas carefully avoid explaining Krishna's special material form, even though both the *Mahābhārata* and the *Śrīmad Bhāgavatam* attest to it in no uncertain terms.

Arjuna would not have said that he resumed his usual attitude and usual nature if Krishna had shown him the two-handed divine form at this stage. In his usual attitude, Arjuna was merely a human being with human senses, so much so that he had to be lectured. If he were using special divine eyes, he would not have identified himself as being earthly or normal (*prakṛtim*).

The *prakṛtim* form of Arjuna or of Krishna or of anyone else is a material form. Lord Krishna identified His special material Form previously in the *Gītā* in Chapter Four, text 6:

ajo'pi sannavyayātmā bhūtānāmīśvaro'pi san
prakṛtiṁ svāmadhiṣṭhāya saṁbhavāmyātmamāyayā (4.6)

Even though I am birthless and My person is imperishable, and even though I am the Lord of the creatures, by controlling My material energies, I become visible by My supernatural power. (4.6)

First of all, the two-armed divine form of Lord Krishna has no interest in fighting battles on the material level. But when Krishna produces a special material form that is adapted from His spiritual body, the material one displays such an interest. Usually the Universal Form relays its interest through empowered limited entities who are called devas (gods). When these gods fail to secure social order, a divine person comes down to the physical level and creates for Himself a special material form which is capable of performing miracles and which can do many supernatural deeds.

श्रीभगवानुवाच
सुदुर्दर्शमिदं रूपं
दृष्टवानसि यन्मम ।
देवा अप्यस्य रूपस्य
नित्यं दर्शनकाङ्क्षिणः ॥११.५२॥
śrībhagavānuvāca
sudurdarśamidaṁ rūpaṁ
dṛṣṭavānasi yanmama
devā apyasya rūpasya
nityaṁ darśanakāṅkṣiṇaḥ (11.52)

śrī bhagavān — The Blessed Lord; uvāca — said; sudurdarsam — difficult to perceive; idam — this; rūpaṁ — form; dṛṣṭvān — having seen; asi — you are; yat — which; mamā — of mine; devā — supernatural rulers; api — also; asya — of this; rūpasya — of the form; nityam — always; darśanakāṅkṣiṇaḥ = darśana — sight + kāṅkṣiṇaḥ — wishing

The Blessed Lord said: This Form of Mine which you saw, is difficult to perceive. Even the supernatural rulers always wish for the sight of this Form. (11.52)

Commentary:

Some Vaishnava commentators are of the opinion that the form under discussion is the two-handed divine form of the Lord. But if we check the Sanskrit closely, we may observe that *dṛṣṭvan* is not a present tense form but rather a past perfect participle verb. This means: having seen. The form that Arjuna saw previously was the four-handed form. Therefore the hard-to-perceive (*sudurdarśam*) form is the four-handed divine one. This is the form the demigods wanted to see and always longed to see, because the demigods wanted to see Lord Vishnu who is the father of *Brahmā*. Even Vasudeva, the father of Krishna, wanted to see the four-handed form of Krishna. The demigods were not impressed with the special two-handed physical form. At the time of the appearance of Krishna, they considered that any two-handed form was an inferior form and was not God's real form.

The information that God has a two-handed form came later on, especially during the advent of Lord Krishna; otherwise the great sages and demigods always looked forward to seeing the four-handed form of God as Vishnu-*Nārāyaṇa* with the lotus, conch, discus and club.

Krishna does have a divine, two-armed form but the demigods did not know much about it. Even when Krishna was in Vrindavana, the leader of the demigods, *Brahmā*, the person who created the forms of the demigods, could not really accept the two-handed, cowherd boy Krishna as God. *Brahmā* tested Krishna. He became convinced when Krishna showed multiple four-armed forms.

This pastime is told in Canto Ten, Chapter Thirteen of *Śrīmad Bhāgavatam*:

Once Lord Krishna went off into the forest without His elder brother Balarāma, but with some of their cowherd friends and their herds. The demigod Brahmā kidnapped the boys and calves. Krishna reacted to Brahmā's action by expanding Himself into the number of missing boys and calves. Later, when Brahmā returned he was surprised to see those boys and calves which he mistook for the ones he previously stole and hid in a cave. Brahmā became worried and perplexed. Noticing this, Lord Krishna showed Brahmā that each of the expanded boys and calves was actually a magical transformation of a four-handed, divine God-form. Seeing this, Brahmā fell flat and acknowledged the supremacy of Lord Krishna, Who acted as a mere cowherder.

With this in mind, readers can take up the study of the *Gītā* with a fresh mind. The four-handed divine form is difficult to see and so is the two-handed divine one, which is even more difficult to see, but Arjuna was not seeing the two-handed divine form any more than a man can see the spirit while he looks at its material body. Arjuna did not get the eyes to see the divine two-handed form, but he did get two sets of vision to see first the supernatural Universal Form and then the four-handed divine form. But he did not see the two-handed divine form at all. Instead he saw the specially-constructed material form of Krsna. But even this material form is not an ordinary form for it is capable of supernatural acts.

नाहं वेदैर्न तपसा
न दानेन न चेज्यया ।
शक्य एवंविधो द्रष्टुं
दृष्टवानसि मां यथा ॥ ११.५३ ॥
nāhaṁ vedairna tapasā
na dānena na cejyayā
śakya evaṁvidho draṣṭuṁ
dṛṣṭavānasi māṁ yathā (11.53)

nāhaṁ = na — neither + aham — I; vedaiḥ — by Vedic study; na — nor; tapasā — by austerity; na — nor; dānena — by charity; na — not; cejyayā = ca — and + ijyayā — by sacrificial ceremony; śakya = śakye — I can; evaṁvidho = evaṁvidhaḥ — in that way; draṣṭuṁ — to see; dṛṣṭavān — having seen; asi — you are; mām — me; yathā — as

Neither by Vedic study, nor by austerity, nor by charity, and not by sacrificial ceremony, can I be seen in the way you saw Me. (11.53)

Commentary:

This is in reference to the four-handed divine Form. Previously, a similar statement was made in reference to the supernatural Universal Form.

na vedayajñādhyayanairna dānair na ca kriyābhirna tapobhirugraiḥ
evaṁrūpaḥ śakya ahaṁ nṛloke draṣṭuṁ tvadanyena kurupravīra (11.48)

Not by Vedic sacrificial ceremonies, nor by Vedic education, not by offering charity as recommended in the Vedic literatures and not by special ritual acts, nor by strenuous austerities, can I be seen in such a form in this world of human beings except through the method used by you, O great hero of the Kurus. (11.48)

From this we can understand that unless a human being is as qualified as Arjuna, he neither sees the Universal Form nor the four-handed divine Form. The perception of each of these visions is different. In seeing the Universal Form one needs supernatural vision. That is a vision within the subtle body of a human being but for the four-handed form, one requires spiritual vision which is not within the capacity of the subtle form, but which is only possible in the spiritual form of a developed soul. Such is the difference. The demigods use their subtle bodies and thus the Universal Form may be seen by any of them whose subtle body is sufficiently energized. But they cannot see the four-handed form unless their spiritual forms are manifested. Lord Krishna implied that they long for the development of the spiritual forms (*nityam darśanakāṅkṣiṇah, 11.52*).

भक्त्या त्वनन्यया शक्य
अहमेवंविधोऽर्जुन ।
ज्ञातुं द्रष्टुं च तत्त्वेन
प्रवेष्टुं च परंतप ॥११.५४॥
bhaktyā tvananyayā śakya
ahamevaṁvidho'rjuna
jñātuṁ draṣṭuṁ ca tattvena
praveṣṭuṁ ca paraṁtapa (11.54)

bhaktyā — by devotion; tu — only; ananyayā — not in another way, undistracted; śakya = śakye — I can; aham — I; evaṁvidho = evaṁvidhaḥ — in that way; 'rjuna = arjuna — Arjuna; jñātuṁ — to be known; draṣṭuṁ — to see; ca — and; tattvena — by reality; praveṣṭuṁ — to communicate with; ca — and; paraṁtapa — scorcher of the enemies

By undistracted devotion only, O Arjuna, can I be known, seen in reality, and communicated with, O scorcher of enemies. (11.54)

Commentary:

It is not just *bhaktyā* but *ananyayā bhaktyā*, which is *undistracted devotion to Krishna.* This qualified Arjuna to have the grace of Krishna through which the divine vision became possible (*mayā prasannena*, 11.47). Readers should note that undistracted devotion is a special type of loving focus on Krishna. Arjuna exhibited this as Krishna's submissive disciple. It appears that the supernatural rulers, though devoted to Krishna, are not sufficiently developed to see His divine forms.

मत्कर्मकृन्मत्परमो
मद्भक्तः सङ्गवर्जितः ।
निर्वैरः सर्वभूतेषु
यः स मामेति पाण्डव ॥११.५५॥
matkarmakṛnmatparamo
madbhaktaḥ saṅgavarjitaḥ
nirvairaḥ sarvabhūteṣu
yaḥ sa māmeti pāṇḍava (11.55)

matkarmakṛt — doing my work; matparamo = matparamaḥ — depending on me; madbhaktaḥ — being devoted to me; saṅgavarjitaḥ = saṅga — attachment + varjitaḥ — abandoned; nirvairaḥ — free from hostility; sarvabhūteṣu — to all beings; yah — who; sa = saḥ — he; mām — to me; eti — comes; pāṇḍava — son of Pāndu

Whosoever does My work, depending on Me, being devoted to Me, abandoning attachment, being freed from hostility towards all beings, comes to Me, O son of Pandu. (11.55)

Commentary:

This is another guarantee of the *Gītā* that is watered down and thrown around by some preachers. This assurance of reaching or coming to Lord Krishna, applies to the devotees who have all the qualifications listed. A devotee who exhibits some of these aspects is not covered in this verse, even though he is definitely a devotee and is covered by other statements.

One must possess all the qualifications listed:

- ✓ *Doing Krishna's work (matkarmakṛt)*
- ✓ *Regarding Krishna as one's top priority (matparamo)*
- ✓ *Being devoted to Lord Krishna (madbhaktah)*
- ✓ *Giving up attachment (saṅgavarjitah)*
- ✓ *Being free from hostility to all creatures (nirvairah sarvabhūteṣu)*

Matkarmakṛt is a combination of three Sanskrit words. When broken down, it is divided into *mat*, *karma*, and *kṛt*. *Mat* means *me*, *karma* means *work*, and *kṛt* means *doing*. *Mat* in this case is Krishna. His work is defined in Chapter Four. We do not need anyone to define this work of Krishna. He explained it clearly in Chapter Four. We do, however, need to work under a superior devotee's direction. In modern times, however, missionaries have used the broad term of *devotional service* as Krishna's *work*.

Strictly speaking, *bhakti* (devotion) is different to *karma* according to the *Gītā*. If we look carefully at the *Gītā*, we will see that Krishna does not interchange the terms *karma* and *bhakti* but some modern teachers and missionaries do. It is clear, however, that Krishna's work in this world was consigned to the kings like *Janaka*. It was taught mainly to the legendary solar rulers like *Manu* and Ikṣvāku. In other words, it was taught to rulers and their sons and not to brahmins or preachers. Nowadays there is a mix-up because the Vaishnavas have little political power. Some of their administrative leaders act as pretend-kings and try to do Krishna's work even though they may not be trained in yoga austerities and they may not have a kingdom except for a few disciples and a temple building.

Krishna's work is defined in the *Gītā* in more than one verse but this statement stands out:

paritrāṇāya sādhūnāṁ vināśāya ca duṣkṛtām
dharmasaṁsthāpanārthāya saṁbhavāmi yuge yuge (4.8)

For protecting the saintly people, to destroy the wicked ones, and to establish righteousness, I come into the visible existence from era to era. (4.8)

This sort of work was the work Arjuna was being urged to do at *Kurukṣetra*. This is the work the Pandavas did for Krishna throughout their adult lives. This was the work the Yadus were doing under Krishna's direction. It is political work. It has little to do with ashramas or temples. It has little to do with monks and their disciples. It is the work of political people who are positioned in governments but who work to help Krishna govern the world in a just way. This kind of work involves police work, as Arjuna was urged to do. It is the work of manifesting judicial violence on those who offend law and order. The first qualification for devotees who fall under the guarantee of this verse is that they must have administrative inclinations or be under the direction of those who do. Such administrators must be in a position of power like Arjuna and Janaka so that they can perform the high-class *karma yoga* that Janaka exemplified.

The question remains as to whether this work of Krishna is *bhakti yoga* devotional service. The answer is that this is a special type of that yoga. It is, in a sense, an indirect form of *bhakti yoga*. Pure devotion to Krishna is the application of purified affections to the Lord while this *karma yoga* is the disciplined application of a man's governing power to a particular type of Krishna's work. Unless a ruler loves or likes Krishna, he cannot help Krishna in this work willingly. This is why this *karma yoga* is a type of *bhakti yoga*. To attain pure devotion, kings like Janaka took steps after retirement, to leave the field of *karma yoga* and to develop the purified affections, which alone, could be applied to pure devotion.

Matparamo, regarding Krishna as one's top priority, was the first requirement indicated by Krishna when Krishna presented Himself as a means of focus. But in this same chapter in text 61, after a long lecture to Arjuna, ascetics were advised to consider Krishna as the priority (*matparah*, 2.61). For regarding Krishna as one's top priority, one needs to be freed from the influence of material nature. If a devotee is still spellbound, his focus on Krishna will be sporadic. Material nature will draw his attention away from Krishna repeatedly. It is undoubtedly a struggle to keep one's mind on Krishna. Even in the presence of Krishna, Arjuna had difficulty in doing this, what to speak of others?

Madbhaktah, being devoted to Krishna, applies widely to anyone who has any devotion to Krishna. Still, a certain percentage of devotion is required to qualify for the guarantee given in this verse. One person might be 1% devoted and another, 70% devoted. Thus the guarantees vary.

Saṅgavarjitah, giving up attachment, is done in varying degrees. Depending on how detached a man is, he is given a certain protection. But Lord Krishna asked Arjuna to be as detached as Janaka was, after Janaka learned yoga, learned its application to worldly life, and took up duties as a king.

Nirvairah sarvabhūteṣu, being free from hostility to all creatures, is only possible if one's life energy is purified. But even if a man's energy has some impurity he will be free from hostility periodically. Lord Krishna did explain in Chapters Five, Six, and Seven how the yogis attain the state of impartiality towards all creatures.

In trying to separate the *Gītā* from its own time and place, and from Krishna and Arjuna, a devotee should not take the *Gītā* too far away from its original intentions. It is definite that the *Gītā* was spoken to Arjuna to get him on the move on the battlefield but the range of topics covered by Lord Krishna, even without Arjuna asking for so much information, indicated that the Lord wanted to say more for the benefit of humanity. The particular path that Arjuna was to follow was the path of *karma yoga*, performed by King Janaka and taught by Krishna through the succession of those yogi kings like *Manu* and *Ikṣvāku*.

Krishna did say that He taught two systems:

śrībhagavānuvāca
loke'smindvividhā niṣṭhā purā proktā mayānagha
jñānayogena sāṁkhyānāṁ karmayogena yoginām (3.3)

The Blessed Lord said: In the physical world, a two-fold standard was previously taught by Me. O Arjuna, my good man. This was mind regulation by the yoga practice of the Sāṁkhya philosophical yogis and the action regulation by the yoga practice of the non-philosophical yogis. (3.3)

It is clear from this that Krishna claimed Himself as the ancient (*purā*) teacher (*proktā*) of a twofold system of spiritual cultivation, one for the philosophically-minded people and one for the administrators. But in the *Gītā*, Lord Krishna especially focused on teaching Arjuna the ideal *karma yoga* which was suited to Arjuna's nature and which empowered Arjuna to complete social duties.

Later on Lord Krishna elaborated on the teaching of *jñāna yoga* to Uddhava. As we stated repeatedly, *bhakti yoga* by the *Gītā* really means the application of our affections to

Krishna in a disciplined yogic way. The broad definition of *bhakti yoga* which is given by modern preachers and missionaries, does not really come from the *Gītā* but rather from historic developments in certain parts of India, particularly from the Bengali history. In trying to understand the *Gītā* in its own time and place, we will have to leave aside those developments for the time being.

CHAPTER 12

The Most Disciplined Yogi*

अर्जुन उवाच
एवं सततयुक्ता ये
भक्तास्त्वां पर्युपासते ।
ये चाप्यक्षरमव्यक्तं
तेषां के योगवित्तमाः ॥ १२.१ ॥
arjuna uvāca
evaṁ satatayuktā ye
bhaktāstvāṁ paryupāsate
ye cāpyakṣaramavyaktaṁ
teṣāṁ ke yogavittamāḥ (12.1)

arjuna — Arjuna; uvāca — said; evaṁ — thus; satatayuktā = satata — constantly + yuktā — disciplined in yoga; ye — who; bhaktāh — devoted; tvam — you; paryupāsate — they cherish; ye — who; cāpi = ca — and + api — also; akṣaram — imperishable; avyaktaṁ — invisible existence; teṣāṁ — of them; ke — which; yogavittamaḥ — those who have the highest knowledge of yoga

Arjuna said: Of those who are constantly disciplined in yoga, being also devoted to You, and those who cherish the imperishable invisible existence, which of these two have the highest knowledge of the yoga techniques? (12.1)

Commentary:

Arjuna's question concerned yoga, the knowledge of yoga (*yogavit*). He asked: Which of the two spiritualists have the best information about yoga, those who are constantly devoted to Krishna or those who focus on the imperishable (*akṣaram*), invisible (*avyaktam*) existence? This is not a contrast between devotees and yogis but rather between devotees to Krishna and devotees of the impersonal absolute. In both groups, those of devotees and those of impersonalists, there are yogis. The idea that every yogi or every person who takes up *haṭha* yoga or *prāṇāyāma* is a non-devotee of Krishna or is an impersonalist, is a false view, but as a missionary tactic, it is propagated. Arjuna did not ask a slanted question nor one that was loaded with missionary intentions. It was a plain contrast between devotees of Krishna and those who are adherents of an impersonal Absolute Truth.

In addition, this contrast does not apply to the *jñānis* who are devotees of Krishna, but only to *jñānis* who aim for the impersonal spiritual energy. Many modern Vaishnavas upset the real meaning of this verse by their polarized missionary interpretations.

**The Mahābhārata contains no chapter headings. This title was assigned by the translator on the basis of verse 2 of this chapter.*

श्रीभगवानुवाच
मय्यावेश्य मनो ये मां
नित्ययुक्ता उपासते ।
श्रद्धया परयोपेतास्
ते.मे युक्ततमा मताः ॥१२.२॥
śrībhagavānuvāca
mayyāveśya mano ye māṁ
nityayuktā upāsate
śraddhayā parayopetās
te me yuktatamā matāḥ (12.2)

śrībhagavān — the Blessed Lord; uvāca — said; mayyāveśya = mayi — on me + āveśya — focusing on; mano = manaḥ — mind; ye — who; māṁ — me; nityayuktā — those who are always disciplined in yoga; upāsate — they worship; śraddhayā — with faith; parayopetās = parayā — with the highest degree; upetāḥ — endowed; te — they; me — to me; yuktatamā — most disciplined; matāḥ — considered.

The Blessed Lord said: Those whose minds are focused on Me, who are always disciplined in yoga, who are always involved in worship of Me, who are endowed with the highest degree of faith, they are considered to be the most disciplined. (12.2)

Commentary:

Arjuna asked about the best of the knowers of yoga (*yogavit*), and Krishna replied not in terms of knowledge of yoga but rather in terms of persistence of practice of yoga disciplines (*yuktatamā*). The knowers of yoga, however, refers not to the theoreticians, but to those who have supernatural experience. This is why the term *vit* is used in the compound *yogavit.* Still Lord Krishna answered by stressing the practice of yoga, indicating that it is His devotees of a particular caliber who are superior. This does not apply to all of His devotees since many devotees of Krishna are not really focused on their Lord. Many are not always involved in the Deity worship of Krishna, some are not always meditating, considering and thinking exclusively of their Lord. Some others are not endowed with the strongest faith in Him. But those who are considered by Krishna (*matāh*) to be the most persistent, the most devoted, are the most disciplined among all the transcendentalists.

ये त्वक्षरमनिर्देश्यम्
अव्यक्तं पर्युपासते ।
सर्वत्रगमचिन्त्यं च
कूटस्थमचलं ध्रुवम् ॥१२.३॥
ye tvakṣaramanirdeśyam
avyaktaṁ paryupāsate
sarvatragamacintyaṁ ca
kūṭasthamacalaṁ dhruvam (12.3)

ye — who; tu — but; akṣaram — imperishable; anirdeśyam — undefinable; avyaktaṁ — invisible; paryupāsate — they cherish; sarvatragam — all-pervading; acintyam — inconceivable; ca — and; kūṭastham — unchanging; acalaṁ — immovable; dhruvam — constant

But those who cherish the imperishable, undefinable, invisible, all-pervading, inconceivable, unchanging, immovable, constant reality, (12.3)

Commentary:

This verse is usually joined with verse 4. These verses, 3 and 4, are connected. Arjuna asked about those who focus on the imperishable, invisible existence (*akṣaram avyaktam*). Lord Krishna defined that abstract existence by using several Sanskrit terms. Some claim that these terms cannot be translated into English but we do not believe that to be true of modern English which is greatly expanded beyond the older English usage.

We gave the equivalent terms above. These identify the focus of certain meditators who avoid a Personality of Godhead and who focus instead on an absolute energy that is not subjected to decay (*akṣaram*), not located in any one place, that cannot be grasped in entirety (*anirdeśyam*), that is invisible (*avyaktam*), that is in all places at once, going in all directions at all times and cannot be tracked effectively (*sarvatragam*), that is unchanging, being absolutely standardized (*kūṭastham*), that does not move or waver (*acalam*), and that is fixed and steady and cannot be budged at all (*dhruvam*).

Anyone who meditates on a topic or subject which fits such a description, is being regarded and identified by Lord Krishna in this verse. He will give His view of their method in the next one.

संनियम्येन्द्रियग्रामं
सर्वत्र समबुद्धयः ।
ते प्राप्नुवन्ति मामेव
सर्वभूतहिते रताः ॥१२.४॥
saṁniyamyendriyagrāmaṁ
sarvatra samabuddhayaḥ
te prāpnuvanti māmeva
sarvabhūtahite ratāḥ (12.4)

saṁniyamyendriyagrāmaṁ = saṁniyamya — controlling + indriyagrāmaṁ — all sensual energies; sarvatra — in all respects; samabuddhayaḥ — even-minded; te — them; prāpnuvanti — they attain; mām — me; eva — also; sarvabhūtahite = sarvabhūta — all creatures + hite — in the welfare; ratāḥ — rejoicing

...by controlling all sensual energies, being even-minded in all respects, rejoicing in the welfare of all creatures, they also attain Me. (12.4)

Commentary:

This type of spiritualist who is involved in the impersonal absolute energy and who regards this as his focus, who does not give much attention to the Personalities of Godhead Who descend to the human plane, does achieve (*te prāpnuvanti*) Lord Krishna. At least this is what He stated. He does not in this verse, express a bias or resentment towards them. However, it is clear that they are required to control the sensual energies absolutely and must be indifferent to everything worldly; otherwise, they will not attain Him. In addition, Krishna Himself has to make clear what He means by their attainment of Him. If He does not clarify this, we are at a loss for an exact view of His ideas. Since He explained His glories and powers as He conceived them, attaining Krishna may include a very wide range of accomplishments. These successful meditators who avoid a Personality of Godhead, are required to find happiness in the welfare of all others.

क्लेशोऽधिकतरस्तेषाम्
अव्यक्तासक्तचेतसाम् ।
अव्यक्ता हि गतिर्दुःखं
देहवद्भिरवाप्यते ॥१२.५॥
kleśo'dhikatarasteṣām
avyaktāsaktacetasām
avyaktā hi gatirduḥkhaṁ
dehavadbhiravāpyate (12.5)

kleśo = kleśaḥ — exertion; 'dhikataraḥ = adhikataraḥ — greater; tesam — of them; avyaktāsaktacetasām = avyakta — invisible existence + āsakta — attached + cetasām — of minds; avyaktā — invisible reality; hi — truly; gatiḥ — goal; duḥkhaṁ — difficult; dehavadbhiḥ — by the human beings; avāpyate — is attained

The mental exertion of those whose minds are attached to the invisible existence is greater. The goal of reaching that invisible reality is attained with difficulty by the human beings. (12.5)

Commentary:

This is a contrast between focus on the Personalities of Godhead Who descend into the human world and are known as historic personalities, and the invisible existence which is not tangible to our normal sense perception. The mental exertion required to focus on the invisible existence is greater. Such a goal is difficult for us, as embodied beings.

ये तु सर्वाणि कर्माणि
मयि संन्यस्य मत्पराः ।
अनन्येनैव योगेन
मां ध्यायन्त उपासते ॥१२.६॥
ye tu sarvāṇi karmāṇi
mayi saṁnyasya matparāḥ
ananyenaiva yogena
māṁ dhyāyanta upāsate (12.6)

ye — who; tu — but; sarvāṇi — all; karmāṇi — actions; mayi — in me; saṁnyasya — deferring: matparāḥ — regarding me as the most important factor; ananyenaiva = ananyena — without another, undistracted + eva — indeed; yogena — with yoga discipline; māṁ — me; dhyayānta — meditating on; upāsate — they worship

But those who defer all actions to Me, regarding Me as the most important factor, who meditate on Me with undistracted yoga discipline, do worship Me. (12.6)

Commentary:

A high standard of Krishna worship is defined herein. Specific guarantees will be given which apply to devotees of Krishna who fit this definition of worship. Some modern teachers reduce these standards and apply the guarantees to their followers, regardless of whether the teachers themselves or their followers reach up to these standards, but the guarantees do not serve those who are below par. All devotees of Krishna are covered in the *Gītā*. The guarantees that apply to each are listed with appropriate descriptions. No one can adjust these arrangements but some spiritual masters do try to do so and give many false impressions.

To be covered in this verse, a devotee of Krishna must meet the specified standards. First he must defer or renounce (*samnyasya*) all his actions to Krishna for Krishna's consideration. This means that he may plan but his planning must be with detachment. A devotee who lacks any of the qualities in this verse is not covered by the guarantee of the following verse.

तेषामहं समुद्धर्ता
मृत्युसंसारसागरात् ।
भवामि नचिरात्पार्थ
मय्यावेशितचेतसाम् ॥१२.७॥
teṣāmahaṁ samuddhartā
mṛtyusaṁsārasāgarāt
bhavāmi nacirātpārtha
mayyāveśitacetasām (12.7)

teṣām — of those; aham — I; samuddhartā — delivered; mṛtyusaṁsārasāgarāt = mṛtyu — death + saṁsāra — reincarnations + sāgarāt — from the vast existence; bhavāmi — I am; nacirāt — soon; pārtha — son of Pṛthā; mayyāveśitacetasām = mayi — in me + āveśita — intently, invested in + cetasām — of thoughts

I am the deliverer of those devotees, rescuing them from the vast existence of death and reincarnation. O son of Pṛthā, I soon deliver those devotees whose thoughts are intently invested in Me. (12.7)

Commentary:

This guarantee does not apply to all devotees nor to all devotees who join a popular Vaishnava spiritual master, but only to the devotees described in the previous verse. *Teṣām* means "of the devotees described". Some modern commentators have haphazardly applied this to many of their followers who do not meet these standards.

Āveśita in the fourth line means *to enter, to occupy*. This is a yogic term. In the time of Krishna and Arjuna, this applied to the practising samkhya yogis, who by deep contemplation (*dhyāyanta*), penetrated the subject of their focus. Krishna said that He would soon (*nacirāt*) deliver those devotees. It is not that other devotees would not be delivered. Elsewhere in the *Gītā*, Krishna says that He would deliver all other devotees, but the word "soon" applies specifically to those great yogi devotees. This particular verse is a favorite among Vaishnavas, but some authorities misuse it, applying it to all their followers even though the *Gītā* itself does not give that broad application.

मय्येव मन आधत्स्व
मयि बुद्धिं निवेशय ।
निवसिष्यसि मय्येव
अत ऊर्ध्वं न संशयः ॥१२.८॥

mayyeva mana ādhatsva
mayi buddhiṁ niveśaya
nivasiṣyasi mayyeva
ata ūrdhvaṁ na saṁśayaḥ (12.8)

mayyeva = mayi — on me + eva — alone; mana — mind; ādhatsva — place; mayi — on me; buddhiṁ — intellect; niveśaya — cause to be absorbed; nivasiṣyasi — you will be focused: mayyeva = mayi — in me + eva — indeed; ata ūrdhvaṁ — from now onwards; na — not; saṁśayaḥ — doubt

Placing your mind on Me alone, causing your intellect to be absorbed in Me alone, you will be focused on Me from now onward. There is no doubt about this. (12.8)

Commentary:

Placing the mind on Krishna completely at all times, putting the intelligence to the task of considering Krishna constantly and focusing on Krishna continuously, is a difficult task. This is not an easy process. A haphazard sporadic focus on Krishna is easy but not a steady continuous attention. It was easy for the practising yogis of Arjuna's time. It was easy for Arjuna who mastered all the eight procedures of the *aṣṭanga* yoga processes. These eight steps are:

1) *yama* — restraints
2) *niyama* — observances
3) *āsana* — postures
4) *prāṇāyāma* — breath control
5) *pratyāhāra* — withdrawal of the senses
6) *dhāraṇā* — concentration
7) *dhyāna* — meditation
8) *samādhi* — unified focus.

The final step of *samādhi*, which is not practised by some modern acharyas, was achieved by Arjuna. It was quite possible for Arjuna to focus on Krishna in the way described in the previous verses. Arjuna was covered by the guarantee. Arjuna is not just a warrior-devotee but he is a yogi-devotee. The entire *Gītā* applies to him because he is qualified with the yoga accomplishments of the samkhya yogis. Arjuna fumbled around with the application of yoga to worldly life. And Lord Krishna initiated him without a fire ceremony. Right there on the battlefield, Krishna taught Arjuna how to apply yoga to worldly life. Even though they are not proficient yogis, many modern devotees claim to be in the disciplic succession from Krishna, just as Arjuna was. However, to be a student of the *karma yoga* Krishna taught in the succession of teachers which passed through *Manu* and others, the saintly kings had to be proficient in yoga as a prerequisite.

Unless a devotee is expert at mind control, he cannot place his mind on Krishna alone (*mayy eva mana*). That comes from yoga practice at concentration. One cannot keep his intelligence on Krishna alone (*ādhatsva mayi buddhim niveśaya*) unless the life force is purified. Otherwise, the life energy will disturb and goad the intelligence periodically, forcing it to chase after sensual pursuits. One cannot dwell upon or be settled on Krishna alone (*nivasiṣyasi mayyeva*) unless the soul energy is freed from association with a scattered mind and impure life force. Arjuna could do it, because he was more than a warrior. He was an accomplished yogi.

अथ चित्तं समाधातुं
न शक्नोषि मयि स्थिरम् ।
अभ्यासयोगेन ततो
मामिच्छाप्तुं धनंजय ॥ १२.९ ॥
atha cittaṁ samādhātuṁ
na śaknoṣi mayi sthiram
abhyāsayogena tato
māmicchāptuṁ dhanaṁjaya (12.9)

atha — if however; cittam — thought; samādhātum — to anchor; na — not; śaknoṣi — you can; mayi — on me; sthiram — steadily; abhyāsayogena = abhyāsa — practice + yogena — by yoga; tato = tataḥ — then; mām — me; icchāptum = iccha — with + āptuṁ — to attain; dhanaṁjaya — conqueror of wealthy countries

If, however, you cannot steadily anchor your thoughts on Me, then by yoga practice, try to attain Me, O conqueror of wealthy countries. (12.9)

Commentary:

Abhyāsayogena means *by the yoga practice* (*abhyāsa*). but some modern commentators erased the word *yoga* and replaced it with *bhakti yoga*. This serves the missionary purpose but it does not help us to understand what Krishna told Arjuna.

If someone was not an expert in yoga concentration, contemplation, and trance of mind, to be as focused on Krishna as He described in the previous verses, that person could immediately,by continued practice of yoga, develop the required expertise. He could, by that mastership, attain Krishna over a period of time, but he would not be delivered soon (*nacirāt*). There would be a delay in deliverance. He would have to continue to be a devotee of Krishna but he would have to take more births and endure the experience of more deaths of the material bodies (*mṛtyusamsārasāgarāt*, 12.7) Instant deliverance would not apply to such a devotee because he did not qualify.

अभ्यासेऽप्यसमर्थोऽसि
मत्कर्मपरमो भव ।
मदर्थमपि कर्माणि
कुर्वन्सिद्धिमवाप्स्यसि ॥ १२.१० ॥
abhyāse'pyasamartho'si
matkarmaparamo bhava
madarthamapi karmāṇi
kurvansiddhimavāpsyasi (12.10)

abhyāse — in practice; 'pi = api — perchance; asamartho = asamarthaḥ — incapable; 'si = asi — you are; matkarmaparamo = matkarmaparamaḥ = matkarma — my work + paramaḥ — be absorbed; bhava — be; madartham — for my sake; api — even; karmāṇi — activities; kurvan — doing; siddhim — perfection; avāpsyasi — you will attain

But if perchance, you are incapable of such practice, then by being absorbed in My work, or even by doing activities for My sake, you will attain perfection. (12.10)

<u>Commentary:</u>

Here is Lord Krishna's idea for those who cannot do yoga practice (*abhyāsayogena*, 12.9). If such a devotee would consider that Krishna's work (*matkarma*) is top priority and if he could do things for Krishna's sake, he would attain perfection that way. This is a type of *karma yoga*, the type of *karma yoga* that is popular in modern times, but this is not the same type of *karma yoga* performed by King Janaka. The type done by King Janaka is the type done by masterful yoga students who returned to worldly life and performed while applying the disciplinary behavior skills they acquired through mind, sense, and life energy control.

The type of *karma yoga* in this verse is an inferior type. It is authorized by Krishna. He described it here in clear words for the first time in the *Gītā*. Before this, it was not mentioned. This is not what King Janaka and Arjuna were doing. We should not confuse the higher and lower type of *karma yoga* because the confusion will cause a misconception whereby we may misconceive that the rapid results of the superior type apply to the inferior method.

What is the difference? Persons like Janaka became liberated rapidly while the lower *karma* yogis become liberated gradually, in slow motion, after many, many, many births and deaths.

If a person is incapable of yoga practice, he should take this advice but he must consider Krishna's work in this world as top priority. What is the work of Krishna? We must go back to Chapter Four to find out:

yadā yadā hi dharmasya glānirbhavati bhārata
abhyutthānamadharmasya tadātmānaṁ sṛjāmyaham (4.7)
paritrāṇāya sādhūnāṁ vināśāya ca duṣkṛtām
dharmasaṁsthāpanārthāya saṁbhavāmi yuge yuge (4.8)

Whenever there is a decrease of righteousness, O son of the Bharata family, and when there is an increase of wickedness, then I show Myself. (4.7)

For protecting the saintly people, to destroy the wicked ones, and to establish righteousness, I come into the visible existence from era to era. (4.8)

If we consider this and if we want to help Krishna in His mission, we could attain perfection through working for this mission of Krishna. A man may also have a spiritual master who works for this mission of the Lord. If he helps that authority, he will be delivered after some time.

अथैतदप्यशक्तोऽसि
कर्तुं मद्योगमाश्रितः ।
सर्वकर्मफलत्यागं
ततः कुरु यतात्मवान् ॥१२.११॥
athaitadapyaśakto'si
kartuṁ madyogamāśritaḥ
sarvakarmaphalatyāgaṁ
tataḥ kuru yatātmavān (12.11)

athaitat = atha — if + etat — this; api — even; aśakto = aśaktaḥ — unable; 'si = asi — you are; kartum — to do; madyogam — my yoga; aśritaḥ — resorting to; sarvakarmaphalatyāgaṁ = sarvakarmaphala — all results of action + tyāgam — abandoning; tataḥ — then; kuru — act; yatātmavān — with restraint

If you are unable to even do this, then resorting to My yoga process, abandoning all results of action, act with self restraint. (12.11)

Commentary:

If a person is not an expert at yoga austerities, then he should first practise the disciplines and then bring it to an expert stage. But if perchance he has no yoga practice to his credit and cannot do it, and if he considers Krishna's work in the material world to be a priority, but cannot help Krishna regardless, the next recommendation is that he should try to learn Krishna's brand of yoga practice (*madyogam*).

Many commentators give different meanings for this verse but *madyoga* is clearly Krishna's special yoga practice and nothing else. We cannot substitute devotional service for these terms. And what is Krishna's yoga? It is already explained in Chapter Four when Krishna told Arjuna that He would instruct him in that yoga of which Krishna is the supreme teacher, which Krishna taught to Vivasvat, and which Arjuna contested since Vivasvat lived many, many years before the time of Krishna. What is Krishna's yoga? It is the application of yoga practice to worldly life, the same process applied expertly by Janaka and which Krishna began to teach Arjuna on the battlefield. This was described in Chapter Four. It is the highest type of *karma yoga*:

śrībhagavānuvāca
imaṁ vivasvate yogaṁ proktavānahamavyayam
vivasvānmanave prāha manurikṣvākave'bravīt (4.1)
evaṁ paraṁparāprāptam imaṁ rājarṣayo viduḥ
sa kāleneha mahatā yogo naṣṭaḥ paraṁtapa (4.2)
sa evāyaṁ mayā te'dya yogaḥ proktaḥ purātanaḥ
bhakto'si me sakhā ceti rahasyaṁ hyetaduttamam (4.3)

The Blessed Lord said: I explained to Vivasvat, this perpetual teaching of controlling the personal energies through yoga. Vivasvat explained it to Manu. Manu imparted it to Ikṣvāku.

Thus, received through a series of teachers, the yogi kings knew this skill of controlling the personal energies. After a long time, here on earth, this yoga application was lost, O burner of enemy forces.

Today, this ancient yoga technique is explained to you by Me, since you are devoted to Me and are My friend. Indeed, this is confidential and is the best teaching. (4.1-3)

How can this writer defy many previous translations and commentaries to make such outlandish statements? What is the proof that this is the highest class of *karma yoga*? Here is the answer. Lines 3 and 4 of this verse read:

sarva karma phala tyāgam/ tatah kuru yatātmavān

Let us consider this word for word and see if it is the yoga that was taught to Vivasvat and which Krishna was about to teach Arjuna on the battlefield or if it is devotional service in the format of an ashram or temple.

sarvakarmaphala --all action results; *tyāgam* --abandoning or renouncing;
tatah —then; *kuru* --you act; *yatātmavān* --self-restrained

This means the skill of acting but with an attitude of detachment or abandonment towards the results of actions and doing so with self-control, soul-control. This process was explained previously to Arjuna in Chapters Three and Four and is explained elsewhere as part of the yoga that was taught to the yogi kings and their sons. Krishna's activities as the son of Prince Vasudeva were, for the most part, political. They were filled with the demonstrations of how to apply yoga to worldly life. Krishna Himself attended Gurukula (school of yoga) under the teaching of Sandipani Muni and Ghora Angirasa and learned the yoga postures and breath restraint methods, as well as other subjects. By His life, Krishna demonstrated the highest type of *karma yoga*.

In giving these alternatives, Krishna never did, at any point, depart from His original basis of yoga austerities as the preliminary step but He did give an allowance for persons who feel for His mission and want to assist Him with it. That allowance is given in text 10.

श्रेयो हि ज्ञानमभ्यासाज्
ज्ञानाद्ध्यानं विशिष्यते ।
ध्यानात्कर्मफलत्यागस्
त्यागाच्छान्तिरनन्तरम् ॥ १२.१२ ॥
śreyo hi jñānamabhyāsāj
jñānāddhyānaṁ viśiṣyate
dhyānātkarmaphalatyāgas
tyāgācchāntiranantaram (12.12)

śreyo = śreyaḥ — better; hi — indeed; jñānam — derived knowledge, experience; abhyāsāt — from the practice; jñānāt — than derived knowledge; dhyānaṁ — meditation; viśiṣyate — is superior; dhyānāt — than meditation; karmaphalatyāgaḥ = karmaphala — results of action + tyāgaḥ — renunciation; tyāgāt — from renunciation; śāntiḥ — spiritual peace; anantaram — instantly

Indeed, derived knowledge is better than practice. Meditation is superior to derived knowledge. Renunciation of results is better than meditation. From such renunciation, spiritual peace is instantly gained. (12.12)

Commentary:

This verse is a reinforcement of the previous verse which advocated Krishna's yoga, the yoga which Krishna taught in the political succession that passed through *Vivasvat* and which Krishna taught again to Arjuna. By that type of yoga practice, a man learned how to apply yoga maturity to a governing situation. It is a yoga that is especially suited to administrators. It was taught to them specifically, since, ideally, they were to govern without bias. Arjuna was such an aristocrat from the governing Kuru family.

This verse is further proof that the yoga taught to Arjuna and *Vivasvat* and which was practiced successfully by Janaka is the advanced *karma yoga*. To prove His point, Lord Krishna explained the first step of this process. First, one must practise yoga. The next step is functional knowledge, the derived knowledge of the experience that comes from the practice. This experience is superior to the practice itself. The question is: Can a man get the experience without the practice? The answer is: No, he cannot. But if a man mastered the practice in a past life and integrated the experience sufficiently, then he certainly may not need to practise again in this life to qualify. It all depends on the continuity of memory of the previous life. Individuals who have such an active memory of their past life are exceptional. They are rare personalities.

After practising and deriving knowledge and experience from the practice, one should meditate on the value of the experience. This is the stage of drawing a conclusion. If at this stage, one does not develop a sense of detachment, he cannot go any further and he will exploit himself by displaying his acquired expertise. He may spoil his advancement or cause himself to become stagnant by the display. If he could renounce the resulting expertise and not expose himself to exploitation, he would gain spiritual peace (*chāntir/śāntih*) His sense of security would greatly increase and he will be self-situated without hankering for popularity.

By explaining this, Krishna proved His original point, that Arjuna should act in a detached manner, not considering the favorable or unfavorable outcome. From such actions, Arjuna would acquire spiritual happiness. This was preached to Arjuna thoroughly in Chapters Three and Four and reinforced elsewhere in the *Gītā*. This is, indeed, Krishna's personal teaching to Arjuna. It is the motivation which Krishna gave for fighting.

This detailed performance is totally distinct from the duality of alternatives. This is the center field of absolute detachment and of sticking to one's duty without considering the positive or negative consequences involved. Of course, in this case, we are dealing with Krishna, a person who makes a claim for Himself as the Supreme Person.

अद्वेष्टा सर्वभूतानां
मैत्रः करुण एव च ।
निर्ममो निरहंकारः
समदुःखसुखः क्षमी ॥ १२.१३ ॥
adveṣṭā sarvabhūtānāṁ
maitraḥ karuṇa eva ca
nirmamo nirahaṁkāraḥ
samaduḥkhasukhaḥ kṣamī (12.13)

adveṣṭā — one who does not dislike; sarvabhūtānāṁ — all creatures; maitraḥ — friendly; karuṇa — compassionate; eva — indeed; ca — and; nirmamo = nirmamaḥ — free from attachment to possessions; nirahaṁkāraḥ — free from the propensity of, "I am the creator of my actions"; samaduḥkhasukhaḥ = sama — equally disposed + duḥkha — pain + sukhaḥ — pleasure; kṣamī — be patient

One who does not dislike any of the creatures, who is friendly and compassionate, free from attachment to possessions, free from the propensity of "I am the creator of my actions," being equally disposed towards pain and pleasure, being patient, (12.13)

Commentary:

This description is one of a person who mastered Krishna's yoga, the application of yoga austerities to worldly life. This type of person is exemplified in King Janaka. Lord Krishna is the supreme teacher of this science of how to apply yoga maturity to worldly life. This teaching centers around dispassion, an even view of life, without bias towards moods or situations.

A person who mastered this, a person like King Janaka, would not be a disliker of any of the creatures. He would be friendly and compassionate, free from attachment even to his own lawfully-acquired possessions, free from the assertive view of egotism and indifferent to his own feelings.

King Janaka did kingly duties. He fought and killed offensive warriors as required. He judged and sentenced criminal elements. He disciplined those who were inimical to law and order. But he acted with detachment, being free from grudges and prejudices.

The foremost example of such a person is Lord Krishna. A reader should read about Krishna's life in Canto 10 of *Śrīmad Bhāgavatam*, to see how Krishna maintained this mood even when killing foes on the battlefield and while chastising arrogant men. This does not mean that every detached ascetic is in the administrative field, or that every ascetic is required to be. Persons who have no such administrative obligation are not duty-bound to use violence constructively. But if one is in a position like Arjuna, he would have to follow Janaka's and Lord Krishna's examples to fulfill these responsibilities.

संतुष्टः सततं योगी
यतात्मा दृढनिश्चयः ।
मय्यर्पितमनोबुद्धिर्
यो मद्भक्तः स मे प्रियः ॥ १२.१४ ॥
saṁtuṣṭaḥ satataṁ yogī
yatātmā dṛḍhaniścayaḥ
mayyarpitamanobuddhir
yo madbhaktaḥ sa me priyaḥ (12.14)

saṁtuṣṭaḥ — contented; satataṁ — always; yogī — yogi; yatātmā — one with a controlled self; dṛḍhaniścayaḥ — determined; mayi — on me; arpitamanobuddhiḥ = arpita — focused + mano = manas — mind + buddhiḥ — intellect; yo = yaḥ — who; madbhaktaḥ — devoted to me; sa = saḥ — he; me — of me; priyaḥ — dear

...the yogi who is always content, who has a controlled self, who is determined, whose mind and intellect are focused on Me, who is devoted to Me, is dear to Me. (12.14)

Commentary:

Some commentators de-emphasize the word *yogi* and replace it with devotee or with the words *bhakta yogi*. However, we cannot follow that tendency to gloss over these words with the flavor of *bhakti*. There is no necessity to do this, because Lord Krishna will Himself include *bhakti* or *bhakta* at His leisure and pleasure.

Only a yogi devotee can actually live and consider life consistently in the way described in this and other verses of this chapter. Modern devotees are mostly pretend yogis, especially if they have not perfected yoga practice in the current life. Some did yoga, failed at it, became disappointed because of not getting instant results, and then left it aside, condemning it. But even though they are devotees, they are not yogi devotees. These verses concern the yogi devotees. The guarantee implied in this verse does not apply to others. Some modern teachers try to extend those guarantees to anyone who agrees to follow their leadership but that is not the original coverage.

A person becomes always content by long yoga practice, not otherwise. If someone is born in that mood and maintains it through good and bad circumstances, people say that he is gifted with it. Otherwise he has to attain it by performing austerities. Some say that a man can change just by association but such changes which occur by association only, are usually cosmetic. They simply do not last. Lasting change in a man comes about by austerities. The *Gītā* itself tells us that for soul purification, we have to perform yoga (6.12). This means austerities. A person may be born with the divine nature and may be able to maintain it but that person is rare, one in many millions of human beings.

To have self-control and to be determined in spiritual practice, to have the mind and intelligence always focused on Krishna, to be constantly devoted to Him, is very, very rare. Nowadays, people join a spiritual society and pretend that they have these qualities. But it is not that simple. In any case, this particular verse applies to the persons like Arjuna, who did perfect yoga disciplines.

यस्मान्नोद्विजते लोको
लोकान्नोद्विजते च यः ।
हर्षामर्षभयोद्वेगैर्
मुक्तो यः स च मे प्रियः ॥१२.१५॥
yasmānnodvijate loko
lokānnodvijate ca yaḥ
harṣāmarṣabhayodvegair
mukto yaḥ sa ca me priyaḥ (12.15)

yasmāt — from whom; nodvijate = na — not + udvijate — is repulsed; loko = lokaḥ — world; lokat — from the world; nodvijate = na — not + udvijate — is repulsed; ca — and; yaḥ — who; harṣāmarṣabhayodvegaiḥ = harṣa — excitement + amarṣa — impatience + bhaya —fear + udvegaiḥ- — with distress; mukto = muktaḥ — freed; yaḥ — who; sa = saḥ — he; ca — and; me — of me; priyaḥ — dear

He from whom the world is not repulsed, and who is not repulsed from the world, who is free from excitement, impatience, fear and distress, is dear to Me. (12.15)

Commentary:

We should not misconstrue that such a man may not at any time frighten anyone. The meaning is that he could not frighten anyone for his own sake. For his duty to God or even to the country, to law and order, he may do so. Just as Janaka did and just as Arjuna did on the battlefield, or just as Lord Krishna did. He would not do it for any petty or selfish motive but he will frighten or scare or even kill someone for the sake of law and order. However, if such a man is not an administrator or if it is not his duty to be a law enforcement officer, he would not be justified in terrorizing as Arjuna did at *Kurukṣetra*.

Some say that they are in the mood described in these verses, but a man who is attached to pleasurable sensations, who always wants the world to go in an easy-going way, does not qualify to be the devotee described above. One must first be freed from the need for happiness. A person who is fearful of pains, does not qualify as any of the persons in these verses, even if he is a devotee of Krishna.

अनपेक्षः शुचिर्दक्ष
उदासीनो गतव्यथः ।
सर्वारम्भपरित्यागी
यो मद्भक्तः स मे प्रियः ॥१२.१६॥
anapekṣaḥ śucirdakṣa
udāsīno gatavyathaḥ
sarvārambhaparityāgī
yo madbhaktaḥ sa me priyaḥ (12.16)

anapekṣaḥ — impartial; śuciḥ — hygienic; dakṣa — competent; udāsīno = udasīnāḥ — indifferent; gatavyathaḥ — one whose anxieties are gone; sarvārambhaparityāgī = sarva — all + ārambha — undertaking + parityāgī — abandoning; yo = yaḥ — who; madbhaktaḥ — devoted to me; sa = saḥ — he; me — of me; priyaḥ — dear

He who is impartial, hygienic, competent, indifferent, whose anxieties are gone, who has abandoned all personal undertakings, and who is devoted to Me, is dear to Me. (12.16)

Commentary:

Unless a man has his mind, body, emotions and life energy under control, he cannot qualify as described in this verse. These verses of the *Gītā* are way beyond our reach. And we must realize this. There is no point in glossing over, reducing, or trying to fit ourselves into these verses, because we have not performed the austerities through which we could get our nature under this much control.

It is, however, of interest to know what sort of person is very dear to Krishna.

The statement regarding the abandonment of all undertakings *(sarvārambhaparityāgī)* refers to personal undertakings. This type of person, being done with material existence, continues to function only as a duty to God and nature and for no other purpose. Thus his liberation from the material world is already manifested. His complete freedom from mundane births is very near. Lord Krishna particularly identifies this person as His devotee, His *bhakta*. This type of ascetic is very dear to Krishna *(sa me priyah)*. Krishna has now added that special word which is very dear to the Vaishnavas, the word *bhaktah*.

यो न हृष्यति न द्वेष्टि
न शोचति न काङ्क्षति ।
शुभाशुभपरित्यागी
भक्तिमान्यः स मे प्रियः ॥१२.१७॥
yo na hṛṣyati na dveṣṭi
na śocati na kāṅkṣati
śubhāśubhaparityāgī
bhaktimānyaḥ sa me priyaḥ (12.17)

yo = yaḥ — who; na — not; hṛṣyāti — rejoice; na — not; dveṣṭi — hates; na — not; śocati — laments; na — not; kāṅkṣati — craves; śubhāśubhaparityāgī = subhasubha — agreeable and disagreeable + parityāgī — leaving aside; bhaktimān — full of devotion; yaḥ — who; sa = saḥ — he; me — of me; priyaḥ — dear

One who does not rejoice, nor hate, nor lament, nor crave, who left aside what is agreeable and disagreeable, who is full of devotion, is dear to Me. (12.17)

Commentary:

Bhaktimān (the quality of being full of devotion) is a very important quality but it is only one of the qualities. It is not the sum total of the qualifications. There are different degrees of purity of devotion. At this stage, the person became so pure that his affections are of the highest quality and Krishna is attracted to him. His purity is thorough. It is so consistent that he feels no need to rejoice for an advantage nor to lament for a disadvantage. He does not crave for anything in the material world. He left behind the agreeable and disagreeable sensations and conditions of this world. Only a person whose life energy is purified, can exist in this way.

समः शत्रौ च मित्रे च
तथा मानावमानयोः ।
शीतोष्णसुखदुःखेषु
समः सङ्गविवर्जितः ॥१२.१८॥
samaḥ śatrau ca mitre ca
tathā mānāvamānayoḥ
śītoṣṇasukhaduḥkheṣu
samaḥ saṅgavivarjitaḥ (12.18)

samaḥ — equally disposed; śatrau — and to an enemy; ca — and; mitre — to friend; ca — and; tathā — similar; mānāvamānayoḥ — in honor and dishonor; śītoṣṇasukhaduḥkheṣu = śīta — cold + uṣṇa — heat + sukha — happiness + duḥkheṣu — in distress; samaḥ — same; saṅgavivarjitaḥ = saṅga — attachment + vivarjitaḥ — freedom from

Being equally disposed to an enemy and a friend, with a similar attitude in honor and dishonor, in cold and heat, happiness and distress, being free from attachment, (12.18)

Commentary:

These states of consciousness are experienced periodically by all creatures, not just by the religiously-inclined people or devotees of the Lord. These attitudes do possess a living entity from time to time. Even criminally-minded persons experience feelings of this nature periodically. The key is the consistency and constancy. This is a description of a person who is equally disposed to everyone in all circumstances and at all times, not just now and again when he is in a good mood. It means that he always sees the spiritual interest of others. This may also mean being violently disposed to another for the person's soul interest. For instance, Lord Krishna Himself, the ultimate Person of such qualities, was violently disposed to enemies but in their spiritual interest. Krishna taught Arjuna how to use violence in the spiritual interest of the warriors at *Kurukṣetra*. These are not sentimental values. They cannot be attained by meek people who do not have the courage to chastise others and who are unwilling to help Krishna in His mission as described in Chapter Four. This is a description of the results of "Krishna's yoga" which was described to an extent in Chapter Four and which is the application of yoga austerities to worldly life. How a devotee like Arjuna can be that dear to himself, dear to all other limited entities, dear to the Supreme Lord and still do violence to others, including uncles and teachers, may be a mystery, but we must understand that in such a stage, the soul is completely removed from material affections. Due to purification of his life energies, his vision is not clouded by emotional sentiments from lower planes. He has no such bias. He can act for the everlasting soul, the spirit. He can afford to act in the interest of the eternal spirit, making long-ranged considerations. He can afford to overlook the sensations of the temporary body. This is the ultimate *ahimsā* (nonviolence).

तुल्यनिन्दास्तुतिर्मौनी
संतुष्टो येन केनचित् ।
अनिकेतः स्थिरमतिर्
भक्तिमान्मे प्रियो नरः ॥ १२.१९ ॥
tulyanindāstutirmaunī
saṁtuṣṭo yena kenacit
aniketaḥ sthiramatir
bhaktimānme priyo naraḥ (12.19)

tulyanindāstutiḥ = tulya — relates to + nindā — condemnation + stutiḥ — glorification; maunī — silent; saṁtuṣṭo = saṁtuṣṭaḥ — content; yena — with what; kenacit = kenacid — with anything; aniketaḥ — without a house; sthiramatiḥ = sthira — steady + matiḥ — mind; bhaktimān — full of devotion; me — of me; priyo = priyaḥ — dear; naraḥ — person

...one who relates equally to condemnation and glorification, who is silent, content with anything, who is unattached to home, who has a steady mind, and who is full of devotion, that person is dear to Me. (12.19)

Commentary:

These are all descriptions of persons who practised yoga to the highest stages and who became so expert in the control of the life energy that they bypassed all social considerations. Such an ascetic must also become *bhaktimān* (full of devotion to Krishna), and must be dear (*priyo*) to Krishna (*me*) as well.

ये तु धर्म्यामृतमिदं
यथोक्तं पर्युपासते ।
श्रद्दधाना मत्परमा
भक्तास्तेऽतीव मे प्रियाः ॥ १२.२० ॥
ye tu dharmyāmṛtamidaṁ
yathoktaṁ paryupāsate
śraddadhānā matparamā
bhaktāste'tīva me priyāḥ (12.20)

ye — who; tu — but; dharmyāmṛtam = dharmya — codes of behavior + amṛtam — life-giving; idam — this; yathoktaṁ = yathā — as + uktaṁ — declared; paryupāsate — they honor; śraddadhānā — having confidence; matparamā — absorbed in me as top priority; bhaktāḥ — be devoted; te — they; 'tīva = atīva — very very; me — to me; priyaḥ — dear

Those who honor these life-giving codes of behavior, who have confidence, being intent on Me as top-priority, being devoted, are very dear. (12.20)

Commentary:

A man may be this or he may be that, but if his life energy is not purified, he will not be free from faults. It is the way of material nature. In contrast, however, is the man who is actually purified and who can easily afford to follow these life-giving (*amṛtam*) codes of behavior (*dharmya*) which apply universally in all dimensions at all times and in all places. If we are unable to follow these codes of behavior at all times and in all places, we cannot get the full guarantee. To have Lord Krishna as the Supreme Focus (*matparamā*) we require a high degree of mental concentration, stability of the mind, and a deep confidence in Krishna (*śraddadhānā*).

CHAPTER 13

Material Nature

The Person

The Living Space*

अर्जुन उवाच
प्रकृतिं पुरुषं चैव
क्षेत्रं क्षेत्रज्ञमेव च ।
एतद्वेदितुमिच्छामि
ज्ञानं ज्ञेयं च केशव ॥१३.१॥
arjuna uvāca
prakṛtiṁ puruṣaṁ caiva
kṣetraṁ kṣetrajñameva ca
etadveditumicchāmi
jñānaṁ jñeyaṁ ca keśava (13.1)

arjuna — Arjuna; uvāca — said; prakṛtiṁ — material nature; puruṣaṁ — person; caiva — and indeed; kṣetraṁ — the living space; kṣetrajñam — the experiencer of the living space; eva — indeed; ca — and; etad — this; veditum — to know; icchāmi — I wish; jñānaṁ — conclusion; jñeyaṁ — what is to be experienced; ca — and; keśava — pretty-haired one

Arjuna said: What is material nature? What is the person? What is the living space? Who is the experiencer of the living space? I wish to know this. What is a conclusion? And what is experienced, O Keshava, pretty-haired One? (13.1)

Commentary:

Arjuna's confidence in Lord Krishna as the Authority is solidified. Arjuna can now ask Krishna any question because any answer he gets from Krishna will be accepted. This was due to the revelation of the Universal Form. To understand the *Gītā* from Chapter Eleven onwards, we have to realize that Arjuna's confidence in Lord Krishna was transformed by the vision of the Universal Form. It is not that Arjuna did not rate Krishna as an authority all along. He certainly did. But all his misgivings and doubts were removed by the vision of the Universal Form. The Form, therefore, and the display of it, as well as the bestowal of supernatural vision to Arjuna, cannot be underrated.

All questions asked of the Lord after Chapter Eleven were asked in a mood of full confidence. All of Arjuna's argumentative stances displayed in Chapter One, and Two in particular, and even in Chapter Four when he contested Krishna's claims as the founder of the disciplic succession which passed from the solar king to his descendants, are gone at this stage. Krishna is the same as He was in the beginning of the discourse but Arjuna is different. Arjuna's mood improved. His submissiveness graduated.

**The Mahābhārata contains no chapter headings. This title was assigned by the translator on the basis of verse 1. of this chapter.*

The questions asked in this Chapter Thirteen are questions we all should ask of the Lord. We do not know the answers to these questions. Only with divine assistance, can we distinguish even the simplest of these factors. Insofar as Krishna's claim to full detachment is valid, Krishna can answer any of these questions perfectly.

श्रीभगवानुवाच
इदं शरीरं कौन्तेय
क्षेत्रमित्यभिधीयते ।
एतद्यो वेत्ति तं प्राहुः
क्षेत्रज्ञ इति तद्विदः. ॥ १३.२ ॥
śrībhagavānuvāca
idaṁ śarīraṁ kaunteya
kṣetramityabhidhīyate
etadyo vetti taṁ prāhuḥ
kṣetrajña iti tadvidaḥ(13.2)

śrī bhagavān — The Blessed Lord; uvāca — said; idaṁ — this; śarīraṁ — earthly body; kaunteya — O son of Kuntī; kṣetraṁ — the living space; iti — thus; abhidhīyate — it is called; etat — this; yo = yaḥ — who; vetti — knows; taṁ — him; prāhuḥ — they declare; kṣetrajña — experiencer of the living space; iti — thus; tadvidaḥ — of those knowledgeable of that

The Blessed Lord said: This, the earthly body, O son of Kuntī, is called the living space. Those who are knowledgeable of this, declare the person who understands this to be the experiencer of the living space. (13.2)

Commentary:

Śarīram means the gross body. There is no other meaning for this word. It definitely refers to the gross body, but in this case it refers to a living gross body. And such a living body is inclusive of the subtle form. The subtle body by itself is known in Sanskrit by many terms, particularly *sukṣma*. The spirit lives in a gross body for a number of years. When that gross form becomes fatally wounded or terminally diseased, the soul is forced to relocate. Unless liberated or elevated, it has to find another gross body for a new living space.

The soul, however, does not move on alone. It carries with it, the subtle form, which consists of life energy, mind and intellect. Only when it becomes liberated from the subtle material nature, does it shed off this subtle form; otherwise it has to carry that by necessity. Generally we think that our living space or environment is the surface of the earth and the atmosphere, but actually that is remote when compared to the earthly and subtle bodies. We live in a combined gross and subtle form, which lives on the earth and in the atmosphere.

क्षेत्रज्ञं चापि मां विद्धि
सर्वक्षेत्रेषु भारत ।
क्षेत्रक्षेत्रज्ञयोर्ज्ञानं
यत्तज्ज्ञानं मतं मम ॥ १३.३
kṣetrajñaṁ cāpi māṁ viddhi
sarvakṣetreṣu bhārata
kṣetrakṣetrajñayorjñānaṁ
yattajjñānaṁ mataṁ mama (13.3)

kṣetrajñam — the experiencer of the living space; cāpi = ca — and + api — also; māṁ — me; viddhi — know; sarvakṣetreṣu — in all living spaces; bhārata — O man of the Bhārata family; kṣetrakṣetrajñayoḥ — of the living space and the experiencer of it; jñānaṁ — information; yat — which; tat — that; jñānaṁ —knowledge; mataṁ -considered; mama — by me

Know also, that I am the experiencer of all living spaces, O man of the Bharata family. Information of the living space and the experiencer of it, is considered by Me to be knowledge. (13.3)

Commentary:

Krishna described the limited soul as being the experiencer of his particular body. A person who knows his body is said to be a wise man. This knowing of his body means the knowing of three bodies, namely the causal, subtle and gross forms. It does not mean knowing the physical body alone. The rating applies to mystic seers who knew that the physical body was energized by the subtle one and the subtle one, by the causal one. As long as the gross body lives, the other two forms are interspaced into it.

There is, on one hand, theoretical knowledge about these bodies. But a man who has theoretical information only and who has not experienced the subtle form objectively, is not really a knower of the body. He is inexperienced. He is not rated as a wise man.

Aside from the limited soul, Krishna makes a claim for Himself as the knower or experiencer of all bodies (*sarvakṣetreṣu*). Arjuna glimpsed that reality of Krishna when the Universal Form was displayed. He saw Krishna as the central figure, energizing and regulating everything by supernatural bodily radiance.

तत्क्षेत्रं यच्च यादृक् च
यद्विकारि यतश्च यत् ।
स च यो यत्प्रभावश्च
तत्समासेन मे शृणु ॥ १३.४॥
tatkṣetraṁ yacca yādṛk ca
yadvikāri yataśca yat
sa ca yo yatprabhāvaśca
tatsamāsena me śṛṇu (13.4)

tat = tad — this; kṣetraṁ — living space; yat — what; ca — and; yadṛk — what kind?; ca — and; yadvikāri = yad — what + vikāri — changes; yataśca = yataḥ — what causes?; ca — and; yat — what; sa = saḥ — he; ca — and; yo = yaḥ — who; yatprabhāvaḥ = yat (yad) — what + prabhāvaḥ — potential + ca — and; tat = tad — that; samāsena — with brevity, in brief; me — of me; śṛṇu — hear

As for this living space, as for what is, as for what kind of environment it is, as for the changes it endures, as to what causes it to change, as for he who is involved, as for his potential, hear from Me of that in brief. (13.4)

Commentary:

The living space or personal environment is the body each soul inhabits. These bodies are called *kṣetram* in the Sanskrit terminology. The common meaning of *kṣetram* is *field*. The field in this case is the material body with facilities which include the subtle form on the psychic plane and the causal form on the plane of super-subtle ideas. All these together are experienced by a common man as himself. We know from the *Gītā*, however, that what a common man regards as himself is a composite form which is comprised of various separate energies.

ऋषिभिर्बहुधा गीतं
छन्दोभिर्विविधैः पृथक् ।
ब्रह्मसूत्रपदैश्चैव
हेतुमद्भिर्विनिश्चितैः ॥ १३.५॥
ṛṣibhirbahudhā gītaṁ
chandobhirvividhaiḥ pṛthak
brahmasūtrapadaiścaiva
hetumadbhirviniścitaiḥ (13.5)

ṛṣibhiḥ — by the yogī sages; bahudhā — many times; gītaṁ — recited; chandobhiḥ — with Vedic hymns; vividhaiḥ — with various; pṛthak — distinctly; brahmasūtrapadaiścaiva = brahmasūtrapadaiḥ — with Brahma-sūtra verses + ca — and, eva — indeed; hetumadbhiḥ — with sound logic; viniścitaiḥ — with definite, conclusive

This was distinctly recited many times with the various Vedic hymns and with the Brahma Sūtras, conclusively with sound logic, by the great yogi sages. (13.5)

Commentary:

Chandobhih refers to the Vedas. *Brahma Sūtra* is also known as Vedanta Sutra. The *Gītā* is based on the Upanishads, the Vedas, the Brahma Sutra, the *Rāmāyāṇa* and some *Purāṇas*. It is claimed that some of these scriptures did not exist in written form in the time of Lord Krishna but such a claim is irrelevant since oral, mouth-to-ear transmission, was the reliable medium in those times. A close study of the Sanskrit language shows that it is quite suited to precise oral transmissions.

महाभूतान्यहंकारो
बुद्धिरव्यक्तमेव च ।
इन्द्रियाणि दशैकं च
पञ्च चेन्द्रियगोचराः ॥ १३.६ ॥
mahābhūtānyahaṁkāro
buddhiravyaktameva ca
indriyāṇi daśaikaṁ ca
pañca cendriyagocarāḥ (13.6)

mahābhūtāni — major elements; ahaṁkāro = ahaṁkāraḥ = ahaṁ — I, person + kāraḥ— doing, initiative to act; buddhiḥ — intellect; avyaktam — unmanifested energy; eva — indeed; ca — and; indriyāṇi — senses; daśaikaṁ = dasa — ten + ekam — one; ca — and; pañca — five; cendriyagocarāḥ = ca — and + indriyagocarāḥ — attractive objects

The major categories of the elements, the personal initiative, the intellect, the unmanifested energy, the ten and one senses, the five attractive objects, (13.6)

Commentary:

This verse is usually combined with verse seven. This sixth verse does not form a sentence. The sentence is completed when verse seven is added.

The major categories of the elements are solids, liquids, combustives and gases, and cosmic spaces.

The personal initiative is the sense of wanting to do something in the material world. *Ahamkāro* means literally: *aham* (I am) and *kāra* (doing). **The intelligence** is still a mystery to modern science and even to some transcendentalists. Some modern scientists call it instinct and others say that it is a combination of instinct and deliberation. Intelligence, however, is a particular tool which is attached to the mind. It is a psychic instrument which can be seen with mystic vision. Modern psychologists confuse instinct and deliberation. Instinct is a form of intelligence but it comes from the life force, while intelligence as named in this verse is a particular psychic tool which is attached to the mind.

The unmanifested factor is the original energy from which these manifested material elements emerged. It may be argued, however, that the personal initiative is something spiritual. However, we must consider that a personal initiative in the material world is spiritual in part only. It is indirectly connected to the spirit. According to the samkhya philosophy which Lord Krishna refers to, the *avyakta* (unmanifested factor) is the primary matter which cannot be seen materially. The material scientists have discovered this unmanifested factor as the energy which is beyond the frequency of light. According to their observations, any material which becomes accelerated beyond the frequency of light becomes invisible. Such an energy, by their definition, has no impact on the material world. To their view, it is not a matter of the existence of such an energy but rather its impact on the physical world. Since it has no impact, they do not rate it as a substantial power. Of course, this is the materialistic outlook. And this is why the soul or spirit is not recognized or acknowledged by the scientists. Without using high frequency detectors, the Upanishadic sages detected the unmanifested energy. They used a highly developed mystic power which they developed by yoga austerities.

The ten and one senses are the five perceiving senses, the five utilizing organs, and the mind. The five perceiving senses are the eye, ear, skin, tongue, and nose. The five utilizing senses are the hand, foot, vocal chord, anus, and genital. The one special sensing tool is the mind, which regulates the other functions. **The five attractive objects** are sound, surface, color, flavor, and odor.

इच्छा द्वेषः सुखं दुःखं
संघातश्चेतना धृतिः ।
एतत्क्षेत्रं समासेन
सविकारमुदाहृतम् ॥१३.७॥
icchā dveṣaḥ sukhaṁ duḥkhaṁ
saṁghātaścetanā dhṛtiḥ
etatkṣetraṁ samāsena
savikāramudāhṛtam (13.7)

icchā — desire; dveṣaḥ — hatred; sukhaṁ — pleasure; duḥkhaṁ — pain; saṁghātaścetanā = saṁghātaḥ — the whole body + cetana — consciousness; dhṛtiḥ — conviction: etat = etad — this; kṣetraṁ — living space; samāsena — with brevity, briefly; savikāram — with changes; udāhṛtam — described

...desire, hatred, pleasure, pain, the whole body, consciousness and conviction; this is described with brevity, as the living space with its changes. (13.7)

Commentary:

Desire, *icchā*, is the converted attention of the spirit. When the spirit is focused in the material direction, desire automatically develops, but only for materialistic things. This desire is, therefore, misleading and it takes the soul further and further away from his well-being.

Hatred or an intense repulsion is part of the response cycle of material existence. In any given circumstance we are apt to respond positively by yearning or negatively by hating or evading. Though we sometimes feel that we are reacting, the scope of it depends on factors in material nature. This is why we react unfavorably to some factors which are in our interest and favorably to other factors which are destructive of our welfare.

Sukham and *duhkham* are **pleasure** and **pain**. Both of these are physical, emotional, and mental. Both occur in the material world on the basis of actions and reactions to the movements of the modes of material nature. A limited being can minimize these but he cannot control them altogether.

Samghātaś means **the whole**, the collective being. Most commentators gave the meaning, *of the body*. However, this includes the subtle and causal forms. It does not mean the physical body alone. A human being, animal, bug or germ is a composite being, comprised of spiritual, psychical, and material parts.

Cetanā is **consciousness** as we know it in the material world. It is the sense of feeling through which we perceive sense objects. Such consciousness is not pure spiritual energy, but is a mixture of spiritual, physical, and psychic force combined.

Dhṛtih is a firm attitude, a **conviction**, a steadiness of the mind and being. This is also a composite feeling. It is not altogether spiritual. In the material world everything is a mixture of the physical, supernatural, and spiritual. It is very hard to distinguish the various proportions of these energies in any given sense object.

All these, listed in this and previous verses, are given as a brief description of the living space (*kṣetram*) with its potential changes. We have to understand that the living space is the body but the body is not just a material, composite whole. It is also a psychological and supernatural formation which comprises various energies.

अमानित्वमदम्भित्वम्
अहिंसा क्षान्तिरार्जवम् ।
आचार्योपासनं शौचं
स्थैर्यमात्मविनिग्रहः ॥१३.८॥
amānitvamadambhitvam
ahiṁsā kṣāntirārjavam
ācāryopāsanaṁ śaucaṁ
sthairyamātmavinigrahaḥ (13.8)

amānitvaṁ — a lack of pride; adambhitvam — freedom from deceit; ahiṁsā — non-violence; kṣāntiḥ — patience; ārjavam — straightforwardness; ācāryopāsanaṁ — sitting near a teacher, attendance to a teacher; śaucaṁ — purity; sthairyam — stability; ātmavinigrahaḥ = ātma — self + vinigrahaḥ — restraint

Lack of pride, freedom from deceit, non-violence, patience, straightforwardness, attendance to a teacher, purity, stability and self-restraint, (13.8)

Commentary:

This listing is partial. The rest will be given in the following verses, through verse 12. This is a listing of experience, as contrasted to inexperience or ignorance.

Qualities which reinforce spiritual existence, which show the soul his natural security as an eternal spirit, are considered to be real experience (*jñānam*), while those qualities or expressions which degrade the soul and make him feel undone, are contributory to ignorance and put him on the plane of inexperience, where he misinterprets the circumstances which confront him.

Since material existence is shifty, a **lack of pride** (*amānitvam*) is appropriate. There is really no sense in being proud of a shifty situation. Humility is therefore the only resort for a limited being who cannot control any phase of the material world. There are so many factors over which we have absolutely no control. And whatever little control we exercise, is wielded for a brief span of time.

In material existence, hardly a person feels secure and thus deceit functions by necessity. This, however, degrades the living being and takes him further away from his innate spiritual glory. Unless a limited person simplifies his existence, he cannot be **freed from deceit** (*adambhitvam).* For a complicated life, for a life which is bigger than our capacity, deceit is necessary.

Ahimsā is **non-violence**. The general definition means *no physical or emotional harm*, but the *Gītā* does advocate violence for the sake of bringing order to the world in a way that Krishna desired. Krishna urged Arjuna to do judicial violence to the corrupt Kurus. Those who advocate an absolute non-injury in the physical and emotional sense, are crazy. Such a view is not practical. It is contradictory to our spiritual development. If we apply little or no physical and emotional disciplines, our spiritual life will be nil. The disciplines are absolutely necessary to bring on our detachment from material nature. As a matter of priority we must, in some circumstances, sacrifice the body for the soul and forsake the emotionally-surcharged feelings in the interest of spiritual discretion.

This world cannot be adjusted without judicial violence. Only a simpleton feels that social order can be maintained without discipline. If we consider this world, its creatures, and the ways of material nature, we will readily understand that order is maintained only with judicial discipline.

Patience *(kṣāntih)* is required because we are limited beings. We cannot fulfill desires without the assistance of others. Our destructive desires need not be fulfilled. But those negative ideas which are manifested, should make us realize our stupidity. A limited being has no alternative but to be patient and tolerant. After all, he is not supreme.

Ārjavam or **straightforwardness** is a quality which enhances spirituality. This quality involves simplicity of living and an ability to stay free of social complications. It is a quality that can be misused by those who are sophisticated and who are straightforward, on occasion, merely to insult and manipulate others. For a simple man, however, who has no financial complications nor social ambitions, it is a wonderful quality.

Sincere service to a teacher, *ācāryopāsanam*, works to help us if we have found a genuine authority. If the teacher is not genuine, we suffer by rendering service to him. The teacher must also be capable. A teacher might be sincere and be ignorant of the ways of salvation. Such a teacher is useless. The teacher must be capable of actual methods of deliverance rather than have mere theoretical knowledge of scripture. He should not be a slogan speaker, who only flashes imaginary methods of salvation. The key to this sincere service of a sincere student to a sincere teacher is given by the word *ācārya*, which means a teacher who teaches by example. But it is difficult to determine who that teacher is. Generally, a student gropes in the dark and does not know the method of salvation. Thus he is greatly reliant on providence to provide him with a gifted teacher, otherwise he is prone to be cheated. If a man can not unmistakenly identify gold, he will more than likely be cheated by jewel dealers.

Purity or *śaucam* has a very wide meaning, all depending on usage. In the *Gītā*, the meanings are given in various verses where Lord Krishna described internal and external purity. Krishna speaks of purity of character, internal purification of the material body by austerities, purity of the mind content by mind control, purity of sensual interest by sensual restrictions, and purity of soul (*ātmaviśuddhaye*, 6.12) by yoga practice. Students of the *Gītā* should look to Krishna Himself for the definitions. The study of the *Gītā* is actually a study of Lord Krishna's ideas. We should not settle for the explanations of writers, even this author, but must search and search, applying ourselves to find Krishna's views.

Stability or *sthairyam* is firmness of mind, steady resolution in spiritual practice. Lord Krishna described this at length in Chapters Three, Four, and Five. He repeatedly used the word sthitam from which *sthairyam* is adapted.

Self-restraint, or *ātmavinigrahah*, soul control, soul regulation, was also described at length by Lord Krishna. He also gave the standard methods used in the time of Arjuna for achieving this.

इन्द्रियार्थेषु वैराग्यम्
अनहंकार एव च ।
जन्ममृत्युजराव्याधि-
दुःखदोषानुदर्शनम् ॥१३.९॥

indriyārtheṣu vairāgyam
anahaṁkāra eva ca
janmamṛtyujarāvyādhi-
duḥkhadoṣānudarśanam (13.9)

indriyārtheṣu — towards the attractive objects; vairāgyam — indifference; anahaṁkāra = an — absence of + ahaṁkāra — motivated initiative; eva — indeed; ca — and; janmamṛtyujarāvyādhi = janma — birth + mṛtyu —death + jarā — old age + vyādhi — disease; duḥkhadoṣānudarśanam = duḥkha — suffering + doṣa — danger + anudarśanam — perception

..indifference towards the attractive objects, absence of motivated initiative, the perception of the danger of birth, death, old age, disease, and suffering, (13.9)

Commentary:

This is a continuation of the qualities of character which reinforce spirituality. Unless we have an **indifferent attitude towards the objects** which are pursued by our senses, we will have no freedom in material existence. If we allow the senses to range over, crave, compete for, and grasp the sense objects haphazardly and impulsively, we will always be preoccupied with materialistic things and will never get a chance to tend to spiritual development.

Ahamkāra is motivated initiative. *Anahamkāra* is the **absence of** this. **Motivated initiative** means the urges for survival in the material world. Whatever we may do for survival is superficial because the soul is eternal. He does not need to commit violence to survive. He will exist regardless. His egotistic needs come into play in the material world because he uses temporary instruments in the form of the various gross and subtle bodies and their sensual gadgets. To keep his body in order, he has to compete with other life forms for basic needs. A human being, for instance, may plant carrots but unless the carrots are protected from rabbits, the human being may never be nourished by the produce. Thus, steps are taken to protect foodstuffs. This causes a sense of false ego (*ahamkāra*) which means that I (*aham*) must do (*kāra*) something for protection. This same tendency, though essential in material existence, is spiritually degrading. Somehow or the other, we have to detach ourselves from this motivated initiative.

In order to minimize and greatly curtail our materially-related egoism, we have to realize that the **process of birth, death, old age, disease, and suffering**, is faulty (*doṣa*). If we accept this process as being part of our psychology we will never get out of the material world. Thus it is necessary to understand that material creature forms are unsuitable for us.

असक्तिरनभिष्वङ्गः
पुत्रदारगृहादिषु ।
नित्यं च समचित्तत्वम्
इष्टानिष्टोपपत्तिषु ॥१३.१०॥

asaktiranabhiṣvaṅgaḥ
putradāragṛhādiṣu
nityaṁ ca samacittatvam
iṣṭāniṣṭopapattiṣu (13.10)

asaktiḥ — non-attachment, social detachment; anabhiṣvaṅgaḥ — absence of emotional affection; putradāragṛhādiṣu = putra — child + dāra — wife + gṛha — home + ādiṣu — beginning with, whatever is related to; nityaṁ — always; ca — and; samacittatvam — even-mindedness; iṣṭāniṣṭopapattiṣu = iṣṭa — desired + aniṣṭa — not wanted + upapattiṣu — in matters

...social and emotional detachment towards a child, a wife, a home and whatever is related to social life, being always even-minded towards what is desired and what is not wanted, (13.10)

Commentary:

Emotional detachment is the crux of a matter when determining whether a householder is advanced or not. Householder life is the test for a transcendentalist since the bond of affection between related bodies is the strongest type of affectionate attachment. By lusty association, a husband and wife become attached to each other. And by their bodily linkage, children are produced. Since the bodies of the children stem directly from the fluids in the parents' forms, there is a strong attachment that binds the parents to each other and to their children. If a man or woman can break this attachment, function as parents as a matter of duty, and still ardently pursue their spiritual interest, they are worthy of recognition as transcendentalists.

Strong cravings for what is desired and intense disliking for what is shunned, is an indication of an uncontrolled life force. When the life force is too impulsively inclined, the soul is drawn into the material world with a greater pull and his spiritual advancement is curtailed.

मयि चानन्ययोगेन
भक्तिरव्यभिचारिणी ।
विविक्तदेशसेवित्वम्
अरतिर्जनसंसदि ॥१३.११॥
mayi cānanyayogena
bhaktiravyabhicāriṇī
viviktadeśasevitvam
aratirjanasaṁsadi (13.11)

mayi — in me; cānanyayogena = ca — and + ananya — no other + yogena — with yoga practice; bhaktiḥ — devotion; avyabhicāriṇī — not wandering away, unwavering; viviktadeśasevitvam = vivikta — secluded + deśa— place + sevitvam — resorting; aratiḥ — having a dislike; janasaṁsadi — in crowds of human beings

...unswerving devotion to Me, with no other discipline but yoga practice, resorting to a secluded place, having a dislike for crowds of human beings, (13.11)

Commentary:

Ananyayogena means **no other discipline or process but yoga**. It does not mean devotional service. Devotion is listed in the second line by its own term, *bhakti*. *Cār* is a Sanskrit term meaning to wander or stray When *avyabhi* is added as a prefix, it means not to wander, not to stray, to be constant or steady. Here Lord Krishna speaks **of applying steady devotion or affection to Him or in Him** (*mayi*), but the process with which to apply that affection is yoga. That is what He recommends. Krishna already defined yoga elsewhere in the *Gītā*. There is no need to change the word yoga into *bhakti* since *bhakti* is listed by Krishna in line two. A solitary confinement is suggested by Krishna. This is consistent with the requirement for performing yoga, a requirement given by Lord Krishna in Chapter Six:

yogī yuñjīta satatam ātmānaṁ rahasi sthitaḥ
ekākī yatacittātmā nirāśīraparigrahaḥ (6.10)

In isolation, the yogi should constantly concentrate on the self. Being alone, he should be of controlled thinking and subdued self without desire and without possessions. (6.10)

Rahasi sthitah ekākī means **remaining in solitude alone**. Yoga was defined in the same Chapter Six. It does not mean devotion, even though many Vaishnava acharyas convert it to that usage. It would be redundant to translate *yogena* into devotional service. Devotional service as it is understood and advocated today includes mixing with the public for preaching and collecting funds. This is contrary to having a **dislike for assemblies of human beings** (*aratirjanasamsadi*). But individual yoga practice is consistent and harmonious with such a disliking for large gatherings.

As we stated previously, yoga is a set of disciplines, mainly as postures, breath nutritions, and mental concentration. *Bhakti* is devotion, affection or love. *Karma* is work. *Jñāna* is either scriptural theory or actual mystic experience. When yoga is applied with either of these in turn, we get *bhakti yoga*, *karma yoga* and *jñana yoga*, which is the yoga discipline having been applied to each of those activities. When we apply our affections by the discipline of yoga it is *bhakti yoga*. When we follow in the footsteps of Janaka or Arjuna and apply our working habits by the disciplinary maturity of yoga, it is *karma yoga*. When we apply our scripturally-based philosophical concepts or ideas by the mental disciplinary methods cultivated through yoga, it is *jñana yoga*. This is the correct understanding of the *Gītā* in its own time and place.

Arjuna was friendly with Lord Krishna. Just before the battle, Arjuna appealed to Krishna in a friendly, way. Arjuna's appeal was rejected because his affections were not being disciplined by yoga (*ananyayogena*). Thus Arjuna was scolded, first verbally and then by the frightening Universal Form. Then Arjuna was directed by Krishna not in the affections (*bhakti*) but in how to work (*karma*) with the disciplined attitude of a yogi (*yogena*). In reading translations of modern Vaishnava acharyas, one has to understand that some of these teachers did not practise yoga. Some who did, renounced the practice before attaining the mastery of it. Even though they may sit on a seat in a half-lotus or an easy posture, a teacher may not be practising yoga as it is defined in Chapter Six and elsewhere in the *Gītā*. Their method of discipline is not yoga but theoretical samkhya. Thus we can readily understand why, in their translations, the word yoga is converted away from the actual meaning given to Arjuna. Even for the *Śrīmad Bhāgavatam*, this type of altered translation is given, changing the original meanings. Each reader should protect himself from this procedure of authorities who come in the disciplic succession. If we want the original meanings, we have to avoid these adjustments.

अध्यात्मज्ञाननित्यत्वं
तत्त्वज्ञानार्थदर्शनम् ।
एतज्ज्ञानमिति प्रोक्तम्
अज्ञानं यदतोऽन्यथा ॥ १३.१२ ॥
adhyātmajñānanityatvaṁ
tattvajñānārthadarśanam
etajjñānamiti proktam
ajñānaṁ yadato'nyathā (13.12)

adhyātmajñānanityatvam = adhyātma — Supreme Spirit + jñana — information + nityatvam — constantly; tattvajñānārthadarśanam = tattva — reality + jñāna — science + artha — value+ darśanam — perceiving; etat — this; jñānam — knowledge; iti — thus; proktam — declared as; ajñānaṁ — ignorance; yat — whatever; ato = ataḥ — to this; 'nyathā = anyathā — otherwise, contrary

...constantly considering information about the Supreme Spirit, perceiving the value of the science of reality; this is declared as knowledge. Whatever is contrary to this, is ignorance. (13.12)

Commentary:

This is an assessment of the value of the material world, at least insofar as Lord Krishna is concerned. To His view, whatever else we derive from the material world is useless. The value of the world is therefore defined by Him in no uncertain terms. Experience which confirms what is listed in texts 8 through 12 is rated by Krishna as being nescience, counterproductive towards spirituality.

Students of the *Gītā* should make a careful study of this listing to see what Krishna proposes as the worth of the material world. This listing is important since the limited entities are trying to exploit the world to extract some value from it. Here Lord Krishna tells us what that value should be.

ज्ञेयं यत्तत्प्रवक्ष्यामि
यज्ज्ञात्वामृतमश्नुते ।
अनादिमत्परं ब्रह्म
न सत्तन्नासदुच्यते ॥ १३.१३ ॥
jñeyaṁ yattatpravakṣyāmi
yajjñātvāmṛtamaśnute
anādimatparaṁ brahma
na sattannāsaducyate (13.13)

jṇeyaṁ — to be known, the desired subject; yat — which; tat — that; pravakṣyāmi — I will explain; yat — which; jñātvā — knowing; 'mṛtam = amṛtam — eternal life; aśnute — he gets in touch with; anādimat — beginningless; paraṁ — supreme; brahma — reality; na — not; sat — substantial; tat — this; nāsat = na — not + asat — non-substantial; ucyate — is said

I will explain that which is to be experienced; knowing this one gets in touch with eternal life. The beginningless Supreme Reality is said to be neither substantial nor unsubstantial. (13.13)

Commentary:

The eternal existence of the living entity is factual. The spirit is eternal, but the awareness of that eternal life is faulty. In material existence, we are robbed of the awareness of spirituality. To become aware of this eternity, one needs a taste of spiritual security. A description of the eternal life and the eternal environment is given in line three: *anādimat param brahma*.

Some commentators divide the word *anādimat* into two words: *anādi* (beginningless) and *mat* (from me). In that case, *anādi* would be an adjective. Sanskrit grammar rules, however, do not allow the word to be divided in that way. If *anādi* were an adjective, its full form would be *anādih*, in the nominative case. When such a word ending with *ih*, is followed by a word beginning with *m*, the *h* in *anādih* would be changed to *r*, making the words: anadir mat.

It is a fact, however, that the word *anadimat* is a logitimate Sanskrit word which carries the same meaning as *anādih*. I translated using *anādimat* as a noun, which matches the other compound noun in that line, namely, *param brahma*.

From the material point of view, the beginningless Supreme Reality (*anādimat param brahma*) appears to be insubstantial (*asat*) while from the spiritual view it is the reality (*sat*).

सर्वतःपाणिपादं तत्
सर्वतोक्षिशिरोमुखम् ।
सर्वतःश्रुतिमल्लोके
सर्वमावृत्य तिष्ठति ॥१३.१४॥
sarvataḥpāṇipādaṁ tat
sarvatokṣiśiromukham
sarvataḥśrutimalloke
sarvamāvṛtya tiṣṭhati (13.14)

sarvataḥ — everywhere; pāṇi — hand; pādaṁ — foot; tat = tad — this; sarvato = sarvataḥ — everywhere; 'kṣiśiromukham= akṣiśiromukham= akṣi — eye + śiraḥ — head + mukham — face; sarvataḥśrutimat = sarvataḥ — everywhere + śrutimat — having hearing ability; loke — in the world; sarvam — all; āvṛtya — ranging over; tiṣṭhati — stands

Everywhere is Its hands and feet, everywhere Its eyes, head and face, everywhere is Its hearing ability in this world; It stands, ranging over all. (13.14)

Commentary:

In verse one of this chapter, Arjuna asked the Lord about *jñeyam*, who is to be experienced or what is to be known. Here the Lord replies that the beginningless Supreme Reality is to be known. In verses 14 through 18, He gives a description of the beginningless Supreme Reality.

Here, there is no distinction given as to whether this Supreme Reality is a person or not but rather the general designation of that Supreme is given as being beginningless and supreme (*anādimat param*). However, insofar as we are told that this Reality has hands, feet, eyes, head and face, we can know that it is a person. We heard of the Universal Form with His thousands of hands, feet, eyes, and faces.

सर्वेन्द्रियगुणाभासं
सर्वेन्द्रियविवर्जितम् ।
असक्तं सर्वभृच्चैव
निर्गुणं गुणभोक्तृ च ॥१३.१५॥

sarvendriyaguṇābhāsaṁ = sarva — all + indriyaḥ — sensual + guṇa — mood + ābhāsaṁ — appearance; sarvendriyavivarjitam = sarva — all + indriya — sensuousness + vivarjitam — freedom

sarvendriyaguṇābhāsaṁ
sarvendriyavivarjitam
asaktaṁ sarvabhṛccaiva
nirguṇaṁ guṇabhoktṛ ca (13.15)

from; asaktaṁ — unattached; sarvabhṛt — maintaining everything; caiva = ca — and + eva — indeed; nirguṇaṁ — free from the influence of material nature; guṇabhoktṛ — experiencer of the modes of material nature; ca — and

It has the appearance of having all sensual moods, and It is freed from sensuousness. Though unattached, It maintains everything. Though free from the influence of material nature, It is the experiencer of that influence nevertheless. (13.15)

Commentary:

This description of the beginningless Supreme Reality is paradoxical, being both sentient and insentient, personal and impersonal, human and inhuman. On one hand it has an appearance with the usual senses and still it is free from sensual influence. It is unattached and still maintains everything. It is free from the modes of material nature. It is aware of the operations of mundane energies.

बहिरन्तश्च भूतानाम्
अचरं चरमेव च ।
सूक्ष्मत्वात्तदविज्ञेयं
दूरस्थं चान्तिके च तत् ॥ १३.१६ ॥
bahirantaśca bhūtānām
acaraṁ carameva ca
sūkṣmatvāttadavijñeyaṁ
dūrasthaṁ cāntike ca tat (13.16)

bahiḥ — outside; antaḥ — inside; ca — and; bhūtānām — of the beings; acaraṁ — non-moving; caram — moving; eva — indeed; ca — and; sūkṣmatvāt — from subtlety; tat — this; avijñeyaṁ — not to be comprehended; dūrasthaṁ — situated far off; cāntike = ca — and + antike — in the location; ca — and; tat = tad — this

It is outside and inside the moving and non-moving beings. Because of Its subtlety, this beginningless Supreme Reality is not comprehended. This Reality is situated far away and it is in the location as well. (13.16)

Commentary:

Because of subtlety, this beginningless Supreme Reality is considered to be insubstantial *(asat)* but actually it is the basis of everything manifested in this world. Due to subtlety, this Reality cannot be seen with normal vision. Arjuna got some supernatural vision. As we heard in Chapter Eleven, he saw that Supreme Reality as the Supreme Personality, Lord Krishna, the central figure in the Universal Form.

अविभक्तं च भूतेषु
विभक्तमिव च स्थितम् ।
भूतभर्तृ च तज्ज्ञेयं
ग्रसिष्णु प्रभविष्णु च ॥ १३.१७॥
avibhaktaṁ ca bhūteṣu
vibhaktamiva ca sthitam
bhūtabhartṛ ca tajjñeyaṁ
grasiṣṇu prabhaviṣṇu ca (13.17)

avibhaktam — undivided; ca — and; bhūteṣu — among the beings: vibhaktam — divided; iva — as if; ca — and; sthitam — remaining; bhūtabhartṛ = bhūta — being + bhartṛ — sustainer; ca — and; tat — this; jñeyaṁ — to be known; grasiṣṇu — absorber; prabhaviṣṇu — producer; ca — and

It is undivided among the beings, but It appears as if It is divided in each. It is the sustainer of the beings and this should be known. It is the absorber and producer. (13.17)

Commentary:

Lord Krishna showed Arjuna evidence of His supremacy and power distribution in the material world, through all forms and energies. This was shown in the Universal Form. Here the Lord spoke of the beginningless Supreme Reality (*anādimat param brahma*), but it is obvious that this Reality is Himself as He projected Himself into the material world, as seen by Arjuna when the Universal Form was displayed.

Most Vaishnava commentators identify this form of Lord Krishna as the *paramātma*, the Supersoul. Here, however, Lord Krishna did not state this but left it to Arjuna to understand what He meant. We must, however, consider this description in terms of what Arjuna saw in the Universal Form since that is the direct context from which this chapter follows.

ज्योतिषामपि तज्ज्योतिस्
तमसः परमुच्यते ।
ज्ञानं ज्ञेयं ज्ञानगम्यं
हृदि सर्वस्य विष्ठितम् ॥१३.१८॥
jyotiṣāmapi tajjyotis
tamasaḥ paramucyate
jñānaṁ jñeyaṁ jñānagamyaṁ
hṛdi sarvasya viṣṭhitam (13.18)

jyotiṣām — of luminaries; api — also; tat — tad — this; jyotiḥ — light; tamasaḥ — of gross or subtle darkness; param — beyond; ucyate — declared to be; jñānaṁ — information; jñeyaṁ — education; jñānagamyaṁ = jñāna — education + gamyam — goal; hṛdi — in the psychological core; sarvasya — of all; viṣṭhitam — situated

This is declared as the light of the luminaries, but It is beyond gross or subtle darkness. It is the information, the education and the goal of education. It is situated in the psychological core of all beings. (13.18)

Commentary:

Arjuna stated something similar about the Universal Form:

tvamādidevaḥ puruṣaḥ purāṇas
tvamasya viśvasya paraṁ nidhānam
vettāsi vedyaṁ ca paraṁ ca dhāma
tvayā tataṁ viśvamanantarūpa (11.38)

You are the First God, the most ancient spirit. You are the knower, You are the supreme refuge of all the worlds. You are that which is to be known. You are the ultimate sanctuary. By You, the universe is pervaded, O Person of Infinite Form. (11.38)

By stating that the Supreme Reality was the light of the luminaries but that it was also beyond darkness *(tamasah param),* Lord Krishna established that the Supreme Reality was beyond the scope of material light and was existing on a plane beyond the speed of light. Such a reality is totally spiritual and will not deteriorate or change. Material light and the frequencies below it, are subjected to alteration in the process of time but what is beyond that, is transcendental, though it is abstract to our senses.

The Supreme Reality is centralized within the psyche of all beings as the ultimate energy source and regulator.

इति क्षेत्रं तथा ज्ञानं
ज्ञेयं चोक्तं समासतः ।
मद्भक्त एतद्विज्ञाय
मद्भावायोपपद्यते ॥ १३.१९ ॥
iti kṣetraṁ tathā jñānaṁ
jñeyaṁ coktaṁ samāsataḥ
madbhakta etadvijñāya
madbhāvāyopapadyate (13.19)

iti — thus; kṣetraṁ — the living space, the psychological environment; tathā — as well as; jñanaṁ — standard knowledge; jñeyaṁ — what is to be known; coktaṁ = ca -and + uktaṁ — described; samāsataḥ — in brief; madbhakta — my devotee; etad — this; vijñāya — experiencing; madbhāvāyopapadyate = madbhāvāya — to my state of being + upapadyate — draws near

Thus the psychological environment as well as the standard knowledge and what is to be known, was described in brief. Experiencing this, My devotee draws near to My state of being. (13.19)

Commentary:

Krishna did not say in any of the verses between texts 13 and 18 of this chapter, that He was giving a description of Himself nor of His Universal Form, nor of His *Paramātma* (Supersoul) feature, but in this verse 19, He did indicate that He was discussing Himself. By stating that an experience of this would transpose His devotee towards His state of being (*madbhāvāyā*), Krishna indicated that the experience of the beginningless Absolute Truth would be an experience of Himself, of Krishna.

प्रकृतिं पुरुषं चैव
विद्ध्यनादी उभावपि ।
विकारांश्च गुणांश्चैव
विद्धि प्रकृतिसंभवान्॥ १३.२० ॥
prakṛtiṁ puruṣaṁ caiva
viddhyanādī ubhāvapi
vikārāṁśca guṇāṁścaiva
viddhi prakṛtisaṁbhavān (13.20)

prakṛtiṁ — material nature; puruṣaṁ — spiritual personality; caiva = ca — and + eva — indeed; viddhi — know; anādī — beginningless; ubhau — both; api — also; vikārān — changes of the living space (see 13.4); ca — and; guṇāṁ — moods; caiva = ca — and + eva — indeed; viddhi — know; prakṛtisaṁbhavān = prakṛti — material nature + saṁbhavān — produced

Know that both material nature and the spiritual personality are beginningless, and know that the changes of the living space and the moods of material nature are produced from material nature. (13.20)

Commentary:

The supposition that nothing can be created nor destroyed was asserted by Lord Krishna, long, long before the modern scientists found sufficient evidence to support the idea. Every perceptible mundane energy is convertible but material nature as a whole is beginningless (*anadi*). Both the limited spirits and material nature are eternal, except that material nature endures endless modifications (*vikārān*). It is important to understand that spirits are not changing as they transmigrate, even though their conceptions and cultural identities are continually being altered. The essential spirits remain the same. The changes are coming from material nature which is being adjusted by a mental pressure from the spirits. In viewing these changes and in being responsive to them, the spirits fall under the notion that they are changing, while, in fact, they do remain the same.

Vikārān in this verse refers to changes in the living space or in the psychological environment, the psyche, but this psyche comprises so much material energy that it is affected by the influences which are and which prevail upon material nature. Readers should check the meaning of *vikārān* in verse 4 of this chapter.

कार्यकारणकर्तृत्वे
हेतुः प्रकृतिरुच्यते ।
पुरुषः सुखदुःखानां
भोक्तृत्वे हेतुरुच्यते ॥ १३.२१ ॥
kāryakāraṇakartṛtve
hetuḥ prakṛtirucyate
puruṣaḥ sukhaduḥkhānāṁ
bhoktṛtve heturucyate (13.21)

kāryakāraṇakartṛtve = kārya — created work + kāraṇa — sensual potency as a cause + kartṛtve — agency; hetuḥ — cause; prakṛtiḥ — material nature; ucyate — is said; puruṣaḥ — the spiritual personality; sukhaduḥkhānāṁ — of pleasure and pain; bhoktṛtve — in terms of experiencing; hetuḥ — cause; ucyate — is said

Material nature is said to be the cause in terms of created work, sensual potency and agency. The spiritual personality is said to be the cause in terms of experiencing pleasure and pain. (13.21)

Commentary:

From the perspective of a social consciousness, it would seem that the spirit is the cause of work and motivation, and that material nature is responsible for imposing certain favorable and unfavorable consequences. But Lord Krishna stated the exact opposite, giving material nature credit for motivation and work, while tagging the spirit for the experiences of pleasure and pain. A careful study, however, would show that Krishna is correct.

पुरुषः प्रकृतिस्थो हि
भुङ्क्ते प्रकृतिजान्गुणान् ।
कारणं गुणसङ्गोऽस्य
सदसद्योनिजन्मसु ॥ १३.२२ ॥
puruṣaḥ prakṛtistho hi
bhuṅkte prakṛtijānguṇān
kāraṇaṁ guṇasaṅgo'sya
sadasadyonijanmasu (13.22)

puruṣaḥ — spirit; prakṛtistho = prakṛtisthaḥ — situated in material nature; hi — indeed; bhuṅkte — experiencing; prakṛtijān — produced on material nature; guṇān — the modes of material nature; kāraṇaṁ — the source; guṇasaṅgo = guṇasaṅgaḥ — attachment to the influence of material nature; 'sya = asya —of it; sadasadyonijanmasu = sad (sat) — reality + asad (asat) — unrealistic + yoni — birth situations + janmasu — birth

The spirit, being situated in material nature, experiences the modes which were produced by that nature. Attachment to the modes is the cause of the spirit's emergence from realistic and unrealistic birth situations. (13.22)

Commentary:

According to the previous verse, the spirits are responsible for the experience. The admittance, therefore, is that material nature does not experience, at least not in the sense of enduring pleasures and pains, as we do. Material nature does vary, not in terms of pleasure and pain, but only in terms of creativity. Thus the rationale of material nature is different from that of the living entities.

Attachment to the modes of material nature *(guṇasaṅgo)* is listed as the cause of the spirit's emergence from various realistic and unrealistic situations. That attachment to the modes affects the operation of the reality-perceiving intellect. Thus, we have misconceptions about reality, misjudge our birth possibilities, and suffer through the reactions.

उपद्रष्टानुमन्ता च
भर्ता भोक्ता महेश्वरः ।
परमात्मेति चाप्युक्तो
देहेऽस्मिन्पुरुषः परः ॥१३.२३॥
upadraṣṭānumantā ca
bhartā bhoktā maheśvaraḥ
paramātmeti cāpyukto
dehe'sminpuruṣaḥ paraḥ (13.23)

upadraṣṭānumantā = upadraṣṭā — observer + anumantā — permitter; ca — and; bhartā — supporter; bhoktā — experiencer; maheśvaraḥ — Supreme Lord; paramātmeti = paramātmā — Supreme Soul + iti — thus; cāpi — and also; ukto = uktaḥ — is called: dehe — in the body; 'smin = asmin — in this; puruṣaḥ — spirit; paraḥ — highest

The observer, the permitter, the supporter, the experiencer, the Supreme Lord, and the Supreme Soul as He is called, is the highest spirit in the body. (13.23)

Commentary:

Besides the limited spiritual person, there is the Supreme Soul, the Supreme Lord, Who acts as an observer to all activities committed, as the permitter to anything that takes place, as the supporter of the overall psychology, and as the ultimate experiencer of existence. He is the highest spiritual person in the body. In this case, body does not mean a material form alone, but it includes such a body if the particular limited spirit possesses one. Body, in this case, means gross, subtle, and causal forms all combined into a creature form, or separated as the case may be. If there is a material body, then the word body means that gross form in addition to a subtle and causal one. If there is no material body but there is a subtle one, body means the subtle one and the causal one, and if there are no gross or subtle forms but there is a causal one only, body means that causal form. Body does not mean the gross form alone.

य एवं वेत्ति पुरुषं
प्रकृतिं च गुणैः सह ।
सर्वथा वर्तमानोऽपि
न स भूयोऽभिजायते ॥१३.२४॥
ya evaṁ vetti puruṣaṁ
prakṛtiṁ ca guṇaiḥ saha
sarvathā vartamāno'pi
na sa bhūyo'bhijāyate (13.24)

ya = yaḥ — who; evaṁ — thus; vetti — knows; puruṣaṁ — spiritual person; prakṛtiṁ — material nature; ca — and; guṇaiḥ — with the variations of material nature; saha — with; sarvathā — in whatever way; vartamāno = vartamānaḥ — existing presently; present condition; 'pi = api — also; na — not; sa = saḥ — he; bhūyo = bhūyaḥ — again; 'bhijāyate = abhijāyate — is born

He who knows the spiritual person and material nature, along with the variations of material nature, is not born again, regardless of his present condition. (13.24)

Commentary:

This assurance is another of the guarantees of the *Gītā* which we need not take cheaply or haphazardly but which we need to study carefully to see who qualifies and who does not fit in.

This knowledge must be one of experience and not just one of theoretical understanding. The theoretical understanding alone will not qualify a person for this guarantee.

ध्यानेनात्मनि पश्यन्ति
केचिदात्मानमात्मना ।
अन्ये सांख्येन योगेन
कर्मयोगेन चापरे ॥ १३.२५॥
dhyānenātmani paśyanti
kecidātmānamātmanā
anye sāṁkhyena yogena
karmayogena cāpare (13.25)

dhyānenātmani = dhyānena — through meditative perception + ātmani — in the spirit; paśyānti — they perceive; kecit — some; ātmānam — by the spirit; ātmanā — the spirit; anye — others; sāṁkhyena — by Sāṁkhya philosophical conclusions; yogena — by yoga practice; karmayogena — by yogically disciplined action; cāpare = ca —and + apare — others

Some perceive the spirit by the spirit through meditative perception of the spirit. Others do so with Sāṁkhya philosophical conclusions and others by yogically disciplined action. (13.25)

Commentary:

In this verse, Lord Krishna spoke of the same spirit which He discussed in verses 20, 21, and 22 as the *puruṣah*. Some Vaishnavas in their eagerness to take us away from our conceited selves to the Supreme Self, have translated *ātman* as the Supersoul in this verse, though there is really no necessity since Lord Krishna discusses the Supersoul separately in text 28 and elsewhere.

The two general paths of spirituality taken for self-realization are listed as *samkhyena yogena* and *karma yogena*. We already knew that Krishna declared Himself as the ancient teacher of both paths but in the *Gītā*, He specifically wanted to teach Arjuna the path of *karma yoga* that was taught to Vivasvat and *Manu* and which was perfected by King Janaka. The path of samkhya yoga was explained to an extent in the *Gītā*, but more elaboration of it was given, not to Arjuna, but rather to Uddhava just before Lord Krishna's departure from this planet. We heard in the *Śrīmad Bhāgavatam* that Maitreya Muni heard all that Lord Krishna was to tell Uddhava about the path of samkhya which is suited to those who do not have administrative duties to perform. Both paths, that of samkhya and that of *karma*, require yoga expertise as a prerequisite. At least this was the requirement in the time of Lord Krishna and Arjuna.

However, in lines one and two of this verse, two other methods of self-realization are listed, namely *dhyānenātmani* and *ātmānam ātmanā*. *Dhyānenātmani* is the process of sheer meditation on the soul itself, while *ātmānam ātmanā* is the process of raw spiritual vision of the soul of itself. These are very advanced processes. The simplest of the four systems listed is *karma yogena* which involves the application of yoga maturity to administrative life. However, a simpler method is given in the next verse.

अन्ये त्वेवमजानन्तः
श्रुत्वान्येभ्य उपासते ।
तेऽपि चातितरन्त्येव
मृत्युं श्रुतिपरायणाः ॥ १३.२६॥
anye tvevamajānantaḥ
śrutvānyebhya upāsate
te'pi cātitarantyeva
mṛtyuṁ śrutiparāyaṇāḥ (13.26)

anye — others; tu — but; evam — thus; ajānantaḥ — not knowing; śrutvānyebhya = śrutvā — hearing + anyebhya — from others; upāsate — they worship; te — they; 'pi = api — also; cātitaranti = ca — and + atitaranti — transcend; eva — indeed; mṛtyuṁ — death: śrutiparāyaṇāḥ = śruti — hearing + parāyaṇāḥ — putting confidence in as the highest

But some, though they are ignorant, hear from others. They worship and by their confidence in what is heard. They also transcend death. (13.26)

Commentary:

This is the easiest of the processes of self-realization. One can hear with great confidence (*parāyanāh*) and experience directly by what is heard, by an affinity for the spiritual authority. This path of hearing is greatly stressed in these times by the Vaishnava spiritual masters. In fact, this one verse in the *Gītā* summarizes the methods used by most devotees in these modern times. It is validated by Krishna in no uncertain terms. Since it relies on a devoted attitude and on sincerity (*parāyanāh*) towards the spiritual teacher, it hinges on the teacher's level of advancement and one's intimate relationship with that personality.

It is, however, a rare person who qualifies under the statement of this verse, for we must remember that Arjuna heard and was not convinced until he saw the vision of the Universal Form. As easy as it sounds, this verse actually applies in the rarest of circumstances. It requires a mystically-experienced spiritual master and a totally-sincere disciple whose nature is absorbent enough to shift to the mystic plane in which the authority perceives the realities as they were described by Lord Krishna.

यावत्संजायते किंचित्
सत्त्वं स्थावरजङ्गमम् ।
क्षेत्रक्षेत्रज्ञसंयोगात्
तद्विद्धि भरतर्षभ ॥ १३.२७
yāvatsaṁjāyate kiṁcit
sattvaṁ sthāvarajaṅgamam
kṣetrakṣetrajñasaṁyogāt
tadviddhi bharatarṣabha(13.27)

yāvat — as for; saṁjāyate — is born; kiṁcit = kiṁcid — anything, whatever; sattvaṁ — existence; sthāvarajaṅgamam = sthāvara — stationary + jaṅgamam — moving; kṣetrakṣetrajñasaṁyogāt = kṣetra — living space + kṣetrajña — experiencer + saṁyogāt — from the synthesis; tat — that; viddhi — know; bharatarṣabha — strong man of the Bharatas

As for anything that is produced in this existence, be it a stationary or moving object, know, O strong man of the Bharatas, that it is produced from a synthesis of the experiencer and the living space. (13.27)

Commentary:

Here is the evidence that the term *ātma* in verse 25 refers to the spiritual person, the limited soul, and not the Supreme Soul. Lord Krishna gave the Sanskrit synonym of the *ātma* which Arjuna listed in the beginning of this chapter as *kṣetrajña* (13.1), the experiencer of living space. Of course, Lord Krishna informed Arjuna about that experiencer and gave more information. Krishna said that He, too, is a super-experiencer with consciousness of all living spaces (*kṣetrajñam sarvakṣetreṣu*).

Everything we perceive with material senses, either of the gross, subtle or causal forms, is a combination of the Supreme Spirit, the spirits, and matter. Generally, however, we may regard the forms as combinations of limited spirits and matter. The Supreme Lord is the detached witness (*upadraṣṭā*. 13.23).

समं सर्वेषु भूतेषु
तिष्ठन्तं परमेश्वरम् ।
विनश्यत्स्वविनश्यन्तं
यः पश्यति स पश्यति ॥ १३.२८॥

samam— similar; sarveṣu—in all; bhūteṣu—in beings; tiṣṭhantaṁ—situated; parameśvaram — Supreme Lord; vinaśyatsu — in disintegration; avinaśyantaṁ— not

samaṁ sarveṣu bhūteṣu
tiṣṭhantaṁ parameśvaram
vinaśyatsvavinaśyantaṁ
yaḥ paśyati sa paśyati (13.28)

perishing; yaḥ—who; paśyati—perceive; sa = saḥ—he; paśyati—really sees

The Supreme Lord is similarly situated in all beings without perishing when they disintegrate. He who perceives that, really sees. (13.28)

Commentary:

Krishna spoke of the Supreme Lord Who is similarly situated in all beings and Who does not perish when their forms decay. Any man (*yah*), the Lord said, who sees this, really perceives. Such a vision is the ultimate vision in the material world and that is why the Vaishnava authorities are so eager for us to achieve it.

समं पश्यन्हि सर्वत्र
समवस्थितमीश्वरम् ।
न हिनस्त्यात्मनात्मानं
ततो याति परां गतिम् ॥१३.२९॥
samaṁ paśyanhi sarvatra
samavasthitamīśvaram
na hinastyātmanātmānaṁ
tato yāti parāṁ gatim (13.29)

samaṁ — same; paśyan — seeing; hi — indeed; sarvatra — everywhere; samavasthitaṃ — same established; īśvaram — Lord; na — not; hinasti — degrade; ātmānātmānaṁ = ātmanā — by the soul + ātmānaṁ — the soul; tato = tataḥ — subsequently; yāti — goes; parām — supreme; gatim — destination

Seeing the same Lord being situated everywhere, he does not degrade the soul by his own soul. Subsequently, he goes to the supreme destination. (13.29)

Commentary:

This verse concerns the vision of the Supersoul and not that of the soul. This concerns Supersoul realization and not self-realization, even though to an extent self-realization is included in that vision. After all, if a spirit cannot perceive itself, he will not be able to see the Supersoul who is much subtler.

By the logic indicated, we will have to agree with the Vaishnava authorities who stress over and over that unless the Supreme Lord is considered, the soul will, of necessity, not be able to elevate himself. The implication of this verse is that if we do not discover that Supersoul, Who is the super-experiencer in all bodies, we will degrade ourselves.

प्रकृत्यैव च कर्माणि
क्रियमाणानि सर्वशः ।
यः पश्यति तथात्मानम्
अकर्तारं स पश्यति ॥१३.३०
prakṛtyaiva ca karmāṇi
kriyamāṇāni sarvaśaḥ
yaḥ paśyati tathātmānam
akartāraṁ sa paśyati (13.30)

prakṛtyaiva = prakṛtya — by material nature + eva — indeed; ca — and; karmāṇi — actions; kriyamāṇāni — performed; sarvaśaḥ — in all cases; yaḥ — who; paśyati — he sees; tathātmānam = tathā — as regarding + ātmānam — self; akartāraṁ — non-doer; sa = saḥ — he; paśyati — truly sees

He who sees that in all cases, the actions are performed by material nature, and who regards himself as a non-doer, truly sees. (13.30)

Commentary:

This basic idea is one of the most difficult views to accept and integrate. We become so much involved in our initiative for actions, that we take ourselves seriously, not realizing the big part played by material nature. But as Lord Krishna explained, the cause of our delusion is the attachments to the modes of material nature, (*guṇasaṅgo*, 13.22).

यदा भूतपृथग्भावम्
एकस्थमनुपश्यति ।
तत एव च विस्तारं
ब्रह्म संपद्यते तदा ॥ १३.३१ ॥
yadā bhūtapṛthagbhāvam
ekasthamanupaśyati
tata eva ca vistāraṁ
brahma saṁpadyate tadā (13.31)

yadā — when; bhūtapṛthagbhāvam = bhūta — being + pṛthak — various + bhāvam — existential state; ekastham — based in one foundation; anupaśyati — he sees; tata — from that conclusion; eva — only; ca — and; vistāraṁ — extending, emanating; brahma — spiritual plane; saṁpadyate — he reaches: tadā — then

When a person sees that all the various states of being are based on a single foundation, and only from that everything emanates, then he reaches the spiritual plane. (13.31)

Commentary:

The single foundation (*ekastham*) or single basis of the various bodies, forms and formations (*bhūtapṛthagbhāvam*) is material nature (*prakṛti*). This was repeatedly stated by Lord Krishna. Even the subtle and causal forms are based on material nature. When a body dies, the departing spirit does not automatically become liberated from this material world. Material nature is subtle. It extends to the place of ideation, the plane of imagination and thinking.

To qualify for the attainment of the spiritual plane as explained in this verse, a person must have direct mystic perception of this truth. Theoretical understanding is insufficient.

अनादित्वान्निर्गुणत्वात्
परमात्मायमव्ययः ।
शरीरस्थोऽपि कौन्तेय
न करोति न लिप्यते ॥ १३.३२ ॥
anāditvānnirguṇatvāt
paramātmāyamavyayaḥ
śarīrastho'pi kaunteya
na karoti na lipyate (13.32)

anāditvāt = due to being without a beginning; nirguṇatvāt — due to being devoid of the influence of material nature; paramātmāyam = paramātmā — Supreme Soul + ayam — this; avyayaḥ — imperishable; śarīrastho = śarīrasthaḥ — situated in the material body; 'pi = api — even though; kaunteya — O son of Kuntī; na — not; karoti — he acts; na — not; lipyate — become contaminated

Since this imperishable Supreme Lord is beginningless and devoid of the influence of material nature, even though He is situated in the material body, O son of Kuntī, He does not act or become contaminated. (13.32)

Commentary:

A distinction is indicated here between the Supreme Soul (*paramātmā*) and the soul (*ātma*). The soul is imperishable just as the Supreme Soul. The soul is beginningless as well, as Krishna stated previously. But so long as the soul is involved in material nature, it exhibits responses to nature's variations. The soul is not fully resistant to it. The soul is not *nirguṇatvāt*. The soul becomes contaminated by a projection of the qualities of material nature into its imagination.

यथा सर्वगतं सौक्ष्म्याद्
आकाशं नोपलिप्यते ।
सर्वत्रावस्थितो देहे
तथात्मा नोपलिप्यते ॥ १३.३३ ॥
yathā sarvagataṁ saukṣmyād
ākāśaṁ nopalipyate
sarvatrāvasthito dehe
tathātmā nopalipyate (13.33)

yathā — as; sarvagataṁ — all-pervading; saukṣmyāt — as by subtlety; ākāśaṁ — sky. nopalipyate = na — not + upalipyate — is polluted; sarvatrāvasthito = sarvatra — all over +avasthitaḥ — situated; dehe — in the body; tathātmā = tathā— so + ātmā—soul; nopalipyate = na — not + upalipyate — affected

As by subtlety, the all-pervading space is not polluted, so the soul, though situated all over the body, is not affected actually. (13.33)

Commentary:

The affection of the soul for the material body and for the modes of material nature is, to a degree, imaginary. The delusion of being identical with the body is a strong impression on the mind of the soul but it is not factual in reality because the soul survives the death of the gross, subtle, and causal bodies. At least this is what we are told in the Vedic literatures. This was the experience of the reality-perceiving sages as explained by Lord Krishna in Chapter Two.

The soul is not evenly situated all over the body but his consciousness is spread throughout the body through the network of nerves. In the subtle body his consciousness is spread by the distribution of *prāṇa* which is super-subtle atomic energy.

The realization of the non-affectation and non-pollution of the soul (*nopalipyate*) is a difficult attainment for persons who are embodied but it can be achieved by the standard methods given elsewhere in the *Gītā*.

यथा प्रकाशयत्येकः
कृत्स्नं लोकमिमं रविः ।
क्षेत्रं क्षेत्री तथा कृत्स्नं
प्रकाशयति भारत ॥ १३.३४ ॥
yathā prakāśayatyekaḥ
kṛtsnaṁ lokamimaṁ raviḥ
kṣetraṁ kṣetrī tathā kṛtsnaṁ
prakāśayati bhārata (13.34)

yathā — as; prakāśayati — illuminates; ekaḥ — one, alone; kṛtsnaṁ — whole; lokam — world; imaṁ — this; raviḥ — sun; kṣetraṁ — living space; kṣetrī — the user of the living space; tathā — so; kṛtsnaṁ — entire; prakāśayati — gives feeling; bhārata — O man of the Bhārata family

As the sun alone illuminates the whole world, O man of the Bharata family, so the user of the living space gives feeling to the entire psyche. (13.34)

Commentary:

The soul causes the body to have feelings (*prakāśayati*). But we must remember that the soul is assisted by the Supreme Soul. The soul is rated as the producer of consciousness but he does this on a minor scale while the Supreme Soul does this on a cosmic level, thus reinforcing His limited partners.

क्षेत्रक्षेत्रज्ञयोरेवम्
अन्तरं ज्ञानचक्षुषा ।
भूतप्रकृतिमोक्षं च
ये विदुर्यान्ति ते परम् ॥ १३.३५ ॥

kṣetrakṣetrajñayorevam
antaraṁ jñānacakṣuṣā
bhūtaprakṛtimokṣaṁ ca
ye viduryānti te param (13.35)

kṣetrakṣetrajñayoḥ — of the experiencer and the living space; evaṁ — thus; antaraṁ = difference; jñānacakṣuṣā = jñāna — perceptive knowledge + cakṣuṣā — intuitive vision; bhūtaprakṛtimokṣaṁ = bhūta — being + prakṛti — material nature + mokṣaṁ — liberation; ca — and; ye — who; viduḥ — they know; yānti — they go; te — they; param — supreme

Those who by intuitive perception know the difference between the living space and the experiencer, as well as the liberation of the living being from material nature, go to the Supreme. (13.35)

Commentary:

Again, this is another verse where we must check the guarantees carefully, since we do not want to indulge in false hopes. A person who qualifies under this verse must have intuitive mystic perception. This does not mean the application of theoretical knowledge but rather the eye of actual experience as attained by the reality-perceiving sages, the *tattvadarśinah* (4.34). It is a mistake to tell readers, listeners and disciples that this means the eye of intellectual or conceptual knowledge. We have to stick to the definitions of the *Gītā*, where Krishna spoke of the samkhya yogis and their attainments. Arjuna could not understand Krishna until he had direct mystic insight into the glories of the Lord, so what can be said about others? It is simply part of a cheating process if we try to convince inexperienced people that they could qualify for these guarantees by intellectual understanding. Of course, Lord Krishna did say that simply by hearing from an authority, one can transcend the death experience. That was stated in this chapter as a process of self-realization:

anye tvevamajānantaḥ śrutvānyebhya upāsate
te'pi cātitarantyeva mṛtyuṁ śrutiparāyaṇāḥ (13.26)

But some, though they are ignorant, hear from others. They worship and by their confidence in what is heard, they also transcend death. (13.26)

And this guarantee about hearing should not be applied at random to other phases of spiritual development. It is unfair to take these certifications and apply them to whatever promises we make to disciples or audiences. We should not warp the *Gītā*.

CHAPTER 14

The Extensive Mundane Reality*

श्रीभगवानुवाच
परं भूयः प्रवक्ष्यामि
ज्ञानानां ज्ञानमुत्तमम् ।
यज्ज्ञात्वा मुनयः सर्वे
परां सिद्धिमितो गताः ॥ १४.१ ॥
śrībhagavānuvāca
paraṁ bhūyaḥ pravakṣyāmi
jñānānāṁ jñānamuttamam
yajjñātvā munayaḥ sarve
parāṁ siddhimito gatāḥ (14.1)

śrī bhagavān — the Blessed Lord; uvāca — said; paraṁ — highest; bhūyaḥ— further; pravakṣyāmi — I will explain; jñānānāṁ — of the knowledges; jñānam — information; uttamam — the very best; yat — which; jñātvā — having experienced; munayaḥ — yogī philosophers; sarve — all; parāṁ — supreme; siddhim — perfection; ito = itaḥ — from here, gatāḥ — done

The Blessed Lord said: I will explain more, giving the highest information of all knowledges, the very best. Having experienced that, all the yogi philosophers went away from here to the Supreme Perfection. (14.1)

Commentary:

Param siddhim means literally, *the Supreme Perfection.* A description of this entails the overall improvement of the condition of the soul as well as his relocation to a non-perishable environment. If we follow the presentation, we might understand that since the soul is eternal, he would require an eternally-manifested environment for his perfection. And he himself would have to be free from fallacies. His leaning towards material nature and his habitual dependence on that energy should be terminated.

Jñātvā means, *having known.* In this case, it is *having experienced.* The yogi philosophers (*munayah*), having that supreme experience, did go away from this temporary environment and were transferred to the spiritual places.

इदं ज्ञानमुपाश्रित्य
मम साधर्म्यमागताः ।
सर्गेऽपि नोपजायन्ते
प्रलये न व्यथन्ति च ॥ १४.२ ॥
idaṁ jñānamupāśritya
mama sādharmyamāgatāḥ
sarge'pi nopajāyante
pralaye na vyathanti ca (14.2)

idaṁ — this; jñānam — experience; upāśritya — resorting to; mama — my; sādharmyam — a nature that is similar; āgatāḥ — transformed into; sarge — at the time of the universal creation; 'pi = api — even; nopajāyante = na — not + upajāyante — they are born; pralaye — at the time of universal dissolution; na — not; vyathanti — disturbed; ca — and

**The Mahābhārata contains no chapter headings. This title was assigned by the translator on the basis of verse 3 of this chapter.*

Resorting to this experience, being transformed into a nature that is similar to My own, they are not born even at the time of the universal creation, nor are they disturbed at the time of dissolution. (14.2)

Commentary:

This is an admittance that it is possible to get totally out of the material world. Persons, therefore, who are interested in a total freedom from material existence, who want to assume an antisocial stance towards this life, may pay strict attention to the information in this chapter. Previously, even in Chapter Two, Lord Krishna spoke of *brahmanirvāṇam* (2.72). Now He will give some details to explain what He meant.

We hear from the *Rāmāyāṇa* scripture, which was existent at least in the oral form during the time of Lord Krishna, that some sages who were met by Lord *Rāma* did reach beyond this material situation and entered into the *brahman* world. Details of what took place in that location are hard to come by. Spiritual sense perception is such a hard achievement that even the accomplished mystics come back from their *brahman samādhi* experience with tales of going to a landscapeless, formless environment. Thus, whatever information we may get from the Lord would be to our benefit. Whatever He would clarify in this chapter of the *Gītā* would be to our interest.

According to the Vedic information, the mass of living entities who are to appear in a material universe come there with God in the very beginning, but they are not manifested immediately. Instead they are reliant on powerful agents of God, especially, on a superior entity named *Brahmā*. This *Brahmā* is a creative super-engineer. When compared to human beings, he functions as a god in his own right. The liberated sages, however, may not return to the material creations over and over again as do the other living entities who are reliant on a particular *Brahmā* for their objective lives in a material world.

Those perfected sages who are in a material universe, may not return to it in the next time cycle. They resort to the transcendental experience. They attain or resume a nature that is similar to Lord Krishna's.

मम योनिर्महद्ब्रह्म
तस्मिन्गर्भं दधाम्यहम् ।
संभवः सर्वभूतानां
ततो भवति भारत ॥१४.३॥
mama yonirmahadbrahma
tasmingarbhaṁ dadhāmyaham
saṁbhavaḥ sarvabhūtānāṁ
tato bhavati bhārata (14.3)

mama — my; yoniḥ — womb; mahat — extensive; brahma — reality; tasmin — into it; garbhaṁ — essence; dadhāmi — I impregnate; aham — I; saṁbhavaḥ — origin; sarvabhūtānāṁ — of all beings; tato = tataḥ — from that; bhavati — comes into being; bhārata — O man of the Bharata family

The extensive mundane reality is My womb. I impregnate the essence into it. The origin of all beings comes from that reality, O man of the Bharata family. (14.3)

Commentary:

Some modern scientists surmise that matter cannot exist beyond the speed of light but the information from the *Gītā* states that matter does exist in that abstract domain. Spirits also exist there. In this verse, Lord Krishna did not use *prakṛti*, the common term for material nature. Instead he used *mahad brahma*, the extensive mundane energy which is the source of material existence. Readers who want more information should learn the samkhya philosophy which was taught by Lord Kapila to His mother Devahuti in Canto Three of the *Śrīmad Bhāgavatam* and which was also taught to Uddhava by Lord Krishna in the

Eleventh Canto of the same text.

Those sages who state that the material existence comes about causelessly, contest this statement of Lord Krishna. He said that He impregnated the extensive mundane reality, thus causing the mergence and evolution of the material world. We may accept or reject that. Since none of us are in a position to prove or disprove this, it remains a matter of our confidence in Krishna or our doubts regarding His claims.

सर्वयोनिषु कौन्तेय
मूर्तयः संभवन्ति याः ।
तासां ब्रह्म महद्योनिर्
अहं बीजप्रदः पिता ॥१४.४॥
sarvayoniṣu kaunteya
mūrtayaḥ saṁbhavanti yāḥ
tāsāṁ brahma mahadyonir
ahaṁ bījapradaḥ pitā (14.4)

sarvayoniṣu — in all wombs; kaunteya — O son of Kuntī; mūrtayaḥ = forms; saṁbhavanti — they are produced; yāḥ — which; tāsāṁ — of them; brahmā — mundane reality; mahat — great; yoniḥ — giving; aham — I; bījapradaḥ — seed-giving; pitā — father

Forms are produced in all types of wombs, O son of Kuntī. I am the seed-giving father. The extensive mundane reality is the great womb. (14.4)

Commentary:

The analogy of man and woman is used by Lord Krishna to explain His relationship with the extensive mundane reality. I had the opportunity to speak to a *Brahmā* Murti we currently have. I asked about the extensive mundane reality, *(brahma mahad):*

"Should I translate this as material nature? What should I do?"

He replied:

"Whatever you do, you will be responsible for the meaning conveyed. I may inform you that mahad brahma does include material nature but it is more than material nature. It is the fabricated formation of material nature and spiritual nature combined. As such, to call it material nature is an understatement. Be careful about it. I myself emerge from this extensive synthesis of material and spiritual energy. In the beginning, however, this entire combination is something spiritual but it is static. When God attends to it, it evolves gradually and the varieties of beings evolve. Persons who want detailed information should check the teachings of Lord Kapila in the Bhāgavat Purāṇa.

"Do not translate it as material nature because it is more than that. The mahad brahma is the combination of the stable material nature and the individual minute spirits. A particular set of these spirits, millions upon millions of them, are then synthesized with a particular portion of material nature. And this artificial combination is evolved by the influence of Lord Vishnu. This much I can tell you."

Readers may analyze some statements of Maitreya Muni:

tato 'bhavān mahat-tattvam avyakāt kāla-coditāt
vijñānātmā 'tma-deha-sthaṁ viśvaṁ vyañjams tamonudaḥ
so 'py aṁśa-guṇa-kālātmā bhagavad-dṛṣti-gocaraḥ
ātmānaṁ vyakarod ātmā viśvasyāsya siṣrksayā

Then the invisible extensive mundane reality came into being, as activated by time. It was essentially intelligence personified and as the dispeller of darkness, it lit up the universe.

It is also personified time, material nature, and a portion of divinity. The purposeful look of the Lord caused it to modify itself for the creation of this universe. (Śrīmad Bhāgavatam 3.5.27-28)

सत्त्वं रजस्तम इति
गुणाः प्रकृतिसंभवाः ।
निबध्नन्ति महाबाहो
देहे देहिनमव्ययम् ॥१४.५॥
sattvaṁ rajastama iti
guṇāḥ prakṛtisaṁbhavāḥ
nibadhnanti mahābāho
dehe dehinamavyayam (14.5)

sattvaṁ — clarity; rajaḥ — impulsion; tama — retardation; iti — thus; guṇāḥ — influences; prakṛtisaṁbhavāḥ = prakṛti — material nature + saṁbhavāḥ — produced of; nibadhnanti — they captivate; mahābāho — O great-armed hero; dehe — in the body; dehinaṁ — embodied soul; avyayam — imperishable

Clarity, impulsion and retardation are the influences produced of material nature. They captivate the imperishable embodied soul in the body, O strong-armed hero. (14.5)

Commentary:

We remind readers that dehe means *the body* but the body in this case means the combination of three separate forms which are interlocked. These forms are the gross body, the subtle body and the causal body of super-subtle ideas. The spirit is captivated (*nibadh*) by the moody variations of material nature. These moods become manifest when the spirit and matter are superficially unified. The meaning is this: Unless the spirits are artificially combined with material nature, there can be no variations of material nature. Thus the emotions within material nature, which are detected through the mind and life energy, are for the most part artificial. These emotions stop as soon as the souls are taken away from the artificial combination brought on by the act of Krishna as described in verses 3 and 4.

तत्र सत्त्वं निर्मलत्वात्
प्रकाशकमनामयम् ।
सुखसङ्गेन बध्नाति
ज्ञानसङ्गेन चानघ ॥१४.६॥
tatra sattvaṁ nirmalatvāt
prakāśakamanāmayam
sukhasaṅgena badhnāti
jñānasaṅgena cānagha (14.6)

tatra — regarding these; sattvaṁ — clarifying influence; nirmalatvāt — relatively free from perceptive impurities; prakāśakam — illuminating; anāmayam — free from disease; sukhasaṅgena = sukha — happiness + saṅgena — by attachment; badhnāti — it binds; jñānasaṅgena = jñāna — knowledge of expertise + saṅgena — by attachment; cānagha = ca — and + anagha — sinless one

Regarding these influences, the clarifying one is relatively free from perceptive impurities. It is illuminating and free from disease, but by granting an attachment to happiness and to expertise, it captivates a person, O sinless one. (14.6)

Commentary:

The influences of material nature occur on the physical, emotional, and mental levels, in plain and irregular patterns. One might be in a lower mode emotionally and be physically in a higher one. Usually, however, a person is affected throughout by the same mode or same combination of modes.

The clarifying influence which is known as the mode of goodness is relatively free of perceptive impurities but it is not completely pure. It causes an attachment to happy conditions, and to the expertise of knowing how best to survive in material existence. If these two attachments are not regulated, they cause degradation.

रजो रागात्मकंविद्धि
तृष्णासङ्गसमुद्भवम् ।
तन्निबध्नाति कौन्तेय
कर्मसङ्गेन देहिनम् ॥१४.७॥
rajo rāgātmakaṁviddhi
tṛṣṇāsaṅgasamudbhavam
tannibadhnāti kaunteya
karmasaṅgena dehinam (14.7)

rajo = rajaḥ — impulsive influence; rāgātmakaṁ — characterized by passion; viddhi — know; tṛṣṇāsaṅgasamudbhavam= tṛṣṇā— desire + saṅga — earnest + samudbhavam — produced from; tat — this; nibadhnāti — it captivates; kaunteya — O son of Kuntī; karmasaṅgena — by attachment to activity; dehinaṁ — the embodied soul

Know that the impulsive influence is characterized by passion. It is produced from earnest desire and attachment. O son of Kuntī, this mode captivates the embodied soul by an attachment to activity. (14.7)

Commentary:

Human existence is mostly controlled by the impulsive mode. The animal world is run by the lower influence which will be discussed in the next verse. Among the human beings, those who are elevated in thought, word, and deed are being conducted mostly by the clarifying mode.

Each of these influences has their advantages and disadvantages as explained by Lord Krishna. Though it provides enthusiasm, the impulsive one promotes impulsive action. This sort of activity makes a person materialistic and proud. It results in an attitude of exploitation which invariably leads to frustration and degradation.

तमस्त्वज्ञानजं विद्धि
मोहनं सर्वदेहिनाम् ।
प्रमादालस्यनिद्राभिस्
तन्निबध्नाति भारत ॥१४.८॥
tamastvajñānajaṁ viddhi
mohanaṁ sarvadehinām
pramādālasyanidrābhis
tannibadhnāti bhārata (14.8)

tamaḥ — depressing mode; tu — but; ajñānajaṁ — produced of insensibility; viddhi — know; mohanam — confusion; sarvadehinām — of all embodied beings; pramādālasyanidrābhiḥ = pramāda — inattentiveness + ālasya — laziness + nidrābhiḥ = sleep; tat — this; nibadhnāti — captivates; bhārata — O man of the Bharata family

But know that the depressing mode is produced of insensibility which is the confusion of all embodied beings. This captivates by inattentiveness, laziness and sleep, O man of the Bharata family. (14.8)

Commentary:

The depressing mode dampens the consciousness of the living entity and makes him insensitive to spiritual interest. In the material world, the depressing mode has a value for inducing inattentiveness, laziness and sleep. It is in sleep, that the gross, subtle and causal bodies take rest and are rejuvenated. When the gross body sleeps, the aches and pains of it are relieved. When the subtle one sleeps, the emotional inharmonies are forgotten, and when the causal form sleeps, the unrealistic ideas subside into nothingness. In this way, the soul is relieved from the struggle for existence.

When the soul misuses the depressive mode, or when he is absorbed in it, he imperils himself by becoming attached to inattentiveness, laziness, and sleep. This increases the tendency of insensitivity. And the soul becomes confused and stupified, not understanding his cultural or spiritual interest.

सत्त्वं सुखे सञ्जयति
रजः कर्मणि भारत ।
ज्ञानमावृत्य तु तमः
प्रमादे सञ्जयत्युत ॥ १४.९ ॥
sattvaṁ sukhe sañjayati
rajaḥ karmaṇi bhārata
jñānamāvṛtya tu tamaḥ
pramāde sañjayatyuta (14.9)

sattvaṁ — clarifying influence; sukhe — in happiness; sañjayati — causes attachment; rajaḥ — impulsive influence; karmaṇi — to action; bhārata — O Bharata family man; jñānam — experience; āvṛtya — obscuring; tu — but; tamaḥ — depressing mode; pramāde — to negligence; sañjayati — causes attachment; uta — even

The clarifying influence causes attachment to happiness. The impulsive one causes a need for action, O Bharata family man. But the depressing mode obscures experience and causes attachment to negligence. (14.9)

<u>*Commentary:*</u>

The disadvantage of each of the modes of material nature is described in turn, as attachment to happiness, impulsive activity, and a lack of concentration. These cause problems for the soul in material existence. They do slow his progress in self-realization.

An attachment to happiness is, in a sense, just as dangerous as a lack of concentration. If a man is attached to happiness, he may violate moral principles to secure enjoyment. Even though initially, a man may be inspired to perform pious acts to reach a happy state of mind, the attachment cultivated causes him to hanker for happiness and prosperity at any cost. Thus he may gradually abandon moral principles and become degraded. An impulsive need for action causes the soul to act regardless of the consequences and so he becomes implicated while exploiting his fellows and material resources. This brings on adverse reactions.

रजस्तमश्चाभिभूय
सत्त्वं भवति भारत ।
रजः सत्त्वं तमश्चैव
तमः सत्त्वं रजस्तथा ॥ १४.१० ॥
rajastamaścābhibhūya
sattvaṁ bhavati bhārata
rajaḥ sattvaṁ tamaścaiva
tamaḥ sattvaṁ rajastathā (14.10)

rajaḥ — impulsiveness; tamaścābhibhūya = tamaḥ — depression + ca — and + abhibhūya — predominating over; sattvaṁ — clarity; bhavati — emerges; bhārata — O Bharata family man; rajaḥ — impulsiveness; sattvaṁ — clarity; tamaścaiva = tamaḥ — depression + caiva — and indeed; tamaḥ — depression; sattvaṁ — clarity; rajaḥ — impulsion; tathā — similarly

When predominating over impulsiveness and depression, clarity emerges, O Bharata family man. Depression rises, predominating over impulsiveness and clarity. Similarly, impulsion takes control over depression and clarity. (14.10)

Commentary:

Each of the modes serves as a part of a three-fold power but on occasion, a part may not be operative. All of the parts form the aggregate total being, which consists of a physical, subtle, and causal body, or a subtle and causal one, or just a causal one alone. In any case, the being has all three modes within it. Any of the energies can expand and dominate the psyche.

Material nature cannot be controlled absolutely by any limited being. It is simply impossible but if we understand how the energy works, we can decrease its leverage. That is the most we can do. If one fails to observe the working of the modes of nature, he loses his status as a *prabhu*, or director of the body, and as a *kṣetrajña*, or objective experiencer of the form. As Lord Krishna explained:

śrībhagavānuvāca
idaṁ śarīraṁ kaunteya kṣetramityabhidhīyate
etadyo vetti taṁ prāhuḥ kṣetrajña iti tadvidaḥ(13.2)

The Blessed Lord said: This, the earthly body, O son of Kuntī , is called the living space. Those who are knowledgeable of this, declare the person who understands this to be the experiencer of the living space. (13.2)

sarvakarmāṇi manasā saṁnyasyāste sukhaṁ vaśī
navadvāre pure dehī naiva kurvanna kārayan (5.13)
na kartṛtvaṁ na karmāṇi lokasya sṛjati prabhuḥ
na karmaphalasaṁyogaṁ svabhāvastu pravartate (5.14)

Renouncing all action with the mind, the embodied soul resides happily within as the director in the nine-gated city, not acting nor causing activity.

The Lord does not create the means of action, nor the actions of the creatures, nor the action-consequence cycle. But the inherent nature causes this. (5.13-14)

The key is to make the impulsive and depressing energies function under the clarifying power.

सर्वद्वारेषु देहेऽस्मिन्
प्रकाश उपजायते ।
ज्ञानं यदा तदा विद्याद्
विवृद्धं सत्त्वमित्युत ॥१४.११॥
sarvadvāreṣu dehe'smin
prakāśa upajāyate
jñānaṁ yadā tadā vidyād
vivṛddhaṁ sattvamityuta (14.11)

sarvadvāreṣu — in all openings; dehe — in the body; 'smin = asmin — in this; prakāśa — clear perception: upajāyate — is felt; jñānaṁ — true knowledge; yadā — when; tadā — then; vidyāt — it should be concluded; vivṛddhaṁ — dominant; sattvam — clarifying mode; iti — thus; uta — indeed

When clear perception, true knowledge, is felt in all openings of the body, then it should be concluded that the clarifying mode is predominant. (14.11)

Commentary:

The openings of the body are the sensual orifices. The highest of these openings, the eyes, allow the body to see outside of itself. The ears allow the body to hear. The nostrils allow the body to smell. The mouth allows the body to taste. The pores of the skin taken collectively as the touching sense, allow the body to feel objects. As partially-perceptive senses, the other two openings of the body are merely extensions of the sense of touch. But those two lower openings, namely the genital and the anus, are used for dispelling and accepting materials into the body. The anus is just for expelling stools, the male sexual organ for expelling urine and semen, and the female sexual organ for the dual purpose of expelling urine, discarding fluids and fetuses and for receiving semen. When these openings of the body are in the best of health, it is to be understood that the body is in the clarifying mode. There are, however, varying degrees of clarity.

लोभः प्रवृत्तिरारम्भः
कर्मणामशमः स्पृहा ।
रजस्येतानि जायन्ते
विवृद्धे भरतर्षभ ॥ १४.१२ ॥
lobhaḥ pravṛttirārambhaḥ
karmaṇāmaśamaḥ spṛhā
rajasyetāni jāyante
vivṛddhe bharatarṣabha (14.12)

lobhaḥ = greed; pravṛttiḥ — over-exertion; ārambhaḥ — rash undertaking; karmaṇām — of action; aśamaḥ — restlessness; spṛhā — craving; rājasī — in impulsiveness; etāni — those; jāyante — are produced; vivṛddhe — in the dominance; bharatarṣabha — strong man of the Bharatas

Greed, overexertion, rash undertakings, restlessness and craving, these are produced when impulsiveness is predominant, O strong man of the Bharatas. (14.12)

Commentary:

An impulsive, blind type of enthusiasm that brings on inconsiderate, rash actions and which causes a person to crave pleasures and to develop vices, is in the mode of passion. Even though a man might decide to curb himself, he may be driven against his will towards degradation by the impulsive life force within his subtle and gross bodies.

अप्रकाशोऽप्रवृत्तिश्च
प्रमादो मोह एव च ।
तमस्येतानि जायन्ते
विवृद्धे कुरुनन्दन ॥ १४.१३ ॥
aprakāśo'pravṛttiśca
pramādo moha eva ca
tamasyetāni jāyante
vivṛddhe kurunandana (14.13)

aprakāśo = aprakāśaḥ — lack of clarity; 'pravṛttiśca = apravṛttiśca = apravṛttiḥ — lack of energy + ca — and; pramādo = pramādaḥ — inattentiveness; mohā — confusion; eva — indeed; ca — and; tamasī — in depression; etāni — these; jāyante — they emerge; vivṛddhe — in the dominance; kurunandana — O dear son of the Kurus

Lack of clarity, lack of energy, inattentiveness and confusion emerge when depression is predominant, O dear son of the Kurus. (14.13)

Commentary:

The energy of the soul is inefficiently absorbed by the depressing mode of material nature. The energy of the soul is constantly being produced, for the soul is, from the mechanical viewpoint, a perpetual energy source. But when in contact with material nature, its energy is absorbed in varying degrees.

यदा सत्त्वे प्रवृद्धे तु
प्रलयं याति देहभृत् ।
तदोत्तमविदां लोकान्
अमलान्प्रतिपद्यते ॥ १४.१४ ॥

yadā — when; sattve — in clarity; pravṛddhe — under the dominance of; tu — but; pralayaṁ — death experience; yāti — he goes; dehabhṛt — the embodied soul; tadottamavidāṁ = tadā — then + uttamavidāṁ — of those who know the supreme;

yadā sattve pravṛddhe tu
pralayaṁ yāti dehabhṛt
tadottamavidāṁ lokān
amalānpratipadyate (14.14)

lokān — worlds; amalān — pure; pratipadyate — he is transferred

When the embodied soul goes through the death experience while under the dominance of the clarifying mode, he is transferred to the pure world of those who know the Supreme. (14.14)

Commentary:

To qualify for such a position in the hereafter one would have to be fully situated in the mode of goodness at the time of death. Any slight flaw would disqualify one for this guarantee of the *Gītā*. The worlds of great yogi sages are those which are known as Maharloka, Janaloka, Tapoloka, and Satyaloka. These residences are far beyond the angelic paradises which are called *svarga* in the Vedic literature and which are known as heavenly places in the Christian religion.

We have to understand that regardless of our view of goodness or clarity, the *Gītā* has a particular definition and the guarantee only covers persons who match the stipulations.

रजसि प्रलयं गत्वा
कर्मसङ्गिषु जायते ।
तथा प्रलीनस्तमसि
मूढयोनिषु जायते ॥१४.१५॥
rajasi pralayaṁ gatvā
karmasaṅgiṣu jāyate
tathā pralīnastamasi
mūḍhayoniṣu jāyate (14.15)

rajasi — in the impulsive mode; pralayam — death experience; gatvā — having gone; karmasaṅgiṣu = karmā — work + saṅgiṣu — among people who are prone; jāyate — is born; tathā — likewise; pralīnaḥ — dying; tamasi — in the depressive mode; mūḍhayoniṣu = mūḍha — ignorant + yoniṣu — in the wombs of species; jāyate — is born

Having gone through the death experience in the impulsive mode, the soul is born among the work-prone people; likewise when dying in the depressive mode, the soul takes birth from the wombs of the ignorant species. (14.15)

Commentary:

Most human beings are in the impulsive mode. Most of what we attribute to be goodness is factually impulsiveness. Thus most human beings will take birth either as human beings again or as animals who are basically ignorant of the value of these life forms.

कर्मणः सुकृतस्याहुः
सात्त्विकं निर्मलं फलम् ।
रजसस्तु फलं दुःखम्
अज्ञानं तमसः फलम् ॥१४.१६॥
karmaṇaḥ sukṛtasyāhuḥ
sāttvikaṁ nirmalaṁ phalam
rajasastu phalaṁ duḥkham
ajñānaṁ tamasaḥ phalam (14.16)

karmaṇaḥ — of action; sukṛtasyāhuḥ = sukṛtasya — of well-performed + āhuḥ — the authorities say; sāttvikaṁ — of the clarifying mode; nirmalaṁ — free of defects; phalam — result; rajasaḥ — of impulsion; tu — but; phalaṁ — result; duḥkham — distress; ajñānaṁ — ignorance; tamasaḥ — of the depressing mode; phalam — consequences

The authorities say that the result of a well-performed action is in the clarifying mode and is free of defects. But the result of an impulsive act is distress, while the consequence of a depressive act is ignorance. (14.16)

Commentary:

Each type of action has a particular result which is invoked within material nature by the motivation and the energy which the action comprises. Material nature accurately rates an activity and then reacts to satisfy and to deny expectations. Instead of studying the course of material nature and understanding her actions and reactions, we work with expectations and are then frustrated by natural laws.

सत्त्वात्संजायते ज्ञानं
रजसो लोभ एव च ।
प्रमादमोहौ तमसो
भवतोऽज्ञानमेव च ॥१४.१७॥
sattvātsaṁjāyate jñānaṁ
rajaso lobha eva ca
pramādamohau tamaso
bhavato'jñānameva ca (14.17)

sattvāt — from clarity; saṁjāyate — is produced; jñānaṁ — factual knowledge; rajaso = rajasaḥ — from impulsion; lobha — greed; eva — indeed; ca — and; pramādamohau — inattentiveness and confusion; tamaso = tamasaḥ — from depression; bhavato = bhavataḥ — they come; 'jñānam = ajñānam — ignorance; eva — indeed; ca — and

Factual knowledge is produced from clarity. Greed comes from impulsion. Inattentiveness, confusion, and ignorance come from depression. (14.17)

Commentary:

It is not so much what a man says about his moods but rather the resulting effects of moods upon his conduct. Thus we have to judge not by appearance or declaration but by the effects in the life of a human being. The laws of material nature operate independently without respect to our expectations. Thus, to judge properly, we must know what sort of result is produced by a particular type of action.

If a man declares that he performed an act in the clarifying mode and if by the result, he becomes greedy and confused or inattentive, we can understand that he was actually under the influence of impulsion and depression. In this way we can rate the moods.

ऊर्ध्वं गच्छन्ति सत्त्वस्था
मध्ये तिष्ठन्ति राजसाः ।
जघन्यगुणवृत्तस्था
अधो गच्छन्ति तामसाः ॥१४.१८॥
ūrdhvaṁ gacchanti sattvasthā
madhye tiṣṭhanti rājasāḥ
jaghanyaguṇavṛttasthā
adho gacchanti tāmasāḥ (14.18)

ūrdhvaṁ — upward; gacchanti — they go; sattvasthā — situated in clarity; madhye — in the middle; tiṣṭhanti — they are situated; rājasāḥ — those who are impulsive; jaghanyaguṇavṛttasthā = jaghanya — lowest + guṇavṛttasthā — situated in the influence of the material energy; adho = adhaḥ — downward; gacchanti — they go; tāmasāḥ those who are retarded

Those who are anchored in clarity, go upward. Those who are impulsive are situated in the middle. Those who are habituated to the lowest influence of the material energy, the retarded people, go downward. (14.18)

Commentary:

In the mundane evolutionary cycle, a living entity evolves, remains stagnant, or moves downward, all depending on his affiliation with the three modes of material nature. The soul is neither his animal form, his human form nor his angelic form but these forms show his relationship with the psychic and physical material nature. An analysis of living entity materialistic affiliation can be misleading, however. We should not judge by the external appearance, but rather by the internal psychic condition of the mind and emotions. A person might have an ugly form externally and be situated in the clarifying mode. A person with a very beautiful external body, might be under the depressive or impulsive mode.

A very attractive and beautifully-feathered bird like a peacock will go to great lengths to find insects like cockroaches. The bird may eat flesh if it can find it. It will chew living worm bodies. But an ugly creature like a buffalo will never eat a piece of meat. This is due to the internal condition of the mind and emotions of the various creatures. We must therefore give up our tendency for external ratings and learn to judge by the internal, emotional, and mental profiles.

Internal purity of emotion and mind takes the soul closer and closer to his natural spiritual constitution, closer and closer to liberation from material bondage, but until he is entirely free from the material association in all its phases, he is at a risk of greater contamination. The solution, therefore, is to put forth all endeavor to get out of the material world.

नान्यं गुणेभ्यः कर्तारं
यदा द्रष्टानुपश्यति ।
गुणेभ्यश्च परं वेत्ति
मद्भावं सोऽधिगच्छति ॥ १४.१९ ॥

nānyaṁ guṇebhyaḥ kartāraṁ
yadā draṣṭānupaśyati
guṇebhyaśca paraṁ vetti
madbhāvaṁ so'dhigacchati (14.19)

nānyaṁ = na — not + anyam — other; guṇebhyaḥ — than the influences of material nature; kartāraṁ — the performer; yadā — when; draṣṭānupaśyati = draṣṭā — observer + anupaśyati — he perceives; guṇebhyaḥ — than the influences of material nature + ca — and; paraṁ — higher; vetti — he knows; madbhāvaṁ — my level of existence; so = saḥ — he; 'dhigacchati = adhigacchati — he reaches

When the observer perceives no performer besides the influences of material nature and knows what is higher than those influences, he reaches My level of existence. (14.19)

Commentary:

This is another one of these difficult-to-comprehend verses of the *Gītā*. From our social perspective, it is difficult to know that material nature is the actor and that the soul is not the functional dignitary. The soul has a token position as the master of his body, just as the passenger in a vehicle is regarded with honor in a car. But in fact, the soul's energies are manhandled by material nature. When he is situated in the clarifying mode, he is least affected and his contributions of energies decrease, but even from that position, the soul is actually misdirected. In the final analysis we should agree with these ideas of Lord Krishna. He explained that the modes of material nature are the actual directors. Once we understand this, we can make that vital thrust to get out of material existence.

गुणानेतानतीत्य त्रीन्
देही देहसमुद्भवान् ।
जन्ममृत्युजरादुःखैर्
विमुक्तोऽमृतमश्नुते ॥ १४.२० ॥

guṇān — the influences of material nature; etān — these; atītya — transcends; trīn — three; dehī — embodied soul; dehasamudbhavān — deha — body + samudbhavān — formulated in; janmamṛtyujarāduḥkhaiḥ = janma — birth + mṛtyu

guṇānetānatītya trīn
dehī dehasamudbhavān
janmamṛtyujarāduḥkhair
vimukto'mṛtamaśnute (14.20)

— death + jarā — old age + duḥkhaiḥ — with distress; vimuktaḥ — released; 'mṛtam = amṛtam — immortality; aśnute — he attains

When the embodied soul transcends these three influences of material nature which are formulated in the body, he is released from birth, death, old age, and distress, and attains immortality. (14.20)

Commentary:

Freedom from material nature has little to do with not having a gross material body. It is a misunderstanding to feel that when a person loses a material body, he is freed from material nature for then he is only freed from one level of it. Some people feel that when their spiritual master gives up his material body, he is automatically freed from material nature, but this is a false assumption. Unless we have mystic vision to see if he relinquished the subtle and causal material forms, we cannot know for sure that he is liberated.

The word *deha* in this verse means: the gross, the subtle, and the causal bodies. It does not mean the gross body alone. The gross form is only a minor part of our mundane psychology. The main problem is the causal form. Usually spiritual masters point a finger at the subtle form as being the cause of our mundane conditioning. This is because it is much easier to realize the subtle body than the causal one which is more abstract. It might be easy to transcend gross matter but it is very difficult to get beyond subtle matter. Many religious people mistake subtle matter for spirit.

अर्जुन उवाच
कैर्लिङ्गैस्त्रीन्गुणानेतान्
अतीतो भवति प्रभो ।
किमाचारः कथं चैतांस्
त्रीन्गुणानतिवर्तते ॥ १४.२१ ॥
arjuna uvāca
kairliṅgaistrīnguṇānetān
atīto bhavati prabho
kimācāraḥ kathaṁ caitāṁs
trīnguṇānativartate (14.21)

arjuna — Arjuna; uvāca — said; kaiḥ — by what; liṅgaiḥ — by features; trīn — three; guṇān — influences; etān — these; atīto = atītaḥ — transcending; bhavati — he is; prabho — respectful Lord; kimācāraḥ = kim — what + ācāraḥ — conduct; kathaṁ — how; caitān = ca — and + etān — these; trīn — three; guṇān — influences; ativartate — he transcends

Arjuna said: In regards to a person who transcended the three influences of material nature, by what features is he recognized, O respectful Lord? What is his conduct? And how does he transcend the three influences? (14.21)

Commentary:

In Chapter Two, Arjuna asked a similar question:

arjuna uvāca
sthitaprajñasya kā bhāṣā samādhisthasya keśava
sthitadhīḥ kiṁ prabhāṣeta kimāsīta vrajeta kim (2.54)

Arjuna said: In regards to the person who is situated in clear, penetrating insight, would you please describe him? Speak of the person who is anchored in deep meditation, O Keśava Krishna. As for the man who is steady in objectives, how would he speak? How would he sit? How would he act? (2.54)

The answer to both questions is similar but the angle of vision regarding each, is different. From the point of view of escaping the influence of material nature, the seeker has to endeavor to get away and from the viewpoint of being situated on the spiritual plane, the seeker has to be stabilized there. Those who are now escaping from material nature are on a lower level than those who have already transcended that influence and who are situated transcendentally as a normality.

श्रीभगवानुवाच
प्रकाशं च प्रवृत्तिं च
मोहमेव च पाण्डव ।
न द्वेष्टि संप्रवृत्तानि
न निवृत्तानि काङ्क्षति ॥१४.२२॥
śrībhagavānuvāca
prakāśaṁ ca pravṛttiṁ ca
mohameva ca pāṇḍava
na dveṣṭi saṁpravṛttāni
na nivṛttāni kāṅkṣati (14.22)

śrī bhagavān — the Blessed Lord; uvāca — said; prakāśaṁ — enlightenment; ca — and; pravṛttiṁ — enthusiasm; ca — and; moham — depression; eva — indeed; ca — and; pāṇḍava — O son of Pāndu; na — not; dveṣṭi — scorns; saṁpravṛttāni — presence; na — nor; nivṛttāni — absence; kāṅkṣati — yearns for

The Blessed Lord said: O son of Pāndu, he does not scorn nor does he yearn for the presence or absence of enlightenment, enthusiasm or depression. (14.22)

Commentary:

Unless a man has mystic vision, he cannot transcend the modes of material nature. It is not a matter of wishful thinking, nor of physical acts alone. One has to avoid material nature on the psychic and physical planes simultaneously. Some feel that a physical endeavor to transcend the modes of material nature is sufficient. But these people indulge themselves in a dangerous and ungainly oversimplification. Material nature, as we hear in the *Gītā*, has a psychic and supernatural counterpart. If we want freedom from those influences, we have to apply methods of restriction on each of those planes.

Enlightenment, impulsion and depression are the alternating modes of material nature. These occur even in the mind of an advanced personality. Even an advanced soul, who is embodied in this world through the modes, must deal with their operations. For instance, a proven saintly man must take hygienic steps to protect his body from disease. Material nature is not that concerned about his body. He has to be cautious. Thus, even though a saintly person avoids the numerous complications and embarrassments brought on by material nature, he must also deal with variations.

How does a saintly man react to nature's variations? This is what Arjuna wanted to find out. Arjuna asked the question broadly as if it were applicable to every man but Arjuna had a special need to know the answer since he was affected by material nature when he gazed on the warriors from the center of the battlefield. He needed a method of transcending material nature's influence.

Lord Krishna gave the solution of being completely observant of and simultaneously detached from the modes. If we are observant, we would know what sort of mode our mind and emotions are influenced by. If we are detached, we can select which modes to reinforce.

दासीनवदासीनो
गुणैर्यो न विचाल्यते ।
गुणा वर्तन्त इत्येव
योऽवतिष्ठति नेङ्गते ॥१४.२३॥
udāsīnavadāsīno
guṇairyo na vicālyate
guṇā vartanta ityeva
yo'vatiṣṭhati neṅgate (14.23)

udāsinavat — detached; āsīnaḥ — sitting, existing; guṇaiḥ — by the influences of material nature; yaḥ — who; na — not; vicālyate — he is affected; guṇā — the mundane influences; vartanta — they operate; iti — thus (thinking that); eva — indeed: yo = yaḥ — who; 'vatiṣṭhati = avatiṣṭhati — he is spiritually situated; neṅgate = na — not + iṅgate — he becomes excited

Being situated in the body, but being detached, not being affected by the influences of material nature, considering that the modes are operating naturally, he who is spiritually-situated, who does not become excited, (14.23)

Commentary:

Even though a man may have mastered the yoga process, he will still have to accept a certain degree of flexibility of the mundane influences. He cannot absolutely control material nature. By the advice of senior ascetics and the Lord, he does his best to minimize agitations. The living entity has a responsibility to keep his life in order but he cannot do so absolutely. Too many of the existential factors are beyond his control. Still, he can develop detachment and save himself from much worry.

समदुःखसुखः स्वस्थः
समलोष्टाश्मकाञ्चनः ।
तुल्यप्रियाप्रियो धीरस्
तुल्यनिन्दात्मसंस्तुतिः ॥१४.२४॥
samaduḥkhasukhaḥ svasthaḥ
samaloṣṭāśmakāñcanaḥ
tulyapriyāpriyo dhīras
tulyanindātmasaṁstutiḥ (14.24)

samaduḥkhasukhaḥ = samā — equally regarded + duḥkha — pain + sukhaḥ — pleasure; svasthaḥ — self-situated; samaloṣṭāśmakāñcanaḥ = samā — regarded in the same way + loṣṭa — lump of clay + aśmā — stone + kāñcanaḥ — gold; tulyapriyāpriyo = tulyapriyāpriyaḥ= tulya — treated equally + priya — loved ones + apriyaḥ — despised person; dhīraḥ — one who is steady of mind; tulyanindātmasaṁstutiḥ = tulya — regarded equally + nindā — condemnation + ātmā — self + saṁstutiḥ — congratulation

...to whom pain and pleasure are equally regarded, who is self-situated, to whom a lump of clay, a stone or gold, are regarded in the same way, by whom a loved one and a despised person are treated equally, who is steady of mind, to whom condemnation and congratulation are regarded equally, (14.24)

Commentary:

This verse 24 is not a sentence. It continues from the previous verse and is linked to the proceeding one. This is a description of the mentality or social mood of the person who is detached from material nature. This is not a pretensive condition, but a psychological state of action which is manifested when one becomes detached from mundane social life. As long as we are depending on social life, we cannot regard life in this way, except on occasion. To be a consistent renouncer, one has to scale down his material existence, keep himself at a distance from the social scene, and get rid of the need for exploitation. So long as we are attracted to any type of exploitation, even for religious purposes, we will be drawn away from the detached, impartial mood described.

If a man needs money for missionary activities, how can he regard clay, stone, and precious metals as the same? He must sort the precious metal, and become involved in commercial ventures. How can a preacher who requires support not despise those who are against his ideas? Thus to live in this way one has to be a yogi who lives in isolation and who does not have to deal with the social scene. If his life is greatly simplified and if he does not require much for maintenance, an ascetic can do this. A preacher who is involved in a worldwide preaching mission, may apply some detachment but only insofar as he does not become involved in too many financial concerns.

मानावमानयोस्तुल्यस्
तुल्यो मित्रारिपक्षयोः ।
सर्वारम्भपरित्यागी
गुणातीतः स उच्यते ॥ १४.२५ ॥
mānāvamānayostulyas
tulyo mitrāripakṣayoḥ
sarvārambhaparityāgī
guṇatītaḥ sa ucyate (14.25)

mānāvamānayoḥ — in honor and dishonor; tulyaḥ — equally-disposed; tulyo = tulyaḥ — impartial; mitrāripakṣayoḥ — to friend or foe; sarvārambhaparityāgī = sarvā — all + ārambha — undertaking + parityāgī — renouncing; guṇatītaḥ = guṇa — mundane influence + atītaḥ — transcending; sa = saḥ — he; ucyate — is said to be

...who is equally disposed to honor and dishonor, who is impartial to friend or foe, who has renounced all undertakings, is said to have transcended the mundane influences. (14.25)

Commentary:

It is for this reason that a genuine *sannyāsi* is said to be socially dead. Most modern *sannyāsis*, however, are fake renunciants. They become involved in social activities in the name of religion. A true *sannyāsi*, by the original definition of the term, gives up all social engagements and just wanders about or remains at one place with a very simple outlay without many disciples.

Unless a man effectively and factually renounces all undertakings (*sarvārambha-parityāgī*), he cannot remain detached from material nature. Thus we find the *sannyāsis* who are not so detached make excuses and polish off their involved life by stating that their material activities are spiritually motivated. It may or may not be, but it is not the full detachment described in this verse. One who is involved and who leaves his body while being deeply entrenched in popularity and disciple management, will carry his attachments with him at the time of death.

Arjuna was not to renounce all undertakings, for he was to become involved in *karma yoga*. This verse is not a description of *karma yoga*. It describes *jñāna* yoga which was practised by the brahmin caste. *Karma yoga*, which is used by the administrative worldly-engaging people, is different. Some powerful, influential modern *sannyāsis*, who are actually administrators in the guise of brahmins, confuse the two paths and try to pretend that they are not neophyte *karma* yogis while, in fact, they are.

मां च योऽव्यभिचारेण
भक्तियोगेन सेवते ।
स गुणान्समतीत्यैतान्
ब्रह्मभूयाय कल्पते ॥ १४.२६ ॥

māṁ — me; ca — and; yo = yaḥ — who; 'vyabhicāreṇa = avyabhicāreṇa — with unwavering; bhaktiyogena — by yogically-disciplincd affection; sevate — serves; sa = saḥ — he; guṇān — the mundane influences;

māṁ ca yo'vyabhicāreṇa
bhaktiyogena sevate
sa guṇānsamatītyaitān
brahmabhūyāya kalpate (14.26)

samatītyaitān = samatītya — transcending + etān — these; brahmabhūyāya — absorbing in spiritual existence; kalpate — is suited

And a person who serves Me with unwavering, yogicly-disciplined affection and who transcends these mundane influences, is suited for absorption in spiritual existence. (14.26)

Commentary:

In this commentary, *bhakti yoga* means the *bhakti* or affections that are applied to Lord Krishna with acquired yogic discipline. Anyone can apply *bhakti* to Lord Krishna. This would mean the application of affections, love, and devotion, but not every devotee could apply that affection with yogic discipline. Only those who have mastered yoga and have acquired the mental and emotional control of their nature can apply devotion with this discipline. It is the same with *karma yoga*, which in this commentary is defined as *karma* (endeavor) applied with yogic discipline by Krishna's directions.

In that case also, anyone can work as advised by Lord Krishna but only a person who mastered yoga and acquired control of his emotional and mental nature can, like Janaka and Arjuna, work with the disciplined attitude, thus performing *karma yoga* rather than just *karma* without yoga.

Karma without yoga is also a recommendation in the *Gītā*. That is recommended in one verse only in Chapter Twelve:

abhyāse'pyasamartho'si matkarmaparamo bhava
madarthamapi karmāṇi kurvansiddhimavāpsyasi (12.10)

But if perchance, you are incapable of such practice, then by being absorbed in My work, or even by doing activities for My sake, you will attain perfection. (12.10)

But this is not the same as the *karma yoga* which King Janaka exemplified and which Krishna taught to Arjuna. And similarly there are grades of *bhakti* or affection to Krishna, but that which is applied by the discipline of yoga is the highest. Even if modern people cannot do this highest devotional yoga, still it is the highest.

Unless one is a yogi or has achieved the mental and emotional detachment that the yogis achieve, one could not apply purified love to Lord Krishna. A person who is not that disciplined in his nature, would not be able to transcend the modes of material nature. He would suffer from numerous distractions. Despite his good intentions, vows, and lofty aims, he would be drawn away from devotion again and again.

Preachers usually hawk on the fall of great yogis like *Viśvāmitra* but the fall of such yogis only proves that if yogis of such magnitude deviate, then everyone else will deviate to a greater degree. Their fall reflects the power of attraction of material nature over our souls.

In this verse, the devotee is required to offer his devotion in a disciplined, non-haphazard, non-impulsive way (*avyabhicāreṇa*) and he must also transcend the modes of material nature. Then he becomes suited for transference to the spiritual plane. But some preachers dismiss this and say that Krishna will grace the devotee if the devotee loves and serves Krishna under their direction.

ब्रह्मणो हि प्रतिष्ठाहम्
अमृतस्याव्ययस्य च ।
शाश्वतस्य च धर्मस्य
सुखस्यैकान्तिकस्य च ॥१४.२७॥
brahmaṇo hi pratiṣṭhāham
amṛtasyāvyayasya ca
śāśvatasya ca dharmasya
sukhasyaikāntikasya ca (14.27)

brahmaṇo = brahmaṇaḥ — of spiritual existence; hi — indeed; pratiṣṭhāham = pratiṣṭhā — basis + aham — I; amṛtasyāvyayasya = amṛtasya — of the immortal + avyayasya — of the imperishable; ca — and; śāśvatasya — of the perpetual; ca — and; dharmasya — of the rules for social conduct; sukhasyaikāntikasya = sukhasya — of happiness + ekāntikasya — of the absolute; ca — and

...for I am the basis of the immortal, imperishable spiritual existence and of the perpetual rules of social conduct and of absolute happiness. (14.27)

Commentary:

This claim of Lord Krishna is denied by some transcendentalists who do not believe that any person could be the basis or foundation (*pratiṣṭha*) of the *brahman* spiritual energy. However, Krishna made the claim for Himself. Some great sages like *Nārada*, Asita Devala, and *Vyāsaji* are supportive of Lord Krishna. And that is sufficient for our notation and understanding.

He also claims to be the basis of eternal law (*śāśvatasya ca dharmasya*). To substantiate that claim, He showed Arjuna the Universal Form and told Arjuna that He arrived at the battlefield to settle that eternal law with the warriors. As the ultimate lawman, Krishna disciplined the most powerful men of His time. This is what Krishna had to say:

śrībhagavānuvāca
kālo'smi lokakṣayakṛt pravṛddho lokānsamāhartumiha pravṛttaḥ
ṛte'pi tvāṁ na bhaviṣyanti sarve ye'vasthitāḥ pratyanīkeṣu yodhāḥ (11.32)
tasmāttvamuttiṣṭha yaśo labhasva jitvā śatrūnbhuṅkṣva rājyaṁ samṛddham
mayaivaite nihatāḥ pūrvameva nimittamātraṁ bhava savyasācin (11.33)
droṇaṁ ca bhīṣmaṁ ca jayadrathaṁ ca karṇaṁ tathānyānapi yodhavīrān
mayā hatāṁstvaṁ jahi mā vyathiṣṭhā yudhyasva jetāsi raṇe sapatnān (11.34)

The Blessed Lord said: I am the time limit, the mighty world-destroying Cause, appearing here to annihilate the worlds. Even without you, all the armored warriors, in both armies will cease to live.

Therefore you should stand up! Get the glory! Having conquered the enemies, enjoy a prosperous country. These fellows are supernaturally disposed by Me already. Be only the agent, O ambidextrous archer.

Droṇa, Bhishma, Jayadratha, and Karṇa, as well as other battle heroes, were supernaturally hurt by Me. You may physically kill them. Do not hesitate. Fight! You will conquer the enemies in battle. (11.32-34)

Some modern Vaishnava acharyas translated or allowed their disciples to translate *dharmasya* in this verse with various meanings which are inconsistent with the *Gītā*. We referred to Chapter Four where Lord Krishna described His activities in this world and where *dharma* is described in detail. Here are the verses:

yadā yadā hi dharmasya glānirbhavati bhārata
abhyutthānamadharmasya tadātmānaṁ sṛjāmyaham (4.7)
paritrāṇāya sādhūnāṁ vināśāya ca duṣkṛtām
dharmasaṁsthāpanārthāya saṁbhavāmi yuge yuge (4.8)

Whenever there is a decrease of righteousness, O son of the Bharata family, and when there is an increase of wickedness, then I show Myself. (4.7)

For protecting the saintly people, to destroy the wicked ones, and to establish righteousness, I come into the visible existence from era to era. (4.8)

Krishna made a claim for Himself as the foundation of ultimate happiness but others say that the brahman spiritual energy is itself that foundation and not Krishna. However, in this commentary, we are merely concerned with what Krishna said and not so much with those who doubt the validity of His claims.

CHAPTER 15

Two Types of Spirits*

श्रीभगवानुवाच
ऊर्ध्वमूलमधःशाखम्
अश्वत्थं प्राहुरव्ययम् ।
छन्दांसि यस्य पर्णानि
यस्तं वेद स वेदवित् ॥ १५.१ ॥
śrībhagavānuvāca
ūrdhvamūlamadhaḥśākham
aśvatthaṁ prāhuravyayam
chandāṁsi yasya parṇāni
yastaṁ veda sa vedavit (15.1)

śṛī bhagavān — The Blessed Lord; uvāca — said; ūrdhvamūlam = urdhva — upward + mūlam — root; adhaḥśākham = adhaḥ — below + śākham — branch; aśvatthaṁ — ashvattha tree; prāhuḥ — the yogī sages say; avyayam — imperishable; chandāṁsi = Vedic hymns; yasya — or what which; parṇāni — leaves; yaḥ — who; taṁ — this; veda — knows; sa = saḥ — he; vedavit — knower of the Vedas

The Blessed Lord said: The yogi sages say that there is an imperishable Ashvattha tree which has a root going upwards and a trunk downwards, the leaves of which are the Vedic hymns. He who knows this is a knower of the *Vedas*. (15.1)

<u>*Commentary:*</u>

In the Katha Upanishad there is a statement about this ashvattha tree. The Katha Upanishad are the teachings of Yamaraja, the judge of sinfully-departed souls. He spoke in that text to Nachiketa. In Section Two, Part Three, there is this statement:

urdhvamūlo 'vākśākha eṣo śvatthaḥ sanātanaḥ tadeva śukraṁ tad brahma
tadevāmṛtamucyate tasmiṁlokāḥ śritāḥ sarve tadu nātyeti kaścana etadvai tat

This is that ancient asvattha tree whose roots are above and branches are below. That alone is the essential factor, the reality, the immortal. All of these worlds are derived from that. None go beyond that. This is certainly that. (Kath. Upa. 2.3.1)

Thus many ideas in the *Gītā* were being taught before the appearance of Lord Krishna. This particular teaching is from the Upanishads. As we hear in this verse, a *vedavit*, a person who really knows the Vedas, is supposed to know about this eternal ashvattha tree but there are many pandits who pass in human society as knowers of the Vedas and who have never even studied the Upanishads, what to speak of having realization or the visual perception of this supernatural tree .

**The Mahābhārata contains no chapter headings .This title was assigned by the translator on the basis of verse 15 of this chapter.*

अधश्चोर्ध्वं प्रसृतास्तस्य शाखा
गुणप्रवृद्धा विषयप्रवालाः ।
अधश्च मूलान्यनुसंततानि
कर्मानुबन्धीनि मनुष्यलोके ॥ १५.२ ॥
adhaścordhvaṁ prasṛtāstasya śākhā
guṇapravṛddhā viṣayapravālāḥ
adhaśca mūlānyanusaṁtatāni
karmānubandhīni manuṣyaloke (15.2)

adhaścordhvaṁ = adhaḥ — downward + ca — and + urdhvam — upward; prasṛtāh — widely spreading; tasya — of it; śākhā — branches; guṇa — mundane influence; pravrddhā — nourished; viṣayapravālāḥ = viṣaya — attractive objects + pravālāḥ — sprouts; adhaśca = adhaḥ — below + ca — and; mūlāni — roots; anusaṁtatāni — stretched out; karmānubandhīni = karmā — action + anubandhīni — promoting; manuṣyaloke = manuṣya — of human being + loke — in the world

Branches spread from it, upwards and downwards. It is nourished by the mundane influences and the attractive objects are its sprouts. The roots are spread below, promoting action in the world of human beings. (15.2)

Commentary:

Even though the main trunk of this supernatural and enduring tree grows downward, other smaller branches, twigs and sprouts are spread in all directions upwards and downwards protruding from the main trunk and from its main branches. The tree may be compared to a massive tangled array of vegetation. As an ashvattha tree and similar trees like the banyan and mangrove send out support roots from the branches, so this supernatural tree, the massive growing organism of the material world, sends out various suction roots for sustenance and support.

Even though the main root grows upwards, still other subsidiary roots grow downwards, feeding on and motivating action of the living beings in this world.

न रूपमस्येह तथोपलभ्यते
नान्तो न चादिर्न च संप्रतिष्ठा ।
अश्वत्थमेनं सुविरूढमूलम्
असङ्गशस्त्रेण दृढेन छित्त्वा ॥ १५.३
na rūpamasyeha tathopalabhyate
nānto na cādirna ca saṁpratiṣṭhā
aśvatthamenaṁ suvirūḍhamūlam
asaṅgaśastreṇa dṛḍhena chittvā (15.3)

na — not; rūpam — form; asyeha = asya — of it + iha — in this dimension; tathopalabhyate = tathā — thus + upalabhyate — it is perceived; nānto = nāntah = na — not + antaḥ — end; na — nor; cādiḥ = ca — and + ādiḥ — end; na — nor; ca — and; saṁpratiṣṭhā — foundation; aśvatthaṁ — ashvattha tree; enam — this; suvirūḍhamūlam = suvirūḍha — well-developed + mūlam — root; asaṅgaśastreṇa = asaṅga — non-attachment + śastreṇa — with the axe; dṛḍhena — with the strong; chittvā — cutting down

Its form is not perceived in this dimension, nor its end, beginning or foundation. With the strong axe of non-attachment, cut down this Ashvattha tree with its well-developed roots. (15.3)

Commentary:

The destruction of the roots of one's materialism requires the special individual action of cutting down the connection between oneself and the material world. The value of the material world is its facility for tangible sense gratification. This means exploitation. But to carry out such a plan, one requires the psychic equipments. These gadgets are the life force, the initiative, the intellect, and the mind. These equipments are faulty. The living entity imperils himself by relying on them.

Since he developed a taste for the satisfaction gained through such tools of experience, he becomes attached to those tools and the exploitive situations. The supernatural tree of the material world is enduring. And therefore it can only be cut down symbolically by detaching ourselves from its facilities.

The tree is eternal and therefore the cutting process applies only to a person's connection with it. When one soul is liberated from it, others who have no effective cutting-action, remain bound to it as parasites and victims simultaneously. They feed on the tree and the tree feeds on them in turn, in a situation of mutual exploitation.

At the beginning of the battle. Arjuna was trapped in a situation of trying to get some emotional nutrients from the tree but on the other hand, the tree held its grip on Arjuna as one of its roots extracted sustenance from him. Thus he was time-bound. Lord Krishna took steps to free Arjuna so that he could follow in the footsteps of the yogi-kings like Janaka, who remained detached even though they were involved in a world which is controlled by the enduring supernatural tree.

Lord Krishna ordered Arjuna to systematically hack away at the tree until his connection with it was severed completely. It is a mistake to think that Arjuna, the hero that he was, could cut down such a tree. The tree is described as being imperishable (*avyayam*). It was even described before the time of Lord Krishna by the accomplished reality-perceiving sages (*tattvadarśinah*) as being a reality unto itself (*brahma*). Thus there is no question of Arjuna or anyone else, cutting down the tree. Arjuna or anyone could cut his or her connection with it but that can only be done when a spirit is detached from craving. For this accomplishment, wishful thinking and religious promises are useless. One has to get that strong axe of non-attachment (*asaṅga*) and hack away consistently at one's connection with the tree.

ततः पदं तत्परिमार्गितव्यं
यस्मिन्गता न निवर्तन्ति भूयः ।
तमेव चाद्यं पुरुषं प्रपद्ये
यतः प्रवृत्तिः प्रसृता पुराणी. ॥ १५.४ ॥

tataḥ padaṁ tatparimārgitavyaṁ
yasmingatā na nivartanti bhūyaḥ
tameva cādyaṁ puruṣaṁ prapadye
yataḥ pravṛttiḥ prasṛtā purāṇī(15.4)

tataḥ — then; padaṁ — place; tat — that; parimārgitavyaṁ — to be sought; yasmin — to which; gatā — some; na — not; nivartanti — they return; bhūyaḥ — again; tam — that; eva — indeed; cādyaṁ = ca — and + ādyaṁ — primal; puruṣaṁ — person; prapadye — I take shelter; yataḥ — from whom; pravṛttiḥ — creation; prasṛtā — emerged; purāṇī — in primeval times

Then that place is to be sought, to which having gone, the spirits do not return to this world again. One should think: I take shelter with that Primal Person, from Whom the creation emerged in primeval times. (15.4)

Commentary:

The supernatural existence of the material world is compared to the enduring ashvattha tree. The advice is to cut down one's connection with the tree with the axe of detachment, but here is the second instruction: One should take shelter of or rely on the *ādyam puruṣam*, the original person, who is said to be the cause of existence, the supreme reliable person. On one hand we should be detached and on the other we have to attach ourselves to the Supreme Person. This is a two-fold action of hacking away at our connection with material nature and establishing our relationship with the world's producer.

निर्मानमोहा जितसङ्गदोषा
अध्यात्मनित्या विनिवृत्तकामाः ।
द्वंद्वैर्विमुक्ताः सुखदुःखसंज्ञैर्
गच्छन्त्यमूढाः पदमव्ययं तत् ॥ १५.५
nirmānamohā jitasaṅgadoṣā
adhyātmanityā vinivṛttakāmāḥ
dvaṁdvairvimuktāḥ
sukhaduḥkhasaṁjñair
gacchantyamūḍhāḥ
padamavyayaṁ tat (15.5)

nirmāna — devoid of pride; mohā — confusion; jita — conquered; saṅga — attachment; doṣa — faults; adhyātmanityā = adhyātma — Supreme Spirit + nityā — constantly; vinivṛtta — ceased; kāmāḥ — cravings; dvandvaiḥ — by dualities; vimuktāḥ — freed; sukhaduḥkha — pleasure-pain; saṁjñaiḥ — known as; gacchanti — they go; amūḍhāḥ — the undeluded souls; padam — place; avyayam — imperishable; tat = tad — that

Those who are devoid of pride and confusion, who have conquered the faults of attachment, who constantly stay with the Supreme Spirit, whose cravings ceased, who are freed from the dualities known as pleasure and pain, these undeluded souls go to that imperishable place. (15.5)

Commentary:

Another of the *Gītā* guarantees is given in this verse. And the qualifications are very high. Not only should one be a devotee of the Supreme Spirit, but one must be devoid of pride, should have conquered the fault of attachment, ceased the cravings within one's nature, be freed from mood variations in relation to dualities like pleasant and unpleasant sensations, and constantly stay in touch with the Supreme Spirit. If one has all of these qualities, he goes to the imperishable place mentioned here and elsewhere in the *Gītā*.

न तद्भासयते सूर्यो
न शशाङ्को न पावकः ।
यद्गत्वा न निवर्तन्ते
तद्धाम परमं मम ॥ १५.६ ॥
na tadbhāsayate sūryo
na śaśāṅko na pāvakaḥ
yadgatvā na nivartante
taddhāma paramaṁ mama (15.6)

na — not; tat — that; bhāsayate — illuminates; sūryo = sūryaḥ — the sun; na — nor; śaśāṅko = śaśāṅkaḥ — moon; na — nor; pāvakaḥ — fire; yat — which; gatvā — having gone; na — never; nivartante — they return; tat — that; dhāmā — residence; paramaṁ — supreme; mama — my

The sun does not illuminate that place, nor the moon, nor the fire. Having gone to that location, they never return. That is My supreme residence. (15.6)

Commentary:

Lord Krishna has now positively identified the anti-material location as His residential habitat. Claiming that the sun, moon, nor fire does not function in that place, He states that the liberated souls go to that location permanently.

ममैवांशो जीवलोके
जीवभूतः सनातनः ।
मनःषष्ठानीन्द्रियाणि
प्रकृतिस्थानि कर्षति ॥ १५.७॥
mamaivāṁśo jīvaloke
jīvabhūtaḥ sanātanaḥ
manaḥṣaṣṭhānīndriyāṇi
prakṛtisthāni karṣati (15.7)

mamaivāṁśaḥ = mama — my + eva — indeed + aṁśaḥ — partner; jīvaloke = jīva — individualized conditioned being + loke — in the world; jīvabhūtaḥ — individual soul; sanātanaḥ — eternal; manaḥ — mind; ṣaṣṭhānindriyāṇi = saṣṭhāni — sixth + indriyāṇi — sense, detection device; prakṛtisthāni — mundane; karṣati — draws

My partner is in this world of individualized conditioned beings. He is an eternal individual soul but he draws to himself the mundane senses of which the mind is the sixth detection device. (15.7)

Commentary:

In the first edition of his *Bhagavad Gītā* translation, *Śrīla* Bhaktivedanta Swami gave *karṣati* as *struggling hard. Śrīla* Sridhara deva Maharaja gave, *attracts* or *carries*. Thus we get variant meanings from these authorities who hail in the Gaudiya Math disciplic succession from Lord Krishna. Both meanings are confirmed in Sanskrit dictionaries. Here are some of the meanings of the Sanskrit root verb *kṛṣ*: to plow, to make furrows, to draw, to pull, to draw away, to tear, to draw to oneself, to attract, to lead an army, to become the master of, to subdue, to overpower, to draw out, to extract, to take away by force.

I have translated *karṣati* as: He draws to himself. *Prakṛtisthāni* means *based on the energies of material nature, something mundane.* But it also means subtle and causal material. It is not just the senses of the gross body but those of the subtle and that of the causal form as well.

शरीरं यद्वाप्नोति
यच्चाप्युत्क्रामतीश्वरः ।
गृहीत्वैतानि संयाति
वायुर्गन्धानिवाशयात् ॥ १५.८॥
śarīraṁ yadavāpnoti
yaccāpyutkrāmatīśvaraḥ
gṛhītvaitāni saṁyāti
vāyurgandhānivāśayāt (15.8)

śarīraṁ — by body; yad — which; avāpnoti — he acquires; yat — which; cāpi — and also; utkrāmatīśvaraḥ = utkrāmati — departs from + īśvaraḥ — master; gṛhītvaitāni = gṛhītvā — taking + etāni — these; saṁyāti — he goes; vāyuḥ — wind; gandhān — perfumes; ivāśayāt = ivā — just as + āśayāt— from source

Regardless of whichever body that master acquires, or whichever one he departs from, he goes taking these senses along, just as the wind goes with the perfumes from their source. (15.8)

Commentary:

Gṛhītvaitāni is a compound of two words, namely *gṛhītvā* and *etāni. Etāni* is a pronoun meaning *these*. This refers to what was listed in the previous verse as *manah ṣaṣthānindriyāṇi* (the mind, the sixth detection device, and the other senses). This mind and the five senses travel along with the spirit. Some say this is a spiritual mind and senses but this is not so. This is the materially-molded mind and senses which evolved in the subtle body on the basis of desires in the causal form. This is why the word *prakṛtisthāni* is used. If it were six spiritual senses it would be *brahmatisthani*, or spirit-based.

Just as the wind carries away a fragrance or aroma from a source, so the spirit carries away from a dead body, the subtle material psychology which energized that form. This subtle energy is mundane (*prakṛtisthāni*).

In this verse the individual spirit (*jīvabhūtah*)is addressed as *īśvarah*, as a director or lord. The individual spirit is given that title because he is held responsible for the activities of the forms he uses.Lord Krishna did, in the previous verse, accredit the spirit as being His shareholder, His partner (*mamaivāmśo, mama eva amśah*).

श्रोत्रं चक्षुः स्पर्शनं च
रसनं घ्राणमेव च ।
अधिष्ठाय मनश्चायं
विषयानुपसेवते ॥ १५.९ ॥
śrotraṁ cakṣuḥ sparśanaṁ ca
rasanaṁ ghrāṇameva ca
adhiṣṭhāya manaścāyaṁ
viṣayānupasevate (15.9)

śrotraṁ — hearing; cakṣuḥ — vision; sparśanaṁ — sense of touch; ca — and; rasanaṁ — taste; ghrāṇaṁ — smell; eva — indeed; ca — and; adhiṣṭhāya — governing; manaścāyaṁ = manaḥ — mind; ca — and + ayaṁ — this; viṣayān — attractive objects; upasevate — becomes addicted

While governing the sense of hearing, vision, touch, taste, smell and the mind, My partner becomes addicted to the attractive objects. (15.9)

Commentary:

This confirms that *etāni* in the previous verse means the five senses and the mind which is the sixth sensing device. Of course these senses embody or are possessed of particular tendencies. When the soul leaves a body, he carries along the subtle senses and mind, along with the tendencies which these developed. In addition the senses include the life force which energizes them. The entity does not travel with dead senses. The dead senses are left behind with the dead form he abandoned. But the living senses of the subtle and causal bodies, proceed with him in a psychic form. And he tries to find a situation through which he would again manifest those tendencies on a gross level.

Adhiṣṭha means *to rule, govern, stand upon, occupy, or control*. While in control or attempting to control those five senses and the mind, the spirit becomes addicted to the sense objects which the senses pursue. Thus he becomes implicated in the activities of the senses. Inasmuch as he can control his senses and mind, that is how much he regulates the activities of the mundane bodies. His failure to control the senses and mind brings on undesirable consequences for which he suffers.

उत्क्रामन्तं स्थितं वापि
भुञ्जानं वा गुणान्वितम् ।
विमूढा नानुपश्यन्ति
पश्यन्ति ज्ञानचक्षुषः ॥ १५.१० ॥
utkrāmantaṁ sthitaṁ vāpi
bhuñjānaṁ vā guṇānvitam
vimūḍhā nānupaśyanti
paśyanti jñānacakṣuṣaḥ (15.10)

utkrāmantaṁ — departing; sthitaṁ — remaining; vāpi = vā — or + api — also; bhuñjānaṁ — exploiting; vā — or; guṇānvitam — under the influence of material nature; vimūḍhā — idiots; nānupaśyanti = na — not + anupaśyanti — they perceived; paśyanti — they perceive; jñānacakṣuṣaḥ — vision of reality

The idiots do not perceive how the spirit departs or remains or exploits under the influence of material nature. But those who have the vision of reality do perceive this. (15.10)

Commentary:

The spirit's departure from a gross body is not seen by a person with theoretical understanding. Only a person with mystic vision, who can visually see on the psychic plane, can see how a soul departs from the body. Others must rely on what they hear from the reliable mystics.

यतन्तो योगिनश्चैनं
पश्यन्त्यात्मन्यवस्थितम् ।
यतन्तोऽप्यकृतात्मानो
नैनं पश्यन्त्यचेतसः ॥ १५.११ ॥
yatanto yoginaścainaṁ
paśyantyātmanyavasthitam
yatanto'pyakṛtātmāno
nainaṁ paśyantyacetasaḥ (15.11)

yatanto = yatantaḥ — endeavoring; yoginaścainaṁ = yoginaḥ — yogis + ca — and + enam — this (spirit); paśyānti — they see; ātmani — in the self; avasthitam — situated; yatanto = yatantaḥ — exertion; 'pi = api — even; akṛtātmāno = akṛtātmānaḥ = akṛta — not in order, imperfect + ātmānaḥ — self; nainaṁ = na — not + enam — this (spirit); paśyanti — they see; acetasaḥ — thoughtless ones

The endeavoring yogis see the spirit as being situated in itself; but even with exertion, the imperfected souls, the thoughtless ones, do not perceive it. (15.11)

Commentary:

By this qualification, thinking of the philosophy of reincarnation is only part of the course of being able to see. One must also be an aspiring yogi (*yatanto yoginas*).

One does not have to be a *bhakta* yogi to see this but one needs to develop his spiritual vision and his psychic subtle vision. That is mysticism. A man does not have to be a devotee (*bhakta*) to see the soul. And a devotee may not be advanced enough to see the soul but may have to rely on belief in a scriptural testimony. In the *Gītā*, we cannot warp the word *yoginah* to mean, *devotee*. It means, *yogi*. When Krishna intends to indicate devotees and to stress that, He does so with the word *bhakta*.

यदादित्यगतं तेजो
जगद्भासयतेऽखिलम् ।
यच्चन्द्रमसि यच्चाग्नौ
तत्तेजो विद्धि मामकम् ॥ १५.१२ ॥
yadādityagataṁ tejo
jagadbhāsayate'khilam
yaccandramasi yaccāgnau
tattejo viddhi māmakam (15.12)

yat — which; ādityagatam — sun-yielding; tejo = tejaḥ — splendor; jagat — universe; bhāsayate— illuminates; 'khitam - akhitam — completely; yat—which; candramasi — in the mood; yat — which; cāgnau - ca — and + āgnau — in fire; tat — that; tejo = tejaḥ — splendor; viddhi — knows; māmakam — mine

That sun-yielding splendor which illuminates the universe completely, which is in the moon and which is in fire; know that splendor to be Mine. (15.12)

Commentary:

Krishna stated that His imperishable place is not illuminated by the sun, moon or fire but at the same time, the splendor of the sun which illuminates this mundane universe, also comes from Krishna. Arjuna got sufficient evidence of that in the vision of the Universal Form, when he saw Krishna with tremendous splendor on all sides, shining wondrously (*tejorāśim sarvato dīptamantam, 11.17*).

गामाविश्य च भूतानि
धारयाम्यहमोजसा ।
पुष्णामि चौषधीः सर्वाः
सोमो भूत्वा रसात्मकः ॥ १५.१३ ॥

gām — the earth; āviśya — penetrating; ca — and; bhūtāni —beings; dhārayāmi — I support; aham — I; ojasā — with potency; puṣṇāmi — I cause to thrive; cauṣadhīḥ = ca — and + auṣadhīḥ — plants; sarvāḥ — all;

gāmāviśya ca bhūtāni
dhārayāmyahamojasā
puṣṇāmi cauṣadhīḥ sarvāḥ
somo bhūtvā rasātmakaḥ (15.13)

somo = somaḥ— moon; bhūtvā — having influenced; rasātmakaḥ — sap-producing

And penetrating the earth, I support all beings with potency. And having influenced the sap-producing moon, I cause all plants to thrive. (15.13)

Commentary:

The subtle influence of Lord Krishna is indicated in this verse by His claim as the supporter of the earthly bodies through mystic penetration (*āviśya*) and by energizing the moon with power for capillary action in plants. *Rasātmakah* means, *consisting of juice* or *sentiment*. And rasa means *sap* or *juice*.

अहं वैश्वानरो भूत्वा
प्राणिनां देहमाश्रितः ।
प्राणापानसमायुक्तः
पचाम्यन्नं चतुर्विधम् ॥ १५.१४॥
ahaṁ vaiśvānaro bhūtvā
prāṇināṁ dehamāśritaḥ
prāṇāpānasamāyuktaḥ
pacāmyannaṁ caturvidham (15.14)

aham—1; vaiśvānaro = vaiśvānaraḥ — Vaiśvānara, a supernatural being, digestive heat; bhūtvā — becoming; prāṇināṁ — of the breathing beings; deham — body; āśritaḥ — entering; prāṇāpānasamāyuktaḥ= prāṇāpāna— inhaled and exhaled breath + samāyuktaḥ— combining; pacāmi — digest; annam— food; caturvidham — four kinds

Becoming the Vaiśvānara digestive heat, I, entering the body of all breathing beings and combining with the inhaled and exhaled breath, digest the four kinds of foodstuffs. (15.14)

Commentary:

Vaiśvānara is one of the deities in the Vedic religion. This deity is supposed to regulate the chemical heat of digestion. Thus Krishna claims to be the ultimate regulator of digestion and respiration.

सर्वस्य चाहं हृदि संनिविष्टो
मत्तः स्मृतिर्ज्ञानमपोहनं च ।
वेदैश्च सर्वैरहमेव वेद्यो
वेदान्तकृद्वेदविदेव चाहम् ॥ १५.१५॥
sarvasya cāhaṁ hṛdi saṁniviṣṭo
mattaḥ smṛtirjñānam apohanaṁ ca
vedaiśca sarvairahameva vedyo
vedāntakṛdvedavideva cāham (15.15)

sarvasya — of all; cāhaṁ = ca — and + aham — I; hṛdi — in the central, psyche; saṁniviṣṭo - saṁniviṣṭaḥ — entered; mattaḥ — from me; smṛtiḥ — memoiy; jñānam — knowledge; apohanaṁ — reasoning; ca — and; vedaiśca = vedaiḥ — by the Vedas + ca — and; sarvaiḥ — by all; aham — I; eva — indeed; vedyo -- vedyaḥ— to be known; vedāntakṛt = vedānta — Vedānta + kṛt — maker, author; vedavit — knower of the Vcdas; eva — indeed; cāham = ca — and + aham — I

And I entered the central psyche of all beings. From Me comes memory, knowledge and reasoning. By all the Vedas, I am to be known. I am the author of Vedānta and the knower of the Vedas. (15.15)

Commentary:

This is a well-known *Gītā* verse. The most frequently used meaning of the word *hṛdi* is, *in the heart. Hṛdayam* is a Sanskrit word meaning: heart, soul, mind, bosom, chest, breast, love, affection, the interior or essence of anything. We gave, *the central psyche*. Krishna entered the central causal space from which the subtle body developed. From the subtle form, the gross one was formulated. Some commentators say that the Lord is in the physical heart. It is, therefore, up to a reader to accept whatever meaning seems appropriate.

Another word of contention is *apohanam,* which is sometimes given as, *forgetfulness*. But Sanskrit dictionaries give these meanings; *denial, reasoning, and objection. Apohanam*, therefore, is the faculty of reasoning through which one raises an objection to some idea or through which one comes to deny something. Forgetfulness is involved in any such denial but the main meaning is the faculty of reasoning.

Apohah, a basic Sanskrit word from which *apohanam* is derived, means: removing, driving away, the removal of doubt by the exercise of the reasoning faculty, arguing and negative reasoning. Readers must, therefore, apply their understanding.

द्वाविमौ पुरुषौ लोके
क्षरश्चाक्षर एव च ।
क्षरः सर्वाणि भूतानि
कूटस्थोऽक्षर उच्यते ॥ १५.१६ ॥
dvāvimau puruṣau loke
kṣaraścākṣara eva ca
kṣaraḥ sarvāṇi bhūtāni
kūṭastho'kṣara ucyate (15.16)

dvau — two; imau — these two; puruṣau — two spirits; loke — in the world; kṣaraścākṣara – kṣaraḥ— affected + ca — and + akṣara — unaffected; eva — indeed; ca — and; kṣaraḥ—affected; sarvāṇi — all; bhūtāni — mundane creatures; kūṭastho = kūṭasthaḥ — stable soul ; 'kṣara - akṣara — unaffected; ucyate — is said to be

These two types of spirits are in this world, namely the affected ones and the unaffected ones. All mundane creatures are affected. The stable soul is said to be unaffected. (15.16)

Commentary:

Two subjects are being discussed in this verse, namely the *puruṣas* and the *bhūtānis*. The *puruṣas* are the spirits. The *bhūtānis* are the mundane bodies used by the spirits. These bodily forms are of three kinds: physical, subtle and causal. The physical and subtle bodies are similar in that they bear limbs and senses while the causal one has no limbs and only carries in it, the sense of ideation and mental responses. Despite its limitation, the causal body is the source of the subtle one. And the subtle form is the source of the physical one.

These three types of mundane bodies (*bhūtānis*) are affected by the modes of material nature. Therefore they are said to be *kṣarah* (affected) by those modes. Even though a particular spirit may make his body somewhat resistant to the modes, his body does, in fact, comprise material nature. He cannot create an absolutely-resistant material form, because by constitution, all mundane forms are subjected to material nature's affectations.

In this verse, Lord Krishna gave detailed information about the spirits. While throughout the *Gītā* He stated that the spirits are transcendental to material existence, here He brings in some startling information that the spirits are of two kinds. One is the affected type (*kṣarah*); the other type is the unaffected (*akṣarah*). But in the last line of this verse, Lord Krishna returned to His original premise which described the spirits as being transcendental to the material power.

This may appear to be a contradiction. Krishna repeatedly said that the spirit is eternal and transcendental to material nature. And then in another statement He said that one type of spirit is affected.

Ucyate means: is said to be, is called, or is declared to be by authorities on the subject.

Before Lord Krishna appeared, it was declared in the Upanishads that the spirits are eternal. Therefore in truth none of them can be affected in real terms. At least their eternality cannot be affected. And since their eternality cannot be affected, what is it about some of them that can be modified? I ask readers to ponder this question.

The unaffected spirits are unaffected in their knowledge of self-realization, while the affected ones are fooled by material nature into thinking that they became the *bhūtānis*, the mundane bodies. And this is why they are called the affected ones (*kṣarah*). It is not their eternal nature that is affected. It is their sense of security. As eternal beings they are secure but their knowledge of that security is insecure.

The meanings given by various translators are variant. We give some standard dictionary meanings as follows:

kṣarah --	*melting away, movable, perishable, being affected*
kṣar --	*to flow, to glide, to send, to stream forth, to drop, to trickle, to waste away, to wane, to perish, to become useless, to have no effect*
akṣarah --	*imperishable, indestructible, the indestructible spirit, being unaffected*
kūţastha --	*staying at the top, occupying the highest place, immovable, perpetually the same, stable.*

उत्तमः पुरुषस्त्वन्यः
परमात्मेत्युदाहृतः ।
यो लोकत्रयमाविश्य
बिभर्त्यव्यय ईश्वरः ॥१५.१७॥
uttamaḥ puruṣastvanyaḥ
paramātmetyudāhṛtaḥ
yo lokatrayamāviśya
bibhartyavyaya īśvaraḥ (15.17)

uttamaḥ — higher: puruṣaḥ — spirit; tu — but; anyaḥ— another; paramātmeti = paramātmā — Supreme Spirit + iti — tims; udāhṛtaḥ — is called; yo = yaḥ— who; lokatrayam — three worlds; āviśya — entering; bibharti — supports; avyaya — eternal; īśvaraḥ — Lord

But the highest spirit is in another category. He is called the Supreme Spirit, Who having entered the three worlds as the eternal Lord, supports it. (15.17)

Commentary:

Krishna now gives us a clear indication of His ideas about the spirits. These indications were also given before the time of Krishna by the Upanishadic sages and by other experts of self-realization. So far we have a listing of the three types of spirits. The most inferior type are the affected ones. The median type are the unaffected ones and the highest type is the Supreme Spirit under discussion in this verse. These types are all eternal but the affected ones are uncertain of their spiritual continuity. They are affected by the modes of material nature, which reinforces their spiritual fears.

The unaffected souls are able to maintain the spiritual perspective even when in contact with the modes of material nature and therefore they are accredited as being *akṣarah* (unaffected). They are emotionally resistant to the modes of material nature. Unlike their fellows, these unaffected entities maintain the spiritual prestige even when using mundane bodies. According to Lord Krishna, both types of souls are His partners or shareholders in existence.

The highest person, the Supreme Personality, stands apart from the affected and unaffected souls because He is the Universal maintainer. His vast influence is incomprehensible.

यस्मात्क्षरमतीतोऽहम्
अक्षरादपि चोत्तमः ।
अतोऽस्मि लोके वेदे च
प्रथितः पुरुषोत्तमः ॥१५.१८॥
yasmātkṣaramatīto'ham
akṣarādapi cottamaḥ
ato'smi loke vede ca
prathitaḥ puruṣottamaḥ (15.18)

yasmāt — since; kṣaram — effected; atīto - atītaḥ — beyond; 'ham - aham — I; akṣarāt — than the unaffected spirits; api — even; cottamaḥ = ca — and + uttamaḥ — higher; ato - ataḥ — hence; 'smi = asmi — I am; loke — in the world; vede — in the Veda; ca — and; prathitaḥ — known as; puruṣottamaḥ — Supreme Person

Since I am beyond the affected spirits and I am even higher than the unaffected ones, I am known in the world and in the *Vedas* as the Supreme Person. (15.18)

Commentary:

There is no doubt that Lord Krishna presented Himself as the Supreme Person (*purusottamah*). Therefore we are to wonder: What happened to all the other personalities who in human history were listed as the Supreme Person? Where do they stand? Readers may form conclusions.

यो मामेवमसंमूढो
जानाति पुरुषोत्तमम् ।
स सर्वविद्भजति मां
सर्वभावेन भारत ॥१५.१९॥
yo māmevamasaṁmūḍho
jānāti puruṣottamam
sa sarvavidbhajati māṁ
sarvabhāvena bhārata (15.19)

yo - yaḥ— who; mām — me; evam — in this way; asaṁmūḍho = asaṁmūḍhaḥ — undeluded; jānāti— knows; puruṣottamam — Supreme Person; sa— he; sarvavit — all-knowing, knowledgeable; bhajati — worships; mām —me; sarvabhāvena — with all being; bhārata — O man of the Bharata family

In this way, he who is undeluded, who knows Me as the Supreme Person, he being knowledgeable, worships Me with all his being, O man of the Bharata family. (15.19)

Commentary:

If a man accepts Lord Krishna's presentation of Himself, that person would naturally worship (*bhajati*) Lord Krishna. If the guarantees offered by Lord Krishna are valid and if a devotee of Krishna can fulfill the pledges indicated, then certainly, everything in the *Gītā* would make perfect sense and the great devotees of Krishna, as described in this verse, would be all-knowing.

इति गुह्यतमं शास्त्रम्
इदमुक्तं मयानघ ।
एतद्बुद्ध्वा बुद्धिमान्स्यात्
कृतकृत्यश्च भारत ॥१५.२०॥
iti guhyatamaṁ śāstram
idamuktaṁ mayānagha
etadbuddhvā buddhimānsyāt
kṛtakṛtyaśca bhārata (15.20)

iti — thus; guhyatamaṁ — most secret; śāstram— teaching; idam — this; uktaṁ— is declared; mayā— by me; 'nagha= anagha — O blameless man; etat — this; buddhvā — having realized; buddhimān —wise; syāt — he should become; kṛtakṛtyaśca = kṛtakṛtyaḥ — with duties accomplished + ca — and; bhārata — O descendant of Bharata

Thus the most secret teaching is declared by Me, O blameless man. Having realized this, O descendant of the Bharatas, one becomes a wise person, whose duties are accomplished. (15.20)

Commentary:

Arjuna had every reason to believe in Lord Krishna. Arjuna had the most convincing proof which was the vision of the Universal Form. Readers of the *Gītā* will, more than likely, not have such proof except in their conceptual acceptance of the revelation received by Arjuna. Thus every reader must form his own opinion about the claims of Krishna.

Persons who are not so certain about these declarations may get more information about Krishna from the *Śrīmad Bhāgavatam*. This scripture is also known as the *Bhāgavata Purāṇa*. We recommend that readers pursue their interest in Krishna to that book. There is another book, however, which gives information about Krishna and that is the *Mahābhārata* of which the *Bhagavad Gītā* is a small but most significant part. As one might carefully remove one special jewel from a heap of gems, so the *Bhagavad Gītā* was removed from the *Mahābhārata*. An interested reader should, if he can, try to understand it in its original setting as part of the *Mahābhārata*.

CHAPTER 16

Two Types of Created Beings*

श्रीभगवानुवाच
अभयं सत्त्वसंशुद्धिर्
ज्ञानयोगव्यवस्थितिः ।
दानं दमश्च यज्ञश्च
स्वाध्यायस्तप आर्जवम् ॥१६.१॥
śrībhagavānuvāca
abhayaṁ sattvasaṁśuddhir
jñānayogavyavasthitiḥ
dānaṁ damaśca yajñaśca
svādhyāyastapa ārjavam (16.1)

Śrī bhagavān — The Blessed Lord; uvāca — said; abhayaṁ — fearlessness; sattvasaṁśuddhiḥ = sattva — existence, being + saṁśuddhiḥ — purity; jñānayogavyavasthitiḥ = jñāna — mental concept + yoga — application of yoga + vyavasthitiḥ — consistence; dānaṁ — charity; damaśca — damaḥ — self-restraint + ca — and; yajñaśca- yajñaḥ— worship ceremony + ca — and; svādhyāyaḥ— recitation of scripture, tapa — austerity; ārjavam — straight-forwardness

The Blessed Lord said: Fearlessness, purity of being, consistency in application of yoga to mental concepts, charity, self-restraint, worship ceremony, recitation of scripture, austerity and straight-forwardness, (16.1)

Commentary:

This is a partial listing which is completed in the next two verses. These are traits of the godly nature. Readers are asked to read verse 3 of Chapter Three, which presents the idea of *jñana yoga*, just as there are explanations about *karma yoga* and *bhakti yoga*. Readers must keep in touch with the meanings of these terms as Krishna explained them to Arjuna.

śrībhagavānuvāca
loke'smindvividhā niṣṭhā purā proktā mayānagha
jñānayogena sāṁkhyānāṁ karmayogena yogināṁ (3.3)

The Blessed Lord said: In the physical world, a two-fold standard was previously taught by Me. O Arjuna, my good man. This was mind regulation by the yoga practice of the Sāṁkhya philosophical yogis and the action regulation by the yoga practice of the non-philosophical yogis. (3.3)

Yoga is a set of practices which came to be known as *yama* (restraints), *niyama* (observances), *āsana* (postures), *prāṇāyāma* (breath control), *pratyāhāra* (withdrawal of senses), *dhāraṇā* (concentration), *dhyāna* (meditation), and *samādhi* (bliss). This is basic yoga. It develops into contemplative disciplines which are known generally as *jñana* yoga or samkhya analysis. Yoga is defined and described in Chapter Six and elsewhere. The application of yoga to our affections is *bhakti yoga*. Whenever one takes yoga disciplines or its disciplinary results and applies them to a certain quality, trait or habit, we get a combined effect in the form of *bhakti yoga, jñana yoga* or *karma yoga*. For instance, Lord Krishna cited Janaka who applied yoga expertise and maturity to administrative duties. Thus Janaka was cited as an expert *karma* yogi. *Karma* means worldly activities. Arjuna was to be an ideal *karma* yogi like Janaka.

**The Mahābhārata contains no chapter headings. This title was assigned by the translator on the basis of verse 6 of this chapter.*

Arjuna cited that he heard the glories of Krishna from *Nārada*. And *Nārada* is rated as the ideal *bhakta* yogi. He applied his yoga expertise to the offering of his affections, love and devotion to Krishna. This is how these various yogas are to be understood. Jñana means knowledge, conception, information, or experience. It also means philosophical ideas. When any of these are regulated by yoga expertise, it is *jñana yoga*. The samkhya philosophers who, according to Lord Krishna, were the experts of *jñana yoga*, were yogi philosophers who researched the psychic and spiritual worlds by mystic penetration. Unlike the *karma* yogis like Janaka, these philosophers were not involved in administrative work but instead worked more on the psychic plane. In the modern societies, their inferior counterparts are known as psychiatrists, psychologists, and philosophers. By using yoga, these ancient samkhya philosophers were able to bring the gross body under a regulation whereby their consciousness switched over to subtle and causal forms. Then they explored the psychic and supernatural worlds which these forms perceive.

अहिंसा सत्यमक्रोधस्
त्यागः शान्तिरपैशुनम् ।
दया भूतेष्वलोलुप्त्वं
मार्दवं ह्रीरचापलम् ॥१६.२॥
ahiṁsā satyamakrodhas
tyāgaḥ śāntirapaiśunam
dayā bhūteṣvaloluptvaṁ
mārdavaṁ hrīracāpalam (16.2)

ahiṁsā — non-violence; satyam — recognition of reality; akrodhaḥ — absence of anger; tyāgaḥ — abandonment of consequences; śāntiḥ — spiritual security; apaiśunam — absence of destructive criticism; dayā — compassion; bhūteṣu — in beings; aloluptvam — freedom from craving; mārdavaṁ — gentleness; hrīḥ — modesty; acāpalam — absence of fickleness

...non-violence, recognition of reality, absence of anger, abandonment of consequences, spiritual security, absence of destructive criticism, compassion for the beings, freedom from craving, gentleness, modesty, absence of fickleness, (16.2)

Commentary:

Non-violence of the *Gītā* is not the type that is usually advocated by meek, compassionate, peace-loving people. Lord Krishna was not a meek individual but was, on occasion, very brazen as the *Mahābhārata* history shows. He was compassionate on occasion and peace-loving too, but He was also warlike. He attacked some persons who were inimical towards Him or antisocial towards the dynasty to which He belonged. The *Bhagavad-Gītā* was spoken to Arjuna to get the hero to fight at *Kurukṣetra*. Arjuna was a meek, compassionate and peace-loving man but Krishna spurred him on with this *Gītā* discourse.

When Arjuna saw the Universal Form, he saw the hostility the Supreme Being hurled at the limited souls who were in opposition, but that occurred on a supernatural level. Arjuna actually saw that the super-people of the Universal Form were biting off heads, crushing faces with fearsome teeth, and blowing fires to burn others to death. Those who say that *ahimsā* (nonviolence) of the *Gītā* means no violence at all, are harboring a misconception.

On the other hand, we hear of the brahmins described by Lord Krishna. This type of individual exhibits no hostility to anyone but neither Krishna nor Arjuna were in the brahmin caste. And therefore, in Krishna's view, the brahmin's way of life did not apply to them. In fact, when Arjuna wanted to go to the forest to join the brahmins for a peace-loving life, Lord Krishna insulted him as a cowardly fellow who wanted to act ignobly. And the Lord used several strong arguments, some of which were purely social, to get Arjuna stirred up enough to draw bow and arrow. Of course, He told Arjuna to remain detached and to act as an administrative law man on the battlefield. It is a great mistake and distortion too, to give the idea that the *Gītā* means non-violence as an absolute pacificism. It does not. If a person believes in such an absolute pacificism, he should say so but he should not falsely accredit it to the *Gītā*, except for the statement about the brahmin ascetics.

Satyam is usually given as truthfulness. I gave, the **recognition of reality**. This is in keeping with the *Gītā* which is not so much concerned with our personal honesty as it is with the truths of reality, as explained by Krishna.

Akrodhas, the **absence of anger**, is an experience of every creature, but it is not a consistent feeling for most beings. Material existence does mean a scramble for mundane resources and an exhibition of an exploitative tendency. Anger is inevitably present whenever we are frustrated in expectations. The *Gītā* does, however, provide recommendations for our freedom from anger. Insofar as we apply the advice, that is how much we would consistently exhibit good qualities. In my honest opinion, I feel that most of these qualities are idealistic. We cannot achieve these easily, nor by any quick method but only by a great simplification of needs. So long as we have mundane desires to fulfill, there will be an exhibition of bad qualities. We can try to minimize these but until we are freed from the need for this material world, the undesirable qualities will remain. We should continue aspiring for a reduction of bad qualities but we should not think that they will vanish overnight. It will require great determination and prolonged endeavor.

Tyāgah is the practice of **abandoning consequences**. In material existence we are presented with many opportunities for enjoyment and many circumstances for enduring suffering. If we become stalled, reacting to each and every presentation of destiny, we will become more and more implicated. A person who is attached to enjoyments is considered to be vice-prone and one who is attached to sufferings is considered to be sadistic. In either case, one should learn how to abandon consequences.

Śāntir (**spiritual peace**) is often confused with the peace a man feels when he is materially secured by health and influence. But that type of security is not *śāntir*. *Śāntir* means the spiritual peace felt while experiencing the eternity of the spirit. This peace eliminates the fear of extinction of one's personality, the fear of death. *Śāntir* also means to understand the relationship between one's spirit and the Supreme Spirit. This relationship is described in detail in the *Gītā*.

Apaiśūnam is the **absence of destructive criticism**. When there is no backbiting, one has reached this stage. Unless we get busy with our own business of spiritual advancement, we will, of necessity, be involved in such backbiting because it is natural to be critical of others when we are not attentive to personal flaws.

Dayā bhūteṣv means **compassion for beings**. In material existence each limited entity is, for the most part, selfish. Even the so-called selfless personalities are selfish, except that they discovered the most practical or operational form of selfishness in the form of selflessness. Those who are immature do not realize that it is in their interest to be selfless. To offset excessive selfishness, one has to exhibit compassion or mercy for others. But one should not exhibit compassion to those who do not require favors. One man might be wealthy but that does not mean that he should offer money to another whose wealth is a thousand times greater than his own. And unless requested, a wealthy man should not offer advice to a philosopher. When compassion is offered in an irregular, inconsiderate way, it brings unfavorable reactions. Compassion is a desirable quality but it brings degradation if it is not tempered with discretion towards the ways of destiny. Bharata, the son of *Ṛṣabha*, exhibited compassion for a deer and took an animal body in the next life. He absorbed the animal's profile by close association.

Aloluptvam means **freedom from cravings**. Many modern seekers feel or are told by authorities that this freedom is merely a matter of willingness to change. Some say that it is merely a matter of desire. Both views are simplistic. A living entity is so limited that his little desire to change and his little, little willingness to go in the right direction, hardly affects anything. Material nature is so powerful of a motivator that she does not give much allowance to our wishes. We are motivated but we do not motivate. We can, however, endeavor to shift ourselves to a higher motivation.

For freedom from cravings, one has to study his psychology and then take steps to purify it. Then the motivations will change. The question is: How do I purify my material nature? The answer is this: Our material nature is purified by purifying the life energy of the subtle body. In the time of Lord Krishna, this was done by *prāṇāyāma*. Modern authorities, especially Vaishnava spiritual masters, claim that one can be purified by mantras and not by *prāṇa*. But this statement has to be substantiated. Before one can purify his material or spiritual nature by mantra, he has to reach a level whereby his system of consciousness and his lower energies become sensitive to mantras, special Sanskrit sounds.

Mantra means sound. We see that in the modern car industry, technicians make a small gadget which can open a car door from thirty feet away. Even without touching the car, the user can press a pad on the gadget to activate the door locks. This is, in effect, a use of a mantra or sound. A sound leaves the gadget, and enters the door to trigger a mechanism which unlocks it. This is not imagination. This actually takes place. Thus if one can make his mantra (sacred sound) change his psychology, then he has found an energy-improving gadget.

Mārdavan or **gentleness**, is opposed to harshness in social dealings. Harshness is appropriate on occasion but as a general feature, one should be gentle towards others. Arjuna wanted to be gentle on the warfield, but Krishna objected. Arjuna's mother, the baroness *Kuntī*, also objected to Yudhishthira's inappropriate gentleness. Thus even this desirable quality can implicate a man if he does not use his intelligence to guide it

Hṛīh or **modesty**, is always appropriate when we face the Supreme. Any limited being has to be modest towards providence. But such modesty also includes being a servant or agent of providence. One should not deny providence when asked to complete a harsh duty, for humility also includes submitting oneself for service to providence.

Acāpalam or the **absence of fickleness**, is a very difficult quality to cultivate. Its development comes in stages as one gradually becomes purified. The impulsiveness of the subtle body is derived from the life energy, which is a system of energy in its own right. Thus one must learn how this system affects the intellect, mind, and senses. One should curb this enthusing power. The best process for curbing this energy is the *prāṇāyāma* discipline.

तेजः क्षमा धृतिः शौचम्
अद्रोहो नातिमानिता ।
भवन्ति संपदं दैवीम्
अभिजातस्य भारत ॥१६.३॥
tejaḥ kṣamā dhṛtiḥ śaucam
adroho nātimānitā
bhavanti saṁpadaṁ daivīm
abhijātasya bhārata (16.3)

tejaḥ — vigor; kṣamā— forbearance; dhṛtiḥ— strong-mindedness; śaucam — purity; adroho = adrohaḥ — freedom from hatred; nātimānitā = na — not + ātimānitā — conceit; bhavanti — they are; saṁpadaṁ — nature; daivīm - godly; abhijātasya — of those born; bhārata — O desendant of Bharata

...vigor, forbearance, strong-mindedness, purity, freedom from hatred, and the freedom from conceit; these are the talents of those born with the godly nature, O descendent of Bharata. (16.3)

Commentary:

Tejah or **vigor**, is the vital power of material life. This power is based on fire or heat. It is a mundane energy surcharged by spiritual force. Each form in the material world has this vital power but only certain forms efficiently reflect it.

Kṣamā or **forbearance**, is the quality of enduring abuse. This quality is best represented in the earth, which is forbearing towards our careless exploitative tendencies. Fruit trees display the quality of forbearance. When children approach a fruit tree, they do not consider its kindness. They yank the fruits off and go away.

Dhṛtih or **strong-mindedness**, is realized as determination to perform a task. Of all spirits in material existence, the Supreme One is the most determined. Still, even God must contend with the other realities. Even the Supreme Spirit has to deal with some of the stubborn traits of the mundane power and of the limited entities whom He supervises. Arjuna saw the struggle in the apparition of the Universal Form.

Śaucam or **purity** by the standards of the *Gītā*, applies physically, emotionally, and mentally. It applies on the subtle and supernatural levels as well. Basic purity, however, which is practical for most human beings, pertains to external cleanliness of the body and a willingness to follow moral principles which keep the living entity from being unfair towards others.

Adroho or **freedom from hatred**, is exhibited periodically by all living beings but its deliberate cultivation produces a rare entity who is equally disposed to all. This type of person is described at length in Chapters Six and Twelve of the *Gītā*. Periodic exhibition of kindness has little to do with cultivated kindness which becomes rooted in every act of an advanced soul.

Nātimānitā or **freedom from conceit**, is another quality which may be exhibited periodically even in a conceited person. When a person reaches the threshold of honesty, through which he can see those qualities which are innate within him and those which are not, he can take steps to cultivate the desirable character traits. In that sense, the material world is our big opportunity for change. These qualities listed in this and the two preceding verses, are said by Krishna to be those of the godly nature. By taking note of these, a human being can endeavor for self-improvement.

दम्भो दर्पोऽतिमानश्च
क्रोधः पारुष्यमेव च ।
अज्ञानं चाभिजातस्य
पार्थ संपदमासुरीम् ॥ १६.४॥

dambho darpo'timānaśca
krodhaḥ pāruṣyameva ca
ajñānaṁ cābhijātasya
pārtha saṁpadamāsurīm (16.4)

dambho = dambhaḥ — deceit; darpo — darpaḥ — arrogance; 'timānaśca -atimānaśca - atimānaḥ — conceit + ca — and; krodhaḥ — anger; pāruṣyam — abusive language; eva — indeed; ca —and; ajñānaṁ — lack of knowledge; cābhijātasya = ca — and + abhijātasya — of those born; pārtha — son of Pṛthā; saṁpadam — tendency; āsurīm — those with a wicked nature

Deceit, arrogance, conceit, anger, abusive language, and lack of knowledge are the tendencies of those born with a wicked nature, O son of Pṛthā. (16.4)

Commentary:

Dambho or **deceit**, means fradulent activities or trickery. This is part and parcel of material existence. Since the life energy of every creature is selfishly motivated, it is a special task for an entity to curtail his mundane needs and thus reduce deceit. There are kind ways to cheat others and hostile ways also. One may cheat another person by being permissive and affectionate towards him. Or one may cheat him by being dictatorial and cruel. It all depends on the motive in dealings. Usually an act is judged by its results, but there is a deeper way of analysis: That of the motive. However, those without mystic insight must rely on the more inaccurate method of judging by results. A person's reaction, however, depends on his maturity and therefore if one is immature he may react unfavorably even to an act which is in his interest.

Darpo or **arrogance**, is the ability to convert an allowance of providence into a display of false supremacy. Opportunities are awarded to living entities on the basis of their past pious acts. The living beings forget most of their past acts but material nature absorbs these and responds to all of them at a later date. If an act is pious, material nature gives an opportunity to do more good but a living entity may instead, become arrogant, rude as it were. Material nature then allows him to use up his merits in a vicious way. But once his merits are exhausted, he loses the controlling power.

'bhimānas (abhimānas) is **conceit** or false pride. When an apostrophe (') is used in English lettering of Sanskrit words, it indicates that an *"a"* is missing. Hence, *'bhimānas* is actually an abbreviated form of *abhimānas*. False pride has value in assisting us with insecurities. It is a way of propping ourselves up existentially. When we find it uncomfortable to rely on others, on material nature, or on providence, we shift to a state of conceit and act accordingly. There are limitations in each one of us. One might become embarrassed when he realizes his incompleteness. Thus a false pride may develop to offset the resulting insecurity.

Krodhah or **anger**, arises from frustration in objectives. Many of our ideas are impractical. Many of our desires are inordinate and unreasonable for ourselves as limited souls. Thus anger is a necessity. It will remain dominant until we can accept limitations.

Pāruṣyam means **abusive language**. It also means the extension of such language. Abusive language begins in the mind as abuse vibrations. These are converted into abusive thoughts. If such ideas are not checked, they are converted into insultive speech. If this is not checked, it is converted into hostile actions. This is part of the range of frustrations. Material existence happens to be our challenge. In this existence, we must either prove ourselves or make the attempt to scale down our role and get out of the world.

Ajñanam is a **lack of knowledge**. This is our symptom of existence. As Lord Krishna told Arjuna:

śrībhagavānuvāca
bahūni me vyatītāni janmāni tava cārjuna
tānyahaṁ veda sarvāṇi na tvaṁ vettha paraṁtapa (4.5)
The Blessed Lord said: Many of My births transpired, and yours, Arjuna. I recall them all. You do not remember, O scorcher of the enemies. (4.5)

This means that we have some enthusiasm or some passion to act in this world but we do not have the sense and recall of experience to grade the effects of different actions. Thus we have to rely on the superior beings for advisories. If we lack superior guidance, we will make mistakes. This is just one aspect of reliance. We have so many incapacities. The only solution is to take the divine association.

There is a middle ground between the godly and the wicked natures. Those of us who are somewhere in between, may evolve our way out of the wicked type into a godly type and so improve the moral status. The first step is to admit particular deficiencies and then work systematically for their curtailment, reduction, and final elimination.

दैवी संपद्विमोक्षाय
निबन्धायासुरी मता ।
मा शुचः संपदं दैवीम्
अभिजातोऽसि पाण्डव ॥१६.५॥
daivī saṁpadvimokṣāya
nibandhāyāsurī matā
mā śucaḥ saṁpadaṁ daivīm
abhijāto'si pāṇḍava (16.5)

daivī — godly; saṁpad — talent; vimokṣāya - to liberation; nibandhāyāsurī = nibandhāyā — to bondage + āsurī — wicked tendency; matā — considered to be; mā — not; śucaḥ -worry; saṁpadaṁ — nature; daivīm — godly; abhijāto = abhijātaḥ — born; 'si = asi — you are; pāṇḍava — son of Pāndu

The godly talent is conducive to liberation. It is considered that the wicked tendencies facilitate bondage. Do not worry. You are endowed with the godly nature, O son of Pāndu. (16.5)

<u>*Commentary:*</u>

The godly talents keep one closer to the clarifying mode of material nature, through which one gets a glimpse of spiritual freedom. The wicked traits take one closer to the depressing mode which brings on more bondage. If one is predominantly good, he will, on occasion, be influenced by impulsion and depression. But his general performance will be in the clarifying mode.

द्वौ भूतसर्गौ लोकेऽस्मिन्
दैव आसुर एव च ।
दैवो विस्तरशः प्रोक्त
आसुरं पार्थ मे श्रृणु ॥१६.६॥
dvau bhūtasargau loke'smin
daiva āsura eva ca
daivo vistaraśaḥ prokta
āsuraṁ pārtha me śṛṇu (16.6)

dvau — two; bhūtasargau = bhūta — being + sargau — two created types; loke — in the world; 'smin = asmin — in this; daiva — godly; āsura — wicked; eva — indeed; ca — and; daivo = daivah— godly type; viṣṭaraśaḥ — in detail; prokta — explained; āsuraṁ— wicked; pārtha— son of Pṛthā; me — from me; śṛṇu — hear

There are two types of created beings in this world, the godly type and the wicked. The godly type was explained in detail. Hear from me of the wicked, O son of Pṛthā. (16.6)

<u>*Commentary:*</u>

Readers should now go back to Chapter 15, text 16 to distinguish the terms *puruṣau* and *bhūtasargau*. *Puruṣau* means *spirit*, and *bhūtasargau* is the same as *bhūtani* which is used extensively in the *Gītā*. It means, *the mundane beings*. This applies to the vehicles or bodily forms used by the spirits. But these forms exist only on the physical and psychic planes.

dvāvimau puruṣau loke kṣaraścākṣara eva ca
kṣaraḥ sarvāṇi bhūtāni kūṭastho'kṣara ucyate (15.16)

These two types of spirits are in this world, namely the affected ones and the unaffected ones. All mundane creatures are affected. The stable soul is said to be unaffected. (15.16)

The two types of spirits, the affected and unaffected ones, use various types of bodies but essentially only two attitudes in bodies are available. These are listed as forms with godly or with vicious inclincations.

We should not, as we usually do, confuse the spirit and the body it uses. A distinction of this is made throughout the *Gītā*, particularly in Chapter Thirteen, verse 2:

śrībhagavānuvāca
idaṁ śarīraṁ kaunteya kṣetramityabhidhīyate
etadyo vetti taṁ prāhuḥ kṣetrajña iti tadvidaḥ(13.2)

The Blessed Lord said: This, the earthly body, O son of Kuntī , is called the living space. Those who are knowledgeable of this, declare the person who understands this to be the experiencer of the living space. (13.2)

However, we must understand that those spirits who are in the affected category (*kṣara*) do adopt the attitude of the particular body being used and do carry the acquired tendencies from one old body to a new one. This means that if an affected spirit takes a body with vicious inclinations, he will, of necessity, carry those predatory instincts to his next body even if the next body is that of a cow or human being. Of course, in a gentle form, he would not exhibit as much viciousness as he did in the predatory form but he would, by instinct, be as vicious as possible. It is, however, different with the unaffected spirits (*akṣara*). Even upon taking vicious forms, they resist the wicked urges. Prahlada is an example. He took a body as a prince in the family of vicious rulers, but he acted piously from the very onset. Thus he is qualified as a spirit who is resistant to the modes of material nature (*akṣara*).

प्रवृत्तिं च निवृत्तिं च
जना न विदुरासुराः ।
न शौचं नापि चाचारो
न सत्यं तेषु विद्यते ॥१६.७॥
pravṛttiṁ ca nivṛttiṁ ca
janā na vidurāsurāḥ
na śaucaṁ nāpi cācāro
na satyaṁ teṣu vidyate (16.7)

pravṛttiṁ— what to do; ca — and; nivṛttiṁ— what not to do; ca — and; janā — people; na — not; viduḥ — they know; āsurāḥ— wicked; na — neither; śaucaṁ— cleanliness; nāpi = na — nor + api — also; cācāro = cācāraḥ = ca — and + ācāraḥ — good conduct; na — nor; satyam — realism; teṣu — in them; vidyate — is found

The wicked people do not know what to do and what not to do. Neither cleanliness or even good conduct, nor realism is found in them. (16.7)

Commentary:

When we are affected by the impulsive and depressing moods, our plans become impractical. We make mistakes. The priorities we have when we are in the clarifying mode vanish when we are overcome by the lower perception. Thus we lose sight of what to do and what not to do. In that confusion, neither cleanliness nor good conduct, honesty nor self respect is found.

असत्यमप्रतिष्ठं ते
जगदाहुरनीश्वरम् ।
अपरस्परसंभूतं
किमन्यत्कामहैतुकम् ॥१६.८॥
asatyamapratiṣṭhaṁ te
jagadāhuranīśvaram
aparasparasaṁbhūtaṁ
kimanyatkāmahaitukam (16.8)

asatyam — unreal; apratiṣṭhaṁ — without a foundation; te — they; jagat — the world; āhuḥ — they say; anīśvaram — without a Supreme Lord; aparasparasaṁbhūtaṁ = aparaspara — without a series of causes + saṁbhūtaṁ — produced; kim — what?; anyat— other cause; kāmahaitukam = kāma — sensual urge + haitukam — caused

They say that the universe is unreal, without a foundation, without a Supreme Lord, without a series of causes. They explain, saying, "Sexual urge is the cause. What other basis could there be?" (16.8)

Commentary:

The theory of creation through lust is an old one, known even in the time of Krishna and Arjuna. And the belief in a Supreme God was present at that time too. Some who feel that the universe evolves through sexual urges, by random selection and combination, do not acknowledge any sort of religious belief and feel that religion is a superimposition.

एतां दृष्टिमवष्टभ्य
नष्टात्मानोऽल्पबुद्धयः ।
प्रभवन्त्युग्रकर्माणः
क्षयाय जगतोऽहिताः ॥१६.९॥
etāṁ dṛṣṭimavaṣṭabhya
naṣṭātmāno'lpabuddhayaḥ
prabhavantyugrakarmāṇaḥ
kṣayāya jagato'hitāḥ (16.9)

etāṁ — this; dṛṣṭim — view; avaṣṭabhya — holding; naṣṭātmāno = naṣṭātmānaḥ = naṣṭa — lost + ātmānaḥ — to their spiritual selves; 'lpabuddhayaḥ = alpabuddhayaḥ = alpa — negligible + buddhayaḥ — intelligence; prabhavanti — they become; ugrakarmāṇaḥ = ugra — cruel + karmāṇaḥ — acts; kṣayāya — to destruction; jagato = jagataḥ — of the world; 'hitāḥ = ahitāḥ — enemies

Holding this view, men who lost track of their spirituality, who have negligible intelligence, who commit cruel acts, become enemies for the destruction of the world. (16.9)

Commentary:

If a man reasons that there is no Supreme Lord, he indicates that there is no accountability for irresponsible acts. Thus, such a person would easily commit criminal actions and exhibit terrorist activities.

A belief in a Supreme God or at least a belief in superior entities is part and parcel of a belief in one's own spirituality. Thus we find that those who do not believe in God are usually disbelieving in a personal spirituality.

काममाश्रित्य दुष्पूरं
दम्भमानमदान्विताः ।
मोहाद्गृहीत्वासद्ग्राहान्
प्रवर्तन्तेऽशुचिव्रताः ॥१६.१०
kāmamāśritya duṣpūraṁ
dambhamānamadānvitāḥ
mohādgṛhītvāsadgrāhān
pravartante'śucivratāḥ (16.10)

kāmam — lusty urge; āśritya — relying; duṣpūraṁ —non-fulfilling; dambhamānamadānvitāḥ = dambba — hypocrisy + māna —pride + mada — intoxicated + anvitāḥ — possessed by; mohāt —from delusion; gṛhītvā — having accepted; 'sadgrāhān = asadgrāhān = asad (asat) — unrealistic + grāhān — views; pravartante — they proceed; 'śucivratāḥ = aśucivratāḥ = aśuci — impure + vratāḥ — objectives

Being reliant on the non-fulfilling lusty urge, possessed of hypocrisy, pride, and intoxication, having accepted unrealistic views, through delusion, they proceed with impure objectives. (16.10)

Commentary:

Kāman āśritya means that a person is reliant on lusty urges, but when *duṣpūram* is added it means that the urges are the type which cannot be fulfilled. These are impractical desires which cause frustration. As Lord Krishna taught in Chapter Two:

dhyāyato viṣayānpuṁsaḥ saṅgasteṣūpajāyate
saṅgātsaṁjāyate kāmaḥ kāmātkrodho'bhijāyate (2.62)
krodhādbhavati saṁmohaḥ saṁmohātsmṛtivibhramaḥ
smṛtibhraṁśādbuddhināśo buddhināśātpraṇaśyati (2.63)

The act of considering sensual objects, creates in a person, an attachment to them. From attachment comes craving. From this craving anger is derived.

From anger, comes delusion. From this delusion, the conscience vanishes. When he loses judgment, his discerning power fades away. Once the discernment is affected, he is ruined. (2.62-63)

Desires manifest in the mind of every man but one should sort between the realistic and non-realistic ones. In this way one may abandon unrealistic hopes and work in a practical way, thus greatly decreasing frustration. Even with realistic desires there might be frustration. We have to consider other factors which contribute to the fulfillment of desires, namely:

adhiṣṭhānaṁ tathā kartā karaṇaṁ ca pṛthagvidham
vividhāśca pṛthakceṣṭā daivaṁ caivātra pañcama (18.14)

The location, the agent, the various instruments, the various movements, and destiny, the fifth factor. (18.14)

'śucivratāh (*aśucivratāh*), the impure objective, arises naturally in the mind of a person who is reliant on insatiable desires. Thus, in trying to carve out a life in this material existence, we may, when we become possessed of madness, act irresponsibly as we are driven by corrupt ideas.

चिन्तामपरिमेयां च
प्रलयान्तामुपाश्रिताः ।
कामोपभोगपरमा
एतावदिति निश्चिताः ॥१६.११॥
cintāmaparimeyāṁ ca
pralayāntāmupāśritāḥ
kāmopabhogaparamā
etāvaditi niścitāḥ (16.11)

cintām — worry; aparimeyāṁ — endless; ca — and; pralayāntām — ending at death; upāśritāḥ — clinging; kāmopabhogaparamā = kāma — lust + upabhoga — enjoyment + paramā — highest aim; etāvat — so much; iti — thus; niścitāḥ — convinced

And clinging to endless worries which end at the time of death, with lusty enjoyment as the highest aim, being convinced that this is all there is, (16.11)

Commentary:

As modern people in a well-developed civilization, we are quite familiar with the habit of clinging to problems and trying day after day to apply solutions which only work in part and which bring on even more problems to which we become attached, producing an endless cycle of worries and emotional stress. The general aim of our modern civilzation is described herein as *kāmopabhoga*, which is the on-going enjoyment of cravings which are spearheaded by sexual and political exploitation.

This writer has many friends who cling to endless worries. These persons, males and females alike, become annoyed if I do not agree to share in problems. And these friends are devotees. They are supposed to be godly people and yet they cling to worries about health, money, status, family relationships, sexual needs, and many other routine necessities. Thus even devotees are afflicted with disturbances. We can just imagine the condition of those persons who do not attempt to cultivate spiritual life.

आशापाशशतैर्बद्धाः
कामक्रोधपरायणाः ।
ईहन्ते कामभोगार्थम्
अन्यायेनार्थसंचयान् ॥१६.१२॥
āśāpāśaśatairbaddhāḥ
kāmakrodhaparāyaṇāḥ
īhante kāmabhogārtham
anyāyenārthasaṁcayān
(16.12)

āśāpāśaśataiḥ = āśāpāśa — frustrating expectations + śataiḥ — by a hundred; baddhāḥ — bound; kāmakrodhaparāyaṇāḥ = kāma — craving + krodha — anger + parāyaṇāḥ — cherishing; īhante — they strive to acquire; kāmabhogārtham = kāma — craving + bhoga — pleasure + artham — fulfillment; anyāyenārthasañcayān = anyāyena — with any other + artha — money + sañcayān — huge sums

...bound by hundreds of frustrating expectations, cherishing craving and anger, using any means, they strive to acquire huge sums of money for the fulfillment of craving and pleasure. (16.12)

Commentary:

This is an accurate description of our modern condition. Krishna stated this about the wicked people, but in the modern era, the godly people are afflicted in this way as well. We must, therefore, ask ourselves if the definition of godliness was adjusted since the time of Krishna. This is an accurate description of our present condition.

इदमद्य मया लब्धम्
इदं प्राप्स्ये मनोरथम् ।
इदमस्तीदमपि मे
भविष्यति पुनर्धनम् ॥१६.१३
idamadya mayā labdham
idaṁ prāpsye manoratham
idamastīdamapi me
bhaviṣyati punardhanam (16.13)

idam — this; adya — today; mayā — by me; labdham — obtained; idaṁ — this; prāpsye — I will fulfill; manoratham — fantasy; idam — this; astīdam = asti — it is + idam — this; api — also; me — mine; bhaviṣyati — willl be; punaḥ — again, also; dhanam — wealth

Thinking: "This was obtained by me today, I will fulfill this fantasy. This is it. This wealth will also be mine. (16.13)

Commentary:

This again, is a description of our condition. We waste so much emotional and mental energy with inordinate, impractical desires, feeling that we can manipulate material nature and bring the supernatural agency under control. And the worst of us are the devotees, who do this in the name of religion. We are those very same people who spearhead this type of crazy, pressurized thinking and hoping.

असौ मया हतः शत्रुर्
हनिष्ये चापरानपि ।
ईश्वरोऽहमहं भोगी
सिद्धोऽहं बलवान्सुखी ॥१६.१४॥

asau — that; mayā — by me; hataḥ — was killed; śatruḥ — enemy; haniṣye — I will kill; cāparān = ca — and + aparān — others; api — as well as; īśvaro = īśvaraḥ — controller; 'ham = aham — I; aham — I;

asau mayā hataḥ śatrur
haniṣye cāparānapi
īśvaro'hamahaṁ bhogī
siddho'haṁ balavānsukhī (16.14)

bhogī — enjoyer; siddho = siddhaḥ — successful; 'ham = aham — I; balavān — powerful; sukhī — happy

"That enemy was killed by me, I will kill others as well. I am the controller. I am the enjoyer. I am successful, powerful and happy. (16.14)

Commentary:

This is a description of a criminal's mentality. But there were instances of modern devotees who assumed this demeanor all in the name of God and religion. Generally, the impious people feel this way about themselves and project pressures in human society for the manifestation of their schemes.

आढ्योऽभिजनवानस्मि
कोऽन्योऽस्ति सदृशो मया ।
यक्ष्ये दास्यामि मोदिष्य
इत्यज्ञानविमोहिताः ॥१६.१५॥
āḍhyo'bhijanavānasmi
ko'nyo'sti sadṛśo mayā
yakṣye dāsyāmi modiṣya
ityajñānavimohitāḥ (16.15)

āḍhyo = āḍhyaḥ — rich; 'bhijanavān = abhijanavān — upper class; asmi — I am; ko = kaḥ — who; 'nyo = anyaḥ — other; 'sti = asti — there is; sadṛśo = sadṛśaḥ — like; mayā — me; yakṣye — I will perform religious ceremony; dāsyāmi — I will give in, donate; modiṣya — I will make merry; iti — thus is said; ajñānavimohitāḥ = ajñāna — ignorance + vimohitāḥ — those who are deluded

"I am rich and upper class. Who is there besides me? I will perform religious ceremony. I will donate. I will make merry." This is what is said by those who are deluded by ignorance. (16.15)

Commentary:

A particular thinking pattern, its motivations and manifestations, is dictated to the living entity by the pushing influence of material nature. We may select which of the three modes we desire to be influenced by but the task only begins there. After the selection, we have to perform certain austerities if we want to live by the influence of the clarifying mode. Without the prescribed austerities, our selection would fail to manifest. Our wishing and thinking is insufficient for results. By prescribed austerities, we move ourselves into a position to act out noble aims.

अनेकचित्तविभ्रान्ता
मोहजालसमावृताः ।
प्रसक्ताः कामभोगेषु
पतन्ति नरकेऽशुचौ ॥१६.१६॥
anekacittavibhrāntā
mohajālasamāvṛtāḥ
prasaktāḥ kāmabhogeṣu
patanti narake'śucau (16.16)

anekacittavibhrāntā = aneka — many + citta — idea + vibhrāntā — carried away; mohajālasamāvṛtāh = moha — delusion + jāla — entanglement + samāvṛtāḥ — occupied by; prasaktāḥ — being attached; kāmabhogeṣu — kāma — craving + bhogeṣu — in enjoyments; patanti — they fall; narake — in hellish condition; 'śucau = aśucau — unclean

Being carried away by many ideas, being occupied by entangling delusions, being attached by cravings and enjoyments, they fall into an unclean, hellish condition. (16.16)

Commentary:

This *narake* (hell) is not something imaginary. According to the Vedic literatures, there are hells which are just as real as the earthly life we presently endure. A person who acts in a socially hostile way, who victimizes others and expresses an exploitative force upon the creation, is sent to certain hells after death. The question of what survives at the time of death is answered simply: The psyche. The thinking and psychic feelings survive. That portion of the human being suffers in a subtle place in the hereafter. But despite this, many suffer in physical prisons which are a type of hell. Some suffer in their minds and feelings which are another type of misery.

If our minds are engrossed in delusive ideas, we are apt to follow crazy schemes. Being occupied with vain hopes and worries, we have no peace of mind. We irritate others and act as nuisances to society.

आत्मसंभाविताः स्तब्धा
धनमानमदान्विताः ।
यजन्ते नामयज्ञैस्ते
दम्भेनाविधिपूर्वकम् ॥१६.१७॥
ātmasaṁbhāvitāḥ stabdhā
dhanamānamadānvitāḥ
yajante nāmayajñaiste
dambhenāvidhipūrvakam (16.17)

ātmasaṁbhāvitāḥ — self-conceited; stabdhā — stubborn; dhanamānamadānvitāḥ = dhanamāna — arrogance of having money + mada — pride + anvitāḥ — possessed with; yajante — they worship in ceremony; nāmayajñaiḥ — with religious ceremony in name only; te — they; dambhenāvidhipūrvakam = dambhena — with hyprocrisy + avidhipurvakam — without reference to Vedic injunction

Self-conceited, stubborn, possessed of pride and the arrogance of having money, with hypocrisy and without reference to Vedic injunctions, they worship in ceremonies that are religious in name only. (16.17)

Commentary:

These qualities are expressed under the impulsive or passionate mode and the depressing or stupifying mode. Under the influence of such energies, the spirit soul loses track of his discerning power and cannot act in self-interest. He must, therefore, take hints from more elevated souls to understand how to get out of the predicament. It is one thing to point a finger, saying, "He is evil." It is another matter to understand that even though I may be pious today, I could be impious tomorrow, all depending on the particular influence which bears upon me.

Let us say, for example, that I am a morally-inclined man. Then I pass from my body. Then I assume birth in a low-class family. I grow up in a criminal environment. I adopt dishonest ways of life. Then, I, the same pious person, would be acting in an immoral way. It is possible.

So much of my good fortune and good behavior depends on social circumstances. It is not that I am absolutely independent in the matter of adopting moral patterns. My so-called free will or self will, is limited. It is conditioned by many other pressures.

अहंकारं बलं दर्पं
कामं क्रोधं च संश्रिताः ।
मामात्मपरदेहेषु
प्रद्विषन्तोऽभ्यसूयकाः ॥१६.१८॥

ahaṁkāraṁ —misplaced self-identity; balam — brute force; darpaṁ — arrogance; kāmaṁ — craving; krodhaṁ — anger; ca — and; saṁśritāḥ — clinging to; mām — me; ātmaparadeheṣu =

ahaṁkāraṁ balaṁ darpaṁ
kāmaṁ krodhaṁ ca saṁśritāḥ
māmātmaparadeheṣu
pradviṣanto'bhyasūyakāḥ (16.18)

ātma — self + para — other + deheṣu — in bodies; pradviṣanto = pradviṣantaḥ — disliking; 'bhyasūyakāḥ = abhyasūyakāḥ — those who are envious

Clinging to a misplaced self-identity, brute force, arrogance, craving and anger, those who are envious dislike Me, in their own bodies and in those of others. (16.18)

Commentary:

One clings to these negative qualities by a strong sense of insecurity, being uncertain of one's continuation. In a state of ignorance, the dislike for the Lord is indeliberate but real, nevertheless. A person with negative qualities senses the Divinity in his own form and in that of others, and keeps a safe distance from the rectifying influence of the Lord. Since, in most cases, the Lord does not force Himself into the consciousness of the soul, a particular personality might exist for a long time, without being adjusted by the divine mercy.

As a blind man may not like the sun even though he has not seen it, so an insecure living entity may dislike the Lord. And therefore a dislike for the influence of God develops. This repulsion can be removed gradually by positive association with saintly persons who understand self-reform. *Samśritāh* means a reliance or dependence upon someone or something. An insecure living entity relies on the lower modes of material nature. Therefore the problems are solved if he is trained to transfer his dependence on higher realities. This transference takes time, lots of time. It requires great care and patience by those doing missionary work.

तानहं द्विषतः क्रूरान्
संसारेषु नराधमान् ।
क्षिपाम्यजस्रमशुभान्
आसुरीष्वेव योनिषु ॥ १६.१९
tānahaṁ dviṣataḥ krūrān
saṁsāreṣu narādhamān
kṣipāmyajasramaśubhān
āsurīṣveva yoniṣu (16.19)

tān — them; aham — I; dviṣataḥ — those who are despising; krūrān — those who are cruel; saṁsāreṣu — in the cycles of rebirth; narādhamān — lowest of humans; kṣipāmi — I hurl; ajasram — constantly; aśubhān — the vicious; āsurīṣu — into the wicked people; eva — indeed; yoniṣu — in the wombs

I constantly hurl the despising, cruel, vicious, lowest of humans into the cycles of rebirth in the wombs of wicked people. (16.19)

Commentary:

This is a most unusual statement, revealing the personal attitude of Krishna towards those souls who are persistently wicked or who remain under the influence of the lower modes. Being dissatisfied with their lack of progress, Lord Krishna stated that He constantly (*ajasram*) hurls them or sends them headlong into degenerate rebirths.

Degradation into bad parental situations occurs automatically. Lord Krishna explained elsewhere that the spirit carries dispositions from one body to another. He takes a new body in a situation that is harmonious with, matching of, his developed demeanor. Still, Lord Krishna explained His action of hurling or sending wicked souls who despise the divine influence.

आसुरीं योनिमापन्ना
मूढा जन्मनि जन्मनि ।
मामप्राप्यैव कौन्तेय
ततो यान्त्यधमां गतिम् ॥ १६.२० ॥
āsurīṁ yonimāpannā
mūḍhā janmani janmani
māmaprāpyaiva kaunteya
tato yāntyadhamāṁ gatim (16.20)

āsurīṁ— the wicked people; yonim — womb; āpannā — entering; mūḍhā — the blockheads; janmani janmani — in birth, in birth again; mām — me; aprāpyaivā = aprāpya — associating + eva — indeed; kaunteya — O son of Kuntī; tato = tataḥ — thence; yānti — they traverse; adhamāṁ — lowest; gatim — route of transmigration

Thus, O son of Kuntī, entering the wombs of the wicked people, the blockheads, after not associating with Me in birth after birth, traverse the lowest route of transmigration. (16.20)

Commentary:

This is another spectacular statement by Lord Krishna. Considering Krishna's urging that Arjuna should fight and chastise the corrupt Kurus, considering what Arjuna saw in the apparition when the Kurus were being sprayed with fire, bitten and chewed, it is not surprising to hear this statement from Krishna.

The lowest route (*adhamām gatim*) is the path to animal life which leads to even lower life forms. This route is the transmigration avenue through which the soul experiences the existence of lower species where his intellectual and spiritual development are stifled.

By this philosophy of Krishna, we may conclude the following:

- An affected entity (*kṣarah puruṣah, 15.16*) is reliant on association with Lord Krishna to remain in a high species of life either as a pious human being or as a celestial personage.
- If the affected spirit is barred that association, he takes birth through criminally-minded, vice-prone parents.
- Such birth causes further degeneration into animal forms, which opens wide the avenues for even lower transmigrations.

Thus we are advised in the next verse:

त्रिविधं नरकस्येदं
द्वारं नाशनमात्मनः ।
कामः क्रोधस्तथा लोभस्
तस्मादेतत्त्रयं त्यजेत् ॥ १६.२१ ॥
trividhaṁ narakasyedaṁ
dvāraṁ nāśanamātmanaḥ
kāmaḥ krodhastathā lobhas
tasmādetattrayaṁ tyajet (16.21)

trividhaṁ — threefold; narakasyedaṁ = narakasya — of hell + idam — this; dvāraṁ — avenues; nāśanam — destructive of, degrading towards; ātmanaḥ — of the self; kāmaḥ — craving; krodhaḥ — anger; tathā— as well; lobhaḥ — greed; tasmāt — therefore; etat — this; trayam — three-fold; tyajet — should abandon

Craving, anger and greed are the three avenues of hell which degrade the soul. Therefore one should abandon this threefold influence. (16.21)

Commentary:

Cravings of all sorts, anger, and greed do corrupt a human being. Even if a man does not believe in a Supreme God, still it stands to reason that cravings discourage self discipline. Anger comes from frustration and causes a person to act irresponsibly, thus bringing on rash reactions from material nature. Greed, which is pushed on by cravings, causes a man to lose his honor. These three which are given by some translators as lust, anger, and greed, do ruin the human being.

एतैर्विमुक्तः कौन्तेय
तमोद्वारैस्त्रिभिर्नरः ।
आचरत्यात्मनः श्रेयस्
ततो याति परां गतिम् ॥१६.२२॥
etairvimuktaḥ kaunteya
tamodvāraistribhirnaraḥ
ācaratyātmanaḥ śreyas
tato yāti parāṁ gatim (16.22)

etair (etaiḥ) — by these; vimuktaḥ — released; kaunteya — son of Kuntī; tamodvārais = tamo (tamaḥ) — depression + dvāraiḥ — by avanues; tribhir (tribhiḥ) — by three; naraḥ — a person; ācaratyātmanaḥ = ācarati — he serves + ātmanaḥ — of the self; śreyaḥ — best interest; tato (tataḥ) — then; yāti — goes; parāṁ — supreme; gatim — destination

Being released from these three avenues of depression, O son of Kuntī, a person serves his best interest and then goes to the highest destination. (16.22)

<u>*Commentary:*</u>

Certainly if any of us were completely released from urges, anger and greed, we would serve our best interest and see something higher as the objective of life. In the meanwhile we struggle to control these impulsions.

यः शास्त्रविधिमुत्सृज्य
वर्तते कामकारतः ।
न स सिद्धिमवाप्नोति
न सुखं न परां गतिम् ॥१६.२३॥
yaḥ śāstravidhimutsṛjya
vartate kāmakārataḥ
na sa siddhimavāpnoti
na sukhaṁ na parāṁ gatim (16.23)

yaḥ — who; śāstravidhim — scriptural injunction; utsṛjya — discarding; vartate — he follows; kāmakārataḥ — impulsion, inclination; na — not; sa = saḥ — he; siddhim — perfection; avāpnoti — attains; na — nor; sukhaṁ — happiness; na — nor; parāṁ — highest; gatim — destination

Whosoever discards the scriptural injunctions, and follows the impulsive inclinations, does not get perfection or happiness or the supreme destination. (16.23)

<u>*Commentary:*</u>

Even though we may not deliberately discard the scriptural injunctions, nor willingly follow the impulsive inclinations, we still may be callous towards morality and accommodating towards vices; thus we will not get perfection until we can come to terms with our base nature.

The scriptural injunctions cited by Lord Krishna are those in the *Gītā* itself and those in texts like the *Manu Samhitā*, books which lay down stipulations for a reformed, religiously-inclined humanity. It will take some time for us to recognize and consistently apply these. The impulsive inclinations are the hardest to curb. The purification of our nature requires more than wishful thinking. As with every other type of natural energy, some force is required to divert it from its natural tendencies. If we want that perfection described by Lord Krishna and if we want the happiness He speaks of and the supreme destination He described, we must come to terms with our nature. It will have to be adjusted.

तस्माच्छास्त्रं प्रमाणं ते
कार्याकार्यव्यवस्थितौ ।
ज्ञात्वा शास्त्रविधानोक्तं
कर्म कर्तुमिहार्हसि ॥१६.२४॥

tasmāt — therefore; śāstram — scripture; pramāṇaṁ — recommendation; te — your; karyākāryavyavasthitau = kārya — duty + akārya — non-duty + vyavasthitau — setting; jñātvā —

tasmācchāstraṁ pramāṇaṁ te
kāryākāryavyavasthitau
jñātvā śāstravidhānoktaṁ
karma kartumihārhasi (16.24)

knowing; śāstravidhānoktaṁ = śāstravidhāna — scriptural rules + uktaṁ — prescribed; karma — action; kartum — to perform; ihārhasi = ihā — here in this world + arhasi — you can

Therefore, setting your standard of duty and non-duty by scriptural recommendation, knowing the scriptural rules prescribed, you should perform actions in this world. (16.24)

Commentary:

Even though the work was an undesirable type. Lord Krishna again urged Arjuna to act on the warfield. Krishna instructed Arjuna to consider duty and non-duty. This would mean that Arjuna had to disregard or deny his base feelings or at least shift himself away from the plane of those emotions, moving to a level where life was perceived merely in terms of duty and non-duty without sentiments. Arjuna was to live by the bare rule of the scriptural injunctions designed for his caste as a prince in the Kuru dynasty.

CHAPTER 17

Three Types of Confidences*

अर्जुन उवाच
ये शास्त्रविधिमुत्सृज्य
यजन्ते श्रद्धयान्विताः ।
तेषां निष्ठा तु का कृष्ण
सत्त्वमाहो रजस्तमः ॥ १७.१ ॥
arjuna uvāca
ye śāstravidhimutsṛjya
yajante śraddhayānvitāḥ
teṣāṁ niṣṭhā tu kā kṛṣṇa
sattvamāho rajastamaḥ (17.1)

arjuna — Arjuna; uvāca — said; ye — who; śastravidhim — scriptural injunction; utsṛjya — disregarding; yajante — they perform religiously-motivated ceremony and austerity; śraddhayānvitāḥ — with full confidence; teṣāṁ — of them; niṣṭhā — position; tu — but; kā — what; kṛṣṇa — O Krishna; sattvaṁ — clarity; āho — is it?; rajaḥ — impulsion; tamaḥ — depression

Arjuna said: Concerning those who disregard scriptural injunction, but who with full confidence perform religiously-motivated ceremonies and austerities, what indeed, is their position, O Krishna? Is it clarity, impulsion or depression? (17.1)

Commentary:

In Arjuna's time in the Kuru provinces and neighboring countries, many people observed the Vedic scriptural injunctions but today most of the population of the world is unconcerned about such stipulations. What then is our position in these modern times? Are we in the clarifying, impulsive, or depressing state?

श्रीभगवानुवाच
त्रिविधा भवति श्रद्धा
देहिनां सा स्वभावजा ।
सात्त्विकी राजसी चैव
तामसी चेति तां शृणु ॥ १७.२ ॥
śrībhagavānuvāca
trividhā bhavati śraddhā
dehināṁ sā svabhāvajā
sāttvikī rājasī caiva
tāmasī ceti tāṁ śṛṇu (17.2)

śrī bhagavān — The Blessed Lord; uvāca — said; trividhā— three types; bhavati — there is; śraddhā— confidence; dehināṁ — of the embodied souls; sā — anyone; svabhāvajā— produced from innate tendency; sāttvikī — clarifying; rājasī — motivating; caiva — and indeed; tāmasī — depression; ceti = ca — and + iti — thus; tāṁ — this; śṛṇu — hear

The Blessed Lord said: According to innate tendency, there are three types of confidences of the embodied souls. These are clarifying, motivating and depressing. Hear about this. (17.2)

**The Mahābhārata contains no chapter headings. This title was assigned by the translator on the basis of verse 2 of this chapter.*

Commentary:

Lord Krishna presented a three-fold division even in regards to confidence or faith. Here again the influence of material nature comes into play.

सत्त्वानुरूपा सर्वस्य
श्रद्धा भवति भारत ।
श्रद्धामयोऽयं पुरुषो
यो यच्छ्रद्धः स एव सः ॥१७.३॥
sattvānurūpā sarvasya
śraddhā bhavati bhārata
śraddhāmayo'yaṁ puruṣo
yo yacchraddhaḥ sa eva saḥ (17.3)

sattvānurūpā = sattva — essential nature + anurūpā — according to; sarvasya — of every person; śraddhā — confidence; bhavati — becomes manifest; bhārata — O man of the Bharata family; śraddhāmayaḥ — made of faith, trend of confidence; 'yaṁ = ayaṁ — this; puruṣo = puruṣaḥ — human being; yo = yaḥ — who; yacchraddhah = yac (yad) — which + chraddhah (śraddhaḥ) — faith; sa = saḥ — he; eva — only; saḥ — he

Confidence becomes manifest according to the essential nature of the person, O man of the Bharata family. A human being follows his trend of confidence. Whatever type of faith he has, that he expresses only. (17.3)

Commentary:

If we live by natural tendency, then how can we adjust ourselves? That is the question. We must therefore admit that our natural state is adjustable *(kṣara)*, otherwise it would be impossible for us to change.

यजन्ते सात्त्विका देवान्
यक्षरक्षांसि राजसाः ।
प्रेतान्भूतगणांश्चान्ये
यजन्ते तामसा जनाः ॥१७.४॥
yajante sāttvikā devān
yakṣarakṣāṁsi rājasāḥ
pretānbhūtagaṇāṁścānye
yajante tāmasā janāḥ (17.4)

yajante — they worship; sāttvikā — clear-minded people; devān — supernatural rulers; yakṣarakṣāṁsi — yakṣa — passionate sorcerers + rakṣāṁsi — to cannibalistic powerful humans; rājasāḥ — impulsive people; pretān — the departed spirits; bhūtagaṇāṁścānye = bhūtagaṇān — hordes of ghosts + ca — and + anye — others; yajante — they petition; tāmasā = retarded; janāḥ — people

The clear-minded people worship the supernatural rulers. The impulsive ones worship the passionate sorcerers and the cannibalistic humans. The others, the retarded people, petition the departed spirits and the hordes of ghosts. (17.4)

Commentary:

Our activities are conditioned by affiliation with a particular mode of material nature. Thus the idea of independence is imaginary. We may, however, attempt a preference of the influences.

अशास्त्रविहितं घोरं
तप्यन्ते ये तपो जनाः ।
दम्भाहंकारसंयुक्ताः
कामरागबलान्विताः ॥१७.५॥
aśāstravihitaṁ ghoraṁ
tapyante ye tapo janāḥ
dambhāhaṁkārasaṁyuktāḥ
kāmarāgabalānvitāḥ (17.5)

aśāstravihitaṁ = aśāstra — not of scripture + vihitaṁ — recommended; ghoraṁ — terrible; tapyante — tbey endure; ye — who; tapo = tapaḥ — austerity; janāḥ — people; dambhāhaṁkārasaṁyuktāḥ = dambha — deceit + ahaṁkāra — misplaced identity + saṁyuktāḥ — enthused with; kāmarāgabalānvitāḥ = kāma — craving + rāga — rage + bala — brute force + anvitāḥ — possessed with

People who endure terrible austerities which are not recommended in the scripture, people who are enthused with deceit and misplaced identity, who are possessed with craving, rage and brute force, (17.5)

Commentary:

This verse and the following one are connected. This is a description of persons who take up austerities while being influenced by the stupifying mode. A man's motivation controls his action. His destiny is based on motivations which are sponsored by the modes of material nature. Usually people do not realize that they are being pushed on by these modes. Being reliant, a living entity may assume that the energies which enthuse him are his own power. Subsequently, he adds impetus to the urges, even though they operate to bring misery.

People are so reliant on material nature that they do not listen to good advice. They remain rooted in the mundane energies. They fight with tooth and nail against any person who might give them the key to their liberation from material bondage.

कर्शयन्तः शरीरस्थं
भूतग्राममचेतसः ।
मां चैवान्तःशरीरस्थं
तान्विद्ध्यासुरनिश्चयान् ॥ १७.६ ॥
karśayantaḥ śarīrasthaṁ
bhūtagrāmamacetasaḥ
māṁ caivāntaḥśarīrasthaṁ
tānviddhyāsuraniścayān (17.6)

karśayantaḥ — torturing, troubling; śarīrasthaṁ — within the body; bhūtagrāmam — collection of elements; acetasaḥ — senseless; māṁ — me; caivantaḥ = ca — and + eva — indeed + antaḥ — within; śarīrasthaṁ — within the body; tān — them; viddhi — know; āsura — wicked + niścayān — intentions

...those who torture the collection of the elements which comprise the body, who also trouble Me within the body, know that they have wicked intentions. (17.6)

Commentary:

Though indeliberate, without any free choice in the matter, and being shown the wicked path by the stupifying mode of material nature, senseless people are held responsible for their actions. Their ignorance (*acetasah*) is due to the absorption of their consciousness by the dulling mode of nature. But as it is in the material world and as Lord Krishna explained, the soul has to take responsibility for the various actions and reactions which come to him, even for insensible acts. The wicked activities are those which are contrary to fairness in social dealings. In truth, the real actor is material nature. The soul is merely a stooge, who like a donkey, carries the load of responsibilities.

आहारस्त्वपि सर्वस्य
त्रिविधो भवति प्रियः ।
यज्ञस्तपस्तथा दानं
तेषां भेदमिमं शृणु ॥ १७.७ ॥
āhārastvapi sarvasya
trividho bhavati priyaḥ
yajñastapastathā dānaṁ
teṣāṁ bhedamimaṁ śṛṇu (17.7)

āhāraḥ — food; tu — but; api — as well; sarvasya — of all; trividho = trividhaḥ — three kinds; bhavati — is; priyaḥ — likes; yajñaḥ — religious ceremony; tapaḥ — austerity; tathā — as; dānaṁ — charity; teṣāṁ — of them; bhedam — difference; imaṁ — this; śṛṇu — hear

But food as well, which is liked by all, is of three kinds, as are religious ceremony, austerity and charity. Hear of the difference between them. (17.7)

Commentary:

Every type of activity is affected by the modes of material nature. Since the materials of nature are involved, one has to deal with the qualities of the materials used. There are also subtle effects. As such, wherever we turn and whatever we may do, comprises a combination of spiritual and mundane reality. It cannot be avoided. We may select a higher mode by putting ourselves in a position to take advantage of it. A man cannot improve himself merely by wishful thinking. So long as he stays in a certain mode, he will be forced to act by the methods of that energy. Thus he must move to a higher existential plane if he wants to act in a nobler way.

आयुःसत्त्वबलारोग्य-
सुखप्रीतिविवर्धनाः ।
रस्याः स्निग्धाः स्थिरा हृद्या
आहाराः सात्त्विकप्रियाः ॥१७.८॥
āyuḥsattvabalārogya-
sukhaprītivivardhanāḥ
rasyāḥ snigdhāḥ sthirā hṛdyā
āhārāḥ sāttvikapriyāḥ (17.8)

āyuḥsattvabalārogya = āyuḥ — duration of life + sattva — spiritual well-being + bala — strength + ārogya — health; sukhaprītivivardhanāḥ = sukha — happiness + prīti — satisfaction + vivardhanāḥ — increasing; rasyāḥ — juicy; snigdhāḥ — milky; sthirā — sustaining; hṛdyā — palatable; āhārāḥ — foods; sāttvikapriyāḥ — dear to the clear-minded people

Foods which increase the duration of the life, the spiritual well-being, strength, health, happiness and satisfaction, which are juicy, milky, sustaining and palatable, are eatables which are dear to the clear-minded people. (17.8)

Commentary:

Food, though a material item, has a psychic counterpart which affects our mind and emotions. Thus the type of food one eats does affect one's attitude to life. Generally speaking, the creatures who eat abominable foods have the worst attitude and take on a carnivorous or cannibalistic demeanor. Since food affects our constitution we should be more selective in eating. But we should not become addicted to any type of food. Even in diet, we should apply detachment. Even preferred foods cause attachment which, in time, could ruin the profile. Any aspect of material nature may cause us to risk ourselves for happiness (*sukha*). We should be alert to use the clarifying mode and not be dominated by it.

कट्वम्ललवणात्युष्ण-
तीक्ष्णरूक्षविदाहिनः ।
आहारा राजसस्येष्टा
दुःखशोकामयप्रदाः ॥१७.९॥
kaṭvamlalavaṇātyuṣṇa-
tīkṣṇarūkṣavidāhinaḥ
āhārā rājasasyeṣṭā
duḥkhaśokāmayapradāḥ (17.9)

kaṭvamlalavaṇātyuṣṇa = kaṭv (kaṭu) — pungent + amla — sour + lavaṇa — salt; atyuṣṇa -peppery; tīkṣnarūkṣavidāhinaḥ = tīkṣṇa — acidic + rūkṣa — dry + vidāhinaḥ — overheated; āhārā — foods; rājasasyeṣṭā = rajasasya — of the passionate people + iṣṭā — desired; duḥkhaśokāmayapradāḥ = duḥkha — pain + śoka — misery + āmaya — sickness + pradāḥ — causing

Foods which are pungent, sour, salty, peppery, acidic, dry and overheated, are desired by the passionate people. These foods cause pain, misery and sickness. (17.9)

Commentary:

A particular type of food produces a particular effect on the gross body. Thus many diseases arise merely on the basis of diet. A greater danger, however, is the tendency acquired by the subtle form. By that tendency one gets his next form. If we are not selective for food, we run the risk of being degraded, since our diet might influence the selection of the next body. Thus we might be drawn to a species of life which is not to our liking.

यातयामं गतरसं
पूति पर्युषितं च यत् ।
उच्छिष्टमपि चामेध्यं
भोजनं तामसप्रियम् ॥ १७.१० ॥
yātayāmaṁ gatarasaṁ
pūti paryuṣitaṁ ca yat
ucchiṣṭamapi cāmedhyaṁ
bhojanaṁ tāmasapriyam (17.10)

yātayāmaṁ — stale; gatarasaṁ — tasteless; pūti — rotten; paryuṣitaṁ — left over; ca — and; yat = yad — which; ucchiṣṭam — rejected; api — also; cāmedhyam = ca — and + amedhyaṁ — unfit for religious ceremony; bhojanaṁ — food; tāmasapriyam — cherished by the depressed people

Food which is stale, tasteless, and rotten, which was left over, as well as that which is rejected or unfit for religious ceremony, is cherished by the depressed people. (17.10)

Commentary:

This selection of foods as well as the other two selections given in verses 8 and 9, are made on the basis of the influence of material nature. This is what we must understand. Any of us may form any of these selections, all depending on the mode which exercises the influence. Thus it is very important that we have some objectivity of the modes and know the symptoms of the various influences of mundane power.

अफलाकाङ्क्षिभिर्यज्ञो
विधिदृष्टो य इज्यते ।
यष्टव्यमेवेति मनः
समाधाय स सात्त्विकः ॥ १७.११ ॥
aphalākāṅkṣibhiryajño
vidhidṛṣṭo ya ijyate
yaṣṭavyameveti manaḥ
samādhāya sa sāttvikaḥ (17.11)

aphalākāṅkṣibhiḥ = aphalā — no benefits + kāṅkṣibhiḥ — desiring; yajño = yajñaḥ — a religious discipline or ceremony; vidhidṛṣṭo - vidhidṛṣṭaḥ = vidhi — scripture + dṛṣṭaḥ — observing; ya — who; ijyate — is offered; yaṣṭavyam — to be sacrificed; eveti = eva — indeed + iti — thus; manaḥ — mind; samādhāya — concentrating; sa — it; sāttvikaḥ — realistic

A religious discipline or ceremony in observance of the scripture, by those who do not desire a benefit and who, while concentrating, think, "This is to be sacrificed," is a ceremony of the realistic type. (17.11)

Commentary:

As stated in Chapter Three, the *Prajāpati* instructed the first human beings to perform certain religious ceremonies:

sahayajñāḥ prajāḥ sṛṣṭvā purovāca prajāpatiḥ
anena prasaviṣyadhvam eṣa vo'stviṣṭakāmadhuk (3.10)

devānbhāvayatānena te devā bhāvayantu vaḥ
parasparaṁ bhāvayantaḥ śreyaḥ paramavāpsyatha (3.11)
iṣṭānbhogānhi vo devā dāsyante yajñabhāvitāḥ
tairdattānapradāyaibhyo yo bhuṅkte stena eva saḥ (3.12)

Long ago, having created the first human beings, along with religious fulfillment and ceremonies, the Procreator Brahmā said: By this worship procedure, you may be productive. May it cause the fulfillment of your desires. (3.10)

By this procedure, you may cause the supernatural rulers to flourish. They, in turn, may bless you. In favorably regarding each other, the highest well-being will be achieved. (3.11)

The supernatural rulers, being manifested through prescribed austerity and religious ceremony, will, indeed, give you the most desired people and things. Whosoever does not offer those given items to them, but who enjoys these, is certainly a thief. (3.12)

Thus, ideally, we are supposed to get instruction from God or from an agent of God; then we should work to satisfy the order of that authority; then return to explain the outcome produced. In the action, our attitude should be that of a duty-bound person.

अभिसंधाय तु फलं
दम्भार्थमपि चैव यत् ।
इज्यते भरतश्रेष्ठ
तं यज्ञं विद्धि राजसम् ॥ १७.१२ ॥
abhisaṁdhāya tu phalaṁ
dambhārthamapi caiva yat
ijyate bharataśreṣṭha
taṁ yajñaṁ viddhi rājasam (17.12)

abhisandhāya — kept in mind; tu — but; phalam — benefit; dambhārtham — for the sake of outsmarting the deity; api — also; caiva — and indeed; yat = yad — which; ijyate — is offered; bharataśreṣṭha — best of the Bhāratas; tam — this; yajñaṁ — disciplined worship; viddhi —know; rājasam — impulsive

But when a benefit is kept in mind and when the motive is to outsmart the deity, know, O best of the Bharatas, that the disciplinary worship offered is based on impulsion. (17.12)

Commentary:

Yajñam means more than religious ceremony or formal religious sacrifice. As we stated, Lord Krishna gave a list of such disciplines in Chapter Four and titled them sacrifice (4.24-32). Any of these processes are considered to be a type of sacrifice of the time and energy of an ascetic. And all have particular motivations, all depending on the mind-set of the performer.

विधिहीनमसृष्टान्नं
मन्त्रहीनमदक्षिणम् ।
श्रद्धाविरहितं यज्ञं
तामसं परिचक्षते ॥ १७.१३ ॥
vidhihīnamasṛṣṭānnaṁ
mantrahīnamadakṣiṇam
śraddhāvirahitaṁ yajñaṁ
tāmasaṁ paricakṣate (17.13)

vidhihīnam — scripture neglected; asṛṣṭānnaṁ = asṛṣṭa — not offered + annam — food; mantrahīnam — Vedic hymn not recited; adakṣiṇam — no fee for the priest; śraddhāvirahitaṁ — confidence lacking; yajñaṁ — disciplinary worship; tāmasaṁ — depressive; paricakṣate — they regard

When scripture is neglected, food is not offered, Vedic hymns not recited, a fee not given to the priest, and confidence is lacking, regard that disciplinary worship as depressive. (17.13)

Commentary:

Strictly speaking, *annam* means food and *asṛṣṭānnam* means unoffered food. This means food items that were not offered by scriptural stipulations. However, *annam* also means the particular type of sustenance being used at the time of the religious discipline. And if that discipline is not a fire sacrifice but is one of the sacrifices listed in Chapter Four, verses 24-32, then in those vows and procedures, the performer should think of and give to the particular deities, the means of sustenance. One must also contribute gifts of money to the priest who performed the ceremony. Whatever has to be done should be done. Otherwise there is a risk that one might not complete the discipline.

देवद्विजगुरुप्राज्ञ-
पूजनं शौचमार्जवम् ।
ब्रह्मचर्यमहिंसा च
शारीरं तप उच्यते ॥१७.१४॥
devadvijagurupräjña-
pūjanaṁ śaucamārjavam
brahmacaryamahiṁsā ca
śārīraṁ tapa ucyate (17.14)

devadvijagurupräjña = deva — supernatural ruler + dvija = those who are qualified by sacred thread ceremony + guru — spiritual teacher + prājña — wise man; pūjanaṁ — reverential respect; śaucam — purity; ārjavam — straightforwardness; brahmacaryam — celibacy; ahiṁsā — non-violence; ca — and; śārīraṁ — body; tapa — austerity; ucyate — is said to be

Reverential respect of the supernatural rulers, of those who are qualified by the sacred thread ceremony, of the spiritual teacher, and of the wise man, purity, straightforwardness, celibacy and non-violence, are said to be austerity of the body. (17.14)

Commentary:

The term *guru* has a particular meaning in the *Gītā*. Readers should check in Chapter Four, verses 24-35, where Lord Krishna explained the disciplines and teachers. The *prājña* are described in the *Gītā* in many verses in Chapters Three, Four, and Five.

Dvija refers to the twice-born people. They are usually of the three higher castes: priests, administrators, and mercantile-minded persons. If any of these take the sacred thread initiation after going through the requirements mentioned in the scriptures, they are considered to be twice-born. In the time of Arjuna, being twice-born was important.

One is required to have reverential respect for the particular deity or supernatural person who supervises the discipline one tries to complete. One may fail if he does not satisfy the deity.

Purity of the mind and body are required. Straightforwardness is required to free the person from bad motivations. Celibacy is required since the sexual energy takes one's mind away from the objective.

Non-violence or harmlessness is required. Religious activities and spiritual disciplines should be for the welfare of everyone. The objective might be personal purification but the outcome should be a reduction in resentment and hostilities.

अनुद्वेगकरं वाक्यं
सत्यं प्रियहितं च यत् ।
स्वाध्यायाभ्यसनं चैव
वाङ्मयं तप उच्यते ॥ १७.१५॥
anudvegakaraṁ vākyaṁ
satyaṁ priyahitaṁ ca yat
svādhyāyābhyasanaṁ caiva
vāṅmayaṁ tapa ucyate (17.15)

anudvegakaraṁ — not causing distress; vākyaṁ — speech; satyam — truthful; priyahitam — agreeable and beneficial; ca — and; yat = yad — which; svādhyāyābhyasanaṁ = svādhyāya — recitation of scripture + abhyasanaṁ — practice, regularity; caiva — and indeed; vāṅmayaṁ — speech-made; tapa — discipline; ucyate — is called

Speech which does not cause distress, and is truthful, agreeable and beneficial, as well as regular recitation of the scriptures is the discipline of speech. (17.15)

Commentary:

Speech expresses the ideas of the mind and the feelings of the life force. Both the mind and life force are somewhat curbed by an austerity in speech as described by Lord Krishna. Curbing the ideas of the mind is the easier accomplishment and curbing the urgings of the life force is the more difficult austerity. More of the *Gītā* is devoted to self-control than to any other discipline.

मनःप्रसादः सौम्यत्वं
मौनमात्मविनिग्रहः ।
भावसंशुद्धिरित्येतत्
तपो मानसमुच्यते ॥ १७.१६ ॥
manaḥprasādaḥ saumyatvaṁ
maunamātmavinigrahaḥ
bhāvasaṁśuddhirityetat
tapo mānasamucyate (17.16)

manaḥprasādaḥ = manah — mind + prasādaḥ — peace; saumayatvaṁ — gentleness; maunam —silence; ātmavinigrahaḥ — self-restraint; bhāvasaṁśuddhiḥ = bhāva — being + saṁśuddhiḥ — purity; iti — thus, etat = etad — this; tapo = tapaḥ — discipline; mānasam — of the mind; ucyate — is called

Peace of mind, gentleness, silence, self restraint, and purity of being, this is called discipline of mind. (17.16)

Commentary:

Discipline of the mind as described in this verse, includes discipline of the senses and life energy. In modern words, this life energy is called consciousness. Consciousness, however, is a vague term in this usage since the life energy comprises the consciousness of the soul in combination with subtle energies which are known as *prāṇa* in the Sanskrit. The consciousness of the soul is a basic energy around which the life energies function and interact.

It is, therefore, simplistic and misleading to say that if we purify our soul consciousness, the problems will be solved. They will not be solved in that way because a man must deal with his subtle life force or subtle material nature which is different to his core spirit. The curbing, reform, or purification of consciousness by meditation or by the various types of will power or imaginative force are partial methods only. These do not completely curb the life force. This is something that many teachers fail to realize.

Meditation means that one tries to influence his consciousness to change by a subtle method. But unfortunately the life force only plays with one's plans for reform through meditation. The various types of will power adaptation include concentration, repetition of special sounds, and the hearing of special types of music or special songs. And even though they amuse and charm the jumpy mind, these disciplines are too weak to curb the life force.

Concentration means that one focuses the mind on a particular object, one tries to hold the mind there or bring it back to that object repeatedly. But this does not curb the life force even though it gives one greater determination and greater power to pursue objectives.

Repetition of special sounds also trains the mind to be satisfied with one idea. Generally the mind is not satisfied unless it shifts itself at every moment. This causes a scattered mentality, which is corrected to a degree by sound repetition. However, the life energy is not that concerned with the disciplines of the mind because the life energy is a totally separate power. Control of the mind affects the life energy a little, but not much. It does not cause a complete re-adjustment of that power.

The deliberate hearing of special types of music or songs serves to push the mind off guard because the mind, like an infant, becomes absorbed in the sound just as a baby becomes absorbed in the sucking action of its mouth on a pacifier. But this also does not curb the life energy. Thus, until the life energy is dealt with directly, there is no question of purity of being.

Silence, another method of keeping the mind from its devilish maneuvers, does not settle the problem of the life energy control, but it may relax the being and save him from creating many inordinate desires.

There are two types of *maunam* (silence). One is external silence. This means that a person who likes to speak, stops and curtails the habit by taking a vow not to speak for a time. Or he lives in isolation where there are no human beings for communication. The isolation practice invokes the need for internal silence. And that is a complicated discipline. For internal silence, one has to sort out his mind from his senses and his senses from his life energy. This requires sense withdrawal, concentration, contemplation and finally trance in meditation.

श्रद्धया परया तप्तं
तपस्तत्त्रिविधं नरैः ।
अफलाकाङ्क्षिभिर्युक्तैः
सात्त्विकं परिचक्षते ॥१७.१७॥
śraddhayā parayā taptaṁ
tapastattrividhaṁ naraiḥ
aphalākāṅkṣibhiryuktaiḥ
sāttvikaṁ paricakṣate (17.17)

śraddhayā — with faith; parayā — with the highest; taptam — performed; tapaḥ — austerity; tat = tad — this; trividham — three-fold; naraih — by people; aphalākāṅkṣibhiḥ — by those who do not aspire for a benefit; yuktaiḥ — by those disciplined in yoga; sāttvikaṁ — realistic; paricakṣate — they consider

When this threefold austerity is performed with the highest faith by yogicly-disciplined people who do not aspire for a benefit, the authorities consider it to be realistic. (17.17)

Commentary:

Discipline of the body, speech, and mind are given by Lord Krishna as the special three-part austerity. Of the three, speech is the chief means of social communication. It represents the relationship between the living entities. The mind, as the *Gītā* denotes, is a special sensing device, listed as the sixth sense. It is the monitor of the five secondary senses. The body, which includes the subtle and causal forms, is the tool for acting morally or immorally.

सत्कारमानपूजार्थं
तपो दम्भेन चैव यत् ।
क्रियते तदिह प्रोक्तं
राजसं चलमध्रुवम् ॥ १७.१८॥
satkāramānapūjārthaṁ
tapo dambhena caiva yat
kriyate tadiha proktaṁ
rājasaṁ calamadhruvam (17.18)

satkāramānapūjārthaṁ = satkāra — reputation +māna — respect + pūjā — reverence + arthaṁ — for the sake of; tapo = tapaḥ — austerity; dambhena — with trickery; caiva — and indeed; yat = yad — which; kriyate — performed; tat — this; iha — in this world; proktaṁ — is declared; rājasaṁ — impulsive; calam — shifty; adhruvam — temporary

Austerity which, in this world is performed with trickery for the sake of reputation, respect and reverence, is declared to be impulsive, shifty and temporary. (17.18)

Commentary:

Respect, honor, and a taste for being revered by others, can all be positive qualities if they are kept within the scope of one's responsibilities. But if any of these are expanded beyond that, and used to exploit simple-minded, human beings, they become negative qualities.

When deceit is present, the activities come from a bad motivation, and as such they are condemned.

मूढग्राहेणात्मनो यत्
पीडया क्रियते तपः ।
परस्योत्सादनार्थं वा
तत्तामसमुदाहृतम् ॥ १७.१९॥
mūḍhagrāheṇātmano yat
pīḍayā kriyate tapaḥ
parasyotsādanārthaṁ vā
tattāmasamudāhṛtam (17.19)

mūḍhagrāheṇātmano = mūḍha — foolish + grāheṇa= by misṭaken ideas + ātmano (ātmanaḥ) — of the self; yat = yad — which; pīḍayā — with torture; kriyate — is performed; tapaḥ — austerity; parasyotsādanārthaṁ = parasya — of someone else + utsādana — harming + artham — purpose; vā — or; tat — that; tāmasam — depressive; udāhṛtam — said to be

Austerity performed with foolish, mistaken ideas, and with torture or for the purpose of harming someone else, is said to be depressive. (17.19)

Commentary:

The spirit is a sensible piece of reality but in the material creation, he is dependent on the psychic equipments which communicate to him, data of the outside world. If he receives the wrong information and gets a foolish conception (*mūdhagrāheṇa*), he draws the wrong conclusion and enters the depressive mode.

It is important, therefore, to keep one's mental and emotional energies in the highest mode of material nature, which is the clarifying energy. Certainly, if a man can, he should go beyond these modes.

दातव्यमिति यद्दानं
दीयतेऽनुपकारिणे ।
देशे काले च पात्रे च
तद्दानं सात्त्विकं स्मृतम् ॥ १७.२०॥
dātavyamiti yaddānaṁ
dīyate'nupakāriṇe
deśe kāle ca pātre ca
taddānaṁ sāttvikaṁ smṛtam (17.20)

dātavyam — to be given; iti — thus; yat — which; dānaṁ — gift; dīyate — is given: 'nupakāriṇe = anupakāriṇe — to one who has not done a prior favor; deśe — in proper place; kāle — at the proper time; ca — and; pātre — to a worthy person; ca — and; tat — that; dānaṁ —gift; sāttvikaṁ — virtuous; smṛtam — remembered as

A gift given to one who has not done a prior favor, in the proper place and time and to a worthy person, is remembered as being virtuous. (17.20)

Commentary:

In all these respects, the motive is examined by Lord Krishna. Thus He teaches us how to analyze everything in great detail, to trace every act to its motive and to determine the intentions by the energy content of an act.

यत्तु प्रत्युपकारार्थं
फलमुद्दिश्य वा पुनः ।
दीयते च परिक्लिष्टं
तद्दानं राजसं स्मृतम् ॥१७.२१॥
yattu pratyupakārārthaṁ
phalamuddiśya vā punaḥ
dīyate ca parikliṣṭaṁ
taddānaṁ rājasaṁ smṛtam (17.21)

yat — which; tu — but; pratyupakārārthaṁ — for a compensation; phalam — a result; uddiśya — pointing to, hoping; vā — or; punaḥ — alternately; dīyate — is given; ca — and; parikliṣṭaṁ — grudgingly: tat — that; dānaṁ — gift; rājasaṁ — impulsive; smṛtam — mentally noted

But the gift which is given grudgingly for a compensation or alternately hoping for a reward, is mentally noted as being impulsive. (17.21)

Commentary:

Anything given with a compensatory motive or given for a stipulated reward, is given with a grudging mood, which might not be displayed by the giver but which will show later and will be remembered by witnesses. Such a thing is done without deep consideration. It is impulsive.

अदेशकाले यद्दानम्
अपात्रेभ्यश्च दीयते ।
असत्कृतमवज्ञातं
तत्तामसमुदाहृतम् ॥१७.२२॥
adeśakāle yaddānam
apātrebhyaśca dīyate
asatkṛtamavajñātaṁ
tattāmasamudāhṛtam (17.22)

adeśakāle — at the wrong place and time; yat — which; dānam — gift; apātrebhyaśca = apātrebhyaḥ — to an unworthy person + ca — and; dīyate — is given; asatkṛtam — without paying respect; avajñātaṁ — without due consideration; tat = tad — that; tāmasam — depressive mode; udāhṛtam — is said to be

That gift which is given in the wrong place and time, to an unworthy person, without paying respect, without due consideration, is said to be of the depressive mode. (17.22)

Commentary:

There are many urgings in material nature with many types of motivations, but none of these can manifest unless a spirit is involved in supplying energy for the core of the operations. Hence the spirit is a crucial factor in the development of the evolution of the world. The spirit, however, is not always in the position to understand the environment, nor can he always stop the use of his energies by material nature. And therefore he might, from time to time, subscribe to operations which are not in his interest. The solution is enlightenment, for without it, he cannot understand the liabilities of his actions.

ओं तत्सदिति निर्देशो
ब्रह्मणस्त्रिविधः स्मृतः ।
ब्राह्मणास्तेन वेदाश्च
यज्ञाश्च विहिताः पुरा ॥१७.२३॥

oṁ tatsaditi nirdeśo
brahmaṇastrividhaḥ smṛtaḥ
brāhmaṇāstena vedāśca
yajñāśca vihitāḥ purā (17.23)

oṁ — Om; tat — Tat; sat — Sat; iti — pronouncement; nirdeśo = nirdeśaḥ — designation; brahmaṇaḥ — of spiritual reality; trividhaḥ — threefold; smṛtaḥ — is known; brāhmaṇāḥ — by the brahmins; tena — by this; vedāsca = vedāḥ — of the Vedas + ca — and; yajñāśca = yajñāḥ — religious disciplines and ceremony + ca — and; vihitāḥ — prescribed; purā — ancient

The pronouncement *Om Tat Sat* is known as the threefold designation of spiritual reality. By this expression, the brahmins, the *Vedas*, and the prescribed religious disciplines and ceremonies were ordained in ancient times. (17.23)

<u>Commentary:</u>

Formerly the spiritual authorities in India used *Om* as the sanctifying word for the religious activities and austerities. Whatever was done was commenced with *Om* and concluded with *Om Tat Sat*. Nowadays, however, different spiritual teachers give different value for these terms.

According to the Chandogya Upanishad, once the demigods were trying to evade death, and they began chanting Vedic mantras in a sacrifice. While they were chanting, they noticed that the controller of death was intending to kill them, so they finished the sacrificial ceremonies and began the chanting of Vedic mantras. Understanding that if they were lax in the sacrificial ceremonies or in the chanting, they would become victims of death, they concentrated on *Om* and became delivered from the threat of death. Thus formerly in India, at least among the adherents of the Vedas, *Om* was an important syllable for pronunciation. Many spiritual teachers of the modern era preached for a reduction in the importance of *Om*. And others who advocate it, fail to explain that its former death-releasing power is not actuated except by those who master meditation. However, let us see how Lord Krishna defines *Om* since His meaning for the term is required for understanding the *Gītā*.

omityekākṣaraṁ brahma vyāharanmāmanusmaran
yaḥ prayāti tyajandehaṁ sa yāti paramāṁ gatim (8.13)

...uttering Om, the one-syllable sound which represents the spiritual reality, meditating on Me, the yogi who passes on, renouncing the body, attains the highest objective. (8.13)

pitāhamasya jagato mātā dhātā pitāmahaḥ
vedyaṁ pavitramoṁkāra ṛksāma yajureva ca (9.17)

I am the father of this universe, the mother, the creator, the grandfather, the subject of education, the purifier, the sacred syllable Om, the Rig, Sama, and Yajur Vedas. (9.17)

In text 8.13 above, *Om* is defined as the one-syllabled term which designates the spiritual reality and in text 9.17, Lord Krishna identified Himself with this *Om*.

From a careful reading of the Upanishads and the *Brahma Sūtra* one will get the idea that ancients took *Om* to be the most important mantra and as the *Gītā* indicated, it was used at the last stages of the practice of meditation by the ascetics, particularly the yogis who were trying for a transfer to the spiritual reality. Many modern Vaishnava spiritual masters, including our authority His Divine Grace A.C. Bhaktivedanta Swami, said that *Om* is an impersonal sound used for an impersonal realization of the Supreme Absolute Truth. He placed importance on the *Hare Krishna* mahamantra:

Hare Krishna Hare Krishna Krishna Krishna Hare Hare

Hare Rama Hare Rama Rama Rama Hare Hare.

Despite the stressing of this mantra, that Hare Krishna recitation does not occur in any verse of the *Gītā*. At no place in the *Gītā* do we see that mantra. Thus to understand the importance of that mantra and the cause of its introduction to the devotees of Krishna, an interested reader would have to pursue his study through the *Śrīmad Bhāgavatam* to the *Chaitanya Charitamrita* which is a Bengali scripture. The religious history of Bengal has much to do with the introduction and popularity of the Hare Krishna mantra. However, insofar as we desire to understand the *Bhagavad Gītā* in its own time and place without projecting it into modern history, we will continue to see how Krishna explains the meaning and usage of *Om Tat Sat*.

तस्मादोमित्युदाहृत्य
यज्ञदानतपःक्रियाः ।
प्रवर्तन्ते विधानोक्ताः
सततं ब्रह्मवादिनाम् ॥१७.२४॥
tasmādomityudāhṛtya
yajñadānatapaḥkriyāḥ
pravartante vidhānoktāḥ
satataṁ brahmavādinām (17.24)

tasmāt — hence; om — the sound Om; iti — thus; udāhṛtya — uttering; yajñadānatapaḥkriyāḥ — yajña — sacrifice + dāna — charity + tapaḥ — austerity + kriyāḥ— acts; pravartante — they begin; vidhānoktāḥ = vidhāna — prescription + uktāḥ — said; satatam — always; brahmavādinām — of the spiritual masters

Hence as prescribed in the *Vedic* scriptures, acts of sacrifice, charity, and austerity always begin by the spiritual masters while uttering the sound *Om*. (17.24)

<u>Commentary:</u>

Formerly, the *Om* mantra could not be uttered by anyone and everyone. It was only uttered by brahmins. The majority of these brahmins were persons born in a lineage of brahmins. Rarely was a man allowed into the confidence of the Vedic mantras if he was not born into a brahmin family. This is an established fact. In other words, in India formerly, only a person who was in a brahmin family was allowed. There are exceptions but these were the exceptions only and not the regular procedure. In the time of Lord *Rāma*, a man was executed because he dared to perform the austerities which were the monopoly of the brahmins.

In the *Vālmīki Rāmāyāṇa*, *Uttara Kanda*, Chapter Seventy-four, it is explained that at the suggestion of the Sage *Nārada*, King *Rāma* executed *Sambuka*, a low-class man who took up severe austerities. The Sage *Nārada* said that by the austerities, the low-class man caused the death of a brahmin's son. However, some modern devotees of Lord *Rāma* disbelieve this story, stating that it is an interpolation.

In a careful study of Vedic literature, we can also observe that persons who were not of the three higher castes, were not even allowed to sit within earshot of chanting of certain confidential mantras. And even the modern spiritual masters from India have confidential mantras which they divulge to their trusted disciples only. Usually there is a double standard where in the public, these spiritual authorities give a view that they have nothing confidential but in private, they reserve certain special mantras for their trusted men. In many cases, *Om* forms a part of the sentence of these confidential sounds.

The Chandogya Upanishad informs us that formerly the demigods used *Om* as a focal point through which they reached the spiritual existence and avoided death. And so, Om has special significance but it must be combined with deep meditation for the effect. For protection the sages used *Om* as a cover under which to enact acts of sacrifice, charity and austerity.

तदित्यनभिसंधाय
फलं यज्ञतपःक्रियाः ।
दानक्रियाश्च विविधाः
क्रियन्ते मोक्षकाङ्क्षिभिः ॥ १७.२५ ॥
tadityanabhisaṁdhāya
phalaṁ yajñatapaḥkriyāḥ
dānakriyāśca vividhāḥ
kriyante mokṣakāṅkṣibhiḥ (17.25)

tat — Tat; iti — saying; anabhisaṁdhāya — without an interest; phalam — benefit; yajñatapaḥkriyāḥ = yajña — sacrifice + tapaḥ — austerity + kriyaḥ — actions; dānakriyāśca = dānakriyāḥ — acts of charity + ca — and; vividhāḥ — various types; kriyante — are performed; mokṣakāṅkṣibhiḥ — by those who desire liberation

While saying *Tat* without an interest in a benefit, acts of sacrifice, austerity and various types of charity are performed by those who are desirous of liberation. (17.25)

Commentary:

Mokṣakāṅkṣibhih refers to those who are very eager for liberation from material existence. Some of these are devotees of Lord Krishna and some are not. Some are interested in a Supreme Personality and some are not. Some are not even interested in continuing their individual existence after liberation. These want to bring an end to their consciousness of material existence by any effective means.

The word *tad* in line one of this verse means *that*. This word appears elsewhere as tat. In the Upanishad, the word denotes the spirit and it denotes the spiritual existence at large. For instance, there is a popular mantra which states *Tat Tvam Asi*. This means literally: You (*tvam*) are (*asi*) a portion of that Spiritual Realilty (*tat*).

In the Upanishad there are stories of disciples of realized sages. These sages would, at a certain stage, inform their inquiring disciples that their spirits were identical to the brahman spiritual reality.

Those who are desirous of liberation from the material world, those who want a complete release, take up specific ritual acts, austerities, and types of charities as terminal actions to end off their material existence. We got a hint of this from Lord Krishna in Chapter Two when He spoke of *brahma nirvāṇa*, the putting out of one's interest in material existence:

eṣā brāhmī sthitiḥ pārtha naināṁ prāpya vimuhyati
sthitvāsyāmantakāle'pi brahmanirvāṇamṛcchati (2.72)

This divine state is required, O son of Pṛthā. If a man does not have this, he is stupefied. At the time of death, the full stoppage of mundane sensuality and the attainment of divinity is attained by one who is fixed in this divine state. (2.72)

सद्भावे साधुभावे च
सदित्येतत्प्रयुज्यते ।
प्रशस्ते कर्मणि तथा
सच्छब्दः पार्थ युज्यते ॥ १७.२६ ॥
sadbhāve sādhubhāve ca
sadityetatprayujyate
praśaste karmaṇi tathā
sacchabdaḥ pārtha yujyate (17.26)

sadbhāve = sad (sat) — reality + bhāve — in meaning; sādhubhāve = sādhu — excellence + bhāve — in meaning; ca — and; sat — reality, that which is productive of reality; iti — thus; etat = etad — this; prayujyate — is used; praśaste — is praiseworthy; karmāṇi — in action; tathā — also; sacchabdaḥ = sat + śabdaḥ — word; pārtha — son of Pṛthā; yujyate — is used

The word *Sat* is used to mean reality and excellence and also for a praiseworthy act, O son of Pṛthā. (17.26)

Commentary:

Lord Krishna defined the very important and over-used Sanskrit word *sat*. This word occurs in line one of this verse as *sad*, which is a variation of the word *sat*.

Sat indicates reality, excellence in performance, or realistic activities. But these aspects are all defined differently by different philosophers. Since this is a study of the *Gītā*, we are obliged to accept Lord Krishna's meanings for these terms.

यज्ञे तपसि दाने च
स्थितिः सदिति चोच्यते ।
कर्म चैव तदर्थीयं
सदित्येवाभिधीयते ॥१७.२७॥

yajñe tapasi dāne ca
sthitiḥ saditi cocyate
karma caiva tadarthīyaṁ
sadityevābhidhīyate (17.27)

yajñe — in sacrifice; tapasi — in austerity; dāne — in charity; ca —and; sthitiḥ — steady application; sat — realism; iti — thus; cocyate = ca — and + ucyate — is designated; karma — action; caiva —and indeed; tadarthīyaṁ — for the purpose of that; sat — realistic; iti — thus; evābhidhīyate = eva — indeed + abhidhīyate — is designated

Steady application in sacrifice, austerity and charity, is also called *Sat*. An action which is supportive of this purpose is also designated as *Sat*. (17.27)

Commentary:

More meanings of *Sat* are given as stability, constancy or persistence in sacrifice, austerity, and charity. The actions which are supportive of such an attitude are also called *Sat*.

This is important because it is beyond the three modes of material nature which Lord Krishna described in great detail. The transcendentalists are supposed to get beyond those three modes and situate themselves consistently in the *Sat* mode. Lord Krishna patiently explained everything about the lower, median and highest grades of life in the material world. Now He presents the way of escape through *Sat* (spiritual reality).

अश्रद्धया हुतं दत्तं
तपस्तप्तं कृतं च यत् ।
असदित्युच्यते पार्थ
न च तत्प्रेत्य नो इह ॥१७.२८॥

aśraddhayā hutaṁ dattaṁ
tapastaptaṁ kṛtaṁ ca yat
asadityucyate pārtha
na ca tatpretya no iha (17.28)

aśraddhayā — with a lack of faith; hutaṁ — oblation; dattaṁ — offered; tapaḥ — austerity; taptaṁ — performed; kṛtaṁ — done; ca — and; yat — which; asat — unrealistic; iti — thus; ucyate — is called; pārtha — son of Pṛthà; na — no; ca — and; tat — that; pretya — hereafter; no = naḥ — to us; iha — here

An oblation offered with a lack of faith and austerity performed in the same way is called asat, unrealistic, O son of Pṛtha. And that has no value to us here or in the hereafter. (17.28)

Commentary:

Regardless of whether one believes in religious ceremonies or in personal upliftment through austerities (*tapas*), one may judge an undertaking by the faith invested in it. If there is a lack of faith, even a valid process becomes unrealistic.

CHAPTER 18

The Most Secret of All Information*

अर्जुन उवाच
संन्यासस्य महाबाहो
तत्त्वमिच्छामि वेदितुम् ।
त्यागस्य च हृषीकेश
पृथक्केशिनिषूदन ॥ १८.१ ॥
arjuna uvāca
saṁnyāsasya mahābāho
tattvamicchāmi veditum
tyāgasya ca hṛṣīkeśa
pṛthakkeśiniṣūdana (10.1)

arjuna — Arjuna; uvāca — said; saṁnyāsasya — of the rejection of opportunity; mahābāho — O strong-armed hero; tattvam — fact; icchāmi — I want; veditum — to know; tyāgasya — of the rejection of consequences; ca — and; hṛṣīkesa — O Hṛṣīkeśa; pṛthak — distinguish; keśiniṣūdāna — slayer of Keshi

Arjuna said: Regarding the rejection of opportunity, O strong-armed hero, I want to know the fact. And regarding the rejection of consequences, O Hṛṣīkeśa, distinguish these, O slayer of Keshi. (18.1)

Commentary:

It is important to understand the difference between rejection of an opportunity and rejection of the consequence of an opportunity which was utilized. Though Western readers usually do not form a distinction between *sannyāsa* and *tyāga*, there is a sharp and clear difference between these terms. *Sannyāsa* means the rejection of opportunities for exploiting material nature. A *sannyāsi* is supposed to be a person who is done with all sorts of mundane cravings and who does not take any more opportunities for exploitation. But some religious societies from India often use the term *sannyāsi* in a convenient way to mean leaders of their particular religious society, even though such leaders are hardly interested in rejecting all exploitive opportunities, especially those having to do with raising money and increasing the number of followers.

Tyāga means rejection of good or bad consequences. A *tyāgi* is a person who practises the rejection of consequences. He still takes opportunities for exploitation but he tries to avoid or disclaim the consequences which trail him from past activities. Obviously, the true *sannyāsi* is the superior to the true *tyāgi*. The *tyāgi* is a preparatory *sannyāsi*. That is how he might be rated.

Why, in this final part of the *Gītā*, was Arjuna interested in this? Arjuna still wanted to know what to do. He was still not convinced completely, even though, for the most part, he already decided to do whatever Krishna would request of him. Arjuna wanted to know if it would have been better to reject the fighting opportunities outright or to fight and then reject the results.

**The Mahābhārata contains no chapter headings. This title was assigned by the translator on the basis of verse 64 of this chapter.*

Let us consider this in detail. Krishna told Arjuna to fight and that in the least, Arjuna would die on the battlefield and gain heaven or would emerge victorious and share a flourishing kingdom. Arjuna was disinclined to this. In Chapter One, he stated that he had no interest in the spoils of war, especially at the expense of dead relatives. And he doubted that he would go to heaven since he believed that he would go to hell for killing off the Kuru elders and for being instrumental in creating a host of husbandless women. Thus he wanted Krishna to explain clearly the subject of the various types of renunciation. Obviously Arjuna wanted to be a *sannyāsi* and not a *tyāgi*. He wanted to renounce fighting opportunity, instead of participating and then rejecting the results later on. But Krishna insisted that Arjuna fight. Krishna wanted Arjuna to be the agent of the Universal Form, Who already destroyed the Kurus on the supernatural level.

It is a great dilemma whether we should serve our own self-interest as we perceive it, or be concerned with the demands of the super-people like Krishna. What should we do? What are our rights in the matter? What is Krishna's authority, whereby He desires that we sacrifice ourselves for His cause? Why should we try to live out Krishna's vision or try to bring to the earthly plane, something that He acted out on the supernatural level? To answer these questions the Vaishnava authorities say that we are servants of Krishna. From their view, it is our position to serve Krishna, even at the expense of our desire.

श्रीभगवानुवाच
काम्यानां कर्मणां न्यासं
संन्यासं कवयो विदुः ।
सर्वकर्मफलत्यागं
प्राहुस्त्यागं विचक्षणाः ॥ १८.२ ॥
śrībhagavānuvāca
kāmyānāṁ karmaṇāṁ nyāsaṁ
saṁnyāsaṁ kavayo viduḥ
sarvakarmaphalatyāgaṁ
prāhustyāgaṁ vicakṣaṇāḥ (18.2)

śrī bhagavān — The Blessed Lord; uvāca — said; śrī kāmyānāṁ — prompted by craving; karmaṇāṁ — of actions; nyāsaṁ — renunciation; saṁnyāsaṁ — rejection of opportunity; kavayo = kavayaḥ — authoritative speakers; viduḥ — know; sarvakarmaphalatyāgaṁ = sarva — all + karma — action + phala — benefit + tyāgaṁ — abandonment; prāhuḥ — they declare; tyāgaṁ — rejection of consequences; vicakṣaṇāḥ — the clear-sighted person

The Blessed Lord said: The authoritative speakers know the rejection of opportunity as renunciation of actions which are prompted by craving. The clear-sighted seers declare the abandonment of the results of benefit-motivated action as the rejection of consequences. (18.2)

Commentary:

The confusion between *sannyāsa* and *tyāga* is cleared up in this verse. Both words mean a rejection, relinquishment, or abandonment, but *sannyāsa* is the abandonment of exploitive opportunities while *tyāga* is the abandonment of the consequences of used-up opportunities.

A comparison may clarify this. One man got an opportunity to make one million dollars in a business venture, but since he assumed a *sannyāsa* mood, he rejected the opportunity. Another man got a similar opportunity; he took up the venture, made the said million in currency, but at that point he assumed the *tyāga* mood and gave the million dollars to a religious organization. The difference shows, since the first man, the *sannyāsi*, rejected or renounced the opportunity to make the money while the second man, the *tyāgi*, took the opportunity but did not use the profit for his personal needs.

त्याज्यं दोषवदित्येके
कर्म प्राहुर्मनीषिणः ।
यज्ञदानतपःकर्म
न त्याज्यमिति चापरे ॥१८.३॥
tyājyaṁ doṣavadityeke
karma prāhurmanīṣiṇaḥ
yajñadānatapaḥkarma
na tyājyamiti cāpare (18.3)

tyājyaṁ — to be abandoned; doṣāvat — full of fault; iti — thus; eke — some; karma — action; prāhur= prāhuḥ — they declare; manīṣaṇaḥ — philosophers; yajñadānatapaḥkarma = yajña — sacrifice + dāna — charity + tapaḥ — austerity + karma — action; na — not; tyājyam — be abandoned; iti — thus; cāpare = ca — and + apare — others

Some philosophers declare that action is to be abandoned, since it is full of faults. Some others say that acts of sacrifice, charity and austerity are not to be abandoned. (18.3)

Commentary:

It appears that Arjuna still thought of going away from the warfield. But Lord Krishna systematically dismantled Arjuna's determination to do so. This is a wonderful view of the relationship between Lord Krishna and His friend Arjuna.

Some ancient philosophers declared that since actions are troublesome and faulty, they should be abandoned. In modern times, we have the example of Lord Buddha. He preached a systematic rejection of rituals but he extolled self-discipline for the sake of cutting loose from sensuality which he felt was productive of repeated births and deaths. Since the time of Buddha, many others adapted a belief in some sort of final conclusion to action, since it is seen that no matter what a man does, there is some fault to be discovered and some pain to be experienced.

निश्चयं शृणु मे तत्र
त्यागे भरतसत्तम ।
त्यागो हि पुरुषव्याघ्र
त्रिविधः संप्रकीर्तितः ॥१८.४॥
niścayaṁ śṛṇu me tatra
tyāge bharatasattama
tyāgo hi puruṣavyāghra
trividhaḥ saṁprakīrtitaḥ (18.4)

niścayaṁ — view; śṛṇu — hear; me — my; tatra — here, on this matter; tyāge — in the abandonment of consequences; bharatasattama — best of the Bharatas; tyāgo (tyāgaḥ) — abandonment of consequences; hi — indeed; puruṣavyāghra — tiger among men; trividhaḥ — three-fold; saṁprakīrtitaḥ — designated

Hear my view on this matter of abandonment of the consequences of action, O best of the Bharatas. The abandonment of consequences, O tiger among men, is designated as being threefold. (18.4)

Commentary:

From this verse 4 through verse 10 of this chapter, Lord Krishnna stressed the word *tyāga*. This means that for Arjuna, He stressed the abandonment of the opportunities. He preached about the selection of opportunities, not the complete rejection of them. Thus Arjuna got no support from Krishna for the *sannyāsa* idea but he did get a promotion for an idea of *tyāga* or the abandonment of the results which come from selected duties. Arjuna lost out in his effort to influence Krishna. Krishna was not interested in allowing Arjuna to do as he desired on this occasion. Instead of discussing *sannyāsa*, or the abandonment of opportunities, Lord Krishna directs Arjuna to be selective in taking opportunities.

Arjuna was to be an ideal *karma* yogi like King Janaka. Such a person cannot be a *sannyāsi* because ideally a *sannyāsi* has nothing to do with any type of positive or negative exploitive opportunities offered by and in material nature. Thus Arjuna had to be a *tyāgi* if he were to act out his duty and caste in life. Under the circumstance, his proposal for *sannyāsa* was absurd. A *karma* yogi cannot be a *sannyāsi* unless he abandons his *karma yoga* practice and takes to full renunciation away from all types of exploitive aims, even those having to do with setting up temples. A true *sannyāsi* has nothing to do with such things. Most of the modern so-called *sannyāsis*, even those who function as great leaders of religious societies, are *tyāgis* but for the sake of prestige they assumed the title of *sannyāsa*, thus blurring the distinction between the two life styles.

यज्ञदानतपःकर्म
न त्याज्यं कार्यमेव तत् ।
यज्ञो दानं तपश्चैव
पावनानि मनीषिणाम् ॥ १८.५ ॥
yajñadānatapaḥkarma
na tyājyaṁ kāryameva tat
yajño dānaṁ tapaścaiva
pāvanāni manīṣiṇām (18.5)

yajñadānatapaḥkarma = yajña — sacrifice + dāna — charity + tapaḥ — austerity + karma — action; na — not; tyājyaṁ — to be abandoned; kāryam — to be performed; eva — indeed; tat = tad — this; yajño = yajñaḥ — sacrifice; dānaṁ — charily; tapaścaiva = tapaḥ — austerity + caiva — and indeed; pāvanāni — purificatory acts; manīṣiṇāṁ — for the wise men

Acts of sacrifice, charity, and austerity are not to be abandoned but should be performed. Sacrifice, charity and austerity are purificatory acts even for the wise men. (18.5)

Commentary:

Lord Krishna dropped this thunderbolt statement on Arjuna to give His final disapproval for Arjuna's *sannyāsa* plans. Krishna wanted Arjuna to be a *tyāgi* only. Still, besides that aim of Lord Krishna, we must consider that a person needs to perform certain activities for his own purification. If, however, he is not selective of the modes under which he performs, the same types of actions will cause contamination.

एतान्यपि तु कर्माणि
सङ्गं त्यक्त्वा फलानि च ।
कर्तव्यानीति मे पार्थ
निश्चितं मतमुत्तमम् ॥ १८.६ ॥
etānyapi tu karmāṇi
saṅgaṁ tyaktvā phalāni ca
kartavyānīti me pārtha
niścitaṁ matamuttamam (18.6)

etāni — these; api — also; tu — but; karmāṇi —actions; saṅgaṁ — attachment; tyaktvā — giving up; phalāni — results; ca — and; kartavyānīti = kartavyāni — to be done + iti — thus; me — my; pārtha — O son of Pṛthā; niścitaṁ — definitely; matam — opinion; uttamam — highest

But these actions are to be performed by giving up attachment to results, O son of Pṛthā. This is definitely My highest opinion. (18.6)

Commentary:

Now this is the final word on the matter. The actions must be performed but one must abandon the attachment one feels and give up the results that come from the action. This is reminiscent of what Krishna explained in Chapter Four when He elaborated on working without a desire for favors or rewards, something for which He praised King Janaka. This is the *karma yoga* that Krishna said He would teach Arjuna and what Krishna claimed to have taught those legendary personalities like *Vivasvan*.

Krishna retained His original idea. And it appears that Arjuna was about to return to his view, even after seeing the scary Universal Form. We will see how Krishna prevailed over Arjuna.

नियतस्य तु संन्यासः
कर्मणो नोपपद्यते ।
मोहात्तस्य परित्यागस्
तामसः परिकीर्तितः ॥१८.७॥
niyatasya tu saṁnyāsaḥ
karmaṇo nopapadyate
mohāttasya parityāgas
tāmasaḥ parikīrtitaḥ (18.7)

niyatasya — of obligation; tu — but; saṁnyāsaḥ — renunciation; karmaṇo (karmaṇaḥ) — of action; nopapadyate = na — not + upapadyate — it is proper; mohāt — from delusion; tasya — of it; parityāgaḥ — rejection; tāmasaḥ — influence of depression; parikīrtitaḥ — is said to be

But renunciation of obligatory actions is not proper. The rejection of it on the basis of delusion, is said to occur by the influence of depression. (18.7)

Commentary:

Sannyāsa is defined as the renunciation of obligatory actions (niyatasya). One has to determine what is obligatory and what is not. Anything that is not an obligation need not be considered. These obligations, however, have to do with cultural improvement while transmigrating. A *sannyāsi* exhibits a reckless attitude toward cultural life because he plans to stop transmigrating. Thus he is exempt from the obligations.

दुःखमित्येव यत्कर्म
कायक्लेशभयात्त्यजेत् ।
स कृत्वा राजसं त्यागं
नैव त्यागफलं लभेत् ॥१८.८॥
duḥkhamityeva yatkarma
kāyakleśabhayāttyajet
sa kṛtvā rājasaṁ tyāgaṁ
naiva tyāgaphalaṁ labhet (18.8)

duḥkham — difficult; ityeva = iti — thus + eva — indeed; yat = yad — which; karma — action; kāyakleśabhayāt = kāya — body + kleśa — suffering + bhayāt — from fear; tyajet — should abandon; sa = saḥ — he; kṛtvā — having performed; rājasaṁ — impulsive influence; tyāgaṁ — renunciation; naiva = na —not + eva — indeed; tyāgaphalam — result of renunciation; labhet — should obtain

He who abandons action because of difficulty or because of a fear of bodily suffering, performs impulsive renunciation. He would not obtain the desired result of that renunciation. (18.8)

Commentary:

This is a warning for one and all, and it is applicable to Arjuna. Arjuna wanted to abandon his duty because of the difficulty involved in battlefield work as well as due to the fear of his own or others' bodily suffering. Such a renunciation of action would be conducted by the impulsive mode of material nature. The escapee, Krishna said,would not obtain the result intended.

As Lord Krishna told Arjuna, people would ridicule Arjuna. Those who were fond of Arjuna would shun him for cowardice. Thus the endearment Arjuna hoped for would be denied.

कार्यमित्येव यत्कर्म
नियतं क्रियतेऽर्जुन ।
सङ्गं त्यक्त्वा फलं चैव
स त्यागः सात्त्विको मतः ॥ १८.९ ॥
kāryamityeva yatkarma
niyataṁ kriyate'rjuna
saṅgaṁ tyaktvā phalaṁ caiva
sa tyāgaḥ sāttviko mataḥ (18.9)

kāryam — to be done; ityeva = iti — thus + eva — indeed; yat — which; karma — action; niyataṁ — disciplinary manner; kriyate — is performed; 'rjuna = arjuna — Arjuna; saṅgaṁ — attachment; tyaktvā — abandoning; phalaṁ — result; caiva — and indeed; sa = saḥ — it; tyāgaḥ — renunciation; sāttviko = sāttvikaḥ — of the clarifying mode; mataḥ — is considered

O Arjuna, when an action is done in a disciplinary manner, because it is to be performed, and with renunciation of the attachment to the results, it is considered to be in the clarifying mode. (18.9)

Commentary:

This type of renunciation was the type recommended for Arjuna. This is the type of renunciation for the *karma* yogis like Janaka. The highest type of such renunciation would take place under the *Sat* principle which is explained at the end of the previous chapter.

Instead of avoiding combat altogether, Arjuna was to act in the disciplinary manner without sentiment (*saṅgam tyaktvā*). That would situate him in the clarifying mode. It may be asked. Why did Krishna not tell Arjuna to enter the *Sat* or spiritual mode immediately? The answer is: Arjuna was situated in the impulsive, passionate energy which was described in the previous verse. He had to evolve gradually to the clarifying mode and then after stabilizing himself there, he would move into the *Sat* position as described in Chapter Seventeen:

yajñe tapasi dāne ca sthitiḥ saditi cocyate
karma caiva tadarthīyaṁ sadityevābhidhīyate (17.27)

Steady application in sacrifice, austerity and charity, is also called Sat. An action which is supportive of this purpose is also designated as Sat. (17.27)

Some modern spiritual masters feel, however, that it is not necessary to transfer oneself first to the clarifying mode or to the mode of goodness. They advocate a hasty and abrupt transfer from any of the modes of material nature to the *Sat* (transcendental) level.

न द्वेष्ट्यकुशलं कर्म
कुशले नानुषज्जते ।
त्यागी सत्त्वसमाविष्टो
मेधावी छिन्नसंशयः ॥ १८.१० ॥
na dveṣṭyakuśalaṁ karma
kuśale nānuṣajjate
tyāgī sattvasamāviṣṭo
medhāvī chinnasaṁśayaḥ (18.10)

na — not; dveṣṭi — hates; akuśalaṁ — disagreeable; karma — action; kuśale — is agreeable; nānuṣajjate = na — not + anuśajjate — is attached; tyāgī — renouncer; sattvasamāviṣṭo = sattva — clarity + samāviṣṭo (samāviṣṭah) — filled with; medhāvi — wise man; chinnasaṁśayaḥ = chinna — removed + saṁśayaḥ — doubt

The renouncer who is filled with clarity, the wise man whose doubts are removed, does not hate disagreeable action, nor is he attached to agreeable performance. (18.10)

Commentary:

As we stated, Lord Krishna was trying to get Arjuna to be in the mode of clarity, the mode of goodness. This is a description of such a person. The highest mode is that of *Sat* (spiritual reality) as described at the end of the last chapter. But that is a giant step away from the impulsive, passionate level Arjuna displayed.

न हि देहभृता शक्यं
त्यक्तुं कर्माण्यशेषतः ।
यस्तु कर्मफलत्यागी
स त्यागीत्यभिधीयते ॥१८.११॥
na hi dehabhṛtā śakyaṁ
tyaktuṁ karmāṇyaśeṣataḥ
yastu karmaphalatyāgī
sa tyāgītyabhidhīyate (18.11)

na — not; hi — indeed; dehabhṛtā — by the body-supported; śakyaṁ — possible; tyaktuṁ — to abandon; karmāṇi — actions; aśeṣataḥ — completely; yaḥ —who; tu — but; karmaphalatyāgī = karma — action + phala — result + tyāgī — remover; sa = saḥ — he; tyāgīti = tyāgī — renunciate + iti — thus; abhidhīyate — is called

Indeed it is not possible for the body-supported beings to abandon actions completely. But whosoever is the renouncer of the results of actions is called a renunciate. (18.11)

Commentary:

This takes us back to the first arguments made by Lord Krishna, where He indicated that even if Arjuna went to the forest for a pacifist life, the thoughts of battle would haunt him. Arjuna would be a pretender. And eventually Arjuna would return to the battlefield to fight since his nature would not allow him to live as a peaceful brahmin.

अनिष्टमिष्टं मिश्रं च
त्रिविधं कर्मणः फलम् ।
भवत्यत्यागिनां प्रेत्य
न तु संन्यासिनां क्वचित् ॥१८.१२॥
aniṣṭamiṣṭaṁ miśraṁ ca
trividhaṁ karmaṇaḥ phalam
bhavatyatyāgināṁ pretya
na tu saṁnyāsināṁ kvacit (18.12)

aniṣṭam — undesired; iṣṭaṁ — desired; miśraṁ — mixed; ca — and; trividham — three types; karmaṇaḥ — of action; phalam — result; bhavati — it is; atyāgināṁ — of those who do not renounce results; pretya — departing; na — not; tu — but; saṁnyāsināṁ — of the renouncers; kvacit — any at all

Undesired, desired and mixed are the three types of results of actions that occur for the departing souls who do not renounce results. But for the renouncers of opportunity, there is no result at all. (18.12)

Commentary:

This verse is usually confused by translators and commentators. Some translators confuse the two words, namely, *sannyāsi* and *tyāgi*. In verse 2 of this chapter, Lord Krishna clearly distinguished these. If we confuse these two terms, we will develop a misunderstanding. Verses 5 through 11 describe a *tyāgi*, a person who renounces the good or bad consequences of his past activities. Such a man does perform selected activities which are prescribed according to his caste. Arjuna, for instance, was to stick to caste duty as a law man. Even though caste has negative connotations in the modern political setting, we cannot avoid its importance if we want to understand the *Gītā* in its own time and place. We cannot hide it because it is plain to see. But if we want to rationalize the *Gītā* in terms of modern concepts of human equality, we may have to twist the *Gītā*. And many did this already.

This verse, unlike verses 5 through 11, is concerned with a comparison between those who are not in the habit of renouncing anything and those who renounce practically everything. Those who renounce even work opportunities are *sannyāsis*. These are not the *karma* yogis or *tyāgis* like Arjuna but rather these persons take the other path of samkhya or *jñana yoga*. Arjuna was on the path of high-class action regulation, *karma yoga*.

śrībhagavānuvāca
loke'smindvividhā niṣṭhā purā proktā mayānagha
jñānayogena sāṁkhyānāṁ karmayogena yogināṁ (3.3)

The Blessed Lord said: In the physical world, a two-fold standard was previously taught by Me. O Arjuna, my good man. This was mind regulation by the yoga practice of the Sāṁkhya philosophical yogis and the action regulation by the yoga practice of the non-philosophical yogis. (3.3)

Here Lord Krishna clarified a very important point, that those who are habituated to attachment of work and attachment of the results of work, do acquire desired, undesired, and mixed results after they leave their bodies while those who renounce practically everything, acquire no results in the mundane world. Arjuna was not in the class of a *sannyāsi*. And he was not supposed to be.

Arjuna wanted a result. He wanted a positive result of being appreciated by his relatives and teachers. Krishna explained that such a result would not be forthcoming if Arjuna left aside duties. It is not that Arjuna did not desire a result. Arjuna is a devotee but he had personal motives. Krishna was to teach Arjuna how to be practical in getting the desired result by working through the grooves of providence. Full renunciation (*sannyāsa*) would not have given Arjuna the result he desired, nor would total attachment. Arjuna had to take up *karma yoga* and be a *tyāgi* to get what he wanted from the battle encounter.

पञ्चैतानि महाबाहो
कारणानि निबोध मे ।
सांख्ये कृतान्ते प्रोक्तानि
सिद्धये सर्वकर्मणाम् ॥१८.१३॥
pañcaitāni mahābāho
kāraṇāni nibodha me
sāṁkhye kṛtānte proktāni
siddhaye sarvakarmaṇām (18.13)

pañcaitāni = pañca — five + tāni — these; mahābāho — O mighty-armed man; kāraṇāni — factors; nibodha — learn; me — from me; sāṁkhye — in Sāṁkhya philosophy; krtānte — in conclusion, in doctrine; proktāni — declared; siddhaye — in accomplishment; sarvakarmaṇām — of all actions

Learn from Me, O mighty-armed man, of the five factors declared in the Sāṁkhya doctrine for the accomplishment of all actions: (18.13)

Commentary:

Arjuna wanted to achieve something. He was not a selfless man, nor was he, at the time of the battle encounter, aiming to be selfless. Arjuna was not a caste brahmin. The brahmin's gentleness was not essential to his nature, otherwise he would not be known as the mighty-armed man or as Dhanamjaya, conqueror of wealthy provinces.

Lord Krishna taught him about the factors which contributed to the formation of actions. If a man understands these and sees them in their proper perspective, he might be successful in endeavors. He would be realisitic in planning.

अधिष्ठानं तथा कर्ता
करणं च पृथग्विधम् ।
विविधाश्च पृथक्चेष्टा
दैवं चैवात्र पञ्चमम् ॥१८.१४॥

adhiṣṭhānaṁ — location; tathā — as well as; kartā — the agent; karaṇaṁ — the instrument; ca — and; prthagvidham — various kinds; vividhāśca = vividhāḥ — various + ca — and; pṛthakceṣṭa —

adhiṣṭhānaṁ tathā kartā
karaṇaṁ ca pṛthagvidham
vividhāśca pṛthakceṣṭā
daivaṁ caivātra pañcama (18.14)

movements; daivam — destiny; caivātra = ca — and + eva — indeed + atra — here in this case; pañcamam — the fifth

The location, the agent, the various instruments, the various movements, and destiny, the fifth factor. (18.14)

Commentary:

Unless these five factors are present, no activity can take place and no result of an activity can be manifested. Usually, however, we ignore four of the contributing factors and pay attention to the kartā (agent). Besides the agent, there must be a location, there must be various instruments for executing the activity, there must be various movements, there must be endeavors, and most of all there must be destiny or supernatural power.

Arjuna was shown that supernatural power in the apparition of the Universal Form. Krishna asserted that whatever took place on that supernatural level would manifest on this earthly plane with or without the agency of Arjuna.

शरीरवाङ्मनोभिर्यत्
कर्म प्रारभते नरः ।
न्याय्यं वा विपरीतं वा
पञ्चैते तस्य हेतवः ॥१८.१५॥
śarīravāṅmanobhiryat
karma prārabhate naraḥ
nyāyyaṁ vā viparītaṁ vā
pañcaite tasya hetavaḥ (18.15)

śarīravāṅmanobhiḥ = śarīra — body + vān(vās) — speech + manobhiḥ — with mind; yat = yad — whatever; karma — project; prārabhate — he undertakes; naraḥ — a human being; nyāyyaṁ — moral; vā — or; viparītam — immoral; vā — or; pañcaite = pañca — five + ete — these; tasya — of it; hetavaḥ — factors

As for whatever project a human being undertakes with body, speech and mind, regardless of it being moral or immoral, these are its five factors. (18.15)

Commentary:

Arjuna was interested in doing something traditional, something moral, something that was approved by the elders and by the Vedas (nyāyyam). But Lord Krishna informed him that regardless of the moral or immoral nature of an action, there must be five factors. This means that destiny or supernatural agency is also supportive of immoral activity. Of course, that sort of support will bring on a reversal or a rash reaction, which is produced by the same supernatural agency.

तत्रैवं सति कर्तारम्
आत्मानं केवलं तु यः ।
पश्यत्यकृतबुद्धित्वान्
न स पश्यति दुर्मतिः ॥१८.१६॥
tatraivaṁ sati kartāram
ātmānaṁ kevalaṁ tu yaḥ
paśyatyakṛtabuddhitvān
na sa paśyati durmatiḥ (18.16)

tatraivaṁ = tatra — here, in this case + evam — thus; sati — in reality, correctly; kartāram — agent; ātmānaṁ — self; kevalam — only; tu — but; yaḥ — who; paśyati — he regards; akṛtabuddhitvāt = akṛta — undone, defective + buddhitvāt — due to intellect; na — not; sa = saḥ — he; paśyati — he perceives; durmatiḥ — idiot

In that case, whosoever regards himself as the only agent, does not perceive correctly. This is due to the defective intellect of the idiot. (18.16)

Commentary:

Arjuna was an agent. He did have a part to play. But his was not the only factor. He was merely one of the factors. He was not the most important one either. His intellect was defective when he first viewed the warriors. In Chapters Three, Four, and Five, where *buddhi* yoga was discussed in great detail, Lord Krishna preached for the correct adjustment of Arjuna's intellect.

यस्य नाहंकृतो भावो
बुद्धिर्यस्य न लिप्यते ।
हत्वापि स इमाँल्लोकान्
न हन्ति न निबध्यते ॥ १८.१७॥
yasya nāhaṁkṛto bhāvo
buddhiryasya na lipyate
hatvāpi sa imāṁllokān
na hanti na nibadhyate (18.17)

yasya — regarding who; nāhaṁkṛto = na — not + ahaṁkṛto (ahaṁkṛtaḥ) — falsely assertive; bhāvo = bhāvaḥ — attitude; buddhiḥ — intellect; yasya — of whom; na — not; lipyate — is clouded; hatvāpi = hatvā — having slain + api — even; sa = saḥ — he; imān — these; lokān — people; na — not; hanti — he slays; na — not; nibadhyate — is implicated

Regarding the person whose attitude is not falsely assertive, whose intellect is not clouded, even after slaying these people, he would not slay or be implicated. (18.17)

Commentary:

Lord Krishna insisted that Arjuna take up the task of a law man. This is to incite Arjuna to fight and to rid Arjuna of the fear of the reactions and of the guilty feelings that Arjuna displayed in Chapter One.

In terms of the philosophy of the *Gītā* which is based on the samkhya system of thinking, this is a piece of valuable information. If while performing one's obligatory duties, one does not assume an assertive, egotistic attitude and if one's attitude is not clouded by false conclusions and by a doership attitude, then even disciplinary actions would not bring on reactions, nor would the actor feel that he was being violent.

This is the practice of *karma yoga* for Arjuna, as he follows in the footsteps of those yogi-kings like Janaka who, through worldly actions, gradually and definitely transferred themselves to the plane of clarity in material nature and then moved to the first spiritual level *Sat* (reality) which was described in the last verses of the previous chapter.

ज्ञानं ज्ञेयं परिज्ञाता
त्रिविधा कर्मचोदना ।
करणं कर्म कर्तेति
त्रिविधः कर्मसंग्रहः ॥ १८.१८॥
jñānaṁ jñeyaṁ parijñātā
trividhā karmacodanā
karaṇaṁ karma karteti
trividhaḥ karmasaṁgrahaḥ (18.18)

jñānaṁ — experience; jñeyaṁ — the item of research; parijñātā — the experiencer; trividhā — three aspects; karmacodanā = karma — action + codanā — impetus for; karaṇaṁ — instrument; karma — action; karteti = kartā — agent + iti — thus; trividhaḥ — three; karmasaṁgrahaḥ = karma — action + saṁgrahaḥ — parts

Experience, the item of research, and the experiencer are the three aspects which serve as the impetus for action. The instrument, the action itself, and the agent are three parts of an action. (18.18)

Commentary:

If we could understand action, we would be free from error to a greater degree. Arjuna needed such an understanding in order to complete duties. Thus Arjuna was given all these details of the samkhya philosophy. As a man of the world, Arjuna needed such information of the science of *karma yoga.* He had to understand the consequences of action if he was to follow in the footsteps of the great yogi-kings like Janaka.

The impetus for action originates on the causal plane which is the zone of ideas. It is the level from which our initial thinking originates. The three aspects which cause an impetus for action are the experiencer, the item to be experienced, and the experience itself. The action takes place on the subtle and physical levels but it is initiated on the subtle plane. There must be an instrument, an action, and the agent. This means that the experiencer acts as the agent or he causes someone else to act in his place.

At *Kurukṣetra*, Arjuna was the experiencer on the causal plane, from which he sought the experience of the battle encounter, in which he would observe the item of research, which was the government.

As for the three parts of the action, Arjuna was the instrument but Lord Krishna, in the Universal Form, was the agent. The action itself was already executed on the supernatural level but it was to be lived out by Arjuna on the physical plane. Lord Krishna was also the experiencer on the causal level, since He told Arjuna that He also was an experiencer of the living space, but He described Himself as the super-experiencer, experiencing in all bodies simultaneously.

ज्ञानं कर्म च कर्ता च
त्रिधैव गुणभेदतः ।
प्रोच्यते गुणसंख्याने
यथावच्छृणु तान्यपि ॥१८.१९॥

jñānaṁ karma ca kartā ca
tridhaiva guṇabhedataḥ
procyate guṇasaṁkhyāne
yathāvacchṛṇu tānyapi (18.19)

jñānaṁ — experience; karma — action; ca — and; kartā — agent; ca — and; tridhaiva = tridha — three types + eva — indeed; guṇabhedataḥ — categorized by the influences of material nature; procyate — is stated; guṇasaṁkhyāne — in the Sāṁkhya analysis of the influences of material nature; yathāvat — correctly; śṛṇu — hear; tāni — these; api — as well

In the Sāṁkhya analysis of the influence of material nature, it is stated that experience, action, and the agent are of three types as categorized by the influence of material nature. Hear correctly of these as well. (18.19)

Commentary:

In Chapter Seventeen and also in this chapter, Lord Krishna explained the three types of categories according to the modes of material nature. This means that one has to understand this thoroughly if he is to master *karma yoga*. The implication is that one cannot effectively and consistently transcend the modes of material nature unless one can instantly recognize each of the modes. One cannot transcend simply by wishful thinking. Unless one can learn how to shift himself to the mode of clarity, one cannot be transferred to the *Sat* mode which was described in the last verses of Chapter Seventeen.

सर्वभूतेषु येनैकं
भावमव्ययमीक्षते ।
अविभक्तं विभक्तेषु
तज्ज्ञानं विद्धि सात्त्विकम् ॥१८.२०॥
sarvabhūteṣu yenaikaṁ
bhāvamavyayamīkṣate
avibhaktaṁ vibhakteṣu
tajjñānaṁ viddhi sāttvikam (18.20)

sarvabhūteṣu — in all beings; yenaikaṁ = yena — by which + ekam — one; bhāvam — being; avyayam — imperishable; īksate — one perceives; avibhaktaṁ — undivided; vibhakteṣu — in the divided; tat — that; jñānaṁ — experience; viddhi — know; sāttvikaṁ — clarifying

That experience by which one perceives one imperishable being in all beings, undivided in the divided, know it to be an experience in clarity. (18.20)

Commentary:

This vision was shown to Arjuna in the Universal Form. This does not mean that the individual spirits are one with God, but rather it means that God supervises the entire situation and has it under control as one realm.

As Sanjaya realized:

tatraikasthaṁ jagatkṛtsnaṁ
pravibhaktamanekadhā
apaśyaddevadevasya
śarīre pāṇḍavastadā (11.13)

There the entire universe existed as one reality divided in many ways. Arjuna Pandava then saw the God of gods in that body. (11.13)

And as Arjuna bowed to that undivided God who prevails over all sections of the undivided world:

namaḥ purastādatha pṛṣṭhataste namo'stu te sarvata eva sarva
anantavīryāmitavikramastvaṁ sarvaṁ samāpnoṣi tato'si sarvaḥ (11.40)

Reverence to You from the front, from behind. Let there be obeisances to You on all sides, O sum total Reality. You are infinite power, immeasurable might. You penetrate everything. In that sense, You are Everything. (11.40)

पृथक्त्वेन तु यज्ज्ञानं
नानाभावान्पृथग्विधान् ।
वेत्ति सर्वेषु भूतेषु
तज्ज्ञानं विद्धि राजसम् ॥१८.२१॥
pṛthaktvena tu yajjñānaṁ
nānābhāvānpṛthagvidhān
vetti sarveṣu bhūteṣu
tajjñānaṁ viddhi rājasam (18.21)

pṛthaktvena — with difference; tu — but; yat — which; jñānaṁ — experience; nānābhāvān = nānā — different + bhāvān — beings; pṛthagvidhān — of different kinds; vetti — realizes; sarveṣu — in all; bhūteṣu — in beings; tat — that; jñānaṁ — experience; viddhi — know; rājasam — of the impulsive mode

But that experience by which one realizes different beings of different kinds with differences in all beings, should be known as experience in the impulsive mode. (18.21)

Commentary:

If one does not see the Supervising God, and if one does not understand that one is merely a servant or agent of that Supervising Super-Person, and that one should minimize one's feelings and get in tune with the desires of that God, then one is apt to see beings of different kinds with differences everywhere. One may think that all beings have absolute rights unto themselves or relative privileges in relation to each other, without seeing that there is an absolute standard which is to be satisfied. Arjuna said this of Krishna:

tvamakṣaraṁ paramaṁ veditavyaṁ tvamasya viśvasya paraṁ nidhānam
tvamavyayaḥ śāśvatadharmagoptā sanātanastvaṁ puruṣo mato me. (11.18)

You are the indestructible Supreme Reality, to be realized. You are the ultimate shelter of all. You are the imperishable, eternal guardian of law. It seems to me that You are the most ancient person. (11.18)

यत्तु कृत्स्नवदेकस्मिन्
कार्ये सक्तमहैतुकम् ।
अतत्त्वार्थवदल्पं च
तत्तामसमुदाहृतम् ॥१८.२२॥
yattu kṛtsnavadekasmin
kārye saktamahaitukam
atattvārthavadalpaṁ ca
tattāmasamudāhṛtam (18.22)

yat = yad — which; tu — but; kṛtsnavat — appears as the whole; ekasmin — in one; kārye — in order of action; saktam — attached; ahaitukam — without due cause; atattvārthavat — without a valid purpose; alpaṁ — petty; ca — and; tat = tad — that; tāmasam — of the depressive influence; udāhṛtam — is said to be

But that experience which appears to be the whole vision, being attached to one procedure without due cause, without a valid purpose, being petty, that is said to be of the depressive influence. (18.22)

Commentary:

We must learn to recognize which mode our vision is being sponsored by. Every man has an opinion, even the people who claim to have no opinion at all, even those who feel that everyone's opinion should carry an equal value. Still, in all cases, we should determine the mode which sponsors the view.

नियतं सङ्गरहितम्
अरागद्वेषतः कृतम् ।
अफलप्रेप्सुना कर्म
यत्तत्सात्त्विकमुच्यते ॥१८.२३॥
niyataṁ saṅgarahitam
arāgadveṣataḥ kṛtam
aphalaprepsunā karma
yattatsāttvikamucyate (18.23)

niyatam — controlled; saṅgarahitam = saṅga — attachment + rahitam — free from; arāgadveṣataḥ — without craving or repulsion; kṛtam — performed; aphalaprepsunā = aphala — without result + prepsunā — desire to get; karma — action; yat = yad — which; tat = tad — such; sāttvikaṁ — of the clarifying influence; ucyate — is said

Action which is controlled, which is free from attachment, which is performed without craving or repulsion, without desire for results, such action is said to be of the clarifying influence. (18.23)

Commentary:

This is the type of action which Krishna recommended for Arjuna. This meant that Arjuna was to relocate from the impulsive mode to the clarifying mode or level. Chapters Three, Four, and Five which are a course for this type of behavior, spell out the preliminary requirements for *karma yoga*.

यत्तु कामेप्सुना कर्म
साहंकारेण वा पुनः ।
क्रियते बहुलायासं
तद्राजसमुदाहृतम् ॥१८.२४॥
yattu kāmepsunā karma
sāhaṁkāreṇa vā punaḥ
kriyate bahulāyāsaṁ
tadrājasamudāhṛtam (18.24)

yat = yad — which; tu — but; kāmepsunā = kāma — craving + ipsunā — desiring to get; karma — action; sāhaṁkāreṇa — with false assertion; vā — or; punaḥ = punar alternatively; kriyate — is performed; bahulāyāsaṁ = bahula — much + āyāsaṁ effort; tat — that; rājasam — of the impulsive influence; udāhṛtam — is said to be

But that action which is performed with a wish for cravings, with false assertion or alternately with much effort, that is said to be of the impulsive influence. (18.24)

Commentary:

If we study Arjuna's attitude and his desire not to fight, it can be analyzed as being a desire for action in the impulsive mode. Arjuna was craving the popularity and approval of elders. He asserted himself without reference to the Universal Form and his energies were dissipated in an emotional breakdown. Lord Krishna took action to lecture, inspire and relocate Arjuna to the clarifying mode, bordering on the *Sat* level which was described in the last verses of the previous chapter.

अनुबन्धं क्षयं हिंसाम्
अनपेक्ष्य च पौरुषम् ।
मोहादारभ्यते कर्म
यत्तत्तामसमुच्यते ॥१८.२५॥
anubandhaṁ kṣayaṁ hiṁsām
anapekṣya ca pauruṣam
mohādārabhyate karma
yattattāmasamucyate (18.25)

anubandhaṁ — consequence; kṣayaṁ — damage; hiṁsām — violence; anapekṣya regardless of; ca — and; pauruṣam — practical power; mohāt — from misconception; ārabhyate — is undertaken; karma — action; yat — which; tat — that; tāmasam — of the depressive mode; ucyate — is said to be

That action which is undertaken from a misconception, regardless of the consequence, the damage and the violence, and without considering one's practical power, is said to be of the depressive mode. (18.25)

Commentary:

Arjuna was not in this depressive mode because he did consider the consequences, liabilities and violence involved. In fact, he described these in Chapter One. However, even if one considers the consequences, one should still submit as an agent for the Universal Form. One should know one's usefulness in any given situation. And one should understand that every endeavor is supervised by the Central Figure in the Universal Form.

मुक्तसङ्गोऽनहंवादी
धृत्युत्साहसमन्वितः ।
सिद्ध्यसिद्ध्योर्निर्विकारः
कर्ता सात्त्विक उच्यते ॥१८.२६॥
muktasaṅgo'nahaṁvādī
dhṛtyutsāhasamanvitaḥ
siddhyasiddhyornirvikāraḥ
kartā sāttvika ucyate (18.26)

muktasaṅgo = muktasaṅgaḥ — freed from attachment; 'nahaṁvādi = anahaṁvādi — free from self praise, free from vanity; dhṛtyutsāhasamanvitaḥ = dhṛty (dhṛti) — consistence + utsāha — perseverance + samanvitaḥ — possessed with; siddhyasiddhyoḥ — in success or failure; nirvikāraḥ — unaffected; kartā — performer; sāttvika — in the clarifying mode; ucyate — is rated to be

A performer who is free from attachment, free from vanity, who is consistent and perseverant, and who is unaffected in success or failure, is rated to be in the clarifying mode. (18.26)

Commentary:

In Chapter One, Arjuna was energetic. Then he was overcome by the depressive mode. He lost enthusiasm. He was affected by the prospect of failure. He was not free from attachment to family and friends. He was involved in a vanity through which he felt that he was in charge of the battle situation. It is not our duty to criticise Arjuna, however, but we must understand his position and then apply the clarification to our situation. Thus ultimately, we may learn to recognize the support we take from material nature.

रागी कर्मफलप्रेप्सुर्
लुब्धो हिंसात्मकोऽशुचिः ।
हर्षशोकान्वितः कर्ता
राजसः परिकीर्तितः ॥१८.२७॥
rāgī karmaphalaprepsur
lubdho hiṁsātmako'śuciḥ
harṣaśokānvitaḥ kartā
rājasaḥ parikīrtitaḥ (18.27)

rāgī — prone to impulsiveness; karmaphalaprepsuḥ = karma — action + phala — result + prepsuḥ — craving; lubdho = lubdhaḥ — greedy; hiṁsāmako = hiṁsāmakaḥ — violent nature; 'śuciḥ = aśuciḥ — unclean; harṣaśokānvitaḥ = harṣa — joy + śoka — sorrow + anvitaḥ — prone to; kartā — performer; rājasaḥ — of the impulsive mode; parikīrtitaḥ — is declared

A performer who is prone to impulsiveness, who craves the results of action, who is greedy, violent by nature, unclean and who is prone to joy or sorrow, is declared to be under the impulsive mode. (18.27)

Commentary:

So long as we are acting without reference to the Universal Form, we are apt to crave favorable results. This means that our actions would be based on desired effects and this would greatly limit us.

If we base our lives on avoidance of sorrow and attraction to joy, we will greatly limit performance. And we would certainly not be interested in working for Lord Krishna since His work might involve unpalatable acts such as discipline of relatives and friends. If we want to give acquiantances unlimited rights of living and freedoms of expression, we will not be able to cooperate with Krishna. It would be difficult, just as it was for Arjuna in Chapter One of the *Gītā*.

अयुक्तः प्राकृतः स्तब्धः
शठो नैष्कृतिकोऽलसः ।
विषादी दीर्घसूत्री च
कर्ता तामस उच्यते ॥१८.२८॥
ayuktaḥ prākṛtaḥ stabdhaḥ
śaṭho naiṣkṛtiko'lasaḥ
viṣādī dīrghasūtrī ca
kartā tāmasa ucyate (18.28)

ayuktaḥ — undisciplined; prākṛtaḥ — vulgar; stabdhaḥ — stubborn; śaṭho = śaṭhaḥ — wicked; naiṣkṛtiko = naiṣkṛtikaḥ — deceitful; 'lasaḥ = alasaḥ — lazy; viṣādī — depressed; dīrghasūtrī — neglectful; ca — and; kartā — performer; tāmasa — in the depressive mood; ucyate — is said to be

A performer who is undisciplined, vulgar, stubborn, wicked, deceitful, lazy, depressed and neglectful, is said to be in the depressive mode. (18.28)

Commentary:

The depressing mode, the mode of ignorance, is the attitude of mind through which we lose objectivity, cannot see clearly what we intend to do, and act haphazardly without caring for the consequences. Generally a person in the depressive mode feels that it does not matter what he does. In other words, he fails to calculate the risks in any venture. In the impulsive or passionate mode, a person begins to calculate but only in terms of immediate gratification and without considering the laws of nature which no living being can successfully circumvent. But in the mode of clarity or goodness, a person considers the laws of nature and tries to alter his plans accordingly.

In each of these modes, the same soul might be involved in the same mind space. What then is the difference? If the same soul can shift from depression, to impulsion, to clarity, then what changed?

The answer is that the life energy changed in quality. In Sanskrit this is called the *prāṇa* but in English it is called sensual or emotional energy. It is also called subtle feeling. To simplify the matter many spiritual authorities say that the consciousness changed. Actually it is not the consciousness but it is rather a mixture of consciousness and life energy. The main force of change is the life energy. When the quality of the life energy improves, a man's vision clears up and he perceives reality. When it deteriorates, his vision becomes clouded and he acts irresponsibly.

In the material world, the spirit cannot function through his own consciousness directly. He uses a mixture of his consciousness and life energy (*prāṇa*). In fact, he cannot all of a sudden transcend the dulling, impulsive, or clarifying power of the life energy, at least not on a consistent basis. Unless he upgrades his life energy, he can only have flashes of enlightenment with no consistent relocation to the *Sat* mode which is briefly described at the end of the last chapter.

बुद्धेर्भेदं धृतेश्चैव
गुणतस्त्रिविधं शृणु ।
प्रोच्यमानमशेषेण
पृथक्त्वेन धनंजय ॥ १८.२९ ॥
buddherbhedaṁ dhṛteścaiva
guṇatastrividhaṁ śṛṇu
procyamānamaśeṣeṇa
pṛthaktvena dhanaṁjaya (18.29)

buddheḥ — intellect; bhedaṁ — difference; dhṛteḥ — determination; caiva — and indeed; guṇataḥ — according to the influences of material nature; trividham — three types; śṛṇu — hear; procyamānam — explained; aśeṣena — thoroughly; pṛthaktvena — distinctly; dhanaṁjaya — a conqueror of wealthy countries

Now, O conqueror of wealthy countries, hear of the three types of intellect and also of determination, explained thoroughly and distinctly, according to their distinctions under the influences of material nature. (18.29)

Commentary:

The intellect is a special psychic tool which is attached to the mind. One's determination is tunneled through the intellect but it is driven by the life energies which we normally experience as inner sensual urges. Anything that is affected by the life energy is subjected to a threefold influence for depression, impulsion, or clarity.

प्रवृत्तिं च निवृत्तिं च
कार्याकार्ये भयाभये ।
बन्धं मोक्षं च या वेत्ति
बुद्धिः सा पार्थ सात्त्विकी ॥ १८.३० ॥

pravṛttiṁ — endeavor; ca — and; nivṛttiṁ — non-endeavor; ca — and; kāryākārye = kārya — what should be done + akārya — what should not be done; bhayābhaye — what is dangerous and what is safe; bandhaṁ — restriction; mokṣaṁ—

pravṛttiṁ ca nivṛttiṁ ca
kāryākārye bhayābhaye
bandhaṁ mokṣaṁ ca yā vetti
buddhiḥ sā pārtha sāttvikī (18.30)

freedom; ca — and; yā — which; vetti — discerns; buddhiḥ — intellectual insight; sā — if, partha — son of Pṛthā; sāttvikī — in the clarifying mode

That intellectual insight which discerns when to endeavor and when not to strive, what should be done and what should not be done, what is dangerous and what is safe, what brings restrictions and what gives freedom, that O son of Pṛthā, is in the clarifying mode. (18.30)

Commentary:

Each mode of nature offers certain guarantees but the lower two show the greater distortion of reality. In each mode a person feels certain of his or her position and feels assured that hopes will come true, but only in the clarifying mode does one stand a chance for minimum frustration. Thus, if one can, one should relocate to the clarifying mode, at least until one can become elevated enough to reach the *Sat* level which is described in the last verses of the previous chapter.

यया धर्ममधर्मं च
कार्यं चाकार्यमेव च ।
अयथावत्प्रजानाति
बुद्धिः सा पार्थ राजसी ॥१८.३१॥
yayā dharmamadharmaṁ ca
kāryaṁ cākāryameva ca
ayathāvatprajānāti
buddhiḥ sā pārtha rājasī (18.31)

yayā — by which; dharmam — right; adharmaṁ — wrong; ca — and; kāryam — duty; cākāryam = ca — and + akāryam — neglect; eva — indeed; ca — and; ayathāvat — mistakenly; prajānāti — is identified; buddhiḥ — intellectual insight; sā — it; pārtha — son of Pṛthā; rājasī — in the impulsive mode

That intellectual insight by which right and wrong, duty and neglect, are mistakenly identified, is, O son of Pṛthā, in the impulsive mode. (18.31)

Commentary:

The mind is supposed to monitor the sensual energies or urges. The soul is supposed to use the intellect to direct the mind. But if the urges are allowed to goad the mind and influence the intellect, the soul becomes responsible for perverse activities.

अधर्मं धर्ममिति या
मन्यते तमसावृता ।
सर्वार्थान्विपरीतांश्च
बुद्धिः सा पार्थ तामसी ॥१८.३२॥
adharmaṁ dharmamiti yā
manyate tamasāvṛtā
sarvārthānviparītāṁśca
buddhiḥ sā pārtha tāmasī (18.32)

adharmaṁ — wrong method; dharmam — right method; iti — thus; yā — which; manyate — it considered; tamasāvṛtā = tamasa — ignorance + āvṛtā — absorbed by; sarvārthān — all values; viparītāṁśca = viparītān — perverted + ca — and; buddhiḥ — intellectual insight; sā — it; pārtha — son of Pṛthā; tāmasī — in the depressive mode

That intellectual insight which is absorbed by ignorance, which considers the wrong method as the right one and perceives all values in a perverted way, is, O son of Pṛthā, of the depressive mode. (18.32)

Commentary:

When the intellectual power is completely absorbed by the urges or sensual feelings and when it does not remain in a governing position over the mind, the spirit perceives in a perverted way that is contrary to reality. Thus he enters the depressive mode in which his good sense is overshadowed.

धृत्या यया धारयते
मनःप्राणेन्द्रियक्रियाः ।
योगेनाव्यभिचारिण्या
धृतिः सा पार्थ सात्त्विकी ॥ १८.३३ ॥
dhṛtyā yayā dhārayate
manaḥprāṇendriyakriyāḥ
yogenāvyabhicāriṇyā
dhṛtiḥ sā pārtha sāttvikī (18.33)

dhṛtyā — by determination; yayā — by which; dhārayate — it holds; manaḥprāṇendriyakriyāḥ = manaḥ — mind + prāṇa — energizing breath + indriyakriyāḥ — senses; yogenāvyabhicāriṇyā = yogena — by yoga practices + avyabhicāriṇyā — unwavering, constant; dhṛtiḥ — determination; sā — it; pārtha — son of Pṛthā; sāttvikī — of the clarifying influence

The determination which holds the mind, the energizing breath, and the senses by constant yoga expertise, that, O son of Pṛthā, is of the clarifying influence. (18.33)

<u>*Commentary:*</u>

To hold the determination firm one has to use *dhāranā* (mental concentration) which is one of the procedures of *aṣṭanga* yoga. These procedures are *yama, niyama, āsana, prāṇāyāma, pratyāhāra, dhāranā, dhyāna*, and *samādhi*.

To hold the vital breath in purity and to direct it efficiently one has to be expert in *prāṇāyāma*, the fourth part of yoga. And to restrain the senses one has to apply *pratyāhāra*, which is a system of reversing the outward flow of the sensual energies, bringing them back to the focal spirit.

***Outward** flow of sensual energies*

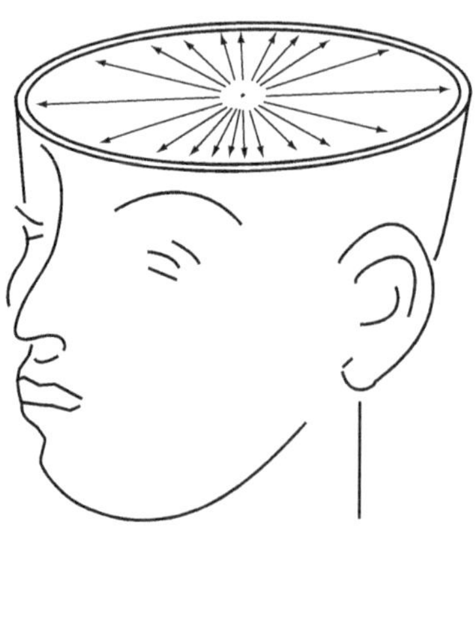

***Reversal** of outward flow of energies*

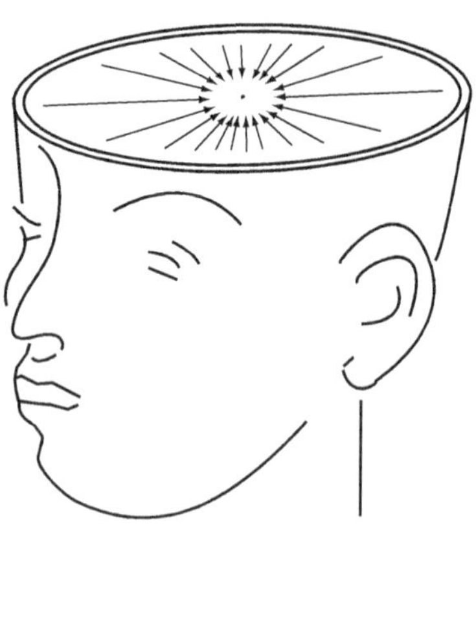

While operating the body, the soul (•) is usually situated in the electrical center of the brain. The soul power normally flows outward for usage in sensual pursuits of the body and mind. In *pratyāhāra*, the soul draws the sensual energies back to itself, the focal spirit.

A person can, however, even if he is not an expert yogi, try his best to keep his determination on spiritual objectives and if he is successful to a degree, he would be able to utilize the clarifying mode.

यया तु धर्मकामार्थान्
धृत्या धारयतेऽर्जुन ।
प्रसङ्गेन फलाकाङ्क्षी
धृतिः सा पार्थ राजसी ॥१८.३४॥

yayā tu dharmakāmārthān
dhṛtyā dhārayate'rjuna
prasaṅgena phalākāṅkṣī
dhṛtiḥ sā pārtha rājasī (18.34)

yayā — by which; tu — but; dharmakāmārthān = dharma — duty + kāma — pleasure + arthān — wealthy; dhṛtyā — with determination; dhārayate — it holds; 'rjuna = arjuna — Arjuna; prasaṅgena — with attachment; phalākāṅkṣī — desiring results; dhṛtiḥ — determination; sā — it; pārtha — son of Pṛthā; rājasī — impulsion

But the determination by which one holds duty, pleasure, and wealth with attachment and with desire for results, is an impulsion, O son of Pṛthā. (18.34)

<u>Commentary:</u>

The primary symptom of the impulsive mode is attachment, which causes a person to hanker for enjoyable, sensuous results. This jars the intellect and prejudices judgement.

यया स्वप्नं भयं शोकं
विषादं मदमेव च ।
न विमुञ्चति दुर्मेधा
धृतिः सा पार्थ तामसी ॥१८.३५॥

yayā svapnaṁ bhayaṁ śokaṁ
viṣādaṁ madameva ca
na vimuñcati durmedhā
dhṛtiḥ sā pārtha tāmasī (18.35)

yayā — by which; svapnaṁ — sleep; bhayaṁ — fear; śokaṁ — sorrow; viṣādaṁ — despair; madam — pride; eva — indeed; ca — and; na — not; vimuñcati — abandons; durmedhā — idiot; dhṛtiḥ — determination; sā — it; pārtha — son of Pṛthā; tāmasī — of the depressive mode

That determination by which an idiot does not abandon sleep, fear, sorrow, despair and pride, is of the depressing mode. (18.35)

<u>Commentary:</u>

The same person who is regarded as an idiot in one circumstance may be regarded as an enthusiastic knowledgeable man in another instance. Thus it is not the person that is under discussion, really, but the influence which prevails. We must, therefore, learn to recognize the various modes and learn how to side-step the lower ones thus situating ourselves in the mode of clarity. From the position of clarity, we can get some idea of how to transcend material nature altogether

Sleep, fear, sorrow, despair, and pride absorb the consciousness of the spirit, inefficiently.These moods should be reduced to a minimum. Sleep cannot be eliminated altogether. It is necessary. Fear, sorrow, despair, and pride will be there to some degree. These should be avoided and minimized. One should find a method to keep the life energies from becoming dissipated by the lower modes.

सुखं त्विदानीं त्रिविधं
शृणु मे भरतर्षभ ।
अभ्यासाद्रमते यत्र
दुःखान्तं च निगच्छति ॥१८.३६॥

sukhaṁ tvidānīṁ trividhaṁ
śṛṇu me bharatarṣabha
abhyāsādramate yatra
duḥkhāntaṁ ca nigacchati (18.36)

sukhaṁ — happiness; tu — but; idānīṁ — now; trividhaṁ — types; śṛṇu — hear; me — from me; bharatarṣabha — O strong man of the Bharatas; abhyāsāt — from habit; ramate — enjoys; yatra — where, through which; duḥkhāntaṁ — end of sorrow; ca — and, or; nigacchati — one comes to

But now hear from Me, O strong man of the Bharatas, regarding the three types of happiness which one either enjoys from habit or through which one comes to the end of sorrow. (18.36)

Commentary:

In contrast to distress, happiness is more of a cause for degradation. Lord Krishna established that, by the mode of goodness, one becomes conditioned to happiness. But from happiness one may develop an addiction through which one may become degraded. It is, therefore, essential that we understand the various types of happiness. Happiness, sadness, soberness, or boredom all produce and provide particular positive or negative habits. But it is only in soberness that one develops some objectivity to understand these influences.

यत्तदग्रे विषमिव
परिणामेऽमृतोपमम् ।
तत्सुखं सात्त्विकं प्रोक्तम्
आत्मबुद्धिप्रसादजम् ॥१८.३७॥
yattadagre viṣamiva
pariṇāme'mṛtopamam
tatsukhaṁ sāttvikaṁ proktam
ātmabuddhiprasādajam (18.37)

yat = yad — which; tat — that; agre — initially; viṣam — poison; iva — like; pariṇāme — in changing; 'mṛtopamam = amṛtopamam = amṛta — nectar + upamam — likeness; tat = tad — that; sukham — happiness; sāttvikaṁ — of the clarifying mode; proktam — is said to be; ātmabuddhiprasādajam = ātmabuddhi — spiritual discernment + prasāda — clarity + jam — produced by

That which initially is like poison but which changes into an experience like nectar, and which is felt through the clarity of spiritual discernment, is said to be happiness in the clarifying mode. (18.37)

Commentary:

Whatever arises from the spiritual discernment (*ātmabuddhi*), and which is sustained in the material nature and influences that nature, directing it to act, performs functions in charity. Spiritual nature is of the *Sat* mode which is described in the last verses of the previous chapter but when the spiritual nature is directed into the material world, it is absorbed by the material energy. If the spiritual nature predominates, we act under the influence of the higher mode, which is the clarifying energy but if it does not, we function under impulsion or depression.

If we are searching for sensation, any decision made from *Sat* or spiritual level, will appear like poison but if we execute the decision anyway, we will, in the future, observe that the distasteful portion of the experience is converted into a mild nectarian pleasure. Spiritually-inspired acts are usually enjoyed after their performance, while impulsive passionate acts give an instant pleasure.

विषयेन्द्रियसंयोगाद्
यत्तदग्रेऽमृतोपमम् ।
परिणामे विषमिव
तत्सुखं राजसं स्मृतम् ॥१८.३८॥
viṣayendriyasaṁyogād
yattadagre'mṛtopamam
pariṇāme viṣamiva
tatsukhaṁ rājasaṁ smṛtam (18.38)

viṣayendriyasaṁyogāt = viṣaya — attractive objects + indriya — sense organs + saṁyogāt — from contact: yat — which; tat — that; agre — in the beginning; 'mṛtopamam = amṛtopamam = amṛta — nectar + upamam — likeness; pariṇāme — changes into; viṣam — poison; ivā — like; tat — that; sukham — happiness; rājasaṁ — impulsion; smṛtam — recognized as

That happiness which in the beginning seems like nectar and which comes from the contact between the sense organs and attractive objects, which changes as if it were poison is recognized as an impulsion. (18.38)

Commentary:

Most human beings aspire for this type of happiness. Most human beings function through impulsion. They helplessly allow their senses to make contact with objects without regards to the consequences.

यदग्रे चानुबन्धे च
सुखं मोहनमात्मनः ।
निद्रालस्यप्रमादोत्थं
तत्तामसमुदाहृतम् ॥ १८.३९ ॥
yadagre cānubandhe ca
sukhaṁ mohanamātmanaḥ
nidrālasyapramādotthaṁ
tattāmasamudāhṛtam (18.39)

yat — which; agre — in the beginning: cānubandhe - ca — and + anubandhe — in consequence; ca—and; sukham — happiness; mohanam — bewildering; ātmanaḥ - of the person: nidrālasyapramādotthaṁ = nidrā — sleep + ālasya — laziness + pramāda — confusion + uttham — comes from; tat = tad — that; tāmasam — depressive mode; udāhṛtam — said to be

And that happiness which in the beginning and in consequence is bewildering to the person, which comes from sleep, laziness and confusion, is said to be of the depressive mode. (18.39)

Commentary:

Human beings who smoke cigarettes, who are habituated to liquor, narcotics and depressants, experience this type of happiness. Human beings who are psychotic, schizophrenic or mad also enjoy this type of happiness. It is their state of mind.

न तदस्ति पृथिव्यां वा
दिवि देवेषु वा पुनः ।
सत्त्वं प्रकृतिजैर्मुक्तं
यदेभिः स्यात्त्रिभिर्गुणैः ॥ १८.४० ॥
na tadasti pṛthivyāṁ vā
divi deveṣu vā punaḥ
sattvaṁ prakṛtijairmuktaṁ
yadebhiḥ syāttribhirguṇaiḥ (18.40)

na — not; tat — that; asti — there is; pṛthivyāṁ — on earth; vā — or; divi — in the supernatural world; deveṣu — among the supernatural rulers; vā — or; punaḥ = punar — even; sattvaṁ — something substantial; prakṛtijaiḥ — produced by material nature; muktaṁ — freed, without; yat — which; ebhiḥ — by these; syāt — it can exist; tribhiḥ — by three; guṇaiḥ — by influence

There is no object on earth nor even in the subtle mundane domains, that can exist without these three modes which were produced from material nature. (18.40)

Commentary:

Thus the modes of material nature are mixed into everything that comprise the gross and subtle material energy.

ब्राह्मणक्षत्रियविशां
शूद्राणां च परंतप ।
कर्माणि प्रविभक्तानि
स्वभावप्रभवैर्गुणैः ॥ १८.४१ ॥

brāhmaṅakṣatriyaviśāṁ = brāhmaṇa — priestly teacher + kṣatriya — ruling sector + viśāṁ — productive managers; śudrāṇāṁ — of the working class; ca — and; paraṁtapa — scorcher of the

brāhmaṇakṣatriyaviśāṁ
śūdrāṇāṁ ca paraṁtapa
karmāṇi pravibhaktāni
svabhāvaprabhavairguṇaiḥ (18.41)

enemy; karmāṇi — activities; pravibhaktāni — allotted; svabhāvaprabhavaiḥ = svabhāva — own nature + prabhavaiḥ — by being produced; guṇaiḥ — by the modes of material nature

The activities of the priestly teachers, the ruling sector, the productive managers and the working class, are allotted by the modes of material nature which arise from natural tendencies. (18.41)

Commentary:

The natural tendencies arise from our association with material nature. This association with material nature is a long drawn-out process. By this association we absorb tendencies which give expression through the subtle body. The subtle body in turn motivates and energizes the gross form to exhibit dispositions. Thus if we put ourselves to the task, we can adjust the subtle form and improve the condition.

शमो दमस्तपः शौचं
क्षान्तिरार्जवमेव च ।
ज्ञानं विज्ञानमास्तिक्यं
ब्रह्मकर्म स्वभावजम् ॥ १८.४२ ॥
śamo damastapaḥ śaucaṁ
kṣāntirārjavameva ca
jñānaṁ vijñānamāstikyaṁ
brahmakarma svabhāvajam (18.42)

śamo = śamaḥ — tranquility; damaḥ — restraint; tapaḥ — austerity; śaucaṁ — cleanliness; kṣāntiḥ — patience; ārjavam — straightforwardness; eva — indeed; ca — and; jñānaṁ — knowledge; vijñānaṁ — discrimination; āstikyaṁ — a belief in God; brahmakarma — work of a priestly teacher; svabhāvajam — based on natural tendencies

Tranquility, restraint, austerity, cleanliness, patience, straightforwardness, knowledge, discrimination and a belief in God, are the work of a priestly teacher based on his natural tendencies. (18.42)

Commentary:

If a man does not have these qualities and wants to acquire them, he can work for their development. He would then require saintly association and an environment in which to practise these qualities consistently. If, however, one has no such desire, still, he would develop these qualities by the flow of evolution, through which one moves from one lower quality to a higher one, over a period of thousands or millions of years.

शौर्यं तेजो धृतिर्दाक्ष्यं
युद्धे चाप्यपलायनम् ।
दानमीश्वरभावश्च
क्षात्रंकर्म स्वभावजम् ॥ १८.४३ ॥
śauryaṁ tejo dhṛtirdākṣyaṁ
yuddhe cāpyapalāyanam
dānamīśvarabhāvaśca
kṣātraṁkarma svabhāvajam (18.43)

śauryaṁ — heroism; tejo = tejaḥ — majesty; dhṛtiḥ — determination; dākṣyaṁ — expertise; yuddhe — in battle; cāpi — and also; apalāyanam — lack of cowardice; dānam — charitable disposition; īśvarabhāvaśca = īśvarabhāvaḥ — governing tendency + ca — and; kṣātraṁ — of the ruling human being; karma — action; svabhāvajam — based on natural tendency

Heroism, majesty, determination, expertise, lack of cowardice in battle, charitable disposition, and governing tendency are the actions of a ruling human being, based on natural tendency. (18.43)

Commentary:

The qualities of the priestly leaders, the governing authorities, the productive sector and the servile people are exihibited in less degree in the animal kingdom. Some species have a more caring attitude. Some have a more governing tendency. Some are more productively-realized. Some are in a more humble position. Even in the animal world, the modes of material nature prevail and serve to condition the spirits who use those forms.

कृषिगोरक्ष्यवाणिज्यं
वैश्यकर्म स्वभावजम्.।
परिचर्यात्मकं कर्म
शूद्रस्यापि स्वभावजम् ॥ १८.४४॥
kṛṣigorakṣyavāṇijyaṁ
vaiśyakarma svabhāvajam
paricaryātmakaṁ karma
śūdrasyāpi svabhāvajam (18.44)

kṛṣigaurakṣyavāṇijyaṁ = kṛṣi — agriculture + gaurakṣya — cow tending + vāṇijyaṁ — trading; vaiśyakarma — action of the productive manager; svabhāvajam — based on natural tendency; paricaryātmakaṁ = paricaryā — service + ātmakaṁ — of natural tendency; karma — action; śudrasyāpi = śudrasya — working class + api — also; svabhāvajam — based on natural tendency

Agriculture, cow-tending and trading are the productive manager's activity based on natural tendency. Service actions are produced of a working class person based on natural tendency. (18.44)

Commentary:

The producers (*vaiśya*) serve human society by providing utilities, foods and services. They are exploiters of social needs. The servile persons (*śūdras*) provide service with their bodies. They exploit our reliance on human services. A man with a particular tendency may work in a contrary occupation if he develops the skill of it but he should be categorized by innate tendency.

स्वे स्वे कर्मण्यभिरतः
संसिद्धिं लभते नरः ।
स्वकर्मनिरतः सिद्धिं
यथा विन्दति तच्छृणु ॥ १८.४५॥
sve sve karmaṇyabhirataḥ
saṁsiddhiṁ labhate naraḥ
svakarmanirataḥ siddhiṁ
yathā vindati tacchṛṇu (18.45)

sve sve — his own, his own, consistent; karmaṇi — in action; abhirataḥ — content; saṁsiddhiṁ — perfection; labhate — attain; naraḥ — human being; svakarmanirataḥ = svakarma — own duty + nirataḥ — satisfied; siddhiṁ — perfection; yathā — of the means; vindati — finds; tat —that; śṛṇu — hear

A human being attains perfection by being content in the consistent execution of his duty. Hear of the means through which a duty-satisfied person finds perfection.(18.45)

Commentary:

Apart from the truth of this statement, this is another tactic of Lord Krishna to inspire Arjuna to complete his duty on the battlefield of *Kurukṣetra*. Arjuna wanted to switch duties and become a renunciant but Lord Krishna insisted that Arjuna remain as a law man and attain perfection (*samsiddim*) in that way.

यतः प्रवृत्तिर्भूतानां
येन सर्वमिदं ततम् ।
स्वकर्मणा तमभ्यर्च्य
सिद्धिं विन्दति मानवः ॥ १८.४६॥

yataḥ — from whom; pravṛttiḥ — origin; bhūtānāṁ — of beings; yena — by whom; sarvam — all; idam — this; tatam — is pervaded; svakarmaṇā — through his duty;

yataḥ pravṛttirbhūtānāṁ
yena sarvamidaṁ tatam
svakarmaṇā tamabhyarcya
siddhiṁ vindati mānavaḥ (18.46)

tam — his; abhyarcya — worshipping; siddhiṁ — perfection; vindati — he finds; mānavaḥ — human being

Through the performance of his own duty, a human being finds perfection by worshipping the Person from Whom the beings originate and by Whom all this is pervaded. (18.46)

Commentary:

This is yet another statement directly intended to inspire Arjuna to give up all reservations and beliefs that are contrary to what Krishna desired. Arjuna was to worship God, not by going to the forest to meditate nor by going away to a temple or an ashrama to sing God's praises and engage in worship ceremonies but rather to stay on the battlefield and fight. Fighting was to be his means of worship. And that God was defined as the person from whom the beings originated and by whom all this reality is pervaded. Arjuna's fight, his completion of battlefield duties, was to be his worship of God.

It is for this reason that the Vaishnava teachers advocate that the *Bhagavad Gītā* is primarily a teaching of *bhakti yoga* (devotional service). In fact, the *Gītā* is primarily a teaching of *karma yoga* but in this verse Lord Krishna sanctified such a course of *karma yoga* as being a form of worship of God. He did this by using the term *abhyarcya* which means worshipping or praising. To identify the person worshipped, Lord Krishna did not say Himself in this verse but identified God as the person from whom all the beings originated and by whom all this reality is pervaded. Krishna will again assert this view in verses 61 and 62 of this chapter.

īśvaraḥ sarvabhūtānāṁ hṛddeśe'rjuna tiṣṭhati
bhrāmayansarvabhūtāni yantrārūḍhāni māyayā (18.61)
tameva śaraṇaṁ gaccha sarvabhāvena bhārata
tatprasādātparāṁ śāntiṁ sthānaṁ prāpsyasi śāśvatam (18.62)

The Lord of all beings is situated in the central psyche, O Arjuna, causing all beings to transmigrate by His mystic power, just as if they were fixed to a spinning machine.

With your whole being, go only to Him for shelter, O descendant of Bharata. You will attain the supreme security and the eternal place by His grace. (18.61-62)

It is clear that Krishna feels that any of us can worship God directly by taking up duties and obligations that are God-approved. But how are we to determine what is permitted and what is not? The Vaishnava teachers simplified that matter by pointing to verse 34 of Chapter Four:

tadviddhi praṇipātena paripraśnena sevayā
upadekṣyanti te jñānaṁ jñāninastattvadarśinaḥ (4.34)

This you ought to know. By submitting yourself as a student, by asking questions, by serving as requested, the perceptive reality-conversant teachers will teach you the knowledge. (4.34)

However, a spiritual master may conveniently distort this verse by replacing *teachers* with *teacher*, thus indicating himself as the sole advisor in our determination of God-approved acts. Of course for Arjuna, the problem was solved because God stood before him on the battlefield. He did not have to risk himself to a teacher who may have misled him.

श्रेयान्स्वधर्मो विगुणः
परधर्मात्स्वनुष्ठितात् ।
स्वभावनियतं कर्म
कुर्वन्नाप्नोति किल्बिषम् ॥ १८.४७॥
śreyānsvadharmo viguṇaḥ
paradharmātsvanuṣṭhitāt
svabhāvaniyataṁ karma
kurvannāpnoti kilbiṣam (18.47)

śreyān — better; svadharmo = svadharmaḥ — own duty; viguṇāḥ — imperfectly; paradharmāt — then another's duty; svanuṣṭhitāt = su + anuṣṭhitāt — well performed, perfectly; svabhāvaniyataṁ = svabhāva — own nature + niyatam — restricted; karma — action; kurvan — performing; nāpnoti = na — not + āpnoti — he acquires; kilbiṣam — sin, fault

Better to attend to one's own duty imperfectly than to heed another's perfectly. By performing actions which are restricted by one's own nature, one does not acquire fault. (18.47)

<u>Commentary:</u>

This is yet another statement to destroy Arjuna's idea of leaving the warfield for a peaceful forest life or just to go away and avoid the battle. By this idea, it is better to stick to one's obligations and perform them, even imperfectly, than to switch and complete the duty of another person satisfactorily.

Krishna flatly stated that one does not acquire sin in trying to execute destined obligations.

सहजं कर्म कौन्तेय
सदोषमपि न त्यजेत् ।
सर्वारम्भा हि दोषेण
धूमेनाग्निरिवावृताः॥ १८.४८॥
sahajaṁ karma kaunteya
sadoṣamapi na tyajet
sarvārambhā hi doṣeṇa
dhūmenāgnirivāvṛtāḥ(18.48)

sahajaṁ — inborn; karma — action; kaunteya — son of Kunti; sadoṣam — with fault; api — even; na —not; tyajet — should abandon; sarvārambhā — all undertakings; hi — indeed; doṣeṇa — with defect; dhumenāgniḥ = dhumena — with smoke + āgniḥ — fire; ivāvṛtaḥ = iva — like + āvṛtaḥ — is shrouded

One should not abandon inborn duty, O son of Kuntī, even if it is faulty. Indeed, all undertakings are with defect, even as fire is shrouded with smoke. (18.48)

<u>Commentary:</u>

Arjuna found some fault in the prospect of completion of obligations to the Pandavas but Krishna pointed out that even if he were to change, there would be faults in whatever occupation he would take up. Krishna already stated that even a stance of non-action is a sort of action that brings consequences. Whatever Arjuna would choose to do, would be faulty, since in Krishna's view, all undertakings carry defects. Krishna presented the conclusion that regardless of the outcome, it is better to stick to duty.

असक्तबुद्धिः सर्वत्र
जितात्मा विगतस्पृहः ।
नैष्कर्म्यसिद्धिं परमां
संन्यासेनाधिगच्छति ॥ १८.४९॥
asaktabuddhiḥ sarvatra
jitātmā vigataspṛhaḥ
naiṣkarmyasiddhiṁ paramāṁ
saṁnyāsenādhigacchati (18.49)

asakta — unattached; buddhiḥ — intellect; sarvatra — in all applications; jitātmā — self-conquered; vigataspṛhah = vigata — disappeared + spṛhaḥ — yearnings; naiṣkarmya — exemption from activities + siddhim — perfection; paramāṁ — supreme; saṁnyāsenādhigacchati = saṁnyāsena — by renunciation of opportunities + adhigacchati — he attains

He whose intellect is unattached in every application, who is self-controlled, whose yearnings disappeared, by the renunciation of opportunities, attains supreme perfection of being exempt from action. (18.49)

Commentary:

Since Lord Krishna used the term *samnyāsena* and not *tyāgena*, we cannot apply this verse to Arjuna. Arjuna was to be a *tyāgi*. Krishna prohibited him from the course of a *sannyāsi*. Readers should recall that Lord Krishna defined *sannyāsa* as the abandonment or renunciation of opportunities while *tyāga* was defined as the renunciation of consequences of action. The difference is technical. The *tyāgi* works as recommended, but he renounces the benefits. On the other hand, the *sannyāsi* does not take up work opportunities in the worldly field. He carefully avoids these. His aim is to abandon the work, the immediate results, and the long-ranged consequences. This is an important distinction. This verse is a description of the state of the true *sannyasi*. We know that Arjuna was confused in the beginning. He asked why Lord Krishna explained both the art of work and the art of renunciation. Arjuna asked for a definite instruction. Lord Krishna told him to work with a detached mind. Arjuna was to take the middle ground between working with a possessive mood and not performing at all. He was to work without a possessive attitude. This is the path of the *tyāgi* renunciant as contrasted to the two extremes of the *kāmakāmī*, pleasure-seeking worker, and the *sannyāsi*, a person who avoids all types of positive or negative involvement.

Lord Krishna wanted Arjuna to understand clearly that this supreme perfection of being exempt from work (*naiṣkarmya*) applied only to the person whose intelligence is unattached in every application, who is already self-controlled and whose yearning for participation has disappeared altogether. For others, an attempt at *sannyāsa* (total renunciation of all involvement) would not be practical. They should take the course of the *tyāgi* who works aggressively but who cultivates detachment in social dealings.

The following verses, 50 though 55, show completely that this *naiṣkarmya* verse applies to yogi devotees and not to Arjuna or persons practicing *karma yoga*. It is wrong to divert the guarantee of this verse to others besides the yogis whose practices are described particularly in verses 51 and 52. We cannot gloss over nor by-pass these verses and derail the *Gītā* into a new, more suitable meaning.

सिद्धिं प्राप्तो यथा ब्रह्म
तथाप्नोति निबोध मे ।
समासेनैव कौन्तेय
निष्ठा ज्ञानस्य या परा ॥१८.५०॥
siddhiṁ prāpto yathā brahma
tathāpnoti nibodha me
samāsenaiva kaunteya
niṣṭhā jñānasya yā parā (18.50)

siddhiṁ — perfection; prāpto = prāptaḥ — attained; yathā — as; brahma — spirituality; tathāpnoti = tathā — thus + āpnoti — attains; nibodha — learn; me — from me; samāsenaiva = samāsena — in brief + eva — indeed; kaunteya — son of Kuntī; niṣṭhā — state; jñānasya — of experience; yā — which; parā — highest

Learn from Me briefly, O son of Kuntī, how a person who attained perfection, also reaches a spirituality which is the highest. (18.50)

Commentary:

Now we will hear how a person who acts perfectly as a *tyāgi*, as a renouncer of results and consequences, may attain the highest experience. We will hear of how a *tyāgi* may attain what a true *sannyāsi* is sure to achieve. Arjuna will hear how, by performing his duty on the battlefield, he can attain the perfection attained by those ascetics who did not have to fulfill worldly obligations and who successfully sidestepped the type of work opportunities that Arjuna was duty-bound to complete.

बुद्ध्या विशुद्धया युक्तो
धृत्यात्मानं नियम्य च ।
शब्दादीन्विषयांस्त्यक्त्वा
रागद्वेषौ व्युदस्य च ॥ १८.५१ ॥
buddhyā viśuddhayā yukto
dhṛtyātmānaṁ niyamya ca
śabdādīnviṣayāṁstyaktvā
rāgadveṣau vyudasya ca (18.51)

buddhyā — with intellect; viśuddhayā — with purified; yukto = yuktaḥ — yogically disciplined; dhṛtyātmānaṁ = dhṛtyā — with firmness + ātmānaṁ — self; niyamya — controlling; ca — and; śabdādīn = śabda — sound + ādīn — beginning with, and others; viṣayān — attractive sensations; tyaktvā — abandoning; rāgadveṣau = rāga — craving + dveṣau — hatred; vyudasya — rejecting; ca — and

Being yogically-disciplined with purified intelligence and controlling the soul, firmly abandoning sound and other attractive sensations, rejecting craving and hatred, (18.51)

Commentary:

This listing is partial. Two following verses will complete the listing.

If Arjuna wanted to be a *sannyāsi*, he would have to satisfy all requirements in order to be sincere, otherwise it could be best for him to act as a *tyāgi* for the time being. One may keep these requirements in mind and gradually move into this position. In fact, the *Mahābhārata* history states that in the end, after the battle and after they ruled for some time, the Pandavas and their wife took full renunciation. It is said that, at the time, Yudhishthira took off his royal clothing and acted as if he heard nothing about government duties. He did, in fact, abandon sound and the other objects of the senses.

The *Śrīmad Bhāgavatam* also informs us of this:

visṛjya tatra tat sarvaṁ dukūla-valayādikam
nirmamo nirahaṅkāraḥ sañchinnāśeṣa-bandhanah
vācaṁ juhāva manasi tat prāṇa itare ca tam
mṛtyāv apānaṁ sotsargaṁ taṁ pañcatve hy ajohavīt
tritve hutvā ca pañcatvaṁ tac caikatve 'juhon muniḥ
sarvam ātmany ajuhavīd brahmaṇy ātmānam avyaye
cīra-vāsā nirāhāro baddha-vāṅ mukta-mūrdhajaḥ
darśayann ātmano rūpaṁ jaḍonmatta-pisācavat
anavekṣamāno niragād aśṛṇvan badhiro yathā
udīcīm praviveśāśāṁ gata-pūrvaṁ mahātmabhiḥ
hṛdi brahma paraṁ dhyāyan nāvarteta yato gataḥ
sarve tam anunirjagmur bhrātaraḥ kṛta-niścayāḥ
kalinādharma-mitrena dṛṣṭvā spṛṣṭaḥ prajā bhuvi
(1.15.40-45)

Discarding everything, his belt, bangles and such things, being non-possessive, non-assertive and completely severing all aspects of attachment,

...he mystically dissolved the speech tendency into the mind, the mind into the vitalizing breath, that vitality into the de-energizing energy with the evacuating function into death, and death into the body which is composed of five elements.

The yogi philosopher then mystically dissolved the body in the three modes of material nature, and that mundane energy into the one primal material potency, that one potency from which all this is produced, into his individual spirit, and he positioned the individual spirit into the unchangeable spiritual existence.

Dressed in tree bark, abstaining from food, not speaking, untying his hair, appearing like a retarded, mad or possessed person, waiting for no one, not hearing, just as a deaf man,

...contemplating the Supreme Spirit in the core of his being wherever he went, going to the north, where the great souls journeyed before, and not returning again,

After deciding, all his brothers followed him, having seen the people on earth being influenced by the friend of vice, the devil Kali. (1.15.40-45)

विविक्तसेवी लघ्वाशी
यतवाक्कायमानसः ।
ध्यानयोगपरो नित्यं
वैराग्यं समुपाश्रितः ॥ १८.५२ ॥
viviktasevī laghvāśī
yatavākkāyamānasaḥ
dhyānayogaparo nityaṁ
vairāgyaṁ samupāśritaḥ (18.52)

viviktasevī = vivikta — is isolated + sevī — living at; laghvāśī = laghv (laghu) — lightly + āśī — eating; yatavākkāyamānasaḥ = yata — controlled + vāk (vāc) — speech + kāya — body + mānasaḥ — mind; dhyānayogaparo = dhyāna — meditation + yoga — yoga + paro (paraḥ) — devoted to; nityam — always; vairāgyam — dispassion; samupāśritaḥ — resorting to

...living in isolation, eating lightly, controlling speech, body and mind, always being devoted to yogic meditation, resorting to dispassion, (18.52)

Commentary:

This is a description of yoga austerities in terms of *āsana* postures , *prāṇāyāma* breath nutrition techniques, drastic diet restrictions, concentration, focus and meditation. These aspects manifested in the life of the Pandavas after they renounced politics. Only then did they take to the *sannyāsa* position. In the meantime, they tried to perfect themselves as *tyāgis*. Some of these isolationist qualities, however, were practiced partially throughout their lives. If one did not cultivate the practice previously, it would be difficult to adopt it in the elderly years.

अहंकारं बलं दर्पं
कामं क्रोधं परिग्रहम् ।
विमुच्य निर्ममः शान्तो
ब्रह्मभूयाय कल्पते ॥ १८.५३ ॥
ahaṁkāraṁ balaṁ darpaṁ
kāmaṁ krodhaṁ parigraham
vimucya nirmamaḥ śānto
brahmabhūyāya kalpate (18.53)

ahaṁkāraṁ — without a misplaced initiative, without a false assertion; balaṁ — brute force; darpaṁ — arrogance; kāmaṁ — cravings; krodhaṁ — anger; parigraham — possessions; vimucya — freeing oneself; nirmamaḥ — unselfish; śānto = śāntaḥ — peaceful; brahmabhūyāya = brahma — spirit + bhūyāyā — to that level, existential; kalpate — is suited

...freeing oneself from a false assertion, from the application of brute force, from arrogance, from craving and from possessiveness, being unselfish and peaceful, one is suited to the spiritual level. (18.53)

Commentary:

Arjuna was eager to attain the spiritual level but Krishna informed him that he would have to work his way towards it by first completing obligations as a member of the Pandava dynasty. Then, by working to attain all these qualities, he would become suited in nature to the spiritual level of existence.

ब्रह्मभूतः प्रसन्नात्मा
न शोचति न काङ्क्षति ।
समः सर्वेषु भूतेषु
मद्भक्तिं लभते पराम् ॥१८.५४॥
brahmabhūtaḥ prasannātmā
na śocati na kāṅkṣati
samaḥ sarveṣu bhūteṣu
madbhaktiṁ labhate parām (18.54)

brahmabhūtaḥ — being absorbed in spiritual existence; prasannātmā = prasanna — peaceful + ātmā — self, spirit; na — not; śocati — laments; na — no; kāṅkṣati — hankers for something; samaḥ — impartial; sarveṣu — in all; bhūteṣu — in the beings; madbhaktiṁ — devotion to me; labhate — attains; parām — supreme

One who is absorbed in the spiritual existence, who has a peaceful spirit, who does not lament or hanker for anything, who is impartial to all beings, attains the supreme devotion to Me. (18.54)

Commentary:

Arjuna did lament in the beginning and did hanker for recognition as a peace-loving man but Krishna informed him that an authentic peaceful spirit does not lament or hanker. Thus Arjuna's behavior in the beginning, at the time of his despair, was not the attitude of a spiritually-focused person.

भक्त्या मामभिजानाति
यावान्यश्चास्मि तत्त्वतः ।
ततो मां तत्त्वतो ज्ञात्वा
विशते तदनन्तरम् ॥१८.५५॥
bhaktyā māmabhijānāti
yāvānyaścāsmi tattvataḥ
tato māṁ tattvato jñātvā
viśate tadanantaram (18.55)

bhaktyā — by devotion; mām — to me; abhijānāti — he realizes; yāvān — how great; yaścāsmi = yaḥ — who + ca — and + asmi — I am; tattvataḥ — in reality; tato = tataḥ — then; mām — me; tattvato = tattvataḥ — in truth; jñātvā — having known; viśate — enters; tadanantaram — immediately

By devotion to Me, he realises how great I am and who I am in reality. Then having known Me in truth, he enters My association immediately. (18.55)

Commentary:

This guarantee like many others in the *Gītā*, does not apply to any and every devotee but rather to devotees who reached the said level of advancement indicated in verses 51 through 55.

सर्वकर्माण्यपि सदा
कुर्वाणो मद्व्यपाश्रयः ।
मत्प्रसादादवाप्नोति

sarvakarmāṇi — in all actions; api — furthermore; sadā — always; kurvāṇo = kurvāṇaḥ — performing; madvyapāśrayaḥ — taking reliance in me; matprasādāt —

शाश्वतं पदमव्ययम् ॥ १८.५६ ॥
sarvakarmāṇyapi sadā
kurvāṇo madvyapāśrayaḥ
matprasādādavāpnoti
śāśvataṁ padamavyayam (18.56)

from my grace; avāpnoti — gets; śāśvataṁ — eternal; padam — abode; avyayam — imperishable

Furthermore, know that while performing all actions, he whose reliance is always on Me, gets by My grace, the eternal imperishable abode. (18.56)

Commentary:

This verse applies to the *tyāgis* like Arjuna. Though they are not as renounced as the true *sannyāsis*, still, while performing actions, if they have full reliance on Krishna always, they do, by His grace, attain the eternal imperishable abode. Thus, Arjuna is again inspired to fight. He is assured repeatedly by Lord Krishna that he would attain the spiritual province.

चेतसा सर्वकर्माणि
मयि संन्यस्य मत्परः ।
बुद्धियोगमुपाश्रित्य
मच्चित्तः सततं भव ॥ १८.५७ ॥
cetasā sarvakarmāṇi
mayi saṁnyasya matparaḥ
buddhiyogamupāśritya
maccittaḥ satataṁ bhava (18.57)

cetasā — by thought; sarvakarmāṇi — all actions; mayi — on Me; saṁnyasya — devoted to me; matparaḥ — devoted to Me; buddhiyogam — disciplining the intellect by yoga practice; upāśritya — relying on; maccittaḥ — thinking of Me; satataṁ — constantly; bhava — be

Renouncing by thought, all actions to Me, being devoted to Me, relying on the process of disciplining the intellect by yoga, be constantly thinking of Me. (18.57)

Commentary:

Arjuna is supposed to complete his duty while applying these disciplines and then relevant guarantees would apply to him. *Bhakti yoga* and *buddhi* yoga are two different disciplines. *Bhakti yoga* means the process of disciplining the affections, the emotions and loving feelings by yoga maturity. *Buddhi* yoga is the procedure for curbing the intellect for yoga maturity.

मच्चित्तः सर्वदुर्गाणि
मत्प्रसादात्तरिष्यसि ।
अथ चेत्त्वमहंकारान्
न श्रोष्यसि विनङ्क्ष्यसि ॥ १८.५८ ॥
maccittaḥ sarvadurgāṇi
matprasādāttariṣyasi
atha cettvamahaṁkārān
na śroṣyasi vinaṅkṣyasi (18.58)

maccittaḥ — thinking of Me; sarvadurgāṇi — all difficulties; matprasādāt — from my grace; tariṣyasi — you will surpass; atha — but; cet = ced — if; tvam — you; ahaṁkārān — false assertion; na — not; śroṣyasi — you will listen; vinaṅkṣyasi — you will be lost

Thinking of Me, you will, by My grace, surpass all difficulties. But if by false assertion, you do not listen, you will be lost. (18.58)

Commentary:

Instead of renouncing the opportunities for battle, Arjuna was to face the problems. Unlike a true *sannyāsi* who turns away from such involvements, he was to take help from

Krishna and by Krishna's grace overcome the difficulties. Otherwise, Krishna predicted failure for Arjuna.

यदहंकारमाश्रित्य
न योत्स्य इति मन्यसे ।
मिथ्यैष व्यवसायस्ते
प्रकृतिस्त्वां नियोक्ष्यति ॥ १८.५९ ॥

yadahaṁkāramāśritya
na yotsya iti manyase
mithyaiṣa vyavasāyaste
prakṛtistvāṁ niyokṣyati (18.59)

yat — which; ahaṁkāram — false assertive attitude; āśritya — relying on; na —not; yotsya — I will fight; iti — thus; manyase — you thing; mithyaiṣa = mithya — mistaken + eṣa — this; vyavasāyaḥ — determination; te — your; prakṛtiḥ — material nature; tvāṁ — you; niyokṣyāti — you will be forced

While relying on a false assertive attitude, you may think, "I will not fight." But that determination is mistaken. Your material nature will force you. (18.59)

Commentary:

We have stuck to the original in the last sentence and have not avoided the words material nature. We have not done like many other translators who use *prakṛtih* in this verse as nature. This is because of what Krishna said earlier about the influence of material nature over every object on the celestial and earthly levels. Arjuna would be forced to fight sooner or later by the pressure of material nature. Regardless of his mental determination, he should take into account the power of material nature and be practical as a *tyāgi* and not try to function as a *sannyāsi* at this stage of his life.

स्वभावजेन कौन्तेय
निबद्धः स्वेन कर्मणा ।
कर्तुं नेच्छसि यन्मोहात्
करिष्यस्यवशोऽपि तत् ॥ १८.६० ॥

svabhāvajena kaunteya
nibaddhaḥ svena karmaṇā
kartuṁ necchasi yanmohāt
kariṣyasyavaśo'pi tat (18.60)

svabhāvajena — of your own natural tendencies; kaunteya — son of Kuntī; nibaddhaḥ — bound; svena — by your own; karmāṇa — obligation; kartuṁ — to perform; necchasi = na — not + icchasi — you want; yan = yad — which; mohāt — from delusion; kariṣyasi — you will do; avaśo = avaśaḥ — against your own will; 'pi = api — also, even; tat = tad — that

By your natural tendencies, being bound by obligations, O son of Kuntī, that which you do not want to perform due to delusion, you will do even if it is against your will. (18.60)

Commentary:

Arjuna had to deal with the nature (*bhāva*) but that nature at this time of Arjuna's life was not just spiritual nature, but spiritual nature and material nature combined. He had not reached the stage of having purged himself of that mundane involvement. And as such, he had to be practical and strive for an action that would work for the time being until he would meet the qualification of a true *sannyāsi* This is why Lord Krishna recommended the course of the *tyāgi*, the lesser neophyte *sannyāsi*, who does the *karma yoga*.

Even against our desire, we are forced into many circumstances to work in and with material nature in a practical way. Until we attain some higher degree of detachment, we will have no alternative but to work in this practical way or be lost in the confusion of false expectations of ourselves, expectations that we cannot possibly complete, until we have advanced further on the path of self-control.

ईश्वरः सर्वभूतानां
हृद्देशेऽर्जुन तिष्ठति ।
भ्रामयन्सर्वभूतानि
यन्त्रारूढानि मायया ॥ १८.६१ ॥
īśvaraḥ sarvabhūtānāṁ
hṛddeśe'rjuna tiṣṭhati
bhrāmayansarvabhūtāni
yantrārūḍhāni māyayā (18.61)

īśvaraḥ — Lord; sarvabhūtānām — of all beings; hṛddeśe = hṛd — central psyche + deśe — in the place; 'rjuna = arjuna — Arjuna; tiṣṭhati — is situated; bhrāmayan — cause to transmigrate; sarvabhūtāni — all beings; yantrārūḍhāni = yantra — machine + ārūḍhāni — fixed to; māyayā — by mystic power

The Lord of all beings is situated in the central psyche, O Arjuna, causing all beings to transmigrate by His mystic power, just as if they were fixed to a spinning machine. (18.61)

Commentary:

This Lord of all beings (*īśvarah sarva bhūtānām*) is supposed to be Lord Krishna. He identified Himself elsewhere in the Gītā:

adhibhūtaṁ kṣaro bhāvaḥ puruṣaścādhidaivatam
adhiyajño'hamevātra dehe dehabhṛtāṁ vara (8.4)

The sum total gross reality is ever-changing nature. The master of the world is the Lord of the supernatural rulers and powers. O best of the embodied souls, I, Who exist here in the body, am the Supreme Regulator of religious ceremonies and disciplines. (8.4)

sarvasya cāhaṁ hṛdi saṁniviṣṭo
mattaḥ smṛtirjñānam apohanaṁ ca
vedaiśca sarvairahameva vedyo
vedāntakṛdvedavideva cāham (15.15)

And I entered the central psyche of all beings. From Me comes memory, knowledge and reasoning. By all the Vedas, I am to be known. I am the author of Vedānta and the knower of the Vedas. (15.15)

The central psyche is the causal body, the most subtle form of ideation, which houses the soul and his initiative. In the *Śrīmad Bhāgavatam*, *Nārada* Muni compared that causal place to the *Mānasa* Lake:

evam sa mānaso haṁso haṁsena pratibodhitaḥ
sva-sthas tad-vyabhicāreṇa naṣṭām āpa punaḥ smṛtim

O great soul, two swans, namely you and I, were residing in the Mānasa Lake. We were separated from that abode for several thousand years. (4.28.64)

तमेव शरणं गच्छ
सर्वभावेन भारत ।
तत्प्रसादात्परां शान्तिं
स्थानं प्राप्स्यसि शाश्वतम् ॥ १८.६२ ॥
tameva śaraṇaṁ gaccha
sarvabhāvena bhārata
tatprasādātparāṁ śāntiṁ
sthānaṁ prāpsyasi śāśvatam (18.62)

tam — to him; eva — only; śaraṇaṁ — shelter; gaccha — go; sarvabhāvena — with all your being; bhārata — O descendant of Bharata; tatprasādāt — from that grace; parāṁ — supreme; śāntiṁ — security; sthānaṁ — place; prāpsyasi — you will attain; śāśvatam — eternal

With your whole being, go only to Him for shelter, O descendant of Bharata. You will attain the supreme security and the eternal place by His grace. (18.62)

Commentary:

Even though Lord Krishna identified Himself as the Supersoul Who resides deep with the psyche, still He tactfully did not mention Himself here. Instead He liberally allowed Arjuna to do the inner consultation by himself. Arjuna would make up his own mind on what to do. Like an expert counselor who presented all advice with due reason, Lord Krishna desisted and allowed Arjuna to decide. Arjuna's doubts were resolved by this inner consultation. It is within the psyche that one gets the supreme inner consultation. It is within the psyche that one gets the supreme security and the eternal place. Valuable consultation needs to be matched with an inspiration, otherwise it bears an oddness and incompleteness. We must go deep within to find the proper match for lofty ideas.

It appears that Arjuna was still a bit doubtful about the instruction of Krishna for the use of violence on the battlefield. Krishna therefore instructed Arjuna to go deeper within, since on the surface level of his inner being, Arjuna would not find the conviction to execute the instructions.

इति ते ज्ञानमाख्यातं
गुह्याद्गुह्यतरं मया ।
विमृश्यैतदशेषेण
यथेच्छसि तथा कुरु ॥१८.६३॥
iti te jñānamākhyātaṁ
guhyādguhyataraṁ mayā
vimṛśyaitadaśeṣeṇa
yathecchasi tathā kuru (18.63)

iti — thus; te — to you; jñānam — information; ākhyātaṁ — was explained; guhyāt — than secret; guhyataraṁ — more secret; mayā— by me; vimṛśyaitat = vimṛśya — having considered + etat — this; aśeṣena — fully; yathecchasi = yathā — as + icchasi — you desire, you please; tathā — in the way; kuru — act

The information that is more secret than secret was explained by Me to you. Having considered this fully, you may act as you please. (18.63)

Commentary:

The final decision must be made by Arjuna.

सर्वगुह्यतमं भूयः
शृणु मे परमं वचः ।
इष्टोऽसि मे दृढमिति
ततो वक्ष्यामि ते हितम् ॥१८.६४॥
sarvaguhyatamaṁ bhūyaḥ
śṛṇu me paramaṁ vacaḥ
iṣṭo'si me dṛḍhamiti
tato vakṣyāmi te hitam (18.64)

sarvaguhyatamaṁ — of all, the most secret; bhūyaḥ — again; śṛṇu — hear; me — of me; paramaṁ — supreme; vacaḥ — discourse; iṣṭo = iṣṭaḥ — loved; 'si = asi — you are; me — of me; dṛḍham — surely; iti — this; tato = tataḥ — hence; vakṣyāmi — I will speak; te — your; hitam — benefit

Hear again of My supreme discourse, the most secret of all information. You are surely loved by Me. Hence I speak for your benefit. (18.64)

Commentary:

Lord Krishna gave seventeen chapters of solid lecture to Arjuna. And still He wants to give Arjuna one last piece of information. The compassion of it! The concern of Krishna for Arjuna!

मन्मना भव मद्भक्तो
मद्याजी मां नमस्कुरु ।
मामेवैष्यसि सत्यं ते
प्रतिजाने प्रियोऽसि मे ॥ १८.६५॥
manmanā bhava madbhakto
madyājī māṁ namaskuru
māmevaiṣyasi satyaṁ te
pratijāne priyo'si me (18.65)

manmanā — be mindful of me; bhava — be; madbhakto = madbhaktaḥ — be devoted to me; madyājī — sacrifice to Me; māṁ — to me; namaskuru — do bow; mām — to me; evaiṣyasi = eva — in this way + eṣyasi — you will come; satyaṁ — in truth; te — to you; pratijāne — I promise; priyo = priyaḥ — dear; 'si = asi — you are; me — of me

Be mindful of Me, be devoted to Me. Sacrifice to Me. Do bow to Me. In this way you will in truth come to Me. I promise, for you are dear to Me. (18.65)

Commentary:

This is a tremendous energy of concern of Krishna for Arjuna. This is more of an exhibition of Krishna's interest than it is an instruction for Arjuna to follow. Krishna does not want Arjuna to make the wrong decision. This is a sincere plea of the Lord to save Arjuna from errors of judgement. This instruction conveys the attachment of Lord Krishna for any devotee who is as dear to Him as Arjuna.

सर्वधर्मान्परित्यज्य
मामेकं शरणं व्रज ।
अहं त्वा सर्वपापेभ्यो
मोक्षयिष्यामि मा शुचः ॥ १८.६६॥
sarvadharmānparityajya
māmekaṁ śaraṇaṁ vraja
ahaṁ tvā sarvapāpebhyo
mokṣayiṣyāmi mā śucaḥ (18.66)

sarvadharmān — all traditional conduct; parityajya — abandoning; mām — in me; ekam —alone; śaraṇaṁ — refuge; vraja — lake; aham — I; tvā — you; sarvapāpebhyo = sarvapāpebhyaḥ— from all sins, of faults; mokṣayiṣyāmi — I will cause you to be freed; mā — not; śucaḥ — worry

Abandoning all traditional conduct, take refuge in Me alone. I will cause you to be freed of all faults. Do not worry. (18.66)

Commentary:

Arjuna cited dharma, traditional conduct, based on moral rulings found in the scripture. He said:

kulakṣaye praṇaśyanti kuladharmāḥ sanātanāḥ
dharme naṣṭe kulaṁ kṛtsnam adharmo'bhibhavatyuta (1.39)

In the destruction of the clan, the ancient family traditions vanish. In the removal of the traditional values, the entire clan is overpowered by lawlessness. (1.39)

Arjuna also stated:

utsannakuladharmāṇāṁ manuṣyāṇāṁ janārdana
narake 'niyataṁ vāso bhavatītyanuśuśruma (1.43)

O Krishna, those who destroy the family customs dwell in hell indefinitely. This was declared repeatedly. (1.43)

But Krishna asked Arjuna not to think of these traditional values nor the scriptural references which were supportive. Arjuna was to follow Krishna's line of reasoning alone. And Krishna displayed the Universal Form to assert that His authority overrides any scriptural or traditional ruling. Krishna assured Arjuna that if he fought as instructed, and if he acted as an instrument as advised, he would be free from reactions. Formerly Krishna told Arjuna:

śrībhagavānuvāca
kālo'smi lokakṣayakṛt pravṛddho lokānsamāhartumiha pravṛttaḥ
ṛte'pi tvāṁ na bhaviṣyanti sarve ye'vasthitāḥ pratyanīkeṣu yodhāḥ (11.32)
tasmāttvamuttiṣṭha yaśo labhasva jitvā śatrūnbhuṅkṣva rājyaṁ samṛddham
mayaivaite nihatāḥ pūrvameva nimittamātraṁ bhava savyasācin (11.33)
droṇaṁ ca bhīṣmaṁ ca jayadrathaṁ ca karṇaṁ tathānyānapi yodhavīrān
mayā hatāṁstvaṁ jahi mā vyathiṣṭhā yudhyasva jetāsi raṇe sapatnān (11.34)

The Blessed Lord said: I am the time limit, the mighty world-destroying Cause, appearing here to annihilate the worlds. Even without you, all the armored warriors, in both armies will cease to live. (11.32)

Therefore you should stand up! Get the glory! Having conquered the enemies, enjoy a prosperous country. These fellows are supernaturally disposed by Me already. Be only the agent, O ambidextrous archer. (11.33)

Droṇa, Bhishma, Jayadratha, and Karṇa, as well as other battle heroes, were supernaturally hurt by Me. You may physically kill them. Do not hesitate. Fight! You will conquer the enemies in battle. (11.34)

Many representatives of Lord Krishna and persons who pretend to be His representatives have quoted this verse 66 over and over again. But we must understand that this freedom from all sins, applied to freedom from sins committed on the battlefield, while Arjuna acted directly under Krishna's directions, doing whatever Krishna indicated. Spiritual masters, however, abuse this statement and apply it to all their valid or mistaken missionary activities. Many disciples are misled by such spiritual masters. This guarantee is not given here to anyone but Arjuna personally, and only for acts that Arjuna would commit directly under Krishna's directions.

इदं ते नातपस्काय
नाभक्ताय कदाचन ।
न चाशुश्रूषवे वाच्यं
न च मां योऽभ्यसूयति ॥१८.६७॥
idaṁ te nātapaskāya
nābhaktāya kadācana
na cāśuśrūṣave vācyaṁ
na ca māṁ yo'bhyasūyati.18.67)

idaṁ — this; te — of you; nātapaskāya = na — not + atapaskāya — to one who does not perform austerity; nābhaktāya = na — not + abhaktāya — to one who is not devoted; kadācana — at any time; na — not; cāśuśrūṣave = ca — and + aśuśrūṣave — one who does not desire to hear; vācyaṁ — what is to be said; na — not; ca — and; mām — me; yo = yaḥ — who; 'bhyasūyati = abhyasūyati — he is critical

This should not be told by you to anyone who does not perform austerity or is not devoted at anytime, or does not desire to hear what is said or is critical of Me. (18.67)

Commentary:

Lord Krishna does not want His guarantees of the *tyāgi* to be shown to persons who are cynical towards Him nor to those who do not perform the austerities recommended in the *Gītā* and who do not worship Krishna as advised.

No one, therefore, is authorized to cheapen or dilute the *Bhagavad Gītā,* nor to attract people to the *Gītā,* who would harm themselves and others in attempts to abuse the guarantees.

य इदं परमं गुह्यं
मद्भक्तेष्वभिधास्यति ।
भक्तिं मयि परां कृत्वा
मामेवैष्यत्यसंशयः ॥१८.६८॥
ya idaṁ paramaṁ guhyaṁ
madbhakteṣvabhidhāsyati
bhaktiṁ mayi parāṁ kṛtvā
māmevaiṣyatyasaṁśayaḥ (18.68)

ya — who; idam — this; paramam — supreme; guhyam — secret; madbhakteṣu — to my devotees; abhidhāsyati — he will explain; bhaktiṁ — devotion; mayi — to me; parām — highest; kṛtvā — having performed; mām — me; evaiṣyati = eva — indeed + eṣyati — he will come; asaṁśayaḥ — without a doubt, certainly

Whosoever, having performed the highest devotion to Me, will explain this supreme secret to My devotees, will certainly come to Me. (18.68)

Commentary:

Only a person who performed the highest devotion as described in the Gita is covered under this guarantee. Anyone can try to explain the Gita, even this writer, but this particular guarantee only applies to those preachers who met all the requirements for the highest devotion that was described by Krishna.

न च तस्मान्मनुष्येषु
कश्चिन्मे प्रियकृत्तमः ।
भविता न च मे तस्माद्
अन्यः प्रियतरो भुवि ॥१८.६९॥
na ca tasmānmanuṣyeṣu
kaścinme priyakṛttamaḥ
bhavitā na ca me tasmād
anyaḥ priyataro bhuvi (18.69)

na — not; ca — and; tasmān — than this person; manuṣyeṣu — among human beings; kaścit — anyone; me — of me; priyakṛttamaḥ = priyaḥ — pleasing + kṛttamaḥ — more in performance; bhavitā — he will be; na — not; ca — and; me — to me; tasmāt — than this person; anyaḥ — other; priyataro = priyataraḥ — more dear; bhuvi — on earth

And no one among human beings is more pleasing to Me in performance than he. And no one on earth will be more dear to Me than he. (18.69)

Commentary:

This only applies to the devotees who satisfy all the standards laid out in the *Gītā* in verses which describe those devotees who perform the highest devotion. Others who claim these promises for themselves misunderstand the guarantees.

अध्येष्यते च य इमं
धर्म्यं संवादमावयोः ।
ज्ञानयज्ञेन तेनाहम्
इष्टः स्यामिति मे मतिः ॥१८.७०॥
adhyeṣyate ca ya imaṁ
dharmyaṁ saṁvādamāvayoḥ
jñānayajñena tenāham
iṣṭaḥ syāmiti me matiḥ (18.70)

adhyeṣyate — he will study; ca - and; ya — who; imaṁ — this; dharmyaṁ — sacred; saṁvādam — conversation; āvayoḥ — of ours; jñānayajñena — by the sacrifice of his knowledge; tenāham = tena — by him + aham — I; iṣṭaḥ — loved; syām — I should be; iti — thus; me — my; matiḥ — opinion

I would be loved by the devotee who by sacrifice of his knowledge, will study this sacred conversation of ours. This is My opinion. (18.70)

Commentary:

A sincere intellectual study of the *Gītā* that is done systematically with intentions to understand Krishna's opinion as I did by translating and writing this commentary, would yield the aspect discussed in this verse. As I looked and looked in the *Gītā*, I found no other verse which gives a guarantee that I may qualify for. This verse may be the verse. There is every hope that I would develop some love for Lord Krishna by this disciplinary study of His philosophy and guarantees.

श्रद्धावाननसूयश्च
शृणुयादपि यो नरः ।
सोऽपि मुक्तः शुभाँल्लोकान्
प्राप्नुयात्पुण्यकर्मणाम् ॥१८.७१॥
śraddhāvānanasūyaśca
śṛṇuyādapi yo naraḥ
so'pi muktaḥ śubhām̐llokān
prāpnuyātpuṇyakarmaṇām (18.71)

śraddhāvān — with confidence; anasūyaśca = anasūyaḥ — without ridiculing + ca — and; śṛṇuyāt — he should hear; api — even; yo = yaḥ — who; naraḥ — the person; so = saḥ — he; 'pi = api — also; muktaḥ — freed; śubhān — happy; lokān — worlds; prāpnuyāt — he should attain; puṇyakarmaṇām – puṇya — pious + karmaṇām — of actions

Even the person who hears with confidence, without ridiculing is freed. He should attain the happy worlds where persons of pious actions reside. (18.71)

Commentary:

And this is the most guarantee we can give to any of our sincere readers of this *Gītā* commentary. To get more of a guarantee from the *Gītā* and from Krishna, a reader would have to qualify as stipulated previously.

कच्चिदेतच्छ्रुतं पार्थ
त्वयैकाग्रेण चेतसा ।
कच्चिदज्ञानसंमोहः
प्रनष्टस्ते धनंजय ॥१८.७२॥
kaccidetacchrutaṁ pārtha
tvayaikāgreṇa cetasā
kaccidajñānasaṁmohaḥ
pranaṣṭaste dhanaṁjaya (18.72)

kaccit — has it?; etat — this; śrutaṁ — was heard; pārtha — son of Pṛthā; tvayaikāgreṇa = tvayā — by you + ekāgreṇa — by one-pointed; cetasā — by mind; kaccit — has it?; ajñānasaṁmohaḥ = ajñāna — ignorance + saṁmohaḥ — confusion; pranaṣṭaḥ — removed; te — your; dhanaṁjaya — conqueror of wealthy countries

Was this heard by you, O son of Pṛthā, with a one-pointed mind? Was your ignorance and confusion removed, O conqueror of wealthy countries? (18.72)

Commentary:

Arjuna was given this opportunity to ask any other questions. At this time, however, he was convinced by Lord Krishna.

अर्जुन उवाच
नष्टो मोहः स्मृतिर्लब्धा
त्वत्प्रसादान्मयाच्युत ।
स्थितोऽस्मि गतसंदेहः
करिष्ये वचनं तव ॥१८.७३॥

arjuna — Arjuna; uvāca — said; nasṭo = naṣṭaḥ — removed; mohaḥ — confusion; smṛtiḥ — memory; labdhā — retrieved; tvat prasādān = tvat — your + prasādān (prasādāt) — from grace; mayācyuta = mayā — by me + acyuta — O unaffected one; sthito

arjuna uvāca
naṣṭo mohaḥ smṛtirlabdhā
tvatprasādānmayācyuta
sthito'smi gatasaṁdehaḥ
kariṣye vacanaṁ tava (18.73)

= sthitāḥ — standing; 'smi = asmi — I am; gatasaṁdehaḥ = gata — gone, cleared away + saṁdehaḥ — doubt; kariṣye — I will execute; vacanaṁ — instruction; tava — your

Arjuna said: Through Your grace, the confusion is removed, memory is retrieved by Me, O unaffected one. I stand clear of doubts. I will execute Your instruction. (18.73)

Commentary:

For Arjuna it was a matter of remembering (*smṛtir*) his former yoga practice and applying all that maturity to conquer over the moods. By the grace of Lord Krishna, that memory was returned and his uncertainty vanished.

Even though Arjuna was proven to be an "affected spirit" (*kṣara puruṣa*), and even though Lord Krishna said that Arjuna was limited in recall of past lives, still, by taking the help Krishna offered, Arjuna gained Krishna's association and became unaffected (*akṣara*).

Thus the course of our liberation was charted out by Lord Krishna and lived out by Arjuna

संजय उवाच
इत्यहं वासुदेवस्य
पार्थस्य च महात्मनः ।
संवादमिममश्रौषम्
अद्भुतं रोमहर्षणम् ॥१८.७४॥
saṁjaya uvāca
ityahaṁ vāsudevasya
pārthasya ca mahātmanaḥ
saṁvādamimamaśrauṣam
adbhutaṁ romaharṣaṇam (18.74)

saṁjaya = Sanjaya; uvāca — said; iti — thus; aham — I; vāsudevasya — of the son of Vasudeva; pārthasya — of the son of Pṛthā; ca — and; mahātmanaḥ — great souled one; saṁvādam — talk; imam — this; aśroṣam — I heard; adbhutaṁ — amazing; romaharṣaṇam — causing hair to stand on end

Sanjaya said: In this way, I heard this talk of the son of Vasudeva and the great-souled son of Pṛthā. It is amazing. It causes the hairs to stand on end. (18.74)

Commentary:

Sanjaya was in a unique position as the first narrator of the *Bhagavad-Gītā*. He was fortunate to see the Universal Form of Lord Krishna. Even though the dialogue is amazing, I am yet to develop that love of Krishna through which my hairs would bristle even after this careful study of the *Bhagavad Gītā*. But Sanjaya naturally reached that plane of devotional excitement which the Vaishnavas categorize as spiritual emotion.

व्यासप्रसादाच्छ्रुतवान्
एतद्गुह्यमहं परम् ।
योगं योगेश्वरात्कृष्णात्
साक्षात्कथयतः स्वयम् ॥१८.७५॥
vyāsaprasādācchrutavān
etadguhyamahaṁ param
yogaṁ yogeśvarātkṛṣṇāt
sākṣātkathayataḥ svayam (18.75)

vyāsaprasādāt = vyāsa — Vyasa + prasādāt — from grace; śrutavān — one who heard; etad — this; guhyam — secret; aham — I; param — supreme; yogaṁ — yoga; yogeśvarāt = yoga — yoga + īśvarāt — from the Lord; kṛṣṇāt — from Krishna; sākṣāt — directly; kathayataḥ — explaining; svayam — himself

By the grace of Vyasa, I am the one who heard this secret information of the supreme yoga from the Lord of yoga, Krishna, who Himself explained it directly. (18.75)

Commentary:

Bhagavad Gītā as Krishna spoke it to Arjuna and as its definitions were given by Krishna without being adjusted to our time and place, is the secret information of the supreme yoga insofar as it applied to Arjuna as a *karma* yogi and insofar as Lord Krishna wanted to give additional details about various types of yoga.

राजन्संस्मृत्य संस्मृत्य
संवादमिममद्भुतम् ।
केशवार्जुनयोः पुण्यं
हृष्यामि च मुहुर्मुहुः ॥ १८.७६ ॥
rājansaṁsmṛtya saṁsmṛtya
saṁvādamimamadbhutam
keśavārjunayoḥ puṇyaṁ
hṛṣyāmi ca muhurmuhuḥ (18.76)

rājan — king; saṁsmṛtya saṁsmṛtya — remembering repeatedly; saṁvādam — talk; imam — this; adbhutam — amazing; keśavārjunayoḥ — of Keśava and Arjuna; puṇyaṁ — holy; hṛṣyāmi — I rejoice; ca — and; muhuḥ muhuḥ — again and again

O King, remembering repeatedly, this amazing and holy talk between Keśava and Arjuna, I rejoice again and again. (18.76)

Commentary:

What a wonderful appraisal by Sanjaya !

तच्च संस्मृत्य संस्मृत्य
रूपमत्यद्भुतं हरेः ।
विस्मयो मे महान्राजन्
हृष्यामि च पुनः पुनः ॥ १८.७७ ॥
tacca saṁsmṛtya saṁsmṛtya
rūpamatyadbhutaṁ hareḥ
vismayo me mahānrājan
hṛṣyāmi ca punaḥ punaḥ (18.77)

tat — this; ca — and; saṁsmṛtya saṁsmṛtya — remembering repeatedly; rūpam — form; atyadbhutaṁ — super-fantastic; hareḥ — of Hari; vismayo = vismayaḥ — astonished; me — my; mahān — great; rājan — O King; hṛṣyāmi — I excitedly rejoice; ca — and; punaḥ punaḥ — again and again

And remembering repeatedly that super-fantastic form of Hari, my astonishment is great, O King, and I excitedly rejoice again and again. (18.77)

Commentary:

The Universal Form was seen directly by Sanjaya. By the grace of his spiritual master, *Śrīla Vyāsaji*, Sanjaya saw that Universal Form repeatedly as he desired. For him, it was not a conceptual idea as experienced by most of us, but a living vision. Thus he had every reason to rejoice in a state of excited joy.

यत्र योगेश्वरः कृष्णो
यत्र पार्थो धनुर्धरः ।
तत्र श्रीर्विजयो भूतिर्
ध्रुवा नीतिर्मतिर्मम ॥ १८.७८ ॥

yatra — wherever; yogeśvaraḥ — the Lord of yoga; kṛṣṇo = kṛṣṇaḥ — Kṛṣṇa; yatra — wherever; pārtho = pārthaḥ — son of Pṛthā; dhanurdharaḥ — bowman; tatra — there; śrīḥ — splendor; vijayo = vijayaḥ— victory;

yatra yogeśvaraḥ kṛṣṇo
yatra pārtho dhanurdharaḥ
tatra śrīrvijayo bhūtir
dhruvā nītirmatirmama (18.78)

bhūtiḥ — prosperity; dhruvā — surely; nītiḥ — morality; matiḥ — opinion; mama — my

Wherever there exists the Lord of yoga, Krishna, wherever there is the son of Pṛthā, the bowman, there would surely be splendor, victory, prosperity and morality. This is my opinion. (18.78)

Commentary:

This is the view of Sanjaya, a person who experienced what Arjuna saw and who had the education and disciplinary background to understand what Krishna said to Arjuna. And this brings us to the end of this translation and commentary of the *Bhagavad Gītā*. Like many readers, I long to be upgraded so that I may qualify for these guarantees given by Lord Krishna. Let no one fool you. The *Gītā* is primarily a treatise on *karma yoga*, the type of yoga King Janaka exemplified. Some modern teachers have said otherwise. In any case, yoga and many of its applications are discussed in the *Gītā* as well. The central teaching was *karma yoga* and the objective of it was to get Arjuna to fight at *Kurukṣetra*. This is the truth of the matter.

I am hopeful of doing a translation of Krishna's instruction to Uddhava since that is a more complex discourse on yoga and the various applications of it, taught by Lord Krishna in ancient times. I believe that everything is in the hands of Lord Krishna. At least this is what I learned from the *Bhagavad Gītā*. May we all acquire more submission to Lord Krishna.

Many commentators set out to give readers devotion (*bhakti*) to Krishna. But in all honesty, I could not give it, since I did not have it. What then was my possession? It was a sincere interest in the *Bhagavad Gītā* and in Lord Krishna and Arjuna. And that alone, I might, by Krishna's grace, impart to a reader.

In 1979, the year of the departure of His Divine Grace A. C. Bhaktivedanta Swami *Śrīla* Prabhupada, I sought formal entry into the Krishna Consciousness Society. I was looking for Krishna. Thus I went, as I heard He could be located there. I did locate Krishna's Deity Form there. And that I appreciate. So with this appreciation, I want to offer my respects and obeisances to His Divine Grace *Śrīla* Prabhupada. Since my formal entry into *Śrīla* Prabhupada's society and my quiet departure from it, I still continue that search for Krishna.

To this point in this body, Krishna displayed Himself to me a few times, but otherwise He eludes me. But I will not give up. I will continue the quest for the time when He will always be right there before me with my perception of Him through spiritual eyes. *Śrīla* Prabhupada's presentation of Krishna's Icon (Deity-Murti) is a most wonderful gift to humanity, something not to be missed by any sane man. But I must move on. I must find Krishna in the spiritual form.

And most of all I have got to see Krishna through natural spiritual eyes. That I consider to be my life's mission. And to all of my readers, I share that urgency of seeking Krishna! Hare Krishna!

Hare Krishna Hare Krishna Krishna Krishna Hare Hare
Hare Rama Hare Rama Rama Rama Hare Hare

OM TAT SAT

Concluding Remarks

The writer took assistance from many translations and commentaries of the *Gītā*. Notably are Winthrop Sargeant's *The Bhagavad Gītā* (State University of New York Press) from which we noted his exact grammar-oriented Sanskrit vocabulary. We also noted the translation and commentary of *Śrīla* Bhaktivedanta Swami's *Bhagavad Gītā As It Is* (Bhaktivedanta Book Trust) and Sridhara Deva Gosvami's *The Hidden Treasure of the Sweet Absolute* (Sri Chaitanya Saraswat Math, India) as well as Sri Swami Sachidananda's *The Living Gītā* (Henry Holt and Co., New York) and Dr. Ramanand Prasad's *Bhagavad Gītā* (Motilal Banarsidass Publishers, India), as well as many other translations and commentaries.

Because of the nature of this edition which explains the *Gītā* in its own time and place, we were unable to utilize much of the missionary material from some of the above publications. In any case, we are grateful to everyone. Overall, this is a successful translation and commentary for the writer. It suits a need that was inspired in him by his Sri Sri Krishna-Balaram deities.

This is not a missionary translation. It is not for starting nor establishing any religious movement. It is only for personal study of the *Gītā* in its own time and place. It does not require to fit into any organisational or missionary schemes. This is not meant for wide distribution nor popularity, nor is it meant to be hailed as an infallible text, but rather, whatever you find here that is true to the view of Lord Krishna, goes to Krishna's credit for having revealed that to Arjuna and ourselves. And whatever you find herein that is a distortion, is simply some mistake in the perception of the writer. As Sanjaya had ability to see what Krishna revealed to Arjuna, so we got some ability but if that ability was partial only, then still, there is no loss. Readers should be on their guard to detect distortions and to take full advantage of any revelations of what Lord Krishna expressed to Arjuna.

Indexed Names of Arjuna

puruṣarṣabha — bull among men, 2.15
bharataśreṣṭha — best of the Bharatas, 17.12
bharatarṣabha — powerful son (strong man) of the Bharatas, bullish man of the Bharata family, 7.11,16; 8.23; 13.27; 14.12
bhārata — man of the Bharata family, descendant of Bharata, 2.18,30; 3.25; 4.7,42; 7.27; 11.6; 13.3,34; 14.3,8,9,10; 15.19,20; 16.3; 17.3; 18.36,62
mahābāho — powerful man, 3.28,43; 5.3; 10.1; 14.5; 18.13
paraṁtapa — burner of enemy forces, scorcher of enemies, 4.2,5; 11.51
kapidhvajaḥ — the man with a monkey insignia (Hanuman), 1.20
Arjuna -- third son of King Pāndu and Queen Kuntī, cousin of Lord Krishna, 1.4; 2.1,4,54; 2.68; 3.1,7,36; 4.4,5,9,37; 5.1; 6.16,32,33,37; 6.46; 7.16; 8.1,16; 10.32,37,39,42; 11.1,36,50,51,54; 13.1; 18.73,76
pāṇḍava — son of Pāndu, 1.14; 4.35; 6.2; 11.13,55; 12.1; 14.21,22; 16.5; 17.1, 18.1,9,34,61
dhanaṁjayaḥ — conqueror of wealthy countries, 1.15; 7.7;11.14; 18.29,72
savyasācin — ambidextrous archer, 11.33
kurusattama — best of the Kurus, 4.31
kurunandana — dear son of the Kurus, 2.41,48; 6.43, 14.13
anagha — blameless one, good man, 3.3
kuruśreṣṭha — best of the Kuru clan, 10.19
pārtha — son of Pṛthā (Kuntī), 1.25,26; 2.3,32,39,42,55,72; 3.16,22,23; 4.11,33; 6.40; 7.1,10; 8.8,14,19,22,27; 9.32; 10.24; 11.5,9; 12.7; 16.4,6; 17.26,28; 18.6,31,33,72,78
dhanurdharaḥ — bowman, 18.78
kaunteya — son of Kuntī (Pṛthā), 1.27; 2.14,21,60; 3.37; 5.22; 6.35; 7.8; 8.16; 9.7,10,23,27,31; 13.2; 14.4; 16.20,22; 18.50,60
puruṣavyāghra — tiger among men, 18.4
tāta — ideal one, 6.40
sakhā — friend, 4.3
bhaktaḥ — devoted person, 4.3
guḍākeśa — the thick-haired baron, conqueror of sleep, 1.24, 11.7
dehabhṛtām vara — best of the embodied souls, 8.4
anagha — sinless one, 14.6
kurupravīra — great hero of the Kurus, 11.48

Indexed Names of Krishna

acyuta, infallible one, 11.42
adhyātma, Supreme Spirit, 15.5
ādidevaḥ, first God, 11.38
ādidevamajaṁ, Primal God, 10.12
ādikartre, original creator, 11.37
ādyaṁ, primal person, 11.31
ajam, birthless, 10.12
akṣaraṁ, imperishable basis of energies, 11.37
akṣaraṁ paramaṁ, indestructible Supreme Person, 11.18
anādimadhyāntam, Person without beginning, middle or ending, 11.19
ananta deveśa, infinite Lord of the gods, 11.37
anantabāhuṁ, Person with unlimited arms, 11.19
anantarūpa, Person of lnfinite Form, 11.38
anantavīryam, Person with infinite manly power, 11.19
anumantā, permitter, 13.23
aprameyam, one who is boundless, 11.42
apratimaprabhāva, person of incomparable splendor, 11.43
asat, sum total temporary existence, 11.37
atyadbhutaṁ hareḥ, super-fantastic form of Hari, 18.77
bhagavān (śrī bhagavān), the Blessed Lord, 2.2,11,55; 3.3,37; 4.1,5;
5.2; 6.1,35,40; 7.1; 8.3; 9.1; 10.1,14,17,19;
11.5,32,47,52; 12.2; 13.2; 14.1,22; 15.1; 16.1; 17.2; 18.2
bhartā, supporter, 13.23
bhavantam, Your lordship, 11.31
bhavānugrarūpo, respected person of terrible form, 11.31
bhoktā, experiencer, 13.23
bhūtabhāvana, one who sustains the existence of all others, 10.15
bhūteśa, Lord of created beings, 10.15
caturbhujena, person with four arms, 11.46
devadeva, God of the gods, 10.15
devam, God, 11.11,14,15,44,45
devavara, best of the gods, 11.31
deveśa (deva-īśa), Lord of all lords, 11.25,45
dīptahutāśavaktraṁ,
Person with the blazing oblation-eating mouth, 11.19
govinda, chief of cowherds, 1.32, 2.9
hariḥ, Hari, the God Vishnu, 11.9; 18.77
hṛṣīkeśa, Master of the sense organs, 1.15,18,24; 18.1
īśam īḍyam, Lord who is to be praised, 11.44
īśvaraḥ, Lord, 4.6

jagannivāsa (jagat-nivāsa),
refuge of the worlds, 11.25
resort of the world, 11.37
shelter of the world, 11.45
jagatpate, Lord of the universe, 10.15
janārdana, motivator of human beings, 1.38;43; 3.1; 11.51
kālo (kālah), time-limit, 11.32
kamalapatrākṣa, Person whose eyes are shaped like lotus petals,11.2
keśava, pretty-haired one, 2.54; 10.14; 11.35; 13.29; 15.17;18.61,75,76
keśiniṣūdāna, slayer of Keshi, 18.1
kṛṣṇa, person with blackish complexion, 1.28,31; 6.34,37,39;
11.35,41; 17.1; 18.75,78
kṣetrajñam (sarva), experiencer of all living spaces, 13.3
mādhava, descendant of Madhu, 1.36
madhusūdana, slayer of Madhu, 1.34; 2.1; 6.33; 8.2
mahābāho, mighty-armed Person, 11.23
mahātma, great personality, 11.20,37
mahātmanaḥ, great personality, 11.12
mahāyogeśvaro, the great master of yoga, 11.9
maheśvara, Supreme Lord, 5.29,13.23
mahīpate, Lord of the earth, 1.21
paraṁ brahma, supreme reality, 10.12
paraṁ dhāma,
supreme refuge, 10.12
ultimate sanctuary, 11.38
paraṁ nidhānam, ultimate shelter, 11.18
paramātmā, Supreme Soul, Supreme Spirit, 13.32,15.17
parameśvara, Supreme Lord, 11.3; 13 28
pavitraṁ paramaṁ, 10.12
prabho (prabhuḥ), respected Lord, 5.14; 11.4; 14.21
prapitāmahaḥ, father of Brahmā, 11.39
pūjyaḥ guruḥ garīyān, gravest spiritual master, 11.43
puruṣaḥ paraḥ, highest spirit, 13.23
puruṣaḥ purāṇaḥ, most ancient spirit, 11.38
puruṣaṁ śāśvataṁ divyam, eternal divine person, 10.12
puruṣottama, Supreme Person, 11.3; 10.15; 15.18,19
rūpaṁ, God-form, 11.45
sahasrabāho, O thousand-armed person, 11.46
sanātanas puruṣo, most ancient person, 11.18
śaśisūryanetram, Person who has sun and moon as eyes, 11.19
śāśvatadharmagoptā, eternal guardian of law, 11.18
sat, sum total permanent life, 11.37
svatejasā viśvamidaṁ tapantam,
Person heating this universe with splendor, 11.19
tatparaṁ, that which is beyond, 11.37
upadraṣṭā, observer, 13.23
vārṣṇeya, clansman of the Vṛṣṇis, 1.40

vāsudevasya, of the son of Vasudeva, 7.19; 11.50; 18.74
vibhum (vibhuḥ), Almighty God, whose influence spreads everywhere, 5.15; 10.12
viṣṇo, Lord Viṣṇu, 11.24,30
viśvamūrte,person of universal dimensions, 11.46
viśvarūpa, form of everything, 11.16
viśvasya paraṁ nidhānam, supreme refuge of all the worlds, 11.38
viśveśvara, Lord of all, 11.16
yādava, family man of the Yadus, 11.41
yogeśvara,
    Lord of yoga disciplines, 18.75,78
    Master of yoga technique, 11.4
yogin, mystic master, 10.17

Names, Places and Things

Ādityas, 10.21
Agni, 10.23; 11.39
Airāvata, 10.27
Ananta, 10.29
Anantavijaya, 1.16
Arjuna,
--see Indexed Names of Arjuna
Aryamā, 10.29
Ashvattha, 10.26
Asita, 10.13
Aśvatthāmā, 1.8
Bhīma, 1.4,10,15
Bhishma, 1.8,10,25; 2.4; 11.26,34
Bhrigu, 10.25
Brahmā, 3.10; 8.16-19; 9.7; 10.33; 11.15,37,39
Brihaspati, 10.24
Cekitāna, 1.5
Chitraratha, 10.26
Dānavāḥ, 10.14
Danu, 10.14
Devadatta, 1.15
Devala, 10.13
Dhātā, 10.33
Dhṛṣṭadyumna, 1.17
Dhṛṣṭaketu, 1.5
Dhṛtarāṣṭra, 1.1,19,20,23
Dhṛti, 10.34
Diti, 10.30
Draupadī,1.6,18
Droṇa, 1.25; 2.4; 11.26,34
Drupada, 1.3,4,18
Duryodhana, 1.2,12
dvijottama, 1.7
Gāṇḍīva, 1.29
Gayatri, 10.35
Hanuman (kapi), 1.20
Hari, 11.9; 18.77
Himalayas, 10.25
Ikṣvāku, 4.1
Indra, 10.22
Jahnu, 10.31
Jayadratha, 11.34
Kamadhuk, 10.28
Kandarpa, 10.28
kapi, 1.20
Kapila, 10.26
Karṇa, 1.8; 11.34
Kāśi, 1.5,17
Kīrti, 10.34
Krishna,
- see Indexed Names of Krishna
Kṣamā, 10.34
Kubera, 10.23
Kuntī, 1.16; 13.2
Kuntibhoja, 1.5
Kuru, 1.12,25
kurukṣetre, 1.1
Manipushpaka, 1.16
Manu, 4.1
Marīci, 10.21
Medhā, 10.34
Meru, 10.23
Nakula, 1.16
Narada, 10.13
narapuṁgavaḥ, 1.5
Pāñcajanya, 1.15
Pandava, 1.2
Pāndu, 1.1,3
Paundra, 1.15
Pavāka, 10.23
Prahlāda, 10.30
Purujit, 1.5
Rāma, 10.31
Rudra, 10.23
Sādhya, 11.22
Sahadeva, 1.16
Śaibya, 1.5
Sāma Veda chants, 10.35
Sāṁkhya, 5.5
Sanjaya, 1.1,2,24; 18.74
Śāśaṅka, 11.39
Sātyaki, 1.17
Shankara, 10.23
Shiva, 10.23
Śikhandī, 1.17
Skanda, 10.24
Smṛti, 10.34
Somadatta, 1.8
Śrī, 10.34
Subhadra, 1.6,18
Sughosha, 1.16
Uccaihśrava, 10.27
Ushana, 10.37
Uttamauja, 1.6
Vaiśvāanara, 15.2
Vajra, 10.28
Vāk, 10.34
Varuṇa, 10.29; 11.39
Vasava, 10.22
Vasudeva, 7.19; 10.37
Vasuki, 10.28
Vasus, 11.22
Vāyu, 11.39
Vikarṇa, 1.8
Vinata, 10.30
Virāṭa, 1.4,17
Vishnu, 10.21; 11.9,24,30
Vishvadevas, 11.22
Vitteśaḥ, 10.23
Vivasvat, 4.1,4
Vṛṣṇis, 1.40, 10.36
Vyasa, 10.13
Vyasa, 10.37; 18.75
Yakshas, 10.23
Yama, 10.29, 11.39
Yudhamanyu, 1.6
Yudhishthira, 1.16
Yuyudhāna, 1.4

Index To Verses: Selected Sanskrit Words

A

ā, 8.16
abhāvayataḥ, 2.66
abhāvo, 2.16
abhipravṛttaḥ, 4.20
abhyāsena, 6.35,44; 8.8;12.9
abhyasūyanto, 3.31
abhyutthānam, 4.7
abuddhayaḥ, 7.24
acalapratiṣṭhaṁ, 2.70
ācaratyātmanaḥ, 16.22
ācāryam, 1.2
ācāryopāsanaṁ, 13.8
acchedyo, 2.24
acetasaḥ, 3.32
acintya, 2,25; 8.9
acireṇādhigacchati, 4.39
adharma, 1.39,40; 4.7; 18.32
ādhāyātmanaḥ, 8.12
adhibhūtaṁ, 8.1,4
adhidaivaṁ, 8.1
adhipatyam, 2.8
adhiṣṭhānam, 3.40; 18.14
adhiṣṭhāya, 4.6
adhiyajñaḥ, 7.30; 8.2,4
adhyātma, 7.29; 13.12
adhyeṣyate, 18.70
ādidevamajaṁ, 10.12
ādityavaj, 5.16
ādityavarṇaṁ, 8.9
ādyantavantaḥ, 5.22
agatāsūṁś, 2.11
aghāyurindriyārāmo, 3.16
āgnidagdha, 4,19
agnirjyotirahaḥ, 8.24
ahaṁ sarvasya, 10.8
ahaṁkāraṁ, 16.18
ahaṁkāraṁ balaṁ, 18.53
ahaṁkāravimūḍhā, 3.27
āhārāḥ, 17.8
ahiṁsā, 10.5; 16.2
ahoratra, 8.17
ajānantaḥ, 7.24
ajñānāṁ, 3.26
ajñānasaṁbhūtaṁ, 4.42
ajñānenāvṛtaṁ, 5.15
ajo, 4.6
akarmakṛt, 3.5
akarmaṇi, 4.18
akartāram, 4.13
ākāśaṁ, 13.33
akhilam, 7.29
ākhyāhi me ko bhavānugrarūpo, 11.31
akīrtikaram, 2.2
akṣara, 3.15; 8.3,11,21; 15.18
akṣayam, 5.21
alpamedhasām, 7.23
ambhasi, 2.67
amṛta, 2.15; 9.19
anabhisnehas, 2.57
anādimatparaṁ, 13.13
anāditvānnirguṇa, 13.32
anahaṁkāra, 13.9
anāmayam, 2.51
anantaṁ, 11.11
ananyacetāḥ, 8.14
ananyamanasaḥ, 9.13
anapekṣya, 18.25
anāryajuṣṭam, 2.2
anāśino, 2.18
anasūyantaḥ, 3.31
anāvṛttim, 8.23
anekacittavibhrāntā, 16.16
anekajanma, 6.45
anekavaktra, 11.10
aniṣṭamiṣṭaṁ, 18.12
anīśvaram, 16.8
aṇīyāṁsam, 8.9
annādbhavanti, 3.14
antakāle, 8.5
antarātmanā, 6.47
anubandhaṁ, 18.25
anucintayan, 8.8
anudvegakaraṁ, 17.15
anusmaran, 8.13
anuśocanti, 2.11
anuśocitum, 2.25
anuśuśruma, 1.43
apahṛta, 2.44
apāne juhvati, 4.29
aparaṁ bhavato, 4.4
apare niyatāhārāḥ, 4.30
apareyamitastvanyāṁ, 7.5
aprameyasya, 2.18
apratiṣṭho, 6.38
apunarāvṛttiṁ, 5.17
āpūryamāṇam, 2.70
arāgadveṣataḥ, 18.23
ārjavam, 16.1
arpitamanobuddhir, 8.7
ārurukṣormuner, 6.3
asaktir, 13.10
asaṁśayaṁ, 6.35; 7.1; 8.7
asaṁyatātmanā, 6.36
asaṅgaśastreṇa, 15.3
asatas, 2.16
asito devalo vyāsaḥ, 10.13
aśraddadhānāḥ, 4.40; 9.3
aśraddhayā, 17.28
aśru, 2.1
asvargyam, 2.2
aśvinau, 11.6
atīndriyam, 6.21
ātiṣṭhottiṣṭha, 4.42
atisvapna, 6.16
ātmabuddhiprasāda, 18.37
ātmānaṁ mat, 9.34
ātmanātmānaṁ, 6.5; 13.29
ātmanyevātmanā, 2.55
ātmasaṁbhāvitāḥ, 16.17
ātmasaṁsthaṁ, 6.25
ātmasaṁyamayogā, 4.27
ātmaśuddhaye, 5.11
ātmatṛptaśca, 3.17
ātmaupamyena, 6.32
ātmavān, 2.45
ātmavantaṁ, 4.41
ātmavaśyair, 2.64
ātmikā, 2.43
avabodhasya, 6.17
avadhyaḥ, 2.30
avaśaṁ, 9.8
avaśiṣyate, 7.2
avatiṣṭhate, 6.18
avibhaktaṁ, 13.17; 18.20
avidhipūrvakam, 9.23
avidvāṁas, 3.25
avināśi, 2.17
āvṛtam, 3.38,39
āvṛttiṁ, 8.23
avyaktaḥ, 2.25,28; 7.24; 12.3

avyaktāsaktacetasām, 12.5
avyavasāyinām, 2.41
avyaya, 2.17; 7.24
avyayātmā, 4.6
ayajñasya, 4.31
āyuḥsattvabalārogya, 17.8
ayuktasya, 2.66

B

bahumataḥ, 2.35
bahūnāṁ janma, 7.19
bahūni me vyatītāni, 4.5
bahuśākhā, 2.41
bahuvidhā, 4.32
balavaddṛḍham, 6.34
balavānsukhī, 16.14
bandhurātmātmanas, 6.6
bhagavanmayā, 10.17
bhagavanvyaktiṁ, 10.14
bhaikṣyam, 2.5
bhakta, 9.23,31; 12.1,20
bhaktiṁ mayi, 18.68
bhaktimānme, 12.19
bhaktimānyaḥ sa, 12.17
bhaktiyogena, 14.26
bhakto'si me sakhā, 4.3
bhaktyā, 8.10,22; 9.29; 11.54; 18.55
bhartā bhoktā, 13.23
bhāṣā, 2.54
bhasmasātkurute, 4.37
bhāvamāśritāḥ, 7.15
bhavantaḥ, 1.11
bhavārjuna, 2.45; 6.46
bhavato, 4.4
bhāvayatā, 3.11
bhinnā, 7.4
bhogā, 1.32; 2.5
bhogaiśvarya, 2.44
bhojanaṁ, 17.10
bhoktā, 9.24
bhoktāraṁ, 5.29
bhoktṛtve, 13.21
bhrāmayansarva, 18.61
bhraṁśāt, 2.63
bhruvoḥ, 5.27; 8.10
bhūmirāpo'nalo, 7.4
bhuñjānaṁ, 15.10
bhuñjate, 3.13
bhuñjīya, 2.5
bhuṅkte, 3.12; 13.22
bhūtabhartṛ, 13.17
bhūtabhāvana, 9.5; 10.15
bhūtabhāvodbhava, 8.3
bhūtabhṛnna, 9.5
bhūtagrāmaḥ, 8.19
bhūtagrāmamimaṁ, 9.8
bhūtamaheśvaram, 9.11
bhūtānāmīśvaro'pi, 4.6
bhūtaprakṛti, 13.35
bhūtapṛthag, 13.31
bhūtasargau, 16.6
bhūteśa, 10.15
bhūtvā, 3.30; 8.19
bījaṁ, 7.10
bījamavyayam, 9.18
boddhavyaṁ, 4.17
brahma, 8.13
brahma brahma, 8.24
brahmabhūto, 5.24
brahmabhuvanāl, 8.16
brahmabhūyāya, 14.26; 18.53
brahmacārivrate, 6.14
brahmacaryaṁ, 8.11
brahmacaryama, 17.14
brahmāgnau, 4.24,25
brahmakarma, 18.42
brahmākṣarasamud, 3.15
brahmaṇaḥ, 6.38
brāhmaṇakṣatriya, 18.41
brahmāṇamīśaṁ, 11.15
brahmaṇastri, 17.23
brahmanirvāṇaṁ, 2.72; 5.24-26
brahmaṇo hi, 14.27
brahmaṇo mukhe, 4.32
brahmaṇyādhāya, 5.10
brahmārpaṇaṁ, 4.24
brahmasaṁsparśam, 6.28
brahmavādinām, 17.24
brahmavidbrahmaṇi, 5.20
brāhmī sthitiḥ, 2.72
brahmodbhavaṁ, 3.15
buddhibhedaṁ, 3.26
buddhigrāhyamatī, 6.20
buddhiḥ, 2.44
buddhimānmanuṣyeṣu, 4.18
buddhimānsyāt, 15.20
buddhimatām, 7.10
buddhināśo, 2.63
buddhi, 2.41,66; 13.6
buddhirbuddhimatām, 7.10
buddhirjñānama, 10.4
buddhirvyatitariṣyati, 2.52
buddhisaṁyogaṁ, 6.43
buddhiyoga, 2.49; 18.57
buddhiyuktā, 2.50,51
buddhvā, 3.43
budhā, 4.19; 10.8

C

cakraṁ, 3.16
calamadhruvam, 17.18
cañcalatvātsthitiṁ, 6.33
cāndramasaṁ, 8.25
caratāṁ, 2.67
caturbhujena, 11.46
cāturvarṇyaṁ mayā, 4.13
caturvidhā, 7.16
cendriyagocarāḥ, 13.6
cetasā, 8.8
chandāṁsi, 15,1
chinna, 5.25; 18.10
cintayet, 6.25

D

daiva, 4.25; 16.6
daivī, 7.14
dakṣiṇāyanam, 8.25
dambha, 16.17; 17.5
daṁṣṭrākarālāni, 11.25, 27
dānakriyāśca, 17.25
dānavāḥ, 10.14
darśanakāṅkṣiṇaḥ, 11.52
darśayātmānamavyayam, 11.4
dehabhṛtāṁ, 8.4
dehasamudbhavān, 14.20
devabhogān, 9.20
devadvijaguru, 17.14
devān, 3.11; 7.23
devarṣirnāradas, 10.13
dhāma, 8.21
dhārayāmyaham, 15.13
dhārayan, 5.8; 6.13
dhārayate, 18.33
dharma, 1.39; 2.7
dharmakṣetre, 1.2
dharmamadharmaṁ, 18.31
dharmasaṁsthā, 4.8
dharmātmā, 9.31
dharmyaṁ, 9.2; 12.20
dhāryate, 7.5
dhātāhaṁ viśvato, 10.33
dhātāram, 8.9
dhīmatām, 6.42
dhṛtigṛhītayā, 6.25
dhruva, 2.27; 12.3; 18.78
dhūmena, 3.38; 18.48
dhūmo rātristathā, 8.25

dhyānātkarma, 12.12
dhyānenātmani, 13.24
dhyāyanta, 12.6
dhyāyataḥ, 2.62
dīpaḥ, 6.19
dīrghasūtrī, 18.28
diśaścānavalokayan, 6.13
divya, 1.14 ; 11.5
doṣa, 1.42; 2.7
dravyas, 4.28, 33
dṛḍhavratāḥ, 7.28, 9.14
dṛṣṭvā lokāḥ, 11.23
dṛṣṭvā rūpaṁ, 11.49
dṛṣṭvādbhutaṁ, 11.20
dṛṣṭvedaṁ, 11.51
duḥkhadoṣā, 13.9
duḥkhahā, 6.17
duḥkhālayam, 8.15
duḥkhaśokāmaya, 17.9
duḥkheṣvanudvigna, 2.56
durāsadam, 3.43
duratyayā, 7.14
durbuddher, 1.23
durgatiṁ, 6.40
durlabhataraṁ, 6.42
durmatiḥ, 18.16
durnigrahaṁ, 6.35
duṣkṛtino, 7.15
duṣprāpa, 6.36
duṣpūreṇānalena, 3.39
dvaṁdvamoha, 7.27,28
dvaṁdvātīto, 4.22
dvārāṇi, 8.12
dveṣṭyakuśalaṁ, 18.10
dvididhā, 3.3
dvijottama, 1.7

E

ekabhaktirviśiṣyate, 7.17
ekākī, 6.10
ekākṣaram, 8.13
ĕśvaraṁ, 11.3

G

gahanā karmaṇo, 4.17
gāmāviśya, 15.13
gandharva, 10.26; 11.22
gāṇḍīvaṁ, 1.29
garbhas, 3.38
garīyase, 11.37
gatāḥ, 8.15
gataprāṇā, 10.9
gatasaṅgasya, 4.23
gatāsūn, 2.11
gatim, 8.13,21
gāyatrī, 10.33
glānirbhavati, 4.7
grasiṣṇu, 13.17
guhyādguhyataraṁ, 18.63
guhyamadhyātma, 11.1
guhyamahaṁ, 18.75
guhyatamam, 9.1; 15.20
guṇabhedataḥ, 18.19
guṇabhoktṛ, 13.15
guṇakarma, 3.28,29; 4.13
guṇamayī, 7.14
guṇasaṁkhyāne, 18.19
guṇātītaḥ, 14.25
gurūn, 2.5

H

hānir, 2.65
hantāraṁ, 2.19
hanyamāne, 2.20
hareḥ, 18.77
hariḥ, 11.9
hatam, 2.19
hitakāmyayā, 10.1
hṛdayadaurbalyaṁ, 2.3
hṛddeśe'rjuna, 18.61
hṛtsthaṁ, 4.42
hutam, 4.24

I

icchā dveṣa, 7.27; 13.6
īkṣaṇam, 2.1
indriyāgniṣu, 4.26
indriyagrāmaṁ, 6.24
indriyāṇi mano, 3.40
indriyāṇīndriyā, 2.58, 68
indriyārāmaḥ, 3.16
indriyārtheṣu, 13.9
indriyasyendriyasy, 3.34
iṣṭakāmadhuk, 3.10
iṣṭānbhogānhi, 3.12
īśvaraḥ sarvabhūtānāṁ
18.61
ivāmbhasi, 2.67

J

jagadavyaktamūrtinā, 9.4
jagadbhāsayate, 15.12
jagadviparivartate, 9.10
jagannivāsa, 11.25,45
jāgarti, 2.69
jagataḥ, 8.26
jagatkṛtsnaṁ, 11.7,13
jagatpate, 10.15
jaghanyaguṇa, 14.18
jāgrato, 6.16
janakādayaḥ, 3.20
jānan, 8.27
jānāti, 15.19
janma, 2.27
janmabandha, 2.51
janma karma ca me, 4.9
janmakarmaphala, 2.43
janmamṛtyujarā, 13.9
janmāni, 4.5
jarāmaraṇamokṣāya, 7.29
jātidharmāḥ, 1.42
jijñāsurapi, 6.44
jitasaṅgadoṣā, 15,5
jitātmanaḥ, 6.7
jīvabhūta, 7.5; 15.7
jñānacakṣuṣa, 13.35; 15.10
jñānadīpena, 10.11
jñānadīpite, 4.27
jñānāgnidagdha, 4.19
jñānāgniḥ, 4.37
jñānaṁ jñeyaṁ, 13.18
jñānamāvṛtya, 3.40; 14.9
jñānamupāśritya, 14.2
jñānamuttamam, 14.1
jñānanirdhūta, 5.17
jñānārthadarśanam, 13.12
jñānasaṅgena, 14.6
jñānāsinātmanaḥ, 4.42
jñānatapasā, 4.10
jñānavānmāṁ, 7.19
jñānāvasthitacetasaḥ, 4.23
jñānavijñāna, 3.41; 6.8
jñānayajña,
4.33; 9.15; 18.70
jñānayoga, 3.3; 16.1
jñānī, 3.38,39; .6.46; 7.18
jñāninastattva, 4.34
jñātavyamavaśiṣyate, 7.2
jñeyo'si niyatātmabhiḥ, 8.2
juhvati, 4.26,27
jvaraḥ, 3.30
jyotir, 8.24

K

kālena, 4.2, 38
kalevaram, 8.5
kalmaṣāḥ, 4.30; 5.17
kalpakṣaye, 9.7
kalyāṇakṛtkaścid, 6.40
kāmabhoga, 16.12,16
kāma, 2.5,62; 7.22
kāmahaitukam, 16.8
kāmaistaistairhṛta, 7.20
kāmakāmā, 2,70; 9.21
kāmakārataḥ, 16.23

kāmakāreṇa, 5.12
kāmakrodhaṁ, 5.26
kāmamāśritya, 16.10
kāmarūpa, 3.39,43
kāmātmānaḥ, 2.43
kāmopabhoga, 16.11
kāmyānāṁ, 18.2
kāṅkṣantaḥ, 4.12
kapidhvajaḥ, 1.20
kāraṇaṁ guṇasaṅgo, 13.22
kāraṇamucyate, 6.3
karmabandhaṁ, 2.39
karmabandhana, 3.9; 9.28
karmabhirna sa, 4.14
karmajā, 4.12
karmajaṁ, 2.51
karmajānviddhi, 4.32
karmākhilaṁ, 4.33
karmānubandhīni, 15.2
karmaṇyabhirataḥ, 18.45
karmaṇyakarma, 4.18
karmāṇyaśeṣataḥ, 18.11
karmaṇyatandritaḥ, 3.23
karmaphala,
4.14; 6.1; 18.27
karmaphalahetur, 2.47
karmaphala, 5.14
karmaphalāsaṅgaṁ, 4.20
karmasamādhinā, 4.24
karmasaṁgrahaḥ, 18.18
karmasaṁjñitaḥ, 8.3
karmasaṁnyāsāt, 5.2
karmasaṅga, 3.26; 14.7,15
karmayoga,
3.3'7; 13.24; 5.2
kārpaṇya, 2.7
karśayantaḥ, 17.6
kartāraṁ, 14.19
kāryakāraṇa, 13.21
kāryākārye, 18.30
kaśmalam, 2.2
kauśalam, 2.50
kavim, 8.9
kāyakleśabhayāt, 18.8
kāyaśirogrīvaṁ, 6.13
keśavārjunayoḥ, 18.76
kevalairindriyairapi, 5.11
khaṁ mano buddhir, 7.4
kiṁ tadbrahma, 8.1
kirīṭinaṁ, 11.17,46
kīrtayanto, 9.14
klaibyaṁ, 2.3
kleśo'dhikataras, 12.5
kraturahaṁ, 9.16
kriyā, 1.41
kriyābhirna, 11.48
kriyamāṇāni, 3.27; 13.30
kriyāviśeṣabahulāṁ, 2.43
krodho, 2.62
kṛpaṇāḥ, 2.49
kṛpayāviṣṭam, 2.1
kṛṣigorakṣya, 18.44
kṛṣṇaḥ, 8.25
kṛtāñjalirabhāṣata, 11.14
kṛtsnakarmakṛt, 4.18
kṛtsna, 7.6,29
kṛtsnavin, 3.29
kṣāntirārjavam, 13.8
kṣaraścākṣara, 15.16
kṣātraṁkarma, 18.43
kṣayāya jagato'hitāḥ, 16.9
kṣetrajña iti tadvidaḥ, 13.3
kṣetrakṣetrajña, 13.,27
kṣetrakṣetrajñayor, 13.3,35
kṣetraṁ kṣetrajñam, 13.1
kṣetraṁ kṣetrī tathā , 13.34
kṣīṇakalmaṣāḥ, 5.25
kṣipraṁ hi mānuṣe, 4.12
kṣudraṁ, 2.3
kuladharmāḥ, 1.39,42,43
kulaghnānāṁ, 1.41,42
kulasya, 1.41
kurukṣetre, 1.1
kurunandana, 2.41
kutaḥ, 2.66
kūṭastho, 6.8; 15.16

L

lāghavam, 2.35
lipyate, 5.6
loka, 2.5; 7.25
lobhopahata cetasaḥ, 1.37
lokamaheśvaram, 10.3
lokasaṁgraham, 3.25
lokastadanuvartate, 3.21
lokatrayamāviśya, 15.17
loke janma, 6.42
luptapiṇḍodaka, 1.41

M

madarpaṇam, 9.26
madasrayah, 7.1
madbhakta, 7.23; 11.55;
12.14; 13.19
madbhakteṣu, 18.68
madbhaktiṁ, 18.54
madbhāva, 4.10; 10.6;
14.19
mādhavaḥ, 1.14
madvyapāśrayaḥ, 18.56
madyājī, 9.25,34; 18.65
madyogamāśritaḥ, 12.11
mahadyonir, 14.4
mahāpāpmā, 3.37
mahārathāḥ, 2.35
maharṣī, 10.2,6
mahāśano, 3.37
mahatā, 4.2
mahātmā, 7.19; 8.15;
9.13; 11.12; 18.74
mahatpāpaṁ, 1.44
mahāyogeśvaro, 11.9
maheśvara, 9.11; 13.23
mama māyā, 7.14
mama yo vetti, 10.7
māmāśritya, 7.29
māmevānuttamāṁ, 7.18
māmupāśritāḥ, 4.10
manaḥ, 6.26; 15.7,9; 17.16
mānasa, 1.46; 17.16
mānāvamānayoḥ, 6.7
manave, 4.1
manīṣiṇām, 18.5
manmanā, 9.34; 18.65
manmayā, 4.10
manogatān, 2.55
mantra, 9.16; 17.13
manuṣya, 3.23; 7.3; 15.2
manyate, 3.27
mārdavaṁ, 16.2
martyalokaṁ, 9.21
matkarma, 11.54; 12.10
matparaḥ, 6.14; 18.57
matparāyaṇaḥ, 9.34
matprasādāt, 18.58
mātrāsparśās, 2.14
matsaṁsthām, 6.15
matsthāni, 9.4
matvā, 3.28
maunamātmaḥ, 17.16
mayādhyakṣeṇa, 9.10
māyayā, 4.6; 7.15
mayi buddhiṁ, 12.8
mayi saṁnyasya, 12.6;
18.57
mayyarpitamano, 8.7
mayyāveśitacetasām, 12.7
mayyāveśya, 12.2
mitrāripakṣayoḥ, 14.25
modiṣya, 16.15
moghaṁ, 3.16
moghāśā, 9.12
mohādārabhyate, 18.25

mohakalilaṁ, 2.52
mohanaṁ, 14.8; 18.39
mohayasi, 3.2
mohinīṁ, 9.12
mohitam, 7.13
mokṣakāṅkṣibhiḥ, 17.25
mokṣaparāyaṇaḥ, 5.28
mokṣayiṣyāmi, 18.66
mokṣyase, 9.1,28
mriyate, 2.20
mṛtyusaṁsāra, 9.3
mucyante, 3.31
mūḍhā, 9.11
mūḍhagrāheṇā, 17.19
mūḍhayoniṣu, 14.15
muhurmuhuḥ, 18.76
muhyati(-yanti), 5.15; 8.27
mukhe, 4.32
mukta, 5.28
muktasaṅga, 3.9; 18.26
muktasya, 4.23
mukto yaḥ, 12.16
mumukṣubhiḥ, 4.15
muniḥ, 2.56
munirbrahma, 5.6
munirmokṣa, 5.28
mūrdhny, 8.12
mūrtayaḥ, 14.4

N

nābhaktāya, 18.67
naiṣkarmya, 3.4; 19.49
naiṣṭhikīm, 5.12
namaskṛtvā, 11.35
namaskuru, 9.34
nānāvarṇākṛtīni, 11.5
narādhama, 7.15; 16.19
narakāya, 1.41,42
nāsābhyantara, 5.27
nāsikāgraṁ, 6.13
nāśitamātmanaḥ, 5.16
nātyaśnatastu, 6.16
navadvāre, 5.13
nāvam, 2.67
nibaddhaḥ, 18.60
nibadhnanti, 4.41
nibadhyate, 4.22
nibandhāyāsurī, 16.5
nibodha, 18.13
nidhanaṁ, 3.35
nidhanāni, 2.28
nidrālasyapramād, 18.39
nigrahaṁ, 6.34
niḥspṛhaḥ, 2.71; 6.18
niḥśreyasakarāv, 5.2
nirahaṁkāraḥ, 2.71; 12.13
nirāhārasya, 2.59
nirāśīr, 3.30, 4.21; 6.10
nirāśrayaḥ, 4.20
nirdeśo, 17.23
nirdhūta, 5.17
nirdoṣaṁ, 5.19
nirdvandvo, 2.45; 5.3
nirguṇaṁ, 13.15
nirmamo, 2.71; 12.13
nirmānamohā, 15.5
nirmuktā, 7.28
nirudhya, 8.12
nirvāṇam, 2.72; 6.15
nirvedaṁ, 2.52
niryogakṣema, 2.45
niścayena, 6.23
niṣṭhā, 3.3
nistraiguṇyaḥ, 2.45
nītirmatirmama, 18.78
nityābhiyuktānāṁ, 9.22
nityajātaṁ, 2.,26
nityaśaḥ, 8.14
nityasaṁnyāsī, 5.3
nityasattvastho, 2.45
nityatṛpto, 4.20
nityavairiṇā, 3.39
nityayukta, 7.17; 8.14; 12.2
nivartate, 2.59; 8.25
nivṛttāni, 14.22
niyamya, 3.7,41; 6.26; 18.51
niyatāhārāḥ, 4.30
niyata, 6.15; 8.2;18.7,9
niyojitaḥ, 3.36
niyokṣyati, 18.59
nyāyyaṁ, 18.15

O

Om, 8.13

P

pacantyātmakāraṇāt, 3.13
padmapatram, 5.10
paṇḍitāḥ, 2.11; 4.19; 5.4,18;
pāpakṛttamaḥ, 4.36
pāpayonayaḥ, 9.32
pāpmānaṁ, 3.41
paradharmā, 3.35; 18.47
paradharmo, 3.35
paraṁ bhūyaḥ, 14.1
paraṁ brahma, 10.12
parāṁ gatim, 6.45
paraṁ janma, 4.4
paramāṁ, 8.13
paramāpnoti, 3.19
paramātmā, 6.7
paramātmety, 15.17
paramavyayam, 7.13
parameśvara, 11.3; 13.28
paramparāprāptam, 4.2
parāṇyāhur, 3.42
parastasmāttu, 8.20
parastāt, 8.9
parataraṁ, 7.7
parāyaṇāḥ, 4.29; 5.17
paricakṣate, 17.17
paridevanā, 2.28
parigrahaḥ, 4.21
parijñātā, 18.18
parikīrtitaḥ, 18.7,27
pariṇāme, 18.38
paripanthinau, 3.34
paripraśnena, 4.34
parisamāpyate, 4.33
paritrāṇāya, 4.8
parjanyāt, 3.14
paryavatiṣṭhate, 2.65
paśya me yogam, 11.8
paśyāmi devāṁ, 11.15
paśyāmi viśveśvara, 11.16
paśyañśṛṇvan, 5.8
paśyantyātmany, 15.11
paśyato, 2.69
patanti, 1.41
patraṁ puṣpaṁ, 9.26
paurvadehikam, 6.43
pavitraṁ, 4.38; 9.2; 10.12
phalahetavaḥ, 2.49
phala, 2.47; 7.23; 17.21
piṇḍa, 1.41
pitāmahaḥ, 9.17
pitaro, 1.41
pitāsi, 11.43
pitṝnyānti, 9.25
prabhāṣeta, 2.54
prabhavaḥ, 7.6
prabhureva, 9.24
prahasann, 2.10
prāhu, 18.2,3
prajāḥ, 3.10
prajahihyenaṁ, 3.41
prajāpatiḥ, 3.10
prajñā, 2.11,57,58,61,67,68
prakāśa, 7.25,14.6,11,22
prakāśayati, 5.16; 13.34
prakṛteḥ, 3.27,29,33; 9.8
prakṛtijair, 3.5; 18.40

prakṛtiṁ, 9.8; 13.1
prakṛtiraṣṭadhā, 7.4
prakṛtisaṁbhavā, 13.20; 14.5
prakṛtisthāni, 15.7
pralayaṁ, 14.14
pralaya, 7.6; 14.2
pralīyante, 8.18,19
pramāda, 11.41; 14.9,17
pramāṇaṁ, 3.21
pramāthīni, 2.60
prāṇakarmāṇi, 4.27
prāṇam, 1.33; 8.12
praṇamya, 11.14
prāṇānprāṇeṣu, 4.30
prāṇāpāna, 5.27; 15.14
pranaṣṭaste, 18.72
praṇaśyāmi, 6.30
praṇaśyati, 2.63; 9.31
praṇavaḥ, 7.8
prāṇāyāma, 4.29
prāṇendriyakriyāḥ, 18.33
prāṇe'pānaṁ, 4.29
praṇipātena, 4.34
prapadyante, 4.11; 7.19,20
prapadyate, 7.19
prapannam, 2.7
prasāda, 2.64,65; 11.43
prasaktāḥ, 16.16
prasaṅgena, 18.34
prasannacetaso, 2.65
prasannātmā, 18.54
praśānta, 6.7,14,27
prasīda deveśa, 11.45
pratiṣṭhita, 2.57,58,61; 3.15; 6.11
pratyavāyaḥ, 2.40
pravakṣyāmi, 4.16
pravakṣye, 8.11
pravartante'śuci, 16.10
pravartitaṁ, 3.16
praveṣṭuṁ, 11.54
pravilīyate, 4.23
pravṛtti, 14.12;15.4; 16.7; 18.30,46
prayāṇakāle, 7.30; 8.2
prītamanāḥ, 11.49
prītiḥ, 1.35
priya, 5.20; 9.29; 10.1; 11.44;17.15; 18.69
priyaḥ priyāyārhasi, 11.44
priyo hi jñānino, 7.17
proktavān, 4.4
pṛthagvidham, 18.14
pūjanaṁ, 17.14
pūjārhāu, 2.4
punarāvartino'rjuna, 8.16
punarbrāhmaṇāḥ, 9.33
punardhanam, 16.13
punarjanma, 4.9; 8.15,16
punaryogaṁ, 5.1
puṇyakarmaṇām, 7.28
puṇyakṛtām, 6.41
puṇyaphalam, 8.28
puṇyo gandhaḥ, 7.9
purāṇamanuśāsitāram, 8.9
purātanaḥ, 4.3
pūrṇa, 2.1
puruṣaḥ, 8.4,22
puruṣottama, 8.1; 15.18,19
pūrvābhyāsena, 6.44
pūrvaiḥ, 4.15
puṣpitāṁ, 2.42

R

rādhanamīhate, 7.22
rāgadveṣau, 2.64, 3.34; 18.51
rahasi, 4.3; 6.10
rajaḥ karmaṇi, 14.9
rājarṣayaḥ, 4.2
rājavidyā, 9.2
rajoguṇa, 3.37
ramanti, 10.9
ramate, 5.22
ratāḥ, 5.25, 12.4
rātri, 8.17,18,25
ripurātmanaḥ, 6.5
ṛksāma, 9.17
romaharṣa, 1.29; 18.74
ṛṣibhirbahudhā, 13.4
ruddhvā, 4.29
rudhirapradigdhān, 2.5
rūpaṁ paraṁ, 11.47
rūpamaiśvaram, 11.9
rūpamatyadbhutaṁ, 18.77

S

śabdabrahm, 6.44
śabdādīnviṣayān, 4.26
śabdaḥ khe, 7.8
sacarācaram, 9.10
sacchabdaḥ, 17.26
sadbhāve, 17.26
sādharmyamāgatāḥ, 14.2
śādhi, 2.7; 7,30
sādhu, 4.8; 6.9
sadityevābhidhīyate, 17.27
sahasra, 7.3; 11.5,46
sahayajñāḥ, 3.10
śakyo'vāptum, 6.36
samabuddhirviśiṣyate, 6.9
samadarśana, 5.18; 6.29
samādha, 2.43,53; 12.9; 17.11
samādhisthasya, 2,54
samaduḥkha, 2.15; 14.24
samagraṁ, 4.23
samāhitaḥ, 6.7
samantataḥ, 6.24
samatītāni, 7.26
saṁbhavaḥ, 3.14; 14.3
saṁbhavāmi, 4.6,8
saṁchinna, 4.41
saṁgraham, 3.20,25
saṁgrāmaṁ, 2.33
samīkṣya, 1.27
saṁjāyate, 2.62
saṁjñake, 8.18
saṁjñārthaṁ, 1.7
saṁkalpa, 6.2,24
saṁkara, 1.41,42; 3.24
sāṁkhya, 2.39; 3.3; 5.4,5; 13.25
saṁmohaṁ, 7.27
sammūḍha, 2.7
saṁniyamyendriya, 12.4
saṁnyāsa, 3.4; 5.1; 9.28, 18.1
saṁnyāsī, 6.1; 18.12
saṁnyasyādhyātma, 3.30
saṁpadvimokṣāya, 16.5
saṁpadyate, 13.31
saṁpaśyan, 3.20
saṁprekṣya, 6.13
samṛddhavegāḥ, 11.29
śaṁsasi, 5.1
saṁśaya, 4.40; 8.5,6
saṁsiddhi, 3.20; 6.43; 8.15
saṁsparśajā, 5.22
saṁstabhyātmānam, 3.43
saṁsthāpana, 4.8
saṁśuddhakilbiṣaḥ, 6.45
saṁtariṣyasi, 4.36
saṁtuṣṭa, 3.17; 4.22; 12.14
samupāśritaḥ, 18.52
saṁvādamimamad, 18.76
saṁyamī, 2.69
saṁyamya, 2.61; 3.6; 4.26; 6.14;8.12
saṁyatendriyaḥ, 4.39
śanaiḥ śanair, 6.25
sanātana, 2.24; 4.31;

7.10; 8.20
sanātanastvaṁ, 11.18
saṅgavivarjitaḥ, 12.18
sañjayatyuta, 14.9
śānti, 2.66; 4.39
śaraṇaṁ, 18.62,66
śarīravāṅmano, 18.15
sarvabhāvena, 15.19
sarvabhūtānāṁ, 5.29; 12.13
sarvabhūtāni, 7.27; 9.7
sarvadharmānpari, 18.66
sarvajñāna, 3.32
sarvakāmebhyo, 6.18
sarvakarma, 12.11; 18.2
sarvaloka, 5.29
sarvāṇīndriya, 4.27
sarvasaṁkalpa, 6.4
sarvatokṣiśiro, 13.14
sarvayoniṣu, 14.4
śaśisūryayoḥ, 7.8
śāśvataṁ, 18.56
śāśvate, 8.26
sasvato, 2.20
sataḥ, 2.16
satataṁ, 9.14
satkāramānapūjā, 17.18
śatruvat, 6.6
sattvamityuta, 14.11
sāttvikaṁ nirmalaṁ, 14.16
sāttvikapriyāḥ, 17.8
saukṣmyād, 13.33
saumyavapur, 11.50
siddhānāṁ, 7.3
siddhasaṁghāḥ, 11.36
siddhāvasiddhau, 4.22
siddhi, 3.4; 4.12; 12.10
siddhyasiddhyoḥ, 2.48; 18.26
śiṣyas, 2.7
śītoṣṇasukha, 2.14; 6.7
smaran, 8.5,6
smarati, 8.14
smṛti, 2.63; 15.15; 18.73
somapāḥ, 9.20
sparśanaṁ, 15.9
sparśānkṛtvā, 5.27
śraddhā, 7.20; 17.3
śraddhāvāṁ, 4.39; 6.47
śraddhāvirahitaṁ, 17.13
śraddhayānvitāḥ, 17.1
śraddhayopeto, 6.37
śreya, 3.11; 4.33; 12.12; 18.47
śrīmatāṁ, 6.41
śrīrvijayo, 18.78
sṛjāmyaham, 4.7
śrotavyasya, 2.52
śrotrādīnīndriyāṇy, 4.26
sṛtī, 8.27
śrutiparāyaṇāḥ, 13.26
śrutivipratipannā, 2.53
srutva, 2.29; 13.26
stena, 3.12
sthāne hṛṣīkeśa, 11.36
sthāvarajaṅgamam, 13.27
sthirabuddhira, 5.20
sthiramāsanam, 6.11
sthitadhīḥ, 2.54, 56
sthitaprajña, 2.54,55
sthitaścalati, 6.21
striyo vaiśyāstathā, 9.32
stutibhiḥ, 11.21
śubhāśubha, 2.57; 9.28
śubhāṁllokān, 18.71
śucīnāṁ, 6.41
sudurlabhaḥ, 7.19
suduṣkaram, 6.34
suhṛnmitrāryudāsīna, 6.9
sukhaduḥkha, 2.14; 13.21; 15.5
sukhamātyantikaṁ, 6.20
sukhasaṅgena, 14.6
sukhī, 5.23
śuklaḥ, 8.24
śuklakṛṣṇe, 8.26
sukṛtaduṣkṛte, 2.50
sukṛtino'rjuna, 7.16
sūkṣmatvāttada, 13.16
sulabhaḥ, 8.14
suniścitam, 5.1
surendralokam, 9.20
susukhaṁ, 9.2
sūtre maṇigaṇā, 7.7
suvirūḍhamūlam, 15.3
svabāndhavān, 1.36
svabhāva, 2.7; 5.14; 18,41,42,47,60
svacakṣuṣā, 11.8
svadharmam, 2.31
svādhyāyā, 17.15
svādhyāyajñāna, 4.28
svajanaṁ, 1.36, 44
svakaṁ rūpaṁ, 11.50
svakarmanirataḥ, 18.45
svāmavaṣṭabhya, 9.8
svanuṣṭhitāt, 3.35
śvapāke, 5.18
svargadvāram, 2.32
svargalokaṁ, 9.21
svargaparā, 2.43
svasyāḥ, 3.33
svatejasā viśvam, 11.19
svayamevātmanā, 10.15

T

tadbhāvabhāvitaḥ, 8.6
tadviddhi, 4.34
tamasaḥ, 8.9
tapasvibhyo, 6.46
tapobhirugraiḥ, 11.48
tapoyajñā, 4.28
tasmādyogī, 6.46
tatraikāgraṁ, 6.12
tattvadarśinaḥ, 4.34
tattvataḥ, 4.9; 6.21; 7.3
tattvavit, 3.28
tejasvinām, 7.10
tejobhirāpūrya, 11.30
tejomayaṁ, 11.47
tejorāśiṁ sarvato, 11.17
titikṣasva, 2.14
traiguṇya, 2.45
trailokya, 1.35
tribhiḥ, 7.13
trīnguṇānativartate, 14.21
trividhaṁ,16.21
tulyanindāstutir, 12.19
tulyapriyāpriyo, 14.24
tyāgaphalaṁ, 18.8
tyāgītyabhidhīyate, 18.11
tyajatyante, 8.6
tyaktasarva, 4.21
tyaktvātmaśuddhaye, 5.11

U

udaka, 1.41
udbhava, 8.3
uddharedātmanā, 6.5
upadhāraya, 7.6
upahata, 2.7
upāyataḥ, 6.36
ūrdhvaṁ, 14.18; 15.1
utkrāmantaṁ, 15.10
utsīdeyurime lokā, 3.24
uttamam, 4.3
uttaram, 6.11
uttarāyaṇam, 8.24

V

vādinaḥ, 2.42
vahnir, 3.38

vairāgya, 6.35; 13.9
vakṣyāmyaśeṣataḥ, 7.2
varṇasaṁkaraḥ, 1.40,42
vartamāno, 6.31
vartmānuvartante, 3.23; 4.11
vāsudevastathoktvā, 11.50
vaśyātmanā, 6.36
vedāntakṛdvedavid, 15.15
vedavādaratāḥ, 2.42
vibhāga, 4.13
vibhuḥ, 5.15
vibhūti, 10.7,16
vicālayet, 3.29
viddhy, 3.37; 4.13
vidheyātmā, 2.64
viduryānti, 13.35
vidvān, 3.26
vidyādduḥkha, 6.23
vidyāvinaya, 5.18
vigatajvaraḥ, 3.30
vigatakalmaṣaḥ, 6.28
vigataspṛhaḥ, 2.56; 18.49
viguṇaḥ, 3.35
vijānataḥ, 2.46
vijānīto, 2.19
vijitātmā jitendriyaḥ, 5.6
vijitendriyaḥ, 6.8
vijñāna, 9.1; 18.42
vijñātumicchāmi, 11.31
vimohayati, 3.40
vimokṣaṇāt, 5.23
vimokṣyase, 4.32
vimūḍho, 6.38
vimuñcati, 18.35
vināśam, 2.17
vināśastasya, 6.40
vinaśyati, 4.40; 13.28
vindatyātmani, 5.21
viniyamya, 6.24
viniyataṁ, 6.18
vipaścitaḥ, 2.60
vipratipannā, 2.53
visargaḥ, 8.3
viṣayān, 2.62,64
viṣayapravālāḥ, 15.2
viṣayendriya, 18.37
viṣīdantam, 2.1,10
viśiṣṭā, 1.7
viśiṣyate, 3.7; 6.9
visṛjāmyaham, 9.7
vistareṇātmano, 10.18
viśuddhātmā, 5.6,7
viśuddhayā, 18.51
viśuddhaye, 6.12
viśvamanantarūpa, 11.38
viśvatomukham, 9.15; 10.33; 11.11
vītarāgabhaya, 2.56; 4.10
vitatā brahmaṇo, 4.32
vivasvataḥ, 4.4
viviktadeśa, 13.11
vivṛddha, 14.11,13
viyogaṁ, 6.23
viyuktānāṁ, 5.26
vratāḥ, 4.28
vṛjinaṁ, 4.36
vyāharan, 8.13
'vyakto'vyaktāt, 8.20
vyāmiśreṇeva, 3.2
vyapāśrayaḥ, 3.18
vyatitariṣyati, 2.52
vyavasāyātmikā, 2.41,43,44

Y

yadā yadā hi, 4.7
yadrājyasukha, 1.44
yadṛccha, 2.32; 4.22
yajanta iha devatāḥ, 4.12
yajjñātvā, 13.13;14.1,12,16,35
yajjuhoṣi, 9.26
yajñabhāvitāḥ, 3.12
yajñakṣapita, 4.30
yajñānayajñāśca, 4.28
yajñārthāt, 3.9
yajñaśiṣṭāmṛtabhujo, 4.31
yajñaśiṣṭāśinaḥ, 3.13
yajñatapasāṁ, 5.29
yajñavido, 4.30
yajñenaivopajuhvati, 4.25
yaṁ yaṁ vāpi, 8.6
yānti devavratā, 9.25
yantrārūḍhāni, 18.61
yatacetasām, 5.26
yatacitta, 4.21; 6.19
yatamānas, 6.45
yatātmānaḥ, 5.25
yatendriyamano, 5.28
yathaidhāṁsi, 4.37
yatīnāṁ, 5.26
yoga, 2.48; 4.1,2; 6.2
yogabalena, 8.10
yogabhraṣṭo, 6.41
yogāccalitamānasaḥ, 6.37
yogadhāraṇām, 8.12
yogāgnau, 4.27,28
yogaḥ proktaḥ, 4.3
yogakṣemaṁ, 9.22
yogaṁ yogeśvarāt, 18.75
yogamaiśvaram, 9.5; 11.8
yogamātmanaḥ, 6.19
yogamavāpsyasi, 2.53
yogamāyāsamāvṛtaḥ, 7.25
yogārūḍha, 6.3,4
yogasaṁjñitam, 6.23
yogasaṁnyasta, 4.41
yogasaṁsiddhaḥ, 4.38
yogasaṁsiddhiṁ, 6.37
yogasthaḥ, 2.48
yogasya, 6.44
yogavittamāḥ, 12.1
yogayukta, 5.6; 6.29; 8.27
yogenāvyabhicāriṇyā, 18.33
yogeśvara, 11.4; 18.75,78
yogī, 3.3; 4.25; 5.11; 6.15,19,32,42,47; 8,14,23
yogī vigatakalmaṣaḥ, 6.28
yogī yuñjīta satatam, 6.10
yonijanmasu, 13.22
yonirmahadbrahma, 14.3
yudhyasva, 2.18; 3.30
yuga, 8.17
yugasahasrāntāṁ, 8.17
yujyasva, 2.50
yukta āsīta matparaḥ, 6.14
yuktacetasaḥ, 7.30
yuktaḥ, 3.26
yuktāhāravihārasya, 6.17
yuktatamo, 6.47
yuñjan, 6.15; 7.1

Index to Translation

A

A--letter, 10.33
abandonment of consequences, 18.4
Abode of Universe, 11.25
absorber God, 13.17
absorption, 14.26
abusive language, 16.4
accomplishment, factors, 18.3
Action/activity,
abandonment?, 18.5, 11
appropriate, 4.17
clarity type, 18.23
conclusion, 4.33
consequence, 5.14
controlled, 18.23
craving, 18.24
deferred to Krishna, 12.6
desireless, 18.23
disciplined, 4.32
distressful, 14.16
essential, 3.8
factors, 18.13-15,18
faulty, 18.3
forceful, 18.60
God created?, 5.14
ignorant, 14.16
implication transcended, 5.7
impulsion, 14.9
impulsive, 18.24
inappropriate, 4.17
incomprehensible, 4.17
Krishna, 4.14
material nature, 3.33; 13.28, 15.2; 18.41
misconception, 18.25
modes, 14.16
mundane energy, 3.27, 28
Action/activity,
nature-produced, 5.14
necessary, 6.1
non-action, 4.18,20
non-defective, 14.16
non-defiling, 5.10
obligatory, 6.1
offering to Krishna, 9.27
parts of, 18.18
performance required, 16.24
questioned, 4.16
reduced, 4.37
regulation, 3.3
results, 2.51
Sat type, 17.27
seer's, 2.54
spiritual, 4.24
transcending, 9.28
types, 18.9,19,23-25
unmotivated, 18.23
yoga mood, 2.48
acts of sacrifice, charity, austerities, 17.24
Ādityas, 10.21
affections,
crippling, 2.57
yogic type, 14.26
agency, 13.21
agent,
factor, 18.14,18
Krishna's 11.33
types, 18.19,26-28
Agni, 11.3
agreeable / disagreeable, 12.17
agriculture, 18.44
air regulation, 4.30
Airāvata, 10.27
airs, 4.29
all-pervasive Form, 11.20
Almighty God,
consequence free, 5.15
Krishna, 6.38; 9.11; 10.3
alone, yogi, 6.10
alphabet, 10.33
alternatives, Arjuna's, 2.6
ambidextrous, 11.33
Ananta, 10.29
anantavijayam, 1.16
ancestors, 9.25
ancient person, 8.9
ancient spirit, 11.38
angel, 11.22
angelic kingdom,
king, 9.20
paradise, 9.21
sovereignty, 2.8
warriors attain, 2.35
anger,
absence of, 16.2
cause, 2.62,63; 5.28
cherished, 16.12
eliminated, 4.10
endured, 5.23
hell, 16.21
tendency, 16.4,18
animals, 10.30
antelope skin, 6.11
anxieties, 2.56,57; 12.16
aquatics, 10.29
Arjuna,
-Also see ***Indexed Names of Arjuna***
agent, 11.33
amazed, 11.14
ambidextrous, 11.33
appreciations, 11.1
bowing, 11.14
bowman, 1.4; 18.78
conch blown, 1.14
confusion, 18.73
death preferred, 1.45
depression, 2.8
devotion, 9.33

Arjuna continued,
disoriented, 11.25
fear-free, 11.49,50
frightened, 11.35
God vision, 11.45
hopelessness, 2.1
instructed, 2.37
intimidation, 2.35
Krishna, 10.37
liberated, 11.1
lost?, 18.58
loved, 18.64,65
majestic form, 11.3
material nature, 18.59
monkey insignia, 1.20
normalized, 11.51
obeisance, 11.39,40
ordered, 11.33,34
overwhelmed, 1.27,46
past birth, 4.5
refuses to fight, 2.9
repulsed, 1.35
request, 1.21,22; 4.42
sense of duty, 2.7
shifty vision, 6.33,34
sickly emotion, 2.2
sinless one, 14.6
sits down, 1.46
stunned, 1.28
submits, 2.7; 18.73
trembles, 1.29, 11.45,48
Universal Form seen, 11.15
work, 4.15
armored warriors, 11.32,34
arms, 11.19, 23
army, destroyed, 11.32,34
arrogance, 16.4,17,18
Aryamā, 10.29
āsana, 6.11-13
ascetic,
Krishna related, 7.9
sacrifice, 4.30
temptations, 2.59
yogi superior, 6.46
Asita, 10.13
assertion, false type, 18.52
assertive attitude, 18.17
assurance, 12.8
astral region, 9.20
aśvattha tree, 10.26; 15.1-3
Aśvatthāmā, 1.8
atmosphere, 7.8
attachment,
as Cause, 13.22
cause, 2.62; 11.55
conquered, 15.5
discarded, 5.10,11
finished, 4.23
freedom from, 3.9; 12.18
idleness, 2.47
attack, superiors, 2.4
attainment, 6.22, 8.21
attention,
drift / restraint, 6.26
Krishna absorbed, 7.1
attractive objects,
addictive, 15.9
detachment, 6.4
living space, 13.6
senses interlocked, 5.9
audiences, 18.67
austerities, enjoyer, 5.29
austerity,
abandoned?, 18.3
asat, 17.28
categories, 17.7-10
faith in, 17.17
godly nature, 16.1
impulsive type, 17.18
ineffective, 11.48,53
invented ones, 17.1
Krishna derived, 7.9; 10.5
mistaken type, 17.19
motivation, 4.23
purificatory, 4.10,30; 18.5
rain, 3.14
realistic type, 17.17
religion, 3.14; 4.23
sacrifice, 4.25
tendency, 18.42
terrible type, 17.5
tricky type, 17.18
types, 17.14-17
Universal Form, 11.48
authority, besides Krishna, 9.30; 10.38
avenues of depression, 16.22
axe, 15.3

B

battle formation, 1.33; 2.31
beasts, 10.30
begetting, 10.28
begging, 2.5
beginning of creation, 7.27
beginningless, Krishna, 10.3
behavior, codes of, 12.20
beings,
disintegration, 13.28
independent, 9.4
influenced, 7.27
Krishna produces, 9.7
Krishna's energy sustains, 9.4
origin / ruination, 11.2
production, 9.8
psychological supremacy, 9.5
relation, 4.35
Supreme Lord inhabits, 13.28
types, 16.6
belief in God, 18.42
belief in Krishna, 3.31
belief in others, 7.21
beliefs of wicked people, 16.8,13-15
bellies, 11.16,23
benefit,
abandoned, 12.11
detachment from 4.20,22; 17.17
disinterest in, 17.25
luck, 4.22
types, 17.11-23; 18.12
best of gods, 11.31
bewitching energy, 7.14
Bhagavad Gītā,
hearing of, 18.67,71
preachers, 18.67
study, 18.70
Bhīma, 1.4,10,15
Bhishma, 1.8,10-12,25;. 2.4; 11.26,34
Bhṛgu, 10.25
Bhṛhat Sama Melody, 10.35
birds, 10.30

birth,
certain, 2.27
rebirth, 4.4,5
liberation from, 5.19; 7.19; 14.20
birthless, Krishna, 10.3,12
blockheads, 16.20
body,
acquirement / departure from, 2.13; 15.8
assumption of, 2.22
detachment, 14.23
head-neck balance, 6.13
living space, 13.2
maintenance, 3.8
purification usage, 5.11
restriction, 3.7
terminal, 2.18
bondage tendencies, 16.5
boys, 10.6
Brahma Sūtras, 13.5
Brahmā,
day / night, 8.17-19; 9.7
Krishna as father, 11.39
Krishna greater, 11.37
Krishna identity, 10.33; 11.39
procreator, 3.10
Universal Form, 11.15
world of, 8.16
brahmin,
compared, 5.18
ordained, 17.23
perceptive, 2.46
praised, 9.33
respected, 17.14
branches of imperishable tree, 15.2
breathing, nature function, 5.8
Bṛhaspati, 10.24
brilliant consciousness, 5.24
brothers, 1.26
brow chakra, 8.10
brute force, 16.18, 17.5
buddy, 11.41,44
business men, 9.32

C

cakes, 1.41
cannibals, 17.4
cardinal points, 11.25
career categories, 4.13
caste, 4.13; 18.41
categories of elements, 13.6
cause,
non-deteriorating, 9.18
destruction, 11.32
elaborated, 13.21
series of, 16.8
Cekitāna, 1.5
celebrity, 3.21
celestial body, 9.19
celestial delights, 9.20
celestial musicians, 11.22
celestial regions, 6.40,41
celestial sea, 10.27
celibacy,
austerity17.14
destination, 8.11
yogi's, 6.14
celibate boys, 10.6
ceremonial articles, 4.24
ceremonial rites, 2.43
-see religious ceremony
cessation, 5.25,26
changes of living space, 13.20
chaos, 3.24
chariot, Arjuna's, 1.21
charitable disposition, 18.43
charity,
abandoned?, 18.3
categories, 16.1; 17.7-10
ineffective, 11.48,53
Krishna derived, 10.5
purificatory, 18.5
Universal Form, 11.48
yogi bypasses, 8.28
cherish the imperishable, 12.3
choice, Arjuna's, 2.6
chum, 11.44
circular process, 3.16
Citraratha, 10.26
clan, 1.37-42
clarity,
captivating, 14.6
disease-free, 14.6
expertise, 14.6
happiness produced by, 14.6,9
illuminating, 14.6
influence, 14.5
lack of, 14.13
clarity continued,
predominating, 14.10,11
class, 1.40,41,42
clay, 6.8; 14.24
cleanliness, 16.7; 18.42
cleansers, 10.31
clear-minded people, 17.8
cloud comparison, 6.38
club, 11.17, 46
cold, 2.14; 6.7
colors, 11.5
command, 2.47
commerce, 18.44
common factor, 5.18
comparative view, 6.33
comparison,
lamp, 6.19
mind / wind, 6.34
yoga methods, 12.1,2,3
compassion, 1.27; 12.13; 16.2
compensation, 17.21
competence, 12.16
compulsion to act, 3.36, 37
conceit, 16.3
concentrated mental focus, 7.30
concentration, lacking, 2.66
concepts, discipline, 9.15
conclusion, 4.33;10.32; 13.1,2
condemnation, resisted, 12.19; 14.24
conditions, 2.15
conduct, 14.21
confidence, 12.10; 17.3,13
confidential teaching, 4.3
confusion,
devoid of, 15.5
impulsion, 14.17
production, 14.13
congratulations, 14.24

consciousness,
detachment, 14.22
Krishna 10.22
living space, 13.7
purifier, 9.2
consequence,
abandonment, 16.2
aftermath, 2.47
Almighty God, 5.15
freedom from 3.31; 9.28
rejection, 18.1,2,4
types, 18.12
contact, happiness, 18.37
contentment, 2.71; 10.5; 12.14
continuation, 10.32
controller, I, 16.14
conviction, 13.7
coping, 2.14
core self, 6.18; 8.12
cosmic destroyers, 10.23
couch, 11.42
cow, 5.18; 10.28; 18.44
cowardice, 2.3; 18.43
craving,
abandoned, 2.55
cause, 2.62; 3.37
cherished, 16.12,16
degrading, 16.18,21
eliminated, 4.10; 8.11; 12.17
endured, 5.23
freedom from, 3.30; 6.18; 16.2
impulsion, 14.11
possession of, 17.5
resisted, 2.70
transcended, 2.70,71
created being, 10.39; 16.6
creation, 10.32; 14.2
creative power, 8.3
creator, 9.17
creature,
disintegrated, 8.20
evolution, 10.6
Krishna knows, 7.26
Krishna related, 7.9
nourishment, 3.14
origination, 7.6
spirit habitat, 6.29
crippling emotions, 2.48, 57
criticism, 16.2
crowds, 13.11
crown, 11.46
culprit, 4.36
cultural activity,
cause of, 3.15
creative power, 8.3
exemption, 3.17; 18.49
inferior, 2.49
Krishna, 4.13,14; 9.9
mandatory, 4.15
mental / physical, 3.1
perfection related, 3.20
production, 3.14
purification usage, 5.11
questioned, 4.16
religious type, 3.9
rewards abandoned, 5.12
social affairs, 3.4
transcended, 4.41
value, 7.29
yoga method, 6.3
cultured man, 2.2
cumulative intellectual interest, 6.43
cutting instrument, 4.42
cycles of rebirth, 16.19
cynical, 9.1

D

dairy farming, 18.44
damage, 18.25
danger of birth/death, 13.9
danger, avoidance, 2.56
Danu, 10.14
dark moon, 8.25
darshan, 11.53
day / night, 8.17-19,24
death,
attainments, 2.72
certainty, 2.27
devotee, 12.7
devotion applied, 8.10
duty, 3.35
eyebrow focus, 8.10
Krishna, 4.9; 8.5; 9.19; 10.34; 15.8
liberation, 7.29; 8.25; 14.20
modes influence, 14.14,15
death continued,
psychology taken 15.8
rebirth, 9.3
repetitive, 8.16
supervisor, 11.39
texture of existence recalled, 8.6
deceit, 13.8; 16.4; 17.5
deceiver, 3.6
December, 10.35
decision, 9.30
deeds of Krishna, 4.9
defeat, victory, 2.38
defect universal, 18.48
deity worship, 7.21
deity, outsmarting, 17.12
deliverer, 12.7
delusion,
banished, 4.35
cause / production, 2.63
experience, 18.22
overpowering, 16.16
saturated mind, 2.52
demigods, 7.23; 11.52; 16.20
-also see supernatural rulers
demons, 11.36; 16.20
- also see wicked people
departed spirits, 1.41; 7.26; 9.25
departure of yogis, 8.23
depressed people, 17.10
depression,
detachment from, 14.22
predominating, 14.10,12
release from, 16.22
desire,
abandoning, 6.24
contrary ones, 7.20
desire for pay-off, 4.14
eliminated, 5.28
freedom from, 6.18
impulsive type, 2.5
living space, 13.7
motivated action, 5.12
productions, 14.8
resistance, 5.20
restrained, 4.19
satisfaction, 2.70

desireless, 6.10
despair, 18.35
destination, highest, 18.50
destiny, factor, 18.14
destroyers, 11.6
destruction, 7.6
detachment,
axe, 15.3
conditions resisted, 6.7
recommended, 3.7,9; 12.19
detection device, 15.7
determination,
tendency, 18.43
types, 18.29, 33-35
yoga practice, 6.23
Devadatta, 1.15
Devala, 10.13
devas,
-see supernatural rulers
deviation, 6.37
devilish people, 9.12
devotee,
categorized, 7.16-18; 12.17
dear, 12.20
delivered, 12.7
guarantees, 18.68-70
Krishna attraction 9.28
Krishna enlightens, 10.11
Krishna protects, 9.22
Krishna's favorite, 9.29
Krishna's proximity, 13.19
offerings, 9.26
ruination, 9.31
yogi, 12.14
devotion,
dear to Krishna, 12.18
extolled, 12.17
great soul's, 9.14
Krishna, 4.3; 11.55; 18.65
offerings related, 9.26
opportunity, 9.33
required, 12.20; 13.11
supreme type, 18.54,55
unique, 11.54
yogic type, 14.26
devotional practice, 12.8-11
devotional relationship, requirement, 8.22
devotional service, 9.27
devotional worship, 9.29
dharmakṣetre, 1.1
Dhātā, 10.33
Dhṛṣṭadyumna, 1.17
Dhṛṣṭaketu, 1.5
Dhṛtaraṣṭra, 1.1,18,35,45; 2.9; 11.26
Dhṛti, 10.34
diet restraint, 4.30
differences, 18.21
digestive heat, 15.14
dimensions beyond, 4.40
dining, 11.42
direction, 11.25
directive self, 6.7
disc, 11.46
discernment,
adjusted, 3.39
constant type, 2.68
maintained, 3.41
senses affected, 2.67
uncontrolled person, 2.66
disciplic succession, 4.34
discipline,
accomplishment, 4.32
body, 17.14
concepts, 9.15
continuous, 6.15
mind, 17.16
offering to Krishna, 9.27
speech, 17.15
types, 17.11-13
disciplined behavior, 3.26
disciplined person, 6.36; 9.26
discredit Krishna, 3.32
discrimination, 2.52; 18.42
discus, 11.17
discussion, 10.10
disease, 13.9
disgrace, 2.2
disgusted / tradition, 2.52
disintegration, 13.28
dislikes / likes, 3.34; 4.22
dispassion, 12.18,19; 18.52
dissolution, 14.2
distinction, 6.9
distress,
cessation, 2.57,65
happiness, 2.38
remover, 6.17
transcended, 12.15; 14.20
distressed person, 7.16
Diti, 10.30
divine form, 11.52, 54
Divine Supreme Person, 8.8,10
divinity, 2.72
doctors, 11.22
dog, 5.18
doubt, 4.40; 6.39
Draupadī, 1.6,18
Droṇa, 1.7,25;2.4; 11.26,34
Drupada, 1.3,4,18
dry food, 17.9
duality, 2.14; 6.7,32
duration of life, 17.8
Duryodhana, 1.2,12
duty,
abandoned?, 18.48
alternatives, 2.31
another's, 3.35
discipline, 6.17
necessary, 3.35; 6.1
neglect, 2.33
perfection, 18.45-48
preferred, 3.19
sin-resistant, 2.38
dying person, 8.5

E

earth, resonated, 1.19; 7.9; 8.15; 15.13
easy to practice, 9 .2
eatables, 17.7-10
eating, yoga method, 5.8; 6.16,17; 9.27
educated people, 3.39
education,
purificatory, 4.10
ineffective, 11.48,53
Krishna, 9.17; 13.18
elements, categories, 13.6
elephant, 5.18; 10.27
embodied soul,
-see also Spirit
nine-gate city, 5.13
embryo, 3.38
emotional detachment, 13.10
emotional distress, 2.65

emotional stability, 2.66
emotional weakness, 2.3
emotions, 1.19; 2.38,48
endeavor,
intention free, 4.19
Krishna, 10.36
righteous type, 2.40
ending, 10.32
enemy killed, 16.14
enemy, passion, 3.37
energizing airs, 4.29
energizing breath, 8.10,12
energy, 7.4-6; 14.13
enjoyable aspects, 1.32
enjoyer, I, 16.14
enjoyment, 2.43,57,58
enlightened parents, 6.42
enlightenment, 14.22
enthusiasm, 14.22
environment of psyche, 13.4
envy-free person, 4.22
equally-disposed, 12.13; 14.25
equanimity, 12.18,19; 14.24,25
era to era, 4.8
essential nature, 17.3
eternal divine person, 10.12
eternal abode, 18.56
eternal life, 9.19; 13.13
eternal peace, 9.31
evacuation, 5.9
even-minded, 12.4; 13.10
everlasting principle, 2.17
evil action forced, 3.36,37
evil-doers, 7.15
evolution, 14.18
example, 3.21
excitement, 2.56,57; 5.20; 12.15; 14.23
exclusive worship, 9.30
exemption, 18.49
exertion, 14.11
exhalation, inhalation, 4.29; 5.27
existence,
ceaseless, 2.12
enduring/ non-enduring, 2.16; 4.24
Krishna originates, 10.5,41
Krishna upholds, 7.7
existential arrangement, 6.29
existential conditions, 10.5
existential residence, 9.18
expectations, 16.12
experience,
depression obscures, 14.9
explained, 13.13
ignorance, 5.16
illuminating, 4.27
impetus, 18.18
incomparable, 4.38
Krishna gave, 7.2
overshadowed, 7.20
spirit's, 13.22
Supreme Spirit, 13.15
types, 7.2; 18.19-22
experiencer, 13.1,2,23,27
expertise, 18.43
eye movement, 5.9
eyebrows, 5.27
eyes, 11.2,10,16,19

F

faces, 11.16
facilities of species, 6.32
factors, five, 18.13-15
failure/ success, 2.48; 4.22
faith,
experience yielding, 4.39
Krishna awards, 7.21
nature based, 17.3
required, 9.3
undisciplined persons, 6.37
faithfulness, 10.34
faithless person, 4.40; 9.3
fallen yogi, 6.37,41
fame, 10.5,34
familiarity, 11.41
family duties, 1.42
family, fallen yogi, 6.41-43
fantasy, 16.13
father, Krishna, 9.17; 11.43; 14.4
fathers, 1.26,33
faults, 3.13; 4.21; 5.17,25; 6.28; 10.3
fear, 2.56; 4.10; 5.28; 10.5; 12.15; 17.20; 18.35
fearlessness, 10.5; 16.1
features, 14.21
fee, 17.13
feelings, 10.34; 13.7
feet, 11.23
feverish mood, Arjuna's, 3.30
fickleness, absence of, 16.2
fig tree, 10.26
financial assets, 1.33
fire ceremony, necessary, 6.1
fire controller, 11.39
fire,
comparison, 18.48
Krishna, 9.16
lust compared, 3.39
universal destruction, 11.25
spirit resists, 2.23
splendor, 15.12
supreme residence 15.6
five factors, 18.13-15
flame, 7.4
flower, Krishna accepts, 9.26
focus on Krishna, 12.2
food, categories, 17.7-10,13
foolish people, 9.11
forbearance, 16.3
forced action, 3.36,37
forgiveness, 11.42
Form of everything, 11.16
Form of Mine, 11.47
formation, 10.32
forms,
Krishna inhabits, 6.30
unlimited, 11.5
womb produced, 14.4
fortune, 10.34
foundation,
material nature, 9.8
future, 10.34
singular, 13.31
yogi compared, 6.38
four celibate boys, 10.6
four kinds/people, 7.16
four-handed Form, 11.52
fresh air, 4.30
friend, 1.26; 3.21; 9.18; 11.41,44; 12.13
friendship, with Krishna, 4.3
fright, 11.35
fruit, 9.26

fulfillments, 7.22
functional work, 4.15
future productions, 10.34

G

gain, 3.18
gambling, 10.36
Gāṇḍīva, 1.29
garlands, 11.11
garments, 2.22; 11.11
Garuḍa, 10.30
gas, 7.4
Gāyatrī, 10.35
geniuses, 7.10
gentleness, 16.2, 17.16
ghastly form, 11.49
ghee, Krishna, 9.16
ghosts, 9.25; 17.4
gift, 17.20-22
glorification, resisted, 12.19
glory, 11.41
goal of invisible reality, 12.5
God form, 11.45
God of gods, 11.13
god of romance, 10.28
God Vishnu, 11.24, 30
God,
    action free, 5.14
    described, 10.12; 11.11; 18.46
    Krishna, 10.15
    location in body, 8.2
    near / far, 13.16
    pervader, 9.4
goddess of counsel, 10.34
goddess of faithfulness, 10.34
goddess of fame, 10.34
goddess of fortune, 10.34
goddess of patience, 10.34
goddess of recollection, 10.34
goddess of speech, 10.34
godly nature, 16.1-3
gods, 7.22
    --see also supernatural rulers
gold, 6.8, 14.24
good feelings, 1.31
good people, 7.18
governing tendency, 18.43
Govinda, 2.9
grace, 11.47
grandfather Krishna, 9.17
grandfathers, 1.26,33
grandsons, 1.26
grasping, 2.45; 4.21
great person, 3.21
Great Personality, 11.12
great soul,
    rare, 7.19
    rebirth exemption, 8.15
    reliance, 9.13
greed, mental obsession, 1.37; 14.11,17; 16.21
grossness, free of, 8.9
grudge, 17.21

H

habits,4.12
hairs on end, 18.74
Hanuman, 1.20
happiness,
    achievement, 2.66
    detachment, 5.23
    distress, 2.38
    endless type, 6.28
    non-fluctuating, 5.21
    production of, 14.6,9
    spiritual type, 5.24
    superior type, 6.27
    types, 18.36-39
    ultimate, 5.2
Hari, 11.9; 18.77
harmony, 6.31
hatred, 16.3
hazy season, 8.25
head posture, 6.13
health, 17.8
hearing
    about soul, 2.29
    austerity, 4.26
    perception, 13.26
    nature function, 5.8
    valid method, 13.26
heat, 2.14; 9.19
heaven,
    attainment, 9.20,21
    material nature, 18.40
    open, 2.31
    sickly emotion, 2.2
hell, avenues, 1.43; 16.16,21
hereafter, 4.31; 14.14,15,18
heroes, 1.9
heroism, 18.43
highest living state, 6.15
highest reality, 5.17
highest well-being, 3.11
Himālaya, 10.25
holding, 5.9
home, 13.10
honor / dishonor, 6.7
honored man, 2.34
hope, 2.41; 4.21
hordes of ghost, 17.4
horses, 10.27
hostility, 11.55; 16.20,21
Hṛṣikeśa, 1.15,21,24; 11.36
human being,
    Brahman realization, 12.5
    creation of, 3.10
    Krishna affects, 4.11
    material nature, 15.2
    perfection, 7.3
    regard for Krishna, 10.3
    world of, 11.48
    worship gods, 4.12
human body of Krishna, 9.11
Brahmā instructed, 3.10,11,12
hygiene, 12.16
hymns, 10.35
hypocrisy, 16.10

I

idea of Krishna, 3.31
ideas, overpowering, 16.16
identity-confusion, 3.27
idiot, 15,1018.16
idleness, 2.47
ignorance,
    defined, 13.12
    doubt, 4.42
    impulsion, 14.17
    knowledge shrouded, 5.15
    Krishna banishes, 10.11
ignorant person, 4.40
Ikṣvāku, 4.1
illusion, 7.14
immortality, 14.20
impartiality, 5.19; 10.5; 12.16; 14.24,25; 18.54
impatience, 12.15

imperishable destination, 8.11
imperishable invisible existence, 12.1,3
impersonal existence, 12.1,3
impetus, 18.18
implication, avoidance, 4.22; 5.3; 9.28
impulsion,
activity produced by, 14.6
attachment, 14.6
desire, 14.6
endured, 5.23
influence, 14.5,10,13
mentality adjusted, 2.60
passion, 14.6
impulsiveness, 2.71
impure objectives, 16.10
impurities, 4.30; 9.1
inattentiveness, 14.8,13,17
inconceivable reality, 12.3
independence, 4.20
indestructible factor, 2.17
indetermination, 3.26
indifference, 5.3;6.9,35; 12.16; 13.9
individual existence, 2.12
individualized
conditioned beings, 15.7
infamy, 10.5
inferior energy, 7.4,5
influence, 10.12; 17.2
information,
God, 13.18
highest, 11.1; 14.1
informed person, 7.16
Krishna's, 7.2; 10.42
liberating, 14.1
secret, 15.20; 18.63,64
Supreme Spirit, 13.12
ultimate, 9.2; 10.1
inhalation, 4.29; 5.27
inherent nature, 18.47
initiate action, 5.8
initiative, 7.4; 13.6,9
innate tendency, 17.2
inner peace, 2.66
inquisitive person, 7.16
insensibility, cause, 14.8
insight,
Arjuna bestowed, 11.8
blocked, 3.38,40
Krishna gives, 10.11
protects, 2.40
reaction-resistant, 2.39
reality-piercing, 2.50
steady type, 2.55
view different, 2.41
instruments, 18.14,18
intellect,
controlled, 5.28
defective type, 18.16
detached type, 18.49
grasped, 6.25
living space, 13.6
self-focused type, 2.44
spiritual happiness, 6.21
types, 18.29-32
intellectual discipline, 2.49
intelligence,
compared, 3.42
grasped, 6.25
Krishna anchored, 8.7
Krishna derived, 10.5
Krishna related, 7.10
mundane, 7.4
passion fostered, 3.40
purification, 5.11
stable, 2.65
intelligent statements, 2.11
intentions,
Krishna's, 11.31
restrained, 4.19
wicked ones, 17.6
interaction, 2.68
interim, 2.28
intoxication, 16.10
introspection, 8.11
intuitive perception, 10.35
invisible existence, 8.18,21;.12.1,3,5;
isolation, 6.10; 13.11; 18.52
item of research, 18.18

J

Jāhnavī, 10.31
Jahnu's daughter, 10.31
Janaka, 3.20
Janārdana, 11.51
japa, 10.25
Jayadrath, 11.34
jinxed, 3.32
joke, 11.42
joy, 5.25
judgment, 6.9

K

Kāmadhuk, 10.28
Kandarpa, 10.28
Kapila, 10.26
karma yoga, 3.7; 4.2
Karṇa, 1.8; 11.26,34
Kaśi, 1.5,17
Keshava, 2.54; 10.14; 13.1; 18.76;
Keśi, 18.1
killed/ killer, 2.19
killing, Arjuna repulsed, 1.34; 18.17
kinfolk, Arjuna, 1.31
king, 4.2; 10.27
king's son, 2.31
Kīrti, 10.34
knower of reality, 5.8
knowledge
clarity produces, 14.17
control, 4.33
defined, 13.8-12
derived, 12.12
experience, 9.1
fiery force, 4.19
Krishna produced, 10.5; 15.15
Krishna represented, 10.38
lack of, 16.4
of Krishna, 4.14
Krishna, Lord,
-also see ***Indexed Names of Krishna***
A – letter, 10.33
actions of, 4.11
Ādityas, 10.21
Agni, 11.39
Airāvata, 10.27,29
Almighty God, 10.3
ancient person, 11.18
appeasers of, 9.25
approach to, 8.15,16
aquatics, 10.29
Arjuna and, 18.78
Arjuna identity, 10 37
Arjuna loved by, 18.64,65
Arjuna's welfare, 10.1

Krishna continued,
armies shown, 1.25
Aryamā, 10.29
ascetics, 7.9
aspiration-free, 3.22
association, 18.55
Aśvattha, 10.26
atmosphere, 7.8
austerity, 7.9
authority, 10.38
basis supreme, 11.37; 14.27
beasts identity, 10.30
beautiful-haired, 1.30
begetting, 10.28
beginningless, 11.19
beings caused by, 9.5
best of gods, 11.31
beyond range, 7.24
birds identity, 10.30
birth transcended, 7.25
birthless, 4.6; 10.12
births, 4.5
body situated, 13.32
Brahmā compared, 10.33; 11.37,39
Bṛhaspati, 10.21
Bṛhgu identity, 10.25
cause of integration, 9.18
cause ultimate, 7.6
celestial sea, 10.27
chanting, 10.25
chariot driver, 1.24
chief of cowherds, 1.32; 2.9
Chitraratha, 10.26
clansman of Vrishnis, 1.40
cleansers, 10.31
commanders, 10.21
conch blown, 1.14
conclusion, 10.32
condition of existence, 8.5
consciousness, identity, 10.22
constant factor, 9.13
continuation, 10.32
contrasting, 11.26
cows identity, 10.28
creations, 10.32
creator, 9.17

Krishna continued,
creatures, 7.9
death producer, 9.19
December, 10.35
dependence on, 7.1,29; 11.55
descendant of Madhu, 1.14 ,36
detachment, 9.9
devoted to, 6.14
devotee approaches, 9.28
devotee delivered by, 12.7
devotee guarantee, 9.31
devotee yogi, 12.16
devotion to, 9.11; 13.11; 18.55
devotional worship 9.29
Dhātā, 10.33
digestion, 15.14
disciplines, 10.25
disliked, 16.18
Diti identity, 10.30
divine form, 11.50
divine glory, 10.7
duty-free / duty-bound, 3.22
earth, 7.9; 15.13
easy to reach, 8.14
education, 9.17
elephants, 10.27
endeavor, 9.27; 10.36
ending identity, 10.32
endless, 11.16
enjoyer, 5.29
entered, 15.15
equally-disposed, 9.29
eternal life, 9.19
everything, 7.19; 11.40
exclusive worship, 9.30
exemplary, 3.23
existential level, 4.10
existential residence, 9.18
exists in body, 8.4
eyes, 11.2,19
fame, 11.36
father, 9.17
father of world, 11.43

Krishna continued,
favorites, 9.29
fig tree identity, 10.26
fire, 9.16
First God, 11.38
focus on, 4.10; 7.30; 8.7; 11.38; 12.8
Form Infinite, 11.16,38
formation, 10.32
foundation, 9.18
four-armed Form, 11.46
fraction, 10.42
friend, 5.29 ; 9.18
gambling, 10.36
garlands, 11.11
garments, 11.11
Garuḍa, 10.30
Gāyatrī, 10.35
geniuses, 7.10
ghastly Form, 11.49
ghee, 9.16
glorified, 9.14; 11.2,9
God of gods, 10.15 ; 11.13
god of romance, 10.28
Govinda, 2.9
grace, 18.56,58
grandfather, 9.17
great souls, 9.13
handsome-haired, 3.1; 11.35
happiness, 14.27
heat producer, 9.19; 11.19
herb, 9.16
higher existence, 7.24; 9.11
highest reality, 7.7
Himalaya, 10.25
honored, 11.39
horses identity, 10.27
Hṛṣikeśa, 1.15
human-like Form, 11.49,51
hurls the wicked, 16.19
hymns identity, 10.35
idea, 3.31
impartial, 9.29
important, 12.6
indifference, 9.9
infallible, 11.42

Krishna continued,
infinite Lord of gods, 11.37
infinite, 11.11,16
influence, 9.6; 10.12
intelligence, 7.10
items accepted, 9.26
Jāhnavī, 10.32
Jahnu's daughter, 10.32
Janārdana, 11.51
japa identity, 10.25
Kāmadhuk, 10.28
Kandarpa, 10.28
Kapila, 10.26
killer of Madhu, 2.1
king identity, 10.27
king of beasts, 10.30
knower, 11.38
knowledge, 10.38
knowledge of, 4.14
known, 7.1
known at death? 8.2
knows Himself, 10.15
Kuvera identity, 10.23
law guardian, 11.18
liberated, 9.9
liberation offered, 18.66
life energy focus, 10.9
life, 7.9
light, 10.21
limitless, 10.19
lion identity, 10.30
logicians, 10.32
longevity, 9.19
Lord of created beings, 10.15
lord of creatures, 4.6
Lord of gods, 11.37
Lord of beings, 7.30
Lord of supernatural rulers and powers, 7.30
Lord of the earth, 1.21
Lord of universe, 10.15
Lord of yoga, 18.75,78
maintainer, 10.15
manifestation, 4.7; 10 40
manliness, 7.9
Marīci, 10.21

Krishna continued,
master of religious ceremony, 9.24
master, 9,18
medicinal herb, 9.16
meditation upon, 8.12; 10.8; 12.6
men, 7.9
mental productions, 10.6
Meru identity, 10.23
mind, identity, 10.22
monitors, 10.30
monsters, 10.31
moon, 7.8; 10.21; 15.13
morality, 7.11; 10.38
mother, 9.17
motivator of humans, 1.38
motivator, 1.38; 10.18
mountain, 10.23
mystic discipline, 10.7
mystic master, 7.25; 10.7,17
Nārada, 10.26
nature of, 14.2
non-dependent, 7.12
non-deteriorating cause, 9.18
not fruitive, 4.14
not recognized, 7.26
not visible, 7.25
November, 10.35
obeisance to, 11.37, 39
objective, 9.18
oblation, 9.16
observer, 9.18
ocean, 10.21
odor, 7.9
offering, 9.27
ointments, 11.11
Oṁ, 7.8; 9.17
omni vision, 9.15
omni-directional, 11.11
one-syllable sound 10.25
opinion, 18.6
opponents, 3.32
opulences, 10.40
origin, 9.18; 10.39
originator, 9.13; 10.8
ornaments, 11.10
Pāṇḍavas, 10.37

Krishna continued,
partner, 15.7
Pāvaka, 10.23
penetrates, 11.40
perfected souls, 10.26
perfumes, 11.11
Person of incomparable splendor, 11.43
Person of universal dimensions, 11.46
plants, 15.13
poets identity, 10.37
Power Infinite, 11.40
Prahlāda, 10.30
praised, 11.44
prayers, 10.25
priests identity, 10.21
Primal God, 10.12
Primal Person, 11.31
primeval cause, 7.10
priority, 12.20
procreators, 10.6
punishment, 10.38
purifier, 9.17
rainfall control, 9.19
Rakṣas identity, 10.23
Rāma identity, 10.31
rarely known, 7.3
recalled at death, 8.5
reciprocates, 4.11
recognizing, 5.29
refuge, 11.38
relation to, 4.35
reliance effective, 9.32
reliance on 4.10; 7.14; 18.56
remembered, 8.7
reproduction, 10.28
research of, 10.17
reservoir of energies, 9.18
residence, 15.6
resort of world, 11.37
respected, 11.31
responsibility, 3.24; 10.20
Rig Veda, 9.17
rivers identity, 10.32
romance, 7.11; 10.28
rulers identity, 10.38
rules of social conduct, 14.27

Krishna continued,
sacrificial ceremony, 9.16
Sāma Veda, 9.17; 10.22,35
sanctified offering, 9.16
sanctuary ultimate, 11.38
Śaśāṅka, 11.39
sciences, 10.32
sea identity, 10.21,27
sea monsters, 10.31
season identity, 10.35
secrets identity, 10.38
self disciplinary, 10.18
self-declaration, 10.13
self-sufficient, 7.12
senses, identity, 10.22
serpents, 10.28
service to, 14.26
shark identity, 10.31
shelter, 9.18; 11.18,43
shielded, 7.25
Shiva identity, 10.23
silence identity, 10.38
Singular Basis, 9.15
Skanda identity, 10.21
slayer of Madhu, 1.34
smiling, 2.10
snakes identity, 10.29
sound, 7.8; 9.16; 10.25
speech about, 10.9
spirits identity, 10.29
spiritual master, 11.43
splendor, 7.10; 10.36,41; 11.19,43
spring identity, 10.35
stars, 10.21
strength, 7.11
subduers, 10.29
sum total, 11.37,40
sun, 10.21
sunlight, 7.8,9
supernatural power, 4.6
supernatural rulers, 10.2,22
supervisor, 9.10
supporter, 9.18
Supreme Being, 9.9
Supreme Form, 11.9
Supreme God, 5.29

Krishna continued,
Supreme Master, 7.30; 8.4
Supreme Objective, 6.14
Supreme Person, 10.15; 15.18,19
Supreme Reformer, 10.12
Supreme Refuge, 10.12
supreme residence, 8.21
Supreme Soul, 10.32
sustains, 9.5
swindlers, 10.36
taste, 7.8
thick-haired, 1.24
think about, 10.10
thinking of, 6.14; 18.57,58
thousand-armed, 11.46
thunderbolt, 10.28
thunderstormers, 10.21
time, 10.30,33
titan identity, 10.30
trend-setter, 3.23
troubled in psyche, 17.6
Uccaiḥśrava, 10.27
unaffected, 1.21; 7.13,25
unbiased, 9.29
uncontaminated, 13.32
under-estimated, 7.24
unique, 11.43
universal father, 9.17
Universal Form, 11.7
universal, 10.12
universal influence, 4.11; 10.39
universally available, 6.30
universe reality, 11.13
unrecognized, 7.13; 9.24
Usana identity, 10.37
Vaiśvānara, 15.13
Vajra identity, 10.28
variety, 9.15
Varuṇa, 10.29; 11.39

Krishna continued,
Vāsava Indra, 10.22
Vāsudeva, 10.37
Vāsuki identity, 10.28
Vasus identity, 10.23
Vāyu, 11.39
Vedas, 7.8; 9.17; 10.22; 15.18
Vedic ritual, 9.16
victory, 10.36,38
Vinata identity, 10.30
Vishnu, 10.21; 11.9,24
Vitteśa identity, 10.23
Vṛṣṇis identity, 10.37
Vyāsa identity, 10.37
water, 7.8
weapon, 10.28,31; 11.10
wind identity, 10.31
wise men, 10.38
word, 10.25,33
work of, 11.55; 12.10
worship, 7.28; 9.14,15,20,22,23,29; 12.6; 15.19
Yajur Veda, 9.17
Yakṣas identity, 10.23
Yama, 10.29; 11.39
yoga master, 11.4,9
yoga process, 12.10
yogi attainment, 12.4
yogi dear, 7.17; 12.14
yogi sages, 10.2,25,26,37
yogi sages' cause, 10.6
Kṣamā, 10.34
Kuvera, 10.23
Kuntī, 1.16,27; 2.14,37,60; 3.9,39; 5.22; 8.16; 9.7; 13.2; 14.4
Kuntibhoja, 1.5
Kuru, 1.25; 2.41; 4.31; 6.43
kurukṣetre, 1.1
kuśa grass, 6.11

L

laborers, facilitated, 9.32
lamentation, 2.25; 12.17
lamp, 6.19
language, 16.4
lawlessness, 1.40
laziness, 14.8
leaf, 9.26

left-over food, 17.10
leisure, 6.17
letters, 10.33
levels of reality, 9.15
liberated person, 4.23; 14.2,23-26
liberation,
dedication to, 5.28
knowers of, 10.35
many births, 6.45
perpetual type, 5.28
described, 13.24
godly talent, 16.5
status, 14.2
life, Krishna, 7.9
life-duration, 9.21
life-giving codes, 12.20
light of luminaries, 13.18
light, 7.8; 10.21; 15.12
liking, 3.34; 4.22; 7.27
lion, 10.30
liquids, 7.4
listeners, 18.67
lives, sacrificed, 1.33
living beings, 2.28; 9.8
living space, 13.1,2,6,7,20,27,35
location of yogi, 6.11
location, 18.14
logic, 13.5
logicians, 10.32
Lord of all beings, 18.61
Lord of gods, 11.25,37,45
Lord of supernatural rulers and powers, 8.4
Lord of yoga, 18.75,78
lotus leaf, 5.10; 11.2
lover, 11.44
low opinion, 9.11
luck, warrior's, 2.32
lust, resistance, 2.71
lusty enjoyment, 16.11
lusty urge, 3.39; 16.10
luxuries, 2.5; 9.21

M

Madhu, 1.14,34; 2.1; 6.33; 8.2
majesty, 18.43
managers, 18.41,44
manifestations, 10.16,19
manifested energies, 4.6; 8.18,19
Maṇipuṣpaka, 1.16
manliness, 7.8
Manu, 4.1
Marīci, 10.21
mass of splendor, 11.17
masses, 2.69
master, Krishna, 8.4; 9.18
master, spirit is, 15.8
masters of philosophical theory, 6.46
material energy, 4.6; 7.14
material existence, cessation, 5.25,26
material nature,
–also see modes of material nature
action bound, 3.9
actions, 9.12
as cause, 13.21
beginningless, 13.20
forces, 18.59
foundation, 9.8
imperceptible, 15.3
influence banished, 10.11; 18.19
inquiry, 13.1
Krishna's womb, 14.3,4
Krishna's, 9.7
moods, 13.20
overpowering, 9.8
performer, 14.19
producer, 9.10
productions, 13.27
reliance on, 9.12
restrictive, 7.20
retrogression into, 9.7
spirit transcends, 14.20
sponsors hopes, 9.12
submission to, 3.33
supernatural level, 9.13
Supreme Spirit, 13.15
universal, 18.40
Medhā, 10.34
meditation,
compared, 12.12
death method, 8.10
deep type, 8.8
energization, 8.10
God as subject, 8.9
on Krishna, 2.61; 9.22; 10.17; 12.8
meditation continued,
pleasure-prone people, 2.44
power-seeking people, 2.44
scriptural information, 2.53
steady type, 2.55-56
superficial type, 3.6
valid type, 3.7
meditator, inquiry of, 2.54
memory,
Krishna produced, 15.15
indulgences, 2.59
men, 7.8; 10.27
mental approach, 3.1
mental concepts, 16.1
mental dominance, 2.54
mercy, 11.1, 25,31,44,45
merit-based world, 9.20
Meru, 10.23
mind
6th device, 15.7
compared, 3.42
control absolute, 8.14
control difficult, 6.34,35
controlled, 5.28; 6.35
drift / restraint, 6.26
impulsive, 6.34
interiorized, 8.8
Krishna anchored, 8.7
passion fostered, 3.40
purification, 5.11
regulation, 3.3
resistant, 6.34
restricted, 8.12
troublesome, 6.34
unsteady, 6.35
wanderings, 6.26
mindal energy, 7.4
minute factor, 8.9
mirror, 3.38
miserable conditions, 2.56
misery-free place, 2.51
misfortune, 6.40
misplaced self identity, 16.18; 17.5
misty season, 8.25
moderation, 6.16,17
modes of material nature, 14.10,23
modesty, 16.2

money, 16.12,17
monitor, 10.30
monkey insignia, 1.20
month, 10.35
moods,
detachment, 14.22
extraction, 2.58
hindrance, 3.34
like / dislike, 3.34
material nature's, 13.20
motivation, 3.29
phases, 2.45
yogic, 5.2
moon
death, 8.24,25
eye, 11.19
Krishna, 7.8; 10.21
lord, 11.39
mundane, 15.6
sap, 15.13
splendor, 15.12
moral action, 3.8
morality, 7.11; 10.38; 18.78
mother, 9.17
motivation, 2.47; 6.4
mountain, 10.23
mourning, 2.11
mouth, 11.10,25
mouth of spiritual existence, 4.32
mouth of Universal Form, 11.19
movement, 18.14
multiplicity, 18.21
multitude of beings, 8.19
mundane affinity, 6.15
mundane energy, 3.5; 7.4
mundane influences, 15.2
musical instruments, 1.13
musicians, 11.22
mystic seers, 2.16

N

Nakula, 1.16
Nārada, 10.13,26
Narāyana Form, 11.46,52
natural resources, 11.22
Nature,
Krishna's, 14.2
producer, 5.14
types, 16.3,4
neck posture, 6.13
nectar, 18.37
needy person, 7.16
negligence, 14.9
nervousness, 3.30
night of Brahmā, 8.17-19
nighttime, death, 8.25
nine-gate city, 5.13
no possessions, 6.10
non-acting factor, 4.18
non-attachment, 3.28; 6.4; 15.3
non-existence, 10.5
non-reliance, 3.18
non-violence, 10.5; 13.8; 16.2; 17.14
northern sun passage, 8.24
nose, breath, 5.27
nose-tip gazing, 6.13
nourishment, 3.14
November, 10.35

O

obeisance, 11.21,35,39,44; 18.65
objective, Krishna, 9.18
oblation, 9.16; 11.19; 17.28
obligatory action, 6.1; 18.7
observer of reality, 14.19
observer, 13.23
ocean, absorption, 2.70
ocean, Krishna represented, 10.24
odor, Krishna related, 7.9
offering, 3.12; 9.16
ointments, 11.11
old age, 13.9, 14.20
Oṁ, 7.8; 8.13; 9.17; 17.24
Oṁ tat sat, 17.23
one imperishable being, 18.20
oneness, 18.20
openings of body, 8.12
opinion of Krishna, 9.11
opportunity,
devotion, 9.33
rejection, 18.1,2
renunciation, 18.49
usage, 5.2
opposite features, 5.3
opulences, 10.40
origin, 9.18; 10.39; 11.2; 14.3
ornaments, 11.10
overheated food, 17.9

P

pacified mind, 2.65
pain,
Krishna derived, 10.5
periodic, 2.14
pleasure related, 5.22
spirit cause, 13.21
pancajanya, 1.15
Pandava, 6.2; 10.37
pandit, 4.19
Pāndu, 1.1,3,14; 4.35; 11.55; 14.22; 16.5
parentage, 9.32
partial insight, 3.29
partner, 15.7
passion,
avoidance, 2.56
emotion, 3.37
insight blocked, 3.38
rooted out, 3.43
ruins discernment, 3.41
squelched, 3.41
warehouse, 3.40
past life impetus, 6.43,44
paths, hereafter, 8.26,27
patience, required, 10.5,34; 12.13; 13.8; 18.42
Pauṇḍra, 1.15
Pāvaka, 10.23
pay-off, 4.20
peace, , 5.12; 12.12; 17.16
pearls, 7.6
peer pressure, 2.34,35
penance, 4.28
people,
deluded, 5.15
four kinds, 7.16
peppery food, 17.9
perception,
clear type, 14.11
dangers, 13.9
hearing method, 13.26
mystic, 13.25; 15.10,11
spiritual, 15.10,11
Supreme Lord, 13.28
perceptive impurities, 14.6
perceptive person, 10.3
perceptive speakers, 5.4
perfected souls, 11.36
perfection,
supreme, 8.15
work, 12.10

performance,
detachment from, 6.4
recommended, 3.8
types, 18.10
performer,
confusion, 3.27
types, 18.19,26-28
perfumes, 11.11; 15.8
permitter, 13.23
Person of universal dimensions, 11.46
Person, knowing everything, 8.9
personal energies,
controlled, 3.43
friend / enemy, 6.6
yoga control, 4.1
personal existence, Supreme Soul, 8.3
personal initiative, 13.6,9
personal undertakings, 12.16
personality, 2.12; 13.1,2
Personified Veda, 3.15
philosophers, 6.3,46
physical activity, 6.1
pious merits, 9.21
pious person, 6.40
piously-departed spirits, 10.29
plants, 15.13
pleasure
cause sin, 1.44
family, 1.32
Krishna derived, 10.5
objective, 9.21
pain, 6.7
poetic quotation, 2.42
sensual contact, 5.22
spirit cause, 13.21
terminal, 5.22
poets, poetry, 10.35,37
poison, 18.37,38
political affairs, 1.1
political power, 1.31,32; 2.43
population, 7.25
possessions,
absent, 6.10
austerity, 4.28
detachment towards, 12.13
freedom from, 2.45
indifference, 2.71
potential, 13.4
power, anger, 3.37
practice, mind control, 6.35
Prahlāda, 10.30
prāṇāyāma, 18.33
pratyāhar, 8.11
prayers, 10.25; 11.14
predominating influences, 14.10
pressure of change, 7.25
pride, 13.8; 15.5; 16,10,17; 18.35
priest, 4.24; 11.22
priestly teachers, 18.41,42
Primal God, 10.12
Primal Person, 11.31; 15.4
primeval unmanifested states, 8.20
priority, 3.2
Procreator Brahmā, - see Brahmā
procreators, 10.6
producer God, 13.17
production, 7.6; 13.27
property control, 4.33
proposal, two-way, 3.2
prosperity, 18.78
prosperous parents, 6.41
prostrations, 11.35
Pṛthā, 1,25,26; 2.3,21,39,42,55,72; 3.16; 4.11; 6.40; 7.1; 8.8,14,19; 9.32; 10.24; 12.7; 18.6
psyche,
described, 13.6,7
directive part, 6.7
friend / enemy, 6.6
God inhabits, 18.61
Krishna entered, 15.15
perceiver different, 10.35
spirit powered, 10.34
psychological core, 13.18
psychological environment, 13.19
psychological perfection, 7.3
psychological power, 8.10
psychological results of sacrifice, 4.31
psychological supremacy, 9.5
psychologically pacified, 6.27
pungent food, 17.9
punishment, 10.38
purificatory acts, 18.5
purified parents, 6.41
purifier,
consciousness, 9.2
experience, 4.38
Krishna, 9.17
purity of being, 16.1; 17.16
purity, 13.8; 17.14
Purujit, 1.5

Q,R

questions, 4.34; 5.1
radiance, 8.9; 11.17
rage, 17.5
rain, 3.14; 9.19
Rakṣas, 10.23
Rāma, 10.31
range of Supreme Spirit, 13.14-18
reactionary work, 4.19
realism, 16.7
Reality,
Krishna highest, 7.7
Krishna represented, 10.36
Krishna's womb, 14.3,4
One, 11.7,13
perceiving person, 3.28
reality-piercing vision, 2.57,58
science, 13.12
undefinable, 12.3
realized knowledge, 4.37,42
reasoning, 15.15
rebels, 11.22
rebirth
avoidance, 5.17
cessation, 15.4,6
exemption, 4.9; 8.15,16
faithless person, 9.3
formula for, 8.6
freedom from, 2.51
heaven prior, 9.21
planetary effect, 8.25
promised, 2.43
repetitive, 8.16
transcended, 13.24

rebirth continued,
wicked peoples', 16.19
yogi's, 6.41
recitation of scripture, 16.1; 17.15
reciters, 2.42,43
recognition of reality, 10.34; 16.2
reference, 5.17
reference, senses, mind, intelligence, spirit, 3.42
reform, 9.31
reformed persons, 9.20
Refuge Supreme, 11.38
regulation,
--see mind regulation,
--see action regulation
reincarnation,
devotee, 12.7
formula for, 8.6
Krishna, 7.26
resisted, 5.17
rejection of consequences, 18.1,2,4
rejection of opportunity, 18.1,2
relation, 5.7
relatives, war field, 1.26
reliance on Krishna, 9.32
religion, 9.24
religious ceremony,
-see also ritual action
austerity, 4.28
categories, 17.7-10
enjoyer, 5.29
false type, 16.17
invented ones, 17.1
Krishna / master, 9.24
ordinances, 3.9,10; 17.23
prescribed, 17.25
purifies, 4.30
sacrifice, 4.25
types, 17.11-13
unapproved type, 9.23
yogi bypass, 8.28
religious fulfillment, 3.9,10
remembering, objects, 3.6
renouncer,
charity, 18.10
consistent type, 5.3
defined, 6.1
renunciation,
compared, 12.12
cultural activity, 5.2
defined, 18.11
insufficient, 3.4
mental type, 5.13
social activity?, 5.1
social opportunities, 5.2
to Krishna, 18.57
types, 18.7-9
yoga applied, 6.2
renunciation of opportunities, 5.6
reproduction, 10.28
repulsion, 12.15
reputation, 2.34-36; 17.18
research, 18.18
reservoir of energies, 9.18
residence, supreme, 15.6
resident of body, 5.13
resort of the world, 11.37
Respected Person, 11.31
restlessness, 14.11
restraint,
bodily limbs, 3.6
questioned, 3.33
tendency, 18.42
result,
best one, 3.2
giving up, 18.6
motivation resisted, 2.47
transcended, 6.1
types, 18.12
yogi bypass, 8.28
retardation, 14.5
retarded people, 14.18; 17.4
retrogression, 9.7
revelation, 11.53
reverence, 11.40,44
reversion, 8.18
reward, 17.21
Rig Veda, 9.17
righteous behavior, 9.3
righteous duty, 3.35
--also see duty
righteous lifestyle, 9.21
righteous method, 9.2
righteous practice, 2.40
righteousness, 4.7
ritual action,
conditional, 4.12
results rapid, 4.12
Universal Form, 11.48
ritual performers, 6.46
ritual regulation, 4.33
rivers, Krishna represented, 10.31
romance, 7.11; 10.28
rotten food, 17.10
ruination, 11.2
rulers, 10.38
ruling sector, 18.41,43

S

sacred thread, 17.14
sacrifice,
abandoned?, 18.3
purificatory, 18.5
results, 4.31
to Krishna, 18.65
types, 17.11-13
value, 4.30
sacrificial ceremony, 9.16; 11.48,53
sacrificial fire, 3.38
sacrificial ingredients, 4.24
Sādhyā, 11.22
Sahadeva, 1.16
Śaibya, 1.5
saint / wicked person, 9.30
saintly people, 4.8
salty food, 17.9
Sāma Veda, 9.12; 10.22,35
sāṁkhya philosophy, 2.39; 13.25; 18.3,19
sāṁkhya, yoga practice, 5.4,5
sanctification, 3.13
sanctified offering, 9.16
sanctuary, 11.38
sanity, 10.5
Sanjaya, 1.1,2,24; 2.1,9; 18.74,76
sannyāsa, 18.2
Śaśaṅka, 11.39
sat, 17.26,27
satisfaction, 2.70; 4.20; 10.18
Sātyaki, 1.17
science of reality, 13.12
sciences, 10.32
scriptural injunctions, 16.23,24; 17.1

scripture, 2.53
sea, 10.24,27
sea monsters, 10.31
seasons, 10.35
seat of yogi, 6.11,12
seclusion, 13.11
secret, 9.1,2; 10.38
security, 6.15; 16.2; 18.62
seeing what was never seen, 11.45,47
seeing, 5.8
seer,
- attainment, 5.25,26
- common factor, 5.18
- destination, 2.51
- inquiry of, 2.54

self,
- concentration on, 6.10
- core, 6.18
- enemy, 6.5
- evaluation, 6.5
- fixed on, 6.25
- friendship, 6.5
- pacified, 6.14

self-composed, 4.41
self-conceited, 16.17
self-content, 2.55
self-control, 5.7; 6.7; 10.5
self-denial, 4.28
self identity, 16.18, 17.5
self-image, 18.16
selfishness, 3.30
self-perception, 6.20
self-purification, 6.12
self-realization, 4.38
self-restraint, 12.11; 13.8; 16.1; 17.16
self-satisfaction, 6.20
self-situated, 3.17
sensations,
- alternating, 2.14
- coping, 2.14
- detachment, 5.21

sense control, 2.69
senseless, 3.32
senses,
- attractive objects, 5.9
- compared, 3.42
- death baggage, 15.8
- Krishna represented, 10.22
- like / dislike, 3.34
- living space, 13.6
- mind affected, 2.67

senses continued,
- passion fostered, 3.40
- purification usage, 5.11
- regulating, 3.41
- restraint, 2.61
- torment ascetic, 2.60
- withdrawn, 2.58

sensual activity, withdrawal, 6.25
sensual contacts, 5.27
sensual energy control, 5.28; 6.12; 12.4
sensual energy, restraint, 4.39; 6.24
sensual feelings, retraction, 2.68
sensual objects, 2.62
sensual potency, 13.21
sensual powers, 4.26
sensual pursuits, 4.26
sensual range, 7.24
sensuality, controlled, 2.61; 5.24
sensuality, perpetual, 7.27
separation, from emotion, 6.23
serpents, 10.28; 11.15
service sector, 18.44
serving, 4.34
sexual intermixture, 1.40
sexual restraint, 6.14
sexual urge, 16.8
Shankara, 10.23
shark, 10.31
shelter, 9.18; 18.62
ship, 2.67
Shiva, 10.23
sickness, 17.9
Śikhandī, 1.17
silence, 10.38; 17.16
simpletons, 3.26; 5.4
sin,
- considered, 1.36,38
- God's resistance, 5.15

sinful propensities, 7.28
singers, 10.26
sins terminated, 5.25
situations, 13.22
sixth device, 15.7
Skanda, 10.24
skills destroyed, 1.42
sky resonated, 1.19
sleep regulator, 10.20
sleep, 5.8; 6.16,17; 14.8; 18.35
smelling, 5.8
smoke, 18.48
smoky season, 8.25
Smṛti, 10.34
snakes, 10.29
social circumstance, 6.41
social life, 13.10
social values, 18.34
society, maintenance, 3.25
solids, 7.4
soma drinkers, 9.20
Somadatta, 1.8
son of charioteer, 11.26
son, 1.26,33; 11.44
sorcerers, 17.4
sorrow, 18.35
soul, embodied, adaptations, 2.13
soul, see spirit
soul-situated, 2.45
sound,
- austerity, 4.26
- Krishna related, 7.8; 10.25
- Oṁ, 17.24

sour food, 17.9
space
- comparison, 9.6; 10.33
- mundane, 7.4
- pervaded, 11.20

species
- as facility, 6.32
- comparison, 5.18
- ignorant type, 14.15
- Krishna inhabits, 6.30; 7.26
- rebirth, 14.15
- spirit caused, 7.6
- spirits inhabit, 15.8

speech,
- control, 18.51,52
- disciplined, 17.15
- Krishna, 10.34

spinning machine, 18.61
spirit
- addicted, 15.9
- affected, 15.16
- amazing, 2.29
- beginningless, 13.20
- body energizer, 10.34
- cannot be killed, 2.19
- cannot kill, 2.19
- captivated, 14.5

spirit continued,
- compared, 3.42
- condition-resistant, 2.23
- confused, 3.40
- considered temporary, 2.26
- creature habitat, 6.29
- death impossible, 2.20,21
- degradation, 16.21
- dry-less, 2.23
- elevate self, 6.5
- eternal, 2.20; 15.7
- experience, 13.22
- fantastic, 2.29
- faultless, 5.19
- going to Krishna, 4.9
- governor of psyche, 15.9
- higher energy, 7.5; 13.23; 15.17
- immeasurable, 2.18
- imperishable, 2.21
- impulsion captivates, 14.6
- incombustible, 2.23
- indestructible, 2.17
- individual, 15.7
- Krishna represented, 10.29
- Krishna's partner, 15.7
- master of body, 15.8
- material nature captivates, 14.5
- material nature transcended, 14.20
- mourning unworthy, 2.30
- movements, 15.10
- non-actor, 5.13
- non-doer, 13.28
- non-killable, 2.30
- not born, 2.26
- not killed, 2.26
- origin of species, 7.6
- perception, 13.25,28
- permanent, 2.24
- primeval, 2.20
- seen / unseen, 15.11
- self upliftment, 13.28
- sensation cause, 13.21
- stable type, 15.16,

spirit continued,
- stable, 2.24; 15.16
- transcendental, 13.33
- types, 15.16
- unaffected ones, 10.33; 15.16
- undetected, 2.28
- undisplayed, 2.25
- unimaginable, 2.25
- universe sustained by 7.5
- unknown, 2.29
- wet-less, 2.23
- wonderful, 2.29

spiritual core self, 6.18
spiritual delight, 5.24
spiritual discernment, 18.37

spiritual existence,
- known, 7.29
- mouth of, 4.32
- sacrifice support, 4.24,25

spiritual level, 5.10
spiritual master, 4.34; 11.43; 17.24; 18.68,69
spiritual peace, 5.29
spiritual perfection, 3.4
spiritual plane, 5.19,20

spiritual reality,
- description, 6.44
- designation, 17.23
- question of, 8.1
- unaffected, supreme, 8.3

spiritual religion, 4.31
spiritual self, 2.55
spiritual teacher, 17.14
spiritual world, 8.20,21,24
spirituality, 5.24-26
spiritually content, 3.17
spiritually-pleased, 3.17
splendor, 7.10; 10.36; 18.78
spring, 10.35
Śrī, 10.34
stability, 13.8
stale food, 17.10
standard position, 6.33
standard, two-fold, 3.3
stars, 10.21
states of being, 7.12; 13.31
status of next life, 8.6
stone, 6.8; 14.24
stormers, 11.22
straightforwardness, 13.8; 16.1; 17.14; 18.42
strength, 7.11
string comparison, 7.6
strong-mindedness, 16.3
stubborn, 16.17
student, 4.34
stupified at death, 2.72
subduers, 10.29
Subhadra, 1.6,18
substantial things, 2.16
subtle body, 9.19
success/ failure, indifference, 2.48; 4.22
suffering, 13.9
Sughoṣa, 1.16
sum total, 8.1,4
summer season, 8.24

sun,
- comparison, 5.16; 10.34
- death affected by, 8.25
- eye, 11.19
- Krishna related, 7.8,9; 10.21
- Krishna's splendor, 15.12
- mundane, 15.6
- thousands, 11.11

super-fantastic form, 18.77
Supermost Personality, 8.1
supernatural destroyers, 11.6
supernatural manifestations, 10.40

supernatural rulers,
- appeasers of, 7.4,.20,23; 9.23,25
- Divine Form not seen, 11.52
- human relation, 3.11,12
- Krishna represented by, 10.22
- Krishna unknown to, 10.2,14
- respect, 17.14
- source, 10.2
- Universal Form, 11.6,15,21

supernatural sight, 11.8
supernatural stormers, 11.6
supernatural wondrous manifestations, 10.16,19

supernatural, material nature, 9.13
supernaturally disposed, 11.33,34
Supersoul,
beings inhabited by, 13.28
described, 13.14-18,23
disliked, 16.18
transmigration, 18.61
troubled, 17.6
supporter, 9.18
Supreme Being, 9.4-6,9; 18.62
-see also Krishna
supreme destination, 13.28; 16.23
Supreme Form, 11.9,47
supreme goal, 6.45; 9.32
Supreme God, 5.29; 16.18
supreme information, 10.1
Supreme Lord, 13.23,28,32; 16.8
supreme objective, 6.14; 7.18; 8.21
supreme peace, 4.39
supreme perfection, 8.15; 14.1
Supreme Person,
action free, 5.14
cause of all causes, 8.22
defined, 15.18
described, 8.9
Krishna, 10.15
reached, 8.8
Supreme Primal State, 8.28
Supreme Reality, 10.12; 11.18; 13.13-18
Supreme Reformer, 10.12
Supreme Refuge, 10.12
Supreme Regulator of religious ceremonies and disciplines, 8.2,4
Supreme Soul / Spirit
association, 15.5
austerity, 3.15
described, 15.17
explained, 11.1
information, 13.12
known, 7.29
Krishna, 10.32
meditate upon, 3.30
Supreme Soul / Spirit continued
mundane world producer, 8.3
permitter, 13.23
personal existence, 8.3
Personified Veda, 3.15
question of, 8.1
religious ceremony, 3.15
supporter, 15.17
Supreme Supernatural Person and Power, 8.1
Supreme Supervisor, 8.9
Supreme truth, 5.16,17
supreme yoga, 18.75
supreme destination, 10.35
Supreme, pure world, 14.14
Surendra, 9.20
surrender, 18.62
sustainer, God, 13.17
svarga angelic world, 2.43
swindlers, 10.36
syllable, 10.25
synthesis, 13.27

T

take note of it, 9.31
talents, 16.3
talking, 5.9
taste, 7.8
tat, 17. 25
teachers,
Gītā, 18.68,69
lineage, 4.2
reality-conversant, 4.34
social, 1.26,33
teaching, best, 4.3; 15.20
teeth, 11.23,25
temptation, 2.59
tendencies,
elaborated, 18.42-44
eliminated, 6.27
innate, 17.2
overcome, 4.36
texture of existence, 8.6
thief, 3.12
thighs, 11.23
thinking,
controlled, 6.10,12
restrained, 5.26
stoppage, 6.20,25
wicked people, 16.13,14
thought controlled, 6.18
thoughts on Krishna, 12.9
threefold influence, 16.21
thunderbolt, 10.28
time, 10.30,33; 11.32
time cycle, 8.17-19
titan, 10.30
tortoise, 2.58
torture, 17.6,19
touching, 5.8
trading, 18.44
tradition,
abandoned, 18.66
Arjuna considers, 1.39
destroyers of, 1.43
disgust with, 2.52
trance, 6.22
tranquility, 10.5; 18.42
transcendent person, 14.21
transformation of psyche, 14.2
transmigration, 18.61
tree, 10.26; 15.1-3
trend, 17.3
trickery, 17.18
truth, 9.1
truthfulness, 10.5
truths of existence, 2.16
tyāga, 18.2

U

Uccaiḥśrava, 10.27
unavoidable circumstance, 2.27
uncles, 1.26
uncontrolled person, 2.66
undisciplined person, 6.36
undivided God, 13.17
unintelligent person, 7.24
universal destruction, 11.25
Universal Form,
displayed, 11.3,5-47
Sanjaya, 18.77
supernatural rulers terrified, 11.21
viewers listed, 11.22
universal integration, 9.18
Universal Soul, 13.14-18

universe,
Krishna supports, 10.42; 11.38
one reality, 11.7
operations, 9.9
production / destruction, 7.6
rejoices, 11.36
spirit sustained, 7.5
three partitions, 11.43
unmanifested energy, 13.6
unmanifested states, 8.20
unpleasant things, 5.20
Upanishads, 13.5
upper class, 16.15
Uśanā, 10.37
Uttamauja, 1.6

V

Vaiśvānara, 15.14
vajra, 10.28
Vāk, 10.34
vanity, 18.26
vapor bodies, 11.22
variations, 3.28,29
variety, 9.15
Varuṇa, 10.29; 11.38
Vāsava, 10.22
vast existence of death, 12.7
Vāsudeva, 7.19; 10.37; 11.50
Vāsuki, 10.28
Vasus, 10.23
Vāyu, 11.39
Veda knower, 8.11; 9.20; 15.1
Veda,
Krishna knows / known, 15.15
Krishna related, 7.8; 10.22
offers of, 2.45
ordained, 17.23
Personified, 3.15
spoken description, 6.44
surpassed, 6.44
Vedānta, 15.15
worth, 2.46
yogi beyond, 8.28
Vedic education, Universal Form, 11.48
Vedic hymns recited, 13.5; 15.1; 17.13
Vedic injunction, 9.21; 16.17
Vedic ritual, 9.16
Vedic ceremonies, 11.48
Vedic study, 11.53
Vedic verses, 2.42
vibration, necessary, 3.5
vices, terminated, 5.25
victory,
defeat, 2.38
Krishna represented, 10.36,38; 18.78
not desired, 1.31
viewers, 2.19
vigor, 16.3
Vikarṇa, 1.8
Vinata, 10.30
violence, 5.10; 18.25
Virāṭa, 1.4,17
virtue, deviation, 9.24
virtuous acts, 6.40
virtuous character, 9.31
virtuous people, 3.13
Vishnu, 10.21
visible world, 8.18,19
vision of reality, 15.10,11
vision of yogi, 2.61
vision, Arjuna given, 11.8
visitation of Krishna, 4.9
visual focus, 5.27
Viśvadeva, 11.22
Vitteśa, 10.23
Vivasvāt, 4.1,4
void, 2.69
vows, ascetics of, 4.28; 7.28; 9.14
Vṛṣṇis, 1.40; 3.36; 10.37
Vyāsa, 10.13,37; 18.75

W

walking, 5.8
war, 2.33,34
warriors,
battle hungry, 1.22
heaven, 2.32
supernaturally disposed, 11.33
water,
Krishna accepts, 9.26
Krishna related, 7.8
lotus leaf, 5.10
master of, 11.39
psychic type, 1.41
weapon carriers, Krishna represented, 10.31
weapons, 2.23; 10.28,31; 11.10
weather, 2.14
welfare of all, 12.4
well (water), 2.46
what to do, 16.7
whole multitude, 9.8
wicked persons, 4.8; 16.7
wickedness, 4.7
wife, 13.10
will power, 18.60
wind
Krishna compared, 9.6; 10.31
mind compared, 6.34
regulator, 11.39
ship, 2.67
spirit compared, 15.8
wise person,
condition-resistant, 2.15
duty, 3.25
immortality, 2.15
Krishna represented, 10.38
realization, 2.13
womb, Krishna's, 14.3,4
wombs of wicked people, 16.20
women, 1.40; 9.32; 10.34
wonders, 11.6
wood, 4.37
word compound, 10.33
work,
discarded, 2.50
material nature, 13.21
tendency, 4.13
working power, 3.30
work-prone people, 14.15
world
action bound, 3.9
God pervades, 9.4
maintenance, 3.20
other, 4.31
production, 8.18,19
spirit pervaded, 2.17
stupefied, 7.13
trembles, 11.20,23
types, 14.14,15
utilized, 4.31
worries, 2.56; 16.10,11
worship
ceremony, 16.1
exclusive, 9.22
God, 18.46

worship continued,
Krishna's, 7.16,28; 12.2
procedure, 3.10-12
supernatural rulers', 9.23
types, 17.4,11-13
worshippers of gods, 7.23
worshippers of Krishna, 7.23
worshippers rated, 9.25
worthless person, 3.16

Y

Yadu family man, 11.41
Yajur Veda, 9.17
Yakṣas, 10.23
Yama, 10.29; 11.38
yearning, 3.39; 18.49
yoga practice,
application lost, 4.2
application, 5.1; 6.2,28;,16.1
austerity, 4.28
celibacy required, 8.11
concentration, 8.12
controlling force, 4.1
cultural activities, 3.7; 4.41
determination, 18.33
deviation, 6.37
distress-remover, 6.17
exertion, 12.5
expertise, 6.3
harmonized, 10.7
indifference, 2.48
insight applied, 2.39
intellectual discipline, 2.49; 18.57
interiorization, 8.8
Krishna worship, 9.22
Krishna's, 11.47; 12.11
mastery, 2.53; 6.23,36
methods, 6.3
moderation, 6.16
mood, 2.48,50
perfected, 4.38; 6.43
performance skill, 2.50
preliminary, 12.9
proficiency, 5.7,8,12; 6.4,18,29
purpose, 6.12
yoga practice continued,
recommended, 7.1;.8.27; 12.9
renunciation, 9.28
required, 13.11
requirements, 12.4
sāṁkhya, 5.4
spiritual plane, 5.21
skill described, 4.18
technique, 4.3,42; 12.2
undistracted, 12.6
yogi,
action austerity, 4.27
actions antiseptic, 5.10
Arjuna, 6.46
attainment, 8.23
austerities bypassed, 8.28
baffled, 6.38
births end, 7.19
breath, 4.27
charity, 8.28
death, 8.10,13,24
defined, 6.1
destination, 4.31; 8.28
deviant, 6.37
devotee, 12.14,17
discipline, 6.8; 18.51
distinguished, 7.17
Divine Supreme Person, 8.10
existential position, 6.15
experience, 6.8
faults ended, 6.28
fond to Krishna, 7.17
happiness, 5.21; 6.28
hearing, 4.26
highest type, 6.32
informed type, 7.17
inquiry, 2.54
intention, 6.2
isolation, 6.10
kings, 4.15; 9.33
knowledge, 4.28
Krishna / everything, 7.19
Krishna attracts, 6.47
Krishna contact, 6.30; 8.14
Krishna devoted, 6.47
Krishna remembrance, 8.13
yogi continued,
Krishna seen, 6.30
Krishna worship, 6.47; 12.6
Krishna's representative, 7.18
Krishna-knowing, 7.30
lamp, 6.19
liberation, 5.26-28; 6.15
meditation, 6.12
memory, 3.6
methods, 12.1,2,3
non-actor, 5.13
past life impetus, 6.43,44
perfection, 6.43
philosophers, 10.37
philosophical / non-philosophical, 3.3
planetary influence, 8.26
possessions, 4.28
proficiency, 6.4
psychologically pacified, 6.27
purification, 5.11
release, 7.29
religion, 4.25
religious ceremonies, 8.28
seat, 6.11
sensual austerity, 4.26
sound austerity, 4.26
spiritual plane, 5.6
steadiness, 6.21
supernatural authority,4.25
supreme primal state, 8.28
tendencies, 6.45
two standards, 3.3
valid type, 3.7
Veda austerity, 4.28
Veda bypassed, 8.28
vision of species, 6.29
yoga austerity, 4.28

yogi sages,
aśvattha tree, 15.1-3
Krishna praised, 10.13; 11.21
Krishna represented, 10.25,26
Krishna unknown, 10.2
seven, 10.6
source, 10.2
Universal Form, 11.15
Yudhāmanyu, 1.6
Yudhiṣṭhira, 1.16
Yuyudhāna, 1.4

Index to Commentary

A

abandonment/consequences, 477
abhimānas, 480
Abhimanyu, 15, 19, 20
abhyarcya, 530
absence of initiative, 430
abstraction, 293
abusive language, 480
acāpalam, 478
acaryopasanam, 429
accountability, 483
aches/ pains, 449
action, choices, 117
action,
  component, 517
  confusion about, 160
  fault-yielding, 509
  God-approved, 530
  jurisdiction of, 134
  liabilities given, 138
five factors, 515
actor, protection, 188
adambhitvam, 428
addiction, meditation, 232
adhamām gatim, 489
Aditi, 351,.352, 359, 369, 381
Āditya, 149, 151
Ādityas, 351, 359, 369, 381
administrative power, 266
administrator, 406
adroho, 479
Advaita Vedantist, 312
affected, 471, 472
affection,
  consciousness, 293
  convertible, 199
  psychic type, 68
  steady, 431
agent, 515, 517
agnihotra, 88
Agnivesha, 13
ahimsā, 421, 428, 476,
Airāvata, 358
ajñanam, 480
akṣarah, 471
alcohol, 99
A-letter, 360
alternatives, 414-416
amānitvam, 428
Ambā, 18, 21
Ambalikā, 21
Ambikā, 21
amśah, 467
anahamkāra, 430
Ananga, 358
Ananta, 358
anantavijava, 28
ananya yogena, 431
anāśino, 66
Aṅga, 22
angelic beings, limited, 405
angelic singers, 357
anger,
  absence of, 477
  degrading, 489
  dormant, 480
  effects, 103
  force, 199
Aṅgirā, 194, 195
Aṅgirasa, 338
animal,
  compared to mind, 237
  composite being, 427
  lowest mode, 449
  subtle forms, 376
animal birth, 489
animal kingdom, 529
anna, 124
antagonistic Godhead, 385
antaryāmi, location, 349
anthropologists, 119
anti-human, 90
anti-material location, 466
anus, 427
apaiśūnam, 477
ape, 119
apohah, 471
apology, 393
apparition, 384, 388
applied yoga, 219
aristocracy, 315
Arisūdana, 54
ārjavam, 429
Arjuna,
  abrupt release, 135
  apology, 393
  apparition called off, 388
  astral travel, 349
  unaffected? 544
  austerities, 129, 140, 234
  believed, 345
  breakdown explained, 53
  conch, 27
  conclusions, 378
  confidence in Krishna, 394
  decision, 539
  desired results, 514
  disempowerment, 54
  emotionally weak, 107
  evidence reviewed, 391
  friendship scrapped, 388
  hack away, 465
  isolation, 116
  karma yoga, 183
  Krishna as, 363
  Krishna's alliance, 49
  man of the moment, 32
  mode influence, 520
  motives, 134
  mystic yogi, 233
  not cynical, 302
  proof of authority, 58
  puruṣarṣabha, 63
  qualifications, 400
  sannyāsa preference, 508
  scared out of his wits, 389
  Shiva, 17
  subtle animals, 376
  Universal Form affected, 423
  vision provided, 368
  yogi, 17
Arnold, Edwin, 354
arrogance, 480
artists, 374
Aryamā, 351, 358
āsana, subtle body, 343
āśaya, 349
ashvattha tree, 464
Ashvinis, 369, 381

Asita Devala, 344, 345, 461
association, crucial, 488
aṣṭanga yoga, 149, 524
astral travel, 228, 476
Asuras, 381
Aśvatthāmā,
16, 20, 22, 23, 129
ātma, defined, 65, 67
ātmamāyayā, 153
ātmanvinigrahah, 429
ātmaśuddhaye, 189
Atri, 194, 338
attachment,
cause? 437
craving fostered by, 102
intellect jarred by, 525
attention focus, 204
attractive objects, 427
austerity,
existential conditions,
336
God as, 174
necessary, 200, 486
three-part, 500
author,
Brahmā Murti, 447
divine favor, 367
liability, 317
prāṇāyāma practice, 173
search for Krishna, 546
sight of Krishna, 546
avatār, 275
avināśi, 65, 66
avyabhi, 431
avyayam, 267
Ayodhyā, 40

B

baby, as old person, 68
back-biting, 477
Balarāma, Lord, 15, 17, 348
Bali, 351
banyan tree, 464
barley, 299
beans, 299
befriend the self, 214
beggar's lifestyle, 56
beginningless Supreme
Reality, 433, 483
belief,
Arjuna's, 530
limited, 329, 330
belief in God, 483
Bengal, 504
Bhagavad Gītā,
basis, 426
distortion, 341
Mahābhārata, 218
study of, 553
universal, 224
Bhāgavata Purāṇa/
Bhāgavatam, Śrīmad,
16, 301, 338, 371
Bhairava, 386
bhakimān, 421, 422
bhaktah, 420
bhakta yogi, Nārada, 476
bhakti, 223, 258, 431, 460
bhakti yoga
buddhi yoga, 101
contrasted, 160, 530
defined, 340, 431, 475
example, 340
karma, 406, 407
Bhaktisastri, 195
Bhaktisiddhanta Sarasvati,
180, 195
Bhaktivedanta Swami,
93, 124, 125, 149, 180,
191, 270 292, 299, 305,
306, 311, 362, 379,
382, 467, 503
—gift to humanity, 346
Bharadvāja, 16
Bharata, 477
bhastrika, 173
bhāsvatā, 343
bhayāvahah, 142
Bhīma, biography,
13,15, 27, 28,
Bhishma, 129,135
biography, 21
conch, 26
Paraśurāma, 55
path of light, 301
Universal Form, 13, 372
wounded, 9
bhogāh, 39
Bhṛgu, 194, 356
Bhūriśravā, 12, 13, 23
bhūta, 241
bhūtānām, 265
bhūtānis, 471, 472
birth/death, 73, 430
birthlessness, 152
blame, 191
boarding schools, 297
body,
attachment to, 70
composite parts, 65
discipline, 500
orifices, 452
types, 425, 439, 471
wealth, 452
Brahmā,
7th. birth, 149
authority, 95
baffled, 174
dependent, 125
faces, 361
god, 446
godhead,318, 328, 338
life history, 291, 292
mental support, 294
mouth of Absolute, 175
Nārāyāṇa taught, 152
night of, 294
questioned, 264
Rudra producer, 353
sons instructed, 121
Universal Form, 376
victimized, 52
Brahmā Murti, 447
Brahma Sutra, 426
brahmacāri, 222
Brahmaloka, 253
brahman, 280, 282
Brahmanirvāṇa, 110
brahman-knowing, 297
brahmaṅo mukhe, 175
brahmarandra, 288
brahmarśis, 338
brahmavid, 196
brāhmī sthitih, 110
brahmin,
degradation, 195
lifestyle, 326
monopoly, 504
breath nutrition, 172
Bṛhad Araṇyaka
Upanishads, 298
brow chakra, 203, 286
Buddha, Gautama,
110, 114, 223, 240, 509

buddhi yoga,
Arjuna? 63
bhakti yoga, 101
defined, 81, 536
purpose of, 516
required, 342, 343
Buddhism, 197
Buddhist, 180
buffalo, 455
bug, 427

C

cactus, 276
calendar, 362
cannibal, 195, 299, 386
capillary action, 470
capitalist, 292
car, 242, 243
cār, 431
career, 158
Castagna, Paul, 139, 210
caste,
animal kingdom, 529
Gītā, 513
prevalence, 82
categories, elements, 426
caturbhujena, 396
causal body,
abstract, 456
described, 471
God inhabits, 538
location, 349
sleep, 449
causal plane, 294, 517
causal space, central, 471
celestial, geography, 300
celibacy,
inefficient type, 21
required, 498
ritual, 314
technique, 287
celibate student, 222
central psyche, 471
cetanā, 427
Chaitanya Charitamrita, 504
Chandogya Upanishad, 150, 195, 282, 297-299, 327, 504
chanting, 170, 174, 224
chariot wheel, 135
charity, 336
Chekitana, 19
chemicals, 186
child, 388
Chitraratha, 357
choice, limited, 145
choristers, 357
Christian, 180
Christianity, 274, 275, 317, 390
cigarettes, 99, 527
civil liberties, 266
clairvoyance, 402
clouds, 381
cockroaches, 455
collective being, 427
combustives, 426
commentators, 80, 81
compassion, 477
compensation, 16, 502
compensatory energy, 18
complications, 303
composite form, 425
conceit, 479-480
confidence in Krishna, 394
conflict, celestial type, 371
consciousness
affection, 293
components, 427
details of, 499
Krishna as, 353
switching, 476
consequences,
abandonment, 477
explained, 138
rejection of, 507
consumer economy, 123
contentment, 336
contributions, 217
convertible affections, 199
conviction, 427, 539
core-self, 67, 204, 471-472
corruption, 57, 85
cosmic spaces, 426
cow, 358
craving, 489
creator Brahmā, 291
criminal devotees, 322, 324
crisis, Arjuna's, 49
criticism, absence of, 477
cultural activity, basic, 124
currency, 329

D

Daitya, 359, 381
daivi, 267
Dakṣa, 149, 194
dambho, 480
darpo, 480
Dāruka, 12
Dasharatha, 225
dear to Krishna, 422
death,
Krishna as, 361
salvation, 172
subtle body, 467
deceit, 428, 480, 501
December, 362
deer rebirth, 477
defects, all action, 531
deity, reverence, 498
deliberation, 426
demigods, 273, 405
departed ancestors, 44
departed soul
material nature, 200
rebirth procedure, 68
transfer, 34
depressants, 527
depressive mode, 520, 524
desire, 123, 427
despair, 525
destination, 167, 290
destiny, 18, 333, 515
detachment,
administrator's, 418
application, 182
basis for, 109
mastery of, 180, 430
necessary, 465
practice, 141
determination, 522
Devadatra, 27
Devahuti, 357, 446
Devakī, 27, 195, 344, 396
devas, influence of, 119
devil's work, 332
devotee
contrasted, 410
criminal type, 322, 324
deviation, 340
guarantee, 320
highest, 269
Krishna tracks, 323
Krishna's approval, 80
livelihood, 320
qualifications, 406
selected, 420
types, 256
worries, 484
yogi ostracized by, 288

devotion,
buddhi compared, 81
degree of purity, 421
first instruction, 101
requirement, 431
singular interest, 269
steady, 431
unpurified type, 289
devotional excitement, 544
devotional love, 375
dhāma, 392
dharma, 540
dhīra, 63
Dhṛṣṭadyumna, 13, 14, 19
Dhṛṣṭaketu, 19
Dhṛtarāṣṭra,
alerted, 370
biography, 14
blind condition, 9
flattered, 29
dhṛtih, 360,479
Dhruva, 278
dhyāna yoga, 439
dictatorship, 123
diet,
necessary, 227
prāṇāyāma, 172, 173
rebirth related, 495, 496
yogi's, 173
digestion, 470
dimensional slips, 291
direct perception, 273
directive self, 215
disciple
management, 459
motivations, 58
/spiritual master, 302
disciplic succession, 150, 327
discipline, 394
disease, 430
disparities, 266
distortion of Gītā, 341
Diti, 23, 352, 359
divine form, 396
divine persons, assist the departed, 297
dog, 299
dog-flesh eater, 195
Dr. Vinay Kumar, 54
Draupadī, 12-14, 17, 20,30
Droṇa,
biography, 16,18
respected, 21
Universal Form, 13, 372
Virāṭa killed by, 13
weapons expert, 11, 129
drugs, 232
Drupada, 12-13
dualistic situations, 214
duhkhahā, 228
Durgā, 95, 273, 355, 386
Duryodhana,
doubts of, 24
Droṇa scolded by, 12
Krishna's alliance, 49
thighs broken, 15
Universal Form, 397
duty,
acclaimed, 530
another's, 142
Krishna style, 90
stressed, 82, 83
dvandva, 360
Dvāpara yuga, 292
Dvāraka, 29

E

$E = mc^2$, 293
ear, 427
eat less, 173
eating, 226
education, 392
Egyptians, 352
Einstein, Albert, 293
ekādaśi, 129
ekastham, 442
elevationists, 299
emotional detachment, 430
emotional energy, 522
emotional inharmonics, 449
emotions, 448, 544
empowerment, 30, 392
endeavors, 515
energy composite, 427
energy of resentment, 18
English, 354
enjoyables, 39
enjoying attitude, 199
enlightenment, 333, 502
enterprise, 162
environment,
permanent, 224
psychological, 425
Equalizer, 16
equipments, 464
escapee, 511
escapist, 210
evading, 427
evidence/Krishna, 391
evolution, 119,158,528
excitement, 544
existential status, 290
existing, 335
experience,
described, 428
impetus, 517
incomparable, 178
required, 86, 193
tools of, 465
experiencer 425, 452
exploitation, 449, 464
extensive reality, 446, 447
external appearance, 455
eye, 427
eyebrow staring, 221

F

factors, five, 515
faculty of reasoning, 471
faith, 179, 271,506
fake renunciants, 459
false pride, 480
fame, 337
farmer, compared, 237
fast of Arjuna, 129
fasting, 100, 173, 228, 314
fear of Krishna, 390
fear, 222, 335, 525
fearlessness, 335
feelings, consistency, 421
fickleness, absence, 478
Final Authority, 336
financial affairs, 459
fire body, 143
fire sacrifice, 88
firmness of mind, 429
five factors, 515
flame-resistant warriors, 388
flash of enlightenment, 333, 522
flavor, 427
focus on Krishna, 414
food
control, 227
modes, 495, 496
offerings, 320
reduction, 173
foot, 427

forbearance, 479
force of Krishna? 324
forced to act, 537
Foremost Reformer, 344
forgetfulness, 471
form of spirit, 153
four faces, 360
Four Kumaras, 338
four-handed form, 396, 401-404
fourteen authorities, 338
fraud, 480
free will, 487
freedom from deceit, 428
freedom from sins, 541
freedom, myth, 145
French, 354
friendship, scrapped, 388
fruit trees, 479
frustration, 480
fulfillments, 121

G

gambling, 362
Gandhari, 14
Gandharvas, 357
Gandhi, 335
Ganesh, 95, 273
Ganga, 360
Ganges, 360
Garbhodakashayi Vishnu, 149, 151, 338
Gargacharya, 371
Garuḍa, 359
gases, 426
Gaudiya Math, 191, 467
Gautama, 150, 327, 328
gāyatrī, 356, 362
gem, 474
genital, 427
gentleness, 478
geography, 233, 300
germ, 427
Ghatotkacha, 22
Ghora Angirasa, 195, 282, 297
ghost food, 44
ghostly plane, 276
Ghritachi, 16
gift, discussed, 502
giram, 356
Gītā
---see Bhagavad Gītā
God
antiseptic, 192
approved acts, 530
charity resistant, 192
human form, 275
integrity, 135
must act, 130
parallel forms, 350, 351
Personality? 380
responsibility, 131
godly talents, 480
gods, 273
gotra, 194
governing science, 328
government corruption, 43
grace, 212, 278
grace of guru, 224
greed, degrading, 489
guarantee,
Krishna's, 551-553
limited, 320, 329, 413
qualifications, 414
quick virtuousness, 322,324
Gudākeśa, 369
guilt, duty, 164
guru,
—-see also spiritual master
----see also teacher
astral type, 22
grace of, 224
service to, 429
gurukula, 297

H

habit,
reform, 100
substitution, 103
hack away, 465
hand, 427
Hanuman, 31, 273
happiness,
addiction, 526
attachment to, 450
degradation cause, 526
depressive type, 527
Hare Krishna mantra, 503, 504
Hari, 370
harshness, 478
hatred, 427, 479
havan, 88
hearing,
defective, 86
faulty, 331
incomplete, 329
heaven,
expiration, 299
hereafter, 314, 315
herbs, 186, 299
hereafter, 297
heroin, 186, 187
Highest Person, 472
Himalaya, 129, 354, 356
Himavat, 129
Hinduism,
critiqued, 347
gods of, 273, 313
Krishna's placement, 318
Hindus, rituals, 121
Hiranyagarbha, 338
historic persons, 69
history, Universal Form, 385
hog, 299
honor, 501
hostilities, 498
hrīh, 478
human being,
composite, 427
impulsive, 449
human form, God's, 275
human psychology, 122
humility, 428

I

icchā, 427
ideas, zone of, 517
ideation level, 294
idiot, 525
ignorance, mode of, 521
immoral devotees, 321, 324
immorality/destiny, 515
immunity, 159
impartiality, 335
impersonalism, 218
impersonalist, 409-411
implications, 178
impulsions, 142
impulsive mode, 449
inaction, 117, 119
inattentiveness, 449
independence, 140, 493
indifference, objects, 429
Indra, 166, 234, 273, 314, 353, 358, 381

inducement, 172
infamy, 337
inherent forces, 191
initiation, 365
initiative,
gadget, 464
living space, 426
motivated, 430
injustices, 372
innate forces, 191
insecure world, 291
insensitivity, 449
insight
development, 63
hereafter, 62,
intellect's, 341
lack of, 343
required, 444
switching, 398
types, 401
yoga, 81
instinct, 426, 482
instinct for yoga, 254
instrument, 517, 515
integrity of God, 135
intellect,
attachment jars, 525
gadget, 464
living space, 426
memory etched by, 232
passion obscures, 143
psychic tool, 522
states of, 84
intelligence, 331, 426
intention,
details, 502
motivation, 162
interest, spiritual type, 421
intimate victimization, 140
invisible world, 293
īśam, 376
Islam, 390
isolation,
conditional, 116
required, 226, 431
item, 517

J

Jahnu, 360
Jaivali, 150, 327
Janaka,
137, 476, 510, 516, 517
Janaloka, 253, 453
japa, 356, 500
Jarāsandha, 28
Jayadratha, 20
Jesus Christ,
95, 274, 275, 317
jīvanam, 264
jñāna yoga,
application, 475
approved, 311
defined, 340, 431, 476
Uddava, 407
jñānadīpena, 343
jñānam, 428
jñani, 167, 256, 269
jñāninah, 179
judging behavior, 455
justice acts, 188

K

Kailash Hill, 22
Kali yuga, 292
Kālī, 273, 386
Kāma, 358
Kāmadhuk, 358
kāmakāmi, 109, 133
kāman āśritya, 483
Kamsa, 153
Kandarpa, 358
kapidhvajah, 31
Kapila Muni, 357, 446
karma yoga,
ancient, 151
Arjuna's training, 185
bhakti compared,
399, 406, 407
defined,
116-117, 340, 431
described, 181, 460
details, 209, 418
inferior type, 415
Janaka's, 47
proficiency, 413
sannyāsa compared, 207
teaching, 327
training, 325
worship compared, 530
yoga required, 183
karma yogi,
compared, 476
contrasted, 216
described, 116-117
karmi, 256
Karṇa, 21, 22, 384
kartā, 515
Karttavirya, 360
karttikas, 355
Karttikeya, 355
Kashi, 19
Kashyapa, 23
Katha Upanishad, 463
Kekayas, 19
kevalam, 164
Kichaka, 13, 28
kirtan songs, 170
Kīrtih, 361
knowledge, 176, 331, 480
Kratu, 194, 338
Krishna,
appearance,
153, 155, 273, 274
approval, 80
basis of all, 263
body, 274
cause non-deteriorating,
314
collapse cause, 314
concern for Arjuna, 540
condition of existence,
284
confusion-less, 329
cooperation with, 521
Deity Ultimate, 313
devotee tracked, 323
distinguished, 318
Education itself, 392
Equalizer, 16
evidence about, 391
exceptional, 329
exempt, 158
experience of all bodies,
425
father, 313
first creation, 265
Foremost Reformer, 344
foundation, 314
friend, 314
Ghora Aṅgiras, 195
God, 313
Godhood question, 380
grandfather of universe,
313
gross actions, 135
immunity granted, 159
integrity, 135
interest in Arjuna, 540
judge, 313
life story, 321
location of Reality, 392
lotus-eyed, 367

Krishna continued,
master, 313
material body, 153, 274
material form, 402, 404
material nature, 269
memory 151, 152
mother, 313
objective, primal, 313
observer, 313
offerings questioned, 319
one-sided influence, 304
origin, 314
Person of Confidence, 60
place, 466
power sampled, 364
producer, 313
promises, 319
proof about, 314
rejected, 268
reservoir of energies, 314
residence, 295
schooling, 282
sexual affection, 266
shelter, 314
spirits contrasted, 153
stressed, 284, 326
sum total Reality, 392
supporter, 313
Supreme Person? 339, 473
Supreme Source, 339
supreme teacher, 208
two-handed form, 402, 403
ultimate aim, 259
ultimate goal of life, 207
unchanging, 267
unerring one, 31
unknown, 276
Upanishads taught by, 195
Vishnu, 370, 383
Vishnu's incarnation, 219
Vishnu's source, 359
warriors contrasted, 389
work, 406
yoga unnecessary, 181
Krishna-Balarāma, Śrī Śrī, 104, 125
Krishna Conscious Society, 546
Krishna Consciousness
course, 363
lessons, 264
resistance, 390
training, 352, 357
Krishna Icon, 546
Kritavarma, 19
kriya masters, 286
kriya practice, 288
kriya yoga, technique, 287
krodhah, 480
Kṛpa, 129
Kṛpacarya, 22
Kṛpi, 22
kṛtsnavit, 136
ksamā, 361, 479
kṣāntih, 428
kṣarah, 471
kṣetrajña, 452
Kumar, Vinay, 54
Kumaras, 167, 176
Kumbhakarna, 386
kundalini yoga, 288
Kuntī, 14, 384
Kuntibhoja, 19
Kuvera, 354

L

lack of knowledge, 480
lack of pride, 428
Lahiri Mahasaya, 286
Lakshmi, 95
law of compensation, 16
law of habit, 172
laziness, 117, 449
legal procedure, 363
legends, 352
liabilities, 138
liberation,
dedication to, 204
life force related, 201
details, 110-111, 297
questioned, 456
rare, 140
requirements, 466
sought, 169
life energy,
control, 277
dissipation, 525
mode changes, 522
life force,
control, 349
curbing, 478
discipline of, 499
gadget, 464
instinct, 426
liabilities of, 201
purification, 332
sleep needs of, 228
light of luminaries, 435
liking/disliking, 141
lineage, 194, 327
lion, 359
liquids, 426
liquor, 527
living space, parts, 427
location,
factor, 515
Krishna, 391
personality gravity, 391
hereafter, 167
spiritual type, 232, 287
Lord of all beings, 538
lotus-eyed, Krishna, 367
LSD, 186, 187
lungs, 170
lust,
creation's cause? 483
degrading, 489
luxury,
acquirement, 253
motivation, 315

M

mad persons, 527
Madhusudana, 52
Madhvācārya, 197
Mādrī, 14
Mahābhārata, 6, 16, 125, 149, 301, 363, 474
mahad brahma, 446, 447
Maharloka, 253, 453
Mahatma Gandhi, 335
mahātma, 290
Maitreya, 439, 447
majesty of God, 371
Mānasa Pake, 538
mangrove, 464
manifestation details, 294
mantra power of, 478
mantra, 170, 237
Manu, 149
manufacturer, 242, 243
Manus, 14, 338
mārdavan, 478

mārgaśīrśo, 362
Marīci, 194, 338, 352
marijuana, 99, 186, 187
Markandeya, 277, 278
marriages, 43
Maruts, 352, 369
Mary, 275
material creation, 261
material existence,
  components, 330, 331
  massive, 464
material nature,
  actor, 494
  all-pervasive, 527
  cause? 437
  detachment from, 465
  dominant, 455
  influences, 308
  intimate, 140
  invisible part, 295
  Krishna's, 270
  prominent, 136
  reality unto itself, 465
  supernatural, 267
  unstable, 283
  worthwhile, 309
matter, abstract type, 446
maunam, 500
Mayans, 352
medhā, 361
meditation,
  addiction, 232
  details, 172
  soul focus, 439
  ultimate type, 285, 286
  useless, 118
memory, 232
mental understanding, 69
mentality, varies, 525
mergence, 167
Meru, 354
mind,
  control, 246
  discipline, 500
  faulty, 331
  gadget, 464
  Krishna as, 353
  penned in, 236
  sense organ, 427
  senses relationship, 146
  sensual monitor, 523
mind-set, 296
missionary, exploitation, 322, 324
mist, 381
modes of material nature,
  contrasted, 522
  guarantees, 523
  attachment to, 450
modesty, 478
modifications, 436
mokṣaparāyanah, 204
monitor, 359, 523
monkey banner, 31
moods,
  actions influenced, 115
  explained, 109
  focus on, 63
  rated, 455
moon,
  destination, 297
  hereafter, 299
  Krishna as, 352
  Krishna supports, 470
  Krishna's searchlights, 378
morality, 34, 363
mother/ son, 77
motivated actions, 180
motivation,
  approval, 312
  controlling force, 493
  details, 502
  human nature, 90
  intention compared, 162
  paramount, 135
  shift of, 478
mouth of spiritual existence, 175
movements, 515
movies, 232
mṛtyuh, 361
Mudgal, 253
mudrās, 286
Mukti, 223
mūlādhāra, 221
muni, defined, 98
music, 232, 499
mystery of Universal Form, 384
mystic
  containers, 19
  insight, 62, 341
  insight, Vedas, 89
  seers, 64
  terrain, 233

N

Nachiketa, 463
Nāga, 358
Nahusha, 28
Nakula, 17
Nanda Gopa, 383
Nārada, 16, 183, 194, 264, 278, 340, 344,.345, 357, 383, 461, 476, 504, 538
Narasingha, 359
Nārāyāṇa, 152, 291, 313, 328, 338, 351, 370, 396
narcotics, 527
nāsikāgram, 221
nātimānitā, 479
nature of one's nature, 213
nirvāṇa, 110, 197, 213, 223
niyatāhārāh, 173
niyatasya, 511
non-diminishing factor, 65
non-existing, 335
nonpossessiveness, 219
non-violence,
  defined, 428
  explained, 128
  Gītā, 92, 335, 476
  judicial violence, 188
  ultimate type, 421
nose focus, 221
nose, 427
November, 362
nyāyyam, 515

O

obeisances, 392
oblation-eating mouths, 379
obligations, faultless? 530
obligatory action, 511
observer, God, 438
odor, 427
offerings, 319, 320
old age, 430
Om Tat Sat, 503, 504
Om, 503-505
Omkār, 356
omnipotence, 371
omnipresence, 371
omniscience, 371
one syllable, 356
oneness, 312, 518
oneness with God, 262, 518
only begotten son, 274, 275
opinion, mode of, 519

opportunity, 507, 509
opposition to Krishna, 390
optical energy focus, 203
oral transmission, 426
organs, utilizing type, 427

P

pacificism, 477, 513
Padmalochana, 28
pain, 334
palm tree, 129
Pampa, 88
Pāñcajanya, 27
Panchala, 13
Pandavas,
biography, 14, 15
politics renounced, 534
Pandit,
modern meaning, 194
qualifications, 463
Pandit Shukracharya, 363
Pandu, 14
pāpena, 188
paradise, 166, 314, 315
paradox, 304
parallel worlds, 294
param brahma, 344
Paramātma, 167
Paramhamsa Yogananda, 172
paramparā, king's, 150
Paraśar Muni, 359
parasites, 465
Paraśurāma, 16, 55, 216, 327, 359, 360
parāyanāh, 440
Parikṣit, 22
parjanya, 124
pāruṣyam, 480
passion,
compared, 526
enemy, 143, 144
force of, 143
misleads, 145
past life memory, 254
Patañjali, 148, 186, 202
paternal desire, 21
patience, 333, 428
Pāvaka, 354
pavitra, 344
peace with God, 222
peace, spiritual, 477
peacock, 455
penance, God as, 174
performer, mode of, 497
permitter, God, 438
perpetual energy, 452
perplexity, 111
Person of Confidence, 60
personal initiative, 426
personalist, 412
personality gravity, 391
Personified Veda, 125
persons, 471
philosophers, 476
piṇḍa, 44
planetary systems, 42
pleasure, 334, 427
political control, 369
political science, 150
political work, 406
popularity, 78, 459
prabhu, 191, 450
Pradyumna, 358
Prahlād, 209-210, 359
prajāpatih, 119
prakṛti, 266
prakṛtim svam, 270
prāṇa, 266, 522
Praṇava, 356
prāṇāyāma, 170-172, 204, 286, 349
Prasad, Ramananda, 9
prasādam, 104
praśānam, 150, 328
Prativindhya, 20
pratyāhār, 99, 107, 524
Pravāhana Jaivali, 150
Pravahana, 327
prayata, 319
predispositions, 482
preference, 182
pride, 428, 480, 525
Primal Cause, 330
Primal God, 402
Primal Person, 377
Primal Vishnu, 402
primitive man, 119
Priyavrata, 278
production, yields 124
proficiency, 246-248
progeny,
mental type, 338
transfer, 34
promise of Krishna,
details, 322, 323, 324
questioned, 319
promises,
religious, 277
warped, 444
property control, 176
Providence,
grace of, 104,105
powerful, 29
pṛthivīpate, 29
psyche
control, 277
central, 471
composites, 215
supreme soul, 283
survives death, 487
psychiatrists, 476
psychic equipments, 464
psychic register, 27
psychic tools, 333
psychologists, 476
psychology,
changes in, 140
survives death, 467
psychotic persons, 527
Pulaha, 194, 338
Pulastya, 194, 338
pundits, 86
punya, 301
Purāṇas, 125, 358, 426
pure devotion, 407
purification,
self, 189
stages, 226, 227
purity, 421, 429, 479
Purujit, 19
Purūrava, 157
puruṣas, 471

Q,R

questions, on God, 281
Rādhā, 21
radical, 210
rahasi sthitah ekākī, 431
Rakshas, 354
Rāma, 40, 88, 128, 225, 273, 359, 360, 504
Ramana Maharshi, 229, 230
Ramanand Prasad, 210
ramate, 199
Rāmāyaṇa, 88, 225, 348, 354, 426, 504
rate of progression, 312
Rāvaṇa, 52, 194, 354, 386
reality, absolute, 333

Reality,
beginningless, 433
recognition of, 477
reasoning, 471
rebirth,
ancestor's, 44
animal life, 489
common type, 453
degenerate type, 488
diet affects, 495, 496
process, 297
yogis, 252, 253
reform, hereafter, 39
reincarnation,
degenerate type, 488
process, 297
responsibility, 62,
relationship
God's, 394
proportional, 316, 317
spiritual type, 293
Supreme Person, 295
variations, 35
reliance, on Krishna 263, 325
religion, 118, 296
religious ceremony
described, 119
mode of, 497
requirements, 498
remorse, duty, 164
renunciant,
fake type, 459
profile, 206
renunciation,
consistent type, 184
motivated actions, 180
yoga, 320
reproduction, 338
repulsion, 427
resentment energy, 18
resentments, 498
reservations, 530
reserved method, 208-210
resistance to Krishna, 390
respect, 501
respiration, 470
responsibility, 263, 494
result-motivated beings, 127
retirement, Pandavas, 534
retrogression, 168, 292
reverence, 373, 501
reversal of tendencies, 487
reward-seeking, 139
rice, 299
Rig Veda, 313
righteousness, 15
ritual technicians, 86
rituals, described, 314
roots of material nature, 464
Ṛṣabha, 477
Rudras, 353, 369, 376

S

sacrifice,
described, 119
eating aspect, 123
Krishna's definition, 205
mode of, 497
particulars, 498
spiritual type, 165
sad, sat, 506
sadistic person, 477
Sahadeva, 17
Saineva, 12
salvation,
death, 172
imaginary? 296
monopoly, 267
worthwhile, 235
Śalya, 52
Sama Veda, 313, 353, 356, 362
samadarśinah, 194, 195
samādhi, details, 172
sambhavāmi, 153
sambhavi mudra, 286
Sambidananda das, 195
Sambuka, 504
same vision, 194, 195
samghātas, 427
Samkhya mystics, 93
samkhya philosophers, 476
samnyāsa,
—see sannyāsa
samnyāsi
—see sannyāsi
samsāra, 20
samsāris, 224
samyama, 236
samyamī, 136, 248
samyatā, 218
Sanaka, 338
Sananda, 338
Sanātana, 338
Sanat-Kumara, 338
sandhi rules, 335
Sandipani Muni, 297
sanity, 332
Sanjaya,
1st narrator, 544
alerted Dhṛtarāṣṭra, 370
biography, 14
clairvoyant, 402
spiritual emotions, 544
Universal Form, 544, 545
sannyāsa,
defined, 507
explained, 508, 510, 514
yoga, 320
sannyāsi,
defined, 321
fake type, 459
profile, 206
Sanskrit literature, 29
Sanskrit, 354-356
Santanu, 22
Santanu, 372
śāntim, 224
śāntir, 477
Sargeant, Winthrop, 191, 261
Sat principle, 512
sat, 506
Satya Nārāyāṇa, 273
Satya yuga, 292
Sātyaki, 12, 13, 23
Satyaloka, 453
satyam, 477
Satyavatī, 33, 344
Saubhari, 238
śaucam, 429, 479
savior, 267
schizophrenic, 105, 527
scripture, theory of, 64
Secretary of State, 14
secrets, 363
seeing the same, 240, 241
selection, 494
self
composites, 215
control, 333
correction, 235
effort, 212, 213
enemy, 214
focus on, 237

self continued,
focus, 224, 229, 230, 236
harnessed, 334
location, 524
lower, 186
purification, 219
realization, 260
restraint, 429
will, 487
selflessness, 477
sense of security, 472
senses,
adjust psyche, 101
hereafter, 472
influence described, 106
perceiving type, 427
supernatural type, 370
ten and one, 427
sensual energy, 522
sensual reliance, 141
sensual retraction, 107
servants of Krishna, 508
service to teacher, 429
sesame, 299
seven sages, 338
sexual affection, 266
sexual restraint, 314
sex-urge, 228
Shaibya, 19
Shankaracharya, 197, 218, 223, 353
Shantanika, 20
Sharabhanga, 225
Sharadvata, 22
shareholder, 467
Shibis, 19
Shiva, 273, 318, 328, 355, 376
Arjuna met, 129
Arjuna, 17
authority, 95
God? 291
Shivananda, 173
Shrutakarma, 20
Shrutakirti, 20
Shuka, 216
Shura, 19
Siddhas, 381
Śikhandī, 13, 14, 18
silence, 363, 500
similarity, 240, 241
singers, celestial, 357
single foundation, 442
Sir Edwin Arnold, 354
Sir Paul Castagna, 139, 162
Sishupala, 17
SltadevI, 128
Skanda, 355
skin, 427
sleep
control, 228
consciousness, 525
subtle body, 449
uses, 449
Smara, 358
smṛtih, 361
solar families, 352
solids, 426
solitude, 431
Soma, king, 299
soma, subtle food, 299
Somadatta, 23
son/mother, 77
songs, 499
sorrow, 525
soul,
—see spirit
sound,
attractive object, 427
medicinal, 363
mystic skills, 186
Om, 356
repetition, 500
space, 426
Spanish, 354
species, rebirth, 299
speech, discipline, 499, 500
spirit,
attachment, 189
cause? 437
composition, 239
consciousness producer, 443
control, 429
defined, 65, 67
dynamic, 118
energy supplier, 190
energy type, 262
focus, 218
form, 153, 198
Krishna contrasted, 153
Krishna's shareholder, 467
location, 524
material energy mind enclosed, 143
perpetual energy source, 452
spirit continued,
psychic affection, 68
purification, 189
responsibility, 62
similar, 194, 195
spiritual nature, on-going, 239
subtle accessories, 424
/supersoul, 195
three kinds, 472
token master, 190
two kinds, 471, 472
unaffected, 443
spiritual advancement, 312
spiritual emotion, 544
spiritual form, 235
spiritual groups, envy, 209
spiritual level, 110
spiritual master,
astral type, 288
cheating, 329
disciple, 302
faith in, 179
finances, 459
grace of, 224
liberated? 456
naïve type, 58
questioned, 139
rare, 440
scriptural theory, 64
service to, 429
specialized, 177
weakness of, 333
yogi type, 288
spiritual objects? 293
spiritual perception, 446
spiritual plane, 198
spiritual world, 466
spoiled child, 388
spring, 362
Śrī Śrī Krishna-Balarāma, 104
Sridhara Maharaja, 118, 135, 166, 180, 191, 305, 306, 338, 358, 361, 362, 467,
śrīh, 361
Śrīmad Bhāgavatam, 125, 194, 264, 321, 432, 474
śruti, 95
stability, 429
sthairyam, 429
sthitaprajña, 110

stimulants, 228
stool odor, 173
storm creators, 352
straight forwardness, 429
striving element, 278
strong-mindedness, 479
struggle of Supreme Spirit, 479
student, teacher, 302
study of Gītā, 553
Subhadra, 17, 30
substitution, 103
subtle body, sleep, 449, 528
subtle plane, 294
subtle stuff, 177
succession, 150, 327
sun, 297, 378
sun god, 300
super experiencer, 517
supernatural level, 385
supernatural people, 380
supernatural sight, 370
supernatural tree, 463, 464
Supersoul
  common factor, 195, 441
  consciousness producer, 443
  contrasted, 442
  equipment provider, 242
  location, 349
  path of, 167
  Supreme Reality, 434-435
  within psyche, 283
Supervising God, 518
support, material nature's, 521
Supreme Focus, 422
Supreme Person, 295
Supreme Spirit,
  described, 285
  struggle of, 479
supreme teacher, 207
supreme yoga, 545
Supreme Personality, 472
Surendra, 314
surface, 427
surrender, 58, 137, 541
Surya, 95, 273
Susharma, 13
Sutasoma, 20
svabhāva, 191
Svargaloka, 166, 234, 362, 453
swindlers, 362

T

tad, tat, 505, 505
taḍāsana, 129
tapa, 224
tapasvis, 256
Tapoloka, 253, 453
tat tvam asi, 505
tattvadarśih, 64, 136, 137
tattvavit, 136
teachers, 177, 302, 429, 530
tejah, 479
tejomayam, 397, 398
tendencies,
  cultivation of, 528
  interchangeable, 487
  origin, 528
texture of existence, 284
theory of creation, 483
thieves, 121, 122
thighs of Draupadi, 15
thinking pattern, 486
thinking control, 218
thunderbolt statement, 510
time,
  calculations, 291
  delay, 385
  Krishna as, 388
  monitor, 359
Titans, 359
tolerance, 429
tongue, 427
tortoise, 100
tradition, 45
trance addiction, 232
tranquility, 334
transcendental form, 153
transfer to Sat, 512
translation, 354
translators, vary, 81
transmigration, 299, 424, 482
transvestite, 18
tree
  growth, 71
  rebirth as, 299
Tretā, yuga, 292
trickery, 362, 480
Trigartas, 13
truthfulness, 333
two word compound, 360
two-handed form, 402
tyāga, 477, 507-510
tyāgi, 320

U

Uchchaihshravah, 357
Uddhava, 183, 407, 439, 446
unaffected, 471, 472
Univeral Form,
  Arjuna clarified by, 395
  Arjuna convinced, 423
  armed, 377
  Bhishma, 16
  celestial beings, 380
  cooperation, 521
  drawing energy, 386
  Droṇa, 16
  Duryodhana,397
  feared, 375
  important, 329
  infinite, 377
  ladies absent, 383
  location, 373
  Primal Person, 377
  qualifications, 400
  revealed, 369
  scary, 511
  shocking, 373
  shunned,383
  viewers, 371, 379
unmani mudra, 286
unmanifest factor, 426
unmanifested existence, 295
upadraṣṭā, 440
Upanishads, 64, 150, 282, 297
Upaplavya, 13
urgency, 325
urges, mind goaded, 523
Urukrama, 351
Urvashi, 157
usefulness to Universal Form, 388
Ushana, 363
Uṣmapās, 381
Uttamauja, 19

V

Vaikuntha, 223
Vaishnava gurus, 406
Vaiśvānara, 470
Vajra, 358
vāk, 361

Vālmīki, 88, 225, 348, 504
Vāmana, 351
Vanih, 143
vapor bodies, 381
varṇa, 158
Varuna, 358
Vāsava, 353
Vasiṣṭha, 128, 194, 358
Vasudeva, 282, 363, 383, 396
Vāsuki, 358
Vasus, 354, 381
Vayuputra, 15
Veda,
- Brahma produced, 125
- critiqued, 254, 255
- manual, 88
- original, 353
- Personified, 125
- split worship, 313
- well compared, 89

Vedanta, 344
Vedanta Sutra, 426
Vedantist, 275
Vedavādis, 84
vedavit, 463
Vedic rites, 194
verbs, 356
Vibhīṣaṇa, 52
vice-prone person, 477
Vichitravirya, 14, 21, 33
victimization, 140
victims, 465
victory, 363
view, mode of, 519
vigor, 479
vikārān, 436
Vikarṇa, 23
Vinata, 359
violence, 188, 421
Virata, 12, 13, 18
Virocana, 351
Vishnu, 125, 174, 318, 328
Vishnu, Purana, 359
Vishvadevas, 381
Vishvamitra,
—see Viśvāmitra
vision switching, 396
vision, types, 401
visual focus, 203, 204
visualizing searchlights, 378
Viśvāmitra, 128, 140, 238, 328, 460
Vitteśa, 354
Vivasvān, 351, 373, 511
Vivasvat, 149, 151
Vivekananda, Swami, 167
vocal cord, 427
vow, 222, 310
Vrikodhara, 15
Vrishni family, 363
vulgarity, 293
Vyāsadeva, 14, 129, 216, 344, 345, 363, 383, 461

W

warriors, Universal Form, 385
weathermen, 352
well, 89
whole, 427
widows, 45
wife, yogi's, 222
wind, purifies, 359
wisdom, 363
wishful thinking, 517
wishing, insufficient, 486
witness, Supreme Lord, 440
women, qualities, 361
word division, 158
words, 356
working power, 137
worlds, adjacent, 294
worries, endless, 484
worship,
- Arjuna's, 530
- deviation, 271
- mistaken type, 318
- mode reliant, 310

writer,
—see author

Y

Yādhava, 12
yajña, defined, 356
yajñārtha, 118
Yajur Veda, 313
Yaksha, 354, 381
Yama, 358
Yamaraja, teachings, 463
yatacittātmā, 218
yatīnām, 202
yearning, perpetual, 144
yield-conscious, 127
yield-hungry beings, 139
yoga groups, 209
yoga of renunciation, 320
yoga practice,
- ancient, I 51
- application, 246
- application, 92, 219, 234, 475
- bhakti contrasted, 216
- defined, 149, 178, 220
- described, 207
- details, 172, 173
- essential discipline, 431
- life force curbed, 228
- lite long, 212
- necessary, 181
- not general, 226
- purpose, 226
- requirements, 217
- reserved method, 210
- standard discipline, 339
- supreme type, 545
- yoga, definite, 232

Yoga Sūtras, 148, 186, 202
Yogananda, 286
yogeshwarananda, 191
yogi,
- advanced type, 288
- destination, 251, 252, 253, 290
- devotee types, 256, 257
- fall, 238, 460
- Krishna contact, 243
- Krishna focus, 289
- Prahlād met, 210
- rebirth, 252, 253
- stressed, 216
- types, 149
- Vedas transcended, 254, 255

yoni mudra, 286
Yudhāmanyu, 19
Yudhishthira,
- biography, 14, 15
- person of righteousness, 28
- total renunciation, 533, 534
- traditional respects, 51, 52
- yogi, 15

Yuyudhāna, 12
Yuyutsū, 52,

Z

zone of ideas, 517

LIST OF TEACHERS

Gaudiya Vaishnava teacher:
Śrīla Bhaktivedanta Swami Prabhupada
Haṭha yoga teacher:
Swami Vishnudevananda
Kundalini yoga teacher:
Mahayogi *Śrī* Harbhajan Singh
Celibacy yoga teachers:
Swami Shivananda,
Śrīla Yogiraj Yogeshwarananda
Purity-of-the-psyche yoga teacher:
Śrīla Yogiraj Yogeshwarananda
***Kriyā* yoga teachers:**
Śrīla Babaji Mahasaya,
Siddha Swami Muktananda
Brahma yoga teacher:
Siddha Swami Nityananda

About the Author

Michael Beloved (Yogi Madhvāchārya) took his current body in 1951 in Guyana. In 1965, while living in Trinidad, he instinctively began doing yoga postures and trying to make sense of the supernatural side of life.

Later on, in 1970, in the Philippines, he approached a Martial Arts Master named Mr. Arthur Beverford, explaining to the teacher that he was seeking a yoga instructor. Mr. Beverford identified himself as an advanced disciple of Rishi Singh Gherwal, an astanga yoga master.

Mr. Beverford taught the traditional Astanga Yoga with stress on postures, attentive breathing and brow chakra centering meditation. In 1972, Madhvāchārya entered the Denver Colorado Ashram of Kundalini Yoga Master Śrī Harbhajan Singh. There he took instruction in Bhastrika Prāṇāyāma and its application to yoga postures. He was supervised mostly by Yogi Bhajan's disciple named Prem Kaur.

In 1979 Madhvāchārya formally entered the disciplic succession of the Brahmā-Madhava Gaudiya Sampradaya through Swami Kirtanananda, who was a prominent sannyāsi disciple of the Great Vaishnava Authority Śrī Swami Bhaktivedanta Prabhupada, the exponent of devotion to Sri Krishna.

After carefully studying and practicing the devotional process introduced by Sri Swami Bhaktivedanta Prabhupada, Madhvacharya was inspired to do this translation of the Bhagavād_Gītā, which initially was published hard bound, under the title of Bhagavad Gītā in Its Own Time and Place, by Asian Printery, Gujarat, India. The translation without commentary is published as Bhagavad Gītā English. The translation with sansikrit text and word-for-word meanings, is published as Bhagavad Gītā Revealed.

This publication does not concern making or controlling disciples. It is designed to give readers insight to what Sri Krishna and Arjuna discussed in the discourse, without any effort to convince or convert. It is free of missionary overtones.

Regarding those who carefully study the Gītā and those who hear it with confidence, Sri Krishna said this:

I would be loved by the devotee who by sacrifice of his knowledge, will study this sacred conversation of ours. This is My opinion. (18.70)

Even the person who hears with confidence, without ridiculing is freed. He should attain the happy worlds where persons of pious actions reside. (18.71)

Publications

English Series

Bhagavad Gita English

Anu Gita English

Markandeya Samasya English

Yoga Sutras English

Uddhava Gita English

These are in 21st Century English, very precise and exacting. Many Sanskrit words which were considered untranslatable into a Western language are rendered in precise, expressive and modern English, due to the English language becoming the world's universal means of concept conveyance.

Three of these books are instructions from Krishna. **In Bhagavad Gita English** and **Anu Gita English**, the instructions were for Arjuna. In the **Uddhava Gita English,** it was for Uddhava. Bhagavad Gita and Anu Gita are extracted from the

Mahabharata. Uddhava Gita was extracted from the 11th Canto of the Srimad Bhagavatam (Bhagavata Purana). One of these books, the **Markandeya Samasya English** is about Krishna, as described by Yogi Markandeya, who survived the cosmic collapse and reached a divine child in whose transcendental body, the collapsed world was existing. Another of these books, the **Yoga Sutras English,** is the detailed syllabus about yoga practice.

My suggestion is that you read **Bhagavad Gita English**, the **Anu Gita English, the Markandeya Samasya English,** the **Yoga Sutras English** and lastly the **Uddhava Gita English**, which is much more complicated and detailed.

For each of these books we have at least one commentary, which is published separately. Thus your particular interest can be researched further in the commentaries.

The smallest of these commentaries and perhaps the simplest is the one for the Anu Gita. We published its commentary as the Anu Gita Explained. The Bhagavad Gita explanations were published in three distinct targeted commentaries. The first is Bhagavad Gita Explained, which sheds lights on how people in the time of Krishna and Arjuna regarded the information and applied it. Bhagavad Gita is an exposition of the application of yoga practice to cultural activities, which is known in the Sanskrit language as karma yoga.

Interestingly, Bhagavad Gita was spoken on a battlefield just before one of the greatest battles in the ancient world. A warrior, Arjuna, lost his wits and had no idea that he could apply his training in yoga to political dealings. Krishna, his charioteer, lectured on the spur of the moment to give Arjuna the skill of using yoga proficiency in cultural dealings including how to deal with corrupt officials on a battlefield.

The second commentary is the Kriya Yoga Bhagavad Gita. This clears the air about Krishna's information on the science of kriya yoga, showing that its techniques are clearly described free of charge to anyone who takes the time to read Bhagavad Gita. Kriya yoga concerns the battlefield which is the psyche of the living being. The internal war and the mental and emotional forces which are hostile to self-realization are dealt with in the kriya yoga practice.

The third commentary is the Brahma Yoga Bhagavad Gita. This shows what Krishna had to say outright and what he hinted about which concerns the brahma yoga practice, a mystic process for those who mastered kriya yoga.

There is one commentary for the **Markandeya Samasya English**. The title of that publication is Krishna Cosmic Body.

There are two commentaries to the Yoga Sutras. One is the Yoga Sutras of Patanjali and the other is the Meditation Expertise. These give detailed explanations of the process of Yoga.

For the Uddhava Gita, we published the Uddhava Gita Explained. This is a large book and requires concentration and study for integration of the information. Of the books which deal with transcendental topics, my opinion is that the discourse between Krishna and Uddhava has the complete information about the realities in existence. This book is the one which removes massive existential ignorance.

Meditation Series

Meditation Pictorial

Meditation Expertise

Core-Self Discovery

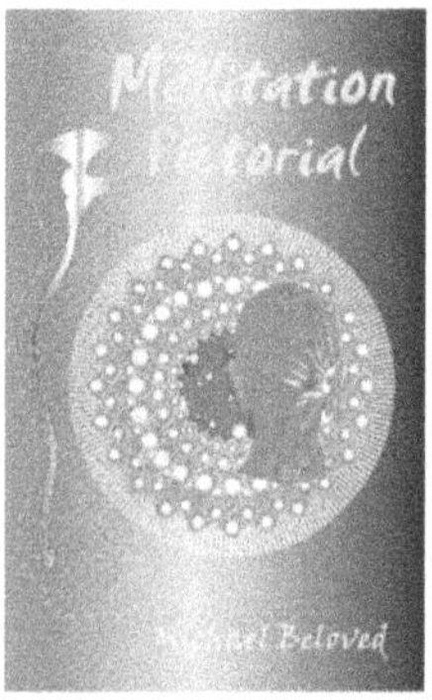

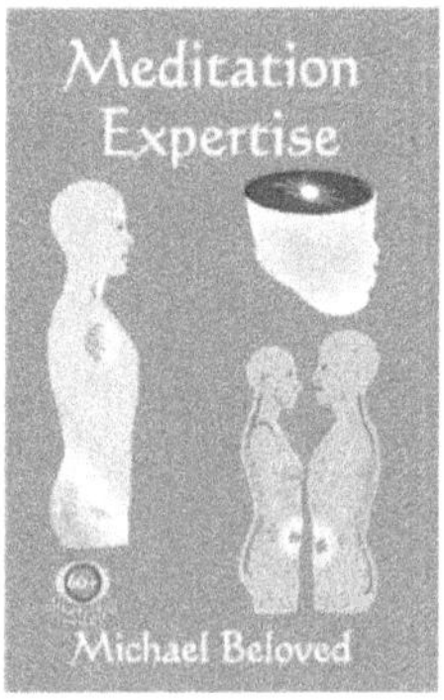

The specialty of these books is the mind diagrams which profusely illustrate what is written. This shows exactly what one has to do mentally to develop and then sustain a meditation practice.

In the **Meditation Pictorial**, one is shown how to develop psychic insight, a feature without which meditation is imagination and visualization, without any mystic experience per se.

In the **Meditation Expertise**, one is shown how to corral one's practice to bring it in line with the classic syllabus of yoga which Patanjali lays out as the ashtanga yoga eight-staged practice.

In **Core-Self Discovery**, one is taken though the course of pratyahar sensual energy withdrawal which is the 5th stage of yoga in the Patanjali ashtanga eight-process complete system of yoga practice. These events lead to the discovery of a core-self which is surrounded by psychic organs in the head of the subtle body. This product has a DVD component for teachers and self-teaching students.

These books are profusely illustrated with mind diagrams showing the components of psychic consciousness and the inner design of the subtle body.

Explained Series

Bhagavad Gita Explained

Uddhava Gita Explained

Anu Gita Explained

The specialty of these books is that they are free of missionary intentions, cult tactics and philosophical distortion. Instead of using these books to add credence to a philosophy, meditation process, belief or plea for followers, I spread the information out so that a reader can look through this literature and freely take or leave anything as desired.

When Krishna stressed himself as God, I stated that. When Krishna laid no claims for supremacy, I showed that. The reader is left to form an independent opinion about the validity of the information and the credibility of Krishna.

There is a difference in the discourse with Arjuna in the Bhagavad Gita and the one with Uddhava in the Uddhava Gita. In fact these two books may appear to contradict each other. In the Bhagavad Gita, Krishna pressured Arjuna to complete social duties. In the Uddhava Gita, Krishna insisted that Uddhava should abandon the same.

The Anu Gita is not as popular as the Bhagavad Gita but it is the conclusion of that text. Anu means what is to follow, what proceeds. In this discourse, an anxious Arjuna request that Krishna should repeat the Bhagavad Gita and again show His supernatural and divine forms.

However Krishna refuses to do so and chastises Arjuna for being a disappointment in forgetting what was revealed. Krishna then cites a celestial yogi, a near-perfected being, who explained the process of transmigration in vivid detail.

Commentaries

Yoga Sutras of Patanjali

Meditation Expertise

Krishna Cosmic Body

Anu Gita Explained

Bhagavad Gita Explained

Kriya Yoga Bhagavad Gita

Brahma Yoga Bhagavad Gita

Uddhava Gita Explained

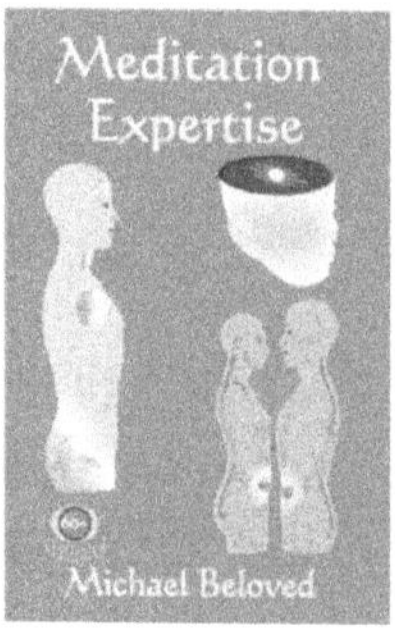

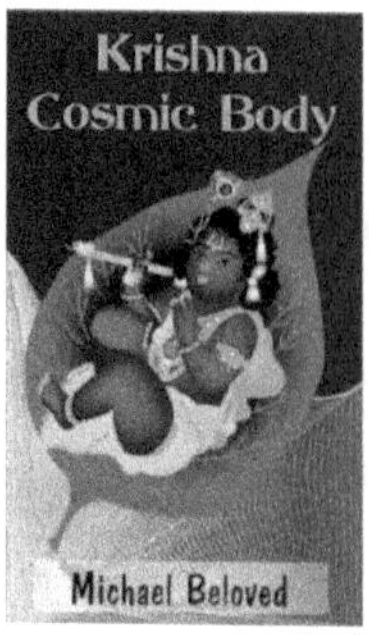

Yoga Sutras of Patanjali is the globally acclaimed text book of yoga. This has detailed expositions of yoga techniques. Many kriya techniques are vividly described in the commentary.

Meditation Expertise is an analysis and application of the Yoga Sutras. This book is loaded with illustrations and has detailed explanations of secretive advanced meditation techniques which are called kriyas in the Sanskrit language.

Krishna Cosmic Body is a narrative commentary on the Markandeya Samasya portion of the Aranyaka Parva of the Mahabharata. This is the detailed description of the dissolution of the world, as experienced by the great yogin Markandeya who transcended the cosmic deity, Brahma, and reached Brahma's source who is the divine infant, Krishna.

Anu Gita Explained is a detailed explanation of how we endure many material bodies in the course of transmigrating through various life-forms. This is a discourse between Krishna and Arjuna. Arjuna requested of Krishna a display of the Universal Form and a repeat narration of the Bhagavad Gita but Krishna declined and explained what a siddha perfected being told the Yadu family about the sequence of existences one endures and the systematic flow of those lives at the convenience of material nature.

Bhagavad Gita Explained shows what was said in the Gita without religious overtones and sectarian biases.

Kriya Yoga Bhagavad Gita shows the instructions for those who are doing kriya yoga.

Brahma Yoga Bhagavad Gita shows the instructions for those who are doing brahma yoga.

Uddhava Gita Explained shows the instructions to Uddhava which are more advanced than the ones given to Arjuna.

Bhagavad Gita is an instruction for applying the expertise of yoga in the cultural field. This is why the process taught to Arjuna is called karma yoga which means karma + yoga or cultural activities done with a yogic demeanor.

Uddhava Gita is an instruction for apply the expertise of yoga to attaining spiritual status. This is why it is explains jnana yoga and bhakti yoga in detail. Jnana yoga is using mystic skill for knowing the spiritual part of existence. Bhakti yoga is for developing affectionate relationships with divine beings.

Karma yoga is for negotiating the social concerns in the material world and therefore it is inferior to bhakti yoga which concerns negotiating the social concerns in the spiritual world.

This world has a social environment and the spiritual world has one too.

Right now Uddhava Gita is the most advanced informative spiritual book on the planet. There is nothing anywhere which is superior to it or which goes into so much detail as it. It verified that historically Krishna is the most advanced human being to ever have left literary instructions on this planet. Even Patanjali Yoga Sutras which I translated and gave an application for in my book, **Meditation Expertise**, does not go as far as the Uddhava Gita.

Some of the information of these two books is identical but while the Yoga Sutras are concerned with the personal spiritual emancipation (kaivalyam) of the individual spirits, the Uddhava Gita explains that and also explains the situations in the spiritual universes.

Bhagavad Gita is from the Mahabharata which is the history of the Pandavas. Arjuna, the student of the Gita, is one of the Pandavas brothers. He was in a social hassle and did not know how to apply yoga expertise to solve it. Krishna gave him a crash-course on the battlefield about that.

Uddhava Gita is from the Srimad Bhagavatam (Bhagavata Purana), which is a history of the incarnations of Krishna. Uddhava was a relative of Krishna. He was concerned about the situation of the deaths of many of his relatives but Krishna diverted Uddhava's attention to the practice of yoga for the purpose of successfully migrating to the spiritual environment.

Specialty

These books are based on the author's experiences in meditation, yoga practice and participation in spiritual groups:

Spiritual Master

sex you!

Sleep **Paralysis**

Astral Projection

Masturbation Psychic Details

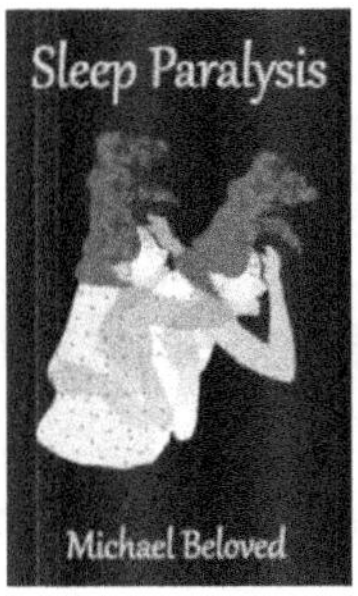

In **Spiritual Master**, Michael draws from experience with gurus or with their senior students. His contact with astral gurus is rated. He walks you through the avenue of gurus showing what you should do and what you should not do, so as to gain proficiency in whatever area of spirituality the guru has proficiency.

sex you! is a masterpiece about the adventures of an individual spirit's passage through the parents' psyches. The conversion of a departed soul into a sexual urge is described. The transit from the afterlife to residency in the emotions of the parents is detailed. This is about sex and you; learn about how much of you comprises the romantic energy of your would-be parents!

Sleep Paralysis clears misconceptions so that one can see what sleep paralysis is and what frightening astral experience occurs while the paralysis is being experienced. This disempowerment has great value in giving you confidence that you can and do exist even if you are unable to operate the physical body. The implication is that one can exist apart from and will survive the loss of the material body.

Astral Projection details experiences Michael had even in childhood, where he assumed incorrectly that everyone was astrally conversant. He discusses the life force psychic mechanism which operates the sleep-wake cycle of the physical form, and which budgets energy into the separated astral form which determines if the individual will have dream recall or no objective awareness during the projections. Astral travel happens on every occasion when the physical body sleeps. What is missing in awareness is the observer status while the astral body is separated.

Masturbation Psychic Details is a surprise presentation which relates what happens on the psychic plane during a masturbation event. This does not tackle moral issues or even addictions but shows the involvement of memory and the sure but hidden subconscious mind which operates many features of the psyche irrespective of the desire or approval of the self-conscious personality.

Online Resources

Visit The Website And Forum

Email:	michaelbelovedbooks@gmail.com axisnexus@gmail.com
Website Forum:	michaelbeloved.com inselfyoga.com

www.ingramcontent.com/pod-product-compliance
Lightning Source LLC
Chambersburg PA
CBHW082107280426
43661CB00090B/925
* 9 7 8 1 9 4 2 8 8 7 9 9 7 *